CONSTRUCTION LAW SERIES

NEW YORK CONSTRUCTION LAW MANUAL

Postner & Rubin
New York, New York

Catherine Kettle Brown, Esq.
Colorado Springs, Colorado

Lawyers Cooperative Publishing™
Aqueduct Building, Rochester, New York 14694

For Customer Assistance Call 1-800-527-0430

Copyright © 1992 by McGraw-Hill, Inc. All rights reserved. Printed in the United States of America. Except as permitted under the United States Copyright Act of 1976, no part of this publication may be reproduced or distributed in any form or by any means, or stored in a data base or retrieval system, without the prior written permission of the publisher.

Information has been obtained by the authors and Shepard's/McGraw-Hill, Inc from sources believed to be reliable. However, because of the possibility of human or mechanical error by our sources, Shepard's/McGraw-Hill, Inc., or others, neither the authors nor Shepard's/McGraw-Hill, Inc. guarantees the accuracy, adequacy, or completeness of any information and is not responsible for any errors or omissions or for the results obtained from use of such information.

Copyright ©1997 West Group

Library of Congress Cataloging-in-Publication Data

Rubin, Robert A.
    New York construction law manual / Robert A. Rubin.
      p. cm. — (Construction law series)
    Includes index.
    ISBN 0-07-172261-0
     1. Construction contracts—New York (State) 2. Construction industry—
Law and legislation—New York (State) I. Title. II. Series.
KFN5224.3.R8 1992
343.747'07869—dc20
[347.47037869]   92-26172
                                                            CIP

ISBN 0-07-172261-0

NYCL

The legal editor for this book was Laurel Cohn.

Foreword

This book is the result of a close collaborative effort between the partners and associates of Postner & Rubin, a firm whose entire practice is devoted to construction matters, and Catherine Brown, a lawyer, professional editor, and writer.

How the book was written may be of some interest to the reader. Postner & Rubin first prepared a detailed chapter-by-chapter outline. Each member of the firm was then assigned to be the coordinator of one or more chapters. The coordinator's role was to assemble materials related to the chapter from the firm's library and files and the attorney's personal files. These materials were sent to Catherine Brown. Catherine would review these materials, do further research, and draft the chapter which would first be reviewed by the coordinator. Catherine would then prepare a second draft. This was reviewed by each member of the firm, followed by a lengthy conference among Catherine and members of the firm. Catherine then would prepare a final draft of the chapter, which was again reviewed by the coordinator.

The goal was to produce a scholarly treatise which, at the same time, reflects the practical experience of the authors. Hence, the reader will notice numerous "Practice Pointers" throughout the text.

Present members of the Postner & Rubin firm who participated in writing the book are:

Robert A. Rubin
William J. Postner
Thomas G. De Luca
Robert J. MacPherson
Lisa A. Banick
Isabel B. Galis-Menendez

Paul R. Schreyer
Jeffrey R. Cruz

Former members of the Postner & Rubin firm who participated in writing the book are:

John E. Osborn, Law Offices of John E. Osborn, P.C.
James F. Forster, Metro-North Commuter Railroad

We are especially grateful to Claire M. Catuogno, legal assistant, for coordinating the overall effort, setting and monitoring time schedules, performing legal research, and checking citations, whose efforts were invaluable in bringing this book to fruition.

Roy Wilson, P.E., and Ed Josiah, Wilson Management Associates, Glen Head, New York, prepared the progress schedule illustrations in Chapter 7.

Robert J. Smith, Esq., Wickwire, Gavin, Madison, Wisconsin, contributed to the portion of Chapter 2 related to construction risk allocation.

Terrell E. Hunt, Esq., formerly of the U.S. Environmental Protection Agency, contributed to the portion of Chapter 14 related to environmental matters.

We thank Bettina Carbajal and Alison Freed, law students, for their assistance in preparing the book outline and legal research.

POSTNER & RUBIN

New York, New York
August 1992

The Authors

ROBERT A. RUBIN is a Partner in the law firm of Postner & Rubin. Mr. Rubin received a Bachelor of Civil Engineering from Cornell University and a Juris Doctor from Columbia University. He is a Fellow of the American College of Construction Lawyers, a Fellow of the American Society of Civil Engineers, and a Fellow of the American Bar Foundation. He is a member of the New York bar and is a licensed professional engineer in the state of New York. In 1984, he served as court-appointed mini-trial referee in the Gilbane-Nemours Foundation Litigation, U.S. District Court, District Court of Delaware.

WILLIAM J. POSTNER is a Partner in the law firm of Postner & Rubin. Mr Postner has practiced construction law since graduating from New York University School of Law and being admitted to the New York bar in 1967. In 1980, with Robert A. Rubin, he founded Postner & Rubin, a law firm whose practice is limited to construction law.

Mr. Postner serves as a Special Master in the Supreme Court of the State of New York, County of New York, and is a member of the American Judges Association, the American College of Construction Lawyers, the Construction Arbitration Panel of the American Arbitration Association, the Defense Research Institute, the New York County Lawyers' Association, the Association of the Bar of the City of New York, and the New York State Bar Association.

THOMAS G. DE LUCA is a Partner in the law firm of Postner & Rubin. He received his Juris Doctor from Seton Hall University. Mr. De Luca is admitted to practice law before various state and federal courts in New York and New Jersey. He is a member of the New Jersey State and American Bar Associations and New York County Lawyers' Association. Mr. De Luca represents contractors, owners, developers, designers, sureties, and insurers in all aspects of construction-related litigation, arbitration, and mediation. He has lectured on topics concerning suretyship, insurance, design liability, and hazardous wastes. Prior to practicing law, he was a senior surety underwriter for Firemans Fund Insurance Company. In addition to his legal counseling, he has served as a financial advisor to construction companies.

ROBERT J. MACPHERSON is a Partner in the law firm of Postner & Rubin. Since he entered the practice of law in 1980, his practice has been limited to construction matters, primarily the resolution of disputes arising out of construction projects.

Prior to joining Postner & Rubin in 1982, Mr. MacPherson served as in-house counsel to a New Jersey-based contractor. He has arbitrated several complex matters, representing suppliers, subcontractors, general contractors, and owners, and has appeared in federal and state courts and administrative hearings in construction-related matters.

He has presented programs on alternative dispute resolution and dispute avoidance to industry groups and other attorneys and has acted as an arbitrator and mediator in private and court-sponsored dispute resolution proceedings.

LISA A. BANICK is a Partner in the law firm of Postner & Rubin. Ms. Banick received a Bachelor of Science, Civil Engineering, from the University of Virginia and a Juris Doctor, Magna Cum Laude, from New York Law School.

Ms. Banick is co-author of "The Hyatt Regency Decision—One View," The Construction Lawyer, ABA, 1986; the chapter "Fixing the Failure and Settling the Dispute," *Construction Failures*, Wiley Law Publications, *1989;* the chapter "Alternative Dispute Resolution Forms," *Construction Industry Forms*, John Wiley & Sons, 1988.

Ms. Banick is a member of the New York and New Jersey Bars. She is an associate member of the American Society of Civil Engineers and a member of the New York County Lawyers' Association, the New York Bar Association, the New Jersey Bar Association, the American Bar Association, and the National Association of Women in Construction.

ISABEL B. GALIS-MENENDEZ is an Associate in the law firm of Postner & Rubin. Ms. Galis-Menendez was born in Havana, Cuba and is fluent in both Spanish and English. She received a Bachelor of Arts Degree in Political Science and Spanish Literature from Fordham University and a Juris Doctor from Fordham University School of Law. Part of her Spanish Literature studies were conducted at the University of Madrid.

Before joining the firm, her practice was in the representation of public owners regarding construction matters. More recently she has represented parties on

all sides of construction cases, as well as serving as an arbitrator on the Construction Arbitration Panel of the American Arbitration Association. Ms. Galis-Menendez has lectured to members of construction organizations and has assisted in teaching a class on construction law at Pratt Institute.
She is admitted to practice law before the state and federal courts of New Jersey and New York.

PAUL R. SCHREYER is an Associate in the law firm of Postner & Rubin. Mr. Schreyer received a Bachelor of Science Degree in Construction cum laude from Bradley University in 1983, and was selected as a member of Sigma Lambda Chi, the national construction honors society.

In 1987, Mr. Schreyer received his Juris Doctor cum laude from University of Bridgeport. He served as lead articles editor for the *University of Bridgeport Law Review.*

Mr. Schreyer is the author of "Construction Managers Liability for Job Site Safety" Vol. 8 No. 1 *University of Bridgeport Law Review* (1987), and co-author of "The Long Arm of Liability" *Civil Engineering* (September 1989).

He is admitted to practice in the states of Connecticut, New Jersey, and New York and before the Federal District Court of the District of New Jersey, and the Southern and Eastern Districts of New York.
Mr. Schreyer is a member of the New York State Bar Association and is an associate member of the American Institute of Constructors.

JEFFREY R. CRUZ is an Associate in the law firm of Postner & Rubin. Mr. Cruz received a Bachelor of Arts in English from Georgetown University, College of Arts and Sciences, in Washington, D.C. He received a Juris Doctor from Fordham University Law School, where he served as a Commentary Editor for the *Fordham Urban Law Journal.*

Mr. Cruz is admitted to practice before the state and federal district courts in New York and New Jersey. He is a member of the American Bar Association, New York State Bar Association, and the New York County Lawyers Association. Mr. Cruz has lectured on construction law matters at Pratt Institute and the Center for Professional Advancement.

JOHN E. OSBORN is currently a partner in the New York City law firm of John E. Osborn, P.C. and a former partner at Postner & Rubin, also of New York City. He practices in the areas of environmental risk and management, construction law, effective contract drafting, real estate litigation, and dispute resolution. He has published and lectured extensively on these subjects and is a faculty member of the New York University Real Estate Institute and Pratt Institute, School of Architecture. He is also an active committee member for numerous professional and trade associations, both national and local. Mr. Osborn received his undergraduate degree in Economics and Political Science from the State University of New York College at New Paltz and earned his law degree from the University of South Carolina Law Center.

JAMES F. FORSTER is associate counsel for Metro-North Commuter Railroad. He was formerly a partner in the New York City law firm of Postner & Rubin. He received his B.A. degree in Political Science from Bradley University and his J.D. from Hofstra University School of Law, where he was an associate editor of the *Hofstra Law Review*. Currently he is a visiting associate professor at Pratt Institute's School of Architecture in Brooklyn, New York. In addition to his teaching at Pratt, Mr. Forster has lectured for many trade associations and engineering societies, and over the last 10 years has represented design professionals, contractors, and owners in contractual, business, and litigation matters. He is licensed to practice law in New York, New Jersey, and Pennsylvania.

CATHERINE KETTLE BROWN is a free-lance author and attorney. She was formerly in private practice, specializing in litigation of real estate and construction related matters. She received a Bachelor of Science in Journalism from the University of Colorado and a Juris Doctor from the University of Denver. She is licensed to practice law in Colorado.

Contents

Summary

Foreword

The Authors

1 Overview of the Contracting Process and Discussion of Some Special Concerns

2 Bidding and Contract Formation

3 The Subcontract

4 Default/Termination

5 Changed Conditions

6 Changes/Extra Work

7 Delays

8 Bonds

9 Mechanics' Liens

10 Insurance

11 Professional's Role and Liability

12 Defects and Failures

13 Construction Safety

14 Environmental Problems in Construction

15 Remedies/Damages

16 Dispute Resolution

17 An Overview of the New York City Procurement Policy Board Rules

Tables

Index

Detailed

Foreword

The Authors

1 Overview of the Contracting Process and Discussion of Some Special Concerns

    §1.01   The Parties
    §1.02   Design Professionals
    §1.03   —Designer Fees
    §1.04   —Architects
    §1.05   —Engineers
    §1.06   —Subconsultants
    §1.07   Owners
    §1.08   —Public Owners
    §1.09   —Private Owners
    §1.10   Contractors
    §1.11   —General Contractors
    §1.12   —Independent Prime or *Trade* Contractors
    §1.13   Construction Managers
    §1.14   Subcontractors
    §1.15   Suppliers and Materialmen

§1.16   Sureties
§1.17   Insurers
§1.18   Types of Contracts
§1.19   —Lump Sum Contracts
§1.20   —Unit Price Contracts
§1.21   —Cost Reimbursable Contracts
§1.22   —Guaranteed Maximum Price Contracts
§1.23   Turnkey/Design-Build
§1.24   Licenses and Codes

Some Special Concerns

§1.25   Abnormally Dangerous Activities
§1.26   The 10-Foot Rule—Lateral Support
§1.27   Call Before You Dig
§1.28   Special Construction Problems in New York City

2 Bidding and Contract Formation

§2.01   Introduction
§2.02   Bidding
§2.03   Bidding on Public Contracts
§2.04   —Lowest Responsible Bidder
§2.05   —Compliance with Bid Documents: Responsiveness
§2.06   —Prequalification of Bidders
§2.07   —Advertising Bids
§2.08   —Specifications
§2.09   —Wicks Law: Separate Specifications for Certain Types of Work
§2.10   —Accepting Bids
§2.11   —Illegal Bids and Contracts
§2.12   —Withdrawal of Bid
§2.13   —Awarding the Bid
§2.14   —Exceptions to Bidding Rules
§2.15   —Challenging an Award or Rejection of Bid

§2.16	—Public Agencies Exempt from Competitive Bidding Requirements
§2.17	Bidding on Private Contracts
§2.18	Mistakes
§2.19	—Excusable and Nonexcusable Unilateral Mistakes
§2.20	—Mutual Mistakes
§2.21	Subcontractor Bids
§2.22	Rejection of Bids
§2.23	Contract Formation
§2.24	—Offer and Acceptance
§2.25	—Mutual Assent/Intent to Be Bound
§2.26	—Certainty of Terms
§2.27	—Statute of Frauds
§2.28	—Illegal Contracts
§2.29	—Authority to Contract (Capacity)
§2.30	—Actual and Apparent Authority
§2.31	Letter of Intent
§2.32	Execution of Contract
§2.33	Negotiating Terms and Conditions
§2.34	Analysis of Boilerplate
§2.35	Evaluating Special Terms
§2.36	Evaluating Risks and Responsibilities
§2.37	—Pricing Risks
§2.38	Risk Allocation in the Best Interest of the Project
§2.39	—Types of Risk
§2.40	—Philosophies for Dealing with Risk
§2.41	—Options for Allocating Risk
§2.42	—Integrating Cost Effective Risk Allocation Language into Contract Documents and Contract Procedures
§2.43	—What Some Owners are Doing to Better Allocate Risks and Reduce Their Total Project Costs

§2.44	—The Role of Counsel: Advocate or Counselor?
§2.45	Subcontract Terms and Conditions
§2.46	Standard Contract Forms
§2.47	Interpreting the Contract
§2.48	—Use of Extrinsic Evidence/Parol Evidence Rule
§2.49	—Conflict Between Contract and Other Documents
§2.50	—Conflict Between Plans and Specifications
§2.51	Incorporation by Reference

3 The Subcontract

§3.01	Introduction
§3.02	Subcontract and Supply Contract Formation
§3.03	"Standard" Subcontract Forms
§3.04	Subcontract Provisions
§3.05	—Boilerplate
§3.06	—Incorporation by Reference
§3.07	—Scope of Work
§3.08	—Time of Performance
§3.09	—Contractor's Duties
§3.10	—Job Site
§3.11	—Warranties
§3.12	—Change Orders and Extras
§3.13	—Hold Harmless and Indemnification Clauses
§3.14	—Sub-subcontractors and Materialmen
§3.15	—Relations with Other Subcontractors
§3.16	—Progress Payments
§3.17	—Retainage
§3.18	—Contingent Payment Clauses
§3.19	—Final Payment

§	
§3.20	—Back Charges
§3.21	—Offsets
§3.22	—Delay Damages
§3.23	—Liquidating Agreements
§3.24	—Default/Termination
§3.25	—Remedies for Non-Payment
§3.26	—Lien Waivers
§3.27	Purchase Orders and Supply Contracts
§3.28	Applicable Law—The UCC
§3.29	Terms of Supply Contract
§3.30	—Time of Performance
§3.31	—Acceptance and Rejection
§3.32	—Price and Terms of Payment
§3.33	—Warranties
§3.34	—Insurance and Shipping
§3.35	Actions for Breach and Damages

4 Default/Termination

§	
§4.01	Introduction
§4.02	Contractual Right of Termination
§4.03	—For Cause
§4.04	—For Convenience
§4.05	—Architect/Engineer Approval
§4.06	Notice Requirements
§4.07	Contractor Default
§4.08	—Failure to Prosecute the Work
§4.09	—Failure to Pay Subcontractors and Suppliers
§4.10	—Failure to Correct Defective Work
§4.11	—Insolvency or Bankruptcy of Contractor
§4.12	Contractor Defenses
§4.13	—Substantial Performance
§4.14	—Owner or Architect/Engineer Interference

§4.15	—Impossibility
§4.16	—Waiver and Estoppel
§4.17	—Non-Payment
§4.18	—Owner's Failure to Follow Contractual Termination Procedure
§4.19	Architect/Engineer Default
§4.20	Rescission
§4.21	Wrongful Termination

5 Changed Conditions

§5.01	Introduction
§5.02	Changed Conditions Defined
§5.03	—Subsurface Conditions
§5.04	—Latent Above-Ground Conditions
§5.05	—Miscellaneous Causes of Changed Conditions
§5.06	Contract Clauses
§5.07	—Changed Conditions Clauses
§5.08	—Disclaimer Clauses
§5.09	—Exculpatory Clauses
§5.10	Owner's Misrepresentation
§5.11	—Owner's Innocent Misrepresentation
§5.12	—Owner's Fraud, Concealment, and Reckless Representation
§5.13	Site Investigation and Other Inquiry
§5.14	Reliance on Owner's Data
§5.15	Contractor's Duty to Perform
§5.16	Remedies
§5.17	Claims
§5.18	—Notice and Documentation
§5.19	Damages
§5.20	—Impact Costs

6 Changes/Extra Work

| §6.01 | Origin of Changes |

§6.02	Basic Clause Coverage
§6.03	—The Contract's Scope of Work
§6.04	—The *Cardinal Change* Doctrine
§6.05	—Deductive Changes v Convenience Terminations
§6.06	Issuing Change Orders
§6.07	Authority to Make Changes
§6.08	The Requirement of a Writing
§6.09	Waiving the Writing Requirement
§6.10	—By Oral Order
§6.11	—By Acquiescence
§6.12	—By Conduct
§6.13	Contractor's Duty to Proceed with Disputed Work
§6.14	—Effect of Failure to Proceed
§6.15	Constructive Changes
§6.16	—Contractor's Duty to Seek Clarification
§6.17	—Owner Interference with Work
§6.18	—Defective Specifications
§6.19	—Owner Nondisclosure of Technical Information
§6.20	—Overmeticulous Inspection
§6.21	—Dictating Performance Methods
§6.22	Performance Specifications v Detailed Specifications
§6.23	Rules of Contract Interpretation Applicable to Scope of Work Disputes
§6.24	Notice, Protest, and Record Keeping Requirements
§6.25	Price Adjustments for Changed Work
§6.26	—Pricing Change-Related Costs
§6.27	—Unit Price
§6.28	—Cost Reimbursement Contracts
§6.29	—Impact Costs
§6.30	—Proving Costs

§6.31 Exculpatory Clauses
§6.32 Claims Preservation and Defense
§6.33 —Accord and Satisfaction
§6.34 Remedies

7 Delays

§7.01 Introduction
§7.02 Determining Delay
§7.03 Time-Money Relationship
§7.04 Scheduling Procedures/Progress Schedules
§7.05 Delay and Disruption Causes
§7.06 Types of Delay
§7.07 Excusable Delay
§7.08 —Acts of God/Force Majeure
§7.09 —Strikes and Labor Disputes
§7.10 —Owner-Caused
§7.11 —Sovereign and Other Acts That Interfere with Construction
§7.12 —Subcontractor's and Supplier's Delays
§7.13 Relevant Contract Clauses
§7.14 —Federal Contracts
§7.15 —State and Local Contracts
§7.16 —Commercial Practice
§7.17 Notice Requirements
§7.18 —Time of Notice
§7.19 —Content
§7.20 Effect of Excuse
§7.21 Noncompensable Delays
§7.22 Compensable Delay
§7.23 —Owner Interference
§7.24 —Denial of Access
§7.25 —Delayed Notice to Proceed
§7.26 —Delays in Inspection/Approval
§7.27 —Defective Design

§	
§7.28	—Contract Changes and Extras
§7.29	—Changed Conditions
§7.30	Nonexcusable Delay
§7.31	Concurrent Delay
§7.32	*No Damage for Delay* Provisions
§7.33	Enforceability of *No Damage for Delay* Clauses
§7.34	General v Specific *No Damage for Delay* Clauses
§7.35	Some Typical *No Damage for Delay* Clauses
§7.36	Exceptions to Enforcement of *No Damage for Delay* Clauses
§7.37	—Uncontemplated Delay
§7.38	—Active Interference
§7.39	—Unreasonable Delay and Abandonment
§7.40	—Willful or Gross Negligence
§7.41	—Fraud or Bad Faith
§7.42	—Breach of Contract
§7.43	Disruption/Interference
§7.44	Acceleration
§7.45	—Actual Acceleration
§7.46	—Constructive Acceleration
§7.47	—Right to Relief
§7.48	Remedies
§7.49	Burden of Proof
§7.50	Apportionment of Responsibility for Delay
§7.51	Waiver
§7.52	Contractor's Damages for Delay
§7.53	—Labor Escalation
§7.54	—Material Escalation
§7.55	—Loss of Productivity
§7.56	—Procurement Costs
§7.57	—Impact Costs
§7.58	—Field Overhead

§7.59	—Idle Equipment	
§7.60	—Home Office Overhead	
§7.61	—Financing Costs	
§7.62	—Inability to Take On Other Work	
§7.63	—Profit	
§7.64	—Interest	
§7.65	Contractor Damage Recovery	
§7.66	Contractor's Other Remedies	
§7.67	Owner's Damages for Delay	
§7.68	—Actual Damages	
§7.69	—Loss of Use	
§7.70	—Interest	
§7.71	—Professional Fees	
§7.72	Liquidated Damages	
§7.73	Owner's Other Remedies	

8 Bonds

§8.01	Difference Between a Bond and Insurance
§8.02	Construing the Bond
§8.03	Parties to the Surety Relationship
§8.04	Bond Types and Terms
§8.05	Bid Bonds
§8.06	—The Surety's Liability
§8.07	—Releasing the Surety
§8.08	Performance Bonds
§8.09	Guaranty and Completion Bonds
§8.10	Who is Protected: Third-Party Beneficiaries and Combination Bonds
§8.11	The Obligee's Obligations
§8.12	The Surety's Obligations and Options
§8.13	—Complete the Work with the Original Contractor
§8.14	—Complete the Work Itself or with a Substitute Contractor
§8.15	—Allow the Obligee to Complete the Work

§8.16	—Pay the Penal Sum to the Obligee
§8.17	Claims by the Obligee
§8.18	—Cost of Completion
§8.19	—Liquidated and Delay Damages
§8.20	—Incidental and Consequential Damages
§8.21	—Attorneys' Fees
§8.22	—Punitive Damages
§8.23	—Interest
§8.24	Surety's Defenses
§8.25	—Lack of or Untimely Notice
§8.26	—Discharge by Modification or Breach of Contract
§8.27	—Discharge by Fraud
§8.28	—Untimely Claim
§8.29	—Liability in Excess of the Penal Sum
§8.30	—The Principal's Defenses and Claims
§8.31	—Party Not Protected by the Bond
§8.32	Payment Bonds
§8.33	Who is Protected
§8.34	—Subcontractors
§8.35	—Suppliers and Materialmen
§8.36	—Architects/Engineers
§8.37	What Items Are Covered
§8.38	—Materials
§8.39	—Rental Equipment
§8.40	Notice of Claim
§8.41	Attorneys' Fees
§8.42	Interest
§8.43	Miller Act Bonds
§8.44	—Persons Protected
§8.45	—Notice of Claim and Limitation of Action
§8.46	—Claimable Items
§8.47	Defenses Available to Surety

§8.48	Claims by the Surety	
§8.49	—Claims Against Obligee	
§8.50	—Claims Against Architect/Engineer	
§8.51	—Claims Against Lending Institutions	
§8.52	—Claims Against Subcontractors, Their Sureties, and Their Insurers	
Appendix 8-1	Payment Bond Notice Provisions	

9 Mechanics' Liens

§9.01	General Principles
§9.02	Liens in the Private Sector
§9.03	—Who May File
§9.04	—Improvement as a Requirement
§9.05	—Owner's Consent
§9.06	—Lien Attaches to Real Property
§9.07	Liens in the Public Sector
§9.08	—Who May File
§9.09	—Improvement as a Requirement
§9.10	—Securing an Interest in Funds
§9.11	What Property is Lienable: Private Property
§9.12	—Condominiums and Cooperatives
§9.13	—Leasehold Interests
§9.14	—Oil and Gas
§9.15	Public Property
§9.16	What Items are Covered by the Lien
§9.17	—Labor
§9.18	—Materials
§9.19	—Rental Equipment
§9.20	—Temporary Works
§9.21	—Overhead and Employee Benefits
§9.22	—Lost Profits and Contract Damages
§9.23	—Extras
§9.24	Lien Waivers
§9.25	Should You File a Notice of Lien?

§9.26	Elements of a Proper Lien Notice for Private Improvements
§9.27	Elements of a Proper Lien Notice for Public Improvements
§9.28	Filing the Notice of Lien—Time and Place
§9.29	—Private Improvement Liens
§9.30	—Public Improvement Liens
§9.31	Service of Notice of Lien
§9.32	Duration and Extension of Lien
§9.33	Amendment of Lien
§9.34	Owner's Response to Notice of Lien
§9.35	—Demand for Statement
§9.36	—Discharge the Lien
§9.37	—Demand to Foreclose
§9.38	Enforcing the Mechanic's Lien
§9.39	—Deadline to Commence Action
§9.40	—Filing of Notice of Pendency
§9.41	—Lien Foreclosure and Arbitration
§9.42	—Venue and Jurisdiction of Action
§9.43	—Courts of Record and Courts not of Record
§9.44	—Necessary Parties
§9.45	—Form of Complaint
§9.46	Answers of Defendant Lienors
§9.47	Defenses to the Foreclosure Action
§9.48	—Defective and Expired Liens
§9.49	—Willful Exaggeration
§9.50	—No Fund to Which Lien Can Attach
§9.51	The Lien Foreclosure Trial
§9.52	Priority of Private Improvement Liens
§9.53	—Building Loan Contracts and Mortgages
§9.54	—Mortgages
§9.55	—Assignment of Moneys Due under Contract for Improvement of Real Property

§9.56	—Miscellaneous Liens
§9.57	—Subsequent Purchasers
§9.58	—Agreements to Subordinate
§9.59	Priority of Public Improvement Liens
§9.60	Parity and Preference among Mechanics' Lienors
§9.61	Obtaining a Judgment
§9.62	—Amount of Judgment
§9.63	Obtaining an Execution
§9.64	Sale upon Execution
§9.65	—Distribution of Proceeds
§9.66	—Deficiency Judgments
§9.67	—Setting Aside a Sale
§9.68	The Trust Fund
§9.69	—Duration of a Trust
§9.70	—Trust Assets
§9.71	—Parties Involved
§9.72	—The Fiduciary Relationship
§9.73	—Record Keeping Requirements
§9.74	—Availability of Records to Claimants
§9.75	—Proper Application of Trust Funds
§9.76	—Notice of Lending
§9.77	—Notice of Assignment
§9.78	—Diversion of Trust Funds
§9.79	—Liability for Diversion
§9.80	—Restoration of the Trust after Diversion
§9.81	Enforcing the Trust Fund
§9.82	—Claims for Relief
§9.83	—Priority and Preference
§9.84	—Judgment

Form 9-1 Notice of Lien
Appendix 9-1 Private v Public Works Liens
Appendix 9-2 Lienable Items

10 Insurance

§10.01 Construction Insurance
§10.02 Understanding Insurance Policies
§10.03 Obtaining the Insurance Needed
§10.04 —Claims Made v Occurrence Policies
§10.05 —Duplicative Coverage
§10.06 Coverage
§10.07 —Liability Coverage
§10.08 —Property Coverage
§10.09 —*Occurrence* or *Accident*
§10.10 Wrap-Up Insurance
§10.11 Professional Liability Insurance
§10.12 Policy Limits
§10.13 Policy Requirements
§10.14 —Premiums
§10.15 —Notice to Insurers
§10.16 What to Do in the Event of an Occurrence
§10.17 Termination
§10.18 Exclusions
§10.19 —Contractor's Own Work
§10.20 —Pollution
§10.21 —Explosion, Collapse, and Underground Damage
§10.22 —Contractual Liability
§10.23 —Care, Custody, or Control
§10.24 Fidelity Insurance
§10.25 Officers' and Directors' Liability
§10.26 Motor Vehicles and Equipment
§10.27 Duty of Defense
§10.28 Limitation of Actions
§10.29 Duty of Cooperation
§10.30 Disclaimers
§10.31 Certificate of Insurance
§10.32 Special Insurance Problems
§10.33 —Design-Build Contracts

§10.34 —Joint Ventures
§10.35 —Construction Managers
Appendix 10-1 Insurance Policies
Appendix 10-2 Glossary of Common Construction Insurance Terms

11 Professional's Role and Liability

§11.01 Introduction
§11.02 Licensing and Qualifying to do Business
§11.03 —Failure to License

Architect/Engineer Liability

§11.04 Generally
§11.05 Liability for Design
§11.06 Liability for Testing
§11.07 Liability for Cost Estimates
§11.08 Liability for Supervision and Inspection
§11.09 Liability for Scheduling and Coordination
§11.10 Liability for Certifying Progress Payments
§11.11 Liability for Dispute Resolution
§11.12 Liability to Third Parties
§11.13 —In Negligence
§11.14 —In Contract Privity

Construction Manager Liability

§11.15 Generally
§11.16 Liability for Design
§11.17 Liability for Cost Estimates
§11.18 Liability for Supervision and Inspection
§11.19 Liability for Scheduling and Coordination
§11.20 Liability for Certifying Progress Payments

§11.21 Liability to Third Parties

General Principles

§11.22 Indemnification and Contribution
§11.23 Statutes of Limitations
§11.24 —Continuous Treatment Doctrine
§11.25 Insurance

12 Defects and Failures

§12.01 Introduction
§12.02 Design Defects
§12.03 Construction Defects
§12.04 Faulty or Improper Materials
§12.05 Improper Installation
§12.06 Divided Responsibility
§12.07 Waiver of Defects
§12.08 Statutes of Limitations
§12.09 Claims Against Bond
§12.10 Indemnification and Contribution
§12.11 —Contractual Indemnification and Contribution
§12.12 Warranty (Guarantee) Clauses
§12.13 —Implied Warranties
§12.14 —Implied Warranties in the Sale of New Homes Subsequent Purchasers
§12.15 —Express Warranties
§12.16 —Exclusive Remedy

13 Construction Safety

§13.01 Introduction
§13.02 Workers' Compensation Laws
§13.03 Owner's Obligations
§13.04 Contractor's Obligations
§13.05 Labor Law §240
§13.06 Labor Law §241
§13.07 General Contractor's Liability under Labor Law §§240 and 241

§13.08 Owner's Liability under Labor Law §§240 and 241
§13.09 —Residential Dwelling Exception
§13.10 Liability of Agents of Owner and General Contractor under Labor Law §§240 and 241
§13.11 —Architect/Engineer
§13.12 —Construction Manager
§13.13 —Subcontractors
§13.14 Affirmative Defenses to Statutory Liability
§13.15 Liability of Architect/Engineer in Negligence
§13.16 Liability of Construction Manager in Negligence
§13.17 Res Ipsa Loquitur: The Thing Speaks for Itself
§13.18 Contribution/Indemnification
§13.19 OSHA

14 Environmental Problems in Construction

§14.01 Introduction
§14.02 Who Should Be Concerned
§14.03 Types of Projects Affected
§14.04 Sources of Environmental Law
§14.05 —Federal Legislation
§14.06 —State Legislation
§14.07 —Local Legislation
§14.08 Managing Environmental Risks
§14.09 Identifying Potential Risks
§14.10 Assigning and Assuming Risk
§14.11 Owner-Contractor Agreement
§14.12 —The Bid
§14.13 —The Contract
§14.14 —Clauses That Cause Trouble for Contractors

§14.15 —Clauses That Are Helpful to Contractors
§14.16 —Industry Standard Forms
§14.17 Owner-Design Professional Agreement
§14.18 —Defining the Role
§14.19 —Industry Standard Forms
§14.20 Insurance
§14.21 —Errors and Omissions Liability Insurance
§14.22 —Comprehensive General Liability Insurance: Exclusions
§14.23 —Claims Made v Occurrence Policies
§14.24 —Hazardous Waste Insurance Coverage
§14.25 Bonds
§14.26 Superfund
§14.27 —Reducing Superfund Risk
§14.28 Asbestos Abatement
§14.29 —Federal Law
§14.30 —New York State Law
§14.31 —Local Law
§14.32 Other Indoor Pollution
§14.33 Underground Storage Tanks
§14.34 Wetlands
§14.35 Trial Preparation
§14.36 —Obtaining Documents
§14.37 —Personal Liability for Environmental Risks
§14.38 Superfund Litigation
§14.39 —Defenses
§14.40 —Consent Decrees
§14.41 Alternative Dispute Resolution
§14.42 —The EPA
§14.43 —Using ADR in Environmental Litigation
§14.44 References

Appendix 14-1 Developer's Environmental Risk Checklist

15 Remedies/Damages

§15.01 Article 78
§15.02 —Procedure
§15.03 —Article 78 in Construction Cases
§15.04 —Standard of Review
§15.05 Injunctions
§15.06 —Preliminary Injunctions
§15.07 —Permanent Injunctions
§15.08 Declaratory Judgment
§15.09 Accounting
§15.10 Breach of Contract v Quantum Meruit
§15.11 Fraud
§15.12 Punitive Damages
§15.13 —Public Contracts
§15.14 Attorneys' Fees
§15.15 Interest
§15.16 Noncontractual Limitations on Damages
§15.17 —Mitigation
§15.18 —Collateral Source Rule
§15.19 —Certainty
§15.20 —Economic Loss Rule
§15.21 UCC Damage and Remedy Provisions
§15.22 Contractual Limitations on Damages
§15.23 Contractual Provisions Regarding Remedies
§15.24 Specific Breaches by Contractor
§15.25 —Failure to Commence Performance
§15.26 —Partial Performance
§15.27 —Substantial Performance
§15.28 —Defective Performance
§15.29 —Cost of Completion v Diminution in Value

§15.30 Specific Breaches by Owner
§15.31 —Failure to Commence Project
§15.32 —Abandonment Following Start of Construction
§15.33 —Nonpayment
§15.34 Breach by Architect/Engineer
§15.35 Breach by Subcontractors
§15.36 Materialmen Remedies
§15.37 —Replevin
§15.38 —Account Stated
§15.39 Specific Performance
§15.40 Rescission and Restitution
§15.41 Reformation

16 Dispute Resolution

§16.01 Introduction
§16.02 Notice of Claim Requirements
§16.03 Freedom of Information Laws
§16.04 Contract Scope of Work Disputes
§16.05 Informal Dispute Resolution
§16.06 —Dispute Review Boards
§16.07 —Mediation
§16.08 —Mediation and "Baseball Arbitration" in Construction Disputes
§16.09 —Minitrials
§16.10 Formal Dispute Resolution
§16.11 —Litigation
§16.12 —Arbitration
§16.13 —Federal Arbitration Act
§16.14 —Agreement to Arbitrate
§16.15 —Conditions Precedent to Arbitration
§16.16 —Arbitration: Is a Surety Bound?
Appendix 16-1 Selected References

17 An Overview of the New York City Procurement Policy Board Rules

§17.01 Negotiating the Maze
§17.02 PPB Rules Chapter Three: Methods of Source Selection
§17.03 PPB Rules Chapter Four: Contract Formation
§17.04 PPB Rules Chapter Five: Contract Award
§17.05 PPB Rules Chapter Six: Contract Administration
§17.06 PPB Rules Chapter Nine: Construction, Architecture, and Engineering Services
§17.07 PPB Rules Chapter Seven: Dispute Resolution
§17.08 —Bidding Disputes
§17.09 —Contract Disputes
§17.10 —Debarment and Suspension
§17.11 —Solicitation or Award of Contract in Violation of PPB Rules
§17.12 —Hearings on Borough President Complaints
§17.13 Questions and Suggestions for PPB Dispute Resolution
§17.14 —Delays
§17.15 —Finality of City Decisions
§17.16 —The Need for Fairness: Some Suggestions

Tables

Cases

Statutes

United States Code

State Statutes
Uniform Commerical Code
Regulations
Code of Federal Regulations
Procurement Policy Board Rules
Authorities
Index

Overview of the Contracting Process and Discussion of Some Special Concerns

§1.01 The Parties
§1.02 Design Professionals
§1.03 —Designer Fees
§1.04 —Architects
§1.05 —Engineers
§1.06 —Subconsultants
§1.07 Owners
§1.08 —Public Owners
§1.09 —Private Owners
§1.10 Contractors
§1.11 —General Contractors
§1.12 —Independent Prime or Trade Contractors
§1.13 Construction Managers
§1.14 Subcontractors
§1.15 Suppliers and Materialmen
§1.16 Sureties
§1.17 Insurers
§1.18 Types of Contracts
§1.19 —Lump Sum Contracts
§1.20 —Unit Price Contracts
§1.21 —Cost Reimbursable Contracts
§1.22 —Guaranteed Maximum Price Contracts
§1.23 Turnkey/Design-Build
§1.24 Licenses and Codes
Some Special Concerns
§1.25 Abnormally Dangerous Activities
§1.26 The 10-Foot Rule—Lateral Support

§1.27 Call Before You Dig
§1.28 Special Construction Problems in New York City

§1.01 The Parties

The parties to a construction project are numerous. There are owners and developers, designers, contractors and builders, construction managers, subcontractors and suppliers, lenders and investors, and insurers and sureties. Not each of these parties is involved in every construction project; a simple project may involve only an owner and a contractor. When any of these parties is part of a project it is by contract, although these parties are not all party to the same contract. Typically, the designer will contract with the owner. The contractor will contract with subcontractors, suppliers, and, perhaps, a surety. Subcontractors will have similar contracts. The lender will contract with the owner and, perhaps, the contractor and surety. Each of these parties has specific roles and duties. In this chapter, these parties and their roles in the construction process are defined, as are basic contract terms.

§1.02 Design Professionals

Today, many construction projects are not designed by an individual but by a team of professionals. The team, usually comprised of an architect and engineer assisted by specialized consultants, attempts to design a facility that satisfies the owner's needs while complying with applicable building codes and state and federal regulations. The more complex and specialized the project, the more members the team may have and the more one type of designer may be needed over another. For instance, if the owner wants a building complex designed, an architect will perform the majority of the design work and will retain a consulting engineer to prepare the structural design. If the owner wants to build a parking facility, an engineer will perform the majority of the design work and may consult an architect for aesthetic help.

Design professionals occupy an integral role in the construction process. They are members of the tripartite delivery team consisting of the owner, designer, and contractors. Their contracts typically are with the owners, although they often have duties which relate to the contract between the owner and general contractor, such as supervision, inspection, and certification of work. A designer's role in the project can vary greatly in scope and range of duties from merely providing a design to being involved in the entire project, from design through final inspection and certification of the completed work. The owner/designer contract must be carefully thought out and drafted to reflect accurately the designer's role and responsibilities in the project and must be consistent with the design professional's duties as spelled out in the owner/contractor or owner/construction manager agreement.

§1.03 —Designer Fees

Design professionals are generally paid through one of three different methods: *lump sum, cost reimbursement,* or *percentage of construction cost.* Under the *lump sum* method, the designer is paid a predetermined sum for all duties plus any reimbursable expenses, extras, and changes. In a lump sum contract, the scope of the designer's duties should be clearly and precisely defined. The designer typically is paid periodically throughout the project according to a schedule set forth in the contract.

Under the *cost reimbursement* method, the designer is compensated for its time and expenses. The contract should specifically set forth which time and expense items are reimbursable and the applicable hourly rates and overtime premiums. The designer typically is paid a retainer before it begins work and bills the owner monthly for its services. The retainer is *in addition to* the hourly fees. Generally, the designer's hourly rates are its direct payroll expenses attributable to the job times a multiplier.

Under the *percentage of construction cost* method, the designer's fee is a percentage of the total cost of the construction project. The contract must specify how and when the cost is established and provide a method for adjusting the fee as the cost estimates change.[1] The contract usually provides a method for making progress payments to the designer based on an estimated total cost and a provision for compensation in the event of delay or work stoppage. When using this method of payment, it is important to define clearly at what point and how costs are determined.

The method chosen to compensate the design professional should be acceptable to both parties and its implications fully understood. Under a lump sum arrangement, the design professional may contemplate little, if any, owner involvement in the various stages of the design, consulting the owner only upon completion of each phase to request approval to proceed to the next. Under an hourly fee basis, the design professional may encourage more owner involvement because the additional time involved will be compensated. The owner, on the other hand, may be surprised to learn that it is expected to pay for what it may have thought was assistance given to the design professional to understand the owner's needs. The percentage of construction cost method may not be appropriate unless the owner has a good idea of its needs and establishes a fair budget in consultation with the designer before work begins.

§1.04 —Architects

The practice of the profession of architecture is defined by statute in New York. To be an architect, one must be licensed in the state of New York and meet statutory requirements of education, experience, age, and examination.[2] An architect renders services which "require the application of the art, science, and aesthetics of design and construction of buildings. . . . Such services

---

[1] *See* AIA Doc B141, arts 3 & 6 (1977 ed).
[2] NY Educ Law §7304 (McKinney 1985 & Supp 1992).

include, but are not limited to consultation, evaluation, planning, the provision of preliminary studies, designs, construction documents, construction management, and the administration of construction contracts."[3]

§1.05 —Engineers

The practice of the profession of engineering is defined by statute in New York and requires one to be licensed in the state of New York and to meet statutory requirements of education, experience, age, and examination.[4] An engineer renders services such as "consultation, investigation, evaluation, planning, design, or supervision of construction or operation in connection with any utilities, structures, buildings, machines, equipment, processes, works, or projects . . . when such service or work requires the application of engineering principles and data."[5] It is the engineer that specifies the required strength of concrete or hydraulic pressure, specifies the type and strength of needed footings or electrical systems, or designs the pitch and banking of a highway system. There are many types of engineers, each of which has a specific area of expertise: electrical, civil, mechanical, soil, structural, etc. New York State does not license subspecialties.

§1.06 —Subconsultants

A subconsultant typically is hired by the project architect or engineer to provide specialized assistance. A geotechnical engineer may be hired to provide subsurface analysis and assistance in designing the foundations for the project. Other subconsultants include surveyors, lighting consultants, acoustical engineers, etc.

§1.07 Owners

The *owner* is the consumer of the construction product. The owner is the person or entity that initiates and pays for the construction project. Owners are a most divergent group; their characteristics, needs, desires, and capabilities vary greatly. A good understanding of the owner can help to ensure a smooth construction project, help to avoid disputes, and, if a dispute arises, help to resolve it. Owners may best be distinguished in two ways: whether they are public or private and whether they are experienced or inexperienced. **Sections 1.08** and **1.09** discuss these types of owners.

---

[3] *Id* §7301.
[4] NY Educ Law §7206 (McKinney 1985 & Supp 1992).
[5] *Id* §7201.

§1.08 —Public Owners

A *public owner* is an owner of a *public improvement*, which is defined as "an improvement of any real property belonging to the state or a public corporation."[6] The *state* is the state of New York and any of its political subdivisions—cities, counties, towns, districts, and municipalities. A *public corporation* is defined as "a municipal corporation or a district corporation or a public benefit corporation as such corporations are defined in section three of the general corporation law."[7]

A public owner's freedom to contract is limited by various laws and regulations. For instance, many public owners are precluded from negotiating construction contracts; they must *award* contracts to the lowest responsible bidder.[8] Similarly, statutes may require a public owner to obtain a payment bond from the successful contract bidder[9] or to include certain terms in its contract.[10] Before submitting a bid on a public contract, it is best to be familiar with all applicable statutes, ordinances, and regulations which govern the public owner, the contracting process, and the construction project.

Most public owners are experienced in construction and have departments or personnel whose full-time job is to administer construction projects.

§1.09 —Private Owners

A *private owner* owns "any improvement of real property not belonging to the state or a public corporation."[11] Private owners are free from the many constraints which affect public owners. For the most part, private owners may contract with whom they wish at what terms they wish. There are, however, statutes which regulate the contractual relationship between home owners and contractors.[12]

Experienced private owners may have in-house management staff who are familiar with the construction process or owners may assemble construction management teams by bringing together persons and firms with whom they have dealt successfully in the past. Experienced owners often have their own contract forms or are thoroughly familiar with the standard form contracts used industrywide. Experienced owners know that the construction process does not always progress smoothly. They know what permits are needed, the difference between acceptable and substandard supplies and work, what their duties are, and what their contractors' duties are.

---

[6] NY Lien Law §2(7) (McKinney 1966).

[7] *Id* §2(6).

[8] See **ch 2** for a discussion of bidding on public contracts.

[9] NY State Fin Law §137 (McKinney 1989 & Supp 1992). See **ch 8** for a complete discussion of payment bonds.

[10] NY Gen Mun Law §106-b (McKinney 1986) (specifies amount of retainage).

[11] NY Lien Law §2(8) (McKinney 1966).

[12] NY Gen Bus Law §§770-776 (McKinney Supp 1992).

Inexperienced owners, on the other hand, know little about the construction process save what they may have read in a weekly news magazine or learned from their neighbors. The inexperienced corporate owner typically can afford to, and will, hire experienced assistance, while the first-time home builder or home owner adding a room onto its home cannot. When dealing with an inexperienced owner, it is best that the contractor explain the construction process thoroughly to the owner (including time frame, when workers will arrive and leave each day, what steps will be taken, and areas of potential delay) and let the owner know what its specific duties are, such as obtaining a plot plan and permits.

§1.10 Contractors

A *contractor* is any person or entity that directly contracts with an owner of real property for its improvement.[13] A written contract generally is not necessary for a party to be a contractor, except for certain home improvement contractors.[14] Typically, the contractor is in charge of a major portion, if not all, of the project, provides labor and materials, and has contracts with subcontractors and suppliers for performance of some of the contract work.

§1.11 —General Contractors

Many projects have one contractor, which contractor is known as the *general contractor*. The general contractor is responsible for the entire project, from contracting with subcontractors and suppliers to scheduling and reviewing their work; ensuring code compliance;[15] worker and job site safety; coordination of work schedules; compliance with contractual deadlines; etc. There are no licensing requirements for general contractors in New York.

§1.12 —Independent Prime or Trade Contractors

On the majority of public contracts there are several contractors, called *independent prime* or *trade contractors,* each of which is responsible for a major portion of the project. For instance, General Municipal Law §101 and State Finance Law §135, called the *Wicks Law,* provide that when the entire cost of contract work for the erection, construction, reconstruction, or alteration of a public building exceeds $50,000, independent prime contracts must be let for the plumbing and gas fitting work; steam heating, hot water heating, ventilating, and air conditioning apparatus; and electrical wiring and standard illuminating fixtures. The general contract includes all other work on the project. Some private owners use independent prime contractors as well.

---

[13] NY Lien Law §2(9) (McKinney 1966).
[14] NY Gen Bus Law §770-776 (McKinney Supp 1992).
[15] *See* AIA Doc A201, art 3.7.3 (1987 ed).

Trade contractors argue that the use of several independent prime contractors can help avoid delay and lower costs since the project usually can proceed if one prime encounters trouble with its labor, suppliers, subcontractors, surety, lender, etc. If there is only one prime contractor—the general contractor—and it encounters any sort of difficulty, an entire project can be ground to a halt until the general contractor resolves its problem or is replaced.

General contractors and public owners, on the other hand, argue that the use of independent prime contractors creates project administration and coordination problems most public owners are unable to handle, leading to delays and increased costs. The absence of one trade contractor can prevent the work of all others from beginning or continuing. Further, general contractors and owners argue that the Wicks Law restricts the means and methods by which public bodies contract and requires the use of harsh one-sided language found in many public works contracts, such as *no damage for delay* clauses.

When using independent prime contractors, the owner has overall responsibility for planning, scheduling, and supervising the project construction. Of course, the owner can hire a construction manager to perform these functions. When using independent prime contractors, it is important that the owner's contracts with each clearly indicate each contractor's duties and scope of work.

§1.13 Construction Managers

The *construction manager* is a relatively new party to the construction process. There is no established definition of who a construction manager is or what a construction manager's responsibilities are or should be; great variations are possible, allowing the role of a construction manager to be tailored to each job. A construction manager is retained by the owner and may be an individual or a firm comprised of a group of professionals. The manager should be experienced in the technical aspects of construction and possess managerial skills; architects and general contractors may serve as construction managers. A construction manager's goal—to reduce the time and cost of the project while safeguarding quality—may be met by acting as the owner's agent in orchestrating the project from start to finish. The construction manager may aid the owner in conceptualizing the project, help the design team produce a coherent and cost efficient set of construction documents, screen and choose contractors, and coordinate and oversee the actual construction.

Generally, the construction manager does not perform any work with its own forces and its sole contract is with the owner. Where there is a construction manager, there generally is not a general contractor; rather, there usually are several independent prime or trade contractors with whom the manager coordinates construction of the project.

§1.14 Subcontractors

A *subcontractor* is any person or entity that contracts with a contractor or a subcontractor for the improvement of the real property and that performs

8 OVERVIEW & SPECIAL CONCERNS

some part of the contractor's contract with the owner.[16] A subcontractor may have subcontractors of its own (called *sub-subcontractors* or *second tier subcontractors*) and may contract with suppliers. A subcontractor typically does not have a contract with the owner and may not look to the owner for payment.

§1.15 Suppliers and Materialmen

A *materialman* or *supplier* is any person or entity that furnishes materials or provides machinery, tools, equipment, vehicles, or other supplies necessary for the project to an owner, contractor, or subcontractor.[17] Typically, a supplier does not perform any labor at the job site.

§1.16 Sureties

A *surety* assures the owner that the owner's contractor is backed by a financially responsible entity and that the contractor's obligation to honor its bid, perform the contract, or pay subcontractors will be met. Typically, the surety is a bonding or an insurance company which issues a bond on the project. The surety's liability is derived from the contractor's obligation to the owner to perform specified duties or pay specified parties.[18]

Most experienced private owners require contractors to obtain bid, payment, and/or performance bonds. The majority of public owners are required by law to obtain bonds.[19]

§1.17 Insurers

It can be said that a construction project is an accident waiting to happen. Laborers work with dangerous equipment and tools in dangerous circumstances. Consequently, contractors and subcontractors often are required to purchase insurance policies covering a variety of occurrences, which policies typically protect not only the contractors but also the owner and design professionals.[20] There are two general types of insurance used by the construction industry—liability and property.

§1.18 Types of Contracts

There are many different types of contracts, distinguished primarily by the method of determining the final contract price. Regardless of the method used,

---

[16] NY Lien Law §2(10) (McKinney 1966); Dorn v Arthur A. Johnson Corp, 16 AD2d 1009, 229 NYS2d 266 (1962).

[17] NY Lien Law §2(12) (McKinney 1966).

[18] United States v Seaboard Sur Co, 817 F2d 956 (2d Cir), *cert denied*, 108 S Ct 161 (1987).

[19] A complete discussion of public bonding requirements is found in **ch 8.**

[20] **Ch 10** discusses insurance.

the goal is the same—quality construction completed on time and to all specifications for the lowest possible price while allowing the contractor an opportunity to make a fair profit. To encourage the parties to meet this goal, several different types of contracts have evolved; the most commonly used pricing methods are discussed in the following four sections. It is important to note that many contracts are hybrids of the types discussed here—features of two or more pricing methods may be used in the same contract, resulting in a "mix and match" contract which meets the parties' needs. The type of contract chosen will depend on several factors, including the identity and relationship, if any, of the owner and contractor; the completeness of the design and its complexity; the type of work being done; and the need or desire for competitive pricing.

§1.19 —Lump Sum Contracts

One form of *fixed price contract*, a *lump sum* contract, is one in which the contractor agrees to do specified construction for a price set forth in the contract. The only changes allowed to the fixed price are for extras or change orders. Lump sum contracts are generally required for public works contracts. Bids are requested on complete plans and specifications, thus allowing for easy comparison of bid prices and fostering competition.

§1.20 —Unit Price Contracts

Another form of fixed price contract, a *unit price contract,* sets forth the price for each *unit* delivered to the contractee (typically the contractor). The unit may be, for example, a pound of nails, a door, a heating system, a modular building, or a cubic yard of excavation. The contract may specify a particular number of units or may state that the supplier will furnish all units needed or a specified percentage of needed units. For example, if the contract is for excavation, it might state that the excavator will be paid five dollars per cubic yard of material excavated from the site. Anything which can be measured in units can be the basis of a unit price contract.

Unit price contracts are most often used in heavy construction and highway contracts, such as for bridge work, tunneling, and rail and transit facilities—situations where it is difficult to calculate quantities in advance.

§1.21 —Cost Reimbursable Contracts

Cost-plus contracts are those in which the contractor is paid its actual costs of the construction plus a specified mark-up to cover overhead and profit. Typically, the contract defines *costs* as including all expenses incurred in the construction, including expenses for materials, labor (including payroll taxes), and subcontractors and suppliers. The contract should specify, in detail, what are and what are not costs. One contract specifies that costs include wages for labor; salaries of field office personnel and support personnel to the extent attributable to the job; payroll taxes and contributions; related travel and subsistence expenses of the contractor and its employees; all materials, supplies, and equipment incorporated into the work and cost of their transportation; payments to subcontractors; cost of materials, supplies, equipment, temporary facilities, and hand tools consumed by the job and cost less salvage value of such items used on, but not consumed by, the job; rental charges or value if owned by the contractor; bond and insurance premiums; sales and use tax; permit fees and royalties; losses not compensated by insurance or otherwise which are related to the job and are not due to the contractor's actions; telephone service at the site, long distance charges, mail charges, and similar petty cash items; debris removal costs; emergency costs; and other costs approved in writing in advance by the owner.[21] The contract also specifies what are not costs for reimbursement purposes. The following discussion sets out several measures of mark-up that are commonly used.

Time and Materials or Cost-Plus Percentage of Cost

In this type of contract, the contractor is paid its actual costs plus a specified percentage of those costs for overhead. Thus, the contract would specifically exclude actual overhead expenses from the definition of costs. To the total of costs and the overhead is then added a specified percentage for profit. A typical cost-plus percentage of cost contract would provide for 10% overhead and 5% profit, resulting in a total 15.5% override to the contractor. Assume that a contractor expended $100,000 in materials and labor to build a home for an owner. The owner would pay the contractor a total of $115,500, computed as follows:

	$100,000	labor and materials
+	10,000	10% overhead
	$110,000	
+	5,500	5% profit
	$115,500	

Cost-Plus Fixed Fee

In this type of contract, the contractor is paid its actual costs plus a fixed fee which is set in advance. The contract may or may not specify that costs include a set daily rate for overhead.

Cost-Plus Incentive Fee

In this type of payment structure, the contract specifies time and quality criteria. If the contractor meets those criteria it is paid its costs plus a set fee. If the contractor exceeds those criteria, perhaps by completing the job early, the contractor is paid an additional fee based on a scale set forth in the contract. If the contractor does not meet those criteria, the fee is less. This type of fee arrangement encourages early, quality work.

---

[21] AIA Doc A111, art 8 (1978 ed).

Cost-plus contracts are appropriate where, due to an incomplete or very complex design, a contractor would be unable to give a lump sum price without including a large contingency for unknown factors.

§1.22 —Guaranteed Maximum Price Contracts

A *guaranteed maximum price contract* is a variation of the cost-plus contract.[22] In this type of contract, the owner and contractor agree that the project will not cost the owner more than a set price, the guaranteed maximum. The contractor is paid on a cost-plus fixed fee or percentage of cost basis, but in no event more than the set maximum price. In some guaranteed maximum price contracts, a *savings clause* provides that if the project costs the owner less than the guaranteed maximum price, the owner and contractor are to split the difference between the costs and the guaranteed maximum price; typical splits are 50%/50% and 60%/40% (owner/contractor). For instance, assume that a contract specifies a guaranteed maximum price of $500,000 and the cost-plus basis turns out to be $400,000. Under a 50%/50% split, the contractor would be entitled to $450,000 for its work.[23] Guaranteed maximum price contracts give contractors great incentive to keep costs as reasonable as possible to ensure themselves as much profit as possible. They also encourage contractors to value engineer the project.

§1.23 Turnkey/Design-Build

Turnkey construction occurs when an owner contracts with one entity to both design and build the project. In some cases, the turnkey builder may even provide the financing. When working with a turnkey builder, the owner first outlines its needs and any particular specifications it requires. In some instances, the turnkey builder produces a preliminary design based on preliminary information provided by the owner and enters into negotiations with the owner to build the project. In other instances, the owner provides all specifications and asks for bids on a lump sum basis; design of the project is up to the builder so long as it meets the owner's specifications. Unlike other approaches to construction, detailed plans and specifications may not be available to the turnkey builder at the time of contracting. It must base its bid on what it understands the owner to want. The owner must choose a turnkey builder based on its initial design and perceived ability to produce the facility within the specified period of time at an agreed price.

The turnkey builder is responsible for every phase of the construction from final design through subcontracting, construction, finishing, and testing. A turnkey builder's duties are over when it has handed the owner the keys to a building which is fully capable of performing as anticipated and meeting the

---

[22] *See* §1.21.

[23] An example of a guaranteed maximum price contract may be found in Tougher Heating & Plumbing Co v State, 73 AD2d 732, 423 NYS2d 289 (1979).

owner's needs as specified. In New York, turnkey building has most often been used for low income housing under Housing and Urban Development (HUD) programs and for commercial or industrial construction—areas where aesthetics are not a major factor.

Turnkey or design-build contracts must be carefully constructed to be valid in New York. In *Charlesbois v JM Weller Associates*,[24] the Court of Appeals by a narrow four-to-three decision upheld the validity of design-build contracts if properly drafted. The contract called for J.M. Weller Associates, to design and construct a new warehouse for Charlebois. The contract, on a standard Associated General Contractors' form, specifically provided that the design services would be furnished by the contractor pursuant to a separate agreement between it and a licensed professional engineer who happened to be the contractor's president. Had the contract provided that the contractor would *perform* design services—considered to be architectural or engineering services which may not be performed without a license[25]—it would have been invalid, resulting in a forfeiture of payment for work performed and potential criminal liability. Because the contract provided that the design services would be performed by a *separately retained* licensed engineer, it was found to be valid. A contractor may not practice engineering or architecture; conversely, an engineer or architect may not engage in contracting while employing its professional suffix. Further, had the engineer rendered the design services as an employee of the contractor and not as a licensed individual or professional service corporation, the contract would have been void. Here, the distinction between the two was minimal as the engineer was also the president of the contractor, but the distinction was present.

The dissent in *Charlebois* vehemently objected to the majority's holding that the contract at issue, or, indeed, any design-build contract, was valid and stated that "in the absence of explicit statutory authorization permitting unlicensed business corporations to practice architecture and engineering through licensees, there is no reasoned basis for inferring that the Legislature intended to permit such practice."[26]

> **PRACTICE POINTER:**
>
> The following precautions are recommended when drafting or reviewing a design-build contract:
>
> (1) The design firm should be independent of the construction firm;
>
> (2) The contract should specifically refer to a separate agreement between the design firm and the construction firm;
>
> (3) A copy of the design contract should be attached as an exhibit to the design-build contract;

---

[24] 72 NY2d 587, 531 NE2d 1288, 535 NYS2d 356 (1988).
[25] NY Educ Law §§7202, 7203, 7209[4] (McKinney 1985).
[26] Charlebois, 72 NY2d at 598, 531 NE2d 1288, 535 NYS2d at 362.

(4) The design contract should specifically make the owner a third-party beneficiary, thus creating direct liability between the owner and designer;

(5) The basis of compensation should not be based on project cost but on some other measurement such as lump sum, hourly fee, or some combination thereof.

§1.24 Licenses and Codes

Construction in New York is governed by a large number of building codes at all levels of government—state, municipal, district, and county. Know what codes are applicable and by what standards the work will be judged. One project may be subject to more than one set of codes. For example, a contract to build a school in New York City might be governed by state, city, and school district codes.

Licenses are required for architects,[27] engineers,[28] electricians,[29] hoisting machine operators,[30] master plumbers,[31] welders,[32] asbestos handlers,[33] home improvement contractors,[34] crane operators,[35] blasters,[36] and land surveyors.[37]

Some Special Concerns

§1.25 Abnormally Dangerous Activities

In 1969, New York joined the great majority of jurisdictions which hold that one who engages in blasting is responsible for *any* injury to neighboring properties caused by the blasting, regardless of fault.[38] The Court of Appeals thus held that absolute liability applied to anyone who was involved in blasting operations. This has been extended to hold general contractors responsible for the blasting operations of their subcontractors[39] and engineers and architects liable

---

[27] NY Educ Law §7301 *et seq* (McKinney 1985).

[28] *Id* §7201 *et seq*.

[29] NY City Admin Code §27-3017 (1986).

[30] *Id* §26-166.

[31] *Id* §26-142.

[32] *Id* §26-154.

[33] NY Lab Law §902 (McKinney 1988 & Supp 1992).

[34] NY City Admin Code §20-387 (1991).

[35] NY Comp Codes R & Regs tit 12, §82.3.

[36] NY Gen Bus Law §482 (McKinney 1984).

[37] NY Educ Law §7204 (McKinney 1985).

[38] Spano v Perini Corp, 25 NY2d 11, 250 NE2d 31, 302 NYS2d 527 (1969). Before 1969, New York judged blasting cases by a negligence standard.

[39] Carmel Assocs v Turner Constr Co, 35 AD2d 157, 314 NYS2d 941 (1st Dept 1970).

for their contractors' dangerous activities.[40]

To determine whether an activity is an abnormally dangerous one, subjecting those involved to absolute liability, the test set forth in *Doundoulakis v Town of Hempstead*,[41] which is based on Restatement (Second) of Torts §§519 and 520, must be applied. The six criteria to consider are:

    1. The existence of a high degree of risk of some harm to the person, land, or chattels of others

    2. The likelihood that resulting harm will be great

    3. An inability to eliminate the risk through the exercise of reasonable care

    4. The extent to which the activity is uncommon

    5. The inappropriateness of the activity to the place where it is performed; and

    6. The extent to which its value to the community is outweighed by its danger

Thus, in New York, there is no list of activities, besides blasting, which are *per se* abnormally dangerous. New York courts apply a variable standard which takes not only the activity into account, but also its location and value. What is determined to be abnormally dangerous in one instance may not be in another.

§1.26 The 10-Foot Rule—Lateral Support

New York common law provides generally that those who excavate upon their own land are not responsible for damage to *structures* on neighboring properties so long as the excavations are done with ordinary care.[42] By code, New York City has amended this rule to apply only to excavations which do not exceed a depth of 10 feet.[43] If it is intended that the excavation exceed 10 feet,[44] the excavator has a responsibility to protect its neighbors' buildings *if* the excavator is given license by its neighbors to enter and inspect adjoining buildings and properties and perform work necessary to protect the buildings. If an owner refuses the excavator's request to enter, the duty to protect the buildings shifts to the owner who then automatically is granted a license to enter and inspect the excavation property.[45]

---

[40] Doundoulakis v Town of Hempstead, 42 NY2d 440, 368 NE2d 24, 398 NYS2d 401 (1977).

[41] *Id.*

[42] Knapp v Cirillo, 133 NYS2d 356 (Westchester 1954); Whitmore v Fago, 93 NYS2d 672 (Steuben 1949); 1 NY Jur *Adjoining Landowners* §16 (1967).

[43] NY City Admin Code §§C26-71.0(b), 1903.1(b)(1) & (2).

[44] Wear v Koehler, 168 AD 115, 153 NYS 773 (1st Dept 1915) (when discussing excavations more than 10 feet deep, it is the excavator's *intended* depth of excavation when it begins digging that is important, not the depth to which it actually digs).

[45] NY City Admin Code §§C26-71.0(b), C26-1903.1(b)(1).

If the excavation does not exceed 10 feet, the adjoining landowner has a right to enter and inspect the excavation so it may protect its property. If the excavation owner refuses to allow inspection, it will be liable for any injury to the adjoining landowner's buildings.[46] It is up to the person who has the right of inspection to request permission to enter; only upon *denial* of a request to inspect will the obligation to protect the adjoining property shift.[47] If license to inspect is denied and the excavator performs work on the adjacent building, perhaps to shore it up, the excavator may be liable in trespass to the owner.[48]

The lateral support rule does not apply to the ground itself. If a neighboring property's lateral support is removed, the person responsible is liable for damages to the ground.[49] The measure of damages in such a case is the lesser amount of (1) the cost of restoring the land and (2) the land's diminished market value.[50]

§1.27 Call Before You Dig

It is a basic rule of construction that before digging a hole of any size in the ground or street, a contractor must make sure that it is not going to strike buried cables, sewer lines, or natural gas pipes. It is not safe to rely on utility markers which are in place, since they might have been moved. In the past, contractors had to call each utility which might have underground lines within an excavation site. Now, however, *One Call* programs exist (or will soon) in all municipalities.[51]

Through a One Call system, a contractor is able to discover the location of all utilities simply by making one telephone call. The contractor calls the system center and tells the operator its proposed excavation location. The center inputs the location information into a central computer that determines which utilities are affected. The center then notifies those utilities affected, which, in turn, notify the contractor of line locations, or mark line locations at the site.

All of this takes time; the sooner a contractor starts the process, the sooner it will have its answer and be able to begin work. The state Industrial Code requires 2 to 10 working days' notice.[52]

For underground utilities information in the 5 boroughs of New York City, the One Call number is 1-800-272-4480. Each municipal area has its own number. Requests may also be sent in by telefacsimile (fax) in some areas, including New York City.

---

[46] *Id* §§C26-71.0(b), C26-1903.1(b)(2).

[47] Dorrity v Rapp, 72 NY 307 (1878).

[48] Ketcham v Newman, 141 NY 206 (1894).

[49] Dorrity v Rapp, 72 NY 307 (1878); Knapp v Cirillo, 133 NYS2d 356 (Westchester 1954).

[50] Knapp v Cirillo, 133 NYS2d 356 (Westchester 1954).

[51] The federal Natural Gas Pipeline Safety Act, 49 USC §§1671-1684 (1976), requires that all municipalities have *One Call* notification systems.

[52] NY State Indus Code Rule 53.

§1.28 Special Construction Problems in New York City

New York City's bureaucracy is legendary. Its many layers and departments can contribute to the confusion and paperwork that swamp every construction project in the permit and inspection stages. The Department of Buildings has the responsibility to enforce all laws that govern the construction, alteration, maintenance, use, safety, mechanical equipment, and inspection of buildings in New York City.[53] Thus, all applications for construction work must be submitted to the Department of Buildings at the appropriate borough office.

In addition to a building department permit, "[f]or virtually all construction projects it is necessary to obtain permits from other City agencies as well."[54] A contractor should consider obtaining permits from the following agencies, among others:

    1. Department of Environmental Protection (sewage disposal and connection, operation of certain types of equipment, incinerators, spray booths)

    2. Department of Transportation (temporary walkways and street closures, placement of building materials and equipment on streets and walkways, pavement work, tree planting, street openings, curb work, sidewalk work, canopies)

    3. Fire Department (blasting, fuel storage, tar kettles, electrical work, fire alarm and detection systems, torch operations, large air compressors)

    4. Department of Ports and Terminals (waterfront property development including dredging, filling, construction)

    5. Department of Health (private drainage systems, solid waste processing and disposal facilities)

    6. Department of General Services, Bureau of Electrical Control (electrical inspections, roadway or sidewalk transformer vault operations)

    7. Transit Authority (if building within 200 feet of an existing transit facility)

    8. Office of Economic Development, Department of Development (if work is within an urban renewal area); and

    9. Landmark Preservation Commission (if work is to be a designated landmark)

This list is not exhaustive.

Controlled Inspections

The New York City Administrative Code requires *controlled inspections* of certain structural construction methods, materials, and assemblies. A controlled inspection is defined as an inspection or testing

---

[53] NY City Charter §643 (1990).
[54] Department of General Services, City of New York, Permit Construction Handbook 11 (1985).

§1.28 SPECIAL PROBLEMS IN NEW YORK CITY   17

to verify compliance with code requirements. . . . [Which is] made and witnessed by or under the direct supervision of an architect or engineer retained by or under the direct supervision of the owner or lessee, who shall be, or who shall be acceptable to, the architect or engineer who prepared or supervised the preparation of the plans; . . . the [testing architect must make a] signed statement that the materials and its use or incorporation into the work comply with code requirements. . . .[55]

Among those matters subject to controlled inspections are: pilings;[56] excavations deeper than 10 feet which require underpinning, cofferdams, caissons, braced excavated surfaces, and other excavations which affect the support of adjacent properties and buildings;[57] certain concrete work;[58] and specified steel weldings and connections, aluminum weldings, laminated wood, plywood, and reinforced and unreinforced masonry.[59]

---

[55] NY City Admin Code §27-132(a) (1991).
[56] *Id* §27-721.
[57] *Id* §27-724.
[58] *Id* §27-586, tables 10-1, 10-2.
[59] *Id* §27-586, table 10-2.

Bidding and Contract Formation   2

§2.01	Introduction
§2.02	Bidding
§2.03	Bidding on Public Contracts
§2.04	—Lowest Responsible Bidder
§2.05	—Compliance with Bid Documents: Responsiveness
§2.06	—Prequalification of Bidders
§2.07	—Advertising Bids
§2.08	—Specifications
§2.09	—Wicks Law: Separate Specifications for Certain Types of Work
§2.10	—Accepting Bids
§2.11	—Illegal Bids and Contracts
§2.12	—Withdrawal of Bid
§2.13	—Awarding the Bid
§2.14	—Exceptions to Bidding Rules
§2.15	—Challenging an Award or Rejection of Bid
§2.16	—Public Agencies Exempt from Competitive Bidding Requirements
§2.17	Bidding on Private Contracts
§2.18	Mistakes
§2.19	—Excusable and Nonexcusable Unilateral Mistakes
§2.20	—Mutual Mistakes
§2.21	Subcontractor Bids
§2.22	Rejection of Bids
§2.23	Contract Formation
§2.24	—Offer and Acceptance
§2.25	—Mutual Assent/Intent to Be Bound
§2.26	—Certainty of Terms
§2.27	—Statute of Frauds

§2.28 —Illegal Contracts
§2.29 —Authority to Contract (Capacity)
§2.30 —Actual and Apparent Authority
§2.31 Letter of Intent
§2.32 Execution of Contract
§2.33 Negotiating Terms and Conditions
§2.34 Analysis of Boilerplate
§2.35 Evaluating Special Terms
§2.36 Evaluating Risks and Responsibilities
§2.37 —Pricing Risks
§2.38 Risk Allocation in the Best Interest of the Project
§2.39 —Types of Risk
§2.40 —Philosophies for Dealing with Risk
§2.41 —Options for Allocating Risk
§2.42 —Integrating Cost Effective Risk Allocation Language into Contract Documents and Contract Procedures
§2.43 —What Some Owners are Doing to Better Allocate Risks and Reduce Their Total Project Costs
§2.44 —The Role of Counsel: Advocate or Counselor?
§2.45 Subcontract Terms and Conditions
§2.46 Standard Contract Forms
§2.47 Interpreting the Contract
§2.48 —Use of Extrinsic Evidence/Parol Evidence Rule
§2.49 —Conflict Between Contract and Other Documents
§2.50 —Conflict Between Plans and Specifications
§2.51 Incorporation by Reference

§2.01 Introduction

Construction law involves the law of contracts. When one agrees to build a house, dig a trench, or pave a road for another in exchange for something of value, the agreement is a contract, whether oral or written. The general principles of contract law apply to construction contracts, including the requirements of offer and acceptance, consideration, meeting of the minds, and capacity, among others. These issues are not discussed in this text, except as they relate specifically to construction law; for example, the concept of offer and acceptance will be discussed because it is uniquely interpreted in construction law, due to the prevalent use of bidding, subcontractors, and the incorporation of subcontractor bids into general contractor bids. The issue of consideration, on the other hand, will not be discussed since it is not uniquely interpreted in construction law.

The beginning of most construction contracts is when an owner, either public or private, determines that something must be built, demolished, or remodeled. For purposes of an example, assume that the owner is a board of education and needs a new elementary school. The board will have specific and detailed plans and specifications drawn by its architects and engineers and set a budget for the school. Once the board has plans and specifications which fit its budget, it will advertise the project and ask for bids from contractors. The contractors will rely on the bid documents provided by the board in estimating the cost to build the school. When submitted, the bids are the contractors' offers to do the work required at the price specified in their bids. Generally, when the board accepts an offer, the winning contractor is bound to honor its bid, subject to fulfillment of specified conditions. Typically, a written contract is executed by the contractor and board a short time after the bid is accepted.

This chapter discusses the bidding process and applicable law, both statutory and common. It then discusses general concepts of construction contracts, including choice of terms, the statute of frauds, and other pertinent issues. Subcontracts are discussed in Chapter 3. Specific terms found in most construction contracts are discussed throughout the book in separate chapters and sections devoted to those terms. For example, Chapter 7 discusses delay clauses, including *no damage for delay* clauses and analysis of other contract terms which concern delay and case law which interprets those terms.

§2.02 Bidding

When choosing a contractor to construct something, most owners solicit price estimates and information from several contractors. Rare is the owner that calls one contractor and gives it the job with no comparison of price, experience, and expertise. Typically, an owner chooses its contractor through a bidding process. In New York, statutes require that most public works contracts be constructed by the lowest responsible, responsive bidder, chosen through competitive bidding. Private contracts, even if competitively bid, are not subject to the same limitations on freedom of contract, and, generally, may be awarded to whatever contractor the owner chooses, so long as the owner reserves the right to do so. Due to this difference, the law of public works bidding will be discussed separately from private bidding.

Bidding on any contract, whether public or private, must be done fairly and independently. A bid which sets its amount as some sum less, such as one dollar, than the lowest bid received is not definite or certain. Allowing such bids would defeat the purpose of competitive bidding. Thus, a bid which is dependent on another's bid for definition is invalid and unacceptable.[1]

---

[1] SSI Investors, Ltd v Korea Tungsten Mining Co, 80 AD2d 155, 438 NYS2d 96 (1981), *affd*, 55 NY2d 934, 434 NE2d 242, 449 NYS2d 173 (1982) (private sale of real property; bid was one dollar higher than highest bid received).

§2.03 Bidding on Public Contracts

Competitive bidding is required by statute on the great majority of public works contracts. General Municipal Law §103 provides that any public works contract, let by a municipality or division of a municipality, which exceeds $7,000 must be awarded to the lowest responsible bidder furnishing the required security following advertisement for sealed bids. What constitutes a municipality or division of a municipality is not always clear. For instance, included in the coverage of §103 are community colleges;[2] not included is the Port Authority of New York.[3] Similar statutes require the state and its subdivisions,[4] towns,[5] counties,[6] and public benefit corporations,[7] and the City University of New York,[8] among other entities, to award their contracts to the lowest responsible bidder following competitive bidding.

The Court of Appeals, in *Jered Contracting Corp v New York City Transit Authority*,[9] stated that competitive bidding statutes were enacted for the benefit of property holders and taxpayers, not bidders, to foster "honest competition in order to obtain the best work or supplies at the lowest possible price. In addition, the obvious purpose of such statutes is to guard against favoritism, improvidence, extravagance, fraud, and corruption."[10] In construing such statutes, a court's sole reference is to the public interest.

Generally, then, to be awarded a public contract, a bid must meet three criteria: it must be *low, responsible,* and *responsive*.

---

[2] DeBonis v Hudson Valley Community College, 55 AD2d 778, 389 NYS2d 647 (1976).

[3] New York City Charter, Inc v Fabber, 73 Misc 2d 859, 343 NYS2d 33 (NY), *affd*, 41 AD2d 821, 343 NYS2d 558 (1973).

[4] NY State Fin Law §135 (McKinney 1989 & Supp 1992).

[5] NY Town Law §122 (McKinney 1987).

[6] NY County Law §625 (McKinney 1991).

[7] Laws covering public benefit corporations which expressly require competitive bidding include: NY Pub Auth Law §2312 (McKinney 1981) (Auburn Industrial Development Authority); NY Pub Auth Law §1779 (McKinney 1981) (Salamanaca Hospital District).

Laws covering public benefit corporations which expressly require both competitive bidding and separate primes include: NY Pub Auth Law §2466(6)(a) & (b) (McKinney 1981) (New York State Sports Authority); NY Pub Auth Law §2620(1) & (2) (McKinney 1981 & Supp 1991) (New York State Regional Development Authority).

Laws covering public benefit corporations which expressly require bidding to be in conformity with NY State Fin Law §135 (McKinney 1989) (Wicks) include: NY Pub Auth Law §1974(4) (McKinney 1981) (Battery Park City Authority); NY Unconsol Law §9606 (McKinney 1974) (United Nations Development Corporation).

[8] NY Educ Law §6218 (McKinney 1988); Michael Mazzeo Elec Corp v Murphy, 137 Misc 2d 853, 522 NYS2d 798 (NY 1987).

[9] 22 NY2d 187, 239 NE2d 197, 292 NYS2d 98 (1968).

[10] *Id* at 192-93, 239 NE2d at 200, 292 NYS2d at 102.

§2.04 —Lowest Responsible Bidder

A public contract governed by a competitive bidding statute must be awarded to the *lowest responsible bidder,* not the lowest bidder. This requirement helps to ensure that contracts are awarded only to those contractors the public owner believes to be capable of satisfactorily performing the work within the specified time for the agreed-upon price. Despite the protection afforded a public owner through required payment and performance bonds, the potential for complications, delay, and poor workmanship by an unqualified or not responsible contractor may offset any savings anticipated by accepting such a contractor, even if a low bidder.

A *lowest responsible bidder* has been defined as a bidder that is pecuniarily responsible, morally worthy, and skilled, and possesses judgment, integrity, and sufficient financial resources;[11] is "accountable or reliable";[12] and has the ability to perform the contract according to its terms.[13]

The issue of responsibility is not whether one bidder is more qualified than another. The issue is whether the lowest bidder is responsible. Thus, where the lowest bidder has never failed to complete any work awarded and never defaulted on any contract, the public owner cannot reject it as not responsible without an investigation and hearing.[14] A bidder may not be rejected as not responsible due to its nonunion status.[15]

A bidder was found to be not responsible when it was a front for an individual and his other construction companies whose public construction activities had brought them into "frequent conflict with the criminal law and its enforcement agencies."[16] Similarly, where a bidder was under indictment for grand larceny in an alleged theft of a state agency's property in the course of public contract work, the bidder was found to be not responsible on a contract bid for that same state agency.[17]

In a case where the references supplied by a bidder did not show that it was responsible—one reference was on a contract completed 10 years earlier and the other reference, when contacted, said that the bidder submitted unsubstantiated and high claims for extras and did substandard work—it was held that the public owner could determine that it was not a responsible bidder and reject

---

[11] Picone v City of NY, 176 Misc 967, 29 NYS2d 539 (NY 1941).

[12] Meyer v Board of Educ, 31 Misc 2d 407, 221 NYS2d 500 (Nassau 1961).

[13] Paccione v Board of Educ, 20 Misc 2d 896, 195 NYS2d 593 (NY 1959).

[14] Seacoast Constr Corp v Lockport Urban Renewal Agency, 72 Misc 2d 372, 339 NYS2d 188 (Erie 1972).

[15] M. Crist, Inc v State Office of Gen Servs, 42 AD2d 481, 349 NYS2d 191 (1973); Long Island Signal Corp v County of Nassau, 51 Misc 2d 320, 273 NYS2d 188 (Nassau 1966). *Contra* Paccione v Board of Educ, 20 Misc 2d 896, 195 NYS2d 593 (NY 1959).

[16] Picone v City of NY, 176 Misc 967, 29 NYS2d 539, 541 (NY 1941).

[17] Zara Contracting Co v Cohen, 23 AD2d 718, 257 NYS2d 118 (1965); *see also* Konski Engrs, PC v Levitt, 69 AD2d 940, 415 NYS2d 509 (3d Dept 1979), *cert denied,* 449 US 840, *affd,* 49 NY2d 850, 404 NE2d 1337, 427 NYS2d 796 (1980); Lord Elec Co v Litke, 122 Misc 2d 112, 469 NYS2d 846 (NY 1983).

its otherwise low bid.[18] Similarly, a public owner had the right to deem a low bidder not responsible where the bidder failed to reveal past penalty assessments on its bid questionnaire and, in past dealings with the bidder, the public owner had encountered delays, lack of cooperation between the bidder and the owner's personnel, and poor work quality.[19]

A public owner's determination that a bidder is not responsible may be based on its evaluation of the bidder's skill, judgment, and integrity and may be the result of an owner's investigation into the bidder's background.[20] So long as the owner's determination is not arbitrary, capricious, or unreasonable, its decision will not be disturbed.[21] The bidder has the burden of showing that it is responsible.[22]

§2.05 —Compliance with Bid Documents: Responsiveness

A bidder may submit the lowest bid, be responsible, and still not win the job if its bid is not *responsive*—i.e., if it does not comply with bid instructions. Strict compliance with bid instructions is always wise and usually necessary.

A public owner may not waive a material noncompliance with a bid specification.[23] The reason for this rule is that waiver of a material specification would give the bidder an unfair advantage, lessens public confidence in the bidding process, may discourage future competitive bidding, and offers the opportunity for manipulation and evasion of bidding statutes.[24] If a bidder fails to include essential information in its bid, it may not later supply that information after the opening of the bids.[25]

A technical noncompliance or mere irregularity may be waived if the waiver does not give the bidder a substantial competitive edge and it is in the best interests of the public owner to do so.[26] No matter how small or trivial the noncompliance, the choice to waive compliance is solely the owner's; it may choose to waive or not to waive noncompliance as it sees fit.[27] A determination that

---

[18] Meyer v Board of Educ, 31 Misc 2d 407, 221 NYS2d 500 (Nassau 1961).

[19] JN Futia v State Office of Gen Servs, 39 AD2d 136, 332 NYS2d 261 (1972).

[20] *Id.*

[21] Meyer v Board of Educ, 31 Misc 2d 407, 221 NYS2d 500 (Nassau 1961).

[22] *Id.*

[23] LeCesse Bros Contracting v Town Bd, 62 AD2d 28, 403 NYS2d 950 (1978), *affd,* 46 NY2d 960, 388 NE2d 737, 415 NYS2d 413 (1979).

[24] *Id.*

[25] *Id.*

[26] Willets Point Contracting Corp v Town Bd, 141 AD2d 735, 529 NYS2d 592, *appeal denied,* 72 NY2d 810, 534 NYS2d 938 (1988).

[27] *In re* CK Rehner, Inc, 106 AD2d 268, 483 NYS2d 1 (1984); Abele Tractor & Equip Co v Department of Pub Works, 74 AD2d 980, 426 NYS2d 186 (1980); LaBarge Bros Co v Town of Cicero, 104 Misc 2d 764, 429 NYS2d 140 (Onondaga 1979); Stage v Whitehouse, 43 Misc 2d 703, 252 NYS2d 142 (Broome 1964).

a noncompliance is not material is within the owner's discretion and must be in the best interests of the public owner and not arbitrary or capricious.[28] Matters which have been upheld as technical noncompliance, and, thus, which may be waived, include failure to include a certificate of noncollusion,[29] failure to supply bid security in the form required by specifications,[30] and substitution of equipment.[31]

§2.06 —Prequalification of Bidders

Some public owners maintain *Bidders' Lists* which are used to give advance notice to prequalified (already deemed responsible) bidders of upcoming contracts for improvements and supplies. These lists do not abrogate the owner's duty to advertise the contracts or to consider bids from parties not included on the list. Generally, these lists are legal, so long as they do not discourage bidding from parties not included on the lists or result in those not listed having an insufficient opportunity to bid.[32]

A party may not be removed from a Bidders' List arbitrarily.[33]

§2.07 —Advertising Bids

The competitive bidding statutes set forth procedures for advertising for bids. General Municipal Law §103, for example, requires that advertisements

---

[28] LeCesse Bros Contracting v Egan, 89 AD2d 640, 453 NYS2d 82 (1982).

[29] AJ Beaudette Constr Co v City of Syracuse, 62 Misc 2d 564, 309 NYS2d 517 (Onondaga), *affd*, 313 NYS2d 356 (App Div 1970) (bidder executed noncollusion certificate immediately upon being notified of its failure to include with its bid); Consolidated Sheet Metal Works, Inc v Board of Educ, 62 Misc 2d 445, 308 NYS2d 773 (Jefferson 1970) (bidder asked to furnish required noncollusion certificate after it submitted its bid but before board considered or acted upon the bids).

[30] LeCesse Bros Contracting v Egan, 89 AD2d 640, 453 NYS2d 82 (1982) (bidder submitted bid bond instead of certified check specified; bidder allowed to cure error by submission of check); Frank Nowak Constr Co v County of Suffolk, 233 NYS2d 627 (Suffolk 1962). Remember that an agency does not have to waive an irregularity. Cases which uphold an agency's right to reject a bid based on a failure to include bid security in the form specified include Stage v Whitehouse, 43 Misc 2d 703, 252 NYS2d 142 (Broome 1964) and LaBarge Bros Co v Town of Cicero, 104 Misc 2d 764, 429 NYS2d 140 (Onondaga 1979) (each bidder submitted bid bonds instead of the cash or certified check specified).

[31] DiNatale Management Co v Finney, 46 AD2d 827, 361 NYS2d 95 (1974) (where manufacturer's literature described backhoe as unable to meet bid performance specifications but low bidder demonstrated that the backhoe could perform to specifications, the court held that there was no abuse of discretion by the agency in awarding the contract to the bidder); *but see* Abele Tractor & Equip Co v Department of Pub Works, 74 AD2d 980, 426 NYS2d 186 (1980) (agency need not consider equipment which does not meet specifications according to manufacturer's information and need not agree to bidder's offer of a trial period).

[32] Orange Front Paint Supply, Inc v Scaramuccia, 59 AD2d 894, 399 NYS2d 52 (1977).

[33] *Id.*

for bids be published in the official newspaper(s) designated for bidding advertisements. An advertisement must state when and where all bids received will be publicly opened and read. The advertisement must be published at least five days before the date designated for the opening and reading of bids.[34] The statutory procedures must be complied with strictly. Compliance with federal advertising provisions on a federally assisted state project is not compliance with state and local advertising requirements; both must be followed.[35] Noncompliance is fatal as any contract awarded in violation of the statute is illegal and void,[36] even where the noncompliance is due entirely to the public owner's error and the winning bidder is unaware of the noncompliance.[37]

The often harsh results of this rule can be seen in the case of *Prosper Contracting Co v Board of Education*.[38] There, the plaintiff was awarded the contract and instructed to proceed immediately. Eight days later, after the plaintiff had done a substantial amount of work, the board rescinded the award, stating that the contract had been advertised improperly. The court held that because the board did not advertise the contract properly, it had no capacity to contract and denied relief to the plaintiff on its implied contract claim, despite the fact that the court recognized the equities of the plaintiff's claim. The court suggested that the plaintiff pursue its claim on equitable grounds through the New York City Administrative Code.[39]

The advertisement must be reasonable; strict compliance with the statute is not always enough. Where, for example, 10 days were given to bid on a complex contract which had 37 single-spaced pages of specifications, the court held that the contract awarded was void. The court found that the 10-day period was not sufficient for a thorough review of the specifications and formulation of bids by any contractor except the one which prepared the specifications.[40]

§2.08 —Specifications

Parties wishing to bid on a contract must base their bids on the bid documents. These documents include not only details about the job itself, such as required supplies, measure of performance, plans and drawings, contract

---

[34] NY Town Law §122 (McKinney 1987) incorporates NY Gen Mun Law §103 (McKinney 1986 & Supp 1992) into town law for town letting of public contracts.

[35] Marvec-All State, Inc v Purcell, 110 Misc 2d 67, 441 NYS2d 618 (Nassau 1981), *affd*, 87 AD2d 593, 450 NYS2d 411 (1982).

[36] *Id*.

[37] Prosper Contracting Co v Board of Educ, 73 Misc 2d 280, 341 NYS2d 196 (App Term 1973), *affd*, 43 AD2d 823, 351 NYS2d 402 (1974).

[38] *Id*.

[39] *Id; see also* Gerzof v Sweeney, 16 NY2d 206, 211 NE2d 826, 264 NYS2d 376 (1965); ST Grand, Inc v City of NY, 32 NY2d 300, 298 NE2d 105, 344 NYS2d 938 (1973); *but see* Gerzof v Sweeney, 22 NY2d 297, 239 NE2d 521, 292 NYS2d 640 (1968) (winner of illegal, completed contract allowed to recover part of its contract price).

[40] McArdle v Board of Estimate, 74 Misc 2d 1014, 347 NYS2d 349 (Westchester 1973), *affd*, 357 NYS2d 1009 (App Div 1974).

terms, and time frame, but also other matters required of the bidder, including bonds, financial information, identification of subcontractors and suppliers, experience questionnaires, and bid security. Bid requirements may be set forth in the bid information, statutes and codes,[41] local rules, etc.

The specifications form the basis of the contract and may later be used to support or defend against a claim for extras. For example, in a case where the specifications on which the contractor bid called for plasterboard, the contractor was entitled to a claim for extras when the city required it to use a more costly lath and plaster method instead, despite a general contract provision requiring the contractor to comply with state rules and regulations.[42] The city was held responsible for the extra charges since it drafted the specifications which did not comply with state law. The contractor was not required to know or research the various laws and building codes and compare them to the specifications; it could rely on the specifications in formulating its bid and in performing the contract.

The specifications should be complied with closely; any failure to comply may result in rejection of the bid. If the written specifications are unclear, ask the owner for written clarification, but do not rely on the speculation of an owner's employee as to what they mean. Ask for a firm clarification from a person with knowledge and authority; the owner's engineer or the party that drafted the specifications may be a good source, unless it also is bidding on the job. Get the clarification in writing. Do not rely on verbal advice from the owner if that advice is in conflict with the written specifications or applicable statutes.[43] The Information for Bidders frequently sets forth the procedures for obtaining clarification. That procedure should be followed; otherwise the owner may not be bound by the clarification.

Once a public bid has been advertised, its specifications can be modified only by notifying all bidders of the change prior to receipt of the bids; a public owner cannot accept bids and recompute them using new, undisclosed specifications.[44] If new specifications are required and even one bid has been received, the owner's choice is to award the contract pursuant to the advertised specifications or reject all bids and readvertise the job with the new specifications.[45] Further, an owner may not make major changes in or additions to an existing

---

[41] For example, see NY Pub Auth Law (McKinney Supp 1992), New York City School Construction Authority Act §1735(3), which requires general contract bidders to submit a sealed list of specified subcontractors with their bids.

[42] Green v City of NY, 283 AD 485, 128 NYS2d 715 (1954).

[43] *See* Marchionne v New York State Dept of Transp, 88 AD2d 655, 450 NYS2d 529 (1982), in which the bidder, relying on verbal advice from an agency employee, submitted one bid deposit although it was bidding on several gas station leases, despite the fact that the specifications and relevant statutes required separate bid deposits for each lease bid.

[44] Progressive Dietary Consultants, Inc v Wyoming County, 90 AD2d 214, 457 NYS2d 159 (1982).

[45] *Id;* Blandford Land Clearing Corp v Davidson, 62 AD2d 1007, 403 NYS2d 775 (1978).

contract without readvertising the changes or additions.[46] Of course, changes which are incidental to the original contract, concern details, or are minor are not subject to rebidding. But where a change or an addition varies so much from the original plan or is of such importance that it constitutes a new undertaking, competitive bidding is necessary.[47] The standard is whether the changes alter the essential identity or purpose of the original contract. If they do, the changes or additions must be competitively bid.

Legality of Specifications

Specifications must be definite and certain enough to foster real competitive bidding. They must afford all interested parties an equal opportunity to bid on the contract offered. They may not be designed to shut out or reduce true competition. For instance, generally, they may not be written in such a way that only one contractor or manufacturer may meet them or such that they eliminate a specific contractor from bidding.

Some specifications which have been found invalid include specifications which establish preconditions to the award of a contract—such as that the contractor have an apprenticeship training program[48]—and specifications which limit potential bidders to those whose facilities are located within a specified county[49] or zoning classification. In *Edenwald Contracting Co v City of New York*,[50] a specification was found invalid which eliminated a bidder based on the zoning of its location. In *Edenwald*, the bidder was an asphalt plant which legally operated at night. Significant numbers of neighbors complained to the city about its night operations. The city, in letting several paving contracts, required night operations but specified that only plants located in areas with a certain zoning designation could bid on the contracts. The bidder was not located in an area with the specified zoning, but was legally operating in full compliance with the zoning applicable to its area. The court found that while eliminating the bidder from night jobs might serve the public good, doing so was not within the public interest protected by competitive bidding statutes; the court found the specification to be invalid.

Specifications which are indefinite are invalid. Any contract awarded pursuant to indefinite specifications will be voided and must be rebid. For instance, specifications stating that a contract is for the "disposal of all refuse" from Brooklyn for five years but leaving many required tasks and details to future determination or the discretion of public officials are invalid. The tendency

---

[46] Albert Elia Bldg Co v New York State Urban Dev Corp, 54 AD2d 337, 388 NYS2d 462 (4th Dept 1976).

[47] *Id.*

[48] Associated Builders & Contractors, Inc v City of Rochester, 67 NY2d 854, 492 NE2d 781, 501 NYS2d 653 (1986). Preconditions to bidding are valid only if the precondition was expressly authorized by statute or local law prior to September 1, 1953. See NY Gen Mun Law §103 (McKinney 1986 & Supp 1992).

[49] Warren Bros Co v Craner, 30 AD2d 437, 293 NYS2d 763 (1968).

[50] 86 Misc 2d 711, 384 NYS2d 338 (NY 1974), *affd*, 47 AD2d 610, 366 NYS2d 363 (1975).

of such indefinite specifications is to restrict competition.[51] Few contractors would wish to bid without knowing whether such a contract includes collection and removal of refuse, how often refuse is to disposed of, permitted methods of disposal, and so forth. The only likely bidders on such a contract are those that are already familiar with the contract offered or those that have an inside source of information.

Specified Materials

Bid specifications often describe required equipment as, for example, "Brand X Crane Model No. 1." Such specifications are legal so long as the words "or equal" follow the model designation and the public owner intends to consider equivalents.[52] An alternate product is considered "equal" and, therefore, acceptable if it possesses all the "salient characteristics" of the specified brand.[53] In other words, the product must possess the "physical properties and performance capabilities that reasonably meet the public project owner's minimum needs for the project."[54] Whether the product meets this standard, however, is often a matter of opinion.[55]

Preclusion of equivalent equipment or materials is allowed only when two-thirds of the awarding board votes to adopt a resolution requiring a specific manufacturer and model based upon its findings that due to reasons of "efficiency or economy, there is need for standardization."[56] The resolution must contain a full explanation of the reasons for its adoption. This two-thirds rule helps to ensure that the owner makes a specific product selection fairly and through exercise of its judgment.[57]

While specifications are not illegal merely because they tend to favor one manufacturer over another, equipment specifications may not be drawn to ensure award of the contract to a particular manufacturer.[58] For instance, specifications which required a 5,000-kilowatt generator of a distinctive design and that the bidder have successfully constructed at least three similar units were found illegal where it was known by the public owner that only one bidder could meet the specifications. The court found that without a clear showing that the specifications were essential to the public interest, they would be illegal. No

---

[51] Brooklyn Ash Removal Co v O'Brien, 238 AD 647, 265 NYS 504 (1933).

[52] *See* NY Gen Mun Law §103(5) (McKinney 1986 & Supp 1992); General Bldg Contractors, Inc v City of Syracuse, 40 AD2d 584, 334 NYS2d 730 (1972) *modified on other grounds*, 32 NY2d 780, 298 NE2d 122, 344 NYS2d 961 (1973); Hodge & Hammond, Inc v Burns, 23 Misc 2d 318, 202 NYS2d 133 (Nassau 1960).

[53] Bruce M. Jervis & Paul Levin, Construction Law Principles and Practice 25 (McGraw-Hill, Inc Book Co 1988).

[54] *Id.*

[55] *Id.*

[56] NY Gen Mun Law §103(5) (McKinney 1986 & Supp 1992).

[57] Hodge & Hammond, Inc v Burns, 23 Misc 2d 318, 202 NYS2d 133 (Nassau 1960).

[58] Gerzof v Sweeney, 16 NY2d 206, 211 NE2d 826, 264 NYS2d 376 (1965).

justification was provided or could be found for requiring the distinctive design.[59]

§2.09 —Wicks Law: Separate Specifications for Certain Types of Work

General Municipal Law §101 and State Finance Law §135, called the *Wicks Law*,[60] provide that when the entire cost of contract work for the erection, construction, reconstruction, or alteration of a building exceeds $50,000, separate specifications must be prepared for the plumbing and gas fitting; steam heating, hot water heating, ventilating, and air conditioning apparatus; and electrical wiring and standard illuminating fixtures; the separate specifications are required in order that they may be separately and independently bid. The purported reason for these statutes is to ensure expertise in these critical areas, rather than leaving the selection to the general contractor, as the ultimate risk of a poor or delayed performance is borne by the public owner.[61]

The Wicks Law applies whenever any one of the three specified types of work is present.[62] The statutes apply only if estimates of cost show that the project will exceed $50,000; they do not apply, and an owner will not be required to readvertise and bid a contract, where bona fide estimates of cost before bidding indicate a total of less than $50,000.[63]

Although the courts are not in complete agreement regarding the applicability of the Wicks Law to various projects, the more reasoned view, based upon

---

[59] *Id; see also* Resco Equip & Supply Co v City Council, 34 AD2d 1088, 313 NYS2d 74 (1970).

[60] Other statutes also incorporate Wicks. These statutes include: NY Gen Mun Law §120-w (McKinney 1986), which governs contracts and agreements for solid waste management, collection, and disposal; NY Unconsol Law §6261 (McKinney 1979), which governs construction contracts for the New York State Urban Development Corp; NY Pub Hous Law §151-a (McKinney 1989), which governs construction contracts in connection with housing projects; NY Pub Auth Law §2722 (McKinney Supplementary Pamphlet 1992), which governs contracts for the Development Authority of North County; NY Pub Auth Law §2768 (McKinney Supplementary Pamphlet 1992), which governs contracts for the Monroe County Airport Authority; NY Pub Auth Law §1045-i (McKinney Supplementary Pamphlet 1992), which governs the construction of water projects for the New York Municipal Water Finance Authority; NY Pub Auth Law §1048-i (McKinney Supplementary Pamphlet 1992), governs water projects for the Buffalo Municipal Water Finance Authority; NY Educ Law §458 (McKinney 1988) which governs construction contracts for the Yonkers Construction Fund.

[61] Nager Elec Co v State Office of Gen Servs, 56 Misc 2d 975, 290 NYS2d 943 (Albany 1967), *affd*, 30 AD2d 626, 290 NYS2d 947, *appeal denied*, 22 NY2d 645, 295 NYS2d 1026 (1968). This is the rationale for the Wicks Law given in the cases. Recent attempts to abolish the Wicks Law have been strenuously resisted by mechanical contractors because of their strong desire *not* to work for general contractors. *See School Subs Decry "Abuse"*, Engineering News Record, Mar 11, 1991, at 11.

[62] AS Reynolds Elec Co v Board of Educ, 46 Misc 2d 140, 259 NYS2d 503 (Queens 1965).

[63] VC Vitanza Sons v Murray, 90 Misc 2d 873, 396 NYS2d 305 (Albany 1977).

the wording of the statutes, is that these statutes apply only to buildings. They should not, for example, apply to contracts for site preparation work required for redevelopment of an area where the contract is for a sewage system to benefit the entire area, not solely for the benefit of buildings included in the redevelopment.[64]

Bid specifications that require the general contract bidder to coordinate and schedule all work on the job, including that of the required separate prime contracts, violate the Wicks Law and are illegal. The responsibility and authority for supervision and coordination of the separate prime contracts are the public owner's, although the owner may contract these responsibilities to another party which is not a prime contractor on the job.[65]

Electrical and mechanical contractors and the labor unions for these groups are the main proponents of the Wicks Law. They contend that the law results in more competition and lower overall bids for public work. On the other hand, general contractors argue that the Wicks Law creates project administration and coordination problems most public bodies are unable to handle, leading to delays and increased costs. Many public officials agree with the general contractors and add that laws like the Wicks Law require the harsh one-sided language found in many public construction contracts, such as *no damage for delay* clauses.

All efforts to repeal the Wicks Law since it was enacted in 1912 have failed, due in large part to the organized and effective lobbying of mechanical and electrical contractors and trade unions. In 1988, however, the New York City School Construction Authority was created and was specifically exempted from compliance with the Wicks Law for five years.[66] Apparently, the legislature intends to study the authority's experience and decide whether to repeal Wicks outright, as the general contractors and public officials hope, or to leave it in place, as electrical and mechanical contractors hope.

§2.10 —Accepting Bids

Awarding agencies may accept bids up to the time set forth in the bid advertisement. They may not accept or consider bids submitted late, even if only

---

[64] Plumbing Contractors Assoc v City of Buffalo, 70 Misc 2d 412, 334 NYS2d 9 (Erie 1972); *cf* AS Reynolds Elec Co v Board of Educ, 46 Misc 2d 140, 259 NYS2d 503 (Queens 1965) (court held that *building* as used in NY Gen Mun Law §101 (McKinney 1986) included construction of any kind and required separate specifications for work which included the demolition and removal of existing bleachers, erection of new bleachers, construction of toilet and storage facilities under the bleachers, alteration of an existing locker room and handball court, and construction of a football field and athletic track).

[65] General Bldg Contractors, Inc v City of Syracuse, 40 AD2d 584, 334 NYS2d 730 (1972) *modified on other grounds,* 32 NY2d 780, 298 NE2d 122, 344 NYS2d 961 (1973), *cf* JA Valenti Elec Co v Board of Educ, 56 AD2d 884, 392 NYS2d 482 (1977).

[66] NY Pub Auth Law §1725 *et seq* (McKinney Supp 1992).

two or three minutes late.[67] Bids may be amended after they are accepted if the amendment or addition is minor, such as the substitution of bid security or the furnishing of a certificate of noncollusion.[68]

§2.11 —Illegal Bids and Contracts

When a public contract has been awarded in violation of the competitive bidding statutes, the contract is null and void.[69] The contractor may not recover for its work or materials upon any theory, whether based in contract or quantum meruit,[70] regardless of the contractor's innocence or the equities of its claim[71] and the fact that the owner has received the benefits of the contract.[72] Further, the public owner may recover any moneys paid to the contractor pursuant to the contract.[73] The application of these harsh remedies is not dependent upon the amount of money involved.[74]

The general rule of complete forfeiture is necessary to deter illegal contracts and only rarely is not followed. For instance, in *ST Grand v City of New York*,[75] the contractor was convicted of a bribery scheme in relation to an award of an "emergency contract." The Court of Appeals ruled that the contractor was not entitled to payment of the $148,000 balance owed on the completed contract and that the city could recover the $689,000 it had already paid the bidder. Similarly, in *D'Angelo v Cole*,[76] a paving contract was found to be void due to noncompliance with the bidding statutes and the municipality was entitled to recover the $8,374.49 it had paid the contractor, even though performance was complete and return of the labor and materials impossible.

In a rare break with the complete forfeiture rule, recovery was allowed to the contractor in the case of *Gerzof v Sweeney*.[77] In *Gerzof*, a village advertised for bids for a 3,500-kilowatt generator. The village commission in charge of

---

[67] Wilton Coach Co v Central High School Dist No 3, 36 Misc 2d 637, 232 NYS2d 876 (Nassau 1962).

[68] See §2.05 on compliance with bid documents.

[69] Resco Equip & Supply Corp v City Council, 34 AD2d 1088, 313 NYS2d 74 (1970).

[70] Jered Contracting Corp v New York City Transit Auth, 22 NY2d 187, 239 NE2d 197, 292 NYS2d 98 (1968).

[71] Prosper Contracting Co v Board of Educ, 73 Misc 2d 280, 341 NYS2d 196 (App Term 1973), *affd*, 43 AD2d 823, 351 NYS2d 402 (1974).

[72] Albany Supply & Equip Co v City of Cohoes, 47 Misc 2d 312, 262 NYS2d 603 (Albany 1965), *affd*, 25 AD2d 700, 268 NYS2d 42, *affd*, 18 NY2d 968, 224 NE2d 716, 278 NYS2d 207 (1966).

[73] D'Angelo v Cole, 67 NY2d 65, 490 NE2d 819, 499 NYS2d 900 (1986).

[74] Gerzof v Sweeney, 16 NY2d 206, 211 NE2d 826, 264 NYS2d 376 (1965); ST Grand, Inc v City of NY, 32 NY2d 300, 298 NE2d 105, 344 NYS2d 938 (1973).

[75] 32 NY2d 300, 298 NE2d 105, 344 NYS2d 938 (1973).

[76] 67 NY2d 65, 490 NE2d 819, 499 NYS2d 900 (1986).

[77] 22 NY2d 297, 239 NE2d 521, 292 NYS2d 640 (1968). A detailed recitation of the facts of the case is found in Gerzof v Sweeney, 16 NY2d 206, 211 NE2d 826, 264 NYS2d 376 (1965).

the project recommended accepting the low bidder. Due to election of a new mayor, however, award of the contract was delayed until the project could be reviewed by the new administration. The new mayor replaced the entire commission and installed a new one, which chose a higher bidder and awarded it the contract. The plaintiff, the replaced low bidder, brought suit and the court ordered the high bidder's contract set aside and the contract awarded "as required by law." The mayor, however, did not award the contract to the plaintiff; rather, he asked the commission for new specifications, which were prepared with the assistance of the higher bidder. The new specifications, for a 5,000-kilowatt generator, were drafted in such a way that only one manufacturer, the higher bidder, could qualify. In fact, the only manufacturer to bid on the new specifications was the higher bidder.

The Court of Appeals found that the new specifications and the resulting contract were illegal because they were not in the public interest but were devised solely to ensure award of the contract to one particular manufacturer. The Court of Appeals, in reciting the general rule of complete forfeiture, chose not to apply it in this case due to the large sum involved (although the court had held in an earlier decision in the same case that the amount of money involved was irrelevant[78]); the fact that the generator was needed by the village and not returnable to the bidder without significant damage to the village; the forfeiture which would result to the bidder; and the unjust enrichment of the village. The village recovered the difference between the cost of the 5,000-kilowatt generator and the low bid on the 3,500-kilowatt generator plus the increased costs borne by the village in installing the larger generator. The bidder was required to return to the village $178,636 of the contract total of $757,625.

Once a contract is shown to have been awarded in violation of the bidding statutes, any taxpayer, including a bidder, is entitled to have the contract set aside; actual injury is irrelevant.[79]

§2.12 —Withdrawal of Bid

If a public contract has not been awarded within 45 days of a public owner's receipt of bids, a bidder may withdraw its bid for whatever reason it chooses, without penalty.[80] The 45-day period is measured from the date the bids are opened by the owner, not from the date the bidder submits its bid. In addition, a bidder may withdraw its bid if it contains an excusable mistake.[81]

---

[78] Gerzof v Sweeney, 16 NY2d 206, 211 NE2d 826, 264 NYS2d 376 (1965).

[79] *Id.*

[80] NY Gen Mun Law §105 (McKinney 1986 & Supp 1992); NY State Fin Law §140 (McKinney 1989); People v John W. Rouse Constr Corp, 26 AD2d 405, 274 NYS2d 981 (1966).

[81] See **§2.19** for a discussion on "Excusable Mistakes."

Failure to withdraw or modify a bid prior to award of the contract will bind a bidder to its bid,[82] except in the case of an excusable and undiscovered mistake. A successful bidder cannot wait past the 45-day period to execute the awarded contract and withdraw its bid upon a claim of right to withdraw due to the lapse of time; the bidder must execute and perform the contract or forfeit its bid security.[83]

> **PRACTICE POINTER:**
>
> When withdrawing a bid, notify the owner in writing of your intent to withdraw the bid and set forth the reason for the withdrawal.

§2.13 —Awarding the Bid

The owner awards the bid or contract to the bidder that has been determined to be the *lowest responsible bidder*. Award of the bid does not necessarily mean that a contract will result between the owner and the bidder; the award binds only the bidder, not the owner. For example, if the contractor awarded the bid fails to meet a condition precedent to contract, such as obtaining a performance bond, the public owner may rescind the award of the bid.[84] Similarly, if the public owner fails to meet a condition precedent, such as providing a certification of available funds by its comptroller, no contract will result.[85] Further, if a public owner has no intent to be bound until a binding formal agreement is executed, it is not bound until all documents and agreements are signed and may reconsider its award of the contract.[86] This rule makes sense because often the complete determination of a bidder's responsibility cannot be made until after a bid has been qualified as lowest and bids often are accepted conditionally.[87]

Once a bidder has been determined to be the lowest responsible bidder, the public owner may seek to reduce the low bid through postbid negotiations with that bidder.[88] It may not ease contract specifications, make changes which materially vary from the advertised specifications,[89] or negotiate with any bidder other than the lowest responsible bidder. The public owner may not attempt

---

[82] Sinram-Marnis Oil Co v City of NY, 74 NY2d 13, 544 NYS2d 119, 542 NE2d 337 (1989).

[83] G&R Elec Contractors, Inc v Egan, 85 AD2d 191, 448 NYS2d 850 (3d Dept), *affd*, 57 NY2d 721, 440 NE2d 795, 454 NYS2d 710 (1982).

[84] City of New York v United States Fidelity & Guar Co, 119 Misc 2d 725, 464 NYS2d 659 (NY 1983).

[85] Kooleraire Serv & Installation Corp v Board of Educ, 28 NY2d 101, 268 NE2d 782, 320 NYS2d 46 (1971).

[86] James H. Merritt Plumbing, Inc v City of NY, 55 AD2d 552, 390 NYS2d 65 (1976).

[87] Tufaro Transit Co v Board of Educ, 79 AD2d 376, 436 NYS2d 886 (1981).

[88] Fischbach & Moore, Inc v New York City Transit Auth, 79 AD2d 14, 435 NYS2d 984 (1981).

[89] LeCesse Bros Contracting v Town Bd, 62 AD2d 28, 403 NYS2d 950 (1978), *affd*, 46 NY2d 960, 388 NE2d 737, 415 NYS2d 413 (1979).

34 BIDDING & CONTRACT FORMATION

to coerce a bidder to make unfair and unwarranted concessions. Permissible postbid negotiations include, but are not limited to, the elimination of duplicative costs, the negotiation of contract terms, such as the addition of liquidated damages, and the repricing of supplies, such as copper, which were priced unusually high at the time of bid preparation and significantly lower at the time of award.[90] Such postbid negotiations benefit the public interest by reducing the total cost of the project, so long as there is no departure from the original specifications and no significant concessions are made to the bidder.[91]

A contract awarded on a bid which, although lowest, exceeds the appropriation for the project is invalid; a subsequent appropriation cannot cure the invalidity.[92] If all responsible bids exceed the project appropriation, the public owner must readvertise for new bids at either the original or the subsequent appropriation amount.

A court cannot compel an owner to award a contract to a particular bidder where the bid specifications give the owner the right to reject any and all bids.[93]

§2.14 —Exceptions to Bidding Rules

Emergency

Competitive bidding is not required when an emergency arises.[94] An emergency situation results from an accident or unforeseen occurrence or condition which affects the public property or citizens of the political subdivision in such a way that immediate action is necessary;[95] for statutory purposes, it must be an unforeseen occurrence or condition which could not have been anticipated or prevented by the exercise of reasonable care.[96] For example, when a fire guts a building and it is in danger of collapse, a city is justified in contracting for demolition of the building on an emergency basis and not advertising for bids.[97]

The emergency must be real; a public owner may not declare an emergency to avoid competitive bidding nor can it neglect to address a situation until it becomes an emergency. For instance, where the need for new garbage trucks was known six months before they were needed, no emergency existed and

---

[90] Fischbach & Moore, Inc v New York City Transit Auth, 79 AD2d 14, 435 NYS2d 984 (1981).

[91] *Id.*

[92] Davis v City of NY, 50 Misc 2d 275, 270 NYS2d 265 (NY 1966).

[93] Marchionne v New York State Dept of Transp, 88 AD2d 655, 450 NYS2d 529 (1982); *but see* Gerzof v Sweeney, 16 NY2d 206, 211 NE2d 826, 264 NYS2d 376 (1965) (court ordered new commission to award contract to lowest responsible bidder chosen by its predecessor).

[94] NY Gen Mun Law §103(4) (McKinney 1986 & Supp 1992).

[95] *Id.*

[96] Rodin v Director of Purchasing, 38 Misc 2d 362, 238 NYS2d 2 (Nassau 1963).

[97] City of NY v Unsafe Bldg & Structure No 97, Columbia Heights, 113 Misc 2d 246, 448 NYS2d 938 (NY 1982).

competitive bidding was required when the appropriate board failed to act on the truck purchase until three weeks before they were needed.[98] Good faith is irrelevant.[99]

Architectural, Engineering, and Surveying Services

Competitive bidding is not required for the state and its subdivisions when acquiring architectural, engineering, and surveying services.[100] These contracts are to be awarded based upon demonstrated competence and qualification for the professional services required at fair and reasonable fees.[101]

§2.15 —Challenging an Award or Rejection of Bid

When a contract has been awarded or a bid rejected in contravention of the bidding statutes, a bidder or any taxpayer may bring an action to set aside award of the contract pursuant to Article 78 of the New York Civil Practice Law and Rules. Typically, such an action will seek a restraining order vacating the award of the project, enjoining the public owner from making any payments to the chosen bidder, and compelling the public owner to award the contract to the petitioner (this is rarely granted) or to readvertise and rebid the contract.

So long as the public owner's decision was not made arbitrarily, capriciously, or unreasonably, however, it will not be disturbed by the courts. This standard holds true when reviewing most bid decisions, including determining that a bidder is not responsible,[102] refusing to waive a bid specification,[103] or waiving a bid irregularity.[104] A public owner's decision to reject any or all bids will not be disturbed except upon a showing of "actual impropriety or unfair dealing" or of a violation of statutory requirements.[105] The burden of proof is on the party challenging an award of a contract, a rejection of any or all bids,[106] or some other public owner determination.[107]

A rejection of a qualified, responsible lowest bidder without an investigation and hearing violates the intent of the competitive bidding statutes and is subject to review by the courts,[108] although review will not always result in an order

---

[98] Rodin v Director of Purchasing, 38 Misc 2d 362, 238 NYS2d 2 (Nassau 1963).

[99] *Id.*

[100] NY State Fin Law §136-a (McKinney 1989 & Supp 1992).

[101] *Id* §136-a(2).

[102] Meyer v Board of Educ, 31 Misc 2d 407, 221 NYS2d 500 (Nassau 1961).

[103] *In re* CK Rehner, Inc, 106 AD2d 268, 483 NYS2d 1 (1984).

[104] LeCesse Bros Contracting v Egan, 89 AD2d 640, 453 NYS2d 82 (1982).

[105] Conduit & Found Corp v Metropolitan Transp Auth, 66 NY2d 144, 149, 485 NE2d 1005, 495 NYS2d 340, 344 (1985).

[106] *Id.*

[107] Meyer v Board of Educ, 31 Misc 2d 407, 221 NYS2d 500 (Nassau 1961).

[108] Warren Bros Co v Crane, 30 AD2d 437, 293 NYS2d 763 (1968); Seacoast Constr Corp v Lockport Urban Renewal Agency, 72 Misc 2d 372, 339 NYS2d 188 (Erie 1972).

36   BIDDING & CONTRACT FORMATION

requiring the contract to be rebid. The standard for awarding a bid is not whether one bidder is more qualified than another, but whether the lowest bidder is responsible.[109]

The usual result of challenging an award is for the project to be readvertised and rebid. Generally, a court cannot force a public owner to accept a bidder, especially where the bid specifications and applicable statutes allow the public owner to reject any and all bids.[110] The only exception to this rule is where the public owner originally chose the petitioner and later, for improper reasons, rejected the petitioner and chose a different bidder.[111]

§2.16   —Public Agencies Exempt from Competitive Bidding Requirements

While most public agencies are required to competitively bid their contracts, several public agencies are exempt from the requirements of competitive bidding statutes. For example, in *Broadway Plus v Metro Transportation Authority*,[112] the court held that under NY Pub Auth Law §1209(5)(a), a contract for renovation work of the Times Square subway station complex could be awarded to a private developer by negotiation without competitive bidding if the private entity agreed to pay at least $1,000,000 toward construction costs, which would include at least 50 per cent of the total cost of the work. As an alternative to competitive bidding, the statute requires that notice be published in at least one newspaper of general circulation. The notice should "identify the parties to the proposed contract and summarize its terms and conditions."[113] The contract is also to be approved by a board of no less than 11 members of the authority.[114]

There are several other public authorities which also are not required to abide by competitive bidding statutes. They include: the trustees of the Westchester Joint Water Works, who may contract for engineering services for a water survey without advertising for bids;[115] the board of cooperative educational services, which is neither a district corporation nor a school district and, therefore, is not subject to provisions of competitive bidding;[116] county farm

---

[109] Seacoast Constr Corp v Lockport Urban Renewal Agency, 72 Misc 2d 372, 339 NYS2d 188 (Erie 1972).

[110] Marchionne v New York State Dept of Transp, 88 AD2d 655, 450 NYS2d 529 (1982).

[111] *See* Gerzof v Sweeney, 16 NY2d 206, 211 NE2d 826, 264 NYS2d 376 (1965); Luboil Heat & Power Corp v Pleydell, 178 Misc 562, 34 NYS2d 587 (NY 1942).

[112] 157 AD2d 453, 549 NYS2d 23 (1st Dept 1990).

[113] NY Pub Auth Law §1209 (McKinney 1982 & Supp 1992).

[114] *Id.*

[115] NY Gen Mun Law §103 n 131 (McKinney 1986 & Supp 1992).

[116] *Id* at n 132.

bureaus and similar groups created under County Law §224;[117] industrial development agencies;[118] municipal hospitals, which may enter into a contract for the purchase of goods, supplies, or services with a hospital association without being subject to competitive bidding requirements;[119] and any authority which is required to do work in a public emergency.[120] Competitive bidding also was not required where a town had the option of leasing or purchasing land and having a building constructed thereon for a municipality, pursuant to which the owner privately constructed the building on his land and leased it to the municipality.[121]

§2.17 Bidding on Private Contracts

Unlike bidding on public contracts, bidding on private contracts is not regulated by the state and, therefore, is free from many of the restrictions of public bidding. A private owner need not advertise for bids or seek bids from more than one party. If a private owner does consider more than one contractor, either as a result of bidding following advertisement or its own selection of bidders, the owner is not bound to choose the lowest bidder or a responsible bidder, unless it expressly stipulates that it will do so.[122] A private owner may draft its contract specifications in any way it chooses and may require specific brands without allowing for substitution of equivalents. It may accept and reject bids when and how it chooses and use whatever means it chooses to evaluate bidders.

Upon notice to the owner, a private general contract bid may be withdrawn without reason at any time the bidder chooses prior to acceptance of the bid by the owner. See §2.21 regarding the withdrawal of subcontractor bids.

§2.18 Mistakes

Mistakes are often made in preparing a bid. Figures are added incorrectly or are transposed when transferred from a calculation sheet to a bid proposal sheet. Specifications are misunderstood or not read carefully. When the mistake results in a *higher* bid than the bidder intended, the bidder's lesson is learned by its failure to win the contract and its being left to ponder "what if." When the mistake results in a bid which is *lower* than intended, problems result when the mistaken bid is also the lowest responsible bid and the bidder is awarded the contract. Then, the question becomes, Under what circumstances will a bidder be held to its mistaken bid? Not all mistakes will relieve a bidder from its bid; in order to do so, the mistake must be an *excusable* one.

---

[117] *Id* at n 134.
[118] *Id* at n 135.
[119] *Id* at n 136.
[120] *Id* at n 137.
[121] *Id* at n 146.
[122] Topping v Swords, 1 ED Smith 609 (CP 1852).

If a bidder makes a mistaken bid and is notified of the mistake, it may choose to stand on its mistaken bid.[123] Of course, it may not then later claim a right to rescind the contract or its bid based on the mistake.

§2.19 —Excusable and Nonexcusable Unilateral Mistakes

An *excusable* mistaken bid is one in which the mistake is of such nature and consequence that the bidder will be relieved of its bid; the bidder will be allowed to withdraw the bid or rescind any contract based on the bid. If the mistake is nonexcusable, the bidder is held to its bid and must enter into and perform the contract or forfeit its bid security and face potential liability for breach of contract.

Generally, a bidder's unilateral mistake will be excusable if it was due to a clerical or mathematical error. This is referred to as an *honest error*. For instance, if a bidder means to reduce its bid by $21,300 but in preparing its bid sheet deducts $213,000, instead, the mistake is clerical and will be excused.[124] Or, if due to a clerical or calculation error a bid is $100,000[125] or $1,000,000 too low,[126] and the bidder promptly notifies the owner of the mistake upon its discovery, the mistake is excusable. Similarly, when transferring figures, if the total number of projected man hours is used, rather than the total projected labor cost, the mistake will be excused, even if the mistake is not noticed until after the bidder is awarded the contract.[127] In each of these cases, the mistake was subject to objective determination (it could be seen upon review and comparison of the calculation sheets and bid proposals), the bidder promptly notified the owner of the mistake and requested amendment or rescission of the bid, and the mistake was material, i.e., it was of such an amount as to make enforcement unconscionable. As the bidders' real bids were not submitted due to the errors, there was no meeting of the minds in any of these cases and no contracts existed.[128]

---

[123] Premier Elec Installation Co v Board of Educ, 20 Misc 2d 286, 191 NYS2d 187 (Suffolk 1959).

[124] City of Syracuse v Sarkisian Bros, 87 AD2d 984, 451 NYS2d 945 (4th Dept), *affd*, 57 NY2d 618, 439 NE2d 880, 454 NYS2d 71 (1982).

[125] Derouin's Plumbing & Heating, Inc v City of Watertown, 71 AD2d 822, 419 NYS2d 390 (1979) (clerical error in transferring total bid amount from calculation sheet to bid proposal).

[126] Jobco, Inc v County of Nassau, 129 AD2d 614, 514 NYS2d 108 (1987) (clerical error).

[127] Union Free School Dist No 1 v Gumbs, 20 Misc 2d 315, 191 NYS2d 183 (Suffolk 1958).

[128] City of Syracuse v Sarkisian Bros, 87 AD2d 984, 451 NYS2d 945 (4th Dept), *affd*, 57 NY2d 618, 439 NE2d 880, 454 NYS2d 71 (1982).

> **PRACTICE POINTER:**
>
> Save all bid work sheets, calculation sheets, adding machine rolls, notes, etc., until the contract has been awarded to another party and performance begun. If you withdraw your bid on a claim of mistake, save these papers indefinitely. If you win the contract, save these papers through the duration of the job, if not beyond.

Overlooking a term of the contract in preparing a bid is not an excusable mistake.[129] For example, in a case where the specifications required the contractor to supply temporary heat and the bidder failed to include the temporary heat when figuring its bid, the bidder was held to its bid and had to choose between performing the contract at its bid price or forfeiting its bid security.[130] The basic rule is that if the error is due to negligence in reviewing the plans and specifications or to an error in exercising business judgment, such as in estimating the total number of man hours required to perform, it will not be excusable.[131]

In addition to deciding whether the mistake itself is excusable, the courts will consider other factors which may result in an otherwise nonexcusable error being excused. In the case of *Brook-Lea Country Club, Inc v Hanover Insurance Co*,[132] the court held that before a bidder will be excused from its bid the following requirements must be met:

1. The mistake must have been of such consequence as to make enforcement unconscionable
2. The mistake must be material
3. The bidder must have exercised ordinary care in compiling its bid; and
4. It must be possible to place the other party in status quo

Application of these requirements can be seen in the case of *Balaban-Gordon*

---

[129] G&R Elec Contractors, Inc v Egan, 85 AD2d 191, 448 NYS2d 850, *affd*, 57 NY2d 721, 440 NE2d 795, 454 NYS2d 710 (1982).

[130] Dierks Heating Co v Egan, 115 AD2d 836, 496 NYS2d 97 (1985).

[131] G&R Elec Contractors, Inc v Egan, 85 AD2d 191, 448 NYS2d 850, *affd*, 57 NY2d 721, 440 NE2d 795, 454 NYS2d 710 (1982); Dierks Heating Co v Egan, 115 AD2d 836, 496 NYS2d 97 (1985). This is the rule most commonly articulated by the courts. Under close scrutiny, however, it does not make complete sense. A computational error should, by all rights, be characterized as negligence. The rule most likely has developed pragmatically. On the one hand, fairness requires that a low bidder not be held to an erroneous bid. On the other hand, the competitive bidding system could be rendered ineffective if the low bidder could easily be relieved by claiming mistake. On balance, clearly demonstrable errors, such as computational errors, form the basis for relief; less demonstrable errors, such as those of judgment, do not.

[132] 61 Misc 2d 896, 306 NYS2d 780 (Monroe 1969); *see also* Balaban-Gordon Co v Brighton Sewer Dist No 2, 41 AD2d 246, 342 NYS2d 435 (1973).

Co v Brighton Sewer District No 2.[133] In that case, the bidder was excused from its bid, despite the fact that the mistake was due to the bidder's negligent misinterpretation of bid specifications and failure to investigate a specification it thought was ambiguous. In *Balaban-Gordon*, the district advertised two sewage projects for bid and invited bids on the general construction, plumbing, heating, and electrical work contracts. The plaintiff was the low responsible bidder for the general construction contract, but the highest bidder for the plumbing contract. Its general contract bid was more than $500,000 lower than the next lowest bid, while its plumbing contract bid was almost $400,000 higher than the lowest plumbing bid.

Upon learning of the difference in the bids, the plaintiff reexamined its work sheets and learned that due to its misinterpretation of specifications it had included some equipment costs in the plumbing contract which should have been included in the general construction contract. The plaintiff notified the district of the mistake immediately and refused to execute or perform the general construction contract.

The court, while noting that the plaintiff's error was not clerical or mathematical, relieved the plaintiff from its bid and stated:

> [I]f the mistake concerns a material matter in an executory contract under circumstances where relief to the bidder results in no damage to the municipality but enforcement results in serious harm to the bidder, rescission will be granted. Manifestly, rescission may be allowed more readily for a mistake made by a bidder which is objectively established and which does not evolve from an inherent risk of business. Even though the mistake is the product of negligence on the part of the bidder, relief should be granted because the assurance exists from the objective proof that the transaction is free from mischief.[134]

An owner that receives an excusable mistaken bid cannot claim that it was damaged by the bidder's rescission of the mistaken bid. The owner is not entitled to the bargain of the mistaken bid, since it cannot claim loss of something to which it was never entitled. Its choice is to award the bid to the second lowest bidder or readvertise the contract for new bids,[135] even though the resulting contract may cost the owner more than if the owner were allowed to enforce the mistaken bid.[136]

---

[133] 41 AD2d 246, 342 NYS2d 435 (1973).

[134] *Id*.

[135] *Id*; City of Syracuse v Sarkisian Bros, 87 AD2d 984, 451 NYS2d 945 (4th Dept), *aff'd*, 57 NY2d 618, 439 NE2d 880, 454 NYS2d 71 (1982); Jobco, Inc v County of Nassau, 129 AD2d 614, 514 NYS2d 108 (1987); Derouin's Plumbing & Heating, Inc v City of Watertown, 71 AD2d 822, 419 NYS2d 390 (1979).

[136] Harper, Inc v City of Newburgh, 159 AD 695, 145 NYS 59 (1913).

§2.20 —Mutual Mistakes

It is basic contract law that when a mistake is mutual and substantial, the resulting contract is voidable. The justification for potential rescission is that if both parties were mistaken as to the content or meaning of the contract or a material term, there could not have been true agreement on the terms, and, hence, there was no meeting of the minds.[137] In construction contracts, true mutual mistake is rare.

In the case of *John West & Sons v West Street Improvement Co*,[138] an excavation contractor tried to rescind its contract based on mutual mistake. The contractor claimed that both parties believed that the soil beneath the job site contained a negligible amount of rock. The owner, however, claimed to be unsure of the exact soil composition and that its uncertainty was reflected in the contract documents. The court denied relief to the contractor on the basis that the mistake was unilateral, not mutual.

If both parties are mistaken and the mistake can be proved, relief from the contract will be granted. For instance, where both the contractor and subcontractor were mistaken as to the time and method of approval for the subcontractor's alternative vacuum cleaning system, the subcontractor was entitled to cancel the contract since the mistake was both mutual and substantial.[139]

§2.21 Subcontractor Bids

When general contractors prepare their bids, they often rely on subcontractors' bids for various portions of the work and incorporate the subcontractors' bids into their general contract bids. As a general rule, courts are unwilling to relieve a subcontractor of its obligation to honor its bid when the general contractor is awarded the contract by the owner. The subcontractor's bid is viewed as a binding promise, despite the lack of consideration. Consistently, the requirement of consideration to make a promise binding is circumvented by the courts through resort to the doctrine of promissory estoppel. Rather than being bound by consideration, the subcontractor is bound by the general contractor's reliance upon the subcontractor's bid by its incorporation into the general contract bid.[140]

The elements of promissory estoppel in the subcontractor bid context are:

---

[137] Brauer v Central Trust Co, 77 AD2d 239, 433 NYS2d 304 (1980).

[138] 149 AD 504, 134 NYS 39 (1912).

[139] Crown NW Equip, Inc v Donald M. Drake Co, 49 Or App 679, 620 P2d 946, 950 (1980); *see also* James H. Merritt Plumbing, Inc v City of NY, 55 AD2d 552, 390 NYS2d 65 (1976); Foundation Co v State, 233 NY 177, 135 NE 236 (1922) (Court of Appeals, in dicta, recognized that mutual mistake may provide basis for relief in changed condition case).

[140] Rochester Plumbing & Supply Co v Burgart, Inc, 49 AD2d 78, 370 NYS2d 716 (1975); James King & Sons v DeSantis Constr No 2 Corp, 97 Misc 2d 1063, 413 NYS2d 78 (NY 1977); Drennan v Star Paving Co, 51 Cal 2d 409, 333 P2d 757 (1958).

42 BIDDING & CONTRACT FORMATION

(1) a promise clear and unequivocal in its terms; (2) reasonable and foreseeable reliance by the general contractor; and (3) the reliance having resulted in injury to the contractor.[141]

While a subcontractor is bound to its bid to a general contractor, a general contractor is not similarly bound. Use of a subcontractor's bid does not bind a general contractor to actually use the subcontractor without a specific promise to do so by the general contractor to the subcontractor.[142]

A subcontractor may be relieved from its bid based on an excusable mistake to the same extent as may a general contractor.[143] Further, a general contractor must notify a subcontractor that it accepts the subcontractor's bid within a reasonable time after it has been awarded the prime contract. A failure to notify a subcontractor of acceptance within a reasonable time will allow a subcontractor to withdraw its bid or treat it as rejected.[144]

§2.22 Rejection of Bids

The soliciting of bids does not always mean that a contract will be awarded. The general rule is that, absent a specific promise or agreement, an owner is under no obligation to award a contract after asking for bids. The freedom with which and reasons for which bids may be rejected depends on whether the owner is private or public.

Private

In New York, a private owner has the right to reject any and all bids. When a private owner solicits bids, it is merely inviting contractors to present offers which the owner may or may not accept as it sees fit; solicitation of bids is not an offer to contract.[145] Bidding on a private contract creates no rights in the bidder until the bid is accepted by the owner.

Public

A public owner's ability to reject bids is restricted by the qualification that it may reject any bid so long as the rejection is supported by a rational basis,

---

[141] James King & Sons v DeSantis Constr No 2 Corp, 97 Misc 2d 1063, 413 NYS2d 78 (NY 1977); Debron Corp v National Homes Constr Corp, 493 F2d 352 (8th Cir 1974). *See also* Restatement (Second) of Contracts §90 (1982).

[142] Cortland Asbestos Prods v J&K Plumbing & Heating Co, 33 AD2d 11, 304 NYS2d 694 (1969).

[143] Edward Joy Co v Noise Control Prods, 111 Misc 2d 64, 443 NYS2d 361 (Onondaga 1981).

[144] Piland Corp v REA Constr Co, 672 F Supp 244 (ED Va 1987) (notifying of acceptance six months after award of the general contract is not within a reasonable time).

[145] SSI Investors, Ltd v Korea Tungsten Mining Co, 80 AD2d 155, 438 NYS2d 96 (1981), *affd*, 55 NY2d 934, 434 NE2d 242, 449 NYS2d 173 (1982); Topping v Swords, 1 ED Smith 609 (CP 1852).

is in the best interests of the public, and is not arbitrary or capricious.[146] Often an invitation to bid will expressly reserve the right of the public owner to reject bids; General Municipal Law §103 specifically allows this.

A public owner may reject all bids if it believes that it would receive a lower bid if the project were readvertised and rebid;[147] if it wishes to change the specifications to include requirements which are essential;[148] or if all bids exceed the amount of public funds appropriated to the project.[149] This list is not meant to be exhaustive; there are many other bases upon which a public owner may reject all bids, including the simplest one of all—that it no longer believes that the project is in the public's best interests. A public owner may not reject all bids merely because its preferred bidder was not the lowest responsible bidder and then later award the contract to its preferred bidder for a small sum less than its original bid.[150]

A public owner may reject any bid which does not strictly comply with bid specifications, no matter how minor the noncompliance may seem.[151]

Finally, if a successful bidder on a contract fails to execute the contract or otherwise defaults in its performance, the public owner may award the contract to the next lowest responsible bidder[152] or reject all other bids and readvertise the project for new bids.[153]

A public owner's decision to reject all bids will not be disturbed except upon a showing of "actual impropriety or unfair dealing" or a violation of statutory requirements.[154] The party challenging the decision to reject has the burden of proof.[155]

§2.23 Contract Formation

Once a bid has been accepted, a contract must be drafted, fine points negotiated, and the final agreement signed. For a valid contract to exist, certain elements must be present: there must be an offer and an acceptance—in construction contracts, this is most often a bid and an acceptance of bid or award of contract; there must be a "meeting of the minds"—the parties must

---

[146] NY Gen Mun Law §103 (McKinney 1986 & Supp 1992); Conduit & Found Corp v Metropolitan Transp Auth, 66 NY2d 144, 485 NE2d 1005, 495 NYS2d 340 (1985); Stisling Elec, Inc v Albany Co, 97 AD2d 631, 469 NYS2d 154 (1983).

[147] Conduit & Found Corp v Metropolitan Transp Auth, 66 NY2d 144, 485 NE2d 1005, 495 NYS2d 340 (1985); Carter v Blake, 63 AD2d 760, 404 NYS2d 728 (1978).

[148] Kings Bay Buses, Inc v Aiello, 100 Misc 2d 1, 418 NYS2d 284 (Kings 1979).

[149] AJ Beaudette Constr Co v City of Syracuse, 62 Misc 2d 564, 309 NYS2d 517 (Onondaga), *affd*, 313 NYS2d 356 (App Div 1970).

[150] Reister v Town of Fleming, 32 AD2d 733, 302 NYS2d 176 (4th Dept 1969).

[151] *See* §2.05.

[152] Tufaro Transit Co v Board of Educ, 79 AD2d 376, 436 NYS2d 886 (1981).

[153] Mar-Mes Constr Co v Gitlow, 24 AD2d 481, 260 NYS2d 703 (2d Dept 1965).

[154] Conduit & Found Corp v Metropolitan Transp Auth, 66 NY2d 144, 149, 485 NE2d 1005, 495 NYS2d 340, 344 (1985).

[155] *Id.*

agree on the main terms of the contract, including the purpose to be achieved and the price to be paid; and there must be consideration—in construction contracts, this typically is the owner's promise to pay the contractor in exchange for the contractor's promise to construct a building for the owner. Other conditions to formation of a valid contract include capacity to contract and a legal objective.

§2.24 —Offer and Acceptance

As discussed earlier in this chapter, a bid is an offer to perform work at a certain price. As an offer, it must be definite and certain so both parties can know what performance is required of them.[156] An owner's asking for bids does not mean that it has to award a contract or build the project upon which bids were sought.[157] If an owner decides to accept a bid (an offer), it may do so by notifying the contractor of its intent to accept the bid. If the owner is a public entity, acceptance may result when the proper body authorizes a public employee to execute the contract.[158] Generally, on a private project, once an offer has been accepted, a contract is formed, despite the parties' intent to later put their agreement in writing.[159] Receipt of a bid typically binds only the bidder, not the owner—see the discussion at §§2.12-2.14.

It is not unusual for an invitation to bid to include not only the plans and specifications that the contractor is asked to bid on, but also the form of the contract, including general conditions. By submitting a bid the contractor may be agreeing to sign the contract form included in the invitation to bid if the owner accepts the bid.

§2.25 —Mutual Assent/Intent to Be Bound

Generally, when a bid is made and accepted, an oral contract exists because there has been mutual assent or a meeting of the minds. If however, the parties do not intend to be bound until a contract is written and fully executed, no contract exists and neither party is bound or has potential liability.[160] The mere fact that the parties intend to reduce their agreement to writing does not make their oral agreement nonbinding—if the parties intend to be bound, they are.[161]

> Generally, where the parties contemplate that a signed writing is required there is no contract until one is delivered. (Citations omitted.) This rule

---

[156] 1 Corbin, Contracts §§95-100 (1952); 1 Williston, Contracts §§38-48 (3d ed 1964).

[157] See §2.22.

[158] Municipal Consultants & Publishers, Inc v Town of Ramapo, 47 NY2d 144, 390 NE2d 1143, 417 NYS2d 218 (1979).

[159] SJ Groves & Sons v LM Pike & Son, 41 AD2d 584, 340 NYS2d 230 (4th Dept 1973). See §2.25.

[160] Scheck v Francis, 26 NY2d 466, 260 NE2d 493, 311 NYS2d 841 (1970); Tebbutt v Niagara Mohawk Power Corp, 124 AD2d 266, 508 NYS2d 69 (3d Dept 1986).

[161] SJ Groves & Sons v LM Pike & Son, 41 AD2d 584, 340 NYS2d 230 (4th Dept 1973).

yields, however, when the parties have agreed on all contractual terms and have only to commit them to writing. When this occurs, the contract is effective at the time the oral agreement is made, although the contract is never reduced to writing and signed. Where all the substantial terms of a contract have been agreed on and there is nothing left for future settlement, the fact, alone, that it was the understanding that the contract should be formally drawn up and put in writing, [does] not leave the transaction incomplete and without binding force, in the absence of positive agreement that it should not be binding until so reduced to writing and formally executed.[162]

If a material element of the contract is not established and is left for future negotiations, there is no contract.[163] If an owner uses the bidding process as a means to select a contractor with which it will enter into further negotiations, the owner will not be bound since it has no intent to be bound, so long as it made clear its intent not to be bound. Determining whether there is a contract depends on the parties' *objective* manifestations of intent, not their subjective intent.[164] "It is necessary that the totality of all the acts of the parties, their relationship, and their objectives be considered in order to determine whether they entered into an oral agreement."[165]

§2.26 —Certainty of Terms

Before a contract can exist, there must be a reasonable certainty as to its terms—if its terms are too uncertain, there cannot be a meeting of the minds and no contract will exist. Such a total failure is rare in construction because an owner typically has plans it wishes the contractor to use in constructing its project and the owner and contractor have agreed upon a basic price. Of more concern is the concept of ambiguity—contract terms or phrases which do not clearly show what the parties intended. This failure of certainty usually is not so great as to defeat the contract, but can be significant enough to cause problems. A typical example of an ambiguity is whether requested work is extra work or contract work. Ambiguity is discussed in §2.47.

§2.27 —Statute of Frauds

It is a widely held misbelief that a contract must be written to be valid. Many people, including experienced contractors, believe that if they have not signed anything, there is no contract. This belief is unfounded, especially in construc-

---

[162] Municipal Consultants & Publishers, Inc v Town of Ramapo, 47 NY2d 144, 148-49, 390 NE2d 1143, 417 NYS2d 218, 219-20 (1979).

[163] Blakey v McMurray, 110 AD2d 998, 488 NYS2d 286 (3d Dept 1985).

[164] PJ Carlin Constr Co v Whiffen Elec Co, 66 AD2d 684, 411 NYS2d 27 (1st Dept 1978).

[165] *Id* 29.

tion contracts. The statute of frauds provides that certain types of contracts are invalid unless they are in writing and signed by the responsible party. These include agreements to reaffirm debts discharged in bankruptcy, contracts which by their terms are not to be performed within one year from the contracts' making,[166] contracts for the sale of real property, agreements to assume the debts of another (e.g., to act as a surety), and contracts for the sale of goods for $500 or more.

Rarely will a construction contract, excluding supply contracts, fall within and be subject to the statute of frauds. Thus, this discussion is brief. For readers seeking an analysis of the New York Statutes of Frauds, NY Gen Oblig Law §§5-701, 5-703, and 15-301, the practice commentary written by Richard A. Givens which immediately follows NY Gen Oblig Law §5-701 in Volume 23A of McKinney's Consolidated Laws of New York will be helpful.

Generally, the statute of frauds does not apply to a construction contract because a construction contract is *capable* of being performed within one year.[167] Contracts for more complex projects which are anticipated to take significantly longer than a year are almost always written and signed as they usually are the result of negotiations or a formal bidding process; rarely are such contracts oral or unsigned. Further, the law in New York is clear: if a contract is at all capable of being performed in one year, it does not come within the statute of frauds, regardless of how improbable such performance may be. The test is one of impossibility, not improbability.[168] A guarantee period which exceeds one year does not change the one-year rule as, technically, a guarantee is a statement of present condition, not a promise of future performance by the promisor.[169] If the contract is for the construction *and sale* of a building and lot, as many new home contracts are, the statute of frauds would apply. If, however, the contract is for the contractor to build a new home on the owner's lot, it is not a contract for the sale of real property and the statute of frauds does not apply.[170]

Uniform Commercial Code

The Uniform Commercial Code (UCC) provides that contracts for the sale of goods for $500 or more must be in writing and signed by the party to be charged.[171] This writing requirement is not strict as the statute specifically provides that the lack of a written contract is not fatal if: the seller has begun manu-

---

[166] Freedman v Chemical Constr Corp, 43 NY2d 260, 372 NE2d 12, 401 NYS2d 176 (1977); Mann v Helmsley-Spear, Inc, 177 AD2d 147, 581 NYS2d 16 (1st Dept 1992).

[167] PJ Carlin Constr Co v Whiffen Elec Co, 66 AD2d 684, 411 NYS2d 27 (1st Dept 1978).

[168] Freedman v Chemical Constr Corp, 43 NY2d 260, 372 NE2d 12, 410 NYS2d 176 (1977); Mann v Helmsley-Spear, Inc, 177 AD2d 147, 581 NYS2d 16 (1st Dept 1992).

[169] PJ Carlin Constr Co v Whiffen Elec Co, 66 AD2d 684, 411 NYS2d 27 (1st Dept 1978).

[170] McCaffrey v Strainer, 81 AD2d 977, 439 NYS2d 773 (3d Dept), *appeal dismissed*, 55 NY2d 700, 431 NE2d 308, 446 NYS2d 947 (1981).

[171] UCC §2-201(1) (McKinney 1964).

facture of goods specially created for the buyer which are unsuitable for sale to other buyers;[172] the charged party admits the existence of the contract in a court document or proceeding;[173] payment has been made and accepted;[174] the goods have been received and accepted;[175] or the parties are merchants and one sends a written confirmation of the contract within a reasonable time and the other party does not make written objection to the confirmation within 10 days.[176]

§2.28 —Illegal Contracts

Courts will not enforce illegal contracts. In construction cases, this principle is best illustrated in instances of illegal bidding, discussed at §2.11. Another aspect of this principle is that courts will not enforce contracts which have illegal objectives, even if a refusal to enforce a contract means that one party benefits to another's detriment.[177] If, however, a court can construe a contract to be performed both lawfully and unlawfully, it will construe the contract in favor of its legality.[178] An example of an illegal provision in a construction contract would be one which requires a contractor to waive any right to file a mechanic's lien prior to the performance of work.[179]

An example of an illegal contract is a home improvement contract where the contractor is not a licensed home improvement contractor.[180] A contractor who does home improvement work without a license, if one is required, may not sue to recover for payment due for the work. Although the homeowner may have signed a contract agreeing to pay the contractor, courts will not enforce the contract if the contractor lacked a required license. As it is difficult to perceive of a construction contract with a wholly illegal objective, this issue will not be discussed further.

§2.29 —Authority to Contract (Capacity)

Capacity, which is one element of authority, typically relates to age and mental competency. Since minors and incompetents rarely enter into construction

---

[172] *Id* §2-201(3)(a).

[173] *Id* §2-201(3)(b). In such cases, the contract is valid only for the quantity of goods admitted to by the person charged.

[174] *Id* §2-201(3)(c).

[175] *Id.*

[176] *Id* §2-201(2).

[177] Braunstein v Jason Tarantella, Inc, 87 AD2d 203, 450 NYS2d 862 (2d Dept 1982).

[178] Galuth Realty Corp v Greenfield, 103 AD2d 819, 478 NYS2d 51 (2d Dept 1984).

[179] *See* NY Lien Law §34 (McKinney 1966 & Supp 1992), providing that any waiver of the right to file a mechanic's lien is void as against public policy; *see also* Clifton Steel v General Elec Co, 80 AD2d 714, 437 NYS2d 735 (3d Dept 1981).

[180] *See* NY City Admin Code §20-387.

contracts, capacity is not discussed here. A similar and often confused concept is the issue of one's authority to contract.

§2.30 —Actual and Apparent Authority

"Authority is the power of the agent to affect the legal relations of the principal by acts done in accordance with the principal's manifestation of consent to him."[181] An agent's authority and powers are no greater than its principal's; i.e., an agent cannot bind its principal to do something the principal lacks the legal capacity to do. For instance, a contractor's foreman would not be able to bind its principal, the contractor, to an agreement to redesign a building if the contractor is not a licensed architect—the contractor cannot legally design or redesign a building; hence, its agent's promise is meaningless.

Actual authority must be contrasted with *apparent authority*. *Apparent authority* is based on a *third person's* reasonable *perception* of the agent's authority based on the principal's actions or manifestations to the third person.[182] *Apparent authority* depends upon appearances, while *actual authority* depends upon facts. If a contractor reasonably believes that an owner's architect has the authority to consent to a change order and in fact the architect does not, the architect's consent might bind the owner. If the contractor has no such belief but the architect has actual authority, the architect's consent will bind the owner, despite the contractor's ignorance of the architect's authority. If the contractor has no reason to believe the architect has authority and, in fact, the architect does not, the architect's actions will not bind the owner.

The actions of the principal which can establish apparent authority need not be directed specifically to the third person who relies on them; they may be directed to the community at large through various means, including written and spoken words, a past course of dealing between the parties, giving someone an impressive title (e.g., "general manager" or "contracting officer"), and failure to repudiate known actions by the employee which reasonably could be interpreted as showing authority.

Who Can Bind Whom

Without actual or apparent authority, the acts of an employee will not bind a corporation.[183]

The persons executing a contract must have authority to enter into a binding agreement on behalf of the parties. In general, a sole proprietor of a business can bind the business. An officer of a corporation can bind the corporation. A general partner can bind a partnership. One member of a joint venture can sometimes bind a joint venture.[184]

---

[181] Restatement (Second) of Agency §7 (1958 & 1984).
[182] *Id* §8.
[183] Kapilow Constr Corp v Prince, 52 AD2d 620, 382 NYS2d 349 (2d Dept 1976).
[184] NY Bus Corp Law § 715 (McKinney 1986 & Supp 1992).

Individuals and corporations can give someone *express* authority to bind the individual or corporation to a contract. Such authority may be written or oral. Corporations can expressly authorize both officers and non-officers to bind the corporation in contract.

Individuals and corporations can also cloak someone with apparent authority to enter into binding contracts. This may be done by a regular course of conduct, or by giving someone an impressive job title such as "Director of Contracts." An individual or corporation can also subsequently elect to affirm a contract which was executed without appropriate authority.

Contracts with the state must be approved by the comptroller in order for them to be binding on the state.[185] In one case, an architect was denied compensation of approximately $13,000 for extra work performed on a public works contract because the contract had never been approved by the State Comptroller as required by statute. Payment to the architect was denied by the court despite the fact that the architect was forwarded a contract by the public owner and the owner paid the architect the agreed fee of approximately $14,000 for his services. The court's ruling denying the architect his fee was based solely on the failure to follow the required statutory procedure.[186] The purpose of such rulings and laws is to prevent state officers, employees, and agents from creating liabilities.[187]

§2.31 Letter of Intent

A letter of intent to enter into a contract does not generally constitute a binding contract. It is simply an agreement to agree on contract terms at some future date. New York courts generally refuse to enforce letters of intent, because on their face they indicate that the parties have not reached agreement on all essential terms,[188] they merely have agreed to make their best effort to complete their contract negotiations at some future date. Thus, it would not be fair for a court to supply terms that are missing from the parties' agreement.

Letters of intent are common in the construction industry. The reasons for entering into a letter of intent often are not altogether clear. Sometimes one party may wish to have a letter of intent to take to its bank to arrange financing; or to take to its surety to arrange for the issuance of payment and performance bonds; or to take to its accountant to support an entry in a financial statement. Other times the parties use it to show good faith—i.e., that they have negotiated the material terms of a contract, that negotiations with other parties have ended, and that all that remains is for the lawyers to draw up the formal agreement. Use of a letter of intent for the latter purpose can be dangerous, however.

---

[185] NY State Fin Law §112(2) (McKinney 1989); Blatt Bowling & Billiard Corp v State, 14 AD2d 144, 217 NYS2d 766 (3d Dept 1961); Deverho Constr Co v State, 94 Misc 2d 1053, 407 NYS2d 399 (Ct Cl 1978).

[186] Dempsey v City Univ, 106 AD2d 486, 483 NYS2d 24 (2d Dept 1984). J. Forster, *Sign the Contract; Then Provide the Service* Consulting Engineer, 1983, at 106-08.

[187] Deverho Constr Co v State, 94 Misc 2d 1053, 407 NYS2d 399 (Ct Cl 1978).

[188] Danton Constr Corp v Bonner, 173 AD2d 759, 571 NYS2d 299 (2d Dept 1991).

In the absence of specific terms to the contrary, if the material terms are spelled out in a so-called letter of intent, the document can be used to show the existence of a contract.[189] Absent a compelling reason to the contrary, parties are better advised to skip the letter of intent and proceed directly to the formal written agreement.

A letter of intent can bind the parties to a contract once performance commences. If the parties are unable to agree on all terms of the contract after performance starts, it is possible that no formal contract will be executed. If this is the case and a dispute arises on the job, it will be the responsibility of some third party, such as a judge or an arbitrator, to determine the parties' intent based on general common law rules, the writings between the parties leading up to performance to date, and their conduct toward each other on this and other jobs.[190]

If the parties do not want to be bound until a formal contract is executed, they should consider stating in the letter of intent that it is not a contract and that they are not bound by any proposed conditions until a formal contract is executed.[191] The letter of intent should also state that if the work proceeds prior to execution of a formal contract, the contractor shall be paid on a time and materials basis for the actual cost of the work performed plus an allowance for overhead and profit.

§2.32 Execution of Contract

Once a city of New York construction contract for work exceeding $15,000 is executed by the contractor, it must be registered with the City Comptroller before it may be executed by a city official.[192] Upon registration, the comptroller certifies that moneys are available to pay for the work or goods.[193] Once the comptroller has registered and certified the contract, the city may execute it. Similar procedures govern state contracts.[194] This process has led to the question of when a competitively bid contract is binding on the government—is the contract formed upon its award to the successful bidder or is it formed upon certification by the comptroller?

In *Kooleraire Service & Installation Corp v Board of Education*,[195] the Court of Appeals considered this question and held that where the comptroller's certification is part of a mandatory, nondiscretionary duty, the contract is formed upon award, if in fact there is enough money to pay for the work. In July, 1965, the plaintiff in *Kooleraire* was awarded a contract for heating and ventilation

---

[189] Nadal Baxendale, Inc v Iannace, 12 AD2d 785, 209 NYS2d 615 (2d Dept 1961).
[190] *Id.*
[191] Aces Mechanical Corp v Cohen Bros Realty & Constr Corp, 136 AD2d 503, 523 NYS2d 824 (1st Dept 1988), *order modified as indicated*, 531 NYS2d 218 (1988).
[192] Rules of the City of NY, Vol 4, tit 9, §5-07 (Lenz & Riecker, Inc 1991).
[193] *Id.*
[194] NY State Fin Law §112 (McKinney 1989 & Supp 1992).
[195] 28 NY2d 101, 268 NE2d 782, 320 NYS2d 46 (1971).

work for a school; the contract was executed by the plaintiff in August and by the defendant the next day. The contract provided that it was not binding unless the comptroller certified that there were sufficient funds to pay the costs of the contract.[196] In November, the defendant rescinded the contract on the grounds that the comptroller had not certified that funds were available. In fact, funds were available and the comptroller's failure to certify this fact was at the request of the defendant. The court found that the comptroller's role was a limited one and that it was never intended that the comptroller would or should have veto power over the contract. Thus, the court refused to allow the defendant Board of Education to avoid its contractual obligations by hiding behind the comptroller's certification powers. "The general rule is, as it has been frequently stated, that a party to a contract cannot rely on the failure of another to perform a condition precedent where he has frustrated or prevented the occurrence of the condition."[197]

The *Kooleraire* case does not, however, stand for the proposition that a contract necessarily exists upon award. If a comptroller does not certify the contract for a valid reason, such as a lack of funds, there is no contract.

§2.33 Negotiating Terms and Conditions

Participation in negotiations will not bind a party.[198] Nor are negotiations admissible to prove an unambiguous contract term; it is presumed that the parties wrote into the contract the result of their negotiations.[199] In most instances, a written contract merges all prior and contemporaneous negotiations.[200]

On competitively bid public projects there can be no negotiation of contract terms and conditions[201]—it would violate the competitive bidding statutes—except to achieve reduction of the low bid chosen.[202] Private contract terms and conditions, however, are frequently negotiated. The extent of negotiation is generally a function of the relative bargaining power of the parties. In some instances, the contract terms and conditions are prepared by the owner's attorney and are given to the architect for inclusion in the bidding documents. In other instances, the architect will prepare terms and conditions, using standard forms, without input from an attorney. The contractor will then prepare a set of exclusions or modifications to the terms and conditions which will be submit-

---

[196] *Id* at 105, 268 NE2d at 783, 320 NYS2d at 47.

[197] *Id* at 106, 268 NE2d at 784, 320 NYS2d at 48.

[198] Tebbutt v Niagara Mohawk Power Corp, 124 AD2d 266, 508 NYS2d 69 (3d Dept 1986).

[199] Collard v Incorporated Village of Flower Hills, 52 NY2d 594, 421 NE2d 818, 439 NYS2d 326 (1981).

[200] John W. Cowper Co v CDC-Troy, Inc, 50 AD2d 1076, 376 NYS2d 754 (4th Dept 1975).

[201] Sinram-Marnis Oil Co v City of NY, 139 AD2d 360, 532 NYS2d 94 (1st Dept 1988), *affd*, 74 NY2d 13, 542 NE2d 337, 544 NYS2d 119 (1989).

[202] Fischbach & Moore, Inc v New York City Transit Auth, 79 AD2d 14, 435 NYS2d 984 (1981); Kick v Regan, 110 AD2d 934, 487 NYS2d 403 (3d Dept 1985); *see* **§2.13**.

ted with its bid. The owner will then negotiate acceptable terms and conditions with the selected bidder.

§2.34 Analysis of Boilerplate

Typically, the construction "agreement" contains little more than the scope of work, names of parties, time of performance, contract sum, and an enumeration of the other documents (sometimes attached and sometimes not) incorporated in the contract, such as plans, specifications, general and special conditions, and geotechnical reports and data. All of the meaty contract terms and conditions are incorporated in the general and special conditions, normally found towards the front of the project specifications book. These contract terms and conditions are commonly referred to as *boilerplate*. These would include: payment terms, retainage, conditions for final payment, changes in the work, differing site conditions, delays and time extensions, guarantees and warranties, indemnities, limitation of actions, arbitration, forum selection, authority of the architect, choice of law, etc. Many contractors do not pay attention to the boilerplate until there are problems on the job, when it is too late to do anything about it. Careful analysis of the boilerplate should be undertaken at the time of preparation of the bid in order to fully understand the risks and responsibilities assumed by each party so that these can be adequately priced and included in the contractor's bid.

§2.35 Evaluating Special Terms

In order to hedge against certain types of risks in a construction contract, a contractor must include contingencies in its bid. The more risks that are imposed upon the contractor, the greater those contingencies should be. One of the major risks in any construction contract is the risk of delay. If a contract provides that the contractor must bear the risk associated with additional costs caused by delays on a project, regardless of fault, the contractor should take this risk into account in calculating the bid.[203] Other risks that must be evaluated by a contractor are addressed throughout this text. Some of these risks include changed conditions, liquidated damages, insurance, design responsibility, and the existence of termination for convenience and dispute resolution clauses.

Prevailing Rate of Wage

Many public contracts provide, by law, that workers must be paid the local *prevailing rate of wage*.[204] The prevailing rate of wage is determined by a "fiscal officer"—most often the state industrial commissioner on state contracts or the comptroller on New York City contracts. In practice, the prevailing rate is almost always the rate required by local union agreements for the same work. The rates are established on a one-year basis, typically from July 1 through

---

[203] Kalisch-Jarcho v City of NY, 58 NY2d 377, 448 NE2d 413, 461 NYS2d 746 (1983).
[204] NY Lab Law §220 (McKinney 1986 & Supp 1992).

June 30. If the prevailing wage changes during the contract period, the contractor bears the increase and may not seek reimbursement from the public owner. Thus, a contractor must make its bid with a contingency for an increase in the wage.[205]

Minority Business Enterprises

Some federal, state, and local contracts on large projects require that contractors perform a specified portion of the work with Minority Business Enterprises (MBEs).[206] An MBE has been defined as

> a business at least 50 percent of which is owned by minority members or, in case of a publicly owned business, at least 51 percent of the stock is owned by minority group members. For purposes of the preceding sentence "minority group members" are citizens of the United States who are Negroes, Spanish-speaking, Orientals, Indians, Eskimos, and Aleuts.[207]

The consequences for violation of MBE regulations can be severe; possible sanctions include monetary damages and being barred from future public works contracts.

§2.36 Evaluating Risks and Responsibilities

Construction is an inherently risky venture. The number and variety of matters that can go wrong seem endless. Workers may strike; weather may be unseasonable; needed supplies may suddenly become unavailable or prohibitively expensive; subsurface conditions may be significantly different from what all parties expected; the plans and specifications may be inaccurate or incomplete. Each of these occurrences can delay, increase the cost of, or make infeasible a construction project. When negotiating a construction contract, the mutual goal of the parties should be to allocate risks and responsibility for risks to the party best able to control and deal with a particular risk.

For instance, when an owner has its architect draw detailed plans and specifications, as between the owner and contractor, the owner bears the risk of any errors in them. The contractor's responsibility is to build the building according to the plans and specifications and to point out any errors it notices; its

---

[205] Meaott Constr Corp v Ross, 76 AD2d 137, 431 NYS2d 207, 208 (3d Dept 1980); *but see* General Elec Co v New York State Dept of Labor, 936 F2d 1448 (2d Cir 1991) (motion for summary judgment denied where NY Labor Law was alleged to violate the Fourteenth Amendment of the US Constitution; the court held that the state's using only privately negotiated union wage rates could make it literally impossible for the state to set fair prevailing wage and supplement rates).

[206] City of Richmond v JA Croson Co, 488 US 469, 109 S Ct 706, 102 L Ed 2d 854 (1989); Fullilove v Klutznick, 448 US 448, 100 S Ct 2758, 65 L Ed 2d 902 (1980).

[207] Noel J. Brunell & Son v Town of Champlain, 95 Misc 2d 320, 407 NYS2d 376 (Clinton 1977), *affd* 64 AD2d 757, 407 NYS2d 447, *revd*, adopting Appellate Division's dissenting opinion, 47 NY2d 745, 390 NE2d 1178, 417 NYS2d 254 (1979).

responsibility is not to ensure that a building built according to the plans and specifications will meet the owner's needs or requirements.[208] The courts have recognized that this is a proper allocation of risk, and in the absence of a contract term to the contrary, the risk of improper or faulty plans or specifications is on the owner.[209]

The law imposes upon the design professional the duty to use that degree of skill, knowledge, and judgment ordinarily used by other designers in the same geographic area. The designer generally does not warrant a result. Contractors, however, sometimes warrant that they will achieve a specific result. If a contract contains a performance requirement instead of a design specification, the contractor assumes the risk if the performance criteria are not achieved.[210]

The risk of faulty plans and specifications cannot be shifted from the party ultimately responsible for creating the risk. For instance, NY Gen Oblig Law §5-324 makes void any contract clause that requires an owner, a contractor, a subcontractor, or a supplier to indemnify an architect, an engineer, or a surveyor from personal injury or property damage liability based on maps, plans, designs, or specifications "prepared, acquired, or used" by the architect, engineer, or surveyor. This statute, does not, of course, prevent an owner from attempting to shift the responsibility for the plans from itself to its contractor. This is most often accomplished by having the contractor guarantee a result, such as a watertight basement, rather than having the contractor agree to build the basement according to the architect's plans.

Generally, the risk of unforeseen difficulties or conditions should be on the owner.[211] In reality, this does not impose any additional burden on the owner since if the risk was known at the time of contracting—e.g., if it was known that soil was unstable, necessitating a large foundation—it would be reflected in the contract price. The owner is in the best position to know about the presence of asbestos or other toxic matter; without expensive and extensive tests, a contractor will not know if toxic matter is present at the work site before it begins performance. Similarly, the owner is in the best position to know subsurface conditions at the job site as it probably had its architects or engineers make test borings of the site prior to preparing the plans and specifications for the project. A contract should address these issues and allocate responsibility for these risks. For instance, if the parties want the owner to bear the risk of unknown subsurface conditions, the contract documents should positively

---

[208] United States v Spearin, 248 US 132 (1918); MacKnight Flintic Stone Co v Mayor of NY, 160 NY 72, 54 NE 661 (1899); Carrols Equities Corp v Villnave, 76 Misc 2d 205, 350 NYS2d 90 (Onondaga 1973), *affd*, 49 AD2d 672, 373 NYS2d 1012 (4th Dept 1975).

[209] United States v Spearin, 248 US 132 (1918); MacKnight Flintic Stone Co v Mayor of NY, 160 NY 72, 54 NE 661 (1899); Carrols Equities Corp v Villnave, 76 Misc 2d 205, 350 NYS2d 90 (Onondaga 1973), *affd*, 49 AD2d 672, 373 NYS2d 1012 (4th Dept 1975).

[210] Schiavone Constr Co v County of Nassau, 717 F2d 747 (2d Cir 1983).

[211] Savin Bros v State, 62 AD2d 511, 405 NYS2d 516 (1978), *affd*, 47 NY2d 934, 393 NE2d 1041, 419 NYS2d 969 (1979).

§2.36 EVALUATING RISKS/RESPONSIBILITIES

describe and represent what the known subsurface conditions are. If the parties intend the contractor to bear the risk, the contract should specify that the representations of the owner regarding the subsurface conditions are for informational purposes only and that the contractor relies upon its own investigation of the site.[212] Such an exculpatory clause relieves the owner of liability for any subsurface conditions which are not as the owner represented and which the contractor would have found during a proper and reasonable inspection.[213] The parties may choose to share the risk of subsurface conditions; for instance, if the contract requires excavation, the contract can set a lump sum but specify that the contractor is entitled to additional compensation measured by unit prices in the event the excavation exceeds a specified quantity.[214]

Risk should be allocated as specifically as possible. Take the case of a home owner wishing to have an in-ground pool; assume that the contract says that the owner is responsible for "pool location." To the normal home owner, this may mean telling the contractor to put the pool in the back left corner of the yard. To the contractor—and, most importantly, the courts—this means that the home owner has a duty to take precautions so that the pool excavation does not disturb utility easements and that the home owner should provide the contractor with a survey showing subsurface structures and easements. Any damages which result from there not being a survey are the owner's responsibility.[215] Similarly, a contract which charges the contractor with "full knowledge of any and all conditions *on, about or above* the site" does not shift the risk of subsurface conditions to the contractor.[216]

Risks which may best be allocated to the owner include:

—Subsurface conditions

—Accuracy of plans and specifications, including code compliance

—Presence of asbestos or other toxic or hazardous materials

—Site access

—Availability and adequacy of financing to pay construction costs

—Delays caused by the owner or its agents

—Building permits and zoning compliance

Risks which may best be allocated to the contractor include:

---

[212] *Id.*

[213] Warren Bros Co v New York State Thruway Auth, 34 AD2d 97, 309 NYS2d 450 (1970), *affd*, 34 NY2d 770, 358 NYS2d 139 (1974).

[214] *See* Depot Constr Corp v State, 19 NY2d 109, 224 NE2d 866, 278 NYS2d 363 (1967) (lump sum contract would be increased by $10 per cubic yard of general rock excavated above 500 cubic yards and by $22 per cubic yard for rock excavated in pier and trench areas above 600 cubic yards).

[215] Miller v Town & Country, Inc, 74 Misc 2d 1038, 346 NYS2d 555 (Suffolk 1973).

[216] Andrew Catapano, Co v City of New York, 116 Misc 2d 163, 455 NYS2d 144 (NY 1980).

—Material and labor availability and price
—Labor strikes by the contractor's employees
—Delay due to minor weather variances
—Subcontractor performance
—Site safety
—Means and method of construction

Risks which may best be shared by the parties include:

—Industrywide labor strikes
—Impossibility of performance due to factors not within the parties' control, such as change of laws, total unavailability or extreme price increase of materials, prolonged unseasonable and extreme weather conditions, etc.

§2.37 —Pricing Risks

Pricing risks are discussed in several chapters in this text, including Chapters 1, 3, and 6.

§2.38 Risk Allocation in the Best Interest of the Project*

by Robert J. Smith
Wickwire Gavin, P.C.
Madison, Wisconsin

Risk is inherent in all of life's undertakings. The construction industry has long been recognized as particularly risk-laden. Some of these risks are fairly predictable; others are totally unforeseen. Some of them are clearly assignable; others are controversial. How these risks are allocated among parties to the

---

* §§2.38-2.44 have been adapted from a paper written by Robert J. Smith, entitled Risk Allocation in the Best Interest of the Project, presented in Atlanta, Georgia at an ABA Forum on Construction Industry (Oct 3-4, 1991).

Robert J. Smith is a shareholder in the law firm of Wickwire Gavin, P.C., in Madison, Wisconsin; Washington, D.C.; and Vienna, Virginia. His practice emphasizes construction contract law, engineering issues, and federal assistance law. He is a frequent lecturer throughout the country on subjects dealing with construction contracts and their administration, contract specifications, construction grants, and architect-engineer professional responsibility. Prior to entering into private practice, Mr. Smith was an Associate Professor of Engineering at the University of Wisconsin and also served as chairman of the Wisconsin Transportation Commission. As a Registered Professional Engineer, Mr. Smith is a member of the American Society of Civil Engineers and past chairman of its National Committee on Construction Contract Administration. He serves as counsel to the Engineers Joint Contract Documents Committee. He is a Fellow of the American College of Construction Lawyers. He earned civil engineering and law degrees from the University of Wisconsin.

contracting process has a direct bearing on *total* project costs. For example, unforeseen conditions or unexpected events may cause the cost and time of performance to increase. The constructed project may not perform as anticipated. The owner may have unrealistic expectations regarding the time and cost of construction, forcing contractors into unrealistic gambles, improvident corner cutting, or commitments that may not be realistic. Add to this the fiercely competitive nature of the construction industry, and it is not surprising that disputes over the rights and obligations of the parties occur. If a dollar loss from an unexpected risk is experienced, relationships become adversarial and energies are directed to things other than getting the job done right, on time, and within budget.

Misallocation and misperception of risks have resulted in owners paying more than necessary for many projects, due to bid contingencies and unanticipated involvement in dispute resolution by owner's staffs, consultants, and attorneys. Improper risk allocation can also cause additional costs in the form of delays to project utilization. Construction projects and their participants will benefit significantly by routinely taking a more systematic, structured, and global view of (and approach to) risk than is sometimes taken at present. Enhanced and broadened cognizance of the wide range of risks that could materialize during the planning, design, and construction phases of a project will result in better-informed and more prudent designs, improved specifications, better-informed bids, improved project relationships and communications, and enhanced construction contract administration practices. It is axiomatic that all of these, of course, should contribute to fewer misunderstandings and unfulfilled expectations, less acrimony, and, therefore, less time and money spent dealing with attempts to mitigate the adverse consequences of unanticipated risks. The end result is that many disputes will be avoided and others will be susceptible to resolution on the job. The entire project benefits.

§2.39 —Types of Risk

Construction contract risks have been categorized in an assortment of ways by various authors. For purposes of the present discussion, it is suggested that risk can be categorized as *contractual* or *construction*. *Contractual risk* emanates from contracts; it is increased with decreased contract clarity as well as imperfect communication and untimely contract administration. There is a very high benefit-to-cost ratio in dealing with contractual risk through improving both contract clarity and contract administration practices.[217] *Construction risk* is an inherent risk which arises from such diverse factors as weather, site conditions, and resource availability. Such risks can be better managed than reduced. Construction risk is often misallocated.[218]

---

[217] C.A. Erikson & M.J. O'Connor, Construction Contract Risk Assignment, Technical Rep P-101, Construction Engineering Research Laboratory, Rep No CERL-TR-P-101, at 9 (1979).

[218] *Id.*

As to what may or should be done with identified risks, one commentator has postulated that there are four methods for "managing" risks, namely: avoidance, abatement, retention, and transfer.[219]

§2.40 —Philosophies for Dealing with Risk

It may be safely stated that:

1. Risks belong with those parties that are best able to evaluate, control, bear the cost of, and benefit from the assumption of risks
2. Many risks and liabilities are best shared
3. Every risk has an associated and unavoidable cost that must be assumed somewhere in the process[220]

The Construction Industry Institute has stated:

> The ideal contract—the one that will be most cost effective—is one that assigns each risk to the party that is best equipped to manage and minimize that risk, recognizing the unique circumstances of the project.[221]

All parties to the design and construction process benefit when modern risk allocation principles and procedures are used. The result is truly a "win-win-win" situation.

Owners will have projects that are more likely to be completed on time, at a fair price, and which meet their needs and expectations. Though this is what every owner strives and hopes for when planning a project, achievement of these goals is often prevented when misallocated risks result in costly and disruptive delays and disputes. Owners that takes a fresh look at risk allocation typically experience reduced total project costs: if the contract says that the owner assumes certain risks and the contractor will get paid *if* certain specified events do or do not occur, the contractor need not include a contingency. In other words, there is a very substantial price to pay if the owner forces the contractor to take too much risk.

Construction contractors also benefit from risk allocation. When already thin profit margins are eroded by uncontrollable, unforeseeable events and unrealistic risk allocation, conflicts occur. Projects employing modern risk allocation typically have a very low rate of such conflicts. The fewer the uncertainties, and the more specific the allocation of risk, the easier it is for competing bidders

---

[219] G.E. Mason, A Quantitative Risk Management Approach to the Selection of Construction Contract Provisions, Technical Rep No 173, The Construction Institute, Department of Civil Engineering, Stanford University at 26-61 (Apr 1973).

[220] II American Socy of Civil Engineers, Construction Risks and Liability Sharing 2 (1980).

[221] *Impact of Various Construction Types and Clauses on Project Performance,* Construction Industry Institute Rep 10 (1986).

to "sharpen their pencils" and provide more competitive bids without contingencies and without the need to use litigation to try to stay solvent.

Design professionals also benefit. Under older philosophies of risk allocation, the design professional is often required to assume types and amounts of risk that are totally out of proportion to either its degree of involvement or its ability to manage or control the risks. On the other hand, modern risk allocation concepts will foster—rather than hinder—a truly professional relationship between the design professional and both the owner and the contractor.

§2.41 —Options for Allocating Risk

There are basically two approaches that the owner can take to address the overall question of risk allocation:

Transfer All Risk of Loss to Other Parties to the Process

Some owners take the view—and adhere to the practice—that they want to transfer all of the risks inherent in construction projects to either the contractor or the design professional or both. These owners believe that there will always be contractors and design professionals willing and available to take those risks and that this approach "locks in" a price at the beginning of the construction. Such an owner is in effect saying, "I will pay the architect or engineer so many dollars for its services and the contractor so many dollars for its services, and if anything unexpected occurs or anything goes wrong, that's their problem, not mine." This logic has some theoretical appeal. However, as a practical matter, things seldom work out this way. For example, if things go wrong and the unexpected occurs, disputes and delays are likely. The owner will find itself spending time and money dealing with problems, and may eventually end up in litigation.

Allocate and Manage Risks in Accordance with Established Principles

The other approach, and one being increasingly used, is to make enlightened risk allocation and contracting procedures part of the owner's standard procedures and documents. (Some specific suggestions are described hereafter.) Owners that take this approach have found that they have fewer delays and disputes and better relationships among all members of the construction team. In addition, they find that they themselves do a better job managing and administering contracts and obtain more competitive bids. At the same time, they report that the incremental costs of allocating risks are quite minimal. Obviously, if a major risk retained by the owner materializes, the owner will pay more. However, if the risk was logically the owner's in the first place, the cost to the owner is no greater.

§2.42 —Integrating Cost Effective Risk Allocation Language into Contract Documents and Contract Procedures

A detailed and sophisticated approach to risk management would have the owner examine its existing contract documents and existing contract practices to determine how they address *each* listed risk. One structured way of addressing some of the more commonly recognized and widely understood risks is to look at them in groups or categories such as the following:

1. Resources and prerequisites to the project (i.e.: adequacy of project funding, adequacy of labor force, permits and licenses, and site access)

2. Performance-related risks (i.e.: sufficiency of plans, underestimation of costs, owner-furnished material and equipment, contractor-furnished material and equipment, means and methods of construction, delay in presenting problems, delay in addressing and solving problems, labor productivity, subsurface conditions, and worker and site safety)

3. Outside-influence risks (i.e.: governmental acts, adverse weather, acts of God, union strife and work rules, and cost escalation)

Each of these risk categories is analyzed in one of the following tables. Table 1 analyzes risks related to project resources and prerequisites; Table 2 analyzes risks related to performance; and Table 3 analyzes risks related to outside influences.

(Text continued on page 63)

TABLE 1
HOW TO ALLOCATE RESOURCE AND PROJECT PREREQUISITE RISKS

RISK	TO WHOM ALLOCATED AND WHY	HOW ALLOCATED/ MITIGATED
Adequacy of Project Funding	Owner—it's the owner's project	Contract language giving contractor right to confirm availability of funds (see American Institute of Architects (AIA), AIA Doc A-201, ¶2.2.1)
Adequacy of Labor Force	Contractor—can best assess at time of bidding	Owner should consider known labor shortage in a particular trade (e.g., ironworkers) in making decisions on alternate materials; owner should consider projected surplus/shortage in determining project schedule
Permits and Licenses	Shared—both parties have some ability to control	Owner should identify all requirements to extent possible; contractor has some lead role in compliance
Site Access	Owner—it's the owner's site	Owner should identify requirements early and then specify them in bidding documents

TABLE 2
HOW TO ALLOCATE PERFORMANCE-RELATED RISKS

RISK	TO WHOM ALLOCATED AND WHY	HOW ALLOCATED/ MITIGATED
Sufficiency of Plans	Owner—funds design	Qualified design professional; adequate design effort[222]
Underestimation of Costs	Contractor—controllable[223]	Competent estimating
Owner-Furnished Material and Equipment	Owner—elects to use this method	Preplanning for purchases, expediting; remedies
Contractor-Furnished Material and Equipment	Contractor—typical scenario	Preplanning for purchases, expediting; remedies
Means and Methods of Construction	Contractor—area of expertise	Using/following "standard" language
Delay in Presenting Problems	Claiming party—controls ability to give notice	Using/following/ enforcing notice provisions
Delay in Addressing and Solving Problems	Party receiving claim—has obligation to respond	Delegating decision-making authority to on-site personnel (also *see* Chapter 16 for discussion on dispute review boards)
Subsurface Conditions	Owner—owns site	Differing site conditions clause; no disclaimers
Worker and Site Safety	Contractor—controls	Clear contract language

---

[222] Often designs are not practical. When this is the case, there may be delays and additional costs incurred to come up with an alternative. By having plans and specifications reviewed for "constructability" before contractors bid on them, owners can modify designs, making construction easier. If planned for in advance, a constructibility review will not add to the time required to do the design, and the cost is minimal.

[223] The majority of this risk is typically assigned to the contractor, but obviously the level of detail on the plans, which is controlled by the design professional and the owner, has an impact here as well.

TABLE 3
HOW TO ALLOCATE OUTSIDE-INFLUENCE RISKS

RISK	TO WHOM ALLOCATED AND WHY	HOW ALLOCATED/ MITIGATED
Governmental Acts	Shared—not foreseeable or controllable	Suspension of work clause
Adverse Weather	Shared—not foreseeable or controllable	Time extension clause
Acts of God	Shared—not foreseeable or controllable	Time extension clause
Cost Escalation	Shared—not foreseeable or controllable	Formula to pay escalation on long-term contracts

§2.43 —What Some Owners are Doing to Better Allocate Risks and Reduce Their Total Project Costs[224]

Contracting procedures and contract documents are the keys to implementing improved risk allocation. To reap the benefits of risk allocation, owners must perform systematic reviews of both their procedures and their documents and compare them with modern practices. Existing procedures and documents are usually the result of incremental additions over the years, with few subtractions. Many times both procedures and documents are "handed down" from one person to another—the "we've always done it this way" approach. Contracts may contain clauses which are unclear or specify procedures which are no longer used.

Owners must ask themselves *how* they allocate risk, *why* they do it that way, and *if* there is a better way.

Including Predefined Adjustment Equations and Procedures

In order to eliminate many sources of disagreement from the contract administration process, some owners specify clear and accurate provisions that establish formulas or methods to predetermine value for disputable items, such as profit on change orders, overhead, equipment rates, change order procedures, and force account procedures. Home office overhead rates, although subject to wider variation within the industry, are also preset in a range acceptable to the owner and contractor. A contract provision is also included to establish a generally accepted manual for determining the equipment rates to be used in pricing any change orders.

---

[224] This section is based in part on portions of *Impact of Various Construction Types and Clauses on Project Performance*, Construction Industry Institute Rep 10 (1986).

It is equally important for the contract to contain very clear provisions with respect to how change orders should be processed and what information should be included in a request for change orders. The same is true for force account provisions, which would enable the contractor to be paid on a timely basis for disputed work, pending negotiation of a change order modification.

Some consideration should be given to include, as a unit price, a per diem value for extended project time. In the event of an owner-caused delay, this amount would be added to any change order, carrying with it entitlement to an extension of time.

§2.44 —The Role of Counsel: Advocate or Counselor?

When attorneys draft contracts for owners, they work from a position of substantial power and influence and may embark on a course of drafting as many pro-owner and anti-contractor clauses as is reasonably possible, or as time permits. Such action is presumably justified by the belief that it is necessary in order to carry out the ethical obligation to represent a client *zealously* within the bounds of the law. Indeed, many current practitioners were schooled and admonished that zealous advocacy was their duty. This is consistent with lawyers' training and conditioning: Be an advocate!

It is submitted that when it comes to construction contract draftsmanship, the lawyer's role should *not* be to draft a contract that in the lawyer's opinion seemingly represents the "best" situation for the client. Rather, in drafting and reviewing construction contract documents, the lawyer is serving his or her client's best interests (and, therefore, the best interests of the project) by acting as a competent advisor. Knowledge of risks and the implications of inappropriate risk allocation are components of competent representation and counseling.

§2.45 Subcontract Terms and Conditions

Subcontract terms are discussed in Chapter 3.

§2.46 Standard Contract Forms

There are several standard contract forms. The most widely used forms in private construction are those of the American Institute of Architects (AIA).[225]

The AIA publishes some 50 standard contracts, ranging from a basic owner-architect agreement for small projects to a sophisticated owner-contractor agreement for major federally assisted projects. These forms are well drafted, mutually consistent, and integrated with one another. Thus, for example, the

---

[225] Standard contract forms published by the AIA may be obtained by writing to: The American Institute of Architects, 1735 New York Avenue, N.W., Washington, D.C. 20006.

§2.46 STANDARD CONTRACT FORMS

owner-architect, owner-contractor, and contractor-subcontractor forms all have consistent terminology and parallel provisions, such that they can each be used on the same project without significant modification. But therein lies the potential trap. Few parties do use these forms without modification because of the perceived inherent bias of these documents. It is not surprising, for example, that it is widely believed by owners that the AIA standard contracts are biased in favor of architects. Some of the clauses referred to in support of this belief provide for the following:

1. There is no time of performance for the architect's services[226]
2. An attempt is made to relieve the architect from responsibility for site safety[227]
3. The architect has the responsibility only to "periodically visit" the site "to become generally familiar with the progress and quality of the work completed and to determine in general if the work is being performed in a manner indicating that the work when completed will be in accordance with the Contract Documents"[228]
4. The architect cannot be required by consolidation or joinder to participate in an arbitration between the owner and the contractor[229]
5. The architect is indemnified and held harmless by the contractor and its subcontractors[230]

Once one of the AIA documents is modified, the other documents have to be reviewed for possible modification. For example, if arbitration is eliminated from the owner-architect agreement, the owner is probably well advised to eliminate arbitration from the owner-contractor agreement. Similarly, in such an event, the contractor would probably wish to eliminate arbitration from the contractor-subcontractor agreements. An alternative is to remove the anticonsolidation language from the various arbitration clauses. For a more complete discussion of dispute resolution clauses, see Chapter 16.

Although often the subject of some debate within the construction industry, there is an expressed belief within the industry that the AIA standard contracts are also somewhat biased in favor of contractors over owners and in favor of subcontractors over contractors.

Thus, the AIA standard contracts are often used as a model or a starting point in drafting contract documents for a particular project; but they are rarely used without some, and often substantial, modification.

Although the AIA standard contracts are perhaps the best known and most widely used standard contracts, other professional and trade organizations have developed and disseminate their own standard contract forms. While the

---

[226] AIA Doc B141, ¶1.1.2 (1987 ed).
[227] *Id* ¶2.6.6.
[228] *Id* ¶2.6.5.
[229] *Id* ¶7.3.
[230] *Id* A201, ¶3.18.1 (1987 ed); *id* A401, ¶4.6.1 (1987 ed).

standard contracts of the AIA are well suited for building construction, those of the Engineers Joint Contract Documents Committee (EJCDC)[231] are believed by some to be better suited to engineered or heavy construction, such as infrastructure, highways, bridges, marine structures, site development, power engineering, and dams.

Similarly, depending upon the bias sought, standard contracts published by the Associated General Contractors of America, Inc (AGC),[232] American Subcontractors Association (ASA),[233] American Society of Foundation Engineers (ASFE),[234] and Construction Management Association of America (CMAA),[235] may be consulted.

Public Contracts

Most larger public entities have their own standard form contracts which they use on construction projects. The form language, terms, and conditions generally are nonnegotiable. Smaller public entities often use the AIA standard forms and standard New York State Specifications.

Regardless of the source of a form contract, it will be construed against the party that decided to use it.[236]

§2.47 Interpreting the Contract

Standard rules of contract interpretation apply to construction contracts,[237] whether they are public or private works contracts.[238] Contracts are construed most strongly against the parties that drafted them.[239] Contracts are interpreted

---

[231] The following organizations are part of the Engineers Joint Contract Documents Committee: National Society of Professional Engineers (NSPE); American Consulting Engineers Council (ACEC); American Society of Civil Engineers (ASCE); The Construction Specifications Institute, Inc. (CSI). Copies of the EJCDC contract forms may be obtained by writing to: The American Society of Civil Engineers, 345 East 47th Street, New York, New York 10017.

[232] Copies of the standard contract forms used by the AGC may be obtained by writing to: The Associated General Contractors of America, 1957 E. Street N.W., Washington, D.C. 20006.

[233] Copies of the standard contract forms used by the ASA may be obtained by writing to: The American Subcontractors Association, 1004 Duke Street, Alexandria, Virginia 22314-3512.

[234] Copies of the standard contract forms used by the ASFE may be obtained from: ASFE, 8811 Colesville Road, Suite G106, Silver Spring, Maryland 20910. Telephone: (301) 565-2733.

[235] Copies of the standard contract forms used by the CMAA may be obtained by writing to: Construction Management Association of America, Inc, 12355 Sunrise Valley Drive, Reston, Virginia. Telephone: (703) 391-1200.

[236] Frye v State, 192 Misc 260, 78 NYS2d 342 (Ct Cl 1948).

[237] Frye v State, 192 Misc 260, 78 NYS2d 342 (Ct Cl 1948).

[238] *Id.*

[239] Deverho Constr Co v State, 94 Misc 2d 1053, 407 NYS2d 399 (Ct Cl 1978).

as of the date of their execution, not the date of their breach.[240]

If a contract is unambiguous, it must be given its fair and reasonable[241] or plain meaning.[242] A court may not use rules of construction to add or delete terms[243] or to relieve a party from a disadvantage it suffers under an unambiguous contract.[244] For instance, where a carefully worded contract plainly gave a village the right to withhold consent for an owner to enlarge its property, the Court of Appeals refused to add a requirement of reasonableness to the village's exercise of power.[245]

A contract is unambiguous if it is not reasonably susceptible to more than one meaning.[246] That a contract is complex and intricate does not mean it is ambiguous.[247] If a contract is ambiguous, it must be construed to give effect to its main purpose[248] and to give the parties' intent its full purpose as reflected by the contract language.[249] Similarly, an ambiguous contract should not be given a literal construction which would defeat the purpose of the contract.[250] Ambiguous contract language should be construed towards what the nondrafter reasonably thought it meant, not what the drafter intended to say.[251]

If a contract has general and specific provisions, the specific provisions control where there is conflict or ambiguity.[252]

Generally, a contract's legal effect is determined by the laws of the state in which it was executed, unless the parties otherwise agreed.[253] Parties may pro-

---

[240] XLO Concrete Corp v John T. Brady & Co, 104 AD2d 181, 482 NYS2d 476 (1st Dept 1984), affd mem, 66 NY2d 970, 489 NE2d 768, 498 NYS2d 799 (1985).

[241] Sutton v East River Sav Bank, 55 NY2d 550, 435 NE2d 1075, 450 NYS2d 460 (1982).

[242] Mazzola v County of Suffolk, 143 AD2d 734, 533 NYS2d 297 (2d Dept 1988).

[243] Shames v Abel, 141 AD2d 531, 529 NYS2d 344 (2d Dept 1988).

[244] Collard v Incorporated Village of Flower Hill, 52 NY2d 594, 421 NE2d 818, 439 NYS2d 326 (1981).

[245] *Id.*

[246] Shames v Abel, 141 AD2d 531, 529 NYS2d 344 (2d Dept 1988).

[247] Goodstein Constr Corp v City of NY, 111 AD2d 49, 489 NYS2d 175 (1st Dept 1985), affd, 67 NY2d 990, 494 NE2d 99, 502 NYS2d 994 (1986), *related Article 78 proceeding,* Goodstein Constr Corp v Gliedman, 117 AD2d 170, 502 NYS2d 136 (1st Dept 1986), affd mem, 69 NY2d 930, 509 NE2d 350, 516 NYS2d 655 (1987).

[248] Cromwell Towers Redev Co v City of Yonkers, 41 NY2d 1, 359 NE2d 333, 390 NYS2d 822 (1976); Christiana Point Dev, Inc v Galesi, 143 AD2d 717, 533 NYS2d 443 (2d Dept 1988).

[249] Goodstein Constr Corp v City of New York, 111 AD2d 49, 489 NYS2d 175 (1st Dept 1985), affd, 67 NY2d 990, 494 NE2d 99, 502 NYS2d 994 (1986), *related Article 78 proceeding,* Goodstein Constr Corp v Gliedman, 117 AD2d 170, 502 NYS2d 136 (1st Dept 1986), affd mem, 69 NY2d 930, 509 NE2d 350, 516 NYS2d 655 (1987).

[250] Tougher Heating & Plumbing Co v State, 73 AD2d 732, 423 NYS2d 289 (3d Dept 1979).

[251] Deverho Constr Co v State, 94 Misc 2d 1053, 407 NYS2d 399 (Ct Cl 1978).

[252] Waldman v New Phone Dimensions, Inc, 109 AD2d 702, 487 NYS2d 29 (1st Dept 1985).

[253] Yager v Rubymar Corp, 34 Misc 2d 704, 216 NYS2d 577 (Kings 1961).

vide that the laws of another state apply so long as the contract has a reasonable relation to that other state,[254] such as a party's headquarters being located there.[255]

§2.48 —Use of Extrinsic Evidence/Parol Evidence Rule

The *parol evidence rule*, which is not a rule of evidence but, rather, of contract construction, provides that oral evidence will not be heard to explain a written contract "unless uncertainty or doubt springs from the written agreement."[256] Thus, if a contract is unambiguous, extrinsic evidence will not be considered[257] for the rather simple reason that if the parties' intent is fully determinable from the contract language, there is no need to resort to outside evidence to interpret it.[258]

That extrinsic evidence is needed to resolve a latent ambiguity does not render the contract invalid. To resolve an ambiguity, a court may look to the parties' intent, the parties' prior dealings, the purpose sought to be effected in the contract, and the means employed.[259] In some instances, a court may use custom and usage to interpret a contract if the custom and usage is

> reasonable, uniform, well-settled, not in opposition to fixed rules of law, not in contradiction of the express terms of the contract, is deemed to form part of the contract, and is deemed to enter into the intention of the parties . . . [to explain phrases used in] a particular sense, by particular persons, as to particular subjects.[260]

To be bound by custom and usage, a party must either know or have reason to know of its existence and nature.

---

[254] Sears, Roebuck & Co v Enco Assocs, 83 Misc 2d 552, 370 NYS2d 338 (Westchester 1975), *affd*, 54 AD2d 13, 385 NYS2d 613 (2d Dept 1976), *affd as modified as to unrelated issue*, 43 NY2d 389, 372 NE2d 555, 401 NYS2d 767 (1977) (dicta).

[255] George Hyman Constr Co v Precision Walls, Inc, 132 AD2d 523, 517 NYS2d 263 (2d Dept 1987).

[256] Benderson Dev Co v Schwab Bros Trucking, Inc, 64 AD2d 447, 448, 409 NYS2d 890, 897 (4th Dept 1978).

[257] West, Weir & Bartel, Inc v Mary Carter Paint Co, 25 NY2d 535, 255 NE2d 709, 307 NYS2d 449 (1969), *remittitur amended*, 26 NY2d 969, 259 NE2d 483, 311 NYS2d 13 (1970).

[258] Teal v Place, 85 AD2d 788, 445 NYS2d 309 (3d Dept 1981).

[259] Frye v State, 192 Misc 260, 78 NYS2d 342 (Ct Cl 1948).

[260] *Id* at 264, 78 NYS2d at 347.

§2.49 —Conflict Between Contract and Other Documents

Agreements executed at essentially the same time, by the same parties, with the same purpose, and which relate to the same subject matter are regarded as contemporaneous and must be read together and incorporated as if one document.[261] Similarly, if several documents constitute part of the same transaction, they must be interpreted together.[262] If the several documents are in agreement, there is no problem. If, however, the documents contradict each other or are inconsistent, there arises the question of which document controls.

The general rule is that a specific document or specific language controls over a more general document or general language. Thus, if two documents control the transaction and one is a general form and one was specifically prepared for the transaction in question, the specifically prepared document takes precedence in the event of inconsistencies.[263]

§2.50 —Conflict Between Plans and Specifications

When plans and technical specifications conflict with each other, claims for extras, delays, and change orders often result. The general rule is that specifications control over plans.[264] An exception to this rule is if the specifications are not truly technical specifications but are merely additional conditions and terms of the parties' agreement or are standard specifications applicable to all contracts. In such cases, the plans, which are specific to the job concerned, would control.[265]

Specifications should be construed as a whole, not in a piecemeal fashion. Further, they should be given the practical interpretation given them by the parties before the dispute arose and should be read in light of recognized trade usage and custom[266] and any prior dealing between the parties.[267] Conflict between performance and detailed specifications is discussed in Chapter 6.

---

[261] BWA Corp v Alltrans Express USA, Inc, 112 AD2d 850, 493 NYS2d 1 (1st Dept 1985); Flemington Natl Bank & Trust Co v Domler Leasing Corp, 65 AD2d 29, 410 NYS2d 75 (1st Dept 1978), *affd*, 48 NY2d 678, 397 NE2d 393, 421 NYS2d 881 (1979).

[262] BWA Corp v Alltrans Express USA, Inc, 112 AD2d 850, 493 NYS2d 1 (1st Dept 1985).

[263] Teal v Place, 85 AD2d 788, 445 NYS2d 309 (3d Dept 1981).

[264] Green v City of NY, 283 AD 485, 128 NYS2d 715 (1st Dept 1954); Byrne Constr Co v New York State Thruway Auth, 30 Misc 2d 980, 221 NYS2d 632 (Ct Cl 1961), *affd*, 19 AD2d 192, 241 NYS2d 58 (4th Dept 1963).

[265] Pallette v State, 266 AD 490, 43 NYS2d 553 (3d Dept 1943), *affd*, 292 NY 657, 55 NE2d 518 (1944); Young Fehlhaber Pile Co v State, 265 AD 61, 37 NYS2d 928 (3d Dept 1942).

[266] Heating Maintenance Corp v State, 206 Misc 605, 134 NYS2d 71 (Ct Cl 1954).

[267] Schubtex, Inc v Allen Snyder Inc, 49 NY2d 1, 399 NE2d 1154, 424 NYS2d 133 (1970).

§2.51 Incorporation by Reference

This issue is discussed in Chapter 3.

The Subcontract

3

§3.01 Introduction
§3.02 Subcontract and Supply Contract Formation
§3.03 "Standard" Subcontract Forms
§3.04 Subcontract Provisions
§3.05 —Boilerplate
§3.06 —Incorporation by Reference
§3.07 —Scope of Work
§3.08 —Time of Performance
§3.09 —Contractor's Duties
§3.10 —Job Site
§3.11 —Warranties
§3.12 —Change Orders and Extras
§3.13 —Hold Harmless and Indemnification Clauses
§3.14 —Sub-subcontractors and Materialmen
§3.15 —Relations with Other Subcontractors
§3.16 —Progress Payments
§3.17 —Retainage
§3.18 —Contingent Payment Clauses
§3.19 —Final Payment
§3.20 —Back Charges
§3.21 —Offsets
§3.22 —Delay Damages
§3.23 —Liquidating Agreements
§3.24 —Default/Termination
§3.25 —Remedies for Non-Payment
§3.26 —Lien Waivers
§3.27 Purchase Orders and Supply Contracts
§3.28 Applicable Law—The UCC

§3.29   Terms of Supply Contract
§3.30   —Time of Performance
§3.31   —Acceptance and Rejection
§3.32   —Price and Terms of Payment
§3.33   —Warranties
§3.34   —Insurance and Shipping
§3.35   Actions for Breach and Damages

§3.01   Introduction

Subcontractors and materialmen are important players in construction projects. Rare is the general contractor that performs all the necessary work and provides all needed materials by itself. The obligations, rights, representations, and warranties of subcontractors and materialmen, both alone and in relation to the prime contract, must be understood. This chapter addresses these contracts and their terms. General principles of formation, consideration, mutuality, statute of frauds, authority to contract, and the like are discussed in Chapter 2. In-depth discussion of many terms typical to subcontracts, supply contracts, and prime contracts is found in other chapters. Thus, the discussion here is brief and is intended to serve as a guide in negotiating subcontracts and supply contracts.

Subcontractors are skilled in one particular trade or work item. By continually performing the same type of work, subcontractors become efficient and cost effective. Subcontractors perform some portion of the prime contract by supplying labor and materials.[1] Their contract is with the general or prime contractor, not with the owner. Thus, subcontractors look to the contractor for payment. It is not unusual for there to be more than one tier of subcontractors. For example, a general contractor usually subcontracts the installation and finishing of drywall. If the drywall subcontractor hires a company to tape, spackle, and sand the drywall, such company is a sub-subcontractor or a second tier subcontractor.

A materialman or supplier merely furnishes materials for the construction project. They do not, as a general rule, do any actual work at the job site. As is discussed in more detail in §3.27, the distinction between suppliers and subcontractors is not always clear.

§3.02   Subcontract and Supply Contract Formation

Subcontract formation often begins before a prime contract exists. When bidding a prime contract, the contractor will contact subcontractors and materialmen and ask them to bid on portions of the prime contract. The price, scope of work, and time of performance are often set in the subcontractor's bid, upon which the contractor relies in making its bid for the prime contract.

---

[1] Dorn v Arthur A. Johnson Corp, 16 AD2d 1009, 229 NYS2d 266 (1962).

As is discussed more thoroughly in Chapter 2, a subcontractor's or materialman's bid may be binding on the subcontractor once a contractor has communicated its acceptance of the bid to the subcontractor or materialman and incorporated it into its prime contract bid.[2] However, the general contractor is under no obligation to award a subcontract to a subcontractor whose bid the general contractor used.

> **PRACTICE POINTER:**
>
> If a general contractor intends to rely on a sub's or supplier's quote in formulating its bid, the general contractor ought to confirm the quote in writing, stating its intent to rely thereon.

§3.03 "Standard" Subcontract Forms

Several "standard" subcontract forms exist which are used by contractors, owners, and architects. The main benefit of a standard form is that, generally, the parties are familiar with the agreement's terms and what modifications, if any, they require. Further, standard subcontract forms, such as American Institute of Architects (AIA) Document 401 and Associated General Contractors of America (AGC) Subcontract Form 600, are used so frequently that often it is known how courts will interpret their terms.

No project is "standard" or "typical." Use of a standard form not tailored to the specific project may cause problems. Drawbacks to these form subcontracts are that they may give one party more or less rights than desired and may provide remedies or powers which seem overexpansive to some parties. For instance, a subcontractor may not wish to be bound to the arbitration terms of the prime contract. If the subcontractor signs an unamended AIA Document 401, it agrees to arbitrate any disputes pursuant to the arbitration terms of the prime contract.[3] Generally, AIA Document 401 is the more favorable standard form from a subcontractor's view, while AGC Subcontract Form 600 is written more in favor of the contractor.

It is important to be thoroughly familiar with the standard form subcontracts. This chapter does not analyze or compare these standard forms. It discusses general and typical subcontract terms which may be found in the forms or in individual subcontracts drafted by contractors, subcontractors, architects, and their attorneys.

§3.04 Subcontract Provisions

Subcontracts should be written and as complete as possible to avoid litigation over what the parties meant or intended. The provisions discussed in §§3.05-3.26 should be included in most subcontracts.

---

[2] Cortland Asbestos Prods, Inc v J&K Plumbing & Heating Co, 33 AD2d 11, 304 NYS2d 694 (1969); Drennan v Star Paving Co, 51 Cal 2d 409, 333 P2d 757 (1958).

[3] AIA Doc A 401, ¶6.1 (1987 ed).

§3.05 —Boilerplate

As in a prime contract, much of a subcontract is *boilerplate*—terms that deal with general matters and do not discuss the specific work to be performed or price to be paid. Boilerplate typically found in subcontracts includes: incorporation by reference of the prime contract; a clause binding the subcontractor to the general contractor to the same extent that the general contractor is bound to the owner; a requirement to comply with all laws and safety regulations; insurance requirements; a duty to proceed with work even if disputed; and dispute resolution provisions. Analysis of boilerplate common to prime contracts and subcontracts is found in Chapter 2.

Section 5-322.2 of the General Obligations Law provides that all subcontracts for the improvement of private property, except those for residential property involving accommodations for less than five families, must contain the full name and address of the owner(s) of the land and buildings and a description of the property by street address; section, block, and lot numbers; or reference to a deed book and page number.[4] If the ownership of the property changes during construction, the owner is required to notify the contractor, who is required to notify the subcontractor, within five days of the change.[5] A failure to comply with the statute has no effect on the validity of the contract.[6]

§3.06 —Incorporation by Reference

It is not unusual for a subcontract to incorporate the prime contract by reference. These clauses, also known as *flow down* and *pass through* clauses, often attempt to bind a subcontractor to all obligations of the prime contract in addition to the obligations of its subcontract. Typically, the subcontractor has not seen the prime contract and is unaware of its provisions for retainage, certification of work completed, notice requirements, termination rights, delay damages, arbitration, etc. Before signing a subcontract that incorporates the prime contract into its terms, a subcontractor should obtain a copy of the prime contract and review it thoroughly. In this way, the subcontractor may exclude, by express language, incorporation of some portions of the prime contract.

Where a subcontract simply states that the terms of the prime contract are incorporated into the subcontract, without specifying any provisions of the prime contract, only those provisions of the prime contract which specifically relate to the scope, quality, or manner of performance of the work by the subcontractor are in fact incorporated into the subcontract and bind the subcontractor.[7] Thus, unless specifically incorporated, a subcontractor is not bound

---

[4] NY Gen Oblig Law §5-322.2(1)(a) and (b), (2) (McKinney 1989).

[5] *Id* §5-322.2(1)(c).

[6] *Id* §5-322.2(4).

[7] United States Steel Corp v Turner Constr Co, 560 F Supp 871 (SDNY 1983).

by the prime contract's forum selection clause,[8] *no damage for delay* clause,[9] or *waiver of damages* clause,[10] or a clause that governs the resolution of claims between the owner and prime contractor.[11] A general incorporation will not bind a subcontractor to an arbitration clause, unless it is specifically agreed to in the subcontract.[12]

Despite the general rule stated above, the standard for specifically incorporating terms of the prime contract into the subcontract is minimal. To specifically include a term of the prime contract, the subcontract need only refer to it or its location in the contract in a general way. Thus, an incorporation of the "General Conditions" of the prime contract will subject a subcontractor to the terms found in the General Conditions.[13]

The fact that the subcontract incorporates the prime contract into its terms does not place the subcontractor in privity of contract with, nor provide the subcontractor with a direct right of action against, the owner.[14] The subcontractor's contract is with the general contractor, despite the incorporation.

Where a subcontract contains a clear requirement and incorporates all prime contract terms related to that requirement, but the prime contract is silent on the issue, the subcontract controls.[15] For instance, in one case, a subcontract specifically provided that all claims and disputes arising out of or in relation to the subcontract or its breach would be resolved by arbitration "in the same manner and under the same procedures as provided in the [general contract]."[16] The general contract did not contain any provision for arbitration. The Appellate Division held that subcontract disputes were bound by the agreement to arbitrate because the parties' intent to be bound by arbitration was clear from the subcontract; the general contract was only to supply the method and manner of the arbitration. Further, where the subcontract incorpo-

---

[8] George Hyman Constr Co v Precision Walls, Inc, 132 AD2d 523, 517 NYS2d 263 (1987); United States Steel Corp v Turner Constr Co, 560 F Supp 871 (SDNY 1983).

[9] S. Leo Harmonay, Inc v Binks Mfg Co, 597 F Supp 1014 (SDNY 1984), *affd*, 762 F2d 990 (2d Cir 1985).

[10] *Id.*

[11] United States Steel Corp v Turner Constr Co, 560 F Supp 871 (SDNY 1983).

[12] *See* Transamerica Ins Co v Yonkers Contracting Co, 49 Misc 2d 512, 267 NYS2d 669 (NY 1966) (surety not bound by arbitration clause in subcontract despite bond's incorporation of subcontract by reference; court held that arbitration is not mandated unless the parties agree to it by clear and unequivocal language); *but see* Pearl St Dev Corp v Conduit & Found Corp, 41 NY2d 167, 359 NE2d 693, 391 NYS2d 98 (1976) (court left it to arbitrators to determine which of two conflicting arbitration clauses applied, the one in the subcontract or the one in the prime contract where the prime contract was generally incorporated into the subcontract).

[13] New York Tel Co v Schumacher & Forelle, Inc, 60 AD2d 151, 400 NYS2d 332 (1977).

[14] Alvord & Swift v Stewart M. Muller Constr Co, 46 NY2d 276, 385 NE2d 1238, 413 NYS2d 309 (1978); Delta Elec, Inc v Ingram & Greene, Inc, 123 AD2d 369, 506 NYS2d 594 (1986).

[15] LA Swyer Co v John W. Cowper Co, 55 AD2d 774, 389 NYS2d 197 (3d Dept 1976).

[16] *Id* 198.

rates the prime contract but the two have different payment terms, the subcontract payment terms control so long as they do not interfere or conflict with pertinent portions of general contract terms regarding the owner's payments to the general contractor.[17] Thus, in a case where the general contract provided one method of payment and retainage and the subcontract another while also incorporating the general contract terms, the court held that the subcontract terms applied to the subcontract parties since the payment terms were not in conflict with the general contract and did not affect the owner's right to retain installments from the general contractor.[18] Where, however, the subcontract contains a clause which is not in total agreement with the incorporated prime contract on the issue, the courts or arbitrators must determine which clause the parties intended would control the issue.[19] In *Pearl Street Development Corp v Conduit & Foundation Corp*,[20] the Court of Appeals was asked to decide which arbitration clause applied—the one in the subcontract, which did not include conditions precedent to arbitration, or the general contract clause, which did include such conditions and was incorporated by reference into the general contract. The court did not reach the issue presented but found that the arbitration clause applied to the issue of which clause applied and, thus, left it to the arbitrators to determine which clause the parties intended to govern their disputes and, if they found the general contract to govern, to determine whether conditions precedent had been met.

§3.07 —Scope of Work[21]

While it is always prudent to define the required work as precisely as possible, this advice is nowhere more important than when drafting a subcontract. If the subcontract states that the subcontractor shall perform "all plumbing work necessary and all related items," the plumbing subcontractor may find itself in a dispute with its contractor regarding who is responsible for preparation work, who is to bear the cost of the fixtures to be installed, and whether two or three sinks were intended. An imprecise description of the work may result in the subcontractor having to perform work or supply materials it did not intend to include in its bid or in being precluded from recovery for what it claims are extras. The use of words such as "required" may cause problems as well; does "required" mean all such work at the site or such work as is directed to be done by the general contractor?[22]

---

[17] Fehlhaber Corp v Unicon Management Corp, 32 AD2d 367, 302 NYS2d 98 (1st Dept 1969), *affd*, 27 NY2d 828, 265 NE2d 257, 316 NYS2d 435 (1970).

[18] *Id.*

[19] Pearl St Dev Corp v Conduit & Found Corp, 41 NY2d 167, 359 NE2d 693, 391 NYS2d 98 (1976).

[20] *Id.*

[21] Analysis of scope-of-work disputes may be found in Robert A. Rubin, *Scope of Work Disputes*, in Construction Litigation 89-114 (K. Cushman ed 1981).

[22] Hansen Excavating Co v Benjamin, 36 Misc 2d 686, 233 NYS2d 589 (Nassau 1962).

The subcontract should include a specific and precise description of the work to be performed and materials to be supplied with reference to specific drawings, plans, specifications, and terms of the prime contract. Further, any agreed-upon additions to or exclusions from the plans or specifications should be enumerated clearly in the subcontract. When a subcontract contains a description of the work to be performed and materials to be installed by the subcontractor, the subcontractor's duties will be limited to those matters included.[23]

> **PRACTICE POINTER:**
>
> A general contractor may include the following scope-of-work terms, which a subcontractor should attempt to remove from the subcontract:
>
> . . . and all related materials
>
> . . . and all related items
>
> . . . as is typical of those in the trade
>
> . . . and all work shown in the plans and specifications
>
> . . . and all work required by the general contract
>
> . . . including all work usually performed by the trade
>
> . . . as are usually performed or furnished in connection with such work
>
> . . . the subcontractor is required to furnish and perform whatever is necessary to make a functioning system, regardless of whether shown in the contract.

§3.08 —Time of Performance

Time of performance typically is expressed in the prime contract in one of two ways: either as (1) a specific date of completion, or as (2) a number of working or calendar days for completion. Most subcontract forms do not state a specific time for performance. Instead, the typical form of the subcontract requires the subcontractor to cooperate and coordinate its work with the prime contractor. This includes the subcontractor's obligation to cooperate with the prime contractor in scheduling and sequencing the work. The American Institute of Architects (AIA) Standard Form of Agreement between Contractor and Subcontractor provides that the subcontractor's work is to be performed in such a way as to "avoid conflict, delay in or interference with the work of the Contractor, other contractors or the Owner's own forces."[24]

From the prime contractor's perspective, the prime must have the ability to control the sequencing of construction in a manner that will be most efficient

---

[23] *See* JN Futia Co v Schenectady Mun Hous Auth, 33 AD2d 591, 304 NYS2d 358 (1969) (plumbing subcontractor not required to install grab bar supports where subcontract obligated plumber to "provide and install" grab bars and no mention was made of grab bar supports in the subcontract although required in the prime contract).

[24] AIA Doc A401, §4.1.1 (1987 ed)

for the overall project. The prime's schedule should not be unreasonably interfered with by a subcontractor because such interference may be detrimental to performance of the prime's work and the work of other subcontractors on the project. The prime must be able to exercise such control even if doing so does not result in the most beneficial manner of performance for an individual subcontractor.

In order to make it clear that the subcontractor shall not be entitled to be paid additional compensation as a result of the prime's sequencing of the subcontractor's work, the subcontract should contain a clause which provides that the subcontractor shall not be entitled to damages for delays occasioned by acts or omissions of the prime contractor. The subcontract should also provide that in the event of delays in the subcontractor's work occasioned by the prime's acts or omissions, the subcontractor's sole remedy would be an extension of time for the subcontractor's performance.

If a subcontractor should happen to have sufficient bargaining power over a prime contractor, the subcontractor may be able to impose certain restrictions on the subcontractor's time for performance. For example, a concrete subcontractor may require that work under the subcontract not be performed when the temperature drops below a certain temperature without the prime contractor incurring additional costs for heat protection. Other subcontractors that possess such bargaining power often include sole source and specialty subcontractors. These kinds of restrictions can be detrimental and very costly to the prime unless the prime is able to pass these costs on to the project owner.

§3.09 —Contractor's Duties

While common law imposes some obligations on contractors under a subcontract, such as not interfering with, hindering, or obstructing the subcontractor's performance[25] and providing a reasonably safe place to work,[26] it is best to state specifically what the contractor's duties are, redundant as that may seem. Thus, while "everyone knows" that a contractor must often do work before the job site is ready for the subcontractor, and that the contractor's work must be scheduled so as not to interfere unreasonably with the subcontractor's work, it is best to refer specifically to the sequence of work performance and preparation work in the subcontract. By doing this, if a contractor fails to have the job site ready for the subcontractor, the subcontractor may have a claim for increased cost or time or a defense to a delay claim.

Contractor duties which should be discussed for specific inclusion or exclusion in the subcontract include: job site security; access to site; job site preparation; clean-up; scheduling; prompt notification of schedule or prime contract changes, hazardous materials presence and handling, and all other information

---

[25] Quaker-Empire Constr Co v DA Collins Constr Co, 88 AD2d 1043, 452 NYS2d 692 (1982); S. Leo Harmonay, Inc v Binks Mfg Co, 597 F Supp 1014 (SDNY 1984), affd, 762 F2d 990 (2d Cir 1985).

[26] NY Lab Law §241(6) (McKinney 1986 & Supp 1992); Gjertsen v Mawson & Mawson, Inc, 135 AD2d 779, 522 NYS2d 891 (1987).

which affects the subcontract; communication of orders and delivery of materials to designated representatives of the subcontractor; providing of certain supplies and facilities, such as equipment, scaffolding, storage areas, and on-site office space and toilets; bond and insurance information; hoisting; and prompt payment.

§3.10 —Job Site

At common law and by statute, the general contractor and owner are required to provide a safe place to work and are responsible for the safe condition of commonly used portions of the job site.[27] Each subcontractor is responsible for safety in areas created by it and "intimately connected with" its work.[28] This division of job site responsibilities may be insufficient to allocate the many areas of possible confusion or controversy. For instance, if the subcontractor uses the contractor's storage shed, may the contractor charge the subcontractor? Who bears the cost if the subcontractor has to remove the contractor's refuse from the site in order to perform the subcontractor's work? Who is to provide the scaffolding required by the subcontractor? If the subcontractor is a welder, must the welder protect surrounding work?[29]

To help ensure smoother and more trouble-free performance, the subcontract should specifically identify the subcontractor's responsibilities in relation to the job site. Specifically, the subcontract should discuss whether the contractor or subcontractor is responsible for: security of the subcontractor's materials, supplies, and partially completed work; removal of hazardous wastes, including asbestos, encountered in the course of the subcontractor's work; removal of refuse created by the subcontractor and other parties; cleanliness; temporary facilities and services, including supplying of and payment for utilities, temporary heat, toilets, cranes, elevators, office space, and telephone service; permits; storage; etc.

Additionally, the subcontract should discuss under what circumstances and at what cost the contractor may supply the subcontractor with some equipment, service, or facility which was the subcontractor's responsibility, such as hoist charges. Such a provision could provide that the subcontractor will pay the contractor's actual cost or actual cost plus some percentage for profit and overhead. The subcontract also should discuss the reverse—under what circumstance and what amount does the contractor pay if the subcontractor performs some job-site-related duty of the contractor.

---

[27] NY Lab Law §241(6) (McKinney 1986 & Supp 1992); Gjertsen v Mawson & Mawson, Inc, 135 AD2d 779, 522 NYS2d 891 (1987).

[28] Freeo v Victor A. Perosi, Inc, 54 AD2d 684, 387 NYS2d 268 (1976).

[29] *See* Jarvis & Spitz, Inc v Federation, 14 AD2d 833, 220 NYS2d 680 (1961), *appeal dismissed,* 11 NY2d 765, 227 NYS2d 15 (1962) (where oral contract for welding did not provide for the furnishing of protection during the welding, the welder had no duty to protect surrounding areas and was not liable for burning and scarring on surrounding tiles and windows).

§3.11 —Warranties

A subcontractor is bound by an implied promise to perform the subcontract in a skillful and workmanlike manner,[30] just as a contractor is so bound to perform its contract. A construction contract or subcontract does not warrant perfect results[31] or guarantee subjective satisfaction with the subcontractor's performance.[32] A discussion of implied warranties applicable to construction contracts is found in Chapter 12. In addition to being subject to the general implied warranties, a supply contract may be subject to the warranties provided by the Uniform Commercial Code (UCC). In determining whether a contract is a subcontract or a supply contract, the general standard is that where a contract includes both sale of a product and service, the primary nature of the contract must be determined including whether the service aspect of the contract was primary or incidental to the sale of goods. If the contract is one primarily for service, such as the design, sale, and installation of a sprinkler system, it is not governed by the UCC warranties but by common law and express contractual warranties.[33] If the contract is one primarily for the sale of goods, such as the sale, delivery, and planting of trees, it is covered by the UCC warranties.[34] See §§3.28 and 3.33.

The warranty issue peculiar to subcontracts is whether the subcontractor's warranty to the contractor is to comply with the contractor's warranty to the owner or whether the subcontractor's warranty is to stand on its own. Either way is common and depends on the parties' agreement. Express warranties that are to be included in the subcontract, if any, should be defined clearly. Incorporation by reference of the prime contract into the subcontract may require the subcontractor to comply with the prime contract warranties. These warranties may be more than the subcontractor can honor or less than the general contractor desires.

General express warranties regarding performance include phrases such as: "the work is guaranteed to be done in a workmanlike manner according to standard practices,"[35] or the work is to be done "in the best workmanlike manner by union skillful craftsmen,"[36] or "all work under this subcontract shall be of good quality, free from faults and defects and in conformance with the Contract Documents."[37] More specific express warranties warrant compliance with specified codes or standards, such as strength tests in the case of concrete.

---

[30] Fairbarn Lumber Corp v Telian, 92 AD2d 683, 460 NYS2d 194 (1983).

[31] Milau Assocs v North Ave Dev Corp, 42 NY2d 482, 368 NE2d 1247, 398 NYS2d 882 (1977).

[32] Grimpel v Hochman, 74 Misc 2d 39, 343 NYS2d 507 (Civ Ct NY 1972).

[33] Milau Assocs v North Ave Dev Corp, 42 NY2d 482, 368 NE2d 1247, 398 NYS2d 882 (1977).

[34] Outdoor Scenes, Inc v Anthony Grace & Sons, 111 Misc 2d 36, 443 NYS2d 583 (Queens 1981).

[35] Guidetti v Pratt Plumbing & Heating, Inc, 55 AD2d 720, 389 NYS2d 170 (1976).

[36] Grimpel v Hochman, 74 Misc 2d 39, 343 NYS2d 507 (Civ Ct NY 1972).

[37] Milau Assocs v North Ave Dev Corp, 42 NY2d 482, 368 NE2d 1247, 398 NYS2d 882 (1977).

Express warranties may also guarantee the work to be free from defect for a specified period of time or guarantee the materials used in the subcontractor's work to be of good quality and new,[38] or suitable for specific purposes or for a period of time.

In addition to express warranties, per se, the subcontract may require the work to comply with a specified code, such as the Albany Plumbing Code. If the completed work violates the code, the subcontractor might be liable for breach of contract.[39] If the contract does not require compliance with a specified code or approval by a specified body, such as the fire department, such a condition will not be implied.[40] In the absence of a specific contract provision, it is not a subcontractor's or contractor's obligation to ensure that the plans and specifications comply with applicable codes; rather, this is the design professional's responsibility.

Due to warranty concerns, the trend is for contract documents to require specialty contractors, such as fire sprinkler contractors, to both design and install their work.

§3.12 —Change Orders and Extras

Changes in the work are a fact of life in the construction industry. Rare is the project that requires no change orders or extras. Thus, the subcontract should address issues related to change orders and extras, such as: how they are issued; who has the authority to issue them; whether the subcontractor can refuse to comply with a change order; adjustment, if any, of the time of performance and amount due the subcontractor; whether change orders or extras must be written;[41] procedures and time for claiming extra compensation; whether the subcontractor's claims for extras will be allowed only to the extent the contractor recovers for the extras from the owner;[42] and procedures for certification of extras by parties other than the contractor or subcontractor, such as the project architect or owner.[43]

Analysis of change orders and extras, including interpretation of contract clauses, is found in Chapter 6.

---

[38] AIA Doc 401, ¶4.5.1 (1987 ed).

[39] Guidetti v Pratt Plumbing & Heating, Inc, 55 AD2d 720, 389 NYS2d 170 (1976); contra Green v City of NY, 283 AD 485, 128 NYS2d 715 (1st Dept 1954).

[40] Bistrian Gravel Corp v Wainscott NW Assocs, 116 AD2d 681, 497 NYS2d 748 (1986).

[41] See Comet Heating & Cooling Co v Modular Technics Corp, 57 AD2d 526, 393 NYS2d 573 (1977).

[42] See Burmar Elec Corp v Starrett Bros, 60 AD2d 561, 400 NYS2d 346 (1977).

[43] See Sturdy Concrete Corp v Nab Constr Corp, 65 AD2d 262, 411 NYS2d 637 (2d Dept 1978), appeal dismissed, 46 NY2d 938, 388 NE2d 349, 415 NYS2d 212 (1979), appeal after remand, 89 AD2d 588, 452 NYS2d 252 (1982).

§3.13 —Hold Harmless and Indemnification Clauses

Labor Law §§240 and 241 hold owners and general contractors liable for certain injuries suffered by workers on the construction site. This duty is non-delegable; it is one, however, against which owners and general contractors may protect themselves through indemnification clauses.[44] It is common for each party to a construction project to require indemnification from those below it. A sub-subcontractor may indemnify its subcontractor, the general contractor, and the owner. The subcontractor might indemnify its general contractor and the owner. The general contractor will usually indemnify the owner.

Thus, many subcontracts include *hold harmless and indemnification* clauses which appear to hold the subcontractor liable to the contractor, owner, and architect for damages suffered by them and to indemnify them from those damages. To the extent such a provision requires the subcontractor to indemnify the contractor or any other party for that party's own negligence, it is void and unenforceable.[45] This prohibition does not mean that a subcontract cannot require the subcontractor to indemnify the contractor for the subcontractor's negligence or for the acts of others.[46] Further, this does not mean that a contractor cannot require that its subcontractor obtain insurance for the contractor, to protect the contractor from its own negligence;[47] an obligation to *insure* the contractor is not an agreement to *indemnify* the contractor.[48] The prohibition is only against indemnification of a party from its own negligence.[49] A finding of liability under NY Lab Law §§240 and 241 is not necessarily a finding of negligence on an owner's or a contractor's part so as to bar indemnification as these statutes impose vicarious liability on owners and contractors.[50] Further, a clause which requires indemnification of the contractor for its own negligence in addition to indemnification for the negligence of others is not entirely void; only that portion of it which requires indemnification for the contractor's own negligence is void.[51]

---

[44] Walsh v Morse Diesel, Inc, 143 AD2d 653, 533 NYS2d 80 (1988); McGurk v Turner Constr Co, 127 AD2d 526, 512 NYS2d 71 (1987).

[45] NY Gen Oblig Law §5-322.1 (McKinney 1989); Quain v Buzzetta Constr Corp, 69 NY2d 376, 507 NE2d 294, 514 NYS2d 701 (1987); County of Onondaga v Penetryn Sys, 84 AD2d 934, 446 NYS2d 693 (1981), *affd*, 56 NY2d 726, 436 NE2d 1340, 451 NYS2d 738 (1982); Tedesco v Niagara Power Corp, 142 AD2d 932, 530 NYS2d 357 (1988).

[46] Magrath v J. Migliore Constr Co, 139 AD2d 893, 527 NYS2d 892 (1988).

[47] Board of Educ v Valden Assocs, 46 NY2d 653, 389 NE2d 798, 416 NYS2d 202 (1979).

[48] Kinney v GW Lisker Co, 76 NY2d 215, 556 NE2d 1090, 557 NYS2d 283 (1990).

[49] Magrath v J. Migliore Constr Co, 139 AD2d 893, 527 NYS2d 892 (1988).

[50] Brown v Two Exch Plaza Partners, 76 NY2d 172, 556 NE2d 430, 556 NYS2d 991 (1990).

[51] Brown v Two Exch Plaza Partners, 146 AD2d 129, 539 NYS2d 889 (1989), *affd*, 76 NY2d 172, 556 NE2d 430, 556 NYS2d 991 (1990).

An indemnification clause may include or be limited solely to personal injury, injury to the work, violation of law or regulation, injury or destruction of personal property including loss of use, patent infringement, or attorneys' fees and costs incurred in defending such claims.

In addition to a clause obligating the subcontractor to indemnify the contractor, the subcontractor may wish to include a clause which requires the contractor to indemnify the subcontractor. Only if the subcontractor has an extremely strong bargaining position can it reasonably expect a general contractor to agree to indemnify it.

In the absence of a contractual indemnity clause, a subcontractor may be liable to its contractor in common law indemnity or contribution,[52] although such liability may not be as extensive as that allowed by contract.

§3.14 —Sub-subcontractors and Materialmen

The subcontract should name any specific sub-subcontractors or materialmen the general contractor requires the subcontractor to use. If there are no specific parties, the subcontract should detail: whether the subcontractor can assign or further subcontract any portion of the subcontract work; approval procedures for sub-subcontractor and materialman selection, work, and payment requests; whether the subcontract or prime contract or portions thereof must be incorporated into the sub-subcontract or supply contract; and insurance and bonding requirements for a sub-subcontractor or materialman.

§3.15 —Relations with Other Subcontractors

Typical subcontracts specify that subcontractors shall not interfere with each other's work or the work of the general contractor, shall protect each other's work, shall cooperate with each other, shall not delay each other, and shall look to each other and not to the general contractor for damages caused by other subcontractors. Generally, these clauses must be included in all subcontracts made on the project or they may not be enforceable.

§3.16 —Progress Payments

To receive monthly progress payments based on a percentage of work completed to date, most subcontracts require that the subcontractor submit a payment requisition to the contractor a specified number of days before the contractor's monthly payment requisition is due to the owner or by a specified date each month. In the alternative, the subcontract may provide that the subcontractor is to apply directly to the owner for payment, thereby bypassing the contractor. As this sort of *direct disbursement* provision limits a contractor's

---

[52] Kemp v Lakelands Precast, Inc, 55 NY2d 1032, 434 NE2d 1077, 449 NYS2d 710 (1982); Glielmi v Toys "R" Us, Inc, 94 AD2d 663, 462 NYS2d 225 (1983), *affd*, 62 NY2d 664, 464 NE2d 981, 476 NYS2d 283 (1984).

hold over a subcontractor and may subject an owner to direct liability to the subcontractor, it is only rarely agreed to by contractors or owners.

Typical progress payment clauses require that the subcontractor's payment requisition set forth the amount and value of the work performed during the period for which payment is sought and an indication of the percentage of work completed to date. Payment generally is conditioned upon the architect's, lender's, and/or owner's approval and certification of percentage of work done.

A subcontractor that submits payment requisitions through its general contractor should request that the subcontract give it the express right to request information directly from the certifying architect or owner regarding percentage of completion and amount certified. Having such a right, the subcontractor can verify that the contractor is paying it all that is due and can communicate directly with the deciding party regarding alleged deficiencies in the work.

The subcontract should provide for amendment of payment requests or the carrying over of a payment to the next month in the event the subcontractor fails to properly or timely request payment.

Progress payments may also be based upon completion of tasks, rather than time of payment request. For instance, if a subcontractor is to supply, install, and paint all the doors in a 25-house development, the subcontract may provide for payment upon completion of each house, rather than payment each month based on the percentage of the total job done.[53]

§3.17 —Retainage

Along with progress payments comes *retainage,* the withholding of a specified percentage of the funds due until the contract work is complete and accepted. The percentage to be retained should be spelled out in the subcontract. From the subcontractor's view, it is best if the contractor's right to retain payment from the subcontractor is based solely upon the owner's withholding of monies from its payment to the contractor attributable to the subcontractor's work; this way, if the contractor receives full payment for the subcontractor's work to date, it will have to pay the subcontractor in full. Similarly, if the owner retains only five per cent from the contractor, the contractor will not be able to retain more than five per cent from the subcontractor. From a contractor's point of view, there may be instances in which it is best to retain a higher percentage, such as where a subcontractor's work requires extensive testing before it can be accepted.

To determine the terms of the contract and amount due or to become due, a subcontractor can obtain a copy of the prime contract or a statement of its terms and the amount due or to become due under the contract by sending the owner a written demand pursuant to NY Lien Law §8. An owner must comply with such demand within 30 days or lose the protection of privity as regards the subcontract and have its property subject to the subcontractor's lien as if

---

[53] *See* Sklar Door Corp v Locoteta Homes, Inc, 33 Misc 2d 299, 224 NYS2d 294 (Nassau 1961).

the subcontractor's labor and materials were furnished directly to the owner. In addition, the owner will be liable to the subcontractor to the extent of its damages as a result of the owner's failure to comply with the demand.

The subcontract should also specify whether the subcontractor is entitled to payment of its retainage upon completion and acceptance of its work or upon completion and acceptance of the entire project. If payment of retainage is not due until completion of the entire project, an early subcontractor, such as an excavator, could wait years until it is entitled to payment in full.

Subcontractors usually prefer clauses which reduce the amount of retainage over the life of the subcontract; the reduction may be stated as a reduction in the percentage retained or by a statement to the effect that a specified percentage shall be retained but in no event shall the total of amounts retained exceed a specified dollar sum. If the true reason for retainage is to ensure complete performance by the subcontractor, and not to provide the owner or contractor with a financing source, the logic for such a provision is irrefutable—the further along subcontract performance is, the less likelihood there is that the subcontractor will not complete.

§3.18 —Contingent Payment Clauses

Many subcontracts contain clauses which condition the contractor's obligation to pay the subcontractor upon the contractor's receipt of payment from the owner. These *contingent payment* clauses have been construed by the courts to be much less effective than they appear. In the leading case of *Schuler-Haas Electric Co v Aetna Casualty & Surety Co*,[54] the New York Court of Appeals held that such clauses are not conditions precedent to payment but, rather, fix the time for payment, in the absence of express language to the contrary. Thus, unless the contingent payment clause specifically states that "payment by the contractor to the subcontractor is expressly contingent upon payment by the owner to the contractor," that "receipt of payment from the owner for the subcontractor's work is a condition precedent to payment by the Contractor to the Subcontractor,"[55] or other words to that effect, a contractor must pay its subcontractor within a reasonable time following the subcontractor's satisfactory performance and it is irrelevant that the owner has not, will not, or cannot pay the contractor.[56]

Despite the numerous cases which hold that such clauses are not conditions precedent, it is best—from a subcontractor's view—to eliminate any such

---

[54] 40 NY2d 883, 357 NE2d 1003, 389 NYS2d 348 (1976), *affg* 49 AD2d 60, 371 NYS2d 207 (1975); *see also* Grossman Steel & Aluminum Corp v Samson Window Corp, 78 AD2d 871, 433 NYS2d 31 (1980), *affd*, 54 NY2d 653, 426 NE2d 176, 442 NYS2d 769 (1981); Kalwall Corp v K. Capolino Design & Renovation, 54 AD2d 941, 388 NYS2d 346 (1976); Colonial Roofing Corp v John Mee, Inc, 105 Misc 2d 140, 431 NYS2d 931 (Queens 1980).

[55] Crown Plastering Corp v Elite Assocs, 166 AD2d 495, 560 NYS2d 694, 695 (2d Dept 1990).

[56] Grossman Steel & Aluminum Corp v Samson Window Corp, 78 AD2d 871, 433 NYS2d 31 (1980), *affd*, 54 NY2d 653, 426 NE2d 176, 442 NYS2d 769 (1981).

clauses so the issue does not arise. By eliminating contingent payment clauses, misunderstandings and problems between the parties can be lessened. From a contractor's view, however, these clauses are vital and should be carefully construed.

§3.19 —Final Payment

It is best if the time for final payment is set forth as so many days following the subcontractor's completion of its work and submission of its application for final payment. Avoid phrases which state that final payment will be made "within a reasonable time" following some event; a subcontractor's opinion of what is reasonable is often very different from a contractor's.

Final payment may be conditioned upon the owner's, lender's, building department official's, or architect's inspection and acceptance of the work; the subcontractor's submitting proof, such as lien waivers, that it has paid its laborers, subcontractors, and materialmen for work and materials related to the subcontract work; the issuance of a certificate of occupancy; or the subcontractor's correcting defects or deficiencies in its work.

§3.20 —Back Charges

Back charges may be passed along to a subcontractor in the same instances as they are charged to a contractor or they may be initiated by the contractor. Subcontractors prefer clauses which limit their exposure to back charge to that amount of back charge actually incurred by the contractor in relation to the subcontractor's work. Additionally, subcontractors should insist on clauses which limit back charges to instances where prompt notice and an opportunity to cure are given.[57]

§3.21 —Offsets

Generally, a contractor cannot offset money or damages due it by a subcontractor on an unrelated contract against funds due the subcontractor of the job in question.[58] Some contracts, however, grant a contractor such a right against its subcontractor:

> Should one or more other contract, now or hereafter, exist between the parties hereto or with any affiliated corporation or company of the

---

[57] *See* Sturdy Concrete Corp v Nab Constr Corp, 65 AD2d 262, 411 NYS2d 637 (2d Dept 1978), *appeal dismissed,* 46 NY2d 938, 388 NE2d 349, 415 NYS2d 212 (1979), *appeal after remand,* 89 AD2d 588, 452 NYS2d 252 (1982).

[58] *See* PS Griswold Co v Cortland Glass Co, 138 AD2d 869, 525 NYS2d 973 (3d Dept 1988); Eli-Dorer Contracting Co v PT&L Constr Co, 85 AD2d 866, 446 NYS2d 457 (3d Dept 1981). *But see* United States v Munsey Trust Co, 332 US 234, 67 S Ct 1599, 91 L Ed 2022 (1946); Williams Press, Inc v States, 45 AD2d 397, 357 NYS2d 920 (3d Dept 1974).

parties, concerning this or any other construction project, then a breach by the subcontractor of any contract, may at the option of the contractor, be considered a breach of all contracts; and in that event the contractor may terminate any or all of the contracts so breached, or may *withhold moneys* due or to become due on any such contracts, and apply the same toward payment of any damages suffered on that or any other such contracts.

The authors are not aware of cases which interpret such clauses and thus cannot authoritatively comment on their validity. Considering, however, basic principles of freedom of contract and the fact that such clauses do not appear to violate any public policies concerns, the authors believe that such clauses are effective.

§3.22 —Delay Damages

Most subcontracts include *liquidated or delay damage* clauses which entitle the contractor to seek damages caused by delay from the subcontractor. At the same time, many of these same subcontracts include *no damage for delay* clauses which attempt to bar the subcontractor from seeking such damages from the contractor. Despite this apparent inequity, there is little most subcontractors can do—short of not accepting jobs with the great majority of contractors whose contracts include such terms. Some comfort can be taken in the fact that if the contractor actively interferes with the subcontractor's job progress or the delay is unreasonably long, the subcontractor may be entitled to delay damages, despite a *no damage for delay* clause.[59]

In what is likely to be regarded as a controversial ruling and a major setback for subcontractors, the New York Court of Appeals, in *Triangle Sheet Metal Works, Inc v James H. Merritt & Co*,[60] affirmed the dismissal of a subcontractor's delay claim against a prime contractor for its failure to offer any evidence that the prime contractor was responsible for any of the delays in question. In reaching its decision, the court relied on a 1910 case which has since been cited infrequently.

The subcontract between Triangle and Merritt did *not* contain the typical *no damage for delay* clause and did not incorporate by reference the general conditions of the prime contract between Merritt and the owner. The court therefore impliedly rejected Triangle's contention that, in the absence of a *no damage for delay* clause, a prime is liable to a subcontractor for owner-caused delay.

The Court of Appeals suggested that "[i]f a subcontractor wants a prime contractor to be a guarantee of job performance, it should bargain for the inclusion in its subcontract of a provision to that effect." In most instances, this will probably be unattainable. Typically, a prime contractor will probably have

---

[59] Ippolito-Lutz, Inc v Cohoes Hous Auth, 22 AD2d 990, 254 NYS2d 783 (1964). Further discussion of this issue is found in ch 7.

[60] 79 NY2d 801, 588 NE2d 69, 580 NYS2d 171 (1991).

the economic clout to insist on a *no damage for delay* clause for all delay other than what the prime can pass off to the owner or others. In such event, whether the subcontractor will be adequately protected by a pari passu clause (e.g., "the prime contractor assumes to the subcontractor all obligations of the owner to the prime contractor under the prime contract documents") remains in question.

The effect of this decision on liquidating agreements is discussed in §3.23.

Subcontractors can protect themselves from outrageous delay or liquidated damages exposure by demanding that the clause limit their liability. A subcontractor should insist that any liquidated daily damage bear some reasonable relation to the damage the contractor will actually incur as a result of *this* subcontractor's delay. One suggestion is to make the daily sum all or some portion of the liquidated damage daily sum in the prime contract. The percentage of the prime contract daily sum applied to the subcontract would depend upon the complexity of and necessity of prompt performance by the subcontractor. For instance, if the subcontractor's work must be done before any other work can be done, such as in the case of an excavator, the liquidated damages penalty should be the same as that suffered by the contractor.

Further, the subcontractor should require that the subcontract specify that its liability for delay or liquidated damages for delay shall not be greater than liquidated or actual damages actually incurred by the general contractor and caused by the subcontractor and its employees, agents, sub-subcontractors, and materialmen. The subcontract should also specify the opposite—that in no instance shall the subcontractor be liable for delays which arise outside the scope of the subcontract.

Another way in which a subcontractor can limit its exposure to delay damages is to specify in the subcontract that the subcontractor will be given access to the job site by a specified date or within a specified number of days of the date of the subcontract and that the access shall be for a minimum stated time. Then, if the subcontractor does not have access to the job site when expected, it may later avoid liability for delay damages caused when, for example, the subcontractor is asked to report to the job site and perform much later than it had anticipated and is unable to begin its work promptly because its laborers and equipment are committed elsewhere.

§3.23 —Liquidating Agreements

In a *liquidating agreement*, the general contractor agrees to reimburse the subcontractor for damages the subcontractor has suffered due to the owner's actions, *but only if, when, and to the extent that* the general contractor receives payment from the owner for the subcontractor's damages; such clauses are valid in New York and the federal Claims Court.[61] Any recovery passes through the

---

[61] Mars Assocs v New York City Educ Constr Fund, 126 AD2d 178, 513 NYS2d 125 (1st Dept 1987); Ardsley Constr Co v Port of NY Auth, 61 AD2d 953, 403 NYS2d 43 (1st Dept 1978); Cable Belt Conveyors, Inc v Alumina Partners, 717 F Supp 1021 (SDNY

general contractor to the subcontractor.[62] Liquidating agreements do not release the general contractor from liability to the subcontractor; in fact, the general contractor must expressly acknowledge liability to the subcontractor for the agreement to be effective.[63] Liquidating agreements liquidate the liability to that amount which can be recovered from other parties[64] and allow the general contractor to sue or negotiate with the owner on behalf of the subcontractor.[65] A liquidating agreement may be part of the contract or a separate agreement entered into after the contract is executed or the job is complete. In essence, a liquidating agreement allows a contractor to seek indemnification for moneys due its subcontractor based on the owner's breach *before* the contractor has paid the damages; hence, a liquidating agreement provides a means by which a party may circumvent the legal principles which prevent an indemnification claim from arising until the primary obligation has been paid.[66]

The efficacy of a liquidating agreement to enable a subcontractor to recover for owner-caused delay has been thrown into question by *Triangle Sheet Metal Works, Inc v James H. Merritt & Co*.[67] In *Triangle*,[68] the Court of Appeals affirmed the dismissal of a subcontractor's delay claim against a prime contractor for its failure to offer any evidence that the prime contractor was responsible for any of the delays in question.

Following *Triangle*,[69] there is a conceptual quandary—namely, how can a prime contractor "confess" a liability to a subcontractor, which the court has said does not exist, and how can a prime contractor recover from an owner for subcontractor claims for which the prime contractor is not independently liable to the subcontractor? For a further discussion, see **§3.22**.

The implied contractual covenant of good faith and fair dealing applies to a liquidating agreement. Such agreements generally require the contractor to "take all reasonable steps so that the [subcontractor's] right to an even-

---

1989); *see also* Degnon Contracting Co v City of NY, 235 NY 481, 139 NE 580 (1923) (In *dicta*, the court recognized that parties may make an arrangement "which would have made the [contractor] liable over to the [subcontractor] for any increased cost and responsible for enforcement against the city for the benefits of its subcontractor of any liability arising through breach of contract." *Id* at 487, 139 NE at 582.).

[62] Lambert Hous Redev Co v HRH Equity Corp, 117 AD2d 227, 502 NYS2d 433 (1986).

[63] Mars Assocs v New York City Educ Constr Fund, 126 AD2d 178, 513 NYS2d 125 (1st Dept 1987).

[64] *Id.*

[65] Whitmyer Bros v State, 63 AD2d 103, 406 NYS2d 617 (1978), *affd*, 47 NY2d 960, 393 NE2d 1027, 419 NYS2d 954 (1979) (contractor sued state owner on subcontractor's behalf for subcontractor's lost profits).

[66] Mars Assocs v New York City Educ Constr Fund, 126 AD2d 178, 513 NYS2d 125, 133 (1st Dept 1987).

[67] 79 NY2d 801, 588 NE2d 69, 580 NYS2d 171 (1991).

[68] *Id.*

[69] *Id.*

tual recovery, if any, from the [owner] will be protected."[70] Thus, a general contractor has a duty to make a good faith effort to present the subcontractor's claim in a fair and serious manner.[71]

§3.24 —Default/Termination

Every subcontract should define what will be a default under the subcontract, should specify who will determine whether there has been a default, and should provide under what circumstances either party may terminate the agreement and the results of the termination. Chapter 4 discusses contractual rights of termination, instances of default, defenses to charges of default, measure of payment upon termination, termination for convenience, etc.

The subcontract issue is what happens to the subcontractor if the prime contract is terminated. The subcontract should address: the measure and time of payment if the subcontractor's work is suspended or terminated due to contractor termination, including lost profits, overhead, and other damages; whether the subcontract can be assigned to the owner or a replacement contractor, and, if so, the successor's obligation to pay the subcontractor for work done before the original contractor's termination; and whether the subcontractor can refuse to complete following contractor termination.

§3.25 —Remedies for Non-Payment

The subcontract should provide that the subcontractor may, upon advance notice to the contractor, stop all work until paid in the event the contractor fails to pay the subcontractor any progress payment within a specified number of days after due, typically 7 to 10 days. It could provide that the subcontractor's right to stop work or choice to return to work does not limit its right to recover lost profits or other consequential damages from the contractor. Further, it could provide that when the subcontractor resumes work on the project it is entitled to its costs of demobilization, delay, and remobilization.[72] It should also provide that the subcontractor may terminate the subcontract for nonpayment of any amount due for a specified period, typically 30 to 90 days. If the amount of payment due is in dispute, the general contractor may want a clause which requires the subcontractor to continue its work and follow the dispute resolution procedures set forth in the contract. Finally, the subcontract should include provisions which discuss whether the subcontractor may recover attorneys' fees or interest, any notice which must be given prior to bringing suit, and the time within which suit must be brought.

---

[70] Martin Mech Corp v Mars Assocs, 158 AD2d 280, 550 NYS2d 681, 682 (1st Dept 1990).

[71] TGI E Coast Constr Corp v Fireman's Fund Ins Co, 534 F Supp 780 (SDNY 1982).

[72] *See* AIA Doc A401, ¶4.7.1 (1987 ed).

§3.26 —Lien Waivers

Blanket lien waivers and "no lien" contract clauses are against public policy, void, and wholly unenforceable.[73] New York recognizes no exceptions, even where the contract specifies that it is to be construed by the laws of a state which allows lien waivers.[74] The Lien Law does, however, permit a contract requirement that a party receiving payment execute a lien waiver with regard to the payment received simultaneous with or after delivery of the payment for work already performed.[75]

§3.27 Purchase Orders and Supply Contracts

Although often the last contract signed or party contacted, the materialman or supplier on a construction project is very important. Even if the contractor is the best in its field and contracts with only the best subcontractors, the project can be ruined by inferior materials or materials which do not match job specifications. If the contractor plans to use top quality materials but fails to lock in a price when bidding on the job, its profits may disappear as it attempts to provide the goods at prices which exceed those in its bid. The purchase order or supply contract is thus an integral part of almost every construction project which should be as fully defined as the subcontract and prime contracts.

Through a thorough understanding of supply contracts and applicable law, a contractor or subcontractor can learn how to lock in favorable prices and purchase terms, how to encourage materialmen to perform, whether it must accept materials which are not as expected, and what its remedies are and how to pursue them in the event of a default or breach by the materialman.

§3.28 Applicable Law—The UCC

As transactions involving the sale of goods, most supply contracts are governed by the Uniform Commercial Code (UCC). Except for identifying the product supplied, the UCC provides almost every other term which is necessary for a supply contract, including imposing an obligation of good faith in performance and enforcement of contracts.[76] Thus, if the parties fail to discuss whether the purchaser is to pick up the ton of bricks ordered or the seller is to deliver them, the UCC provides that the buyer must pick up its bricks at the seller's business.[77] Similarly, if the parties have not settled on a price or time of delivery, the UCC provides that the price shall be a "reasonable

---

[73] NY Lien Law §34 (McKinney 1966 & Supp 1992). This issue is more fully discussed in ch 9.

[74] Clifton Steel Corp v General Elec Co, 80 AD2d 714, 437 NYS2d 734 (1981).

[75] NY Lien Law §34 (McKinney 1966 & Supp 1992).

[76] UCC §1-203 (McKinney 1964).

[77] Id §2-308 (McKinney 1964 & Supp 1992).

price at the time of delivery"[78] and that the goods shall be delivered within a "reasonable time."[79] The UCC also defines what is a justified excuse for a materialman's failure to perform.[80]

Not all contracts which appear to be supply contracts are, in fact, supply contracts and thus governed by the UCC. Only those which are for the *sale of goods* are governed by the UCC. All others are governed by common law contract principles. Hybrid contracts, which call for the sale of goods and services, may be construed as supply contracts (for the sale of goods) or service contracts (what is typically referred to as a subcontract in the construction industry). To determine which laws apply to a hybrid contract, it must be determined whether the contract is one primarily for the sale of goods or the rendering of a service. If the services provided are incidental or collateral to the sale of goods, the contract is one for the sale of goods and would be governed by the UCC.[81] If the goods provided under the contract are not the emphasis of the contract, such as in a plumbing contract,[82] the contract is one primarily for services and is governed by common law contract principles.

A contract to design, sell, and install a sprinkler system is primarily a service contract; the furnishing of the needed pipes is incidental to the main purpose of the contract.[83] Similarly, contracts for the sale and installation of a swimming pool[84] or a roof[85] are primarily service contracts. The UCC would apply, however, to the equipment portion of those subcontracts between the subcontractor and materialman.[86] Conversely, a contract for the sale, delivery, and planting of trees is one primarily for the sale of goods,[87] as is one for the sale and delivery of screened sand and gravel.[88] The service portion of those contracts, delivery, planting, and screening, is incidental to the product purchased.

---

[78] *Id* §2-305.

[79] *Id* §2-309(1).

[80] *Id* §2-615.

[81] Sawyer v Camp Dudley, 102 AD2d 914, 477 NYS2d 498 (1984).

[82] Geelan Mech Corp v Dember Constr Corp, 97 AD2d 810, 468 NYS2d 680 (1983); *see also* Schenectady Steel Co v Bruno Trimpoli Gen Constr Co, 43 AD2d 234, 350 NYS2d 920 (1974), *affd mem*, 34 NY2d 939, 316 NE2d 875, 359 NYS2d 560 (1976) (contract to furnish and erect structural steel necessary for bridge was not a contract for the sale of goods).

[83] Milau Assocs v North Ave Dev Corp, 42 NY2d 482, 368 NE2d 1247, 398 NYS2d 882 (1977).

[84] Ben Constr Co v Ventre, 23 AD2d 44, 257 NYS2d 988 (1965).

[85] County of Chenango v Lockwood Greene Engrs, Inc, 114 AD2d 728, 494 NYS2d 832 (1985).

[86] *Id;* Pecker Iron Works, Inc v Sturdy Concrete Co, 96 Misc 2d 998, 410 NYS2d 251 (Queens 1978) (UCC applied to contract for the furnishing and erecting of structural steel where contract was not fully performed and suit brought on sales portion of contract only).

[87] Outdoor Scenes, Inc v Anthony Grace & Sons, 111 Misc 2d 36, 443 NYS2d 583 (Queens 1981).

[88] Sawyer v Camp Dudley, 102 AD2d 914, 477 NYS2d 498 (1984).

To determine if a contract is one for services or goods, it may help to look at the title of the contract, the basis of compensation, and the amount of goods sold as opposed to service rendered.[89]

The courts of New York are uncertain whether the UCC applies to a lease of equipment. Some cases hold that it does;[90] some hold that it does not.[91]

The distinction between sales and service contracts is important due to the far-reaching consequences of the UCC. Under the UCC, there are shorter statutes of limitations, stricter standards for judging performance, more and broader implied warranties, etc. Unless the sales contract specifically exempts the transaction from the operation and effect of specific UCC provisions, they will apply and may materially affect the purchaser's and materialman's relationship.

§3.29 Terms of Supply Contract

Despite the fact that the Uniform Commercial Code (UCC) will supply missing terms in a supply contract,[92] it is best to discuss and agree to certain material terms so that the parties—not the UCC—will determine how to judge compliance with the supply contract, the price of the materials, payment terms, warranties, etc.

When purchasing goods, it is important for the seller to read the entire purchase order and for the purchaser to read the entire confirmation order. Either party may impose terms by including them on these forms.[93] Thus, for example, a purchaser that hasn't read the forms might, without having meant to, agree to arbitration[94] or a shorter statute of limitations.[95]

§3.30 —Time of Performance

Time of performance is merely the specification of when the materialman must make the goods sold available to the purchaser. If the contract calls

---

[89] *See* Triangle Underwriters, Inc v Honeywell, Inc, 604 F2d 737 (2d Cir 1979) (computer purchase contract).

[90] Eisert v Ermco Erectors, Inc, 60 AD2d 903, 401 NYS2d 553 (1978) (rental of cranes used in construction); Industrial Automated & Scientific Equip Corp v RME Enters, 58 AD2d 482, 396 NYS2d 427 (1977) (lease was really in nature of sales contract as it provided for a lump sum purchase price equal to four months rent at the end of the five-year lease); Hertz Commercial Leasing Corp v Transportation Credit Clearing House, 59 Misc 2d 226, 298 NYS2d 392 (Civ Ct NY 1969), *revd on other grounds*, 64 Misc 2d 910, 316 NYS2d 585 (1970) (UCC governs lease to the "extent applicable").

[91] Owens v Patent Scaffolding Co, 50 AD2d 866, 376 NYS2d 948 (1975), *revg* 77 Misc 2d 992, 354 NYS2d 778 (Kings 1974).

[92] *See* §3.28.

[93] UCC §§2-201, 2-207 (McKinney 1964 & Supp 1992).

[94] *See* Trafalgar Square, Ltd v Reeves Bros, 35 AD2d 194, 315 NYS2d 239 (1970).

[95] *See* American Tempering, Inc v Craft Architectural Metals Corp, 107 AD2d 565, 483 NYS2d 304 (1985).

for delivery, it is the date delivery is required. If the contract does not call for delivery, it is the date the materialman must have the goods at its place of business, ready to be picked up by the purchaser.[96]

If the contract does not specify a time of performance, the Uniform Commercial Code (UCC) implies a "reasonable time."[97] What is considered to be a reasonable time depends upon the nature, purpose, and circumstances of the product, sale, and order.[98]

§3.31 —Acceptance and Rejection

Absent contractual provisions to the contrary, the Uniform Commercial Code (UCC) provides specific procedures for acceptance and rejection of materials. Rejection may be because the goods are defective, nonconforming (such as they are the wrong color), or late. If a purchaser fails to notify the materialman of its intent to reject within a reasonable time, the purchaser is deemed to have accepted the goods. What is a reasonable time depends upon the type of goods. For example, if the materialman supplied concrete, the purchaser can wait until the concrete has hardened sufficiently for strength tests to be performed; it need not accept or reject the concrete upon its pouring or initial hardening.[99] Terms may be placed in the supply contract which specify when the goods must be rejected or be deemed accepted. By specifying a time period, the parties can avoid arguments about what is a reasonable time.

Pursuant to the UCC, to reject the goods, the purchaser must notify the materialman and make the goods available to the materialman; it need not physically return them. Thus, if the materialman sold and installed carpet, which the purchaser later rejects as defective, the purchaser does not have to rip the carpet off its floors and return it to the materialman. Despite the fact that the carpet is on its floors, the purchaser has not accepted the carpet by using it; the purchaser has no choice but to use the carpet until the materialman removes it.[100] The parties may wish to provide alternate terms which provide that the purchaser must physically return the goods to the materialman or must inspect and accept or reject the goods prior to installation. Further, the parties may wish to include a damages clause which entitles the purchaser to liquidated delay damages in the event of rejection, in addition to the replacement cost damages provided by the UCC.

---

[96] UCC §§2-308, 2-503 (McKinney 1964 & Supp 1992).

[97] UCC §2-309 (McKinney 1964 & Supp 1992).

[98] *Id* §1-204(2).

[99] Barrett Paving Materials, Inc v United States Fidelity & Guar Co, 118 AD2d 1039, 500 NYS2d 413 (1986).

[100] Garfinkel v Lehman Floor Covering Co, 60 Misc 2d 72, 302 NYS2d 167 (Nassau 1969).

Acceptance of nonconforming goods does not mean that the purchaser cannot recover damages for breach of contract and warranty.[101] If a purchaser decides to accept nonconforming goods it should promptly notify the materialman of the nonconformity so its damage claim will be preserved. Further, if the purchaser accepts nonconforming goods it must pay the contract price for the goods accepted, but may seek damages from the materialman.[102] Damages in excess of the contract purchase price are not *per se* excessive if the breach creates special circumstances which warrant a replacement cost measure of damages, as opposed to a breach of warranty measure which would award the purchaser the difference between the value of the goods as accepted and as warranted.[103] An example of a special circumstance which would entitle a purchaser to replacement cost is where the goods are custom-made unique goods not bought or sold on the open market, such as custom-made and -designed cabinetry.[104] If a purchaser accepts late delivery of goods, it does not waive its right to seek damages caused by the delay.[105]

Repudiation is not rejection. Repudiation is when the purchaser breaches the contract by notifying the materialman before delivery that it will not accept the goods[106] or the materialman breaches the contract by notifying the purchaser that it will not deliver the goods.[107] Rejection, on the other hand, refers to the rejection of goods because of a breach by the materialman in furnishing defective or nonconforming goods.

If a materialman must delay or cancel delivery, it will not be in breach of its contract if its performance was made impracticable by unforeseen supervening circumstances, outside the parties contemplation at the time of contracting, including failure of presumed conditions and changes in law.[108] Generally, an increase in the price of performance alone does not excuse performance.[109] An example of a contingency failure which would excuse performance is if a

---

[101] Gem Jewelers, Inc v Dykman, 160 AD2d 1069, 553 NYS2d 890 (3d Dept 1990); V. Zappala & Co v Pyramid Co, 81 AD2d 983, 439 NYS2d 765 (1981).

[102] Nassau Suffolk White Trucks, Inc v Twin County Transit Mix Corp, 62 AD2d 982, 403 NYS2d 322 (1978).

[103] Gem Jewelers, Inc v Dykman, 160 AD2d 1069, 553 NYS2d 890 (3d Dept 1990); UCC §2-714(2) (McKinney 1964 & Supp 1992).

[104] Gem Jewelers, Inc v Dykman, 160 AD2d 1069, 553 NYS2d 890 (3d Dept 1990); UCC §2-714(2) (McKinney 1964 & Supp 1992).

[105] Beacon Plastic & Metal Prods, Inc v Corn Prods Co, 57 Misc 2d 634, 293 NYS2d 429 (App Term NY 1968).

[106] Feinberg v J. Bongiovi Contracting, Inc, 110 Misc 2d 379, 442 NYS2d 399 (Suffolk 1981).

[107] Robert Mfg Co v South Bay Corp, 82 Misc 2d 250, 368 NYS2d 413 (Nassau 1975).

[108] UCC §2.615(a) (McKinney 1964 & Supp 1992).

[109] Maple Farms, Inc v City School Dist, 76 Misc 2d 1080, 352 NYS2d 784 (Chemung 1974); *but see* Moyer v City of Little Falls, 134 Misc 2d 299, 510 NYS2d 813 (Herkimer 1986) (performance excused when cost of performance of public sanitation rose 666% due to government action creating a monopoly in landfill operations).

supply is available only from one source and that source fails, or if the parties anticipated obtaining the good from a particular source and that source fails.[110]

§3.32 —Price and Terms of Payment

In the absence of a specific price term, the Uniform Commercial Code (UCC) will imply that the parties intended the price of the goods to be a "reasonable price" at the time of delivery.[111] Obviously, this is insufficient in most construction cases where the contractor's bid for the entire project typically is given many months, if not several years, before some materials are needed or provided. Thus, it is essential that the parties agree, in writing, to a price for the goods prior to their delivery. Three methods of pricing are used most often: fixed price, cost-plus, and escalation clauses.

Fixed price contracts very simply provide that the materialman will furnish the specified goods at price X, regardless of when furnished, market conditions, or availability of the goods. Purchasers prefer this type of price clause because it provides cost stability and enables them to bid accurately. Materialmen, on the other hand, prefer not to give a fixed price if their bid is made a significant time before they will be required to supply the goods. If providing a fixed price on a long-term bid, the materialman would have to anticipate future prices or include the current price plus the cost of storage until delivery.

Cost-plus contracts provide that the purchaser will pay the materialman its cost for the goods plus a specified percentage for profit and overhead. Purchasers do not like cost-plus contracts because they place all risk of increased prices on them. Materialmen prefer cost-plus contracts because their profits are guaranteed regardless of what happens in the marketplace.

Escalation clauses allocate the risk of price increase between the purchaser and the materialman by providing that if there is a significant delay or increase in price, the price of the goods will be equitably adjusted. Under such a clause, the purchaser bears the risk of a significant increase, the materialman the risk of a slight increase. It is best if the parties define in the contract what is meant by a significant increase in price: 10%? 20%? Similarly, it is wise if the parties define what is to be considered a significant delay which will entitle the materialman to increase its price. For instance, the contract may state that the price of the materials is guaranteed so long as delivered by a specified date and that if not delivered by that date, the price to the purchaser will increase if the materialman's cost increases plus a specified percentage for profit and overhead.

The contract also should discuss any discounts or rebates to which the purchaser is entitled.[112]

The parties would also do well to specify the terms of payment—cash on delivery, within 30 days, on purchaser's credit account, etc. The UCC provides

---

[110] Davis Co v Hoffman-LaRoche Chem Works, 178 AD 855, 166 NYS 179 (1917); International Paper Co v Rockefeller, 161 AD 180, 146 NYS 371 (1914).

[111] UCC §2-305 (McKinney 1964 & Supp 1992).

[112] Eisert v Ermco Erectors, Inc, 60 AD2d 903, 401 NYS2d 553 (1978).

that payment is due at the time and place of acceptance of the goods by the purchaser.[113] On many construction projects, this would cause problems for the purchaser that may not have the funds to pay the supplier until its payment application is approved at the end of the month. Thus, it is advised that the purchaser specify payment terms that correspond with its right to payment under its contract on the project.

§3.33 —Warranties

The Uniform Commercial Code (UCC) provides that all goods, unless otherwise specified in the sales contract, are covered by implied warranties—those of merchantability,[114] course of dealing or usage of trade,[115] and fitness for a particular purpose.[116] In addition, goods may be covered by express warranties, which may arise without the materialman necessarily intending to grant express warranties.[117] Thus, it is important for the materialman to specifically exclude its goods from any or all of these warranties as is appropriate and to specifically indicate what warranties, if any, apply. If the parties want more warranties than the UCC provides, the contract should say so expressly. If the parties want fewer, the contract must say so expressly and conspicuously.

To exclude the UCC warranties, the contract must indicate, in *conspicuous writing*, disclaimer of any intent to offer a warranty of merchantability or fitness,[118] or any warranty, express or implied, which is not in writing and made a part of the contract. Conspicuous writing is writing which is larger than the rest of the contract or product label[119] and is in bold letters.[120] While language such as *as is, with all faults,* or otherwise will effectively disavow any implied warranties,[121] the use of more detailed exclusions of warranty effectively shows the parties' true agreement as to what warranties apply; either party would be hard pressed to sustain an argument that the warranties are not as are written in the contract.

Purchasers often are concerned that the goods comply with their contracts on the project and ask that materialmen agree to warrant that the goods are as specified in the relevant general contract or subcontract. The materialman can incorporate those specifications into its sales contract and warrant

---

[113] UCC §§2-307, 2-310 (McKinney 1964 & Supp 1992).

[114] *Id* §2-314.

[115] *Id* §2-314(3).

[116] *Id* §2-315.

[117] *Id* §2-313.

[118] *Id* §2-316(2).

[119] Nassau Suffolk White Trucks, Inc v Twin County Transit Mix Corp, 62 AD2d 982, 403 NYS2d 322 (1978).

[120] Basic Adhesives, Inc v Robert Matzkin Co, 101 Misc 2d 283, 420 NYS2d 983 (Civ Ct NY 1979).

[121] UCC §2-316(3)(a) (McKinney 1964 & Supp 1992).

98 SUBCONTRACT

compliance with them.[122] To ensure that the parties' intent is interpreted through the supply contract, the materialman should review the relevant general contract specifications and add language to its contract which warrants the goods in specific terms agreeable to the purchaser. This precaution should prevent the interpretation of the materialman's duties by the general contract, a contract several tiers removed which may be couched in vague terms.

§3.34 —Insurance and Shipping

If the sales contract is silent as to delivery of the goods, the Uniform Commercial Code (UCC) presumes that the purchaser is to take possession at the seller's place of business, unless usage of trade indicates otherwise.[123] This presumption is inconvenient for most construction purchasers. A builder may not have the special equipment necessary to deliver plate glass windows or the time or inclination to have its laborers load and transport several tons of bricks across town.

The supply contract should specify that responsibility for the materials, including protection from the weather, ends with delivery to the purchaser at a particular place[124] or a specified time after the goods are made available for pick-up by the purchaser. Under the UCC, a seller remains responsible for and bears the risk of loss to the goods until the goods are actually received by the purchaser where the contract requires the purchaser to take delivery at the seller's place of business, even if the purchaser has fully paid for the goods and has been notified that they are available for pick-up.[125]

The sales contract should also specify when, where, and to whom the goods must be delivered if the seller is responsible for delivery of the goods to the purchaser. For instance, it should name, by title or actual name, those individuals whom the purchaser has authorized to sign for the goods. If the goods may be delivered to the job site and left there with anyone's signature, the contract should so state. Under the UCC, the goods must be delivered to the purchaser or the purchaser's agent, not to a mere laborer of the purchaser or some other person who happens to be on the job site when the goods are delivered.[126]

---

[122] *See* Horn Waterproofing Corp v Horn Constr Co, 104 AD2d 851, 480 NYS2d 367 (1984).

[123] UCC §2-308 (McKinney 1964 & Supp 1992).

[124] Jewish Bd of Guardians v Grumman Allied Indus, 96 AD2d 465, 464 NYS2d 778 (1983), *aff'd*, 62 NY2d 684, 465 NE2d 42, 476 NYS2d 535 (1984).

[125] UCC §2-509 (McKinney 1964 & Supp 1992); Ramos v Wheel Sports Center, 96 Misc 2d 646, 409 NYS2d 505 (Civ Ct NY 1978); La Casse v Blaustein, 93 Misc 2d 572, 403 NYS2d 440 (Civ Ct NY 1978).

[126] National Plumbing Supply Co v Castellano, 118 Misc 2d 150, 460 NYS2d 248 (Westchester 1983).

§3.35 Actions for Breach and Damages

An action for breach of a contract for the sale of goods must be brought within four years of when the breach occurred, regardless of knowledge of the breach.[127] By contract, the parties may shorten the limitations period to as little as one year, but may not extend it.[128]

Actions may be arbitrated, if the parties agreed to arbitration either expressly or impliedly. A party may inadvertently agree to arbitration by failing to object to an arbitration provision on an order confirmation which follows an oral purchase order.[129]

The Uniform Commercial Code (UCC) provides measures of damages for breach of a sales contract. For example, if the buyer breaches the contract by refusing to purchase the goods and the seller justifiably withholds delivery, the UCC provides that the seller's measure of damages is liquidated damages per the parties' agreement or, if there is no liquidated damages agreement, the lesser of $500 or 20% of the buyer's total contract performance price.[130] Another measure provided by the UCC is that if the seller breaches the contract, the buyer may purchase substitute goods and recover from the seller any increased cost of purchase plus its incidental or consequential damages.[131]

If the parties wish to provide other remedies or measures of damages, either as alternatives or additions, they may do so.[132] One addition purchasers could include is a provision for delay or liquidated damages. If a subcontractor's performance is delayed due to a materialman's failure to deliver needed materials on time, the subcontractor should be able to pass any delay damages it suffers on to the materialman. A provision a materialman may want to include regards special orders. If a materialman makes a product to the purchaser's special order, the materialman may wish to make the entire contract price the measure of damages in the event of purchaser repudiation.

---

[127] UCC §2-725(1), (2) (McKinney 1964 & Supp 1992).

[128] Id §2-725(1); Reiss v Pacific Steel Pool Corp, 73 Misc 2d 78, 341 NYS2d 364 (Albany 1973).

[129] Trafalgar Square, Ltd v Reeves Bros, 35 AD2d 194, 315 NYS2d 239 (1970).

[130] UCC §§2-708, 2-718(2) (McKinney 1964 & Supp 1992); Feinberg v J. Bongiovi Contracting, 110 Misc 2d 379, 442 NYS2d 399 (Suffolk 1981).

[131] UCC §§2-712, 2-713 (McKinney 1964 & Supp 1992).

[132] Id §2-719.

Default/Termination 4

§4.01 Introduction
§4.02 Contractual Right of Termination
§4.03 —For Cause
§4.04 —For Convenience
§4.05 —Architect/Engineer Approval
§4.06 Notice Requirements
§4.07 Contractor Default
§4.08 —Failure to Prosecute the Work
§4.09 —Failure to Pay Subcontractors and Suppliers
§4.10 —Failure to Correct Defective Work
§4.11 —Insolvency or Bankruptcy of Contractor
§4.12 Contractor Defenses
§4.13 —Substantial Performance
§4.14 —Owner or Architect/Engineer Interference
§4.15 —Impossibility
§4.16 —Waiver and Estoppel
§4.17 —Non-Payment
§4.18 —Owner's Failure to Follow Contractual Termination Procedure
§4.19 Architect/Engineer Default
§4.20 Rescission
§4.21 Wrongful Termination

§4.01 Introduction

It is rarely advisable for a contractor to walk off a job or for an owner to terminate a contract. The only time either party should consider such drastic remedies is if the problems are enormous and apparently unresolvable. Termination is ill advised because in the real world, regardless of the facts or applicable law, sureties rarely step in to complete the job; the owner will incur higher costs and delays; mechanic's liens will be filed by subcontractors and suppliers; and costly litigation with the terminated contractor probably will follow. Similarly, when a contractor walks off a job, it usually does not have another job it can turn to immediately, its reputation and bondability may be damaged, and it probably will have to sue the owner to recover any moneys due with little chance of a true full recovery. In most instances, default is the fault of both parties to some extent—unforeseen conditions are encountered, changes are ordered, designs are poorly drawn, mistakes are made, etc. A small default by one party leads to a larger default by the other which leads to a still larger one by the first party, and so on, eventually resulting in a terminated contract.

To avoid defaults and prevent termination, clear lines of communication must be established; parties must respond promptly and fairly to problems, questions, and claims; complete records must be kept; and all parties must strictly adhere to contract provisions. An owner should not assume that a contractor's failure to pay its subcontractors is because the contractor is dishonest; perhaps the contractor is dissatisfied with the subcontractor's work or disagrees with its payment requisitions. Similarly, a contractor should not assume that an owner is trying to get work for free when its architect refuses to authorize a change order; perhaps the architect is reluctant to approve the change order because it is needed due to a design defect. If the underlying cause of the default can be found, it will be easier to resolve and termination may be avoided. The most typical defaults of a contractor are failure to perform the work in accordance with the schedule, failure to pay subcontractors and suppliers, and performing defective work and failing to correct it. The most typical owner defaults are failure to make payments when due, failure to issue extensions of time and price adjustments for change orders, and interference with the contractor's work.

As you read this chapter, you will notice that it has a decided bent—it primarily discusses default and termination from an owner's viewpoint. This slant is because it is unusual for a contractor voluntarily to terminate a contract; contractors need work to survive and do not lightly default on jobs or terminate contracts. If a contractor does terminate a contract with an owner, it may be because the contractor has greatly underbid the job or, most often, may be in response to something it believes an owner has done or not done, such as grossly interfering with the contractor's work or not paying the contractor. This is not to say contractors never breach contracts—defects and failures are discussed in Chapter 12.

Elimination of work due to changed conditions is discussed in Chapter 6.

§4.02 Contractual Right of Termination

The law implies in every contract a covenant on each party to provide the other with the opportunity to perform.[1] Without a termination clause, an owner or a contractor may terminate a contract in the event of a material breach; most

---

[1] Zadek v Olds, Wortman & King, 166 AD 60, 151 NYS 634 (1st Dept 1915).

contracts, however, specify reasons for which a party may terminate the contract. Some construction contracts, primarily public works contracts, go so far as to provide that the owner may terminate the contract at its convenience or at will, without any reason or cause. These *termination for convenience* clauses are discussed separately from *termination for cause* clauses.

§4.03 —For Cause

Most contracts provide a list of causes which will justify an owner's terminating a contract. The causes typically are contractor defaults, although an owner may specify other reasons for termination, such as an owner's inability to obtain financing. The justification for termination must be real; it may not be a pretense.[2] Further, a party may not terminate a contract for a cause which is not included in the termination clause, unless the cause is so related to the contract that it frustrates the very purpose of the contract.[3]

This "purpose of the contract" basis for terminating a contract is strictly construed. Consider a city of New York contract for construction of a school which the city anticipated would be needed when the state built a new housing project. The state canceled the housing project plans; consequently, the city believed it no longer needed the school. Faced with financial circumstances so dire that the state declared the city to be in a financial emergency, the city chose to terminate the school contract rather than some other capital projects. The court found this termination to be unjustified and awarded the contractor its damages. The court found that the planned and canceled housing project was not so intimately related to the school contract that the failure of the housing project frustrated the basic purpose of the school contract. The court reasoned that if the city believed that the two were intimately connected, it could have made the school contract contingent on the housing project.[4]

The American Institute of Architects (AIA) contract between an owner and a contractor, General Conditions of the Contract for Construction (AIA A201) provides:

> 14.2.1 The Owner may terminate the Contract if the Contractor:
>
> .1 persistently or repeatedly refuses or fails to supply enough properly skilled workers or proper materials;
>
> .2 fails to make payments to Subcontractors for materials or labor in accordance with the respective agreements between the Contractor and the Subcontractors;
>
> .3 persistently disregards laws, ordinances, or rules, regulations or orders of a public authority having jurisdiction; or

---

[2] Langan Constr Corp v State, 110 Misc 177, 180 NYS 249 (Ct Cl 1920).

[3] Pettinelli Elec Co v Board of Educ, 56 AD2d 520, 391 NYS2d 118 (1st Dept), *affd mem*, 43 NY2d 760, 372 NE2d 799, 401 NYS2d 1011 (1977).

[4] *Id.*

.4 otherwise is guilty of substantial breach of a provision of the Contract Documents.

14.2.2 When any of the above reasons exist, the Owner, upon certification by the Architect that sufficient cause exists to justify such action, may without prejudice to any other rights or remedies of the Owner and after giving the Contractor and the Contractor's surety, if any, seven days' written notice, terminate employment of the Contractor and may, subject to any prior rights of the surety:

.1 take possession of the site and all materials, equipment, tools, and construction equipment and machinery thereon owned by the Contractor;

.2 accept assignment of subcontracts pursuant to Paragraph 5.4; and

.3 finish the Work by whatever reasonable method the Owner may deem expedient.

14.2.3 When the Owner terminates the Contract for one of the reasons stated in Subparagraph 14.2.1, the Contractor shall not be entitled to receive further payment until the Work is finished.

14.2.4 If the unpaid balance of the Contract Sum exceeds costs of finishing the Work, including compensation for the Architect's services and expenses made necessary thereby, such excess shall be paid to the Contractor. If such costs exceed the unpaid balance, the Contractor shall pay the difference to the Owner. The amount to be paid to the Contractor or Owner, as the case may be, shall be certified by the Architect, upon application, and this obligation for payment shall survive the termination of the Contract.[5]

Under the same contract, if the work is stopped for 30 days for a specified reason—through no fault of the contractor or its subcontractors or agents, the contractor may terminate the contract. Specified reasons for termination by the contractor include the work stoppage being due to: court or public authority order; government act which makes material unavailable; failure of the project architect to issue a certificate of payment or to give a reason for withholding the certificate; failure of the owner to pay; excessive delays, suspension, or interruptions; or the owner's failing to provide the contractor with evidence that it has the financial means to fulfill its payment obligations under the con-

---

[5] AIA Doc A201, ¶14.2 (1987 ed). Reproduced by permission of The American Institute of Architects under license number 92095. Permission expires July 31, 1993. FURTHER REPRODUCTION IS PROHIBITED. Because AIA Documents are revised from time to time, users should ascertain from the AIA the current edition of this document. Copies of the current edition of this AIA document may be purchased from The American Institute of Architects or its local distributors. The text of this document is not "model language" and is not intended for use in other documents without permission of the AIA.

tract.[6] If the work is stopped for 60 days through no fault of the contractor, its subcontractor, or its agents, the contractor may terminate the contract if the owner has "persistently failed to fulfill [its] obligations under the Contract Documents with respect to matters important to the progress of the Work. . . ."[7] To terminate, the contractor must give seven days' written notice to the owner and architect. A terminating contractor is entitled to recover payment for work performed and "proven loss with respect to materials, equipment, tools, and construction equipment and machinery, including reasonable overhead, profit and damages."[8]

Analysis of the specific causes and standards by which termination by an owner is justified is found at §§4.03 through 4.04. Justification for default or termination by a contractor is discussed at §§4.12 through 4.18.

§4.04 —For Convenience

If a contract provides the owner with a unilateral right to terminate the contract at will or at its convenience, the right to terminate is *absolute* and wholly enforceable in New York, regardless of the owner's good faith, or lack thereof,[9] so long as the contract requires written notice to the contractor of the termination.[10] Federal contracts are subject to a good faith and changed circumstances requirement, as discussed below.

In the absence of a convenience termination clause, an owner must allow a contractor to complete the work or pay the contractor its damages for termination, unless cause for termination exists. The right to terminate for convenience must be explicit and will not be implied.[11] A fairly typical termination clause provides that the owner has the right to ". . . abandon, postpone, or terminate the work or any part thereof for any . . . reason, including the failure of the [contractor] and [owner] to agree upon the pricing of the work in accordance with [the contract] . . ." upon proper notice to the contractor.[12] Similarly, a state of New York contract provides:

> The Director may terminate this Contract whenever in his judgment the public interest so requires by delivering to the Contractor a notice of termination specifying the extent to which performance of the work under

---

[6] *Id* ¶14.1.1.

[7] *Id* ¶14.1.3.

[8] *Id* ¶14.1.2.

[9] New York Tel Co v Jamestown Tel Corp, 282 NY 365, 373, 26 NE2d 295, 298 (1940); Taylor-Warner Corp v Minskoff, 167 AD2d 382, 561 NYS2d 797 (2d Dept 1990); Alco Standard Corp v Schmid Bros, 647 F Supp 4 (SDNY 1986).

[10] Niagara Mohawk Power v Graver Tank & Manu Co, 470 F Supp 1308 (NDNY 1979); Taylor-Warner Corp v Minskoff, 167 AD2d 382, 561 NYS2d 797 (2d Dept 1990) (citing *Niagara*).

[11] Baker v State, 77 AD 528, 78 NYS 922 (3d Dept 1902).

[12] Desco Vitro Glaze, Inc v Mechanical Constr Corp, 159 AD2d 760, 552 NYS2d 185, 186 (3d Dept 1990).

the Contract is terminated and the date upon which such termination becomes effective. Upon receipt of the notice of termination, the Contractor shall act promptly to minimize the expenses resulting from such termination.[13]

" 'Convenience' may be defined as the quality of being personally convenient or 'suitable or well adapted to one's easy action or performance of functions,' or the saving of trouble."[14] A party's motive under a convenience termination clause is rarely relevant. Indeed, such a clause has been held to encompass the right to terminate a contract due to an error in specifications[15] and to terminate one contract and substitute another for essentially the same services or materials.[16] Pursuant to Canal Law §32, every contract for the improvement, maintenance, or repair of the state canal system must reserve to the commissioner of transportation the right to suspend or cancel the contract if the commissioner determines that the "work is not being performed according to the contract or *for the best interests of the state*" and the right to readvertise and relet the work.

Under a fairly typical termination for convenience clause, a contractor's recovery is limited to:

> (a) the costs actually incurred up to the effective date of such termination, plus
> (b) the cost of settling and paying claims arising out of the termination of work under subcontracts or orders . . . [and]
> (c) the rate of profit and overhead on (a) and (b) as prescribed by this Contract. . . .[17]

Under such a clause, the terminated contractor is not entitled to recovery of the profit or overhead allocable to the work not performed.[18] A current city of New York contract provides that upon termination for the city's convenience, the contractor is to be paid only for that amount of work completed at termination and if the work is being done on a unit price basis, that will be the measurement for payment; thus, under a city of New York contract, a termi-

---

[13] G&R Elec Contractors, Inc v State, 130 Misc 2d 661, 663, 496 NYS2d 898, 900 (Ct Cl 1985).

[14] *Id* at 665, 496 NYS2d at 902 (quoting The Compact Edition of the Oxford English Dictionary 934-35 (Jan 1984).

[15] G&R Elec Contractors, Inc v State, 130 Misc 2d 661, 496 NYS2d 898 (Ct Cl 1985).

[16] Desco Vitro Glaze, Inc v Mechanical Constr Corp, 159 AD2d 760, 552 NYS2d 185, 186 (3d Dept 1990).

[17] G&R Elec Contractors, Inc v State, 130 Misc 2d 661, 663, 496 NYS2d 898, 900 (Ct Cl 1985).

[18] Affirmative Pipe Cleaning, Inc/Edenwald Contracting Co v City of NY, 159 AD2d 417, 553 NYS2d 324 (1st Dept 1990); G&R Elec Contractors, Inc v State, 130 Misc 2d 661, 496 NYS2d 898 (Ct Cl 1985).

nated contractor is not even entitled to its start-up costs, much less overhead and lost profit, even if the amount paid under the unit price does not fully compensate the contractor.[19]

Owners argue that termination for convenience clauses are necessary to protect themselves from having to continue with a job if financing falls through, regulations change significantly, or the economy changes so that the project is no longer economically sound. In fact, if owners wish protection from such events, they may provide that the contract is terminable for cause upon their occurrence. Under New York law, due to lack of a good faith requirement, a convenience termination clause effectively allows an owner to cancel a contract because a better deal comes around or because it decides, late in the process, that it does not like the contractor.

An owner cannot use a contractual right of *suspension* for convenience as a termination for convenience clause. A suspension clause allows an owner to postpone *temporarily* the work for reasons set forth in the contract and provides for adjustment of the contract price upon resumption of the work.[20] Abandonment of the project and resulting termination for convenience of the contract are not permitted under a suspension for convenience clause.[21]

Some contracts also contain clauses which provide that if a contractor is terminated for cause and later

> it is determined for any reason that the Contractor was not in default under the provisions of this clause . . . the rights and obligation of the parties shall, if the contract contains a clause providing for termination for convenience of the [Owner], be the same as if the notice of termination had been issued pursuant to such clause.[22]

The authors have used a similar clause which provides:

> If it shall later be determined that a termination for cause . . . by the Owner was not for cause, then the termination shall be deemed to have been for convenience under [the termination for convenience clause] and any amounts due the Contractor arising out of the termination shall be determined by [the termination for convenience clause].

Termination of a contract and elimination of work due to changed conditions is discussed in Chapter 6.

Federal Contracts

Most construction contracts with the federal government contain termination for convenience clauses which allow the government to terminate a con-

---

[19] Affirmative Pipe Cleaning, Inc/Edenwald Contracting Co v City of NY, 159 AD2d 417, 553 NYS2d 324 (1st Dept 1990).
[20] *See* AIA Doc A201 ¶14.3 (1987 ed).
[21] Baker v State, 77 AD 528, 78 NYS 922 (3d Dept 1902).
[22] Federal Form 23A, General Provisions, ¶5(e).

tract when the contracting officer determines that a termination "is in the Government's interest."[23] The federal courts have construed these clauses more narrowly than New York courts have construed similar clauses, and, generally, have held that the government's right to terminate for convenience is restricted by an implied requirement of good faith, thus effectively limiting convenience terminations to situations in which substantial changes in the original contracting conditions have taken place. In *Torncello v United States*,[24] the Court of Claims held that an unrestricted right of termination clause would make a contract illusory for lack of consideration. The court, instead of invalidating the majority of federal contracts, held that a termination for convenience clause includes a "changed circumstance restriction." Examples of changed circumstances which would justify termination include a national emergency or some other drastic change in the circumstances under which the parties entered into the contract.

§4.05 —Architect/Engineer Approval

Most contracts condition termination for cause upon an architect/engineer's certification that sufficient cause exists to terminate the contract. Depending upon the extent of the architect's powers under the contract, its decision regarding cause may or may not be binding on the contractor.[25]

§4.06 Notice Requirements

If a party truly believes that it has no choice but to abandon a job or terminate a contract it must follow contract procedures precisely. A failure to follow contractual termination procedures may turn a justified termination into a breach of contract. The default must be declared, notice must be given, and an opportunity to cure must be provided, if specified in the contract, for a termination to be effective. Notice provisions are closely read and literally construed.[26] In one case, for example, an owner was not required to give advance notice of intent to terminate when the contract specified that the owner must, upon certification of the architect, give the contractor three days' written notice of a *default* before providing labor and materials itself, but specified that termination of the contract would be effective simply upon a proper certificate of the architect.[27]

---

[23] Federal Acquisition Regulation §§52.249-1 to -5, 48 CFR ch 1.

[24] 681 F2d 756 (Ct Cl 1982).

[25] *See* **§16.04**.

[26] Casale v August Bohl Contracting Co, 26 AD2d 974, 275 NYS2d 140 (3d Dept 1966).

[27] Midtown Contracting Co v Goldsticker, 165 AD 264, 150 NYS 809 (1st Dept 1914).

§4.07 Contractor Default

Contractor default sufficient to justify termination of the contract may occur through many events. The most common are discussed here and include failure to prosecute the work, failure to pay subcontractors and suppliers, failure to correct defective work, and insolvency or bankruptcy (*but see* **§4.11**). Not every default by a contractor justifies termination; the default must be material and of consequence.

> **PRACTICE POINTER:**
>
> The conventional wisdom in deciding whether to declare a contractor in default and terminate the contract is *DON'T*. Taking the matter a little further, however, the following rules of thumb may be helpful:
>
> (1) In the first trimester of the job, termination may make some sense.
>
> (2) In the second trimester of the job, termination makes less sense.
>
> (3) In the final trimester of the job, termination hardly ever makes sense.

An owner must be wary when terminating a contractor; it faces the risk of a court's later finding that the contractor was not in default and that the termination was wrongful. The consequences of wrongful terminations are discussed in **§4.21**.

If a contractor is terminated due to its breach, it loses all right to additional compensation unless it can show that it had substantially performed the contract prior to termination.[28] See **§4.13** for a discussion of substantial performance. Further, any recovery it may be entitled to must be in quantum meruit, not contract, since the termination of the contract makes the contract level of compensation irrelevant.[29] Of course, if the contract provides a measure of compensation upon termination or that the contract price and payment terms shall survive termination, such provision would control. American Institute of Architects (AIA) AIA Doc A201 ¶14.2.4 shows such a reservation; it is quoted in **§4.03** above.

§4.08 —Failure to Prosecute the Work

If a contractor does not provide a job with sufficient labor or materials, does not work on the project steadily, or fails to complete the work on time, it may be in default for a failure to prosecute the work, and termination may be justi-

---

[28] Triple M Roofing Corp v Greater Jericho Corp, 43 AD2d 594, 349 NYS2d 771 (2d Dept 1973). See **§4.13** for a discussion of substantial performance.

[29] Midtown Contracting Co v Goldsticker, 165 AD 264, 150 NYS 809 (1st Dept 1914).

fied.[30] Not every delay is a default, however. Whether performance has been delayed beyond a reasonable time so as to constitute a default is a question of fact. Factors to consider include: ". . . the subject matter of the contract, the situation of the parties, their intentions, what they contemplated at the time the contract was made, and the circumstance attending performance."[31] For instance, a contractor was held to be justified in terminating its subcontractor when an already late subcontractor failed to give the contractor an often-requested definite schedule or completion date but merely promised to do the work with "all possible speed," did not make sufficient progress on the work, and did not perform within a reasonable time.[32]

In another instance, the trial court found that an owner was justified in terminating its contract when the contractor was unreasonably late with completion. The contract provided that the contractor would construct a home for the owner to be completed by March 1. On June 1, the contractor claimed that it needed three more months to complete. The home was not complete on September 1, nor on October 14 when the owner terminated the contract and asked for its deposit back.[33]

§4.09 —Failure to Pay Subcontractors and Suppliers

The issue of when a subcontractor or supplier is entitled to be paid, including the effectiveness of contingent payment clauses, is discussed in Chapter 3 on subcontracts.

> **PRACTICE POINTER:**
>
> Often, a contractor's failure to pay subcontractors is due to financial difficulties. When faced with unpaid subcontractors and suppliers, an owner should ask the contractor why. If the contractor admits to financial difficulties, the owner should ask what the source of the difficulties is and might explore ways of helping the contractor, including helping finance the contractor's work, perhaps by making progress payments more often and payment by joint check for items attributable to subcontractor and supplier work. An owner should avoid advancing the contractor's payroll or it may risk being liable for payroll taxes. Further, an owner should avoid dealing directly with subcontractors and suppli-

---

[30] Triple M Roofing Corp v Greater Jericho Corp, 43 AD2d 594, 349 NYS2d 771 (2d Dept 1973); Midtown Contracting Co v Goldsticker, 165 AD 264, 150 NYS 809 (1st Dept 1914).

[31] Lake Steel Erection v Egan, 61 AD2d 1125, 403 NYS2d 387, 389 (4th Dept 1978); Young v Whitney, 111 AD2d 1013, 490 NYS2d 330 (3d Dept 1985).

[32] Schenectady Steel Co v Bruno Trimpoli Gen Constr Co, 43 AD2d 234, 350 NYS2d 920 (3d Dept), *affd mem*, 34 NY2d 939, 316 NE2d 875, 359 NYS2d 560 (1974).

[33] Tupper v Wade Lupe Constr Co, 39 Misc 2d 1053, 242 NYS2d 546 (Schenectady 1963).

ers or it could face direct liability or inadvertently void its contractor's performance bond. If the contractor is bonded, the owner should obtain the surety's written consent to any arrangements it makes with the contractor to help it perform; otherwise, the surety may be discharged.

§4.10 —Failure to Correct Defective Work

Determining who is responsible for a defect or failure can be difficult. Architects and engineers tend to believe the fault is with the contractor or the materials, while contractors like to believe the fault is with the original plans and specifications. Before terminating a contractor for defective work, an owner must be certain that the contractor is in fact responsible for the defect and that the defect is significant enough to constitute a material breach of the contract. A contractor is responsible only for its performance of the construction contract[34] and the performance of its subcontractors. If a contractor performs in a workmanlike manner according to the plans and specifications, it is not liable even if the construction is defective.[35] A contractor's duty is to follow the plans and specifications.[36] If they are defective, it is not the contractor's fault. Chapter 12 discusses defects in more detail.

> **PRACTICE POINTER:**
>
> Deficient or shoddy work can be avoided or remedied by careful inspection by the project architect and the retention of funds until deficiencies are corrected.

§4.11 —Insolvency or Bankruptcy of Contractor

Clauses in contracts that provide that an owner may terminate a contractor because it files for bankruptcy protection are void. Federal bankruptcy laws give the bankrupt contractor or bankruptcy trustee the option to affirm or disavow the contract.[37] Thus, the choice is not really the owner's, but is the trustee's or the contractor's, depending upon the type of bankruptcy filed. If an owner validly terminates a contractor *before* it files for bankruptcy, the trustee may not resurrect the contract.

---

[34] Carrols Equities Corp v Villnave, 76 Misc 2d 205, 350 NYS2d 90 (Onondaga 1973), *affd mem*, 49 AD2d 672, 373 NYS2d 1012 (4th Dept 1975).
[35] *Id.*
[36] MacKnight Flintic Stone Co v Mayor of NY, 160 NY 72, 54 NE 661 (1899).
[37] 11 USC §365.

§4.12 Contractor Defenses

There are always two sides to every story. As often as an owner claims that a contractor is in default, a contractor claims that the default originally was caused by the owner or some intervening factor which excuses the default. Some of the items discussed as defenses are also grounds upon which a contractor may justifiably terminate its contract with an owner. Discussed here are the primary defenses; this list is not exhaustive—there is always a new theory to be tried or a unique set of facts which creates its own defense.

If the contractor abandons the work in response to an owner's breach, it may choose whether to sue in quantum meruit or on the contract.[38] Where the contract is terminated due to an owner's breach, the owner may not recover its excess costs of completion from the contractor.[39]

§4.13 —Substantial Performance

If the contract is *substantially completed* at the time of termination, the contractor is entitled to the contract price plus extras, less the costs of correcting any defects, furnishing missing materials, and completing the contract work.[40] Determining whether a contractor has substantially performed is not dependent on the number of defects or per cent of the work remaining to be done; the question is *did the owner get essentially what it bargained for?* In other words, is the project sufficiently complete so the owner may use it for the purpose intended? Thus, a roofer that was terminated for failure to complete on time was found not to have substantially performed its contract when 15 per cent of one building's roof remained to be completed, and 30 per cent of another roof was not complete.[41]

Substantial performance (also called substantial completion) is also discussed in Chapter 12.

§4.14 —Owner or Architect/Engineer Interference

If an owner interferes with the progress of the work, a contractor cannot be blamed for delay due to the owner's interference. If the interference is significant enough, a contractor will be justified in terminating the contract. It is

---

[38] Greenspan v Amsterdam, 145 AD2d 535, 536 NYS2d 90 (2d Dept 1988); Zadek v Olds, Wortman & King, 166 AD 60, 151 NYS 634 (1st Dept 1915).

[39] Greenspan v Amsterdam, 145 AD2d 535, 536 NYS2d 90 (2d Dept 1988).

[40] Pilgrim Homes & Garages, Inc v Fiore, 75 AD2d 846, 427 NYS2d 851 (2d Dept), *appeal dismissed,* 51 NY2d 702, 431 NYS2d 1030 (1980); Gem Drywall Corp v C. Scialdo & Sons, 42 AD2d 1045, 348 NYS2d 643 (4th Dept 1973), *affd mem,* 35 NY2d 781, 320 NE2d 867, 362 NYS2d 152 (1974); Turk v Look, 53 AD2d 709, 383 NYS2d 937 (3d Dept 1976).

[41] Triple M Roofing Corp v Greater Jericho Corp, 43 AD2d 594, 349 NYS2d 771 (2d Dept 1973).

112 DEFAULT/TERMINATION

not always clear when an owner has so interfered with a contract that a contractor's default is excusable or its termination of the contract justified. Obviously, if the contractor can show that an action taken by the owner or its architect caused a certain delay or defect, the contractor's "default" should be excused. The more difficult question is when does the interference rise to such a level that the contractor is justified in stopping work on the contract and entitled to recovery for work done, despite the lack of substantial performance.

For example, in one case, a contractor was justified in stopping work when the owner locked it out of the work site.[42] Similarly, a contractor was justified in abandoning the work when the owner of the site, a mental hospital, failed and refused to keep mental patients out of the work area and away from the contractor's tools, equipment, and laborers.[43] In another instance, a contractor was allowed to recover from the owner when the owner prevented it from completing the contract by failing and refusing to furnish it with details and information needed to complete the work.[44] The interference need not be as obvious and dramatic as the above examples for the contractor to justifiably abandon the work. For instance, in one case, the court found that a contractor was justified in stopping work due to the owner's hindrance of and interference with the contractor's work by: issuing 70 revised drawings after work had begun; refusing to acknowledge the contractor's right to extra compensation due to the numerous changes required by the 70 revised drawings; failing to obtain needed building permits; misrepresenting the suitability of excavated matter as roadway fill; and failing to coordinate the work of other contractors. The contractor was allowed to recover the value of its work; the owner was not allowed its costs of completion.[45]

If a contractor is in default and has abandoned the job, an owner does not have the obligation to preserve the contractor's right to remedy its default;[46] i.e., the owner need not make it possible for the contractor to return to complete the contract work.

Interference is also discussed in Chapter 7.

§4.15 —Impossibility

The defense or excuse of impossibility of performance is available only if the contract performance truly is rendered impossible. Just because a contract is more difficult or expensive to perform does not mean that doing so is impos-

---

[42] Greenspan v Amsterdam, 145 AD2d 535, 536 NYS2d 90 (2d Dept 1988).

[43] Farrell Heating, Plumbing & Air Conditioning Contractors v Facilities Dev & Improvement Corp, 68 AD2d 958, 414 NYS2d 767 (3d Dept 1979).

[44] Zadek v Olds, Wortman & King, 166 AD 60, 151 NYS 634 (1st Dept 1915).

[45] Felix Contracting Corp v Oakridge Land & Prop Corp, 106 AD2d 488, 483 NYS2d 28 (2d Dept 1984), *appeal denied*, 66 NY2d 606, 519 NYS2d 1025 (1985).

[46] Iervolino v Best Built Homes Holding Corp, 56 Misc 2d 343, 288 NYS2d 724 (Kings 1968).

sible.[47] Further, the event which caused the impossibility must not have been foreseeable.[48] Of course, if the parties wish to specify in their contract that a specific event will excuse performance, they may do so. For instance, if the owner needs federal funds to finance a project, it must state in the contract that performance is dependent on federal funds in order for its nonperformance to be excused.

§4.16 —Waiver and Estoppel

If an owner waives a contractor's default, it may be estopped from using the default as a basis to justify termination. Most often, waiver is found when a contractor has not completed the work by the completion date. The owner, not wishing to lose even more time by terminating and replacing the contractor, does not terminate the contract immediately, but allows the contractor to continue performance and insists on completion. By such actions, the owner has waived the contractor's default and converted the contract from one with a definitive completion date to one to be completed within a reasonable time.[49] What is a reasonable time is discussed in §4.08. The owner does retain the right to seek damages for delay.

An owner may not, after allowing a completion date to pass, summarily terminate the contract; it must give the contractor an opportunity to perform.[50] It may reinstate a definite time element by giving the contractor notice of its intent to reinstate a deadline and by calling for performance within a reasonable time.[51] What is a reasonable time for completion depends on the circumstances of the case. For instance, in one case, where the owner had waived the initial completion date and the contractor, as part of the contract to build a home, built a well in compliance with applicable regulations, but the well was inspected after new regulations had been passed and was failed, the owner could not demand completion within 10 days because such was not a sufficient period of time to remove the original well and build a new one.[52]

§4.17 —Non-Payment

Common sense would suggest that if one is not being paid for its work, it may quit working. However, this is not always the case. Generally, if an owner

---

[47] Ogdensburg Urban Renewal Agency v Moroney, 42 AD2d 639, 345 NYS2d 169 (3d Dept 1973).

[48] *Id.*

[49] General Supply & Constr Co v Goelet, 241 NY 28, 148 NE 778 (1925); Schenectady Steel Co v Bruno Trimpoli Gen Constr Co, 43 AD2d 234, 350 NYS2d 920 (3d Dept), *affd mem*, 34 NY2d 939, 316 NE2d 875, 359 NYS2d 560 (1974); Schneider v Rola Constr Co, 16 Misc 2d 556, 183 NYS2d 955 (Suffolk 1959).

[50] Realty Adv & Supply Co v Hickson, 184 AD 168, 171 NYS 455 (1st Dept 1918).

[51] Schenectady Steel Co v Bruno Trimpoli Gen Constr Co, 43 AD2d 234, 350 NYS2d 920 (3d Dept), *affd mem*, 34 NY2d 939, 316 NE2d 875, 359 NYS2d 560 (1974).

[52] Schneider v Rola Constr Co, 16 Misc 2d 556, 183 NYS2d 955 (Suffolk 1959).

fails to make timely progress payments, the contractor may regard the contract as terminated by the owner and recover either in contract or in quantum meruit.[53] Further, a contractor may be justified in leaving a job if it learns that the owner has exhausted its financing and will be unable to make future payments.[54] If, however, the contract provides for dispute resolution, including disputes regarding entitlement to payment, a contractor that terminates because of non-payment faces the possibility of finding itself to be the party in default and without a remedy.[55] Contractual dispute resolution clauses are discussed in Chapter 16.

The right to terminate for non-payment may be exercised properly only if the contractor is in fact entitled to payment. If it has failed to submit proper requisitions, it may not be entitled to payment, and may be unable to terminate for failure to pay.[56] Further, if a contractor has accepted late payments in the past, it may have waived its right to prompt payment and cannot terminate for late payment without resurrecting the time element. "If one party acquiesces in the other's late payments throughout the period of the contract, the tardy party is entitled to unequivocal notice that timely payment will be required in the future."[57] This does not mean that a contractor must abandon a job when its progress payment is not paid on the exact day when due. A contractor will not waive an owner's failure to pay by continuing work until it is certain that it will not be paid.[58] Finally, a contractor cannot cease work on one contract due to an owner's failure to pay it on another contract, where the two contracts are separate and are not contingent upon one another.[59]

A contractor that fails to pay its subcontractors because it has not been paid by the owner cannot expect them to continue working;[60] they would be justified in terminating work[61] and entitled to recovery in contract[62] or quantum meruit,[63] unless there is a valid contingent payment clause.[64]

---

[53] Paterno & Sons v Town of Windsor, 43 AD2d 863, 351 NYS2d 445 (2d Dept 1974).

[54] Turk v Look, 53 AD2d 709, 383 NYS2d 937 (3d Dept 1976) (contractor justified in leaving job when it learned that home owner's mortgage bank would not make further advances).

[55] *See* Keyway Contractors, Inc v Leek Corp, 189 Ga App 467, 376 SE2d 212, *cert denied*, 189 Ga App 912 (1988).

[56] Granite Computer Leasing Corp v Travelers Indem Co, 702 F Supp 415 (SDNY 1988), *vacated on other grounds*, 894 F2d 547 (2d Cir 1990).

[57] Tri-Mar Contractors, Inc v Itco Drywall, Inc, 74 AD2d 601, 424 NYS2d 737, 739 (2d Dept 1980).

[58] Serena Constr Corp v Valley Drywall Serv, 45 AD2d 896, 357 NYS2d 214 (3d Dept 1974).

[59] Waters v Glasheen, 103 AD2d 1043, 478 NYS2d 437 (4th Dept 1984).

[60] This issue is discussed in some detail at §3.18.

[61] Louis N. Picciano & Son v Olympic Constr Co, 112 AD2d 604, 492 NYS2d 476 (3d Dept), *appeal dismissed*, 66 NY2d 854, 489 NE2d 253, 498 NYS2d 366 (1985).

[62] *Id*.

[63] Serena Constr Corp v Valley Drywall Serv, 45 AD2d 896, 357 NYS2d 214 (3d Dept 1974).

[64] Discussed at §3.18.

§4.18 —Owner's Failure to Follow Contractual Termination Procedure

If an owner terminates a contract without following all contractual termination procedures *to the letter*, the termination may be invalid and entitle the contractor to recover damages from the owner, despite the fact that the contractor was at fault. Whether an owner has followed termination procedures properly is a question of fact.[65]

§4.19 Architect/Engineer Default

Architect and engineer defaults are discussed in Chapter 11 on professional liability.

§4.20 Rescission

If a contract was procured through fraud, the innocent party may rescind the contract if the parties can be placed in the position they were in prior to contracting. Similarly, if one party so materially breaches the contract so as to *substantially* defeat the purpose of the contract, there may be rescission with the remedy based in restitution, not compensation.[66] In the event of a substantial breach, the wronged party has the option to seek rescission in law and sue for consideration paid, to affirm the contract and sue for damages, or to seek rescission in equity and a return to the status quo.[67] If substantial restoration to the status quo is not possible, an equitable action in rescission will not lie.[68] In most construction cases, rescission is a difficult remedy once performance has begun.

Rescission is a drastic remedy which will be granted only if: (1) the party seeking rescission acts promptly to cancel the agreement after discovery of the grounds for rescission; (2) it is possible to restore the parties to their original position; and (3) the injury cannot be practically compensated by monetary damages.[69] Using these criteria, rescission was not granted to a home buyer from its builder when the builder built its garage driveway so it ran across a neighbor's property. The home owner was able to get one car in its two-car garage without driving on the neighbor's property. The court denied the home owner's plea for rescission because the garage was partially usable, the defect affected the home value by only 10 per cent, and the home owner had made

---

[65] Aetna Cas & Sur Co v City of NY, 160 AD2d 561, 554 NYS2d 210 (1st Dept 1990).

[66] Strand Bldg Corp v Russell & Saxe, Inc, 36 Misc 2d 339, 232 NYS2d 384 (Kings 1962), *affd mem*, 240 NYS2d 948 (2d Dept 1963) (a contract to purchase stock).

[67] *Id*.

[68] Tarelton Bldg Corp v Spider Staging Sales Co, 26 AD2d 809, 274 NYS2d 43 (1st Dept 1966).

[69] Fink v Friedman, 78 Misc 2d 429, 358 NYS2d 250 (Nassau 1974).

changes to the home so that it was difficult to return either party to the status quo.[70]

If the parties voluntarily enter into a termination agreement that rescinds the contract, it will operate as an accord and satisfaction of any claims the parties may have, unless a claim is expressly or impliedly reserved in the agreement.[71]

Rescission is further discussed in Chapter 15.

§4.21 Wrongful Termination

If an owner wrongfully terminates a contract, it is not entitled to seek redress from the contractor's surety[72] or its excess costs of completion from the contractor. The wrongfully terminated contractor may be entitled to its lost profits, value of work done to date, and start-up expenses.[73] The contractor may choose between recovery in contract or quantum meruit.[74] In quantum meruit, its measure of damages is the value of work completed; in contract, the measure is the contract price less payments made less the *contractor's*, not the owner's, anticipated cost of completion.[75]

If a contractor wrongfully terminates a contract or abandons a job, it loses its right to lost profits. The owner may recover the cost of completing the contractor's work, to be offset by the amount due the contractor for work performed.[76]

---

[70] *Id.*

[71] MJ Posner Constr Co v Valley View Dev Corp, 118 AD2d 1001, 499 NYS2d 997 (3d Dept 1986).

[72] Farrell Heating, Plumbing & Air Conditioning Contractors v Facilities Dev & Improvement Corp, 68 AD2d 958, 414 NYS2d 767 (3d Dept 1979).

[73] Peru Assocs v State, 70 Misc 2d 775, 334 NYS2d 772 (Ct Cl 1971), *affd mem*, 335 NYS2d 373 (3d Dept 1972); Baker v State, 77 AD 528, 78 NYS 922 (3d Dept 1902).

[74] New Era Homes Corp v Forster, 299 NY 303, 86 NE2d 757, 22 ALR2d 1338 (1949); Paterno & Sons v Town of New Windsor, 43 AD2d 863, 351 NYS2d 445 (2d Dept 1974).

[75] New Era Homes Corp v Forster, 299 NY 303, 86 NE2d 757, 22 ALR2d 1338 (1949).

[76] Tri-Mar Contractors, Inc v Itco Drywall, Inc, 74 AD2d 601, 424 NYS2d 737 (2d Dept 1980).

Changed Conditions 5

§5.01 Introduction
§5.02 Changed Conditions Defined
§5.03 —Subsurface Conditions
§5.04 —Latent Above-Ground Conditions
§5.05 —Miscellaneous Causes of Changed Conditions
§5.06 Contract Clauses
§5.07 —Changed Conditions Clauses
§5.08 —Disclaimer Clauses
§5.09 —Exculpatory Clauses
§5.10 Owner's Misrepresentation
§5.11 —Owner's Innocent Misrepresentation
§5.12 —Owner's Fraud, Concealment, and Reckless Representation
§5.13 Site Investigation and Other Inquiry
§5.14 Reliance on Owner's Data
§5.15 Contractor's Duty to Perform
§5.16 Remedies
§5.17 Claims
§5.18 —Notice and Documentation
§5.19 Damages
§5.20 —Impact Costs

§5.01 Introduction

The phrase *changed conditions* is misleading.[1] It generally does not refer to a change in condition but to a change of knowledge about an existing condi-

---

[1] M. Greenberg, *Problems Relating to Changes and Changed Conditions on Public Contracts,* 3 Pub Cont LJ 135 (1970).

tion—a condition which existed at the time the contract was executed but of which the contractor was unaware or which was not reasonably to be expected by either party.[2] United States government contracts refer to them as *differing site conditions*,[3] while the American Institute of Architects (AIA) refers to them as *concealed or unknown conditions*.[4] They might also be referred to as *unforeseen conditions* or *unanticipated conditions*. A typical example of a changed condition is when subsurface conditions vary from what was expected, such as when a tunneler encounters solid rock, expecting to encounter compact dirt, or when a contractor furnishes much less fill than the contract led it to believe would be needed.[5]

Despite many contractors' beliefs to the contrary, there is no implied right to extra compensation for changed conditions. A changed conditions claim exists only by express contract or in the event of fraud or misrepresentation by the owner.[6]

Many public authorities in New York, including New York City, use changed condition clauses. New York State and the Port Authority of New York and New Jersey rarely use these clauses. Changed condition clauses are intended to protect contractors from damage due to unforeseen and unanticipated conditions. Before such clauses were used, contractors were forced to guard against changed conditions by including contingency factors in their bids to cover increased costs which *might* have resulted if an unforeseen condition arose. If one did not arise, the contractor pocketed the contingency factor as a windfall. If one did arise, the contractor had to hope it had provided a large enough factor in its bid; if it had not, it more often than not sued the owner anyway. Although no project is surprise-free, *significant* unforeseen conditions do not arise on most projects. The result of including contingency factors in the bids was that construction bids were driven up and costs destabilized. By using a changed conditions clause, however, an owner reallocates the risk of unanticipated conditions, taking some of it on itself, and, in return, receives more accurate and lower bids, at least in theory. A 1976 Wisconsin decision best explains the rationale behind shifting the risk from the contractor to the owner by using a changed conditions clause:

> The changed condition clause is a contractual innovation designed for the mutual benefit of both the government and the contractor. The government benefits by use of such a clause because the contractor no longer

---

[2] Rarely, a changed condition will occur during construction. In Dawco Constr, Inc v United States, 18 Cl Ct 682 (1989), *modified on other grounds*, 930 F2d 872 (Fed Cir 1991), a contractor was awarded damages due to a changed condition when an eight-month contract suspension caused the contractor to encounter much deeper weed roots than anticipated.

[3] Federal Acquisition Regulations, 48 CFR §52.243.5.

[4] AIA Doc A201, ¶4.3.6 (14th ed 1987).

[5] John Arborio, Inc v State, 41 Misc 2d 145, 245 NYS2d 274 (Ct Cl 1963).

[6] Weston v State, 262 NY 46, 186 NE 197, 199, 88 ALR 1219 (1933); M. Simon, Construction Contracts and Claims 135 (1979).

needs to add large contingency sums to his bid in order to cover risk of encountering adverse subsurface conditions. The contractor benefits because he is awarded extra compensation if adverse subsurface conditions are encountered which materially differ from those indicated in the contract. Thus, much of the gamble is taken out of underground construction. The government does not have to pay the contractor a windfall price when only normal conditions are encountered, and the contractor suffers no disaster when unanticipated conditions arise. Furthermore, both parties benefit by the existence of an informal machinery for resolving problems through negotiation rather than litigation.[7]

§5.02 Changed Conditions Defined

Regardless of the term by which a contract refers to them, *changed conditions* are perhaps best described in United States government contracts as

> (1) subsurface, latent, or physical conditions at the site materially different from those indicated in the contract or (2) unknown physical conditions at the site of an unusual nature, differing materially from those ordinarily encountered and generally recognized as inhering in work of the character provided for in the contract.[8]

Type I and Type II Changed Conditions

There are two basic types of changed conditions, generally referred to as *Type I* and *Type II*. These designations are derived from the above clause. Type I changed conditions involve a misrepresentation in the contract documents as to site conditions by the owner; the misrepresentation may be innocent or intentional, the contractual representations express or implied.[9] Type II changes involve surprise: the physical site conditions are not what one normally expects to encounter. "Type II conditions apply when the owner has not included specifications in the contract."[10]

Behavioral Changed Conditions

Another type of changed condition classification is a *behavioral* changed condition. The distinction between behavioral and traditional changed conditions can best be seen in a subsurface example. To recover for a traditional changed condition, the contractor would have to encounter a different *kind* of ground—it was expecting soft dirt and encountered solid rock. A behavioral changed condition is encountered when the ground *behaves* differently than

---

[7] Metropolitan Sewage Comm v RW Constr, Inc, 72 Wis 2d 365, 370, 241 NW2d 371, 376 (1976).

[8] Federal Acquisition Regulations, 48 CFR §52.243.5.

[9] Shank-Artukovich v United States, 13 Cl Ct 346, 350 (1987), *aff'd*, 848 F2d 1245 (Fed Cir 1988) (unpublished opinion).

[10] *Id.*

what was expected. For instance, it may be expected by all parties that the ground will stand long enough for advance of a boring machine; however, part way through the job the contractor encounters loose sand which stops progress because it will not stand and requires a more complicated tunneling method using different equipment. If the contractor keeps good records and carefully pleads its case, it may be able to recover for this behavioral changed condition.[11]

Materiality

Regardless of the type of changed condition, in order for a contractor to recover, the condition must be *materially* different from what was anticipated, be reasonably unforeseeable on the basis of all information available to the contractor,[12] and *materially* affect the cost of the work or time needed to complete the work.[13]

There are several different types of changed conditions which may face a contractor. The list of possibilities is probably endless. An unscrupulous owner may conceal almost any problem. Perhaps the easiest way to discuss changed conditions is to break them into two basic categories: subsurface and latent above-ground conditions. In either location the conditions may be manmade or natural. Weather is not a changed condition but is an act of God and a risk generally accepted by a contractor,[14] although it may be the basis of an excusable delay claim. What happens *as a result* of the weather, however, may be a changed condition, such as when unusually heavy rains cause the soil to become excessively wet.[15] A changed condition typically involves the presence of something unanticipated, but it may also involve the absence of something anticipated. For instance, changed conditions were found when a contractor on a unit price contract was required to provide much less borrow than anticipated[16] and when a quarry did not have sufficient quantities of usable rock.[17]

§5.03 —Subsurface Conditions

Unanticipated subsurface conditions may include ground water, subterranean caverns, foundations of previous buildings, underground storage tanks, rock, extensive root growth, etc. Any physical condition located under the sur-

---

[11] *See* J. Smyth, *Behavioral Differing Site Conditions Claims,* 11 Constr Litig Rep 158 (1990); Shank-Artukovich v United States, 13 Cl Ct 346, 352 (1987), *affd,* 848 F2d 1245 (Fed Cir 1988) (unpublished opinion); *In re* S&M—Traylor Bros, ENG BCA Nos 3878, 3943, 32-1 BCA ¶15,484.

[12] Mojave Enters v United States, 3 Cl Ct 353, 357 (1983).

[13] *See* Andrew Catapano Co v City of NY, 116 Misc 2d 163, 455 NYS2d 144 (NY 1980).

[14] AG Concrete Breakers, Inc v State, 16 Misc 2d 511, 185 NYS2d 455 (Ct Cl), *affd,* 9 AD2d 995, 194 NYS2d 743 (3d Dept 1959).

[15] Bolander Co v United States, 186 Ct Cl 398 (1968); *but see* AG Concrete Breakers, Inc v State, 16 Misc 2d 511, 185 NYS2d 455 (Ct Cl), *affd,* 9 AD2d 995, 194 NYS2d 743 (3d Dept 1959).

[16] John Arborio, Inc v State, 41 Misc 2d 145, 245 NYS2d 274 (Ct Cl 1963).

[17] Kaiser Indus Corp v United States, 340 F2d 322 (Ct Cl 1965).

face of the earth may be a changed condition *if* it was not anticipated or reasonably capable of anticipation.

Changed conditions have been found and recovery allowed a contractor where: there was a significant difference between the rock elevations upon which the state based its designs and actual elevations;[18] the state misrepresented the amount of rock to be excavated,[19] creek bed elevations,[20] and the amount of necessary fill and borrow;[21] the city significantly miscalculated the location of bedrock;[22] weed roots grew significantly during a work suspension ordered by the government;[23] and the state failed to reveal the presence of large amounts of hardpan in the soil,[24] an underground swamp,[25] and underground obstructions placed by its agent.[26]

Changed subsurface conditions have not been found where: the builder assumed that a job completed 15 years earlier was built according to specifications;[27] the contract provided unit prices for excavation work;[28] the contractor failed to survey the site and later encountered public utility lines;[29] and excavated materials were unsuitable for fill.[30]

§5.04 —Latent Above-Ground Conditions

Changed conditions are found above ground as well as under the surface of the earth, although not as often. For instance, if a contractor were to encounter previously unknown asbestos while demolishing a building, it would look to the changed conditions clause of its contract for relief. Other latent above-

---

[18] Grow Constr Co v State, 56 AD2d 95, 391 NYS2d 726 (3d Dept 1977).

[19] County Asphalt, Inc v State, 40 AD2d 26, 337 NYS2d 415 (3d Dept 1972); Rusciano Constr Corp v State, 37 AD2d 745, 323 NYS2d 21 (3d Dept 1971).

[20] Young Fehlhaber Pile Co v State, 265 AD 61, 37 NYS2d 928 (3d Dept 1942).

[21] John Arborio, Inc v State, 41 Misc 2d 145, 245 NYS2d 274 (Ct Cl 1963).

[22] Faber v City of NY, 222 NY 255, 118 NE 609 (1918).

[23] Dawco Constr, Inc v United States, 18 Cl Ct 682 (1989), *modified on other grounds*, 930 F2d 872 (Fed Cir 1991).

[24] Jackson v State, 210 AD 115, 205 NYS 658 (4th Dept 1924), *affd*, 241 NY 563, 150 NE 556 (1925).

[25] Cauldwell-Wingate Co v State, 276 NY 365, 12 NE2d 443 (1938).

[26] LI Waldman & Co v State, 41 NYS2d 704 (Ct Cl 1943).

[27] Warren Bros Co v New York State Thruway Auth, 34 AD2d 97, 309 NYS2d 450 (3d Dept 1970), *affd*. 34 NY2d 770, 314 NE2d 878, 358 NYS2d 139 (1974).

[28] Depot Constr Corp v State, 19 NY2d 109, 224 NE2d 866, 278 NYS2d 363 (1967); Weston v State, 262 NY 46, 186 NE 197, 88 ALR 1219 (1933); Arthur A. Johnson Corp v City of NY, 162 Misc 665, 295 NYS 547 (NY 1936), *affd*, 251 AD 811, 298 NYS 188 (1937). *Contra* Faber v City of NY, 222 NY 255, 118 NE 609 (1918); Andrew Catapano Co v City of NY, 116 Misc 2d 163, 455 NYS2d 144 (NY 1980).

[29] Delma Engg Corp v 6465 Realty Co. 39 AD2d 846, 332 NYS2d 841, *affd*, 31 NY2d 816, 291 NE2d 587, 339 NYS2d 464 (1972); *but see* Frank Nordone Contracting Co v City of NY, 269 AD 1035, 59 NYS2d 256 (1945), *affd*, 295 NY 985, 68 NE2d 61 (1946).

[30] Savin Bros v State, 62 AD2d 511, 405 NYS2d 516 (4th Dept 1978), *affd*, 47 NY2d 934, 393 NE2d 1041, 419 NYS2d 969 (1979).

ground conditions might include the presence or absence of plumbing in walls and ceilings;[31] the number of plies of roofing on a roof;[32] the strength and fitness for use of an existing bridge support;[33] and the lack of suitable rock in a quarry designated as acceptable in the contract.[34]

Changed conditions were not found when a contractor assumed that bid earthwork sheets included after-strip quantities of fill when in fact they did not[35] or when a contractor removed less sod than it had anticipated being necessary.[36]

§5.05 —Miscellaneous Causes of Changed Conditions

Some of the items contractors have claimed to be changed conditions defy classification. For instance, in *Triangle Steel, Inc v Sarkisian Bros*,[37] a contractor tried to show that a significant increase in the cost of steel was a changed condition. The court rejected this argument based upon the fact that the contract provided a mechanism for the parties to split the cost of steel price increases. In another case, a contractor argued that the unanticipated unavailability of a rail line was a changed condition. The court rejected this argument, holding that the cost of transporting materials to a job site is a risk contractors take and that the state could not be held liable for a third party's decision to cease rail service.[38]

A contractor on a federal job was able to prove that a labor shortage was a changed condition. The United States Court of Claims, agreeing with the contractor's argument, based its decision on the facts that the government knew that its activities in the area would cause a significant labor shortage and increased labor costs, that the contractor did not know these facts and had no way of knowing them, and that the government failed to warn the contractor.[39]

§5.06 Contract Clauses

There are many variations of changed conditions and related clauses. Some are very general, others specific. Typically, changed conditions are dealt with in three types of clauses found in bid documents or the contract: *changed condi-*

---

[31] Jarcho Bros v State, 179 Misc 795, 39 NYS2d 867 (Ct Cl 1943).

[32] Laura Roofing & Renovating Co v Board of Educ, 57 AD2d 586, 393 NYS2d 593 (2d Dept 1977).

[33] Collins v State, 259 NY 200, 181 NE 357 (1932).

[34] Kaiser Indus Corp v United States, 340 F2d 322 (Ct Cl 1965).

[35] Chemical Bank v State, 64 AD2d 755, 406 NYS2d 633 (3d Dept 1978).

[36] John Arborio, Inc v State, 41 Misc 2d 145, 245 NYS2d 274 (Ct Cl 1963).

[37] 70 AD2d 698, 416 NYS2d 391, *appeal denied*, 47 NY2d 710, 393 NE2d 1050, 419 NYS2d 1027 (1979).

[38] John Arborio, Inc v State, 41 Misc 2d 145, 245 NYS2d 274 (Ct Cl 1963).

[39] JA Jones Constr Co v United States, 390 F2d 886 (Ct Cl 1968).

tions clauses which create the right to make claims; *disclaimer* and *site investigation* clauses which limit the right to make claims; and *exculpatory* clauses which attempt to prevent claims.[40]

§5.07 —Changed Conditions Clauses

Typical *changed conditions* clauses provide procedures for identification of changed conditions and modification of the contract if additional work is necessary due to unanticipated conditions.[41]

The city of New York has used the following changed conditions clause which relates solely to subsurface conditions. A disclaimer clause in the same contract specifically disclaims city responsibility for the majority of surface changed conditions.

> Section No. 4-(Examination) Viewing of Site and Consideration of Other Sources of Information
>
> (b) Changed Conditions—Should the Contractor encounter during the progress of the work, subsurface conditions at the site materially differing from any shown on the Contract Drawings or indicated in the specifications or such subsurface conditions as could not reasonably have been anticipated by the Contractor and were not anticipated by the City, which conditions will materially affect the cost of the work to be done under the contract, the attention of the Commissioner must be called immediately to such conditions before they are disturbed. The Commissioner shall thereupon promptly investigate the conditions. If he finds [a changed condition] . . ., the contract may be modified. . . .[42]

The American Institute of Architects (AIA) General Conditions[43] include the following clause which contains Type I and Type II conditions[44] but does not limit the location of the condition:

---

[40] Construction Litigation: Representing the Owner 278, §126 (Practising Law Institute R. Cushman & K. Cushman eds 1984).

[41] *See* Wrecking Corp of Am v Memorial Hosp for Cancer & Allied Diseases, 63 AD2d 615, 405 NYS2d 83, 85 (1st Dept), *appeal dismissed*, 45 NY2d 774, 380 NE2d 335, 408 NYS2d 509 (1978).

[42] Andrew Catapano Co v City of NY, 116 Misc 2d 163, 164-65, 455 NYS2d 144 (NY 1980).

[43] AIA Doc A201 (1987 ed). Reproduced by permission of The American Institute of Architects under license number 92095. Permission expires July 31, 1993. FURTHER REPRODUCTION IS PROHIBITED. Because AIA Documents are revised from time to time, users should ascertain from the AIA the current edition of this document. Copies of the current edition of this AIA document may be purchased from The American Institute of Architects or its local distributors. The text of this document is not "model language" and is not intended for use in other documents without permission of the AIA.

[44] *See* §5.02.

4.3.6 Claims for Concealed or Unknown Conditions.

> If conditions are encountered at the site which are (1) subsurface or otherwise concealed physical conditions which differ materially from those indicated in the Contract Documents or (2) unknown physical conditions of an unusual nature, which differ materially from those ordinarily found to exist and generally recognized as inherent in construction activities [typical to the contract work] . . ., then notice by the observing party shall be given to the other party promptly before conditions are disturbed and in no event later than 21 days after first [observed]. The Architect will promptly investigate . . ., and if they differ materially and cause an increase or decrease in the Contractor's cost of, or time required for, performance of any part of the Work, will recommend an equitable adjustment, in the Contract Sum or Contract Time, or both.

The federal government uses a similar clause:

> Differing Site Conditions
>
> (a) The Contractor shall promptly and before such conditions are disturbed notify the Contracting Officer in writing of [Types I and II changed conditions]. . . . The Contracting Officer shall promptly investigate the conditions, and if he finds that such conditions do materially so differ and cause an increase or decrease in the Contractor's cost of, or the time required for, performance of any part of the work under this contract, whether or not changed as a result of such conditions, an equitable adjustment shall be made and the contract modified in writing accordingly.[45]

A changed condition clause is not always called by that name. For instance, a clause which provides for the parties to share the cost of any increased prices due to inflation has been construed as a changed condition clause.[46] Similarly, a clause which provides for contract price adjustment for excavation in excess of a stated amount is akin to a changed condition clause because it allocates the risk of changed conditions among the parties.[47]

§5.08 —Disclaimer Clauses

Of necessity, owners must provide contractors with information for bid formulation. To avoid responsibility for incorrect or incomplete information, bid

---

[45] Stuyvesant Dredging Co v United States, 834 F2d 1576, 1580 (Fed Cir 1987), *affg* 11 Cl Ct 853 (1987). For a discussion of Type I and Type II changed conditions, see **§5.02.**

[46] *See* Triangle Steel, Inc v Sarkisian Bros, 70 AD2d 698, 416 NYS2d 391, *appeal denied*, 47 NY2d 710, 393 NE2d 1050, 419 NYS2d 1027 (1979).

[47] *See* Depot Constr Corp v State, 19 NY2d 109, 224 NE2d 866, 278 NYS2d 363 (1967).

specifications and contracts often include *disclaimers*. Such clauses generally require the contractor to investigate the site and determine the risks associated with the job, state that the owner does not warrant the information it provides, and state that the information is provided for estimation purposes only. For instance, the state has used a clause which claims to prevent a contractor "from pleading misunderstanding or deception because of estimates of quantities, character, location, or other conditions. . . ."[48] The state has also used the following clause effectively:

> This information is intended for State Design purposes only, and is made available to bidders only that they may have access to identical subsurface information available to the State. It is presented in good faith, but is not intended as a substitute for personal investigations, interpretations or judgments of the Contractor.[49]

However, the state's attempt to disclaim liability with a very similar clause was unsuccessful when it did *not* provide the contractor with access to the same information it had, despite its claim to have done so in its disclaimer clause.[50]

The city of Watervliet effectively used this clause in a unit price contract:

> It is supposed that the location, size of pipes, drains, etc., are correctly shown on contract drawings, but the commission does not so guarantee and no claim shall be made by the contractor on account of any structure being found in a position other than shown on the plans.[51]

Similarly, the city of New York had success with the following clause in a unit price contract for construction of a subway:

> The Special and Standard Specifications, taken in connection with the other provisions of this contract, are intended to be full and comprehensive, and to show all the work required to be done. But in a work of this character the soil and other conditions cannot be fully explored or determined in advance and it is therefore impossible either to show all details or precisely forecast all exigencies.[52]

Some contracts include more than one disclaimer. For instance, a contract between a wrecking company and a hospital included a clause which stated: "No representation is made by the General Contractor, Owner, Architect or Engineer in any contract regarding the existing sub-surface conditions." Another clause in the same contract provided: "The Owner, Architect and Con-

---

[48] Young Fehlhaber Pile Co v State, 265 AD 61, 37 NYS2d 928, 929 (3d Dept 1942).

[49] Depot Constr Corp v State, 19 NY2d 109, 114, 224 NE2d 866, 278 NYS2d 363, 366 (1967).

[50] Public Constructors, Inc v State, 55 AD2d 368, 390 NYS2d 481 (3d Dept 1977).

[51] Leary v City of Watervliet, 222 NY 337, 118 NE 849 (1918).

[52] Arthur A. Johnson Corp v City of NY, 162 Misc 665, 295 NYS 547, 551 (NY 1936), *affd*, 251 AD 811, 298 NYS 188 (1937).

126 CHANGED CONDITIONS

sulting Engineer make no representations regarding the character and extent of the soil data or other surface conditions to be encountered during the work and no guarantee as to their accuracy or interpretation is made or intended."[53]

To a certain extent, a disclaimer is effective to protect an owner from a contractor's claim of changed conditions. How may a contractor claim that it reasonably relied on bid information if the owner disclaims the accuracy of that information and requires the contractor to make its own investigation? For instance, in a case in which bid information did not include borrow requirements on the earthwork summary, the earthwork summary stated that it was not a warranty or representation of actual field conditions or quantities, and the bid information warned that borrow might be necessary despite the fact that it was not shown on the excavation table, the contractor was precluded from claiming that it was entitled to compensation beyond the contract price for borrow it provided.[54] Further, if a site inspection would have shown true conditions, a disclaimer will protect the owner.[55]

Disclaimers will not, however, insulate an owner from all liability for changed conditions. Liability may attach if conditions are not as represented by the owner and "(1) inspection would have been unavailing to reveal the incorrectness of the representations . . . or (2) the representations were made in bad faith [citations omitted]."[56]

Disclaimer clauses are strictly construed against owners. For instance, in a case where a contract disclaimed owner responsibility for conditions "*on, about or above* the site," the trial court held that the owner had not disclaimed responsibility for *subsurface* conditions, especially in light of a changed conditions clause which provided for adjustments in the event of unanticipated subsurface conditions.[57]

Site Investigation Clauses

Another form of disclaimer clause is a *site investigation* clause. This type of clause attempts to place the risk of changed conditions on the contractor by requiring it to investigate the site before bidding and to familiarize itself with all conditions under which the job will be performed. For instance, a site investigation clause in bid information may direct bidders to " 'examine the site and

---

[53] Wrecking Corp of Am v Memorial Hosp for Cancer & Allied Diseases, 63 AD2d 615, 405 NYS2d 83 (1st Dept), *appeal dismissed*, 45 NY2d 774, 380 NE2d 335, 408 NYS2d 509 (1978).

[54] Twin Village Constr Corp v State, 53 NY2d 724, 421 NE2d 827, 439 NYS2d 335 (1981).

[55] Warren Bros v New York State Thruway Auth, 34 AD2d 97, 309 NYS2d 450 (3d Dept 1970), *affd*, 34 NY2d 770, 314 NE2d 878, 358 NYS2d 139 (1974).

[56] *Id* at 99, 309 NYS2d at 452. *See also* Foundation Co v State, 233 NY 177, 184-85, 135 NE 236 (1922); Faber v City of NY, 222 NY 255, 260, 118 NE 609, 610 (1918); Young Fehlhaber Pile Co v State, 265 AD 61, 37 NYS2d 928, 929 (3d Dept 1942); Jackson v State, 210 AD 115, 205 NYS 658, 661 (4th Dept 1924), *affd*, 241 NY 563, 150 NE 556 (1925).

[57] Andrew Catapano Co v City of NY, 116 Misc 2d 163, 165, 455 NYS2d 144 (NY 1980).

form their own conclusions as to the exact elevations of the existing grades, the exact elevations of the ground water, the exact formation and character of the underlying rock and all other existing soil conditions.' "[58] A site investigation clause in a contract may state that the contractor " 'shall be held to have visited the site prior to the submission of his proposal for the work, and to have made all necessary investigations and measurements, and to have appraised the conditions under which the work is to be executed.' "[59]

Generally, such clauses are judged by the same standards as are any other disclaimers. Thus, under a site investigation clause, a contractor is held to knowledge of any conditions that it could have obtained from a reasonable site investigation.[60] A site investigation clause does not necessarily, however, prevent recovery of damages due to changed conditions if the owner knew of the condition but failed to disclose it.[61] Further, a site investigation clause does not obligate a contractor to undertake expensive or lengthy tests or other means of investigation where the owner has done them. The investigation required of a contractor is that which is reasonable in light of the nature of the job and the difficulty, time, and cost of investigation. See §5.13 for more discussion of site investigations.

§5.09 —Exculpatory Clauses

Exculpatory clauses, which attempt to relieve an owner of liability for the accuracy of data it provides and for damages incurred due to changed conditions, are common in construction contracts. Generally, exculpatory clauses are valid and enforceable, even when they are intended to relieve the owner of responsibility for its own negligence. They are not, however, favored by the courts and are strictly construed against those benefited by them. Thus, to be enforced, they must be clear and unequivocal.[62] Generally, where the language is express, the clause is effective and evidence of trade custom and usage is not admissible.[63]

The state has used an exculpatory clause titled "Examination of Documents and Site" which states that the contractor agrees "that he will make no claim against the State by reason of estimates, tests or representations of any officer

---

[58] TJW Corp v Board of High Educ, 251 AD 405, 296 NYS 693 (1st Dept 1937), *affd*, 276 NY 644, 12 NE2d 800 (1938).

[59] Niewenhous Co v State, 248 AD 658, 288 NYS 22, 23 (3d Dept), *affd*, 272 NY 484, 3 NE2d 880 (1936).

[60] Delma Engg Corp v 6465 Realty Co, 39 AD2d 846, 332 NYS2d 841, *affd*, 31 NY2d 816, 291 NE2d 587, 339 NYS2d 464 (1972); Niewenhous Co v State, 248 AD 658, 288 NYS 22, 23 (3d Dept), *affd*, 272 NY 484, 3 NE2d 880 (1936).

[61] LI Waldman & Co v State, 41 NYS2d 704 (Ct Cl 1943).

[62] Gross v Sweet, 49 NY2d 102, 400 NE2d 306, 424 NYS2d 365 (1979).

[63] Michael J. Torpey, Inc v Consolidated Edison Co, 99 AD2d 484, 470 NYS2d 426 (1984), *appeal dismissed*, 66 NY2d 915, 489 NE2d 773, 498 NYS2d 1027 (1985).

or agent of the State."[64] Similarly the city of Watervliet has used a bid specification which states that the information is not guaranteed and that "no claim shall be made by the contractor on account of any structure being found in a position other than that shown on the plans."[65]

"[A]n exculpatory agreement, no matter how flat and unqualified its terms, will not exonerate a party from liability under all circumstances."[66] As regards changed conditions, an exculpatory clause is not effective if it "places the burden to investigate the site and to discover potential problems wholly upon [the contractor], when the [owner] is chargeable with knowledge of their existence and location."[67] Further, an exculpatory clause will not insulate an owner from liability when the owner intentionally misrepresents conditions;[68] when the owner gives *positive*, but inaccurate, bid specifications (such as subsurface information) that it intends the contractor to use in making its bid;[69] or if the bidder is allowed insufficient time to make a thorough personal investigation.[70]

§5.10 Owner's Misrepresentation

An owner will be liable to its contractor, despite contract clauses which provide otherwise, if the owner misrepresents or conceals true job conditions. The law in New York is set forth most clearly in *AS Wikstrom, Inc v State*:[71]

> In *Rusciano Construction Corp v State*,[72] one of the questions involved the State's failure to make available all soil testing information and to provide in the contract plans for the possibilities of unstable subsurface material which contributed to a delay in completing the project. We held that "[t]he exculpatory clauses in the contract and in the invitation to bid do not insulate the State from liability where the conditions are not as represented in the contract and inspection by the contractor would not reveal the representations to be false." . . . Additionally, in *Warren Brothers Co v*

---

[64] Weston v State, 262 NY 46, 186 NE 197, 199, 88 ALR 1219 (1933); Savin Bros v State, 62 AD2d 511, 405 NYS2d 516, 520 (4th Dept 1978), *aff'd*, 47 NY2d 934, 393 NE2d 1041, 419 NYS2d 969 (1979).

[65] Leary v City of Watervliet, 222 NY 337, 118 NE 849, 850 (1918).

[66] Kalisch-Jarcho, Inc v City of NY, 58 NY2d 377, 384, 448 NE2d 413, 461 NYS2d 746, 749 (1983).

[67] Laura Roofing & Renovating Co v Board of Educ, 57 AD2d 586, 393 NYS2d 593, 594 (2d Dept 1977).

[68] Rusciano Constr Corp v State, 37 AD2d 745, 323 NYS2d 21 (3d Dept 1971). See discussion regarding an owner's fraud and concealment at §5.12.

[69] Hollerbach v United States, 233 US 165, 34 S Ct 553, 58 L Ed 898 (1915).

[70] Young Fehlhaber Pile Co v State, 265 AD 61, 37 NYS2d 928, 929 (3d Dept 1942); John Arborio, Inc v State, 41 Misc 2d 145, 245 NYS2d 274 (Ct Cl 1963).

[71] 52 AD2d 658, 381 NYS2d 1010, 1012 (3d Dept 1976).

[72] 37 AD2d 745, 746, 323 NYS2d 21, 24 (3d Dept 1971).

New York State Thruway Authority,[73] we said: "In a construction contract between the State and an individual, which contains representations as to existing conditions affecting work thereunder as well as an exculpatory clause relieving the State of liability and requiring personal inspection of the contract site, liability, nevertheless, may attach to the State if said conditions are not as represented and (1) inspection would have been unavailing to reveal the incorrectness of the representations (*Foundation Co v State*;[74] *Faber v New York*[75]), or (2) the representations were made in bad faith (*Young Fehlhaber Pile Co v State*;[76] *Jackson v State*[77]) [citations omitted]."

Thus, an owner may be liable for both innocent and intentional misrepresentations; under either theory, the misrepresentation must be material.[78]

Whether there has been a representation of fact is judged by a reasonably prudent contractor standard.[79] Any assumption made by a contractor must be justifiable.[80] For instance, a contractor failed in its claim that the state misrepresented rock excavation quantities when the contract was a lump sum contract which provided for unit pricing for all excavated rock above the amount set forth in the contract; the state took only 17 borings for a project which would have 216 pier footings of 25 square feet each; and the bid information contained a disclaimer clause. The Court of Appeals held that the risk of quantity of rock to be excavated was on the contractor and that the allocation of risk was plainly set forth in the contract. The court further held that no reasonable person would have believed that the contract set forth maximum rock quantities or that the state had done a complete investigation.[81]

§5.11 —Owner's Innocent Misrepresentation

If an owner innocently misrepresents conditions, perhaps through its engineer's honest or negligent mistake in evaluating borings,[82] recovery is based on the contract. "When no claim of deception, inequality, or inequity is pres-

---

[73] 34 AD2d 97, 99, 309 NYS2d 450, 452 (3d Dept 1970), *affd*, 34 NY2d 770, 314 NE2d 878, 358 NYS2d 139 (1974).

[74] 233 NY 177, 184-85, 135 NE 236, 238 (1922).

[75] 222 NY 255, 260, 118 NE 609, 619 (1918).

[76] 265 AD 61, 37 NYS2d 928 (3d Dept 1942).

[77] 210 AD 115, 205 NYS 658 (4th Dept 1924), *affd*, 241 NY 563, 150 NE 556 (1925).

[78] AS Wikstrom, Inc v State, 52 AD2d 658, 381 NYS2d 1010 (3d Dept 1976); Eastern Tunneling Corp v Southgate Sanitation Dist, 487 F Supp 109 (D Colo 1980).

[79] Depot Constr Corp v State, 19 NY2d 109, 224 NE2d 866, 278 NYS2d 363 (1967).

[80] Mojave Enters v United States, 3 Cl Ct 353 (1983).

[81] Depot Constr Corp v State, 19 NY2d 109, 224 NE2d 866, 278 NYS2d 363 (1967).

[82] Arthur A. Johnson Corp v City of NY, 162 Misc 665, 295 NYS 547 (NY 1936), *affd*, 251 AD 811, 298 NYS 188 (1937).

ented [a contractor] is bound by the terms of his contract."[83] If the contract or bid specifications contain positive representations of fact, a "bidder may rely upon them, even though it be provided that he shall satisfy himself by personal inspection and investigation as to their truth, where because of time or situation such investigation would be unavailing...."[84] Thus, if an owner innocently misrepresents a fact *and* inspection by the contractor would not have shown the misrepresentation, the owner may be liable. Further, a party cannot make "reckless inaccurate representations" and escape liability for damages incurred by another who relied on those representations.[85]

The central issue in misrepresentation cases is whether a representation of fact has been made. Not all information supplied to a bidder by an owner is a representation. Disclaimer notices on plans or test results may mean that the plans or test results are not representations and that the contractor takes the risk of any inaccuracies if it relies on them.[86] For instance, the following things have been found not to be representations by owners: "typical" layouts;[87] dam plans which did not show foundation depths;[88] and plans not incorporated into bid specifications or the contract but which were obtained from detail sheets in the Department of Public Works.[89]

In *Faber v New York*,[90] the court found that the city owner had represented fact when its bid specifications for a bridge tower stated that the detailed plans which accompanied them were part of the specifications and that bids were to be based upon the depth of excavation indicated on the plans. These plans showed bridge caissons being sunk to bedrock and that bedrock was located eight-to-nine feet lower than it actually was. The contractor was required to excavate to the depth shown on the plans, despite the higher bedrock level, so the caissons would be sunk to the depth originally specified. The court, in finding that the city had misrepresented the level of the bedrock, stated that

> it would be wholly inequitable to hold that under such circumstances, where the contractor had no reasonable opportunity of discovering the truth, and where the other party had made the examination and asked for bids upon plans showing the results of such examination, the latter

---

[83] Weston v State, 262 NY 46, 186 NE 197, 199, 88 ALR 1219 (1933).

[84] Foundation Co v State, 233 NY 177, 135 NE 236, 238 (1922).

[85] John Arborio, Inc v State, 41 Misc 2d 145, 245 NYS2d 274, 277 (Ct Cl 1963).

[86] Foundation Co v State, 233 NY 177, 135 NE 236, 238 (1922).

[87] Michael J. Torpey, Inc v Consolidated Edison Co, 99 AD2d 484, 470 NYS2d 426 (1984), *appeal dismissed*, 66 NY2d 915, 489 NE2d 773, 498 NYS2d 1027 (1985) (contract contained exculpatory clause and layout stated it was for "example" purposes only).

[88] Foundation Co v State, 233 NY 177, 135 NE 236 (1922) (the information for bidders included a "preliminary estimate of quantities" which stated that the estimates were approximate and that bidders were required to form their own judgment of the work by personal investigation).

[89] John Arborio, Inc v State, 41 Misc 2d 145, 245 NYS2d 274 (Ct Cl 1963).

[90] 222 NY 255, 118 NE 609 (1918).

can be heard to say that it is not responsible should those plans wholly misrepresent the fact.[91]

The contract did not contain an effective exculpatory or disclaimer clause.

Generally then, the New York rule is that if the contract places the risk of changed conditions on the contractor, recovery will not be awarded, unless:

(1) the owner made a positive, good faith representation of a material fact, (2) that fact was incorrect, (3) the contractor could not have discovered the mistake, and (4) no effective exculpatory or disclaimer clause applies.[92]

The federal rule is more lenient. If the federal government makes a positive statement of material fact concerning the nature of the work and the fact is false, the federal government is liable to the contractor.[93] General exculpatory clauses which disclaim responsibility for accuracy of the data are of no effect if positive specifications made by the federal government were intended to be used by contractors in formulating their bids.[94]

Even where the contract places all risk of changed conditions on the contractor, a contractor may be able to convince an owner that an equitable apportionment of increased costs due to the changed condition is merited, especially where the owner's misrepresentation was innocent and the resulting costs are significant.

§5.12 —Owner's Fraud, Concealment, and Reckless Representation

An owner may be liable for damages due to changed conditions if the owner made representations in bad faith[95] or concealed true conditions,[96] even where exculpatory and disclaimer clauses would otherwise bar a changed conditions

---

[91] *Id* at 260, 118 NE at 610.

[92] Chemical Bank v State, 64 AD2d 755, 406 NYS2d 633 (3d Dept 1978); Arthur A. Johnson Corp v City of NY, 162 Misc 665, 295 NYS 547 (NY 1936), *affd*, 251 AD 811, 298 NYS 188 (1937); *but see* Frank Nordone Contracting Co v City of NY, 269 AD 1035, 59 NYS2d 256 (1945), *affd*, 295 NY 985, 68 NE2d 61 (1946) (contractor allowed to recover additional compensation due to changed subsurface condition despite fact it did no real site investigation and found condition within one-to-two hours of beginning work, the bid specifications provided that the information was not guaranteed, the contract specified that any loose rock excavated was to be included in the contract price, and the city was not shown to have actual knowledge of the condition; the court's decision may have been based on the fact that the city's agent or predecessor created the condition many years earlier); *see also* Laura Roofing & Renovating Co v Board of Educ, 57 AD2d 586, 393 NYS2d 593 (2d Dept 1977) (if owner chargeable with knowledge of condition, an exculpatory clause will not be effective).

[93] Hollerbach v United States, 233 US 165, 34 S Ct 553, 58 L Ed 898 (1915).

[94] *Id*.

[95] Young Fehlhaber Pile Co v State, 265 AD2d 61, 37 NYS2d 928 (3d Dept 1942); Jackson v State, 210 AD 115, 205 NYS 658 (4th Dept 1924), *affd*, 241 NY 563, 150 NE 556 (1925).

[96] Young Fehlhaber Pile Co v State, 265 AD 61, 37 NYS2d 928 (3d Dept 1942).

claim. In order for there to be a misrepresentation, there must be a representation of fact. This principle holds true in fraudulent misrepresentation cases as well as in innocent misrepresentation cases.[97]

Misrepresentation was found in a case in which the state's bid information showed that the material to be excavated was "sand, sand and clay, sand and gravel, red sand, black sand, gravel filling, rock, sand and stone" when, in fact, the material was "hard and compact," resulting in the excavation being significantly more difficult and expensive than anticipated. The Appellate Division found this to be a "representation of a fact entirely contrary to the actual known fact" and held the state liable despite exculpatory language and disclaimers.[98] Similarly, when the state misrepresented to a completion contractor that work had been done which in fact had not been, it could not avoid liability through exculpatory and disclaimer clauses.[99]

In another case, the state was unprotected by contractual exculpatory clauses when it provided bidders with results of only 71 test holes when it had 657 more and knew of the presence of unsuitable materials and unstable soil conditions but failed to notify bidders about these conditions.[100] Similarly, when the federal government failed to warn bidders that its planned extensive construction activities would cause labor shortages and increased labor costs, it was liable to the contractor.[101] Thus, an owner has a duty to reveal relevant, material information and may be liable not only for active misrepresentation but also for failing to disclose material information.[102]

In *Young Fehlhaber Pile Co v State,*[103] the Appellate Division found "a clear case of fraud and misrepresentation on the part of the state" when the state failed to notify bidders on a bridge construction job that the creek bottom had been dredged. The contractor relied on the plans and specifications furnished all bidders in making its bid and suffered greatly increased costs when it found the creek bottom to be four-and-one-half feet lower than shown on the plans. The state attempted to avoid liability by relying on disclaimer and exculpatory clauses in the bid information and contract. The court rejected this argument and stated:

---

[97] Mojave Enters v United States, 3 Cl Ct 353 (1983).

[98] Jackson v State, 210 AD 115, 205 NYS 658 (4th Dept 1924), *affd,* 241 NY 563, 150 NE 556 (1925); *see also* Public Constructors, Inc v State, 55 AD2d 368, 390 NYS2d 481 (3d Dept 1977).

[99] Jarcho Bros v State, 179 Misc 795, 39 NYS2d 867 (Ct Cl 1943).

[100] Rusciano Constr Corp v State, 37 AD2d 745, 323 NYS2d 21 (3d Dept 1971); *see also* County Asphalt, Inc v State, 40 AD2d 26, 337 NYS2d 415 (3d Dept 1972) (state omitted pertinent information from bid packet and drastically reduced estimated quantities of certain materials without justification); Commercial Mech Contractors, Inc, ASBCA 25695, 83-2 BCA ¶16768.

[101] JA Jones Constr Co v United States, 390 F2d 886 (Ct Cl 1968).

[102] AS Wikstrom, Inc v State, 52 AD2d 658, 381 NYS2d 1010 (3d Dept 1976); JA Jones Constr Co v United States, 390 F2d 886 (Ct Cl 1968).

[103] 265 AD 61, 37 NYS2d 928 (3d Dept 1942).

§5.12 FRAUD & RECKLESS REPRESENTATION

> The state should not be thus permitted by general provisions in its specifications, instructions or contract from escaping liability for its direct and patent misrepresentations. The bidder could properly rely upon the clear and unequivocal information contained in the plans, otherwise they would serve no useful purpose. They should reasonably depict the work to be done and where they are definite and plain the contractor is entitled to rely upon them. . . . Here there was clear misrepresentation by the state. . . . [T]he state must accept full responsibility for the falsity of its plans, for it is clear that it had ample knowledge that its contour lines were inaccurate.[104]

The court also rejected the state's argument that the contractor failed to adequately inspect the site, finding that physical site conditions and the limited time allowed for inspection by the state prevented thorough investigation by the contractor.

Similarly, an owner may be barred from reliance on exculpatory and disclaimer clauses when its representations are recklessly inaccurate. For instance, where a unit price contract provided that the contractor would supply over 400,000 cubic yards of borrow and the contractor had to supply only 56,775 cubic yards, the trial court held the state to its representations which it found to be "recklessly inaccurate" and stated that while reasonable variation is acceptable, "[t]he difference between the represented quantities and the actual quantities is so great that the State cannot escape the consequences of its misleading and deceptive statements to the financial detriment of an innocent bidder. . . ."[105]

Finally, it is not necessarily the claimant's contract which must contain the misrepresentation. In *Cauldwell-Wingate Co v State*,[106] the claimant was the contractor for construction of a superstructure. The excavation and foundation work was to be done by another contractor. Cauldwell-Wingate could not begin work until the excavation and foundation contractor finished its work. The excavation and foundation contractor experienced significant difficulty and delay when it encountered an unexpected underground swamp and other obstacles, thus delaying Cauldwell-Wingate. The Court of Appeals allowed Cauldwell-Wingate to recover its damages suffered due to the changed conditions encountered by the excavation and foundation contractor, reasoning that the damages suffered by it were due to acts or failures of the state and through no fault of its own.[107]

A contractor may waive an owner's misrepresentation, even an intentional one. For instance, in a case where a contractor encountered substantially different conditions than what the owner led it to expect but entered into a new contract with full knowledge of the inaccuracies, it was barred from recovery

---

[104] Young Fehlhaber Pile Co v State, 265 AD 61, 37 NYS2d 928, 929-30 (3d Dept 1942).

[105] John Arborio, Inc v State, 41 Misc 2d 145, 245 NYS2d 274, 278 (Ct Cl 1963).

[106] 276 NY 365, 12 NE2d 443 (1938).

[107] *Id* at 375, 12 NE2d at 446.

134 CHANGED CONDITIONS

based on the difference of conditions. By agreeing to enter into a new contract, after it knew of the misrepresentation, the contractor, in effect, waived the misrepresentation and was barred from claiming a changed condition.[108]

§5.13 Site Investigation and Other Inquiry

The duty imposed on a contractor by site investigation clauses, exculpatory clauses, and disclaimers is not absolute. A contractor is not always expected to discover everything an owner knows about the site. A bidder is not expected to discover in a limited time period the extent of information which an owner possesses after months and, often, years of testing and planning.[109] For instance, three weeks has been held to be an insufficient time to conduct subsurface exploration,[110] and a contractor was held not to be barred by exculpatory provisions and disclaimers when it would have taken at least six months to do an independent subsurface soils investigation.[111] Further, a contractor's duty to investigate relates to its contract only; it does not have a duty to investigate specifications and site conditions which relate to another contractor's job, even when its work is dependent on the completion of the other contractor's work. In *Cauldwell-Wingate Co v State*,[112] the claimant was the contractor for construction of the superstructure. The excavation and foundation work was to be done by another contractor. The Court of Appeals allowed the superstructure contractor to recover its damages suffered due to the changed conditions encountered by the excavation and foundation contractor, reasoning that the damages suffered by it were due to acts or failures of the state, through no fault of Cauldwell-Wingate.[113] The court held that the superstructure contractor did not have an obligation to make site tests and review plans which concerned the foundation contract.[114]

Where an inspection would have revealed true conditions, a contractor is held to know that which it would have discovered had it made a reasonable inspection[115] and is estopped from claiming a changed condition.[116] The standard for what is reasonable depends on the job involved; exhaustive inspection of deep subsurface jobs is rarely required while the opposite holds true for

---

[108] A&R Constr Co v New York State Elec & Gas Corp, 23 AD2d 450, 261 NYS2d 482 (1965); *see also* AG Concrete Breakers, Inc v State, 16 Misc 2d 511, 185 NYS2d 455 (Ct Cl), *affd*, 9 AD2d 995, 194 NYS2d 743 (3d Dept 1959).

[109] Young Fehlhaber Pile Co v State, 265 AD 61, 37 NYS2d 928 (3d Dept 1942); Public Constructors, Inc v State, 55 AD2d 368, 390 NYS2d 481 (3d Dept 1977).

[110] County Asphalt, Inc v State, 40 AD2d 26, 337 NYS2d 415 (3d Dept 1972).

[111] Grow Constr Co v State, 56 AD2d 95, 391 NYS2d 726 (3d Dept 1977).

[112] 276 NY 365, 12 NE2d 443 (1938).

[113] *Id* at 375, 12 NE2d at 446.

[114] *Id*.

[115] Warren Bros Co v New York State Thruway Auth, 34 AD2d 97, 309 NYS2d 450 (3d Dept 1970), *affd*, 34 NY2d 770, 314 NE2d 878, 358 NYS2d 139 (1974).

[116] Mojave Enters v United States, 3 Cl Ct 353 (1983).

surface jobs such as sod removal.[117] A reasonable inspection may include not only a physical site investigation and usual tests,[118] but also discussions with operators on adjacent sites,[119] review of boring logs and soil samples,[120] and review of records of previous operations at the site.[121]

An owner is not responsible or liable for information which a contractor discovers in its investigation and chooses to rely on. For instance, in a case where a contractor reviewed detail sheets in the Department of Public Works office and those sheets were not part of the plans incorporated into the bid documents or contract, the owner was not responsible for the accuracy, or inaccuracy, of those plans.[122] Further, a contractor should not assume that conditions encountered on a previous job will apply to a new one[123] or that plans accurately show rock quantities when they do not purport to do so.[124]

A contractor is held to know that which it could have discovered given the nature of the job, the time available for inspection, the type of inspection typically made, the physical conditions at the job site, and the time that the owner had to inspect the site and plan the project. It is the contractor's burden to prove that it made a reasonable investigation.[125] If the contractor failed to make a reasonable investigation, any damages it incurs are its own fault and responsibility.[126]

§5.14 Reliance on Owner's Data

A contractor must be careful when relying on an owner's data because such reliance may be barred by an effective exculpatory or disclaimer clause. For example, in a case in which an earthwork summary specifically stated that it was not a warranty or representation of actual conditions or quantities and that

---

[117] John Arborio, Inc v State, 41 Misc 2d 145, 245 NYS2d 274 (Ct Cl 1963).

[118] Niewenhous Co v State, 248 AD 658, 288 NYS 22 (3d Dept), *affd*, 272 NY 484, 3 NE2d 880 (1936).

[119] Weeks Dredging & Contracting, Inc v United States, 13 Cl Ct 193 (1987), *affd mem*, 861 F2d 728 (Fed Cir 1988).

[120] Wrecking Corp of Am v Memorial Hosp for Cancer & Allied Diseases, 63 AD2d 615, 405 NYS2d 83 (1st Dept), *appeal dismissed*, 45 NY2d 774, 380 NE2d 335, 408 NYS2d 509 (1978).

[121] Stuyvesant Dredging Co v United States, 11 Cl Ct 853, *affd*, 834 F2d 1576 (Fed Cir 1987).

[122] John Arborio, Inc v State, 41 Misc 2d 145, 245 NYS2d 274 (Ct Cl 1963).

[123] Stuyvesant Dredging Co v United States, 834 F2d 1576 (Fed Cir 1987).

[124] Mojave Enters v United States, 3 Cl Ct 353 (1983).

[125] Wrecking Corp of Am v Memorial Hosp for Cancer & Allied Diseases, 63 AD2d 615, 405 NYS2d 83 (1st Dept), *appeal dismissed*, 45 NY2d 774, 380 NE2d 335, 408 NYS2d 509 (1978); Stuyvesant Dredging Co v United States, 11 Cl Ct 853, *affd*, 834 F2d 1576 (Fed Cir 1987).

[126] Delma Engg Corp v 6465 Realty Co, 39 AD2d 846, 332 NYS2d 841, *affd*, 31 NY2d 816, 291 NE2d 587, 339 NYS2d 464 (1972).

"[b]orrow may be necessary even when not shown on the excavation table," the contractor was not entitled to rely on the summary and was not entitled to compensation beyond that provided in the contract payment schedule.[127]

In limited circumstances, however, a contractor may rely on data supplied it by the owner and incorporated into bid documents and the contract. For instance, a contractor may rely on information incorporated into the bid documents and contract if conditions are not as represented and inspection would not reveal the falsity of the representations,[128] such as when the contractor does not have time to make an independent investigation.[129] Site investigation clauses do not prevent recovery of damages due to an owner's failure to disclose.[130] A discussion of the effectiveness of disclaimer, site investigation, and exculpatory clauses in barring reliance on an owner's data is found in §§5.08 and 5.09.

A bidder has a right to rely upon "clear and unequivocal information contained in the plans"[131] and "the fact that the [owner] made its own studies reasonably accurate. . . ."[132] Thus, in a case where the state's contract provided that earth to be excavated would be suitable for fill, but, in fact, it was not, the court found that the contractor had a right to rely on the information in the contract and granted its claim for extras. The court said that the fact that the contractor examined the site was irrelevant.[133]

Federal courts allow a contractor to rely more extensively upon an owner's data. The federal government is liable to a contractor when it makes *positive* statements of material facts concerning the nature of the work and those facts are false.[134] General exculpatory clauses which attempt to disclaim responsibility for the accuracy of data are of no effect if positive specifications given by the government were intended to be used by contractors in formulating their bids.[135] To recover for a misrepresentation two conditions must be met: (1) the bidder must not have been reasonably able to discover the true facts itself and (2) the misrepresentation must have been material.[136] Thus, a federal government owner is bound by positive descriptions of subsurface conditions if the contractor could not have discovered inaccuracies in those descriptions.[137] Fur-

---

[127] Twin Village Constr Corp v State, 53 NY2d 724, 421 NE2d 827, 439 NYS2d 335 (1981).

[128] County Asphalt, Inc v State, 40 AD2d 26, 337 NYS2d 415 (3d Dept 1972).

[129] Young Fehlhaber Pile Co v State, 265 AD 61, 37 NYS2d 928 (3d Dept 1942); John Arborio, Inc v State, 41 Misc 2d 145, 245 NYS2d 274 (Ct Cl 1963).

[130] LI Waldman & Co v State, 41 NYS2d 704 (Ct Cl 1943).

[131] Young Fehlhaber Pile Co v State, 265 AD 61, 37 NYS2d 928, 929 (3d Dept 1942).

[132] John Arborio, Inc v State, 41 Misc 2d 145, 245 NYS2d 274 (Ct Cl 1963).

[133] Dolomite Prods Co v State, 258 AD 294, 17 NYS2d 48 (4th Dept 1939).

[134] Hollerbach v United States, 233 US 165, 34 S Ct 553, 58 L Ed 898 (1915).

[135] *Id.*

[136] Eastern Tunneling Corp v Southgate Sanitation Dist, 487 F Supp 109 (D Colo 1980).

[137] City of Reading v Rae, 106 F2d 458 (3d Cir), *cert denied,* 308 US 607, 60 S Ct 145, 84 L Ed 508 (1939).

ther, a contractor is entitled to rely upon contract specifications.[138]

A contractor's reliance upon an owner's data must be reasonable; if the data is clearly incomplete or inadequate, a contractor cannot rely on it as though it were complete.[139]

If a contractor is barred from recovery from the owner for inaccurate information, it may be able to obtain some relief from the soils engineer, architect, or other party that furnished the owner with the inaccurate study or data.[140]

§5.15 Contractor's Duty to Perform

Generally, it is a contractor's responsibility to perform the contract at the agreed price.[141] In the absence of a compensable changed condition, any extra costs or damages are the contractor's responsibility.[142]

If a contractor discovers a changed condition before it begins performance but after its bid is accepted, it may repudiate the contract or demand an agreement to extras.[143] If the contractor begins work without an agreement to its demand for extras, it may be held to have waived the changed condition and any alleged misrepresentation.[144]

§5.16 Remedies

When a contractor encounters a changed condition, it has several remedies and theories under which it may pursue compensation for its increased costs, both in tort and in contract.[145] It may claim mutual mistake if neither party knew

---

[138] Shank-Artukovich v United States, 13 Cl Ct 346 (1987), *affd*, 848 F2d 1245 (Fed Cir 1988) (unpublished opinion).

[139] Weeks Dredging & Contracting, Inc v United States, 13 Cl Ct 193 (1987), *affd mem*, 861 F2d 728 (Fed Cir 1988).

[140] *See* Berkel & Co Contractors v Providence Hosp, 454 So 2d 496 (Ala 1984); Biankanja v Irving, 49 Cal 2d 647, 320 P2d 16 (1958); Rhodes-Haverty, Etc v Robert & Co, 163 Ga App 88, 293 SE2d 876 (1982), *affd*, 250 Ga 680, 300 SE2d 503 (1983); Davidson & Jones, Inc v County of New Hanover, 41 NC App 661, 255 SE2d 580, *cert denied*, 259 SE2d 911 (1979). *See also* Ossining Union Free School Dist v Anderson LaRocca Anderson, 73 NY2d 417, 539 NE2d 91, 541 NYS2d 335 (1989); Credit Alliance Corp v Anderson & Co, 65 NY2d 536, 483 NE2d 110, 493 NYS2d 435 (1985); and the discussion regarding privity of contract at **ch 8**.

[141] Delma Engg Corp v 6465 Realty Co, 39 AD2d 846, 332 NYS2d 841, *affd*, 31 NY2d 816, 291 NE2d 587, 339 NYS2d 464 (1972).

[142] *Id.*

[143] AG Concrete Breakers, Inc v State, 16 Misc 2d 511, 185 NYS2d 455 (Ct Cl), *affd*, 9 AD2d 995, 194 NYS2d 743 (3d Dept 1959); *see also* A&R Constr Co v New York State Elec & Gas Corp, 23 AD2d 450, 261 NYS2d 482 (1965).

[144] AG Concrete Breakers, Inc v State, 16 Misc 2d 511, 185 NYS2d 455 (Ct Cl), *affd*, 9 AD2d 995, 194 NYS2d 743 (3d Dept 1959); *see also* A&R Constr Co v New York State Elec & Gas Corp, 23 AD2d 450, 261 NYS2d 482 (1965).

[145] Jackson v State, 210 AD 115, 205 NYS 658 (4th Dept 1924), *affd mem*, 241 NY 563, 150 NE 556 (1925).

of the condition, although a contract clause which debars a claim of mistake may prevent such a claim.[146] If the owner intentionally misrepresents conditions either actively or by concealment, a contractor is entitled to have the contract set aside as fraudulent or to a claim for extra and additional work not included in the contract.[147]

The general rule regarding recovery of damages for additional work due to changed conditions was set forth in *Borough Construction Co v City of New York*.[148] In that case, the court upheld a contractor's right to sue for damages in breach of contract and stated that

> within certain limits, a contractor who is ordered by the proper representatives of the municipality to furnish materials or do work which the former thinks [is] . . . not called for by his contract may under protest do as directed and subsequently recover damages . . . even though it should turn out that the contractor was right and the official had no right to call on him to furnish such materials and do such labor under his contract.

Contractors with changed conditions claims have successfully sued for breach of implied warranty,[149] for breach of contract by requiring additional work not contemplated,[150] and for rescission of the contract and recovery of damages in fraud,[151] as well as under other theories.

To prevail on a claim for changed conditions, a contractor must prove that conditions encountered were materially different from those indicated in the contract, that the conditions were reasonably unforeseeable at the time of bidding, that the contractor reasonably investigated the site, that its interpretation of the contract data was reasonable, and that it was damaged as a result of the changed conditions.[152]

A contractor may sue the owner for damages incurred by its subcontractor in performing extra work due to changed conditions.[153]

---

[146] Weston v State, 262 NY 46, 186 NE 197, 88 ALR 1219 (1933).

[147] Jarcho Bros, Inc v State, 179 Misc 795, 39 NYS2d 867 (Ct Cl 1943).

[148] 200 NY 149, 93 NE 480, 482 (1910).

[149] Jackson v State, 210 AD 115, 205 NYS 658 (4th Dept 1924), *aff'd mem*, 241 NY 563, 150 NE 556 (1925).

[150] Collins v State, 259 NY 200, 181 NE 357 (1932); Borough Constr Co v City of NY, 200 NY 149, 93 NE 480 (1910); County Asphalt, Inc v State, 40 AD2d 26, 337 NYS2d 415 (3d Dept 1972).

[151] City of Reading v Rae, 106 F2d 458 (3d Cir), *cert denied*, 308 US 607, 60 S Ct 145, 84 L Ed 508 (1939).

[152] Stuyvesant Dredging Co v United States, 834 F2d 1576, 1581 (Fed Cir 1987).

[153] Dolomite Prods Co v State, 258 AD 294, 17 NYS2d 48 (4th Dept 1939). See discussion regarding liquidating agreements in **ch 3**.

§5.17 Claims

Preserving a claim for the extra costs and expenses associated with changed conditions is crucial. If contract procedures are not followed, legitimate claims may be lost. Typically, the procedures to preserve and recover on a changed conditions claim are the same as those for extras and change orders, although a contract may contain a specific procedure to modify the contract in the event additional work is necessary due to unanticipated conditions.[154] The discussion here is brief; readers are referred to Chapter 6 for a more detailed treatment of this issue.

§5.18 —Notice and Documentation

To recover for a changed condition, a contractor must comply with contractual notice provisions and keep thorough documentation of its costs, including costs of changed methods of performance and increased labor hours and materials. A contract may require that a change order be written or that a contract modification be executed in order for a contractor to be compensated for additional work performed due to a changed condition. A failure to obtain the required documentation can be fatal to a contractor's recovery.[155]

Notice provisions are required to enable an owner to investigate the condition while it is still visible and decide whether a true changed condition exists and what to do about it—i.e., abandon the project, change construction methods, authorize the contractor's proposed solution, if any, etc. Notice provisions may be contractual, statutory, or both. Notice requirements are discussed in more detail in Chapter 17.

In the case of *Buckley & Co v City of New York*,[156] the contractor encountered unanticipated subsurface conditions. The contract provided a procedure for modification of the contract in the event of extra work. The contract also provided a procedure for work under protest. The contractor failed to follow either procedure; consequently, the court barred the contractor's claim for compensation. Due to a *no damage for delay* clause in the contract, the court also barred the contractor's claim for delay damages that was based upon the delay caused by the unanticipated conditions. If the contractor had preserved its changed conditions claim by following those procedures set forth in the contract, its claim might not have been barred. The *Buckley* decision must be criticized as one which discourages the use of changed conditions clauses by holding, in effect, that the inclusion of a changed conditions clause means that any changed conditions encountered were contemplated for purposes of assessing delay damages. See Chapter 7 for more discussion of *Buckley*.

The federal government's standard changed conditions clause, found in Federal Acquisition Regulations 48 CFR §52.243.5 (formerly known as Article 4, "Differing Site Conditions" of the General Provisions, Standard Form 23A),

---

[154] Buckley & Co v City of NY, 121 AD2d 933, 505 NYS2d 140 (1st Dept 1986).
[155] Buckley & Co v City of NY, 121 AD2d 933, 505 NYS2d 140 (1st Dept 1986).
[156] *Id.*

provides that a contractor must promptly notify the contracting officer, in writing, of changed conditions before disturbing them. The officer must then promptly investigate the conditions and make an "equitable adjustment" if appropriate and modify the contract. The contract provides: "No claim of the Contractor under this clause shall be allowed unless the Contractor has given the notice required. . . ."[157] The contract also provides procedures for notice of protest if the officer does not agree that a changed condition has been encountered.[158]

If a contractor does not know that it has a changed condition until after the contractor has disturbed it, the contractor's claim is protected so long as the contractor notifies the owner or its designated agent immediately.

When executing supplemental agreements or modifications of contract, it is important for a contractor, if it believes that the modification or supplement does not fairly compensate it for changed conditions, to preserve claims for damages by notifying the owner in writing of its intent in all possible ways, including executing the agreements subject to submission of verified claims.[159] If a contractor executes a new contract without preserving its right to claim for the changed condition or without reaching an agreement as to compensation for the changed condition, it will be considered to have waived the changed condition, including any underlying misrepresentation.[160]

§5.19 Damages

A contractor faced with changed conditions may be entitled to damages calculated in one of several ways, including: damages equal to its additional costs and expenses incurred;[161] the difference between the value of work shown in the plans and contract and that actually performed;[162] the increased cost of performance;[163] or the value of materials and work furnished.[164] In addition, a contractor is entitled to appropriate amounts of profit and overhead.[165] If the contract was a unit price contract, the contractor's proper measure of damages generally is the unit price set forth in the contract for additional work.[166]

A contractor should not expect a court to award it every increased cost that it suffered in the construction. Damages are apportioned between those caused

---

[157] Federal Acquisition Regulations, 48 CFR §52.243.5.

[158] *Id.*

[159] *See* County Asphalt, Inc v State, 40 AD2d 26, 337 NYS2d 415 (3d Dept 1972).

[160] A&R Constr Co v New York State Elec & Gas Corp, 23 AD2d 450, 261 NYS2d 482 (1965); AG Concrete Breakers, Inc v State, 16 Misc 2d 511, 185 NYS2d 455 (Ct Cl), *affd,* 9 AD2d 995, 194 NYS2d 743 (3d Dept 1959).

[161] County Asphalt, Inc v State, 40 AD2d 26, 337 NYS2d 415 (3d Dept 1972).

[162] Jackson v State, 210 AD 115, 205 NYS 658 (4th Dept 1924), *affd mem,* 241 NY 563, 150 NE 556 (1925).

[163] Kaiser Indus v United States, 340 F2d 322 (Ct Cl 1965).

[164] Borough Constr Co v City of NY, 200 NY 149, 93 NE 480 (1910).

[165] Kaiser Indus v United States, 340 F2d 322 (Ct Cl 1965).

[166] Leary v City of Watervliet, 222 NY 337, 118 NE 849 (1918).

by the changed conditions and those caused by other factors, such as the contractor's errors.[167]

§5.20 —Impact Costs

In addition to extra costs and expenses, a contractor often suffers other damages called *impact costs*. As a result of changed conditions, a contractor may be required to use more laborers, more and different equipment, and different methods than anticipated,[168] and to accelerate performance.[169] Changed conditions often result in delay and in damages often classified as delay damages, including increased wages and benefits, loss of efficiency, materials storage costs, increased materials costs,[170] costs of acceleration,[171] etc. For example, when an excavation contractor on a lump sum contract encountered water, sewer, drainage, and electrical lines not shown on the plans and was significantly delayed when it had to resort to hand excavation rather than machine excavation, it recovered as damages its extra foreman wages, the value of its equipment during the extra days, the fair and reasonable value of the excess hand excavation, plus 5 per cent overhead and 10 per cent profit.[172]

Classification of impact costs is important. If a contractor makes a claim for delay damages when it is actually seeking its damages, including impact costs, due to changed conditions, it may be barred from recovery by a *no damage for delay* clause.[173] Impact costs are different from delay damages, although some of the terminology used is similar, such as overhead, loss of efficiency, higher labor costs, and so forth.

---

[167] LI Waldman & Co v State, 41 NYS2d 704 (Ct Cl 1943).

[168] Grow Constr Co v State, 56 AD2d 95, 391 NYS2d 726 (3d Dept 1977).

[169] County Asphalt, Inc v State, 40 AD2d 26, 337 NYS2d 415 (3d Dept 1972).

[170] *See* Cauldwell-Wingate Co v State, 276 NY 365, 12 NE2d 443 (1938).

[171] County Asphalt, Inc v State, 40 AD2d 26, 337 NYS2d 415 (3d Dept 1972).

[172] LI Waldman & Co v State, 41 NYS2d 704 (Ct Cl 1943).

[173] *See* Buckley & Co v City of NY, 121 AD2d 933, 505 NYS2d 140 (1st Dept 1986) and discussion of *no damage for delay* clauses in **ch 7**.

Changes/Extra Work   6

§6.01 Origin of Changes
§6.02 Basic Clause Coverage
§6.03 —The Contract's Scope of Work
§6.04 —The *Cardinal Change* Doctrine
§6.05 —Deductive Changes v Convenience Terminations
§6.06 Issuing Change Orders
§6.07 Authority to Make Changes
§6.08 The Requirement of a Writing
§6.09 Waiving the Writing Requirement
§6.10 —By Oral Order
§6.11 —By Acquiescence
§6.12 —By Conduct
§6.13 Contractor's Duty to Proceed with Disputed Work
§6.14 —Effect of Failure to Proceed
§6.15 Constructive Changes
§6.16 —Contractor's Duty to Seek Clarification
§6.17 —Owner Interference with Work
§6.18 —Defective Specifications
§6.19 —Owner Nondisclosure of Technical Information
§6.20 —Overmeticulous Inspection
§6.21 —Dictating Performance Methods
§6.22 Performance Specifications v Detailed Specifications
§6.23 Rules of Contract Interpretation Applicable to Scope of Work Disputes
§6.24 Notice, Protest, and Record Keeping Requirements
§6.25 Price Adjustments for Changed Work
§6.26 —Pricing Change-Related Costs
§6.27 —Unit Price

§6.28 —Cost Reimbursement Contracts
§6.29 —Impact Costs
§6.30 —Proving Costs
§6.31 Exculpatory Clauses
§6.32 Claims Preservation and Defense
§6.33 —Accord and Satisfaction
§6.34 Remedies

§6.01 Origin of Changes

It is probably safe to say that there has never been a building built exactly as envisioned, a home remodeled precisely as planned, or a foundation poured with the exact amount of concrete estimated. Every project—no matter how standard the design—is unique in that it has never been built in the same location under the same conditions. Changes are inevitable in construction, whether they are simple, such as changing the color of carpet to be laid or the type of cement to be used, or major, such as moving a building site[1] or redesigning a central component of a project due to unforeseen conditions. An extension of time to perform a contract is also a change.[2] Changes are not always additions or extras; the elimination of work originally included in a contract can be a change,[3] typically called a *credit*.

Changes occur and extras are needed because of changed or unforeseen conditions,[4] an owner's changing wishes, unclear or conflicting specifications,[5] design changes,[6] defective designs or specifications,[7] new specifications,[8] and so forth. Whether simple or complicated, changes do not have to result in disputes, threats to shut down the job, or lawsuits. If handled in a reasonable, cooperative way in which all parties communicate fully and abide by the contract, changes can be effected with a minimum amount of delay and negative impact. If, however, an owner tries to obtain changes without paying for them or a contractor tries to obtain extra compensation for contract work or corrective measures,[9] hard feelings and difficult dealings may result, often leading to delay, increased costs, lost profits, and litigation.

---

[1] *See* United States v Rice, 317 US 61, 63 S Ct 120, 87 L Ed 53 (1942).

[2] Bush Constr Co, ASBCA No 8573, 1963 BCA ¶3657.

[3] *See* Trimpoli v State, 20 AD2d 933, 249 NYS2d 154 (3d Dept 1964) (design change resulted in elimination of portion of sewer system contract).

[4] See ch 5 on changed conditions.

[5] Anderson Constr Co v United States, 289 F2d 809 (Ct Cl 1961).

[6] Trimpoli v State, 20 AD2d 933, 249 NYS2d 154 (3d Dept 1964).

[7] Buckley & Co v City of NY, 121 AD2d 933, 505 NYS2d 140 (1st Dept 1986).

[8] Hedden Constr Co v Rossiter Realty Co, 136 AD 601, 121 NYS 64 (1st Dept 1910), *affd mem*, 202 NY 522, 95 NE 1130 (1911).

[9] *See* Savin Bros v State, 62 AD2d 511, 405 NYS2d 516 (4th Dept 1978), *affd mem*, 47 NY2d 934, 393 NE2d 1041, 419 NYS2d 969 (1979) (contractor could not recover for "extras" incurred when it was required to correct its work to meet contract standards).

Extra work or *extras* have been defined as work which "was not embraced within the plans and specifications originally prepared, in existence at the time of making of the contract, and with reference to which both parties acted"[10] and, more simply, as work not included in the original contract[11] or "something necessarily required in the performance of the contract which could not be anticipated."[12] Thus, in a case where a subcontractor had a unit price contract to rake topsoil estimated at 4,620 cubic yards and the general contractor spread almost 90,000 cubic yards pursuant to change orders in the general contract, which 90,000 cubic yards the subcontractor raked, the court held that the additional topsoil was not an extra because the subcontractor was hired to rake all areas needing topsoil and the additional topsoil could not be considered unanticipated.[13] The subcontractor was paid for the additional topsoil raking at contract unit prices.

Additional Work v Extra Work

Some cases make a distinction between *extra work* and *additional work* when evaluating claims for additional compensation. *Extra work* has been classified as "work arising outside and entirely independent of the contract—something not required in its performance. . . ."[14] *Additional work* has been characterized as

> something necessarily required in the performance of the contract and without which it could not be carried out. The necessity for this additional work might arise from conditions which could not be anticipated and which were not open to observation and could not be discovered until the specified work under the contract was actually undertaken.[15]

This definition is markedly similar to one of the definitions of extra work given above. To see the often hazy distinction between extra and additional work, consider a contract to renovate an apartment. Extra work would be furnishing new kitchen appliances; additional work would be furnishing new subflooring because the existing one is not repairable. Similarly, in a contract to build a home, changing the roof elevation would be additional work or an alteration

---

[10] Hedden Constr Co v Rossiter Realty Co, 136 AD 601, 121 NYS 64, 66 (1st Dept 1910), *affd mem*, 202 NY 522, 95 NE 1130 (1911).

[11] EH Smith Contracting Co v City of NY, 240 NY 491, 148 NE 655, 659 (1925).

[12] Savin Bros v State, 62 AD2d 511, 405 NYS2d 516, 519 (4th Dept 1978), *affd mem*, 47 NY2d 934, 393 NE2d 1041, 419 NYS2d 969 (1979); but see Shields v City of NY, 84 AD 502, 82 NYS 1020 (1st Dept 1903), which classified such necessary work as *additional work*, not as *extra work*.

[13] Seebold v Halmar Constr Corp, 146 AD2d 886, 536 NYS2d 871 (3d Dept 1989).

[14] Shields v City of NY, 84 AD 502, 82 NYS 1020, 1021 (1st Dept 1903).

[15] *Id*; but see Savin Bros v State, 62 AD2d 511, 405 NYS2d 516 (4th Dept 1978), *affd mem*, 47 NY2d 934, 393 NE2d 1041, 419 NYS2d 969 (1979), which calls this *extra work*.

since it was always intended that the house would have a roof and, thus, the change was within the contract, but adding a medicine closet not shown on the plans or specifications would be an extra and thus not within the contract.[16]

The distinction has also been made in contracts. For example, a state of New York contract provided that additional work was to be compensated at contract rates, while extra work was to be compensated at a price to be agreed upon by the parties.[17]

The distinction has also been used to determine whether a contractor is entitled to additional compensation despite its failure to comply with a writing requirement. For instance, if a contract requires a written order for extra work but not for additional work, a contractor may recover additional compensation if it can successfully argue that the work was additional and not extra.[18] Not all courts recognize this distinction;[19] the more recent trend is to treat them the same, thus relegating the distinction to legal history. It is best if a contractor complies with all contract requirements, whether it believes itself faced with a demand to perform extra or additional work.

For ease of reference, the terms *changes* and *extras* are used to refer to additions, alterations, extras, changes, deductions, and whatever other terms a variation in work performed may be called.

§6.02 Basic Clause Coverage

The contract documents, which include the specifications, determine whether a contractor is entitled to additional compensation for changes or extra work.[20] Generally, a contractor is obligated to do the work specified in the contract documents at its bid price. In the absence of a *changes* clause in the contract, a contractor need not perform any work different from or beyond that specified in the contract documents. Thus, most contracts have clauses which permit owners to make changes and order extras as necessary and provide mechanisms for approval of and payment for changes and extras.

---

[16] Fetterolf v S&L Constr Co, 175 AD 177, 161 NYS 549 (2d Dept 1916).

[17] *See* Amadeus, Inc v State, 55 Misc 2d 27, 284 NYS2d 620, 624 (Ct Cl 1967), *affd as modified*, 36 AD2d 873, 320 NYS2d 677 (3d Dept), *appeal dismissed*, 29 NY2d 634, 324 NYS2d 458 (1971).

[18] *See* Shields v City of NY, 84 AD 502, 82 NYS 1020 (1st Dept 1903).

[19] *See* Buckley & Co v City of NY, 121 AD2d 933, 505 NYS2d 140, 143 (1st Dept 1986), in which the court stated:

> This distinction between "extra" and "additional" work seems tenuous in the extreme since the contract defines "extra work" as "work other than that required by the contract at the time of its execution," which definition would seem to be inclusive of "additional" work. . . . [R]egardless of the manner in which "additional work" incurred due to changed subsurface conditions differs from "extra work," it is compensable only by means of a contract modification pursuant to contract section 4(b).

[20] Savin Bros v State, 62 AD2d 511, 405 NYS2d 516 (4th Dept 1978), *affd mem*, 47 NY2d 934, 393 NE2d 1041, 419 NYS2d 969 (1979).

A typical changes clause provides that the owner has the right to make changes in the work; that the contractor must perform owner ordered changes; that the change order must be written and signed; and how the change is priced.

A changes clause used by the state, titled "Additions-Deductions-Deviations," provides that "the State, without invalidating the contract, may make changes by altering, adding to or deducting from the work, the contract sum being adjusted accordingly."[21] In another contract, the state—apparently concerned about impossibility or impracticability of performance due to unforeseen conditions—reserved the right to "alter plans or omit any portion of the work as it may deem reasonably necessary for the public interest. . . ."[22]

Another changes clause, unique in that it provides for changes by "mutual consent," states:

> Changes in the work, or in the performance of the contract, either by alterations, additions to, or deductions from work, may be made by mutual consent, the same to be in written form, which shall include compensation and allowances to be made for such additions, corrections and deductions. The furnishing of extras shall be governed by this provision, and there shall be no charge therefor unless the same are furnished at the request of the Owners, in writing, with agreements as to prices therefor.[23]

Part of an American Institute of Architects (AIA) form contract between an owner and a contractor "Changes in the Work" article provides that the "Owner may by Construction Change Directive, without invalidating the Contract, order changes in the Work within the general scope of the Contract consisting of additions, deletions or other revisions, the Contract Sum and Contract Time being adjusted accordingly."[24]

The exercise of authority to order changes and add or delete work must be done within the conditions set forth in the contract. Thus, if the contract states that changes may be made if "necessary," the ordered change must indeed be necessary.[25] "The necessity need not be absolute, but must be reasonable . . . [,]" such as, for example, if it is impractical to build a project as planned due to unforeseen unstable soil conditions.[26]

Changes clauses typically include requirements that any orders for changes, extras, or additions be in writing. Such clauses may also provide a mechanism

---

[21] Trimpoli v State, 20 AD2d 933, 249 NYS2d 154 (3d Dept 1964).

[22] D'Angelo v State, 7 Misc 2d 783, 166 NYS2d 378, 385 (Ct Cl 1957); *see also* Whitmyer Bros v State, 63 AD2d 103, 406 NYS2d 617, 619 (3d Dept 1978), *affd*, 419 NYS2d 954, 393 NE2d 1027, 47 NY2d 960 (1979).

[23] LA Rose v Backer, 11 AD2d 314, 203 NYS2d 740, 743, *judgment amount modified*, 11 AD2d 969, 207 NYS2d 258 (3d Dept 1960), *affd*, 11 NY2d 760, 226 NYS2d 695 (1962).

[24] AIA Doc A201, ¶7.3.1 (1987 ed).

[25] Kinser Constr Co v State, 204 NY 381, 97 NE 871 (1912); D'Angelo v State, 7 Misc 2d 783, 166 NYS2d 378 (Ct Cl 1957).

[26] Kinser Constr Co v State, 204 NY 381, 97 NE 871 (1912).

for a contractor to reserve its right to make a claim for additional compensation if it is ordered to do work which the owner or its agent contends is contract work but which the contractor believes is extra work. Writing requirements are discussed in §§6.08-6.12; protest procedures are discussed in §§6.13-6.14 and 6.24.

§6.03 —The Contract's Scope of Work

Payment for changes is available only if the contractor performed work beyond that or different from that specified in its contract, generally referred to as the contractor's *scope of work*. The contract documents are the ultimate guide in determining whether extra work has been performed. For example, in a case in which a contractor encountered a badly rotted roof and walls when building a home addition, it was entitled to extra compensation for the bridging and reconstruction work it had to do on the rotted portions of the home to complete the addition; the reconstruction was not shown on the plans and neither party anticipated the rot.[27] Similarly, in a case where the contract required the owner to furnish "all materials except welding rod and cinch anchors," the contractor was entitled to a contract price adjustment when the project engineer determined that the contract required the contractor to provide some piping.[28]

Conversely, where a contract required the contractor to demolish, clear, fill where needed, compact, and grade the site, each as a distinct responsibility, it could not claim that compaction of the entire site, as opposed to just fill areas, was extra work.[29] A contractor cannot recover extra compensation for remedial work it was required to perform when its original work failed to meet the contract standards.[30] Similarly, in the absence of bad faith by the owner, a contractor cannot recover a higher unit cost when it is required to excavate more than estimated in the contract documents; generally, excess excavation is not an extra but is work within the contract.[31]

Determining whether work is within the scope of the contract is not always simple. For example, in *Green v City of New York*,[32] the contract specifications provided that the contractor could use plaster board partitions in a bathroom. The contract required the contractor to comply with state rules and regulations and stated that this compliance requirement took precedence over

---

[27] Herzog v Williams, 139 Misc 2d 18, 526 NYS2d 329 (Ossining Justice Ct 1988).

[28] Joseph Davis, Inc v Merritt-Chapman & Scott Corp, 27 AD2d 114, 276 NYS2d 479 (4th Dept 1967).

[29] Valente v Two Guys from Harrison, NY, Inc, 35 AD2d 862, 315 NYS2d 220 (3d Dept 1970).

[30] Savin Bros v State, 62 AD2d 511, 405 NYS2d 516 (4th Dept 1978), *affd mem*, 47 NY2d 934, 393 NE2d 1041, 419 NYS2d 969 (1979).

[31] Depot Constr Corp v State, 19 NY2d 109, 224 NE2d 866, 278 NYS2d 363 (1967); Yonkers Contracting Co v New York State Thruway Auth, 25 AD2d 811, 270 NYS2d 16 (4th Dept 1966), *affd*, 23 NY2d 856, 245 NE2d 800, 298 NYS2d 67 (1969).

[32] 283 AD 485, 128 NYS2d 715 (1st Dept 1954).

the specifications if there were a conflict. In fact, the specifications did not comply with a state law which required more costly plaster-over-lath bathroom partitions. Despite a contract requirement that the contractor comply with all laws and codes, the court awarded the contractor the extra cost that it incurred when it complied with a change order that substituted plaster-over-lath for the plaster board partitions, finding that the contractor based its bid on the specifications and was not required to ensure that the specifications complied with the law.

§6.04 —The *Cardinal Change* Doctrine

An owner's right to make changes under a changes clause is limited by the general scope of the work described in the contract.[33] An owner may not make changes of such magnitude that the essential or main purpose of the contract is altered. When it does, a *cardinal change* has occurred and the contract has been breached by the owner. There is no precise definition of cardinal change or means to determine when one has occurred. It has been said that a cardinal change occurs when the changes made are "radical,"[34] "of such magnitude that they [are] . . . not within the scope of the original contract but rather constitute a breach thereof,"[35] or "change the scope of the work originally contemplated under the contract. . . ."[36]

"The test to be applied is whether the supplemental work [or change] ordered so varied from the original plan, was of such importance, or so altered the essential identity or main purpose of the contract that it constitutes a new undertaking."[37] Thus, one must look at the essential identity or main purpose of the contract to determine whether a cardinal change has occurred. If the addition or omission is incidental, there is no cardinal change.[38] Whether a change is incidental does not depend upon the percentage of work or cost involved but on the *character* of the work.[39] Thus, elimination of 10 per cent[40] and even 41 per cent[41] of the work has been allowed, while elimination of 2-½ per cent of the work has not.[42]

A clear example of cardinal change was found where, due to poor engineering, substantial redesign of a project was needed resulting in hundreds of changes (many before construction began), over 16,000 hours of redesign

---

[33] McMaster v State, 108 NY 542, 15 NE 417 (1888).

[34] Westcott v State, 264 AD 463, 36 NYS2d 23 (3d Dept 1942).

[35] Luria Bros & Co v United States, 369 F2d 701, 707 (Ct Cl 1966).

[36] C. Norman Peterson Co v Container Corp of Am, 172 Cal App 3d 628, 639, 218 Cal Rptr 592, 598 (1985).

[37] Albert Elia Bldg Co v New York State Urban Dev Corp, 54 AD2d 337, 388 NYS2d 462, 467 (4th Dept 1976).

[38] Del Balso Constr Corp v City of NY, 278 NY 154, 15 NE2d 559 (1938).

[39] *Id.*

[40] *Id.*

[41] Kinser Constr Co v State, 204 NY 381, 97 NE 871 (1912).

[42] Litchfield Constr Co v City of NY, 244 NY 251, 155 NE 116 (1926).

work, over 250 disputes between the owner and contractor concerning changes, and the contractor's spending almost twice as much as the original contract price.[43] In a less obvious case, the court found a "radical change" in the plans and design of the work, and, thus, breach of a bridge building contract, when the state required the contractor to use much longer piles than called for in the contract. This change required types of lumber that were different than the shorter piles contemplated in the original contract and increased transportation, material, and labor costs and prolonged the time of performance.[44]

Cardinal change was not found in a case where an owner required its contractor to use excavated material as fill despite a contract provision that the contractor was to supply and install clean sand as fill. The court held that the deletion was not substantial enough to alter the essential purpose of the contract, especially in light of a contract provision giving the owner the right to omit work.[45]

Accepting a Cardinal Change

In private construction, a contractor may perform or "accept" a cardinal change if it chooses. The performance of a cardinal change either results in a new agreement or is a breach or an abandonment of the contract by the owner.[46] If breach or abandonment is found, the contractor may be able to recover in quantum meruit, a measure of damages which may exceed the contract price. Further, contract damages limitations, including *no damage for delay* clauses, and other exculpatory clauses may be inapplicable.[47]

In public construction, acceptance or performance of a cardinal change may result in a contractor doing work for free.[48] If a change is cardinal, it may be barred by applicable competitive bidding statutes. A public owner may order changes within the general scope of the work, but it may not make a different or new contract without complying with competitive bidding statutes.[49] Thus, where a tunnel was added to a contract to construct a convention center and the tunnel originated as a modification of a different project and not as an alternative to a structure within the convention center, the court held that the work should have been competitively bid. Rather than cause the contractor to forfeit totally its compensation for the tunnel work, the court required it to refund

---

[43] C. Norman Peterson Co v Container Corp of Am, 172 Cal App 3d 628, 218 Cal Rptr 592 (1985).

[44] Westcott v State, 264 AD 463, 36 NYS2d 23 (3d Dept 1942).

[45] De Foe Corp v City of NY, 95 AD2d 793, 463 NYS2d 508 (2d Dept 1985), *appeal dismissed*, 66 NY2d 759, 497 NYS2d 1028 (1985).

[46] C. Norman Peterson Co v Container Corp of Am, 172 Cal App 3d 628, 218 Cal Rptr 592 (1985).

[47] *See* Westcott v State, 264 AD 463, 36 NYS2d 23 (3d Dept 1942).

[48] Albert Elia Bldg Co v New York State Urban Dev Corp, 54 AD2d 337, 388 NYS2d 462 (4th Dept 1976).

[49] *Id* at 342, 388 NYS2d at 467.

the difference between the price it charged and the price which would have resulted had there been competitive bidding.[50]

In a public contract, the risk of performing a cardinal change is wholly on the contractor despite the fact that there is a breach of contract by the owner. When faced with what it believes to be a cardinal change, a public works contractor may either perform the change under protest or refuse to perform it and, if wrong, face termination for cause by the owner and consequential loss of the profits that it could have made had it completed the job.[51] If the contractor performs the change and a court later determines that the change was cardinal and *so clearly* outside the scope of the contract that the contractor should have known it was unauthorized, the contractor may not be entitled to payment for the extra work.[52] If the contractor performs a cardinal change which was not clearly so and the dispute is an honest one, the contractor will be entitled to recover for its work.[53] If the change is, in fact, cardinal and the contractor refuses to perform, it will be entitled to its lost profits.[54]

> **PRACTICE POINTER:**
>
> When faced with an apparent cardinal change on a public job, contractors should consult their attorneys before proceeding. Performing under protest may not be enough to preserve a right to compensation.[55]

When a cardinal change is deductive in nature, a contractor is entitled to its lost profits and other damages.[56] If a deductive change is not cardinal and is allowable under the contract changes clause, the contractor is without recourse to recover its lost profits.[57]

§6.05 —Deductive Changes v Convenience Terminations

At times, owners may decide that they do not wish to complete their projects or that they wish to eliminate large portions of them. Along with such decisions

---

[50] Albert Elia Bldg Co v New York State Urban Dev Corp, 54 AD2d 337, 388 NYS2d 462 (4th Dept 1976).

[51] Kinser Constr Co v State, 204 NY 381, 97 NE 871 (1912).

[52] *See* Borough Constr Co v City of NY, 200 NY 149, 93 NE 480 (1910) (city demand "so preposterous that there could be no reasonable doubt that it exceeded the obligations of the contract"; contractor was not justified in doing the work); Albert Elia Bldg Co v New York State Urban Dev Corp, 54 AD2d 337, 388 NYS2d 462 (4th Dept 1976).

[53] Collins v State, 259 NY 200, 181 NE 357 (1932).

[54] Langan Constr Corp v State, 110 Misc 177, 180 NYS 249 (Ct Cl 1920).

[55] A declaratory judgment action may resolve the issue. *See* City of Rochester v Vanderlinde Elec Corp, 56 AD2d 185, 392 NYS2d 167 (1977); *but see* Kalisch-Jarcho, Inc v City of NY, 72 NY2d 727, 533 NE2d 258, 536 NYS2d (1988).

[56] McMaster v State, 108 NY 542, 15 NE 417 (1888).

[57] Trimpoli v State, 20 AD2d 933, 249 NYS2d 154 (3d Dept 1964).

is the desire to avoid additional expense, including paying their contractors' lost profits or termination damages. To avoid termination damages, some owners attempt to eliminate significant portions of work through change orders. If the contract expressly reserves to the owner the right to terminate or abandon the work at any stage, a contractor may not claim lost profits since there would be no breach due to the owner's termination of the contract[58] or elimination of a large portion of the work.[59] In the absence of such a reservation, however, an owner is obligated to allow a contractor to complete its work; any preemptory termination or unfounded elimination of work is a breach of contract entitling the contractor to damages.[60]

An owner may not, through the issuance of change orders, abandon its contract. For instance, in *McMaster v State*,[61] the contractor was to furnish and cut the stone necessary for the Buffalo State Asylum for the Insane. The asylum was to contain an administration building, five male wards, five female wards, and certain out-buildings. The state issued change orders which changed the exterior of the buildings from stone to brick with stone trim and, later, halted further work. The five female wards were never built. The Court of Appeals held that the state's changes clause did not give it the right to omit entirely any buildings or to change the buildings from stone to brick. The contractor was allowed to recover its lost profits.

Under many contracts, the deduction or elimination of work from a project is governed by a requirement of necessity. Such changes clauses reserve the right to delete work as "may be necessary"[62] or as the owner "deems necessary."[63] In such cases, a contractor is entitled to its lost profits for any work eliminated where the elimination was not founded upon necessity.[64] "There must be a rational and just ground for deeming a change necessary."[65] Thus, in a case where an enlargement of a reservoir shed area made paving of the reservoir's side slopes unnecessary and permitted elimination of a second dam, and these eliminations did not affect the use of the reservoir, the changes were proper and necessary and did not change the substantial character of the work.[66] Similarly, elimination of a large portion of a contractor's work was allowed where natural conditions prevented performance of the work as planned and made it necessary to change the location of a canal lock.[67]

---

[58] Baker v State, 77 AD 528, 78 NYS 922 (3d Dept 1902).

[59] Kinser Constr Co v State, 204 NY 381, 97 NE 871 (1912).

[60] McMaster v State, 108 NY 542, 15 NE 417 (1888); Baker v State, 77 AD 528, 78 NYS 922 (3d Dept 1902).

[61] 108 NY 542, 15 NE 417 (1888).

[62] Kinser Constr Co v State, 204 NY 381, 97 NE 871, 872 (1912).

[63] Langan Constr Corp v State, 110 Misc 177, 180 NYS 249, 251 (Ct Cl 1920).

[64] AE Ottaviano, Inc v State, 202 Misc 532, 110 NYS2d 99 (Ct Cl 1952); Dunbar & Sullivan Dredging Co v State, 34 NYS2d 848 (Ct Cl 1942), *after remand from* 259 AD 440, 20 NYS2d 127 (4th 1940), *rev'g* 34 NYS2d 848 (Ct Cl 1939).

[65] Langan Constr Corp v State, 110 Misc 177, 180 NYS 249, 252 (Ct Cl 1920).

[66] Kingsley v City of Brooklyn, 78 NY 200 (1879).

[67] Kinser Constr Co v State, 204 NY 381, 97 NE 871 (1912).

Necessity was not found and the state was held to be in breach of its contract in a case in which it canceled the asphalt portion of a paving contract—some 43 per cent of the contract work. The work was eliminated when the state discovered that an existing macadam road was not sufficient to be the base of the contractor's asphalt. The state asked the contractor to make the old road sufficient and proposed prices. The contractor replied that it could not do the work at the state's price and offered to do it for a higher price. The contractor later offered to discuss the price when the state balked at its offer. Rather than discuss the price, the state notified the contractor that the asphalt portion of its contract was eliminated, leaving the contractor with the concrete and macadam portions of its contract—little more than half of the contract. This deletion removed "most, if not all" of the work on which the contractor could make a profit. The contractor refused to perform the remaining portions of the contract and sued for breach and lost profits. The court found a breach by the state, ruling that there was no need to remove the asphalt portion of the contract and, in effect, that the elimination was retaliatory. The state itself could have made the macadam road sufficient and allowed the contractor to lay the asphalt paving as the contract contemplated, reached an agreement with the contractor to make the road base sufficient, or canceled the contract and become liable for damages. The court awarded the contractor its lost profits.[68]

§6.06 Issuing Change Orders

When a public board or commission, such as a board of education, is involved in a construction project, there may be several steps for issuance of a change order. Under one scenario, the contractor submits a claim for extra work to the project architect. If the architect approves the claim, it recommends approval of the claim to the board. If the board approves the claim, it passes a resolution. The contractor is then notified of the resolution and may submit a requisition for the extra the following month.[69]

In a private contract, the same steps may be involved, with the architect submitting the claim to the owner for approval rather than to a board. For instance, American Institute of Architects (AIA) contract form A201 provides that the contractor must submit a written claim for additional cost or time to the architect, and that the architect will review the claim within 10 days. If it approves the claim, it recommends approval by the owner; the owner then either agrees or disagrees with the architect.[70]

---

[68] Langan Constr Corp v State, 110 Misc 177, 180 NYS 249 (Ct Cl 1920).
[69] *See* Board of Educ v Bernard Assocs No 3, 230 NYS2d 509 (Westchester 1962).
[70] AIA Doc A201, ¶¶4.3.7, 4.3.8, 4.4.1 (1987 ed).

§6.07 Authority to Make Changes

Most contract changes clauses specify who has the authority to order changes. It may be the owner's architect,[71] engineer, or husband,[72] the owner and architect jointly,[73] or simply the owner. In public construction, it may be the town engineer,[74] the public agency,[75] board,[76] or commission that contracted for the work, the comptroller, specified city officials, or any other person or office designated in the contract. Regardless of whom the contract designates to review work or supervise day-to-day operations, the *only* person who can issue and authorize change orders is the person specifically designated in the changes clause as having the authority and power to do so. If the contract is silent, the general rule is that only an owner can authorize a change.

Thus, where a changes clause provides that an order to perform extra work is valid only if "issued in writing and signed by the commissioner," neither the resident engineer nor the relevant department head has the power to order extra work.[77] A contractor that performs extra work ordered by anyone other than the designated person may be barred from receiving payment for that extra work.[78] In public construction, the issue is not whether the public entity benefited from the work or whether it is morally obligated to pay for it; the issue is the public entity's *legal* obligation. Generally, on public projects, if the prescribed procedure is not followed, recovery for improperly ordered work is not available in contract or quantum meruit.[79] Private contracts are not as strictly construed; however, this is not to imply that they are leniently construed.

In public construction, the authority to order changes is not limitless. Just as the contracting agency's power to change a project is restricted by the project appropriation[80] and competitive bidding statutes,[81] so too is the designated

---

[71] Fetterolf v S&L Constr Co, 175 AD 177, 161 NYS 549 (2d Dept 1916).

[72] Walter v Horowitz, 60 NYS2d 327 (Westchester), *affd*, 271 AD 802, 65 NYS2d 672 (2d Dept 1946).

[73] AIA Doc A201, ¶12.1.2 (1987 ed).

[74] AJ Cianciulli, Inc v Town of Greenburgh, 12 Misc 2d 931, 172 NYS2d 233 (Westchester 1958).

[75] Albert Elia Bldg Co v New York State Urban Dev Corp, 54 AD2d 337, 388 NYS2d 462 (4th Dept 1976).

[76] Lutes v Briggs, 64 NY 404 (1876) (board of public works of the city of Rochester).

[77] Joseph F. Egan, Inc v City of NY, 17 NY2d 90, 215 NE2d 490, 268 NYS2d 301 (1966).

[78] *Id;* RH Cunningham & Sons Co v State, 52 NYS2d 65 (Ct Cl 1944), *affd*, 270 AD 864, 60 NYS2d 206 (3d Dept 1946).

[79] Lutzken v City of Rochester, 7 AD2d 498, 184 NYS2d 483 (4th Dept 1959).

[80] AJ Cianciulli, Inc v Town of Greenburgh, 12 Misc 2d 931, 172 NYS2d 233 (Westchester 1958).

[81] *See* Albert Elia Bldg Co v New York State Urban Dev Corp, 54 AD2d 337, 388 NYS2d 462 (4th Dept 1976).

154 CHANGES/EXTRA WORK

person's authority limited.[82] A public entity may make only those changes which are incidental to and reasonably necessary to complete the project. It may change the way the work is to be done,[83] but may not change the character of the work. If a public ordered change exceeds the agent's or entity's authority, the contractor may be barred from payment, despite its good faith.[84]

The authority of an owner's agent to order changes is limited by the terms of the agency. If the owner authorizes the agent to order changes in writing, the agent is without authority to order changes orally and waive the writing requirement.[85] "An agent cannot enlarge his own powers by waiving the limitations thereon."[86]

§6.08 The Requirement of a Writing

Construction contract changes clauses usually require that all orders for changes or extra work be in writing and signed by the owner and architect or other designated person(s). In general, such provisions are designed to protect the owner from unexpected costs or unjustified claims for additional compensation.[87] Absent a waiver, a contract provision requiring a written order is binding and will bar recovery for extra work or changes performed without one.[88] A failure to follow contract requirements regarding extra work is, in effect, a waiver of a claim for compensation for that work.[89]

There may be some question as to what constitutes a writing. The answer depends upon the particular contractual requirements and the facts of each case. If the contract is clear and rigid in its definition of what will suffice, little else will do. More often, the contract is not definite and there is room to argue that there is a written order despite the apparent absence of one. For instance, revised specifications accepted and approved by the owner in writing *may* be

---

[82] AJ Cianciulli, Inc v Town of Greenburgh, 12 Misc 2d 931, 172 NYS2d 233 (Westchester 1958).

[83] Lutes v Briggs, 64 NY 404 (1876).

[84] *See* AJ Cianciulli, Inc v Town of Greenburgh, 12 Misc 2d 931, 172 NYS2d 233 (Westchester 1958); Manshul Constr v Board of Educ, 551 NYS2d 497 (App Div 1st Dept 1990). See the discussion regarding cardinal change in **§6.04**.

[85] Langley v Rouss, 185 NY 201, 77 NE 1168 (1906); Kelly v St Michael's Roman Catholic Church, 148 AD 767, 133 NYS 328 (2d Dept 1912).

[86] Langley v Rouss, 185 NY 201, 77 NE 1168, 1170 (1906).

[87] Langley v Rouss, 185 NY 201, 77 NE 1168 (1906); *but see* Arrow Plumbing Co v Dare Constr Corp, 212 NYS2d 438 (Nassau 1961) (court found writing requirement was for protection of plumber, not owner).

[88] Langley v Rouss, 185 NY 201, 77 NE 1168 (1906); Comet Heating & Cooling Co v Modular Technics Corp, 57 AD2d 526, 393 NYS2d 573 (1st Dept 1977); Valente v Two Guys from Harrison, NY, Inc, 35 AD2d 862, 315 NYS2d 220 (3d Dept 1970).

[89] De Foe Corp v City of NY, 95 AD2d 793, 463 NYS2d 508 (2d Dept 1983), *appeal dismissed*, 66 NY2d 759, 497 NYS2d 1028 (1985).

a written order for extras.[90] On the other hand, plans or drawings of proposed alterations unsigned by the owner do not constitute a written order within the meaning of most construction contracts.[91]

§6.09 Waiving the Writing Requirement

Like any contract requirement, a requirement for written orders may be waived by a party[92] or a party's agent, *if* the agent has the authority to do so.[93] Rarely will an agent have the authority to waive a writing requirement,[94] and an owner is not bound by its agent's unauthorized waiver.[95] A party may waive a writing requirement inserted for its protection[96] but may not waive a writing requirement intended to protect another party—for example, a contractor may not waive a writing requirement that is intended to protect the owner; rather, the owner would have to waive it. A writing requirement may be waived in three ways: by oral order; by acquiescence; or by conduct.

§6.10 —By Oral Order

Waiver may be inferred from an owner's oral order to do extra work when the owner promises to pay the contractor for the work.[97] For instance, in *Clark v Harris*,[98] a plumber was working as a prime contractor on a plumbing and gas fitting contract. When the general prime contractor abandoned the project, the owner asked the plumber to complete the job and perform extra work. The court allowed the plumber to recover for the extras despite its failure to comply with a contractual writing requirement, holding that "having ordered the work

---

[90] Hedden Constr Co v Rossiter Realty Co, 136 AD 601, 121 NYS 64 (1st Dept 1910), *affd mem*, 202 NY 522, 95 NE 1130 (1911); *contra* Fetterolf v S&L Constr Co, 175 AD 177, 161 NYS 549 (2d Dept 1916) (working plans and sketches may not be regarded as an order).

[91] Fetterolf v S&L Constr Co, 175 AD 177, 161 NYS 549 (2d Dept 1916).

[92] Scribner v Cottone, 284 AD 1007, 135 NYS2d 280 (3d Dept 1954); *see also* Joseph F. Egan, Inc v City of NY, 17 NY2d 90, 215 NE2d 490, 268 NYS2d 301 (1966).

[93] Langley v Rouss, 185 NY 201, 77 NE 1168 (1906).

[94] Buckley & Co v City of NY, 121 AD2d 933, 505 NYS2d 140 (1st Dept 1986); National Bank of Commerce v City of Watervliet, 97 Misc 121, 160 NYS 1072 (Albany 1916), *affd mem*, 178 AD 944, 164 NYS 1103 (3d Dept 1917).

[95] Rainbow Elec Co v Bloom, 132 AD2d 539, 517 NYS2d 273 (2d Dept 1987).

[96] Arrow Plumbing Co v Dare Constr Corp, 212 NYS2d 438 (Nassau 1961).

[97] Louis N. Picciano & Son v Olympic Constr Co, 112 AD2d 604, 492 NYS2d 476 (3d Dept), *appeal dismissed*, 66 NY2d 854, 489 NE2d 253, 498 NYS2d 366 (1985) (general contractor orally ordered subcontractor to perform extras and promised to pay); Howdy Jones Constr Co v Parklaw Realty, Inc, 76 AD2d 1018, 429 NYS2d 768 (3d Dept 1980), *affd mem*, 53 NY2d 718, 421 NE2d 846, 439 NYS2d 354 (1981).

[98] 53 Misc 556, 103 NYS 785 (App Term 1907).

156 CHANGES/EXTRA WORK

done and received the benefit of plaintiff's services, defendant can hardly hide behind this provision. . . ."[99]

> **PRACTICE POINTER:**
>
> To avoid inadvertently waiving a writing requirement, an owner should confirm all oral discussions in writing and instruct its personnel to do the same. Further, an owner should respond in writing to all of its contractor's assertions, oral or written, with which it disagrees.

§6.11 —By Acquiescence

An owner who is present during changes or alterations may be precluded from claiming that the work was not properly authorized because a contractually required written order was not obtained.[100] For instance, in a case where the contractor and owner discussed construction of a pond, the contractor installed the pond, and the owner knew of its installation but "expressed no dissatisfaction," the owner could not avoid paying for the pond by relying on the contractor's failure to obtain written authorization.[101]

A city was held to have waived its writing requirement when its project engineer included the contractor's claimed amount for extras in its monthly estimates and the city paid the estimates, including the extras, without objection.[102]

§6.12 —By Conduct

The parties' conduct may establish a waiver of a writing requirement.[103] For example, waiver may be found if the parties consistently do not follow contract procedures for review and approval of change orders and extra work.[104] Thus, waiver by conduct was found where testimony showed that a city's plans required constant revision, that the city bureau in charge of processing change orders was behind schedule, that work was done before the issuance of change

---

[99] Id at 557, 103 NYS at 786.

[100] Perry v Levenson, 82 AD 94, 81 NYS 586 (1st Dept 1903), affd, 178 NY 559, 70 NE 1104 (1904).

[101] Miller v McMahon, 135 AD2d 1030, 523 NYS2d 185 (3d Dept 1987).

[102] National Bank of Commerce v City of Watervliet, 97 Misc 121, 160 NYS 1072 (Albany 1916), affd mem, 178 AD 944, 164 NYS 1103 (3d Dept 1917).

[103] FW Carlin Constr Co v New York & Brooklyn Brewing Co, 149 AD 919, 134 NYS 493 (2d Dept 1912) (dicta); Peter A. Camilli & Sons v State, 41 Misc 2d 218, 245 NYS2d 521 (Ct Cl 1963).

[104] Joseph F. Egan, Inc v City of NY, 17 NY2d 90, 215 NE2d 490, 268 NYS2d 301 (1966); Howdy Jones Constr Co v Parklaw Realty, Inc, 76 AD2d 1018, 429 NYS2d 768 (3d Dept 1980), affd mem, 53 NY2d 718, 421 NE2d 846, 439 NYS2d 354 (1981); D'Onofrio Bros Constr Corp v Board of Educ, 72 AD2d 760, 421 NYS2d 377 (2d Dept 1979).

orders to avoid delay, and that over 400 change orders were issued after work was done and were subsequently confirmed by the commissioner.[105]

§6.13 Contractor's Duty to Proceed with Disputed Work

Disputed work issues arise when the owner or its agents order the contractor to perform work that the contractor believes to be extra work but the owner contends is contract work. Most contracts give the owner or its architect or engineer the right to direct the contractor to proceed with disputed work. For instance, Article 27 of New York City's standard contract provides:

> If the Contractor is of the opinion (1) that any work ordered to be done as contract work by the Commissioner, the Engineer or the Resident Engineer, is extra work and not contract work, or (2) that any determination or order of the Commissioner, Engineer or Resident Engineer violates the terms and provisions of this contract, he must promptly, and before proceeding with such work and complying with such determination or order, or simultaneously therewith notify the Commissioner in writing of the reasons for his opinion with respect thereto, and request a final determination thereon.
>
> If the Commissioner determines that the work in question is contract work and not extra work, or that the determination or order complained of is proper, he will so notify the Contractor to proceed, and the Contractor must promptly comply. However, in order to reserve his right to claim compensation for such work or damages resulting from such compliance, the contractor must, within five days after receiving notice of the Commissioner's determination and direction, notify the Commissioner in writing that the work is being performed, or that the determination or direction is being complied with, under protest.[106]

Under such a clause, the contractor must proceed (unless the work in question is so far beyond the scope of the contract as to be a cardinal change[107]) and give notice that it is working under protest, reserving its right to make a claim for payment for the work.[108] If the contractor refuses to proceed, it can be held in default and its contract terminated.[109] Once the job is completed, the con-

---

[105] Joseph F. Egan, Inc v City of NY, 17 NY2d 90, 215 NE2d 490, 268 NYS2d 301 (1966).

[106] Kalisch-Jarcho, Inc v City of NY, 135 AD2d 262, 525 NYS2d 190 (1st Dept) (Sandler, J. dissenting), *revd.* 72 NY2d 727, 533 NE2d 258, 536 NYS2d 419 (1988).

[107] Cardinal changes are discussed at **§6.04**.

[108] Amadeus, Inc v State, 55 Misc 2d 27, 284 NYS2d 620 (Ct Cl 1967), *affd as modified,* 36 AD2d 873, 320 NYS2d 677 (3d Dept), *appeal dismissed,* 29 NY2d 634, 324 NYS2d 458 (1971).

[109] Ferguson Contracting Co v State, 202 AD2d 27, 195 NYS 901 (3d Dept 1922), *affd,* 237 NY 186, 142 NE 580 (1923).

tractor, assuming that it has reserved its right to make a claim by giving all contractually and statutorily required notices (see Chapter 16), may bring suit against the owner to recover its damages due to the disputed work.[110]

Generally, a contractor does not have a right to a prior judicial determination of whether it must perform disputed work when its contract provides a means to resolve such disputes.[111] Provisions such as that quoted above do not violate public policy. In fact, they were designed to protect the public interest by avoiding costly and disruptive delays during public works projects.[112]

§6.14 —Effect of Failure to Proceed

If a contractor refuses to proceed, it faces the risk of being considered in default and having its contract terminated. Even if the contractor is later found to have been correct—i.e., the work is found to have been extra work and to have entitled the contractor to extra compensation—its failure to proceed under protest can result in a loss of its claim for lost profits.[113]

If the contract does not contain a clause similar to Article 27 of the New York City contract quoted in §6.13, a contractor does not have a duty to proceed with disputed work and can refuse to perform the work until it receives a written and signed change order.[114] Similarly, where the change is deductive in nature and clearly and radically changes the contractor's work, the contractor may refuse to proceed with the remaining contract work and sue the owner for damages, including lost profits.[115]

§6.15 Constructive Changes

Constructive changes are changes caused by the owner but not acknowledged by it as changes. The term *constructive change* developed under federal construction contracts and is often used by lawyers in New York, but less often by the courts. Simply put, it is a breach of the contract by the owner. In a constructive change, the contractor asserts that an action or order of the owner or its architect or engineer amounts to a change which requires an adjustment of time or money; the owner denies that there is a change. Typically, a constructive change arises from a dispute in contract language interpretation. When an owner requires a contractor to perform work or use materials which the con-

---

[110] Collins v State, 259 NY 200, 181 NE 357 (1932).

[111] Kalisch-Jarcho, Inc v City of NY, 72 NY2d 727, 533 NE2d 258, 536 NYS2d 419 (1988).

[112] *Id.*

[113] John W. Johnson, Inc v Basic Constr Co, 292 F Supp 300 (DDC 1968), *affd*, 429 F2d 764 (DC Cir 1970).

[114] *Id.*

[115] *See* Langan Constr Corp v State, 110 Misc 177, 180 NYS 249 (Ct Cl 1920). The doctrine of cardinal change is discussed in **§6.04**. The issue of an owner's ability to deduct work from a project is discussed in **§6.05**.

tractor considers to be different from that required by the contract but will not issue a formal change order, the contractor may treat the order as a constructive change order and later make a claim for additional compensation under the changes clause of the contract.[116]

A constructive change might be found where an owner insists that concrete work meet a higher standard than the contractor believes the contract requires. The owner's standard may be more rigorous than customarily accepted local standards or that accepted by the American Concrete Institute. Unless the contract specifications clearly define concrete standards, the owner's insistence upon the higher standard would obligate it to pay the extra costs incurred by the contractor in meeting the higher standard.[117]

A constructive change may result from owner interference with the work, defective specifications, owner nondisclosure of technical information, overmeticulous inspection, owner dictation of performance methods, or contradictions between performance and detailed specifications.

§6.16 —Contractor's Duty to Seek Clarification

The potential government contractor has the duty to seek clarification of ambiguities which may exist in the contract prior to the submission of its bid. Even if a court believes that the contractor's interpretation of contract language is reasonable, it will still bar recovery for the contractor if that interpretation grows out of an ambiguity that is clear on the face of the contract.[118] This requirement is intended to protect the government from a contractor that intentionally submits a low bid in order to make claims for extras later on by claiming ambiguities during performance.

While no New York law appears to be directly on this point, federal case law clearly sets forth this duty of clarification for government contractors. In 1963, the United States Court of Claims in *Beacon Construction Co v United States*[119] recognized and upheld the contractor's duty to seek clarification where a clause in the contract required prospective bidders to immediately inform the contracting officer of discrepancies in the drawings or specifications.

The court stated that if the bidder is on notice of a problem involving the language of the contract but chooses to ignore it, the bidder cannot later rely on the fact that ambiguities in contracts written by the government are held against the drafter. In fact, the bidder is under an affirmative obligation to call attention to the ambiguity or omission if it intends to interpret it in the bidder's

---

[116] Ets-Hokin Corp v United States, 420 F2d 716 (Ct Cl 1970).

[117] R. Rubin, S. Guy, A. Maevis, & V. Fairweather, Construction Claims: Analysis, Presentation, Defense 37 (1983); *see also* Clemente Contracting Co v State, 89 NYS2d 453 (Ct Cl 1944) (contractor recovered extra compensation when state made it erect stone walls and building additions of a better quality than required by contract).

[118] Ralph C. Nash, Jr, Government Contract Changes 233 (1981).

[119] 314 F2d 501 (Ct Cl 1963).

favor. Otherwise, the bidder's failure "to resort to the remedy proffered by the Government" in regard to an obvious discrepancy will be interpreted against the bidder.[120]

Soon after *Beacon* was decided, another case out of the Court of Claims, *WPC Enterprises v United States*,[121] restated the *Beacon* rule, but this time there was no clause in the contract requiring clarification. However, the court emphasized that if a particular provision in a government contract is usually interpreted a particular way and the contractor reasonably interprets it that way, the interpretation will be adopted. While the contractor may have some duty to inquire about a major discrepancy, stated the court, it is not normally required to seek clarification of all ambiguities.[122]

Today, it is held that the duty to request clarification is "inherent" in bidding on government contracts if a bidder is faced with a "major patent discrepancy, obvious omission or drastic conflict in provisions."[123] The existence of a provision in a contract requiring clarification of ambiguities is not determinative of whether clarification will be held to be required in a particular instance. The test used is whether a reasonable businessperson would have recognized the discrepancy or ambiguity during bidding.[124] A contractor can get around the rule if it can convince the court that its interpretation was made in a good faith effort to make sense out of the entire package of specifications and drawings.[125] In addition, a contractor must submit requests for clarification in a timely manner in order to recover.[126]

§6.17 —Owner Interference with Work

A contractor was entitled to an equitable adjustment based upon a change in its manner or method of performance when the owner made the contractor remove a painting subcontractor, who was previously approved and whose work was sufficient. The Court of Claims allowed the contractor to recover the higher cost of a replacement subcontractor.[127]

Owner interference may also entitle a contractor to recover extras when it is required to repair damage to its work caused by other contractors hired by the owner.[128]

---

[120] Ralph C. Nash, Jr, *supra* note 118, at 234.

[121] 323 F2d 894 (Ct Cl 1963).

[122] *Id*.

[123] Ralph C. Nash, Jr, *supra* note 118, at 235 (citing Merritt-Chapman & Scott Corp v United States, 458 F2d 42 (Ct Cl 1972)).

[124] *Id* 235.

[125] *Id* (citing Tenney Engg, Inc, ASBCA 7352, 1962 BCA ¶6189).

[126] *Id* 235.

[127] Liles Constr Co v United States, 455 F2d 527 (Ct Cl 1972).

[128] Clemente Contracting Co v State, 89 NYS2d 453 (Ct Cl 1944).

§6.18 —Defective Specifications

When specifications are defective and a contractor is ordered to perform as though the specifications are accurate, a constructive change may result. For instance, where a contractor constructed a tunnel according to specifications but the tunnel moved, splintered, and broke, the contractor was entitled to recover for the extra work and materials it provided to repair the tunnel.[129] Similarly, a constructive change results where the specifications are interpreted by the contracting officer to require work that the contractor believes is not included in the specifications and the contractor's interpretation is later found to be the reasonable one.[130]

The basic principle was perhaps best stated by the Court of Appeals in *MacKnight Flintic Stone Co v Mayor of NY*,[131] when it said that "the fault of the defendant's plan should not prevent the plaintiff from recovering payment for good work done and good materials furnished precisely as the defendant required." Some courts have held that if the faulty plan or design is the contractor's, the contractor is not entitled to compensation for correcting the work, even where the owner has approved the plan.[132]

§6.19 —Owner Nondisclosure of Technical Information

The failure of an owner to reveal relevant technical information, such as a subsurface condition or the strength of a bearing wall, may result in a constructive change. If the nondisclosure was intentional, it may constitute fraud or misrepresentation. If it was an innocent mistake but the owner contends that the information does not change the work, a constructive change may result.[133] This issue is discussed in some depth in Chapter 5 on changed conditions.

§6.20 —Overmeticulous Inspection

A constructive change might result if an owner improperly rejects the contractor's work. For instance, if an owner rejects plumbing work because of a

---

[129] McEligot v State, 246 AD 121, 284 NYS 646 (3d Dept 1936); *see also* Seglin-Harrison Constr Co v State, 267 AD 488, 46 NYS2d 602 (3d Dept), *affd*, 293 NY 782, 58 NE2d 521 (1944) (contractor laid floor pursuant to specifications; when floors cracked contractor was required to repair them; contractor recovered for repairs as extras because cracking was due to faulty specifications, not poor work).

[130] Anderson Constr Co v United States, 289 F2d 809 (Ct Cl 1961); *see also* Green v City of NY, 283 AD 485, 128 NYS2d 715 (1st Dept 1954) (city required compliance with code rather than specifications; contractor recovered its extras due to change).

[131] 160 NY 72, 84, 54 NE 661 (1899).

[132] Community Science Tech Corp, ASBCA 20244, 77-1 BCA 12,352 (1977); Dawson Constr Co, GSBCA 3685, 72-2 BCA ¶9758 (1972); Whitney Bros Plumbing & Heating, Inc, ASBCA 16876, 72-1 BCA 9448 (1972).

[133] R. Rubin, S. Guy, A. Maevis, & V. Fairweather, Construction Claims: Analysis, Presentation, Defense 38-39 (1983).

cosmetic defect which will not be visible, the owner's order to repair the cosmetic defect might be a constructive change if it is unreasonable in terms of normal trade practices. Absent a contract clause to the contrary, a contractor has a right to assume that its work must meet customary standards and that reasonable deviations are permitted; no one does perfect work. If an owner or its engineer or architect insists on compliance with more restrictive standards than are customary, a contractor may be entitled to recover compensation for the extras it incurs in making its work comply with the stricter standards imposed.[134]

Inspections by different members of an owner's team might create a constructive change. For example, a constructive change may occur if an owner inspects the work and directs correction of a defect in one way, and, later, after correction has been begun, the owner's architect directs that the correction be done differently.

§6.21 —Dictating Performance Methods

An owner's dictating to its contractor how it is to perform its work may be a constructive change. For example, a change in construction procedure was found in a case when a contractor was not allowed to simply excavate to the elevations shown on drawings but was required by the owner's engineers to excavate one or two feet at a time and to level and trim the excavation into finished form so the excavation could be inspected at each stage.[135] Similarly, a contractor was awarded damages when the state made it wait until a floor had been laid to install an underfloor duct system (thereby requiring the contractor to cut through the floors), rather than letting it install the system before the floors were laid.[136]

A constructive change may also result where the contract documents are silent on an issue and the owner or its agent directs performance different from that planned by the contractor. In one case, the contractor was to backfill an area with "suitable material." The contract did not define "suitable material" nor did the project architect make any determination of the suitability of excavated earth as fill. The contractor was awarded compensation for the extra work it performed when the owner required it to remove the excavated earth it used as backfill and replace it with porous or select fill.[137]

Constructive change may also result where the owner, project engineer, or architect misinterprets the specifications and requires the contractor to do something more or different than that specified. A project engineer or architect

---

[134] Kenneth Reed Constr Corp v United States, 475 F2d 583 (Ct Cl 1973).

[135] Luria Bros & Co v United States, 369 F2d 701 (Ct Cl 1966).

[136] Jandous Elec Equip Co v State, 158 Misc 238, 285 NYS 385 (Ct Cl 1936).

[137] Frank A. Scibetta Plumbing & Heating Corp v M&W Ltd Partnership, 90 AD2d 956, 456 NYS2d 544 (4th Dept 1982), affd, 58 NY2d 1092, 449 NE2d 742, 462 NYS2d 848 (1983).

generally has the power to interpret the contract documents;[138] a constructive change may result when it misuses that power or misinterprets the documents.[139] For instance, in a case where a project engineer interpreted the specifications and drawings to require a contractor to install reinforcing steel, the contractor was awarded the cost of purchasing and installing the steel, including overhead and profit, when the court determined that the engineer was in error.[140]

§6.22 Performance Specifications v Detailed Specifications

Performance specifications set forth the standard to which a contractor's work is held, such as requiring that the contractor provide air conditioning equipment which can maintain a 70-degree indoor temperature on a 95-degree day. *Detailed specifications* state how the contractor is to perform the work or what specific materials it is to provide, such as specifying that the contractor install a model 1 Brand X air conditioner.[141] In one federal contract, the performance specification set forth the allowed moisture content for an embankment while the detailed specifications set forth how many passes of a specified roller should have been made over the embankment; the court found that the performance specification was impossible to meet for all practical purposes, as doing so required the use of much additional equipment and time.[142]

Where the specifications are complementary there should be no problems. Where they are not, however, constructive change may result. In one case, a performance-type specification required the contractor to comply with building codes, while the detailed specifications set forth how the work was to be done. The contractor bid the job based on the work as shown in the detailed specifications, which allowed plaster board partitions, but later was required to use plaster over lath (a more expensive method) to meet state building codes. The court held that the detailed specifications took precedence over the performance specification and awarded the contractor the extra charges it incurred.[143] In a similar case, a sign maker was awarded its contract price when it made a sign consisting of 319 lamp sockets as shown on the plans, not the 359 lamp

---

[138] *See* §6.23.

[139] *See* Joseph Davis, Inc v Merritt-Chapman & Scott Corp, 27 AD2d 114, 276 NYS2d 479 (4th Dept 1967) (engineer's improper determination that specifications required the contractor to furnish piping entitled contractor to extra compensation for the cost of the pipe).

[140] Seglin-Harrison Constr Co v State, 267 AD 488, 46 NYS2d 602 (3d Dept), *affd*, 293 NY 782, 58 NE2d 521 (1944).

[141] R. Rubin, *Scope-of-Work Disputes*, in Construction Litigation, 89 (Practising Law Institute K. Cushman ed 1981).

[142] Tombigbee Constructors v United States, 420 F2d 1037 (Ct Cl 1970); R. Rubin, S. Guy, A. Maevis, & V. Fairweather, Construction Claims: Analysis, Presentation, Defense 38 (1983).

[143] *See* Green v City of NY, 283 AD 485, 128 NYS2d 715 (1st Dept 1954); *see also* MacKnight Flintic Stone Co v Mayor of NY, 160 NY 72, 54 NE 661 (1899).

sockets specified in the contract. The court held that the plans controlled because they were more specific, showing not only the number of sockets but also their exact location.[144]

§6.23 Rules of Contract Interpretation Applicable to Scope of Work Disputes

Standard rules of contract interpretation apply to construction contracts and *scope of work* disputes.[145] Those rules of particular relevance to construction law are discussed in Chapter 2. In scope of work disputes, the issue is not so much which rule of interpretation applies but who has the power to determine what the contract documents mean. Many contracts, particularly those for public works, provide that in the event of a disagreement over what the contract, plans, and specifications require, the project engineer or architect will resolve any factual disputes.[146] In most instances, the legal meaning of the contract is for the courts to determine; engineers do not have the power to construe the contract,[147] unless expressly given that power in the contract.

A contract may provide that the engineer's decision is final where it involves the "quantity or quality of materials, classification or amount of work performed, or a calculation as to a final estimate."[148] So long as its determination is free from "fraud, bad faith or palpable mistake, the decision of the [owner's] engineer is conclusive and binding upon the contractor."[149] Thus, an engineer may decide whether working with a specific type of pipe is more difficult than working with cast iron pipe,[150] whether the plans require steel reinforcement in basement walls,[151] what is meant by "standard cast iron fittings,"[152] upon what basis change order work should be paid,[153] and any other factual issues.

---

[144] American Sign Co v Rundback, 161 NYS 228 (1st Dept 1916).

[145] Frye v State, 192 Misc 260, 78 NYS2d 342 (Ct Cl 1948).

[146] *See* Borough Constr Co v City of NY, 200 NY 149, 93 NE 480, 481 (1910) ("the chief engineer of sewers shall in all cases determine the amount or the quantity of the several kinds of work . . ., all questions in relation to said work and the construction thereof, and . . . every question which may arise relative to the execution of this contract on the part of the contractor, and his estimate and decision shall be final and conclusive upon said contractor"); Ardsley Constr Co v Port Authority, 54 NY2d 876, 429 NE2d 414, 444 NYS2d 907 (1981).

[147] Joseph Davis, Inc v Merritt-Chapman & Scott Corp, 27 AD2d 114, 117, 276 NYS2d 479, 483 (4th Dept 1967).

[148] *Id* at 117-18, 276 NYS2d at 483.

[149] Tufano Contracting Corp v Port of NY Auth, 18 AD2d 1001, 238 NYS2d 607 (2d Dept), *affd mem*, 13 NY2d 848, 192 NE2d 270, 242 NYS2d 489 (1963).

[150] Joseph Davis, Inc v Merritt-Chapman & Scott Corp, 27 AD2d 114, 276 NYS2d 479, 483 (4th Dept 1967).

[151] Seglin-Harrison Constr Co v State, 267 AD 488, 46 NYS2d 602 (3d Dept), *affd*, 293 NY 782, 58 NE2d 521 (1944).

[152] Frye v State, 192 Misc 260, 78 NYS2d 342 (Ct Cl 1948).

[153] Tufano Contracting Corp v Port of NY Auth, 18 AD2d 1001, 238 NYS2d 607 (2d Dept), *affd mem*, 13 NY2d 848, 192 NE2d 270, 242 NYS2d 489 (1963).

§6.23 SCOPE OF WORK DISPUTES

An engineer may interpret the specifications; it may not construe the contract,[154] unless its powers of arbitration are unlimited.[155]

In *Thomas Crimmins Contracting Co v City of New York*,[156] the Court of Appeals held that absent an *explicit and unequivocal* agreement, a project engineer's decision is not final and binding as to legal determinations. The clause in question read:

> To prevent disputes and litigations, the Engineer shall in all cases determine the classification, amount, quality, acceptability and fitness of the several kinds of work and materials which are to be paid for under this contract, shall determine every question in relation to the Works and the construction thereof and shall determine every question which may arise relative to the fulfillment of this contract on the part of the Contractor. His determination shall be final and conclusive upon the Contractor. . . .[157]

The court found that the clause did not unequivocally and explicitly empower the engineer to decide *legal* issues, including contract construction. Its decision was further based on the historical background of the clause in New York City contracts, the presence in the contract of conditions precedent to litigation, and several clauses which discussed "engineer determinations," each in the context of factual issues.[158] The court specifically noted that it did not have to decide the issue of whether the sort of dispute resolution contemplated by the contract was "so skewed in [the city's] favor as to be unenforceable as a matter of public policy."

Where the decision is without basis[159] or is incorrect and outside the realm of the engineer's expertise,[160] the contractor may recover for extras.

> [I]f there appears no reasonable basis for the engineer's action, if it is patently erroneous, then the courts have found the equivalent of bad faith and the contractor is not bound by the engineer's decision. Similarly, the contractor is not bound by the engineer's erroneous construction of law in interpreting the contract.[161]

---

[154] Charles S. Wood & Co v Alvord & Swift, 232 AD 603, 251 NYS 35 (1st Dept 1931), *affd mem*, 258 NY 611, 180 NE 354 (1932).

[155] Maross Constr, Inc v Central NY Regional Transp Auth, 66 NY2d 341, 488 NE2d 67, 497 NYS2d 321 (1985).

[156] 74 NY2d 166, 542 NE2d 1097, 544 NYS2d 580 (1989).

[157] *Id* at 169, 542 NE2d at 1098, 544 NYS2d at 581.

[158] *Id* at 172-73, 542 NE2d at 1099-1100, 544 NYS2d at 582-83.

[159] Degnon Contracting Co v City of NY, 235 NY 481, 139 NE 580 (1923), *affg in part & revg in part*, 202 AD 390, 196 NYS 63 (1st Dept 1922).

[160] Joseph Davis, Inc v Merritt-Chapman & Scott Corp, 27 AD2d 114, 276 NYS2d 479 (4th Dept 1967).

[161] Savin Bros v State, 62 AD2d 511, 405 NYS2d 516, 519 (4th Dept 1978), *affd mem*, 47 NY2d 934, 393 NE2d 1041, 419 NYS2d 969 (1979); *see also* EH Smith Contracting Co v City of NY, 240 NY 491, 148 NE 655 (1925).

166 CHANGES/EXTRA WORK

Thus, an engineer's decision was reversed where it wrongly construed the specifications to require the contractor to furnish pipe when the contract clearly stated that the owner was to furnish all materials except welding rods and cinch anchors.[162] Similarly, where the engineer wrongly construed the contract basis of measurement, its decision was overruled by the court.[163]

Comfort should not be taken in the fact that the courts will reverse an engineer's or architect's decision if it is not supported by the contract or is clearly erroneous. The standard is a strict one; decisions which appear to be obviously improper and erroneous have been upheld. Nowhere is the strictness of the standard better seen than in *Maross Construction, Inc v Central New York Regional Transportation Authority*.[164] Maross was a contractor that entered into a contract with the Authority to construct a liquid handling system in a public bus garage. The Authority awarded separate prime contracts for other work on the project. The bid specifications required the systems contractor to supply and install tanks while certain contract documents indicated that the tanks were the responsibility of the general contractor. Maross asked for a clarification before submitting its bid and was told that the bid specifications took precedence. After winning the bid, Maross added a paragraph to the contract which stated that Maross was not responsible for the "supplying and installing of fiberglass . . . , as the drawings specifically place such responsibility with the general contractor."[165] Maross did not notify the Authority of its addition to the contract nor did it modify any other contract provisions which pertained to the same matter. After making the change, Maross signed the contract and returned it to the Authority which signed the contract without making any protests, corrections, or deletions. Not surprisingly, a dispute arose concerning responsibility for the tanks. The dispute was submitted to the project architect pursuant to a dispute resolution clause in the contract. The clause provided that the architect could decide *"all questions of any nature whatsoever"* related to the contract and that its decision would be "conclusive, final, and binding on the parties."[166] The architect reviewed evidence submitted by the parties and concluded that the systems contractor was required to supply and install the tanks.

Maross refused to comply with the architect's orders and sought a court declaration that it was not responsible for the tanks. The court, upon reviewing the contract documents, found that the contract dispute resolution clause did not limit the architect's powers to resolution of only factual questions, "but, rather, include[d] within its scope the interpretation of the legal meaning of

---

[162] Joseph Davis, Inc v Merritt-Chapman & Scott Corp, 27 AD2d 114, 276 NYS2d 479 (4th Dept 1967).

[163] Oscar Daniels Co v City of NY, 196 AD 856, 188 NYS 716 (1st Dept 1921).

[164] 66 NY2d 341, 488 NE2d 67, 497 NYS2d 321 (1985).

[165] *Id* at 343, 488 NE2d at 68, 497 NYS2d at 322.

[166] *Id* at 344, 488 NE2d at 69, 497 NYS2d at 323.

the contract."[167] Because the parties did not limit the architect's arbitral authority to factual disputes or matters which fell within its expertise, its authority was unlimited. The court also found that the architect's decision was not totally irrational. "Notwithstanding the disclaimer provision added by Maross," the architect's decision had a rational basis in the fact that Maross knew before entering its bid that it was responsible for the tanks and that the two drawings showing the opposite were erroneous.[168] It does not matter that a court would have reached a different conclusion or been bound by judicial rules of contract construction; the architect's decision need only have been rational.

This issue is further discussed in Chapter 16.

§6.24 Notice, Protest, and Record Keeping Requirements

When a contractor is directed to perform work that it believes to be extra work without a change order or adjustment of contract price or time, most contracts require the contractor to give the owner notice of the contractor's contention and that it is working under protest and to keep detailed records of the disputed work. For instance, one state contract required a contractor to give the state written notice if it believed it was ordered to perform extra work. The contractor was to continue its work and keep daily records of the labor, materials, and equipment used in the disputed work.[169] Under such a clause, a contractor cannot recover unless: it gave written notice and kept the required records;[170] the owner waived strict compliance with the clause;[171] or the change was cardinal.[172]

Generally, the form of the notice of protest is not crucial; neither is its wording. What is important is that the contractor notify *in writing* the party designated in the contract that it considers the work to be disputed or extra and is performing under protest.[173] The only exception is where the manner or form of a notice of claim is specified by law. For instance, Education Law §3813 requires that a verified notice of claim be submitted to the relevant board of education within three months of the claim's accrual. Strict compliance with

---

[167] *Id* at 347, 488 NE2d at 71, 497 NYS2d at 325.

[168] *Id*.

[169] *See* Amadeus, Inc v State, 55 Misc 2d 27, 284 NYS2d 620, 626 (Ct Cl 1967), *affd as modified*, 36 AD2d 873, 320 NYS2d 677 (3d Dept), *appeal dismissed*, 29 NY2d 634, 324 NYS2d 458 (1971); D'Angelo v State, 7 Misc 2d 783, 166 NYS2d 378, 387 (Ct Cl 1957).

[170] D'Angelo v State, 7 Misc 2d 783, 166 NYS2d 378 (Ct Cl 1957).

[171] Amadeus, Inc v State, 55 Misc 2d 27, 284 NYS2d 620 (Ct Cl 1967), *affd as modified*, 36 AD2d 873, 320 NYS2d 677 (3d Dept), *appeal dismissed*, 29 NY2d 634, 324 NYS2d 458 (1971) (dicta); see discussion regarding waiver of writing requirements at §§6.09-6.12.

[172] See discussion at §6.04.

[173] Amadeus, Inc v State, 55 Misc 2d 27, 284 NYS2d 620 (Ct Cl 1967), *affd as modified*, 36 AD2d 873, 320 NYS2d 677 (3d Dept), *appeal dismissed*, 29 NY2d 634, 324 NYS2d 458 (1971).

such statutes is required. For example, in one case, a contractor's requisition to a board's architect which included its claims for extra work did not comply with the statute.[174] Notices of claims are discussed more thoroughly in Chapter 17.

§6.25 Price Adjustments for Changed Work

When a change occurs or extra work is ordered, often the issue is not whether the contractor is entitled to compensation for that work but, rather, the measure of compensation. The price adjustment for changed work is dependent on the type of contract involved (i.e., does it provide for lump sum, unit price, cost-plus, or some other method of pricing changes) and the nature of the changed or extra work. Generally, an owner must pay for extra work required due to its actions or orders and a contractor is entitled to payment based on a computation method which "adequately and, as nearly as possible, fully compensates" the contractor for its work.[175]

Where the contract does not specifically address the means of pricing change orders but gives the engineer the power to decide issues relating to change orders, the decision of the project engineer as to how a change order should be priced is controlling in the absence of fraud, bad faith, or palpable mistake.[176] Thus, an engineer's decision that change order work would be paid for on a cost-plus basis was controlling, despite the fact that it meant less compensation than the contractor would have received under its preferred method of computation.[177] Similarly, it is for the project engineer to determine whether the extra work falls into a contract work classification—and, hence, the rate of compensation due—where the contract provides that extra work which falls into a contract work classification will be compensated at contract specified unit prices, whether or not the extra work was indicated on the plans, and that work which does not come within a contract work classification will be compensated on a cost-plus basis.[178]

Means of pricing changed work include the cost of labor and materials used plus profit and overhead percentages,[179] the contractual unit price,[180] the contractual unit price plus profit and overhead,[181] quantum meruit measurements

---

[174] Board of Educ v Bernard Assocs No 3, 230 NYS2d 509 (Westchester 1962).

[175] AE Ottaviano, Inc v State, 202 Misc 532, 110 NYS2d 99 (Ct Cl 1952).

[176] Tufano Contracting Corp v Port of NY Auth, 18 AD2d 1001, 238 NYS2d 607 (2d Dept), *affd mem*, 13 NY2d 848, 192 NE2d 270, 242 NYS2d 489 (1963).

[177] *Id.*

[178] *See* EH Smith Contracting Co v City of NY, 240 NY 491, 148 NE 655 (1925).

[179] Seglin-Harrison Constr Co v State, 267 AD 488, 46 NYS2d 602 (3d Dept), *affd*, 293 NY 782, 58 NE2d 521 (1944).

[180] Camarco Contractors, Inc v State, 33 AD2d 717, 305 NYS2d 207 (3d Dept 1969), *modified on other grounds*, 28 NY2d 948, 271 NE2d 917, 323 NYS2d 434 (1971). *See* §6.33.

[181] LG DeFelice & Son v State, 63 Misc 2d 357, 313 NYS2d 21 (Ct Cl 1970).

if a cardinal change has occurred,[182] lost profits on deleted work,[183] lost profits due to extra work,[184] and cost plus impact costs.[185]

The American Institute of Architects (AIA) contract forms, federal contracts, and many other contracts provide that changes shall result in an "equitable adjustment" of the contract price. An equitable adjustment may be an increase or decrease. It is intended to "keep a contractor whole when the [owner] modifies a contract."[186] It is not intended to provide a windfall for either the owner or the contractor. The general measure is not the value of work received by the owner but "must be more closely related to and contingent upon the altered position in which the contractor finds himself by reason of the modification," i.e., the reasonable cost.[187] Reasonable cost may be the actual cost, the fair market value, or the historical cost, but is more often determined through an objective test. Elements used to determine reasonable cost include the contractor's situation at the time the cost was incurred, the exercise of the contractor's business judgment, and the contractor's costs. There is a presumption that actual costs paid are reasonable. The presumption must be overcome by the party which alleges that actual cost is unreasonable.[188]

§6.26 —Pricing Change-Related Costs

If unit prices are not applicable to the changed work, it is best for the parties to agree on a firm price for the change *before* the work is begun. Each side should estimate the cost of the change and negotiate any difference, with each thoroughly analyzing the other's estimate in good faith. The agreed pricing method may be lump sum, unit price, cost-plus, guaranteed maximum, or any other arrangement upon which the parties are able to agree.

Impact costs must also be considered. If the change will disrupt the contractor's other work on the project or significantly delay the work, these problems should be addressed and appropriate compensation made. A contractor should not look to make an unexpected windfall, but neither should an owner fail to consider the real and total cost of the change. If the parties cannot agree on the impact costs or, due to the emergency nature of the change, do not have time to fully consider them, the change order should specifically state that the issues of impact costs and adjustment of contract time are reserved for later

---

[182] Kole v Brown, 13 AD2d 920, 215 NYS2d 876 (1st Dept 1961); C. Norman Peterson Co v Container Corp of Am, 172 Cal App 3d 628, 218 Cal Rptr 592 (1985).

[183] McMaster v State, 108 NY 542, 15 NE 417 (1888); Dunbar & Sullivan Dredging Co v State, 34 NYS2d 850 (Ct Cl 1942), *after remand from* 259 AD 440, 20 NYS2d 127 (4th Dept 1940), *revg* 34 NYS2d 848 (Ct Cl 1939); AE Ottaviano, Inc v State, 202 Misc 532, 110 NYS2d 99 (Ct Cl 1952).

[184] Whitmyer Bros v State, 63 AD2d 103, 406 NYS2d 617 (3d Dept 1978), *affd,* 47 NY2d 960, 393 NE2d 1027, 419 NYS2d 954 (1979).

[185] See discussion at §6.29.

[186] Bruce Constr Corp v United States, 324 F2d 516, 518 (Ct Cl 1963).

[187] *Id.*

[188] *Id.*

determination and that the contractor does not waive its right to claim them. If the parties agree that impact costs are not appropriate or that the agreed-upon price is to be full compensation for the change, the change order should specifically state that it represents full compensation for all costs arising out of or in connection with the change, including delay, disruption, and impact costs.

§6.27 —Unit Price

In a unit price contract, the changes clause may provide that additional work will be compensated at the contractual unit price. In one contract, it was provided that excavation below a certain number of units would be compensated at one price and excavation above a certain number of units would be compensated at another.[189] Generally, in a unit price contract, the contractor is not entitled to more compensation than the contractual unit price for extra work unless the contractor can show bad faith or concealment of relevant information by the owner.[190] Where, however, the increase in quantities of materials is not simply a numerical increase in materials required under the contract, unit prices do not apply. As the Court of Appeals put it:

> It is perfectly true that steel is steel. But it is also true that when it is to be used in a manner totally different from that originally proposed on the basis of which bids were made and necessarily costing far more per ton, it may not reasonably, fairly, and in good faith be classified as similar.[191]

Similarly, where the increase or decrease is so large as to be more accurately characterized as *qualitative* rather than *quantitative*, contractual unit prices may not apply.

Quantitative v Qualitative Change

Generally, if a contractor's sole basis for requesting a higher unit price is that the amount of work is greater or less than that anticipated, the contractor may not recover—it is held to have assumed the risk of a variance in quantity.[192] Similarly, an owner may be held to a unit price if it contends that it is entitled

---

[189] Depot Constr Corp v State, 19 NY2d 109, 224 NE2d 866, 278 NYS2d 363 (1967) (lump sum contract with unit prices for excavation less than or greater than specification estimate).

[190] Yonkers Contracting Co v New York State Thruway Auth, 25 AD2d 811, 270 NYS2d 16 (4th Dept 1966), *affd*, 23 NY2d 856, 245 NE2d 800, 298 NYS2d 67 (1969).

[191] EH Smith Contracting Co v City of NY, 240 NY 491, 148 NE 655, 659 (1925).

[192] 10 NY Jur §284 (1960); Depot Constr Corp v State, 19 NY2d 109, 224 NE2d 866, 278 NYS2d 363 (1967).

§6.27 UNIT PRICE

to a lesser unit price due to an increase in quantity.[193] If the change is *qualitative*, and not merely *quantitative*, however, the contractor may be entitled to compensation calculated differently. "If a mere quantitative change is involved the contract provisions would apply. . . . On the other hand, if there is a qualitative change the [contractor] would be entitled to compensation for the extra work on a quantum meruit basis."[194] The distinction is based upon the court's opinion that "it would be inequitable to confine the bidder to a unit bid made to meet entirely different conditions."[195]

As the Appellate Division pointed out in *Tufano Contracting Corp v State*, in one sense, a change in quantity in a unit price contract is "simply a quantitative increase over the number of [units] envisioned at the time of contracting"; where, however, "the additional involvement was not originally contemplated by the parties[,]" a qualitative change may result.[196] In *Tufano*, the contract called for the construction of 28 temporary road detours; 123 to 128 detours were actually constructed. The court held that an increase this great was not within the parties' contemplation and was qualitative, entitling the contractor to recover on a quantum meruit basis, not on the contractual unit price. The quantum meruit recovery applied only to the extra work, not to the 28 detours contemplated in the contract; those were compensated at the contractual unit price.

To determine whether a change is quantitative or qualitative, a close analysis of the contract and specific factual situation involved is necessary. A simple review of applicable cases can be misleading and confusing. For instance, it has been held that a 400 per cent increase in the amount of topsoil to be provided was a qualitative change, entitling the contractor to profit and overhead on top of its unit price,[197] while a 1300 per cent increase in the amount of grout provided was not, meaning that the contractor was paid its unit price for the additional grout.[198]

There are some determining factors which, *generally*, apply when analyzing whether a quantitative or qualitative change has occurred. *First*, if the contract specifically discusses different unit prices for different quantities of work or materials, the contractor will probably be held to the prescribed unit price. In *Depot Construction Corp v State*,[199] the contractor agreed to excavate a given quantity of work for a lump sum. Any excess or shortage was to be paid on

---

[193] DeFoe Constr Corp v Beame, 75 Misc 2d 309, 347 NYS2d 626 (NY 1973); *see also* Kingsley v City of Brooklyn, 78 NY 200 (1879) (owner not entitled to reduction in contract price where contractor drove piles to a shallower depth than required at direction of owner).

[194] Depot Constr Corp v State, 23 AD2d 707, 708, 257 NYS2d 230 (3d Dept 1965), *affd*, 19 NY2d 109, 224 NE2d 866, 278 NYS2d 363 (1967).

[195] Foundation Co v State, 233 NY 177, 135 NE 236, 239 (1922).

[196] Tufano Contracting Co v State, 25 AD2d 329, 269 NYS2d 564, 566 (3d Dept 1966), *affd*, 26 NY2d 823, 257 NE2d 901, 309 NYS2d 355 (1970).

[197] LG DeFelice & Son v State, 63 Misc 2d 357, 313 NYS2d 21 (Ct Cl 1970).

[198] DeFoe Constr Corp v Beame, 75 Misc 2d 309, 347 NYS2d 626 (NY 1973).

[199] 19 NY2d 109, 224 NE2d 866, 278 NYS2d 363 (1967).

172 CHANGES/EXTRA WORK

a per-cubic-yard basis—excavation over 600 cubic yards was to be paid for at $22 per cubic yard. The total excavation was 2,982 cubic yards, almost 5 times the contract estimate. The Court of Appeals held that the contract placed the risk of the quantity on the contractor and limited the contractor's recovery to the unit price. Similarly, where a contract provided that a change in quantity would not result in a change of unit price, the contractor was not entitled to lost profits or a higher unit price when the amount of sheathing was reduced.[200] *Second,* if the change in quantity was due to an honest error by the owner, it is more probable that the change will be considered quantitative.[201] *Third,* to be qualitative, the increase or decrease must be very large, although a large change may merely be quantitative.[202] For instance, an 11 per cent change is quantitative,[203] while a 400 per cent increase *may* be qualitative.[204] *Finally,* a change of method is usually a qualitative change. For example, if the depth of excavation is increased, and that increase requires the contractor to blast rather than mechanically dig, a qualitative change may result.

§6.28 —Cost Reimbursement Contracts

In most cost reimbursement contracts, including cost-plus contracts, the measure of compensation for changed work is no different than the contract measure. That is, if the contract provides for the contractor to be paid its actual cost plus 10 per cent overhead and 5 per cent profit for contract work, changed work generally is compensated in the same manner.[205]

In a unit price or lump sum contract, changes may be priced in a cost reimbursement manner. The contractor recovers its actual costs plus an agreed percentage for profit and overhead. Sometimes it is difficult to allocate accurately the cost of a change or an extra which is inextricably interwoven with contract work. For example, suppose the contract provides for two-wire light switches

---

[200] Camarco Contractors, Inc v State, 33 AD2d 717, 305 NYS2d 207 (3d Dept 1969), *modified on other grounds,* 28 NY2d 948, 271 NE2d 917, 323 NYS2d 434 (1971); *see also* Leary v City of NY, 222 NY 337, 118 NE 849 (1918) (actual rock excavation was 2,200 or 2,400 cubic yards, estimate was 1,800); Farub Found Corp v City of NY, 138 Misc 636, 49 NYS2d 922 (NY 1944) (city used 13% of materials it estimated would be needed resulting in greatly increased unit price; contractor held to contract unit price).

[201] *See* Yonkers Contracting Co v New York State Thruway Auth, 25 AD2d 811, 270 NYS2d 16 (4th Dept 1966), *affd,* 23 NY2d 856, 245 NE2d 800, 298 NYS2d 67 (1969) (actual excavation 11% more than estimate); EG DeLia & Sons Constr Corp v State, 1 AD2d 732, 146 NYS2d 757 (3d Dept 1955) (state estimated 4,850 feet of piling would be used; over 2,000 feet left at end of job); Farub Found Corp v City of NY, 138 Misc 636, 49 NYS2d 922 (NY 1944) (city used 13% of materials it estimated it would need).

[202] *See* Seebold v Halmar Constr Corp, 146 AD2d 886, 536 NYS2d 871 (3d Dept 1989) (unit price applied where subcontractor raked almost 90,000 yards of topsoil on contract which estimated 4,620 yards).

[203] Yonkers Contracting Co v New York State Thruway Auth, 25 AD2d 811, 270 NYS2d 16 (4th Dept 1966), *affd,* 23 NY2d 856, 245 NE2d 800, 298 NYS2d 67 (1969).

[204] LG DeFelice & Son v State, 63 Misc 2d 357, 313 NYS2d 21 (Ct Cl 1970).

[205] EH Smith Contracting Co v City of NY, 240 NY 491, 148 NE 655, 656 (1925).

and the owner changes the switches to three-way before any work is done on the switches. How much does the small amount of extra wire cost? How much extra time does it take to wire a switch as a three-way rather than as a two-way? For this reason, cost-plus pricing of change orders may not be advisable. If the parties do not intend the overhead and profit percentages to cover impact costs, they should specifically provide so and the contractor should reserve the right to claim impact costs.

§6.29 —Impact Costs[206]

When a change occurs, the parties may be affected beyond the cost of making the change. *Impact costs* are the additional costs or damages incurred in performing the unchanged items of the contract that were affected by the change. These may include delay damages, loss of productivity, increased materials costs, increased labor costs, etc. For instance, if an owner orders that the excavation area be enlarged, thereby postponing the time when the contractor can begin pouring the foundation until winter weather and cold conditions interfere with its concrete work, the contractor's increased costs to pour the foundation would be impact costs.

Most owners prefer that a change order state that it is in full compensation for *all costs due to, arising out of, or in relation to* the change and that any additional claims are released, thereby absolving the owner of liability for impact costs. Most contractors, however, prefer that the change order state that it does not include allowance for impact costs and that any such claims are *specifically reserved*. Obviously, compromise typically is needed. Perhaps the best way to avoid work stoppage due to a pricing disagreement is for the contractor to specifically reserve its right to claim impact costs after the job is complete, for the parties to agree on what records the contractor will keep to document impact costs, and for the owner to agree, at least in principle, to objectively review those records. Proving impact costs can be difficult; thorough records are essential.[207]

> **PRACTICE POINTER:**
>
> To substantiate a claim for impact costs, it is suggested that contractors keep thorough records including daily reports, time cards, materials invoices, diaries, and field reports. The daily reports should be verified by the project engineer or owner on a daily basis.

Where changed work requires a contractor to complete a part of its contract

---

[206] Impact costs and damages are more fully discussed in **ch 7**.

[207] *See* Hart, *The Ripple Effect: Proving Contractor's Losses*, 3 Litig 12 (1976); Wickwire, Hurlbut, & Lerman, *Use of Critical Path Method Techniques in Contract Claims: Issues and Developments, 1974 to 1988*, 18 Pub Cont LJ 338 (1989); Wickwire & Smith, *The Use of Critical Path Method Techniques in Contract Claims*, 7 Pub Cont LJ 1 (1974).

out of sequence, reducing normal efficiency, it may be entitled to recover its increased performance costs.[208] Similarly, where the changes significantly delay the contractor's work, a contractor may be able to recover its delay damages.[209]

In federal cases, prior to the adoption of Form 23A, the government contract provision allowing for an "equitable adjustment" of the contract price due to changes was not considered broad enough to include delay or other consequential damages.[210] More recent cases, based on the current federal form, have allowed recovery of delay damages[211] due to changed work, including home office overhead[212] and loss of labor force productivity.[213]

§6.30 —Proving Costs

When forced to prove costs due to changed work, either informally to the owner or engineer or formally in a court, the more complete a contractor's records are, the better chance it has of recovering its actual costs. Extra costs cannot be proven merely by comparing the bid to the job's actual costs.[214] Records must be maintained while the job is in progress. It is difficult, if not impossible, to accurately reconstruct and allocate labor usage, down time, supervision, and miscellaneous supply usage several months or years after a job or change order is completed. To prove not only the direct costs of the change but the impact costs as well, separate daily records should be maintained of disputed work, including labor, materials, equipment, and supplies used. The records should be countersigned by the contractor and owner or its engineer on a daily basis. Project supervisors should maintain diaries that specify what work was done when, oral directions received, the impact of changed work on contract work, labor allocation, etc. Keeping photographs of changed conditions or extra work and before-and-after pictures can be an excellent way to document the true nature and extent of the disputed work performed.

§6.31 Exculpatory Clauses

The effectiveness of various exculpatory clauses is discussed in Chapters 5 and 7. Exculpatory clauses of particular relevance to changes and extras are contractual requirements that an order for an extra be in writing (discussed at §§6.08-6.12) and that daily records be maintained in order for there to be

---

[208] AE Ottaviano, Inc v State, 202 Misc 532, 110 NYS2d 99 (Ct Cl 1952); Coley Props Corp, PSBCA 291, 75-2 BCA ¶11,514 (1975).

[209] Westcott v State, 264 AD 463, 36 NYS2d 23 (3d Dept 1942).

[210] United States v Rice, 317 US 61, 63 S Ct 120, 87 L Ed 53 (1942).

[211] Anderson Constr Co v United States, 289 F2d 809 (Ct Cl 1961).

[212] Luria Bros & Co v United States, 369 F2d 701 (Ct Cl 1966); Anderson Constr Co v United States, 289 F2d 809 (Ct Cl 1961).

[213] Luria Bros & Co v United States, 369 F2d 701 (Ct Cl 1966).

[214] Novak & Co v Facilities Dev Corp, 116 AD2d 891, 498 NYS2d 492 (1986).

recovery (discussed at §6.24), and those relating to performing work under protest (discussed at §§6.13, 6.14, and 6.24).

§6.32 Claims Preservation and Defense

A contractor can have the most clear-cut case of an extra which entitles it to compensation but lose its right to that compensation if it has not preserved its right to make a claim. Contractual notice provisions must be strictly adhered to; releases and waivers of claims must be carefully read and tailored so they release only what the contractor intends them to release; claims must be timely filed, with the proper entity, and contain the proper information; final payment must not be accepted if a claim is still outstanding. The potential pitfalls are numerous and easily catch an unwary contractor and its attorney.

It is not unusual for an owner to require that a contractor waive its claim for damages in exchange for an extension of time to complete the contract. If a contractor executes such an agreement without specifically exempting its claims for extras, those claims will be forfeited.[215] Obviously, if a contractor executes a release that specifically mentions but does not reserve change orders on which the contractor intends to make further claim, the contractor will be held to its release regardless of the merit of its claim for additional compensation.[216]

Many private contracts include notice of claim requirements and specify when notice must be given and to whom. A failure to follow contractual notice provisions can be fatal to a claim for extra compensation. In public works, there may be statutory, in addition to contractual, notice requirements. For instance, Education Law §3813 details to whom, in what form, and when any claim for damages must be made. A failure to fully and strictly comply with its provisions will defeat the great majority of claims for extras.[217] In rare instances, it has been found that statutory notice provisions were waived. For instance, a contractor's failure to file a timely claim for extras with a school board was not fatal where the project architect assured the contractor that the board had misinterpreted the contract and that it would be paid, asked the contractor to stay and complete its contract, and said that it would issue one blanket change order to cover all excess excavation. After the job was completed the board refused to pay for the extra excavation. The court found a waiver of statutory notice requirements based on the architect's conduct, the contractor's reliance, and the fact that the contract specifically gave the architect the authority to interpret the contract and decide disputes and made the architect the board's representa-

---

[215] EM Substructures, Inc v City of NY, 73 AD2d 608, 422 NYS2d 444 (2d Dept 1979), *appeal dismissed*, 49 NY2d 878, 405 NE2d 233, 427 NYS2d 990 (1980).

[216] Najjar Indus v City of NY, 86 AD2d 573, 446 NYS2d 302 (1st Dept), *affd*, 57 NY2d 647, 439 NE2d 874, 454 NYS2d 65 (1982).

[217] Central School Dist No 1 v Double M Constr Corp, 41 AD2d 771, 341 NYS2d 905 (2d Dept 1973), *affd mem*, 34 NY2d 695, 312 NE2d 479, 356 NYS2d 296 (1974); *In re* Board of Educ, 226 NYS2d 300 (Westchester 1962).

tive.[218] This case is the exception, not the rule. Notice of claim issues are more fully discussed in Chapter 17.

§6.33 —Accord and Satisfaction

One of the most frequent ways that a changed work claim is lost is through the doctrine of accord and satisfaction. Acceptance of "final payment" may operate as a release of claims for extras, even if it clearly is not the contractor's intention to release its claims.[219] If the contract specifies that acceptance of final payment operates as a release of the owner from all liability, the contractor's acceptance of the final payment will have that effect. Its attempts to accept the final payment while unilaterally reserving the right to claim for extras will be ineffective, even if the owner knew of the contractor's claim before it issued the final payment.[220] Under such a clause, a separate general release is unnecessary.[221]

However, there is some statutory authority to the contrary. Specifically, under a state contract,

> [n]o provision contained in a construction contract awarded by any state department or agency shall bar the commencement of any action for breach of contract on the sole ground of the contractor's acceptance of final payment . . . provided that a detailed and verified statement of claim is served upon the public body not later than forty days after the mailing of such final payment.[222]

Therefore, in some specified areas, the legislature has preserved the contractor's right to claim for extras after accepting final payment, even if an express provision of the contract makes acceptance of final payment a release of all claims.

In the absence of a clause making acceptance of final payment a release, a contractor may cash a check designated as final or full while still preserving its rights to make claims for extra compensation by noting in its check endorsement that the check is cashed "under protest" or other words to that effect which show an explicit reservation of the right to make further claim against the payor.[223]

Generally, contractual release provisions may not be waived by anyone except the owner or authorizing entity. For example, neither a comptroller's

---

[218] Welsch v Gindell & Johnson, 50 AD2d 971, 376 NYS2d 661 (3d Dept 1975).

[219] Buffalo Elec Co v State, 14 NY2d 453, 201 NE2d 869, 253 NYS2d 537 (1964).

[220] Id.

[221] Oakhill Contracting Co v City of NY, 262 AD 530, 30 NYS2d 567 (1st Dept 1941).

[222] NY State Fin Law §145 (McKinney 1989).

[223] See Horn Waterproofing Corp v Bushwick Iron & Steel Co, 66 NY2d 321, 488 NE2d 56, 497 NYS2d 310 (1985), in which the Court of Appeals held that the provisions of UCC §1-207 apply to acceptance of any check for contract debt regardless of whether the contract was for the sale of goods.

§6.33 ACCORD & SATISFACTION

clerk nor the comptroller itself has the power to waive a final payment release provision and a contractor cannot claim that it accepted a final payment in reliance on one of their statements that a unilateral reservation would be effective.[224] Similarly, it has been found that it was of no effect that a transit authority resolution called a comptroller's attention to a contractor's claim for extras where the transit authority did not have the power to modify a city contract and did not approve the claim but merely drew the comptroller's attention to it.[225]

While a unilateral reservation of claims by a contractor is ineffective, an agreement between the contractor and owner reserving claims will avoid operation of a final payment clause. For instance, an acceptance of final payment clause was not applicable in a case where the parties, following months of negotiations, jointly executed a "final" agreement after the contract was performed which provided for payment of all uncontested sums to the contractor and specifically stated that it was "without prejudice to the [contractor's claim] for additional payments" for work and materials in the amount of $40,000, which claim was specifically reserved by the contractor. The reservation was effective because it was not unilateral and was executed by proper representatives of the state owner.[226]

Typically, the cashing of a final payment check is acceptance of final payment. If, however, the contractor can show that it did not intend to accept final payment and that deposit of the check was in error, and promptly attempts to return the final payment, its claim for extras will not be barred. Thus, in *Dalrymple Gravel & Contracting Co v State*,[227] the court found that there was not an acceptance of final payment where: the contractor notified the state of its claim for extras, which the state denied; the contractor refused to sign and returned to the state the "final agreement" drafted by the state which set forth the state's view of the final amount due; the state sent the contractor a check for the amount the state claimed was due without any accompanying letter or notation that specified it was a final payment, the name of the job, or a job number; the check was endorsed with a rubber stamp by a clerical employee and was deposited; the contractor sent the state a certified check 13 days later in the amount of the state's check, which the state returned. The court found that the deposit of the check was a "simple mistake" and not acceptance of final payment.[228] Of particular importance was the contractor's promptness in returning the check. In a similar case, a contractor tried to assert a claim for extras following its assignee's acceptance of a final payment check. Its claim was unsuccessful—despite the fact that neither the state nor the assignee noti-

---

[224] Oakhill Contracting Co v City of NY, 262 AD 530, 30 NYS2d 567 (1st Dept 1941).
[225] Brandt Corp v City of NY, 14 NY2d 217, 199 NE2d 493, 250 NYS2d 407 (1964).
[226] Poirier & McLane Corp v State, 13 Misc 2d 858, 178 NYS2d 925 (Ct Cl 1958).
[227] 23 AD2d 418, 261 NYS2d 566 (3d Dept 1965), *affd mem*, 19 NY2d 644, 225 NE2d 210, 278 NYS2d 616 (1967).
[228] *Id*.

178 CHANGES/EXTRA WORK

fied the contractor of the payment—in part because the contractor waited 6 months to make its claim.[229]

Acceptance of a "final payment" check which is less than the amount certified by the appropriate authority will not operate as a release or an accord and satisfaction. In public projects, this is especially true where acts of the comptroller show that the payment was not intended to be final.[230] In a case where the project engineer certified that the contractor was owed $72,760.16, but the comptroller issued a check for $71,000, the contractor could accept this partial payment of the final payment without releasing its claims for extras above and beyond the balance of the certified amount not paid.[231]

Acceptance of payment tendered following a partial summary judgment is not acceptance of a final payment which would release an owner from a contractor's claims for extras.[232]

§6.34 Remedies

Generally, to be entitled to recover for extras, a contractor must have substantially performed its contract.[233] It may sue for extras under the contract, for breach of contract, or in quantum meruit, depending upon the work done and the contract.[234]

Changed work is compensated according to the contract or in quantum meruit. Quantum meruit is available only if the contract has been repudiated, abandoned, or waived.[235] This is not to say that the measure of damages available under the contract or for breach of contract may not appropriately be a quantum meruit measure,[236] but that the contractor's theory of recovery cannot be based in quantum meruit unless the contract is not applicable. Further, if the extra work was so outside the contract as to exceed it (i.e., a cardinal change occurred) and no new contract was made, the contractor must make its claim in quantum meruit; it may not recover in contract.[237]

---

[229] L. Rosenman Corp v State, 32 AD2d 603, 299 NYS2d 652 (3d Dept 1969).

[230] Bronx Asphalt Corp v City of NY, 35 NYS2d 7 (App Term 1942).

[231] Oscar Daniels Co v City of NY, 196 AD 856, 188 NYS 716 (1st Dept 1921).

[232] Tufano Contracting Corp v Port of NY Auth, 33 Misc 2d 1028, 227 NYS2d 707 (Queens 1962), *affd*, 18 AD2d 832, 237 NYS2d 562 (2d Dept 1963); *see also* D'Angelo v State, 7 Misc 2d 783, 166 NYS2d 378 (Ct Cl 1957) (contractor's acceptance of admitted balance owed while judicially pursuing its claims for extra compensation did not release state).

[233] Turk v Look, 53 AD2d 709, 383 NYS2d 937 (3d Dept 1976).

[234] Gearty v Mayor of NY, 171 NY 61, 63 NE 804 (1902); Borough Constr Co v City of NY, 200 NY 149, 93 NE 480 (1910); see discussion regarding additional versus extra work at §6.01.

[235] LA Rose v Backer, 11 AD2d 314, 203 NYS2d 740 (3d Dept), *judgment amount modified*, 11 AD2d 969, 207 NYS2d 258 (3d Dept 1960), *affd*, 11 NY2d 760, 226 NYS2d 695 (1962).

[236] Savin Bros v State, 62 AD2d 511, 405 NYS2d 516 (4th Dept 1978), *affd mem*, 47 NY2d 934, 393 NE2d 1041, 419 NYS2d 969 (1979).

[237] Kole v Brown, 13 AD2d 920, 215 NYS2d 876 (1st Dept 1961).

Before a contractor may file suit upon its claim for extras, its claim must be ripe. If the contract provides a procedure through which claims for extras are evaluated, the contractor must follow that procedure; for example, if the contract provides for a review and determination by the project engineer, the contractor must await the engineer's determination before its claim is ripe.[238]

---

[238] Sturdy Concrete Corp v Nab Constr Corp, 65 AD2d 262, 411 NYS2d 637 (2d Dept 1978), *appeal dismissed,* 46 NY2d 938, 388 NE2d 349, 415 NYS2d 212 (1979).

Delays 7

§7.01 Introduction
§7.02 Determining Delay
§7.03 Time-Money Relationship
§7.04 Scheduling Procedures/Progress Schedules
§7.05 Delay and Disruption Causes
§7.06 Types of Delay
§7.07 Excusable Delay
§7.08 —Acts of God/Force Majeure
§7.09 —Strikes and Labor Disputes
§7.10 —Owner-Caused
§7.11 —Sovereign and Other Acts That Interfere with Construction
§7.12 —Subcontractor's and Supplier's Delays
§7.13 Relevant Contract Clauses
§7.14 —Federal Contracts
§7.15 —State and Local Contracts
§7.16 —Commercial Practice
§7.17 Notice Requirements
§7.18 —Time of Notice
§7.19 —Content
§7.20 Effect of Excuse
§7.21 Noncompensable Delays
§7.22 Compensable Delay
§7.23 —Owner Interference
§7.24 —Denial of Access
§7.25 —Delayed Notice to Proceed
§7.26 —Delays in Inspection/Approval
§7.27 —Defective Design
§7.28 —Contract Changes and Extras

§7.29	—Changed Conditions
§7.30	Nonexcusable Delay
§7.31	Concurrent Delay
§7.32	*No Damage for Delay* Provisions
§7.33	Enforceability of *No Damage for Delay* Clauses
§7.34	General v Specific *No Damage for Delay* Clauses
§7.35	Some Typical *No Damage for Delay* Clauses
§7.36	Exceptions to Enforcement of *No Damage for Delay* Clauses
§7.37	—Uncontemplated Delay
§7.38	—Active Interference
§7.39	—Unreasonable Delay and Abandonment
§7.40	—Willful or Gross Negligence
§7.41	—Fraud or Bad Faith
§7.42	—Breach of Contract
§7.43	Disruption/Interference
§7.44	Acceleration
§7.45	—Actual Acceleration
§7.46	—Constructive Acceleration
§7.47	—Right to Relief
§7.48	Remedies
§7.49	Burden of Proof
§7.50	Apportionment of Responsibility for Delay
§7.51	Waiver
§7.52	Contractor's Damages for Delay
§7.53	—Labor Escalation
§7.54	—Material Escalation
§7.55	—Loss of Productivity
§7.56	—Procurement Costs
§7.57	—Impact Costs
§7.58	—Field Overhead
§7.59	—Idle Equipment
§7.60	—Home Office Overhead
§7.61	—Financing Costs
§7.62	—Inability to Take On Other Work
§7.63	—Profit
§7.64	—Interest
§7.65	Contractor Damage Recovery
§7.66	Contractor's Other Remedies
§7.67	Owner's Damages for Delay
§7.68	—Actual Damages
§7.69	—Loss of Use
§7.70	—Interest
§7.71	—Professional Fees

§7.72　Liquidated Damages
§7.73　Owner's Other Remedies

§7.01　Introduction

Delays are common in construction; as common as extras and change orders. Rare is the construction project that is complete by the date specified in the contract. Thus, delay damage claims are frequently made by contractors, subcontractors, and owners. A party claims delay damages when the project is not complete at the time expected. The cause of the delay can be many different things—an unusually cold winter, lack of site access, poor planning, a limited labor pool, owner interference; etc. Regardless of the reason for the delay, its effect is the same—increased costs for all parties involved. The cause of the delay is important in determining who, if anyone, is entitled to damages and the measure of those damages.

Typically, a suit for delay damages is a claim of breach of contract. This basic fact can be difficult to recognize because of the many causes of delay and results. Delay can be caused by negligence, intentional wrongdoing, misrepresentation, etc., each of which could be a theory for relief if the basic action did not sound in contract. It is also easy to confuse delay claims with claims for extras and changes, since, often, extras and changes are what lead to delay. For example, if an owner makes so many changes in the plans and specifications that the project is delayed, the contractor may be entitled to the direct cost of those changes as well as its consequential damages due to the delay, such as increased materials and overhead costs.

This chapter discusses delays—their causes, consequences, and costs. Changed conditions are discussed in Chapter 5; changes and extras are discussed in Chapter 6.

§7.02　Determining Delay

To determine whether a project has been delayed, it must first be established whether time was *of the essence* to the contract. If a contract does not specify a completion date, time is not of the essence and a reasonable time for completion is implied.[1] What is reasonable depends on the contract subject matter, the parties' intention, the parties' contemplation at the time the contract was entered into, and the circumstances surrounding performance.[2]

Simply designating a date upon which the contract is to be completed does not *necessarily* make time of the essence.[3] For instance, a contract that stated that the work would be done "on or about" March 1, 1960, but did not state that time was of the essence, was not automatically considered a contract in

---

[1] Young v Whitney, 111 AD2d 1013, 490 NYS2d 330 (3d Dept 1985).

[2] *Id;* Lake Steel Erection, Inc v Egan, 61 AD2d 1125, 403 NYS2d 387 (4th Dept), *appeal dismissed,* 44 NY2d 848, 378 NE2d 124, 406 NYS2d 761 (1978).

[3] Ring 57 Corp v Litt, 28 AD2d 548, 280 NYS2d 330 (2d Dept 1967).

which time was of the essence; a court must look at the parties' actions to determine whether they intended time to be of the essence.[4] Acquiescence in delays and giving a party repeated opportunities to perform can result in a waiver of time as being of the essence to the contract. To reestablish time as of the essence, a party must demand performance by a "clear, distinct, and unequivocal" notice fixing a reasonable time for performance.[5]

Time provisions are also affected if one party causes the other's performance to be delayed. For instance, if the contractor performs extra work at the owner's request and that extra work delays completion, the owner cannot claim delay damages from the contractor.[6] In such a case, time for completion is extended a reasonable time to allow for completion of the additional work. Similarly, a party cannot insist on strict performance as to time when it has not itself strictly complied with time provisions.[7] Thus, "[a] failure on the part of the party demanding performance to do the preliminary work required in order to enable the other party to complete its obligations within the time limit operates as a waiver of the time provision in the contract."[8]

Just because a project is completed on time or early does not mean that there could not have been compensable delay. For instance, in *Grow Construction Co v State*,[9] the contractor finished its work more than nine months early. The court allowed the contractor to recover delay damages based on its finding that *but for* state interference, the contractor would have finished even earlier and at less cost to the contractor. Similarly, in another case, a contractor that completed the contract work on time was allowed to recover delay damages when it proved that it would have completed the contract ahead of schedule if not for the state's delay in the initial stages of the contract.[10]

Since a claim cannot accrue until damages are ascertainable, a determination of whether a delay claim exists cannot be made until completion. Unless the

---

[4] Tupper v Wade Lupe Constr Co, 39 Misc 2d 1053, 242 NYS2d 546 (Schenectady 1963).

[5] Ring 57 Corp v Litt, 28 AD2d 548, 280 NYS2d 330 (2d Dept 1967).

[6] Janowitz Bros Venture v 25-30 120th St Queens Corp, 75 AD2d 203, 429 NYS2d 215 (2d Dept 1980).

[7] Fifty States Management Corp v Niagara Permanent Sav & Loan Assn, 58 AD2d 177, 396 NYS2d 925 (4th Dept 1977).

[8] Staten Island Supply Co v Beverly-Glenwood Richmond Corp, 96 AD2d 553, 465 NYS2d 232 (2d Dept 1983); Fifty States Management Corp v Niagara Permanent Sav & Loan Assn, 58 AD2d 177, 396 NYS2d 925, 928 (4th Dept 1977).

[9] 56 AD2d 95, 391 NYS2d 726 (1977); *see also* D'Angelo v State, 41 AD2d 77, 341 NYS2d 84 (3d Dept), *appeal dismissed*, 32 NY2d 896, 300 NE2d 155, 346 NYS2d 814 (1973), *order modified*, 34 NY2d 641, 311 NE2d 509, 355 NYS2d 377 (1974); Shore Bridge Corp v State, 186 Misc 1005, 61 NYS2d 32 (Ct Cl), *affd*, 271 AD 811, 66 NYS2d 921 (1946).

[10] D'Angelo v State, 41 AD2d 77, 341 NYS2d 84 (3d Dept), *appeal dismissed*, 32 NY2d 896, 300 NE2d 155, 346 NYS2d 814 (1973), *modified*, 34 NY2d 641, 311 NE2d 509, 355 NYS2d 377 (1974); Shore Bridge Corp v State, 186 Misc 1005, 61 NYS2d 32 (Ct Cl), *affd*, 271 AD 811, 66 NYS2d 921 (1946).

contract provides otherwise, this determination is based on *substantial*, not total, completion.[11]

Of course, damages are not recoverable for delays that occur *before* a contract is awarded,[12] is executed,[13] or is certified and registered by the comptroller, if a public contract where such is required for the validity of the contract.[14] If a contractor contemplates that it will incur delay damage prior to the award or execution of the contract—perhaps due to increased costs—its remedy is to refuse to sign the contract unless the amount of the contract price is adjusted.[15]

§7.03 Time-Money Relationship

To each party in a construction project, time is money. The sooner an owner gains possession of its building, the sooner it can rent it, sell it, or move into it. The sooner a contractor finishes a project, the more profit it will make and the sooner it can collect its moneys and move on to another job and another opportunity to make a profit. The longer an owner is without its new building, the longer it must pay rent or interest. The longer a contractor is involved in a job, the greater risk it faces for increased labor and materials costs. Due to the value of time, parties to a construction project try to avoid delay and, when delay occurs, assign blame for it to someone besides themselves in hopes of recovering compensation for their losses due to the delay.

§7.04 Scheduling Procedures/Progress Schedules

Most construction contracts contain provisions that require the contractor to prepare and submit to the owner a schedule showing how the contractor intends to perform the work in order to complete it by the contract completion date. The requirement for a schedule forces the contractor to think out how it will perform the myriad tasks necessary to make the project come together on time and permits the owner to monitor the contractor's progress. Just as anyone taking a trip in a foreign country would use a map to find his or her way, a contractor will use a progress schedule as a road map through the project.

In hopes of avoiding delay, some parties go to great lengths in attempting to schedule precisely work progress. One method, the *Critical Path Method*

---

[11] See §7.18 for further discussion of this subject.
[12] Jaffie Contracting Co v Board of Educ, 90 AD2d 163, 456 NYS2d 375 (1st Dept 1982).
[13] McKay Constr Co v City of Oneida Hous Auth, 70 AD2d 993, 417 NYS2d 808 (3d Dept 1979).
[14] Jaffie Contracting Co v Board of Educ, 90 AD2d 163, 456 NYS2d 375 (1st Dept 1982).
[15] McKay Constr Co v City of Oneida Hous Auth, 70 AD2d 993, 417 NYS2d 808 (3d Dept 1979).

(*CPM*), is used by contractors to "plan, schedule, coordinate, and control work activities on projects in such a manner to enable the contract to be completed in the quickest and most economical fashion possible."[16] CPM schedules show the interrelationships of contractors' work and time frames and the interdependencies of one contractor's work on another's. See Figure 7-1. CPM schedules have proven useful not only in facilitating efficient construction but in substantiating contract claims as well.[17]

A less sophisticated, but more easily managed, scheduling tool is a *bar chart*. A bar chart plots specific tasks on a time graph with job tasks listed on the vertical line and the time span portrayed on the horizontal line. See Figure 7-2.

Other scheduling aids include flow charts and Program Evaluation and Review Technique (PERT) charts.

§7.05 Delay and Disruption Causes

Delay can be caused by many factors. An owner may cause delay by failing to make the work site available on time,[18] failing to clear the site,[19] redesigning the project,[20] allowing one contractor to interfere with another's work,[21] using the project prior to its completion,[22] unreasonably delaying in preparing, reviewing, and approving drawings and designs,[23] failing to coordinate work by various contractors,[24] failing to demand prompt performance by other contractors,[25] issuing extensive change orders,[26] concealing true conditions,[27]

---

[16] Wickwire & Smith, *The Use of Critical Path Method Techniques in Contract Claims*, 7 Pub Cont LJ 1 (1974).

[17] *See* Wickwire, Hurlbut, & Lerman, *Use of Critical Path Method Techniques in Contract Claims: Issues and Developments, 1974 to 1988*, 18 Pub Cont LJ 338 (1989); Wickwire & Smith, *supra* note 16.

[18] *See* Fehlhaber Corp v State, 65 AD2d 119, 410 NYS2d 920 (3d Dept 1978); Carlo Bianchi & Co v State, 17 AD2d 38, 230 NYS2d 471 (3d Dept 1962), *affd*, 28 NY2d 536, 268 NE2d 121, 319 NYS2d 439 (1971).

[19] Fehlhaber Corp v State, 65 AD2d 119, 410 NYS2d 920 (3d Dept 1978).

[20] *Id* (redesign of superstructure for a large mall); Klein v Young, 168 NYS 526 (App Div 1918) (owner added a room to the building).

[21] Fehlhaber Corp v State, 65 AD2d 119, 410 NYS2d 920 (3d Dept 1978).

[22] Rao Elec Equip Co v State, 36 AD2d 1019, 321 NYS2d 670 (4th Dept 1971) (state opened hospital before its completion); Johnson v State, 5 AD2d 919, 172 NYS2d 41 (3d Dept 1958) (state opened road to traffic before its contractor's work was complete); Seglin-Harrison Constr Co v State, 30 NYS2d 673 (Ct Cl 1941), *affd as modified*, 264 AD 466, 35 NYS2d 940 (1942) (state inhabited building prior to its completion).

[23] Grow Constr Co v State, 56 AD2d 95, 391 NYS2d 726 (3d Dept 1977); Walter Sign Corp v State, 31 AD2d 729, 297 NYS2d 45 (4th Dept 1968).

[24] Forest Elec Corp v State, 30 AD2d 905, 292 NYS2d 589 (3d Dept 1968).

[25] *Id*.

[26] Rao Elec Equip Co v State, 36 AD2d 1019, 321 NYS2d 670 (4th Dept 1971) (336 change orders costing over $1,000,000).

[27] Rusciano Constr Corp v State, 37 AD2d 745, 323 NYS2d 21 (3d Dept 1971).

186   DELAYS

Figure 7-1

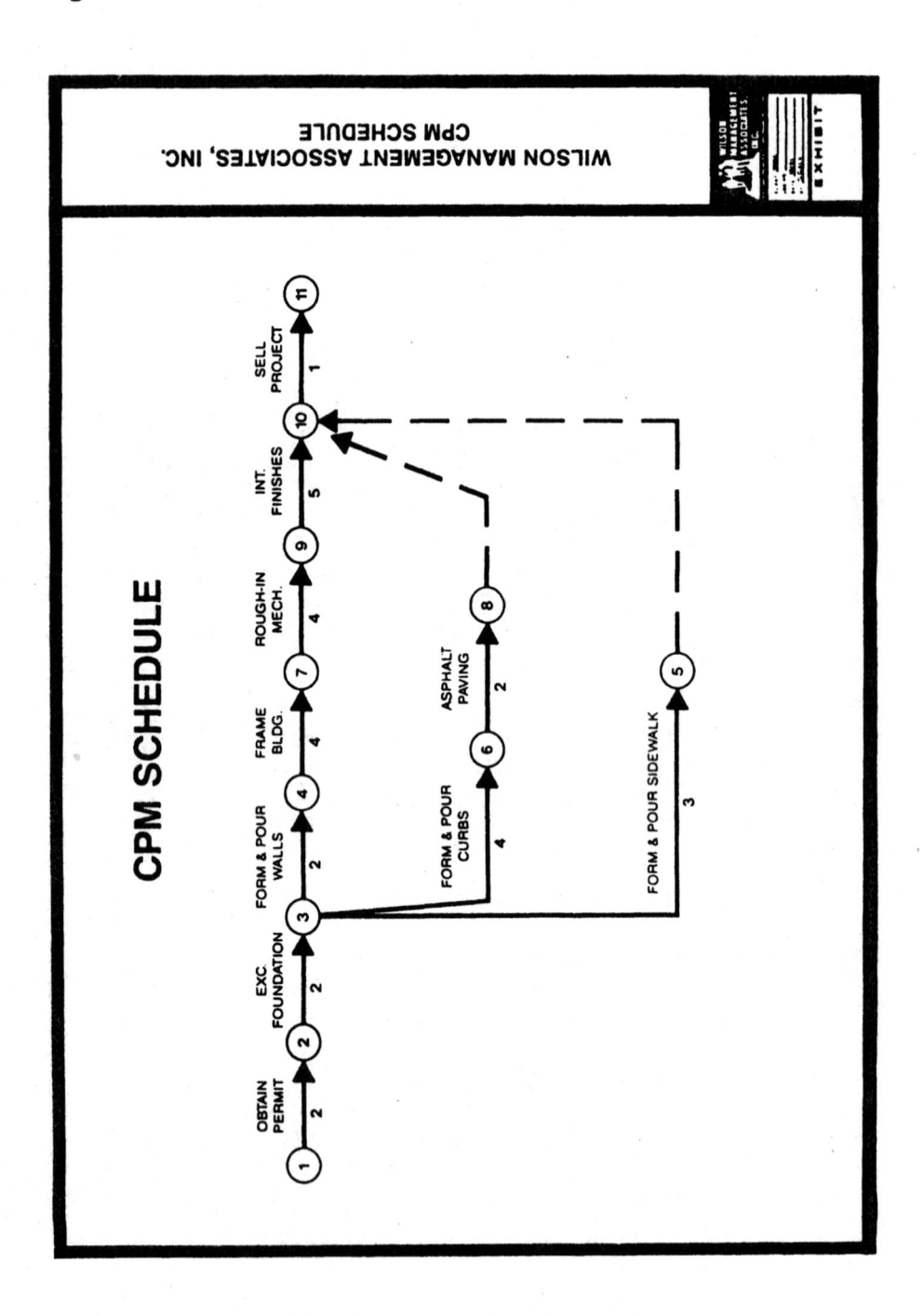

Figure 7-2

Bar Chart for Swimming Pool Construction

Permits	XXX
Site Layout	XXX
Excavation	XXXXX
Plumbing	XXX
Lateral Support	XX
Pour Form	XXXX
Tile	XXX
Finish decking, sanding, painting	XXXXX

- -

Time in Weeks   0   1   2   3   4   5   6

failing to promptly order work to commence,[28] etc. The methods by which an owner can delay a project are countless. One of the most unusual causes of delay occurred when an owner failed to control the patients in its mental hospital and allowed them to interfere with the contractor's work.[29]

A contractor can cause delay in innumerable ways as well, including by failing to assign enough labor to the job,[30] beginning work later than allowed in the contract,[31] submitting drawings late,[32] generally slow progress,[33] not grouting concrete flooring slabs at the proper time,[34] removing its equipment from the job site,[35] erroneous measurements,[36] and poor work.[37] Subcontractors and suppliers can cause delay as well by not supplying the needed materials on time or by delaying as a contractor might delay.

Delay can be caused by factors that are not attributable to any party, including strikes,[38] protesters,[39] lawsuits,[40] and weather.[41] A project may be disrupted by these same factors. The causes of delay and disruption are varied and numerous. What is important is whether the delay is excusable or not and whether it is compensable or not. These issues are discussed in relevant sections following.

§7.06 Types of Delay

Delays fall into one of two categories: excusable and nonexcusable. Put very simply, *excusable* delays are all delays defined as excusable in the contract.

---

[28] Bernmil Contracting Corp v City of NY, 80 AD2d 869, 437 NYS2d 17 (2d Dept 1981).

[29] Farrell Heating & Plumbing & Air Conditioning Contractors, Inc v Facilities Dev & Improvement Corp, 68 AD2d 958, 414 NYS2d 767 (3d Dept 1979).

[30] Walter Sign Corp v State, 31 AD2d 729, 297 NYS2d 45 (4th Dept 1968).

[31] Erecto Corp v State, 29 AD2d 728, 286 NYS2d 562 (3d Dept 1968).

[32] *Id.*

[33] Mount Vernon Contracting Corp v State, 56 AD2d 952, 392 NYS2d 726 (3d Dept 1977); Herbert G. Martin, Inc v City of Yonkers, 54 AD2d 971, 388 NYS2d 673 (2d Dept 1976), *appeal dismissed,* 43 NY2d 946, 374 NE2d 1246, 403 NYS2d 895 (1978).

[34] Lake Steel Erection, Inc v Egan, 61 AD2d 1125, 403 NYS2d 387 (4th Dept), *appeal dismissed,* 44 NY2d 848, 378 NE2d 124, 406 NYS2d 761 (1978).

[35] Tibbetts Contracting Corp v O&E Contracting Co, 15 NY2d 324, 206 NE2d 340, 258 NYS2d 400 (1965).

[36] Quaker-Empire Constr Co v DA Collins Constr Co, 88 AD2d 1043, 452 NYS2d 692 (3d Dept 1982).

[37] *Id.*

[38] City of NY v Local 333, Marine Div, Intl Longshoremen's Assn, 79 AD2d 410, 437 NYS2d 98 (1st Dept 1981), *affd.* 55 NY2d 898, 433 NE2d 1277, 449 NYS2d 29 (1982).

[39] Slattery Assocs v City of NY, 98 AD2d 686, 469 NYS2d 758 (1st Dept 1983).

[40] Mount Vernon Contracting Corp v State, 56 AD2d 952, 392 NYS2d 726 (3d Dept 1977).

[41] Camarco Contractors, Inc v State, 33 AD2d 717, 305 NYS2d 207 (3d Dept 1969), *affd as modified,* 28 NY2d 948, 271 NE2d 917, 323 NYS2d 434 (1971); Bero Constr Corp v State, 27 AD2d 974, 278 NYS2d 658 (4th Dept 1967).

Typically, these are delays that are not caused by the contractor. In addition, delays caused by the owner's breach are excusable as regards the contractor, regardless of whether defined as such in the contract. *Nonexcusable* delays are those attributable to the contractor. Excusable delays entitle the contractor to extra time for completion and, sometimes, to extra money. Excusable delays may be compensable or noncompensable. Nonexcusable delays will never entitle a contractor to extra time and, instead of entitling the contractor to extra money, may subject it to compensating the owner or another party to the project, termination of the contract, or a demand for acceleration.

This chapter will first discuss the causes of excusable delay and relevant contract clauses, including notice requirements. It will then discuss the effect of an excusable delay on the contractor, owner, and project, and the difference between compensable and noncompensable delay. It will then discuss nonexcusable delay.

§7.07 Excusable Delay

The general rule is that a party must fulfill its contractual obligations within the contract period *unless* performance is rendered impossible by an act of God, the law, or some other party. Unforeseen difficulties do not excuse performance.[42] To protect themselves from unexpected contingencies beyond those allowed at common law, contractors place exculpatory clauses in their contracts. One common exculpatory clause provides for excusable delay. An excusable delay clause expressly provides that a failure or delay in performance will not subject the contractor to default action or damages if the delay was due to a cause beyond the control and without the fault or negligence of the contractor. The primary function of an excusable delay provision is to protect the contractor from sanctions for late performance. To the extent that it is excused, a contractor is protected from default termination, liquidated damages, actual damages, and excess costs of reprocurement and completion. Excusable delay entitles a contractor to an extension of time to complete the work to be done under the contract. For a delay to be excusable, it must directly affect the ability of the contractor to complete the job as scheduled, i.e., the delay must fall on the *critical path*.[43] For an excusable delay to be compensable in addition to entitling a contractor to extra time, it must be extraordinary and not reasonably contemplated by the parties.[44] It is important to remember, however, that not every extraordinary or uncontemplated delay is compensable.

The contract is ultimately controlling in defining what is an excusable delay and in allocating risk for delays caused by various factors. For instance, if the contract states that unusual weather conditions shall *not* affect time of completion, the contractor bears the risk of an unseasonably cold winter or wet sum-

---

[42] Dermott v Jones, 2 Wall (69 US) 1 (1864).
[43] *See* **§7.04.**
[44] LG DeFelice & Son v State, 63 Misc 2d 357, 313 NYS2d 21 (Ct Cl 1970).

mer and should schedule its work and price its bid accordingly. Whether a delay is excusable is usually a jury question.[45]

§7.08 —Acts of God/Force Majeure

It is inevitable for most construction projects to be affected by the weather and other forces beyond the control of the parties. Much of the work is done outside, in all seasons. Generally, *unusual* weather and physical conditions are bases for excusable delay, unless the contract says otherwise. A contractor assumes all risk of normal local weather conditions. If hurricanes are the expected norm in September, a contractor must anticipate them in its bid and schedule. Examples of problems that can result in delay caused by unusual weather include frozen ground,[46] unusually wet subgrade conditions,[47] and being required to work in winter when the contract says otherwise or the contract schedule provides otherwise.[48]

No party is responsible for—i.e., causes—delay due to unusual weather. The issue is, who bears the risk of bad weather? Typically, a contractor is allowed extra time to complete its work but is not afforded extra compensation for its increased costs caused by the weather delay.[49] When a job is stalled due to weather, a contractor may move its equipment to another job until it is able to return to work on the subject job; in such an instance, moving the equipment is not abandonment of the job and does not entitle the owner to damages for delay.[50] Thus, each party assumes its own cost consequences of such a delay.

Three basic rules can be used to determine whether or not weather justifies a time extension under a severe/abnormal conditions clause. In order for it to do so:

> (1) The work impacted by the weather must be identified as controlling the overall completion of the project, i.e., it must affect work on the *critical path*.[51]
>
> (2) The controlling work must be shown to have been delayed by the weather.

---

[45] Philip Zweig & Sons v Tuscarora Constr Co, 50 AD2d 1069, 376 NYS2d 761 (4th Dept 1975).

[46] Tibbetts Contracting Corp v O&E Contracting Corp, 15 NY2d 324, 206 NE2d 340, 258 NYS2d 400 (1965).

[47] Martin Mech Corp v PJ Carlin Constr Co, 132 AD2d 688, 518 NYS2d 166 (2d Dept 1987).

[48] Norelli & Oliver Constr Co v State, 30 AD2d 992, 294 NYS2d 35 (3d Dept 1968), *affd,* 32 NY2d 809, 298 NE2d 691, 345 NYS2d 556 (1973).

[49] *Id; but see* Martin Mech Corp v PJ Carlin Constr Co, 132 AD2d 688, 518 NYS2d 166 (2d Dept 1987); Camarco Contractors, Inc v State, 33 AD2d 717, 305 NYS2d 207 (3d Dept 1969), *affd as modified,* 28 NY2d 948, 271 NE2d 917, 323 NYS2d 434 (1971) (state found liable for delay caused by *stop work* order that delayed work so frost permeated sewage disposal fields and made excavation impossible).

[50] Tibbetts Contracting Corp v O&E Contracting Co, 15 NY2d 324, 206 NE2d 340, 258 NYS2d 400 (1965).

[51] *See* §7.04.

(3) The weather must be shown to have been unforeseeable, i.e., abnormally severe.

Using these criteria, it can be seen that foul weather will not always excuse delay. For instance, blizzards during the time a project is supposed to be wired will not excuse late performance as most of the electrical work is performed indoors. Further, if a contractor delays in good weather and later is faced with bad weather, it cannot blame its delay on the bad weather and claim that it prevented work that could and should have been done earlier.[52]

§7.09 —Strikes and Labor Disputes

Labor disputes are not uncommon in New York and, generally, if industry-wide, are defined as excusable delay in contracts, thereby granting a contractor extra time in which to perform the contract,[53] with neither party being responsible for the damages caused by the strike and each bearing its own damages.[54]

If the contract is silent as to performance during a strike, the issue is for the fact-finder—was the strike an unforeseen circumstance such as would excuse delay?[55] If a party is shown to have caused the strike, it may be held responsible for the delay damages caused thereby.[56]

§7.10 —Owner-Caused

Owner-caused delay entitles a contractor to extra time, at a minimum. When a contractor experiences delay due to the owner (or contractee), the contract completion date becomes inoperative and the contractor is afforded a reasonable time extension for completion of the work. Thus, when an owner delays work due to a dispute with an adjoining landowner, the contractor is entitled to an extension of time.[57] Similarly, a contractor is entitled to extensions of time when: the owner significantly changes the plans so the original deadline cannot be met;[58] the owner orders extras not contemplated in the original con-

---

[52] Erecto Corp v State, 29 AD2d 728, 286 NYS2d 562 (3d Dept 1968).

[53] LG DeFelice & Son v State, 63 Misc 2d 357, 313 NYS2d 21 (Ct Cl 1970).

[54] Terry Contracting, Inc v State, 42 AD2d 619, 344 NYS2d 583 (3d Dept 1973); Forest Elec Corp v State, 30 AD2d 905, 292 NYS2d 589 (3d Dept 1968) (strike responsible for 25% of delay); Kleinhans v State, 17 AD2d 905, 233 NYS2d 134 (4th Dept 1962).

[55] City of NY v Local 333, Marine Div, Intl Longshoreman's Assn, 79 AD2d 410, 437 NYS2d 98 (1st Dept 1981), *affd*, 55 NY2d 898, 433 NE2d 1277, 449 NYS2d 29 (1982).

[56] Kleinhans v State, 17 AD2d 905, 233 NYS2d 134 (4th Dept 1962).

[57] Smith v Vail, 53 AD 628, 65 NYS 834 (1st Dept 1900), *affd*, 166 NY 611, 59 NE 1125 (1901).

[58] Rao Elec Equip Co v State, 36 AD2d 1019, 321 NYS2d 670 (4th Dept 1971) (336 change orders worth over $1,000,000); Smith v Vail, 53 AD 628, 65 NYS 834 (1st Dept 1900), *affd*, 166 NY 611, 59 NE 1125 (1901) (different cornices ordered and additional work).

tract;[59] the owner fails to properly coordinate the work or supplies;[60] the owner delays in issuing the order to commence work;[61] extra work is required because the owner breached the contract;[62] the designs of the owner or its architect or engineer are negligent or defective;[63] the owner provides misleading bidding information;[64] the owner or its architect or engineer delays in reviewing, approving, and providing plans and designs;[65] etc.

An owner that is responsible for delay cannot terminate its contractor for failing to comply with the contract time provisions, even where the contractor is responsible for some delay.[66] To demand strict performance from a contractor, an owner must give strict performance.

§7.11 —Sovereign and Other Acts That Interfere with Construction

Construction may be delayed by a government act making the project illegal, impossible, or significantly more difficult. For instance, if an ordinance were to place a moratorium on road construction during tourist season, it would prevent a paver from proceeding with its repair work of a highway until tourist season was over. A new Occupational Safety and Health Act regulation that changed ventilation requirements would delay construction of a new plant until a new system could be designed. The discovery of a rare and unusual snail in a field scheduled to be turned into a parking lot could halt construction until it could be determined whether the snail was entitled to protection.

Similarly, construction may be delayed when a contractor is served with a restraining order forcing it to stop its work pending outcome of a lawsuit by those opposed to the project,[67] when community groups opposing the project block access to the site,[68] or when protesters invade the work site.[69]

---

[59] Klein v Young, 168 NYS 526 (1918) (owner ordered additional room on roof of building).

[60] Forest Elec Corp v State, 30 AD2d 905, 292 NYS2d 589 (3d Dept 1968); Smith v Vail, 53 AD 628, 65 NYS 834 (1st Dept 1900), affd, 166 NY 611, 59 NE 1125 (1901).

[61] Mount Vernon Contracting Corp v State, 56 AD2d 952, 392 NYS2d 726 (3d Dept 1977).

[62] Id (contractor required to do extra work, which delayed completion of the project, when the state failed to provide required fill disposal areas); Rao Elec Equip Co v State, 36 AD2d 1019, 321 NYS2d 670 (4th Dept 1971) (opening hospital before work was substantially complete).

[63] Grow Constr Co v State, 56 AD2d 95, 391 NYS2d 726 (3d Dept 1977).

[64] Id.

[65] Walter Sign Corp v State, 31 AD2d 729, 297 NYS2d 45 (4th Dept 1968).

[66] Id.

[67] Mount Vernon Contracting Corp v State, 56 AD2d 952, 392 NYS2d 726 (3d Dept 1977) (town opposed to widening of parkway sued state and temporarily enjoined further work on project).

[68] Blau Mech Corp v City of NY, 158 AD2d 373, 551 NYS2d 228 (1st Dept 1990).

[69] Slattery Assocs v City of NY, 98 AD2d 686, 469 NYS2d 758 (1st Dept 1983).

Generally, such delays are neither party's fault and entitle the contractor to an extension of time and payment for extras if they are required. Delay damages are not available, unless one of the parties concealed the factor causing the delay,[70] directly caused it, or had the duty and ability to prevent it.[71]

§7.12 —Subcontractor's and Supplier's Delays

Projects are often delayed because materials are late in arriving or subcontractors fail to perform on time. If the materialman or subcontractor causing the delay is not the contractor's agent, it is excusable delay and the contractor should be allowed additional time to complete the work.[72] On the other hand, if it is the contractor's subcontractor that is causing the delay, it would not be excusable,[73] as a contractor is considered to be in control of its subcontractors and materialmen. Of course, if the subcontractor or materialman delay was due to an excusable reason, such as weather or impossibility of performance, the delay would be excusable for the contractor as well.

§7.13 Relevant Contract Clauses

Many contracts have clauses that specifically set forth the circumstances under which a contractor will be entitled to an extension of time, the length of the extension, and the procedures and time to make a claim for and be allowed an extension. Included below in the following three sections are some typical clauses.

§7.14 —Federal Contracts

The federal government has added a clause to its standard construction contract to deal with "Time Extensions." This Federal Acquisition Regulation (FAR) language, found at 48 CFR §52.212-6, reads as follows:

> Notwithstanding any other provisions of this contract, it is mutually understood that the time extensions for changes in the work will depend upon the extent, if any, by which the changes cause delay in the completion of the various elements of construction. The change order granting

---

[70] Mount Vernon Contracting Corp v State, 56 AD2d 952, 392 NYS2d 726 (3d Dept 1977) (state did not have obligation to notify contractor of lawsuit where state did not conceal it).

[71] Blau Mech Corp v City of NY, 158 AD2d 373, 551 NYS2d 228 (1st Dept 1990) (city not liable for disruption due to protesters without a showing that its failure to provide police protection was grossly negligent or intentional); Slattery Assocs v City of NY, 98 AD2d 686, 469 NYS2d 758 (1st Dept 1983) (city does not have a duty to stop protesters).

[72] *See* Smith v Vail, 53 AD 628, 65 NYS 834 (1st Dept 1900), *affd.* 166 NY 611, 59 NE 1125 (1901).

[73] Norcross v Wills, 198 NY 336, 91 NE 803 (1910).

the time extension may provide that the contract completion date will be extended only for those specific elements so delayed and that the remaining contract completion dates for all other portions of the work will not be altered and may further provide for an equitable readjustment of liquidated damages under the new completion schedule.[74]

The federal government has also incorporated a clause on excusable delays into its standard construction contract. The FAR language on excusable delays may be found at 48 CFR §52.249-14. It reads as follows:

(a) Except for defaults of subcontractors at any tier, the Contractor shall not be in default because of any failure to perform this contract under its terms if the failure arises from causes beyond the control and without the fault or negligence of the Contractor. Examples of these causes are (1) acts of God or the public enemy, (2) acts of the government in either its sovereign or contractual capacity, (3) fires, (4) floods, (5) epidemics, (6) quarantine restrictions, (7) strikes, (8) freight embargoes, and (9) unusually severe weather. In each instance, the failure to perform must be beyond the control and without the fault or negligence of the Contractor.[75]

§7.15 —State and Local Contracts

Excusable delay clauses can also be found in state and local contracts. The New York City Department of Transportation contract at Article 13, paragraph 3, reads as follows:

The Contractor shall be entitled to an extension of time for delay in completion of the work caused solely: (1) By the acts or omissions of the City, its officers, agents, or employees; or (2) By the acts or omissions of the other Contractors on this project; or (3) By supervening conditions entirely beyond the control of either party hereto (such as, but not limited to, Acts of God or the public enemy, excessive inclement weather, war or other national emergency making performance temporarily impossible or illegal, or strikes or labor disputes not brought about by any act or omission of the Contractor.

§7.16 —Commercial Practice

American Institute of Architects Document A201 contains a clause that addresses excusable delays. Paragraph 8.3.1 of AIA-A201 reads as follows:

If the Contractor is delayed at any time in progress of the Work by an act or neglect of the Owner or Architect, or of an employee of either,

---

[74] 48 CFR §52.212-6.
[75] *Id* §52.249-14.

or of a separate contractor employed by the Owner, or by changes ordered in the Work, or by labor disputes, fire, unusual delay in deliveries, unavoidable casualties or other causes beyond the Contractor's control, or by delay authorized by the Owner pending arbitration, or by other causes which the Architect determines may justify delay, then the Contract Time shall be extended by Change Order for such reasonable time as the Architect may determine.[76]

§7.17 Notice Requirements

Construction contracts often contain provisions that require prompt written notice of any act or event that allegedly caused delay as a condition precedent to request an extension of time, to not complete the work within the specified time, or for damages due to the delay. The purpose of notice provisions is to provide the owner with prompt notice of claims so efficient investigation may be made, the validity of the claim determined, and steps taken to avoid or minimize the delay.[77] Typically, substantial compliance with a notice provision is a condition precedent to a contractor's right to an extension of time and damages,[78] unless the owner has actual knowledge of the delay and only contractual, not statutory, notice provisions apply. These notice requirements should be complied with as closely as possible.

For public construction projects, notice requirements are set forth in statutes. For example, State Finance Law §145 sets forth notice requirements for claims against the state. These statutes and their requirements are automatically part of every contract made by a school district or the state.[79] Contractual terms specifying procedures for filing a claim do not, as a general rule, replace statutory requirements as conditions precedent.[80] Compliance with statutory notice provisions is mandatory to maintain a claim.[81] Notice of claims issues are more fully discussed in Chapter 16.

---

[76] AIA Doc A201, ¶8.3.1 (1987 ed). Reproduced by permission of The American Institute of Architects under license number 92095. Permission expires July 31, 1993. FURTHER REPRODUCTION IS PROHIBITED. Because AIA Documents are revised from time to time, users should ascertain from the AIA the current edition of this document. Copies of the current edition of this AIA document may be purchased from The American Institute of Architects or its local distributors. The text of this document is not "model language" and is not intended for use in other documents without permission of the AIA.

[77] Board of Educ v Wager Constr Corp, 37 NY2d 283, 333 NE2d 353, 372 NYS2d 45 (1975).

[78] Vanderlinde Elec Corp v City of Rochester, 54 AD2d 155, 388 NYS2d 388 (4th Dept 1976).

[79] Anderson Constr Co v Board of Educ, 229 NYS2d 337 (Suffolk 1962).

[80] Public Improvements, Inc v Board of Educ, 81 AD2d 537, 438 NYS2d 305 (1st Dept 1981), affd, 56 NY2d 850, 438 NE2d 876, 453 NYS2d 170 (1982).

[81] Id.

§7.18 —Time of Notice

Typically, a notice of claim is due within a specified number of days after a claim arises. Contract notice provisions vary from as few as 5 days to as many as 90. Similarly, statutory notice provisions vary as well; contractors on state contracts have 40 days from the mailing of the final payment,[82] while contractors on school contracts have 3 months from the accrual of their claim.[83] To determine whether notice was timely given, it must be determined when the time frame for notice began to run. Sometimes this determination is simple, such as when the contract is one for state improvements. It is easy to count 40 days from the day the final payment was mailed.[84] More often, however, the time frame begins to run from the "accrual of the claim"[85] or the date the "claim arose."[86] When considering delay damages, it can be difficult to ascertain the date when a claim arose or accrued.

A delay damage claim arises when the contract is *substantially* completed[87] or when the contract is terminated or work ceases.[88] The main point is that a claim cannot accrue until damages are ascertainable;[89] generally, it does not matter when the event occurred that caused the delay. The reasoning behind this standard is simple: if a notice provision is supposed to give an owner an opportunity to evaluate the contractor's damage claim, it would do little good to give notice before the damages are ascertainable. Of course, if the contract requires notice of each incident of delay (as compared to notice of a damage claim), the notice period begins to run when the event that caused the delay occurred. Similarly, if a contractor plans to request an extension of time, it is best to give notice of this intent as soon as an excusable delay occurs; monetary damage information can be given later, when known.

Generally, damages have been found to be ascertainable when the contract was substantially complete so that the contractor could itemize a large portion of and realistically estimate the remainder of its damages.[90] It is irrelevant when the owner internally certifies the project as substantially complete.[91] Similarly,

---

[82] NY State Fin Law §145 (McKinney 1989 & Supp 1992).

[83] NY Educ Law §3813(1) (McKinney 1981).

[84] NY State Fin Law §145 (McKinney 1989 & Supp 1992).

[85] NY Educ Law §3813(1) (McKinney 1981).

[86] Vanderlinde Elec Corp v City of Rochester, 54 AD2d 155, 388 NYS2d 383 (1976).

[87] Crescent Elec Installation Corp v Board of Educ, 72 AD2d 760, 421 NYS2d 376 (2d Dept 1979), *affd,* 50 NY2d 780, 409 NE2d 917, 431 NYS2d 443 (1980).

[88] Nyack Bd of Educ v K. Capolino Design & Renovation, Ltd, 114 AD2d 849, 494 NYS2d 758 (2d Dept 1985), *affd,* 68 NY2d 647, 496 NE2d 233, 505 NYS2d 74 (1986).

[89] Board of Educ v Wager Constr Corp, 37 NY2d 283, 333 NE2d 353, 372 NYS2d 45 (1975).

[90] *Id* (claim accrued when contractor able to itemize half its damages and "almost precisely" estimate the rest).

[91] Castagne & Son v Board of Educ, 151 AD2d 392, 542 NYS2d 622 (1st Dept 1989).

the original contract completion date is irrelevant.[92] Another focal point is when the contractor asserts that it has substantially completed the work. Punch lists and minor repairs do not extend the date from which the notice period begins to run.[93]

Depending on the statute or contract involved, a notice of claim filed before accrual of the claim may be premature and ineffective.[94] If a notice is filed early, the problem may be remedied by filing a new notice of claim after the claim has accrued, so long as the new notice is not filed late.

Late claims will not always be rejected, although their acceptance should not be expected. In deciding whether a late claim should be rejected, a court is to consider whether the board had actual knowledge of the essential facts of the claim during the notice period and "all other relevant facts and circumstances," including the claimant's ability to give notice, whether there was justifiable reliance on settlement representations made by an authorized representative of the board, and whether the delay in giving notice substantially prejudiced the district or school board.[95]

§7.19 —Content

A notice of delay damage claim should contain all relevant information that the contractor has regarding its claim. State Finance Law §145 requires a "detailed and verified statement of claim" that should "specify the items upon which the claim will be based."[96] Education Law §3813 requires a "written verified claim." At a bare minimum, whether the claim is under a private or public contract, it should:

1. Identify the contract
2. State original contract commencement and completion dates and actual dates
3. Identify the date, duration, and cause of delay
4. Identify all involved parties
5. Estimate or state delay damage amount and how it was calculated

---

[92] Shalman v Board of Educ, 31 AD2d 338, 297 NYS2d 1000 (3d Dept 1969).

[93] Castagne & Son v Board of Educ, 151 AD2d 392, 542 NYS2d 622 (1989).

[94] Anderson Constr Co v Board of Educ, 229 NYS2d 337 (Suffolk 1962).

[95] NY Educ Law §3813(2)(a) (McKinney Supplementary Pamphlet 1992).

[96] A claim that stated the following was held to be in compliance with NY State Fin Law §145 (McKinney 1989 & Supp 1992): (1) that the breach of contract was due to extraordinary delay caused by the misfeasance and malfeasance of the state; (2) that the damages were increased costs of labor and materials; (3) the critical dates (the date the contract was signed, the date the contract work was supposed to have begun, the date it was actually done, the date the contract work was supposed to have been completed, and the date it actually was completed); and (4) that the delays were due to the state's actions. *See* A&M Wallboard, Inc v Facilities Dev Corp, 97 Misc 2d 434, 411 NYS2d 492 (Albany 1978).

6. Request a specific amount of additional time, if appropriate; and
7. Be verified

§7.20 Effect of Excuse

An *excusable* cause of delay entitles a contractor to an extension of time and may entitle it to monetary damages. Essentially, an excusable delay relieves the contractor of exposure to termination for default and to an owner's claim of actual or liquidated delay damages.[97] Further, the grant of an extension of time to a contractor by an owner carries with it the presumption that the delays resulted through no fault of the contractor.[98]

Whether a contractor is entitled to monetary damages in addition to an extension of time depends on whether the excusable delay is noncompensable or compensable to the contractor. Noncompensable and compensable delays are discussed in §§7.21-7.29.

§7.21 Noncompensable Delays

An excusable delay that entitles a contractor to an extension of time *only*, is called a *noncompensable excusable delay*. Typically, this type of delay is caused by something beyond the control of either the contractor or the owner. Examples of noncompensable delay are acts of God, unusual weather, labor disputes, and so forth. Additional time to complete the work is the contractor's only remedy.

A contractor may agree to make a compensable delay into a noncompensable one by waiving its right to delay damages in exchange for an extension of time. Generally, such waivers are valid.[99] Further, if the contract specifies that a particular delay shall not be compensable[100] or has an applicable and valid *no damage for delay* provision,[101] the delay is noncompensable for all practical purposes.

§7.22 Compensable Delay

Another type of excusable delay is the *compensable delay*. Absent a *no damage for delay* clause (discussed in §§7.32-7.42), compensable delays entitle a contrac-

---

[97] Smith v Vail, 53 AD 628, 65 NYS 834 (1st Dept 1900), *affd*, 166 NY 611, 59 NE 1125 (1901); New Again Constr Co v City of NY, 76 Misc 2d 943, 351 NYS2d 895 (Kings 1974).

[98] JD Hedin Constr Co v United States, 347 F2d 235 (Ct Cl 1965).

[99] Mars Assocs v City of NY, 70 AD2d 839, 418 NYS2d 27 (1st Dept 1979), *affd*, 53 NY2d 627, 420 NE2d 971, 438 NYS2d 779 (1981); Naclerio Contracting Co v EPA, 86 AD2d 793, 447 NYS2d 4 (1st Dept 1982); *but see* New Again Constr Co v City of NY, 76 Misc 2d 943, 351 NYS2d 895 (Kings 1974).

[100] Jaffie Contracting Co v Board of Educ, 90 AD2d 163, 456 NYS2d 375 (1st Dept 1982) (contract specified that board not responsible for delay of up to 90 days in delivering site).

[101] *No damage for delay* provisions are discussed at §§7.32-7.42.

tor to a time extension *and* additional compensation. Typically, a compensable delay is due to some act or omission of the owner. The delay must be more than ordinary delay to be compensable; it must be extraordinary and not reasonably contemplated by the parties.[102] If the delay is of the sort typical to the type of construction involved, the delay is noncompensable.[103] Compensable delay can be caused by many factors, the most common of which are owner interference, denial of access, delayed notice to proceed, delays in inspection and approval, defective designs, contract changes and extras, and changed conditions. These are discussed in §§7.23-7.29.

§7.23 —Owner Interference

Every contract carries an implied obligation that neither party will interfere with the other and, specifically, that the owner will not interfere with the prosecution of its contractor's work.[104] Thus, in most instances, owner interference will entitle a contractor to compensation in addition to time extensions, in the absence of a *no damage for delay* clause.

An owner may interfere with the contractor's work in any number of ways. Owner liability for contractor delay damages has been found where an owner issued stop work orders,[105] failed to keep mental patients from interfering with the contractor's work,[106] refused to allow a contractor to use an acceptable procedure consistently allowed in the past,[107] did not clear the site of obstructions,[108] required the contractor to fabricate steel necessary for a bridge long before it was needed,[109] failed to keep its agreement to provide temporary heat at the building construction site,[110] occupied and used the building prior to completion of the work,[111] and opened the road on which the contractor was working to traffic for the use of other contractors and a college.[112]

---

[102] Forest Elec Corp v State, 30 AD2d 905, 292 NYS2d 589 (3d Dept 1968); LG DeFelice & Son v State, 63 Misc 2d 357, 313 NYS2d 21 (Ct Cl 1970).

[103] Charles H. Sells, Inc v New York State Thruway Auth, 27 AD2d 893, 278 NYS2d 162 (3d Dept 1967).

[104] Shalman v Board of Educ, 31 AD2d 338, 297 NYS2d 1000 (3d Dept 1969).

[105] Camarco Contractors, Inc v State, 33 AD2d 717, 305 NYS2d 207 (3d Dept 1969), *affd as modified*, 28 NY2d 948, 271 NE2d 917, 323 NYS2d 434 (1971).

[106] Farrell Heating, Plumbing & Air Conditioning Contractors, Inc v Facilities Dev & Improvement Corp, 68 AD2d 958, 414 NYS2d 767 (3d Dept 1979).

[107] Johnson, Drake & Piper, Inc v State, 31 AD2d 980, 297 NYS2d 754 (3d Dept 1969).

[108] Columbia Asphalt Corp v State, 70 AD2d 133, 420 NYS2d 36 (3d Dept 1979).

[109] American Bridge Co v State, 245 AD 535, 283 NYS 577 (3d Dept 1935); *see also* United States Steel Corp v Missouri Pac RR, 668 F2d 435 (8th Cir 1982).

[110] DeRiso Bros v State, 161 Misc 934, 293 NYS 436 (Ct Cl 1937).

[111] Seglin-Harrison Constr Co v State, 30 NYS2d 673 (Ct Cl 1941), *modified on other grounds*, 264 AD 466, 35 NYS2d 940 (1942).

[112] Johnson v State, 5 AD2d 919, 172 NYS2d 41 (3d Dept 1958).

Owner interference that rises to the level of *active interference* may entitle a contractor to compensation despite the existence of a *no damage for delay* clause. (*See* §7.38.)

Owner interference may also be found in the acts of those under the owner's control. The primary example of this is when an owner fails to coordinate the work of the owner's other prime contractors so that their work does not hinder the claimant contractor's work.[113] An owner has an obligation to regulate and coordinate the activities of its several prime contractors.[114] Further, an owner must make a "serious and substantial effort to progress and coordinate the work" and has a responsibility to pressure and threaten its delaying contractor into more prompt performance.[115] Thus, an owner may be liable for delay damages when it allows one contractor to perform its work in a disjointed manner over the claimant's objections, thereby disrupting the claimant's schedule, causing it to proceed in a disjointed manner, and preventing it from using economical methods.[116] Of course, if the contract relieves the owner of this duty or provides that the owner will not be liable for delay or damage caused by other contractors, it will not be liable for delay damages despite a failure to coordinate.[117]

Lack of coordination is not automatically a compensable cause of delay. For instance, an owner may not have an obligation to terminate or impose other severe sanctions against a delaying contractor, especially where such an action would result in the project and the complaining contractor being even more delayed.[118]

An owner may not escape responsibility for delay by delegating its supervisory duties to its architect or to one of its independent prime contractors.[119]

§7.24 —Denial of Access

If a contractor is denied access to the work site, it should be entitled to compensation in addition to a time extension. One of the fundamental contractual obligations of an owner to its contractor is to make an unobstructed work site available so the contractor can do its work.[120] Thus, delay in furnishing an unob-

---

[113] Forest Elec Corp v State, 30 AD2d 905, 292 NYS2d 589 (3d Dept 1968).

[114] Websco Constr Corp v State, 57 Misc 2d 9, 292 NYS2d 315 (Ct Cl 1966).

[115] Forest Elec Corp v State, 30 AD2d 905, 292 NYS2d 589 (3d Dept 1968) (seven meetings over a two-year period is not a "serious and substantial" effort).

[116] RH Baker Co v State, 267 AD 712, 48 NYS2d 272 (3d Dept 1944), *affd*, 294 NY 698, 60 NE2d 847 (1945).

[117] Gottlieb v City of NY, 86 AD2d 588, 446 NYS2d 311 (1st Dept 1982), *affd*, 58 NY2d 1051, 449 NE2d 422, 462 NYS2d 642 (1983).

[118] Norelli & Oliver Constr Co v State, 30 AD2d 992, 294 NYS2d 35 (3d Dept 1968), *affd*, 32 NY2d 809, 298 NE2d 691, 345 NYS2d 556 (1973); Websco Constr Corp v State, 57 Misc 2d 9, 292 NYS2d 315 (Ct Cl 1966).

[119] Norman Co v County of Nassau, 27 AD2d 936, 278 NYS2d 719 (2d Dept 1967), *on remand*, 63 Misc 2d 965, 314 NYS2d 44 (Nassau 1970).

[120] Fehlhaber Corp v State, 65 AD2d 119, 410 NYS2d 920 (3d Dept 1978).

structed work site may be compensable so long as the delay was not contemplated.[121]

Contractors have recovered delay damages when: an owner failed to clear the site in time for the contractor to begin its work;[122] an owner allowed another contractor access to the site before permitted by contract, thereby interfering with the claimant's site access;[123] a board of education failed to clear structures from a school site for over a year, preventing the contractor from beginning its work;[124] and an owner failed in its obligation to obtain title to the work site or make it available to the contractor so it could begin its work.[125]

A delay caused by a denial of access must not be inconsequential. For instance, a 12-day delay in making a site available was found to be neither unreasonable nor extraordinary so as to entitle the contractor to delay damages therefor.[126] Further, the delay in delivery of the site must be due to a factor within the owner's control. For example, the state was found not liable for delay in site delivery due to its failure to obtain title to properties where the bid documents warned that the state was engaged in eminent domain proceedings.[127] In this instance, not only did the owner not have control over the delay, but also the bid documents warned of the potential problem, making the delay somewhat contemplated.

§7.25 —Delayed Notice to Proceed

Many construction contracts set forth the date on which a notice to proceed will be issued to the contractor instructing it to begin its work. In formulating bids, contractors rely on this date to determine labor and materials costs and in scheduling other jobs. If the notice to proceed is not issued within a reasonable time after the date set forth in the contract, the contractor may face increased labor and material costs; higher insurance and interest costs; lost opportunities for other jobs; and so forth. Its equipment and laborers may sit idle, costing money but producing nothing. Because of these problems, an unreasonably delayed notice to proceed is a compensable delay.

In *Bernmil Contracting Corp v City of New York*,[128] the contract provided that the order to commence work would be given within 60 days after contract execution. When more than 60 days had passed without an order to commence, the contractor withdrew from the project as was permitted by the contract. The

---

[121] *Id.*

[122] Rusciano Constr Corp v State, 37 AD2d 745, 323 NYS2d 21 (3d Dept 1971).

[123] Peter A. Camilli & Sons v State, 41 Misc 2d 218, 245 NYS2d 521 (Ct Cl 1963).

[124] John T. Brady Co v Board of Educ, 222 AD 504, 226 NYS 707 (1st Dept 1928).

[125] Carlo Bianchi & Co v State, 17 AD2d 38, 230 NYS2d 471 (3d Dept 1962), *affd*, 28 NY2d 536, 268 NE2d 121, 319 NYS2d 439 (1971).

[126] Norelli & Oliver Constr Co v State, 30 AD2d 992, 294 NYS2d 35 (1968), *affd*, 32 NY2d 809, 298 NE2d 691, 345 NYS2d 556 (1973).

[127] Peckham Road Co v State, 32 AD2d 139, 300 NYS2d 174 (3d Dept 1969), *affd*, 28 NY2d 734, 269 NE2d 826, 321 NYS2d 117 (1971).

[128] 80 AD2d 869, 437 NYS2d 17 (2d Dept 1981).

city of New York rejected the withdrawal and ordered the contractor to proceed, which the contractor did under protest. The court awarded the contractor its damages incurred due to the city's delay in ordering work to commence. Similarly, a contractor was awarded its delay damages when the owner delayed in awarding a separate prime contract upon which the claimant contractor's work depended.[129]

If the contract provides that the owner shall *not* be responsible for a delay of up to 90 days in site delivery, a contractor cannot recover damages for delay if the site is delivered within the 90-day period.[130]

A delayed notice to proceed should not be confused with delay prior to execution of the contract. The first is compensable; the second is not.[131] Generally, delay damages are not recoverable for any period before a contract is awarded, certified, or executed.[132]

§7.26 —Delays in Inspection/Approval

Often, a contractor's ability to perform certain steps in a project depends upon the owner or the owner's architect or engineer inspecting preliminary work or approving contractor submittals. For example, a contract may provide that "no work called for by said working or shop drawings shall be done until the approval of the engineer be obtained, which must be given or refused within twenty (20) working days after delivery to him at his office."[133] Under such a clause, prompt performance by the owner, its engineer, or architect is required; it is impossible for a contractor to perform timely its duties without the cooperation of the owner or its architect or engineer. An owner is liable for the delay of its architect or engineer; it is so liable even where the architect or engineer is an independent contractor because, by its contract with the contractor, an owner takes responsibility that the architect or engineer will perform according to the contract.[134]

To recover for delay in inspection or approval, a contractor must prove that the owner or its agents unnecessarily delayed, that the delays constituted a breach of contract, and that the contractor was damaged due to the breach.[135] The delay must not be inconsequential; it is doubtful that a few days' delay in approving plans is actionable.

---

[129] New Again Constr Co v City of NY, 76 Misc 2d 943, 351 NYS2d 895 (Kings 1974).

[130] Jaffie Contracting Co v Board of Educ, 90 AD2d 163, 456 NYS2d 375 (1st Dept 1982).

[131] McKay Constr Co v City of Oneida Hous Auth, 70 AD2d 993, 417 NYS2d 808 (3d Dept 1979).

[132] Jaffie Contracting Co v Board of Educ, 90 AD2d 163, 456 NYS2d 375 (1st Dept 1982).

[133] Litchfield Constr Co v City of NY, 244 NY 251, 155 NE 116, 118 (1926).

[134] Norman Co v County of Nassau, 27 AD2d 936, 278 NYS2d 719 (2d Dept 1967), *on remand*, 63 Misc 2d 965, 314 NYS2d 44 (Nassau 1970); Litchfield Constr Co v City of NY, 244 NY 251, 155 NE 116, 118 (1926).

[135] Metropolitan Paving Co v United States, 163 Ct Cl 420 (1963).

Thus, a contractor is entitled to compensation when an owner delays *unreasonably* in preparing and approving plans and making decisions.[136] For example, the state was found liable for delay when it took three months to approve sign designs on a contract that was to take only three months to perform.[137] Similarly, the state was found liable when it delayed making necessary tests, which then delayed test results that showed where and in what amounts topsoil would be needed, which then delayed the contractor until the following spring and summer.[138]

§7.27 —Defective Design

In most contracts, the contractor works from plans and designs supplied by the owner. An owner is deemed to represent the adequacy of its designs. A bidding contractor has the right to assume that the plans upon which its bid is based describe a structure properly designed by competent engineers.[139] Thus, if a project is defectively designed, the owner should compensate the contractor for the damages it incurred waiting for a good design in addition to its extra costs associated with the new design. Owners have been found liable to contractors for delay damages incurred due to: incorrect drainage provisions and plans that interfered with existing utilities;[140] inadequately and defectively designed cofferdams;[141] differences between actual rock elevations and the elevations the owner's designs were based on;[142] erroneous field measurements;[143] impossible welding technique specifications;[144] and so forth.

§7.28 —Contract Changes and Extras

Changes and extras are common in construction projects. Recovery for extra costs associated with them is discussed in Chapter 6, as are contract clauses concerning changes and extras, authority to make changes, duty to proceed, and other related topics. A contractor will be entitled to *delay* damages[145] due to changes and extras where the changes and extras are excessive; reasonable

---

[136] Grow Constr Co v State, 56 AD2d 95, 391 NYS2d 726 (3d Dept 1977).
[137] Walter Sign Corp v State, 31 AD2d 729, 297 NYS2d 45 (4th Dept 1968).
[138] LG DeFelice & Son v State, 63 Misc 2d 357, 313 NYS2d 21 (Ct Cl 1970).
[139] Grow Constr Co v State, 56 AD2d 95, 391 NYS2d 726 (3d Dept 1977).
[140] Rusciano Constr Co v State, 37 AD2d 745, 323 NYS2d 21 (3d Dept 1971).
[141] Grow Constr Co v State, 56 AD2d 95, 391 NYS2d 726 (3d Dept 1977).
[142] *Id.*
[143] Quaker-Empire Constr Co v DA Collins Constr Co, 88 AD2d 1043, 452 NYS2d 692 (3d Dept 1982).
[144] Lee Turzillo Contracting Co v State, 24 AD2d 548, 261 NYS2d 387 (4th Dept 1965).
[145] It is not inconsistent for a contractor to be awarded its claim for extras while its claim for delay damages based upon those extras is denied. Conduit & Found Corp v State, 52 NY2d 1064, 420 NE2d 397, 438 NYS2d 516 (1981).

changes and extras rarely allow a contractor to recover delay damages (as opposed to payment for extra work) as some change is considered to be expected.[146] A contractor's entitlement to extra time to perform extras or changes is rarely questioned.

> **PRACTICE POINTER:**
>
> When negotiating a change order, a contractor should not waive its right to be compensated for impact costs attributable to the items covered by the change order. At the time of the change order, it may be difficult to determine the ultimate effect of the change order on completion time as well as on total costs. It is advisable for contractors to include a "reservation clause" in the change order. This clause should state that the change order covers only direct costs of the changed work, and does not include any impact costs or extensions of contract time, which are specifically reserved until such time as they can be fully ascertained.

To recover delay damages for extras and changes, the extras and changes must be substantial in number in relation to the project.[147] The time taken to perform them is generally irrelevant, as is the timing of the change or extra.[148] The mere fact that performance time was extended is immaterial, as the contractor can claim its increased costs for the added work.[149]

Owners have been held liable for delay damages due to extras and changes where they were substantial. Thus, the state was held liable for its contractor's delay damages when the state redesigned 70-to-80 per cent of the entire job.[150] Similarly, owners were found liable for delay damages where they issued 336 change orders costing over $1,000,000[151] and revised contract drawings 266 times.[152] An owner who issued 33 changes was not found liable; this number was considered reasonable in light of the contract size.[153]

Owners may also be liable for delay damages when they change the order or manner in which work under the contract must be performed.[154]

---

[146] Slattery Contracting Co v State, 56 Misc 2d 111, 288 NYS2d 126 (Ct Cl 1968); JD Hedlin Constr Co v United States, 347 F2d 235 (Ct Cl 1965).

[147] JD Hedlin Constr Co v United States, 347 F2d 235 (Ct Cl 1965).

[148] *Id.*

[149] *Id.*

[150] Slattery Contracting Co v State, 56 Misc 2d 111, 288 NYS2d 126 (Ct Cl 1968).

[151] Rao Elec Equip Co v State, 36 AD2d 1019, 321 NYS2d 670 (4th Dept 1971).

[152] Fehlhaber Corp v State, 65 AD2d 119, 410 NYS2d 920 (3d Dept 1978).

[153] JD Hedlin Constr Co v United States, 347 F2d 235 (Ct Cl 1965).

[154] Johnson, Drake & Piper, Inc v State, 31 AD2d 980, 297 NYS2d 754 (3d Dept 1969); LG DeFelice & Son v State, 63 Misc 2d 357, 313 NYS2d 21 (Ct Cl 1970).

§7.29 —Changed Conditions

Most construction contracts include *changed conditions* clauses that specify a contractor's remedies in the event that it encounters changed conditions. These clauses are discussed in detail in Chapter 5. The terms *changed conditions* and *differing site conditions* refer to situations in which physical construction conditions are different from those represented in the contract documents and from what the parties reasonably could have expected. A common changed condition occurs when actual subsurface conditions vary from what the borings and site investigation reveal. Another common, although less innocent, changed condition is when the owner misrepresents the true conditions, either intentionally or negligently. Whether the contractor is entitled to delay damages often depends on the contract. If the contract allocates the risk of changed conditions to the owner, the contractor may be entitled to delay damages. If the contract allocates this risk to the contractor, it may be precluded from delay damages, unless the owner misrepresented conditions or failed to disclose information in its possession that indicated the actual conditions.[155]

Thus, in one case, the state was found liable to its contractor for delays that the contractor encountered when it found unstable soil conditions at the site despite the fact that the contract contained an exculpatory clause making the contractor responsible for subsurface conditions.[156] In this case, the court held the state liable for the changed conditions due to its misrepresentation—the state knew of the unstable conditions, did not reveal the same in its bid information or the contract, and did not give the contractor access to all test borings.[157]

The state was also found liable to its contractor for delays due to changed site conditions when rock elevations turned out to be significantly different from those upon which the state based its designs, thereby requiring redesign of the project.[158]

§7.30 Nonexcusable Delay

Nonexcusable delay is delay caused by the contractor. A contractor responsible for delay is not entitled to an extension of time or delay damages for the delay it caused. Causes of nonexcusable delay include failing to submit shop drawings in a timely manner,[159] failing to commence work at the time required by contract,[160] poor workmanship, improper allocation of labor and materials, lack of proper equipment, failing to progress the work,[161] failing to coordinate work,

---

[155] Rusciano Constr Corp v State, 37 AD2d 745, 323 NYS2d 21 (3d Dept 1971).
[156] *Id.*
[157] *Id.*
[158] Grow Constr Co v State, 56 AD2d 95, 391 NYS2d 726 (3d Dept 1977).
[159] Erecto Corp v State, 29 AD2d 728, 286 NYS2d 562 (3d Dept 1968).
[160] *Id.*
[161] Herbert G. Martin, Inc v City of Yonkers, 54 AD2d 971, 388 NYS2d 673 (2d Dept 1976), *appeal dismissed*, 43 NY2d 946, 374 NE2d 1246, 403 NYS2d 895 (1978).

failing to perform the work on time,[162] and so forth.

A contractor guilty of nonexcusable delay may be liable to the owner for delay damages suffered by it, either on an actual[163] or a liquidated damages basis.[164] Further, nonexcusable delay can be the basis for rescission or termination[165] of the contract or an order of acceleration.[166]

§7.31 Concurrent Delay

Often there is more than one reason for delay. When one event causes delay simultaneously with another event, *concurrent delay* results. For instance, if an owner fails to provide site access for 20 days and there is unusually severe rain for 10 of the 20 days, there was concurrent delay for 10 days. Had there been normal weather, the contractor could have recovered for 20 days of delay. Due to the rain, however, the contractor is limited to 10 days of compensable delay since it would not have been able to work those 10 days even if the site had been available. Thus, the owner benefits from the rain. See Figure 7-3.

Concurrent delay can work to a contractor's benefit as well. For instance, if an owner fails to provide site access during the same period that the contractor has not procured needed equipment, the delays cancel each other and the contractor is entitled to an extension of time only. See Figure 7-4. Similarly, if the contractor fails to procure the equipment for 20 days and it rains heavily for 10 of those 20 days, the contractor would be liable to the owner for only 10 days of nonexcusable delay. See Figure 7-5.

An example of a concurrent delay clause can be found in the New York City Department of Transportation contract. Article 13, paragraph 5, of the New York City contract reads as follows:

> The Contractor shall not be entitled to receive a separate extension of time for each one of several causes of delay operating concurrently, but, if at all, only for the actual period of delay in completion of the work as determined by the Commissioner or the Board irrespective of the number of causes contributing to produce such delay. If one of several causes of delay operating concurrently results from any act, fault or omission of the Contractor or of his subcontractors or materialmen, and would of itself (irrespective of the current issues) have delayed the work no extension of time will be allowed for the period of delay resulting from such act, fault or omission.

---

[162] Lake Steel Erection, Inc v Egan, 61 AD2d 1125, 403 NYS2d 387 (4th Dept), *appeal dismissed*, 44 NY2d 848, 378 NE2d 124, 406 NYS2d 761 (1978).

[163] Cooperstein v Patrician Estates, 117 AD2d 774, 499 NYS2d 423 (2d Dept 1986).

[164] *See* Melwood Constr Corp v State, 126 Misc 2d 156, 481 NYS2d 289 (Ct Cl 1984), *affd*, 119 AD2d 734, 501 NYS2d 604 (1986); §7.72.

[165] Tupper v Wade Lupe Constr Co, 39 Misc 2d 1053, 242 NYS2d 546 (Schenectady 1963).

[166] *See* §7.44.

Figure 7-3
Concurrent Delay

```
Days 0————————10————————20-
     ——Owner fails to provide site access——       Type of Delay
                    ——Severe rain——               Compensable
     [ ——compensable—— ]                          Excusable
                    [ ——excusable—— ]
```

Result: Contractor gets compensation for first 10 days of delay. Second 10 days noncompensable.

Figure 7-4
Concurrent Delay

Days 0——————10——————20-
————Owner fails to provide site access————
————Contractor fails to procure equipment————

Type of Delay
Compensable
Nonexcusable

Result: Delays cancel each other, contractor gets time extension only.

Figure 7-5

Days 0——————10——————20-
————Contractor fails to procure equipment————
————————severe rain————
[——nonexcusable——] [——excusable——]

Type of Delay
Nonexcusable
Excusable

Result: Contractor liable for 10 days nonexcusable delay.

§7.32 No Damage for Delay Provisions

In an effort to relieve owners of monetary exposure due to delay, many construction contracts contain *no damage for delay* clauses. These *exculpatory clauses* purport to excuse an owner from contractual liability for damages due to delay caused by itself, its agents, or other contractors under its employ. Contractors who are faced with *no damage for delay* clauses in a general or prime contract often include them in their contracts with subcontractors, either by inclusion of a *no damage for delay* clause or by a specific incorporation-by-reference of the prime contract's delay damage provisions.[167] A *no damage for delay* clause in a subcontract is judged by the same standards as is one in a prime contract.[168] For ease of reference in the following discussion, the party protected by such a clause will be called an owner and the party against whom the clause operates will be called a contractor.

Pros & Cons of the *No Damage for Delay* Clause

Pros

Advocates for the *no damage for delay* clause believe that the clause is a necessary and positive aspect of a construction contract.[169] They claim several purposes are fulfilled by the use of the clause, the first one being the achievement of fiscal stability and integrity by ensuring that the owner knows at the outset substantially the full cost that it will incur on any construction project. In exchange for this certainty and the avoidance of a multitude of claims, the owner is willing to accept, if it must, the possibility of higher bids.

Second, such clauses attempt to deflect vexatious litigation over whether delays were reasonable or unreasonable, or who was at fault and by how much. Delay cases tend to be time consuming, which, of course, leads to high litigation costs. For example, the case of *Kalisch-Jarcho v City of New York*[170] on retrial took four months and ended in a hung jury.

Third, *no damage for delay* clauses are intended to protect the public bidding process by ensuring that the "lowest" bid is actually the lowest bid. If contractors take into account the cost of delays in their bid prices, they will not later have the need to compensate (by imposing numerous other claims) for the bid they used only to underbid competitors.

Finally, if a contractor knows that it alone will bear the cost of delay regardless of fault, it may think twice about delaying the job itself and later attempting to extract delay claim money from the owner. The *no damage for delay* provision provides incentive to all contractors on the job to cooperate with one another in the expeditious completion of the project.

---

[167] Martin Mech Corp v Mars Assocs, 158 AD2d 280, 550 NYS2d 681 (1st Dept 1990); see 13 Am Jur 2d *Building & Construction Contracts* §52 (1964). See discussion regarding incorporation-by-reference in **ch 2**.

[168] Martin Mech Corp v Mars Assocs, 158 AD2d 280, 550 NYS2d 681 (1st Dept 1990).

[169] Parts of this section have been adapted from J. Grubin, *No-Damage-For-Delay Clauses: Fair or Foul—The Owner's Perspective*, 78 Mun Engineer's J issue 2, at 1 (1990).

[170] 58 NY2d 377, 448 NE2d 413, 461 NYS2d 746 (1983).

Cons

On the other hand, those against the *no damage for delay* clause believe that where a contract is competitively bid, the contractor, in calculating its bid, is forced to increase the "contingency factor." Any contract price given by the contractor must take into account foreseeable contingencies, such as inclement weather, increased heating costs in winter months, etc. To the extent that such uncertainties can be foreseen and reasonably quantified, the contractor's bid can reflect their cost. If the contract contains a *no damage for delay* clause, contractors are likely to bid even higher in order to account for any unforeseen contingencies.

Some contractors simply will not engage in the competition under such terms. This shrinks the field of willing contractors, often by the elimination of those most desirable. The risk of contractor default is significantly increased if delays for which compensation is barred are actually experienced. If contractor default does not occur, certainly the contractor can be expected to try to make up on the loss in other ways, such as through reduced quality control, increased claims, and general uncooperativeness, often further delaying the project.

If *no damage for delay* clauses are strictly enforced, what can be expected to occur over a period of time is instability of the local construction industry through contractor defaults and large financial losses, a reduced field of willing bidders, often the least qualified or reliable, unnecessarily high bid prices, a multitude of claims for expenses not including delay, overall reduced quality of construction, and many projects long delayed in completion.

On balance, the authors believe, in most cases, that the owners' interests are better served by not including a *no damage for delay* clause in construction contracts.

§7.33 Enforceability of *No Damage for Delay* Clauses[171]

Generally, *no damage for delay* clauses are valid and enforceable in New York, so long as the basic requirements for a valid contract are present.[172] A *no damage for delay* clause can prevent recovery for damages caused by a wide range of both reasonable and unreasonable behavior by the owner if the behavior or cause of the delay was contemplated by the parties at the time they entered into the contract. If the cause of the delay was contemplated, but the delay was due to the owner's intentional wrongdoing, the provision will not be enforced.[173] Exceptions to enforcement are discussed in §§7.36-7.42.

---

[171] *See* Maurice Brunner, Annotation, *"Validity and Construction of "No Damage" Clause With Respect to Delay in Building or Construction Contract,"* 74 ALR3d 187 (1976).

[172] Corinno Civetta Constr Corp v City of NY, 67 NY2d 297, 493 NE2d 905, 502 NYS2d 681 (1986).

[173] Kalisch-Jarcho, Inc v City of NY, 58 NY2d 377, 448 NE2d 413, 461 NYS2d 746 (1983).

A *no damage for delay* clause will be strictly construed against the party seeking to avoid liability[174] and must be construed in light of all relevant proof relating to the nature of the job and circumstances surrounding the signing of the contract.[175] The party seeking to avoid operation of the clause has the burden of proving the clause inapplicable.[176] Each case involving a *no damage for delay* clause must be judged upon its own facts[177] and requires exploration of the parties' knowledge and intent.[178]

§7.34 General v Specific *No Damage for Delay* Clauses

No damage for delay clauses may be general or specific. General clauses attempt to prevent recovery for any delay caused by any act of the owner; despite the attempt of general clauses to exempt the owner from delay damages for contemplated and *un*contemplated delays, the courts consistently have refused to read them literally and do allow recovery for uncontemplated owner-caused delays. General clauses are construed to bar recovery for contemplated delays only. Even where a delay is contemplated, however, a contractor may still be entitled to recover delay damages if the delay was due to willful or grossly negligent conduct by the owner, as is discussed below in §§7.36-7.42.

Specific clauses prevent recovery of damages due to specified causes, such as the owner's failure to acquire timely title to the property,[179] to make the work site available,[180] or to properly coordinate and sequence work schedules.[181] Such specific clauses have been relied upon by the courts in holding that a particular delay was contemplated.

§7.35 Some Typical *No Damage for Delay* Clauses

There are countless versions of *no damage for delay* clauses. As discussed above, they may be general or specific, simple or complex. Typical clauses are

---

[174] Vanderlinde Elec Corp v City of Rochester, 54 AD2d 155, 388 NYS2d 388 (1976); Ippolito-Lutz, Inc v Cohoes Hous Auth, 22 AD2d 990, 254 NYS2d 783 (3d Dept 1964).

[175] Bradley Envtl Constr v Village of Sylvan Beach, 98 AD2d 973, 470 NYS2d 214 (4th Dept 1983).

[176] Vanderlinde Elec Corp v City of Rochester, 54 AD2d 155, 388 NYS2d 388 (1976).

[177] *Id*; JR Stevenson Corp v County of Westchester, 113 AD2d 918, 493 NYS2d 819 (2d Dept 1985); Martin Mech Corp v Mars Assocs, 158 AD2d 280, 550 NYS2d 681 (1st Dept 1990).

[178] Dal Constr Corp v City of NY, 108 AD2d 892, 485 NYS2d 774 (2d Dept 1985).

[179] *See* John T. Brady & Co v Board of Educ, 222 AD 504, 226 NYS 707 (1st Dept 1928).

[180] Thomason & Perry, Inc v State, 38 AD2d 609, 326 NYS2d 246 (3d Dept 1971), *affd*, 30 NY2d 836, 286 NE2d 465, 335 NYS2d 81 (1972).

[181] *Id.*

found in New York case law. For example, Article 13 of the city of New York's public works contract provides this general clause:

> The Contractor agrees to make no claim for damages for delay in the performance of this contract occasioned by any act or omission to act of the City or any of its representatives, and agrees that any such claim shall be fully compensated for by an extension of time to complete performance of the work as provided herein.[182]

Perhaps the most outrageous *no damage for delay* clause was found in a short-lived 1987 version of Article 13 of the New York City contract. So outrageous was the clause that when it was circulated by the city many contractors protested and promised to refuse to bid on jobs on which the clause would be used. Sureties said they would refuse to bond contracts containing the clause. The volume of discussion and controversy convinced the city to withdraw the clause. The most objectionable portions of the "infamous" article 13 read as follows:

> D. *Specifically Contemplated Uncompensable Delays.*
>
> The following Delay Causes, whether Excusable or not, are hereby agreed by the Contractor and the City to be specifically contemplated . . . and accordingly are not compensable under any circumstances:
>
> 1. Inability to secure, or delays in securing, permissions, approvals, actions or consents by or with respect to any utilities affecting (or affected by) the Work;
>
> 2. The fact that the City has entered into, or delayed entering into, contracts separately for electrical, plumbing, heating, ventilating and air conditioning work, general construction work, and/or other kinds or areas of work;
>
> 3. The action or inaction of other contractors (including failure to organize and integrate their work with the Contractor's Work) or the failure or delay of the City to resolve or remedy such problems or to default or replace any contractor;
>
> 4. Errors or inaccuracies in the Contract Drawings and Specifications proposed by an outside consultant, or errors of design committed by an outside consultant, either in this contract or in any other contract for work on this Project; . . .
>
> 6. Unavailability or defectiveness of material, equipment or products whether or not specified by the Contract or the City;
>
> 7. Site, soil or subsurface conditions differing from those indicated in plans, drawings or specifications;

---

[182] Corinno Civetta Constr Corp v City of NY, 67 NY2d 297, 493 NE2d 905, 502 NYS2d 681, 685 n 1 (1986); Kalisch-Jarcho, Inc v City of NY, 58 NY2d 377, 448 NE2d 413, 461 NYS2d 746, 747 (1983); Buckley & Co v City of NY, 121 AD2d 933, 505 NYS2d 140, 142 (1st Dept 1986).

> 8. Purported changes in the Work, including alleged changes in scope, except when, and to the extent compensable [elsewhere];
>
> 9. Alleged delay by the City in responding to any request from the Contractor (i) to conduct any inspection or test, (ii) to review and approve any materials, documents, drawings or other matter in connection with the Work or (iii) to make any decision, issue any clarification or otherwise reply to the Contractor after request therefor by Contractor; . . .
>
> 12. The (a) approval by the City of a defective or incorrect Progress Schedule or other schedules of work or (b) a change in the planned sequence of performance of the Work allegedly caused by the City;
>
> 13. The occurrence of circumstance productive of Delay which, although not within one of the specific categories listed above in this subparagraph 13.D, were or could have been anticipated because (i) such circumstances are referred to elsewhere in this contract or arise out of the nature of the work being done; (ii) the Contractor has experienced such circumstances on prior construction contracts; and/or (iii) such circumstances were discussed as possibilities between representatives of the parties prior to the Bid Date, or were otherwise foreseen or should have been foreseen by the Contractor.

The city of New York Board of Education has used the following clause, which is both specific and general:

> If the work be delayed by an act or omission of the City or the Board or for any reason that the City or the Board does not own or has not obtained possession of, or the right to enter upon the land upon which the work is to be performed, or because of any act or omission of any employee or agent of the City or of the Board . . . the Board . . . shall then extend the time for the completion of the work for such period as the Superintendent shall certify that the work has been delayed. No allowance whatsoever as damages or otherwise shall be claimed by or made to the contractor because of any such delays.[183]

The Cohoes Housing Authority has used this general clause:

> No payment of compensation of any kind shall be made to the Contractor for damages because of hindrance or delay from any cause in the progress of the work, whether such hindrances or delays be avoidable or unavoidable.[184]

Finally, the state of New York has used this specific clause in its bid documents:

---

[183] John T. Brady & Co v Board of Educ, 222 AD 504, 505, 226 NYS 707, 709 (1st Dept 1928).

[184] Ippolito-Lutz, Inc v Cohoes Housing Auth, 22 AD2d 990, 254 NYS2d 783 (3d Dept 1964).

> Delays in availability of any part of the site or any delays due to interference between the several contractors and utility owners shall be compensated for by the Superintendent of Public Works solely through granting an extension of time in which to complete the work of the Contract without Engineering changes. The Contractor in submitting his bid hereby agrees that he shall have no claim against the State of New York for any damages due to such delays or interference other than extended time in which to complete the work itself.[185]

Despite the fact that each of these examples is from a public construction project, be aware that similar clauses may be found in private contracts[186] and are most likely to be construed in the same way as public contract clauses.

The validity of these clauses depends on the particular fact situation involved. Generally, these clauses are valid and will bar many delay damage claims. The exceptions to enforcement are few and are strictly applied.

§7.36 Exceptions to Enforcement of *No Damage for Delay* Clauses

The leading case in establishing exceptions to enforcement of *no damage for delay* clauses is *Corinno Civetta Construction Corp v City of New York*.[187] In *Corinno*, the Court of Appeals reaffirmed contractors' rights to sue for delay damages despite *no damage for delay* clauses. The court stated:

> Generally, even with such a clause, damages may be recovered for: (1) delays caused by the contractee's bad faith or its willful, malicious, or grossly negligent conduct, (2) uncontemplated delays, (3) delays so unreasonable that they constitute an intentional abandonment of the contract by the contractee, and (4) delays resulting from the contractee's breach of a fundamental obligation of the contract.[188]

Corinno did not address a number of questions, such as the standard to be applied in determining whether a delay was contemplated and whether abandonment is to be determined from the contractee's actual intent or the contractor's reasonable interpretation of the contractee's actions.

It is clear that a *no damage for delay* clause is not absolute and will not be enforced under all circumstances, "no matter how flat and unqualified its

---

[185] Thomason & Perry, Inc v State, 38 AD2d 609, 610, 326 NYS2d 246, 248 (3d Dept 1971), *affd,* 30 NY2d 836, 286 NE2d 465, 335 NYS2d 81 (1972).

[186] *See* Wilson & English Constr Co v New York Cent RR Co, 240 AD 479, 269 NYS 874 (2d Dept 1934).

[187] 67 NY2d 297, 493 NE2d 905, 502 NYS2d 681 (1986).

[188] *Id,* 67 NY2d at 309, 493 NE2d 905, 502 NYS2d at 686.

§7.36 EXCEPTIONS TO *NO DAMAGE FOR DELAY*

terms."[189] Basically, a *no damage for delay* clause is not enforceable when the conduct that caused the delay "smacks of intentional wrongdoing."[190]

> **PRACTICE POINTER:**
>
> Practitioners must be careful when faced with a *no damage for delay* clause. The law in this area is unsettled, primarily because of *Kalisch-Jarcho, Inc v City of New York*,[191] which was believed by many attorneys and lower courts to stand for the proposition that *no damage for delay* clauses bar any claim for delay damages and that the exceptions are so narrowly drawn that no factual situation could meet them. Some members of the legal community considered the case to have wiped out nearly all *no damage for delay* clause cases that were decided before it. After *Kalisch-Jarcho*, nearly every case that considered delay damages where there was a *no damage for delay* clause rejected the claim. In *Corinno Civetta*, the Court of Appeals stated that *Kalisch-Jarcho* simply reaffirmed the existing rule regarding *no damage for delay* clauses, including the existence of exceptions, and implied that the decision had been misread. The question now is, which cases are good law? Were pre-*Kalisch-Jarcho* cases revived by *Corinno Civetta*? Are any cases decided between the two of value? All that is clear is that exceptions exist to *no damage for delay* clauses. It is not clear how narrowly those exceptions will be drawn. The practical effect of the confusion has been that many public bodies refuse to settle delay claims.

To determine whether delay damages may be recovered despite a *no damage for delay* clause, a two-step inquiry must be made:

(1) Was the cause of the delay contemplated by the parties at the time the contract was executed? If the delay was uncontemplated, no further inquiry is necessary; damages are recoverable, so long as the duration of the delay is not inconsequential.[192] If the cause of the delay was contemplated, the second inquiry must be made.

(2) Can an exception be proven? Was the cause of the delay such that it makes the clause inapplicable? Damages may be recovered for contemplated delay caused by the owner's active interference, abandonment,

---

[189] Kalisch-Jarcho, Inc v City of NY, 58 NY2d 377, 385, 448 NE2d 413, 461 NYS2d 746, 749 (1983); *see also* Martin Mech Corp v Mars Assocs, 158 AD2d 280, 550 NYS2d 681 (1st Dept 1990) (an exculpatory clause is not an absolute bar but raises a question of fact).

[190] Kalisch-Jarcho, Inc v City of NY, 58 NY2d 377, 448 NE2d 413, 461 NYS2d 746 (1983); *see also* Martin Mech Corp v Mars Assocs, 158 AD2d 280, 550 NYS2d 681 (1st Dept 1990) (an exculpatory clause is not an absolute bar but raises a question of fact); Corinno Civetta Constr Corp v City of NY, 67 NY2d 297, 493 NE2d 905, 502 NYS2d 681 (1986).

[191] 72 NY2d 727, 533 NE2d 258, 536 NYS2d 419 (1988).

[192] *See* §7.26 hereof.

willful or gross negligence, fraud or bad faith, or breach of a fundamental obligation of the contract.

> **PRACTICE POINTER:**
>
> Beating a *No Damage for Delay* Clause[193]
>
> (1) *Select a theme.* The theme is not a legal argument but a persuasive one that the court can use to find the clause inapplicable or unenforceable. It should emphasize the injustice of enforcing the clause by convincing the court that:
>
> —the contractor did not cause or have control over the delay;
>
> —the owner did cause or have control over the delay;
>
> —neither the cause nor length of the delay was contemplated or foreseeable (i.e., the contractor did not contractually accept the risk of the delay).
>
> (2) *Select a legal theory that allows the court flexibility in interpreting the contract* and to use its discretion to judge the facts on a case-by-case basis.
>
> Traditional theories:
>
> —active interference
>
> —fraud and material misrepresentation
>
> —unreasonable delay/abandonment
>
> —delay uncontemplated
>
> —contract theories, including waiver, strict construction of exculpatory clauses against drafter, inconsistent clauses, etc.
>
> Nontraditional theories:
>
> —cardinal change of obligation
>
> —drafter's breach of a material contract term prevents its reliance on exculpatory clause.

§7.37 —Uncontemplated Delay

If a delay is found not to have been contemplated by the parties at the time the contract was executed, a *no damage for delay* clause will not apply. "[C]ontemplation of parties involves only such delays as are reasonably foreseeable, arise from the contractor's work itself during performance, or other

---

[193] This Practice Pointer is based upon an article by Richard Gary Thomas & Fred D. Wilshusen, *How to Beat a 'No Damage For Delay' Clause*, 9 Construction Law 17 (1989) and is included here with the permission of the authors and the Forum on the Construction Industry of the American Bar Association, publisher of *The Construction Lawyer*.

§7.37 UNCONTEMPLATED DELAY

delays specifically mentioned in the contract."[194] Based on a reading of the relatively few cases available, it appears that the courts apply an *objective* standard to determine what was contemplated. The courts will examine the contract, concentrating on its specific clauses, and related documents to see if the cause of the delay was addressed; if so, the delay will be deemed to have been contemplated, no matter how unlikely, on a subjective level, the delay might have seemed when the contract was executed.[195]

This objective standard was applied in *Buckley & Co v City of New York*.[196] Buckley was the general contractor on a project to build a pumping station. Construction was due to be completed in June, 1968. Soon after construction began problems arose with a cofferdam designed by the city. The cofferdam proved ineffective at preventing seepage into the excavation. Progress on the project was delayed until the city could design an alternative. The project was finally completed in June, 1976, some eight years late. Based on a *no damage for delay* clause, the Appellate Division rejected Buckley's claim for delay damages and ruled that the subsurface conditions that caused the problems were contemplated. This holding was based on a changed conditions clause that provided a procedure to modify the contract should additional work be necessary due to "unanticipated subsurface" conditions. The court stated that "while the conditions themselves may not have been anticipated, the possibility, however unlikely, of their arising was contemplated and addressed by the parties in their agreement."[197] The court, in effect, issued a self-contradicting holding by ruling that unanticipated conditions were contemplated.

The decision in *Buckley* applies an unreasonably strict standard that is inconsistent with the rationale behind a changed conditions clause—namely to encourage lower bids by inducing contractors to eliminate contingency allowances. In effect, the court, by using a changed conditions clause to indicate what the parties contemplated, penalized the general contractor for not including in its bid a contingency for changed conditions, despite the existence of a contract mechanism to compensate the contractor for changed conditions. Such a decision discourages parties from drafting and signing specific contracts that attempt to address and provide a mechanism to resolve problems before they arise.

A similarly strict objective standard was applied in a case where a contract contained a change order clause. The court ruled that because the contract contained a change order clause and provided compensation for extra work

---

[194] Peckham Road Co v State, 32 AD2d 139, 300 NYS2d 174 (3d Dept 1969), *affd*, 28 NY2d 734, 269 NE2d 826, 321 NYS2d 117 (1971).

[195] Buckley & Co v City of NY, 121 AD2d 933, 505 NYS2d 140 (1st Dept 1986).

[196] *Id; see also* Blau Mech Corp v City of NY, 158 AD2d 373, 551 NYS2d 228 (1st Dept 1990).

[197] Buckley & Co v City of NY, 121 AD2d 993, 505 NYS2d 140, 142 (1st Dept 1986); *see also* Blau Mech Corp v City of NY, 158 AD2d 373, 551 NYS2d 228 (1st Dept 1990); Earthbank Co v City of NY, 145 Misc 2d 937, 549 NYS2d 314 (NY 1989).

required by change orders, all change orders were contemplated by the parties, even ones that significantly delayed the project.[198]

Despite the use of the objective standard, courts should still examine the parties' actual knowledge and intent at the time the contract was signed to determine whether the cause of the delay was contemplated.[199]

An example of the difference between uncontemplated and contemplated delay is found in *WL Waples Co v State*.[200] In that case, the contract was to clean, paint, and waterproof the State Capitol Building in Albany. Progress was delayed by two things. First, the state delayed in testing the waterproofing the contractor planned to use. The court denied recovery of delay damages for the few weeks' delay, stating that reasonable delay in the important testing and selection of waterproofing materials was within the parties' contemplation under a clause exempting damage for delay due to any acts of "state authorities." The second delay was caused when the state legislature required the contractor to stop sandblasting because the noise interfered with an impeachment hearing. The court held that the contractor's increased labor costs due to this delay were recoverable because work cessation due to legislative hearings was not contemplated, although it was, technically, due to an act of state authorities.

Causes of delay that have been held to be *uncontemplated* include: failure of the city to obtain excavation permits that it was required to obtain by contract;[201] a general contractor's erroneous field measurements, improper grading, paving, and curb work, and insistence that the subcontractor work through the winter despite subcontract provisions to the contrary;[202] failure of the owner to obtain necessary rights-of-way, provide required materials, and furnish bridge plans on time as required by the contract;[203] failure of the state to furnish temporary heat required by contract so the contractor could work through the winter;[204] defective plans and specifications;[205] occupation of the building and monopolization of the elevator before the building was complete, despite a contract clause allowing pre-completion occupation;[206] and cessation

---

[198] Blau Mech Corp v City of NY, 158 AD2d 373, 551 NYS2d 228 (1st Dept 1990). The case is not explicit as to the magnitude of changes.

[199] Dal Constr Corp v City of NY, 108 AD2d 892, 485 NYS2d 774 (2d Dept 1985).

[200] 178 AD 357, 164 NYS 797 (3d Dept 1917); *see also* Wright & Kremers, Inc v State, 263 NY 615, 189 NE 724 (1934) (claimant allowed to recover delay damages due to state's failure to clear the building site, but not due to the changes made by the state in the plans and specifications).

[201] Earthbank Co v City of NY, 145 Misc 2d 937, 549 NYS2d 314 (NY 1989).

[202] Quaker-Empire Constr Co v DA Collins Constr Co, 88 AD2d 1043, 452 NYS2d 692 (3d Dept 1982).

[203] Wilson & English Constr Co v New York Cent RR, 240 AD 479, 269 NYS 874 (2d Dept 1934).

[204] DeRiso Bros v State, 161 Misc 934, 293 NYS 436 (Ct Cl 1937).

[205] Cauldwell-Wingate Co v State, 276 NY 365, 12 NE2d 443 (1938).

[206] Seglin-Harrison Constr Co v State, 30 NYS2d 673 (Ct Cl 1941), *modified on other grounds*, 264 AD 466, 35 NYS2d 940 (1942).

of work due to a city's failure to appropriate funds necessary for portions of the work.[207]

Delays found to have been *contemplated* include: cessation of work to investigate materials where the contract allowed cessation if it was in the best interests of the city;[208] delays caused by other contractors;[209] obstruction caused by underground utility lines where the contract gave the contractor the burden of checking for underground obstructions;[210] failure of the state to obtain title to properties where the bid documents warned that the state was engaged in eminent domain proceedings;[211] and delay caused by hospital operations where the contract stated that the contract work was not to interfere with hospital services.[212]

§7.38 —Active Interference

The *active interference* exception to enforcement of *no damage for delay* clauses stems from the uncontemplated delay exception, although the delay need not have been uncontemplated for the contractor to recover delay damages. Often, cases discuss the same delay as being both uncontemplated and caused by active interference.[213] Since every contract carries an implied obligation that neither party will interfere with the other and, specifically, that the owner will not interfere with the prosecution of its contractor's work,[214] it is natural to assume that active interference by the owner is not capable of being contemplated at the time of contract. Thus, a *no damage for delay* clause will not bar the contractor from recovery where the owner actively interferes with the work.

Active interference requires some affirmative act by the owner that is "reprehensible," "unreasonable," and in bad faith.[215] The act must be in collision with or run at cross-purposes to the work of the contractor.

---

[207] Johnson v City of NY, 191 AD 205, 181 NYS 137, *affd*, 231 NY 564, 132 NE 890 (1920) (the contract included a clause permitting the borough president to suspend the work if it was deemed in the best interests of the city; the court held that a failure to appropriate funds was not reasonably contemplated).

[208] Mechanic's Bank v City of NY, 164 AD 128, 149 NYS 784 (2d Dept 1914); *compare* Ryan v City of NY, 159 AD 105, 143 NYS 974 (1st Dept 1913) (contract right of city to suspend work without delay compensation did not preclude delay damage recovery where delay was due to failure of other contractors to complete their work on time).

[209] FN Lewis Co v State, 132 Misc 688, 230 NYS 517 (Ct Cl 1928).

[210] Davis Constr Corp v County of Suffolk, 149 AD2d 404, 539 NYS2d 757 (2d Dept 1989).

[211] Peckham Road Co v State, 32 AD2d 139, 300 NYS2d 174 (3d Dept 1969), *affd*, 28 NY2d 734, 269 NE2d 826, 321 NYS2d 117 (1971).

[212] Phoenix Contracting Corp v New York City Health & Hosp Corp, 118 AD2d 477, 499 NYS2d 953 (1st Dept), *appeal denied*, 68 NY2d 606, 498 NE2d 151, 506 NYS2d 1031 (1986).

[213] *See* WL Waples Co v State, 178 AD 357, 164 NYS 797 (3d Dept 1917).

[214] Shalman v Board of Educ, 31 AD2d 338, 297 NYS2d 1000 (3d Dept 1969).

[215] Corinno Civetta Constr Corp v City of NY, 67 NY2d 297, 493 NE2d 905, 502 NYS2d 681 (1986).

A good example of active interference is found in *American Bridge Co v State*.[216] The plaintiff was to build the superstructure of a bridge. It could not begin until the substructure contractor completed its work. The substructure contractor encountered serious difficulties that obviously would delay significantly the date on which the plaintiff would be able to begin its work. The state required the plaintiff to fabricate the steel, despite the fact that neither party had a place to store the steel until it was needed, some 21 months later. There were two consequences to the state's insistence that the plaintiff fabricate the steel early: the plaintiff incurred storage expenses, and the paint on the stored steel deteriorated, requiring extra painting. The court allowed the plaintiff to recover its damages based on the plaintiff's position that it sought damages not for the delay but for the state's active and unnecessary interference in requiring the plaintiff to fabricate the steel despite the delay.

Active interference has been found and damages for delay recoverable where: an owner failed to keep its agreement to provide temporary heat at the building construction site;[217] an owner occupied and used the building prior to completion of the work;[218] an owner opened the road on which the contractor was working to traffic for the use of other contractors and a college;[219] and an owner allowed one contractor to perform its work in a disjointed manner over the claimant's objection, thereby disrupting the claimant's schedule, subjecting it to water damage, causing it to proceed in a disjointed manner, and preventing it from using economical methods.[220]

Active interference may be found in an owner's several acts combined. For instance, active interference was found when the court considered several actions by the state, including: its occupation of the building prior to its completion causing undue interference in the contractor's work progression; its refusal to give the contractor prompt access to the transformer site; its lethargy in selecting artists to prepare ornamentation models; its slowness in furnishing full-size detail and working drawings; and its delay in delivering the entire building site.[221] Any one of these alone probably would not have been enough to allow the contractor to recover delay damages; but taken together, they showed active interference.

Active interference is not bad contract administration[222] or inaction, faulty

---

[216] 245 AD 535, 283 NYS 577 (3d Dept 1935); *see also* United States Steel Corp v Missouri Pac RR, 668 F2d 435 (8th Cir 1982).

[217] DeRiso Bros v State, 161 Misc 934, 293 NYS 436 (Ct Cl 1937).

[218] Seglin-Harrison Constr Co v State, 30 NYS2d 673 (Ct Cl 1941), *modified on other grounds*, 264 AD 466, 35 NYS2d 940 (1942).

[219] Johnson v State, 5 AD2d 919, 172 NYS2d 41 (3d Dept 1958).

[220] RH Baker Co v State, 267 AD 712, 48 NYS2d 272 (3d Dept 1944), *affd*, 294 NY 698, 60 NE2d 847 (1945).

[221] Seglin-Harrison Constr Co v State, 30 NYS2d 673 (Ct Cl 1941), *modified on other grounds*, 264 AD 466, 35 NYS2d 940 (1942).

[222] Martin Mech Corp v PJ Carlin Constr Co, 132 AD2d 688, 518 NYS2d 166 (2d Dept 1987).

work, or defaults by other contractors hired by the owner.[223] It is not found when an owner estimates that a job will take less time than it actually does or when an owner refuses to grant a time extension in response to its contractor's request.[224]

Often, the active interference is the owner's breach of a material obligation of the contract.[225]

§7.39 —Unreasonable Delay and Abandonment

Another exception to enforcement of a *no damage for delay* clause is if "the delays are so unreasonable as to constitute an intentional abandonment of the contract by the owner."[226] This exception does not apply to all unreasonable delays, as exculpatory clauses are intended to cover some unreasonable behavior.[227] The exception applies only to delays that are so unreasonably lengthy that they connote a relinquishment or abandonment of the contract by the owner with the intent of *never* resuming it.[228]

There is no steadfast rule as to how much time must elapse before the delay becomes so unreasonable as to be compensable. The particular facts of each case are important in determining whether the clause applies. What is unreasonably lengthy delay in one case may not be in another.

A delay sufficient to avoid operation of a *no damage for delay* clause was found when a board of education failed to clear structures from a school site for over a year and, thus, prevented the contractor from beginning its work.[229] The court found the delay so unreasonable as to strike at the heart of the contract. Similarly, a delay of more than 3 years on a contract that was to take only 120 days was found to be so unreasonable as to make the *no damage for delay* clause inapplicable.[230] A delay of 6 months was found not to constitute abandonment;[231] neither was a delay of over 2 years where the city attempted to remedy the problem that delayed the contractor.[232]

---

[223] Gottlieb Contracting, Inc v City of NY, 86 AD2d 588, 446 NYS2d 311 (1st Dept 1982), *affd*, 58 NY2d 1051, 449 NE2d 422, 462 NYS2d 642 (1983).

[224] Taylor-Fichter Steel Constr Co v Niagara Frontier Bridge Commn, 261 AD 288, 25 NYS2d 437 (1st Dept), *affd*, 287 NY 669, 39 NE2d 290 (1941).

[225] *See* DeRiso Bros v State, 161 Misc 934, 293 NYS 436 (Ct Cl 1937); **§7.42**.

[226] Corinno Civetta Constr Corp v City of NY, 67 NY2d 297, 309, 493 NE2d 905, 502 NYS2d 681, 686 (1986).

[227] Mack v State, 122 Misc 86, 202 NYS 344 (Ct Cl), *affd without opinion*, 211 AD 825, 206 NYS 931 (1923).

[228] *Id;* Kalisch-Jarcho, Inc v City of NY, 58 NY2d 377, 448 NE2d 413, 461 NYS2d 746 (1983); Foulke v New York Consol RR, 228 NY 269, 127 NE 237 (1920).

[229] John T. Brady v Board of Educ, 222 AD 504, 226 NYS 707 (1st Dept 1928).

[230] Wells & Newton Co v Craig, 232 NY 125, 133 NE 419 (1921).

[231] Endres Plumbing Corp v State, 198 Misc 546, 95 NYS2d 574 (Ct Cl 1950), *affd mem*, 285 AD 1107, 139 NYS2d 319 (3d Dept 1955).

[232] Corinno Civetta Constr Corp v City of NY, 67 NY2d 297, 493 NE2d 905, 502 NYS2d 681 (1986).

222   DELAYS

Meeting this exception is difficult. If an owner has several independent prime contractors and permits them each to proceed slowly with its work and resolves problems in a lackadaisical fashion, making the project take much longer than anyone could have expected, it may be impossible for any one contractor to claim that the delay was so unreasonable as to indicate abandonment because the owner kept work progressing, albeit very slowly.[233] The strict standard employed in unreasonable delay/abandonment cases is perhaps best seen in the *Honeywell, Inc v City of New York* portions of the *Corinno Civetta* case.[234] Honeywell had a contract with the city to install and maintain a complex computer system at the city's sewage treatment plants. The contract was executed in August, 1973, and provided that installation was to be completed in February, 1977. In February, 1979, Honeywell terminated its work with installation work still not completed. Honeywell attempted to avoid operation of the contract's *no damage for delay* clause by arguing that it did not seek delay damages but damages for the city's abandonment or breach of contract. The Court of Appeals did not reject this attempt outright; it recognized the potential for a party to avoid a *no damage for delay* clause by arguing abandonment and stated:

> [T]o avoid the risk of the exculpatory clause and recover on the ground of abandonment, a contractor must establish that the contractee is responsible for delays which are so unreasonable that they connote a relinquishment of the contract by the contractee with the intention of never resuming it.[235]

Honeywell based its claims on the city's failure to remedy wiring problems at two of the sewage plants, which problems remained when Honeywell left the job, two years after its original completion date. The wiring problems were caused primarily by the city's electrical contractor, another city contractor. The city did attempt to remedy the problems through design changes and working with the contractor. Almost one year after Honeywell left the job, the wiring problems had not been remedied, although the city estimated that the wiring would be completed "in the near future." Wiring was finally completed in August, 1979, two-and-one-half years after the contract date for completion of installation. Because the city pursued resolution of the wiring problems throughout contract performance and because the contract provided that Honeywell would not look to the city but to other contractors if their work caused Honeywell damage, the court denied Honeywell's claim. It held that the wiring problems were not uncontemplated; that the city's conduct was not malicious, in bad faith, grossly negligent, or so unreasonable that it connoted abandonment or avoided operation of the *no damage for delay* clause; and that the city had not breached the contract. Thus, it appears that so long as an owner makes some effort to progress a job, a contractor will be precluded from claim-

---

[233] *Cf* Wells & Newton Co v Craig, 232 NY 125, 133 NE 419 (1921).

[234] Corinno Civetta Constr Corp v City of NY, 67 NY2d 297, 493 NE2d 905, 502 NYS2d 681 (1986).

[235] *Id* at 313, 493 NE2d at 912, 502 NYS2d at 688.

ing abandonment or breach of contract where a *no damage for delay* clause applies.

It is unclear whether the courts will use a subjective or an objective test to determine whether an owner's actions connote abandonment. If an owner does not work on its project for two years and then completes it with a different contractor, will the first contractor's claim for delay damages based on this exception stand? Will the court look at what the contractor reasonably believed to be the owner's intent regarding abandonment, or will it look at what the owner actually intended and later did? These questions cannot be answered at this time. When faced with a lengthy delay, it may be best to argue both the unreasonable delay/abandonment exception and that the owner breached a material obligation of the contract (as is discussed in §7.42).

§7.40 —Willful or Gross Negligence

Another exception to enforcement of a *no damage for delay* clause occurs when the delays are caused by the owner's "willful, malicious, or grossly negligent conduct."[236] This exception, like the others, is narrowly construed. Delays caused by an owner's poor administration of the contract[237] or its failure to coordinate contractors' work and ensure prompt and proper performance by all contractors[238] do not rise to the level of willful or gross negligence. A city-owner's failure to provide adequate police protection to prevent protesters[239] or strikers[240] from disrupting the contractor's work is not willful or gross negligence by the city-owner.

While no cases could be found in which an owner's conduct fit the standard required by this exception, the Court of Appeals in *Kalisch-Jarcho, Inc v City of New York*[241] indicated that gross negligence would be established if, on retrial, the contractor could prove that the city's misconduct caused an extraordinarily long delay, an immense number of drawing revisions, and lack of coordination of contractors. The court stated that if these facts could be proven they would "have to establish that the city's conduct amounted to gross negligence," even in the absence of any evidence of malice.[242]

---

[236] Corinno Civetta Constr Corp v City of NY, 67 NY2d 297, 309, 493 NE2d 905, 502 NYS2d 681, 686 (1986).

[237] Martin Mech Corp v PJ Carlin Constr Co, 132 AD2d 688, 518 NYS2d 166 (2d Dept 1987).

[238] Novak & Co v New York City Hous Auth, 108 AD2d 612, 485 NYS2d 68 (1st Dept 1985), *appeal dismissed*, 67 NY2d 1027, 494 NE2d 457, 503 NYS2d 326 (1986), *second appeal dismissed*, 72 NY2d 1002, 531 NE2d 297, 534 NYS2d 665 (1988).

[239] Blau Mech Corp v City of NY, 158 AD2d 373, 551 NYS2d 228 (1st Dept 1990).

[240] Slattery Assocs v City of NY, 98 AD2d 686, 469 NYS2d 758 (1st Dept 1983).

[241] 58 NY2d 377, 448 NE2d 413, 461 NYS2d 746 (1983).

[242] *Id* at 385, 448 NE2d at 417, 461 NYS2d at 750.

In *Castagna & Son v Board of Education*,[243] the Supreme Court of New York indicated that "willful, malicious, or grossly negligent conduct" would be established if the contractor, Castagna, could present sufficient evidence to prove that delay damages were, in fact, caused by the Board of Education's deliberately concealing from the contractor knowledge that the plans and specifications for the project were defective, incomplete, and not in compliance with the Board of Education standards and building codes.[244]

§7.41 —Fraud or Bad Faith

A *no damage for delay* clause may be avoided if a contractor can prove fraud or bad faith by the owner.[245] When there is fraud or bad faith, the necessary meeting of the minds is absent. Courts cannot enforce an exculpatory provision when the delay stems from the owner's false or misleading statements.

A contractor avoided dismissal of his delay damage claim by his allegation that the owner misrepresented that it had obtained a wetland excavation permit when, in fact, it had not.[246] Similarly, a contractor avoided dismissal by summary judgment of its claim by its allegations that the county misrepresented ground water conditions, drainage systems, and the presence of underground electrical lines.[247]

Delay damages were allowed when the state provided erroneous subsurface information that increased the excavation time from an estimated three weeks to almost a year. The court found that the state's engineers had misrepresented subsurface conditions.[248]

§7.42 —Breach of Contract

The final exception to enforcement of a *no damage for delay* provision is if the delay results from the owner's breach of a fundamental contract obligation.[249] This exception is applied to an "especially narrow range of circumstances."[250] The breach must be of a *fundamental, affirmative* obligation expressly imposed on the owner by the contract.

In *Corinno*, the Court of Appeals explained that the reason for such a narrow exception is that the purpose of a *no damage for delay* clause is to protect the

---

[243] 151 AD2d 392, 542 NYS2d 622 (1st Dept 1989).

[244] *Id.*

[245] Corinno Civetta Constr Corp v City of NY, 67 NY2d 297, 309, 493 NE2d 905, 502 NYS2d 681, 686 (1986).

[246] Earthbank Co v City of NY, 145 Misc 2d 937, 549 NYS2d 314 (NY 1989).

[247] JR Stevenson Corp v County of Westchester, 113 AD2d 918, 493 NYS2d 819 (2d Dept 1985).

[248] Cauldwell-Wingate Co v State, 276 NY 365, 12 NE2d 443 (1938).

[249] Corinno Civetta Constr Corp v City of NY, 67 NY2d 297, 309, 493 NE2d 905, 502 NYS2d 681, 686 (1986).

[250] *Id* at 312, 493 NE2d at 912, 502 NYS2d at 688.

owner from "claims for delay damages resulting from its failure of performance in ordinary, garden variety ways."[251] The court said that an example of a breach meeting the exception is when an owner fails in its obligation to obtain title to the work site or to make it available to the contractor so it can begin its work.[252]

Other examples of fundamental breaches of contract were found when an owner failed to furnish temporary heat as required by contract so the contractor could work through the winter (the court also called this *active interference*);[253] an owner failed to obtain a wetland excavation permit (the court also called this *misrepresentation* and *uncontemplated cause of delay*);[254] and when an owner delayed the project because it failed to appropriate necessary funds.[255]

§7.43 Disruption/Interference

Similar to a delay claim is a claim of *disruption or interference*. This claim essentially asserts that the owner or its agents disrupted or interfered with the contractor's work to such an extent that the work was made more costly. The claim is based on an owner's implied duty not to interfere with the contractor's work progress[256] or to hinder or obstruct its performance.[257] Interference or disruption may be found in an owner's refusal to allow the contractor to do its work in the sequence or manner originally planned[258] or when an owner allows other contractors to work in the claimant-contractor's work area before it is ready and thereby disrupt the claimant-contractor's work.[259] Examples of disruption and interference can be found in the sections on owner interference at §7.23 and active interference at §7.38.

Many claims fail to distinguish between claims for disruption and interference and claims for delay. While the disruption or interference may often cause a delay and thus give rise to a delay claim, the increased cost of performing

---

[251] *Id.*

[252] *Id; see also* Carlo Bianchi & Co v State, 17 AD2d 38, 230 NYS2d 471 (3d Dept 1962), *affd*, 28 NY2d 536, 268 NE2d 121, 319 NYS2d 439 (1971).

[253] DeRiso Bros v State, 161 Misc 934, 293 NYS 436 (Ct Cl 1937).

[254] Earthbank Co v City of NY, 145 Misc 2d 937, 549 NYS2d 314 (NY 1989).

[255] Johnson v City of NY, 191 AD 205, 181 NYS 137, *affd*, 231 NY 564, 132 NE 890 (1920).

[256] Shalman v Board of Educ, 31 AD2d 338, 297 NYS2d 1000 (3d Dept 1969).

[257] Quaker-Empire Constr Co v DA Collins Constr Co, 88 AD2d 1043, 452 NYS2d 692 (3d Dept 1982).

[258] American Bridge Co v State, 245 AD 535, 283 NYS 577 (1935) (owner required contractor to fabricate steel long before needed); *see also* United States Steel Corp v Missouri Pac RR, 668 F2d 435 (8th Cir 1982); Quaker-Empire Constr Co v DA Collins Constr Co, 88 AD2d 1043, 452 NYS2d 692 (3d Dept 1982) (contractor required to work through winter months despite contract which said otherwise).

[259] Peter A. Camilli & Sons v State, 41 Misc 2d 218, 245 NYS2d 521 (Ct Cl 1963); *see also* Rao Elec Equip Co v State, 36 AD2d 1019, 321 NYS2d 670 (4th Dept 1971) (state opened hospital before contractor done with work).

the work in a disjointed manner gives rise to a claim independent of any delay claim.

The following hypothetical may help to illustrate the difference between the two types of claims.

> An excavation contractor intends to excavate a site in 30 days, using machinery to excavate the northern half in the first 15 days and only hand tools to excavate the southern half in the last 15 days. After 5 days of machine excavation, the owner orders the contractor to change the sequence of its operation and to excavate from south to north. The contractor hand excavates the southern half in 15 days as contemplated and then completes the machine excavation of the northern half in another 10 days. The excavation has been completed in 30 days as scheduled; there has been no delay. However, the contractor has a claim for the increased cost of having the machinery on the site for 30 days rather than 15 days.

It is important to distinguish disruption and interference claims from delay claims. If damages are couched as delay damages, they may be barred by a *no damage for delay* clause, whereas if the damages are couched as disruption or interference damages, they may survive a *no damage for delay* clause.[260]

§7.44 Acceleration

Acceleration is the means by which work that is behind schedule "catches up" to the contract completion date. Acceleration can be achieved by placing extra laborers on the job, working overtime, acquiring more equipment, using more efficient equipment, and so forth. Whatever method a contractor employs to accelerate its performance, it is bound to be costly. The central issue surrounding acceleration is which party bears the extra cost.

Generally, if the contractor is responsible for the delay, and thus the needed acceleration, it will be responsible for the costs of acceleration.[261] Similarly, if the contractor voluntarily accelerates to finish the job early or on time to avoid liquidated damages, it will not be entitled to extra compensation but will bear responsibility for the costs. On the other hand, if an owner directs completion before the contract completion date or demands timely completion despite the occurrence of excusable delay, the contractor would be entitled to recovery of its acceleration costs.

In a case where another subcontractor causes the delay in the project, the general contractor will be held liable for the acceleration costs of the subcontractor who, because of the delay, is unable to begin work until much later than

---

[260] *See* US Indus, Inc v Blake Constr Co, 671 F2d 539 (DC Cir 1982).
[261] Merritt-Chapman & Scott Corp v State, 54 AD2d 37, 386 NYS2d 894 (3d Dept 1976), *affd*, 43 NY 690, 371 NE2d 790, 401 NYS2d 28 (1977).

scheduled.[262] Also, it has been held that where both the owner and the general contractor are equally responsible, due to early delays, for the subcontractor's losses, they are both equally liable for the subcontractor's acceleration costs.[263]

§7.45 —Actual Acceleration

Actual acceleration occurs when an owner orders the contractor to finish the contract work before the completion date set by the contract or orders the contractor to complete the work before the revised completion date and acknowledges that it is accelerating completion. The contractor is entitled to its increased costs due to the acceleration.

§7.46 —Constructive Acceleration

Constructive acceleration occurs when an owner orders a contractor to complete the work by the contract completion date despite the existence of excusable delay or the addition of extra work that entitles the contractor to an extension of time. When an owner fails to recognize that the contractor is entitled to an extension of time it forces the contractor to perform the work in a shorter period of time than would have been available had an extension been given.

There are five elements of constructive acceleration:

1. The contractor encountered excusable delay or was ordered to perform extra work affecting the *critical path*[264]
2. The owner had knowledge of the excusable delay[265] or extra work and that it affected the critical path
3. The owner failed or refused to grant the contractor's request for an extension of time
4. There was some act or statement by the owner that could be construed as an acceleration order, such as reference to liquidated damages
5. The contractor accelerated performance

To recover on a claim of constructive acceleration, a contractor must prove each of these elements.

An owner can order acceleration directly or indirectly. A direct order is usually obvious. What is not so obvious is whether an owner intends to accelerate a job when it asks the contractor to adhere to the original schedule despite

---

[262] Wolff & Munier, Inc v Whiting-Turner Contracting Co, 946 F2d 1003 (2d Cir 1991).

[263] Mobil Chem Co v Blount Bros Corp, 809 F2d 1175 (5th Cir 1987).

[264] *See* **§7.04.**

[265] An owner typically gains knowledge of excusable delay through a request for an extension of time. Knowledge may be implied; for example, if work was delayed due to an exceptionally heavy and lengthy blizzard, an owner would have difficulty asserting that it did not know of the excusable delay.

extra work or excusable delay,[266] stresses the urgency of the project,[267] or threatens the contractor with termination or liquidated damages.[268]

To avoid inadvertently giving an order of acceleration, an owner should avoid threatening language when discussing delays with its contractor. When concerned that work is lagging, an owner should write as neutral a letter as possible using language such as, "I am concerned. . . ." Then, the contractor cannot claim that it was unaware of the problem, nor can it claim that it was threatened and accelerated to avoid the threatened behavior.

> **PRACTICE POINTER:**
>
> To avoid inadvertent constructive acceleration, an owner should:
> —use neutral language;
> —avoid threats;
> —promptly respond to requests for extensions of time;
> —be reasonable when evaluating requests for extensions of time; and
> —work with the contractor toward prompt completion.

§7.47 —Right to Relief

Damages due to acceleration should be distinguished from damages due to delay to avoid operation of *no damage for delay* provisions. Acceleration damages are for increased labor costs due to increased numbers of craftspersons working on the job and overtime, not because of increased labor rates. Similarly, loss of productivity damages may result when more laborers than can efficiently work together are required to work in a limited area so the job can be completed sooner. Procurement costs may have increased because a contractor had to pay extra for early delivery of materials, not because the passage of time made them cost more. Extra supervision costs are incurred because of the need for more foremen to supervise the extra laborers, not because the same supervi-

---

[266] Raymond Intl, Inc, ASBCA 13121, 70-1 BCA ¶8341 (1970) (contractor required to perform more than twice as much earthwork as specified in the contract within original contract time when government refused to allow extension of time for extra work; court held adherence to original schedule despite changed condition constituted an order to accelerate).

[267] Electronic & Missile Facility, Inc, ASBCA 9031, 1964 BCA ¶4338 (1964) (acceleration order found when government refused to grant extension of time, insisted on original schedule, and stressed project's urgency through statements to the effect that the entire project was dependent on the contractor's completion on time and that it was "paying for time on this job and [had] deadline dates to meet").

[268] Pathman Constr Co, ASBCA 14285, 71-1 BCA ¶8905 (1971) (extension of time refused following strike, government stressed the urgency of the job, and read the contract liquidated damages provision at a meeting).

sors had to work on the job longer.[269] Thus, acceleration damages are due to increased direct and indirect costs *during* performance, while delay damages are due to increased direct and indirect costs due to performance later than anticipated.

§7.48 Remedies

When delay occurs, contractors and owners have several different remedies available to them. Primarily, contractors seek their actual damages, although they may be entitled to terminate the contract. Owners similarly may be entitled to their actual damages and contract termination. Alternatively, they may be entitled to recover liquidated damages.

§7.49 Burden of Proof

As in any case, the party claiming the injury has the burden of proving its damages. Delay damages are often difficult to prove with absolute certainty. Impossibility of precise computation of damages or their apportionment does not bar recovery of delay damages,[270] although the damages cannot be wholly speculative.[271]

To recover damages for delay, a plaintiff must show

> that defendant was responsible for the delay; that these delays caused delay in completion of the contract (eliminating overlapping or duplication of delay); [and] that the plaintiff suffered damages as a result of these delays; and plaintiff must furnish some rational basis for the court to estimate those damages, although obviously a precise measure is neither possible nor required.[272]

The mere fact that items of cost were incurred after the scheduled completion date does not necessarily mean that they were additional costs or due to delay.[273] A party must prove that there was an increase in costs and that the increase was due to the delay.[274]

Damages cannot be based solely on a comparison of bid estimates with actual costs, due to the inherent unreliability of the elements in a bid[275] and the fact that the owner may not have been responsible for all increased costs.

---

[269] *See* Contracting & Material Co v City of Chicago, 20 Ill App 3d 684, 314 NE2d 598 (1974), *revd,* 64 Ill 2d 21, 349 NE2d 389 (1976).

[270] Rusciano Constr Corp v State, 37 AD2d 745, 323 NYS2d 21 (3d Dept 1971).

[271] Hirsch Elec Co v Community Servs, 145 AD2d 603, 536 NYS2d 141 (2d Dept 1988).

[272] Manshul Constr Corp v Dormitory Auth, 79 AD2d 383, 436 NYS2d 724, 728 (1st Dept 1981).

[273] *Id.*

[274] *Id.*

[275] Novak & Co v Facilities Dev Corp, 116 AD2d 891, 498 NYS2d 492 (3d Dept 1986).

Total Cost Method

One method of calculating delay damages is the *total cost* method. The total cost approach essentially seeks to convert a standard fixed-price construction contract into a cost reimbursement arrangement.[276] The total cost method subtracts the total estimated cost of performance from the total actual cost of performance.[277] Since a contractor's total cost figure generally represents only its actual direct expenses, overhead and profit,[278] based upon percentages that the court regards as fair and reasonable,[279] are usually added.

In order to implement the total cost method, a contractor must establish that:

1. The nature of the particular losses makes it impossible or highly impracticable to determine them with a reasonable degree of accuracy
2. The plaintiff's bid or estimate was realistic
3. The plaintiff's actual costs were reasonable; and
4. The plaintiff was not responsible for the added expense[280]

However, the total cost method of computing damages is not favored by the courts. It fails to assign specific damages to specific delays.[281] It makes no allowance for delays caused by the contractor itself.

The almost universal rule is that a total cost proof of damages will only be accepted in certain limited circumstances.[282] It is generally considered to be a method of last resort.[283]

New York permits resort to a total cost basis of proof despite the contractor's responsibility for some of the damages incurred.[284]

In *Westcott v State*,[285] proof of damages by the total cost method was permitted because a more precise mathematical basis for computation of damages was not available. More recent cases have not explicitly required the unavailability

---

[276] R. Cushman & D. Carpenter, Proving and Pricing Construction Claims 136 (1990).

[277] *Id* 119.

[278] D'Angelo v State, 41 AD2d 77, 341 NYS2d 84 (3d Dept 1973).

[279] *See* Westcott v State, 264 AD 463, 465-66, 36 NYS2d 23, 25 (3d Dept 1942) (court awarded 15% for overhead and profit); Columbia Asphalt Corp v State, 70 AD2d 133, 137, 420 NYS2d 36, 39 (3d Dept 1979), *appeal denied*, 49 NY2d 702, 426 NYS2d 1027 (1980) (court awarded 10% for overhead and an additional 10% for profit).

[280] Cushman & Carpenter, *supra* note 276, at 36.

[281] *Dealing with Damages* 388 (Itzkoff, ed 1983).

[282] Simon, *Construction Contracts and Claims* 144 (McGraw-Hill Book Co 1979).

[283] Cushman & Carpenter, *supra* note 276, at 119.

[284] *See* Columbia Asphalt Corp v State, 70 AD2d 133, 420 NYS2d 36 (3d Dept 1979), *appeal denied*, 49 NY2d 702, 426 NYS2d 1027 (1980); Fehlhaber Corp v State, 69 AD2d 362, 419 NYS2d 773 (3d Dept 1979).

[285] 264 AD 463, 36 NYS2d 23 (3d Dept 1942).

of a more precise method of damage calculation as a condition to using the total cost method.[286]

Jury Verdict Method

The *jury verdict* method of assessing damages is similar to that of the *total cost* method; however, there are some differences. In the *jury verdict* method, the triers of fact weigh the various elements of a contractor's claim and derive a total value for the claim, often expressed as a lump sum.[287] From this lump sum, the court deducts a percentage that it believes represents the damages attributable to the contractor's own delays or to causes not chargeable to the owner. The remainder of the lump sum constitutes the contractor's compensable loss.[288]

In awarding damages on a jury verdict basis, the courts must be persuaded that:

1. Entitlement exists
2. There is no more reliable method for computing damages; and
3. The record affords a basis for a fair and reasonable approximation of damages[289]

The jury verdict method of determining damages is favored over the total cost method of computing damages, but also is generally not accepted by the courts.

§7.50 Apportionment of Responsibility for Delay

It is rare that only one factor or one party causes a project to be delayed. Delay of a project may be caused by labor disputes, the weather, the owner, and the contractor.[290] It is reversible error for a trial court to fail to allocate responsibility for delay where more than one factor is responsible.[291] In such cases, the court must apportion liability for the delay,[292] typically by determining the cause and length of each delay, to whom (if anyone) it should be

---

[286] *See* Fehlhaber Corp v State, 69 AD2d 362, 419 NYS2d 773 (3d Dept 1979); Whitmyer Bros v State, 63 AD2d 103, 406 NYS2d 617 (3d Dept 1978), *affd,* 47 NY2d 960, 393 NE2d 1027, 419 NYS2d 954 (1979).

[287] Cushman & Carpenter, *supra* note 276, at 163-64. Reprinted with permission from Cushman, *Proving and Pricing Construction Claims,* © 1990 John Wiley & Sons, Inc., New York, New York.

[288] *Id* 164.

[289] *Id.*

[290] Bero Constr Co v State, 27 AD2d 974, 278 NYS2d 658 (4th Dept 1967).

[291] Rusciano Constr Corp v State, 37 AD2d 745, 323 NYS2d 21 (3d Dept 1971); Tully & DiNapoli, Inc v State, 34 AD2d 439, 311 NYS2d 941 (3d Dept 1970).

[292] Grow Constr Co v State, 56 AD2d 95, 391 NYS2d 726 (3d Dept 1977) (contractor found 75% responsible for delay, state 25%).

charged, and the net amount of damages due.[293] Of course, precise determination is impossible.[294]

Apportionment is made in percentages. For example, in one case, the state was found liable for 15 per cent of the delay and the contractor for the other 85 per cent.[295] In another, the state was found 95 per cent responsible and the contractor 5 per cent responsible.[296] Responsibility for a portion of the delay is not an absolute bar to recovery of damages, no matter how much the party seeking recovery contributed to the delay. Thus, a contractor found 85 per cent liable for the delay can recover 15 per cent of its damages from the owner who was responsible for only 15 per cent of the delay.

To determine damages due a contributing contractor, the courts will determine total damages due to delay regardless of fault, subtract any credits or offsets due the owner for such things as defective work or changes, and apportion the resulting sum by the liability percentages.[297] Apportionment must be made *after* credits and offsets for such things as defective work or changes are subtracted from the total delay damage sum.[298] Thus, where the contractor's delay damages were shown to be $60,567, the contractor that was 5 per cent responsible for the delay was awarded 95 per cent of this sum, or $57,538.[299]

§7.51 Waiver

As in any other type of case, damages for delay may be waived, either before they are incurred, as was discussed in §7.32 on *no damage for delay* clauses, or afterward through execution of a waiver of claims. Generally, a waiver of claims is valid. For instance, when a contractor sought an extension of time to complete the contract and agreed to waive its claim for delay damages in exchange, the waiver was upheld.[300] A similar waiver was upheld in another case, despite the fact that the contractor had initiated suit on its delay claims.[301] The court stated that the fact that suit had been initiated was irrelevant, based on the waiver which made no mention of the suit and stated that the contractor agreed to "waive and release all claims which [it] may have . . . arising out of the aforesaid contract" and excepted claims for change orders and work under pro-

---

[293] Bero Constr Co v State, 27 AD2d 974, 278 NYS2d 658 (4th Dept 1967).

[294] Manshul Constr Corp v Dormitory Auth, 79 AD2d 383, 436 NYS2d 724 (1st Dept 1981).

[295] Columbia Asphalt Corp v State, 70 AD2d 133, 420 NYS2d 36 (3d Dept 1979), *appeal denied,* 49 NY2d 702, 426 NYS2d 1027 (1980).

[296] Manshul Constr Corp v Dormitory Auth, 79 AD2d 383, 436 NYS2d 724 (1st Dept 1981).

[297] Columbia Asphalt Corp v State, 70 AD2d 133, 420 NYS2d 36 (3d Dept 1979), *appeal denied,* 49 NY2d 702, 426 NYS2d 1027 (1980).

[298] *Id.*

[299] Manshul Constr Corp v Dormitory Auth, 79 AD2d 383, 436 NYS2d 724 (1st Dept 1981).

[300] Naclerio Contracting Co v EPA, 86 AD2d 793, 447 NYS2d 4 (1st Dept 1982).

[301] Mars Assocs v City of NY, 70 AD2d 839, 418 NYS2d 27 (1st Dept 1979), *affd,* 53 NY2d 627, 420 NE2d 971, 438 NYS2d 779 (1981).

test.[302] Claims for delay damages may also be lost if a contractor fails to comply with notice and record-keeping requirements.[303]

A waiver will not always be upheld. A trial court held a waiver invalid when it found that the owner extracted the waiver by refusing to grant the contractor an extension of time and pay it if it did not execute a waiver of its claim. The court held that it was unconscionable of the owner to require the contractor to abandon its legitimate claims, especially where the delays were due wholly to the owner.[304]

§7.52 Contractor's Damages for Delay

A contractor's damages for delay are recovered most often through a breach of contract claim. Delay damages based in quantum meruit are available in limited circumstances but never to avoid operation of a *no damage for delay* clause.[305] A contractor may recover in quantum meruit where it has been terminated[306] or has justly abandoned the contract.[307] Further, the courts have awarded delay damages measured on quantum meruit bases, allowing contractors to recover their actual job costs plus reasonable overhead and profit.[308] A contractor is never required to abandon a contract due to an owner's breach; it may choose to complete the contract and sue for damages.[309]

Pursuant to a liquidating agreement, a contractor may bring suit on behalf of its subcontractor for delay damages suffered by its subcontractor. Under such an agreement, the contractor is liable to its subcontractor in the amount of delay damages it recovers from the owner on the subcontractor's behalf, even if the contractor itself directly suffered no delay damages.[310]

There are many elements to a contractor's delay damages. The major ones are discussed in the relevant sections following. Do not let this discussion limit a contractor's search for compensation; it is not exhaustive. If an injury is real and the loss documented, a contractor should not be deterred from claiming it as an element of its damages, even if the element is not found here or in other literature, previously may have been tried and lost, or has never been tried.

---

[302] *Id* at 839, 418 NYS2d at 27.

[303] *See* §§7.17-7.19 and ch 15.

[304] New Again Constr Co v City of NY, 76 Misc 2d 943, 351 NYS2d 895 (Kings 1974).

[305] Buckley & Co v City of NY, 121 AD2d 933, 505 NYS2d 140 (1st Dept 1986).

[306] Fehlhaber Corp v State, 65 AD2d 119, 410 NYS2d 920 (3d Dept 1978).

[307] Farrell Heating, Plumbing Air Conditioning Contractors, Inc v Facilities Dev & Improvement Corp, 68 AD2d 958, 414 NYS2d 767 (3d Dept 1979).

[308] *See* Whitmyer Bros v State, 47 NY2d 960, 393 NE2d 1027, 419 NYS2d 954 (1979), *affg* 63 AD2d 103, 406 NYS2d 617 (1978); D'Angelo v State, 41 AD2d 77, 341 NYS2d 84 (3d Dept), *appeal dismissed*, 32 NY2d 896, 300 NE2d 155, 346 NYS2d 814 (1973), *modified*, 34 NY2d 641, 311 NE2d 509, 355 NYS2d 377 (1974).

[309] Shalman v Board of Educ, 31 AD2d 338, 297 NYS2d 1000 (3d Dept 1969).

[310] American Standard, Inc v New York City Transit Auth, 133 AD2d 595, 519 NYS2d 701 (2d Dept 1987). Liquidating agreements are discussed in **ch 3** on subcontracts.

§7.53 —Labor Escalation

It is natural for there to be increased labor costs when a contract takes longer to perform than was planned. Many construction contracts provide for a two- or three-year performance period; delay can push that period to five years or more. It is only to be expected that a labor hour in the fifth year will cost more than a labor hour in the second year. Increased labor cost includes not only direct pay but also increased expenditures on indirect labor costs, such as benefits, payroll taxes, social security, insurance, etc.

A claim for increased labor costs cannot be based solely on a comparison of total labor costs with the bid estimate for labor.[311] A contractor must prove which elements of its labor costs were increased due to the owner's actions[312] and the extent to which the delay carried the work into a period of higher wage costs.[313] Proof may be made through payroll records or check copies that show the actual cost incurred; this amount can then be compared with estimated costs of labor (as opposed to the bid estimate).[314] The point is that bid estimates are considered to be inherently unreliable as proof of what a job would have cost but for the delay—bid estimates are often hurriedly made at a time when few facts are known. Estimates for proving damages are best made after the job is begun or has been completed when more facts are known upon which a realistic estimate can be based.

§7.54 —Material Escalation

It is natural for the cost of materials used in a project to increase during a period of delay. Sometimes, materials that would have been available become unavailable or more difficult and costly to obtain due to shortages that would not have been encountered but for the delay. In the event of acceleration, materials may cost more because of earlier delivery, because of the necessity of using a different supplier, or because they have to be purchased in small quantities locally rather than in bulk with a long lead time from a national supplier. The measure of damages is the difference between what the materials would have cost if performance was timely and what they actually cost due to the compensable delay, plus reasonable overhead and profit.[315]

§7.55 —Loss of Productivity

When bidding on contracts, contractors assume that most of the work will progress in an orderly fashion that minimizes duplication of effort and idleness of labor and equipment and makes use of the most efficient methods and sched-

---

[311] Manshul Constr Corp v Dormitory Auth, 79 AD2d 383, 436 NYS2d 724 (1st Dept 1981).

[312] Novak & Co v Facilities Dev Corp, 116 AD2d 891, 498 NYS2d 492 (3d Dept 1986).

[313] JL Young Engg Co v United States, 98 Ct Cl 310 (1943).

[314] Litchfield Constr Co v City of NY, 244 NY 251, 155 NE 116 (1926).

[315] Fehlhaber Corp v State, 65 AD2d 119, 410 NYS2d 920 (3d Dept 1978).

ules. When delay occurs, efficiency is often lost resulting in lower productivity of the contractor. For example, a delayed contractor might complete only 41 per cent of a job during the original contract period but expend 100 per cent of its anticipated equipment and operating costs.[316] Such a contractor is entitled to recover what it actually expended; not merely the amount allocable to the percentage of work completed.

Similarly, a contractor may experience loss of productivity if the owner forces, either directly or indirectly through delay, the contractor to use a less efficient method of doing the job. For instance, in one case, a contractor recovered its increased cost of performance due to loss of productivity when the state's engineer delayed in approving the contractor's choice of method and required drawings for so long that the contractor was unable to obtain needed structural steel (World War I significantly reduced the availability of steel for civil construction), which steel was plentiful at the time when it originally would have been purchased but for the engineer's delay. Due to the inability to obtain the steel, the contractor was forced to use less efficient and more costly methods in excavating and erecting a subway line.[317]

Proving the amount of damage due to loss of productivity is difficult. Loss of productivity damages may not be based solely on a comparison of precontract estimates with actual costs[318] and must be proven through showing that the work had to be completed in an irregular and inefficient manner due to the delay.[319] One way to show loss of productivity is for a contractor's expert to prepare an analysis that demonstrates what the job would have cost in labor hours had there not been a delay and compares it with what the actual costs were.[320]

§7.56 —Procurement Costs

In addition to higher materials costs, the cost of subcontract work and equipment and tool purchase or rental may increase due to a delay.

§7.57 —Impact Costs

Impact costs may include loss of productivity, materials escalation, and other items of damage discussed in this chapter. In addition, impact costs include the increased cost of performance, such as when specific future operations are impacted by a delay. Assume that a delay in excavating a foundation occurs, pushing the time to pour the concrete from fall, when the weather does not

---

[316] *See* Fehlhaber Corp v State, 65 AD2d 119, 410 NYS2d 920 (3d Dept 1978).

[317] Litchfield Constr Co v City of NY, 244 NY 251, 155 NE 116 (1926).

[318] Manshul Constr Corp v Dormitory Auth, 79 AD2d 383, 436 NYS2d 724 (1st Dept 1981).

[319] JL Young Engg Co v United States, 98 Ct Cl 310 (1943).

[320] For analysis of other methods of proving loss of productivity, see T. Shea, *Proving Productivity Losses in Government Contracts*, 18 Pub Cont LJ 414 (Mar 1989).

cause a problem, to winter, when precautions must be taken to ensure that the concrete will set properly. The extra costs of pouring the concrete—heaters, more expensive mix, measures to protect the concrete from winter weather while setting—would be impact costs. Careful records must be kept to prove most impact costs.

§7.58 —Field Overhead

The longer a contractor must work on a job, the higher are its field overhead costs, including field office personnel costs (supervisors, site engineers, etc.)[321] and field office expenses.[322] A contractor is entitled to award of expenses incurred in field overhead where the delay caused the contractor to incur expense above that which would have been incurred but for the delay.[323] Of course, if the delay is noncompensable, field overhead is not recoverable.[324]

When proving increased field overhead, it is not enough to simply show that field overhead costs were incurred after the original completion date.[325] A contractor must prove that there was in fact an increase in field overhead *due to delay.*

§7.59 —Idle Equipment

Another damage that may be incurred as a result of delay is the cost of equipment, machinery, and plant facilities lying idle. The measure of damages is the fair and reasonable rental value of the equipment for the period it was idle.[326] Rental rates may be those actually paid or, if the contractor owns the equipment, the damage amount may be based on local rental rates or rates published in, or determined in accordance with, an acceptable rate guide, such as the Associated Equipment Dealers Manual[327] or the Associated General Contractors method for computing ownership expense.[328]

---

[321] LG DeFelice & Son v State, 63 Misc 2d 357, 313 NYS2d 21 (Ct Cl 1970).

[322] Manshul Constr Corp v Dormitory Auth, 79 AD2d 383, 436 NYS2d 724 (1st Dept 1981) (field overhead claim disallowed as duplicative and not proven).

[323] Johnson, Drake & Piper, Inc v State, 31 AD2d 980, 297 NYS2d 754 (3d Dept 1969).

[324] Charles H. Sells, Inc v New York State Thruway Auth, 27 AD2d 893, 278 NYS2d 162 (3d Dept 1967).

[325] Manshul Constr Corp v Dormitory Auth, 79 AD2d 383, 436 NYS2d 724 (1st Dept 1981) (field overhead claim disallowed as duplicative and not proven).

[326] Shore Bridge Corp v State, 186 Misc 1005, 61 NYS2d 32 (Ct Cl), *affd,* 271 AD 811, 66 NYS2d 921 (1946); Country Excavation, Inc v State, 44 Misc 2d 1057, 255 NYS2d 708 (Ct Cl 1964).

[327] Fehlhaber Corp v State, 65 AD2d 119, 410 NYS2d 920 (3d Dept 1978).

[328] Robert A. Rubin, Sammie D. Guy, Alfred C. Maevis & Virginia Fairweather, Construction Claims: Analysis, Presentation, Defense 85 (VanNostrand Reinhold 2d ed 1992)

The fact that the contractor owns the idle equipment does not preclude a contractor from recovery of its reasonable rental value.[329] If the contractor could have made use of the equipment but for the fact that it had to be kept at the job site, there has been damage and the contractor should recover. If the contractor moves the equipment and uses it elsewhere during the delay period, however, it may not recover the rental value during the time when the equipment was used elsewhere, but may recover during the time it was being moved and may recover the cost of demobilizing and remobilizing the equipment.[330]

§7.60 —Home Office Overhead

Similar to a field overhead claim,[331] but more difficult to prove,[332] is a claim for home office overhead. This type of overhead includes every cost involved in operating an office: building rent or depreciation, office equipment rent or depreciation, utilities, telephone, office staff, stationery, payroll costs, taxes, etc.[333] As with any element of damage, a contractor has the burden of proving that there was an increase in home office overhead in relation to the contract's being delayed.[334] For instance, a showing that the delay caused engineering or design problems that required central office staff consideration would prove that there was an increase.[335] These costs can be allocated to the delay through use of office records normally kept for tax purposes.

The amount of office overhead is difficult to calculate and unavoidably somewhat uncertain. This does not mean, however, that an injured contractor will be denied recovery because its damage is difficult to measure.[336] Due to the problems of quantifying office overhead and proving what percentage of those costs was due to the delay (since the office would have been open regardless of the delay, an owner is not responsible for all office overhead that arises dur-

---

[329] Fehlhaber Corp v State, 65 AD2d 119, 410 NYS2d 920 (3d Dept 1978); Shore Bridge Corp v State, 186 Misc 1005, 61 NYS2d 32 (Ct Cl), affd, 271 AD 811, 66 NYS2d 921 (1946).

[330] Columbia Asphalt Corp v State, 70 AD2d 133, 420 NYS2d 36 (3d Dept 1979), appeal denied, 49 NY2d 702, 426 NYS2d 1027 (1980).

[331] See §7.58.

[332] Berley Indus v City of NY, 45 NY2d 683, 687, 385 NE2d 281, 412 NYS2d 589, 591 (1978).

[333] A thorough analysis of the many elements of home office overhead and how to prove that a contractor is entitled to recovery of delay damages for them is found in R. Lane, *Recovering Delay Damages for Home Office Overhead*, 89-13 Construction Briefings 1 (1989).

[334] Berley Indus v City of NY, 45 NY2d 683, 385 NE2d 281, 412 NYS2d 589 (1978); Manshul Constr Corp v Dormitory Auth, 79 AD2d 383, 436 NYS2d 724 (1st Dept 1981).

[335] Manshul Constr Corp v Dormitory Auth, 79 AD2d 383, 436 NYS2d 724 (1st Dept 1981).

[336] Berley Indus v City of New York, 45 NY2d 683, 385 NE2d 281, 412 NYS2d 589 (1978).

ing a period of delay), the courts look to allocate these damages through the use of formulas or by application of contract percentages.

Mechanical application of the *Eichleay formula*,[337] which focuses solely on the length of the delay without independent substantiating evidence and does not consider any other factor, has been rejected in New York. In *Berley Industries v City of New York*,[338] the Court of Appeals held that it was error to submit the *Eichleay* formula to the jury and found it to be an artificial measure of damages that could easily result in an overreaching and arbitrary award and that, at best, produces an award with a chance relationship to actual damages.[339] The main problem with the Eichleay formula is that it bases overhead damages partially on the portion of work *not* delayed, resulting in a potential windfall to the contractor.[340]

New York's rejection of *Eichleay* has been criticized as confusing the concept of *extended overhead* with that of *unabsorbed overhead*.[341] Unabsorbed overhead in many cases may be merely viewed as the flip side of extended overhead. It is conceivable that when a project is delayed, fewer home office resources are used during the base contract period and, instead, those same resources are used during the extended period. When used on the delayed project during the extended period, they are not available for the contractor's use on other projects. There may, in fact, be no net increase in home office resources utilization caused by the delay, but merely a shift in the period of utilization. How is the contractor to be compensated for the underutilization of its home office resources during the base contract period, assuming that it was unable to find another project to fill that slot? When a project is delayed, the contractee (e.g., the owner) receives the benefit of the availability of the contractor's home office resources for a prolonged period, although the contractor may not be able to prove damage in the form of increased home office expenses or inability to secure or perform other projects. Should the law require compensation for

---

[337] The formula is a three-step formula:

1. $\dfrac{\text{Contract billings}}{\text{Total billings for contract period}} \times \begin{array}{l}\text{Total overhead}\\ \text{for contract period}\end{array} = \begin{array}{l}\text{Overhead}\\ \text{allocable to}\\ \text{the contract.}\end{array}$

2. $\dfrac{\text{Allocable overhead}}{\text{Days of performance}} = \text{Daily contract overhead.}$

3. Daily contract overhead × No. days delay = Amount claimed.

Eichleay Corp, ASBCA No 5183, 61-1 BCA ¶2894 (1960), *affg*, ASBCA No 5183, 60-2 BCA ¶2688 (1960). The Eichleay formula is evaluated in H. Reynolds, *Is Eichleay the Answer? An In-Depth Look at Home Office Overhead Claims*, 7 Construction Law 1 (1987) and J. Ernstrom & K. Essler, *Beyond the Eichleay Formula: Resurrecting Home Office Overhead Claims*, 3 Construction Law 1 (1982).

[338] 45 NY2d 683, 385 NE2d 281, 412 NYS2d 589 (1978).

[339] *Id* at 688-89, 385 NE2d at 284, 412 NYS2d at 592.

[340] *Manshul Constr Corp v Dormitory Auth*, 79 AD2d 383, 436 NYS2d 724 (1st Dept 1981).

[341] M. McElroy, Construction Litigation §11.0.2[2][a][ii] (S. Stein, ed 1987).

§7.60 HOME OFFICE OVERHEAD   239

a benefit conferred or merely recompense for a damage sustained? The authors believe that the answer to this question, not specifically addressed in the cases, underlies the approach taken by different courts to the issue of home office overhead as an element of delay damages.

The *Eichleay formula* is accepted in many federal courts in its original and modified forms.[342] The Court of Appeals of the Federal Circuit, the circuit that has jurisdiction of all final decisions of federal agencies and the United States Claims Court,[343] accepts *Eichleay*.[344]

The rejection of the *Eichleay formula* by the New York Court of Appeals does not mean that formulas may not be used to establish home office overhead. Use of a formula is appropriate where actual damages are unavoidably uncertain and the proposed formula constitutes a reasonable basis to calculate actual damages.[345] A formula may be acceptable if it is tailored to the facts of the specific case,[346] considers factors in addition to the length of the delay, such as cost of completion and the percentage of work complete on the original completion date, and does not base overhead damages on the portion of work *not* delayed.[347] For instance, in *Manshul Construction Corp v Dormitory Authority*,[348] the Appellate Division applied the following formula:

> (1) Estimate the actual cost of the work done after the scheduled completion date by deducting from the contract price the portion allocable to overhead and profit.
>
> (2) Allocate a percentage of this cost for overhead, and allow this as excess cost due to delay.
>
> (3) Add to this a profit percentage based on this excess overhead.
>
> (4) Take the proper damage allocation figure percentage of the sum of (2) and (3) and award as delay damages.[349]

The application of this formula can be more easily seen through the use of real numbers:

In *Manshul*, the authority was found to be responsible for 95% of the delay, the contractor for the other 5%. The court assumed that the overhead and profit portion of the contract price was 15%, 7.25% for each. The payment requisition for the delay period was $895,785. The formula works as follows:

---

[342] *See* Luria Bros v United States, 369 F2d 701 (Ct Cl 1966); JD Hedin Constr Co v United States, 347 F2d 235 (Ct Cl 1965).

[343] 28 USC §1295 *et seq*.

[344] Capital Elec Co v United States, 729 F2d 743 (Fed Cir 1984).

[345] Wayne County Vinegar & Cider Corp v Schorr's Famous Pickled Prods, 118 Misc 2d 52, 460 NYS2d 209 (Kings 1983).

[346] Manshul Constr Corp v Dormitory Auth, 111 Misc 2d 209, 444 NYS2d 792 (Kings 1981).

[347] *Dicta* Berley Indus v City of NY, 45 NY2d 683, 385 NE2d 281, 412 NYS2d 589 (1978).

[348] 79 AD2d 383, 436 NYS2d 724 (1st Dept 1981).

[349] *Id* at 391-92, 436 NYS2d at 731.

(1) Estimated cost of work done after completion date is 100/115 of the delay cost, or $778,943.

(2) 7.25% overhead of $778,943 is $56,473, the portion of overhead due to delay.

(3) 7.25% profit of the additional overhead of $56,473 is $4094.

(4) The sum of (2) and (3) is $60,567 in overhead and profit. The sum attributable to the delay for home office overhead is thus $57,538 (95% of $60,567).[350]

Damages for overhead may also be calculated simply by the addition of the appropriate overhead percentage to the actual cost of the contract in a quantum meruit basis[351] or, in a contract basis, to the amount of additional expense proved to be due to the delay.[352]

> **PRACTICE POINTER:**
>
> How to Prove a Home Office Overhead Claim in New York
>
> (1) Never mention the *Eichleay* formula.
>
> (2) Have a person familiar with the home office applications, such as the office manager, testify to exactly what the home office staff did during the delay period and the costs involved in running the home office.
>
> (3) Have an expert present a formula and testify that the particular formula is the best measure of damages in your case, giving reasons why—e.g., the formula demonstrates the actual home office cost of running the delayed project and takes into account the large amount of supervision required, length of delay compared to project duration, impact of delay on other jobs, etc.

> **PRACTICE POINTER:**
>
> How to Defeat a Home Office Overhead Claim in New York
>
> (1) Argue that the formula proposed is the contractor's attempt to use the *Eichleay* formula without acknowledging the source of the formula.
>
> (2) Argue that the formula used has no relationship to the contractor's actual experience on the job concerned.
>
> (3) Establish that there was little home office involvement during the delay period by demonstrating that the contractor's overall volume of work remained constant or increased yet the contractor did not add home office staff.

---

[350] *Id* at 392-93, 436 NYS2d at 731-32.

[351] *See* D'Angelo v State, 41 AD2d 77, 341 NYS2d 84 (3d Dept 1973), *appeal dismissed*, 32 NY2d 896, 300 NE2d 155, 346 NYS2d 814 (1973), *order modified*, 34 NY2d 641, 311 NE2d 509, 355 NYS2d 377 (1974).

[352] *See* LG DeFelice & Son v State, 63 Misc 2d 357, 313 NYS2d 21 (Ct Cl 1970); AE Ottaviano, Inc v State, 202 Misc 532, 110 NYS2d 99 (Ct Cl 1952).

> (4) Argue that the claimant has not laid a sufficient evidentiary foundation for its claim and use of its proposed formula by showing that the claimant has not presented sufficient factual evidence as to the effect of the delay on the home office, that the claimant has provided insufficient financial evidence as to the amount of home office overhead, and that its expert did not establish that the formula is one which will fairly allocate home office overhead based on the actual overhead. Present your own expert to support your attack of the formula.

§7.61 —Financing Costs

Theoretically, higher financing costs may be an element of delay damage. Assume that a contractor had to borrow money to perform a job, which money it would not have had to borrow but for the delay. The cost of borrowing the money would be damages attributable to the delay. This type of damage would be very difficult to prove—the contractor would have to trace the loan to the specific project and prove that the high cash requirements of the job required the contractor to get a loan.

§7.62 —Inability to Take On Other Work

Often during a period of delay, other jobs come up for bidding. A delayed contractor may be unable to bid on these jobs because its laborers and equipment are unavailable due to the delay or because it cannot obtain a bond. Generally, a claim for damages based on the inability to obtain other jobs due to delay is too speculative and recovery of actual damages is prohibited. Such a claim assumes that the contractor would have been the lowest qualified bidder, would have received the job, and would have earned the lost profit claimed. Such inferences upon inferences cannot be the basis of an actual damages claim, although such a contractor would be entitled to nominal damages.[353]

Loss of Bondability

Sometimes other work cannot be taken on because a contractor cannot get a job due to its inability to obtain a bond. A contractor's ability to obtain a bond is vital to its ability to enter into many contracts. Without the ability to procure bid, performance, and payment bonds, a contractor would be shut out from bidding on many jobs. When a contractor is delayed on a job, its access to bonds for new jobs may be restricted because sureties may be wary of issuing bonds to a delayed contractor. Generally, such a loss is not recoverable because it is deemed to be too speculative and based upon assumptions and inferences.[354]

---

[353] Hirsch Elec Co v Community Servs, 145 AD2d 603, 536 NYS2d 141 (2d Dept 1988).

[354] *Id.*

§7.63 —Profit

A contractor's bid includes a reasonable amount of profit. For example, a cost reimbursable contract will specify that the contractor shall be entitled to its costs plus a percentage for overhead plus an overall percentage for profit. Where excess costs are incurred due to delay, a contractor is entitled to profit on those excess costs in addition to the costs themselves.[355]

§7.64 —Interest

A contractor is not entitled to damages for loss of use of, or interest on, unpaid retainage, despite the fact that but for the delay the retainage would have been paid earlier.[356] The reasoning behind this rule is that, despite a delay, retainage is not earned until a job is complete.[357]

A contractor is entitled to interest on amounts that are not paid when due. Thus, a contractor was awarded interest on its claim for two years before its application for last payment where the owner could have determined the amount due the contractor earlier than the final payment application.[358]

A contractor is also entitled to interest on delay damages in a breach of contract action. Normally, this type of interest is computed from the date of the damage or the date that the cause of action accrued. However, where the date of the breach is indeterminable, the interest on recovery is to be determined from the date of commencement of the action.[359]

§7.65 Contractor Damage Recovery

Recovery of the elements of delay damages is not automatic. Proper notice must be given as required by the contract or applicable statutes. Damages must be substantiated. Only by keeping thorough, accurate books can a contractor hope to recover its actual damages due to delay. Careful records of labor overtime and the reason for the overtime should be maintained, as should records of equipment allocation and materials purchases. Schedules must be kept current, and each version should be saved in the event it becomes necessary to show the cause and impact of a delay.

---

[355] Novak & Co v Facilities Dev Corp, 116 AD2d 891, 498 NYS2d 492 (3d Dept 1986); AE Ottaviano, Inc v State, 202 Misc 532, 110 NYS2d 99 (Ct Cl 1952).

[356] Litchfield Constr Co v City of NY, 244 NY 251, 155 NE 116 (1926); AE Ottaviano v State, 202 Misc 532, 110 NYS2d 99 (Ct Cl 1952).

[357] Litchfield Constr Co v City of NY, 244 NY 251, 155 NE 116 (1926).

[358] Fehlhaber Corp v State, 65 AD2d 119, 410 NYS2d 920 (3d Dept 1978).

[359] S. Leo Harmonay, Inc v Binks Mfg Co, 597 F Supp 1014 (SDNY 1984) (applying New York law).

§7.66 Contractor's Other Remedies

A contractor may be entitled to terminate a contract delayed by the owner if the contract so provides or if the delay is unreasonably long. For example, in a case where an owner failed to issue an order to commence work within 60 days of the contract execution as provided in the contract, it was held that the contractor was justified in withdrawing from the contract.[360] When the contractor, under protest, honored the owner's demand that it proceed, the court allowed the contractor to recover its damages for the delay in issuing the order to commence. Contract termination is discussed in Chapter 4.

§7.67 Owner's Damages for Delay

Owners are also damaged by delay. Where the delay is caused by the contractor, an owner may look to the contractor for recovery of damages. An owner may recover its actual or liquidated damages, depending on the contract; generally, it may not recover both[361] and does not have the choice of which to pursue.

Elements of owner damages for delay are discussed in the following sections.

§7.68 —Actual Damages

An owner's actual delay damages can have many measures; they depend upon the unique situation of the owner involved. For instance, if the contract is for the addition of a garage onto a home and it is delayed, the owner may be entitled to recover its loss of use damages, including extra wear and tear to its car due to weather or for garage rent. If the contract is for a public parking garage, the owner may be entitled to damages for lost net revenues, higher interest on its construction loan, and items of specific damage, such as extra insurance premiums and supervision.

§7.69 —Loss of Use

Often, an owner has a building built because it intends to use it itself. When a contract is delayed, the owner is unable to use the building as soon as it should have. Thus, an owner may be entitled to damages for loss of use and enjoyment of property.[362] These damages typically include costs incurred in renting or using substitute space.

---

[360] Bernmil Contracting Corp v City of NY, 80 AD2d 869, 437 NYS2d 17 (2d Dept 1981).

[361] *But see* Melwood Constr Corp v State, 126 Misc 2d 156, 481 NYS2d 289 (Ct Cl 1984), *affd*, 119 AD2d 734, 501 NYS2d 604 (1986) (state allowed to recover liquidated damages and actual damages in the form of engineering charges).

[362] Cooperstein v Patrician Estates, 117 AD2d 774, 499 NYS2d 423 (2d Dept 1986).

Another element of loss of use is lost profits. These are recoverable to the extent they are not speculative.[363]

§7.70 —Interest

Typically, construction loans are short-term and carry higher rates of interest than does permanent financing. The higher interest rates and interest charges incurred beyond the reasonable completion date due to delay should be recoverable.[364] Interest on actual increased costs is payable from the date of the loss.[365]

In addition, an owner may recover damages for increased interest rates it is forced to pay on its permanent financing as a result of the delay.[366] For instance, if the prevailing mortgage rate at the time of expected completion was 10 per cent and the rate at the time of actual completion was 12 per cent, the owner could recover its future increased costs due to the increase in rates.

§7.71 —Professional Fees

Another common element of owner damages for delay is the increased fees due its architects and engineers. These are recoverable to the extent the extra work was necessary and was occasioned by the contractor's wrongful delay.[367]

§7.72 Liquidated Damages

Parties to construction contracts often seek to avoid the difficult task of proving loss due to delay by using liquidated damages clauses in their contracts. Typically, these clauses specify a daily sum that a contractor will be charged for each day the project is delayed past the contract completion date and any extensions. A very few contracts contain clauses that work both ways—i.e., the contractor pays the owner liquidated damages for each day the project is delayed and the owner pays the contractor a bonus for each day the project is completed prior to the contract completion date.[368]

There is a pervasively held belief within the construction community that a liquidated damages clause for delay is not enforceable in the absence of a corresponding bonus clause for early completion and that a bonus/penalty

---

[363] Lake Steel Erection, Inc v Egan, 61 AD2d 1125, 403 NYS2d 387 (4th Dept), *appeal dismissed*, 44 NY2d 848, 378 NE2d 124, 406 NYS2d 761 (1978).

[364] *See* Stein, *Construction Law* 11, ¶11.02 [6][c] (1991).

[365] Webster v Culver Roadways, Inc, 79 Misc 2d 256, 359 NYS2d 863 (Monroe 1974).

[366] Cooperstein v Patrician Estates, 117 AD2d 774, 499 NYS2d 423 (2d Dept 1986).

[367] Erecto Corp v State, 29 AD2d 728, 286 NYS2d 562 (3d Dept 1968).

[368] City of Elmira v Larry Walter, Inc, 150 AD2d 129, 546 NYS2d 183 (3d Dept 1989), *affd*, 76 NY2d 912, 564 NE2d 655, 563 NYS2d 45 (1990) (contract provided that the contractor would pay the city $1,000 per day that the project was late and that the city would pay the contractor $1,000 per day that the project was completed early).

clause is enforceable. The origin of this belief is uncertain. The authors are not aware of any jurisdiction in which it is correct. It is certainly not correct in New York.

A liquidated damages clause is valid in New York so long as the clause does not attempt to penalize a party. If the clause attempts to assess a penalty rather than approximate actual damages, it generally will be void and unenforceable. "[I]f the damage presumed to result from nonperformance of a contract is uncertain and incapable of exact assessment, the sum fixed by the parties is deemed to be liquidated damages and is recoverable. . . . ."[369] If, however, the liquidated damages clause bears "no reasonable relationship" to the amount of damages that may be sustained, the clause will be deemed a penalty.[370] Generally, a penalty is void and unenforceable.[371]

To determine whether a liquidated damages clause is valid, it must be considered in light of the time the contract was executed.[372] For a clause to be enforceable, actual damages must be shown to be potentially difficult to determine and the liquidated sum must not be obviously disproportionate to the possible loss.[373] The clause must be intended as compensation to the injured party and must bear a reasonable relationship to actual damages likely to result from default.[374] If the clause goes beyond compensation and serves to coerce a party's performance, it will be deemed a penalty.[375] In a doubtful case, New York courts tend to favor construction of the contract as imposing a penalty rather than liquidated damages.[376]

In private construction, liquidated damages clauses usually are upheld. Private owners face potential lost profits, construction loan interest, loss of use, etc. Thus, liquidated damages clauses provide a reasonable estimation of potential loss and a way for an owner to recoup its losses caused by delay without having to prove them.

---

[369] Associated Gen Contractors v Savin Bros, 45 AD2d 136, 139, 356 NYS2d 374 (3d Dept 1974), affd, 36 NY2d 957, 335 NE2d 859, 373 NYS2d 555 (1975).

[370] Id.

[371] Clauses that are penalties are not *per se* illegal and void. In Associated Gen Contractors, id, a clause used in a collective bargaining agreement was enforced, despite the fact that the court deemed it to be a penalty, because the parties had clearly agreed to the imposition of a penalty and because of the prior knowledge of the resulting serious damage to the association's bargaining power if the contractor were to breach the collective bargaining agreement.

[372] XLO Concrete Corp v John T. Brady & Co, 104 AD2d 181, 482 NYS2d 476 (1st Dept 1984), affd, 66 NY2d 970, 489 NE2d 768, 498 NYS2d 799 (1985).

[373] Walter E. Heller & Co v American Flyers Airline Corp, 459 F2d 896 (2d Cir 1972).

[374] City of Rye v Public Serv Mut Ins Co, 34 NY2d 470, 315 NE2d 458, 358 NYS2d 391 (1974); Melwood Constr Corp v State, 126 Misc 2d 156, 481 NYS2d 289 (Ct Cl 1984), affd, 119 AD2d 734, 501 NYS2d 604 (1986).

[375] City of Rye v Public Serv Mut Ins Co, 34 NY2d 470, 315 NE2d 458, 358 NYS2d 391 (1974); Melwood Constr Corp v State, 126 Misc 2d 156, 481 NYS2d 289 (Ct Cl 1984), affd, 119 AD2d 734, 501 NYS2d 604 (1986).

[376] Associated Gen Contractors v Savin Bros, 45 AD2d 136, 356 NYS2d 374 (3d Dept 1974), affd, 36 NY2d 957, 335 NE2d 859, 373 NYS2d 555 (1975).

In public construction, however, potential loss is not so easy to show. There are no lost profits and rarely are there construction loans. Increased personnel time devoted to a project and lost tax revenues may be too insignificant to substantiate a liquidated damages clause.[377] Public entities can recover liquidated damages, however, despite their difficulty in showing economic loss. For instance, in *Melwood Construction Corp v State*,[378] the state was allowed to recover liquidated damages of $500 per day for 111 days of delay by arguing that the liquidated damages clause was intended as compensation for inconvenience suffered by the public due to the contractor's delay in removing bridge obstructions and not as compensation for loss suffered directly by the state. In addition to the liquidated damages, the state was allowed, pursuant to specific contract provisions, to assess actual engineering charges and watchmen service charges against the contractor to compensate the state for certain of its expenses incurred due to the delay. This case is unusual as liquidated damages, if provided, are generally the exclusive remedy available. The result was possible because of the unusual contract provisions that allowed this "double" recovery.

Liquidated damages clauses will not be enforced if enforcement would be unconscionable or unjust. The best example of unjust enforcement is found when both the owner and the contractor are responsible for the delay. If the owner causes some of the delay and the contract does not include a provision whereby the contract period may be extended for causes beyond the contractor's control, such as owner-caused delay, the liquidated damages clause will not be enforced. An owner, otherwise entitled to liquidated damages, is limited to its actual damages, not to exceed the stipulated liquidated damages. However, if the contract does provide for extensions of time for causes beyond the contractor's control, such as owner-caused delay, the owner will be entitled to liquidated damages for the period after the contract completion date as extended. It would be unusual to find a contract without a time extension provision since most standard form contracts include one.

The cases do not provide a clear answer to the following hypothetical:

> The contract contains a liquidated damages clause. There is a 100-day delay for which the contractor is entitled to a 50-day extension of time. Of the 50 days for which the contractor is entitled to an extension of time, 25 days of delay resulted from causes over which neither party had control, and the other 25 days resulted from owner-caused delay. Is the contractor entitled to offset the damages it sustained from the 25 days of owner-caused delay against the 50 days of liquidated damages to which the owner is entitled? The authors believe that, in such circumstances, the owner should not be allowed to escape liability for the delay it caused and that the contractor is entitled to the offset.

---

[377] City of Rye v Public Serv Mut Ins Co, 34 NY2d 470, 315 NE2d 458, 358 NYS2d 391 (1974) (city was unable to show that the $200 per day liquidated damages bore any relationship to potential loss; total delay was over 500 days).

[378] 126 Misc 2d 156, 481 NYS2d 289 (Ct Cl 1984), *affd,* 119 AD2d 734, 501 NYS2d 604 (1986).

PRACTICE POINTER:

Setting Amounts for Liquidated Damages

In setting a liquidated damages figure, an owner should keep in mind that setting too high an amount may cause the contractor to include a large contingency amount in the contract price in order to offset the possibility of having to pay liquidated damages. In addition, a liquidated damages provision setting too high a figure may be seen as a penalty and not enforced by the court. The following are some factors to take into consideration when setting amounts for liquidated damages:

(1) Extra rental of other premises that might be required because the one being built is not completed.

(2) Extra maintenance and utility costs that may be incurred either in the continued use of old high-cost buildings or equipment or in the maintenance of a new area before beneficial use.

(3) Interest on the investment of borrowed capital.

(4) Extended supervision inspection or engineering cost.

(5) Additional operating costs that may result from the continued use of an inefficient facility or inefficient equipment.

(6) Extra costs of split operations resulting from partial occupancy or use of equipment.

(7) Loss of revenue expected from the completed facility.[379]

Liquidated damages begin to accrue from the contract completion date or from any extensions of time given the contractor by the owner;[380] they end at substantial completion. A waiver of time as being of the essence does not mean that the owner has waived its right to liquidated damages for the delay.[381] Thus, where an owner allowed its contractor to continue the contract work despite the fact that the contract completion date had passed, the owner was allowed to recover its liquidated damages for the contractor's delay. The court found that the contractor breached the contract by failing to complete the work on the contract completion date, which gave rise to a claim for breach of contract damages. By its actions, the owner waived the default but not its claim for damages.[382]

PRACTICE POINTER:

Once the contract completion date arrives and the contractor has not substantially completed, the owner must determine whether the delay

---

[379] Robert A. Rubin, Sammie D. Guy, Alfred C. Maevis & Virginia Fairweather, Construction Claims 122-23 (Van Nostrand Reinhold 2d ed 1992).

[380] Mosler Safe Co v Maiden Lane Safe Deposit Co, 199 NY 479, 93 NE 81 (1910).

[381] General Supply & Constr Co v Goelet, 241 NY 28, 148 NE 778 (1925).

[382] *Id.*

> warrants a time extension. If the owner believes that the delay is not excusable, the contractor should be put on notice that liquidated damages will be assessed. The owner should be prepared to back up this determination with records indicating what work remains to be completed and that this work is substantial, that the owner's actions have not caused the delay, and that the owner has fulfilled its obligations.

A liquidated damages clause does not apply if the contractor abandons the project prior to the stipulated completion date.[383] In such a case, the owner may pursue its actual damages. However, if the parties intend that the liquidated damages clause should apply in the event of abandonment, the clause should so specify.[384]

§7.73 Owner's Other Remedies

In addition to delay damages, an owner may rescind or terminate the contract and recover its excess cost of completion when the delay is unreasonable. For instance, an owner was allowed to rescind its contract for a new home when the builder failed to complete the home within the original three-month period and within seven additional months.[385]

Similarly, an owner may be awarded specific performance of a construction contract in addition to its delay damages,[386] although it is difficult to understand why an owner would seek specific performance from a contractor who has delayed to such an extent that a lawsuit was necessary.

---

[383] City of Elmira v Larry Walter, Inc, 150 AD2d 129, 546 NYS2d 183 (3d Dept 1989), affd, 76 NY2d 912, 564 NE2d 655, 563 NYS2d 45 (1990).

[384] Id.

[385] Tupper v Wade Lupe Constr Co, 39 Misc 2d 1053, 242 NYS2d 546 (Schenectady 1963).

[386] Cooperstein v Patrician Estates, 117 AD2d 774, 499 NYS2d 423 (2d Dept 1986).

Bonds

8

§8.01 Difference Between a Bond and Insurance
§8.02 Construing the Bond
§8.03 Parties to the Surety Relationship
§8.04 Bond Types and Terms
§8.05 Bid Bonds
§8.06 —The Surety's Liability
§8.07 —Releasing the Surety
§8.08 Performance Bonds
§8.09 Guaranty and Completion Bonds
§8.10 Who is Protected: Third-Party Beneficiaries and Combination Bonds
§8.11 The Obligee's Obligations
§8.12 The Surety's Obligations and Options
§8.13 —Complete the Work with the Original Contractor
§8.14 —Complete the Work Itself or with a Substitute Contractor
§8.15 —Allow the Obligee to Complete the Work
§8.16 —Pay the Penal Sum to the Obligee
§8.17 Claims by the Obligee
§8.18 —Cost of Completion
§8.19 —Liquidated and Delay Damages
§8.20 —Incidental and Consequential Damages
§8.21 —Attorneys' Fees
§8.22 —Punitive Damages
§8.23 —Interest
§8.24 Surety's Defenses
§8.25 —Lack of or Untimely Notice
§8.26 —Discharge by Modification or Breach of Contract
§8.27 —Discharge by Fraud

§8.28 —Untimely Claim
§8.29 —Liability in Excess of the Penal Sum
§8.30 —The Principal's Defenses and Claims
§8.31 —Party Not Protected by the Bond
§8.32 Payment Bonds
§8.33 Who is Protected
§8.34 —Subcontractors
§8.35 —Suppliers and Materialmen
§8.36 —Architects/Engineers
§8.37 What Items Are Covered
§8.38 —Materials
§8.39 —Rental Equipment
§8.40 Notice of Claim
§8.41 Attorneys' Fees
§8.42 Interest
§8.43 Miller Act Bonds
§8.44 —Persons Protected
§8.45 —Notice of Claim and Limitation of Action
§8.46 —Claimable Items
§8.47 Defenses Available to Surety
§8.48 Claims by the Surety
§8.49 —Claims Against Obligee
§8.50 —Claims Against Architect/Engineer
§8.51 —Claims Against Lending Institutions
§8.52 —Claims Against Subcontractors, Their Sureties, and Their Insurers
Appendix 8-1 Payment Bond Notice Provisions

§8.01 Difference Between a Bond and Insurance

There is a fundamental distinction between a bond and insurance which often is not understood. Confusion may arise because insurance policies and bonds physically resemble one another and some major insurance companies and many insurance agents issue both insurance policies and bonds. The philosophies and mechanics of the two are vastly different. Insurance companies assume risk; bonding companies guarantee credit. An insurance policy is a two-party contract that generally does not allow for a third-party direct right of action against the insurance company; a third-party typically sues the insured, and the insured is then defended by its insurer. A bond, on the other hand, is a three-party contract that allows for direct right of action against the bonding company by specified third parties.

Insurance companies, for a premium, assume the risk of certain losses. Premiums are based on the calculable odds of the risk insured against occurring and spreading that risk among all those insured. An insurance company tries to collect enough money from its insureds to pay for the losses that occur, its overhead, and a reasonable profit. When faced with a claim, an insurance company checks to make sure that the claim is covered under the policy and is legitimate. If these criteria are met, the claim is paid. Often, an insurance company will not try to recover its losses from third parties unless there is clear liability. Typically, an insurer is precluded from seeking recovery from its insured.

Bonding companies, for a fee, extend credit on behalf of their principals. The premium for a surety bond is a fee paid to the bonding company for investigating and guaranteeing the credit of its principal. A bonding company acts much like a bank issuing a letter of credit. It will issue the bond only when it feels certain that the principal is financially able to perform the contract secured or, in the event of the principal's default, is financially able to repay any losses the bonding company may suffer due to a claim under the bond. Like a bank, a bonding company will avoid all possible losses and make substantial efforts to collect its losses. Thus, most bonding companies require personal indemnifications to assure themselves that, if the principal experiences financial difficulty, they can recover their losses from their indemnitors.

When faced with a claim, a bonding company first notifies its principal and indemnitors and demands that they satisfy the claim if they admit its validity. If the principal and indemnitors assert that the claim is invalid, the bonding company turns over the claim to them and instructs them to honor or defend the claim without cost to the bonding company. A bonding company will pay a claim only when it finds no legitimate alternative, e.g., when its principal and indemnitors are insolvent or refuse to perform, there is no defense to the claim, or a judgment has been entered against it. The reason for a bonding company's reluctance to pay an unproven or unadmitted claim is simple—if it were to pay a claim without justification, it could be deemed to be a volunteer and lose its subrogation and indemnification rights. Once a bonding company honors a claim, it seeks reimbursement from its principal and indemnitors.

§8.02 Construing the Bond

Bonds are construed in the same way as any contract.[1] The same principles of construction apply. Thus, where a bond is unambiguous, it must be given its "plain, ordinary, and proper meaning."[2] Generally, ambiguities are resolved in the obligee's favor,[3] but where no interpretation of a bond's language is required, a surety's obligations and rights are construed *strictissimi juris* in the surety's favor.[4]

---

[1] State v Peerless Ins Co, 108 AD2d 385, 489 NYS2d 213 (1985), *affd*, 67 NY2d 845, 492 NE2d 779, 501 NYS2d 651 (1986).

[2] Dupack v Nationwide Leisure Corp, 73 AD2d 903, 424 NYS2d 436, 439 (1980).

[3] *Id.*

[4] Mendel-Mesick-Cohen-Architects v Peerless Ins Co, 74 AD2d 712, 426 NYS2d 124 (1980).

Bonds attach to and are construed in conjunction with the underlying contract[5] and applicable law or statute.[6]

§8.03 Parties to the Surety Relationship

Typically, there are four parties to the surety relationship that arises upon the execution of a bond: principal; indemnitor; obligee; and surety.

The Principal

The *principal* is the entity that typically obtains the bond, and the bond secures the principal's performance of specified duties. For the purposes of this discussion, the bond is usually obtained by the contractor and secures the contractor's obligation to enter into a contract based upon its bid, complete its contract, or pay its subcontractors. Typically, the principal is also the surety's indemnitor and is liable to the surety for any damage suffered by the surety or any payment made by the surety to the obligee. The principal may be found to be the surety's indemnitor even in the absence of the principal's express consent.[7]

The Indemnitor

Indemnitors are responsible for any obligation owed by the principal to the surety as a result of the principal's default under the contract secured. In addition to the principal, there often are other indemnitors, such as when a surety requires personal guaranties of a corporation's officers and their family members.

The Obligee

The *obligee* is the beneficiary of the bond and the party to which the principal has promised the specified performance. Typically, the owner of the construction project is the obligee, whether the project is owned by the state or a private entity; additionally, contractors are often obligees of performance and payment bonds obtained by their subcontractors, just as subcontractors are often third-party beneficiaries of their contractor's payment bonds. There may be multiple obligees to one bond.

The status of obligee is generally limited to those parties specifically mentioned in the bond as beneficiaries of the bond, although unnamed parties have

---

[5] Hall & Co v Continental Cas Co, 34 AD2d 1028, 310 NYS2d 950 (1970), *affd*, 30 NY2d 517, 280 NE2d 890, 330 NYS2d 64 (1972).

[6] Town of Chester v Republic Ins Co, 89 AD2d 959, 454 NYS2d 107 (1982); Town of Shawangunk v Goldwill Properties, Inc, 61 AD2d 693, 403 NYS2d 784 (1978).

[7] *See* Carrols Equities Corp v Villnave, 57 AD2d 1044, 395 NYS2d 800 (1977), in which the court upheld an indemnity judgment against the principal and in favor of the surety despite the facts that the principal did not sign the bond and no implied consent was found. The court held that where a party becomes a surety at an obligee's request, it is subrogated to the obligee's rights against the principal.

been granted third-party beneficiary status in certain instances.[8] The standard to determine whether a party is a third-party beneficiary is whether the bond "manifests a clear intent to grant that right to the third party."[9]

The Surety

The surety secures the principal's obligation to perform the contract or pay its subcontractors; typically, the surety is the bonding or insurance company that issued the bond. The surety's liability is derived from the principal's obligation to the obligee to perform the specified duties or pay the specified parties.[10]

There are compensated and uncompensated sureties. As their titles imply, compensated sureties are paid for their agreement to secure the principal's performance, while uncompensated sureties are not. This chapter discusses compensated sureties because rarely, if ever, does an uncompensated surety issue a construction bond.

§8.04 Bond Types and Terms

There are three basic types of bonds used in the construction industry: bid; performance; and payment. *Bid* bonds secure the obligation of the successful bidder on a job to enter into the contract at the bid price. *Performance* bonds secure the obligation of the contractor to perform its contract. Performance bonds sometimes are also known as completion bonds and may include guaranty bonds, although they are not, technically, the same things.[11] *Payment* bonds secure the obligation of the contractor to pay its subcontractors, laborers, and materialmen for their work on the specified project.[12]

It is not unusual for a contractor to be required to provide all three types of bonds on the same project.

§8.05 Bid Bonds

The majority of public owners, and many private owners, require contractors to submit *bid* bonds with their bids. *Bid* bonds secure the obligation of the successful bidder to enter into the contract as bid. A bid bond is "required of . . .

---

[8] In Novak & Co v Travelers Indem Co, 56 AD2d 418, 392 NYS2d 901 (1977), there is an excellent discussion of the leading cases on the issue of third-party beneficiaries to bonds.

[9] *Id* at 423, 392 NYS2d at 903.

[10] United States v Seaboard Sur Co, 817 F2d 956 (2d Cir), *cert denied*, 484 US 855, 108 S Ct 161 (1987).

[11] The technical distinctions between these three bonds are discussed in **§8.09**.

[12] There is also a bond known as a *lien discharge* bond that typically is posted by an owner when a mechanic's lien is filed against its property to discharge the lien from the property and transfer it to the bond. These bonds are discussed in **ch 9**.

prospective bidders so that reparations are available to an [obligee] in the event a successful bidder refuses to sign the contract."[13]

The amount of the bid bond is set by statute or the obligee and, usually, is specified in the bid instructions. Generally, bid bonds are 5 or 10 per cent of the total bid price, although some bid bonds provide for payment to the obligee of the difference between the defaulting contractor's bid and the next lowest responsible bid, not to exceed the penal sum of the bond.[14] Failure to follow all written directions regarding bond requirements may cause the bid to be disqualified.[15] Nonmaterial errors or "mere irregularities," however, may be waived by the owner if it chooses to do so.[16] Be forewarned that waiver of a minor error is never required; thus, it is wise to follow every instruction regarding the bond and to clarify any unclear areas.[17] For instance, if the bidding instructions call for submission of a certified check, the owner is not required to accept a bid bond instead and may refuse to consider the bid.

§8.06 —The Surety's Liability

The surety does not become liable on a *bid* bond unless and until the contractor has a legal obligation to enter into the specified contract and fails to meet that obligation.[18] Thus, the general rule is: if the contractor is awarded the contract based on its bid but unjustifiably refuses to execute the contract, the surety is liable to the owner. For instance, if the contractor made an unexcusable error in its bid and refuses to execute the contract, the surety becomes liable to the owner; the contractor may choose to forfeit its bond and be liable to its surety for the amount the surety is liable to the owner, where that choice will damage the contractor less than performing the work at the contract price.[19] Similarly, if the contractor is precluded from entering into the contract by failure to meet a condition precedent, such as obtaining a performance bond, the surety will be held liable under the bid bond.[20]

The surety's liability is expressly limited to the amount set forth in the bond—the *penal sum*—regardless of the owner's actual damages or lack there-

---

[13] Superior Hydraulics, Inc v Town Bd, 88 AD2d 404, 453 NYS2d 711, 715 (1982).

[14] A principal may be liable to the owner beyond the amount of the bond for any losses suffered by the owner not covered by the bond sum.

[15] Marchionne v Department of Transp, 88 AD2d 655, 450 NYS2d 529 (1982); LaBarge Bros Co v Town of Cicero, 104 Misc 2d 764, 429 NYS2d 140 (Onondaga 1979).

[16] Frank Nowak Constr Co v County of Suffolk, 233 NYS2d 627 (Suffolk 1962).

[17] As is discussed more thoroughly in **ch 2**, all bid instructions should be followed carefully. Refer to **ch 2** for a complete discussion of when an owner may reject a bid for failure to follow bid instructions.

[18] Jobco, Inc v County of Nassau, 129 AD2d 614, 514 NYS2d 108 (1987); Balaban-Gordon Constr Co v Brighton Sewer Dist No 2, 41 AD2d 246, 342 NYS2d 435 (1973).

[19] G&R Elec Contractors, Inc v Egan, 85 AD2d 191, 448 NYS2d 850, *affd*, 57 NY2d 721, 440 NE2d 795, 454 NYS2d 710 (1982).

[20] City of New York v United States Fidelity & Guar Co, 119 Misc 2d 725, 464 NYS2d 659 (NY 1983).

of.[21] Further, a surety that provides a bid bond to a contractor is under no obligation to provide performance or payment bonds on the same project, even where the surety's failure to issue a performance or payment bond causes the contractor to be unable to enter into the contract and lose its bid bond.[22] The surety's duties, and thus its liability, are limited to those duties and that liability specifically set forth in the bid bond.

§8.07 —Releasing the Surety

A surety is released from its obligation when the contractor fulfills its obligations under the *bid* bond. Thus, when the selected bidder enters into a contract with the owner, the contractor's bid bond is discharged and the surety has no further liability with respect to the contract. Similarly, when a contract is awarded or all bids are rejected, all unsuccessful bidders and their bid bonds are discharged.[23] If a bidder is allowed to withdraw its bid, either due to an excusable error or due to the passage of time,[24] the bond is discharged and the surety released from its obligation.

The most common ways a surety can be released from its bid bond obligation are by an alteration of the obligation, a failure to award the contract, and an excusable bidding error.

Altering the Obligation

When a surety decides whether to issue a *bid* bond to a contractor for a project, the surety relies on the bid documents. Its bid bond secures the successful bidder's obligation to enter into a contract that is in accordance with the bid. If the contract tendered by the owner is inconsistent with the bid documents, the surety is discharged from its bond obligations. The reasoning behind this principle is that the surety agreed to bond a specific bid; by altering the terms of the contract awarded in response to that bid, the owner is, in effect, demanding that the surety be bound by an agreement neither it nor its contractor contemplated.[25] Thus, "a surety is discharged by any alteration of the contract to

---

[21] *Id.* If the surety wrongly defaults in paying the bond, its liability is increased to include interest from the time of the default. NY Gen Oblig Law §7-301 (McKinney 1989 & Supp 1992). A principal may be liable beyond the amount of the bond to the owner for any losses suffered by the owner not covered by the bond sum.

[22] Travelers Indem Co v Buffalo Motor & Generator Co, 58 AD2d 978, 397 NYS2d 257 (1977).

[23] *In re* PJ Panzeca, Inc, 56 Misc 2d 460, 288 NYS2d 813 (Nassau), *affd,* 30 AD2d 640, 292 NYS2d 1007 (1968).

[24] If a public owner fails to award a contract within 45 days of its receipt and opening of bids, any bidder may withdraw its bid and have its bond or deposit released. NY State Fin Law §140 (McKinney 1989 & Supp 1992); NY Gen Mun Law §105 (McKinney 1986 & Supp 1992). See **ch 2** for a more complete discussion.

[25] Hall & Co v Continental Cas Co, 34 AD2d 1028, 310 NYS2d 950 (1970), *affd,* 30 NY2d 517, 280 NE2d 890, 330 NYS2d 64 (1972).

256 BONDS

which the guaranty applied, whether the alteration is material or not."[26]

Similarly, a bid bond is valid only for the bid specified in the bond; any new bid, even if on the same project, requires a new bond as if it were a new obligation.[27]

Failure to Award Contract

If a public owner fails to award a contract within the statutory period and the contractor chooses to withdraw its bid,[28] the bond is discharged and the owner cannot recover against it.[29] Similarly, when the obligee awards the contract, all unsuccessful bidders and their bonds are released,[30] unless the bidding instructions otherwise provide.

Excusable Bidding Error

Finally, where the contractor has made an *excusable* bidding error, it may withdraw its bid,[31] thereby releasing itself and its surety from all bid and *bid* bond obligations. For instance, in a case where a clerical error resulted in a bid being far too low and the contractor notified the city obligee immediately of the error, the bid was rescinded. The city could not award the contractor the job and recover on the bid bond when the contractor refused to enter into the contract.[32] Thus, in cases where, through calculation or clerical error, bids were $100,000 low[33] and $1,000,000 low[34] and the contractors promptly notified the obligees, the bids were rescinded and the bonds discharged.

Where, however, the error is due to a contractor's negligence in failing to

---

[26] William J. Morris, Inc v Lanzilotta & Teramo Constr Corp, 63 AD2d 969, 405 NYS2d 508 (1978), *affd*, 47 NY2d 901, 393 NE2d 488, 419 NYS2d 494 (1979).

[27] *In re* PJ Panzeca, Inc, 56 Misc 2d 460, 288 NYS2d 813 (Nassau), *affd*, 30 AD2d 640, 292 NYS2d 1007 (1968) (bid bond found of no effect where owner rejected all bids, later readvertised same job, and awarded contract to bidder that submitted new bid but used bid bond from its original bid).

[28] If a public obligee fails to award a contract within 45 days of its receipt and opening of bids, any bidder may withdraw its bid, and its bond or deposit must be released. NY State Fin Law §140 (McKinney 1989 & Supp 1992); NY Gen Mun Law §105 (McKinney 1986 & Supp 1992). An obligee can shorten the acceptance time if it chooses. People v John W. Rouse Constr Co, 26 AD2d 405, 274 NYS2d 981 (1966). See **ch 2** for a more complete discussion.

[29] People v John W. Rouse Constr Co, 26 AD2d 405, 274 NYS2d 981 (1966).

[30] *In re* PJ Panzeca, Inc, 56 Misc 2d 460, 288 NYS2d 813 (Nassau), *affd*, 30 AD2d 640, 292 NYS2d 1007 (1968).

[31] The standards for determining whether a bid may be withdrawn on the basis of mistake are discussed in **ch 2**. *See also* Balaban-Gordon Co v Brighton Sewer Dist No 2, 41 AD2d 246, 342 NYS2d 435 (1973).

[32] City of Syracuse v Sarkisian Bros, 87 AD2d 984, 451 NYS2d 945, *affd*, 57 NY2d 618, 439 NE2d 880, 454 NYS2d 71 (1982).

[33] Derouin's Plumbing & Heating, Inc v City of Watertown, 71 AD2d 822, 419 NYS2d 390 (1979).

[34] Jobco, Inc v County of Nassau, 129 AD2d 614, 514 NYS2d 108 (1987).

include a specified item in its bid[35] or its failure to read the job specification carefully,[36] the contractor has the choice of honoring its mistaken bid or forfeiting its bond.

Bidding and bidding errors are discussed in detail in Chapter 2.

§8.08 Performance Bonds

A *performance* bond secures the obligation of the principal to perform the work in accordance with the contract. When the principal defaults in that performance, by failing to complete the contract or by a defective performance, both it and the surety are liable to the obligee in the amount needed to correct the default, within certain limits.[37] The obligee on a performance bond is typically the owner of the property, although a general contractor may require a performance bond of its subcontractors listing it as the obligee. Performance bonds are regularly used in both private and public improvements. Often, performance bonds are required by ordinance or statute. The majority of federal projects require performance and payment bonds pursuant to the Miller Act, 40 USC §270a-270f, discussed below in **§§8.43-8.46**. Where a bond is required by law, it is interpreted in light of the requiring legislation.[38]

Generally, the amount of the bond—the *penal sum*—is equal to the contract price, although it may be any amount the obligee requires. An obligee may require less than a 100% bond where the contract price is very large or where the principal will pass the savings in obtaining a lesser bond on to the obligee in the form of a lower contract price. Whether to agree to accept a performance bond in a penal sum less than the contract price is a difficult decision for the obligee. The decision depends on many factors, including: bond premium savings, if any; degree of complexity of the contract work; financial strength of the contractor; reliability and knowledge of the contractor; and market conditions affecting replacement of a defaulting contractor.

§8.09 Guaranty and Completion Bonds

Guaranty bonds and *completion* bonds are often called *performance* bonds due to their similarities. However, there are technical differences that must be understood to ensure that the parties to a bond receive the protection desired.

Guaranty bonds guarantee to the obligee that the principal will remedy any defects in its work for a specified time. A guaranty bond is not needed if the

---

[35] Dierks Heating Co v Egan, 115 AD2d 836, 496 NYS2d 97 (1985).

[36] G&R Elec Contractors, Inc v Egan, 85 AD2d 191, 448 NYS2d 850, *affd,* 57 NY2d 710, 440 NE2d 795, 454 NYS2d 721 (1982).

[37] Carrols Equities Corp v Villnave, 57 AD2d 1044, 395 NYS2d 800 (1977); People v Massachusetts Bonding & Ins Co, 182 AD 122, 169 NYS 693 (1918); Board of Educ v Matthew L. Carroll, Inc, 157 NYS2d 775 (Cattaraugus 1956).

[38] Town of Chester v Republic Ins Co, 89 AD2d 959, 454 NYS2d 107 (1982); Town of Shawangunk v Goldwill Properties, Inc, 61 AD2d 693, 403 NYS2d 784 (1978).

obligee has a performance bond and the contract requires the principal/contractor to guarantee its work for a specified time.

Even where an owner has a performance bond from its prime contractor, it may wish to obtain guaranty bonds from key subcontractors, guaranteeing to the owner the subcontractors' work. Suggested subcontractors to consider requiring guaranty bonds from are roofing, electrical, plumbing, HVAC, and other important component suppliers and installers. It is important to know the difference between a guaranty bond and a subcontractor's guaranty. The first has a surety that ensures payment or correction of the defect if the principal/subcontractor is found at fault; the second has only the subcontractor's word that it will correct its work if necessary.

Completion bonds are different from *performance* bonds in one material respect. Under a *performance* bond, the surety may choose to complete the work, regardless of its penal sum (the amount of the bond), or to pay the cost of completion up to its penal sum. Under a true *completion* bond, the surety has no choice: it must finish the work regardless of the amount of its bond. In effect, there is no penal sum. Completion bonds are rare but may be required, most often by public entities that wish to ensure that the job will be done at the contract price. For example, a town may wish to ensure that a subdivision will be built properly and require the contractor to post a completion bond to secure its agreement to install and provide utility connections, streets, sewer lines, etc., for the subdivision. This type of completion bond is known as a *subdivision* bond. By requiring a completion bond, the town is assured of having the subdivision begun properly and is protected from any increases in labor and materials.

§8.10 Who is Protected: Third-Party Beneficiaries and Combination Bonds

Usually under a *performance* bond, the named obligee is the only party protected by the bond. Some confusion arises, however, when a bond purports to secure performance *and* payment. These *combination* bonds,[39] like simple performance bonds, typically secure the obligation of the principal to an owner/obligee to perform the underlying contract; where the contract includes the obligation of the contractor to pay its subcontractors, laborers, and materialmen, the bond is said to secure the principal's obligation to pay as one aspect of the principal's performance owed under the contract. Some combination bonds specify that the security provided by the surety includes payment of all liens and encumbrances[40] or of claims by subcontractors, laborers, materialmen, etc.[41]

At first glance, it may seem that an unpaid subcontractor should have the right to sue the surety for payment under a combination bond. The bond

---

[39] *Combination* bonds are also referred to as *single instrument performance and payment* bonds.

[40] Scales-Douwes Corp v Paulaura Realty Corp, 24 NY2d 724, 249 NE2d 760, 301 NYS2d 980 (1969).

[41] Merchants Mut Cas Co v United States Fidelity & Guar Co, 253 AD 151, 2 NYS2d 370 (4th Dept 1938).

appears to secure the principal's obligation to pay much as a *payment* bond does; under a *payment* bond, the basic right of a subcontractor to recover as a named or an intended third-party beneficiary cannot be disputed. With combination bonds, however, the law is almost the opposite.

> The rule has developed with relation to combined payment and performance bonds that third parties have no direct cause of action thereon, unless it is established that there was an intent to confer such right of action. Fosmire v National Surety Co, 229 NY 44, 127 NE 472 (1920). The question remains . . . as to what the dominant purpose of the instrument was and whether there was an intent to confer a right to sue upon third parties.[42]

This *dominant purpose* rule is premised upon the belief that when an obligee requires a combination bond, its primary intent is to protect itself and ensure the completion of its project. In the leading case of *Fosmire v National Surety Co*,[43] the court reasoned that if a third party could recover against the bond in question, the obligee would be left unprotected. For instance, if third-party suits were allowed, a third party could bring suit on the bond before the project was complete, resulting in the diminution or possible exhaustion of the bond penal sum. The obligee would be deprived of the full protection it sought in requiring the bond. The court held that the bond, when read in its entirety, did not intend to grant third parties a right to sue on the bond. Where the intention to grant the right is absent, the right to sue is denied.[44] Thus, the dominant purpose of such bonds is to protect the obligee, not third parties.[45]

Even where combination bonds grant third parties the right to sue, the right has been held subordinate to the obligee's right to the protection provided it under the bond. Third-party beneficiaries cannot recover on a combination bond until the dominant purpose of the bond has been fulfilled,[46] i.e., unless and until the obligee has received substantial performance of the contract[47] or its rights have been satisfied.[48] Thus, if the penal sum of the bond is exhausted in satisfying the performance obligations of the principal to the owner, the bond will not afford any protection to unpaid subcontractors.

---

[42] J&J Tile Co v Feinstein, 43 AD2d 529, 530, 348 NYS2d 783, 784 (1973).

[43] 229 NY 44, 127 NE 472, *amended,* 229 NY 564, 128 NE 130 (1920).

[44] *Id.*

[45] *Id;* J&J Tile Co v Feinstein, 43 AD2d 529, 348 NYS2d 783 (1973); William S. Van Clief & Sons v City of NY, 141 Misc 216, 252 NYS 402 (NY 1931).

[46] Samson Elec Co v Buffalo Elec Co, 234 AD 521, 256 NYS 219 (1932).

[47] EJ Eddy, Inc v Fidelity & Deposit Co, 265 NY 276, 192 NE 410 (1934).

[48] Johnson Serv Co v EH Monin, Inc, 253 NY 417, 171 NE 692, *remanded for remittitur,* 254 NY 551, 173 NE 862 (1930) (obligee sued in its own interest and on behalf of third-party beneficiaries; third-party beneficiaries entitled to surplus recovery after obligee's damages were satisfied); New York Plumbers Specialties Co v Columbia Cas Co, 13 AD2d 449, 211 NYS2d 824 (1961) (bond specified that subcontractor's benefit under bond was "subject to Obligee's priority").

When faced with a combination bond, the wise course is to demand a copy of the bond and serve a notice of claim upon the surety, contractor, and obligee. Doing this will protect bond benefits if the claimant is an intended beneficiary, as third-party beneficiaries are held to a bond's terms and requirements, including notice provisions and limitation periods.[49] The surety may set forth its position regarding the claimant's right to sue under the bond in its reply to the notice of claim. If the surety asserts that the claimant does not have the right to sue, the claimant should pressure the contractor and obligee for payment, through demand letters and a mechanic's lien. The claimant should also ask the obligee to sue the surety on its behalf, although the obligee has no obligation to do so.[50] A surety's response to a notice of claim should never be construed as a waiver of any condition of the bond or right of the surety under the bond, including limitation periods.

§8.11 The Obligee's Obligations

Typically, an obligee is not a signatory to a bond; it is a beneficiary of the bond. Thus, its "obligations" are limited to what it must do to gain the benefits of the bond. First, an obligee must perform its duties under the contract and not make any modifications to it without the surety's approval, unless the surety has expressly waived notification of modifications in the bond itself. An obligee's failure to perform the contract, such as failing to pay the contractor, or to obtain approval of a change order could result in the surety's discharge.[51] Second, an obligee must comply with all notice and limitation provisions of the bond. A failure to timely and properly notify a surety of a claim under a bond or to timely bring suit can bar the claim or suit.[52] Finally, as must any party, an obligee must mitigate its damages.[53]

Unless the bond otherwise provides, an obligee has no duty to keep the surety informed of the project's status[54] or of the principal's financial condition or performance.[55]

---

[49] Timberline Elec Supply v Insurance Co of N Am, 72 AD2d 905, 421 NYS2d 987 (1979), *affd*, 52 NY2d 793, 417 NE2d 1248, 436 NYS2d 707 (1980); John Johnston Concrete Gutter Co v American Empire Ins Co, 81 AD2d 1004, 440 NYS2d 107 (1981).

[50] Johnson Serv Co v EH Monin, Inc, 253 NY 417, 171 NE 692, *remanded for remittitur*, 254 NY 551, 173 NE 862 (1930); William S. Van Clief & Sons v City of NY, 141 Misc 216, 252 NYS 402 (NY 1931).

[51] See discussion at **§8.26.**

[52] See **§§8.25 and 8.28.**

[53] Federal Ins Co v Walker, 53 NY2d 24, 422 NE2d 548, 439 NYS2d 888 (1981).

[54] Hunt v Bankers & Shippers Ins Co, 60 AD2d 781, 400 NYS2d 645 (1977).

[55] State v Peerless Ins Co, 108 AD2d 385, 489 NYS2d 213 (1985), *affd*, 67 NY2d 845, 492 NE2d 779, 501 NYS2d 651 (1986).

§8.12 The Surety's Obligations and Options

A surety's obligations are set forth in its bond as interpreted through the contract or relevant law. Under the typical performance bond, in the event of its principal's default, a surety's duties are to complete the contract or pay the obligee the amount due under the bond in a timely fashion, and to act fairly. Its duties and liabilities are limited to those of its principal[56] and, unless expressly exempted, include all obligations undertaken by the principal in the contract.[57] The surety has no other duties. Thus, unless the bond provides otherwise, the surety is not required to supervise an obligee's performance under the contract or to notify an obligee of its default, even where that default may result in the surety's discharge.[58]

When a claim is made under a performance bond, usually because the obligee asserts that the principal failed to complete the contract or that the principal's performance was defective, the surety may have several options. It may convince the principal to complete the contract with its assistance; complete the contract itself or with a substitute contractor; allow the obligee to complete the contract; or refuse to complete the contract, and pay the obligee. Of course, if the surety believes that it is not obligated under the bond—perhaps because it does not believe that its principal has defaulted or because it believes itself to have been discharged—it will refuse the claim. The surety's choice among these options may affect its liability and exposure to increased liability. These options are discussed below in §§8.13-8.16.

§8.13 —Complete the Work with the Original Contractor

If the principal lets the surety know that it is having, or will have, trouble completing the contract, the surety has the option of rendering financial, technical, or other assistance to the principal. This option is often the least expensive for both the surety and the principal. Finding replacement contractors can be expensive and time consuming. By helping the principal complete the work, the surety helps to ensure minimal delay in completing the contract and permits the principal to go on to other jobs with a relatively clean reputation, thereby making it more likely that the principal will be able to reimburse the surety. Further, the surety may be able to lower completion costs and its out-of-pocket expenses through better management of the principal's operations. Finally, this option is usually most attractive to the principal as it may be accomplished without notice to the obligee. Any sums the surety expends in helping its principal complete the work *do not* reduce the penal sum of the bond.

A surety that fails to assist its principal in completing a contract cannot complain that the replacement contract's costs were too high and that it is not

---

[56] Lamparter Acoustical Prods v Maryland Cas Co, 64 AD2d 693, 407 NYS2d 579 (1978).

[57] Benderson Dev Co v Schwab Bros Trucking, 64 AD2d 447, 409 NYS2d 890 (1978).

[58] Birnant v Aetna Cas & Sur Co, 28 AD2d 978, 283 NYS2d 393 (1967).

responsible for all increased costs incurred by the obligee (who has the duty to mitigate),[59] up to the penal sum of the bond.

§8.14 —Complete the Work Itself or with a Substitute Contractor

Upon default by the principal, the surety may choose to complete the job itself by acting as the prime contractor or may contract with a replacement contractor to undertake completing the original contract. If the surety chooses to complete the work, either by itself or with another contractor, its potential liability is not limited by the penal sum of the bond. Once it chooses to complete, it must do so, regardless of cost.[60] Thus, if a surety or its substitute contractor later fails to complete the work, the surety is liable to the obligee in the full penal sum; it does not reduce the penal sum by expending money toward completion. The obligee must pay the surety any sums that would have been due the original contractor had there not been a default.[61]

Unless the bond otherwise provides, the choice to complete, and with whom to complete, the contract is the surety's.[62] It is important that an obligee notify the surety of default and allow the surety to make its choice before the obligee undertakes completion.

§8.15 —Allow the Obligee to Complete the Work

A surety may choose to allow the obligee to complete the work when the principal defaults on the contract. If a surety makes no choice but refuses to complete the work or pay the penal sum (the amount of the bond), it has, effectively, made the choice to allow the obligee to complete. Whether the surety affirmatively chooses this option or the obligee chooses to complete following the surety's default, the surety's liability is the same, except that the surety in default is liable for interest.[63] If the obligee does not complete the work, the measure of the surety's liability may include the obligee's consequential damages, including its loss of the use of the premises and lost profits on the sale of unfinished premises. A surety is liable for the damages which reasonably

---

[59] Tynan Incinerator Co v International Fidelity Ins Co, 117 AD2d 796, 499 NYS2d 118 (1986).

[60] NY Gen Oblig Law §7-301 (McKinney 1989 & Supp 1992) implies that a surety's liability on a performance bond is limited to the penal sum only if the surety chooses payment rather than performance.

[61] Spancrete NE, Inc v Travelers Indem Co, 112 AD2d 571, 491 NYS2d 848, *appeal dismissed*, 66 NY2d 909, 489 NE2d 762, 498 NYS2d 793 (1985); Firemen's Ins Co v State, 65 AD2d 241, 412 NYS2d 206 (1979); O'Brien v Fago, 54 Misc 2d 203, 282 NYS2d 295 (Erie 1967).

[62] Village of Warwick v Republic Ins Co, 104 Misc 2d 514, 428 NYS2d 589 (Orange 1980).

[63] NY Gen Oblig Law §7-301 (McKinney 1989 & Supp 1992).

and naturally flow from the breaches of it and its principal.[64] The only limit to the surety's liability is the penal sum plus interest if the surety defaulted.

Regardless of how the obligee ends up completing the work, the basic measure of the surety's liability is the same. In most cases, it is the obligee's actual completion costs less the contract balance unearned by the principal at the time of the principal's default.[65] Thus, the surety may be liable in an amount over the original contract price.[66] This is not the only measure of liability, however; a surety may be liable for delay[67] or other consequential damages. Again, however, the surety's liability is limited to the penal sum plus interest if the surety defaults.

§8.16 —Pay the Penal Sum to the Obligee

The surety may pay the penal sum of the bond to the obligee upon notice of the principal's default. A surety might make this choice if it appears that completion costs will far exceed the bond amount, perhaps because of deficient work or because its principal grossly underbid the contract. Of course, a surety is free to and usually will bargain with the obligee in an attempt to get it to accept less than the full penal sum. An obligee's decision to accept less than the full bond amount should be based on the stage of the work; anticipated completion costs; the urgency of completion; the obligee's willingness to undertake litigation, which often is expensive and lengthy, if necessary; the obligee's financial strength; and such other factors as may be pertinent to the job in question. Regardless of the amount agreed to, once the surety pays the obligee, what the obligee spends to complete the contract or whether the obligee in fact completes the work is irrelevant. The surety's liability with regard to the project ends upon its payment to the obligee.

§8.17 Claims by the Obligee

When an obligee makes its initial claim under a performance bond, it usually seeks completion of the work by the surety or funding of its anticipated completion costs. When a surety refuses an obligee's demand, perhaps because it believes that the obligee has materially breached the contract or that its principal is not in default, the obligee may suffer damages as a result. The obligee may incur, or believe itself entitled to, delay damages, liquidated damages, attorneys' fees, incidental or consequential damages, punitive damages, and

---

[64] Hunt v Bankers & Shippers Ins Co, 73 AD2d 797, 423 NYS2d 718 (1979), affd, 50 NY2d 938, 409 NE2d 928, 431 NYS2d 454 (1980).

[65] Norris v Depew Paving Co, 14 AD2d 117, 217 NYS2d 203 (1961), affd, 11 NY2d 812, 182 NE2d 109, 227 NYS2d 436 (1962); United States v Glens Falls Ins Co, 534 F Supp 109 (NDNY 1981).

[66] Maltin v Maryland Cas Co, 24 AD2d 419, 260 NYS2d 194 (1965).

[67] Id (delay damages permitted by the contract); cf Village of Canton v Globe Indem Co, 201 AD 820, 195 NYS 445 (1922) (delay damages against surety not allowed).

264 BONDS

interest. As was discussed above, however, regardless of the measure of damages, the surety's liability generally is limited to the bond's penal amount plus interest in the event of default.[68] Further, the surety is liable to the obligee only to the extent its principal would have been liable.[69] If the principal would not have been liable to the obligee for delay damages, the surety cannot be liable for them.

§8.18 —Cost of Completion

The obligee is entitled to recover from the surety its actual excess cost of completion up to the penal amount of the bond. The measure of recovery is not what it would have cost the original contractor to complete the contract[70] nor what might be "fair and reasonable."[71] If the obligee seeks reimbursement following a principal's defective performance, the surety is liable to the obligee in the amount necessary to correct the defect.[72]

§8.19 —Liquidated and Delay Damages

In a case where a contract provided for liquidated damages based on a daily sum for each day of delay caused by the contractor/principal and the contractor abandoned the work, the surety was not liable to the obligee for liquidated damages. The court reasoned that the principal did not delay but, rather, abandoned the work.[73] This result seems absurd. Typically, time of completion is delayed when a principal defaults, whether that default is delay or abandonment. The obligee suffers damage due to the delay, a damage for which it provided itself with a remedy in the very contract the surety secured.

A surety may, however, be liable for an obligee's *actual* delay damages if the underlying contract expressly provides for delay damages;[74] but if the contract is silent or expressly provides that there will be no delay damages,[75] the surety cannot be held liable. Further, if the delay is by mutual agreement of the obligee and principal or if the *bond* expressly exempts the surety from liability for delay damages, the surety will not be liable.[76]

---

[68] *See* §8.15.
[69] County of Rockland v Aetna Cas & Sur Co, 129 AD2d 606, 514 NYS2d 102 (1987); Lamparter Acoustical Prods v Maryland Cas Co, 64 AD2d 693, 407 NYS2d 579 (1978).
[70] Tynan Incinerator Co v International Fidelity Ins Co, 117 AD2d 796, 499 NYS2d 118 (1986).
[71] LG Defelice & Son v Globe Indem Co, 189 F Supp 455 (SDNY 1960).
[72] Board of Educ v Matthew L. Carroll, Inc, 157 NYS2d 775 (Cattaraugus 1956).
[73] Village of Canton v Globe Indem Co, 201 AD 820, 195 NYS 445 (1922).
[74] Maltin v Maryland Cas Co, 24 AD2d 419, 260 NYS2d 194 (1965).
[75] Lamparter Acoustical Prods v Maryland Cas Co, 64 AD2d 693, 407 NYS2d 579 (1978).
[76] Village of Canton v Globe Indem Co, 201 AD 820, 195 NYS 445 (1922).

On a multi-prime construction project, one prime contractor may suffer delay damages as a result of another prime's actions. The damaged prime contractor may not recover delay or any other damages against the other prime contractor's surety, except in the rare instance when it is a member of a class specifically intended to be a third-party beneficiary of the bond.[77]

§8.20 —Incidental and Consequential Damages

It is not unusual for an obligee, another prime contractor, or a subcontractor to suffer consequential damages as a result of a principal's breach of contract. If the surety performs under the bond either by completion or by payment, it is not liable for these consequential damages. When a surety breaches its duties under the bond by failing to complete the work or pay the penal sum of the bond, the surety may be liable to the obligee for those damages that "reasonably and naturally" flow from the principal's breach as well as the surety's breach. The case of *Hunt v Bankers & Shippers Insurance Co*[78] illustrates how far this rule may go.

In *Hunt*, the principal/contractor abandoned its work, which involved building several restaurants for the obligee. The surety refused to complete the restaurants or pay its penal sum. The obligee was forced to sell the partially completed restaurants at reduced prices. The court found the surety liable for the obligee's loss of the use of the premises and the lower sales prices of the restaurants, as losses which reasonably and naturally flowed from the surety's default and its principal's breaches. By refusing to complete the restaurants or pay for their completion, the surety exposed itself to greater liability.[79] In effect, the court held that the surety chose to incur higher damages and failed to mitigate its own damages.

§8.21 —Attorneys' Fees

A surety will not be liable for attorneys' fees incurred by an obligee, regardless of the provisions of the underlying contract,[80] and even if the obligee incurred attorneys' fees solely due to the surety's default.[81] A surety will be liable for an obligee's attorneys' fees only if the contract and bond specifically establish liability therefor.[82] The primary reason for this principle is that under

---

[77] Novak & Co v Travelers Indem Co, 56 AD2d 418, 392 NYS2d 901 (1977).

[78] 73 AD2d 797, 423 NYS2d 718 (1979), *affd*, 50 NY2d 938, 409 NE2d 928, 431 NYS2d 454 (1980).

[79] Of course, the court did not hold the surety liable for damages over the bond amount except to the extent that interest caused the damage award to exceed the bond amount.

[80] Davis Acoustical Corp v Hanover Ins Co, 22 AD2d 843, 254 NYS2d 14 (1964).

[81] Tynan Incinerator Co v International Fidelity Ins Co, 117 AD2d 796, 499 NYS2d 118 (1986) (attorneys' fees and bond premiums incurred by obligee in discharging mechanics' liens were not recoverable from the surety).

[82] Robbins v Melbrook Realty Co, 28 Misc 2d 1076, 213 NYS2d 403 (Queens 1961).

266 BONDS

New York law, attorneys' fees generally are not recoverable except by specific contractual agreement.[83]

§8.22 —Punitive Damages

Of course, like any party to a contract, a surety may be liable for punitive damages which exceed the bond amount where the surety shows "extraordinary bad faith" in refusing to honor a claim under its bond. The standard is the same as for any breach of contract: the wrong must be "morally culpable or actuated by evil and reprehensible motives."[84]

No New York cases have been found which discuss whether a surety may be liable to the obligee for punitive damages that have been awarded against the principal in the obligee's favor. The authors believe that a surety should not be liable for its principal's bad faith actions. The public policy behind awarding punitive damages—to deter similar conduct by others and to punish the wrongdoers—would not be met by requiring the surety to pay punitive damages based on its principal's actions. Further, a surety secures a principal's obligation to perform the contract, not the principal's moral character or manner of doing business.

§8.23 —Interest

Generally, a surety is not liable for interest due an obligee. The only exception to this rule is that a defaulting surety is liable for interest on the amount that it should have paid the obligee from the time of default by the surety.[85] Interest due is measured from the time of the surety's default in honoring a claim under the bond, not its principal's default.[86]

§8.24 Surety's Defenses

A surety will pay a claim or take over completion of a contract only when it perceives, in good faith, that it has no legitimate alternative. It will not pay over the objection of its principal or indemnitors for fear of being caught in the middle; a surety that wrongfully honors an obligee's claim may be deemed to be a volunteer and lose its right to recover its loss from its principal or indemnitors.

---

[83] Davis Acoustical Corp v Hanover Ins Co, 22 AD2d 843, 254 NYS2d 14 (1964).

[84] Spancrete NE, Inc v Travelers Indem Co, 112 AD2d 571, 491 NYS2d 848, *appeal dismissed*, 66 NY2d 909, 489 NE2d 762, 498 NYS2d 793 (1985).

[85] NY Gen Oblig Law §7-301 (McKinney 1989 & Supp 1992). Hunt v Bankers & Shippers Ins Co, 73 AD2d 797, 423 NYS2d 718 (1979), *affd*, 50 NY2d 938, 409 NE2d 928, 431 NYS2d 454 (1980); Carrols Equities Corp v Villnave, 57 AD2d 1044, 395 NYS2d 800 (1977).

[86] Tynan Incinerator Co v International Fidelity Ins Co, 117 AD2d 796, 499 NYS2d 118 (1986).

When faced with a claim, a surety notifies its principal and indemnitors. If they admit that the claim is valid, the surety instructs them to satisfy the claim. If they deny the claim and their denial appears to have merit, the surety will instruct them to defend the claim at no expense to the surety. Only if the principal and indemnitors fail to satisfy a claim and there are no defenses available to the surety will it honor a claim.

The most typical defenses of a surety are that it was not given timely notice of the obligee's claim; that it was discharged from its bond obligations by a breach, modification, or voiding of the contract; that the obligee did not bring suit within the limitation period; that the obligee seeks to hold the surety liable in excess of its penal sum (the amount of the bond); its principal's defenses; and that the claimant is not a beneficiary of the bond. In addition, sureties have available to them most standard defenses, including failure to mitigate damages.[87] Because the defenses available to a surety are not always dependent upon the type of bond involved, the discussion that follows (§§8.25-8.31) concerns both performance and payment bonds.

§8.25 —Lack of or Untimely Notice

The majority of performance bonds contain notice clauses that specify when an obligee must notify the surety of the principal's default. Typical clauses provide that the notice must be in writing and delivered in person or by certified or registered mail within 30-to-90 days of the day the default occurred. A failure to substantially comply with a notice provision is fatal to any later suit on the bond.[88] While precise compliance with a bond's notice requirements is not required,[89] the wise claimant provides full notice early and often. The notice should include all information required by the bond's provisions, including identification of the contract and bond claimed upon, the date and nature of the default, and other information which may be necessary to fully explain the scope and possible consequences of the default. Further, the notice should clearly specify that it is a notice of claim or default under the bond and should be served as specified in the bond. A failure to serve the notice as required can be fatal to a claim.[90]

A bond claimant is held to a bond's notice requirements regardless of its

---

[87] Federal Ins Co v Walker, 53 NY2d 24, 422 NE2d 548, 439 NYS2d 888 (1981).

[88] Coleman Capital Corp v Travelers Indem Co, 443 F2d 47 (2d Cir 1971).

[89] Village of Warwick v Republic Ins Co, 104 Misc 2d 514, 428 NYS2d 589 (Orange 1980).

[90] *See* Ulster Elec Supply Co v Maryland Cas Co, 35 AD2d 309, 316 NYS2d 159 (1970), *affd*, 30 NY2d 712, 283 NE2d 622, 332 NYS2d 648 (1972) (interpreting notice service requirements of NY State Fin Law §137 (McKinney 1989 & Supp 1992) before its amendment); *but see* Fleisher Engg & Constr Co v United States *ex rel* Hallenbeck, 311 US 15, 61 S Ct 81, 85 L Ed 12 (1940) (where receipt of a notice of a Miller Act claim mailed by regular mail was admitted by surety, court held service was valid).

knowledge of the bond.[91] Similarly, an assignee of a claim under a bond must comply with its notice provisions regardless of knowledge.[92]

§8.26 —Discharge by Modification or Breach of Contract

When an obligee substantially breaches or modifies the terms of the contract without the surety's consent, the surety may be discharged, regardless of actual damage to the surety or principal.[93] Modifications that have discharged sureties include reducing the amount of retainage required[94] and payment to the principal before it was earned or required by the contract, although advance payment will not always release a surety.[95] An obligee's breach by failing to make timely payments to the principal will discharge the surety.[96]

While older cases discharge a surety for minor modifications, the modern trend is for the surety *not* to be wholly discharged due to a modification or breach, unless the modification or breach is so substantial as to materially change the underlying contract and, hence, the surety's obligation or risk. The surety is released *pro tanto*, in the amount that it was impaired by the modification or breach. (See discussion below.)

Further, where the contract specifies that the owner may make changes and specific alterations without invalidating the contract, the surety is deemed to have assented to and is not released by any modification made pursuant to such a provision.[97] The general rule is that where changes are contemplated by the contract, a surety is bound by changes which are reasonably within the contemplation of the contract.[98]

Similarly, not all variations from the contract payment schedule are breaches that will discharge a surety. The guiding principle is that if the surety's collateral (here, the contract funds unpaid) is impaired by, for instance, advance payment, the surety is released either completely or *pro tanto*—in the amount of

---

[91] John Johnston Concrete Gutter Co v American Empire Ins Co, 81 AD2d 1004, 440 NYS2d 107 (1981); Coleman Capital Corp v Travelers Indem Co, 443 F2d 47 (2d Cir 1971).

[92] Ferrante Equip Co v Charles Simkin & Sons, 30 AD2d 525, 290 NYS2d 246 (1968).

[93] Page v Krekey, 137 NY 307, 33 NE 311 (1893).

[94] Schooley Enter v Paso Contracting Corp, 33 AD2d 981, 307 NYS2d 388 (1970) (retainage reduced by mutual agreement of obligee and principal from $15,000 to $2,500).

[95] Advance payments do not always discharge a surety, especially where the advances encourage and allow a principal to continue its performance under the contract. *See* Village of Canton v Globe Indem Co, 201 AD 820, 195 NYS 445 (1922).

[96] Hunt v Bankers & Shippers Ins Co, 60 AD2d 781, 400 NYS2d 645 (1977).

[97] Carrols Equities Corp v Villnave, 57 AD2d 1044, 395 NYS2d 800 (1977).

[98] Village of Newark v James F. Leary Constr Co, 118 Misc 622, 194 NYS 212 (Wayne 1922). In this case, the court found that the surety was bound by changes, despite the fact that change orders were not written as required by the contract. The court held that the failure to give written change orders was a "technical deviation" that did not release the surety.

the impairment—depending on the size and nature of the advance and the increased risk borne by the surety.[99] This principle is based upon the belief that retainage and payment for work done, as opposed to advance payment, encourage a contractor to fully perform its contractual duties so it will be paid.[100] Thus, if advance payments are made, there is less incentive for the contractor to continue performance, especially if the contractor has been paid in full or more than due for its partial performance. Not all advance payments have this effect, however, and, thus, will not serve automatically to discharge the surety. For instance, in a case where an obligee paid its principal in advance so the principal could stay in business, the court found that the advance payments encouraged and allowed the principal to further perform the contract and, thus, did not release the surety.[101] Similarly, in a case where an obligee voluntarily paid its contractor's employees after the contractor abandoned the contract, the court found that the payment was made independent of the contract for the purpose of avoiding future labor problems. The court found that the payment did not adversely affect the surety or have any negative effect upon the contract and, therefore, that the surety was not discharged. The court further held, however, that the obligee could not recover the payment from the surety as it was made at the obligee's risk and was not a part of the cost of the building.[102]

As mentioned above, if an obligee fails to pay its principal in a timely manner, the surety will be discharged unless the surety consents to the delay in payment.[103]

§8.27 —Discharge by Fraud

A surety is liable only where there is a valid contract between the obligee and principal. Thus, where a contract is void for fraudulent inducement, the surety is discharged.[104] Where the fraud is in the *performance* of the contract, however, the surety is not necessarily discharged. For example, in a case where a principal installed inferior materials and misrepresented the quality of the materials to the obligee to induce acceptance and the obligee overpaid the principal due to the misrepresentation, the surety was not discharged but was liable to the obligee for its principal's defective performance.[105] Such fraud by the principal does not, however, extend the obligee's time to sue; the limitation period begins to run upon the obligee's acceptance of the performance, despite

---

[99] St John's College v Aetna Indem Co, 201 NY 335, 94 NE 994 (1911); Globe Indem Co v Southern Pac Co, 30 F2d 580 (2d Cir 1929). *See also* 17 Am Jur 2d *Contractor's Bonds* §31 (1990).

[100] St John's College, Fordham v Aetna Indem Co, 201 NY 335, 94 NE 994 (1911).

[101] Village of Canton v Globe Indem Co, 201 AD 820, 195 NYS 445 (1922).

[102] St John's College, Fordham v Aetna Indem Co, 201 NY 335, 94 NE 994 (1911).

[103] Hunt v Bankers & Shippers Ins Co, 60 AD2d 781, 400 NYS2d 645 (1977).

[104] Taylor & Jennings, Inc v Bellino Bros Constr Co, 106 AD2d 779, 483 NYS2d 813 (1984).

[105] People v Massachusetts Bonding & Ins Co, 182 AD 122, 169 NYS 693 (1918).

the fact that the acceptance was based upon the principal's fraud.[106] If the obligee participates in the principal's fraud in performing the contract, the surety should be discharged.[107]

§8.28 —Untimely Claim

In addition to containing notice provisions, a bond usually specifies time limits in which suit may be brought on claims under the bond. A failure of an obligee or third-party beneficiary to meet a bond's limitation period will cause its suit to be dismissed.[108] Bond limitation periods are typically shorter than applicable statutes of limitation and are triggered by different events. So long as the bond limitation period is not unreasonably short, the period will be valid.[109] A one-year period generally is considered reasonable.[110]

Thus, it is important for obligees and their attorneys to keep careful watch of a bond's limitation period. It is neither wise nor prudent to wait patiently for a contractor or subcontractor to perform its obligations or pay its suppliers, or to wait for a surety to decide what to do, when that patience may result in the obligee's losing the only true security it has—the surety's promise to perform or pay if the contractor does not.

Bond limitation periods are construed strictly against the surety to provide obligees and third-party beneficiaries every opportunity to seek legal remedies.[111] Thus, where a bond provided that suit under the bond must begin no more than two years from the date final payment became due under the subcontract, but the contractor paid the subcontractor before final payment was due, the court held that the time to sue did not begin to run with payment of the subcontractor but on the later date, when the subcontractor *should* have been paid.[112]

---

[106] Town of Esopus v Brinnier & Larios, PC, 135 AD2d 935, 522 NYS2d 337 (1987).

[107] *See* BG Equip Co v American Ins Co, 61 AD2d 247, 402 NYS2d 478 (1978), in which the principal and obligee were closely related corporations and the obligee acquiesced in the principal's fraud.

[108] Yeshiva Univ v Fidelity & Deposit Co, 116 AD2d 49, 500 NYS2d 241 (1986). Third-party beneficiaries are bound by all terms of the bond, including limitation periods. Timberline Elec Supply Corp v Insurance Co of N Am, 72 AD2d 905, 421 NYS2d 987 (1979), *affd*, 52 NY2d 793, 417 NE2d 1248, 436 NYS2d 707 (1980).

[109] Timberline Elec Supply Corp v Insurance Co of N Am, 72 AD2d 905, 421 NYS2d 987 (1979), *affd*, 52 NY2d 793, 417 NE2d 1248, 436 NYS2d 707 (1980).

[110] *Id;* York Concrete Corp v Northwood Projects, Inc, 57 AD2d 950, 395 NYS2d 98 (1977); *see also* NY State Fin Law §137 (McKinney 1989 & Supp 1992), which provides a one-year limitation period for suit on a public payment bond.

[111] Clyde-Savannah Cent School Dist v Naetzker, Thorsell & Dove, 73 AD2d 810, 424 NYS2d 67 (1979).

[112] *Id* (subcontractor was not due its final payment until its work was accepted by the owner or its architect, which occurred some time after the contractor paid the subcontractor). *But see* Yeshiva Univ v Fidelity & Deposit Co, 116 AD2d 49, 500 NYS2d 241 (1986).

§8.28 UNTIMELY CLAIM

This strict construction of bond limitation periods can result in decisions which seem to indicate that some limitation periods never begin to run. For instance, where a bond required suit to be brought within one year of the date the Federal Housing Administration Chief Underwriter signed a final project inspection report, but a report was not signed, the court held that the limitation period had not begun to run.[113] Similarly, where a principal abandoned its work, final payment under the contract never came due, and the court held that the two-year limitation period, which was to be triggered by final payment coming due, never began to run.[114] Such strict construction has been criticized in recent cases as, in effect, allowing obligees to keep sureties forever exposed to liability by withholding formal acceptance of work.[115]

Many performance bonds avoid the problems inherent in limitation periods triggered by final payments by providing that the limitation period begins when the principal *ceases work* under the contract. Under these clauses, the period begins when the *principal* either completes[116] or abandons[117] its work under the contract, not when final payment is due. Completion by the surety or its substitute contractor does not extend the limitation period.[118] A principal *ceases work* on the contract when the construction project itself ceases or when labor and the supplying of materials directly related to the project cease. Typically, *work* does not include the contractor's administrative tasks, such as securing releases and lien waivers. Under such clauses, the limitation period begins to run when actual construction by the principal or claimant stops.[119] The fact that a performance is defective does not mean that the principal never completed its work or that final payment never became due.[120] Thus, fraud by a contractor in performing its contract does not extend a bond's limitation period, even where the fraud causes the obligee to accept defective performance and the limitation

---

[113] York Concrete Corp v Northwood Projects, Inc, 57 AD2d 950, 395 NYS2d 98 (1977); *but see* Phillips Constr Co v City of NY, 61 NY2d 949, 463 NE2d 585, 475 NYS2d 244, *reargument denied*, 62 NY2d 646, 464 NE2d 990, 476 NYS2d 1028 (1984) (in a case not involving a surety, the Court of Appeals held that the statute of limitations, NY Civ Prac L & R §213(2) (McKinney 1990 & Supp 1992), began to run upon completion of actual physical work, not when the city finally certified or refused the contractor's final payment voucher).

[114] Stanley R. Benjamin, Inc v Fidelity & Cas Co, 72 Misc 2d 742, 340 NYS2d 578 (Nassau 1972).

[115] Yeshiva Univ v Fidelity & Deposit Co, 116 AD2d 49, 500 NYS2d 241 (1986).

[116] Whitacre Constr Specialties, Inc v Aetna Cas & Sur Co, 86 AD2d 972, 448 NYS2d 287 (1982), *affd*, 57 NY2d 1018, 443 NE2d 953, 457 NYS2d 479 (1984).

[117] Timberline Elec Supply Corp v Insurance Co of N Am, 72 AD2d 905, 421 NYS2d 987 (1979), *affd*, 52 NY2d 793, 417 NE2d 1248, 436 NYS2d 707 (1980).

[118] Town of Esopus v Brinnier & Larios, PC, 135 AD2d 935, 522 NYS2d 337 (1987).

[119] Whitacre Constr Specialties, Inc v Aetna Cas & Sur Co, 86 AD2d 972, 448 NYS2d 287 (1982), *affd*, 57 NY2d 1018, 443 NE2d 953, 457 NYS2d 479 (1984).

[120] Yeshiva Univ v Fidelity & Deposit Co, 116 AD2d 49, 500 NYS2d 241 (1986). Where defects are latent, the obligee is not without recourse—it may sue the principal directly.

period to begin to run.[121] The time to sue the surety dates from when the principal defaults and ceases its work on the contract, regardless of how or why it stops working on the contract.

Of course, determining when work *ceases* or when final payment *is due* is dependent on interpretation of both bond and contract language or the law and may be difficult. The wise course is to bring suit within the limitation period as it relates to the particular claim, regardless of when final payment is due or whether the principal is still performing under the contract, if the claim regards a subcontractor's work. By doing this, a claimant should be in compliance with a bond limitation period.

§8.29 —Liability in Excess of the Penal Sum

A surety's liability on its bond is specifically limited and cannot exceed the penal sum (the amount of the bond) plus interest from the time of the surety's default, if any,[122] regardless of the obligee's actual damages or completion costs.[123] Interest due is measured from the surety's default in honoring a claim under the bond, not from its principal's default.[124] If a surety opts to fund completion of the contract it remains liable to the obligee for the full penal sum of the bond; payments made to persons other than the obligee generally do not reduce the penal sum.

Of course, like any party to a contract, a surety may be liable for punitive damages which exceed the bond amount where it shows "extraordinary bad faith" in refusing to honor a claim under its bond. The standard is the same as for any breach of contract: the wrong must be "morally culpable or actuated by evil and reprehensible motives."[125]

§8.30 —The Principal's Defenses and Claims

The questions of when a surety may defend against an obligee's claims by raising a defense or claim of its principal and which defenses and claims it may raise are not easily answered. The Court of Appeals held in *Walcutt v Clevite*

---

[121] Town of Esopus v Brinnier & Larios, PC, 135 AD2d 935, 522 NYS2d 337 (1987).

[122] NY Gen Oblig Law §7-301 (McKinney 1989 & Supp 1992). Hunt v Bankers & Shippers Ins Co, 73 AD2d 797, 423 NYS2d 718 (1979), *affd,* 50 NY2d 938, 409 NE2d 928, 431 NYS2d 454 (1980); Carrols Equities Corp v Villnave, 57 AD2a 1044, 395 NYS2d 800 (1977).

[123] Norris v Depew Paving Co, 14 AD2d 117, 217 NYS2d 203 (1961), *affd,* 11 NY2d 812, 182 NE2d 109, 227 NYS2d 436 (1962). This rule is not applicable where the surety is bound to complete the project regardless of cost (as in a *completion* bond) or where the surety chooses to complete the contract itself.

[124] Tynan Incinerator Co v International Fidelity Ins Co, 117 AD2d 796, 499 NYS2d 118 (1986).

[125] Spancrete NE, Inc v Travelers Indem Co, 112 AD2d 571, 491 NYS2d 848, *appeal dismissed,* 66 NY2d 909, 489 NE2d 762, 498 NYS2d 793 (1985).

Corp[126] that a surety may not raise the defense of fraud in the inducement or the defense of breach of warranty by the obligee without the principal's consent when a surety is sued alone. The court went on to state, and, thereby, confuse the issue, that a surety may "always" assert a total or partial failure of consideration and may raise the defense that the obligee defaulted in its performance to the principal. The Appellate Division cases that discuss these issues contradict each other. Some cases seem to hold that a surety may assert *any* defense the principal may have against the obligee that is related to the contract;[127] other cases hold that a surety may not assert its principal's defenses without consent.[128] Consent has been found in the principal's decision to sue the obligee or defend against an obligee's claims and in its use of certain theories in its case.[129]

There are some principles on which the cases seem to be in agreement:

1. The surety may assert any defense that the principal either asserts itself or consents to the surety's asserting
2. The surety may assert a failure of consideration in the contract, such as nonpayment by the obligee
3. Without the principal's consent, the surety may not assert a claim of the principal against the obligee that is unrelated to the underlying contract
4. The surety may always assert that, through some action of the obligee, it was fraudulently induced to issue the bond[130]

The authors believe that those cases that hold that a surety may assert any defense of the principal misinterpret *Walcutt*. Despite this belief, however, it is wise when representing a surety to raise every good faith defense or claim that the surety or its principal may have against the obligee on the underlying contract. The case law is there to support this position.[131]

Of course, the problem can be avoided completely by an assignment by the principal to the surety of all of the defenses and claims the principal has or may have against the obligee on the underlying contract. The assignment may be in the bond, the indemnity agreement, or a separate document.

---

[126] 13 NY2d 48, 191 NE2d 894, 241 NYS2d 834, *remittitur amended*, 13 NY2d 903, 193 NE2d 511, 243 NYS2d 903 (1963).

[127] Spancrete NE, Inc v Travelers Indem Co, 112 AD2d 571, 491 NYS2d 848, *appeal dismissed*, 66 NY2d 909, 489 NE2d 762, 498 NYS2d 793 (1985); Construction Management Corp v Brown & Root, Inc, 35 Misc 2d 223, 229 NYS2d 70 (NY 1962).

[128] Taylor & Jennings, Inc v Bellino Bros Constr Co, 57 AD2d 42, 393 NYS2d 203 (1977).

[129] *Id*.

[130] General Motors Acceptance Corp v Kalkstein, 101 AD2d 102, 474 NYS2d 493 (1984).

[131] *See* Spancrete NE, Inc v Travelers Indem Co, 112 AD2d 571, 491 NYS2d 848, *appeal dismissed*, 66 NY2d 909, 489 NE2d 762, 498 NYS2d 793 (1985); Construction Management Corp v Brown & Root, Inc, 35 Misc 2d 223, 229 NYS2d 70 (NY 1962).

§8.31 —Party Not Protected by the Bond

A party that is not an obligee or beneficiary of a bond cannot recover against the surety on the bond. If a party is not a named obligee or beneficiary or an intended third-party beneficiary, it has no rights against the surety, even though it may have been damaged by the principal's performance of the contract or it may not have been paid. Thus, one prime contractor was denied recovery on another prime contractor's performance bond, despite the fact that it was damaged by the bonded contractor's delayed performance; the injured prime contractor was not a third-party beneficiary of the bond.[132]

An interesting twist to the protection afforded third-party beneficiaries is that a party may be protected under more than one bond. This is true most often in the case of payment bonds.[133]

Discussions regarding which parties are protected under performance and payment bonds are found in **§§8.10, 8.33-8.36,** and **8.43-8.44.**

§8.32 Payment Bonds

In most construction projects, the general contractor uses subcontractors, laborers, and materialmen in performance of the contract. A *payment* bond secures the obligation of the general contractor to pay those parties for their work on the general contract. The purpose of the bond is to protect the obligee against the claims of unpaid parties[134] and to facilitate payment for labor done and materials furnished for an improvement. Thus, in addition to the obligee, beneficiaries of a payment bond may include subcontractors, laborers, materialmen, and all others who supply labor and materials to the contractor or a subcontractor, or who are specifically identified as beneficiaries of the bond. It is rare for a *payment* bond to be required without a *performance* bond also being required, and vice versa.

> **PRACTICE POINTER:**
>
> If the general contractor has provided a performance bond, there is probably a payment bond as well. A subcontractor should ask the general contractor for a copy of any and all bonds it has provided on the job.

If a private project has a payment bond, the owner of the project must file a copy of the bond with the county clerk of the city where the project is located if the contract is in excess of $100,000. The bond must be filed within 30 days of the owner's receipt of the bond. A private owner does not have a duty to obtain a bond, but if it does have one and fails to file it, the owner will be liable for attorneys' fees incurred by a successful bond claimant.[135]

---

[132] Novak & Co v Travelers Indem Co, 56 AD2d 418, 392 NYS2d 901 (1977).

[133] *See* §8.33.

[134] HNC Realty Co v Bay View Towers Apts, Inc, 64 AD2d 417, 409 NYS2d 774 (1978).

[135] NY Gen Oblig Law §5-322.3 (McKinney 1989 & Supp 1992).

In New York, all public improvements undertaken by the state, municipal corporations, public benefit corporations, and commissions appointed by law require payment bonds (hereinafter *§137 bonds*) which secure payment to all persons who furnish labor or materials to the contractor or its subcontractor.[136] Section 137 bonds were designed to supplement the Lien Law by extending additional protection to parties that improve public property by ensuring payment of money due on public improvements.[137] Other public entities and improvements, for example, town highway improvements,[138] sewer systems,[139] and canals,[140] also require payment bonds pursuant to statute. Additionally, public entities can require payment bonds in the absence of requiring law.[141] When a payment bond is demanded by a public entity but is not required by law, the bond is interpreted by common law, independent of statute, as though it were a private bond,[142] unless the bond specifically incorporates a statute into its terms.

Typically, contract bid specifications detail whether and what sort of a payment bond is required for the job. Prior to bidding, it is wise to review not only the bid specifications but also the applicable statute, ordinance, or law, if any, which requires the bond. By doing this, a bidding contractor can ensure that it will be able to provide the bond required if awarded the job and thus avoid loss of its bid bond.

Many private improvements also require payment bonds. It is rare for a payment bond to be required where a performance bond is not. As a surety usually will not charge extra to issue a payment bond on the same project to the same principal it has already issued a performance bond to, it is wise for an owner to require a payment bond as a matter of course where it has chosen to require a performance bond. When deciding whether to require only a payment bond, a private obligee should consider the contractor's financial condition; the contractor's payment history; the complexity and length of the job; the number of potential subcontractors, materialmen, and laborers; the willingness of the corporate contractor's officers to furnish personal guaranties of payment; etc. The benefits of a payment bond—the assurance of an ever-solvent surety to pay—must be weighed against its typical cost of 90-cents-to-2-dollars per 1,000 dollars of contract price. Whether it is the obligee or contractor that pays the bond premium directly to the surety, it is the obligee that ultimately pays the cost.

---

[136] NY State Fin Law §137 (McKinney 1989 & Supp 1992).

[137] Chittenden Lumber Co v Silberblatt & Lasker, Inc, 288 NY 396, 43 NE2d 459 (1942).

[138] NY High Law §193 (McKinney 1979 & Supp 1992).

[139] NY Village Law §17-1718(5) (McKinney 1973 & Supp 1992).

[140] NY Canal Law §30(6) (McKinney 1939 & Supp 1992).

[141] Clark Plastering Co v Seaboard Sur Co, 237 AD 274, 260 NYS 468 (1932).

[142] Sullivan Highway Prods Corp v Edward L. Nezelek, Inc, 52 AD2d 986, 383 NYS2d 463 (1976); Clark Plastering Co v Seaboard Sur Co, 237 AD 274, 260 NYS 468 (1932).

§8.33 Who is Protected

In addition to covering the obligee, the typical *payment* bond covers those parties that are protected by the Lien Law and are below the bond principal in the project hierarchy. Thus, when a general contractor is the principal, the bond protects the subcontractors, laborers, and materialmen. It is not unusual to find that a contractor will require payment bonds of its subcontractors, especially in a complex contract where it is known that the subcontractor will have numerous subcontractors and materialmen working for it. The applicable principles of law are the same whether the obligee is an owner, a contractor, or some other party. If the principal fails to pay its subcontractors, the surety is liable to the obligee directly or to the subcontractors as third-party beneficiaries up to the penal sum of the bond.

The protection afforded by a private payment bond depends on its specific language and the parties' intent in requiring and furnishing the bond. Private payment bonds are strictly interpreted. Typically, they benefit the same class of persons protected by the Lien Law, although the parties may limit the bond's protection as they choose. For instance, where a bond specifically limits the class of beneficiaries to those who have contracts with the principal or its subcontractor, a remote subcontractor is not protected and cannot claim under the bond, even if such a subcontractor may have been entitled to file a mechanic's lien.[143]

Private bonds may expand the class of beneficiaries as well, although it is doubtful that all findings of expansion have been intended by the parties. For instance, in a case where a payment bond specified merely that the bond protected those who performed work in "furtherance of the contract," the court allowed a party to recover under the bond despite the fact that the party performed its work for the principal *before* the bond was obtained. The court held that because the bond did not exclude previously performed work, the claimant was protected under the bond as one who fell within the class specified by the bond.[144]

Section 137 bonds[145] protect those parties that are protected by the Lien Law applicable to public improvements,[146] whether or not there is a lien fund[147]

---

[143] American Indus Contracting Co v Travelers Indem Co, 54 AD2d 679, 387 NYS2d 260 (1976), *affd*, 42 NY2d 1041, 369 NE2d 762, 399 NYS2d 206 (1977).

[144] Davis Wallbridge, Inc v Aetna Cas & Sur Co, 103 AD2d 1010, 478 NYS2d 389 (1984).

[145] In New York, all public improvements undertaken by the state, municipal corporations, public benefit corporations, and commissions appointed by law require payment bonds that secure payment to all persons who furnish labor or materials to the contractor or its subcontractor. NY State Fin Law §137 (McKinney 1989 & Supp 1992).

[146] Chittenden Lumber Co v Silberblatt & Lasker, Inc, 288 NY 396, 43 NE2d 459 (1942).

[147] Ingalls Iron Works Co v Golden, 32 Misc 2d 426, 224 NYS2d 158 (NY 1961).

or the bond claimant filed a lien.[148] The general rule is that if a party can file a public improvement lien, that party is protected under a §137 bond.[149] Thus, like the Lien Law, the bond protects only first and second tier subcontractors, and their laborers, materialmen, etc., on public improvements. A full discussion of what parties, actions, and items are protected by and properly included in a public improvement mechanic's lien is found in Chapter 9.

Where a bond specifies that other parties are intended beneficiaries but their benefits are "subject to the obligee's priority," the beneficiaries have no rights under the bond and no cause of action against the surety until the obligee's rights are satisfied.[150] Thus, under such a bond, if a contractor/obligee were to pay its subcontractor's materialmen after the subcontractor/principal abandoned the job, the contractor/obligee would be entitled to recover from the surety before the subcontractor's other unpaid materialmen.

A party may be a beneficiary of more than one payment bond on the same project. For instance, if a contractor has a payment bond that specifically benefits a subcontractor's materialman and the subcontractor has a payment bond, required by the contractor, that also specifically benefits the materialman, the materialman may recover from whichever surety it chooses. It need not join its subcontractor's surety in its suit against the contractor's surety. If judgment is obtained against the contractor's surety, it may seek recovery against the subcontractor's surety as it would be subrogated to the materialman's right of recovery against the subcontractor's surety.[151]

As the class of persons protected by payment bonds is typically the same as that class protected by the Lien Law, the definitions of included persons, activities, and materials will not be repeated here. These matters are discussed in depth in Chapter 9 on mechanics' liens. A good understanding of the principles discussed there is necessary to understand the class of parties protected by bonds. The discussions which follow in this chapter are intended to emphasize certain principles only.

§8.34 —Subcontractors

Under §137 bonds[152] and most other bonds required on public projects, subcontractors and sub-subcontractors are protected; subcontractors beyond the

---

[148] Honeywell, Inc v Trico Sheet Metal, Inc, 60 Misc 2d 1049, 304 NYS2d 530 (Albany 1969).

[149] Hub Oil Co v Jodomar, Inc, 176 Misc 320, 27 NYS2d 370 (Monroe 1941).

[150] New York Plumbers Specialties Co v Columbia Cas Co, 13 AD2d 449, 211 NYS2d 824 (1961); Samson Elec Co v Buffalo Elec Co, 234 AD 521, 256 NYS 219 (1932).

[151] Huber Lathing Corp v Aetna Cas & Sur Co, 132 AD2d 597, 517 NYS2d 758 (1987).

[152] In New York, all public improvements undertaken by the state, municipal corporations, public benefit corporations, and commissions appointed by law require payment bonds that secure payment to all persons who furnish labor or materials to the contractor or its subcontractor. NY State Fin Law §137 (McKinney 1989 & Supp 1992).

second tier are not within the class of bond beneficiaries.[153]

Under most private *payment* bonds, however, any number of tiers of subcontractors are intended beneficiaries. Where, however, a bond specifically limits its protection to those who have a contract directly with the contractor or *its* subcontractor, a remote subcontractor is not within the bond's class of beneficiaries and is unprotected.[154]

§8.35 —Suppliers and Materialmen

Suppliers, also known as *materialmen*, generally are beneficiaries of *payment* bonds, whether public or private, so long as they supply the materials to a subcontractor or contractor, the materials supplied are necessary for the work done, and the materials supplied are incorporated into the project, consumed by the work, or specifically made for the project.[155] This standard is the same as that used in determining whether materials supplied may be claimed in a mechanic's lien. If the materials are not within the category of materials defined by the Lien Law at §2(12), the cost of the materials is not recoverable under a payment bond.[156] Of course, a private bond may exclude suppliers or limit their recovery to specific types of materials.

§8.36 —Architects/Engineers

Generally, architects and engineers work directly for the owner of the property and would not be protected by a *payment* bond unless specifically named as an intended beneficiary. Where an architect or engineer works for the contractor, however, it should be entitled to recover under a payment bond as one that performed labor for the contractor.

§8.37 What Items Are Covered

Payment bonds, whether for public or for private improvements, are for the payment of labor and materials. Thus, they do not cover a beneficiary's lost

---

[153] Section 137 provides that "[e]very person who has furnished labor or material, to the contractor or to a subcontractor of the contractor" may claim payment under the bond. This language specifically excludes subcontractors beyond the second tier from claiming under the bond. *See* Cameron Equip Corp v People, 31 AD2d 299, 297 NYS2d 326 (1969), *affd*, 27 NY2d 634, 261 NE2d 668, 313 NYS2d 763 (1970) (interpreting similar language found in §5 of the Lien Law).

[154] American Indus Contracting Co v Travelers Indem Co, 54 AD2d 679, 387 NYS2d 260 (1976), *affd*, 42 NY2d 1041, 369 NE2d 762, 399 NYS2d 206 (1977).

[155] Zipp v Fidelity & Deposit Co, 73 AD 20, 76 NYS 386 (1902) (coal used to fuel boilers needed for excavation work was properly included in a bond claim).

[156] Norris v Depew Paving Co, 14 AD2d 117, 217 NYS2d 203 (1961), *affd*, 11 NY2d 812, 182 NE2d 109, 227 NYS2d 436 (1962). *See* **ch 9.**

profits or delay damages[157] or damages a beneficiary suffers due to a principal's negligence.[158] The items for which a §137 bond[159] allows recovery are the same as may be properly included in a mechanic's lien.[160] Similarly, most private bonds' coverage is interpreted in light of the Lien Law,[161] although a private bond may limit its coverage by its terms.[162] A thorough review of the bond and the underlying contract is necessary to discover what items are covered by a private bond.

As the class of items covered under most payment bonds generally is the same as that class allowed by the Mechanic's Lien Law, the definitions of included items will not be repeated here. These items include labor, materials, rental equipment, temporary works, employee benefits, and extras, and are discussed in depth in Chapter 9 on mechanics' liens. A good understanding of the principles discussed there is essential to understand what is covered under a bond. The discussions that follow in this chapter are intended to emphasize certain principles only and do not discuss every type of item that may be covered by a bond. Indeed, there is always room for inclusion of another item as covered by a payment bond; case law is ever expanding.

§8.38 —Materials

The standard for determining whether the cost of materials supplied is covered under a bond is the same as that used in determining whether materials supplied may be claimed in a mechanic's lien. If the materials are not within the category of materials defined by NY Lien Law §2(12), the cost of the materials is not recoverable under a *payment* bond.[163] If the materials supplied could be used by the contractor in another job, such as tires and tubes for the contractor's vehicles, the supplier does not have a bond claim.[164]

---

[157] Concrete Constr Corp v Commercial Union Ins Co, 68 AD2d 866, 414 NYS2d 703 (1974) (the claimant can recover from the surety increased costs incurred due to the delay; it cannot recover its lost profits).

[158] Gerosa Crane Serv v International Prods, 70 Misc 2d 176, 332 NYS2d 536 (Civ Ct NY 1972).

[159] In New York, all public improvements undertaken by the state, municipal corporations, public benefit corporations, and commissions appointed by law require payment bonds that secure payment to all persons who furnish labor or materials to the contractor or its subcontractor. NY State Fin Law §137 (McKinney 1989 & Supp 1992).

[160] Hub Oil Co v Jodomar, Inc, 176 Misc 320, 27 NYS2d 370 (Monroe 1941).

[161] Norris v Depew Paving Co, 14 AD2d 117, 217 NYS2d 203 (1961), *affd*, 11 NY2d 812, 182 NE2d 109, 227 NYS2d 436 (1962).

[162] American Indus Contracting Co v Travelers Indem Co, 54 AD2d 679, 387 NYS2d 260 (1976), *affd*, 42 NY2d 1041, 369 NE2d 762, 399 NYS2d 206 (1977).

[163] Norris v Depew Paving Co, 14 AD2d 117, 217 NYS2d 203 (1961), *affd*, 11 NY2d 812, 182 NE2d 109, 227 NYS2d 436 (1962).

[164] *Id.* See **ch 9** on mechanics' liens.

§8.39 —Rental Equipment

Do not confuse materials supplied with equipment leased to a contractor. The rental value of leased equipment used in an improvement is a proper claim under a *payment* bond.[165]

§8.40 Notice of Claims

As is true with performance bonds, notice provisions in a *payment* bond or statute must be complied with or the claim will be denied, regardless of its merit. Private payment bond claim requirements and deadlines vary depending on the surety; so long as they are reasonable, they will be upheld. An assignee of a claim under a bond must comply with the bond's notice provisions applicable to its assignor.[166]

Time and Necessity of Notice

State Finance Law §137[167] provides that a claimant that contracted directly with the contractor and has not been paid in full within 90 days of the day on which the claimant last performed labor or supplied materials may sue the surety without prior notice of its claim. If the claimant contracted with a subcontractor and not the contractor, the claimant must give notice of its claim to the contractor within 120 days of the day on which the claimant last performed labor or supplied materials.[168] The notice must be served personally on the contractor or by registered mail.[169] If the notice is actually received by the contractor, the manner of service is irrelevant.[170] The burden of proof of establishing actual receipt of a notice of claim is on the claimant.

---

[165] Vigliarolo Bros v Lanza Contracting Corp, 127 Misc 2d 965, 487 NYS2d 979 (Civ Ct NY 1985). See **ch 9** on mechanics' liens. *See also* BG Equip Co v American Ins Co, 61 AD2d 247, 402 NYS2d 479, *affd,* 46 NY2d 811, 386 NE2d 833, 413 NYS2d 922 (1978) (rental value claim not allowed due to fraudulent collusion between contractor and supplier).

[166] Ferrante Equip Co v Charles Simkin & Sons, 30 AD2d 525, 290 NYS2d 246 (1968).

[167] In New York, all public improvements undertaken by the state, municipal corporations, public benefit corporations, and commissions appointed by law require payment bonds that secure payment to all persons who furnish labor or materials to the contractor or its subcontractor. NY State Fin Law §137 (McKinney 1989 & Supp 1992).

[168] NY State Fin Law §137(3) (McKinney 1989 & Supp 1992). Federal courts construe similar language in the Miller Act, 40 USC §§270a-270f, to mean that the period begins to run on the last day work was done as part of the original contract; correction of defects or repairs following inspection of the work will not extend the notice period. United States *ex rel* Magna Masonry, Inc v RT Woodfield, Inc, 709 F2d 249 (4th Cir 1983).

[169] NY State Fin Law §137(3) (McKinney 1989 & Supp 1992).

[170] *Id.*

> **PRACTICE POINTER:**
>
> Make every effort to serve the notice personally or by registered mail. Such methods provide readily acceptable proofs of service and eliminate the issue of whether the contractor actually received notice.

If making a claim under a public bond other than a §137 bond, refer to the requiring law or to the bond if there is no applicable statute or ordinance. When a payment bond is not required by law but is demanded by a public entity, and does not incorporate any statute, the bond is interpreted by common law as though it were a private bond.[171]

Private payment bonds also contain notice provisions, which provisions are strictly construed. For instance, a payment bond in one case specified that the time period began to run when the "work mentioned in the contract" was complete. When the principal defaulted and the obligee completed the work, the court held that time did not begin to run until the obligee completed the work detailed in the contract.[172]

If a claimant provides additional labor or materials that are a necessary portion of the contract work, a new notice period begins to run from the last day of the additional work.[173] Similarly, if a significant gap exists between deliveries under a series of purchase orders, a separate notice should be filed for each series.[174]

> **PRACTICE POINTER:**
>
> To avoid loss of a claim when work is interrupted—as with a series of deliveries, additional work, or delayed work—serve a separate notice of claim for each portion of work whenever it appears that the time between work may be the same as or longer than the prescribed time to file a notice of claim.

Contents of Notice

Section 137 bond claims must state with "substantial accuracy" the amount claimed and the name of the party to whom material was furnished or for whom labor was performed. This requirement has been interpreted both strictly and liberally. For example, a letter which stated that the claimant was proceeding

---

[171] Sullivan Highway Prods Corp v Edward L. Nezelek, Inc, 52 AD2d 986, 383 NYS2d 463 (1976); Clark Plastering Co v Seaboard Sur Co, 237 AD 274, 260 NYS 468 (1932).

[172] Davis Wallbridge, Inc v Aetna Cas & Sur Co, 103 AD2d 1010, 478 NYS2d 389 (1984).

[173] Triangle Erectors, Inc v James King & Son, 41 Misc 2d 12, 244 NYS2d 433 (Suffolk 1963).

[174] *See* United States *ex rel* JA Edward & Co v Peter Reiss Constr Co, 273 F2d 880 (2d Cir 1959), *cert denied*, 362 US 951, 80 S Ct 864, 4 L Ed 2d 869 (1960) (claimant delivered two series of materials, one series ended in December, next began in April; court held that notice filed within required 90 days of last delivery of April series was ineffective as to December deliveries).

with a lien against the job was held not to be a notice of claim, despite the claimant's intent that it be so;[175] but when a claimant signed a waiver of lien form provided by the contractor in order to receive final payment, the court held that the §137 notice requirement was met because the waiver form included the information required for a notice of claim.[176]

This requirement is simple and should be complied with as much as possible. It is wise to make it clear in the notice that it is a notice of claim under the bond; this notation can be in the form of a title of a document, such as "Notice of Claim upon Payment Bond," or set out as a regarding line in a letter. Clearly set forth the amount claimed, the work done, the job address, the name, including any known aliases, of the party with whom the claimant contracted, and any other information required or which would be of help in identifying the claim.

§8.41 Attorneys' Fees

Attorneys' fees may be recovered under a private *payment* bond in the same instances as under a private performance bond—if they are provided for in the bond and underlying contract.[177]

State Finance Law §137[178] provides that attorneys' fees may be awarded to any party if it had to defend against a claim or defense which was "without substantial basis in fact or law."[179]

§8.42 Interest

A payment bond surety will be liable for interest above the penal sum of the bond if it defaults in paying a legitimate claim under the bond.[180] Interest is calculated from the time of the refusal to pay the claim.

Where there are several parties claiming under a bond or where the claims exceed the amount of the bond, the surety may interplead the penal sum into the court and let the claimants litigate the issue of which party is entitled to it. The surety is not in default in such a case and the parties are not entitled to interest from the surety.[181]

---

[175] Ulster Elec Supply Co v Maryland Cas Co, 30 NY2d 712, 283 NE2d 622, 332 NYS2d 648 (1972).

[176] Vigliarolo Bros v Lanza Contracting Corp, 127 Misc 2d 965, 487 NYS2d 979 (Civ Ct NY 1985).

[177] *See* §8.21.

[178] In New York, all public improvements undertaken by the state, municipal corporations, public benefit corporations, and commissions appointed by law require payment bonds that secure payment to all persons who furnish labor or materials to the contractor or its subcontractor. NY State Fin Law §137 (McKinney 1989 & Supp 1992).

[179] NY State Fin Law §137(4)(c) (McKinney 1989 & Supp 1992).

[180] NY Gen Oblig Law §7-301 (McKinney 1989 & Supp 1992).

[181] Gould, Inc v Pension Benefits Guar Corp, 589 F Supp 164 (SDNY 1984).

§8.43 Miller Act Bonds[182]

The Miller Act[183] applies to almost every federal government construction project over $25,000.[184] The Miller Act requires separate payment[185] and performance[186] bonds on each prime contract and allows the contracting agency to require such other bonds as it chooses.[187] While the act does not provide a remedy if a federal agency awards a contract without the required Miller Act bonds, the agency may be liable directly to a party who would have been protected under the required payment bond *if* the agency has waived its sovereign immunity, i.e., if the agency has the power to sue and be sued, as has, for example, the Postal Service.[188] Further, regarding any agency that waived immunity, after construction work is completed, the Postal Service may be liable directly to a potential bond claimant for funds in the Postal Service's hands due the prime contractor, even when the underlying contract is bonded as required by the Miller Act.[189]

The Miller Act was intended to be highly remedial and is to be construed liberally.[190] The act provides separate protections for separate parties. A Miller Act *performance* bond is intended to benefit the United States; there are no other beneficiaries of the performance bond. A Miller Act *payment* bond is intended

---

[182] As this text is on New York construction law, only a brief discussion on Miller Act bonds is included. If faced with a Miller Act question, refer to the United States Code Annotated.

[183] 40 USC §§270a-270f.

[184] Exempt from the Miller Act requirements are certain army, navy, air force, and coast guard contracts, 40 USC §270e; certain transportation contracts entered into pursuant to the Merchant Marine Act, 1936, 46 USC §1101 *et seq*, and the Merchant Ship Sales Act of 1946, 50 USC app §1735 *et seq*, 40 USC §270f; and contracts performed in certain foreign countries, 40 USC §270a(b).

[185] 40 USC §270a(a)(2). If the total contract price is $1,000,000 or less, the payment bond must be 50% of the contract price. If the total contract price is more than $1,000,000 but less than $5,000,000, a 40% bond is required. If the total contract price is more than $5,000,000, a $2,500,000 bond is required. Contractors may pledge security in place of a surety payment bond. Acceptable forms of replacement security include certified and cashier's checks, post office money orders, and cash. 48 CFR §28.203.

[186] 40 USC §270a(a)(1). The amount of the performance bond is set by the awarding officer.

[187] *Id* §270a(c).

[188] Kennedy Elec Co v United States Postal Serv, 508 F2d 954 (10th Cir 1974) (court allowed a subcontractor to directly recover from the Postal Service under an equitable lien theory and based upon the right of the Postal Service to sue and be sued pursuant to 39 USC §401 *et seq*). The Postal Service has the same liability as any other business. Franchise Tax Bd v United States Postal Serv, 467 US 512, 104 S Ct 2549, 81 L Ed 2d 446 (1984).

[189] Active Fire Sprinkler Corp v United States Postal Serv, 811 F2d 747 (2d Cir 1987) (the suing subcontractor, which could have made claim under the bond, sued the Postal Service directly after the subcontractor failed to bring suit within the one-year Miller Act limitation period).

[190] Fleisher Engg & Constr Co v United States *ex rel* Hallenbeck, 311 US 15, 61 S Ct 81, 85 L Ed 12 (1940).

to benefit those who perform labor or furnish materials.[191] Thus, one that furnishes materials must make its claim under the payment bond; such a party cannot recover under the performance bond.[192]

§8.44 —Persons Protected

Much like a §137 bond,[193] the right to bring suit on a Miller Act bond is limited to those who deal directly with the prime contractor or the prime contractor's subcontractor.[194] Thus, a third-tier subcontractor is too remote to recover on the bond,[195] as are a materialman who supplies a materialman[196] and a sub-subcontractor's laborers.[197]

The federal courts have construed *subcontractor* somewhat broadly. A subcontractor under the Miller Act is one "who performs for and takes from the prime contractor a specific part of the labor or material requirements of the original contract, thus excluding ordinary laborers and materialmen."[198] Under the courts' interpretations, one who makes custom materials, not generally available in an open market, to a contractor's specifications is a *subcontractor*, not a *materialman*, even where the specially made materials are not delivered to or installed at the job site by their maker.[199] Thus, one who supplies such a subcon-

---

[191] United States Fidelity & Guar Co v American State Bank, 372 F2d 449 (10th Cir 1967).

[192] United States Fidelity & Guar Co v A&A Mach Shop, Inc, 330 F Supp 1403 (SD Tex 1971); Sun Ins Co v Diversified Engrs, Inc, 240 F Supp 606 (D Mont 1965); *but see* Houston Fire & Cas Ins Co v EE Cloer Gen Contractor, Inc, 217 F2d 906 (5th Cir 1954) (court held that Miller Act performance bond required surety to stand responsible for payment of materials; there was no payment bond).

[193] In New York, all public improvements undertaken by the state, municipal corporations, public benefit corporations, and commissions appointed by law require payment bonds that secure payment to all persons who furnish labor or materials to the contractor or its subcontractor. NY State Fin Law §137 (McKinney 1989 & Supp 1992).

[194] JW Bateson Co v United States *ex rel* Board of Trustees, 434 US 586, 98 S Ct 873, 55 L Ed 2d 50 (1978); Clifford F. MacEvoy Co v United States *ex rel* Calvin Tomkins Co. 322 US 102, 64 S Ct 890, 88 L Ed 1163 (1944); United States *ex rel* Wellman Engg Co v MSI Corp, 350 F2d 285 (2d Cir 1965).

[195] United States *ex rel* Powers Regulator Co v Hartford Accident & Indem Co, 376 F2d 811 (1st Cir 1967).

[196] Clifford F. MacEvoy Co v United States *ex rel* Calvin Tomkins Co, 322 US 102, 64 S Ct 890, 88 L Ed 1163 (1944).

[197] JW Bateson Co V United States *ex rel* Board of Trustees, 434 US 586, 98 S Ct 873, 55 L Ed 2d 50 (1978).

[198] Clifford F. MacEvoy Co v United States *ex rel* Calvin Tomkins Co, 322 US 102, 109, 64 S Ct 890, 894, 88 L Ed 1163 (1944); United States *ex rel* Hasco Elec Corp v Reliance Ins Co, 390 F Supp 158 (EDNY 1975).

[199] United States *ex rel* Wellman Engg Co v MSI Corp, 350 F2d 285 (2d Cir 1965) (designer and manufacturer of hydraulic system for opening and closing missile launcher roofs was a subcontractor); United States *ex rel* Consol Pipe & Supply Co v Morrison-Knudsen Co, 687 F2d 129 (6th Cir 1982) (manufacturer and supplier of pipe custom-made to prime contract specification was a subcontractor).

§8.45 NOTICE OF CLAIM/LIMITATION OF ACTION 285

tractor/materialman is entitled to recover under a Miller Act payment bond as a materialman to a subcontractor; such a supplier's claim would not be barred as one of a materialman to a materialman.

§8.45 —Notice of Claim and Limitation of Action

A party with a direct contractual relationship with the prime contractor need not give notice of its claim prior to bringing suit against a Miller Act *payment* bond. The claim is ripe when 90 days have passed from the last day the claimant performed the labor or furnished the materials upon which the claim is based.[200]

Those parties that lack an express or implied contractual relationship with the prime contractor, but that have a direct contractual relationship with a subcontractor, must give notice to the contractor of their claim for payment within 90 days from the date they last performed the labor or supplied the materials upon which their claim is based.[201] If a gap of more than 90 days exists between deliveries of materials under a series of purchase orders, a separate notice must be served for each series within 90 days of the day of last delivery of each series. Thus, in a case where one series of deliveries ended in December and the next series did not begin until April, separate notices should have been served for the December and April series, with each notice served within 90 days of the last delivery of the series.[202]

The notice of claim must state with "substantial accuracy" the amount claimed and for whom the labor was performed or materials supplied.[203] The notice must show that it is intended to be a presentation of a claim against the contractor and the surety.[204] It must be served upon the prime contractor by registered mail or personal service.[205] The requirement of service by registered mail or personal service is not strictly enforced, however; if receipt of the notice is admitted by the contractor or can be otherwise shown, the manner of service is irrelevant.[206]

An action to compel payment from the surety must be brought within one

---

[200] 40 USC §270b(a).

[201] *Id;* United States *ex rel* Harris Paint Co v Seaboard Sur Co, 437 F2d 37 (5th Cir 1971).

[202] United States *ex rel* JA Edward & Co v Peter Reiss Constr Co, 273 F2d 880 (2d Cir 1959), *cert denied,* 362 US 951, 80 S Ct 864, 4 L Ed 2d 869 (1960); United States *ex rel* I. Burack, Inc v Sovereign Constr Co, 338 F Supp 657 (SDNY 1972).

[203] 40 USC §270b(a).

[204] United States *ex rel* Edwards v Thompson Constr Corp, 273 F2d 873 (2d Cir 1959), *cert denied,* 362 US 951, 80 S Ct 864, 4 L Ed 2d 869 (1960). *See* 78 ALR2d 421.

[205] 40 USC §270b(a). Specifically, the statute provides that service may be had by registered mail or in a manner in which a United States Marshal of the district may serve a summons.

[206] Fleisher Engg & Constr Co v United States *ex rel* Hallenbeck, 311 US 15, 61 S Ct 81, 85 L Ed 12 (1940).

year of the day on which the claimant completed its primary work on the project,[207] not the repairs of its work following inspection.[208]

§8.46 —Claimable Items

Labor and Materials

Generally, if a claim for materials would be allowed under a §137 bond,[209] it will be allowed under a Miller Act bond, including leased equipment.[210] The Miller Act provides that labor and materials that are "furnished in the prosecution of the work" are claimable. There is no all-inclusive definition that determines whether a particular material falls within this category. The facts and circumstances of each case require individual consideration and determination.[211] One factor to consider is whether the parties *expected* the materials to be substantially consumed on the job; *actual* consumption or use is not necessary.[212] Thus, a claim for tires used on heavy earth movers and replaced constantly throughout a job is proper, while a claim for highway truck tires is not.[213]

Delay Damages

A Miller Act surety is liable for actual increased costs due to delay not caused by the claimant. Proper elements of those increased costs, if provable, include: increased labor costs due to an increase in wages during delay; increased materials cost; increased labor costs due to inefficient use of labor caused by the piecemeal, disjointed method of work necessitated by the delay; increased field operations cost; and increased overhead.[214] Lost profits due to delay are *not* recoverable.[215] The criterion for determining whether the delay costs are recoverable is whether the labor and materials were actually used in performance of the contract work.[216]

---

[207] 40 USC §270b(b).

[208] United States *ex rel* Magna Masonry, Inc v RT Woodfield, Inc, 709 F2d 249 (4th Cir 1983).

[209] In New York, all public improvements undertaken by the state, municipal corporations, public benefit corporations, and commissions appointed by law require payment bonds which secure payment to all persons who furnish labor or materials to the contractor or its subcontractor. NY State Fin Law §137 (McKinney 1989 & Supp 1992).

[210] Illinois Sur Co v John David Co, 244 US 376, 37 S Ct 614, 61 L Ed 1206 (1917).

[211] United States *ex rel* JP Byrne & Co v Fire Assoc, 260 F2d 541 (2d Cir 1958).

[212] *Id;* United States *ex rel* I. Burack, Inc v Sovereign Constr Co, 338 F Supp 657 (SDNY 1972).

[213] United States *ex rel* JP Byrne & Co v Fire Assoc, 260 F2d 541 (2d Cir 1958); United States *ex rel* I. Burack, Inc v Sovereign Constr Co, 338 F Supp 657 (SDNY 1972).

[214] United States *ex rel* Mariana v Piracci Constr Co, 405 F Supp 904 (DDC 1975).

[215] United States *ex rel* Otis Elevator Co v Piracci Constr Co, 405 F Supp 908 (DDC 1975) (a companion case to *Mariana* cited in footnote 214 above).

[216] United States *ex rel* Mariana v Piracci Constr Co, 405 F Supp 904 (DDC 1975).

If the underlying contract states that delay damages are not available, increased costs due to delay are not recoverable under the bond.[217]

Taxes

The Miller Act specifically provides that the performance bond includes the prime contractor's payment of federal employment taxes.[218] The act provides specific provisions the United States must follow in making a claim for wage taxes due.

Attorneys' Fees

Attorneys' fees are not recoverable under a Miller Act bond, regardless of state law.[219]

Interest

Interest from the time of the surety's default forward is recoverable against a Miller Act surety, if provided for in state law.[220]

§8.47 Defenses Available to Surety

A surety to a *payment* bond has many of the same defenses to payment of a claim as does a *performance* bond surety. These defenses are: that the party is not protected by the bond and is not a proper claimant;[221] that the claimant did not give proper or timely notice of its claim;[222] that suit on the claim was not brought in a timely manner;[223] that the surety was discharged by a breach or modification of the underlying contract;[224] that the surety has or will suffer liability in excess of the penal sum of the bond;[225] that the surety

---

[217] United States v Rice, 317 US 61, 63 S Ct 120, 87 L Ed 53 (1942).

[218] 40 USC §270a(d); United States v Fidelity & Deposit, 690 F Supp 905 (D Haw 1988).

[219] FD Rich Co v United States ex rel Indus Lumber Co, 417 US 116, 94 S Ct 2157, 40 L Ed 2d 703 (1974); *cf* United States ex rel Sherman v Carter, 353 US 210, 77 S Ct 793, 1 L Ed 2d 776 (1957) (Miller Act surety liable for attorneys' fees where provided for in collective bargaining agreement).

[220] Aetna Cas & Sur Co v BBB Constr Corp, 173 F2d 307 (2d Cir), *cert denied*, 337 US 917, 69 S Ct 1158, 93 L Ed 1726 (1949) (applying New York law).

[221] *See* §§8.10, 8.31, 8.33-8.36, and 8.44.

[222] *See* §8.25; Coleman Capital Corp v Travelers Indem Co, 443 F2d 47 (2d Cir 1971).

[223] *See* §8.28; John Johnston Concrete Gutter Co v American Empire Ins Co, 81 AD2d 1004, 440 NYS2d 107 (1981); Gerosa Crane Serv v International Prods, 70 Misc 2d 176, 332 NYS2d 536 (Civ Ct NY 1972).

[224] *See* §8.26; Hall & Co v Continental Cas Co, 34 AD2d 1028, 310 NYS2d 950 (1970), *aff'd*, 30 NY2d 517, 280 NE2d 890, 330 NYS2d 64 (1972) (surety discharged by alteration of contract that extended principal's time of performance); Schooley Enters v Paso Contracting Corp, 33 AD2d 981, 307 NYS2d 388 (1970) (surety discharged when retainage reduced without its consent).

[225] *See* §8.29.

was discharged by fraud;[226] and some of its principal's defenses.[227]

§8.48 Claims by the Surety

Once a surety has honored or defended against a claim on its bond, it seeks to recover its losses. A surety is entitled to full indemnity against the consequences of its principal's default.[228] Thus, a surety is entitled to reimbursement not only for what it cost to discharge the principal's obligation, but also for all related and reasonable expenses.[229] This reimbursement includes the costs and attorneys' fees that a surety incurs in defending an obligee's action on a bond,[230] including a surety's defense of its principal in a groundless action brought by an obligee.[231] However, a surety is not entitled to recover from the principal or the indemnitors its attorneys' fees incurred in pursuing reimbursement, unless the indemnity agreement specifically provides for such recovery.[232]

When seeking reimbursement, a surety primarily looks to its principal and indemnitors. For a party to be liable as an indemnitor, it must have agreed specifically to indemnify the surety against losses incurred by the surety due to the principal. For a principal to be liable to a surety, however, it need not have agreed or consented, either expressly or impliedly. Where a party becomes a surety at the request of the obligee, it is subrogated to the obligee's rights against the principal, regardless of the principal's consent.[233]

Generally, a surety must suffer an actual loss to be entitled to indemnification. Often a surety that is sued on its bond will crossclaim against its principal for indemnification. When judgment is entered against the surety, it is entitled to judgment in an equal amount against its principal or indemnitors. Such judgments are conditioned upon the surety's first satisfying the judgment against it.[234]

Some indemnity agreements, however, allow the surety to recover if it is actually *liable;* the surety need suffer no actual loss to recover under such bonds. To recover in such cases, the surety must show its liability through proof of

---

[226] See §8.27.

[227] See §8.30.

[228] Leghorn v Ross, 53 AD2d 560, 384 NYS2d 830 (1976), affd, 42 NY2d 1043, 369 NE2d 763, 399 NYS2d 206 (1977).

[229] Thompson v Taylor, 72 NY 32 (1878).

[230] Bank of NY, Albany v Hirschfeld, 59 AD2d 976, 399 NYS2d 329 (1977); Continental Cas Co v Chrysler Constr Co, 80 Misc 2d 552, 363 NYS2d 258 (Orange 1975).

[231] Lori-Kay, Inc v Lassner, 61 NY2d 722, 460 NE2d 1097, 472 NYS2d 612 (1984).

[232] Bank of NY, Albany v Hirschfeld, 59 AD2d 976, 399 NYS2d 329 (1977); Carrols Equities Corp v Villnave, 57 AD2d 1044, 395 NYS2d 800 (1977).

[233] Carrols Equities Corp v Villnave, 57 AD2d 1044, 395 NYS2d 800 (1977).

[234] Town of Wappinger v Republic Ins Co, 89 AD2d 621, 452 NYS2d 674 (1982).

judgment or an admission of liability by the surety in favor of the obligee.[235] Where there is not a judgment against the surety, the surety must show that its admitted liability is reasonable and that it had no defense against the obligee's valid claims.[236] If the surety is free to contest any claims against it, it is not yet entitled to indemnification.

An indemnitor or principal is bound by the surety's defense of claims against the bond—including its decision to settle a claim, so long as the settlement was prudent and made in good faith, and there were no valid defenses against the claim.[237]

In addition to seeking recovery from its principal and indemnitors, a surety may look for recovery of some or all of its damages from the obligee, the project architect or engineer, lending institutions, a lien discharge bond, or subcontractors. These categories are not intended to be exclusive. The underlying principle is that if a surety is injured by a third party's wrongful or fraudulent actions, the surety may have a claim against that party sounding either in contract, as a third-party beneficiary, or in negligence.[238]

§8.49 —Claims Against Obligee

A surety may assert its principal's claims against the obligee in certain instances—for example, by subrogation or assignment. Where an obligee's actions cause the surety damage but are not sufficient to discharge the surety, the surety may be entitled to some recovery—for example, where retainage is paid before due, the surety may be entitled to recover from the obligee the amount of retainage wrongfully paid.[239]

If an obligee refuses to pay the surety all retainage held and funds due under the contract, the surety may sue the obligee for those funds. A *performance* bond surety's right to funds due under its principal's contract upon completion of the contract is absolute;[240] a *payment* bond surety's right to funds due its principal arises upon the surety's payment of the claims of subcontractors, laborers, and materialmen,[241] and is subject to the obligee's possible right of set-off.[242]

Other potential areas of obligee liability to a surety include liability due to

---

[235] Maryland Cas Co v Straubinger, 19 AD2d 26, 240 NYS2d 228 (1963).
[236] *Id.*
[237] Home Indem Co v Wachter, 115 AD2d 590, 496 NYS2d 252 (1985).
[238] 72 CJS *Principal & Surety* §257 (1987).
[239] *See* Village of Canton v Globe Indem Co, 201 AD 820, 195 NYS 445 (1922) (in which court refused to discharge surety despite excessive advance of retainage by obligee to principal) *and* State *ex rel* National Sur Corp v Malvaney, 221 Miss 190, 72 So 2d 424 (1954) (architect held liable to surety when it prematurely released retainage).
[240] Security Ins Co v United States, 428 F2d 838 (Ct Cl 1970); Trinity Universal Ins Co v United States, 382 F2d 317 (5th Cir 1967), *cert denied*, 390 US 906 (1968).
[241] Prairie State Bank v United States, 164 US 227, 17 S Ct 142, 41 L Ed 412 (1896).
[242] United States v Munsey Trust Co, 332 US 234, 67 S Ct 1599, 91 L Ed 2022 (1947).

subrogation for breach of the contract by the obligee, design defects, increased costs due to delay caused by the obligee, and claims for extra work required by the obligee that were outside the scope of the contract.[243]

§8.50 —Claims Against Architect/Engineer

A complete discussion of when and under what theories a design professional may be held liable to a surety is beyond the scope of this chapter. An excellent discussion of the theories and case law in this area is found in the article *The Liability of Design Professionals to the Surety*.[244] This section briefly discusses the basic theories under which sureties have been successful.

There are several theories upon which a surety may recover damages from an architect, an engineer, a construction manager, or some other design or supervisory professional (hereinafter *architect*). While no New York cases have been found that recognize or discuss the liability of an architect to a surety, the principle that an architect owes a duty to a contractor's surety in certain instances is well established in most jurisdictions. The principle is based upon the belief that the architect-surety relationship is one which approaches privity. The authors believe that the principle is one which eventually will be adopted in New York.[245]

Indeed, the Court of Appeals has taken the necessary steps in two cases. In the case of *Credit Alliance Corp v Anderson & Co*,[246] the Court of Appeals held that accountants could be liable to noncontractual parties if the relationship of the parties approached that of privity. *Credit Alliance* was expanded in the case of *Ossining Union Free School District v Anderson LaRocca Anderson*.[247] In that case, the Court of Appeals held that a school district, which contracted with an architect, could sue engineers hired by the architect for damages suffered as a result of the engineers' negligence and malpractice. The issue addressed by the court was whether privity of contract is required in a negligent misrepresentation case that produces only economic injury. The court held that what is required is not actual privity of contract but a relationship so close as to be

---

[243] R. Cushman & C. Meeker, Construction Defaults: Rights, Duties, and Liabilities §§1.11, 6.8 (1984).

[244] Michael Chapman, *The Liability of Design Professionals to the Surety*, 20 Forum 591 (1984-85).

[245] The groundwork for recognizing this liability was laid in Glanzer v Shepard, 233 NY 236, 135 NE 275 (1922), in which Justice Cardozo discussed privity of contract and recognized a party's right of action based on a contract to which the party was not in privity where the party's relationship with the contracting parties was so close as to approach that of privity. Many of the cases that recognize an architect's liability to a surety cite the *Glanzer* case. *See* State ex rel National Sur Co v Malvaney, 221 Miss 190, 72 So 2d 424 (1954); Westerhold v Carroll, 199 F Supp 951 (D Minn 1961).

[246] 65 NY2d 536, 483 NE2d 110, 493 NYS2d 435 (1985).

[247] 73 NY2d 417, 539 NE2d 91, 541 NYS2d 335 (1989).

the "functional equivalent of contractual privity."[248] The court laid out a three-prong test which requires: (1) that the design professional be aware that its reports are to be used for a *particular purpose;* (2) that a *known person* rely on the reports in furtherance of that purpose; and (3) that there be some *conduct* by the design professional *linking* it to the reliant person and evidencing its understanding of the reliance.

Although the New York Court of Appeals construed the close-to-privity relationship more narrowly than other jurisdictions—for instance, the injured, reliant party must be more than merely foreseeable—it has taken the necessary first steps toward recognizing a surety as one that would meet the three-prong test. Of course, the burden would be upon the surety to allege in its complaint and prove at trial the three necessary facts.[249]

In other jurisdictions, architects are most frequently held liable to a surety when they improperly certify progress payments[250] or prematurely release retainage.[251] Courts have recognized that a surety relies upon the professional competence and unbiased position of a project architect in managing the project's construction. When an architect certifies progress payments and allows payment before due or prematurely releases retainage, the surety is damaged as its principal's incentive to complete the project is lessened or removed.

The surety's measure of damages is, in the case of a *performance* bond, the amount necessary to complete the project, or, in the case of a *payment* bond, the amount for which the surety is liable to the obligee or bond beneficiaries. Another measure of damages that has been used is the amount of retainage wrongfully released less the funds still retained.[252] This last measure of damage seems to give the architect a windfall while artificially limiting the surety's recovery—but for the architect's premature release of retainage or negligent certification of payment, the principal would have completed the project. The surety's damages easily can exceed the retainage, especially where the surety must complete the project. The better measure of damages is the surety's actual loss; i.e., the amount necessary to complete the project or the amount of the surety's liability to the obligee and unpaid beneficiaries.

Other potential grounds for architect liability to the surety are negligent supervision and inspection of the contractor's work,[253] negligent interpretation

---

[248] *Id* at 419, 539 NE2d at 91, 541 NYS2d at 335.

[249] *See* William Iselin & Co v Landau, 71 NY2d 420, 522 NE2d 21, 527 NYS2d 176 (1988); Westpac Banking Corp v Deschamps, 66 NY2d 16, 484 NE2d 1351, 494 NYS2d 848 (1985).

[250] Hall v Union Indem Co, 61 F2d 85 (8th Cir), *cert denied,* 287 US 663, 53 S Ct 222, 77 L Ed 572 (1932).

[251] State *ex rel* National Sur Corp v Malvaney, 221 Miss 1900, 72 So 2d 424 (1954).

[252] American Fidelity Fire Ins Co v Pavia-Byrne Engg Corp, 393 So 2d 830 (La Ct App 1981); R. Cushman & T. Bottum, Architect and Engineer Liability: Claims Against Design Professionals §11.6 (1987).

[253] Aetna Ins Co v Hellmuth, Obata & Kassabaum, Inc, 392 F2d 472 (8th Cir 1968) (architect held liable to surety for failing to inspect and ensure correction of surety's

of plans and specifications,[254] and undercertification of payments due.[255]

§8.51 —Claims Against Lending Institutions

A surety that has performed its obligations under the bond has priority to receive contract funds over a bank holding an assignment from the principal[256] or that has an Article 9, Uniform Commercial Code, security interest in the contract funds.[257] If a bank seizes contract funds that should have been paid to the surety, the surety may bring suit against it for return of the funds.

§8.52 —Claims Against Subcontractors, Their Sureties, and Their Insurers

When extra work is required because of a subcontractor's actions, the surety responsible for payment or performance of that extra work may have a cause of action against the subcontractor, its performance bond surety, or, if the extra work is required because of the subcontractor's damage to another party's work, its liability insurer.[258]

Further, where a contractor's default is caused by a subcontractor's breach, the contractor's performance bond surety may be allowed to seek recovery against the subcontractor and its performance bond surety on a cause of action sounding in contract.[259] In addition to stating a contract claim, the surety's complaint should include a common law indemnification claim against the subcontractor and its surety, although the indemnification claim may be denied. There is some question regarding the extent to which New York courts will allow a party that actively participated in the construction to seek common law indem-

---

principal's work; this decision, in effect, allowed the surety to recover for its principal's breach, the very damage from which the surety was supposed to protect the obligee); Navajo Circle, Inc v Development Concepts, 373 So 2d 689 (Fla Dist Ct App 1979) (condominium association suit against architect based on alleged third-party beneficiary status); cf Durham v Reidsville Engg Co, 255 NC 98, 120 SE2d 564 (1961).

[254] Fett Roofing & Sheet Metal Co v Seaboard Sur Co, 294 F Supp 112 (ED Va 1968).

[255] James Acret, Architects & Engineers 375-77 (Shepard's/McGraw-Hill 2d ed 1984). Mr. Acret remarks that, from the surety's point of view, the architect's certification of the amount due "should be exactly right."

[256] Henningsen v United States Fidelity & Guar, 208 US 404, 28 S Ct 389, 52 L Ed 547 (1908); Prairie State Bank v United States, 164 US 227, 17 S Ct 142, 41 L Ed 412 (1896).

[257] National Shawmut Bank v New Amsterdam Cas Co, 411 F2d 843 (1st Cir 1969).

[258] See R. Cushman & C. Meeker, Construction Defaults: Rights, Duties, and Liabilities §6.8 (1984).

[259] Menorah Nursing Home, Inc v Zukov, 153 AD2d 13, 548 NYS2d 702 (2d Dept 1989).

nification against other parties actively engaged in the construction.[260] By seeking relief under both contract and indemnification theories, the surety's complaint should withstand a motion to dismiss on standing grounds.

---

[260] *See* SSDW Co v Feldman-Mistopoulos Assocs, 151 AD2d 293, 542 NYS2d 565 (1989) (architect denied common law indemnification from contractor and window supplier because architect, as designer of windows, actively participated in the construction process).

Appendix 8-1

Payment Bond Notice Provisions

Claimant	§137 Bond	Miller Act Bond
Bond		
First tier	none; right to bring suit after 90 days following last work claimed	same
Second tier	within 120 days of last work claimed	within 90 days of last work claimed
Service of Notice		
On whom	prime contractor	same
Method	personally or by registered mail, but method irrelevant if notice actually received	same
Limitations Period	one year from date final payment becomes due under claimant's subcontract	one year from date of last work claimed

Mechanics' Liens

9

§9.01 General Principles
§9.02 Liens in the Private Sector
§9.03 —Who May File
§9.04 —Improvement as a Requirement
§9.05 —Owner's Consent
§9.06 —Lien Attaches to Real Property
§9.07 Liens in the Public Sector
§9.08 —Who May File
§9.09 —Improvement as a Requirement
§9.10 —Securing an Interest in Funds
§9.11 What Property is Lienable: Private Property
§9.12 —Condominiums and Cooperatives
§9.13 —Leasehold Interests
§9.14 —Oil and Gas
§9.15 Public Property
§9.16 What Items are Covered by the Lien
§9.17 —Labor
§9.18 —Materials
§9.19 —Rental Equipment
§9.20 —Temporary Works
§9.21 —Overhead and Employee Benefits
§9.22 —Lost Profits and Contract Damages
§9.23 —Extras
§9.24 Lien Waivers
§9.25 Should You File a Notice of Lien?
§9.26 Elements of a Proper Lien Notice for Private Improvements
§9.27 Elements of a Proper Lien Notice for Public Improvements
§9.28 Filing the Notice of Lien—Time and Place

§9.29 —Private Improvement Liens
§9.30 —Public Improvement Liens
§9.31 Service of Notice of Lien
§9.32 Duration and Extension of Lien
§9.33 Amendment of Lien
§9.34 Owner's Response to Notice of Lien
§9.35 —Demand for Statement
§9.36 —Discharge the Lien
§9.37 —Demand to Foreclose
§9.38 Enforcing the Mechanic's Lien
§9.39 —Deadline to Commence Action
§9.40 —Filing of Notice of Pendency
§9.41 —Lien Foreclosure and Arbitration
§9.42 —Venue and Jurisdiction of Action
§9.43 —Courts of Record and Courts Not of Record
§9.44 —Necessary Parties
§9.45 —Form of Complaint
§9.46 Answers of Defendant Lienors
§9.47 Defenses to the Foreclosure Action
§9.48 —Defective and Expired Liens
§9.49 —Willful Exaggeration
§9.50 —No Fund to Which Lien Can Attach
§9.51 The Lien Foreclosure Trial
§9.52 Priority of Private Improvement Liens
§9.53 —Building Loan Contracts and Mortgages
§9.54 —Mortgages
§9.55 —Assignment of Moneys Due under Contract for Improvement of Real Property
§9.56 —Miscellaneous Liens
§9.57 —Subsequent Purchasers
§9.58 —Agreements to Subordinate
§9.59 Priority of Public Improvement Liens
§9.60 Parity and Preference among Mechanics' Lienors
§9.61 Obtaining a Judgment
§9.62 —Amount of Judgment
§9.63 Obtaining an Execution
§9.64 Sale upon Execution
§9.65 —Distribution of Proceeds
§9.66 —Deficiency Judgments
§9.67 —Setting Aside a Sale
§9.68 The Trust Fund
§9.69 —Duration of a Trust
§9.70 —Trust Assets

§9.71 —Parties Involved
§9.72 —The Fiduciary Relationship
§9.73 —Record-Keeping Requirements
§9.74 —Availability of Records to Claimants
§9.75 —Proper Application of Trust Funds
§9.76 —Notice of Lending
§9.77 —Notice of Assignment
§9.78 —Diversion of Trust Funds
§9.79 —Liability for Diversion
§9.80 —Restoration of the Trust after Diversion
§9.81 Enforcing the Trust Fund
§9.82 —Claims for Relief
§9.83 —Priority and Preference
§9.84 —Judgment
Form 9-1 Notice of Lien
Appendix 9-1 Private v Public Works Liens
Appendix 9-2 Lienable Items

§9.01 General Principles

Many attorneys shudder or yawn when they think of mechanics' liens. They imagine complicated schemes and nit-picking requirements that serve only to frustrate clients, whether a client is an owner, a builder, a contractor, a lender, or any other of a number of potential parties. In fact, the mechanic's lien law in New York is understandable, although it is very detailed and provides limited actual protection to those whom it is supposed to protect.[1]

It must first be remembered that mechanics' liens ostensibly were created to protect those who improve real property. Sufficient protection was not afforded the contractor or laborer by common law or equity. Mechanics' liens are premised upon the theory that the lienor, by labor or materials, has added value to the real property of another.[2] Mechanics' liens provide a remedy whereby the lienor may be able to recover the value added to the real property, now unrecoverable due to physical or practical considerations.[3] A simple example is when someone asks an architect to design a home for him or her and then fails to pay the architect after the house is built. The architect cannot recover the plans—they have been used. By filing a mechanic's lien, however, the architect's interest in the property can be protected.

Unfortunately, due to the priorities afforded most lenders over mechanics' lienors, the protections provided by the Lien Law are not as great as they seem.

---

[1] This chapter discusses all of arts 1, 2, 3, and 3A of the NY Lien Law (§§1 through 79-a), except §6 which relates to railroad construction labor. This chapter does not discuss any matters covered in arts 4 through 10B of the NY Lien Law.

[2] JC Whritenour Co v Colonial Homes Co, 209 AD 676, 205 NYS 299 (1924).

[3] PT&L Constr Co v Winnick, 59 AD2d 368, 399 NYS2d 712, 713 (1977).

In fact, most of the benefits are illusory. This is not to say that it is useless to file a mechanic's lien; mechanics' liens do encourage owners and contractors to pay their debts, whether because they act as a notice to lenders, sureties, and other subcontractors that the project is not meeting its obligations in a timely manner, because they notify an owner that its contractor may be experiencing cash flow difficulties, or because they interfere with sale of the property.

As creatures of statute,[4] mechanics' liens must strictly comply with the statute to be valid,[5] although the statute is construed liberally.[6] This chapter provides an overview of the New York Mechanics' Liens Law and its application to real property located in New York. The Lien Law does not apply to property located in New York but owned by the United States or any agency thereof.[7]

There are three primary areas that must be discussed in any consideration of New York mechanics' liens—private improvements, public improvements, and trust funds. The law provides different remedies, rights, and obligations depending on whether one is a lienor of private or of public improvements. The discussion here will focus first on basic private improvement issues, next on basic public improvement issues, then on principles applicable to both (scope of permissible claims, filing and notice requirements, etc.), on foreclosure and enforcement of the lien, and, finally, on the trust fund.

§9.02 Liens in the Private Sector

Section 3 of the NY Lien Law permits members of a defined class who have worked or provided materials for the *improvement of real property* to file liens upon that real property. *Improvement of real property* is defined as "any improvement of real property not belonging to the state or a public corporation."[8] Liens for improvements of real property belonging to the state or a public corporation are treated differently and are discussed generally in §§9.07-9.10 of this chapter.

Through a private improvement lien, certain parties may enforce their rights and recover against an owner of improved property, regardless of privity of contract. To avail oneself of the protections of a private improvement lien, a lienor must fall within a defined list of claimants and *improve* real property with the *owner's consent.* Who these potential claimants are and what they must do to file their liens are issues that are not always as clear as they first may appear.

---

[4] Umbaugh Builders, Inc v Parr Co, 86 Misc 2d 1036, 385 NYS2d 698 (Suffolk 1976).

[5] Ausable Chasm Co v Hotel Ausable Chasm & Country Club, 263 AD 486, 33 NYS2d 427 (1942); Mineola Road Oil Corp v Walsh, 137 NYS2d 342 (Suffolk 1954).

[6] NY Lien Law §23 (McKinney 1966 & Supp 1992).

[7] I. Burack, Inc v Simpson Factors Corp, 21 AD2d 481, 250 NYS2d 989 (1964), *affd,* 16 NY2d 604, 261 NYS2d 58 (1965). Claimants on federal government contracts are protected by the Miller Act, 40 USC §§270a, 270b. This case is no longer applicable to the United States Postal Service which has the power "to sue and be sued" by the provisions of the 1970 Postal Reorganization Act. 30 USC §401(1).

[8] NY Lien Law §2(8) (McKinney 1966).

§9.03 —Who May File

Section 3 of the NY Lien Law lists those parties that may file mechanics' liens on privately owned real property: "[a] contractor, subcontractor, laborer, materialman, landscape gardener, nurseryman or person or corporation selling fruit or ornamental trees, . . . who performs labor or furnishes materials for the improvement of real property. . . ." More important than what a potential lienor is called is whether the lienor has improved another's property. "What parties call themselves and each other is not controlling, the facts constituting the relationship are determinative."[9] Generally, the party must be licensed to do the required work[10] and authorized to do business in the state of New York in order to be able to foreclose a mechanic's lien.[11]

Contractor

A *contractor* is anyone who directly contracts with an owner of real property for its improvement.[12] A written contract is not necessary for a party to be a contractor.

Subcontractor

A *subcontractor* is anyone who contracts with a contractor or a subcontractor for the improvement of the real property and who performs some part of the contractor's contract with the owner (hereinafter, the *general contract*).[13] There does not appear to be a limit to the number of tiers of subcontractors who can file liens against a private improvement.[14]

Laborer

A *laborer* is a natural person who performs labor or services upon the improvement.[15]

Materialman

A *materialman* is anyone who furnishes materials or provides machinery, tools, equipment, vehicles, and other supplies necessary for the improvement *to an*

---

[9] Carl A. Morse, Inc v Rentar Indus Dev Corp, 85 Misc 2d 304, 379 NYS2d 994, 999 (Queens 1976), *affd*, 56 AD2d 30, 391 NYS2d 425 (1977), *affd*, 43 NY2d 952, 375 NE2d 409 (1978).

[10] Mortise v 55 Liberty Owners Corp, 102 AD2d 719, 477 NYS2d 2, *affd*, 63 NY2d 743, 469 NE2d 529, 480 NYS2d 208 (1984); Millington v Rapoport, 98 AD2d 765, 469 NYS2d 787 (1983).

[11] Engineering Corp v Scott-Paine, 29 Misc 2d 508, 217 NYS2d 919 (Columbia 1961).

[12] NY Lien Law §2(9) (McKinney 1966).

[13] *Id* §2(10); Dorn v Arthur A. Johnson Corp, 16 AD2d 1009, 229 NYS2d 266 (1962).

[14] *Cf* Cameron Equip Corp v People, 31 AD2d 299, 297 NYS2d 326 (1969), *affd mem*, 27 NY2d 634, 261 NE2d 668, 313 NYS2d 763 (1970). (Public improvement liens are limited to sub-subcontractors.)

[15] NY Lien Law §2(11) (McKinney 1966).

owner, a contractor, or a subcontractor.[16] Not everyone who furnishes materials that are incorporated into an improvement are materialmen pursuant to this statute. If a gravel pit sells gravel to a trucker who delivers and dumps the gravel at the construction site, the gravel pit cannot file a lien since it did not supply the gravel to an owner, a contractor, or a subcontractor, but to a materialman; however, the trucker may file a lien as a materialman.[17] Similarly, if a lumberyard supplies a carpenter regularly, without regard to a specific project, the lumberyard is not a materialman and cannot lien the building into which its lumber was incorporated. To be entitled to file a lien, the lumberyard must supply the lumber for a specific project.[18]

Landscape Gardener, Nurseryman, Etc.

The Lien Law provides no definitions for this class of potential lienors as it is self-explanatory and includes "landscape gardener, nurseryman or person or corporation selling fruit or ornamental trees, roses, shrubbery, vines and small fruits."[19]

Successors in Interest

In addition to the above-defined lienors, those who succeed to a lienor's rights by assignment of a filed, valid notice of lien are *successors in interest* and are entitled to the same protections afforded the original lienor.[20] A pre-filing assignment of lien rights is ineffective. Section 14 of the Lien Law sets forth the requirements for a valid assignment of a lien.

Architects, Engineers, Surveyors, and Construction Managers

Although not specifically listed in NY Lien Law §3, architects,[21] engineers,[22] and surveyors[23] who prepare plans, specifications, or surveys for the improvement of a specific piece of real property are protected under the statute. Further, one who supervises the improvement of real property at the request of

---

[16] *Id* §2(12).

[17] Dorn v Arthur A. Johnson Corp, 16 AD2d 1009, 229 NYS2d 266 (1962).

[18] *See In re* Berlanti, 198 Misc 543, 103 NYS2d 418 (Westchester 1950). This is the only case the authors could find on this point. If the materialman can identify its goods in the improvement, the authors believe it should be entitled to file a lien.

[19] NY Lien Law §3 (McKinney 1966 & Supp 1992).

[20] Tisdale Lumber Co v Read Realty Co, 154 AD 270, 138 NYS 829 (1912).

[21] NY Lien Law §2(4) (McKinney 1966 & Supp 1992); Di-Com Corp v Active Fire Sprinkler Corp, 36 AD2d 20, 318 NYS2d 249 (1971).

[22] *See* NY Lien Law §2(4) (McKinney 1966 & Supp 1992), in which an engineer's drawings are considered improvements.

[23] *Id.*

the owner, such as a construction manager, performs work that may form the basis of a mechanic's lien.[24]

§9.04 —Improvement as a Requirement

To be eligible for a mechanic's lien, the party's labor or materials must have improved the real property.[25] In NY Lien Law §2(4), the term "improvement" is defined as "the demolition, erection, alteration or repair of any structure upon, connected with, or beneath the surface of, any real property and any work done upon such property or materials furnished for its permanent improvement. . . ." Section 2(4) details several items that are improvements for the purposes of the mechanic's lien law: lighting fixtures;[26] architect's, engineer's, and surveyor's plans and drawings, including preliminary plans;[27] the reasonable rental value of equipment actually used;[28] the value of compressed gasses used by welders; the value of fuel and oil used by machinery at the construction site or in transporting materials to or from the site; and the service of real estate brokers, pursuant to a written contract, in obtaining a nonresidential lessee for at least a three-year term to all or part of the real property. This list is not exhaustive and is expanded continually through case law.

Perhaps the primary criterion for judging whether the labor or material furnished is an improvement is whether it results in a permanent change in the property. For example, the planting of a tree is an improvement, but the trimming of trees, mowing of lawns, and spraying of insecticides is not.[29] *Permanent* does not indicate that the improvement will last for a span of years, but, rather, indicates that the improvement becomes a part of the realty.[30] Thus, decorating and repair work usually are improvements; the wallpaper is attached to the property as is the paint.[31]

Materials that were specifically manufactured for a property are *improvements,*

---

[24] Carl A. Morse, Inc v Rentar Indus Corp, 85 Misc 2d 304, 379 NYS2d 994 (Queens 1976), *affd,* 56 AD2d 30, 391 NYS2d 425 (1977), *affd,* 43 NY2d 952, 375 NE2d 409 (1978).

[25] NY Lien Law §3 (McKinney 1966 & Supp 1992).

[26] Light fixtures are improvements; light bulbs are not. Waring v Burke Steel Co, 69 NYS2d 399 (Monroe 1947).

[27] *In re* Bralus Corp, 282 AD 959, 125 NYS2d 786 (1953), *affd,* 307 NY 626, 120 NE2d 829 (1954).

[28] Mobile trailers (shanties) rented to a subcontractor and used for material storage and offices at a construction site are lienable items. PJ Carlin Constr Co v A to Z Equip Corp, 31 AD2d 546, 295 NYS2d 239 (1968).

[29] *In re* Magowan, 203 NYS2d 35 (Suffolk 1960).

[30] Sica & Sons v Ciccolo, 39 Misc 2d 698, 241 NYS2d 923 (Westchester 1963).

[31] *Id;* New York Artcrafts, Inc v Marvin, 29 Misc 2d 774, 215 NYS2d 788 (Nassau 1961) (repair and painting of ceiling is an improvement); Campagna Dev Corp v UCM Interior Designs, Inc, 75 Misc 2d 191, 347 NYS2d 253 (NY 1973) (carpeting placed over subflooring is an improvement, while carpeting placed over an existing floor is not).

whether or not delivered to or incorporated into the construction.[32] Thus, one who makes a custom cabinet for an office but is stopped from delivering it by a breach of contract can lien the real property for the contract price.

§9.05 —Owner's Consent

The final hurdle to being entitled to file a lien is whether the owner of the real property consented to the improvement. Section 3 of the NY Lien Law states that those who improve real property "with the consent or at the request of the owner thereof, or of his agent, contractor or subcontractor shall have a lien. . . ." If owner consent cannot be shown, no lien may be had.

An *owner* is defined in §2(3) of the NY Lien Law and includes the "owner in fee of real property, or of a less estate therein, a lessee for a term of years, a vendee in possession, and all persons having any right, title or interest in such real property. . . ." This definition is misleading, however, as each owner's consent affects its interest in the property only and, does not affect a co-owner's interest without consent of that co-owner. Thus, where a lessee has improvements made to a building without the owner of the building consenting to the improvements, the lienor cannot lien the real property and can only lien the lessee's estate, a term of years.[33]

An owner's consent may be actual or implied and may be given by one authorized by the owner, such as an agent, a contractor, a subcontractor, or a lessee. Consent is not freely implied; mere knowledge and acceptance of the improvements is not enough to imply consent.[34] Generally, the owner must have indicated, through some affirmative act, a willingness to have the improvement made. Lack of objection to an improvement does not mean that an owner has consented.[35] Thus, where an owner watched a contractor excavate his back yard for a pool, when both the owner and the contractor knew that the owner had not received the necessary financing, the owner was found not to have consented to the work and the contractor's lien was voided.[36]

The scope of an owner's consent cannot be expanded without additional consent. Thus, where an owner contracted for certain improvements at a stated price and the subcontractors' billings exceeded that price, the owner's liability was limited to the contract price.[37] If, before a lien is filed, the owner has paid

---

[32] NY Lien Law §§2(3), 3 (McKinney 1966 & Supp 1992).

[33] As regards a life tenant's right to consent to improvements that subject the whole to a mechanic's lien, see J.M.H., Annotation, *Right to Mechanics' lien against fee for work or material furnished under contract with, or consent of, life tenant,* 97 ALR 870 (1935).

[34] P. Delay & Co v Duvoli, 278 NY 328, 16 NE2d 354 (1938); Cowen v Paddock, 137 NY 188, 33 NE 154 (1893).

[35] P. Delay & Co v Duvoli, 278 NY 328, 16 NE2d 354 (1938).

[36] Seaboard Pools, Inc v Freeman, 46 Misc 2d 508, 259 NYS2d 999 (Nassau 1965).

[37] Tibbetts Contracting Corp v O&E Contracting Co, 15 NY2d 324, 258 NYS2d 400 (1965); Central Valley Concrete Corp v Montgomery Ward & Co, 34 AD2d 860, 310 NYS2d 925 (1970).

the contractor but the contractor has failed to pay the subcontractor, the subcontractor's remedy is to look to the contractor.[38]

Generally, "actual consent for the particular work done" is required to hold an owner responsible for another's consent; the exceptions are so numerous, however, that determining whether an owner has consented is best done on a case-by-case basis.[39] The following discussions are intended to serve as guides only; they are not an exhaustive listing of every fact that has been held to indicate owner consent.

Owner's Agent

The owner's agent may take any form; the important facts that must be determined are whether the agent has actual or implied authority and the scope of that authority. General agency, partnership, and corporate law principles apply in making these determinations. An individual who is also a member of a partnership does not necessarily have the authority to consent to improvements on behalf of the partnership.[40] For purposes of the mechanic's lien law, spouses are presumed to be each other's agents. Thus, the consent of one spouse to improvements on joint or separate property is deemed consent by the other spouse, unless within 10 days of learning of the contract, the other spouse gives the contractor written notice of refusal to consent.[41]

A receiver is not an owner or an owner's agent; improvements made at a receiver's request are not lienable items.[42]

Contractor or Subcontractor

The contractor's and subcontractor's authority to consent on behalf of an owner comes into play when dealing with sub- and sub-subcontractors. The scope of authority is limited by the terms of the original contract with the owner and any owner-authorized changes thereto.[43] Thus, where a subcontract is not within the purview of the general contract (the contractor's contract with the owner), the subcontractor does not have a lien for that portion of the subcon-

---

[38] Central Valley Concrete Corp v Montgomery Ward & Co, 34 AD2d 860, 310 NYS2d 925 (1970).

[39] Met Painting Co v Dana, 90 Misc 2d 289, 394 NYS2d 392, 393 n 1 (Civ Ct NY 1977).

[40] See Contelmo's Sand & Gravel v J&J Milano, Inc, 96 AD2d 1090, 467 NYS2d 55 (1983); Tech Heating & Mechanical, Inc v First Downstream Serv Corp, 126 Misc 2d 85, 481 NYS2d 201 (NY 1984). In a similar vein, see Mathies Wheel & Pump Co, v Plainview Jewish Center, 42 Misc 2d 569, 248 NYS2d 441 (Nassau 1964), where the center's consent was implied by its board of trustees' taking title to the improvements following a board member's contracting for the installation of an air conditioning system. The board member alone did not have authority to contract for the improvement.

[41] NY Lien Law §3 (McKinney 1966 & Supp 1992).

[42] Eno v Rapp, 169 Misc 473, 7 NYS2d 513 (NY 1938).

[43] Custer Builders, Inc v Quaker Heritage, Inc, 41 AD2d 448, 344 NYS2d 606 (1973).

tract that is outside the general contract.[44] For instance, if the subcontractor's lien includes extras that the general contractor asked the subcontractor to perform, but the owner did not consent or agree to the extras, the subcontractor would not have a valid lien against the owner for the extras.[45]

Lessee

The consent issue is most complicated and litigated when it involves lessees who improve the leased premises. Unless the lessee has the lessor/owner's express or implied consent to improve the property, a contractor's lien is available only on the lessee's leasehold interest and, like any creditor, his or her personal property. Consent by the owner can be found in the lease language or the owner's actions; as in other scenarios, however, some affirmative language or action on the part of the lessor is generally required. In the leading case of *Paerdegat Boat & Racquet Club, Inc v Zarrelli*,[46] it was held that under no circumstances, regardless of the facts, are there private mechanics' liens rights where a private lessee of a public property has improved the property.[47]

General lease language obligating a lessee to repair and maintain the property does not constitute owner consent;[48] something more is needed. Where a lease stated that the lessee could erect temporary or permanent structures as needed for its business and that any permanent structures became the lessor's property at the end of the lease term, owner consent was found.[49] The right to improve the property or erect structures does not necessarily mean that an owner has consented, however. For instance, where a lessee had the right, under a land lease, to improve the property but any improvement was required to be removed at the conclusion of the lease term, no owner consent was found.[50]

A lessor's granting a lessee of an apartment the right to decorate the apartment does not always indicate owner consent. But, in a case where the lessor gave the lessee a rent concession based on intended decorations, express consent was found.[51]

---

[44] *Id.* See also Annotation, 62 ALR3d 288 (1975).

[45] Forman v Pala Constr Co, 124 AD2d 453, 507 NYS2d 553 (1986).

[46] 83 AD2d 444, 449-52, 445 NYS2d 162, 166-68 (1981) (Hopkins, J. dissenting), revd, 57 NY2d 966, 443 NE2d 477, 457 NYS2d 229 (1982). The Court of Appeals, in reversing the Appellate Division's decision, adopted the reasons stated in Justice Hopkins's dissent.

[47] *See also* Albany County Indus Dev Agency v Gastinger Ries Walker Architects, Inc, 144 AD2d 891, 534 NYS2d 823 (1988); TNT Coatings, Inc v Nassau, 114 AD2d 1027, 495 NYS2d 466 (1985); Niagra Venture v Sicoli & Massaro, 77 NY2d 175, 565 NYS2d 449 (1990) (sale and leaseback arrangement).

[48] Eisenson Elec Serv Co v Wien, 30 Misc 2d 926, 219 NYS2d 736 (NY 1961).

[49] Osborne v McGowan, 1 AD2d 924, 149 NYS2d 781 (1956); Otis v Dodd, 90 NY 336 (1882).

[50] Backstatter v Berry Hill Bldg Corp, 56 Misc 2d 351, 288 NYS2d 850 (Nassau 1968).

[51] Met Painting Co v Dana, 90 Misc 2d 289, 394 NYS2d 392 (Civ Ct NY 1977).

Even where it is found that the owner consented to the improvements, it does not always follow that the consent was to the amount charged for the work. Where the owner does not consent to the contract price, the lien against the lessor's property is for the reasonable value of the labor and materials added to the property, not the contract price agreed to by the lessee.[52]

Vendee (Purchaser) in Possession

Many of the same considerations reviewed in the lessee discussion above apply in vendee improvement situations. Some affirmative act on the part of the vendor/owner is required to subject the vendor's interest to a mechanic's lien.[53] Thus, in a case where a purchaser living in the premises under an installment contract of sale had improvements made and was later evicted for nonpayment of an installment payment, there was no lien as the vendor did not consent to the work.[54]

§9.06 —Lien Attaches to Real Property

In private liens, the lien is filed against "the real property improved or to be improved and upon such improvement,"[55] and becomes attached to them. Herein lies the most pronounced distinction between private and public liens: with public liens, the lien attaches to the funds appropriated to the project. This distinction affects filing requirements and foreclosure and execution procedures.

§9.07 Liens in the Public Sector

Generally, §5 of the NY Lien Law permits those who have performed labor or furnished materials for the construction or demolition of a *public improvement* to file a lien upon the "moneys of the state or such public corporation applicable to the construction or demolition." A *public improvement* is defined as ". . . an improvement of any real property belonging to the state or a public corporation."[56]

Public policy considerations require that public property be immune from execution and seizure.[57] Instead of a lien on the real property improved, the statute has provided that a lien for public improvements attaches solely to the funds of the public entity that are due under the contract for the improve-

---

[52] Umbaugh Builders, Inc v Parr Co, 86 Misc 2d 1036, 385 NYS2d 698 (Suffolk 1976).

[53] P. Delay & Co v Duvoli, 278 NY 328, 16 NE2d 354 (1938).

[54] Utica Plumbing Supply Co v Home Owner's Loan Corp, 267 AD 779, 45 NYS2d 452 (1943).

[55] NY Lien Law §3 (McKinney 1966 & Supp 1992).

[56] NY Lien Law §2(7) (McKinney 1966).

[57] Leonard v Brooklyn, 71 NY 498 (1877).

ment.[58] This distinction is needed to ensure that public entities retain control over their property and that the properties are used for the good of the public. Imagine what would happen if an electrician could lien a police station, foreclose that lien, and move into the police station. The public's interest in police protection must outweigh the electrician's interest.[59]

Public improvements belong to the state or a public corporation. The *state* is the state of New York and any of its political subdivisions—cities, counties, towns, districts, and municipalities. A *public corporation* is defined as "a municipal corporation or a district corporation or a public benefit corporation as such corporations are defined in section three of the general corporation law."[60] This definition is strictly interpreted.[61]

Generally, a public corporation is an instrumentality of and is owned by a government entity.[62] Where it is unclear whether the improvements made are public or private, courts consider many factors, including legislative intent,[63] profit structure, capital gains benefits, lien law definitions, and general corporate law definitions.

Like private improvement liens, public liens have specific requirements as to who can file them, what must be done to be entitled to file them, and to what they attach.

§9.08 —Who May File

To file a lien for work done on a public improvement, one must be a "person performing labor or furnishing materials to a contractor, his subcontractor or legal representative, . . . pursuant to a contract by such contractor with the

---

[58] John Kennedy & Co v New York World's Fair 1939, Inc, 260 AD 386, 22 NYS2d 901 (1940), *affd*, 288 NY 494, 41 NE2d 789 (1942); Lincoln First Bank, NA v Spaulding Bakeries, Inc, 117 Misc 2d 892, 459 NYS2d 696 (Broome 1983).

[59] Hempstead Resources Recovery Corp v Peter Scalamandre & Sons, 104 Misc 2d 278, 428 NYS2d 146 (Nassau 1980).

[60] NY Lien Law §2(6).

[61] *In re* Edgerton Estates, 78 Misc 2d 961, 359 NYS2d 88 (Onondaga 1974). Edgerton Estates was a Limited Profit Housing Company that contracted with a public benefit corporation ("UDC") to build housing. UDC advanced 95% of the costs of the improvement, held the mortgage on the development, and was the pledgee and holder of all stock of Edgerton, although Edgerton retained the right to receive dividends, which were limited in amount and payment by state law. The court found that although Edgerton was a subsidiary of a public benefit corporation, it was not itself a public benefit corporation and thus was not immune to mechanics' liens filed against the real property. *See also* Milbank-Frawley Hous Dev Fund Co v Marshall Constr Co, 71 Misc 2d 42, 335 NYS2d 598 (NY 1972).

[62] *Id.*

[63] See the New York City Housing Development Corporation Act, NY Priv Hous Fin Law §650 (McKinney's 1991), in which the legislature specifically designated housing development companies organized pursuant to its articles as public benefit corporations.

state or a public benefit corporation. . . ."[64] Generally, the same parties that would be entitled to a private improvement lien would be entitled to a public improvement lien,[65] except that the general contractor cannot file a lien nor can subcontractors, materialmen, and laborers that are removed more than two times from the general contractor. See §9.03 for definitions of the parties.

Due to the statute's use of the phrase "his subcontractor" following "contractor" in §5, the courts have held that only those parties in privity with the contractor, his or her subcontractor, or legal representative are entitled to file a lien. Thus, a sub-subcontractor may file a public improvement lien, but a sub-sub-subcontractor may not.[66] Similarly, only those who are materialmen to first tier subcontractors or the general contractor may file public improvement liens.[67]

§9.09 —Improvement as a Requirement

The only distinction between what the lienor must have done to be entitled to a public lien as opposed to a private lien is that the labor performed or materials furnished must have been for the construction or demolition of a public improvement. The same definitions found in NY Lien Law §2(4) and standards apply. (See §9.04.)

§9.10 —Securing an Interest in Funds

Unlike a private lien, a public lien is not filed against the owner of the property; rather, it is filed against the funds due the contractor, subcontractor, or legal representative who entered into the public works contract with the state or public corporation.[68]

Public liens attach to the funds appropriated by the state or public corporation for the public improvement and due or to become due under the contract for the improvement.[69] Where the public owner has paid the general contractor in full, no lien attaches as there are no funds owed the general contractor.

The fact that the lien attaches to funds, rather than real property, affects filing requirements and foreclosure and enforcement procedures. These differ-

---

[64] NY Lien Law §5 (McKinney 1966 & Supp 1992).

[65] *See id* §§2(9), (10), (11) and (12).

[66] Cameron Equip Corp v People, 31 AD2d 299, 297 NYS2d 326 (1969), *affd mem*, 27 NY2d 634, 261 NE2d 668, 313 NYS2d 763 (1970).

[67] A&J Buyers, Inc v Johnson, Drake & Piper, Inc, 25 NY2d 265, 303 NYS2d 841 (1969); Gernatt Asphalt Prod v Bensal Constr, Inc, 90 AD2d 993, 456 NYS2d 590 (1982), *affd as modified*, 60 NY2d 871, 458 NE2d 821, 470 NYS2d 362 (1983); Dorn v Arthur A. Johnson, Inc, 16 AD2d 1009, 229 NYS2d 266 (1962).

[68] NY Lien Law §5 (McKinney 1989 & Supp 1991).

[69] John Kennedy & Co v New York World's Fair 1939, Inc, 260 AD 386, 22 NYS2d 901 (1940), *affd*, 288 NY 494, 41 NE2d 789 (1942); First Bank, NA v Spaulding Bakeries, Inc, 117 Misc 2d 892, 459 NYS2d 696 (Broome 1983).

ences are discussed in each relevant section following. The major differences can be seen in Appendix 9-1.

§9.11 What Property is Lienable: Private Property

Despite the statute's language that seems to indicate otherwise, not all real property or an owner's interest therein is lienable. The exceptions are few but noteworthy, and are discussed in the relevant sections following.

Generally, all private interests in real property are lienable, although it may be difficult to realize an interest in, or to foreclose effectively a lien against, such interests. Any ownership of real property is lienable so long as the ownership is "a right, title or interest in such real property, which may be sold under an execution."[70] Properties that require special attention are condominiums and cooperatives, leasehold interests, and oil and gas properties. These are discussed in the following three sections.

§9.12 —Condominiums and Cooperatives

Condominiums and cooperatives provide unique examples of real property that is not necessarily subject to mechanics' liens. The application of the Lien Law to condominiums is fairly clear. Unfortunately, the same cannot be said of cooperatives.

Condominiums

Under the Condominium Act,[71] once a required declaration of condominium status of a project is filed, no lien may be filed against the common elements of a condominium project without the unanimous consent of unit owners.[72] Thus, where a contractor improves common elements of a condominium by installing landscaping, no lien is available.[73] A contractor in this situation is not without a remedy, however, as all common charges collected by the condominium board of managers constitute trust funds for the purpose of paying for labor and materials supplied at the board's express consent.[74]

Any work done prior to the recording of a condominium declaration is not bound by this restriction and a lien may be filed as though the project were any other improvement. Thus, if a contractor were involved in the building of a new condominium project, a lien could be filed against the common ele-

---

[70] NY Lien Law §2(3). An interesting discussion of unusual interests that have been held subject to mechanics' liens may be found at §§38-49 of E. Marks, Jensen on the Mechanics' Lien Law (4th ed 1963, Supp 1983).

[71] NY Real Prop Law, art 9-B, §§339-d through 339-ii.

[72] Condominium Act §339-1; subsection 2 of §339-1 provides for trust fund provisions for any common charges moneys in the control of the condominium board of managers.

[73] Country Village Heights Condo v Mario Bonito, Inc, 79 Misc 2d 1088, 363 NYS2d 501 (Rockland 1975).

[74] Condominium Act §339-1(2).

ments because the owner would have consented through its contract. Once the declaration is filed, the lien would then be valid against all units waiting to be sold. Further, any mechanic's lien would be valid against the common elements after the declaration is recorded until such time as even one unit is sold. Once one unit is sold, the contractor should list in its lien those units that are still owned by the developer; a "blanket lien" that attempts to lien the entire project would fail.[75]

If an owner of a condominium unit requests or consents to improvement of his or her unit, a lien may be filed against that owner's interest in his or her unit only, not against his or her interest in the common elements. Owner consent to improvement is not necessary when emergency repairs to an owner's unit are necessary.[76]

Cooperatives

Unlike condominium mechanics' liens, there are no statutes or clear cases that discuss when and under what circumstances a mechanic's lien may be available against a cooperative's common elements or an individual cooperative unit. Thus, this section discusses what the authors believe the law to be, based on related cases and statutes.

As the sole owner of a cooperative's land and buildings, the cooperative corporation may contract for debts, may sell or mortgage the property, and has all powers, rights, and privileges necessary to operate the cooperative.[77] Thus, if the corporation, through a majority vote of its board, enters into a contract to improve the property, such as installing a security system or repairing the ventilation system, the owner of the property—the board—consented to the improvement and the contractor should be entitled to a mechanic's lien against the entire project—the common elements (the fee) and all individual units.[78]

An individual unit "owner" is a shareholder in the corporation that owns the cooperative and is a tenant in the building owned by the cooperative. The unit owner has a lease and is without power to encumber either its unit or the cooperative fee. Further, a cooperative unit is not indexed on the property tax rolls. Thus, a unit owner's interest in the cooperative is personal, not real, property.[79] The unit owner's interest is most akin to a lessee's interest. Thus, a contractor who improves the unit would be in the same position as one who improves a lessee's property; if the owner—the cooperative corporation—consents to the improvement, the contractor may be entitled to file a mechanic's lien against the unit and perhaps the fee.[80] The unit could be sold,

---

[75] Advanced Alarm Tech, Inc v Pavilion Assocs, 145 AD2d 582, 536 NYS2d 127 (1988).

[76] Condominium Act §339-1(1), (2).

[77] NY Coop Corp Law §§14(o), (q), (r) (McKinney 1951 & Supp 1992).

[78] *See* Susskind v 1136 Tenants Corp. 43 Misc 2d 588, 251 NYS2d 321 (Civ Ct NY 1964).

[79] *See id; but see* Lacille v Feldman, 44 Misc 2d 370, 253 NYS2d 937 (NY 1964) (court, in determining whether a tax lien could attach to a cooperative unit, held that a cooperative unit owner has a quasi-real property interest).

[80] Dash Contracting Corp v Slater, 142 Misc 2d 512, 537 NYS2d 736 (NY 1989).

subject to the cooperative rules, much as a leasehold interest is sold subject to the lease terms.[81]

§9.13 —Leasehold Interests

The New York Lien Law specifically includes lessees of private property as owners against whose interests liens may be created.[82] Thus, a lienor may ignore the owner/lessor interest and assert a lien against the lessee's interest.[83] Upon successful foreclosure, the lienor controls the remainder of the lessee's lease term and it is sold at the execution sale to a third party. The interest sold is restricted by the terms of the lease between the original lessee and lessor.[84] Of course, if the lienor had the owner/lessor's consent to the improvement, it may lien the whole property and not just the lessee's interest.[85]

A private leasehold of public property is never subject to a mechanic's lien.[86]

§9.14 —Oil and Gas

The New York Lien Law specifically includes oil and gas properties as real property subject to liens.[87] The statute includes as real property all oil and gas wells and all connected structures and fixtures, any lease of oil lands, and any right to produce oil or gas from land. Specific provision for oil and gas properties appear at §§4(2) and (4) of the NY Lien Law.

§9.15 Public Property

Real property owned by the state or a public corporation is never subject to a mechanic's lien, even where that property is leased to a private lessee.[88] A contractor who improves real property at the request of a private lessee of public property cannot assert a mechanic's lien. In *Paedergat Boat*, the Court

---

[81] See §§9.05 and 9.13.

[82] NY Lien Law §2(3) (McKinney 1966).

[83] Schwartz & Co v Aimwell Co, 204 AD 769, 198 NYS 838, *affd*, 236 NY 672, 142 NE 330 (1923); Ingram & Greene, Inc v Wynne, 47 Misc 2d 200, 262 NYS2d 663 (Queens 1965).

[84] Cornell v Barney, 94 NY 394 (1884).

[85] See §9.05.

[86] Paedergat Boat & Racquet Club, Inc v Zarrelli, 83 AD2d 444, 449-52, 445 NYS2d 162, 166-68 (1981) (Hopkins, J. dissenting), *revd*, 57 NY2d 966, 443 NE2d 477, 457 NYS2d 229 (1982). The Court of Appeals, in reversing the Appellate Division's decision, adopted the reasons stated in Justice Hopkins's dissent. Albany County Indus Dev Agency v Gastinger Ries Walker Architects, Inc, 144 AD2d 891, 534 NYS2d 823 (1988).

[87] NY Lien Law §2(2) (McKinney 1966).

[88] Paedergat Boat & Racquet Club, Inc v Zarrelli, 83 AD2d 444, 449-52, 445 NYS2d 162, 166-68 (1981) (Hopkins, J. dissenting), *revd*, 57 NY2d 966, 443 NE2d 477, 457 NYS2d 229 (1982). The Court of Appeals, in reversing the Appellate Division's decision, adopted the reasons stated in Justice Hopkins's dissent.

of Appeals based its decision on its belief that the public interest is best served by the state's controlling the identity of the parties to whom its property is leased.[89]

§9.16 What Items Are Covered by the Lien

As was discussed above in §9.04, a lien is available solely for labor and materials provided in the improvement of real property. Those expenses that are properly included in a lien and may be claimed by the lienor are many. The major categories are discussed below and are intended to serve as a guide only. The list of items that may and may not be included in a lien is ever changing through case law. Care must be taken in including questionable items; a lien that is willfully exaggerated may be voided in full by the court and may subject the lienor to a damage award in favor of the owner.

§9.17 —Labor

Labor costs are properly included in a lien to the extent that the labor was done in direct benefit to the property. For example, labor expended to manufacture materials to be used in an improvement cannot be claimed in the lien. Labor used to install the materials in the improvement, however, may be claimed.[90] Presumably, this distinction is because the cost of the labor expended in manufacturing the materials is included in the price of the materials. Further, a laborer for a materialman would be too far removed from a contractor or subcontractor to be entitled to file a lien. (See the discussion at §9.03.)

Supervision is properly included in a lien where the supervision is of the actual construction and is performed at the request of the owner.[91] The procurement of bids, negotiation of contracts, and procurement of permits are not part of such supervision and may not be included in a lien, unless performed by the contractor or architect.[92]

---

[89] *Id. See also* John Kennedy & Co v New York World's Fair 1939, Inc, 260 AD 386, 22 NYS2d 901 (1940), *affd*, 288 NY 494, 41 NE2d 789 (1942); Hempstead Resources Recovery Corp v Peter Scalamandre & Sons, 104 Misc 2d 278, 428 NYS2d 146 (Nassau 1980).

[90] Kingston Trust Co v State, 57 Misc 2d 55, 291 NYS2d 208 (Ulster 1968).

[91] Carl A. Morse, Inc v Rentar Indus Dev Corp, 85 Misc 2d 304, 379 NYS2d 994 (Queens 1976), *affd*, 56 AD2d 30, 391 NYS2d 425 (1977), *affd*, 43 NY2d 952, 375 NE2d 409 (1978).

[92] Henry & John Assoc v Demile Constr Corp, 137 Misc 2d 354, 520 NYS2d 341 (Queens 1987).

§9.18 —Materials

The delivery of materials to the site is sufficient for a lien; materials need not be incorporated into an improvement to be claimed on a lien.[93] Further, materials accepted by the owner or contractor but stored off-site are properly included in a lien.[94] Finally, as specified in the Lien Law, materials actually manufactured for but not delivered to a specific piece of real property are lienable items.[95]

§9.19 —Rental Equipment

Prior to the 1937 amendments to the Lien Law, equipment rented to improve real property was not properly included in a lien.[96] The current law, however, specifically includes the reasonable rental value of machinery, tools and equipment as *materials*[97] and, therefore, as lienable items.

§9.20 —Temporary Works

Works of a temporary nature that are necessary to complete an improvement are lienable items. For example, costs incurred in the construction of a temporary roadbed that is required in a contract for road expansions are properly included in a notice of lien.[98]

§9.21 —Overhead and Employee Benefits

The Lien Law specifically provides that the following costs of doing business are properly included in a mechanic's lien: employee benefits and wage supplements,[99] including health, welfare, and retirement benefits, nonoccupational disability, life insurance, and holiday and vacation pay;[100] payroll taxes;[101] and unemployment insurance.[102]

---

[93] American Blower Corp v James Talcott, Inc, 18 Misc 2d 1031, 194 NYS2d 630 (NY 1959), *affd mem,* 11 AD2d 654, 203 NYS2d 1018 (1960), *affd,* 10 NY2d 282, 219 NYS2d 263 (1961).

[94] Charles E. Gates & Co v John F. Stevens Constr Co, 220 NY 38, 115 NE 22 (1917).

[95] NY Lien Law §3 (McKinney 1966 & Supp 1992).

[96] Troy Pub Works v City of Yonkers, 207 NY 81, 100 NE 700 (1912).

[97] NY Lien Law §2(12) (McKinney 1966).

[98] Berger Mfg Co v City of NY, 206 NY 24, 99 NE 153 (1912); Charles E. Gates & Co v John F. Stevens Constr Co, 220 NY 38, 115 NE 22 (1917).

[99] NY Lien Law §3 (McKinney 1966 & Supp 1992).

[100] *Id* §2(5-a) (McKinney 1966).

[101] *Id* §2(5).

[102] *Id.*

§9.22 —Lost Profits and Contract Damages

A lienor's lost profits due to an owner's breach of contract may not be included in a lien; neither are breach of contract damages,[103] including delay damages. Sections 2(4), (5), (5)(a), (12), 3, and 9 of the NY Lien Law set forth those items that may be included in a lien. Lost profits and contract damages are not listed in any of those sections. Of course, extra charges incurred because of a party's breach may be included.[104]

§9.23 —Extras

Extras and change orders are properly included in a lien when the owner has consented to them. To recover for extras, however, they should be itemized and stated separately from original contract work in the notice of lien.[105] A subcontractor's extras are also properly included in a lien where the extra labor and materials are required due to a contractor's abandonment of the contract.[106]

§9.24 Lien Waivers

Blanket lien waivers and "no lien" contract clauses are against public policy, void, and wholly unenforceable.[107] There are no exceptions, even where the contract specifies it is to be construed by the laws of a state that allows lien waivers.[108] The statute does, however, permit a contract requirement that a party receiving payment execute a lien waiver with regard to the payment received simultaneous with or after delivery of the payment.[109]

§9.25 Should You File a Notice of Lien?

A mechanic's lien can be an effective way to protect one who has improved the real property of another. If an unreasonable owner refuses to pay its debts, a town council disagrees on the need and cost of an improvement approved by its predecessor, or a contractor misapplies payments received, a mechanic's lien helps to ensure that a lienor receives the value of its work. Yet, it is not always wise nor prudent to file a notice of lien at the first possible moment. A mechanic's lien is a potentially powerful remedy that may have effects far

---

[103] Schenectady Homes Corp v Greenside Painting Corp, 37 NYS2d 53 (Schenectady 1942).

[104] See §9.23.

[105] 819 Sixth Ave Corp v T&A Assoc, 24 AD2d 446, 260 NYS2d 984 (1965). In re Pinckney, 13 AD2d 806, 216 NYS2d 19 (1961).

[106] LB Foster Co v Terry Contracting, 34 AD2d 638, 310 NYS2d 76 (1970).

[107] NY Lien Law §34 (McKinney 1966 & Supp 1992).

[108] Clifton Steel Corp v General Elec Co, 80 AD2d 714, 437 NYS2d 734 (1981).

[109] NY Lien Law §34 (McKinney 1966 & Supp 1992).

beyond the immediate relationship between the lienor and the owner or contractor and can have unintended consequences.

Often, the filing of a lien stops all payments from a construction lender to the owner or general contractor until the lien is satisfied, vacated, or discharged. Further, when a lien is filed, an owner or the state usually stops payment to the general contractor until the matter is resolved. If an owner were to make payments to his or her general contractor after a lien was filed, the owner would do so at his or her own peril; the extent of the owner's liability is set at the date of the filing of the notice of lien. If an owner paid his or her general contractor who then failed to pay the lienor, the owner may be liable for the same moneys twice.[110]

Any decision to file a lien must be made carefully and only where there is a strong belief that it is necessary to ensure payment. This decision must be made promptly, however, as delay may result in: there being no liability of the owner to the general contractor; in case of insolvency, there being so many liens ahead of the lienor's lien that the lienor's lien is of low priority with little chance of receiving payment; or the expiration of time to file a lien.

Contractors of public improvements who have a direct contract with the public entity may not file a mechanic's lien.[111] A general contractor's remedy is to sue the public entity on the contract.

§9.26 Elements of a Proper Lien Notice for Private Improvements

Section 9 of the NY Lien Law lists those items that must be included in the notice of lien for a private improvement. These items are:

1. The name and residence of the lienor (or if the lienor is a business, its business address)
2. The name and address of the lienor's attorney, if any
3. The name of the owner and extent of its interest in the property
4. The name of the person for whom the lienor worked or to whom it furnished materials (i.e., the person with whom the lienor contracted)
5. A description of the work performed or materials furnished and the price
6. The amount owing
7. The dates when the first and last work was performed or materials furnished; and
8. A description of the property subject to the lien

The notice of lien must be verified by the lienor or its agent to the effect that the notice is true to its knowledge, except for those matters that are designated in the notice to be true to the best of its information and belief. Those items

---

[110] *Id* §11.
[111] *Id* §5.

§9.26 LIEN NOTICE/PRIVATE IMPROVEMENTS

that cause difficulty to lienors are discussed below. It is important to remember, when considering a notice of lien, that the Lien Law is to be liberally construed; a substantial compliance with its provisions is sufficient.[112] Thus, as is shown in the discussion below, failure to fully provide each element listed in NY Lien Law §9 is not always fatal to the notice of lien.

Information included in a notice of lien that is "surplusage"—items that are not required to be included in a notice of lien—will not cause a lien to be defective. For example, if a notice of lien lists a wrong address for the owner of the property, the lien is valid. The law does not require that a notice of lien include the owner's address and, so long as no one is prejudiced by the inclusion of wrong information, the notice of lien will be valid.[113]

Pre-printed forms are available which aid greatly in the preparation of the notice of lien and help ensure the inclusion of all necessary material. See Form 9-1 for an example of a typical notice of lien form. Of course, every form must be checked for compliance with the statute and any changes thereto.

Identifying the Owner

Although NY Lien Law §9(2) requires that a notice of lien include the owner's name and interest in the property "as far as known to the lienor," the statute also states that "a failure to state the name of the true owner . . . or a misdescription of the true owner, shall not affect the validity of the lien."[114] This qualification is not absolute. The purpose of a notice of lien is to notify interested parties of the lien. A total failure to name the true owner or a misidentification of the owner so extreme that the true owner is not discernible will render a lien invalid.

When an owner is not described perfectly, the question becomes, how wrong can you be and still be right? Naming the spouse of the true owner is not sufficient,[115] nor is naming a previous owner.[116] While there is no set definition of how wrong the description can be, the standard appears to be that so long as the description of the owner provides substantially the same information as the actual name would, the lien is valid.[117]

The safest way to make sure that a lien names the proper owner of the property is to check the real property records. A lienor is entitled to rely upon the

---

[112] NY Lien Law §23.

[113] Griffin Bldg & Constr Corp v RHD Constr Corp, 133 Misc 2d 335, 507 NYS2d 116 (Albany 1986).

[114] NY Lien Law §9(7) (McKinney 1966 & Supp 1992).

[115] LoForte v Omel, 50 Misc 2d 178, 269 NYS2d 924 (Erie 1966).

[116] See DiPaolo v HBM Enters, 95 AD2d 794, 463 NYS2d 511 (1983), where the notice of lien named a corporation as owner when the property was owned by an individual. Three months later the lienor filed another notice that named the individual as the owner. Unfortunately for the lienor, the individual transferred ownership of the property to the corporation one day before the lienor filed his second lien.

[117] Marshall Constr Co v Brookdale Hosp Center, 68 Misc 2d 20, 324 NYS2d 806 (Kings 1971) (lien held valid and amendable where it listed The Brookdale Hospital Center Nursing Home Co, Inc as owner, but true owner was The Brookdale Hospital Center).

real property records for the name of the owner, as that record stands on the date of filing of the notice of lien; an unrecorded transfer of property will not affect the lien.[118]

Identifying the Person for Whom the Work Was Performed

The requirement that the person for whom the work was performed be identified on the notice of lien is qualified by subsection 7 of §9 of the Lien Law: a notice of lien will not be invalidated for a failure to state the true name. Thus, where a notice of lien listed "Morris Margowitz, president of Grossman Construction Corporation," as a contractor when the contractor was actually the corporation, not its president, the lien was found valid.[119] Similarly, where a lien named an employee of the corporation as the contractor and as the person to whom materials were delivered, the lien could have been amended to show the true contractor.[120] In a case where there was a total failure to name any person with whom the lienor contracted or to whom he furnished labor or materials, the lien was found invalid and incapable of correction by amendment.[121]

Stating the Work Performed and the Price

Section 9(4) of the NY Lien Law requires a statement of "the labor performed or materials furnished and the agreed price or value thereof, or materials actually manufactured for but not delivered to the real property and the agreed price or value thereof." This requirement is not one for a detailed listing of each task performed and nut and bolt supplied. Rather, it requires a description sufficient to inform interested persons of the character and extent of the lien claim.

Thus, a notice of lien was found valid which described the work as that required pursuant to contract to "renovate and remodel a portion of the premises for use as a beauty salon."[122] A mere reference to a contract without any description of the work done, however, was not sufficient;[123] nor was a statement that the work performed was "equipment and machinery."[124]

Similarly, a notice of lien that described the work done but failed to state the agreed price of the work was found to have substantially complied with

---

[118] Admiral Transit Mix Corp v Sagg-Bridgehampton Corp, 56 Misc 2d 47, 287 NYS2d 751 (Suffolk 1968).

[119] Lichtenstein v Grossman Constr Corp, 221 AD 527, 225 NYS 118, *modified on other grounds*, 248 NY 390, 162 NE 292 (1928).

[120] San Marco Constr Corp v Gillert, 15 Misc 2d 208, 178 NYS2d 137 (Westchester 1958). The lienor failed to amend his notice of lien, however, and the action to foreclose the lien was dismissed as the lienor could not prove his lien.

[121] Houseknecht v Reeve, 108 NYS2d 917 (Oneida 1951).

[122] Meo v Skellyway Constr Co, 30 AD2d 606, 290 NYS2d 516 (1968).

[123] Toop v Smith, 181 NY 283, 73 NE 1113 (1905).

[124] San Marco Constr Corp v Gillert, 15 Misc 2d 208, 178 NYS2d 137 (Westchester 1958).

the statute and to be amendable because the notice stated that the "amount unpaid of the agreed price is $1,750.00."[125] Further, a notice of lien was found valid which described the work done and stated the "agreed and owing" price for contract work, but stated only the amount owing for extras. The court found that the lien apprised interested persons of the extensive work performed and that the amount owing was for contract work and extras.[126]

Amount Owed

If the amount due is not evident from the face of the lien, the lien will be found invalid. It is important to be as accurate as possible in stating the amount due for two reasons. First, the amount of a lien and a lienor's recovery in a lien foreclosure action is limited by the amount claimed due in the lien; a lien that claims less than is owed may place a ceiling on the lienor's recovery.[127] Second, a lien that is found to have been willfully exaggerated will be declared void and will subject the lienor to paying damages to the very party against whom the lien was filed.[128]

Dates of Performance

A statement of when the work was performed is essential to a valid lien.[129] Once again, the reason for this requirement is to allow interested parties to determine from the face of the lien what the lienor's interest is and whether the lien is invalid for being filed too late.

Where a notice of lien listed the date when labor was last provided but not when it was first provided, the court held that the notice of lien could be amended to show the date when labor was first provided.[130] Where that same notice of lien failed to list any dates with respect to the furnishing of materials, however, the notice of lien could not be amended as there was no indication on the face of the notice of lien that materials were furnished.

It is important to list the *actual* date that work first began; where a notice of lien states a first date that is later than the actual first date, it cannot include sums due for labor or materials provided prior to the date listed in the notice.[131] Although the notice of lien should be as accurate as possible, it need not be

---

[125] Nimke v Inta-State, Inc, 34 AD2d 675, 310 NYS2d 462 (1970).

[126] Forman v Pala Constr Co, 124 AD2d 453, 507 NYS2d 553 (1986).

[127] It is difficult to amend a lien to increase the amount claimed due. *See* Scriven v Maple Knoll Apts, Inc, 46 AD2d 210, 361 NYS2d 730 (1974); Perrin v Stempinski Realty Corp, 15 AD2d 48, 222 NYS2d 148 (1961); *In re* O'Neill, 182 Misc 838, 45 NYS2d 564 (Wayne 1943); *In re* Upstate Builders Supply Corp, 63 Misc 2d 35, 310 NYS2d 862 (Onondaga 1970).

[128] NY Lien Law §§39, 39-a (McKinney 1966 & Supp 1992). See discussion at **§9.52.**

[129] NY Lien Law §9(6) (McKinney 1966 & Supp 1992).

[130] Bennett Bros v Bracewood Realty No 1, Inc, 31 Misc 2d 284, 220 NYS2d 38 (Queens 1961).

[131] RG Equip Corp v Gursha, 60 Misc 2d 240, 303 NYS2d 275 (Montgomery 1969).

exact; in one case, a court allowed a lienor to amend his notice of lien which stated only the months and years of first and last work but omitted the dates of each month.[132]

When filing a lien while work is in progress or has not been completed for some other reason, the notice of lien must show that it was filed during the progress of the lienor's work or within the applicable time period following the last item of work performed or materials furnished.[133]

Identifying the Property Improved

The property improved must be described sufficiently so that the property is identifiable with reasonable certainty to the exclusion of all other parcels.[134] A correct description in an attached rider or cover sheet will not correct an incorrect description in the notice of lien.[135]

In counties where the county clerk indexes liens in a block index, each notice of lien must include the number of every block affected by the lien.[136] Generally, it is best to describe the property by all means available: block and lot, metes and bounds, and street address. A notice of lien that lists correct block and lot numbers but gives incorrect metes and bounds may be valid and amendable,[137] as may be a notice of lien that gives the correct street address but the wrong lot number.[138]

A lien that failed to provide any geographic coordinates and that incorrectly stated that the property was on the west side of the road, when it was on the north side of the road, was found invalid.[139] Similarly, describing adjacent property renders a notice of lien wholly invalid and incapable of amendment.[140]

If too little property is included in a notice of lien, the lien is fatally defective; if too much property is included, the lien claim will be limited to that property

---

[132] *In re* Refrod Realty Corp, 216 NYS2d 564 (Kings 1961).

[133] *In re* Koch, 98 NYS2d 109 (Erie 1950). It is not sufficient for the notice of lien to state that the last work has not been done and cannot be done until another subcontractor's work is done.

[134] Contelmo's Sand & Gravel, Inc v J&J Milano, Inc, 96 AD2d 1090, 467 NYS2d 55 (1983); Hudson Demolition Co v Ismor Realty Corp, 62 AD2d 980, 403 NYS2d 327 (1978).

[135] Hudson Demolition Co v Ismor Realty Co, 62 AD2d 980, 403 NYS2d 327 (1978).

[136] NY Lien Law §10(2) (McKinney 1966 & Supp 1992).

[137] Marshall Constr Co v Brookdale Hosp Center, 68 Misc 2d 20, 324 NYS2d 806 (Kings 1971) (metes and bounds included in a rider attached to notice, not on notice's face).

[138] Fremar Bldg Corp v Sand, 104 AD2d 1025, 480 NYS2d 945 (1984) (lot number on notice was same as that listed in contract).

[139] Contelmo's Sand & Gravel v J&J Milano, Inc, 96 AD2d 1090, 467 NYS2d 55 (1983) (property described as "on west side of Wheeler Hill Road, Town of Wappinger, Duchess County, New York").

[140] Avon Elec Supplies, Inc v Goldsmith, 54 AD2d 552, 387 NYS2d 1 (1976).

on which improvements were made.[141] Thus, if the property is 50' × 75' but is described as 25' × 75', the lien is invalid;[142] conversely, if the property is 25-feet wide but is described in the lien as 50-feet wide, the lien will be valid.[143] Of course, the fact that a court may allow a lien that includes too much property to stand does not mean that the lienor may not be subject to a slander of title claim if its lien hinders an unrelated party's property.

If improvements are made to several separate and distinct properties owned by the same owner, separate notices of lien should be filed for each property.[144]

Where, however, a contractor performs improvements to a portion of a unified tract of land and the owner conveys the improved portion, in good faith, prior to the filing of a lien, the lien attaches to the unimproved portion that the owner retained, even though the contractor did not perform any improvements on that portion.[145] The requirement of separate liens does not apply in such a case because there is a single transaction, involving a single tract of land, which is divided only after the improvements are completed.

§9.27 Elements of a Proper Lien Notice for Public Improvements

The requirements for a notice of lien for a public improvement are similar to those for a private improvement lien. The differences, though few, are important. A notice of lien for a public improvement must include the following:

1. The lienor's name and residence or business address if the lienor is a business
2. The name of the contractor or subcontractor for whom the labor was performed or materials furnished, if known
3. The amount due or to become due
4. The date when due
5. A description of the public improvement

---

[141] Blackman-Shapiro Co v Salzberg, 8 Misc 2d 972, 168 NYS2d 590 (Queens 1957).

[142] Sprickerhoff v Gordon, 120 AD 748, 105 NYS 586 (1907), affd, 194 NY 77, 88 NE 1132 (1909); LA Storch & Co v Marginal Realty Corp, 109 Misc 669, 180 NYS 611 (NY 1919) (lot was 100' × 98', lien invalid which described lot as 50' × 98').

[143] Hall v Thomas, 111 NYS 979 (NY 1908). See also Jannotta v Noslac Realty Corp, 231 AD 864, 246 NYS 510 (1930) (lien valid which included more land than was directly benefited by improvement, where all land liened was owned by same owner); but see Advanced Alarm Tech v Pavilion Assoc, 145 AD2d 582, 536 NYS2d 127 (1988) (blanket lien against condominium project invalid where some units had been sold by developer after work done but before lien filed).

[144] Twin County Transit Mix, Inc v Ingula Builders Corp, 27 AD2d 939, 278 NYS2d 990 (1967).

[145] Niagra Venture v Sicoli & Massaro, Inc, 77 NY2d 175, 565 NYS2d 449 (1990).

6. The kind of labor performed and materials furnished, or manufactured for the project but not delivered; and
7. A general description of the public improvement contract

The public improvement notice of lien must be verified by the lienor or the lienor's agent to the same extent as is done in a private notice of lien. Those items that are included in a private improvement notice of lien will not be discussed separately as the standards are the same for describing the work performed, materials furnished or specifically manufactured, and amount due, although not the amount to become due. A discussion of private improvement notice of lien requirements is found in §9.26.

Amount Due or to Become Due

Unlike a private lien, a lien for public improvements may include not only amounts that are due but also amounts that are to become due.

Description of the Public Improvement

The description of the public improvement is best done simply. For example, a lienor that supplied and installed windows in a courthouse could describe the public improvement as "Construction of the Broome County Courthouse."

Description of the Contract

In the description of the contract for the public improvement, it is wise to include more information than a general description. It is the contract between the public entity and the general contractor that must be described, not the contract between the lienor and the general contractor. It is best when describing the contract to include the contract number, if any, as well as its official title. The lienor may obtain this information from the general contractor,[146] from public records, or through a request under freedom of information law. Thus, a lienor providing the windows for a courthouse might describe the contract as "Broome County Contract Registration No. CH-51559 dated June 12, 1989, for construction of the Broome County Courthouse, Department of Justice Contract No. 30-C."

The statute[147] requires only a "general" description of the contract sufficient to advise the filing officer and other interested parties of the lien.[148] However, it is advisable that lienors provide as much information as possible. A failure to sufficiently describe the contract can result in discharge of the lien.

§9.28 Filing the Notice of Lien—Time and Place

If a notice of lien is not filed timely and in the proper place, it will not be valid. There are no exceptions. The differences between private and public

---

[146] NY Lien Law §8 (McKinney 1966 & Supp 1992).

[147] Id §12.

[148] Davis Lumber Co v Blanchard, 175 AD 256, 161 NYS 474 (1916).

improvement liens are most marked in these two areas; see the following two sections for discussions of the filing of these different liens.

§9.29 —Private Improvement Liens

Section 10 of the New York Lien Law specifies that a notice of lien may be filed "at any time during the progress of the work and the furnishing of materials . . ." or within eight months after "completion of the contract, or the final performance of the work, or the final furnishing of materials. . . ." The eight-month period is dated from the last item of work performed or materials furnished by the lienor.[149] If the improvement is a single family dwelling, the notice of lien must be filed within four months after completion of the work.[150]

Completion and *final performance* refer to the last work done on the contract or approved extras. Repair or warranty work done after completion of the contract will not extend the time to file a notice of lien.[151] Where a contract has been abandoned, the time to file runs from the date of abandonment;[152] any work done after the abandonment cannot be used to extend the time period as it would not have been done in furtherance of the contract.[153]

A notice of lien for a private improvement must be filed in the clerk's office of the county or counties in which the property improved is located.[154] The county clerk is then required to enter the lien in his or her "lien docket." A failure by the clerk to properly docket a lien shall not cause the lien to be invalid; it is the filing of the lien that creates the lien.[155]

§9.30 —Public Improvement Liens

In sharp contrast to the time afforded a lienor of private property, NY Lien Law §12 provides that a lien for public improvements may be filed at any time before the completion and acceptance of a public improvement, but in no instance later than 30 days following completion *and* acceptance by the state or the public corporation. The improvement must be both completed and accepted before the 30-day period begins to run.[156] Thus, where a subcontrac-

---

[149] NY Lien Law §10 (McKinney 1966 & Supp 1992).

[150] *Id;* Griffin Bldg & Constr Corp v RHD Constr Corp, 133 Misc 2d 335, 507 NYS2d 116 (Albany 1986) (*single family dwelling* refers to a single residence, not to a development of many single family residences).

[151] Nelson v Schrank, 273 AD 72, 75 NYS2d 761 (1947); Bradley v Kostanoski, 101 NYS2d 767 (Nassau 1950).

[152] Locke v Goode, 10 Misc 2d 65, 174 NYS2d 435 (1957).

[153] *Id.*

[154] NY Lien Law §10 (McKinney 1966 & Supp 1992).

[155] Manton v Brooklyn & Flatbush Realty Co, 217 NY 284, 111 NE 819 (1916); Hurley v Tucker, 128 AD 580, 112 NYS 980 (1908), *affd,* 198 NY 534 (1910).

[156] Miliken Bros v City of NY, 201 NY 65, 94 NE 196 (1911).

tor finished its work in June and the project was completed in December but not accepted until March, the 30-day period to file a notice of lien did not expire until April.[157]

The contrast in time allowed for filing a public versus a private lien may be seen in comparing when a building foundation excavator, often the first subcontractor to work on a job, must file its lien. On the private project, the excavator lien would have to be filed within 8 months of the time when the excavator completed its work; on the public project, however, the excavator could wait until 30 days after the entire building was completed and accepted to file its lien.

The question of what is acceptance arises frequently. If the public entity moves into the building, is there acceptance? If the public entity issues a certificate of final inspection, is there acceptance? The answers to these questions are not as easy as may appear. The answers depend on the terms of the contract between the public entity and the general contractor. If an acceptance procedure is specified in the contract, it must be followed as set forth in order for there to be acceptance.[158] As in private improvements, abandonment or termination of the contract is equivalent to completion and acceptance for purposes of determining filing deadlines.[159]

Generally, a contractor is not required to notify a subcontractor or materialman that there has been completion and acceptance.[160] A subcontractor would be wise to demand that it be notified promptly of acceptance and completion by the state through the provisions of §11-a of the NY Lien Law, despite the fact that a total failure by the state to notify a party pursuant to such demand does not extend the time to file the notice of lien or give rise to any cause of action, right, or duty.[161]

A notice of lien for a public improvement is not filed with the county clerk; rather, it must be filed with

> the head of the department or bureau having charge of such construction or demolition *and* with the comptroller of the state or with the financial officer of the public corporation, or other officer or person charged with the custody and disbursements of the state or corporate funds applicable to the contract under which the claim is made. (Emphasis added.)[162]

---

[157] Reynolds Metals Co v People, 41 Misc 2d 694, 245 NYS2d 890 (NY 1963), *affd mem*, 259 NYS2d 1006 (1965).

[158] NW Developers, Inc v Jeremiah Burns, Inc, 55 AD2d 580, 389 NYS2d 865 (1976); Biondo v City of NY, 18 AD2d 78, 238 NYS2d 7 (1963); Lehigh Portland Cement Co v City of NY, 179 AD 368, 166 NYS 454 (1917).

[159] Ferran Concrete Corp v Avon Elec Supplies Corp, 128 AD2d 527, 512 NYS2d 459 (1987).

[160] Ingalls Iron Works Co v Fehlhaber Corp, 29 AD2d 29, 285 NYS2d 369 (1967), *affd mem*, 24 NY2d 862, 301 NYS2d 95 (1969).

[161] NY Lien Law §11-a(4) (McKinney 1966 & Supp 1992).

[162] *Id* §12.

The notice of lien must be filed with two separate offices or agencies: with the one in charge of the construction of the improvement and with the one in charge of paying for it.[163]

The requirement that the lien be filed with the "head of the department" does not mean that the head of the department must acquire physical possession of the notice. It is enough if the notice is filed with the department head's designated custodian.[164]

The possibilities and variations of proper filing locations are almost limitless. Thus, only a few examples of filings that have been upheld by the courts are mentioned here. A notice of lien for a contract to erect a school for a city should be filed with the city council president (the entity that approved and administered the contract) and the city treasurer.[165] Similarly, if work is done for a village and the contract is confirmed by the village board of trustees, a notice filed with the mayor and treasurer of the village is proper. Of course, if the contract is with a state department, the notice may be filed with the State Comptroller and head of the state department; but, it is also permissible for the notice to be filed with the regional director of the department and the regional financial officer of the department.[166]

§9.31 Service of Notice of Lien

Private Improvement Liens

Private improvement liens are served upon the owner of the property,[167] the general contractor, and, if applicable, the subcontractor with whom the lienor contracted or worked if the lienor did not have a direct contractual relationship with the general contractor.[168] The notice must be served within 30 days after filing the notice of lien or the lien will be invalid.[169] It must be served on the contractor and subcontractor by certified mail.[170]

Proof of service must be filed with the county clerk within 35 days after the notice of lien is filed or the lien will become invalid.[171] It is wise to serve the

---

[163] Jensen's §210 (on Mech Lien Law, by E. Marks; 1963 & Supp 1983).

[164] Albany Builders Supply Co v Eastern Bridge & Structural Co, 235 NY 432, 139 NE 565 (1923) (notice filed with city clerk, where city clerk was the designated clerk of the city council and custodian of its records, was a valid filing; if the lien were "filed" with the president of the council—the department head in this instance—his duty would be to give it to the city clerk for docketing).

[165] Id.

[166] In re Callanan Indus, 88 Misc 2d 802, 389 NYS2d 80 (Albany 1975) (department of transportation).

[167] NY Lien Law §11 (McKinney 1966 & Supp 1992).

[168] Id §11-b.

[169] Id §11, 11-b.

[170] Id §11-b.

[171] Id §11.

owner as soon as possible because an owner without knowledge of the lien is protected in any payments made in good faith.[172]

Public Improvement Liens

Since a public improvement lien is filed with the responsible parties, the "owners," there is no need to also serve a copy of the notice on the same parties. Simultaneously with filing the notice, a copy must be served by certified mail on the general contractor and subcontractor, if applicable, with whom the lienor dealt.[173] Proof of service must be noted on the notice of lien itself or filed with the notice, or the lien will be invalid.[174]

§9.32 Duration and Extension of Lien

Private Improvement Liens

Private improvement liens are valid for one year from the date of filing.[175] A notice of lien is automatically extended when a foreclosure action is begun[176] and a notice of pendency filed. Failure to file a notice of pendency will cause a lien to expire after the one-year period has lapsed, regardless of the status of the foreclosure action,[177] unless the lien has been extended or discharged through a bond or cash deposit (see §9.37).

A lien may be extended for one year by the filing and service of an extension to lien within one year of the original notice of lien.[178] The extension must contain the lienor's name, the owner's name, a brief description of the property, the amount of the lien, and the date of the filing of the original notice of lien.[179] If an additional one-year extension is needed, a lienor, upon good cause shown, may obtain an order from a court of record continuing the lien and re-docket the lien with reference to the order.[180] The self-filed extension

---

[172] *Id.*

[173] *Id* §11-c.

[174] *Id.*

[175] NY Lien Law §17.

[176] A foreclosure action must be begun properly for the lien to be automatically extended; proper parties must be included and served, venue must be proper, filing fees must be paid, etc.

[177] Mineola Road Oil Corp v Walsh, 137 NYS2d 342 (Suffolk 1954) (lienor commenced foreclosure action within one year of filing lien, but did not file pendency notice nor court order continuing lien until after one year; lien expired after one year). *See also* Jensen's §292 (on Mech Lien Law, by E. Marks; 1963 & Supp 1983).

[178] NY Lien Law §17 (McKinney 1966 & Supp 1992). A lien on a single family dwelling may not be self-extended; it may be extended only by court order.

[179] *Id.*

[180] *Id.* There is some question whether a lien may be extended by an *ex parte* order of court. The statute itself, §17, does not expressly require notice, and some courts have held that it is within the court's discretion to require notice or to allow an *ex parte* extension. *See In re* Lycee Francais de NY, 26 Misc 2d 374, 204 NYS2d 490 (NY 1960).

of lien is good for one time only, for one year only. A court-ordered extension is good for one year only, but a new order may be granted and docketed for successive one-year periods.

Public Improvement Liens

Public improvement liens are valid for six months from the time of filing, unless continued by an extension or unless a foreclosure action is begun *and* a notice of pendency is filed.[181] Public lien extensions must be filed within six months of the filing of the original notice of lien and are valid for one year. Extensions must include the lienor's name, the name of the party with whom the lienor contracted, a description of the public improvement, the amount of the lien, and the date of filing of the original notice of lien. Self-filed extensions are valid for one year only and may not be renewed. A lien may be further extended for one year through an order of a court of record.[182] If the extension is granted, the lien must be re-docketed, showing its continuance by court order.[183] A court-ordered extension is not valid for more than one year, although a new order may be granted and the lien re-docketed in successive years.

§9.33 Amendment of Lien

Within 60 days of filing a notice of lien, a lienor may reduce its lien through amendment, with 20 days' notice to the owner and any mortgagees or lienors.[184] Any other amendment of a lien must be done by court order with notice to the owner and any mortgagees or lienors.[185] No amendment will be granted which prejudices an existing mortgagee, lienor, or purchaser in good faith.[186] Amendments are available only after the statutory time period to file a notice of lien has expired; a lienor may file as many liens as it wishes during the statutory filing period.[187]

However, it has also been held that the statute "implicitly contains a requirement of notice to the property owner-lienee when motion is made to continue a mechanic's lien past the initial one-year period." *In re* Barnes Constr Co, 131 Misc 2d 285, 499 NYS2d 867, 870 (Cattaraugus 1986).

[181] Both the notice of pendency and the extension are filed with the same persons as is the notice of lien. NY Lien Law §18.

[182] As with private liens, it is not clear whether an extension may be granted *ex parte*.

[183] NY Lien Law §18.

[184] *Id* §12-a(1). Amendment to reduce a willfully exaggerated lien will not remove the potential cause of action.

[185] *Id* §12-a(2).

[186] NY Lien Law §12-a(2).

[187] Berger Mfg Co v City of NY, 206 NY 24, 99 NE 153 (1912); *In re* O'Neill, 182 Misc 2d 838, 45 NYS2d 564 (Wayne 1943).

326 MECHANICS' LIENS

To allow an amendment, the court must first find that a valid lien was filed.[188] A lienor cannot, by amendment, validate a wholly invalid notice of lien, since no lien exists unless there has been substantial compliance with the statute.[189] As was discussed in §9.26, what is substantial compliance depends upon which element of the notice of lien is sought to be amended.

While any interested party may oppose an amendment, only those parties that are enumerated in NY Lien Law §12-a(2) may oppose an amendment on the grounds of prejudice; an owner is not one of those parties.[190]

It is important to amend a notice of lien that is in any way inaccurate. A lienor must prove the validity of the notice of lien as it exists at trial; a failure to amend a notice of lien to correct it may result in the lien being found unenforceable at trial.[191]

§9.34 Owner's Response to Notice of Lien

When an owner receives a notice of lien from a subcontractor, the owner should stop all further payments to the contractor that employed the subcontractor or withhold enough money from the contractor to cover the amount of the lien, interest, and court costs. An owner's liability for a lien is limited to the amount of money due or to become due the contractor on the contract at the time of receipt of the notice of lien or at the time the owner has knowledge of the lien;[192] this pool of money is called the *lien fund*. If an owner, following receipt of a notice of lien, were to make additional payments to the contractor, the lien fund would not be diminished and the owner would remain liable to the subcontractor/lienor even though the owner paid the contractor in full.

When faced with a lien, an owner typically will insist that the contractor pay or bond the lien, or will set aside from moneys due the contractor one and one-half times the lien amount. An owner also has other steps it may take to protect its interests before the lien is resolved; some of these are discussed in §§9.35-9.37.

---

[188] Tri-Quality Mechanical Corp v Chappastream Corp, 138 AD2d 610, 526 NYS2d 194 (1988); Empire Pile Driving Co v Hylan Sanitary Serv, 32 AD2d 563, 300 NYS2d 434 (1969); Sbarro Holding Corp v Lamparter Acoustical Prods, 87 Misc 2d 556, 386 NYS2d 920 (Nassau 1976).

[189] Houseknecht v Reeve, 108 NYS2d 917 (Oneida 1951).

[190] Carboline Co v Gold, 94 AD2d 921, 463 NYS2d 341 (1983); Commander Elec, Inc v Lerner, 54 AD2d 698, 387 NYS2d 294 (1976). *But see In re* Upstate Builders Supply Corp, 63 Misc 2d 35, 310 NYS2d 862 (Onondaga 1970) (court denied amendment to increase amount of lien on grounds that owner and mortgagee would be prejudiced because they had released moneys in reliance on the amount of the lien).

[191] San Marco Constr Corp v Gillert, 15 Misc 2d 208, 178 NYS2d 137 (Westchester 1958).

[192] NY Lien Law §4; Van Clif v Van Vechten, 130 NY 571, 29 NE 1017 (1892); Trustees of Hanover Square Realty Investors v Weintraub, 52 AD2d 600, 382 NYS2d 110 (1976); Central Valley Concrete Corp v Montgomery Ward & Co, 34 AD2d 860, 310 NYS2d 925 (1970).

§9.35 —Demand for Statement

An owner or a contractor may demand an itemized statement of the lienor setting out specifically the items of labor and materials furnished and the terms of the contract under which they were furnished.[193] Through an itemized statement, an owner, or the owner's contractor, can check the lienor's claim.[194] The itemized statement must be verified[195] and must present detailed descriptions. It is not enough for a lienor to submit unsigned and unverified handwritten notes of tasks performed[196] or to attach copies of invoices that show all materials furnished.[197] The statement is required only for matters disputed by the owner. If the owner agrees with some of the lien claim, the lienor need supply itemization only for those items and amounts that are disputed.[198]

In *Sperry v Millar*,[199] the court set forth the standard by which an itemized statement should be judged. The statement should specify the types of labor used, skilled and unskilled, and the number of hours worked by each type of laborer and hourly rates; it should specify the types of materials and quantity and cost of each; and it should set forth the provisions of the contract whereby such labor and materials were furnished.[200]

If the lien is for a lump sum or fixed price contract that has been substantially completed, however, the lienor does not have to provide an itemized statement for those matters included in the contract.[201] If the lien includes extras or changes in addition to the lump sum, the extras must be itemized.[202] If the lump sum contract has not been substantially completed, itemization is required.[203]

§9.36 —Discharge the Lien

A lien may be removed from the real property or public funds by a discharge of the lien. There are four basic ways of discharging a lien: the lienor discharges the lien, usually because the lienor has been paid; the lien is discharged by a bond or deposit; the lien is discharged because it is defective on its face; and

---

[193] NY Lien Law §38.
[194] Callipari v 516 E 11th St Corp, 166 Misc 2d 79, 1 NYS2d 384 (NY 1937).
[195] *Id.*
[196] DePalo v McNamara, 139 AD2d 646, 527 NYS2d 283 (1988).
[197] *In re* Seid, 31 Misc 2d 316, 219 NYS2d 962 (Onondaga 1961).
[198] Solow v Bethlehem Steel Corp, 60 AD2d 826, 401 NYS2d 227 (1978).
[199] 254 AD2d 819, 5 NYS2d 249 (1938).
[200] *Id.*
[201] FJC Cavo Constr, Inc v Robinson, 81 AD2d 1005, 440 NYS2d 106 (1981); 819 Sixth Ave Corp v T&A Assocs, 24 AD2d 446, 260 NYS2d 984 (1965); *In re* Pinckney, 13 AD2d 806, 216 NYS2d 19 (1961).
[202] FJC Cavo Constr, Inc v Robinson, 81 AD2d 1005, 440 NYS2d 106 (1981); 819 Sixth Ave Corp v T&A Assocs, 24 AD2d 446, 260 NYS2d 984 (1965); *In re* Pinckney, 13 AD2d 806, 216 NYS2d 19 (1961).
[203] *In re* Borysko, 2 Misc 2d 621, 149 NYS2d 53 (Kings 1956).

328 MECHANICS' LIENS

the lien is discharged because it is procedurally defective.[204]

If all or part of a lien is paid, either before or during a foreclosure action,[205] the lienor should be required to furnish a complete or partial satisfaction or release of the lien. When this is filed, the lien is completely or partially discharged. Once a foreclosure judgment has been entered, payment is shown by filing a satisfaction of judgment.[206] Similarly, if judgment in a foreclosure action is rendered for the owner, the lien is discharged by filing a transcript of the judgment.[207] The three remaining methods of discharging a lien require discussion.

File a Bond or Deposit

To discharge a lien, an owner or a contractor may file a bond or undertaking (hereinafter *bond*)[208] with the financial officer of the public entity or clerk of the county in which the lien was filed in an amount set by the court, but in no event in an amount less than the lien claim,[209] or in an amount set by stipulation with the lienor.

Where a lien covers two parcels of property, a bond to discharge a lien on one parcel only may not be for less than the amount of the lien. While a lien may be partially satisfied and discharged, it may not be partially bonded.[210]

The bond may be executed with individual[211] or corporate sureties.[212] Upon notice to the lienor or its attorney, the court may enter an order discharging the lien.[213] The lien then "shifts" from the property to the bond and the lienor must prove the lien as though there were no bond.[214]

An owner or contractor may also file a bond before there is a lien claim through §37 of the NY Lien Law and thereby prevent any liens from being

---

[204] *See* NY Lien Law §§19, 20, 21, 37, 55, and 59.

[205] *Id* §§19(1) (private liens), 21(1) (public liens).

[206] *Id* §§19(1) (private lien), 21(3) (public liens).

[207] *Id* §21(5).

[208] A detailed analysis of discharging a lien through a bond is found at §§250-272 of *Jensen's* (on Mech Lien Law, by E. Marks; 1963 & Supp 1983).

[209] NY Lien Law §§19(4), 37 (private lien), 21(5) (public lien). Where an owner owes less on the general contract than the amount of the lien claim, a bond may be set by the court at the amount owed on the general contract. Trustees of Hanover Square Realty Investors v Weintraub, 52 AD2d 600, 382 NYS2d 110 (1976); *contra In re* Rockefeller Center, 238 AD 736, 265 NYS 546 (1933).

[210] Sieburg v Paddell, 134 NYS 403 (NY 1912).

[211] The individual sureties (two or more are required) must be deemed "sufficient" by the court and together justify at least twice the amount of the lien. The lienor must be given five days' notice of an attempt to discharge a lien through a bond guaranteed by individual sureties. NY Lien Law §19(5).

[212] There need only be one corporate surety, so long as it is a fidelity or surety company authorized to transact business in the state. *Id* §§19(4) (private lien), 21(5) (public lien).

[213] *Id* §19(4).

[214] Miliken Bros v City of NY, 201 NY 65, 94 NE 196 (1911).

filed against the property. The amount of the bond is set by the court and is not to be less than the amount unpaid on the contract.[215] This type of bond may not be used on a public improvement.[216]

An owner[217] or a contractor[218] may discharge a lien by the deposit of money with the court or state financial officer, in an amount set by the court. The deposit must be, at a minimum, the amount of the lien plus interest and costs and expenses. Generally, courts set bond and deposit amounts at 10-to-15 per cent over the face amount of the lien. If a foreclosure action has begun, the deposit may be in cash or "securities," subject to the lienor's approval, and must be sufficient to satisfy any judgment that may be rendered in the lienor's favor.[219]

A discharge of a lien by bond or deposit is not an admission of liability. A lienor is not automatically entitled to payment from the bond or deposit; the lien must be judicially established for the lienor to recover from the fund.[220] The lienor must foreclose the lien and follow the same procedures it would have had there been no bond or deposit;[221] however, there are slight procedural differences: the surety becomes a necessary party;[222] the mortgagee, if any, is no longer a necessary party,[223] although the owner still is;[224] the prayer for relief and judgment direct the surety to pay;[225] and a notice of pendency is no longer necessary in a private lien action.[226]

A bond or deposit covers only those liens that were specifically discharged thereby. Thus, where an owner discharged a general contractor's lien by a bond, a subcontractor, whose lien was filed after the bond discharged the general contractor's lien, could not claim against the bond fund.[227]

---

[215] NY Lien Law §37(1).

[216] Most public works contracts require that general contractors post performance bonds that guarantee not only the completion of the job, but also payment of subcontractors, materialmen, and laborers. These bonds are discussed in **ch 8**.

[217] NY Lien Law §20.

[218] *Id* §20 (private lien), §21(4) (public lien).

[219] *Id* §§20, 55 (private lien), 21(4) (public lien).

[220] Cooper v Emmanuele, 25 AD2d 809, 270 NYS2d 99 (1966).

[221] Martirano Constr Corp v Briar Contracting Corp, 104 AD2d 1028, 481 NYS2d 105 (1984).

[222] Morton v Tucker, 145 NY 244, 40 NE 3 (1895).

[223] Bryant Equip Corp v A-1 Contracting Corp, 51 AD2d 792, 380 NYS2d 705 (1976).

[224] Harlem Plumbing Supply Co v Handelsman, 40 AD2d 768, 337 NYS2d 329 (1972).

[225] *Id;* Martirano Constr Corp v Briar Contracting Corp, 104 AD2d 1028, 481 NYS2d 105 (1984).

[226] Bargabos Constr Co v Realty Intl, Inc, 96 Misc 2d 1028, 410 NYS2d 263 (Onondaga 1978). A pendency notice is still necessary in a public lien foreclosure.

[227] 101 Park Ave Assoc v Trane Co, 99 AD2d 428, 470 NYS2d 392, *affd mem*, 62 NY2d 734, 465 NE2d 359, 476 NYS2d 820 (1984) (private lien); Bethlehem Fabricators, Inc v Wills Taylor & Mafera, 248 AD 331, 289 NYS 96 (1936) (public lien); *cf* First Fed Sav & Loan Assoc v Burdett Ave Properties, Inc, 41 AD2d 356, 343 NYS2d 271 (1973) (where owner deposited money into court to discharge liens, subsequent lienors were not entitled to payment from the deposit until the prior lienors had been paid in full;

An owner or contractor that deposits cash may replace it with a bond, upon court approval and notice to the lienor[228] or by stipulation with the lienor. But in a case where the court approved the discharge of a lien through a bond, the owner whose interest was liened, one of several tenants-in-common, could not substitute an escrow fund held by a title insurance company for the bond as the money in the escrow was not solely the owner's property.[229] Presumably, a bond may be replaced by a cash deposit.

Defects on the Face

Where a lien is facially defective due to the character of labor or materials furnished or for a failure to comply with the notice provisions of §9, 11, or 12 of the NY Lien Law, it may be discharged by court order upon application by any interested party.[230] The defect must be obvious from the face of the notice of lien or it cannot be summarily discharged, even where there is uncontroverted evidence that the lien is invalid.[231] Usually where extrinsic proof is necessary to prove that a lien is invalid, it is necessary to wait until the lienor forecloses the lien or it expires, to bond the lien, or to compel the lienor to commence a foreclosure action.[232] Courts may consider an itemized statement furnished by a lienor in response to a NY Lien Law §38 request in determining whether a lien may be summarily discharged,[233] and have considered a lienor's attachments to its notice of lien as well.[234]

Procedural Defects

Where a lien is defective for not being filed within the statutory period, for not being filed in the proper place, or for not being continued in a timely fashion, it may be discharged. A discharge because the lien has lapsed is self-executing and no court action is necessary.[235] Discharge for any other defect requires a court order.

---

any surplus becomes an Article 3-A trust asset or is held for the benefit of subsequent lienors).

[228] *In re* Tumac Realty Corp, 203 Misc 649, 123 NYS2d 642 (Kings 1952).

[229] Melniker v Grae, 82 AD2d 798, 439 NYS2d 409 (1981).

[230] NY Lien Law §§19(6) (private lien), 21(7) (public lien).

[231] Melniker v Grae, 82 AD2d 798, 439 NYS2d 409 (1981); Di-Com Corp v Active Sprinkler Corp, 36 AD2d 20, 318 NYS2d 249 (1971) (lienor unlicensed); Milbank-Frawley Hous Dev Fund Co v Marshall Constr Co, 71 Misc 2d 42, 335 NYS2d 598 (NY 1972) (lien had been waived); *contra* DiCamillo v Navitsky, 90 Misc 2d 923, 396 NYS2d 585 (Putnam 1977) (court discharged lien that was facially valid but proved invalid through extrinsic evidence where lienor made no request to amend).

[232] DiCamillo v Navitsky, 90 Misc 2d 923, 396 NYS2d 585 (Putnam 1977).

[233] *In re* Oster, 31 Misc 2d 253, 219 NYS2d 988 (Oneida 1961).

[234] Piston v Lincoln Supply Co, 37 Misc 2d 1003, 239 NYS2d 20 (Onondaga 1963).

[235] NY Lien Law §§19(2) (private lien), 20(2) (public lien). An owner is entitled to an order cancelling an expired lien of record if it desires. Bretzfelder v Froman, 76 Misc 2d 1063, 352 NYS2d 549 (Westchester 1973) (notice of the motion to cancel must be given to the lienor's attorney); *In re* Jericho Jewish Center, 28 Misc 2d 458, 210 NYS2d

To discharge a lien for a failure to file it within the statutory time period or for its not being filed in the proper county or with the proper state authorities, the defect must be evident from the face of the lien.[236] Even where uncontroverted evidence establishes that the lien is invalid, it cannot be summarily cancelled unless the defect is obvious on the lien's face.[237]

§9.37 —Demand to Foreclose

Rather than wait for a lienor to let the lien expire or foreclose it, an interested party may demand that the lienor foreclose the lien or show cause why it should not be canceled.[238] The demand must be served personally on the lienor. The only questions before a court at a show cause hearing following a demand to foreclose motion are whether the lienor complied with the demand and, if not, whether the lienor can show good cause why not; the validity of the lien is not at issue.[239] The lienor is entitled to at least 30 days following service of the notice of demand to commence foreclosure of the lien. The notice must be specific and contain all elements required by §59 or §21-a of the NY Lien Law or the notice will be ineffective and the lien will not be canceled.[240]

To comply with the demand, the lienor must start a foreclosure action; an action seeking damages only does not comply with the demand and will result in the lien being canceled.[241]

A lien does not automatically fail by reason of a lienor's noncompliance with a demand to foreclose. A court has the power to excuse a lienor for not commencing the foreclosure action within the time stated in the notice.[242] Thus, in a case where the parties entered into settlement discussions following service of the notice, the court excused the lienor's failure to foreclose within the time period.[243]

---

77 (1960) (lienor must be served with order to show cause why the lien should not be canceled).

[236] NY Lien Law §§19(6) (private lien), 21(7) (public lien).

[237] Melniker v Grae, 82 AD2d 798, 439 NYS2d 409 (1981); Country Village Heights Condominium v Mario Bonito, Inc, 79 Misc 2d 1088, 363 NYS2d 501 (NY 1975).

[238] NY Lien Law §§59 (private lien), 21-a (public lien).

[239] In re Selwyn Realty Corp, 184 AD 355, 170 NYS 491 (1918).

[240] In re Euclid Concrete Corp, 279 AD 594, 107 NYS2d 237 (1951); Drake Constr Corp v Kenn Equip Co, 274 AD 809, 79 NYS2d 747 (1948).

[241] Miller v TA & JM Gen Contractors, Inc, 124 Misc 2d 273, 476 NYS2d 449 (Kings 1984); Department of Health v East Minster Realty Corp, 53 Misc 2d 957, 280 NYS2d 63 (NY 1967).

[242] Kim Kevin Corp v A&A Gibel Co, 20 AD2d 807, 248 NYS2d 741 (1964) (lienor given an extra 20 days to commence foreclosure); In re Empress Apts Inc, 26 Misc 2d 852, 203 NYS2d 972 (Kings 1960) (lienor commenced action 9 days late, but before show cause hearing); In re Rosen, 172 Misc 134, 13 NYS2d 1019 (Queens 1939) (29-day delay excused).

[243] In re Lasa Corp, 27 Misc 2d 495, 203 NYS2d 731 (Queens 1960) (lienor began foreclosure immediately after settlement discussions ended).

§9.38 Enforcing the Mechanic's Lien

A notice of mechanic's lien is only security for the underlying debt owed to the party claiming the lien. The lienor may sue on the underlying debt, foreclose the lien, or do both. The ultimate objective is the same: to make the lienor whole by obtaining payment of the money due for the services performed or materials supplied.

The procedure to enforce a lien is wholly statutory. An action to recover the debt can take any form recognized by statute or common law. While the actions are procedurally different, they stem from the same claim and can be brought in the same or separate actions, although it is not possible for a party to recover twice on the same claim.[244] An action on the debt will not bar a subsequent foreclosure action; conversely, an action to foreclose will not bar a subsequent action on the debt.

Placing aside the action on the debt, this chapter will focus on the foreclosure of a lien. The statute's provisions must be followed closely or foreclosure may be denied.

In an enforcement action, private liens are foreclosed against the real property improved or against the lien discharge bond surety and personal judgment is sought against any person liable for the debt upon which the lien is founded.[245] Public liens, however, are foreclosed against the funds of the public entity for which the improvement was made and against the contractor or subcontractor liable for the debt.[246] Although these differences affect some aspects of the foreclosure actions, both are enforced by a civil action in the same courts and manner.[247]

§9.39 —Deadline to Commence Action

An action to foreclose must be commenced[248] within the time the lien is valid or the lien will expire.[249] An action to foreclose cannot be commenced after the lien has expired. The action must be commenced with respect to each defendant for it to continue the lien against that defendant.[250]

---

[244] Smith v Fleischman, 23 AD 355, 48 NYS 234 (1897) ("where a lienor has chosen to bring an action at law, that does not affect his right to continue a lien and, any time before the satisfaction of the judgment, resort to a foreclosure of the lien. It is declared to be a cumulative remedy.").

[245] NY Lien Law §41.

[246] Id §42.

[247] Id.

[248] NY Civ Prac L & R §304; In re Selwyn Realty Corp, 184 AD 355, 170 NYS 491 (1st Dept), affd, 224 NY 559, 120 NE 876 (1918); Reliable Constr Corp v Relide Realty Corp, 6 Misc 2d 857, 162 NYS2d 550 (NY 1957).

[249] See §9.32 hereof for discussion of the duration of private and public liens.

[250] SCM Corp v Hudson Overlook Co, 58 AD2d 578, 395 NYS2d 663 (1977).

§9.40 —Filing of Notice of Pendency

To properly commence an action, a lienor must file a notice of pendency, or *lis pendens*, within the applicable lien duration period, or the lien will expire (unless the lien is a private lien that has been bonded, in which case a notice of pendency is not required). The notice is filed with the county court of the county in which the notice of lien was filed[251] or, in the case of a public lien, with the State Comptroller or financial officer with whom the notice of lien was filed.[252]

A notice of pendency may not be filed when a private lien has been discharged through a bond or deposit.[253] A public lien always requires a notice of pendency.

§9.41 —Lien Foreclosure and Arbitration

Commencing an arbitration action is not the same as commencing a foreclosure action and will not stop a lien from expiring. Arbitration cannot determine the validity of a lien or what amount, if any, can be charged against the liened property; these issues can be determined only in a lien foreclosure.[254] Similarly, arbitration cannot determine whether a lien has been willfully exaggerated.[255] It is not unusual, however, for a lienor to be required to address the claim underlying the lien through arbitration due to an arbitration clause in its contract. In such cases, the arbitrators usually determine the validity of the basic lien claim, while the foreclosure action is postponed pending the arbitrators' decision.[256] Once the arbitrators rule on the validity and value of the amount claimed due the lienor, the lienor may initiate or renew the foreclosure action and seek the equitable remedies available.[257]

Filing a notice of lien is never a waiver of a party's right to arbitrate,[258] nor is commencing a foreclosure action.[259]

---

[251] NY Lien Law §17.

[252] *Id* §18.

[253] Bargabos Constr Co v Realty Intl, Inc, 96 Misc 2d 1028, 410 NYS2d 263 (Onondaga 1978).

[254] Brescia Constr Co v Walart Constr Co, 264 NY 260, 190 NE 484 (1934).

[255] Reeve Serv Corp v Raab, 64 AD2d 826, 407 NYS2d 315 (1978).

[256] If a foreclosure action has begun, it is usually stayed through court order until the arbitration is completed. If an action has not begun, the lienor can continue its lien through extensions until arbitration is completed.

[257] NY Lien Law §35.

[258] *Id*.

[259] A. Burgart, Inc v Foster-Lipkins Corp, 63 Misc 2d 930, 313 NYS2d 831 (Monroe), *affd*, 38 AD2d 779, 328 NYS2d 856, *affd* 30 NY2d 901, 287 NE2d 269, 335 NYS2d 562 (1970); DMC Constr Corp v A. Leo Nach Steel Corp, 50 AD2d 560, 375 NYS2d 18 (1975).

§9.42 —Venue and Jurisdiction of Action

Private lien foreclosures are brought "in the supreme court or in a county court otherwise having jurisdiction, regardless of the amount of such debt, or in a court which has jurisdiction in an action founded on a contract for a sum of money equivalent to the amount of such debt."[260] Typically, this means that the action is brought in the county in which the real property improved is located since foreclosure of a mechanic's lien is an action affecting real property. Where the lien has been discharged through a bond, the action may be brought in any county that has personal jurisdiction. Public lien foreclosures are brought "in the same court and in the same manner" as private foreclosures.[261]

§9.43 —Courts of Record and Courts Not of Record

Under the New York Lien Law, a mechanic's lien may be enforced in either a court of record[262] or a court not of record.[263] The distinction is important as the different courts require that different parties be named, may address different issues, and may affect the owner's interest differently. A court of record has legal and equitable powers;[264] a court not of record has legal powers only. A foreclosure action in a court not of record is based upon the contractual liability of the defendant, not upon mechanic's lien theories of the lienor's work benefiting the property. In a court not of record, a lienor is barred from recovery from the real property improved and is limited to recovery from the obligor on the contract, even where a subsequent purchaser has full knowledge of the lien.[265]

Public lien foreclosures are brought "in the same court and in the same manner" as private lien foreclosures,[266] although it is not clear whether a public lien foreclosure may be brought in a court not of record.[267]

---

[260] NY Lien Law §41.

[261] *Id* §42 (McKinney 1966 & Supp 1992).

[262] NY Lien Law §43.

[263] *Id* §46.

[264] Not all courts of record have full equitable powers and are able to foreclose mechanics' liens. Generally, all supreme courts of the state and the county courts have the full powers necessary to enforce mechanics' liens. Local courts of record, such as the city courts, generally are not able to fully foreclose the liens and are limited to the same powers as courts not of record. The exceptions to this rule are the New York Civil Court and the Yonkers City Court, which have full equitable powers and are able to enforce fully a mechanics' liens, within their monetary jurisdictional limits. *See Jensen's* §§336-340 (on Mech Lien Law, by E. Marks; 1963 & Supp 1983).

[265] La May & Poudrier, Inc v Smith, 3 Misc 2d 843, 150 NYS2d 71 (Suffolk 1956).

[266] NY Lien Law §42.

[267] See brief discussion at 76 NY Jur 2d §156 (1989).

Special provision for service, return, default judgments, and execution in courts not of record is provided in the Lien Law.[268] This chapter discusses actions brought in courts of record as they are the majority of lien foreclosures. Further, it is prudent to foreclose liens in a court of record as a matter of course.

§9.44 —Necessary Parties

Section 44 of the NY Lien Law lists those entities that are necessary parties to a lien foreclosure action in a court of record. Those parties that must be named as defendants are:

1. All mechanics' lienors of record (upon the same real property) as of the filing of the notice of pendency;[269] if no notice of pendency is required, all mechanics' lienors[270]
2. All subsequent lienors and claimants, "by judgment, mortgage, or otherwise, filed, docketed or recorded" prior to filing of the notice of pendency;[271] if no notice of pendency is required, all subsequent lienors and claimants[272]
3. All owners of record, regardless of the nature of their ownership.[273]
4. The state, when the lien is filed against funds of the state[274]
5. The surety on the discharge bond, if any[275]

Failure to join a necessary party is not always fatal. The missing party may later be joined through court order;[276] or, where the objection to nonjoinder is not made promptly and the missing defendant has such a limited interest that the issues can be completely determined without that defendant, joinder is not necessary.[277]

Section 62 of the NY Lien Law provides a means whereby a mechanic's lienor,[278] not originally joined because its lien was filed after the foreclosure action

---

[268] NY Lien Law §§46-53.

[269] NY Lien Law §44(1).

[270] Id §44(4).

[271] Id §44(2).

[272] Id §44(4).

[273] Id §44(3). *Owner* includes the public entity that owns the public improvement. RE Crist, Inc v Lasker-Goldman Corp, 27 Misc 2d 552, 203 NYS2d 493 (NY 1960).

[274] NY Lien Law §44(6).

[275] Morton v Tucker, 145 NY 244 (1895).

[276] Spitz v M. Brooks & Sons, 210 AD 438, 206 NYS 313 (1924).

[277] Hawkins v Mapes-Reeve Constr Co, 178 NY 236, 70 NE 783 (1904).

[278] This section is specifically related to mechanics' lienors. Mercury Paint Corp v Seaboard Painting Corp, 112 Misc 2d 529, 447 NYS2d 191 (NY 1981) (a judgment creditor is not a mechanic's lienor and may not be joined later); Hurley Sand & Gravel Co v Italian-American Civil Rights League, 76 Misc 2d 305, 350 NYS2d 837 (Ulster 1973) (a judgment creditor who improved the property may not be added per this section).

336   MECHANICS' LIENS

was begun, may join the action at any time up to the day of trial upon application to the plaintiff's attorney or by application of any other party to the court that the omitted lienor be joined.[279] The joinder of the new party shall not cause substantial delay in the trial or cause prejudice to the proceedings.[280]

§9.45 —Form of Complaint

In a complaint to foreclose a mechanic's lien, the plaintiff must allege all facts essential to its right to recover. The complaint should allege sufficient facts to show:

1. Typical introductory allegations, including jurisdiction, venue, and capacity and identity of parties, including corporate status, licenses, etc.
2. Ownership and description of the property[281]
3. The terms of the contract between the general contractor and the owner or public entity[282]
4. Existence of a lien fund (money owing from owner/public entity to general contractor) at the time of filing of the lien
5. The terms of the agreement or contract by which the plaintiff improved the real property
6. That the plaintiff improved the real property pursuant to the agreement or contract listed in number 5 above and the specific way that the plaintiff improved the property (e.g., delivery of described materials to subcontractor A)
7. That money is due the plaintiff and was due at the time the lien was filed[283]
8. Particulars of the lien, including its substance, filing, and service[284]
9. That the lien was not paid or otherwise released or discharged, or, if it was discharged by bond or deposit, the facts of such discharge
10. That the named defendants have claims or interest in the real property[285]
11. That plaintiff has named all parties with claims or interests in the real property, or fund, if a public lien; and
12. A prayer for relief that requests that the plaintiff's lien be deemed valid and to have priority over all other liens and claims against the real property or fund, that the property be sold and the plaintiff's lien paid from

---

[279] NY Lien Law §62.
[280] Id.
[281] Entenman v Anderson, 106 AD 149, 94 NYS 45 (1905).
[282] Id. The owner's consent to the improvement must be shown.
[283] Lehmann v Kingston Plaza, Inc, 44 Misc 2d 63, 252 NYS2d 964 (Albany 1964).
[284] Miller v TA & JM Gen Contractors, Inc, 124 Misc 2d 273, 476 NYS2d 449 (Kings 1984).
[285] Entenman v Anderson, 106 AD 149, 94 NYS 45 (1905).

the proceeds (or that the plaintiff be paid from the fund, bond, or deposit), a deficiency judgment, personal judgment on the contract, and such other and further relief as the court deems proper.[286]

The complaint must be verified.[287]

§9.46 Answers of Defendant Lienors

A defendant that is also a lienor must affirmatively set forth its lien in its answer or the lien will be deemed to be waived.[288] The answer must be served on every party and, in a public improvement lien foreclosure, upon the state or public entity involved.[289] A lienor defendant need not respond to the answers and assertions of liens of other lienor defendants, as they are deemed denied.[290]

§9.47 Defenses to the Foreclosure Action

In addition to traditional defenses to construction contract actions, such as breach of contract, nonperformance, failure to correct defective work, delay, design defects, etc., there are several defenses to mechanics' liens actions that are unique and often more powerful than typical construction defenses. These defenses can result in a lien's being declared void and removed from the property, although they will not necessarily remove personal liability where it exists.

§9.48 —Defective and Expired Liens

As was discussed in §§9.26, 9.27, and 9.36 hereof, there are many ways in which a lien may be defective. It may have been filed or foreclosed too late, it may name the wrong owner, it may be for work that is not lienable, or it may have been improperly filed. Where the defect is substantial and the lien cannot be said to comply with the statute, it must be voided as invalid and ineffective.[291]

---

[286] For a detailed discussion of each of these components, see *Jensen's* §§383-403 (on Mech Lien Law, by E. Marks; 1963 & Supp 1983); 76 NY Jur 2d §§244-271, Mechanics' Liens (1989).

[287] Sherman v Freuhaff, 177 Misc 2d 727, 32 NYS2d 945 (Queens 1941).

[288] NY Lien Law §44(5). The only exception is where the lien is admitted in the complaint and is not contested by any other defendant. As this cannot be expected as a matter of course, it is prudent to set forth the lien in the answer, even where the complaint admits the lien. By doing this, no delay will occur, and no amendment will be necessary in the event a defendant, such as the owner, contests the lien.

[289] *Id* §63. The state must be served within 40 days after the defendant was served with the complaint.

[290] *Id* §44(5).

[291] For discussion of each manner in which a lien may be defective, review the applicable sections of this chapter. Requirements and standards for adjudicating the validity of mechanics' liens are discussed throughout §§9.02-9.24, 9.26-9.33, and 9.36.

§9.49 —Willful Exaggeration

The affirmative defense or counterclaim of willful exaggeration, available under both private and public lien foreclosure actions, is a powerful weapon. A lien found to be willfully exaggerated not only is void, but also subjects the lienor to liability to the owner or general contractor.[292] The purpose of the statute is to "punish willful exaggeration and not honest differences . . . and to protect an owner or contractor from fictitious, groundless, and fraudulent lienors."[293] A failure by a lienor to prove all items comprising the lien amount does not, of itself, establish a willful exaggeration.[294]

The defense and counterclaim is a two-step process: first, the lien is found to be willfully exaggerated and is voided; second, the defendant owner or contractor is awarded damages from the lienor. The remedy and liability provided by statute are exclusive.[295]

Section 39-a of the NY Lien Law provides that the damages awarded to an owner or a contractor shall include any premium paid to obtain a bond to discharge the lien, the interest on any money deposited to discharge the lien, reasonable attorneys' fees incurred in discharging the lien or in voiding the lien for willful exaggeration, and the amount of the exaggeration. The amount of the exaggeration is also deducted, as an offset, from the amount the court finds the lienor is due. Thus, the lienor suffers a double loss due to its exaggeration. The following case example illustrates the workings and interaction of §§39 and 39-a of the NY Lien Law.

In *Grimpel v Hochman*,[296] the court declared a lien void for willful exaggeration. The lien claimed that $5,102.00 was due the lienor; the lien amount should have been $3,985.05. Thus, the lien was exaggerated by $1,116.95 or by 20%. The court awarded the defendant owner the following damages:

$1,116.95	-	amount of exaggeration
86.20	-	20% of the premiums charged on the bond to discharge the lien
+ 408.16	-	20% of the owner's attorneys' fees
$1,611.31	-	damages to owner

The contractor lost his lien but was awarded damages as follows:

$2,737.19	-	amount due under contract (this is less than the amount of lien found legitimate due to reductions for poor work)

---

[292] NY Lien Law §§39, 39-a.

[293] E-J Elec Installation Co v Miller & Raved, Inc, 51 AD2d 264, 265, 380 NYS2d 702, *appeal dismissed*, 39 NY2d 898, 352 NE2d 584, 386 NYS2d 397 (1976).

[294] A&E Plumbing, Inc v Biedoff, 66 AD2d 455, 413 NYS2d 776 (1979).

[295] E-J Elec Installation Co v Miller & Raved, Inc, 51 AD2d 264, 265, 380 NYS2d 702, *appeal dismissed*, 39 NY2d 898, 352 NE2d 584, 386 NYS2d 397 (1976).

[296] 74 Misc 2d 39, 343 NYS2d 507 (NY 1972).

<u>-1,611.31</u> - damages to owner for lien exaggeration
$1,125.88 - damages to contractor

Thus, the dishonest contractor, who was due $2,737.19 for work done, owes the defendant owner $485.43.

Willful exaggeration was found in a case where the plaintiff performed some work pursuant to the alleged contract with the state to cut brush and trees in a state park and then brought an action to foreclose a lien in the amount of $2,000.00 for moneys due a subcontractor, when it was determined that the greatest amount that could be due was $1,500.00.[297] Willful exaggeration was found where the plaintiff contractor failed to deduct four concededly omitted items of work claimed in its notice of lien to be the amount owed under the contract; the defendant owner was entitled to recover.[298] Where the contract price for work to be done is less than the mechanic's lien filed by the plaintiff, it is an indication of willful exaggeration.[299] Willful exaggeration was also found in a case where the party seeking the mechanic's lien upon real property for installing a boiler had tampered with the evidence, thereby increasing the price of the boiler by $1,000.00.[300] Finally, in a case where the contractor had billed the owner for an unpaid balance of $3,985.05 and then two months later filed a lien for $5,482.10, the court found the exaggeration to be deliberate and allowed the owner to recover damages.[301]

However, willful exaggeration was not established in a case where the contractor made a claim against the owner in good faith for the reasonable value of material and labor, including a percentage for overhead and profit.[302] In a case where the plaintiff subcontractor still owed the contractor $2,000.00 for work to be done even after he filed an $11,000.00 mechanic's lien, no willful exaggeration was found since the subcontractor was still entitled to a lien for $1,629.00 in extras.[303] A mere inaccuracy in the amount of a lien does not amount to willful exaggeration.[304]

§9.50 —No Fund to Which Lien Can Attach

As has been discussed throughout this chapter, an owner's liability to a subcontractor is strictly limited to the amount of the *lien fund*—that amount of

---

[297] Northern Tree Serv v Donovan Tree Serv, 36 AD2d 22, 318 NYS2d 638 (3d Dept 1971).

[298] Soundwall Constr Corp v Moncarol Constr Corp, 290 NYS2d 363 (1968).

[299] Aluminum Fair, Inc v Abdella, 90 AD2d 603, 456 NYS2d 184 (3d Dept 1982).

[300] A&E Plumbing, Inc v Budoff, 66 AD2d 455, 413 NYS2d 776 (3d Dept 1979).

[301] Grimpel v Hochman, 74 Misc 2d 39, 343 NYS2d 507 (NY 1972).

[302] PJ Panzeca, Inc v Alizio, 52 AD2d 919, 383 NYS2d 396 (2d Dept 1976).

[303] Hansen Excavating Co v Benjamin, 36 Misc 2d 686, 233 NYS2d 589 (Nassau 1962).

[304] Goodman v Del-Sa-Co Foods, Inc, 15 NY2d 191, 257 NYS2d 142 (1965).

money owed the general contractor.[305] If a subcontractor cannot prove that money was due, or thereafter became due, from the owner to the contractor at the time the notice of lien was filed, there is no fund to which the subcontractor's lien can attach and the lien is void. Similarly, if a materialman cannot prove that money was due, or thereafter became due, from the contractor to the subcontractor with whom the materialman dealt, there will be no fund to which the materialman's lien can attach. Each tier of subcontractors, materialmen, and laborers has its own lien fund and may look only to its own lien fund for recovery. A lien attaches only to funds owed to the party directly above the lienor.[306] The fact that there is a lien fund that benefits a subcontractor does not mean necessarily that there is a lien fund that benefits that subcontractor's materialmen.

§9.51 The Lien Foreclosure Trial

In many ways, the lien foreclosure trial is like any other trial: the same rules regarding discovery and evidence apply; there are pre-trial, trial, and post-trial motions, interim hearings, testimony, and findings and judgments. Each party has to prove the allegations that make that party's cause of action, affirmative defense, crossclaim, or counterclaim.[307]

The lien foreclosure trial is often more complicated than other trials, however, due to the number of parties with claims involved. Each party's claims must be adjudicated as though its claims were raised in the complaint. Once the validity of the plaintiff's lien is determined, the action does not cease. The validity of other mechanics' liens must be determined, as must the validity of liens claimed through mortgage or judgment.[308] Further, when a lienor fails to prove that its lien is valid, it may still be entitled, in the same action, to judgment against any party on the basis of money due or in contract[309] or quantum meruit.[310]

A mechanic's lien foreclosure action, as an equitable action, is not triable to a jury; nor are issues raised in counterclaims to a lien foreclosure.[311] There have been exceptions to this rule, however, such as in a case where the com-

---

[305] NY Lien Law §4; Van Clif v Van Vechten, 130 NY 571, 29 NE 1017 (1892); Trustees of Hanover Square Realty Investors v Weintraub, 52 AD2d 600, 382 NYS2d 110 (1976); Central Valley Concrete Corp v Montgomery Ward & Co, 34 AD2d 860, 310 NYS2d 925 (1970). See discussion at §9.34 hereof.

[306] Philan Dept of Borden Co v Foster-Lipkins Corp, 39 AD2d 633, 331 NYS2d 138 (1972).

[307] Generally, the lienor has the burden of proof on those matters set forth in the lienor's complaint, answer, crossclaim, or counterclaim. See §9.45 for a discussion of those matters that a lienor must allege.

[308] See NY Lien Law §§44(2), (4), and (5), 45.

[309] Id §54.

[310] EJ Dayton, Inc v Brock, 120 AD2d 560, 502 NYS2d 53 (1986).

[311] NY Lien Law §45.

plaint included eight causes of action that sought money damages on contract claims and there were nine counterclaims for money damages on contract and tort claims.[312]

It is wise to resolve as many issues as possible prior to trial, whether by motion, stipulation, or admission. This general rule of litigation is nowhere more important than in a lien foreclosure action. In an action with so many parties and such potential for numerous and confusing claims and theories crisscrossing among the parties, the elimination of as many issues and parties as possible before trial should ultimately result in a quicker and less expensive resolution.

§9.52 Priority of Private Improvement Liens

The priority of mechanics' liens is the most confusing issue in mechanic's lien practice. It is important to consider a lienor's priority in deciding whether to foreclose a lien. It does a lienor no good to foreclose a lien upon a property if that property has so many other encumbrances that have priority over the mechanic's lien that the mechanic's lienor would receive nothing from a sale of the property. Following are some basic rules that, subject to exception, are helpful in determining the priority of a lien:

1. Generally, a mechanic's lien has priority over any claim that was filed against the real property after the notice of lien was filed, except claims of others who improved the property or other mechanics' lienors.[313]

2. Among mechanics' liens of the same class there is parity, regardless of when the notice of lien was filed.[314] There are statutory preferences for laborers over all other lienors and for subcontractors and materialmen over their contractors.[315]

3. A recorded purchase money mortgage has priority over all subsequently filed claims, including liens.[316]

4. A mortgage, building loan mortgage, or conveyance of any kind, if recorded before the improvement began, has priority over any lien to the extent of advances made prior to the filing of the notice of lien.[317]

5. A lien has priority over any mortgage, building loan mortgage, or convey-

---

[312] John W. Cowper Co v Buffalo Hotel Dev Venture, 99 AD2d 19, 471 NYS2d 913 (1984) (the court held that the action was not "essentially" one for foreclosure and that therefore, the defendant did not waive its right to a jury trial by its assertion of legal counterclaims).

[313] NY Lien Law §13(1).

[314] Id.

[315] Id; NY Lien Law §§25(3), (4), 56.

[316] Shilowitz v Wedler, 237 AD 330, 261 NYS 351 (1932); NY Lien Law §13(4).

[317] Id §13(1-a), (2), (3).

ance of any kind recorded more than four months after completion of the improvement.[318]

6. A mortgage, building loan mortgage, or conveyance that was recorded after the improvement began but within four months of its completion has priority over a lien only if the mortgage or conveyance includes a trust covenant.[319]

7. A lien never has priority over an assignment of moneys due, or to become due, under a contract for the improvement of real property; at best, the lien has parity.[320]

8. A lien always has priority over a creditor whose debt is not based upon an improvement of the property, regardless of whether the claim is based on an assignment, an attachment, or a judgment, and regardless of the time of recording of the claim.[321]

9. A lien has priority over any advances made under any contract or mortgage after the notice of lien was filed.[322]

Each of these rules assumes that the lien, claim, mortgage, conveyance, etc., is valid and has been properly recorded and filed, pursuant to all applicable statutes.

Sections 9.53-9.58 contain more detailed discussions of the relative priority of building loan contracts and mortgages, mortgages, assignments of money due under contracts for the improvement of real property, miscellaneous liens, and subsequent purchasers in relation to a mechanic's lien, and subordination of liens.

§9.53 —Building Loan Contracts and Mortgages

A *building loan contract* is defined as a contract in which a lender agrees to make advances to an owner for the improvement of real property, such advances to be secured by a mortgage.[323] A *building loan mortgage* is a mortgage made pursuant to a building loan contract and may include consolidation of the new loan with an existing mortgage on the property.[324]

---

[318] *Id.* Although this is the way the statute reads, it must be questioned whether this four-month period is the result of an oversight by the legislature. In 1982 when the legislature extended the time a lienor has to file a lien from four to eight months (on all but single family dwellings), see NY Lien Law §10, it did not amend the priorities sections.

[319] *Id* §13(1-a), (2), (3); also see preceding footnote.

[320] *Id* §13(1-a), (6).

[321] *Id* §13(1).

[322] *Id.*

[323] NY Lien Law §2(13).

[324] *Id* §2(14).

A building loan mortgage delivered and recorded has priority over a mechanic's lien to the extent of advances actually made prior to the filing of the lien,[325] *if* the building loan mortgage or contract contains the trust covenant required by NY Lien Law §13(3)[326] *and* the contract was filed as required by NY Lien Law §22.[327] Advances made after a lien is filed do not have priority.

§9.54 —Mortgages

A purchase money mortgage recorded before improvement of the property began has priority over any mechanic's lien. This rule is based upon the common law principle of "first in time, first in right."[328] Equally simple, a mortgage recorded more than four months after the improvement is completed has no priority over a mechanic's lien.[329] The only issue regarding priority of a mortgage arises if the mortgage is recorded after work began on the improvement but before the improvement had been completed for four months.

In such an instance, the mortgage is prior to subsequently filed mechanics' liens to the extent of advances made before the notice of lien was filed, if the mortgage includes a trust covenant, discussed in **§9.53** above,[330] or reference to the trust provision of NY Lien Law §13.[331]

Pursuant to NY Lien Law §7, a mortgage made for the purpose of defeating liens is void and of no effect against a lien.

§9.55 —Assignment of Moneys Due under Contract for Improvement of Real Property

An assignment of money due, or to become due, under a contract for the improvement of real property (in this section only, hereinafter referred to as *assignment*) pursuant to §§15 and 26 of the NY Lien Law is afforded priority

---

[325] Monroe Sav Bank v Stark-Center Corp, 79 Misc 2d 952, 361 NYS2d 839 (Seneca 1974).

[326] The trust covenant must specify that the party, whether owner or contractor, receiving the advances and entitled to receive advances will hold them as a trust fund that will be applied first to pay for the cost of the improvement. This covenant does not obligate the lender to make sure that advances are applied properly. If the contract or mortgage contains the phrase "subject to the trust fund provisions of section thirteen of the lien law," the covenant is deemed to have been made. NY Lien Law §13(3).

[327] The contract must be in writing, be verified, show the consideration paid, or to be paid, for the loan and all other loan expenses, and show the net sum available to the borrower. The contract must be filed in the county clerk's office of each county in which the property is located, on or before the date the building loan mortgage is recorded. Any modifications to the contract must be filed within 10 days. Failure to file the contract causes the mortgage to lose its priority over subsequently filed mechanics' liens. NY Lien Law §22.

[328] Shilowitz v Wadler, 237 AD 330, 261 NYS 351 (1932).

[329] NY Lien Law §13(1).

[330] *Id* §13(2).

[331] *Id* §13(3).

over mechanics' liens in special instances. An assignment, properly made and filed,[332] has priority over subsequently filed mechanics' liens to the extent of moneys advanced before *any* mechanic's lien or other assignment is filed, if the assignment contains a trust covenant.[333] Advances made after a mechanic's lien or some other assignment is filed are treated as mechanics' liens.[334] An assignment filed after any mechanic's lien or other assignment is filed is considered in parity with mechanics' lienors as to pre- and post-filing advances.[335]

§9.56 —Miscellaneous Liens

Judgments

Judgments for matters not related to the improvement of the real property are always subordinate to a mechanic's lien, regardless of when they were filed.[336] Judgments for matters related to the improvement of real property—whether for the performance of labor, furnishing of materials, or lending of money—may or may not be prior to mechanics' liens. The Lien Law statute seems to imply that a mechanic's lien is on a par with any claimant whose claim is based upon the improvement of real property.[337]

Tax Liens

A mechanic's lien filed prior to a state or federal tax lien has priority over

---

[332] For an assignment to be valid as a prior obligation, a notice of assignment meeting the requirements of NY Lien Law §15(2) must be filed within 10 days of the assignment in the county clerk's office of each county in which the real property to be improved is located. In lieu of a notice of assignment, the contract assigned, or a statement containing the substance of the contract assigned, along with a copy of the assignment, must be filed within 10 days of the assignment in the county clerk's office of each county in which the real property to be improved is located.

[333] NY Lien Law §13(1-a), (6).

[334] *Id.*

[335] *Id* §13(1-a).

[336] NY Lien Law §13(1).

[337] *See id. But see* Anderman v 1395 E 52nd St Realty Corp, 60 Misc 2d 437, 303 NYS2d 474 (Sullivan 1969) (where judgment creditor received judgment for value of materials furnished but failed to file a mechanic's lien, court held that its status was that of a judgment creditor and not a lienor); *and* City & County Sav v Oakwood Holding Corp, 88 Misc 2d 198, 387 NYS2d 512 (Chemung 1976) (when a personal judgment was obtained by a mechanic's lienor prior to the filing of other mechanics' liens, the court held that the judgment was prior to subsequently filed mechanics' liens, thereby allowing a mechanic's lienor to better his priority, from parity with other mechanics' lienors to superiority; the court held that the silence of the statute as regards improvement judgments docketed prior to the filing of a lien required the application of the common law rule of "first in time, first in right"; here, the judgment lienor filed a mechanic's lien on July 7, 1973, but also received and docketed a judgment on the debt on November 7, 1973; another party's mechanic's lien was filed on November 9, 1973); *see also* Cobleskill Sav & Loan Assn v Rickard, 15 AD2d 286, 223 NYS2d 246 (1962).

the tax lien.[338] Thus, in a case where property was sold through foreclosure of a federal tax lien, the property was sold subject to the mechanics' liens thereon and the purchaser had to either satisfy those liens or face foreclosure.[339] Further, due to the Lien Law's doctrine of parity among a class of lienors, any lien that is of the same class as the first filed mechanic's lien is prior to the tax lien. For example, if a materialman files a mechanic's lien on March 19, a federal tax lien for withholding taxes due for labor on the subject contract is filed on May 6, and a second materialman files a mechanic's lien on June 17, both of the materialmen's liens are prior to the tax lien.[340] Of course, a mechanic's lien filed *after* a tax lien has no priority.

Attorneys' Fees Lien

In a case where an attorney was due fees for successfully representing a contractor against an owner on a contract to improve real property, the attorney's charging lien was awarded priority over subcontractors' liens filed subsequent to the attachment of the attorney's lien, which was held to attach from the beginning of the action.[341]

§9.57 —Subsequent Purchasers

Those who purchase improved property after the improvement has begun but within four months of its completion and who record the conveyance have priority over subsequently filed mechanics' liens, if the conveyance contains a trust covenant clause. Similarly, a vendee under an executory contract for sale of the property has priority over subsequently filed liens if the contract was properly recorded[342] and specifies the total amount of payments due the vendor before title will be conveyed. The vendee's priority is to the extent of money paid by the vendee to the vendor prior to the filing of the lien.[343]

---

[338] Mercury Paint Corp v Seaboard Painting Corp, 112 Misc 2d 529, 447 NYS2d 191 (NY 1981). The priority of a federal tax lien is determined by federal law, which generally follows the "first in time, first in right" rule, unless that rule is varied by statute as is done by NY Lien Law §25(4) which provides parity among lienors of the same class. See also 26 USC §6323, which provides that most rights in property that arise prior to a tax lien are protected and are prior to the tax lien, including pre-tax lien mechanics' liens.

[339] Peter K. Freuh, Inc v Kass, 120 Misc 2d 330, 465 NYS2d 841 (Albany 1983).

[340] Mercury Paint Corp v Seaboard Painting Corp, 112 Misc 2d 529, 447 NYS2d 191 (NY 1981).

[341] Travis v Nansen, 176 Misc 44, 26 NYS2d 590 (Broome 1941). This principle did not apply where an attorney represented a defendant who won no award and against whom a deficiency judgment was entered. *In re* Morsillo, 17 AD2d 894, 233 NYS2d 689 (1962).

[342] NY Real Prop Law §294 (McKinney 1989 & Supp 1991).

[343] NY Lien Law §13(2).

§9.58 —Agreements to Subordinate

While it is difficult to imagine why a lienor would wish to lower any priority it may have, the Lien Law provides that a lienor may agree to subordinate its liens to a trust mortgage,[344] an assignment of building loan proceeds,[345] a subsequent mortgage,[346] or a subsequent purchase.[347] Subordination requires the consent of the lienors of at least 55 per cent of the aggregate amount of lien claims and execution and recording of the consent. Such consent subordinates not only consenting and nonconsenting lienors,[348] but also judgment and attachment claimants. Thus, the obtaining, execution, and filing of consents to subordination must be done properly.

Where there is subordination to a subsequent mortgage or purchase, a specified amount is deposited with the clerk of the county. In such cases, the lienor may still foreclose its lien; the court directs the application of the deposit to all claims established in the foreclosure action.[349]

§9.59 Priority of Public Improvement Liens

The relative priorities of public improvement liens are simple when compared to private ones. The only claimants that need to be prioritized are mechanics' lienors and assignees of moneys due under contracts for public improvements; these priorities are determined in the same way as for private liens.

Thus, mechanics' liens claimants have parity within their class[350] and assignees have or do not have priority, depending on when they come into existence. The assignee has priority to the extent of advances made before any mechanic's lien or other assignment was filed, if the assignment contains a trust covenant.[351] Advances made after liens or other assignments are filed and all advances made on any assignment other than the first filed assignment are on a parity with mechanics' lienors, if the assignments contain trust covenants.[352]

---

[344] NY Lien Law §26.
[345] *Id*.
[346] *Id* §29.
[347] *Id* §31.
[348] Laborers' liens are not subject to subordination without their express consent. *Id* §33.
[349] *Id* §29.
[350] NY Lien Law §25.
[351] *Id* §25(1), (5).
[352] *Id* §25(1), (2), (5).

§9.60 Parity and Preference among Mechanics' Lienors

All mechanics' lienors, and other claimants whose recorded claims[353] are based upon an improvement of the real property and are necessary or joined parties to the action to foreclose, have the same priority in relation to other claims, regardless of when their liens were filed.[354] They do not, however, have complete parity among themselves. The Lien Law statute provides preference to certain lienors over others. Essentially, this preference is best stated as follows: The first payment to mechanics' lienors paid out of foreclosure proceeds is paid to the tier of lienors furthest removed from the owner or state.[355] Lienors at the same level share pro rata in any proceeds.

Thus, in *private* liens, the order of preference is as follows: (1) laborers for daily and weekly wages;[356] (2) subcontractors and materialmen who supplied other subcontractors; (3) subcontractors and materialmen who supplied the general contractor; and (4) the general contractor and others who directly contracted with the owner.

In *public* liens, the order of preference is the same, except there is no fourth tier.

It is important to remember the concept of the *lien fund* in considering preference among lienors.[357] If Lienor A filed his lien when there was $5,000 in the lien fund, and Lienor B filed her lien after the lien fund was exhausted, Lienor B's lien is without preference because it could not attach to any lien fund.

§9.61 Obtaining a Judgment

Private Lien Foreclosure

The judgment in a *private* lien foreclosure action is very similar to the judgment in a mortgage foreclosure. In fact, the Lien Law provides that the provisions of the Real Property Actions and Proceedings Law relating to real property mortgage foreclosures, sales, and distributions of proceeds apply to mechanics' liens foreclosures in courts of record.[358]

Following trial of the matter, the court enters judgment for the prevailing lienors and orders that the property be sold by the county sheriff or court ref-

---

[353] Williamson & Adams, Inc v McMahon-McEntegart, Inc, 256 AD 313, 10 NYS2d 37 (1939) (unrecorded claimants have neither priority nor parity).

[354] Drachman Structurals, Inc v Anthony Rivara Contracting Co, 78 Misc 2d 486, 356 NYS2d 974 (Nassau 1974).

[355] NY Lien Law §56.

[356] A laborer is not necessarily one who does physical labor. JV Vrooman Sons Co v Pierce, 179 AD 436, 165 NYS 929 (1917).

[357] *See* §9.34.

[358] NY Lien Law §43.

348 MECHANICS' LIENS

eree to satisfy the liens against it plus sale expenses and costs of the action.[359] If the liens have been discharged by deposit or bond, the judgment orders satisfaction of the liens from the fund[360] and enters personal judgment against the surety, if named as a party.[361]

Obviously, the goal of a foreclosure action is the speedy and inexpensive recovery of moneys owing the lienor. Through a judgment of personal liability, for sale of the property, and for a deficiency, a lienor can realize its goal. It is often easier and quicker to realize satisfaction on the personal judgment, through garnishment or attachment of cash or money-equivalent assets, such as stocks and bonds, rather than to pursue a sale of the property. Thus, it is wise to demand information regarding the debtor's assets through postjudgment debtor interrogatories as soon as possible following the judgment. This chapter assumes that foreclosure is necessary and does not discuss collection of personal or deficiency judgments.

Once a judgment of foreclosure has been entered, an owner may avoid sale of its property by paying the adjudicated amount or by agreeing to deliver or deposit "bills, notes, securities, or other obligations or any other property" as substitution for the real property.[362]

Public Lien Foreclosure

In a *public* lien foreclosure, the judgment is much the same as a judgment against a bond or deposit. First, the court determines the amount due on the contract by the public entity to the general contractor, then it determines the amount owed by the general contractor to each subcontractor, and, finally, from each subcontractor to its subcontractors, materialmen, and laborers. The judgment orders the public entity to pay the lienors directly the sums found due with interest and costs, to the extent of the sum found owed by the public entity to the general contractor.[363]

§9.62 —Amount of Judgment

A judgment in a lienor's favor should include all costs of the improvement[364] as determined due less any offsets and counterclaims. The Lien Law statute

---

[359] The form and contents of the judgment are set forth at NY Real Prop Acts Law §1351 (McKinney 1979 & Supp 1992).

[360] *See* §9.34.

[361] Coppola Bros Excavating Corp v Melnick & Co, 55 AD2d 522, 389 NYS2d 7 (1976), *affd as modified*, 56 AD2d 524, 391 NYS2d 121, *affd*, 43 NY2d 752, 372 NE2d 797, 401 NYS2d 1009 (1977). If the surety on a bond has not been named, the foreclosing lienors may have to bring an action against the surety to recover the judgment.

[362] NY Lien Law §57.

[363] *Id* §60.

[364] NY Lien Law §2(5).

specifically includes interest[365] and costs[366] as part of the amount due a successful lienor. Although the amount of costs awarded rests in the court's discretion, a denial of interest and costs without any equitable reason is an abuse of discretion.[367]

The costs and expenses of the foreclosure sale are also recoverable.[368] As this amount cannot be determined before the sale, the judgment will leave the amount of sale costs blank with directions to the court clerk to enter the proper amount following the sale.

§9.63 Obtaining an Execution[369]

Before the property can be sold in a foreclosure sale, a notice of sale must be served upon all parties with an interest in the real property, published immediately preceding the sale either once a week for four consecutive weeks or twice a week for three consecutive weeks in a newspaper published in the county in which the real property is located, and posted on the property and in other public places.[370] The notice must contain a description of the property, the details of the judgment, and the time and exact place of sale.[371] In addition to the state rules found in the Real Property Actions and Proceedings Law, there are local rules in some counties that must be followed.

§9.64 Sale upon Execution

The foreclosure sale is conducted by the sheriff or referee, who reads the terms of the sale and then opens the bidding.[372] The successful bidder signs an agreement as to his or her purchase and acceptance of the terms of the purchase, pays a deposit to secure his or her bid, and schedules a closing date for transfer of title.[373]

---

[365] *Id* §§3, 5; CD Perry & Sons v Sarkisian Bros, 53 AD2d 932, 385 NYS2d 191 (1976).

[366] NY Lien Law §53.

[367] Macro M. Frisone, Inc v Paul Borg Constr Co, 40 AD2d 589, 334 NYS2d 590 (1972).

[368] NY Lien Law §53; NY Real Prop Acts Law §1354.

[369] Rarely will a lienor actually foreclose its lien against the property. Typically, the lender has priority and takes the property in satisfaction of the debt or the owner pays the judgment amount once it realizes it cannot postpone the inevitable any longer. Thus, the discussion here is brief and serves only as a basic introduction to the mechanisms of a foreclosure sale.

[370] The exact requirements for the notice of sale are found in §231 of the Real Prop Acts Law.

[371] *Id* §§231, 1351.

[372] NY Real Prop Acts Law §231.

[373] *Id* §1353.

§9.65 —Distribution of Proceeds

Foreclosure sale proceeds are paid first to satisfy the costs and expenses of the sale, including referee or sheriff fees, then to the party with first priority, and down through parties with lesser priorities until the proceeds are exhausted.[374] Surplus moneys are paid to parties claiming them through the court.[375]

§9.66 —Deficiency Judgments

Both the Lien Law[376] and the mortgage foreclosure law[377] provide for the award of deficiency judgments when the foreclosure sale proceeds are insufficient to meet the claims of all creditors. The presumption is that a foreclosure sale satisfies fully the debt against the property.[378] Thus, deficiency judgments are available only upon application to the court, and a failure to apply for a deficiency judgment causes the creditor to lose its right to pursue other assets of the debtor.[379]

Deficiency judgments may be awarded only against those parties who are personally liable on the debt and were personally served in the action.[380] Thus, in a public lien action, a deficiency may be awarded against the general contractor but not the public entity.

§9.67 —Setting Aside a Sale

Generally, a foreclosure sale will not be set aside where it was fair and free from fraud. The setting aside of a sale is within the court's discretion, which may be exercised under special circumstances upon application by any person whose rights and interests were "injuriously affected" by the foreclosure sale.[381] Factors that a court will consider include adequacy of notice, price, and conduct of sale.[382] A motion to set aside a sale must be brought within one year after the sale.[383]

---

[374] NY Real Prop Acts Law §1354.

[375] *Id* §1361.

[376] NY Lien Law §58.

[377] NY Real Prop Acts Law §1371.

[378] *Id* §1371(3); Pomperaug Realty Corp v Schulte Real Estate Co, 182 Misc 1080, 50 NYS2d 238 (NY 1944).

[379] NY Real Prop Acts Law §1371(3); Pomperaug Realty Corp v Schulte Real Estate Co, 182 Misc 1080, 50 NYS2d 238 (1944).

[380] NY Lien Law §58; NY Real Prop Acts Law §1371; Moore Golf, Inc v Lakeover Golf & Country Club, Inc, 49 AD2d 583, 370 NYS2d 156 (1975) (lessor who consented to lessee's improvements was not liable on a deficiency judgment resulting from the sale of his property); Tager v Healy Ave Realty Corp, 14 AD2d 584, 218 NYS2d 679 (1961).

[381] Goodell v Harrington, 76 NY 547 (1879).

[382] McCoy v Bailey, 24 Misc 2d 875, 209 NYS2d 550 (Nassau 1960).

[383] NY Real Prop Acts Law §231.

Inadequacy of price alone is not enough reason to vacate a sale, unless the price paid is so low as to shock the court's conscience.[384]

§9.68 The Trust Fund

The Lien Law provides a second and separate method to ensure payment for the improvement of real property: the trust fund.[385] The remedies provided by the trust fund provision are separate from those provided in the lien sections of the Lien Law. A party need not have a mechanic's lien to have trust fund rights.

The trust fund provisions of the Lien Law provide that all funds paid to an owner, a contractor, or a subcontractor for the improvement of private or public real property constitute trust funds that are held by the party receiving them, the trustee, on behalf of the parties who provided labor and materials to the trustee. As was stated in the leading case of *Aquilino v United States*,[386] "the only purpose for which the contractor may use the funds are trust purposes."[387] The contractor does not have a beneficial interest in the trust funds until all claims of all beneficiaries have been settled.[388] The contractor does not own the funds and has no property rights in them. Thus, because of the trust fund provisions of the Lien Law, a contractor cannot take the money it received to build a house and pay its secretary's salary or its office rent.[389] The money must first be used to pay its subcontractors, laborers, materialmen, various taxes, and insurance costs. Only after all claimants who are due money for work on the house have been paid can the contractor pay its overhead or other debts not related to construction of the house.[390] Further, the contractor cannot pay Paul with Peter's money (i.e., the proceeds from one project cannot be used to satisfy obligations incurred on another project). Nor can the federal government seize

---

[384] Frank Buttermark Plumbing & Heating Corp v Sagarese, 119 AD2d 540, 500 NYS2d 551 (1986) (sale of property at 30% of protester's uncorroborated opinion of value is not unconscionable); *but see* Home Owners Loan Corp v Vangerow, 277 AD 774, 96 NYS2d 861 (1950) (in a mortgage foreclosure case, sale was set aside when debtor proved it produced a purchaser before the sale who offered almost double the bank's sale bid; the property was resold upon the debtor's purchaser's terms).

[385] Article 3-A, Definition and Enforcement of Trusts, of the Lien Law, §§70 through 79-a.

[386] 10 NY2d 271, 219 NYS2d 254 (1961), *on remand from*, 363 US 509, 80 S Ct 1277, 4 L Ed 2d 1365 (1960).

[387] *Id* at 280, 219 NYS2d at 261.

[388] *Id*.

[389] "[A] contractor does not have a sufficient beneficial interest in the monies, due or to become due from the owner under the contract, to give him a property right in them, except insofar as there is a balance remaining after all subcontractors and other statutory beneficiaries have been paid." Aquilino v United States, 10 NY2d 271, 219 NYS2d 254, 263 (1961).

[390] Niaztat Iron Works, Inc v Tri-Neck Constr Corp, 62 Misc 2d 228, 308 NYS2d 427 (Kings 1970).

the trust funds to satisfy a tax lien of the contractor not related to the construction.[391]

The purpose of the trust fund provisions of the Lien Law is to ensure that funds obtained to finance an improvement and funds received in payment of work done on an improvement are used to pay for the work.[392] "The problem sought to be remedied was the diversion of said monies to other uses since such diversion had the potential and often actual consequence of leaving . . . protected persons . . . unpaid. The remedy chosen to attempt to prevent this was the trust."[393] Thus, the law creates a fiduciary relationship and imposes a responsibility upon the receiver of moneys intended to pay for improvements. The law prohibits diversion of trust funds to purposes that are not directly related to the particular improvement for which the funds were received and, in the event of diversion, imposes liability upon trustees and knowing transferees of trust funds.

The protections and requirements of the trust fund are automatic[394] and cannot be waived.[395] A trustee's responsibilities arise with the first payment received and continue until the last claimant is paid or the fund is exhausted.[396] Similarly, trust beneficiaries are automatically created and protected by law; they need not file any claims or be specifically named to achieve their beneficiary status.[397]

Not all funds received by an owner, a contractor, or a subcontractor are trust funds, and not all parties who improve real property are beneficiaries of all trusts. It is necessary to understand which funds are trust assets and who the beneficiaries of those assets are before the rights and responsibilities of the trust fund provisions of the Lien Law can be understood.

§9.69 —Duration of a Trust

A trust commences once a trust asset comes into a trustee's hands; the existence of a beneficiary is irrelevant.[398] The trust does not end until every trust claim has been paid or the fund has been exhausted in payment of trust obliga-

---

[391] Aquilino v United States, 10 NY2d 271, 219 NYS2d 254 (1961), *on remand from*, 363 US 509, 80 S Ct 1277, 4 L Ed 2d 1365 (1960).

[392] Teman Bros v New York Plumbers' Specialties Co, 109 Misc 2d 197, 444 NYS2d 337 (NY 1981).

[393] *Id* at 200, 444 NYS2d at 340.

[394] NY Lien Law §70(4).

[395] Allerton Constr Corp v Fairway Apts Corp, 26 AD2d 636, 272 NYS2d 867 (1966); *In re* Primiano Constr Co, 117 Misc 2d 523, 458 NYS2d 147 (Nassau 1982).

[396] Raisler Corp v Uris 55 Water St Co, 91 Misc 2d 217, 397 NYS2d 668 (NY 1977).

[397] Seville Iron Works, Inc v Devine Constr Co, 32 Misc 2d 797, 224 NYS2d 321 (Queens 1962).

[398] NY Lien Law §70(3); Eljam Mason Supply, Inc v IF Assocs Corp, 84 AD2d 720, 444 NYS2d 96 (1981); Seaboard Sur Co v Massachusetts Bonding & Ins Co, 17 AD2d 795, 232 NYS2d 809 (1962). See **§9.68** for discussion of the trust fund.

tions.[399] Once all claims have been paid, any remaining trust assets become the property of the trustee.[400]

§9.70 —Trust Assets

The trust assets consist of funds actually received by an owner, a contractor, or a subcontractor and "any right of action for any such funds due or earned or to become due or earned."[401] Only those moneys received, due, or earned by a trustee in a manner specified in the Lien Law are trust assets.[402] Further, the trust assets are those funds left after all valid mechanics' liens have been paid.[403]

The Owner's Trust

New York Lien Law §70(5) provides that the trust of which an owner is trustee consists of the following funds, including any right of action to receive these funds:

1. Building loan contract and mortgage proceeds[404]
2. Home improvement loan proceeds
3. Proceeds of any mortgage recorded after the improvement was begun but within four months of its completion[405]
4. Sale proceeds recorded after the improvement was begun but within four months of its completion[406]

---

[399] NY Lien Law §70(3); Raisler Corp v Uris 55 Water St Co, 91 Misc 2d 217, 397 NYS2d 668 (NY 1977).

[400] NY Lien Law §70(3).

[401] Id §70(1). See §9.68 for discussion of the trust fund.

[402] Seaboard Sur Co v Massachusetts Bonding & Ins Co, 17 AD2d 795, 232 NYS2d 809 (1962).

[403] The perfection of a mechanic's lien removes any trust assets subject to the lien from the trust and thus diminishes the trust. Hall v Blumberg, 26 AD2d 64, 270 NYS2d 539 (1966); Onondaga Commercial Dry Wall Corp v Clinton St, Inc, 25 NY2d 106, 250 NE2d 211, 302 NYS2d 795 (1969).

[404] The source of the mortgage proceeds is unimportant in determining whether the proceeds are trust assets. Thus, where a private individual is the mortgagee, the trust fund provisions apply. Costello v Geffen, 36 Misc 2d 895, 236 NYS2d 93 (Nassau 1962). The trust fund is that portion of the loan actually received by the owner. Caledonia Lumber & Coal Co v Chili Heights Apartments, 70 AD2d 766, 417 NYS2d 536 (1979).

[405] Mortgages that are given to secure antecedent debt not related to the improvement do not give rise to trust assets as no value is exchanged. In re CH Stuart, Inc, 17 BR 400 (WDNY 1982).

[406] The funds need not be in the owner's hands to be trust assets. See People v Rallo, 46 AD2d 518, 363 NYS2d 851 (1975), affd, 39 NY2d 217, 347 NE2d 633, 383 NYS2d 271 (1976), in which closing proceeds held by a corporate owner's attorney were found to be trust assets.

5. Consideration for or assignment of rents of existing or future leases on the property being improved, if the assignment is executed after the improvement was begun but within four months of its completion and if the assignment contains an express promise to make the improvement
6. Insurance proceeds payable due to destruction of the property being improved by casualty, less sums paid by the owner as premiums for the policy; and
7. Executory contract sale proceeds where the contract includes the improvement of the real property[407]

In addition, common elements charges received by a condominium's board of managers are trust funds of which the board is the trustee.[408] An owner holds these assets in trust for anyone with whom it contracts for the improvement of the property, including architects, engineers, contractors, materialmen, and laborers.

The owner's trust does not include money loaned to the owner that is not secured by a mortgage on the real property[409] or an owner's own funds used to pay for the improvement.[410] Proceeds of surety payment bonds[411] are not always trust assets, such as where a bond is given to a landlord to secure a tenant's payment of construction costs and the surety agreement specifically provides that it is for the benefit of the landlord[412] and excludes other parties from having any right to sue for benefits under the bond.[413]

It has been held that where an owner improves several parcels at the same time with the same contractor but each parcel is sold to a different purchaser, a separate trust exists with respect to each parcel.[414]

---

[407] Glazer v Alison Homes Corp, 62 Misc 2d 1017, 309 NYS2d 381 (Kings 1970) (where the contract vendee turned mortgage proceeds over to the contract vendor/owner to pay for improvements, the proceeds became trust funds in the owner's control).

[408] Condominium Act §339-1(2) (Real Property, McKinney 1989 & Supp 1991); Mario Bonito, Inc v Country Village Heights Condo, 79 Misc 2d 1094, 363 NYS2d 508 (Rockland 1975).

[409] Kingston Trust Co v Catskill Land Corp, 43 AD2d 995, 352 NYS2d 514 (1974).

[410] Bristol, Litynski, Wojcik, PC v Elliott, 107 Misc 2d 1005, 436 NYS2d 190 (Albany 1981); G&B Lab Installation, Inc v Beekman Downtown Hosp, 66 Misc 2d 441, 321 NYS2d 175 (NY 1971).

[411] It may include monies in the hand of a performance bond surety where the surety has completed a defaulting contractor's performance. Tri-City Elec Co v People, 96 AD2d 146, 468 NYS2d 283 (1983).

[412] Glantz Contracting Corp v 1955 Assocs, 20 AD2d 535, 245 NYS2d 129 (1963), affd, 14 NY2d 931, 200 NE2d 867, 252 NYS2d 328 (1964) (the fact that the landlord and tenant were joint venturers did not affect the court's decision, which said that the contractor could sue the landlord in contract, but could not claim the settlement funds received by the landlord from the surety as though they were trust assets).

[413] York Corp v 1955 Assocs, 20 AD2d 538, 245 NYS2d 131 (1963). This case was a companion case to the *Glantz* case cited in the preceding note.

[414] Matnel Constr Corp v Robert Homes, Inc, 221 NYS2d 889 (Nassau 1961).

The Contractor's Trust

New York Lien Law §70(6) provides that a contractor's trust consists of the following funds, including any right of action to receive these funds:

1. Payments under a contract for the improvement of public or private real property and for home improvement
2. Assignments of funds due, earned, or to become due or earned, under the contracts; and
3. Insurance proceeds payable due to destruction of the improvement by casualty, less premiums paid by the contractor

Basically, any funds that a contractor receives or is owed from the owner or the public entity due to the contractor's improvement of the real property are trust assets. A contractor holds these assets in trust for those parties with whom the contractor directly contracts, including subcontractors, materialmen, and laborers. A performance bond surety is substituted for the contractor as trustee when the surety has completed the contractor's performance.[415]

The Subcontractor's Trust

New York Lien Law §70(7) provides that a subcontractor's trust consists of the following funds, including any right of action to receive these funds:

1. Payments under the subcontract
2. Assignments of funds due, earned, or to become due or earned, under the subcontract; and
3. Insurance proceeds payable due to destruction of the improvement by casualty, less premiums paid by the subcontractor

Basically, like a contractor, any funds a subcontractor receives or is owed on the subcontract are trust assets. A subcontractor holds these trust assets for those parties with whom it directly contracts, including sub-subcontractors, materialmen, and laborers.

§9.71 —Parties Involved

Trustees

Owners, contractors, and subcontractors, as defined in **§§9.03, 9.05, 9.08, and 9.70** hereof, who receive funds specified as trust assets in the statute are

---

[415] Tri-City Elec Co v People, 96 AD2d 146, 468 NYS2d 283 (1983).

trustees.[416] Generally, no other parties are trustees.[417] Lenders are not trustees because they are not specified as such;[418] owners who improve their property with their own funds are not trustees of their own money because they did not receive the money in a way specified in the statute.[419]

The trustee has no interest or property right in the trust funds. Thus, a trustee's creditors cannot execute against trust funds until all statutory beneficiaries have been paid.[420]

Beneficiaries

Generally, trust beneficiaries are those parties owed money for the improvement of the property, regardless of when their efforts improved the property and with whom they contracted.[421] The class of trust beneficiaries is the same class of persons who are given the right to file a mechanic's lien,[422] with some additions.

The United States and state of New York are proper beneficiaries where their claims are for employment taxes, including withholding taxes, unemployment insurance, and social security deductions, to the extent that the taxes are owed for employment in the improvement of the specific real property that is the subject of the trust.[423] Further, an executory contract vendee is a trust beneficiary as to trust assets that come into the hands of the vendor/owner for the improvement of the property,[424] although the vendee's trust claims are subordinate to claims of other trust beneficiaries.[425]

---

[416] See §9.68 for discussion of the trust fund.

[417] One exception to this rule is in the case of a condominium board of managers that collects common charges and contracts for the improvement of the common elements. Per Condominium Act §339-1(2) (Real Property, McKinney 1989 & Supp 1991), the board of managers are trustees of the common charges and hold the common charges for the purpose of paying for labor and materials supplied at its express request or with its consent.

[418] Caledonia Lumber & Coal Co v Chili Heights Apartments, 70 AD2d 766, 417 NYS2d 536 (1979); ALB Contracting Co v York-Jersey Mortgage Co, 60 AD2d 989, 401 NYS2d 934 (1978) (mortgagee did not "step into the shoes" of the owner/contractor and thus become a trustee when it withheld funds due the owner; only those parties specified by statute can be trustees).

[419] Bristol, Litynski, Wojcik, PC v Elliott, 107 Misc 2d 1005, 436 NYS2d 190 (Albany 1981); G&B Lab Installation, Inc v Beekman Downtown Hosp, 66 Misc 2d 441, 321 NYS2d 175 (NY 1971).

[420] NY Lien Law §72(2); Sousie v Williams, 97 Misc 2d 532, 411 NYS2d 861 (Rensselaer 1979).

[421] St Paul Fire & Marine Ins Co v State, 99 Misc 2d 140, 415 NYS2d 949 (Ct Cl 1979).

[422] See discussion at §§9.03 and 9.08.

[423] Harman v Fairview Assocs, 25 NY2d 101, 302 NYS2d 791 (1969). Thus, while a tax claimant is not entitled to a mechanic's lien, it is a trust beneficiary and is entitled to first priority in distribution of any trust assets remaining after valid mechanic's lien claimants have been paid. Onondaga Commercial Dry Wall Corp v Clinton St, Inc, 25 NY2d 106, 250 NE2d 211, 302 NYS2d 795 (1969).

[424] Glazer v Alison Homes Corp, 62 Misc 2d 1017, 309 NYS2d 381 (Kings 1970).

[425] Schwadron v Freund, 69 Misc 2d 342, 329 NYS2d 945 (Rockland 1972).

A party cannot be both trustee and beneficiary of the same trust fund. Thus, a contractor is the beneficiary of the owner's trust only; the contractor is not also a beneficiary of the trust it controls on behalf of its subcontractors,[426] although the contractor may reimburse itself for proper trust expenditures.[427]

A party is the beneficiary only of the trust held by the party with whom the beneficiary contracted or by a party "obligated" to the beneficiary.[428] Thus, a contractor is the beneficiary of the owner's trust; a subcontractor is the beneficiary of the contractor's trust, but not of the owner's trust; and so forth.[429] Each trust is separate and distinct in terms of assets, trustees, and beneficiaries.[430]

§9.72 —The Fiduciary Relationship

A trustee of a NY Lien Law Article 3-A trust has the same basic fiduciary duties and loyalties as has the trustee of any trust. It has

> a duty of loyalty to the beneficiaries, a duty to keep and render accounts for the beneficiaries, and [to] keep trust funds separate from [its] own; a duty to furnish beneficiaries information and to permit them to examine the trust accounts; and a duty to take proof of the trust assets and to enforce claims on behalf of the trust.[431]

Unlike traditional trustees, an Article 3-A trustee is not required to act impartially in paying beneficiaries and has discretion in determining the order and manner of payment of trust claims.[432]

A trustee's fiduciary responsibility does not include the obligation to make certain that beneficiaries distribute their trust proceeds properly, nor does it include a guarantee of payment to beneficiaries' creditors. Thus, an owner has no obligation to see that its contractor disburses trust funds solely to proper trust beneficiaries.[433]

---

[426] Niaztat Iron Works, Inc v Tri-Neck Constr Corp, 62 Misc 2d 228, 308 NYS2d 427 (Kings 1970).

[427] Fentron Architectural Metals Corp v Solow, 101 Misc 2d 393, 420 NYS2d 950 (NY 1979).

[428] *See* NY Lien Law §71(2), (3), and (4).

[429] Onondaga Commercial Dry Wall Corp v Sylvan Glen Co, 26 AD2d 130, 271 NYS2d 523 (1966), *affd*, 21 NY2d 739, 234 NE2d 840, 287 NYS2d 886 (1968).

[430] NY Lien Law §70(2).

[431] Frontier Excavating, Inc v Sovereign Constr Co, 30 AD2d 487, 294 NYS2d 994, 998 (1968), *motion denied*, 24 NY2d 991, 250 NE2d 228, 302 NYS2d 820 (1969) (citations omitted from quote). *See also* NY Lien Law §72(3)(a) regarding a trustee's obligations to defend against application of trust funds for nontrust purposes.

[432] NY Lien Law §74(1); Teman Bros v New York Plumbers' Specialties Co, 109 Misc 2d 197, 444 NYS2d 337 (NY 1981).

[433] Eminon Acoustical Contractor's Corp v Richkill Assocs, 89 Misc 2d 992, 392 NYS2d 1007 (Queens 1977).

§9.73 —Record-Keeping Requirements

A trustee's books of account must show the allocation of income and expenses to each trust it administers.[434] While a trustee need not maintain a separate bank account for each improvement's trust funds, a trustee's books must clearly show what funds were received and paid on each trust. Separate books must be maintained on each improvement,[435] which are separate also from the trustee's office overhead expense books.[436]

The trust books are to include the following entries:

1. Trust assets receivable, including who owes the money and upon what contract or transaction, the amount now due from such person, and the date due[437]

2. Trust accounts payable, including to whom the money is owed and upon what contract or transaction, the amount owed, and the date owed[438]

3. Trust funds received, including who paid such funds, in what form they were paid (cash, check, etc.), the date and amount of the payment received, and, if applicable, the name and address of the bank where the funds are deposited[439]

4. Trust payments made with trust assets including to whom, when, where, and the amount and manner of payment, the reason for the payment, the contract date and price if applicable, a description of the item of the improvement the payment relates to, and, if such payment was made with funds received per an assignment, a statement of the amount of the funds so used, the date of the assignment, and the name and address of the assignee;[440] and

5. Transfers made as repayment of or to secure advances made pursuant to a notice of lending, including to whom a transfer was made, the date and amount of the transfer, a description of the trust asset transferred, the amount of the consideration for the transfer or advance, and when and how such consideration was paid[441]

Failure to keep the records required is presumptive evidence that the trustee diverted or consented to the diversion of trust funds for nontrust purposes.[442]

---

[434] NY Lien Law §75(1).

[435] Schwadron v Freund, 69 Misc 2d 342, 329 NYS2d 945 (Rockland 1972).

[436] Matnel Constr Corp v Robert Homes, Inc, 221 NYS2d 889 (Nassau 1961).

[437] NY Lien Law §75(3)(A).

[438] Id §75(3)(B).

[439] Id §75(3)(C).

[440] Id §75(3)(D).

[441] Id §75(3)(E).

[442] Id §§75(4), 79-a(3). Frontier Excavating v Sovereign Constr Co, 30 AD2d 487, 294 NYS2d 994 (1968); Schwadron v Freund, 69 Misc 2d 342, 329 NYS2d 945 (Rockland 1972). This presumption is constitutional; in criminal cases it is treated as a permissible inference that does not shift the burden of proof as to criminal intent. People v

§9.74 —Availability of Records to Claimants

Lien Law §76 provides for an informal accounting[443] by permitting trust beneficiaries to examine trust books and records or to demand verified statements as to trust activities from the trustee. It is the beneficiary's choice between examining the books and records or obtaining a verified statement.[444] It is wise to first request a verified statement of the trustee; then, the trustee will have the duty of organizing its books and reducing them into a readily examinable form. If the beneficiary is not satisfied with the statement furnished, it can examine the trustee's books itself at a later date or move the court for an order compelling the trustee to furnish a complete statement. It may also be wise to request statements from the trustee's trustees (i.e., the subcontractor's contractor or the owner with whom the contractor has dealt), so that records of payment may be verified.

To examine the books or receive a verified statement, the beneficiary's trust claim must be at least 30 days past due and the request must be made and served in the manner specified by the statute. A failure to follow the statute as to the time,[445] form,[446] or service[447] of the request can make the request void and ineffective.

The request must be made by a verified statement[448] in writing and served upon the trustee, either personally or by registered or certified mail.[449] It must contain the name and address of the beneficiary; a description of the improvement, not just a description of the real property upon which the improvement is located,[450] and a description of the trust claim, including the work performed, the amount due, and the date due.[451] A new request

---

Rosano, 50 NY2d 1013, 409 NE2d 1357, 431 NYS2d 683 (1980). *See also* Raisler Corp v Uris 55 Water St Co, 91 Misc 2d 217, 397 NYS2d 668 (NY 1977).

[443] A request for an examination or a verified statement should not be confused with the accounting available under NY Lien Law §77. They are separate procedures, both of which may be pursued by a beneficiary with regard to the same improvement and trustee. *Id* §76(6). *See also* Fentron Architectural Metals Corp v Solow, 48 AD2d 820, 370 NYS2d 58 (1975), in which a trust enforcement action request for an accounting was preceded by a request to examine the trustee's books and records.

[444] East Coast Wholesalers, Inc v John J. Moran Co, 42 AD2d 605, 345 NYS2d 115 (1973).

[445] Isadore Rosen & Sons v Conforti & Eisele, Inc, 40 AD2d 794, 338 NYS2d 39 (1972) (a premature request will be denied); Hansen Excavating Co v Comet Constr Corp, 14 AD2d 911, 222 NYS2d 233 (1961).

[446] Warebak Realty Corp v Enros Constr Co, 39 Misc 2d 298, 240 NYS2d 193 (1963).

[447] Ciavarella v People, 36 Misc 2d 1083, 234 NYS2d 15 (Albany 1962).

[448] The statement and verification must be made by the beneficiary, not its agent or attorney. Hansen Excavating Co v Comet Constr Corp, 14 AD2d 911, 22 NYS2d 233 (1961).

[449] NY Lien Law §76(2).

[450] Warebak Realty Corp v Enros Constr Co, 39 Misc 2d 298, 240 NYS2d 193 (Queens 1963).

[451] NY Lien Law §76(2).

may be served no more than once a month.[452]

A beneficiary's right to examine the books or receive a verified statement is almost limitless. It does not matter if the beneficiary is in privity with the trustee.[453] It is irrelevant whether a lien has been filed, whether the beneficiary has begun or failed to begin any action against the trustee,[454] whether the beneficiary's performance is in dispute,[455] whether conditions precedent have been met,[456] or whether the lien has been bonded.[457] A beneficiary does not have to prove or even allege a diversion of trust funds to be entitled to examine the books or to receive a verified statement.[458]

In response to a request, the trustee has two choices: within 10 days after service it must either comply with the request or apply to the court for an order vacating the request.[459] A trustee is not entitled to a protective order[460] and the only grounds upon which the courts will vacate a request for an examination or a verified statement are if the request is procedurally incorrect, as discussed above, or if the party making the request is a "mere interloper" who has no right to the information requested.[461] The cost to the trustee of complying with the request is irrelevant.[462]

To comply with the request, the trustee must include all information required to be kept by a trustee pursuant to NY Lien Law §75. The beneficiary is entitled to information concerning the whole trust and the whole improve-

---

[452] *Id* §76(1).

[453] Travers v Kronenberg's Inc, 32 Misc 2d 141, 230 NYS2d 768 (Erie 1961). *See also* Radory Constr Corp v Arronbee Constr Corp, 24 AD2d 573, 262 NYS2d 389 (1965) (subcontractor entitled to verified statement from owner).

[454] The beneficiary need not have begun a trust enforcement action, Ciavarella v People, 36 Misc 2d 1083, 234 NYS2d 15 (Albany 1962), or a mechanic's lien foreclosure action, *In re* Silverstein, 30 Misc 2d 510, 219 NYS2d 389 (Queens 1961).

Similarly, it is irrelevant if the beneficiary has begun a trust enforcement action, Harry J. Kangieser, Inc v Palm Beach Realty Co, 223 NYS2d 38 (Suffolk 1961), sued the trustee for breach of contract, *In re* Silverstein, 30 Misc 2d 510, 219 NYS2d 389 (Queens 1961), or has other remedies at law not pursued, Frontier Excavating, Inc v Sovereign Constr Co, 30 AD2d 487, 294 NYS2d 994 (1968).

[455] Conforti & Eisele, Inc v R. Salzstein & Co, 56 AD2d 292, 392 NYS2d 430 (1977); Cadin Constr Corp v Adam Jay Assocs, 86 Misc 2d 407, 382 NYS2d 671 (Nassau 1976); Fontaine Bleau Swimming Pool Corp v Aquarama Swimming Pool Corp, 27 Misc 2d 315, 210 NYS2d 634 (Nassau 1961).

[456] Conforti & Eisele, Inc v R. Salzstein & Co, 56 AD2d 292, 392 NYS2d 430 (1977).

[457] Merv Blank, Inc v Dwyer, 50 AD2d 563, 374 NYS2d 676 (1975); Radory Constr Corp v Arronbee Constr Corp, 24 AD2d 573, 262 NYS2d 389 (1965).

[458] Cadin Constr Corp v Adam Jay Assocs, 86 Misc 2d 407, 382 NYS2d 671 (Nassau 1976).

[459] NY Lien Law §76(5).

[460] G&B Lab Installation, Inc v Beekman Downtown Hosp, 66 Misc 2d 441, 321 NYS2d 175 (NY 1971).

[461] Fontaine Bleau Swimming Pool Corp v Aquarama Swimming Pool Corp, 27 Misc 2d 315, 210 NYS2d 634 (Nassau 1961). A "mere interloper" is one who has not supplied materials or labor or who has no other grounds for being an Article 3-A trust beneficiary.

[462] Ciavarella v People, 36 Misc 2d 1083, 234 NYS2d 15 (Albany 1962).

ment, not just information relating to that beneficiary.[463] Thus, a trustee that reproduces select pages from its books does not comply with a request for a verified statement. Further, a beneficiary is entitled to receive information not only on the contract but also on claims based on delay damages and extra work, even where the extras are not confirmed by change orders.[464]

If a trustee fails to comply with a request, the beneficiary may apply to the court for an order compelling the trustee to comply.[465] No sanctions are provided for a failure to comply with a request, except in the case of a lender under a notice of lending.[466]

§9.75 —Proper Application of Trust Funds

The Lien Law specifically provides how trust funds may be used, whether the trustee is an owner,[467] a contractor,[468] or a subcontractor.[469] Generally, an owner may use trust funds to pay the "cost of the improvement";[470] usually, any payment to a contractor, subcontractor, materialman, laborer, or building loan mortgage holder is appropriate, *if* the payment is directly related to improvement of the real property in issue. Under the statute, payment of Federal Housing Administration (FHA) inspection and examination fees and legal and accounting fees are proper disbursements of trust funds where they are "intrinsically related" to the procurement of building loan financing.[471]

Generally, a contractor or subcontractor may use trust funds to pay claims of subcontractors, laborers, and materialmen, payroll taxes, sales taxes, employment taxes, benefits and wage supplements, and surety bond and insurance premiums, *if* the payment is related to the improvement.[472] Payment of office overhead expenses is not a proper application of trust funds.[473]

It is important to realize that not all sums that may be claimed under a mechanic's lien are proper trust claims. For instance, payment of interest due

---

[463] Poly Constr Corp v Oxford Hall Co, 44 Misc 2d 82, 252 NYS2d 971 (Kings 1964); In re M. Leiken & Sons, 39 Misc 2d 156, 240 NYS2d 73 (Queens 1963).

[464] Stewart M. Muller Constr Co v Alvord & Swift, 50 AD2d 572, 375 NYS2d 27 (1975).

[465] NY Lien Law §76(5).

[466] See **§9.76**.

[467] NY Lien Law §§71(1), (3)(a), 71-a.

[468] *Id* §71(2), (3)(b).

[469] *Id.*

[470] *Id* §71(1). *Cost of improvement* is defined at *id* §2(5) and has been discussed in **§§9.17-9.24** and **9.27** of this chapter.

[471] The Lien Law includes "fair and reasonable sums" paid to obtain financing as a cost of improvement. NY Lien Law §2(5). Cadin Constr Corp v Adam Jay Assocs, 112 AD2d 395, 492 NYS2d 55 (1985).

[472] NY Lien Law §71(2).

[473] Niaztat Iron Works, Inc v Tri-Neck Constr Corp, 62 Misc 2d 228, 308 NYS2d 427 (Kings 1970).

a claimant for an overdue bill is not a proper use of trust funds, although it is properly included in a lien claim.[474]

Further, the right to receive a trust disbursement is not automatic for all claimants. Lenders and assignees of moneys due the trustee must comply with certain statutory requirements or any trust assets they receive in payment will be considered inappropriate or a diversion of trust funds, and will subject them to possible liability. A lender or an assignee must file a notice of lending or a notice of assignment to protect its right to receive trust assets.

§9.76 —Notice of Lending

Where a lender advances money to a trustee for trust purposes, a notice of lending must be filed to protect the lender's right to repayment from trust funds. Section 73 of the Lien Law provides that a notice of lending is effective as to advances made as early as five days before the filing, on the day of filing, and after the filing through the specified termination date. Where advances will be made after the termination date, a notice of lending may be continued by the filing of a subsequent notice entitled "second notice of lending" or "third notice of lending" at least 60 days before the termination date of the prior notice.[475]

A notice of lending must include the following information:

1. The name and address of the lender
2. The name, address, and status (owner, contractor, or subcontractor) of the person on whose behalf the advances are made
3. A description of the improvement and real property
4. The dates of any advance made on or prior to filing for which the notice is supposed to be effective
5. The termination date if the notice relates to several or undetermined improvement projects, but in no event shall the termination be more than two years from the date the notice was filed; and
6. The maximum balance of advances outstanding[476]

A second notice of lending must refer to the prior notice and conform to the above-listed requirements.[477] A notice of lending that does not substantially meet the requirements of §73 will be ineffective and will subject the lender to a charge of diversion of trust assets.[478]

---

[474] Northern Structures, Inc v Union Bank, 57 AD2d 360, 394 NYS2d 964, *amended as to judgment amount*, 396 NYS2d 1021 (1977); Gruenberg v United States, 29 AD2d 527, 285 NYS2d 962 (1967).

[475] NY Lien Law §73(3)(c) (McKinney 1966 & Supp 1992).

[476] *Id* §73(3)(b).

[477] *Id* §73(3)(c).

[478] Schreiber Hauling Co v Schwab Bros Trucking, 54 Misc 2d 395, 283 NYS2d 69 (Erie 1967).

The notice of lending is filed where a mechanic's lien on the improvement would be filed—in the case of a private improvement, in the county where the real property is located; in the case of a public improvement, with the department head and financial officer of the public entity.[479]

The loan contract or mortgage upon which the notice of lending is based must contain a trust covenant that affirmatively binds the trustee to use the funds advanced for trust purposes.[480]

Failure to comply with the provisions of §73 can cause a transfer by a trustee to its lender to be set aside as a diversion, even where the transfer was otherwise a proper repayment of a loan advance made on the improvement.[481] While this result may seem unfair, a lender has the means to protect itself through compliance with the statute; a lender that fails to take advantage of that protection does so at its risk.[482] Due to the serious repercussions of failing to file a notice of lending, lenders are wise to automatically file a notice whenever they loan money or approve a line of credit to a party involved in the construction business.

A notice of lending does not make all transfers of trust assets to the lender *per se* proper. It provides the lender with an affirmative defense to a charge of diversion and allows the lender to show that the transfer of trust assets was made in repayment of advances made pursuant to the notice of lending[483] and that the transfers were applied in payment of proper trust purposes as specified in NY Lien Law §71.[484] Establishment of the defense provides the lender with a credit against any liability for diversion, to the extent of advances made that do not exceed the maximum amount specified in the notice of lending.[485] If a lender fails to respond to a trust beneficiary's written request for a verified statement regarding advances made, the lender will not be entitled to the credit, effectively losing its affirmative defense.[486]

§9.77 —Notice of Assignment

Where a trustee has assigned its right to receive moneys due under a contract, the assignee may protect its right to receive trust assets as part of that assignment by filing a notice of assignment as set forth in §15 of the NY Lien Law. A notice of assignment that meets the requirements of §15 is deemed

---

[479] NY Lien Law §73(3)(a) (McKinney 1966 & Supp 1992).

[480] *Id* §73(1).

[481] Eljam Mason Supply Co v Glazer, 74 AD2d 912, 426 NYS2d 69 (1980); Raisler Corp v Uris 55 Water St Co, 91 Misc 2d 217, 397 NYS2d 668 (NY 1977).

[482] Caristo Constr Corp v Diners Fin Corp, 21 NY2d 507, 289 NYS2d 175 (1968); American Blower Corp v James Talcott, Inc, 10 NY2d 282, 219 NYS2d 263 (1961).

[483] NY Lien Law §73(1) (McKinney 1966 & Supp 1992).

[484] *Id* §73(2).

[485] *Id*.

[486] *Id* §73(4).

a notice of lending for trust purposes and provides an assignee with the same protection and duties that a lender receives under a notice of lending.[487]

Assignees are advised always to file a notice of assignment when accepting an assignment from any party involved in the construction business. By doing so, the assignee may be able to defeat a claim of diversion.

§9.78 —Diversion of Trust Funds

Any payment of trust assets for a purpose that is not allowed by the statute (Article 3-A of the NY Lien Law) before all trust claims are paid is a diversion of trust assets, regardless of whether trust claims exist at the time of the diversion[488] and regardless of the trustee's or transferee's intent or good faith.[489] The fact that the transferee is actually owed money by the trustee is irrelevant in determining whether a diversion has occurred; if the money is not owed for a trust purpose, any transfer of trust funds is a diversion.[490]

It is not a diversion when a holder in due course of a negotiable instrument or a good faith purchaser for value accepts a transfer of trust assets without notice that the funds are trust funds.[491] Further, in a case where the trustee commingled trust and nontrust funds in its bank account, the fact that nontrust claims were paid from that account did not establish a diversion.[492] Similarly, where a trustee used trust funds to pay for past debts but was still able to pay all trust beneficiaries and no beneficiary was prejudiced by the payment of past debts, the trustee was not liable for a diversion.[493]

Finally, where the amount actually spent on an improvement exceeds the amount of the trust, there is no diversion, regardless of the fact that some beneficiaries may be unpaid.[494]

§9.79 —Liability for Diversion

A transferee who knowingly accepts, or a trustee who knowingly applies, trust funds in payment of nontrust purposes takes the payment subject to the claims

---

[487] NY Lien Law §73(3)(d) (McKinney 1966 & Supp 1992).

[488] NY Lien Law §72(1) (McKinney 1966 & Supp 1992).

[489] People v Rallo, 46 AD2d 518, 363 NYS2d 851 (1975), *affd*, 39 NY2d 217, 347 NE2d 633, 383 NYS2d 271 (1976).

[490] *See* Northern Structures, Inc v Union Bank, 57 AD2d 360, 394 NYS2d 964, *amended as to judgment amount*, 396 NYS2d 1021 (1977) (bank that seized trust funds in trustee's undesignated checking account to pay trustee's unsecured loan found liable for diversion of funds where bank knew funds were construction loan proceeds and trust funds); Merit Plumbing & Heating v Eastern Natl Bank, 221 NYS2d 143 (Suffolk 1961).

[491] NY Lien Law §72(1) (McKinney 1966 & Supp 1992).

[492] BG Equip Co v American Ins Co, 61 AD2d 247, 402 NYS2d 479, *affd*, 46 NY2d 802, 386 NE2d 833, 413 NYS2d 922 (1978).

[493] General Crushed Stone Co v State, 23 AD2d 250, 260 NYS2d 32 (1965).

[494] Fentron Architectural Metals Corp v Solow, 101 Misc 2d 393, 420 NYS2d 950 (NY 1979).

of the trustee and the rights of the beneficiaries and is liable to the beneficiaries in conversion for the amount of the transfer, plus interest.[495] The transferee, trustee, or trust fund may be liable for the beneficiaries' attorneys' fees, if a representative action is actually brought.[496] Additionally, if the diversion is done in flagrant disregard of Lien Law trust fund provisions, the person responsible (whether individuals or a corporation), may be liable for punitive damages.[497]

Where the transferee or trustee is a corporation, the officers, directors, shareholders, and agents of the corporation may be found personally liable for the diversion, if the individuals had knowledge and actively participated in the diversion.[498] An individual trustee or corporate trustee officer, director, or agent who applies or consents to the application of trust funds for nontrust purposes is guilty of larceny and subject to criminal penalties.[499]

The requirement of knowledge for liability to exist is *not* one of *actual* knowledge. Knowledge will be found if there are sufficient facts to put a "reasonably intelligent and diligent" person on inquiry and require him or her to investigate, which investigation would lead to facts that would have shown that the funds transferred were the subject of a trust and that the transfer was in violation of that trust.[500] Simply put, a transferee or trustee will be liable if it knew or should have known that the transfer was a breach of the trust.[501]

§9.80 —Restoration of the Trust after Diversion

The return of an alleged diversion by a *transferee* to the trust is a recognized defense that may relieve the transferee of liability.[502] It is debatable whether a *trustee* can escape civil liability for a diversion by restoring the trust.[503] How-

---

[495] NY Lien Law §77(3)(a)(i) (McKinney 1966 & Supp 1992); Fleck v Perla, 40 AD2d 1069, 339 NYS2d 246 (1972).

[496] *See* Caristo Constr Corp v Diners Fin Corp, 21 NY2d 507, 289 NYS2d 175 (1968).

[497] Sabol & Rice, Inc v Poughkeepsie Galleria Co, 147 Misc 2d 641, 557 NYS2d 253 (Dutchess 1990).

[498] People v Rosano, 69 AD2d 643, 419 NYS2d 543 (1979); Fleck v Perla, 40 AD2d 1069, 339 NYS2d 246 (1972). Diversion is not established by the mere fact that the defendant was a corporate officer or an agent at the time of the diversion. Ace Hardwood Flooring Co v Glazer, 74 AD2d 912, 426 NYS2d 69 (1980).

[499] NY Lien Law §79-a (McKinney 1966 & Supp 1992).

[500] *Id.*

[501] Gerrity Co v Bonacquisti Constr Corp, 136 AD2d 59, 525 NYS2d 926 (1988).

[502] Travelers Indem Co v Central Trust Co, 47 Misc 2d 849, 263 NYS2d 261 (Monroe 1965), *affd*, 27 AD2d 803 (4th Dept 1967); Raisler Corp v Uris 55 Water St Co, 91 Misc 2d 217, 397 NYS2d 668 (NY 1977); Schwadron v Freund, 69 Misc 2d 342, 329 NYS2d 945 (Rockland 1972).

[503] See discussion in Schwadron v Freund, 69 Misc 2d 342, 329 NYS2d 945, 951-52 (Rockland 1972) regarding restoration of trust funds and its effect on the civil liability of trustees and transferees.

ever, it would appear that if a trustee expends sums equal to or in excess of the original trust assets, any diversion would become academic as a beneficiary would have difficulty establishing damage or prejudice due to the diversion.[504]

Restoration or repayment does provide a trustee with a defense to a criminal larceny charge if the diversion was to repay an advance of funds actually applied for trust purposes, whether those funds were advanced by a lender or the trustee.[505]

§9.81 Enforcing the Trust Fund

Any beneficiary or trustee of a trust fund may bring an action to enforce the fund. The action is brought as a representative action, similar to a class action, with the party bringing the suit seeking relief on behalf of all beneficiaries of the fund.[506] Thus, once an action has begun on a trust, a beneficiary must assert its claims in the existing suit; it cannot begin a new one.[507] Once an enforcement action is begun, it cannot be settled, dismissed, or discontinued without court approval.[508]

The action may be brought at any time during construction of the improvement or up to one year from its completion.[509] If a subcontractor or materialman brings the suit, it may be brought up to one year after the improvement's completion or up to one year after the final payment of its claim is due, whichever is later.[510] An action not brought within one year will be dismissed.[511] Unlike in a mechanic's lien foreclosure action, an abandonment of the improvement or termination of the contract is not the same as a completion, and the

---

[504] General Crushed Stone Co v State, 23 AD2d 250, 260 NYS2d 32 (1965) (where beneficiary can show no prejudice from trustee's payment of trust assets for nontrust purposes, no liability for diversion will be found); Fentron Architectural Metals Corp v Solow, 101 Misc 2d 393, 420 NYS2d 950 (NY 1979) (where sums expended on the improvement exceed the amount of the trust fund, no diversion can be found).

[505] NY Lien Law §79-a(2) (McKinney 1966 & Supp 1992).

[506] NY Lien Law §77(1), (3)(b) (McKinney 1966 & Supp 1992); Glazer v Alison Homes Corp, 62 Misc 2d 1017, 309 NYS2d 381 (Kings 1970).

[507] Premier Elec Constr Corp v Security Natl Bank, 39 AD2d 967, 334 NYS2d 199 (1972).

[508] NY Lien Law §77(7).

[509] Completion is measured from the time the entire project is completed, not when a substantial portion of the work is completed, Northern Structures, Inc v Union Bank, 57 AD2d 360, 394 NYS2d 964, *amended as to judgment amount*, 396 NYS2d 1021 (1977), and not upon completion of the beneficiary's portion, Wynkoop v Mintz, 17 Misc 2d 1093, 192 NYS2d 428 (Kings 1958).

[510] Completion is measured from the time the entire project is completed, not when a substantial portion of the work is completed, Northern Structures, Inc v Union Bank, 57 AD2d 360, 394 NYS2d 964, *amended as to judgment amount*, 396 NYS2d 1021 (1977), and not upon completion of the beneficiary's portion, Wynkoop v Mintz, 17 Misc 2d 1093, 192 NYS2d 428 (Kings 1958).

[511] AD Walker & Co v Shelter Programs Co, 84 AD2d 536, 443 NYS2d 96 (1981).

statute of limitation does not begin to run as to a beneficiary until that beneficiary knows or should know of the abandonment or termination.[512]

An action by a trustee for a final settlement and discharge of the trust is not bound by the one-year limitation,[513] and trust beneficiaries may assert their claims in a trustee's action for settlement, even if the one-year period has expired.[514]

Venue lies in the county where the improvement is located or in the county of the petitioner's residence.[515]

§9.82 —Claims for Relief

A trust enforcement action may seek any or all of the many different forms of relief provided by the trust fund provisions of the Lien Law statute. The action may seek:

1. An accounting by the trustee[516]
2. Identification, enjoinment, tracing, setting aside, and recovery of trust diversions from the hands of any transferee[517]
3. Damages for breach of trust[518]
4. Enforcement of any right of action the trust may have[519]
5. Determination of the validity of a trust claim[520]
6. An order limiting or terminating the trustee's authority[521]

---

[512] Putnins Contracting Corp v Winston Woods, Inc, 72 Misc 2d 987, 340 NYS2d 317 (Nassau), affd, 43 AD2d 667, 349 NYS2d 652 (1973), affd, 36 NY2d 679, 365 NYS2d 853 (1975); Forest Elec Corp v Century Natl Bank & Trust Co, 70 Misc 2d 190, 333 NYS2d 644NY (1970).

[513] Putnins v Contracting Corp v Winston Woods, Inc, 72 Misc 2d 987, 340 NYS2d 317 (Nassau), affd, 43 AD2d 667, 349 NYS2d 652 (1973), affd, 36 NY2d 679, 365 NYS2d 853 (1975); Forest Elec Corp v Century Natl Bank & Trust Co, 70 Misc 2d 190, 333 NYS2d 644 (1970); Harman v Fairview Assocs, 25 NY2d 101, 302 NYS2d 791 (1969).

[514] Id.

[515] Costello v Geffen, 36 Misc 2d 895, 236 NYS2d 93 (Nassau 1962).

[516] NY Lien Law §77(3)(a)(i) (McKinney 1966 & Supp 1992). Proof of diversion is not necessary for a party to be entitled to an accounting; it need show only that what happened to all trust funds is uncertain. Fentron Architectural Metals Corp v Solow, 48 AD2d 820, 370 NYS2d 58 (1975).

[517] Id; NY Lien Law §77(3)(a)(vi)(McKinney 1966 & Supp 1992).

[518] Id §77(3)(a)(i).

[519] Id §77(3)(ii).

[520] Id §77(3)(iii).

[521] Id §77(3)(iv); Frontier Excavating, Inc v Sovereign Constr Co, 30 AD2d 487, 294 NYS2d 994 (1968).

7. An order requiring the trustee to post security to ensure proper distribution of trust assets[522]
8. An order for distribution of trust assets[523]
9. Discharge of the trustee;[524] and
10. Such other and further relief as the court deems necessary and proper,[525] including attorneys' fees if the beneficiary actually brings a representative action.[526]

A party may pursue these claims in addition to its mechanic's lien claims,[527] although it is important to remember that the actions are distinct and dependent upon different statutory provisions.[528]

§9.83 —Priority and Preference

Not all trust beneficiaries are created equal. Mechanics' lienors have priority over all trust beneficiaries who do not have mechanics' liens.[529] Trust claimants have preference with respect to distribution of trust assets pursuant to order or judgment in the following order:[530]

1. Claims for employment taxes, unemployment insurance, and social security related to the contract[531]

---

[522] NY Lien Law §77(3)(a)(v) (McKinney 1966 & Supp 1992); Palm Beach Realty Co v Harry J. Kangieser, Inc, 36 Misc 2d 1058, 233 NYS2d 641 (NY 1962), affd, 19 AD2d 862, 243 NYS2d 413 (1963) (a trustee who asserts "dominion and control" over trust assets and is not protecting trust beneficiaries may be required to post a surety bond).

[523] NY Lien Law §77(3)(a)(vi) (McKinney 1966 & Supp 1992).

[524] Id §77(3)(a)(viii).

[525] Id §77(3)(a)(ix). This may include consolidation of a trust action with other actions that concern the same issues. For example, consolidation of a trust enforcement action was proper with a suit for partnership dissolution and accounting where the issue central to each claim was whether there was a wrongful diversion of funds. Fleck v Putterman, 60 AD2d 904, 401 NYS2d 556 (1978).

[526] Caristo Constr Co v Diners Fin Corp, 21 NY2d 507, 289 NYS2d 175 (1968) (where beneficiary was only unpaid claimant of trust, it was not entitled to an award of attorneys' fees because it was not required to bring a representative action). It appears that the attorneys' fees are paid from the trust fund. See id at 515, 289 NYS2d at 181.

[527] Poughkeepsie Iron & Metal Co v Ermco Erectors, Inc, 79 Misc 2d 142, 359 NYS2d 634 (Duchess 1974).

[528] Scriven v Maple Knoll Apartments, Inc, 46 AD2d 210, 361 NYS2d 730 (1974).

[529] Onondaga Commercial Dry Wall Corp v Clinton St, Inc, 25 NY2d 106, 250 NE2d 211, 302 NYS2d 795 (1969); Hall v Blumberg, 26 AD2d 64, 270 NYS2d 539 (1966) (a perfected mechanic's lien removes any assets of the trust that are subject to the lien).

[530] Before judgment or order, the trustee has discretion to apply trust funds to legitimate trust purposes as it chooses. NY Lien Law §74(1) (McKinney 1966 & Supp 1992); Teman Bros v New York Plumbers' Specialties Co, 109 Misc 2d 197, 444 NYS2d 337 (NY 1981).

[531] NY Lien Law §77(8)(a) (McKinney 1966 & Supp 1992). The preference afforded tax claimants in trust fund cases is in sharp contrast with a tax claimant's treatment

2. Laborers' claims for daily and weekly wages[532]
3. Benefits and wage supplement claims[533]
4. Garnishers and assignees of laborers' daily and weekly wages who are entitled to be paid directly from the laborers' wages by deduction[534]
5. Materialmen, subcontractors, and contractors
6. Vendees of executory contracts for the sale and improvement of real property[535] and
7. Creditors of the trustee who did not improve the real property[536]

Within each preferred class, claimants share pro rata any trust assets.[537]

§9.84 —Judgment

Once a beneficiary obtains a judgment against the trustee, it cannot execute the judgment upon any trust asset for its sole benefit. Any execution must be for the benefit of the entire class of beneficiaries.[538] This provision does not apply to the enforcement of mechanics' liens.[539]

---

under the mechanic's lien statute. Onondaga Commercial Dry Wall Corp v Clinton St, Inc, 25 NY2d 106, 250 NE2d 211, 302 NYS2d 795 (1969).

[532] NY Lien Law §77(8)(b) (McKinney 1966 & Supp 1992).

[533] Id §77(8)(c).

[534] Id §77(8)(d).

[535] Glazer v Alison Homes Corp, 62 Misc 2d 1017, 309 NYS2d 381 (Kings 1970).

[536] Gerosa Haulage & Warehouse Corp v Prospect Iron Works, Inc, 197 NYS2d 936 (Nassau 1959).

[537] NY Lien Law §77(8) (McKinney 1966 & Supp 1992).

[538] NY Lien Law §78 (McKinney 1966).

[539] Id §§78, 79 (McKinney 1966 & Supp 1992).

Form 9-1 Notice of Lien

NOTICE UNDER MECHANIC'S LIEN LAW
TO THE CLERK OF THE COUNTY OF [NEW YORK] AND ALL OTHERS WHOM IT MAY CONCERN:

PLEASE TAKE NOTICE, that [CLAIMANT], as lienor, has and claims a lien on the real property hereinafter described as follows:

1. The name of the lienor is [CLAIMANT], a [corporation]. The business address and principal place of business of the lienor is [_____].

The name, address, and telephone number of the lienor's attorneys are [_____].

2. The owner of the real property is [ADVERSARY I] and the interest of the owner as far as known to the lienor is [fee simple].

3. The name of the person by whom the lienor was employed is [ADVERSARY II]. The name of the person to whom the lienor furnished or is to furnish materials and form whom the lienor performed or is to perform labor is [ADVERSARY II]. The name of the person with whom the contract was made is [ADVERSARY II].

4. The labor performed was labor necessary to perform [general construction, plumbing, heating and ventilating, and electrical work]. The material furnished was [material necessary to perform general construction, plumbing, heating and ventilating, and electrical work]. The agreed price and value of the labor performed and the agreed price and value of the materials furnished is [TWO MILLION] ($2,000,000.00]) DOLLARS and the total agreed price and value is [TWO MILLION] ($2,000,000.00]) DOLLARS.

5. The amount unpaid to the lienor for the said labor performed and the amount unpaid to the lienor for the said material furnish is [ONE MILLION] ($1,000,000.00]) DOLLARS and the total amount for which this lien is filed is [ONE MILLION] ($1,000,000.00]) DOLLARS.

6. The time when the first item of work was performed and the time when the first item of material was furnished was [February 30, 1990]. The time when the last item of work was performed and the time when the last item of material was furnished was [March 32, 1990].

7. The property subject to the lien is situated in [the Borough of Manhattan, County of New York, City and State of New York, being known as _____ Avenue (Block _____, Lot _____). A more complete description is annexed hereto, marked Exhibit "1"].

The said labor and materials were performed and furnished for and used in the improvement of the real property hereinbefore described. Eight (8) months have not elapsed dating from the last item of work performed or from the last item of material furnished or since the completion of the contract or since the final performance of the work or since the final furnishing of the material for which this lien is claimed.

Dated: New York, New York
    [April 31, 1990]   [CLAIMANT]

By: _____
[John A. Client],
[President]

[AFFIX VERIFICATION HERE]

Appendix 9-1

Private v Public Works Liens

Topic	Private	Public
Lien attaches	to real property	to funds appropriated for project
Who can file	contractor, unlimited tiers of subcontractors, laborers, materialmen	subcontractors, sub-subcontractors, laborers, materialmen
Against whom is lien filed	owner	funds owing the contractor
When must lien be filed	within 8 months or 4 months if single family residence after lienor completes its work	within 30 days of project completion and acceptance
Where lien filed	county real property records	department head and state comptroller or department financial officer
Duration of lien	1 year	6 months
Lien extensions	1 year	1 year
Enforcement	suit for damages, foreclosure, or both	suit against funds and contractor

Appendix 9-2

Lienable Items
Items that are always lienable:

Architect's and engineer's plans
Light fixtures
Fixtures
Paint and other decorating

Items that are never lienable:

Light bulbs
Warranty work
Property maintenance

Items that may be lienable:

Carpeting
Supervision

Insurance

10

§10.01 Construction Insurance
§10.02 Understanding Insurance Policies
§10.03 Obtaining the Insurance Needed
§10.04 —Claims Made v Occurrence Policies
§10.05 —Duplicative Coverage
§10.06 Coverage
§10.07 —Liability Coverage
§10.08 —Property Coverage
§10.09 —*Occurrence* or *Accident*
§10.10 Wrap-Up Insurance
§10.11 Professional Liability Insurance
§10.12 Policy Limits
§10.13 Policy Requirements
§10.14 —Premiums
§10.15 —Notice to Insurers
§10.16 What to Do in the Event of an Occurrence
§10.17 Termination
§10.18 Exclusions
§10.19 —Contractor's Own Work
§10.20 —Pollution
§10.21 —Explosion, Collapse, and Underground Damage
§10.22 —Contractual Liability
§10.23 —Care, Custody, or Control
§10.24 Fidelity Insurance
§10.25 Officers' and Directors' Liability
§10.26 Motor Vehicles and Equipment
§10.27 Duty of Defense
§10.28 Limitation of Actions

§10.29   Duty of Cooperation
§10.30   Disclaimers
§10.31   Certificate of Insurance
§10.32   Special Insurance Problems
§10.33   —Design-Build Contracts
§10.34   —Joint Ventures
§10.35   —Construction Managers
Appendix 10-1   Insurance Policies
Appendix 10-2   Glossary of Common Construction Insurance Terms

§10.01   Construction Insurance

The subject of construction insurance is complicated and difficult to explain simply. Different companies offer different policies and coverages for different rates. What one insurer covers under a general liability policy, another may exclude. Thus, this chapter is very general. Its goal is to familiarize the reader with the basic coverages available, teach the reader how to read and gain a basic understanding of its insurance policies, and discuss court interpretations of policy language, requirements, and general rules of construction of policies. At the end of the chapter is a chart that attempts to show the most typical policies used in construction and their coverages, exclusions, and extensions (Appendix 10-1). Following the chart is a glossary of common construction insurance terms (Appendix 10-2). The reader is advised to review both the chart and the glossary before and while reading this chapter.

§10.02   Understanding Insurance Policies

Insurance policies often seem to be written in the "doublespeak" of George Orwell's *1984*. For instance, an "all risks" property insurance policy typically excludes coverage for damage due to risks such as flood, earthquake, defective design and workmanship, vandalism, testing, and theft, leaving one to wonder what risks an "all risks" policy covers. There is some recent effort on insurers' parts to use "plain language" in the hopes of reducing confusion.

Confusion as to the scope of insurance coverage, exclusions, and extensions is further created by the physical form of most policies. Most policies consist of numerous separate pieces of thin paper covered with fine print. Reading an insurance policy is like putting together a jigsaw puzzle with one important difference—it is difficult to tell if any insurance pieces are missing. Furthermore, most policies are poorly written; sentences ramble on for entire paragraphs, with so many commas and clauses that it is difficult to tell what clause modifies which word or phrase. Within an exclusion there may be an exception—an exclusion to the exclusion.

Very simply, a policy works this way: the main policy grants coverage; exclusions take coverage away; extensions give back coverage taken away by exclusions or add coverage to the main policy; endorsements may either take away or expand coverage; riders may expand or exclude coverage.

> **PRACTICE POINTER:**
>
> To determine whether a particular potential risk or actual injury is covered, review applicable insurance policies in this way:
>
> (1) Does general policy language indicate coverage? Does the risk or injury fit within policy definitions of covered events? If so, go to number (2); if not, go to number (3).
>
> (2) Do *any* exclusions apply to bar coverage? Does the risk or injury come within an exclusion? If so, go to number (3); if not, there is coverage.
>
> (3) Does the risk or injury fit within any of the policy extensions, endorsements, or riders? If so, there is coverage; if not, there is not coverage.
>
> For the visually minded reader, Figure 10-1 provides a flow chart that attempts to show this process of policy analysis.

Confusion as to coverage is further created by the insurers' frequent changing of policy language to meet new industry standards, avoid the consequences of adverse court decisions, and comply with requirements imposed by statutes. The constant changes make it difficult to interpret policy language consistently. What was defined as an *occurrence* in a contractor's policy last year may not be an occurrence this year. A case that interprets what a policy means by *occurrence* may not be applicable to an understanding of what it means under a different policy. Generally, any change in policy language tends to limit the coverage provided. Rarely, if ever, do insurers voluntarily expand coverage to insure more risks.

Another source of confusion is the fact that there are few standard policies or exclusions. Construction insurance is not offered by every company. The policies offered and coverages available vary greatly. There is a standard policy issued by the Insurance Services Organization (ISO) that is gaining acceptance and more common usage. If a potential insured is familiar with the standard ISO policy and knows that an insurance company uses it, the insured knows generally what the policy exclusions and coverages available under the policy are. It is difficult to compare one policy with another without the help of an expert who has a thorough understanding of both the construction and the insurance businesses.

§10.03 Obtaining the Insurance Needed

Unfortunately, the same care that an owner pays to the design of its project and selection of its contractor is not always given to obtaining the insurance it needs. Either the contract requires too much or too little insurance of the contractor; rarely does it require just the right amount. The principal reason for this failure is that few of the parties involved in a typical construction project, including architects and engineers, are adequately informed or understand construction insurance. Indeed, many insurance brokers and agents do not really understand construction insurance. If a broker sells life, home, health,

Figure 10–1

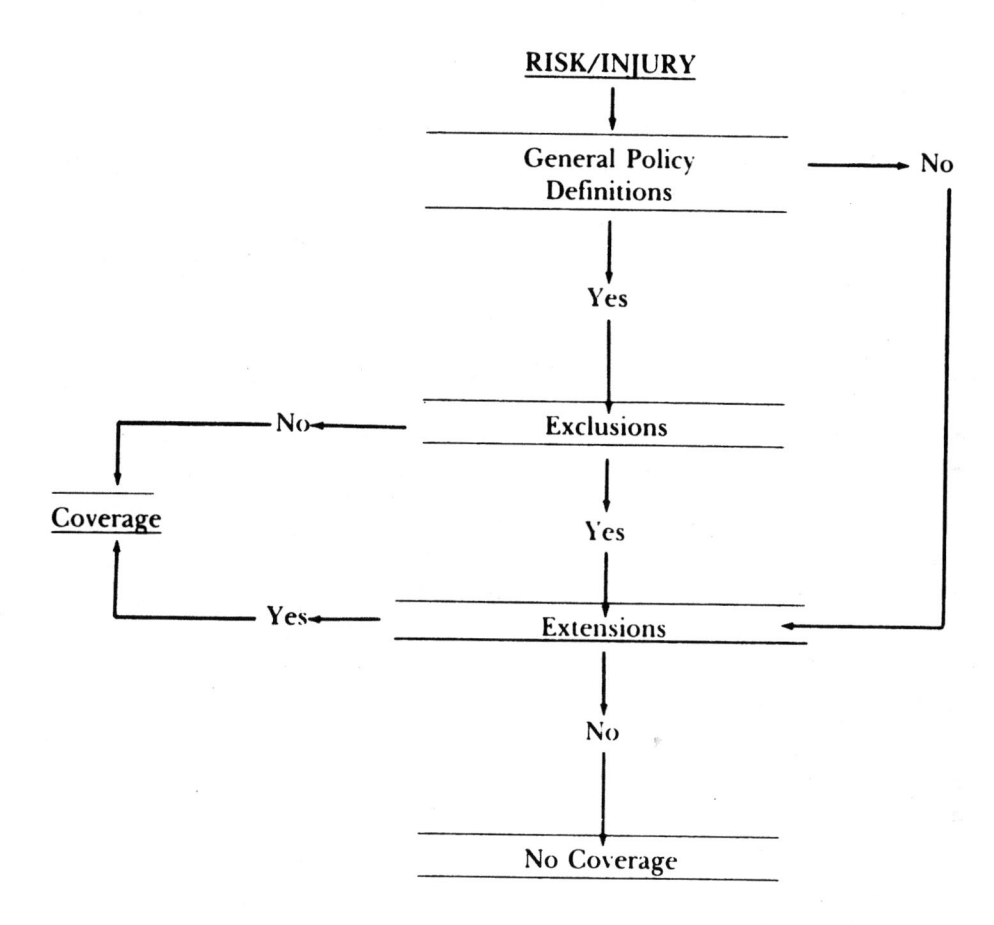

```
                    RISK/INJURY
                         │
                         ▼
                ┌──────────────────┐
                │  General Policy  │──────► No
                │   Definitions    │          │
                └──────────────────┘          │
                         │                    │
                         ▼                    │
                        Yes                   │
                         │                    │
                         ▼                    │
                ┌──────────────────┐          │
          No ◄──│    Exclusions    │          │
          │     └──────────────────┘          │
          │              │                    │
          ▼              ▼                    │
      ┌────────┐        Yes                   │
      │Coverage│         │                    │
      └────────┘         ▼                    │
          ▲     ┌──────────────────┐          │
          │ Yes │    Extensions    │ ◄────────┘
          └─────└──────────────────┘
                         │
                         ▼
                         No
                         │
                         ▼
                ┌──────────────────┐
                │   No Coverage    │
                └──────────────────┘
```

automobile, and general business insurance on behalf of several companies, when will it have had the time to understand the construction business and construction insurance sufficiently to fully advise a construction client?

Little comfort should be taken in the fact that if an agent misleads a client into believing that coverage is provided for a specified risk, when, in fact, it is not, the client may, nevertheless, have insurance. Consider what happened to a plumber. It was awarded a contract to connect an entire subdivision to a city sewer system and told its insurance agent that it needed "full coverage."[1] The policy application prepared by the agent described the hazard to be insured as "plumbing," despite the fact that it knew or should have known that its company's standard plumbing liability policy contained an exclusion for underground property damage and that the plumber was depending on the agent to obtain complete coverage for its operations. The agent did not tell the plumber of the exclusion, but merely sent the policy on to the plumber. When an accident happened and the plumber was sued, the insurer disclaimed coverage by virtue of the policy exclusions. Finally, after arguing with the insurance company and its agent, the plumber filed suit. The Appellate Division ruled in the plumber's favor and required the insurer to provide a defense to the plumber and indemnify it to the policy limits due to the agent's negligence and the insurer's responsibility for its agent's actions under basic principal/agent doctrines. If the plumber had obtained its insurance from a broker instead of an agent, the court probably would have found that the plumber did not have coverage.[2] Even though the plumber was found to have coverage, one can only imagine the strain the lawsuits put on the plumber's business and the damage the initial denial of coverage did to its reputation. Certainly the plumber would have been better off if it had used an agent who really knew the construction business and its insurance needs. There are such agents and brokers—insurance professionals who specialize in construction and other high risk industries. Truly objective advice can be obtained from an independent risk management consultant.

Risk Management Consultants

To obtain an objective and thorough review of insurance needs, an owner planning to build a large project, or a major contractor or subcontractor, would be wise to use a risk management consultant. One who is experienced in the construction industry can review a client's business operations or a particular project, evaluate the many policies and coverages available, advise the client on the value and effectiveness of the policies as compared with premium rates, and review contracts on specific jobs to ensure that they require each party to provide appropriate insurance, hence avoiding unnecessarily overlapping and excessive coverage. If the consultant is an insurance agent or broker, its services may be without cost in hopes that the client will buy the insurance

---

[1] Neil Plumbing & Heating Constr Co v Providence Wash Ins Co, 125 AD2d 295, 508 NYS2d 580 (2d Dept 1986).

[2] *See* Security Mut Ins Co v Acker-Fitzsimons Corp, 31 NY2d 436, 293 NE2d 76, 340 NYS2d 902 (1972).

through it. If the consultant is not a broker or an agent (and, hence, truly independent), its fee generally will be money well spent in terms of reduced premiums, elimination of duplicate coverage, lower contract prices, and more complete insurance coverage.

§10.04 —Claims Made v Occurrence Policies

Historically, most commercial general liability policies have been written on an *occurrence* basis. A claim is covered regardless of when filed so long as the occurrence took place during the policy period. As the courts began to interpret this policy language broadly, underwriters reacted by offering certain coverage on a *claims made* basis—i.e., coverage is based on when the claim is made, rather than on when the occurrence happened. In the mid-1970s, an insurance "crisis" arose due to several events—the most significant from a construction standpoint concerned asbestos litigation. Courts found that occurrence-based policies issued decades before an asbestos claim was made provided coverage. As a result, insurers switched to offering coverage on claims made bases to protect themselves.

Claims made coverage can cause a number of practical problems for some parties. If a building is found to be structurally unsound 10 years after it was built and all involved parties had claims made coverage during construction, the architect and the contractor may not have insurance protection. Under a claims made policy, an insured has little reason to believe that premiums paid today will offer any protection for a claim that may be made for latent defects discovered years in the future. There will be insurance protection only if (1) the same policy is maintained through the years and the construction company and the insurance company are still viable; (2) the current policy has sufficient prior acts coverage; or (3) the construction policy had a sufficient extended reporting period. Insureds are advised to keep copies of all old policies, as an insured seeking coverage many years after a policy period has passed must be able to identify who its insurer was for each potential period of injury or incident and discover the terms of its coverage during those periods. This process is made more difficult if the insured changed insurance carriers.

When a policy is written on a claims made basis, the insured must exercise great care to be certain that there are no gaps in coverage. For example, if a prior policy, also written on a claims made basis, is being replaced, the insured must be certain that the retroactive date on the new policy is far enough in the past to ensure that the present policy will provide coverage for a claim due to a past occurrence. Alternatively, the insured should purchase a tail (extended reporting period) of sufficient length on the replaced policy to be certain that the claim is covered by the older policy.

Occurrence coverage provides protection for accidents that occur during the policy period. It is irrelevant when a claim is made, a lawsuit is filed, or the insured first learns of the claim. Most commercial general liability policies are occurrence based.

An insured must be aware of what type of coverage it has. The fact that insurance is called *occurrence* coverage does not mean that it is any more helpful than *claims made* coverage. Some insurers include clauses in an occurrence policy that provides that the policy reverts to claims made after several years; this is called a "sunset clause."

§10.05 —Duplicative Coverage

Many specific risk insurance policies, such as fire insurance, extend coverage to the insured's property "not otherwise covered by insurance"[3] or specifically exclude coverage for property and risks covered by other insurance. Such policies or exclusions prevent recovery only if there is an *identity of interest* in the property covered, i.e., when one insured has more than one coverage on the same property.[4] Thus, if the same property is covered but by different insureds, such an exclusion would not apply. For instance, in one case, a scaffolding company leased scaffolding to a resort. A fire at the resort damaged the scaffolding. The scaffolding company had insurance on its scaffolding, while the resort had several fire insurance policies that extended coverage to builders' equipment that was not otherwise covered by insurance. The court held that the scaffolding company's insurance did not affect the resort's right to recover from its fire insurer because the two parties had separate and distinct insurance interests.[5] This does not mean that there is a double recovery from insurance carriers. The owner's policy will respond only if the owner is found liable for the loss to the scaffolding company. One insurance company will simply be paying another insurance company.

See §10.10 on wrap-up insurance for a discussion on how to avoid unnecessarily duplicative coverage.

§10.06 Coverage

Standard construction contracts typically specify risks for which a contractor is required to provide insurance and dollar limits of such coverage. Types of insurance specified generally include workers' compensation and employee injury; death or bodily injury; and damage or destruction of property. *Liability* coverage (also known as *third-party coverage*) is needed for contractors, subcontractors, and owners to insure against bodily injury and property damage claims by third persons. *Property* coverage (also known as *first-party coverage*), such as fire insurance, is needed to protect the premises under construction. The principal distinction between liability and property insurance is that liability insurance covers one's liability to *others* for bodily injury or property damage, while property insurance covers damage to one's *own* property.

Insurance is intended to cover loss caused by *accidents*, i.e., sudden, unexpected events. It will not cover intended results of intentional acts or poor

---

[3] Modern Scaffold Co v Karell Realty Corp, 28 AD2d 581, 279 NYS2d 436 (3d Dept 1967).

[4] *Id.*

[5] *Id.*

workmanship or design. For instance, if a heater is poorly designed and will not adequately heat the building, liability insurance will not cover the deficiency. If, however, the poor design causes the heater to explode, the damage to persons and property caused by the explosion would be covered by insurance.

§10.07 —Liability Coverage

Liability insurance furnishes a legal defense and responds in damages to suits by third parties. Insurance carriers are quick to point out that their only obligation under the policy is to defend lawsuits commenced against the insured and, if there is coverage, pay any judgment. The insurer's duty to defend is much broader than the duty to pay.[6] The insurer does not have a duty to settle a case in order to help its insured if a job has been stopped due to an accident or coverage dispute. Of course, an insurer does have a duty of good faith towards its insured.

Contractors should be aware that many policies exclude coverage if the insured provides construction management services. This exclusion is intended to preclude coverage for liability arising from the errors and omissions of construction managers. Thus, if a contractor agrees to serve as a construction manager for a project, it must have the exclusion removed before it performs any construction manager services.

> **PRACTICE POINTER:**
>
> When representing a contractor or subcontractor, it may be wise to include in the contract a clause that provides that payment may not be withheld on account of a claim if the claim is covered by insurance.

§10.08 —Property Coverage

For the most part, property insurance is written on two bases. One provides coverage for specific risks, such as fire, lightning, theft, malicious mischief, etc. The second provides "all risks" coverage, subject to the exclusion of numerous risks.

§10.09 —*Occurrence* or *Accident*

Most policies state that they provide coverage for an *occurrence*, which is typically defined as "[a]n accident, including injurious exposure to conditions, which results, during the policy period, in bodily injury or property damage,

---

[6] McGroarty v Great Am Ins Co, 36 NY2d 358, 329 NE2d 172, 368 NYS2d 485 (1975). The duty to defend is discussed in §10.27.

neither expected nor intended from the standpoint of the insured."[7] To determine whether an accident caused the damage complained of (and, thus, whether there is coverage), the chain of events must be considered as a whole. This "transaction as a whole" test was first established in 1921 by Justice Cardozo who wrote that the "character of the liability is not to be determined by analyzing the constituent acts, which, in combination, make up the transaction, and viewing them distributively. It is determined by the quality and purpose of the transaction as a whole."[8] It is the *results* that are viewed, not the causes of the results. While the act may be intentional, insurance liability is avoided only if the result of the act was intended.[9] The courts have distinguished between damages which "flow directly and immediately from an intended act, thereby precluding coverage, and damages which accidentally arise out of a chain of unintended though expected or foreseeable events that occurred after an intentional act."[10] The issue of whether a particular event is an accident is a question of fact, not a question of law.[11]

"It is not legally impossible to find accidental results flowing from intentional causes, i.e., that the resulting damage was unintended although the original act or acts leading to the damage were intentional."[12] To deny coverage under the definition of *occurrence*, a fact-finder must find that the insured intended to cause damage or expected its action to result in damage; the damage must have been more than reasonably foreseeable.[13] Neither ordinary negligence nor a calculated risk shows intent to cause damage[14] and may result in an accident.[15]

This definition of *accident* can be seen in the case of an excavator that, knowing that its work might damage a garage on adjacent property, took a calculated risk that damage would not occur and chose to continue its operation without altering its methods despite the adjacent property owner's claims that the excavation methods chosen threatened its property.[16] The resulting damage to the adjacent property was found to be an accident; taking a calculated risk does not make the results of an insured's action intentional. Similarly, consider the

---

[7] Continental Ins Co v Colangione, 107 AD2d 978, 484 NYS2d 929, 930 (3d Dept 1985). See also General Acc Ins Co of Am v Manchester, 116 AD2d 790, 497 NYS2d 180 (3d Dept 1986); American Motorists Ins Co v ER Squibb & Sons, 95 Misc 2d 222, 406 NYS2d 658 (NY 1978).

[8] Messersmith v American Fidelity Co, 232 NY 161, 133 NE 432, 433 (1921).

[9] McGroarty v Great Am Ins Co, 36 NY2d 358, 329 NE2d 172, 368 NYS2d 485 (1975).

[10] Continental Ins Co v Colangione, 107 AD2d 978, 484 NYS2d 929, 930 (3d Dept 1985).

[11] McGroarty v Great Am Ins Co, 36 NY2d 358, 329 NE2d 172, 368 NYS2d 485 (1975); Continental Ins Co v Colangione, 107 AD2d 978, 484 NYS2d 929 (3d Dept 1985).

[12] McGroarty v Great Am Ins Co, 36 NY2d 358, 364, 329 NE2d 172, 177, 368 NYS2d 485, 490 (1975).

[13] General Acc Ins Co of Am v Manchester, 116 AD2d 790, 497 NYS2d 180 (3d Dept 1986).

[14] *Id.*

[15] McGroarty v Great Am Ins Co, 36 NY2d 358, 329 NE2d 172, 368 NYS2d 485 (1975).

[16] *Id.*

case of a subcontractor hired to perform work in a theater.[17] The work required laborers to cross the theater ceiling, although no work was to be done on the ceiling. Although expressly warned not to walk on the ceiling but told to walk on planks placed across the ceiling, the subcontractor's laborers did walk on the ceiling, causing it to crack and eventually fall. The court held that the damage was caused by a series of accidents, that the laborers did not walk on the ceiling intending to damage it or to sabotage the theater but did so accidentally, temporarily and carelessly forgetting their instructions not to walk on the ceiling.

An occurrence may be gradual; it need not be a sudden or catastrophic event. For instance, an occurrence was found when steel gradually rusted over a period of time.[18] Similarly, an accident was held to have occurred when the plaintiff's building cracked and settled over a several-month period due to excavation by the insured.[19]

Finally, under the typical definition of occurrence, coverage is provided if the injury or damage occurs during the policy period.[20]

Insurance issues relative to environmental concerns are discussed in **Chapter 14.**

§10.10 Wrap-Up Insurance

Construction insurance is rarely written in a vacuum. Generally, on one project, the owner, contractor, subcontractors, and architects/engineers have their own ongoing insurance programs. Each party's insurance is tailored to meet its specific needs. A construction project is a short-term enterprise that has specific insurance needs that must be superimposed on the ongoing insurance needs of each party. Each party's permanent insurance program needs to be analyzed and a custom policy specially written for the project; there are bound to be overlaps and gaps in coverage if standard policies are used to meet individual project requirements. To mitigate the problem, many insurance agents and brokers recommend that additional coverage be purchased by owners and contractors with clearly duplicative coverages in order to fill as many gaps as possible; this is a great solution from the agent's point of view—more premiums on which to earn commissions. From the insured's point of view, however, this results in multiple premiums for duplicative coverage, often without really increasing coverage or eliminating the feeling (and, often, the reality) that there are gaps in coverage, i.e., that all of the risks that should be covered are not.

When an accident occurs, there is one occurence regardless of the number of victims that the accident may have created. It is an appealing idea to have

---

[17] AT Morris & Co v Lumber Mut Cas Ins Co, 163 Misc 715, 298 NYS 227 (Queens 1937).

[18] TJ Picozzi Constr Co v Exchange Mut Ins Co, 138 AD2d 907, 526 NYS2d 652 (3d Dept 1988).

[19] McGroarty v Great Am Ins Co, 36 NY2d 358, 329 NE2d 172, 368 NYS2d 485 (1975).

[20] American Motorists Ins Co v ER Squibb & Sons, 95 Misc 2d 222, 406 NYS2d 658 (NY 1978).

only one insurance company covering all damage and the potential liability of each party to the construction process. Such coverage is known as *wrap-up insurance*. There would be only one premium for the risks insured, one policy commission, one administrative expense for the insurance company, and, if a loss occurred, one attorneys' fee for defending the interests of all parties. There would not be suits between insurers arguing over who had to cover the loss or defend the suit. These are some of the rationales behind wrap-up insurance.

Wrap-up insurance is legal in New York by statute for private works; wrap-up insurance on certain public contracts is not allowed.[21] An owner or contractor may provide all insurance on a project and require that bidders provide a credit that reflects the amount that the bidding contractor or subcontractor would otherwise add if it had provided its own insurance as required in the bid specifications.[22] If an owner or a contractor chooses to provide all insurance, it may not require its contractor or subcontractors to pay premiums or other charges for such policies obtained by the owner or contractor.[23] Generally, wrap-up insurance is not cost effective on projects where the anticipated construction costs are less than $100 million. Wrap-up insurance should include builder's risk property coverage, professional liability coverage, workers' compensation and employee injury insurance coverage, and liability and property coverages. It should not include automobile, employee fidelity, valuable papers, or other miscellaneous coverages.

There is much controversy surrounding wrap-up insurance; arguments both in favor of and against wrap-up insurance have merit. Arguments favoring wrap-up insurance include:

1. It provides the potential for uniform high level insurance expertise that is applied to a projectwide program of risk and safety management.

2. As there is only one carrier, coverage disputes between carriers are eliminated. Not only does this make the insured more secure but it also facilitates quicker settlement of third-party claims.

3. Premium rates should be the lowest overall when compared with multiple policies, since wrap-up insurance avoids multiple coverages, defense costs, and commissions.

Arguments against wrap-up insurance include:

1. Without careful administration of an owner's wrap-up insurance program, a contractor's loss records for workers' compensation and liability insurance can be adversely affected. Specifically, the contractor is not represented in the determination of liability and settlement negotiation. Anticipating that its overall insurance experience record will be adversely

---

[21] NY Ins Law §2504 (McKinney 1982).
[22] *Id* §§2502(c), 2505(b).
[23] *Id* §2505(a).

affected by experiences allocated to it by the owner's insurance provider, a contractor may add extra costs to its bid to cover the extra expense it will incur in higher premiums on its policies.
2. A reduction in a contractor's or subcontractor's total policy and premium volume with its own insurance company may increase insurance costs on its other work. This increase will be reflected in its bid.
3. Contractors and subcontractors may have less incentive to reduce their liability costs and exercise care. This increased exposure is shown in the premium risk rating for wrap-up insurance.
4. Smaller contractors and subcontractors do not separate insurance costs from overhead costs and will not or cannot accurately reflect a credit in their bids if wrap-up insurance is provided.
5. Wrap-up insurance can interfere with a contractor's or subcontractor's ability to obtain coverage for its other operations at a reasonable rate. For instance, wrap-up insurance may not cover a paving contractor's plant and equipment; insurance solely for the plant and equipment may not be available at a reasonable rate. Thus, a contractor may have to purchase duplicative coverage to protect itself, defeating the purpose of wrap-up insurance.

Each side's arguments can be convincing. Depending upon the parties and project concerned, wrap-up insurance may or may not reduce an owner's or a contractor's overall insurance cost for a project. The solution to the dilemma is for owners to make a comprehensive insurance cost analysis for each project to determine which approach most economically provides adequate coverage.

If an owner or a contractor decides to provide wrap-up insurance, its contractors' or subcontractors' workers' compensation premium refunds should be returned to them as they are earned (rather than held by the owner) to provide an incentive to promote safety. If the wrap-up insurance covers a contractor's or subcontractor's plant and equipment, a high deductible should apply to any claims involving such plant and equipment. The contractor or subcontractor is thus provided with catastrophe insurance without removing responsibility for its plant and equipment. The contractor or subcontractor can insure the deductible if it chooses. Similarly, liability coverage for contractors and subcontractors should carry a realistic deductible for each occurrence, to give them an incentive to minimize third-party damage. If professional liability insurance is included in the wrap-up for the project architects and engineers, it should carry a substantial deductible which can be separately insured by each designer if it chooses.

§10.11 Professional Liability Insurance

Architects' and engineers' professional liability insurance is intended to cover loss due to an error, an omission, or a negligent act of the professional in its professional capacity. The coverage is very restrictive and is available virtually only on a *claims made* basis.[24] Policies contain numerous exclusions, particularly for contractual liability, and have high deductibles. Many policies require the insurance to be in effect both when the negligent act occurred (i.e., a design error) and when the injury occurred (such as a roof collapse several years later). If the professional has changed insurance companies, it may be without coverage for projects that it built earlier, unless it obtains prior acts coverage under its new policy or had a very long tail (extended reporting period) on its prior policy.

Contractors and owners who are not licensed engineers or architects probably will not be able to obtain professional liability insurance. Thus, if an accident happens due to failure of a contractor's design, there would not be insurance coverage. A good example of this is when a contractor "designs" a trench wall bracing system to hold back earth when excavating.

> **PRACTICE POINTER:**
>
> Licensed professionals who are employed by contractors should obtain their own professional liability policies if they perform professional design services as part of their jobs. Unfortunately, this may be difficult to obtain, as such coverage is not generally available to employed engineers. If there is a collapse or failure with resulting personal injury or property damage, the professional engineer who sealed the drawings can expect to be sued. The contractor's commercial general liability carrier will generally not provide a defense or cover the loss on behalf of the professional engineer. If the contractor has gone out of business or the professional engineer has left its employ, the professional engineer can be left holding the bag. Employed professional engineers are therefore usually well advised not to seal drawings for their contractor-employers.

While the law does not require that design professionals have insurance, it does regulate the insurance available, including placing limits on the amount of defense costs an insurer may charge against the policy limits. (See the discussion in §10.12.)

§10.12 Policy Limits

Policy limits are the maximum amount an insurer will pay on behalf of an insured, on either an occurrence or an annual basis. See the glossary (Appendix 10-2) for a complete definition and explanation of policy limits.

Generally, the cost of defending an action may not be counted against the policy limits in determining funds available to pay damages, although the new trend is to count defense costs against policy limits. For instance, assume that a contractor has a $1,000,000 per occurrence policy limit and is sued for $975,000. The insurance company pays $60,000 defending the action and

---

[24] *See* §10.04.

loses, resulting in an award to the plaintiff of $975,000. The $60,000 spent on the defense would not reduce the policy limits; the insurer would pay the plaintiff the $975,000. Thus, the insurer would pay $1,035,000 on a policy with a $1,000,000 per occurrence limit.

Under certain professional liability policies that meet minimum policy limit standards, up to 50 per cent of the policy limits may be applied toward legal defense costs.[25] Under such a policy, the insurer in the above example could offset all of the legal defense costs against the $1,000,000 policy limit, leaving only $940,000 to pay the plaintiff's damages. (The net result being that the insured must pay the remaining $35,000). Such an offset provision may be included in liability policies that have policy limits of at least $1,000,000 for director and officer liability and employee benefit liability and policy limits of at least $500,000 for architect and engineer liability.[26]

§10.13 Policy Requirements

Under an insurance policy, an insured has certain duties it must perform to have coverage. The three most important are paying the premium (discussed in §10.14), notifying the insurer of occurrences and claims (discussed in §10.15), and cooperating with the insurer in the investigation and defense of the claims (discussed in §10.29).

§10.14 —Premiums

Premiums must be paid when due. If an insured risks paying its insurance late and a claim occurs in the interim, it may find itself without coverage.[27] Premium notices should be sent to an insured well before they are due so the insured has ample notice and time to pay the premium or seek alternative insurance if it chooses. By statute, insurers must give notice of cancellation due to nonpayment before cancellation becomes effective.[28]

Premiums are based on the coverage provided, the particular insured's loss record and risk management programs, the deductibles chosen, and the risks insured against—e.g., a high risk contractor, such as a demolition contractor, will pay a higher premium than will a contractor involved in a relatively low risk enterprise, such as a painter.

Premiums are computed or rated in different ways. For example, some policies are rated *retrospectively*, which means that after the policy term is ended, the insurer reviews the actual experience during the policy term and adjusts the premium for the expired policy to reflect the claims actually made. Such premiums are subject to pre-agreed minimum and maximum amounts.

---

[25] NY State Ins Reg 107 (11 NYCRR 71) (Lenz & Riecker, Inc).
[26] *Id.*
[27] Brecker v Mutual Life Ins Co, 120 AD2d 423, 501 NYS2d 879 (1st Dept 1986).
[28] NY Ins Law §3426 (McKinney 1985 & Supp 1992).

§10.15 —Notice to Insurers

The great majority of insurance policies set forth under what conditions and at what point of time an insured must give the insurer notice of an accident or occurrence and a claim or potential claim. A policy may require that notice be given to the insurer "as soon as practicable" after an occurrence and "immediately" upon knowledge of a claim being made or a suit being brought.[29] Compliance with a notice provision is a condition precedent to an insurer's liability under the policy[30] and, hence, is essential for coverage of a claim. If the insurance agreement is silent, New York law implies an obligation on the insured to notify the insurer within a reasonable period of time.[31] If a notice provision requires written notice within a specified number of days, give written notice. A failure to comply with a notice provision without a valid excuse will relieve the insurer of its obligations under the policy in relation to the claim.[32] An insurer need not show prejudice to assert the defense of noncompliance with a notice provision.[33] Be forewarned that a delay in giving notice need not be lengthy for it to relieve the insurer of its obligations. For instance, delays as short as 29,[34] 51,[35] and 56 days[36] have been found unreasonable and held to excuse the insurer from providing coverage.

If an insured really believes, in good faith, that it would not be liable for the occurrence or claim, its failure to give timely notice may be excused if its belief in its nonliability is *reasonable under all circumstances*.[37] For instance, in one case, it was not reasonable for a contractor to believe that it was not potentially liable for a pedestrian's injuries when the pedestrian tripped and fell within 5-to-10 feet of the contractor's work area.[38] When determining whether a belief is reasonable, it is appropriate to examine the extent of an insured's investigation and inquiry into the occurrence.[39] A failure to conduct any investigation

---

[29] *See* Empire City Subway Co v Greater NY Mut Ins Co, 35 NY2d 8, 315 NE2d 755, 358 NYS2d 691 (1974).

[30] Commercial Union Ins Co v International Flavors & Fragrances, Inc, 822 F2d 267, 271 (2d Cir 1987).

[31] Ell Dee Clothing Co v Marsh, 247 NY 392, 160 NE 651 (1928); Allstate Ins Co v Kashkin, 130 AD2d 744, 516 NYS2d 43 (2d Dept 1987).

[32] Allstate Ins Co v Kashkin, 130 AD2d 744, 516 NYS2d 43 (2d Dept 1987).

[33] Reliance Ins Co v Garsart Bldg Corp, 131 AD2d 828, 517 NYS2d 189 (2d Dept 1987); State Farm Mut Auto Ins Co v Romero, 109 AD2d 786, 486 NYS2d 297 (2d Dept 1985).

[34] Government Employees Ins Co v Elman, 40 AD2d 994, 338 NYS2d 666 (2d Dept 1972).

[35] Deso v London & Lancashire Indem Co, 3 NY2d 127, 143 NE2d 889, 164 NYS2d 689 (1957).

[36] Power Auth v Westinghouse Elec Corp, 117 AD2d 336, 502 NYS2d 420 (1st Dept 1986).

[37] Empire City Subway Co v Greater NY Mut Ins Co, 35 NY2d 8, 315 NE2d 755, 358 NYS2d 691 (1974).

[38] *Id.*

[39] Security Mut Ins Co v Acker-Fitzsimons Corp, 31 NY2d 436, 293 NE2d 76, 340 NYS2d 902 (1972).

upon learning of an occurrence would be unreasonable. The insured has the burden of proving that its failure to give timely notice should be excused.[40]

When an insured is served with a complaint or receives notice of a claim, the insured has a duty to exercise reasonable care and diligence to learn the facts behind the claim and evaluate its potential liability.[41] The safest course is to give notice as soon as one learns of an occurrence, receives a letter demanding recompense, or is served with a complaint.

Agents and Brokers

Be wary when giving notice to anyone but the insurance company. The person through whom the policy was purchased may not have the authority to accept notice on the insurer's behalf. Notice to an insurance broker generally is not notice to the insurer,[42] while notice to an insurance agent is. The best advice is to deal only with knowledgeable *construction* insurance professionals.

Without a real or an apparent agency relationship with the insurance carrier, a broker is not an insurer's representative, but represents the insured;[43] generally, an agent represents the insurer and a broker represents the insured.[44] To be found to be an agent, there must be "evidence of some action on the insurer's part, or facts from which a general authority to represent the insurer may be inferred."[45] Whether an insurance salesperson is a broker or an agent is determined by the circumstance of the case, not by statutory definitions.[46] A good indication of whether one is an agent or a broker is whether one is able to issue a policy without seeking specific authority.[47] If one has to make a telephone call or receive a letter of authorization before issuing a binder, he or she probably is a broker, not an agent.

> **PRACTICE POINTER:**
>
> Because of the difficulty in determining whether an insurance salesperson is an agent or a broker, it is best to review your policy notice provisions when notice of a claim is required. Do not rely upon your salesperson to forward your notice of claim to the insurer.

---

[40] Reliance Ins Co v Garsart Bldg Corp, 131 AD2d 828, 517 NYS2d 189 (2d Dept 1987).

[41] Empire City Subway Co v Greater NY Mut Ins Co, 35 NY2d 8, 315 NE2d 755, 358 NYS2d 691 (1974); Security Mut Ins Co v Acker-Fitzsimons Corp, 31 NY2d 436, 293 NE2d 76, 340 NYS2d 902 (1972).

[42] Security Mut Ins Co v Acker-Fitzsimons Corp, 31 NY2d 436, 293 NE2d 76, 340 NYS2d 902 (1972); Gabriel v Attigliato, 60 Misc 2d 536, 303 NYS2d 399 (Rockland 1968).

[43] Gabriel v Attigliato, 60 Misc 2d 536, 303 NYS2d 399 (Rockland 1968).

[44] American Motorists Ins Co v Salvatore, 102 AD2d 342, 476 NYS2d 897 (1st Dept 1984).

[45] Matco Prods v Boston Old Colony Ins Co, 104 AD2d 793, 480 NYS2d 134 (1984).

[46] Price v Lawrence-Van Voast, Inc, 58 AD2d 727, 396 NYS2d 296 (3d Dept 1977).

[47] Moshiko, Inc v Seiger & Smith, Inc, 137 AD2d 170, 529 NYS2d 284 (1st Dept), *affd mem*, 72 NY2d 945, 529 NE2d 420, 533 NYS2d 52 (1988).

§10.16 What to Do in the Event of an Occurrence

When something happens that may give rise to an insurance claim:

1. *Give timely notice.* As soon as *anything* happens that *might possibly* give rise to a claim, notify your own insurance company and the owner, architect, contractor, subcontractors, and each of their insurance companies *in writing* and by *certified* or *registered* mail. Do not rely upon another party to notify their insurer as they may not do so, hoping to avoid an unfavorable premium adjustment or believing themselves not liable. Do not let someone else's error harm your ability to recover for damages you have suffered.

2. *Do nothing that might prejudice the rights of the insurance company.* Always act as though your own money is at stake. Do not admit you were at fault. Do not give oral statements or discuss the occurrence with the injured party or its attorneys without first informing your insurance company. Do not sign written statements without obtaining the *written* consent of your insurer.

3. *Cooperate with the insurer in defense of the suit or in investigation of the claim.* Assist the insurer in gathering documents, photographs, exhibits, plans, specifications, and correspondence. Attend depositions and hearings if asked to by the insurer.

4. *Preserve your right to sue your insurer.* As soon as a potentially covered loss occurs, review the policy and note when a proof of loss must be filed and when a lawsuit must be commenced against the insurer in the event it does not honor the claim.

§10.17 Termination

Policies may be terminated by insureds without cause and by insurers for cause. If an insurer wishes to cancel a policy it must comply with all applicable statutory requirements.[48] Of course, if an insured requests cancellation, the insurer does not have to comply with statutory notice requirements.[49] A request for cancellation by an insured is not effective until it is *received* by the insurer or its agent, regardless of the date the insured requested that termination be effective.[50]

Within the first 60 days that a commercial or professional liability policy is in force, an insurer may cancel the policy for any specific reason upon 20 days' written notice, but it must notify the insured why the policy is being terminat-

---

[48] Cancellation procedures are found in NY Ins Law §§3425 (fire and automobile insurance), 3426 (commercial and professional liability insurance), 3427 (products liability insurance), 3429 (fire insurance), and 3431 (notice provisions for termination) (McKinney 1985 & Supp 1992).

[49] Zulferino v State Farm Auto Ins Co, 123 AD2d 432, 506 NYS2d 736 (2d Dept 1986).

[50] Savino v Merchants Mut Ins Co, 44 NY2d 625, 378 NE2d 1038, 407 NYS2d 468 (1978).

ed.[51] After the first 60 days, a policy may be canceled only for one of the reasons set forth in the statute, including nonpayment of premium.[52] When a policy is up for renewal and an insurer does not wish to renew, it must comply with the same statutory requirements as if it were terminating the policy; it may not simply bill a renewal premium and permit coverage to terminate without a notice of cancellation or grace period for payment.[53] In the absence of a notice of nonrenewal, renewal is automatic upon the billing of a premium for the renewal term.[54]

A notice of cancellation or termination is effective so long as the insurer complies with all statutory and policy notice provisions, regardless of whether the insured actually receives the notice.[55]

§10.18 Exclusions

The number and extent of exclusions in insurance policies are ever changing. This chapter and its chart (Appendix 10-1) and glossary (Appendix 10-2) discuss the more common exclusions and their effects. When reading a policy's exclusions, it is important to realize that each exclusion must be read individually, not cumulatively. Absent an endorsement or a rider, if any one exclusion applies, there is no coverage; one exclusion cannot be regarded as inconsistent with another.[56]

To be relieved of a duty to defend or indemnify the insured, the insurer has the burden of proving that the claim comes *wholly* within an exclusion.[57] Exclusions are strictly construed against the insurer. For instance, a "sistership" clause is designed to exclude coverage of losses caused by withdrawal of work or product "from the market or from use because of any known or suspected defect or deficiency therein."[58] Such a clause was found not to bar recovery for damages to a house caused by urea formaldehyde insulation that had to be removed and replaced. The court found that the damages and removal and replacement costs were not due to a withdrawal from the market or use as specified in the exclusion.[59]

---

[51] NY Ins Law §3426(b) (McKinney 1985 & Supp 1992); Sinclairs Deli, Inc v Associated Mut Ins Co, 163 AD2d 296, 559 NYS2d 15 (2d Dept 1990).

[52] Gannon v New York Mut Underwriters, 78 AD2d 399, 435 NYS2d 163 (3d Dept), *affd mem*, 55 NY2d 641, 430 NE2d 1318, 446 NYS2d 265 (1981).

[53] Victor v Turner, 113 AD2d 490, 496 NYS2d 761 (2d Dept 1985).

[54] NY Ins Law §3425 (McKinney 1985 & Supp 1992).

[55] Fichtner v State Farm Fire & Cas Co, 148 Misc 2d 194, 560 NYS2d 94 (Cattaraugus 1990).

[56] Zandri Constr Co v Firemen's Ins Co, 81 AD2d 106, 440 NYS2d 353 (3d Dept), *affd mem*, 54 NY2d 999, 430 NE2d 922, 446 NYS2d 45 (1981).

[57] International Paper Co v Continental Cas Co, 35 NY2d 322, 320 NE2d 619, 361 NYS2d 873 (1974).

[58] Truax & Hovey, Ltd v Aetna Cas & Sur Co, 122 AD2d 563, 504 NYS2d 934, 934-35 (4th Dept 1986).

[59] *Id.*

§10.19 —Contractor's Own Work

Insurance policies are not performance bonds or warranties.[60] Under the terms of most policies and exclusions, they do not protect a contractor or an owner against poor workmanship except to the extent that the poor workmanship damages something or someone else. Thus, insurance does not provide coverage for a contractor's defective work product or for damage to the contractor's work or materials.[61] For instance, a contractor was without coverage when it was sued by the owners of a church it had constructed. The church alleged that the church building was so poorly built that it had to conduct services elsewhere at considerable additional expense and that "great sums of money" would be needed to make the building safe for occupancy.[62] The court held that the insurance policies carried by the contractor clearly excluded coverage for damage to the insured's work product due to its failure to perform in a workmanlike manner or its breach of warranty of fitness or quality. The court found that the risk that the insurance covered was that the completed work product (here the church building) might cause bodily injury or damage to property other than the completed work product itself.

The exclusion for a contractor's own work does not usually bar coverage for damage to other parts of the building or its contents. If a contractor installs a boiler improperly and it blows up, the cost of replacing the boiler, including its installation, generally would not be covered; the contractor would bear this loss itself. If the boiler explosion causes a fire that damages the building and burns a laborer who was laying floor tile near the boiler when it exploded, insurance would cover these losses. If the building was completed at the time of the explosion, there would be no coverage from the contractor's insurance policy, unless it had completed operations coverage.

Similarly, if a roof is negligently installed and its defects cause damage to the remainder of the building and the occupant's possessions, the contractor may have coverage for the damages that it owes the owner of the building and its occupant.[63]

Liability insurance generally excludes coverage for damages done to the contractor's own work. For example, if a wall collapses and causes damage to an automobile parked near it, the contractor's liability insurance will pay on account of the damage to the automobile, but will not pay to replace the wall because the wall was the contractor's own work.

Until recently, a general contractor's *own work* excluded work performed by a subcontractor. For example, a general contractor's policy would not pay to repair the electrical subcontractor's work; it would pay only to repair the damage to other property caused by an electrical failure.

---

[60] JGA Constr Corp v Charter Oak Fire Ins Co, 66 AD2d 315, 414 NYS2d 385 (4th Dept 1979).

[61] Zandri Constr Co v Firemen's Ins Co, 81 AD2d 106, 440 NYS2d 353 (3d Dept), affd mem, 54 NY2d 999, 430 NE2d 922, 446 NYS2d 45 (1981).

[62] *Id* at 107, 440 NYS2d at 354.

[63] *See* Marine Midland Servs Corp v Samuel Kosoff & Sons, 60 AD2d 767, 400 NYS2d 959 (4th Dept 1977).

The most recent Insurance Services Organization (ISO) policy form, however, does not define a subcontractor's work as the general contractor's own work. Therefore, under the latest policy form, the general contractor's policy would pay to repair the electrical subcontractor's work.

§10.20 —Pollution

This exclusion is discussed in **Chapter 14** on environmental problems in construction.

§10.21 —Explosion, Collapse, and Underground Damage

A common exclusion is the "x,c,u" exclusion; it is discussed in the glossary (Appendix 10-2).

§10.22 —Contractual Liability

Often insurance agreements exclude coverage for "liability assumed by the insured under any contract or agreement."[64] When coupled with many contractors' contractual duties to indemnify owners for others' actions, it appears that contractors are without coverage for a potentially large area of liability. The courts, however, have read this exclusion very closely. Thus, if a contractor is sued in common law *and* contractual indemnity, the insurer must defend. Similarly, if the insured contractor is liable to the owner under either the construction contract's indemnity provision or in tort, independent of the contract, the exclusion is not applicable and there would be coverage. "Where the facts are such that an insured's liability exists on one theory as well as another and one of the theories brings the liability within coverage, the insured may avail itself of the coverage."[65]

§10.23 —Care, Custody, or Control

The "care, custody, or control" exclusion has been the source of many suits between insureds and insurers. The new wording of the exclusion that limits its application (see Appendix 10-2) may help make the issue clearer. At the time this was written, the authors knew of no cases interpreting the new care, custody, or control exclusion.

One version of the "old" exclusion provided coverage for damage to any property except

---

[64] Aetna Cas & Sur Co v Lumbermens Mut Cas Co, 136 AD2d 246, 527 NYS2d 143, 144 (4th Dept 1988).

[65] *Id* at 248, 527 NYS2d at 145; C.T. Drechsler, Annotation, *Scope and Effect of Clause in Liability Policy Excluding From Coverage Liability Assumed Under Contract Not Defined in Policy, Such as One of Indemnity*, 63 ALR2d 1122 (1959).

property in the care, custody, or control of the insured or property as to which the insured for any purpose is exercising physical control.[66]

Generally, a contractor does not have care, custody, or control of property merely because it is working there. Control of a property is indicated by occupation of the premises exclusive of the control of anyone else.[67] Thus, if a contractor is on the premises to repair or remodel the premises, there typically is not care, custody, or control of the property sufficient to make the exclusion applicable. However, if the contractor is the only party responsible for a particular operation and is in sole control of the portion of the site when an accident occurs, it may not have coverage by virtue of this exclusion. For instance, in one case, the exclusion was held to apply to an iron subcontractor. The subcontractor was to erect iron roof beams. The beams collapsed in the middle of the erection and the insurer disclaimed coverage based on the care, custody, or control exclusion. The court found care, custody, and control of the site by the subcontractor—and, hence, no coverage—based on the following: the subcontractor was exercising "physical control" over the roof beams when they collapsed; the erection of the beams was in progress when they collapsed; the beams were to be clustered and each cluster attached to each other as work was completed; and the subcontractor's laborers were physically active on the site and in sole control of the site when the collapse occurred.[68] The court stated that proof that the insured knew that it was not covered was found in the fact that it had procured supplemental insurance from another insurance company.

§10.24 Fidelity Insurance

As with any business that handles large amounts of cash or checks, a construction company may wish to purchase fidelity insurance on its employees involved in processing incoming and outgoing cash and checks. Fidelity insurance insures a business against embezzlement by its own employees.

§10.25 Officers' and Directors' Liability

Any corporation and each of its officers and directors are well advised to consider obtaining officer and director insurance. Such insurance protects corporate officers and directors individually against suits by shareholders and third parties for damages caused by decisions made by officers or directors in their official capacities. Premiums are typically based on the number of share-

---

[66] North Am Iron & Steel Co v Isaacson Steel Erectors, Inc, 36 AD2d 770, 321 NYS2d 254 (2d Dept 1971), *affd mem*, 30 NY2d 640, 331 NYS2d 667 (1972).

[67] AT Morris & Co v Lumber Mut Cas Ins Co, 163 Misc 715, 298 NYS 227 (Queens 1937).

[68] North Am Iron & Steel Co v Isaacson Steel Erectors, Inc, 36 AD2d 770, 321 NYS2d 254 (2d Dept 1971), *affd mem*, 30 NY2d 640, 331 NYS2d 667 (1972).

to meet this burden of proof.[72] The only way that a court can conclude that there is not a duty to defend is if it can conclude that there is no possible factual or legal basis by which the insurer could be required to indemnify the insured under any policy provision.[73] Any doubts must be resolved in favor of the insured, against the insurer.[74] For instance, in a case where the policy excluded damage to the insured's work product and the complaint alleged that the contractor/insured breached its contract by negligent performance, resulting in a defective roof, the insurer was required to defend the insured because the plaintiff in the damage suit sought damages in excess of the value of the roof and for damages to the building (as distinct from the roof).[75] An insurer must honor its duty to defend until it is "unequivocally established that the harm caused . . . was not within the coverage afforded by the [insurer]."[76]

Despite this strict standard, insurers have been found not to have a duty to defend. For instance, an insurer was not required to defend a suit that sought to enforce warranties made by the contractor/insured where the policy specifically excluded failure of the work performed by the insured to "meet the level of performance, quality, fitness or durability warranted or represented by the named insured."[77] Further, an insurer may be relieved of its duty to defend if its insured breaches its duty of cooperation, discussed at §10.29. Although it is difficult for an insurer to establish noncooperation sufficient to relieve it of its duty to defend,[78] it can be done.

If an insurer breaches its duty to defend, it is liable in damages to the insured. Its failure to defend does not create coverage, however. The only way an insurer has a duty to indemnify its insured is if there is coverage under the policy.[79]

If an insurer believes that it does not have a duty to defend and its insured asserts that it does, an insurer's wisest course is to bring a declaratory judgment action to determine the issue. Otherwise, an insurer may be liable for the attorneys' fees its insured pays in bringing an action to force the insurer to defend, as well as the insured's costs and fees in the initial action.[80]

---

[72] *Id.*

[73] JGA Constr Corp v Charter Oak Fire Ins Co, 66 AD2d 315, 414 NYS2d 385 (4th Dept 1979).

[74] TJ Picozzi Constr Co v Exchange Mut Ins Co, 138 AD2d 907, 526 NYS2d 652, 653 (3d Dept 1988); Muhlstock & Co v American Home Assurance Co, 117 AD2d 117, 502 NYS2d 174 (1st Dept 1986).

[75] Marine Midland Servs Corp v Samuel Kosoff & Sons, 60 AD2d 767, 400 NYS2d 959 (4th Dept 1977).

[76] *Id* at 770, 400 NYS2d at 962.

[77] Willets Point Contracting Corp v Hartford Ins Group, 75 AD2d 254, 429 NYS2d 230 (2d Dept 1980), *affd mem*, 53 NY2d 881, 423 NE2d 42, 440 NYS2d 619 (1981).

[78] Hartford Fire Ins Co v Masternak, 55 AD2d 472, 390 NYS2d 949 (4th Dept 1977).

[79] Servidone Constr Corp v Security Ins Co of Hartford, 64 NY2d 419, 477 NE2d 441, 488 NYS2d 139 (1985).

[80] McGroarty v Great Am Ins Co, 36 NY2d 358, 329 NE2d 172, 368 NYS2d 485 (1975); Pavarini Constr Co v Liberty Mut Ins Co, NYLJ, Dec 21, 1990, at 23, col 4.

holders, the type of business concerned, and the impact of business operations on third parties.

§10.26 Motor Vehicles and Equipment

Just as an individual insures his or her automobiles, so too should a company insure its motor vehicles and equipment for property and personal injury damage. These coverages may be rolled into the company's general liability policy if specifically endorsed or may be covered under separate policies. For complete protection, *any* automobile or equipment that is owned or leased by the company or used for company business should be covered. Similarly, *any* driver of a company automobile or of any automobile for a company purpose and *any* user of equipment for a company purpose should be covered.

§10.27 Duty of Defense

Liability policies typically include a duty of the insurer to defend the insured against claims of damage that fall within the policy coverage. One policy stated the duty thus:

> The company will pay on behalf of the insured all sums which the insured shall become legally obligated to pay as damages because of . . . Coverage B property damage to which this insurance applies, caused by an occurrence, and the company shall have the right and duty to defend any suit against the insured seeking damages on account of such . . . property damage, even if any of the allegations of the suit are groundless, false or fraudulent, and may make such investigation and settlement of any suit or claim it deems expedient. . . .[69]

Under such a clause, an insurer's duty to defend a lawsuit against its insured is much broader than its obligation to pay a claim on behalf of its insured. The duty to defend arises whenever a complaint alleges facts and circumstances which, if only some of them were proved, would fall within the risks covered by the policy. The duty to defend is measured against allegations in pleadings, but the duty to pay is determined based on the insured's actual liability to a third person.[70] The burden is on the insurer to prove that an alleged loss is not and could not be covered by the policy.[71] The insurer must prove that the loss comes entirely within a policy exclusion or is clearly not covered for it

---

[69] Marine Midland Servs Corp v Samuel Kosoff & Sons, 60 AD2d 767, 400 NYS2d 959 (4th Dept 1977).

[70] Servidone Constr Corp v Security Ins Co, 64 NY2d 419, 477 NE2d 441, 488 NYS2d 139 (1985).

[71] *Id.*

> **PRACTICE POINTER:**
>
> If it is in the best interest of the insured for it, and not the insurer, to select counsel and control the defense of a covered claim, the insured should not hesitate to ask the insurer's consent to do so. For example, if, when pursuing a claim against an owner, a general contractor is faced with a counterclaim by the owner that may be covered under its liability insurance, the contractor should notify the carrier of the counterclaim and request the insurer to appoint the attorney prosecuting the claim to also handle the defense of the counterclaim. This will allow for a coordinated response on behalf of the contractor to the owner and most likely a reduction of legal fees for both the contractor and the insurer.

§10.28 Limitation of Actions

An insurance agreement may specify that suit on the policy must be brought within a specified time after a claim arises, coverage is denied, or an occurrence happens. Most policies provide a one- or two-year period within which suit may be brought. As with any contractual limitation, so long as the time allowed is reasonable, it will be enforced. Most policies contain a one-year limitation period. In the absence of a contractual time limitation, the applicable statutory time limitation is six years.[81]

§10.29 Duty of Cooperation

An insured has a duty to cooperate with its insurer when a claim is made. Generally, it must assist its insurer with any investigation, be available for examinations before trial, testify at trial, and do nothing to prejudice the insurer's case. It need not, however, be at an insurer's beck and call. Indeed, the courts have been very lenient in defining a breach of the duty of cooperation sufficient to allow an insurer to disclaim coverage.

To justify a disclaimer of liability on the basis of noncooperation, an insurer must meet a heavy burden and show that: (1) it acted diligently in seeking to bring about the insured's cooperation; (2) its efforts were reasonably calculated to bring about cooperation; and (3) the insured's attitude after cooperation was sought was one of "willful and avowed obstruction."[82] Simple nonaction by the insured is not enough.[83] Further, making false statements to a claims investigator, encouraging the injured party to sue and use the insured's lawyer, and informing the insurer's attorney that it wants the case settled probably do

---

[81] NY Civ Prac L&R 213 (McKinney 1990 & Supp 1992).

[82] Thrasher v United States Liab Ins Co, 19 NY2d 159, 225 NE2d 503, 278 NYS2d 793 (1967); Flans v Martini, 136 AD2d 498, 523 NYS2d 819 (1st Dept 1988); Van Opdorp v Merchants Mut Ins Co, 55 AD2d 810, 390 NYS2d 279 (4th Dept 1976).

[83] Flans v Martini, 136 AD2d 498, 523 NYS2d 819 (1st Dept 1988).

not indicate a lack of cooperation sufficient to relieve an insured of its duty to defend. Where, however, these same acts were coupled with the insured's refusal to be examined before trial and stated refusal to attend trial, breach of the duty of cooperation was found, relieving the insurer of its duty to defend.[84] An insurer need not show prejudice to its case to allege an insured's failure to cooperate.[85]

§10.30 Disclaimers

If an insurer wishes to disclaim coverage because of an insured's failure to comply with policy provisions, it must do so promptly or it may be found to have waived its right to disclaim coverage. If there is no coverage under the policy or its endorsements, an insurer cannot waive disclaimer of coverage merely by delay in disclaiming.[86]

§10.31 Certificate of Insurance

It is wise to require a certificate of insurance from all parties to a project to ensure that all have coverage. It is even wiser to require a copy of all policies, *in addition to* the certificates of insurance. Only by requiring both can one really ascertain what coverage a party has—its exclusions, limits, defense duties, and so forth.

§10.32 Special Insurance Problems

Unusual construction projects require special insurance. Rarely do form policies provide a unique project with the protection it needs; a job- or party-specific policy, typically known as a "manuscript policy," is needed. Three such unique projects and possible solutions to their insurance problems are discussed briefly in the following three sections. When faced with an insurance problem, dealing with an experienced construction insurance professional is a must to obtain the tailor-made coverage needed.

§10.33 —Design-Build Contracts

Typical construction policies exclude design work. Thus, a "manuscript policy"[87] is needed to provide the design coverage that the contractor and owner need in a design-build contract.

---

[84] Employers-Commercial Union Ins Cos of Am v Buonomo, 41 AD2d 285, 342 NYS2d 447 (4th Dept 1973).

[85] *Id.*

[86] Interboro Mut Indem Ins Co v Karpowic, 116 Misc 2d 947, 456 NYS2d 967 (Kings 1982).

[87] *See* §10.32.

§10.34 —Joint Ventures

Standard liability policies exclude coverage for claims that arise from projects on which the insured is a joint venturer. Thus, it is necessary to have the exclusion removed or to obtain insurance for the joint venture itself, as well as the individual joint venturers.

§10.35 —Construction Managers

Normal construction liability insurance specifically excludes liability for design, inspection, and supervision, tasks performed by construction managers, although some insurers may allow a construction manager to be added as an additional insured to an owner's or a contractor's commercial general liability policy and the exclusions to be removed. Far better would be for a construction manager or an owner to obtain insurance specifically fitted to a construction manager, a hybrid sort of professional liability insurance. While few companies offer specific construction manager insurance, it is available. If it cannot be found, an owner must carefully consider its project's insurance requirements and obtain coverage for each of its elements where it may, typically through a hodgepodge of policies.

Appendix 10-1 Insurance Policies

POLICY NAME	RISKS COVERED	PARTY THAT USUALLY PROVIDES COVERAGE	COMMON EXCLUSIONS	COMMON EXTENSIONS	COMMENTS
Protective Liability	Insured's liability for bodily injury and property damage to third persons.	Owner and contractor generally provide own coverage; coverage can be obtained by either and extended to the other by rider.	1. Property of the insured or which belongs to others but is in the care, custody, or control of the insured. Exclusion is limited to that particular part of the real property being worked on if the loss arises out of that operation. 2. Contractual liability - another's legal liability which the insured agrees to assume by a hold-harmless or indemnification agreement.	1. None. Used to be extended through Broad Form Property Damage extension. More precise wording of exclusion makes extension unnecessary. 2. Extension obtainable either for specific contracts or Blanket Contractual Liability coverage which excludes "broad form" indemnify and typically has 18 other exclusions. Extension is not available to cover professional liability.	Independent Contractors Protective Liability coverage is generally included in the basic policy. It protects the insured against contingent liability arising out of the negligence of independent contractors and subcontractors. Policy limits are expressed as $0000/$0000, meaning coverage per occurrence/total coverage per policy period or project.

INSURANCE POLICIES 401

3. <u>Completed operations</u> - basic coverage ends when work is completed or the owner takes beneficial occupancy, whichever occurs first. Normal one-year guarantee period is not included. If an occurrence policy, coverage is provided for events during the policy period, regardless of when suit is brought.

4. <u>Professional liability</u> - preparation of plans, surveys, specifications, etc.; also excludes professional supervisory, inspection, or engineering services. Excludes most services offered by construction managers and design/build contractors.

5. "x,c,u" excludes primary liability (but not contingent liability) coverage for

3. Extension to make coverage last as long as policy is in effect, subject to other policy exclusion. Overlaps owner's permanent property and liability insurance.

4. Coverage is not available for owner's or contractors. Special policies are written for construction managers and design/build contractors.

5. Coverage is written for specific activities. Can be costly.

Recent ISO Form changes include "x,c,u" coverage.

POLICY NAME	RISKS COVERED	PARTY THAT USUALLY PROVIDES COVERAGE	COMMON EXCLUSIONS	COMMON EXTENSIONS	COMMENTS
			most demolition, excavation, pile driving, and foundation work and damage to underground facilities. 6. Personal injury - excludes coverage for libel, slander, etc. 7. Employee injuries. 8. Automobiles and mobile equipment. 9. Nuclear hazard, war, aircraft, watercraft, contamination, pollution, and asbestos. 10. <u>Contractor's own work</u> - to the property out of which the occurrence arose—excludes coverage for replacing the contractor's work if a defect in that work caused the loss.	6. Personal injury. 7. Workers' Compensation and Employer's Liability as an extension or separate policy. 8. Comprehensive Business Automobile Liability as an extension or separate policy. 9. These risks can be separately insured, often at great cost. 10. Builder's Risk or Installation Floater.	

INSURANCE POLICIES 403

Umbrella excess liability	Excess limits of insurance for risks covered by primary insurance. Can also provide primary coverage for risk not otherwise insured.	Owner or contractor.	1. Legal defense. 2. Contractual liability - see Protective Liability policy discussion above.	Typically a $10,000 to $25,000 deductible applies to risks not otherwise insured against.
Workers' Compensation and Employer's Liability	Injuries to employees.	Each employer covers its own employees.		Required by statute. If not provided by independent contractor, owner must pay benefits.
Fire Insurance Vandalism and Malicious Mischief Extended Coverage			1. Policy covers only those risks specifically enumerated.	1. Extended coverage (windstorm, hail, explosion, riot, civil commotion, aircraft, vehicles, smoke).	Coverage is too narrow for most construction projects, although should be considered for inclusion in any business insurance program.
Builder's Risk "All Risk" Installation Floater	Covers damage to property owned by the insured or in the care, custody, or control of the insured. Covers "all risks," except those specifically excluded.	Owner or contractor. One will generally have to supplement basic coverage provided by others.	1. Flood. 2. Earthquake, landslide, volcanic eruption, and other catastrophes. 3. Plate glass damage by vandalism. 4. Failure of electrical apparatus unless fire ensues.	1. Flood. 2. Earthquake and Volcanic Eruption. 4. Electrical Apparatus.	Customary for named insureds to be the owner, contractors, and subcontractors, as their interests may appear. Waiver of subrogation endorsement generally obtained. Typically, there are separate policy limits and deductibles for different classes of property.

APPENDIX 10-1

POLICY NAME	RISKS COVERED	PARTY THAT USUALLY PROVIDES COVERAGE	COMMON EXCLUSIONS	COMMON EXTENSIONS	COMMENTS
	There is separate coverage for different classes of property: 1. Property in the course of construction. 2. Materials and equipment at job site awaiting installation. 3. Materials and equipment on others' premises. 4. Materials and equipment in transit.		5. Defective design, workmanship, or testing unless fire ensues. 6. Explosion or failure of steam boilers or machinery, unless fire ensues. 7. Delays, loss of market, loss use, consequential damages. 8. Theft. 9. Collapse.	5. Defective design, workmanship, and testing. 6. Boiler and Machinery. 7. Business Interruption, or loss of use. 8. Theft. 9. Collapse.	If owner procures the policy, contractor should obtain separate coverage for its equipment and uninstalled materials. Usual policy time limits are: 1) Notice to insurer of damage—on occurrence. 2) Proof of loss statements—on occurrence. 3) Suit against insurer—one year from occurrence.
Professional Liability Errors and Omissions	Covers negligence in preparation of plans and specifications, construction inspection, and other usual professional activities.	Architects and Engineers.	Policy exclusions vary greatly: 1. Prior acts which give rise to occurrences or claims during the policy period. 2. Contractual Liability.	1. Prior acts coverage. Retired Professional Liability covers damage or injury after the policy period for those who are no longer active in the profession.	In general, the policy must be in effect both when the negligent act occurred and when the damage occurred. Policies tend to have very high deductibles which vary greatly, anywhere from $1,000 to $100,000.

2. Contractual Liability.

3. Intentional, malicious, dishonest or fraudulent acts.
4. Insolvency of the insured or others.
5. Cost estimates.
6. Advice or recommendations on insurance or bonds.
7. Libel and slander.
8. Failure to complete plans and specifications or to approve shop drawings on time.
9. Services not customary to an engineer or architect.

7. Personal Injury Liability.

High limits of liability are recommended in light of large risk exposure.

Special coverage is required for joint ventures of two architectural or engineering firms.

POLICY NAME	RISKS COVERED	PARTY THAT USUALLY PROVIDES COVERAGE	COMMON EXCLUSIONS	COMMON EXTENSIONS	COMMENTS
			10. Ground testing and surveys.	10. Separate coverage is available.	
			11. Construction management activities.	11. Separate coverage is available.	
			12. Express warranties and guarantees.	13. Separate coverage is available.	
			13. Temporary structures for exhibits and fairs.	14. Separate coverage is available.	
			14. Tunnels, bridges, and dams.		

Appendix 10-2
Glossary of Common Construction Insurance Terms

Accident See occurrence. A sudden, unexpected, and unintended event causing injury or damage traceable to a definite time or place. It is not the act that must be unexpected but the *result* of the act.

Additional Insured Basic policies protect the named insureds and provide coverage for any executive officer, director, or stockholder acting within the scope of its duties. Generally, other employees can be added for a nominal premium. The most typical additional insureds are an owner on a contractor's policy or a contractor on a subcontractor's policy; the typical purpose behind contractual requirements of additional insured status is to reinforce the intent of an indemnification provision. Such additional insureds must be added to the policy by an endorsement or be specifically provided for in the insurance policy.[xx]

Additional Named Insured An "additional insured" is a party added as an insured to a liability insurance policy of another party by an endorsement. An additional insured generally does not have the same rights and obligations under a liability policy as the named insured. The additional insured endorsement generally contains restrictions and limitations that apply to the additional insured. This type of endorsement generally restricts coverage for the additional insured to liability arising out of the operations or premises that are the subject of the contract. Also, coverage for the additional insured is often restricted to acts or omissions of the additional insured in connection with its general supervision of the named insured. Thus, the additional insured often is not covered for its own negligence.

The term "additional named insured" is generally not defined in liability insurance policies. Some insurers apply the same restrictions and limitations to an additional named insured as are applied to an additional insured. In such cases, there may be little or no distinction between the two. Other insurers take the position that in order to be an additional named insured, there must be an endorsement that contains no additional restrictions or limitations on the additional named insured.

The most common difference between the two types of insureds is that an additional named insured is covered for liability arising out of its own sole negligence while an additional insured is covered only for vicarious liability due to actions of the named insured. Depending on the language of the endorsement that is used, however, this may not always be correct. There are two standard forms of endorsements that are used to provide additional insured status. They are sometimes referred to as Form A and Form B. The distinction between the two forms is subtle and not always clear. In that most owners do

---

[xx] Donald S. Malecki & Jack P. Gibson, The Additional Insured Book 1 (1991).

not require a contractor to provide copies of insurance policies, the owner will never know which form of endorsement has been used. One way to avoid this problem might be to require a specific form of endorsement in the construction contract, in addition to requiring the contractor to submit copies of the entire insurance policy to the owner.[89]

Aggregate Limit The maximum sum the insurer can be called upon to pay, regardless of the number of occurrences. Insurance policies typically include a "per occurrence" limit, which is the maximum sum the insurer can be called upon to pay, regardless of the number of persons injured in a given accident. Absent an "aggregate limit," there is no limit on the number of times the insurer can be called upon to pay the "per occurrence" limit for different accidents. There are several problems posed by aggregate limits in contractors' Commercial General Liability (CGL) policies. These are created by the fact that such policies typically provide coverage for all the contractor's operations and are not limited to a specific project. An owner who wishes its contractor to have $10 million in CGL coverage cannot be sure how much of the policy's aggregate limit may be used up by the time there is an accident on the owner's project. This becomes particularly significant where "additional insureds" and "indemnitees" are depending upon a certain level of coverage, which may not be available when it is needed. One way to deal with this problem is to require the insurance to be written with a per project aggregate limit.

All Risks This form of property insurance covers "all risks" except those specifically excluded. The exclusions to the typical "all risk" policy are so numerous that the policy might more accurately be called "many, but not all risks."

Blanket Contractual Liability See contractual liability. This liability policy *extension* is applicable to all contracts but is subject to numerous exclusions. In particular, it excludes contractual liability based on broad form indemnification.

Broad Form Property Damage This liability policy coverage *extension* amends and clarifies the usual "care, custody, or control" exclusion. It defines *how much* of the property being worked on is covered by the exclusion. Under this extension, the "care, custody and control" exclusion applies only to "that particular part" of the property being worked on by the insured at the time of the loss. Some more recent policies do not offer this extension but, instead, more precisely define the care, custody, or control exclusion to exclude only "that particular part" of the property being worked on if the loss arises out of that operation.

Care, Custody, *or* Control An *exclusion* in liability policies for damage to real and personal property. Generally, if the exclusion discusses *property*, it means real property. The term *personal property* refers to any other property. This exclusion excludes coverage for real property owned, leased, or occupied

---

[89] For a more detailed analysis of the distinctions between Additional Insureds and Additional Named Insureds, see Donald S. Malecki & Jack P. Gibson, The Additional Insured Book (1991).

by the insured. Property insurance policies are available to cover losses to an insured's real property. Coverage is also excluded for damage to personal property in the insured's care, custody, or control. Typically, this means no coverage for damage to property that belongs to others but is temporarily in the insured's care, custody, or control.

Certificate of Insurance A form issued by an insurance company that certifies the fact that the insured has current insurance of the type and limits specified. A certificate is often required by owners from their contractors, to make sure that the contractors have the insurance required by the contracts. Similarly, a contractor may require certificates of its subcontractors. A typical certificate will contain a provision that the policy described will not be canceled until at least 30 days prior written notice has been given to the party to whom the certificate was issued. Most certificates do not set forth exclusions. A certificate is binding on the insurance company only if issued by an authorized agent. Note that most insurance brokers are *not* authorized agents of the insurer but are deemed to be agents of the insured.

CGL Policy Commercial general liability policy. This policy protects the contractor against third-party bodily injury and property damage liability claims arising from the contractor's operations, the products and completed operations of the contractor, and the actions of the contractor's independent contractors (e.g., subcontractors and sub-subcontractors). It may also cover the bodily injury and property damage liability of others that the contractor assumes in a contract. Additionally, the policy can insure against liability arising from certain personal injury and advertising injury perils (libel, slander, false arrest). The policy will pay monetary damages for which the contractor is liable (up to policy limits), defense and investigations costs, and certain other specified supplementary payments.[90]

Claims Made Policy A type of policy that must be in effect at the time an actual claim is asserted against the insured for there to be coverage, even if the occurrence giving rise to the claim took place prior to the effective date of the policy.

Completed Operations This extension of a contractor's liability coverage begins as soon as the contractor completes its work or the owner takes beneficial occupancy, whichever comes first. The extension is subject to the same exclusions as the contractor's basic liability coverage. The extension does not include the removal, repair, or replacement of the work itself; it covers damage caused by the work. This coverage often overlaps the owner's permanent property and liability insurance.

Contingent Liability The derivative or secondary liability one has for another's acts. Most owner and contractor liability policies automatically include coverage for contingent liability. Thus, if a pedestrian is injured by a contractor's blasting—an ultrahazardous activity that imposes strict liability on a landowner even if an independent contractor does the blasting—an owner's contingent liability coverage would provide the owner with a defense

---

[90] I Construction Risk Management vi.C.1, Intl Risk Mgmt Inst (1990).

and pay any judgment obtained, within policy limits. Although by law (and usually by contract) the owner would have a claim against its contractor for the damage caused by the blasting, contingent liability coverage provides the sometimes substantial benefits of the cost of the legal defense against the pedestrian's action and prosecution of the contribution claim against the contractor, as well as payment of the damages, without the owner having to hope the contractor has sufficient resources to compensate the owner for its loss.

Contractual Liability A typical *exclusion* to liability policies that excludes coverage for an insured's agreement to assume another party's legal liability in tort, most often under an indemnification or hold harmless provision in the construction contract. Extensions are generally available to negate the effect of this exclusion.

Coverage Whether there is insurance for a particular risk. Coverage is distinguished from "policy limits" or "limits of liability," defined below. For example, assume an owner purchases an "all risks" property insurance policy with a $500,000 policy limit. A flood causes $20,000 damage and a fire causes $650,000 damage. There is no coverage for the flood as it is usually excluded under an all risks policy. There is coverage for the fire up to the policy limits of $500,000.

Deductible The amount of the loss the insured pays. Insurance companies claim that deductibles provide incentives to insureds to exercise care in preventing loss.

Designated Carrier If an owner or a contractor requires its contractor and subcontractors to purchase their insurance policies from the insurance company the owner or contractor designates, the chosen company is called the designated carrier. With limited exceptions, it is illegal in New York for a public or private owner or a contractor to require that its contractors and subcontractors use a designated carrier.[91]

Endorsement An amendment to the policy that may either grant or exclude coverage. An extension is a form of endorsement.

Errors and Omissions Another name for professional liability coverage.

Extended Coverage A common policy *extension* for fire insurance policies that adds coverage for the perils of wind, storm, hail, explosion, riot, civil commotion, aircraft, vehicles, and smoke.

Extended Reporting Period (Also known as "Tail.") On a claims made policy, an additional period of time beyond the basic policy term, during which period, if a claim is made, the policy will provide coverage. Many policies contain an automatic 60-day extended reporting period; longer periods may be purchased for an additional premium.

Extension An addition of coverage to a policy. Typically, extensions remove specified perils from policy exclusion, thus making them covered.

Floater A separate policy, rather than a rider, that provides additional coverage beyond that provided in the main policy.

---

[91] NY Ins Law §§2504, 2502 (McKinney 1982).

Hold Harmless See contractual liability.

Indemnification See contractual liability.

Limits of Liability The maximum sum the insurer will be required to pay for covered risks. Policy limits are often expressed as $0000/$0000, defined as $ per occurrence/$ aggregate per policy year or project. For instance, a property insurance policy may have a $50,000/$150,000 limit; the insurance company would pay up to $50,000 for each occurrence but no more than $150,000 during the policy year or on the particular project covered. Also known as policy limits.

Named Insured The party or parties named in the policy as the insured. Naming the proper insured is particularly important in property insurance as each insured is entitled to recover only to the extent of its insurable interest in the property. If a contractor is incorporated but gets insurance in its president's name, it is conceivable that there would be no recovery since the corporation, not its president, owns the property insured; the president would have no insurable interest in the property. Naming the proper insureds is also important when considering subrogation. Where there are several named insureds, the insurer has no right of subrogation against named insureds.

Occurrence The insurance policy term for an event giving rise to coverage. Typical policies define occurrence as: "an accident, including continuous or repeated exposure to conditions, which results in bodily injury or property damage neither expected nor intended from the standpoint of the insured." Case law has interpreted this definition to mean that the *results* of an action must be neither expected nor intended; the action itself may be willful. Thus, while a contractor may intentionally excavate land and such excavation causes damage to an adjacent property, there is coverage as the damage was neither expected nor intended, although the act that caused the damage was.[92]

Occurrence Based Policy A policy that must be in effect at the time that the occurrence that gives rise to a claim takes place, even if the claim is not asserted against the insured until after the expiration date of the policy.

Owner's Protective Liability Policy A policy that protects the owner from injury or damage claims caused by the operations of the general contractor or any of the subcontractors. Owner's protective liability insurance has the owner as the named insured. It covers the owner's contingent liability for personal injury, including death, or property damage that may occur during the construction operations of independent contractors and subcontractors. This policy also pays legal expenses associated with the owner's defense.[93]

Policy The contract of insurance between the insured and insurance company that sets forth the coverage, policy limits, exclusions, and coverage extensions and endorsements, and includes the basic insuring agreement, including notice requirements and limitation periods.

---

[92] McGroarty v Great Am Ins Co, 36 NY2d 358, 329 NE2d 172, 368 NYS2d 485 (1975).

[93] Richard H. Clough, *Construction Contracting* 205 (4th ed 1981).

Policy Extension A rider providing coverage for property or risks otherwise excluded in the main policy.

Policy Limits See limits of liability.

Policy Period The period of time the policy is in effect. Particularly important when there are two dates that govern coverage. For instance, many professional liability policies provide coverage only if the policy is in effect on the date of the negligent act and the date of damage.

Professional Liability Exclusion A typical exclusion to liability policies for faulty designs, maps, plans, specifications, and professional inspection and supervision. Professional liability extensions are generally not obtainable by owners and contractors. Generally, coverage is issued only to practicing engineers and architects. Assume that a pedestrian is injured when a trench wall collapses. If the trench sheeting and bracing were designed by an engineer, there should be coverage under its professional liability policy. If, however, the sheeting and bracing were designed by the contractor, there would not be coverage because of the professional liability exclusion to its policy.

Reservation of Rights A written statement from the insurance company to its insured that states that the insurance company will provide the insured with a legal defense but reserves its right to assert that there is no coverage for one or more of the claims asserted or that the claims exceed policy limits. The insurer thus reserves the right to refuse to pay claims for which there is no coverage or which exceed policy limits, or to withdraw from defense of the action if it becomes clear that there would not be coverage.

Retroactive Date The earliest occurrence date to which a claims made policy will provide coverage. If the occurrence took place prior to the retroactive date, a claims made policy will not provide coverage even if the claim arising from the occurrence is made during the policy period.

Rider A form or endorsement physically attached to an insurance policy altering the coverage, policy limits, named insured, right of subrogation, notice of cancellation, or any other matter.

Strict Liability One's legal responsibility for damage to another regardless of one's own fault. Also referred to as absolute liability. For example, an owner and a contractor are strictly liable for any damage to third persons from blasting and other ultra hazardous activities, regardless of fault and regardless of who actually did the blasting work.

Subrogation The legal right of an insurer to "stand in the shoes of" its insured after paying a loss on its behalf and to pursue a claim in the insured's name against anyone legally responsible for the loss. For instance, after paying a fire loss, an owner's insurance company may seek to recover from the subcontractor whose negligence started the fire.

Tail See extended reporting period.

Umbrella Excess Liability A liability insurance policy that provides limits of liability and coverage in excess of other primary policies. Legal defense is not always included, particularly for coverage not provided in primary policies.

Most have large deductibles for risks for which there is no primary coverage. Policy does not provide coverage unless other primary policies' coverage has been or could be exhausted by a claim.[94]

Waiver of Subrogation A rider to property insurance where the insurance company waives its right of subrogation, typically for an additional premium. Absent such a waiver, multiple coverage by each party for the same risk would have to be obtained—ultimately at additional cost to the owner. The same result can be had by naming all contractors and their subcontractors as additional insureds on the property insurance. Another method to prevent subrogation is for each contract and subcontract to provide that each party waives all rights it has against all other parties for damages caused by fire or other perils to the extent covered by insurance.

Workers' Compensation Insurance Coverage mandated by statute to assure that an employer is financially capable to respond to compensation claims. This coverage is provided through private insurance carriers as well as the New York State Insurance Fund.

Wrap-Up Insurance An overall insurance program provided by the owner, which covers the owner, architect/engineer, and all prime contractors and their subcontractors for a particular construction project. Under wrap-up insurance, the owner normally provides coverage for workers' compensation and employer's liability; personal injury, bodily injury, and property damage liability; and "all risks" property insurance. It typically does not include bonds or insurance for the contractors' or subcontractors' equipment, automobiles, off-site property, or property prior to installation. Contractors may also provide wrap-up insurance.

"x,c,u" A typical exclusion in liability insurance for property damage arising out of explosion, collapse, or underground damage during excavation, pile driving, and other foundation work underground. Coverage can be obtained by an extension for an additional premium. Recent Insurance Services Organization (ISO) policies do not have this exclusion.

---

[94] Willets Point Contracting Corp v Hartford Ins Group, 75 AD2d 254, 429 NYS2d 230 (2d Dept 1980), *affd mem.* 53 NY2d 881, 423 NE2d 42, 440 NYS2d 619 (1981).

Professional's Role and Liability

11

§11.01 Introduction
§11:02 Licensing and Qualifying to Do Business
§11.03 —Failure to License

Architect/Engineer Liability

§11.04 Generally
§11.05 Liability for Design
§11.06 Liability for Testing
§11.07 Liability for Cost Estimates
§11.08 Liability for Supervision and Inspection
§11.09 Liability for Scheduling and Coordination
§11.10 Liability for Certifying Progress Payments
§11.11 Liability for Dispute Resolution
§11.12 Liability to Third Parties
§11.13 —In Negligence
§11.14 —In Contract

Construction Manager Liability

§11.15 Generally
§11.16 Liability for Design
§11.17 Liability for Cost Estimates
§11.18 Liability for Supervision and Inspection
§11.19 Liability for Scheduling and Coordination
§11.20 Liability for Certifying Progress Payments
§11.21 Liability to Third Parties

General Principles

§11.22 Indemnification and Contribution

§11.23   Statutes of Limitations
§11.24   —Continuous Treatment Doctrine
§11.25   Insurance

§11.01   Introduction

In New York, engineers, architects, and land surveyors must be licensed by the state; contractors and construction managers are not licensed by the state. Most municipalities require licenses of home improvement contractors and electrical and plumbing contractors. A listing of other construction-related professions that require licensing is found in **Chapter 1**. This chapter discusses the potential liabilities of architects, engineers, and construction managers. This chapter does not attempt to be an exhaustive discussion of this area; such a discussion itself can easily fill a book. Indeed, there are numerous books that adequately deal solely with the liability of construction professionals.[1]

Contractor and subcontractor liabilities are discussed throughout this text, and particularly in **Chapter 12** on defects and failures and **Chapter 4** on default and termination.

Architect and engineer (hereinafter collectively referred to as A/Es) and construction manager liability merits separate discussion because of its nature—these professionals are judged by a different standard based on their role and responsibilities, not a reasonable person standard. Often, liability is imposed for the failures of others, such as when a defect results because the A/E failed to supervise a contractor's work carefully. Further, unlike contractors and subcontractors, an A/E or construction manager has many roles and responsibilities on a project, from its design and cost estimates through construction and certificates of payment and completion. Each role and responsibility exposes the professional to potential liability to the owner, contractors, subcontractors, and other third parties, including subsequent owners and remote users of the building.

§11.02   Licensing and Qualifying to Do Business

Before a person can practice the profession of architecture or engineering in New York, he or she must be licensed or registered by the state of New York. Licensure by another state is irrelevant to one's ability to practice architecture or engineering in New York.[2] The purpose of licensing is to safeguard the life,

---

[1] There are numerous books on the subject. Some the authors have found useful include J. Acret, Architects and Engineers (Shepard's/McGraw-Hill 2d ed 1984); Avoiding Liability in Architecture, Design and Construction (R. Cushman ed 1983); H. Streeter, Professional Liability of Architects and Engineers (1988), and J. Sweet, Legal Aspects of Architecture, Engineering and the Construction Process (1985).

[2] *See* Wormuth v Lower Eastside Action Project, Inc, 71 Misc 2d 314, 335 NYS2d 896 (App Term 1st Dept 1972). Architects and engineers who are not New York

health, and property of New York residents.[3] An architect's license is required if one wishes to render or offer to render services that include

> the art, science, and aesthetics of design and construction of buildings, groups of buildings, including their components and appurtenances and the spaces around them wherein the safeguarding of life, health, property, and public welfare is concerned. Such services include, but are not limited to consultation, evaluation, planning, the provision of preliminary studies, designs, construction documents, construction management, and the administration of construction contracts.[4]

Similarly, an engineer's license is required if one wishes to perform professional services such as "consultation, investigation, evaluation, planning, design or supervision of construction or operation in connection with any utilities, structures, buildings, machines, equipment, processes, works, or projects...."[5] Thus, it has been held that a license was needed for a person to prepare plans and drawings for a restaurant[6] and to prepare bid documents.[7] It is the individual person that must be a licensed architect or engineer, not the corporation or partnership.[8]

Contractors and builders who perform construction management do not need licenses in New York and are specifically exempted from the licensing requirements to practice architecture and engineering.[9] Despite the fact that this exemption was added to the statutes in 1972, there are no known cases that define what the practice of construction management is and set out how

---

residents and who are licensed in another state or country may obtain a limited permit to practice architecture (NY Educ Law §7305 (McKinney 1985 & Supp 1992)) or engineering (NY Educ Law §7207 (McKinney 1985 & Supp 1992)) for a limited time on a specific project if they meet statutory qualifications.

[3] Vereinigte Osterreichische Eisen & Stahlwerke, AG v Modular Bldg & Dev Corp, 64 Misc 2d 1050, 316 NYS2d 812 (NY 1970), affd as modified, 37 AD2d 525, 322 NYS2d 976 (1st Dept 1971).

[4] NY Educ Law §7301 (McKinney 1985 & Supp 1992).

[5] Id §7201 (McKinney 1985).

[6] Wineman v Blueprint 100, Inc, 75 Misc 2d 665, 348 NYS2d 721 (Civ Ct NY 1973).

[7] PC Chipouras & Assocs v 212 Realty Corp, 156 AD2d 549, 549 NYS2d 55 (2d Dept 1989).

[8] This is not the case with some home improvement contractor licensing ordinances. For instance, the Town of East Hampton Code provides that no person may conduct a home improvement under a name other than that in which the license has been obtained. East Hampton Town Code §89-40. This has been construed to mean that a corporation must have its own license; the license of the corporate president will not suffice. See Robert M. Padden Constr, Inc v Reitkopf, 146 Misc 2d 272, 550 NYS2d 523 (Suffolk 1989).

[9] Neither licensing article affects contractors or builders or prevents them "from engaging in construction management and administration of construction contracts." NY Educ Law §§7208(p), 7306(1)(g) (McKinney 1985).

much true architecture and engineering one may practice under the guise of construction management without violating licensing requirements.

Loss of License

An architect's or engineer's license can be revoked, temporarily suspended, or placed on probation if the architect or engineer practices its profession without due care or engages in improper conduct relating to its profession—such as when an architect lost its license because it offered to bribe zoning officials on behalf of a client.[10] In most cases, licenses are lost for poor and incomplete work or for fraud. Consider, for instance, the case of a man who was a licensed engineer and land surveyor.[11] His surveyor's license was revoked and his engineer's license suspended for one year (which suspension was stayed pending successful completion of a one-year probation period) when it was found that he practiced both professions with gross negligence, fraudulently, and unprofessionally. Specifically, on one job he incorrectly calculated boundary lines, incorrectly described the parcel's square footage and the location and outline of an existing structure, showed a nonexistent ravine, made incorrect descriptions on the topographical survey, and committed traverse closure errors. The fraud charge was based on the fact that the engineer falsely advertised that he was associated with other licensed engineers and surveyors. The engineer's errors were found to be gross and substantial and of sufficient magnitude to justify the discipline given.[12]

In another case, an engineer's license was suspended for six months for his performance of a contract to test a building's ventilation system for building department rule compliance.[13] The engineer certified that the building was in compliance despite several easily discoverable violations. The state licensing board found the engineer guilty of gross negligence, incompetence, and misconduct in the practice of engineering and unprofessional conduct based on the engineer's failure to test the entire system, to make inspections and tests himself, and to correct his certifications when he learned of the errors. The engineer had his two sons run the tests—one son was still in training, the other had been licensed only six months at the time the work was done. They did not test the entire system; indeed, they did not even look in the building's basement where many components of the system were located. Further, when the engineer discovered that his certifications were in error, he failed to notify either the owner or the city of the system's serious defects.[14]

§11.03 —Failure to License

Generally, the lack of a license precludes recovery for services performed, no matter how competently the services were rendered or how satisfied the

---

[10] Daub v Board of Regents, 33 AD2d 964, 306 NYS2d 869 (3d Dept 1970).
[11] Brew v State Educ Dept, 73 AD2d 743, 423 NYS2d 271 (3d Dept 1979).
[12] *Id.*
[13] Shapiro v Board of Regents, 29 AD2d 801, 286 NYS2d 1001 (3d Dept 1968).
[14] *Id.*

person receiving the services was.[15] This rule especially holds true when the owner promptly disavows the contract upon learning of the architect's or engineer's lack of a license.[16] Further, the rule precludes recovery for services that are incidental to the design contract, such as consultation; generally, such services are part of an indivisible contract and, as such, recovery is barred.[17]

Architect/Engineer Liability

§11.04 Generally

An architect's or engineer's (collectively referred to as A/Es) liability may be in either contract or negligence depending upon who was damaged and the basis of the claim. An owner who had a direct contract with an A/E may seek redress in either contract or tort at the owner's option.[18] If the owner chooses to sue in negligence, the action generally is called a claim for malpractice.[19] Thus, despite the fact that the relationship is founded in contract, an owner may sue an A/E simultaneously for breach of contract and negligent performance of contract; it is, of course, limited to one recovery.[20]

Contract-Based Claims

When judging breach of contract claims against A/Es, the courts apply a standard based in negligence—i.e., to recover against an A/E in contract, one must show that the A/E failed to perform in accordance with the standard of professional care usually exercised by such professionals in the community.[21] Of course, the contract is controlling—if it specifies what the A/E is to do and the standard for its performance, the A/E is judged by the contract require-

---

[15] Bujas v Katz, 133 AD2d 730, 520 NYS2d 18 (2d Dept 1987).

[16] PC Chipouras & Assocs v 212 Realty Corp, 156 AD2d 549, 549 NYS2d 55 (2d Dept 1989); Wineman v Blueprint 100, Inc, 75 Misc 2d 665, 348 NYS2d 721 (Civ Ct NY 1973).

[17] Gordon v Adenbaum, 171 AD2d 841, 567 NYS2d 777 (2d Dept 1991). There is some difference of opinion as to whether an owner should be allowed to benefit from an unlicensed architect's or engineer's services if the owner knew of the lack of a license when it contracted for the services. For instance, where the owner knew—before the work was contracted for—that the architect was licensed in Louisiana, but not in New York, and raised the issue after the architect's work was completed as a means to avoid paying the architect, the court found that the owner was estopped from invoking the licensing defense because the parties were equally in the wrong. *See* Wormuth v Lower Eastside Action Project, Inc, 71 Misc 2d 314, 335 NYS2d 896 (App Term 1st Dept 1972). *Contra* DJL Gen Contractor, Inc v Harrison, NYLJ Apr 9, 1991, at 29, col 6 (Nassau 1991) (unlicensed home improvement contractor); Robert M. Padden Constr, Inc v Reitkopf, 146 Misc 2d 272, 550 NYS2d 523 (Suffolk 1989).

[18] Naetzker v Brocton Cent School Dist, 41 NY2d 929, 363 NE2d 351, 394 NYS2d 627 (1977).

[19] Hotel Utica, Inc v Armstrong, 62 AD2d 1147, 404 NYS2d 455 (4th Dept 1978).

[20] *Id.*

[21] *Id.*

ments. Consider, for instance, a case in which an architect advised an owner on the use of a ballasted roof. The architect had two acceptable alternate methods of analysis it could use to evaluate the issue. The architect used only one of the two methods and reached the conclusion that a ballasted roof would not meet the building code; the other method would have shown that it was acceptable. The court ruled that if the contract required the architect to discover whether a ballasted roof *could* be used, the architect committed malpractice. On the other hand, if the contract required the architect to determine whether a ballasted roof *should* be used, there was no malpractice.[22]

A/E contracts typically contain exculpatory language to the effect that the A/E is not responsible for construction means or methods or contractors' acts or omissions. Such clauses do not immunize A/Es from liability that flows from breaches of their duties to owners. Such provisions have been interpreted to be

> "nothing other than an agreement that the architect is not the insurer or guarantor of the general contractor's obligation to carry out the work in accordance with the construction documents." It does not diminish the Architect's "non-construction responsibility . . . to visit, to familiarize, to determine, to inform, and to endeavor to guard."[23]

Thus, notwithstanding such clauses, contractual liability claims have been asserted against A/Es for failing to complete projects on time,[24] for work improperly done by others,[25] for leaking roofs,[26] and for shrinking woodwork.[27]

In contract, an A/E may be liable to the party with which it had a direct contract, to third-party beneficiaries, and to any other person whose relationship with the A/E approached privity.[28]

Warranty Claims

In New York, there is no recognized cause of action for breach of an implied warranty against an architect or engineer.[29] Further, as a warranty claim is the

---

[22] Westmount Intl Hotels, Inc v Sear-Brown Assocs, 65 NY2d 618, 480 NE2d 739, 491 NYS2d 150 (1985).

[23] Diocese of Rochester, NY v R-Monde Contractors, Inc, 148 Misc 2d 926, 562 NYS2d 593, 596 (Monroe 1989) (quoting Hunt v Ellisor & Tanner, Inc, 739 SW2d 933, 937 (Tex Ct App 1987)).

[24] Steiner v Wenning, 43 NY2d 831, 373 NE2d 366, 402 NYS2d 567 (1977).

[25] *Id.*

[26] Board of Educ v Celotex Corp, 88 AD2d 713, 451 NYS2d 290 (3d Dept), *affd,* 58 NY2d 684, 444 NE2d 1006, 458 NYS2d 542 (1982).

[27] Lindeberg v Hodgens, 89 Misc 454, 152 NYS 229 (App Term 1st Dept 1915).

[28] *See* §11.14.

[29] Sears Roebuck & Co v Enco Assocs, 43 NY2d 389, 372 NE2d 555, 401 NYS2d 767 (1977); Milau Assocs v North Ave Dev Corp, 42 NY2d 482, 368 NE2d 1247, 398 NYS2d 882 (1977); Paver & Wildfoerster v Catholic High School Assoc, 38 NY2d 669, 345 NE2d 565, 382 NYS2d 22 (1976).

basis for a strict products liability claim, there is no cause of action in strict products liability for damages due to the negligent performance of professional services.[30] An A/E may, however, by contract agree to guarantee a result for which the A/E could be liable for breach of express warranty if the A/E fails to produce the result guaranteed, even if the A/E meets the applicable standard of care.[31]

Tort-Based Claims

When evaluating negligent performance of contract (or malpractice) claims by owners against A/Es, courts apply a test of ordinary and reasonable skill usually exercised by a member of the profession.[32] To prove malpractice, an owner must present expert evidence to show the standard of care by which an A/E's competence may be judged and that the A/E did something, or failed to do something, that violated accepted standards of architectural or engineering practice,[33] except in the very rare case when the alleged malpractice falls within a lay jury's ability to evaluate the alleged malpractice through its common experience and observation.[34]

In tort, in addition to the owner, an A/E may be liable to pedestrians and users of and visitors to the building who are physically injured, to workers injured on the job site,[35] or to contractors or subcontractors on interference with contractual relationship claims.

The distinction between contract and tort claims by an owner against its A/E is important when considering an owner's ability to recover damages, discussed in §11.23. For purposes of an A/E's liability, however, there is no true distinction. The thin line between owner claims in contract and in tort against A/Es is further blurred by the use of less-than-precise wording by courts in their opinions; too often, any wrong by an A/E is called malpractice, even if the owner sues in contract. Technically, a malpractice claim is a negligence claim asserted by an owner, not a contract claim. Because of this mixing of claims and the difficulty in distinguishing between tort and contract claims by owners against A/Es, liability issues will not be divided on the basis of legal theory, but rather on the basis of the A/E's alleged wrongdoing or failure. The choice to discuss alleged shortcomings on this basis is further justified by the way most complaints against A/Es are drafted—an alleged wrong is described and this

---

[30] Queensbury Union Free School Dist v Jim Walter Corp, 91 Misc 2d 804, 398 NYS2d 832 (Warren 1977).

[31] Horgan & Slattery v City of New York, 114 AD 555, 100 NYS 68 (1st Dept 1906).

[32] 530 E 89 Corp v Unger, 43 NY2d 776, 373 NE2d 276, 402 NYS2d 382 (1977), affg 54 AD2d 848, 388 NYS2d 284 (1st Dept 1976).

[33] John Grace & Co v State Univ Constr Fund, 99 AD2d 860, 472 NYS2d 757, 760 (3d Dept) (J. Levine concurring in part and dissenting in part opinion), affd as modified, 64 NY2d 709, 475 NE2d 105, 485 NYS2d 734 (1984) (adopting J. Levine's concurring/dissenting opinion).

[34] 530 E 89 Corp v Unger, 43 NY2d 776, 373 NE2d 276, 402 NYS2d 382 (1977), affg 54 AD2d 848, 388 NYS2d 284 (1st Dept 1976).

[35] Discussed in **ch 13**.

same wrong used as the basis for breach of contract, negligent performance of contract, general negligence, and malpractice claims. The most common bases of A/E liability are found in the design, the performance of tests, cost estimation, supervision and inspection, scheduling and coordination of work, certification of progress payments, and disputes resolution. These are discussed in §§11.05-11.11.

§11.05 Liability for Design

The law does not expect perfection from an architect or engineer (collectively referred to as A/Es) in designs and plans.[36] Unless the parties have contractually agreed to a higher standard, an A/E's work is judged by the rule of ordinary and reasonable skill usually exercised by a licensed professional.[37] Generally, the more complex and unusual the design, the more latitude an A/E is allowed.[38] If plans are wholly defective and unfit for use, the A/E is not entitled to any payment for the plans.[39] If an architect hires an engineer to prepare a portion of a design, the architect is liable to the owner for any defects in the engineer's plans that the architect approves.[40]

The A/E may not be liable for deviations that a contractor or materialman makes from the designs if the A/E does not have reason to know of the deviations. For instance, in *John Grace & Co v State University Construction Fund*,[41] the engineer was relieved of liability for leaks in a hot water system that occurred because of a materialman's use of incompatible metals in internal parts of sealed heat exchangers. The engineer's drawings and plans did not call for the use of incompatible metals, neither did the materialman's shop drawings approved by the engineer show that use of these metals was contemplated.

In rare instances, a party not in privity of contract with an A/E may recover for poor design. For instance, a materialman's claims in contribution against an A/E were allowed to stand.[42] In that case, a subcontractor sued the A/E and the materialman, alleging that it incurred damages when it was required to replace installed pipe because of the architect's faulty designs and the materialman's pipe, which did not meet contract specifications. The materialman claimed it was entitled to contribution from the A/E toward the subcontractor's recovery from it, if any, due to the faulty plans and the A/E's failure to properly

---

[36] Milau Assocs v North Ave Dev Corp, 42 NY2d 482, 368 NE2d 1247, 398 NYS2d 882 (1977).

[37] Major v Leary, 241 AD 606, 268 NYS 413 (2d Dept 1934).

[38] *Id*.

[39] Dunne v Robinson, 53 Misc 545, 103 NYS 878 (App Term 1907).

[40] Italian Econ Corp v Community Engrs, Inc. 135 Misc 2d 209, 514 NYS2d 630 (NY 1987).

[41] 99 AD2d 860, 472 NYS2d 757, 760 (3d Dept) (J. Levine concurring in part/dissenting in part opinion), *affd as modified*, 64 NY2d 709, 475 NE2d 105, 485 NYS2d 734 (1984) (adopting J. Levine's concurring/dissenting opinion).

[42] Haseley Trucking Co v Great Lakes Pipe Co. 101 AD2d 1019, 476 NYS2d 702 (4th Dept 1984).

advise it of contract requirements. Similarly, if an A/E's design defects or survey deficiencies cause delays that injure contractors or subcontractors, they may have a claim against the A/E.[43]

§11.06 Liability for Testing

It is not unusual for architects or engineers (collectively referred to as A/Es) to be retained to inspect existing buildings for compliance with building codes, structural soundness, or fitness for habitation prior to purchase. Under agreements for such tasks, the A/E must perform its tests and make its report with the care usually exercised by other professionals. Liability for a faulty report may go beyond the owner or person to whom the report was directly made and be extended to a party whom the A/E knew or should have known would rely upon the report.[44]

If an A/E or land surveyor is hired to survey an owner's property, it is not an insurer of the accuracy of its survey, but must "exercise that duty of care which a surveyor or civil engineer 'of ordinary skill and prudence would exercise under similar circumstances and may be held responsible for such damages as are sustained due to [its] negligence and lack of skill.' "[45] Under this standard, a civil engineer/land surveyor was held liable for an owner's increased construction costs when it was forced to relocate a partially completed structure's sewer line and septic tank and incurred additional expenses due to the engineer's failure to properly note the location of a water line, as the engineer did not resolve obvious discrepancies in the water line location revealed by various maps it examined and the owner had made it clear to the engineer at the outset that discovering the true location of the water line was very important.[46]

An A/E's inspection duties do not arise only in the context of construction. Often, A/Es are retained to inspect structures for a potential purchaser. These issues are discussed in §11.06. In one case, a potential home owner hired an engineering firm to inspect a home it was hoping to purchase.[47] The engineer reported some water seepage in the basement, a fair-to-poor ground slope, and several low spots on the property. The report disclaimed liability for every defect, save those which could be examined visually. After the client purchased the home, it discovered that the home was surrounded by a virtual "lake" when-

---

[43] Northrup Contracting, Inc v Village of Bergen, 139 Misc 2d 435, 527 NYS2d 670 (Monroe 1986), *affd mem as modified on other grounds*, 129 AD2d 1002, 514 NYS2d 306 (4th Dept 1987).

[44] Ossining Union Free School Dist v Anderson LaRocca Anderson, 73 NY2d 417, 539 NE2d 91, 541 NYS2d 335 (1989), discussed at §11.21.

[45] RH Bowman Assocs v Danskin, 72 Misc 2d 244, 338 NYS2d 224, 226 (Schenectady 1972), *affd mem*, 43 AD2d 621, 349 NYS2d 655 (3d Dept 1973) (quoting 19 NY Jur *Engineers & Surveyors* §§13, 556 (1961)).

[46] *Id.*

[47] Della Corte v Incorporated Village of Williston Park, 60 AD2d 639, 400 NYS2d 357 (2d Dept 1977).

ever there was a substantial rainfall. The owner sued the engineer for what it alleged to be a negligent inspection and report. The court, ruling on the engineer's motion for summary judgment based on the disclaimer, found that ground drainage and sewage problems were specifically disclaimed as areas not inspected as not being capable of visual examination. The court found, however, that the engineer may be liable if the report were to be found to be incomplete based on whether the engineer should have further elucidated potential problems with the home due to the visual signs observed by the engineer. The court held that the disclaimer could not exempt the engineer from liability for negligence in inspecting and reporting visually perceptible items.[48]

§11.07 Liability for Cost Estimates

If an architect or engineer (collectively referred to as A/Es) grossly miscalculates the cost of a project, it may be liable to the owner or may lose its right to compensation for the work. For instance, an architect was retained by the city of New York armory board to prepare plans and specifications for an armory building to cost "well within the sum of $450,000" in building costs, including the architect's fees.[49] Bids were asked on the plans and specifications; bids received ranged from over $650,000 to almost $750,000, well above the $450,000 appropriated for the work. In reviewing the architect's claim for payment, the court stated:

> If the plaintiff substantially performed its contract, which we think was to furnish plans and specifications for an armory which could be erected within the sum of $450,000, then it is entitled to recover thereon the customary price.... This, however, the plaintiff did not do.... [T]he excess cost was so great that it cannot be said plaintiff substantially performed its contract.[50]

A substantial discrepancy between the A/E's estimate and the bids received is not, alone, proof of negligence nor does it permit an inference of negligence. The discrepancy must be shown to be due to the A/E's failure to estimate costs, as it could just as easily be due to changed market conditions or other factors.[51]

Many contracts include a clause limiting an A/E's liability for cost estimates.

---

[48] *Id.*

[49] Horgan & Slattery v City of NY, 114 AD 555, 100 NYS 68 (1st Dept 1906).

[50] *Id* at 559, 100 NYS at 71-72 (the architect was allowed to recover the quantum meruit value of some of its work, as it made preliminary plans and sketches which were used by the board to decide the size and character of the armory).

[51] Pipe Welding Supply Co v Haskell, Conner & Frost, 61 NY2d 884, 462 NE2d 1190, 474 NYS2d 472 (1984) (A/E's estimated building cost was far too low, bids received exceeded estimate by 33% to 45%).

§11.08 Liability for Supervision and Inspection

If an architect or engineer (collectively referred to as A/Es) assumes supervision and inspection duties under the contract, the A/E "is bound to exercise due care in the performance of such duties."[52] The A/E must be diligent in inspecting and supervising the work, but is not obligated to discover every defect in a contractor's or subcontractor's work and will not be liable for defects so long as they are not attributable to carelessness, negligence, or inattention on the A/E's part.[53] In an attempt to avoid assumption of inspection and supervision duties, recent contracts obligate architects only to "observe":

> The Architect shall visit the site at intervals appropriate to the stage of construction to become generally familiar with the progress and quality of the completed Work and to determine in general if the Work is proceeding in accordance with the Contract Documents. However, the Architect shall not be required to make exhaustive or continuous on-site inspections.... On the basis of such on-site observations as an architect, the Architect shall endeavor to guard the Owner against defects and deficiencies in the Work of the Contractor.[54]

Based on such observations, the Architect often is obligated to issue certificates of payment that serve as a representation by the A/E to the owner

> that the Work has progressed to the point indicated; that to the best of the Architect's knowledge, information, and belief, the quality of the Work is in accordance with the Contract Documents ... and that the Contractor is entitled to payment in the amount certified.[55]

The same contract includes a disclaimer that states that the A/E is not responsible for "construction means, methods, techniques, sequences or procedures, ... for the acts or omissions of the Contractor, Subcontractors, or other persons performing any of the Work, or for the failure of any of them to carry out the Work in accordance with the Contract Documents."[56]

---

[52] Lindeberg v Hodgens, 89 Misc 454, 152 NYS 229, 231 (App Term 1st Dept 1915); Straus v Buchman, 96 AD 270, 89 NYS 226, 228 (1st Dept 1904), *affd mem*, 184 NY 545, 76 NE 1109 (1906) (A/E must exercise "reasonable care and diligence in supervising the work").

[53] Petersen v Rawson, 34 NY 370 (1866).

[54] AIA Doc B141(CM) Contract between Owner and Architect, ¶1.5.4 (1980 ed), *as quoted in* Diocese of Rochester, NY v R-Monde Contractors, Inc, 148 Misc 2d 926, 562 NYS2d 593, 595 (Monroe 1989).

[55] AIA Doc B141(CM) Contract between Owner and Architect, ¶1.5.8 (1980 ed), *quoted in* Diocese of Rochester, NY v R-Monde Contractors, Inc, 148 Misc 2d 926, 562 NYS2d 593, 595 (Monroe 1989).

[56] AIA Doc B141(CM) Contract between Owner and Architect, ¶1.5.5 (1980 ed), *as quoted in* Diocese of Rochester, NY v R-Monde Contractors, Inc, 148 Misc 2d 926, 562 NYS2d 593, 595 (Monroe 1989).

The primary purpose of inspection and supervision provisions is to impose an obligation on the A/E to assure to the owner prior to acceptance of the work that the work has been completed in accordance with the plans and specifications.[57] Owners hire A/Es to inspect and supervise work as a means to protect themselves against defects and improper workmanship.[58] Hence, a disclaimer does not relieve an A/E from an obligation to perform a contractual duty; it merely shows the parties' agreement that the A/E is not the guarantor of the general contractor's obligation to do its work properly. Before an A/E certifies work as complete, the A/E must, at a minimum, generally inspect the work. It is no defense for an A/E to claim that important work was performed and covered between visits,[59] that it would have been difficult to inspect the work,[60] that the A/E lacked specialized knowledge needed to properly inspect and supervise the work,[61] or that the owner had its own clerk of the works that approved work progress.[62]

> [The architect] is an expert in carpentry, in cements, in mortar, in the strength of materials, in the art of constructing walls, the floors, the staircases, the roofs, and is duty bound to possess reasonable skill and knowledge as to all these things; and when, in the progress of civilization, new conveniences are introduced into our homes, and become, not curious novelties, but the customary means of securing the comfort of the unpretentious citizen, why should not the architect be expected to possess the technical learning respecting them that is exacted of him with respect to other and older branches of his professional studies?[63]

It is not yet known how New York will construe observation clauses. One court has held that while such clauses do not require exhaustive or continuous inspections, they do impose some inspection duties on an A/E, including the duties to

> visit the site periodically in order to be familiar with the progress and quality of the work, to determine generally if the work was proceeding in accordance with the contract documents, to keep [the owners]

---

[57] Welch v Grant Dev Co, 120 Misc 2d 493, 498, 466 NYS2d 112 (Bronx 1983).

[58] Straus v Buchman, 96 AD 270, 89 NYS 226 (1st Dept 1904), *affd mem*, 184 NY 545, 76 NE 1109 (1906).

[59] *Id.*

[60] Diocese of Rochester, NY v R-Monde Contractors, Inc, 148 Misc 2d 926, 562 NYS2d 593 (Monroe 1989).

[61] Hubert v Aitken, 2 NYS 711 (CP 1888), *affd on reargument*, 5 NYS 839 (CP 1889), *affd mem*, 123 NY 655 (1890).

[62] Central School Dist No 2 v Flintkote Co, 56 AD2d 642, 391 NYS2d 887 (2d Dept 1977).

[63] Hubert v Aitken, 2 NYS 711, 712-13 (CP 1888), *affd on reargument*, 5 NYS 839 (CP 1889), *affd mem*, 123 NY 655 (1890).

informed about the progress and quality of the work, and to guard against defects in the work.[64]

If an A/E breaches contractual obligations and such breach is a proximate cause of a failure to discover a defect, the A/E may be liable to the owner for damages incurred due to the A/E's breach.[65] Generally, the measure of damages is the cost to remedy the defects.[66]

An A/E hired to periodically inspect and report on construction progress to a mortgagee does not owe a duty to subsequent owners of the property for allegedly deficient inspections—the A/E's sole purpose was to protect the mortgagee's interest in the property during construction.[67] Further, an A/E's duty to inspect and supervise does not relieve a contractor from its duties to perform its work properly and to ensure that its subcontractors' work is properly done.[68]

An A/E's inspection duties do not arise only in the context of construction. Often, A/Es are retained to inspect structures for a potential purchaser. These issues are discussed in §11.06.

§11.09 Liability for Scheduling and Coordination

An architect or engineer (collectively referred to as A/Es) may be liable for breach of contract to an owner if the project is not completed on time.[69] As regards contractors and subcontractors, however, the duty of scheduling and coordination is ultimately the owner's. Unless the owner has fully delegated these duties *and* the power to enforce scheduling decisions to the A/E, the A/E should not be liable to contractors and subcontractors who are damaged due to poor scheduling or coordination; the liability is more properly the owner's.[70]

§11.10 Liability for Certifying Progress Payments

Architects may be held liable to owners when they improperly certify a prog-

---

[64] Diocese of Rochester v R-Monde Contractors, Inc, 148 Misc 2d 926, 562 NYS2d 593, 596 (Monroe 1989).

[65] *Id.*

[66] Nieman-Irving & Co v Lazenby, 263 NY 91, 188 NE 265 (1933); Schwartz v Kuhn, 71 Misc 149, 126 NYS 568 (App Term 1911).

[67] Gordon v Holt, 65 AD2d 344, 412 NYS2d 534 (4th Dept), *appeal denied*, 47 NY2d 710, 419 NYS2d 1026 (1979).

[68] John W. Cowper Co v Buffalo Hotel Dev Venture, 72 NY2d 890, 528 NE2d 1214, 532 NYS2d 742 (1988).

[69] Steiner v Wenning, 43 NY2d 831, 373 NE2d 366, 402 NYS2d 567 (1977) (court implied that negligent performance claim not valid).

[70] *See* ch 7.

ress payment or prematurely release retainage.[71] Courts recognize that owners rely upon the professional competence and unbiased position of a project architect in approving payments. When an architect certifies progress payments and allows payment before due or prematurely releases retainage, the owner may be damaged as its contractor's incentive to complete the project is lessened or removed.

An engineer may be liable to a subcontractor for its refusal to certify work done so payment can be made, regardless of a contract between the architect or engineer and subcontractor or a total lack of privity, if the subcontractor can show that the refusal to certify work done was willful and wrongful.[72]

§11.11 Liability for Dispute Resolution

Often, architects and engineers (collectively referred to as A/Es) serve as the initial deciders of disputes between the owner and contractor. Contractual clauses obligating A/Es to such duties typically specify that the A/E is to be impartial, that disputes must be referred to the A/E before arbitration or litigation can be begun, and that the owner or contractor may appeal an A/E's decision. Such clauses place the A/E in a position that is rife with potential conflicts of interest. The A/E is under contract to the owner and may be called upon to interpret its own plans and specifications and review its own prior decisions and inspections. It is not surprising that contractors often claim that the A/E's decision was unfair or biased and, as a result, seek review of the decision. The issue of pertinence here is whether an A/E may be liable for its resolution of contractual disputes. New York case law, at this time, provides no real guidance on this issue.

Generally, so long as the A/E's decision was made in good faith and within the scope of its contractual authority, it should face no additional liability because its decision was incorrect.[73] Of course, if the A/E's decision acknowledges its responsibility for a defect or some other wrong, it could be liable on grounds other than as a decider of disputes. If, however, the decision was made in bad faith or was fraudulent, the A/E should be liable to those parties damaged by the decision.[74] Further, if the A/E unreasonably delays in taking action or making a decision, and hence has breached its contractual obligations as a resolver of disputes, it may be liable for damages caused due to its delay.[75]

---

[71] *See* State v Malvaney, 221 Miss 190, 72 So 2d 424 (1954); *see also* W.E. Shipley, Annotation, Liability of Architect or Engineer for Improper Issuance of Certificates, 43 ALR2d 1227.

[72] Unity Sheet Metal Works, Inc v Farrell Lines, Inc, 101 NYS2d 1000 (NY 1950), *revd*, 108 NYS2d 919 (1st Dept 1951) (plaintiff failed to allege sufficient facts but was given leave to replead), *affd*, 304 NY 639, 107 NE2d 164 (1952).

[73] *E.g.*, Blecick v School Dist No 18, 2 Ariz App 114, 406 P2d 746 (1965).

[74] *Contra* Wilder v Crook, 250 Ala 424, 34 So 2d 832 (1938).

[75] EC Ernst, Inc v Manhattan Constr Co, 551 F2d 1026 (5th Cir 1977), *cert denied*, 434 US 1067 (1978).

428   PROFESSIONAL'S ROLE & LIABILITY

In reality, however, it is difficult to imagine that these damages would be of any significance, as most clauses provide that either the owner or the contractor may seek arbitration or litigation 10 days after the evidence supporting the claim was presented to the A/E, whether the A/E has rendered a decision or not.[76]

If an A/E is called upon to act as a decider when it appears that the problem is the A/E's fault, the A/E should make a preliminary determination as to whether the dispute or claim falls within the dispute resolution clause requiring initial submission of disputes to the A/E. An A/E could reasonably conclude that such a dispute, which in essence relates to the adequacy of the A/E's performance, does not fall within the clause and advise the parties, promptly in writing, that it will not render a decision because the dispute does not come within its authority, and inform the parties that they are free to pursue other remedies under the contract.

If the A/E believes that the dispute does come within the clause, but the dispute allegedly involves the A/E's acts or omissions, the A/E could decline to render a decision, on the basic principle that one cannot act as one's own judge, *nemo potest esse simul actor et judex*. Indeed, some courts have held that, notwithstanding such clauses, a party is not required to submit a dispute to an A/E if the dispute involves the A/E's acts or omissions.[77] This is an idealized solution. In practice, A/Es rarely decline to render decisions on questions that concern their own work. In fact, the American Institute of Architects (AIA) General Conditions of the Contract for Construction empower A/Es to judge their own work.[78]

§11.12 Liability to Third Parties

In addition to owners, other parties often seek redress from architects and engineers (collectively referred to as A/Es) for damages suffered as a result of their actions or failures to act. As was discussed in §11.10, a subcontractor may seek redress from a project A/E for its failure to issue a certificate so payment can be made. An A/E's liability to contractors, subcontractors, and others for defects and failures is discussed throughout Chapter 12. An A/E's liability to laborers on the job site is discussed in Chapter 13. A/Es probably have been sued by a representative member of every imaginable class of persons who are involved with the construction of the project, live close to or pass by the project during construction, or make some use of the project after its completion. Generally, New York courts have been reluctant to make A/Es ultimately responsible for a third party's injuries. This should not be read to imply that liability will not be imposed on an A/E where it is the party responsible for the defect

---

[76] AIA Doc A201, ¶4.5.4 (1987 ed).

[77] Pashen Contractors, Inc v John J. Colnan Co, 13 Ill App 3d 485, 300 NE2d 795 (1973); *see also* County of Rockland v Priamiano Constr Co, 51 NY2d 1, 409 NE2d 951, 431 NYS2d 478 (1980) (only disputes relating to the execution or progress of the work or interpretation of the contract documents initially must be submitted to A/E).

[78] AIA Doc A201, ¶4.3.2 (1987 ed).

or if reliance by the injured party on an act or report of the A/E can be shown. Third-party claims against A/Es perhaps are best discussed in terms of actions founded in either negligence or contract. In reality, pleadings of parties with a quasi-contractual relationship are often couched in terms of both; these will be discussed in §11.14, where the concept of *privity* plays an important role.

§11.13 —In Negligence

True negligence claims against architects and engineers (collectively referred to as A/Es) are brought when individuals suffer physical injury or property damage in, on, or near a building if it appears that the injury or damage was due, at least in part, to a design defect. When restaurant patrons walk through plate glass windows or doors, they often sue the A/E who specified the door or window in the building plans and specifications, alleging a design defect. When tenants slip on wet laundry room floors[79] or fall off narrow stoops,[80] they may claim that the injury was due to a design defect—the floor should have drained better or the stoop should have been wider. Generally, even where there is a design defect, an A/E will not be liable for a remote user's injuries if the defect was not hidden or concealed; if the defect is patent, the A/E is not liable.[81] Some more recent cases reject the latent/patent distinction and simply examine whether the architect had a duty to the claimant and breached the duty by failing to exercise due care in preparing the plans for the project.[82]

The issues are different when considering A/E liability to injured workers. Despite their erosion in some areas of tort, the concepts of malfeasance and nonfeasance are still important when considering A/E tort liability to injured workers. Malfeasance or misfeasance is an affirmative wrongful act that results in harm; today it is more often called active negligence. Nonfeasance, on the other hand, relates to the nonperformance of a contract that results in harm to one not in privity of contract with the wrongdoer. When discussing A/E liability, some courts retain these distinctions and refuse to "impose liability on a [supervising] engineer . . . for an injury sustained by a worker at a construction site unless active malfeasance exists or such liability is imposed by a clear contractual provision, creating an obligation explicitly running to and for the benefit of workers."[83] Chapter 13 discusses safety more thoroughly.

---

[79] Cubito v Kreisberg, 69 AD2d 738, 419 NYS2d 578 (2d Dept 1979), *affd mem*, 51 NY2d 900, 415 NE2d 979, 434 NYS2d 991 (1980).

[80] Inman v Binghamton Hous Auth, 3 NY2d 137, 143 NE2d 895, 164 NYS2d 699 (1957).

[81] *Id;* DiPerna v Roman Catholic Diocese, 30 AD2d 249, 292 NYS2d 177 (3d Dept 1968).

[82] Cubito v Kreisberg, 69 AD2d 738, 419 NYS2d 578 (2d Dept 1979), *affd mem*, 51 NY2d 900, 415 NE2d 979, 434 NYS2d 991 (1980).

[83] Conti v Pettibone Cos, 111 Misc 2d 772, 445 NYS2d 943, 945-46 (1981); *see also* Hamill v Foster-Lipkins Corp, 41 AD2d 361, 342 NYS2d 539 (3d Dept 1973); Ramos v

§11.14 —In Contract

Despite the fact that architects and engineers (collectively referred to as A/Es) rarely contract with any party save the owner, they often find themselves sued in contract or quasi-contract actions. Generally, where only economic loss damages have occurred,[84] a party cannot recover against an A/E directly, in the absence of a contract or a "bond between [the parties] so close as to be the functional equivalent of contractual privity."[85] This discussion does not concern contribution and indemnification, which are discussed in §11.22.

It is not unusual for a mortgagee to hire an A/E to periodically inspect and report on construction progress to it. In such a case, the A/E does not owe a duty to subsequent owners of the property for allegedly deficient inspections; the A/E's sole purpose is to protect the mortgagee's interest in the property during construction.[86]

An A/E's potential liability to a surety is discussed in Chapter 8.

Privity

The Court of Appeals has held that privity of contract is no longer a requirement for a party to recover economic loss damages from a professional for negligent misrepresentation. In *Credit Alliance Corp v Anderson & Co*,[87] the Court of Appeals held that accountants could be liable to noncontractual parties if the relationship of the parties approached that of privity. For a period of time, some thought that the *Credit Alliance* rule applied only to claims against accountants.[88] This notion was dispelled in the case of *Ossining Union Free School District v Anderson LaRocca Anderson*.[89] In that case, the Court of Appeals held that a school district, which contracted with an architect, could sue engineers hired by the architect for damages suffered as a result of the engineers' negligence and malpractice. The issue addressed by the court was whether, in a negligent misrepresentation case that produces only economic injury, privity of contract is required. The court held that what is required is not actual privity of contract but a relationship so close as to be the "functional equivalent of contractual privity."[90] The court laid out a three-prong test, which requires: (1) that the design professional be aware that its reports were to be used for a *particular purpose*; (2) that a *known person* rely on the reports in furtherance

---

Shumavon, 21 AD2d 4, 247 NYS2d 699 (1st Dept), *affd*, 15 NY2d 610, 203 NE2d 912, 255 NYS2d 658 (1964).

[84] A discussion of the economic loss doctrine is found in **ch 15**.

[85] Ossining Union Free School Dist v Anderson LaRocca Anderson, 73 NY2d 417, 419, 539 NE2d 91, 541 NYS2d 335, 335 (1989).

[86] Gordon v Holt, 65 AD2d 344, 412 NYS2d 534 (4th Dept), *appeal denied*, 47 NY2d 710, 419 NYS2d 1026 (1979).

[87] 65 NY2d 536, 483 NE2d 110, 493 NYS2d 435 (1985).

[88] *E.g.*, Northrup Contracting, Inc v Village of Bergen, 139 Misc 2d 435, 527 NYS2d 670 (Monroe 1986), *affd mem as modified on other grounds*, 129 AD2d 1002, 514 NYS2d 306 (4th Dept 1987).

[89] 73 NY2d 417, 539 NE2d 91, 541 NYS2d 335 (1989).

[90] *Id* at 419, 539 NE2d at 91, 541 NYS2d at 335.

of that purpose; and (3) that there be some *conduct* by the design professional *linking* it to the reliant person and evidencing its understanding of the reliance.

Since this test was laid down, there has been little guidance as to what meets its three prongs and what is or is not the functional equivalent of privity sufficient to allow the recovery of economic loss damages in the absence of true privity.[91] Some claims by contractors against A/Es for economic loss damages have been allowed for defective designs and misleading bid documents, as it can be shown that an A/E knows when preparing bid documents that prospective bidders, including the ultimately successful bidder, will rely on those documents.[92] A contractor's claim against an A/E that had inspection duties was dismissed when the court found a lack of privity or of any bond approaching privity; the A/E's sole responsibility was to inspect and approve work for the benefit of the owner—it could not be liable to the contractor for approving the contractor's faulty work.[93] It is unclear how the courts will view an A/E's contractual duties of supervision and scheduling as a basis for liability to contractors and subcontractors; much will depend upon the particular contract language used.

Other potential grounds for architect liability to third parties are negligent supervision and inspection of the contractor's work[94] and negligent interpretation of plans and specifications.[95]

An architect's liability to a surety is discussed in Chapter 8.

Construction Manager Liability

§11.15 Generally

At the present time, it is a difficult task to define accurately the potential

---

[91] *See* Industrial Temperature Sys v Tishman Interiors, NYLJ, Nov 8, 1991, at 22, col 2, Sup Ct NY.

[92] Northrup Contracting, Inc v Village of Bergen, 139 Misc 2d 435, 527 NYS2d 670 (Monroe 1986), *affd as modified on other grounds,* 129 AD2d 1002, 514 NYS2d 306 (4th Dept 1987); J. McKinney & Son v Lake Placid 1980 Olympic Games, Inc, 92 AD2d 991, 461 NYS2d 483 (3d Dept 1983), *affd as modified,* 61 NY2d 836, 462 NE2d 137, 473 NYS2d 960 (1984).

[93] Briar Contracting Corp v City of NY, 156 AD2d 628, 550 NYS2d 717 (2d Dept 1989).

[94] Aetna Ins Co v Hellmuth, Obata & Kassabaum, Inc, 392 F2d 472 (8th Cir 1968) (architect held liable to surety for failing to inspect and ensure correction of contractor's (surety's principal) work); Navajo Circle, Inc v Development Concepts, 373 So 2d 689 (Fla Dist Ct App 1979) (condominium association suit against architect based on alleged third-party beneficiary status); *cf* Durham v Reidsville Engg Co, 255 NC 98, 120 SE2d 564 (1961).

[95] Fett Roofing & Sheet Metal Co v Seaboard Sur Co, 294 F Supp 112 (ED Va 1968).

liability of construction managers.[96] They have been part of the construction process for a relatively short period of time, resulting in there being few reported cases that concern construction manager liability. Further, not all construction managers operate under the same arrangements as all others—the two most common arrangements are, first, that the construction manager acts solely as the owner's agent, does not enter into contracts with trade or subcontractors, and performs no actual construction, and, second, that the construction manager essentially acts as a general contractor, subcontracting to the trades and providing the owner with additional services.[97] A construction manager's duties can, and, in practice, do vary widely and may include design consultation and review, construction scheduling and coordination, supervision, payment certification, cost estimations, and bid review; its knowledge and the services it provides are both technical and managerial.[98] Liability can arise from a construction manager's improper performance of any of these tasks. Where the construction manager has undertaken duties that traditionally are undertaken by an architect or engineer (collectively referred to as A/Es), such as supervision and payment certification, its standard of care and potential liabilities should be the same as an A/E's.[99] When the duties are more akin to those traditionally performed by general contractors, the standard of care should be the same as a contractor's.[100] A construction manager's liability for safety is discussed in Chapter 13.

§11.16 Liability for Design

Rarely will a construction manager design a project. Typically, its role in the design process is to communicate the owner's desires, financing limitations, and project scope to the architect or engineer and to review the design for compliance with these desires, and for feasibility and obvious defects. It may also review the design for constructability, ways to improve it through value engineering, materials selection, and choice of appropriate construction methods. Where the construction manager's actions have resulted in a defect, it

---

[96] Various authors have addressed construction manager liability. A wholly arbitrary and nonexhaustive selection of articles on the issue includes: Sneed, *What Is My Liability as Construction Manager?*, in Avoiding Liability in Architecture, Design and Construction 111 (R. Cushman ed 1983); C.A. Foster, *Construction Management and Design-Build/Fast Track Construction*, 46 Law & Contemp Probs 95 (1983); Partridge & Noletto, *Construction Management: Evolving Roles and Exposure of Construction Managers and Architects/Engineers*, 12 Am J Trial Advoc 55 (1988); Note, *Construction Manager's Liability for Job-Site Safety*, 8 U Bridgeport L Rev 105 (1987); and Note, *Professional Construction Management: Developments in Legal Liability*, 32 Loy L Rev 447 (1986).

[97] *See* O'Mara Org, Inc v Plehn, 579 NYS2d 48 (1st Dept 1992).

[98] Note, *supra* note 96, at 110.

[99] Sneed, *supra* note 96, at 112.

[100] *Id.*

should be liable to the owner damaged by its actions.[101]

§11.17 Liability for Cost Estimates

If a construction manager is responsible for estimating costs, it should be liable in the same manner that an architect is. The authors are not aware of any reported New York cases that discuss liability of a construction manager for cost estimates.

Where a construction manager's contract is a guaranteed maximum price contract, it should not be entitled to recover an amount over and above its guarantee[102] unless the excess cost is due to some action or misrepresentation of the owner or an unforeseen condition.

§11.18 Liability for Supervision and Inspection

Some construction manager contracts provide that the construction manager must perform all supervision not provided by trade contractors or the owner.[103] These contracts usually are fairly specific in delineating the construction manager's duties and responsibilities; any shortcomings by the construction manager or defects due to lackadaisical supervision would be a breach of contract.

§11.19 Liability for Scheduling and Coordination

Typically, one of the prime responsibilities of a construction manager is scheduling and coordinating job progress. Where the construction manager merely has the power to make a schedule and recommend enforcement to the owner but does not have the ability to control performance, the owner would retain ultimate responsibility for scheduling and coordination and should bear any delay damages suffered by trade contractors and subcontractors.[104] Where, however, the owner has expressly delegated its scheduling and coordination duties and the construction manager has assumed such duties *and* has the ability to enforce scheduling decisions, the construction manager's legal responsibility to both the owner and the trade contractors and subcontractors should fol-

---

[101] Sneed, *What Is My Liability as Construction Manager?*, in Avoiding Liability in Architecture, Design and Construction 111, 115-19 (R. Cushman ed 1983); First Natl Bank v Cann, 503 F Supp 419 (ND Ohio 1980), *aff'd*, 669 F2d 415 (6th Cir 1982).

[102] Riva Ridge Apts v Robert G. Fisher Co, 745 P2d 1034 (Colo Ct App 1987).

[103] *See* AIA Doc B801, ¶1.2 (1980 ed); AGC Doc No 8d Owner/Construction Manager Agreement §2.2.2 (1979 ed).

[104] Note, *Professional Construction Management: Developments in Legal Liability*, 32 Loy L Rev 447, 459-67 (1986); Bagwell Coatings, Inc v Middle S Energy, Inc, 797 F2d 1298 (5th Cir 1986) (contractor not in privity with construction manager could not recover damages for delay from construction manager, although construction manager caused the delays).

low,[105] so long as there are no other impediments to recovery, such as *no damage for delay* clauses.[106]

§11.20 Liability for Certifying Progress Payments

As this duty traditionally is one performed by architects and engineers (collectively referred to as A/Es), a construction manager's performance should be judged by the same standard that an A/E's is.[107]

§11.21 Liability to Third Parties

Generally, the authors believe that a construction manager's liability to third parties should be the same as an architect's/engineer's, an owner's, or a general contractor's liability, depending upon the role played by the construction manager. Of course, if the construction manager acts as a general contractor and directly contracts with the trade contractors, it will be liable to those contractors and potentially to their subcontractors. The number of New York cases dealing with construction manager liability to third parties is too small to provide an opportunity for true analysis; liability may be predicated upon a negligence or a third-party beneficiary basis. In *McKinney & Son v Lake Placid Olympic Games*,[108] for example, a subcontractor's claims of negligence and fraud against a "project manager" survived a motion to dismiss. The project manager's contract required it to manage, supervise, and inspect the construction, review contract drawings and specifications, review redesign work, and identify defects in the design. The court found that these duties "inure[d] to the benefit of the subcontractors as well as the owner, for the former are 'members of a lim-

---

[105] Note, *supra* note 104; Bagwell Coatings, Inc v Middle S Energy, Inc, 797 F2d 1298 (5th Cir 1986) (contractor not in privity with construction manager could not recover damages for delay from construction manager, although construction manager caused the delays). Green Plumbing & Heating Co v Turner Constr Co, 500 F Supp 910 (ED Mich 1980), *affd*, 742 F2d 965 (6th Cir 1984); Edward J. Dobson, Jr, Inc v Rutgers State Univ, 157 NJ Super 357, 384 A2d 1121 (1978), *affd*, 180 NJ Super 350, 434 A2d 1125 (1981), *affd*, 90 NJ 253, 447 A2d 906 (1982). *Contra* Bagwell Coatings, Inc v Middle S Energy, Inc, 797 F2d 1298 (5th Cir 1986) (contractor not in privity with construction manager could not recover damages for delay from construction manager although construction manager caused the delays).

[106] Bates & Rogers Constr Corp v Greeley & Hansen, 109 Ill 2d 225, 486 NE2d 902 (1985). *Contra* RS Noonan, Inc v Morrison-Knudsen Co, 522 F Supp 1182 (ED La 1981) (prime contractor recovered delay damages from construction manager despite *no damage for delay* clause in contract between them).

[107] Sneed, *What Is My Liability as Construction Manager?*, in Avoiding Liability in Architecture, Design and Construction 111, 134-35 (R. Cushman ed 1983).

[108] 92 AD2d 991, 461 NYS2d 483 (3d Dept 1983), *affd as modified*, 61 NY2d 836, 462 NE2d 137, 473 NYS2d 960 (1984) (the subcontractor's claim later was dismissed due to a release executed by the subcontractor's surety).

ited class' whose reliance upon the project manager's ability is clearly foreseeable."[109]

General Principles

§11.22 Indemnification and Contribution

The principles of indemnification and contribution are discussed throughout this text; specifically, they are discussed in Chapters 3, 12, and 13. A surety's right to indemnifications from its principal is discussed in Chapter 8.

A professional's right to indemnification and contribution is not significantly different from any other construction party's right. Similarly, the issue of when a professional can be sued for indemnification or contribution is not significantly different from the issue of when other parties can be sued. Each may seek common law indemnification or contribution against any other party that has caused the harm complained of and each may be sued by any other party harmed, limited by general principles of law applicable to each. For instance, contribution is not available for purely economic loss resulting from breach of contract.[110]

Thus, an architect or engineer (collectively referred to as A/Es) sued by an owner to recover damages that the owner was required to pay to persons injured by highly combustible "fireproof" materials could seek common law indemnification or contribution against the materialman that supplied[111] the combustible materials.[112] An A/E could not seek contribution from a contractor who installed a defective roofing system where the damage suffered by the owner was only economic loss and there was no personal injury or property damage.[113]

To avoid the limitations of contribution and indemnification, A/Es and construction managers are advised to require indemnification clauses in their contracts with owners, which include recovery of attorneys' fees incurred in third-party claims for property damage and personal injury. They are further advised to require clauses in owner-contractor agreements that provide for indemnification of the A/Es.

In contractual indemnification and contribution, the parties' recovery rights are limited only by the clauses they choose and the restriction of NY Gen Oblig Law §5-322.1 and §5-324 against indemnifying a party against its own negli-

---

[109] *Id* at 993, 461 NYS2d at 486.

[110] Hudson City Bd of Educ v Sargeant, Webster, Crenshaw & Folley, 71 NY2d 21, 517 NE2d 1360, 523 NYS2d 475 (1987).

[111] State Univ Constr Fund v United Tech Corp, 78 AD2d 748, 432 NYS2d 653 (3d Dept 1980).

[112] Greenberg v City of Yonkers, 45 AD2d 314, 358 NYS2d 453 (2d Dept 1974), *affd on opinion*, 37 NY2d 907, 340 NE2d 744, 378 NYS2d 382 (1975).

[113] Hudson City Bd of Educ v Sargeant, Webster, Crenshaw & Folley, 71 NY2d 21, 517 NE2d 1360, 523 NYS2d 475 (1987).

gence.[114] A wholly innocent A/E sued by an injured worker may seek contractual indemnification from the general contractor and those subcontractors that contractually agreed to indemnify the A/E and hold it harmless.[115]

A claim for contribution and indemnification accrues when payment of the underlying liability has been made.[116]

§11.23 Statutes of Limitations

Owners' claims against architects and engineers (collectively referred to as A/Es) for defective construction, regardless of how denominated, generally accrue upon completion of the project[117] or issuance of the final payment certificate[118]—the typical termination of the professional relationship.[119] (The continuous treatment doctrine is discussed in §11.24.) Essentially, the rule is that an owner's claim against an A/E accrues when the professional relationship between the two is over with respect to the construction at issue. The A/E's attention to minor details after completion of all physical work on the project, such as adjustment of contract price due a general contractor due to delays and change orders, does not postpone the date on which the statute of limitation begins to run.[120] Similarly, if an owner is responsible for the issuance of the final certificate, the statute of limitation begins to run upon completion of the contract work.[121] If an owner asserts a claim of fraud, it, too, accrues upon completion, if the fraud was in the performance of the contract and was not extraneous to it.[122] Owners' claims against A/Es for negligent performance of contract or for malpractice are essentially contract actions and are subject to the six-year statute of limitation applicable to contract actions, no matter how denominated.[123] A third party's breach of contract claim accrues at the same time that an owner's does.[124]

---

[114] Discussed in **ch 3**. Also, see **ch 15**.

[115] Drzewinski v Atlantic Scaffolding & Ladder Co, 70 NY2d 774, 515 NE2d 902, 521 NYS2d 216 (1987) (memorandum opinion).

[116] Cubito v Kreisberg, 69 AD2d 738, 419 NYS2d 578 (2d Dept 1979), *affd mem*, 51 NY2d 900, 415 NE2d 979, 434 NYS2d 991 (1980); Alside, Inc v Spancrete NE, Inc, 84 AD2d 616, 444 NYS2d 241 (3d Dept 1981).

[117] Farash Constr Corp v Standco Dev, Inc, 139 AD2d 899, 527 NYS2d 940 (4th Dept 1988), *appeal dismissed*, 73 NY2d 918, 539 NYS2d 301 (1989).

[118] Board of Educ v Celotex Corp, 88 AD2d 713, 451 NYS2d 290 (3d Dept), *affd*, 58 NY2d 684, 444 NE2d 1006, 458 NYS2d 542 (1982).

[119] Sosnow v Paul, 43 AD2d 978, 352 NYS2d 502 (2d Dept 1974), *affd mem*, 36 NY2d 780, 330 NE2d 643, 369 NYS2d 693 (1975).

[120] State v Lundin, 91 AD2d 343, 459 NYS2d 904 (3d Dept), *affd*, 60 NY2d 987, 459 NE2d 486, 471 NYS2d 261 (1983).

[121] *Id*.

[122] Lewis v Axinn, 100 AD2d 617, 473 NYS2d 575 (2d Dept 1984).

[123] Paver & Wildfoerster v Catholic High School Assoc, 38 NY2d 669, 345 NE2d 565, 382 NYS2d 22 (1976).

[124] Board of Managers v Vector Real Estate Corp, 172 AD2d 303, 568 NYS2d 391 (1st Dept), *appeal denied*, 78 NY2d 854, 578 NE2d 442, 573 NYS2d 644 (1991).

The distinction between an owner's claim for breach of contract and for malpractice or negligent performance of contract, both based on the same conduct, becomes important when considering the remedies available to the owner. Despite the fact that an owner's breach of contract claim is subject to the six-year statute of limitation, its right to avail itself of different remedies can be affected by the three-year statute of limitation applicable to malpractice claims[125] and negligence actions.[126] In the case of *Sears, Roebuck & Co v Enco Associate, Inc*,[127] the Court of Appeals stated that "claims by owners against architects arising out of the performance or nonperformance of obligations under contracts between them are governed by the six-year contract Statute of Limitation (CPLR 213, subd. 2), except with respect to the issue of damages. . . ."[128] In *Sears*, the owner, seeking tort and contract damages, brought suit four years after the work was completed. The court ruled:

> [P]roof on the issue of damages should be limited to that admissible under the law of damages for contract liability. Had the action been commenced within the three-year period applicable to tort claims, the owner would have been free to elect to sue in contract or in tort as it saw fit and to offer appropriate proof of damages. . . . [T]he claim is not barred because the six-year statute is applicable, but damages that may be recovered are limited because the three-year statute is also applicable.[129]

Thus, if an owner wishes to receive a negligence measure of damages (which may provide a greater and broader recovery than a contract measure[130]), it must bring its suit within the negligence/malpractice three-year statute of limitation. If an owner brings suit more than three years but less than six years after its claim accrues, it will be limited to a contractual measure of damages.

A simple negligence action against an A/E (brought by a physically injured third party) accrues at the time of the injury[131] and is subject to the three-year statute of limitation applicable to negligence actions.[132] In a personal injury action, it is irrelevant when the project was completed.

Public Works Contracts

The state is exempt from the operations of statutes of limitations unless the contract provides a limitations period or a statute make the state subject to a limitations period; i.e., if the state is not named in a limitations statute, it

---

[125] NY Civ Prac L&R 214(6) (McKinney 1990 & Supp 1992).

[126] *Id* 214(4) (McKinney 1990).

[127] 43 NY2d 389, 372 NE2d 555, 401 NYS2d 767 (1977).

[128] *Id* at 395, 372 NE2d at 558, 401 NYS2d at 770.

[129] *Id* at 396-97, 372 NE2d at 558-59, 401 NYS2d at 771-72.

[130] Palsgraf v Long Island RR, 248 NY 339, 162 NE 99 (1928); Hadley v Baxendale, 156 Eng Rep 145, 9 Ex 341 (Ex 1854).

[131] Cubito v Kreisberg, 69 AD2d 738, 419 NYS2d 578 (2d Dept 1979), *affd mem*, 51 NY2d 900, 415 NE2d 979, 434 NYS2d 991 (1980).

[132] NY Civ Prac L&R 214 (McKinney 1990 & Supp 1992).

is not affected by it.[133] Most limitations statutes in New York expressly apply to actions by the state.[134]

§11.24 —Continuous Treatment Doctrine

The *continuous treatment doctrine* provides that an owner is entitled to an extension or *tolling* of the statutory period applicable to its potential causes of action[135] against a professional for as long as the professional relationship continues. The doctrine, which was first applied in medical malpractice cases,[136] is applied in architectural and engineering malpractice cases to prevent architects and engineers from concealing the cause of defects until the statutory period has passed.[137] Most often, the doctrine is applied when an architect or engineer (collectively known as A/Es) engages in postconstruction activities on behalf of the owner in attempts to discover the cause of and to remedy known defects. For instance, in *County of Broome v Vincent J. Smith, Inc,*[138] the first case to apply the doctrine to architects, the project architect engaged in a great deal of activity on the county owner's behalf after a building was completed in an attempt to correct a roof that began leaking immediately after the building was completed. The roof was constructed under the architect's supervision. The county's claim against the architect did not accrue until the architect stopped working on the roof problem and the professional relationship between the county and architect ended. The court reasoned that the continuing relationship between the two probably "lulled the County into an unfounded assurance that the problem would be corrected. It is clear that the professional relationship between these parties continued through the entire period that [the architect] acted in the County's behalf with respect to the problem of the leaking roof."[139]

In similar instances, the continuous treatment doctrine has been applied where A/Es: actively continued their contractual responsibilities by working for and with owners for several years after completion trying to analyze and

---

[133] *In re* Smathers' Will, 249 AD 523, 293 NYS 314 (2d Dept 1937), *limited on other grounds*, 262 NYS2d 352, 357; Commissioner of Welfare v Jones, 73 Misc 2d 1014, 343 NYS2d 661 (Queens 1973) (citing Guaranty Trust Co v United States, 304 US 126 (1938)).

[134] NY Civ Prac L&R §201 (McKinney 1990 & Supp 1992).

[135] The doctrine is not limited to negligence actions but is also applicable to other causes of action, including actions for equitable relief. Greene v Greene, 56 NY2d 86, 436 NE2d 496, 451 NYS2d 46 (1982).

[136] Borgia v City of NY, 12 NY2d 151, 187 NE2d 777, 237 NYS2d 319 (1962).

[137] Board of Educ v Thompson Constr Corp, 111 AD2d 497, 488 NYS2d 880 (3d Dept 1985); County of Broome v Vincent J. Smith, Inc, 78 Misc 2d 889, 358 NYS2d 998 (Broome 1974).

[138] 78 Misc 2d 889, 358 NYS2d 998 (Broome 1974).

[139] *Id* at 893, 358 NYS2d at 1003.

identify the causes of an insulation problem and to devise a remedy;[140] and learned of a roof defect during construction but failed to notify the owner and, pursuant to the contract, inspected the roof following completion over several years but again and again did not reveal the defect.[141]

The A/E's involvement in the project after its completion must concern the work itself in order for the doctrine to apply; postcompletion negotiations as to prices to be paid for extra work or other equitable adjustments do not constitute continuous treatment by the A/E.[142] Further, the involvement must closely follow the project completion; where a three-and-one-half year gap existed between completion and an A/E's attempts to resolve a roof leak problem, the doctrine was held not to apply.[143]

It is not clear whether the continuous treatment doctrine is applicable to construction managers. The doctrine applies only to *professional* relationships and has been held not to apply to an owner's action against its contractor.[144] The answer probably depends upon whether the construction manager performs duties more akin to an A/E's or to a general contractor's and upon the degree of reliance the owner places on the construction manager's expertise.

§11.25 Insurance

Professional liability insurance is discussed in Chapter 10.

---

[140] Greater Johnstown City School Dist v Cataldo & Waters, Architects, 159 AD2d 784, 551 NYS2d 1003 (3d Dept 1990).

[141] Board of Educ v Thompson Constr Corp, 111 AD2d 497, 488 NYS2d 880 (3d Dept 1985).

[142] State v Lundin, 91 AD2d 343, 459 NYS2d 904 (3d Dept), *affd,* 60 NY2d 987, 459 NE2d 486, 471 NYS2d 261 (1983).

[143] Naetzker v Brocton Cent School Dist, 50 AD2d 142, 376 NYS2d 300 (4th Dept 1975); *revd on other grounds,* 41 NY2d 929, 363 NE2d 351, 394 NYS2d 627 (1977).

[144] Board of Educ v Thompson Constr Corp, 111 AD2d 497, 488 NYS2d 880 (3d Dept 1985).

Defects and Failures   12

§12.01 Introduction
§12.02 Design Defects
§12.03 Construction Defects
§12.04 Faulty or Improper Materials
§12.05 Improper Installation
§12.06 Divided Responsibility
§12.07 Waiver of Defects
§12.08 Statutes of Limitations
§12.09 Claims Against Bond
§12.10 Indemnification and Contribution
§12.11 —Contractual Indemnification and Contribution
§12.12 Warranty (Guarantee) Clauses
§12.13 —Implied Warranties
§12.14 —Implied Warranties in the Sale of New Homes
§12.15 —Express Warranties
§12.16 —Exclusive Remedy

§12.01 Introduction

Defects and failures are not rare occurrences in construction. Nothing man-made is ever perfect. Indeed, the law does not require perfection.[1] Construction is judged by the standard of ordinary and reasonable skill that is usually exercised by architects, engineers, contractors, subcontractors, materialmen, and laborers in their work. Thus, when discussing defects and failures, it is important to remember that not every imperfection has a remedy. It is also important to note that not all failures are as spectacular and sudden as the collapse of the suspended walkways at the Hyatt Regency Hotel in Kansas City,

---

[1] Major v Leary, 241 AD 606, 268 NYS 413 (2d Dept 1934).

Missouri in 1981.[2] Most defects and failures either are readily apparent or manifest slowly, becoming apparent only through the passage of time.

Defects and failures may be due to many different factors but, regardless of the actual cause, the root of a defect or failure is usually in poor design, faulty construction, improper or faulty materials, or improper installation. Responsibility for the defect or failure may rest with the owner, designer, builder, or supplier. In rare instances, a building inspector also may be held liable for a defect or failure. Determining who is responsible for a defect or failure can be difficult. Architects and engineers tend to believe that the fault is with the builder or materials, while contractors like to believe that the fault is with the original plans and specifications. Materialmen tend to believe that their products were not installed properly, not that the materials themselves were defective. Basically, when a failure occurs or a defect is discovered, each party usually points its finger at another party, and rarely at itself. Even when it is clear that the fault is due to poor construction, for example, it is not unusual for the liable contractor to assert that the supervising architect should bear some of the responsibility for not making the contractor perform according to the plans and specifications. Similarly, when the fault lies clearly with poor plans and specifications, it is not unusual for the architect or engineer to assert that the contractor is at least partially responsible because it did not point out the defect to the design professional.

Latent and Patent Defects

Latent defects are defects that are concealed or are not obvious or readily discoverable upon inspection; they are unknown and generally undiscoverable defects. They appear only through the passage of time, such as when a basement wall cracks or a roof leaks. Foundation settlement due to inadequate backfilling and improperly welded pipes may be examples of latent defects.

Patent defects are defects that are obvious upon inspection. An example of a patent defect is the lack of a handrail on a stairway.

Sometimes the difference between latent and patent defects is hard to see—it is not always clear whether a particular defect is latent or patent.

§12.02 Design Defects

Defects and failures due to poor or faulty design or redesign manifest themselves in many ways. Pipes may burst,[3] children may fall down steps,[4] houses

---

[2] This failure is discussed thoroughly by Matthew A. Victor in *The Hyatt Collapse—A Post Mortem*, 10 Constr Law 7 (1990). The revocation of the engineers' licenses is discussed by Robert A. Rubin & Lisa A. Banick in *The Hyatt Regency Decision—One View*, 6 Constr Law 1 (Aug 1986).

[3] Village of Endicott v Parlor City Contracting Co, 51 AD2d 370, 381 NYS2d 548 (3d Dept 1976).

[4] Inman v Binghamton Hous Auth, 3 NY2d 137, 143 NE2d 895, 164 NYS2d 699 (1957).

may sink or be flooded with ground water,[5] parking ramps may crack,[6] basements may not be watertight,[7] roads may be too steep or narrow,[8] etc. The ways and places in which design defects appear and their results are countless. Generally, however, a design professional is liable only if it failed to perform in accord with the standard of professional care typically exercised by similar professionals in the community.[9] Of course, if the contract holds the designer to a higher standard, the contractual standard will be used to judge the designer's performance. For instance, if a designer guarantees a certain result, the law will hold it to this higher standard. Similarly, a higher standard of care may be imposed on the designer by law, such as by a statute, code, or regulation.[10]

Typically, it is the owner that sues an architect or engineer for a design defect in a malpractice action which may contain allegations of negligence and breach of contract.[11] A remote user, such as a building tenant or public invitee, may sue an architect or engineer for personal injury or property damages due to a design defect if the defect is latent, i.e., hidden or concealed.[12] A designer may also be liable in strict liability to parties who are harmed by abnormally dangerous activities undertaken by the designer.[13]

Generally, a contractor is not liable to an owner for design defects, despite the fact that the contractor may have warranted the structure to be free from defects or may have specifically guaranteed some aspect of the structure, such as that it would make the structure watertight.[14] The duty to design a structure properly rests with the design professional; a contractor cannot be liable to an owner for a breach by the designer of this duty—it may be liable only for

---

[5] Doundoulakis v Town of Hempstead, 42 NY2d 440, 368 NE2d 24, 398 NYS2d 401 (1977).

[6] Sears, Roebuck & Co v Enco Assocs, 43 NY2d 389, 372 NE2d 555, 401 NYS2d 767 (1977).

[7] MacKnight Flintic Stone Co v Mayor of NY, 160 NY 72, 54 NE 661 (1899).

[8] Manniello v Dea, 92 AD2d 426, 461 NYS2d 582 (3d Dept 1983).

[9] Hotel Utica, Inc v Armstrong, 62 AD2d 1147, 404 NYS2d 455 (4th Dept 1978). See also 530 E 89 Corp v Unger, 43 NY2d 776, 373 NE2d 276, 402 NYS2d 382 (1977), affg 54 AD2d 848, 388 NYS2d 284 (1st Dept 1976), which went so far as to hold that an architect does not guarantee that its plans will be acceptable to a local building department, in the absence of a specific agreement that they will be. This holding is probably limited to the facts of the case which concerned an owner's need for rapid building department approval in order to avoid operation of soon-to-be changing zoning regulations.

[10] NY Admin Code §27-730 (1986), construction required for or affecting the support of adjacent properties or buildings.

[11] Hotel Utica, Inc v Armstrong, 62 AD2d 1147, 404 NYS2d 455 (4th Dept 1978).

[12] Inman v Binghamton Hous Auth, 3 NY2d 137, 143 NE2d 895, 164 NYS2d 699 (1957); DiPerna v Roman Catholic Diocese, 30 AD2d 249, 292 NYS2d 177 (3d Dept 1968).

[13] Doundoulakis v Town of Hempstead, 42 NY2d 440, 368 NE2d 24, 398 NYS2d 401 (1977).

[14] MacKnight Flintic Stone Co v Mayor of NY, 160 NY 72, 54 NE 661 (1899).

breaches of its own duty.[15] A contractor's duty is to build a structure according to the design it is given; it does not warrant the adequacy of the design.[16] Thus, if the defect is due to poor design, a contractor is entitled to full payment for its work, unless it had reason to believe that the design was defective, failed to raise the issue, and followed it nevertheless.[17] If a contractor is required to perform extra work to correct a design defect, it is entitled to extra compensation for that work.[18] Logically, the owner should be entitled to recover its increased costs from the designer.

An owner may be liable for a design defect to third parties if the defect is latent and was the cause of a personal injury to a third party, such as a tenant[19] or public invitee.[20]

When faced with a design defect, an owner is entitled to that measure of damages which will put it in as good a position as it would have been in if the design contract had been properly performed.[21] Thus, an owner may be entitled to only nominal damages where the defect is minor, to repair costs if the defect is repairable, to lost value if the defect is not remediable but the structure is usable, to its increased cost of construction due to the design defect, or to the cost of total reconstruction if the defect is not remediable and the structure is not usable.[22] If the owner's real property has been permanently injured, the owner may be entitled to recover the lesser of the cost to restore the property to its original condition or the amount of diminution of the property's market value.[23]

Architect and engineer responsibilities, including supervision duties, are further discussed in Chapter 11 on professional liability.

§12.03 Construction Defects

Construction defects range from a contractor's simple failure to complete the contract to deviations from the plans and specifications to outright defective work that results in a structure being wholly unsafe. A foundation may

---

[15] Carrols Equities Corp v Villnave, 76 Misc 2d 205, 350 NYS2d 90 (Onondaga 1973), affd mem, 49 AD2d 672, 373 NYS2d 1012 (4th Dept 1975).

[16] MacKnight Flintic Stone Co v Mayor of NY, 160 NY 72, 54 NE 661 (1899).

[17] Rubin v Coles, 142 Misc 139, 253 NYS 808 (City Ct Kings 1931); see also Caceci v DiCanio Constr Corp, 132 AD2d 591, 517 NYS2d 753 (2d Dept 1987), affd, 72 NY2d 52, 526 NE2d 266, 530 NYS2d 771 (1988).

[18] Seglin-Harrison Constr Co v State, 267 AD 488, 46 NYS2d 602 (3d Dept), affd, 293 NY 782, 58 NE2d 521 (1944).

[19] Inman v Binghamton Hous Auth, 3 NY2d 137, 143 NE2d 895, 164 NYS2d 699 (1957).

[20] Thomassen v J&K Diner, Inc, 152 AD2d 421, 549 NYS2d 416 (2d Dept 1989), appeal dismissed, 76 NY2d 771, 559 NE2d 673, 559 NYS2d 979 (1990).

[21] Manniello v Dea, 92 AD2d 426, 461 NYS2d 582 (3d Dept 1983).

[22] Id.

[23] Id.

444 DEFECTS & FAILURES

settle,[24] a roof may leak,[25] steps may be too narrow or small for safe passage,[26] rooms and windows may not be symmetrical,[27] archways may fall,[28] and ice rinks may not freeze.[29] Such defects may be caused by a contractor's failure to follow plans and specifications, shoddy workmanship, use of improper materials, etc. Defects due to poor design are discussed in §12.02; defects due to poor materials or improper installation are discussed in §§12.04-12.05.

The existence of a defect does not always mean that the contractor is responsible. A contractor is responsible only for its performance of the construction contract[30] and the performance of its subcontractors. If a contractor performs in a workmanlike manner according to the plans and specifications, it is not liable even if the building is defective.[31] A contractor's duty is to follow the plans and specifications; it does not warrant or guarantee that those plans and specifications are correct or defect-free.[32] A contractor does, however, have some responsibility for interpreting the plans and specifications. If it has reason to believe that they are defective and follows them without pointing out the defects to the owner or designer, a contractor may be found liable for the resulting defects.[33] For instance, in a case where the plans and specifications did not indicate that any special foundation work was necessary, a contractor was nonetheless liable for foundation settlement of a home it built on poor soil that obviously was comprised of significant amounts of organic material, including tree limbs.[34] Similarly, the American Institute of Architects (AIA) standard contract between owner and contractor provides that the contractor shall not be responsible for design defects unless it recognized the error, failed to report it to the architect, and did the work in accordance with the defective design.[35]

A contractor's work is judged by the standards of the community or by the

---

[24] Caceci v DiCanio Constr Corp, 132 AD2d 591, 517 NYS2d 753 (2d Dept 1987), affd, 72 NY2d 52, 526 NE2d 266, 530 NYS2d 771 (1988).

[25] Board of Educ v Sargent, Webster, Crenshaw & Folley, 71 NY2d 21, 517 NE2d 1360, 523 NYS2d 475 (1987); Ralston Purina Co v Arthur G. McKee & Co, 158 AD2d 969, 551 NYS2d 720 (4th Dept 1990).

[26] Inman v Binghamton Hous Auth, 3 NY2d 137, 143 NE2d 895, 164 NYS2d 699 (1957); Thomassen v J&K Diner, Inc, 152 AD2d 421, 549 NYS2d 416 (2d Dept 1989), appeal dismissed, 76 NY2d 771, 559 NE2d 673, 559 NYS2d 979 (1990).

[27] Petersen v Rawson, 34 NY 370 (1866).

[28] Lake v McElfatrick, 139 NY 349, 34 NE 922 (1893).

[29] City of NY v Kalisch-Jarcho, Inc, 161 AD2d 252, 554 NYS2d 900 (1st Dept 1990).

[30] Carrols Equities Corp v Villnave, 76 Misc 2d 205, 350 NYS2d 90 (Onondaga 1973), affd mem, 49 AD2d 672, 373 NYS2d 1012 (4th Dept 1975).

[31] Id.

[32] MacKnight Flintic Stone Co v Mayor of NY, 160 NY 72, 54 NE 661 (1899).

[33] Rubin v Coles, 142 Misc 139, 253 NYS 808 (City Ct Kings 1931).

[34] Caceci v DiCanio Constr Corp, 132 AD2d 591, 517 NYS2d 753 (2d Dept 1987), affd, 72 NY2d 52, 526 NE2d 266, 530 NYS2d 771 (1988).

[35] AIA Doc A201, ¶3.2.1 (1987 ed).

§12.03 CONSTRUCTION DEFECTS

standard set forth in the contract.[36] At a minimum, a contractor is bound by an implied promise to perform the contract work in a skillful and workmanlike manner.[37] If the parties wish the work to be judged by a higher standard or by the owner's subjective standards, the contract must say so.[38]

If the "defect" is simply that the contractor did not finish the contract work, an owner need not pay the contractor the full contract price. A contractor's failure to fully perform is not automatically a bar to its right to payment. If the contract is *substantially completed*, the contractor is entitled to the contract price less the costs of correcting any defects and completing the contract work.[39] The contractor has the burden of proving its substantial completion to be entitled to any recovery,[40] including proving the value of work not performed.[41] Determining whether a contractor has substantially performed is not dependent on the number of defects or percentage of the work remaining to be done; the question is, *did the owner get essentially what it bargained for?* In other words, is the project sufficiently complete so the owner may use it for the purpose intended? If so, there is substantial performance despite numerous defects.[42] To recover under the substantial performance doctrine, a contractor must also prove that its departures from the specifications were not "willful nor substantial in view of the entire project."[43] Thus, in a contract to remodel a kitchen, the installation of significantly defective cabinets did not prevent the contractor's recovery for substantial completion as the cabinets were only part of the contract for extensive remodeling of the kitchen.[44]

If the owner did not get essentially what it bargained for, there was not substantial performance and the contractor is not entitled to compensation. For instance, in a case where a road built by a contractor immediately developed potholes and required significant repairs due to the contractor's failure to remove clay and loam when it subgraded the roadbed, the appellate court held that the contractor had not substantially performed, finding that the building of a new road that breaks up shortly after completion is neither full nor

---

[36] Grimpel v Hochman, 74 Misc 2d 39, 343 NYS2d 507 (Civ Ct NY 1972).

[37] Fairbairn Lumber Corp v Telian, 92 AD2d 683, 460 NYS2d 194 (3d Dept 1983).

[38] Grimpel v Hochman, 74 Misc 2d 39, 343 NYS2d 507 (Civ Ct NY 1972).

[39] Pilgrim Homes & Garages, Inc v Fiore, 75 AD2d 846, 427 NYS2d 851 (2d Dept), *appeal dismissed*, 51 NY2d 702, 431 NYS2d 1030 (1980); Gem Drywall Corp v C. Scialdo & Sons, 42 AD2d 1045, 348 NYS2d 643 (4th Dept 1973), *affd mem*, 35 NY2d 781, 320 NE2d 867, 362 NYS2d 152 (1974); Turk v Look, 53 AD2d 709, 383 NYS2d 937 (3d Dept 1976).

[40] Pilgrim Homes & Garages, Inc v Fiore, 75 AD2d 846, 427 NYS2d 851 (2d Dept), *appeal dismissed*, 51 NY2d 702, 431 NYS2d 1030 (1980).

[41] Spence v Ham, 163 NY 220, 57 NE 412 (1900).

[42] Pilgrim Homes & Garages, Inc v Fiore, 75 AD2d 846, 427 NYS2d 851 (2d Dept), *appeal dismissed*, 51 NY2d 702, 431 NYS2d 1030 (1980).

[43] Lewis v Barsuk, 55 AD2d 817, 389 NYS2d 952, 953 (4th Dept 1976).

[44] Mayfair Kitchen Center, Inc v Nigro, 139 AD2d 885, 527 NYS2d 613 (3d Dept 1988).

substantial completion.[45] The appellate court reversed the trial court's award of the balance of the contract price and awarded the owner its cost of repairs.

Typically, it is the owner that sues the contractor for a construction defect, although a remote user of the structure may seek redress from a contractor for personal injury or property damage if the defect is latent.[46] Further, an owner may sue a subcontractor for damages due to defective work by the subcontractor, despite the lack of privity between owners and subcontractors.[47] If an owner is an intended third-party beneficiary of a subcontract, it may sue the subcontractor for breach of contract and express warranty.[48] An owner cannot sue a subcontractor for breach of implied warranty, strict liability, or negligence where its damages are for economic loss due to a defective product.[49]

In addition to liability for a design defect, an architect or engineer may also be held liable to the owner for a construction defect if it can be shown that the defect is due to the architect's failure to properly supervise the contractor's work and that the architect had a duty of supervision.[50] In very limited circumstances, a lender that takes an active role in the construction of a project may be liable for construction defects.[51] Finally, in rare instances, a building inspector may be personally liable for a construction defect if it fraudulently, willfully, or wantonly issued a permit or certificate of occupancy despite an obvious defect.[52]

An owner may be liable for a construction defect if the defect is latent and concealed and was the cause of a personal injury to a third party, such as a

---

[45] Gifford Constr Co v Lever Management Corp, 78 AD2d 869, 432 NYS2d 897 (2d Dept 1980).

[46] Inman v Binghamton Hous Auth, 3 NY2d 137, 143 NE2d 895, 164 NYS2d 699 (1957); Thomassen v J&K Diner, Inc, 152 AD2d 421, 549 NYS2d 416 (2d Dept 1989), *appeal dismissed*, 76 NY2d 771, 559 NE2d 673, 559 NYS2d 979 (1990).

[47] Ralston Purina Co v Arthur G. McKee & Co, 158 AD2d 969, 551 NYS2d 720 (4th Dept 1990); City of NY v Kalisch-Jarcho, Inc, 161 AD2d 252, 554 NYS2d 900 (1st Dept 1990).

[48] Ralston Purina Co v Arthur G. McKee & Co, 158 AD2d 969, 551 NYS2d 720 (4th Dept 1990); City of NY v Kalisch-Jarcho, Inc, 161 AD2d 252, 554 NYS2d 900 (1st Dept 1990).

[49] Schiavone Constr Co v Elgood Mayo Corp, 56 NY2d 667, 436 NE2d 1322, 451 NYS2d 720 (1982), *adopting the dissenting opinion of Silverman, J. in*, 81 AD2d 227, 439 NYS2d 933 (1st Dept 1981).

[50] Lake v McElfatrick, 139 NY 349, 34 NE 922 (1893) (architect did not have duty of supervision; defect due to contractor's failure to follow plans); Petersen v Rawson, 34 NY 370 (1866) (architect had duty to supervise and performed it adequately; defects not due to architect's carelessness, negligence, or inattention).

[51] *See* C. Ferguson, *Lender's Liability for Construction Defects*, 11 Real Est LJ 310 (1983).

[52] *See* P. Blawie, *Legal Liability of Building Officials for Structural Failures*, 57 Conn BJ 211 (1983); Rottcamp v Young, 21 AD2d 373, 249 NYS2d 330 (2d Dept 1964), *aff'd*, 15 NY2d 831, 205 NE2d 866, 257 NYS2d 944 (1965) (inspector not held liable for failure to issue permit).

tenant or public invitee.[53] "[T]he doctrine of respondeat superior renders the owners of places of public assembly subject to vicarious liability for the negligence of their independent general contractors even if the construction has been completed and possession of the premises has been turned over to the property owners."[54]

The party alleging the defect has the burden of proof. Generally, to prove that a problem is due to faulty construction, an owner should present expert testimony as to the cause of the defect. Take, for example, the case of a home owner who had a fireplace and chimney built. Whenever the owner used it, smoke backed up into the house. The owner presented himself and a neighbor as witnesses that the fireplace caused smoke to fill the house, but did not present an expert to testify that the problem was due to faulty construction. The contractor suggested other possible causes of the problem and the court ruled that the owner did not meet his burden of proof.[55]

Defects in the work do not result in a forfeiture of a contractor's right to be compensated; they diminish the amount to which the contractor is entitled.[56] If the defects are reasonably remediable, even if substantial, the measure of damages is the market price of completing or correcting performance.[57] If the contract provides that the contractor shall remedy defects, it must do so, even if the defects are due to its subcontractor's faulty workmanship or materials.[58]

§12.04 Faulty or Improper Materials

If a structure is built with all the care and precision possible but the wrong materials are used, it will not be what the owner wanted. If faulty or defective materials are used, it may be of no or limited use. When a structure is defective due to the materials used, any number of parties may be responsible—the architect or engineer for specifying improper materials that are incapable of doing the job required,[59] the contractor for wrongfully substituting materials,[60] the

---

[53] Inman v Binghamton Hous Auth, 3 NY2d 137, 143 NE2d 895, 164 NYS2d 699 (1957); Thomassen v J&K Diner, Inc, 152 AD2d 421, 549 NYS2d 416 (2d Dept 1989), *appeal dismissed*, 76 NY2d 771, 559 NE2d 673, 559 NYS2d 979 (1990).

[54] Thomassen v J&K Diner, Inc, 152 AD2d 421, 549 NYS2d 416, 417 (2d Dept 1989), *appeal dismissed*, 76 NY2d 771, 559 NE2d 673, 559 NYS2d 979 (1990).

[55] Trentacosti v Materesa, 67 AD2d 1025, 413 NYS2d 236 (3d Dept 1979).

[56] Arc Elec Constr Co v George A. Fuller Co, 24 NY2d 99, 247 NE2d 111, 299 NYS2d 129 (1969).

[57] VanDeloo v Moreland, 84 AD2d 871, 444 NYS2d 744 (3d Dept 1981).

[58] A-1 Camp Chair Serv Co v William L. Crow Constr Co, 24 AD2d 623, 262 NYS2d 166 (2d Dept 1965).

[59] Village of Endicott v Parlor City Contracting Co, 51 AD2d 370, 381 NYS2d 548 (3d Dept 1976).

[60] Jacob & Youngs v Kent, 230 NY 239, 129 NE 889 (1921).

subcontractor for supplying goods that do not meet contract specifications,[61] or the materialman for supplying defective goods or goods that do not perform as warranted.[62] The most commonly alleged defect in construction due to materials (judging by the reported cases) appears to be the construction of leaky roofs.[63]

"In the area of products liability, New York has recognized that, depending upon the factual context in which the claim arose, a plaintiff may assert causes of action based upon breach of express or implied warranty, negligence, . . . strict products liability[,]" and breach of contract.[64] Under such theories, an owner may sue any one of the responsible parties (including a subcontractor or materialman as a third-party beneficiary[65]), limited only by concepts of privity and appropriateness of remedies. Generally, a direct purchaser may sue a supplier for defective goods on any number of theories. The more remote the ultimate purchaser and user is, the less opportunity it has of recovering from the manufacturer. In New York, a remote purchaser does not have a strict products liability claim against a manufacturer that made no representations to the remote purchaser and had no privity of contract with the remote purchaser where the only damages alleged by the remote purchaser are economic loss (as opposed to personal injury or property damage) and the product was not unduly dangerous.[66] For a remote user to recover for a defective product, it must allege in its complaint and prove at trial that the defect was latent.[67]

If defective materials are supplied, the proper measure of damages is the cost of repairing or replacing the defective goods and any damages due to

---

[61] Bellevue S Assocs v HRH Constr Corp, 160 AD2d 189, 553 NYS2d 159 (1st Dept 1990); Barrett Paving Materials, Inc v United States Fidelity & Guar Co, 118 AD2d 1039, 500 NYS2d 413 (3d Dept 1986).

[62] Ralston Purina Co v Arthur G. McKee & Co, 158 AD2d 969, 551 NYS2d 720 (4th Dept 1990); Bellevue S Assocs v HRH Constr Corp, 160 AD2d 189, 553 NYS2d 159 (1st Dept 1990); City School Dist v McLane Constr Co, 85 AD2d 749, 445 NYS2d 258 (3d Dept 1981).

[63] Bulova Watch Co v Celotex Corp, 46 NY2d 606, 389 NE2d 130, 415 NYS2d 817 (1979); Ralston Purina Co v Arthur G. McKee & Co, 158 AD2d 969, 551 NYS2d 720 (4th Dept 1990); Queensbury Union Free School Dist v Jim Walter Corp, 82 AD2d 204, 442 NYS2d 650 (3d Dept), appeal dismissed, 55 NY2d 745, 431 NE2d 642, 447 NYS2d 157 (1981); County of Broome v Vincent J. Smith, Inc, 78 Misc 2d 889, 358 NYS2d 998 (Broome 1974).

[64] Chenango Indus Dev Agency v Lockwood Greene Engrs, Inc, 114 AD2d 728, 494 NYS2d 832, 833 (3d Dept 1985), appeal dismissed, 67 NY2d 757, 490 NE2d 1233, 500 NYS2d 1027 (1986).

[65] Bellevue S Assocs v HRH Constr Corp, 160 AD2d 189, 553 NYS2d 159 (1st Dept 1990); Ralston Purina Co v Arthur G. McKee & Co, 158 AD2d 969 551 NYS2d 720 (4th Dept 1990).

[66] Schiavone Constr Co v Elgood Mayo Corp, 56 NY2d 667, 436 NE2d 1322, 451 NYS2d 720 (1982), adopting the dissenting opinion of Silverman, J. in, 81 AD2d 227, 439 NYS2d 933 (1st Dept 1981).

[67] DiPerna v Roman Catholic Diocese, 30 AD2d 249, 292 NYS2d 177 (3d Dept 1968).

§12.04 FAULTY OR IMPROPER MATERIALS

breach of warranty on the goods.[68] The measure of damages for improper materials (or substitution of materials) was set forth in one of the most widely read New York construction cases: *Jacob & Youngs, Inc v Kent*,[69] the "Reading pipe" case studied by law students across the United States. In *Jacob & Youngs*, Kent contracted with Jacob & Youngs, Inc to build Kent a home. The contract specified that all wrought-iron pipe was to be "galvanized, lap welded pipe of the grade known as 'standard pipe' of Reading manufacture."[70] Nine months after Kent moved into the home, he discovered that not all of the pipe used in his home was Reading pipe; Jacob & Youngs had unintentionally used another brand of pipe of the same quality and cost as Reading pipe. Much of the substitute pipe was encased within the walls of the home and could not be replaced without tearing down and rebuilding those walls. Kent asked that the builder be required to replace the non-Reading pipe throughout the house or pay him the cost of replacement. The court, by Justice Cardozo, recognized that in most cases the measure of damages is the cost of replacement, unless the cost is "grossly and unfairly out of proportion to the good to be attained. When that is true, the measure is the difference of value."[71] Thus, the court ruled that in a case such as this where the quality of the substituted goods is as good as that of the goods specified in the contract, the proper measure of damages is "not the cost of replacement, which would be great, but the difference in value, which would be either nominal or nothing."[72] The court stated:

> Substitution of equivalents may not have the same significance in fields of art on the one side and in those of mere utility on the other. Nowhere will change be tolerated, however, if it is so dominant or persuasive as in any real or substantial measure to frustrate the purpose of the contract.... [Citation omitted.] We must weigh the purpose to be served, the desire to be gratified, the excuse for deviation from the letter, the cruelty of enforced adherence.... [T]he law will be slow to impute the purpose, in the silence of the parties, where the significance of the default is grievously out of proportion to the oppression of the forfeiture.[73]

In a unique case, the cost of replacement was awarded to a school district when it was supplied with functional roof beams which were aesthetically different from those specified in its contract.[74] The contract was for a swimming pool building which was to be a "showplace." The roof was of a dramatic design of natural wood decking supported by exposed, laminated wood beams. The

---

[68] Mayfair Kitchen Center, Inc v Nigro, 139 AD2d 885, 527 NYS2d 613 (3d Dept 1988).
[69] 230 NY 239, 129 NE 889 (1921).
[70] *Id* at 240, 129 NE at 890.
[71] *Id* at 244, 120 NE at 891.
[72] *Id*.
[73] *Id* at 243-44, 120 NE at 891.
[74] City School Dist v McLane Constr Co, 85 AD2d 749, 445 NYS2d 258 (3d Dept 1981).

beams were to be maintenance-free and as perfect in appearance as possible. The subcontractor purchased the beams from a materialman that was fully aware of the plans and specifications for the beams. Nevertheless, the materialman had the beams treated in a way that it knew would stain and discolor them and failed to clean them before treatment so dirt permeated the wood. When the beams were delivered, the materialman's representative told the school district that the beam discoloration was road grime and cleanable, inducing the school district to accept them. Of course, the beams were not cleanable and, if the materialman's proposed repair efforts were allowed, would require constant maintenance over their 40-year life expectancy. The school district asked that it be awarded the cost of replacement of the beams, a measure significantly higher than the cost of repair or difference in value of the building. The court agreed with the school district's arguments that the suggested repair methods were unsatisfactory or impractical and would require maintenance of the beams over their life expectancy. Further, the court agreed that diminished value damages were inapplicable because the building was a specialty with no real market value. Finally, the materialman's bad faith and the importance of the defective beams to the overall structure precluded it from claiming the lesser measure of damages.

§12.05 Improper Installation

If the materials used in a construction project are of good quality but improperly installed, problems can result. Consider for instance, the problems that resulted in a case where a plumbing subcontractor sloped sewage pipes toward an apartment building rather than toward the street and main sewer line—backups occurred in first floor apartments, often flooding the apartments and damaging carpets and floors. This installation was a clear violation of the local plumbing code, despite the fact that the city plumbing inspector approved the work. The plumber was held liable to the owner of the apartment building for correction costs and the costs of clean-up and related necessary repairs incurred by the owner due to the backups.[75]

In some cases, defective installation can lead to death, as was seen in a case where a worker was killed when a steel column fell after anchor bolts were improperly installed.[76] The engineer, general contractor, or steel contractor may have been found liable, depending upon the chain of causation. The court upheld a jury award in favor of the plaintiff and against the engineer, who knew of the faulty installation and failed to remedy it properly, and the general contractor, who performed the faulty installation of the anchor bolts.

For a remote user to recover for a defect in installation, it must allege in its complaint and prove at trial that the defect was latent.[77]

---

[75] Guidetti v Pratt Plumbing & Heating, Inc, 55 AD2d 720, 389 NYS2d 170 (3d Dept 1976).

[76] Clemens v Benzinger, 211 AD 586, 207 NYS 539 (4th Dept 1925).

[77] Diperna v Roman Catholic Diocese of Albany, 30 AD2d 249, 292 NYS2d 177 (3d Dept 1968).

§12.06 Divided Responsibility

Generally, a party is responsible for that portion of the project over which it has control. Thus, a contractor who follows a design is not responsible for defects in the design[78] unless it expressly warrants the design. If, however, the contractor fails to disclose obvious defects in the plans and follows them despite the obvious defects, it may be liable.[79]

In some instances, more than one party may be responsible for the same defect. For instance, a contractor and engineer were found liable for a worker's death caused by the collapse of a steel column when the contractor failed to properly install anchor bolts and the engineer, who learned of the improper installation, attempted to solve the defect and did so negligently.[80] Similarly, if a landowner engages in an abnormally dangerous activity, it, its engineers or architects who design the project, and its contractors who implement the activity may be held jointly liable for any damages caused as a result of the activity.[81] Thus, not only landowners but also blasting[82] and dredging[83] contractors and project engineers or architects may be held liable for damage to another's property.

The parties may, through contract clauses, allocate responsibility for defects. For instance, the American Institute of Architects (AIA) standard contract between owner and contractor provides that the contractor shall not be responsible for design defects unless it recognized the error, failed to report it to the architect, and did the work despite the defect.[84]

§12.07 Waiver of Defects

Generally, when a party accepts the work and pays for it, defects in performance are waived.[85] Defects that are obvious or easily discoverable upon inspection are waived when an owner takes occupancy of the premises, accepts the work, and pays for it. Of course, the parties may avoid this automatic—and often unintentional—waiver by providing in their contract that the contractor will remedy any defects that appear within one year of acceptance. Such *guarantee* or *warranty* clauses are discussed in **§§12.12-12.16**. Further, there is no waiver if an owner is induced to accept defective work by a misrepresentation that the defect is remediable and that the responsible party will remedy it.[86]

---

[78] MacKnight Flintic Stone Co v Mayor of NY, 160 NY 72, 54 NE 661 (1899).

[79] Rubin v Coles, 142 Misc 139, 253 NYS 808 (City Ct Kings 1931).

[80] Clemens v Benzinger, 211 AD 586, 207 NYS 539 (4th Dept 1925).

[81] Doundoulakis v Hempstead, 42 NY2d 440, 368 NE2d 24, 398 NYS2d 401 (1977).

[82] Spano v Perini Corp, 25 NY2d 11, 250 NE2d 31, 302 NYS2d 527 (1969).

[83] Doundoulakis v Hempstead, 42 NY2d 440, 368 NE2d 24, 398 NYS2d 401 (1977).

[84] AIA Doc A201, ¶3.2.1 (1987 ed).

[85] Village of Endicott v Parlor City Contracting Co, 51 AD2d 370, 381 NYS2d 548 (3d Dept 1976).

[86] City School Dist v McLane Constr Co, 85 AD2d 749, 445 NYS2d 258 (3d Dept 1981).

If the defect is latent or not obvious prior to purchase or occupancy, such as a drainage problem, occupancy will not operate as a waiver.[87]

When a subcontractor is responsible for the defect, there may be an issue of whether acceptance by the owner is acceptance by the general contractor. In most cases, it is not. Consider, for instance, the case of *Barrett Paving Materials, Inc v United States Fidelity & Guaranty Co*,[88] in which concrete supplied by a subcontractor did not meet strength tests specified in the contract. The owner agreed to accept and pay for the concrete after many meetings were held, the project architect expressed its belief that the concrete would perform adequately, and the subcontractor assured the general contractor that the rest of its concrete work would pass the strength test. The general contract provided that payment by the owner would not excuse contract noncompliance.

Concrete is somewhat unique—it cannot be fully tested until it has hardened sufficiently, typically a minimum of 28 days after it is poured. The court ruled that use of the concrete was not acceptance because it is impossible to test it fully until after its use. Further, the court held that the owner's payment to the general contractor was not acceptance because although it acknowledged substantial completion, the owner did not relieve the general contractor of liability for defective work. Finally, the court held that acceptance by the owner was not acceptance by the general contractor, especially where the general contractor asked the subcontractor to guarantee the concrete work for two years, which it refused to do, and warned the subcontractor that it would hold the subcontractor responsible if the owner later disapproved the concrete or demanded repair.

A party may waive its right to recover the cost of substantial reconstruction if it occupies a substantially defective building and makes remedial repairs. In such a case, the owner would be entitled to recover its remedial repair costs.[89]

§12.08 Statutes of Limitations

The clearest case of construction defect and failure will be lost if it is not timely brought. Statute of limitation defenses are not unique to construction law but merit discussion because they are uniquely applied in construction cases. It is simple to determine when a cause of action arises on a promissory note or some other contract-based action; similarly, accrual of a personal injury action may be easy to determine. Determining when a construction-related claim accrues is not so easy. It depends not only on the nature of the claim but also against whom it is asserted. Three entirely different limitations periods may apply to one defect if an owner has a claim against the architect/engineer, the general contractor, and the materialman. Thus, it is important to have a basic understanding of the various statutes of limitations applicable in construction cases and when and where they apply.

---

[87] Ting-Wan Liang v Malawista, 70 AD2d 415, 421 NYS2d 594 (2d Dept 1979).

[88] 118 AD2d 1039, 500 NYS2d 413 (3d Dept 1986).

[89] VanDeloo v Moreland, 84 AD2d 871, 444 NYS2d 744 (3d Dept 1981).

§12.08 STATUTES OF LIMITATIONS 453

Generally, a construction-related cause of action for a defect or failure (except personal injury), regardless of the theory of liability, accrues when the project is *substantially completed*.[90] Substantial completion may be when an owner takes occupancy,[91] actual physical work is completed,[92] a certificate of substantial completion is issued by an architect or engineer,[93] or final payment is made. If it is the owner, and not an architect or engineer, that controls issuance of the final certificate, the owner cannot postpone the date when the statute of limitation begins to run by refusing to issue a certificate of completion. In such cases, the controlling date is when actual physical work is complete,[94] excluding incidental matters such as repair work[95] and the completion of punch list items;[96] this and other incidental work generally will not extend the accrual date. Of course, if the contract specifies when the statute of limitation begins to run, the contract is controlling.

If the claim is against an architect who also was responsible for supervision and inspection and issuance of final certificates of completion and payment, a cause of action will not accrue until the final certificate of payment is issued, the point at which the architect-owner relationship is terminated.[97] This *continuous treatment doctrine* is discussed in Chapter 11 on professional liability.

Most construction claims by owners against contractors and designers are governed by NY Civ Prac L&R §213 which provides a six-year statute of limitation for breach of contract actions,[98] including warranty actions[99] and breach of contract and professional malpractice claims against architects and engineers.[100] There are some different applications of statutes of limitations as

---

[90] The only real exceptions to this rule are when remote users of a structure are injured or when an architect or engineer continues its *professional* relationship with the owner in regard to the project after substantial completion.

[91] Bayridge Air Rights, Inc v Blitman Constr Corp, 160 AD2d 589, 554 NYS2d 528 (1st Dept 1990).

[92] Cabrini Medical Center v Desina, 64 NY2d 1059, 479 NE2d 217, 489 NYS2d 872 (1985); Phillips Constr Co v City of NY, 61 NY2d 949, 463 NE2d 585, 475 NYS2d 244 (1984).

[93] Cabrini Medical Center v Desina, 64 NY2d 1059, 479 NE2d 217, 489 NYS2d 872 (1985).

[94] State v Lundin, 60 NY2d 987, 459 NE2d 486, 471 NYS2d 261 (1983).

[95] Cabrini Medical Center v Desina, 64 NY2d 1059, 479 NE2d 217, 489 NYS2d 872 (1985).

[96] Phillips Constr Co v City of NY, 61 NY2d 949, 463 NE2d 585, 475 NYS2d 244 (1984).

[97] Board of Educ v Celotex Corp, 88 AD2d 713, 451 NYS2d 290 (3d Dept), *affd*, 58 NY2d 684, 444 NE2d 1006, 458 NYS2d 542 (1982).

[98] Video Corp of Am v Frederick Flatto Assocs, 58 NY2d 1026, 448 NE2d 1350, 462 NYS2d 439 (1983).

[99] Bulova Watch Co v Celotex Corp, 46 NY2d 606, 389 NE2d 130, 415 NYS2d 817 (1979).

[100] Board of Educ v Thompson Constr Corp, 111 AD2d 497, 488 NYS2d 880 (3d Dept 1985).

regard architects and engineers and available remedies;[101] Chapter 11 on professional liability discusses those issues. In most defects and failure cases, allegations of fraud or negligence are incidental to a contract claim and are considered within it; they cannot extend the life of a claim.[102]

If the claim relates to defective materials and the contract with the materials supplier was predominantly one for the sale of goods, it is governed by the Uniform Commercial Code (UCC) four-year statute of limitation.[103] The fact that the contract includes performance of some services, including installation, supervision, and testing of the equipment, does not convert a contract for the sale of goods into one for services. If the sale of goods was incidental to the main purpose of the contract, it will be governed by the six-year statute of limitation applicable to contract actions. The distinction between contracts for services and contracts for the sale of goods is more thoroughly discussed in Chapter 3.

The party alleging that a claim is barred by the statute of limitation has the burden of proof.[104]

Although many states have statutes of repose that relate to construction activities, New York offers no such protection. Thus, to protect oneself from being barred from asserting a claim based on a latent defect that is discovered after the limitation period has expired, owners and contractors should obtain guarantees against defective designs and construction from their contractors, subcontractors, designers, and materialmen for a period of longer than six years. Further protection may be obtained through a precisely worded indemnification clause in the contract; for instance, a subcontractor would agree in such a clause to indemnify the contractor against any loss or damages caused to the contractor due to the subcontractor's defective performance.[105] Indemnification and contribution are further discussed in §§12.10-12.11.

---

[101] *See* Sears, Roebuck & Co v Enco Assocs, 43 NY2d 389, 372 NE2d 555, 401 NYS2d 767 (1977), which distinguishes between statutes of limitations applicable to negligence and contract based actions against architects as limiting the remedies available to a plaintiff, not as *absolute* bars to recovery.

[102] Cabrini Medical Center v Desina, 64 NY2d 1059, 479 NE2d 217, 489 NYS2d 872 (1985); Lewis v Axinn, 100 AD2d 617, 473 NYS2d 575 (2d Dept 1984); Banks v Demillo, 145 AD2d 903, 536 NYS2d 284 (4th Dept 1988). *But cf* Queensbury Union Free School Dist v Jim Walter Corp, 82 AD2d 204, 442 NYS2d 650 (3d Dept), *appeal dismissed*, 55 NY2d 745, 431 NE2d 642, 447 NYS2d 157 (1981) (negligence claim held to accrue when "injury" occurred, i.e., when roof deterioration first manifested); Durant v Grange Silo Co, 12 AD2d 694, 207 NYS2d 691 (3d Dept 1960) (negligent construction claim held to accrue when silo collapsed, not when silo completed).

[103] JI Hass Co v Frank A. Kristal Assocs, 127 AD2d 541, 512 NYS2d 104 (1st Dept), *appeal denied*, 69 NY2d 611, 517 NYS2d 1025 (1987).

[104] Suffolk County Water Auth v JD Posillico, Inc, 145 AD2d 623, 536 NYS2d 149 (2d Dept 1988); Banks v DeMillo, 145 AD2d 903, 536 NYS2d 284 (4th Dept 1988).

[105] L. Cantor, *The Application of Statutory Limitation Periods on Latent Construction Defects*, 18 NY St BA Real Prop L Sec Newsl 13 (July 1990).

Agreements to Waive, Extend, or Postpone Statutes of Limitations

General Obligations Law §17-103 provides that statutes of limitations may be waived or extended if the promise relates to an action arising out of an express or implied contract and is "made after the accrual of the cause of action and made, *either with or without consideration,* in a *writing signed by the promisor* or his agent...."[106] Such a written promise prevents use of a statute of limitation defense within the time "that would be applicable if the cause of action had arisen at the date of the promise, or within such shorter time as may be provided in the promise."[107] The promise is enforceable by those to whom the promise was made *and* those for whose benefit it was expressly made.[108] If the agreement does not fully comply with the statute, it will be void and unenforceable.[109]

§12.09 Claims Against Bond

Often, owners and contractors require *guaranty* bonds, also known as *repair* or *maintenance* bonds. Guaranty bonds guarantee to the obligee that the principal will remedy any defects in its work for a specified time. The surety ensures payment or correction of the defect if the principal is found at fault and does not itself remedy the defect. If the owner/obligee has a performance bond and the contract requires the principal/contractor to guarantee its work for a specified time, the owner may be able to seek redress from the surety if its bond is in force when the default occurs.[110]

Even where an owner has a performance bond from its prime contractor, it may wish to obtain guaranty bonds from key subcontractors, guaranteeing to the owner the subcontractors' work. For example, owners often require bonds from roofing contractors guaranteeing that they will repair any leaks caused by defects in workmanship and materials and ordinary wear and tear by the elements. Such guaranty bonds are agreements to repair, not express warranties of the future performance of the roof.[111] A contractual warranty is separate from a bond agreement on the same work.[112]

---

[106] NY Gen Oblig Law §17-103(1) (McKinney 1989 & Supp 1992) (emphasis added).

[107] *Id.*

[108] *Id* §17-103(2).

[109] Bayridge Air Rights, Inc v Blitman Constr Corp, 160 AD2d 589, 554 NYS2d 528 (1st Dept 1990).

[110] See for instance, Carrols Equities Corp v Villnave, 57 AD2d 1044, 395 NYS2d 800 (4th Dept 1977), in which a performance bond surety was held liable to an owner for "differential settlement" of a restaurant that occurred when its principal, the contractor, failed to place the foundation footings properly. The contractor was also held liable to the owner.

[111] Queensbury Union Free School Dist v Jim Walter Corp, 101 AD2d 992, 477 NYS2d 475 (1984), *affd mem,* 64 NY2d 964, 477 NE2d 1106, 488 NYS2d 652 (1985).

[112] Bulova Watch Co v Celotex Corp, 46 NY2d 606, 389 NE2d 130, 415 NYS2d 817 (1979).

A claim on a guarantee bond accrues with each breach of the surety of its bond obligations, i.e., each time the surety refuses to repair that which it bonded.[113] The statute of limitation runs separately for damages incurred each time a breach of an obligation under the bond occurs.[114]

§12.10 Indemnification and Contribution

Indemnification and *contribution* are often-confused principles through which a party held liable to another may recover its loss from a third party. For example, through one of these principles, a contractor held liable to an owner may seek recovery from its subcontractor. Despite the similarities of the two concepts, each is appropriate in different situations.

Indemnification

Indemnity involves an attempt to shift the entire loss from one who is compelled to pay for a loss, without regard to his own fault, to another party who should more properly bear responsibility for that loss because it was the actual wrongdoer. The right to indemnification may be created by express contract, or may be implied by law to prevent an unjust enrichment or an unfair result.[115]

Thus, through indemnification, a party may recover 100 per cent of the loss it has incurred due to another's fault.

If a party is sued by another and believes that others are *wholly* responsible for the damages, it may seek indemnification from the others only if it could be held liable to the plaintiff. For example, if an owner sues a contractor because its building is defective, the contractor may try to bring in the architect as a third-party defendant if the contractor believes the defects are due to design problems rather than construction defects. If it alleges that the defect is due to poor design, it alleges a theory under which it could not possibly be liable to the owner and, hence, has no *implied* right of indemnification from the architect;[116] its third-party claim against the architect would be dismissed. If, however, the contractor could be held liable to the owner, despite its lack of fault (under a strict liability, vicarious liability, or nondelegable duty theory, perhaps), the contractor could seek common law indemnification from the architect.[117] If the party seeking implied or common law indemnification actu-

---

[113] *Id.*

[114] *Id.*

[115] Trustees of Columbia Univ v Mitchell/Giurgola Assocs, 109 AD2d 449, 492 NYS2d 371, 374 (1st Dept 1985).

[116] *See* Carrols Equities Corp v Villnave, 76 Misc 2d 205, 350 NYS2d 90 (Onondaga), *affd mem*, 49 AD2d 672, 373 NYS2d 1012 (4th Dept 1975).

[117] Trustees of Columbia Univ v Mitchell/Giurgola Assocs, 109 AD2d 449, 492 NYS2d 371 (1st Dept 1985); *see also* City of Rochester v Holmsten Ice Rinks, 155 AD2d 939, 548 NYS2d 959 (4th Dept 1989).

ally participated in wrongdoing, it cannot seek indemnification; it may, however, be entitled to contribution.[118]

Contribution

When *contribution* is sought, liability for a wrong is apportioned among wrongdoers.

> The right to *contribution* and apportionment of liability among alleged multiple wrongdoers arises when they each owe a duty to plaintiff or each other and by breaching their respective duties they contribute to plaintiff's ultimate injuries. This is so regardless of whether the parties are joint tortfeasors, or whether they are liable under different theories, so long as their wrongdoing contributes to the damage or injury involved.[119]

If a party is sued by another and believes that others are partially responsible for the damages for injury to property, it may seek contribution from the others. Although the word *contribution* may imply a voluntary act, it rarely is. Typically, the party sued crossclaims or brings a third-party action against those it believes may be liable in contribution, although one need not wait until one is sued or a judgment rendered to claim a right to contribution.[120] A contributor may be compelled to contribute no more than its equitable share of the judgment recovered by the injured party; a party's equitable share is based on the relative culpability of each person liable for contribution.[121]

Contribution is available only for damages due to "personal injury, injury to property, or wrongful death."[122] Purely economic loss that typically results from breach of contract has been held not to constitute an "injury to property" that would entitle one to seek contribution.[123] "The existence of some form of tort liability is a prerequisite to application of the [contribution] statute."[124] Of course, parties are free to create contractual rights of contribution that allow contribution for economic loss.[125]

---

[118] Trustees of Columbia Univ v Mitchell/Giurgola Assocs, 109 AD2d 449, 492 NYS2d 371 (1st Dept 1985).

[119] *Id* at 454, 492 NYS2d at 376.

[120] NY Civ Prac L&R 1401 (McKinney 1976 & Supp 1992). This statute is part of the Uniform Contribution among Tortfeasors Act. The significance of this act to settlement of failure cases is discussed in William J. Postner, Robert A. Rubin & Lisa A. Banick, *Fixing the Failure and Settling the Dispute,* in Construction Failures 313 (Cushman, Richter, & Rivelis, eds 1989).

[121] NY Civ Prac L&R 1402 (McKinney 1976 & Supp 1992).

[122] *Id* 1401.

[123] Board of Educ v Sargent, Webster, Crenshaw & Folley, 71 NY2d 21, 517 NE2d 1360, 523 NYS2d 475 (1987); City of Rochester v Holmsten Ice Rinks, Inc, 155 AD2d 939, 548 NYS2d 959 (4th Dept 1989).

[124] Board of Educ v Sargent, Webster, Crenshaw & Folley, 71 NY2d 21, 28, 517 NE2d 1360, 523 NYS2d 475, 478 (1987).

[125] *Id.*

§12.11 —Contractual Indemnification and Contribution

Often contracts contain *indemnification* and *contribution* clauses through which a party seeks to protect itself from damages for others' wrongs and to avoid the strict common law interpretations of indemnification and contribution. For instance, a housing authority clause provided:

> The Contractor shall be the insurer of the Authority . . . and hold [it] harmless against . . . (b) The risk of causing injuries to persons, wrongful death, and property damages, direct or consequential, to the Authority . . . arising out of or in connection with the performance of the Work, whether sustained before or after Final Payment. . . . (c) The risk of liability or losses suffered by, or claims and demands, just or unjust, made by, third persons, whether made before or after Final Payment, against the Authority . . . arising or alleged to arise out of performance of the Work.[126]

Similarly, the American Institute of Architects (AIA) in its Standard Form Agreement between Owners and Contractors provides:

> ¶3.18.1 To the fullest extent permitted by law, the Contractor shall indemnify and hold harmless the Owner, Architect, Architect's consultants, and agents and employees of any of them from and against claims, damages, losses and expenses, including but not limited to attorneys' fees, arising out of or resulting from performance of the Work provided that such claim, damage, loss or expense is attributable to bodily injury, sickness, disease or death, or to injury to or destruction of tangible property (other than the Work itself) including loss of use resulting therefrom, but only to the extent caused in whole or in part by negligent acts or omissions of the Contractor, a Subcontractor, anyone directly or indirectly employed by them or anyone for whose acts they may be liable, regardless of whether or not such claim, damage, loss or expense is caused in part by a party indemnified hereunder. . . .
>
> ¶3.18.2 In claims against any person or entity indemnified under the Paragraph 3.18 by an employee of the Contractor, a Subcontractor, anyone directly or indirectly employed by them or anyone for whose acts they may be liable, the indemnification obligation under this Paragraph 3.18 shall not be limited by a limitation on amount or type of damages, compensation or benefits payable by or for the Contractor or a Subcontractor under workers' or workmen's compensation acts, disability or other employee benefit acts.
>
> ¶3.18.3 The obligations of the Contractor under the Paragraph 3.18 shall not extend to the liability of the Architect, the Architect's consultants, and agents and employees of any of them arising out of (1) the prepara-

---

[126] Inman v Binghamton Hous Auth, 3 NY2d 137, 147, 143 NE2d 895, 164 NYS2d 699, 706 (1957).

tion or approval of maps, drawings, opinions, reports, surveys, Change Orders, designs or specifications, or (2) the giving of or failure to give directions or instructions by the Architect, the Architect's consultants, and agents and employees of any of them provided such giving or failure to give is the primary cause of the injury or damage.[127]

Such clauses are strictly construed to limit liability of the indemnitor[128] and do not relieve a party of liability to an injured third party. They provide for relief between potentially responsible parties and are legally irrelevant to an unrelated injured party.[129] Chapter 3 discusses indemnification clauses in more detail.

§12.12 Warranty (Guarantee) Clauses

It is only natural that a party contracting for work expects that work to be done to certain standards and to be free of defects for a period of time. Often, it may ask that the party doing the work warranty or guarantee its work against defects or failures for a specified time. Warranties may be either expressly given or implied through conduct or operation of the law.

A contractual warranty or guarantee period in a contract is not a limitation of the time in which a party may bring suit for defects or for breach of other contractual obligations.[130] A guarantee provision typically provides a period in which the contractor has a duty to correct defects through supplemental performance. Without a specific statement that the parties intend to shorten the period in which suit may be brought, a guarantee clause does not shorten the statute of limitation[131] or bar an owner from bringing suit on a defect.

In the absence of any express or implied warranties, New York law provides that construction contracts are governed by the six-year statute of limitation.[132] A cause of action for breach of a construction contract accrues upon completion

---

[127] AIA Doc A201, ¶3.18 (14th ed 1987). Reproduced by permission of The American Institute of Architects under license number 92095. Permission expires July 31, 1993. FURTHER REPRODUCTION IS PROHIBITED. Because AIA Documents are revised from time to time, users should ascertain from the AIA the current edition of this document. Copies of the current edition of this AIA document may be purchased from The American Institute of Architects or its local distributors. The text of this document is not "model language" and is not intended for use in other documents without permission of the AIA.

[128] Inman v Binghamton Hous Auth, 3 NY2d 137, 147, 143 NE2d 895, 164 NYS2d 699, 706 (1957).

[129] Thomassen v J&K Diner, Inc, 152 AD2d 421, 549 NYS2d 416 (2d Dept 1989), *appeal dismissed*, 76 NY2d 771, 559 NE2d 673, 559 NYS2d 979 (1990).

[130] Ting-Wan Liang v Malawista, 70 AD2d 415, 421 NYS2d 594 (2d Dept 1979).

[131] Carrols Equities Corp v Villnave, 57 AD2d 1044, 395 NYS2d 800 (4th Dept 1977).

[132] NY Civ Prac L&R, 213 (McKinney 1990). *See* §12.08.

of construction.[133] Contracts for the sale of goods are governed by the Uniform Commercial Code (UCC). UCC §2-725 provides that any action for breach of a contract for the sale of goods must be commenced within four years after the cause of action accrues. According to the UCC, a cause of action for breach accrues at the time of the breach of warranty. This is generally deemed to be when tender of delivery is made, except when a warranty explicitly extends to future performance.

Thus, assuming that no further warranties have been made by a contractor or a supplier, an action for breach of contract or warranty can be commenced at any time within six years of substantial completion of construction or four years of delivery of the materials that have been purchased. There are no other specific warranty periods provided for under New York law. Therefore, it could turn out that the absence of any express warranty in a contract could be more advantageous to an owner than a contract that provides for an express warranty limited to a shorter period of time than the applicable statute of limitation.

The question of whether a contractor or supplier has made express warranties that extend to future performance is generally very fact specific and must be considered on a case-by-case basis. Some of the factors that could be involved include representations made by the contractor or supplier in its literature, brochures, or advertising. For example, does the contractor's or supplier's advertising state that it "stands behind" its work or product for "x" years, or does it state that the work or product has an "average in-service life" of "x" years? Some of these types of representations may be found to be warranties, and others may be considered "puffing."

Similarly, a contractor or a supplier may limit the duration of a warranty, and thus the time during which a claim for breach of that contractual obligation can be made, by setting forth a shorter warranty period in the contract or purchase order. Thus, if a contractor or supplier expressly states that all materials and workmanship are warranted for a period of one year from the date of delivery, the owner must make its claim within that one-year period of time. If the owner fails to make a claim within that one-year period, the claim may be barred.

§12.13 —Implied Warranties

Implied warranties may arise by virtue of the law or the parties' conduct. For instance, an implied warranty may arise if a contractor makes representations regarding its work, such as in a case where the Appellate Division found an implied warranty in a contract to install a septic system. The court found an implied warranty to provide a workable septic system in the builder's representations that it knew the area and was familiar with the swampy condition of the land, its assuring the home owner that there would be no problems,

---

[133] Sears Roebuck & Co v Enco Assocs, 43 NY2d 389, 372 NE2d 555, 401 NYS2d 767 (1977).

and its bidding extra for the work because it anticipated taking extra precautions due to the swampy nature of the land.[134]

To recover solely economic loss damages due to breach of an implied warranty, the injured party must be in privity with the party allegedly responsible.[135] For instance, when a building owner sued the manufacturer and installer of its defective roof solely for economic loss under a claim of breach of implied warranty, its claim was dismissed due to the lack of privity between the owner and the manufacturer and between the owner and the subcontractor that installed the roof.[136] The owner was allowed to sue the subcontractor for breach of express warranty as the subcontract expressly extended its warranties to the owner, thus allowing it to sue as an intended third-party beneficiary.[137] Similarly, if the owner had relied on specific representations of the supplier in advertisements or sales literature in agreeing to the subcontractor's choice of the roof, it would have had a breach of express warranty claim.[138] There is no privity requirement if the injured party seeks tort-based damages.

The Uniform Commercial Code (UCC) provides that all goods, unless otherwise specified in the sales contract, are covered by implied warranties—those of merchantability,[139] course of dealing or usage of trade,[140] and fitness for a particular purpose.[141] In addition, goods may be covered by express warranties, which can arise without the materialman necessarily intending to grant express warranties.[142] Warranties on the sale of goods are further discussed in Chapter 3.

§12.14 —Implied Warranties in the Sale of New Homes

In 1988, the Court of Appeals, in *Caceci v DiCanio Construction Co*,[143] recognized a "Housing Merchant" warranty that applies to new home construction: "There is an implied term in the express contract between the builder-vendor and purchasers that the house to be constructed would be done in a skillful

---

[134] Lange v Blake, 58 AD2d 1034, 397 NYS2d 290 (4th Dept 1977).

[135] Coffey v United States Gypsum Co, 149 AD2d 960, 540 NYS2d 92 (4th Dept), *appeal denied*, 74 NY2d 610, 545 NE2d 868, 546 NYS2d 554 (1989); Chenango Indus Dev Agency v Lockwood Greene Engrs, Inc, 114 AD2d 728, 494 NYS2d 832 (3d Dept 1985), *appeal dismissed*, 67 NY2d 757, 490 NE2d 1233, 500 NYS2d 1027 (1986).

[136] Ralston Purina Co v Arthur G. McKee & Co, 158 AD2d 969, 551 NYS2d 720 (4th Dept 1990).

[137] *Id* at 970, 551 NYS2d at 722.

[138] *See* Chenango Indus Dev Agency v Lockwood Greene Engrs, Inc, 114 AD2d 728, 494 NYS2d 832 (3d Dept 1985), *appeal dismissed*, 67 NY2d 757, 490 NE2d 1233, 500 NYS2d 1027 (1986).

[139] UCC §2-314.

[140] *Id* §2-314(3).

[141] *Id* §2-315.

[142] *Id* §2-313.

[143] 72 NY2d 52, 526 NE2d 266, 530 NYS2d 771 (1988).

manner free from material defects."[144] The court rejected the notion that the rule of *caveat emptor* is appropriate in new home sales, stating that "[c]ommon sense dictates that the purchasers were entitled to expect, without necessarily stating the obvious in the contract, that the house being purchased was to be a habitable place."[145]

Shortly thereafter, the legislature enacted Article 36-B of the General Business Law which established automatically created warranties upon the sale of a new home.[146] It has been argued that the act supplements and does not repeal the common law implied warranty and that the act sets forth minimum, not exclusive, standards for new home warranties.[147] The act's warranties include that the home will meet or exceed the "specific standards of the applicable building code"; if the code does not have a specific relevant standard, the home must be constructed with workmanship and materials that meet or exceed locally accepted building practice standards.[148] Specifically, the act provides that a housing merchant implied warranty shall mean that:

> a. one year from and after the warranty date the home will be free from defects due to a failure to have been constructed in a skillful manner;
>
> b. two years from and after the warranty date the plumbing, electrical, heating, cooling and ventilation systems of the home will be free from defects due to a failure by the builder to have installed such systems in a skillful manner; and
>
> c. six years from and after the warranty date the home will be free from material defects.[149]

Unless the parties indicate otherwise, the implied warranty does not extend to discoverable patent defects if the buyer inspected or refused to inspect the home prior to taking title[150] or to defects that are *not* due to the designs, workmanship, or materials of the builder or its agents, of the designer, or of the subcontractors.[151] The warranty does extend to goods sold incidentally with the home, such as refrigerators and stoves.

Before bringing suit on the implied warranties, the home owner must give the builder notice and a reasonable opportunity to repair the defect.[152] An action may be commenced as late as one year from the end of the applicable warranty period or four years from the date the warranty began, whichever

---

[144] *Id* at 56, 526 NE2d at 267, 530 NYS2d at 772.

[145] *Id* at 61, 526 NE2d at 270, 530 NYS2d at 772.

[146] NY Gen Bus Law §777 *et seq* (McKinney 1984 & Supp 1992).

[147] *See* R. Givens, *Practice Commentaries*, 19 McKinney's Consol L of NY 260; Schuster v City of NY, 5 NY2d 75, 154 NE2d 534, 180 NYS2d 265 (1958).

[148] NY Gen Bus Law §777(3) (McKinney 1984 & Supp 1992).

[149] *Id* §777-a(1).

[150] *Id* §777-a(2)(b).

[151] *Id* §777-a(2)(a).

[152] *Id* §777-a(4)(a).

is later.[153] Thus, if the defect falls within the one-year warranty, the home owner would have four years from its acceptance of the property to bring a claim; if the two-year warranty applies, it would also have four years; if the six-year warranty applies, the home owner would have up to seven years from the date of acceptance to bring a suit. If a builder makes repairs, the limitation period is extended for one year after the last date on which repair work was performed.[154] The measure of damages for breach of the warranties is the reasonable cost of repair or replacement and consequential damage to the home, not to exceed the replacement costs of the home (excluding the value of the land).[155] A court may award the diminished value of the home due to the defect if it finds that to be a more equitable measure of damages.[156]

The implied warranties may be excluded or modified only if the builder offers the buyer a limited warranty that complies with the statute.[157]

Subsequent Purchasers

In New York, the new home warranty has been extended to subsequent purchasers who purchase a home within the warranty periods set forth in the statute.[158] Thus, in the absence of an effective disclaimer, a subsequent purchaser who purchases a home within one year of its occupancy by or title transfer to the original purchaser will have a warranty that the home will be free from latent defects due to unskillful construction; within two years of occupancy or transfer, a warranty on the home's plumbing, electrical, heating, cooling, and ventilation systems; and within six years, a warranty that the home will be free from latent material defects.[159] The Supreme Court of Illinois has extended the implied warranty of habitability to subsequent purchasers of homes for latent defects.[160] The court extended the implied warranty for a "reasonable" time period following construction for latent defects discovered by subsequent purchasers.[161] Other states that similarly have extended the implied warranty by

---

[153] *Id* §777-a(4)(b).

[154] *Id.*

[155] *Id* §777-a(4)(b).

[156] *Id.*

[157] *Id* §777-b(3).

[158] Under *id* §777(6), the definitions portion of the act that codified Warranties on the Sale of New Homes, *owner* is defined as "the first person to whom the home is sold and, during the unexpired portion of the warranty period, each successor in title to the home and any mortgagee in possession."

[159] *Id* §777-a(1)(a), (b), (c).

[160] Redarowicz v Ohlendorf, 92 Ill 2d 171, 441 NE2d 324 (1982).

[161] *Id* at 185, 441 NE2d at 331. This case is analyzed in *Latent Defects in Home Construction: The Illinois Supreme Court Redefines Legal Options for the Subsequent Purchaser*, 59 Chi-Kent L Rev 1099 (1983). A similar Texas case is analyzed in Lloyd E. Ferguson, *Gupta v Ritter Homes, Inc: Extending the Implied Warranty of Habitability to Subsequent Purchasers—An Honorable Result Based on Unsound Theory*, 35 Baylor L Rev 670 (1983).

court decision include Indiana,[162] Wyoming,[163] South Carolina,[164] and Oklahoma.[165]

§12.15 —Express Warranties

For an express warranty to exist, a party must have made a specific, express promise or representation to the party attempting to assert a breach of express warranty claim.[166] Most often the warranty is given in a written contract and specifically states what is warranted and for how long. For instance, a warranty clause may provide:

> The Contractor warrants to the Owner that materials and equipment furnished under the Contract will be of good quality and new unless otherwise required or permitted by the Contract Documents, that the Work will be free from defects not inherent in the quality required or permitted, and that the Work will conform with the requirements of the Contract Documents.

The same contract may further provide:

> If, within one year after the date of Substantial Completion of the Work or designated portion thereof, or by terms of an applicable special warranty required by the Contract Documents, any Work is found to be not in accordance with the requirements of the Contract Documents, the Contractor shall correct it promptly after receipt of written notice from the Owner to do so.

When a contractor gives such a warranty, it generally does not warrant the accuracy or sufficiency of plans or design of the building prepared by someone else; it warrants its execution of the plans.[167]

Although express warranties are most commonly given in contracts, they also arise if a party that sells goods makes representations that are relied upon by another party in deciding to purchase or use the goods. Such warranties can arise through advertisements[168] and sales literature.[169]

---

[162] Barnes v MacBrown & Co, 264 Ind 227, 342 NE2d 619 (1976).

[163] Moxley v Laramie Builders, Inc, 600 P2d 733 (Wyo 1979).

[164] Terlinde v Neely, 275 SC 395, 271 SE2d 768 (1980).

[165] Elden v Simmons, 631 P2d 739 (Okla 1981).

[166] Coffey v United States Gypsum Co, 149 AD2d 960, 540 NYS2d 92 (4th Dept), *appeal denied*, 74 NY2d 610, 545 NE2d 868, 546 NYS2d 554 (1989).

[167] MacKnight Flintic Stone Co v Mayor of NY, 160 NY 72, 54 NE 661 (1899).

[168] Chenango Indus Dev Agency v Lockwood Greene Engrs, Inc, 114 AD2d 728, 494 NYS2d 832 (3d Dept 1985), *appeal dismissed*, 67 NY2d 757, 490 NE2d 1233, 500 NYS2d 1027 (1986).

[169] *Id.*

When [a manufacturer's] representations expressed and disseminated in the mass communications media and on labels (attached to the goods themselves) prove false and the user or consumer is damaged by reason of his reliance on those representations, . . . it is highly unrealistic to limit a purchaser's protection to warranties made directly to him by his immediate seller. The protection he really needs is against the manufacturer whose published representations caused him to make the purchase.[170]

Express warranties are specifically construed and will not be expanded to provide more protection than is specified. For instance, in a case where the contractor guaranteed a home's basement "against seepage through foundation walls," the court dismissed the home owner's claim for a breach of warranty due to water damage and leakage from the basement back door stoop into the basement, as the seepage was not through the basement *walls*.[171]

§12.16 —Exclusive Remedy

A warranty or guarantee will not be construed as a party's exclusive remedy unless the contract specifically indicates the parties' intent that there be no recourse save through the warranty or guarantee provision.[172] Thus, in a case where a contract provided a one-year period following substantial completion in which the contractor would correct defects, but did not specifically state that the correction remedy was exclusive, the correction remedy was not exclusive and the owner had a right to seek damages for defects. Further, the one-year period was not a limitation on the time within which the owner was required to sue; because the contract did not *specifically* limit the owner's time to sue, it had six years as provided by statute.[173]

Similarly, a repair bond provided pursuant to a construction contract will not be an owner's exclusive remedy if the contract does not specifically indicate that it is.[174]

The distinction between an action based on a breach of warranty and one based on a breach of contract becomes significant if privity is lacking, such as when materials, rather than workmanship, are defective. In such a case, an owner can bring an action directly against the manufacturer of the materials on a breach of warranty theory. If the workmanship is defective, the contractor is obligated to correct it up until the warranty period expires. If privity does exist, however, the owner should also sue for breach of contract, in view of the fact that express warranties are very strictly construed.

---

[170] Randy Knitwear, Inc v American Cyanamid Co, 11 NY2d 5, 12-13, 181 NE2d 399, 226 NYS2d 363, 367-68 (1962).

[171] Gomes v Ern-Roc Homes, Inc, 72 Misc 2d 410, 339 NYS2d 401 (Civ Ct Queens 1973).

[172] Carrols Equities Corp v Villnave, 57 AD2d 1044, 395 NYS2d 800 (4th Dept 1977).

[173] John W. Cowper Co v Buffalo Hotel Dev Venture, 115 AD2d 346, 496 NYS2d 127 (4th Dept 1985), *affd*, 72 NY2d 890, 528 NE2d 1214, 532 NYS2d 742 (1988).

[174] *See* Queensbury Union Free School Dist v Jim Walter Corp, 101 AD2d 992, 477 NYS2d 475 (3d Dept 1984), *affd mem*, 64 NY2d 964, 477 NE2d 1106, 488 NYS2d 652, (1985).

Construction Safety 13

§13.01 Introduction
§13.02 Workers' Compensation Laws
§13.03 Owner's Obligations
§13.04 Contractor's Obligations
§13.05 Labor Law §240
§13.06 Labor Law §241
§13.07 General Contractor's Liability under Labor Law §§240 and 241
§13.08 Owner's Liability under Labor Law §§240 and 241
§13.09 —Residential Dwelling Exception
§13.10 Liability of Agents of Owner and General Contractor under Labor Law §§240 and 241
§13.11 —Architect/Engineer
§13.12 —Construction Manager
§13.13 —Subcontractors
§13.14 Affirmative Defenses to Statutory Liability
§13.15 Liability of Architect/Engineer in Negligence
§13.16 Liability of Construction Manager in Negligence
§13.17 Res Ipsa Loquitur: The Thing Speaks for Itself
§13.18 Contribution/Indemnification
§13.19 OSHA

§13.01 Introduction

Safety is an important issue on any construction site. The potential for serious and, often, fatal accidents to workers, passers-by, and site visitors is everywhere. Bricks fall on passing pedestrians, workers fall off scaffolds, children stray onto construction sites and fall into excavations, nails ricochet and strike people, trenches collapse—the possibilities are countless, as are the causes. A complete discussion of the personal injury law aspects of construction safety is beyond the scope of this book, as is an in-depth discussion of workers' compensation, labor law, negligence, specific regulations governing construction site and worker safety, or many other related topics. This chapter merely attempts to alert construction parties to their duties, rights, and potential liabilities, and to some means by which potential liabilities may be shifted or possible exposures lessened.

It is important to note that New York's Labor Law may govern construction projects that are not located within the state. In *Calla v Shulsky*,[1] the First Department found that New York's Labor Law applied when a worker, a New York resident employed by a New York contractor, was injured on a job in New Jersey. The individual owners of the work site were New York residents; the corporate owner of the site and the contractor were New York corporations with their principal places of business in New York. The construction contract was executed in New York. The court found that "[i]t is not inherently unfair to impose the provisions of the New York Labor Law on the [owners'] contract with the [contractor] where the significant contacts of the transaction are all within this State."[2] The opposite result was reached by the Fourth Department.[3]

§13.02 Workers' Compensation Laws

Workers' compensation laws[4] provide a means by which an injured employee's damages are measured and compensated. The statutes provide guidelines for compensation for various injuries, including death. Typically, a workers' compensation award is substantially less than what an injured worker could recover in tort. However, the injured employee is entitled to benefits under workers' compensation laws if the injury occurred in the course of his or her employment, even if the injury did not result from the employer's negligence. If an employee is injured in the course of his or her employment, generally, the employee's sole, exclusive remedy against his or her employer is under the workers' compensation laws—i.e., the worker cannot sue his or her employer for those injuries.

In theory, workers' compensation benefits are supposed to wholly compensate workers for their injuries. In practice, however, it is an ineffective system in New York because the benefits are far too low to provide a measure of relief that even approaches a realistic compensation. Rather than simply increasing a worker's potential benefits to a realistic level and making workers' compensation a worker's sole remedy against any party, the legislature has, through the Labor Laws, allowed workers to seek additional compensation from owners,

---

[1] 148 AD2d 60, 543 NYS2d 666 (1st Dept 1989). *Contra* Brewster v Baltimore & Ohio RR, 167 AD2d 908, 562 NYS2d 277 (4th Dept 1990).

[2] Calla v Shulsky, 148 AD2d 60, 543 NYS2d 666 (1st Dept 1989). *Contra* Brewster v Baltimore & Ohio RR, 167 AD2d 908, 562 NYS2d 277 (4th Dept 1990).

[3] Brewster v Baltimore & Ohio RR, 167 AD2d 908, 562 NYS2d 277 (4th Dept 1990).

[4] NY Work Comp Law §1 *et seq* (McKinney 1965 & Supp 1992).

contractors, and other parties that are not the worker's employer.[5] These other parties invariably implead the employer for contribution. It is the authors' belief that all parties would be better served by a system that would permit a worker to recover *fair and adequate* compensation from his or her employer and bar all other worker remedies for job-related injuries.

Determining whether someone is an employee for workers' compensation purposes is not as simple as one might think. For instance, it is not unusual for a contractor to "borrow" a subcontractor's employee for a specific purpose or period of time. If the worker is injured during this time, who is the worker's employer? The issue is an important one because the restriction against seeking redress other than workers' compensation applies only as between the worker and his or her employer. If a subcontractor's employee is injured by a fall from a scaffold, the employee may seek only workers' compensation from his or her employer, the subcontractor, but may be able to sue a wholly nonnegligent general contractor by virtue of the Labor Laws. Factors to consider when determining by whom an injured worker is employed include the right to control the worker's tasks, how the worker is paid and by whom, who furnishes the tools and equipment used by the worker, who has the right to discharge the worker, and the relative nature of the work itself.[6] The issue is a factual one for the Workers' Compensation Board to decide.[7]

One exception to the exclusive remedy provisions provided by the workers' compensation law is when the injury was caused by the employer's intentional tort. It should be noted here that a violation of NY Lab Law §240 or §241 (discussed at §§13.05-13.14), is not a *per se* intentional tort.[8]

§13.03 Owner's Obligations

An owner, as the party with ultimate responsibility for a construction project, has common law and statutory obligations to workers on its projects. Its general obligation is to protect workers from accidents that are capable of being anticipated. An owner does not have a common law or statutory duty to protect workers from freak accidents[9] or from their own unforeseeable, dangerous acts.[10] Further, an owner's duty extends only to the workplace and does not necessarily include access to the workplace.[11]

---

[5] Federal Employer's Liability Act, 45 USC §51 *et seq* (1908).

[6] Schaff v William C. Maunz Co, 144 AD2d 109, 534 NYS2d 447 (3d Dept 1988).

[7] *Id.*

[8] Rarick v Samal Constr Co, 137 Misc 2d 953, 522 NYS2d 829 (Albany 1987).

[9] Herman v Lancaster Homes, Inc, 145 AD2d 926, 536 NYS2d 298 (4th Dept 1988) (carpenter struck in eye by ricocheting nail).

[10] Mack v Altmans Stage Lighting Co, 98 AD2d 468, 470 NYS2d 664 (2d Dept 1964).

[11] Wolf v New York State Elec & Gas Corp, 142 Misc 2d 774, 538 NYS2d 188 (Niagara 1989) (issue of fact whether road part of workplace). *Contra* Derion v Buffalo Crushed Stone, Inc, 135 AD2d 1105, 523 NYS2d 322 (4th Dept 1987) (roadway owned by quarry owner which lead to quarry not place of work).

Common Law

At common law, an owner has a duty to furnish a safe place to work as far as *its* facilities are concerned; i.e., it is responsible for the commonly used portions of the premises,[12] but it does not have a duty to make sure that its contractor's plant or equipment is safe or that the work the contractor is performing is done in a safe manner.[13]

An owner is not responsible for safety matters concerning a *detail of the work.* "Where . . . negligence as to a detail of the work causes injury, or the prosecution of the work itself necessitates or creates the risk, the 'safe place to work' doctrine is not applicable."[14] An owner's common law duty to provide a safe place to work is not breached if an injury is due to a defect in the contractor's plant, tools, and methods, or due to a negligent act of the contractor relating to a *detail of the work.*[15] For example, owners have been found not liable when trenches collapsed[16] and when trees being felled struck workers.[17]

The general rule is that "one who engages an independent contractor to do work is not liable for the latter's negligence in performance."[18] Following are the exceptions to this rule:

1. An owner is responsible for dangerous conditions created by the contractor of which the owner had actual or constructive knowledge (an owner has a duty to make reasonable inspections, but a failure to inspect does not conclusively establish liability unless an inspection would have disclosed the defect that caused the injury)[19]

2. An owner is liable if injuries will result *unless* precautions are taken, i.e., the work is inherently dangerous to others and the owner reasonably should have anticipated the danger[20]

3. An owner is liable if it failed to use due care when selecting its contractor[21]

4. An owner is liable if the owner exercises a significant level of control over the project, by controlling work methods and retaining the power to order changes, inspect work, and choose subcontractors;[22] the owner's

---

[12] Freeo v Victor A. Perosi, Inc, 54 AD2d 684, 387 NYS2d 268 (2d Dept 1976).

[13] Ortiz v Uhl, 39 AD2d 143, 332 NYS2d 583 (4th Dept 1972), *aff'd mem*, 33 NY2d 989, 309 NE2d 425, 353 NYS2d 962 (1974).

[14] Freeo v Victor A. Perosi, Inc, 54 AD2d 684, 387 NYS2d 268, 269-70 (2d Dept 1976).

[15] Persichilli v Triborough Bridge & Tunnel Auth, 16 NY2d 136, 145, 209 NE2d 802, 262 NYS2d 476 (1965).

[16] Freeo v Victor A. Perosi, Inc, 54 AD2d 684, 387 NYS2d 268 (2d Dept 1976).

[17] Dube v Kaufman, 145 AD2d 595, 536 NYS2d 471 (2d Dept 1988).

[18] Kojic v City of NY, 76 AD2d 828, 428 NYS2d 305, 307 (2d Dept 1980).

[19] Kennedy v McKay, 86 AD2d 597, 446 NYS2d 124 (2d Dept 1982).

[20] Kojic v City of NY, 76 AD2d 828, 428 NYS2d 305 (2d Dept 1980).

[21] Janice v State, 201 Misc 915, 107 NYS2d 674 (Ct Cl 1951).

[22] Gallo v Supermarkets Gen Corp, 112 AD2d 345, 491 NYS2d 796 (2d Dept 1985).

retention of a *general* power of supervision does not change its common law liabilities"[23]

Thus, an owner may be liable if its inspector notices a dangerous condition but does not make sure that it is made safe.[24] Similarly, on a demolition contract, an owner was held liable when it selected a wholly inexperienced demolition contractor that failed to erect warnings or barriers of any kind around the building demolition site.[25]

An owner also has obligations to authorized and unauthorized visitors who come onto the premises to protect them from danger, such as injury from blasting[26] or falling into unfenced excavations.[27]

Statutory

An owner's statutory duties are much greater than its common law duties. New York Labor Law §200 codifies an owner's common law obligations to provide a safe workplace;[28] additionally, it makes those obligations nondelegable and expands the owner's obligations to include the tools and equipment necessary to make the workplace complete.[29] This does not mean that an owner is responsible for all tools used on the job—it is responsible only for those tools and equipment that it furnishes and over which it has control. Where an owner assumes control of safety, by imposing safety rules for instance, Labor Law §200 imposes on an owner a duty to protect the workers' health and safety and to make reasonable inspections to detect unsafe conditions.[30] An owner's obligations under §200 are governed by negligence principles,[31] and alleged violations are subject to the owner's defense of the injured worker's comparative negligence.[32]

New York Labor Law §§240 and 241 greatly expand an owner's obligation to provide and ensure a safe working environment for workers who perform services at the owner's property. While these laws are briefly discussed here, they are discussed more thoroughly in §§13.05-13.14.

Generally, under Labor Law §240, an owner has a *nondelegable* duty to provide and erect safe scaffolding and to provide other safety equipment to protect

---

[23] *Id.*
[24] Kojic v City of NY, 76 AD2d 828, 428 NYS2d 305 (2d Dept 1980).
[25] Janice v State, 201 Misc 915, 107 NYS2d 674 (Ct Cl 1951).
[26] Petluck v McGolrick Realty Co, 240 AD 61, 268 NYS 782 (1st Dept 1934).
[27] Amerman v Lizza & Sons, 45 AD2d 996, 358 NYS2d 220 (2d Dept 1974).
[28] Dube v Kaufman, 145 AD2d 595, 536 NYS2d 471 (2d Dept 1988).
[29] Olsen v Chase Manhattan Bank, 10 AD2d 539, 205 NYS2d 60 (2d Dept 1960), *affd mem*, 9 NY2d 829, 175 NE2d 350, 215 NYS2d 773 (1961).
[30] DaBolt v Bethlehem Steel Corp, 92 AD2d 70, 459 NYS2d 503 (4th Dept), *appeal dismissed*, 60 NY2d 554, 467 NYS2d 1029 (1983).
[31] Shaheen v International Business Mach Corp, 157 AD2d 429, 557 NYS2d 972 (3d Dept 1990).
[32] Siragusa v State, 117 AD2d 986, 499 NYS2d 533 (4th Dept 1986).

laborers working at heights, i.e., above floor level on elevated devices.[33] The duty runs to workers only, and is one for which an owner may require indemnification from its contractor and subcontractors.[34] A question must be asked: Why does the contractor have to pay workers' compensation premiums if it will also have to pay a tort measure of damages to the owner through an indemnification clause?[35]

Under NY Labor Law §241, an owner has an obligation to comply with requirements designed to protect workers from falls through open floors, shafts, elevators, etc., and from being struck by falling matter, and to provide "reasonable and adequate protection and safety"[36] to protect them from the "usual dangers of construction."[37]

Typically, an owner tries to pass these statutory obligations on to its contractor by contractual clauses that make the contractor responsible for job safety. Such clauses are effective between the owner and contractor only; they do not affect an injured worker's right to seek redress from an owner since the owner's responsibility for safety is absolute and nondelegable.[38]

§13.04 Contractor's Obligations

A contractor's obligations are similar to an owner's, but more extensive. Not only is the contractor obligated to provide a safe job site, but it also must provide workers with safe equipment, tools, and safety devices. A contractor's common law obligations have been greatly expanded by statute and regulations that not only specify general safety precautions that must be taken, but also specify, in detail, what safety devices must be made available and under what conditions. Like an owner, a contractor is not responsible for freak accidents under either common or statutory law.[39]

Common Law

Like an owner, a contractor's responsibility for the safe condition of the work site does not extend to areas created by and intimately connected with a sub-

---

[33] Yaeger v New York Tel Co, 148 AD2d 308, 538 NYS2d 526 (1st Dept 1989).

[34] See discussion at §13.18.

[35] The ability of an owner to require indemnification can tend to defeat the benefits a contractor receives from workers' compensation laws—instead of having to pay only its workers' compensation premiums, the contractor ends up paying the worker's tort damages as well.

[36] NY Lab Law §241(6) (McKinney 1986 & Supp 1992).

[37] Yaeger v New York Tel Co, 148 AD2d 308, 538 NYS2d 526, 529 (1st Dept 1989).

[38] Haimes v New York Tel Co, 46 NY2d 132, 385 NE2d 601, 412 NYS2d 863 (1978); Allen v Cloutier Constr Corp, 44 NY2d 290, 376 NE2d 1276, 405 NYS2d 630 (1978).

[39] Herman v Lancaster Homes, Inc, 145 AD2d 926, 536 NYS2d 298 (4th Dept 1988).

contractor's work, i.e., the *details* of the subcontractor's work.[40] Further, a contractor for general construction is not responsible for the safety conditions of an independent prime contractor's work where the contractor for general construction has no actual or contractual authority to control the prime's work or enforce safety standards.[41]

If, however, a subcontractor's employee is injured while under the control and supervision of the general contractor, the general contractor will be liable for the employee's injuries.[42] Similarly, if a general contractor assumes responsibility for the method of work performed, it cannot assert that the injury was caused during performance of a detail of the work.[43] Further, if a known, unsafe condition exists and an unrelated subcontractor's worker is injured, the party responsible for the unsafe condition may be liable in common law negligence to the injured worker.[44]

A contractor's duty to maintain a safe work site is not limited to workers; it extends to invitees[45] and trespassers.[46]

Statutory

A contractor, like an owner, may be liable to an injured worker, including one employed by someone else, under NY Lab Law §§200, 240, and 241, discussed in §§13.05-13.14. Under §200, a general contractor is not liable for the manner in which subcontract operations are carried out unless it has control over the subcontractor's work or assumes direct responsibility for the method used.[47] Simply checking to make sure that work is progressing and being done properly does not automatically mean that a contractor has assumed control.[48]

Under NY Lab Law §§240 and 241, a contractor's obligations are identical to an owner's—they are absolute and nondelegable. Like an owner, a contractor may attempt to pass responsibility for safety on to its subcontractors, typically through clauses in each subcontract obligating the subcontractor to provide all necessary safety measures, absolving the contractor of responsibility for safety, and providing for indemnification and contribution of the contractor by the subcontractor. Such measures are effective only between the

---

[40] Wright v Belt Assocs, Inc, 14 NY2d 129, 198 NE2d 590, 249 NYS2d 416 (1964); Freeo v Victor A. Perosi, Inc, 54 AD2d 684, 387 NYS2d 268 (2d Dept 1976). *See* §13.03.

[41] Nowak v Smith & Mahoney, PC, 110 AD2d 288, 494 NYS2d 449 (3d Dept 1985).

[42] Broderick v Cauldwell-Wingate Co, 301 NY 182, 93 NE2d 629 (1950); LaCroix v J. Migliore Constr Co, 142 AD2d 980, 530 NYS2d 401 (4th Dept 1988).

[43] Lagzdins v United Welfare Fund-Sec, Div Marriott Corp, 77 AD2d 585, 430 NYS2d 351 (2d Dept 1980). *See* §13.03.

[44] Magrath v J. Migliore Constr Co, 139 AD2d 893, 527 NYS2d 892 (4th Dept 1988) (suit by painting subcontractor's injured employee against steel subcontractor).

[45] Petluck v McGolrick Realty Co, 240 AD 61, 268 NYS 782 (1st Dept 1934).

[46] Amerman v Lizza & Sons, 45 AD2d 996, 358 NYS2d 220 (2d Dept 1974).

[47] Lagzdins v United Welfare Fund-Sec, Div Marriott Corp, 77 AD2d 585, 430 NYS2d 351 (2d Dept 1980).

[48] *Id.*

contractor and subcontractor; they do not limit an injured worker's right to seek damages from the contractor under NY Lab Law §§240 and 241.[49]

§13.05 Labor Law §240

New York Labor Law §240 provides, in part:

> (1) All contractors and owners and their agents ... in the erection, demolition, repairing, altering, painting, cleaning or painting of a building or structure shall furnish or erect, or cause to be erected for the performance of such labor, scaffolding, hoists, stays, ladders, slings, hangers, blocks, pulleys, braces, irons, ropes, and other devices which shall be so constructed, placed and operated as to give proper protection to a person so employed.

The law goes on to specify that scaffolding more than 20 feet from the ground or floor must have a safety rail,[50] the size of the rail,[51] and the minimum load bearing capacity of a scaffold.[52] These specifications do not mean that scaffolding lower than 20 feet need not have a guardrail; if a rail or some other safety device is necessary to protect workers, it is mandated by §240.[53] The primary purpose of §240 is to protect workers from injuries due to falls from scaffolds or other safety devices used when working at heights and from injuries due to the collapse of such, and to protect workers from objects falling from elevated heights.[54] Thus, in addition to §240 liability having been imposed for falls from scaffolding and other structures,[55] it has been imposed when a worker was struck in the head by a loosened "come along" (a device used to tighten

---

[49] Haimes v New York Tel Co, 46 NY2d 132, 385 NE2d 601, 412 NYS2d 863 (1978); Allen v Cloutier Constr Corp, 44 NY2d 290, 376 NE2d 1276, 405 NYS2d 630 (1978).

[50] NY Lab Law §240(2) (McKinney 1986 & Supp 1992).

[51] *Id.*

[52] *Id* §240(3).

[53] Bland v Manocherian, 66 NY2d 452, 488 NE2d 810, 497 NYS2d 880 (1985); Heath v Soloff Constr, Inc, 107 AD2d 507, 487 NYS2d 617 (4th Dept 1985).

[54] There is some division as to how broadly §240 should be construed. The Third Department found liability when a scaffold fell *on* a worker, Smith v Jesus People, 113 AD2d 980, 493 NYS2d 658 (3d Dept 1988), and possible liability for a failure to provide a hoist to move equipment, Gregory v General Elec Co, 131 AD2d 967, 516 NYS2d 549 (3d Dept 1987), while the First and Fourth Departments have held that it applies only when the worker is working at an elevated height. Yaeger v New York Tel Co, 148 AD2d 308, 538 NYS2d 526 (1st Dept 1989); DaBolt v Bethlehem Steel Corp, 92 AD2d 70, 459 NYS2d 503 (4th Dept), *appeal dismissed,* 60 NY2d 554, 467 NYS2d 1029 (1983).

[55] Young v Casabonne Bros, 145 AD2d 244, 538 NYS2d 348 (3d Dept 1989) (scaffolding collapsed); Blair v Rosen-Michaels, Inc, 146 AD2d 863, 536 NYS2d 577 (3d Dept 1989) (fall from roof); Conway v New York State Teachers' Retirement Sys, 141 AD2d 957, 530 NYS2d 300 (3d Dept 1988) (fall from beam); Kojic v City of NY, 76 AD2d 828, 428 NYS2d 305 (2d Dept 1980) (scaffolding collapsed).

scaffolding cables)[56] and when a worker jumped from a steel beam to avoid being hit in the head by a 10-ton pipe.[57] The statute has been construed to require safe access to, from, and among scaffolding.[58]

The statute has been liberally construed to apply to many types of devices in addition to scaffolds. For example, §240 has been held to apply to workers who performed their work while standing on platforms raised by fork lifts,[59] wooden refrigerator boxes,[60] freezers,[61] braced trusses,[62] and a structure comprised of 10' × 2-½" planking, resting on structural steel on one end and, on the other end, on a 3-½'-long piece of 4" × 4" which rested on structural steel.[63] Generally, the standard is that §240 applies to anything that a worker stands on while working.[64] Under a similar reading of the statute, a crane was held to be a hoist within the meaning of §240,[65] and a hoist was held to be an "other device" so as to impose liability.[66] In a most unusual construction of the statute, the Third Department held that §240 liability could result from a contractor's failure to provide workers with a hoist to move two 300-pound jacks more than 60 feet and up a flight of stairs.[67]

Liability under §240 does not automatically result every time a worker is injured while on or near a scaffold. If safety devices were present, liability applies only if the worker can show that safety devices supplied were inadequate to protect the worker and that their inadequacy was the proximate cause of the worker's injury. If no safety device was supplied, there is absolute liability if the lack of a safety device caused the injury.[68]

As mentioned, two issues arise if a safety device was supplied, the inquiry becoming: (1) was the device adequate, and, if not, (2) was the inadequacy of the device the proximate cause of the injury?[69] In making such inquiries, courts

---

[56] Koumianos v State, 141 AD2d 189, 534 NYS2d 512 (3d Dept 1988).

[57] Lockwood v National Valve Mfg Co, 143 AD2d 509, 533 NYS2d 44 (4th Dept 1988).

[58] Klien v General Foods Corp, 148 AD2d 968, 539 NYS2d 604 (4th Dept 1989); Vanoni v New York State Gas & Elec Corp, 141 Misc 2d 680, 533 NYS2d 846 (Niagara 1988).

[59] Klien v General Foods Corp, 148 AD2d 968, 539 NYS2d 604 (4th Dept 1989).

[60] Kennedy v McKay, 86 AD2d 597, 446 NYS2d 124 (2d Dept 1982).

[61] Vincenty v Davis, 43 AD2d 534, 349 NYS2d 376 (1st Dept 1973).

[62] Lagzdins v United Welfare Fund-Sec, Div Marriott Corp, 77 AD2d 585, 430 NYS2d 351 (2d Dept 1980).

[63] Evans v Nab Constr Corp, 80 AD2d 841, 436 NYS2d 774 (2d Dept), *appeal dismissed*, 54 NY2d 605, 443 NYS2d 1027 (1981).

[64] Kennedy v McKay, 86 AD2d 597, 446 NYS2d 124 (2d Dept 1982).

[65] Camillo v Olympia & York Props Co, 136 Misc 2d 315, 518 NYS2d 702 (NY 1987).

[66] Koumianos v State, 141 AD2d 189, 534 NYS2d 512 (3d Dept 1988).

[67] Gregory v General Elec Co, 131 AD2d 967, 516 NYS2d 549 (3d Dept 1987). *Contra* Staples v Town of Amherst, 146 AD2d 292, 540 NYS2d 926 (4th Dept 1989).

[68] Zimmer v Chemung County Performing Arts, Inc, 65 NY2d 513, 482 NE2d 898, 493 NYS2d 102 (1985).

[69] Antunes v 950 Park Ave Corp, 149 AD2d 332, 539 NYS2d 909 (1st Dept 1989); Blair v Rosen-Michaels, Inc, 146 AD2d 863, 536 NYS2d 577 (3d Dept 1989).

have found that whether §240 liability should apply was a question of fact when a worker slipped and fell from a ladder that was not broken,[70] and that §240 liability did apply when an ironworker fell from a beam.[71] The ironworker was wearing his own safety belt which was attached to a 10-foot-long monkey line. The monkey line was not attached to a life line or other safety support because it was too short to allow the worker to do his work; it furnished inadequate protection. There were no other safety devices. The contractor's duty was to furnish equipment to protect its workers properly; it is not enough that the contractor supplied a safety device—the device must be appropriately placed or erected and provide adequate protection against the dangers inherent to the job.[72]

Further, it is not enough for an owner or a contractor to supply adequate safety devices at the job site; the owner or contractor must require workers to use them.[73] This does not mean that an owner or a contractor has an affirmative duty to *compel* workers to use safety equipment, however. Section 240 does not protect workers who refuse to use available, adequate safety equipment.[74]

If safety devices provided were inadequate but their inadequacy did not cause the injury, there is no liability. For instance, §240 liability was not imposed in a case where a worker was injured descending from a roof. In that case, wind had blown over a ladder that led to the roof. The failure to brace the ladder to prevent its falling was a violation of §240. However, the worker was injured when an old, worn rope he found on the roof and used to climb down on broke. The court held that the worker's conduct was unforeseeable and was the cause of his injuries. There was no emergency that required his descent from the roof and he failed to wait for a passer-by to ask for help; if he had, he probably would not have suffered any injuries.[75]

Section 240 does not apply to every injury that befalls a worker at elevated heights, regardless of the presence of safety devices. If a worker is struck in the eye by a ricocheting nail while on a scaffold, §240 does not impose liability as the injury was not due to a breach of a §240 duty.[76] Similarly, §240 has been found not to apply, despite the fact that the workers were working on elevated structures, when a worker's hand was crushed in a conveyor[77] and when a worker was stuck in the eye by a wire suspended from a ceiling.[78] The injury must be related to a hazard due to working at an elevated height—generally, the falling of a worker or some object from a height. Section 240 was found

---

[70] Antunes v 950 Park Ave Corp, 149 AD2d 332, 539 NYS2d 909 (1st Dept 1989).

[71] Conway v New York State Teachers' Retirement Sys, 141 AD2d 957, 530 NYS2d 390 (3d Dept 1988).

[72] *Id.*

[73] Heath v Soloff Constr, Inc, 107 AD2d 507, 487 NYS2d 617 (4th Dept 1985).

[74] Koumianos v State, 141 AD2d 189, 534 NYS2d 512 (3d Dept 1988).

[75] Mack v Altmans Stage Lighting Co, 98 AD2d 468, 470 NYS2d 664 (2d Dept 1984).

[76] Amedure v Standard Furniture Co, 125 AD2d 170, 512 NYS2d 912 (3d Dept 1987).

[77] DaBolt v Bethlehem Steel Corp, 92 AD2d 70, 459 NYS2d 503 (4th Dept), *appeal dismissed*, 60 NY2d 554, 467 NYS2d 1029 (1983).

[78] Shaheen v IBM Corp, 157 AD2d 429, 557 NYS2d 972 (3d Dept 1990).

not to apply, for example, to a worker injured when an excavation trench collapsed, despite the absence of safety devices.[79]

There has developed over the years a significant difference of opinion between the Appellate Divisions as to the scope of coverage afforded by §240. A much awaited decision by the Court of Appeals in *Rocovich v Consolidated Edison Co*,[80] may provide the needed guidance. In that case the court held that the application of §240 is for risks inherent in a task because of the "relative elevation" at which the task is performed or at which materials or loads are positioned or secured. The court explained its reasoning as follows:

> The contemplated hazards are those related to the effects of gravity where protective devices are called for either because of a difference between the elevation level of the required work and a lower level or a difference between the elevation level where the worker is positioned and the higher level of the materials or load being hoisted or secured.[81]

In *Rocovich*, the court decided that §240 did not apply to a worker injured when he stepped into a shallow, rooftop trough carrying hot industrial oil.

Once liability is found, it is strict and absolute. Agreements between parties as to which party is responsible for safety are irrelevant to the injured worker. An injured worker may recover from the owner, contractor, and their statutory agents, regardless of these parties' actual fault. Further, it is irrelevant: that the worker's injuries were due to his own negligence or assumption of risk;[82] whether the owner or contractor had control over the work performed;[83] or that the injured worker was a self-employed independent contractor.[84]

Regulatory provisions may be used as evidence of proper standards and devices, but they are not conclusive where §240 is concerned; it is self-executing and does not defer to rule-making powers.[85]

§13.06 Labor Law §241

New York Labor Law §241 provides, in part:

---

[79] Staples v Town of Amherst, 146 AD2d 292, 540 NYS2d 926 (4th Dept 1989). *Contra* Gregory v General Elec Co, 131 AD2d 967, 516 NYS2d 549 (3d Dept 1987).

[80] 78 NY2d 509, 577 NYS2d 219 (1991).

[81] 577 NYS2d at 222.

[82] Koumianos v State, 141 AD2d 189, 534 NYS2d 512 (3d Dept 1988); Heath v Soloff Constr, Inc, 107 AD2d 507, 487 NYS2d 617 (4th Dept 1985); Lagzdins v United Welfare Fund-Sec, Div Marriott Corp, 77 AD2d 585, 430 NYS2d 351 (2d Dept 1980).

[83] Haimes v New York Tel Co, 46 NY2d 132, 385 NE2d 601, 412 NYS2d 863 (1978); Klien v General Foods Corp, 148 AD2d 968, 539 NYS2d 604 (4th Dept 1989).

[84] Haimes v New York Tel Co, 46 NY2d 132, 385 NE2d 601, 412 NYS2d 863 (1978); Crawford v Leimzider, 100 AD2d 568, 473 NYS2d 498 (2d Dept 1984).

[85] Blair v Rosen-Michaels, Inc, 146 AD2d 863, 536 NYS2d 577 (3d Dept 1989). *Contra* Zimmer v Chemung County Performing Arts, 65 NY2d 513, 482 NE2d 898, 493 NYS2d 102 (1985).

All contractors and owners and their agents . . . when constructing or demolishing buildings or doing any excavating in connection therewith shall comply with the following requirements:

(1) [F]looring or filling shall be completed as the building progresses.

(2) [U]nder flooring shall be laid on each story as the building progresses.

(3) If double floors are not to be used, the floor two stories immediately below the story where work is being performed shall be kept planked over.

(4) If the floor beams are of iron or steel, the entire tier of iron or steel beams . . . shall be thoroughly planked over, except places reasonably required . . .

(5) If elevators, . . ., or hod-hoisting apparatus are used in the course of construction, . . ., the shafts . . . shall be enclosed or fenced in. . . .

(6) All areas . . . shall be so constructed, shored, equipped, guarded, arranged, operated, and conducted as to provide reasonable and adequate protection and safety.

Section 241 goes on to provide that the "commissioner" may make rules[86] to be complied with by owners, contractors, and their agents to carry into effect subdivision 6, for the protection of workers,[87] and for the reasonable and adequate protection of passers-by in cities with populations of less than one million.[88] Such regulatory provisions are evidence of proper standards of safety,[89] and an allegation of a violation of a specific rule or standard may be necessary for recovery under §241(6).[90]

Like §240, the first five subsections of §241 are construed to prevent certain types of injuries. The first five subsections concern the safeguarding of openings in floors and shafts and the planking over of open spaces to prevent people and things from falling through those spaces.[91] Thus, a worker could not recover under these subsections of §241 for injuries he received when an oxygen bottle fell from a crane.[92] Subsection 6 provides a duty to protect workers from the "usual dangers of construction."[93]

Liability under the first five sections of §241 is absolute and nondelegable; if the statute is violated and the violation was the proximate cause of the worker's injuries, there is liability, regardless of the worker's own negligence or who

---

[86] Regulations are found at NY Comp Codes R & Regs tit 12, pt 23.

[87] NY Lab Law §241(7) (McKinney 1986 & Supp 1992).

[88] Id §241(8).

[89] Blair v Rosen-Michaels, Inc, 146 AD2d 863, 536 NYS2d 577 (3d Dept 1989).

[90] Simon v Schenectady N Congregation of Jehovah's Witnesses, 132 AD2d 313, 522 NYS2d 343 (3d Dept 1987).

[91] Ortiz v Uhl, 39 AD2d 143, 332 NYS2d 583 (4th Dept 1972), *affd mem*, 33 NY2d 989, 309 NE2d 425, 353 NYS2d 962 (1974); see also NY Lab Law §241 (a nondelegable duty to provide planking across openings above and below work areas).

[92] Id.

[93] Yaeger v New York Tel Co, 148 AD2d 308, 538 NYS2d 526 (1st Dept 1989).

controlled the work.[94] In sharp contrast is §241(6), which imposes a more generally worded duty upon owners, contractors, and their agents. Its standards are set through administrative rules, a breach of which does not establish negligence as a matter of law, thus making an injured worker's negligence relevant.[95] The duties imposed by §241(6) may not be delegated,[96] but they may be defended against if the worker's contributory negligence or assumption of risk can be shown. It is irrelevant for purposes of §241(6) liability, however, that one had no control over the work.[97]

To recover under §241(6), a worker should allege violation of a specific standard set forth in implementing regulations adopted by the commissioner.[98] A breach of such a standard does not automatically create liability—it is only evidence of negligence.[99] The worker must prove that the breach was the proximate cause of his or her injury.

§13.07 General Contractor's Liability under Labor Law §§240 and 241

A general contractor's liability under NY Labor Law §§240 and 241[100] extends to work of its employees, its subcontractors' and suppliers' employees, and their subcontractors' and suppliers' employees for injuries that occur on the job site, regardless of the general contractor's control over their work. The purpose of these statutes is to place responsibility where it ultimately lies and to encourage the selection of safe, responsible subcontractors.[101] The liability of the contractor for general construction does not extend to employees of other general contractors on the same site or to employees of independent prime contractors with whom the contractor for general construction does not have a relationship and over whose work it has no control.[102] Without actual

---

[94] Long v Forest-Fehlhaber, 55 NY2d 154, 433 NE2d 115, 448 NYS2d 132 (1982); Joyce v Rumsey Realty Corp, 17 NY2d 118, 216 NE2d 317, 269 NYS2d 105 (1966).

[95] Long v Forest-Fehlhaber, 55 NY2d 154, 160, 433 NE2d 115, 448 NYS2d 132, 134 (1982).

[96] Zimmer v Chemung County Performing Arts, 65 NY2d 513, 482 NE2d 898, 493 NYS2d 102 (1985).

[97] Allen Cloutier Constr Corp, 44 NY2d 290, 376 NE2d 1276, 405 NYS2d 630 (1978).

[98] Simon v Schenectady N Congregation of Jehovah's Witnesses, 132 AD2d 313, 522 NYS2d 343 (3d Dept 1987).

[99] O'Leary v Raymond LeChase, Inc, 125 AD2d 991, 510 NYS2d 389 (4th Dept 1986).

[100] See §§13.05-13.06.

[101] Allen v Cloutier Constr Corp, 44 NY2d 290, 376 NE2d 1276, 405 NYS2d 630 (1978).

[102] Russin v Louis N. Picciano & Son, 54 NY2d 311, 429 NE2d 805, 445 NYS2d 127 (1981) (prime contractor not liable for injuries suffered by employee of contractor for general construction); Nowak v Smith & Mahoney, PC, 110 AD2d 288, 494 NYS2d 449 (3d Dept 1985) (contractor for general construction not liable for injuries suffered by prime contractor's employee).

or implied authority to enforce safety standards, there is no liability.[103]

A general contractor may protect itself somewhat by including indemnification and contribution clauses in its contracts with subcontractors and by choosing subcontractors that have the financial means and adequate insurance to make such clauses worthwhile.[104]

§13.08 Owner's Liability under Labor Law §§240 and 241

An owner's liability under NY Labor Law §§240 and 241[105] is not dependent upon the owner's implied, contractual, or actual right to control, supervise, or direct the work; it is absolute and its duties are nondelegable.[106]

Whether a party is an owner is not always clear, nor is it dependent upon the owner's actual ability to control its property. Take, for example, a case where an owner leased its property, Penn Central Station, to the Metropolitan Transit Authority for a 60-year term. The owner had no right of repair or maintenance; indeed, it did not even have the right of access. Yet, as it was the owner of the fee, it was held liable under §241 as the owner.[107] In another case, however, the owner of the fee was found not to be an owner for §241 purposes when it owned the land above a *condemned* tunnel easement.[108] The Appellate Division reasoned that the owner of a condemned easement does not have the power to impose restrictions and stated, in *dicta*, that if the surface owner had granted the easement, it might have been liable under the statute.[109]

An owner should seek protection against damages it may suffer by requiring its contractors to provide a comprehensive safety program and adequate insurance, including contractual liability insurance, of all parties, by requiring indemnification and contribution clauses in its contracts, and by insisting on similar insurance and indemnification and contribution clauses in its contractors' contracts with subcontractors and suppliers.[110]

---

[103] Russin v Louis N. Picciano & Son, 54 NY2d 311, 429 NE2d 805, 445 NYS2d 127 (1981); Nowak v Smith & Mahoney, PC, 110 AD2d 288, 494 NYS2d 449 (3d Dept 1985).

[104] *See* §13.18.

[105] *See* §§13.05-13.06.

[106] Haimes v New York Tel Co, 46 NY2d 132, 385 NE2d 601, 412 NYS2d 863 (1978).

[107] Sperber v Penn Cent Corp, 150 AD2d 356, 540 NYS2d 877 (2d Dept 1989); *see also* Kerr v Rochester Gas & Elec Corp, 113 AD2d 412, 496 NYS2d 880 (4th Dept 1985) (owner and lessor of property held liable for injuries suffered by worker of contractor hired by lessee).

[108] Fox v Jenny Engg Corp, 122 AD2d 532, 505 NYS2d 270 (4th Dept 1986), *affd mem*, 70 NY2d 761, 514 NE2d 1374, 520 NYS2d 750 (1987).

[109] *See* Celestine v City of NY, 86 AD2d 592, 446 NYS2d 131 (2d Dept 1982), *affd mem*, 59 NY2d 938, 453 NE2d 548, 466 NYS2d 319 (1983).

[110] *See* §13.18.

§13.09 —Residential Dwelling Exception

Both §240 and §241 of the NY Labor Law[111] provide an exception for "owners of one- and two-family dwellings who contract for but do not direct or control the work. . . ."[112] Determining whether a home owner fits within this exception is a factual issue; it depends upon the degree of supervision the owner exercised over the method and manner in which work was performed.[113]

For purposes of this exception, the word *dwelling* has been strictly interpreted in more recent cases. For instance, in a 1991 case, the Court of Appeals held that the exemption is dependent on the building's function and that the exemption does not apply to "encompass homeowners who use their one- or two-family premises entirely and solely for commercial purposes. . . ."[114] In this case, the defendants owned a four-bedroom house which was used solely for rental to college students. The court refused to allow the owners to take advantage of the family dwelling exemption. In an even stricter reading in 1985, the Third Department refused to allow a home owner to use the exception because her husband, a physician, used the basement of the home as his office.[115]

§13.10 Liability of Agents of Owner and General Contractor under Labor Law §§240 and 241

New York Labor Law §§240 and 241[116] impose liability upon "owners, contractors, and their agents."

> When the work giving rise to [the duties imposed by the statutes] has been delegated to a third party, that third party then obtains the concomitant authority to supervise and control that work and becomes a statutory "agent" of the owner or general contractor. Only upon obtaining the authority to supervise and control does the third party fall within the class of those having nondelegable liability as an "agent" under sections 240 and 241. . . .
>
> [This] interpretation of the statutory "agent" language appropriately limits the liability of a contractor as agent for a general contractor or owner for job site injuries to those areas and activities within the scope of work delegated or, in other words, to the particular agency created.[117]

---

[111] *See* §§13.05-13.06.
[112] NY Lab Law §§240(1), and 241(6)-(8) (McKinney 1986 & Supp 1992).
[113] Ennis v Hayes, 152 AD2d 914, 544 NYS2d 99 (4th Dept 1989).
[114] Van Amerogen v Donnini, 78 NY2d 880, 573 NYS2d 443 (1991).
[115] Zahn v Pauker, 107 AD2d 118, 486 NYS2d 422 (3d Dept 1985).
[116] *See* §§13.05-13.06.
[117] Russin v Louis N. Picciano & Son, 54 NY2d 311, 318, 429 NE2d 805, 445 NYS2d 127, 130 (1981).

Under this definition, an independent prime heating contractor is an owner's agent only with respect to its work, and is not an agent with respect to an injury that might occur within the scope of the general construction contract work.[118]

The parties most often looked to as agents under the statutes are architects and engineers, construction managers, and subcontractors. It should be noted that the fact that an agent for statutory purposes is found provides direct benefit only to the injured worker; it gives the worker an additional source for potential damage recovery. The only benefit to an owner or a general contractor may be through indemnification or contribution.

§13.11 —Architect/Engineer

New York Labor Law §§240 and 241[119] specifically state:

> No liability pursuant to this subdivision for the failure to provide protection to a person employed shall be imposed on professional engineers . . ., architects . . . or landscape architects . . . who do not direct or control the work for activities other than planning and design. This exception shall not diminish or extinguish any liability . . . arising under the common law or any other provisions of law.[120]

An architect/engineer will not be liable if it has no authority to supervise or control the injured worker or the construction procedures or safety measures employed by the worker's employer.[121] A duty to the owner to monitor construction to ensure compliance with the contract documents does not translate into control by an architect/engineer.[122] Absent a duty to supervise laborers and absent responsibility for safety precautions, an architect/engineer is not an agent for §240 and §241 purposes.[123] Indeed, without the ability to stop work if unsafe conditions exist, an architect/engineer is without the ability to ensure compliance with safety requirements.[124] Thus, in New York, absent a clear assumption of a duty to supervise *and control* the work, including safety, an architect/engineer is not liable under §§240 and 241 to an injured worker.[125]

---

[118] *Id.*

[119] *See* §§13.05-13.06.

[120] NY Lab Law §§240(1), 241(9) (McKinney 1986 & Supp 1992).

[121] Kerr v Rochester Gas & Elec Corp, 113 AD2d 412, 496 NYS2d 880 (4th Dept 1985).

[122] *Id.*

[123] Fox v Jenny Engg Corp, 122 AD2d 532, 505 NYS2d 270 (4th Dept 1986), *affd mem*, 70 NY2d 761, 514 NE2d 1374, 520 NYS2d 750 (1987); Kerr v Rochester Gas & Elec Corp, 113 AD2d 412, 496 NYS2d 880 (4th Dept 1985); Conti v Pettibone Cos, 111 Misc 2d 772, 445 NYS2d 943 (NY 1981), *affd mem*, 90 AD2d 708, 455 NYS2d 689 (1st Dept 1982); Welch v Grant Dev Co, 120 Misc 2d 493, 466 NYS2d 112 (Bronx 1983).

[124] Davis v Lenox School, 151 AD2d 230, 541 NYS2d 814 (1st Dept 1989).

[125] Welch v Grant Dev Co, 120 Misc 2d 493, 466 NYS2d 112 (Bronx 1983).

482 CONSTRUCTION SAFETY

An architect/engineer may be liable to an *owner* for a worker's injury, even if it is not liable to the worker. Liability may result if the architect/engineer does not carefully draft its contract with the owner to state that it has no responsibility with respect to safety and will not be liable to any party—including the owner—for injuries suffered by any party with which it does not have a contract.[126]

Once construction has been completed, an architect's potential liability as an agent has passed. It does not, for example, have any obligation to someone attempting to repair work performed under its original supervision.[127]

An architect's/engineer's common law obligations and liabilities are discussed in §13.15.

§13.12 —Construction Manager

A construction manager typically is an agent or a contractor for purposes of §§240 and 241 of the NY Labor Law.[128] For instance, agency was found in a case where the contract provided that the manager would represent the owner in the performance of the work and delegated authority to the construction manager over "all phases of the construction project," including safety.[129] Under a similar contract, the manager was found to be both a contractor and an agent for §240 and §241 purposes where it had the power and responsibility to provide design consultation, monitor project costs, schedule project efficiency for design and construction phases, review design, and coordinate and supervise construction activities.[130]

Like an owner or a contractor, a construction manager may protect itself with indemnification and contribution clauses in its contracts with other parties.[131] A construction manager's common law obligations and liabilities are discussed later in this chapter.[132]

§13.13 —Subcontractors

Under previous versions of NY Labor Law §§240 and 241,[133] subcontractors

---

[126] Olsen v Chase Manhattan Bank, 10 AD2d 539, 205 NYS2d 60 (2d Dept 1960), *affd mem*, 9 NY2d 829, 175 NE2d 350, 215 NYS2d 773 (1961); Welch v Grant Dev Co, 120 Misc 2d 493, 466 NYS2d 112 (Bronx 1983).

[127] Jaroszewicz v Facilities Dev Corp, 115 AD2d 159, 495 NYS2d 498 (3d Dept 1985).

[128] *See* §§13.05-13.06.

[129] Kenny v George A. Fuller Co, 87 AD2d 183, 189-90, 450 NYS2d 551, 556 (2d Dept 1982).

[130] Carollo v Tishman Constr & Research Co, 109 Misc 2d 506, 440 NYS2d 437 (NY 1981).

[131] *See* §13.18.

[132] *See* §13.16.

[133] *See* §§13.05-13.06.

were specifically listed as responsible parties.[134] Current versions deleted subcontractors; thus, a subcontractor may be held liable only if it is found to be an agent for statutory purposes. To have liability, a subcontractor must be shown to have supervision and control over the activity which resulted in the worker's injury[135] or over the work area where the injury occurred.[136] The injured worker has the burden of proving the subcontractor's control and supervision.[137]

A subcontractor may be liable in common law to an injured worker who is not its employee. For instance, if a subcontractor creates a dangerous condition and fails to guard against injuries or warn known users of the danger, it may be liable in negligence.[138] A subcontractor's employee's remedy for injury caused during his or her work for the subcontractor is found in the workers' compensation law.[139]

§13.14 Affirmative Defenses to Statutory Liability

Liability under NY Labor Law §240(1) and §241, subsections (1) through (5),[140] is strict and absolute and is not subject to affirmative defenses of contributory or comparative negligence, regardless of the injured worker's negligence.[141] If an injured worker can show that the statute was violated and that the violation was a *proximate* cause of his or her injury, he or she is entitled to recover against the owner, contractor, and their agents.[142] Of course, if the violation was not the proximate cause of the accident, there is no liability under the statute.[143] For instance, liability under §240 was not found in a case where the court held that the worker's conduct was unforeseeable and was the proximate cause of his injuries.[144] In that case, the wind blew over a ladder which led to the roof on which the worker was working. The failure to anchor the ladder was a violation of §240(1). Rather than waiting for someone to notice

---

[134] *See* Allen v Cloutier Constr Corp, 44 NY2d 290, 376 NE2d 1276, 405 NYS2d 630 (1978).

[135] Magrath v L. Migliore Constr Co, 139 AD2d 893, 527 NYS2d 892 (4th Dept 1988).

[136] Headen v Progressive Painting Corp, 160 AD2d 319, 553 NYS2d 401 (1st Dept 1990).

[137] *Id.*

[138] Magrath v J. Migliore Constr Co, 139 AD2d 893, 527 NYS2d 892 (4th Dept 1988).

[139] *See* §13.02.

[140] *See* §§13.05-13.06.

[141] Zimmer v Chemung County Performing Arts, Inc, 65 NY2d 513, 482 NE2d 898, 493 NYS2d 102 (1985); Berndt v Aquavello, 139 AD2d 920, 527 NYS2d 910 (4th Dept 1988); Conway v New York State Teachers' Retirement System, 141 AD2d 957, 530 NYS2d 300 (3d Dept 1988).

[142] Zimmer v Chemung County Performing Arts, Inc, 65 NY2d 513, 482 NE2d 898, 493 NYS2d 102 (1985); Blair v Rosen-Michaels, Inc, 146 AD2d 863, 536 NYS2d 577 (3d Dept 1989).

[143] Mack v Altmans Stage Lighting Co, 98 AD2d 468, 470 NYS2d 664 (2d Dept 1984).

[144] *Id.*

his plight or calling to a passer-by, the worker tried to climb down from the roof using an old, noticeably worn rope he found on the roof; it broke. As there was no emergency compelling the worker to leave the roof, the court held that the worker's unforeseeable reaction to the ladder falling caused the injuries, not the violation of the statute.[145]

The strict liability of owners and contractors holds true even if sufficient safety equipment was available but the worker failed to use it.[146] This does not mean that an owner or a contractor has an affirmative duty to *compel* workers to use safety equipment; a worker who *refuses* to use available safety equipment will not find protection in Labor Law §240. An owner or contractor has the burden to prove that a worker refused, not merely failed, to use safety equipment.[147]

Claims under NY Labor Law §§200 and 241(6), however, are subject to the affirmative defense of comparative negligence.[148]

§13.15 Liability of Architect/Engineer in Negligence

If an architect/engineer does not have a contractual right or duty to supervise and control construction work, including safety, it cannot be held liable to a worker for injuries which were due to a failure of supervision, since the architect/engineer owed no duty to the worker, either directly or as a third-party beneficiary.[149] Further, the authority to stop work if the contractor fails to correct unsafe conditions—in the absence of authority to supervise and control a worker or direct construction or safety measures—does not create a duty from an architect/engineer to a worker; the duty runs to the owner.[150] For a worker to recover from an architect/engineer in negligence, the professional must have breached a duty imposed by contract or by law, or the professional must have been actively negligent with regard to a duty that it voluntarily assumed[151]—for instance, in a contract with an owner, an engineer agreed to " 'ensure' that the construction contractor would provide a safe environment

---

[145] *Id.*

[146] Koumianos v State, 141 AD2d 189, 534 NYS2d 512 (3d Dept 1988).

[147] *Id.*

[148] Long v Forest-Fehlhaber, 55 NY2d 154, 433 NE2d 115, 448 NYS2d 132 (1982); Siragusa v State, 117 AD2d 986, 499 NYS2d 533 (4th Dept 1986). Contributory negligence is a defense to claims brought under NY Lab Law §§200 and 241(6) on injuries which occurred prior to 1975.

[149] Welch v Grant Dev Co, 120 Misc 2d 493, 466 NYS2d 112 (Bronx 1983).

[150] Fox v Jenny Engg Corp, 122 AD2d 532, 505 NYS2d 270 (4th Dept 1986), *affd mem*, 70 NY2d 761, 514 NE2d 1374, 520 NYS2d 750 (1987).

[151] Ramos v Shumavon, 21 AD2d 4, 247 NYS2d 699 (1st Dept), *affd mem*, 15 NY2d 610, 203 NE2d 912, 255 NYS2d 658 (1964); Roy v Poquette, 147 Vt 332, 515 A2d 1072 (1986).

§13.15 ARCHITECT/ENGINEER NEGLIGENCE 485

'for both workers and the general public.' "[152] In the absence of clear contractual duties or active negligence or malfeasance on an architect's/engineer's part, there is no common law duty that runs from an architect/engineer to a worker.[153]

> It is well settled in New York that liability may not be imposed upon an engineer, who is engaged to assure compliance with construction plans and specifications, for an injury sustained by a worker, unless the engineer commits an affirmative act of negligence or such liability is imposed by a clear contractual provision.[154]

In one case, an engineer was found liable for the death of one child and for the injuries of two others when they fell through the ice on a pool of water at a construction site. The 42"-to-47" deep pool was the result of excavation work and was unfenced and unguarded. On one side of the pool was a large, steep pile of dirt. Both the engineer and general contractor had seen children playing on the pile of dirt and done nothing to stop them or to guard against falls into the pool of water. Based on the engineer's contractual duties, which included *inspecting* for safety compliance, the engineer was held liable as was the general contractor.[155]

With the careful drafting of architect/engineer contracts and 1987 revisions of the standard American Institute of Architects (AIA) contracts, it will be difficult for a worker to recover from an architect/engineer without active negligence on the professional's part. Newer contracts make it clear that the professionals are not responsible for safety, that they have no supervisory duties or powers, and that exclusive control over the construction work and responsibility for safety rest with the general contractor.[156]

The absence of a duty and liability to the worker does not necessarily mean that the architect is not liable to the owner for damages the owner suffered as a result of the worker's injuries.[157]

> [I]f an independent obligation can be found on the part of [the architect/engineer] to prevent foreseeable harm, he should be held responsi-

---

[152] *See* Ostrower, *The Absolutely Worst Contract I Ever Saw*, Consulting Engineer 24 (July 1985).

[153] Fox v Jenny Engg Corp, 122 AD2d 532, 505 NYS2d 270 (4th Dept 1986), *affd mem*, 70 NY2d 761, 514 NE2d 1374, 520 NYS2d 750 (1987); Jaroszewicz v Facilities Dev Corp, 115 AD2d 159, 495 NYS2d 498 (3d Dept 1985).

[154] Brooks v A. Gatty Serv Co, 127 AD2d 553, 511 NYS2d 642 (2d Dept 1987); *see also* Davis v Lenox School, 151 AD2d 230, 541 NYS2d 814 (1st Dept 1989); Hamill v Foster-Lipkins Corp, 41 AD2d 361, 342 NYS2d 539 (3d Dept 1973).

[155] Amerman v Lizza & Sons, 45 AD2d 996, 358 NYS2d 220 (2d Dept 1974).

[156] *See* Welch v Grant Dev Co, 120 Misc 2d 493, 466 NYS2d 112 (Bronx 1983) (court analyzes AIA standard architect/owner agreement as an "effort to avoid liability" 466 NYS2d at 114).

[157] Welch v Grant Dev Co, 120 Misc 2d 493, 466 NYS2d 112 (Bronx 1983).

ble [to the owner] for the portion of the damage attributable to his negligence, despite the fact that the duty violated was not one owing directly to the [injured worker].[158]

Thus, if the architect's/engineer's contract requires it to "guard the Owner against defects and deficiencies in the Work of the Contractor," it would have a duty to report known safety hazards to the owner and may be liable to an owner if it fails to do so.[159]

Chapter 11 discusses professional liability more fully.

§13.16 Liability of Construction Manager in Negligence

Unlike an architect or engineer, a construction manager's contract often requires it to supervise construction, ensure compliance with safety procedures, and otherwise act as the owner's agent and represent its interests on the job site. Often, construction managers are responsible for the creation and maintenance of a job site safety program. A worker may be a third-party beneficiary of the contract between the owner and construction manager, if it can be shown that the worker was an intended beneficiary of that agreement.[160] If the worker cannot show third-party beneficiary status, he or she may still be able to recover in tort if he or she can show that the construction manager owed the worker a duty to provide a safe work site and breached that duty. The duty may be shown by the construction manager's assumption of control.[161]

§13.17 Res Ipsa Loquitur: The Thing Speaks for Itself

Res ipsa loquitur is Latin for "the thing speaks for itself." This doctrine is a means by which a plaintiff may prove negligence by saying, in essence, "The negligence is clear from the injury, let the defendant explain it away," thereby effectively shifting the burden of proof from the plaintiff to the defendant, who must then try to rebut the presumption of negligence imposed by the doctrine. The best example of a res ipsa loquitur case is when a person awakens from surgery to learn that surgical instruments were left inside him or her. In con-

---

[158] Garrett v Holiday Inns, Inc, 58 NY2d 253, 447 NE2d 717, 460 NYS2d 774 (1983).

[159] Welch v Grant Dev Co, 120 Misc 2d 493, 466 NYS2d 112, 117 (Bronx 1983).

[160] *See* Schreyer, *Construction Managers' Liability for Job-Site Safety*, 8 U Bridgeport L Rev 105, 116-19 (1987).

[161] Disalvatore v United States, 456 F Supp 1079 (ED Pa 1978); Hammond v Bechtel, Inc, 606 P2d 1269 (Alaska 1980); *see* Kenny v George A. Fuller Co, 87 AD2d 183, 189-90, 450 NYS2d 551, 556 (2d Dept 1982) (liability imposed on construction manager as statutory agent of owner); Carollo v Tishman Constr & Research Co, 109 Misc 2d 506, 440 NYS2d 437 (NY 1981) (liability imposed on construction manager as statutory agent of owner).

struction accidents, the doctrine is not easily used as it may be difficult for a plaintiff to discover who caused the accident. Imagine a building on which a general contractor, an electrician, a mason, a brick materialman, and a painter are working at the same time. A passing pedestrian is struck on the head by a falling brick. Clearly, the pedestrian is without fault, but who is at fault? The doctrine of res ipsa loquitur applies and relieves the pedestrian of proving duty of care and breach of care; those issues are clear. What is not clear, and is not resolved by the doctrine, is *who* is responsible. It would not be fair or just to make the several potentially liable parties show that they are not responsible and bear legal costs to defend an action when there is no proof that they are responsible. "When there is no proof where the brick came from except that it came from the building and nothing to identify the person who set it in motion, it cannot be said that the plaintiff has made out a case for the jury."[162]

The doctrine generally requires that the plaintiff prove that the person charged with negligence was in *sole* control of the thing that caused the harm and that the event that caused the harm does not normally occur in the absence of negligence.[163] However, if more than one person can be shown to have been in control of the thing that caused the damage, the doctrine may be applied. For instance, as stated in one case, where "one or some or all three interdependent defendants [owner, owner's contractor, and tenant's contractor] are in control and burdened with supervision of a street barricade, it is for them to explain their action and conduct when it collapses with resultant damage to another."[164]

§13.18 Contribution/Indemnification

New York Labor Law §§240 and 241[165] hold owners and general contractors liable for certain injuries suffered by workers on the construction site. This duty is nondelegable; it is one, however, against which owners and general contractors may protect themselves through indemnification clauses.[166] It is common for each party to a construction project to require indemnification from those below it. A sub-subcontractor may indemnify its subcontractor, the general contractor, architect, and owner. The subcontractor might indemnify its general contractor, architect, and the owner. The general contractor will often indemnify the architect and owner. Indemnification clauses may also be used

---

[162] Wolf v American Tract Socy, 164 NY 30, 33-34, 58 NE 31 (1900).

[163] Lagzdins v United Welfare Fund-Sec, Div Marriott Corp, 77 AD2d 585, 430 NYS2d 351 (2d Dept 1980).

[164] Schroeder v City & County Sav Bank, 293 NY 370, 57 NE2d 57, 59 (1944).

[165] *See* **§§13.05-13.06.**

[166] Allen v Cloutier Constr Corp, 44 NY2d 290, 376 NE2d 1276, 405 NYS2d 630 (1978); Francavilla v Nagar Constr Co, 151 AD2d 282, 542 NYS2d 557 (1st Dept 1989); Walsh v Morse Diesel, Inc, 143 AD2d 653, 533 NYS2d 80 (2d Dept 1988); McGurk v Turner Constr Co, 127 AD2d 526, 512 NYS2d 71 (1st Dept 1987); Kenny v George A. Fuller Co, 87 AD2d 183, 450 NYS2d 551 (2d Dept 1982).

to protect owners, architects, contractors, and others from claims based in common law.

In the absence of indemnification clauses, parties may seek protection through common law indemnification and contribution.[167] For instance, assume that a subcontractor was solely responsible for a worker's injuries but the general contractor was held liable under Labor Law §240. As the general contractor's liability was purely vicarious, it is entitled to common law indemnification from the responsible subcontractor.[168] If, however, a subcontractor's employee is injured while under the control of the general contractor, the general contractor is not entitled to indemnification, either contractual or common law, from the wholly nonnegligent subcontractor.[169]

Chapters 3, 11, and 12 discuss indemnification and contribution clauses.

§13.19 OSHA

The Occupational Safety and Health Act (OSHA)[170] promulgates standards and regulations that govern an employer's responsibilities as regards the safety of its employees. The obligations imposed by OSHA run solely between an employer and its employee and cannot be used to establish liability of an owner.[171] OSHA does not provide an injured worker with a civil remedy.[172]

The volume of construction safety material is quite great. Some publications that are of use in construction-related safety matters are listed below. These publications are available through the Associated General Contractors of America (AGC). This list is by no means exhaustive.

Manual of Accident Prevention in Construction

AGC Guidelines for a Basic Safety Program

OSHA Safety and Health Standards for the Construction Industry

Guide for Voluntary Compliance with OSHA

AGC Safety Videotapes

Caught In Time: Fall Protection In Construction

Controlling The Field: Jobsite Safety Inspections

---

[167] Kelly v Diesel Constr Div of Carl Morse, Inc, 35 NY2d 1, 315 NE2d 751, 358 NYS2d 685 (1974).

[168] Conway v New York State Teachers' Retirement Sys, 141 AD2d 957, 530 NYS2d 300 (3d Dept 1988).

[169] LaCroix v J. Migliore Contr Co, 142 AD2d 980, 530 NYS2d 401 (4th Dept 1988).

[170] 29 USC §651 *et seq*.

[171] Herman v Lancaster Homes, Inc, 145 AD2d 926, 536 NYS2d 298 (4th Dept 1988).

[172] 29 USC §653(b)(4).

Environmental Problems in Construction*   14

§14.01   Introduction
§14.02   Who Should Be Concerned
§14.03   Types of Projects Affected
§14.04   Sources of Environmental Law
§14.05   —Federal Legislation
§14.06   —State Legislation
§14.07   —Local Legislation
§14.08   Managing Environmental Risks
§14.09   Identifying Potential Risks
§14.10   Assigning and Assuming Risk
§14.11   Owner-Contractor Agreement
§14.12   —The Bid
§14.13   —The Contract
§14.14   —Clauses That Cause Trouble for Contractors
§14.15   —Clauses That Are Helpful to Contractors
§14.16   —Industry Standard Forms
§14.17   Owner-Design Professional Agreement
§14.18   —Defining the Role
§14.19   —Industry Standard Forms
§14.20   Insurance
§14.21   —Errors and Omissions Liability Insurance
§14.22   —Comprehensive General Liability Insurance: Exclusions
§14.23   —Claims Made v Occurrence Policies

---

* This chapter is partially adapted from materials prepared by the authors for a 1989 Cambridge Institute seminar entitled "Managing the Environmental Risks of Construction and Real Estate Development in New York." This adaptation is with the consent of the Cambridge Institute.

§14.24 —Hazardous Waste Insurance Coverage
§14.25 Bonds
§14.26 Superfund
§14.27 —Reducing Superfund Risk
§14.28 Asbestos Abatement
§14.29 —Federal Law
§14.30 —New York State Law
§14.31 —Local Law
§14.32 Other Indoor Pollution
§14.33 Underground Storage Tanks
§14.34 Wetlands
§14.35 Trial Preparation
§14.36 —Obtaining Documents
§14.37 —Personal Liability for Environmental Risks
§14.38 Superfund Litigation
§14.39 —Defenses
§14.40 —Consent Decrees
§14.41 Alternative Dispute Resolution
§14.42 —The EPA
§14.43 —Using ADR in Environmental Litigation
§14.44 References
Appendix 14-1 Developer's Environmental Risk Checklist

§14.01 Introduction

In addition to worrying about compliance with environmental laws at their own plants and facilities, parties involved in a construction project must be concerned with environmental issues that affect their job sites.

This chapter is designed to provide a *very* basic overview of environmental considerations that should be reviewed before renovation, demolition, or new construction, or its design, is begun.[1] A selected reference section is provided at the conclusion of this chapter, listing several sources for more information. There are, literally, hundreds of articles, books, statutes, laws, ordinances, and regulations that pertain to this area of the law. This chapter does not attempt to discuss them all.

The potential environmental liability that faces all participants in the development of and construction on real property requires that all parties become aware of and examine environmental concerns before entering into contracts to purchase or construct property. Parties not only must investigate the details of the building site and attempt to limit or shift liability, but also must recognize and confront the risks that remain after investigation and liability shifting and

---

[1] Postner & Rubin, Managing the Environmental Risks of Construction and Real Estate Development in New York (Cambridge Institute Seminar 1989).

avoidance have occurred. Each party to construction must keep in mind that it could bear full liability for environmental violations, even though it may bear little blame.

An owner of a property is responsible for environmental hazards that exist on its property, regardless of who caused the hazard and whether the activities that caused it were legal at the time the hazard was created. Often, owners try to shift responsibility for hazards to others: prior owners, purchasers, dumpers, engineers, architects, and contractors. Those involved in the construction process should not allow an owner to shift unspecified or unidentified environmental risk to them. While an owner may be justified in shifting a portion of the risk to a contractor who knows of it, contract clauses that wholly shift all risk are inappropriate from a contractor's point of view. For instance, a contractor may agree to remove *known* asbestos from a school, but a contract that requires the contractor to remove *all* asbestos would expose the contractor to unnecessary, and probably unintended, risk. To avoid such pratfalls, parties to construction agreements should understand the environmental risks they may face.

§14.02 Who Should Be Concerned

Developers/Owners

Current owners of real property bear the brunt of legal responsibility for environmental risk. When evaluating a property for purchase and development, a developer should keep this in mind and structure the purchase or joint venture agreements so that the seller indemnifies the developer/purchaser and secures that indemnification with a letter of credit or bond. Then, a developer/purchaser still may be primarily responsible, but would have recourse against its seller or joint venturers.

Contractors and Construction Managers

Both contractors and construction managers must be careful not to assume more environmental liability than they intend to or should at the behest of an owner/developer. Seasoned owners may try to insert contract clauses that make parties working on a site responsible for yet unknown problems they may encounter. Where hazards are known to exist and that knowledge is shared, all parties are better able to allocate responsibilities. The more a contractor or construction manager knows about a site, its history, and the owner and its way of doing business, the safer a contractor or construction manager will be in evaluating and avoiding environmental hazard liability.

Subcontractors

Subcontractors, generally, know less about the presence of environmental risks than do their contractors. Often, subcontractors are called upon, as bid conditions, to take on those environmental risks that the owner foisted onto the contractor. As subcontract terms are often not negotiable, it is important for subcontractors to gather at least basic information about the site and owner, and, thus, the risk to which it may be exposing itself, *before* bids are submitted.

Suppliers and Materialmen

Suppliers and materialmen should not be required to assume responsibility for environmental risk at the site since they rarely perform work there.

Insurers

Insurers have increasingly been looked to as a source of funds to address environmental risks, often unsuccessfully. With the widening of potential liability in the 1970s, insurers developed *pollution exclusions* that exempt coverage of most environmental problems. As is discussed later in this chapter, the issue of coverage often hinges on whether it is *claims made* or *occurrence* coverage.

Sureties

As a performance bond surety may be called upon to step into the shoes of its principal, it is susceptible to being caught in the same web of potential liability as is a contractor or subcontractor.

Architects and Engineers

As are contractors, design professionals are apt to be recipients of the transfer of risk from owner/developers. Blanket assumption of environmental risk should be avoided.

Officers, Directors, and Shareholders

A corporation's officers, directors, and shareholders may become personally liable for environmental hazards, in both civil and criminal contexts. Before an officer or a director signs a document, gives an order, or approves a procedure, all environmental ramifications must be considered.

§14.03 Types of Projects Affected

The type of project involved shapes the type of problems that may be encountered. When one embarks upon the development or building of an environmentally troubled site or project, the array of risks is usually apparent and can be dealt with in the initial stages. Where there is no prior indication of environmental problems, however, the parties are left to discover what the problems might be and devise solutions at the time discovered, often in the middle of a job. Thus, different issues must be considered for different types of projects.

New Construction

When an entirely new facility is being built, the largest initial issue is whether subsurface conditions will cause problems. Are there underground storage tanks? Is hazardous waste buried on the site? Is contaminated ground water present?

Renovation and Demolition

A wide array of environmental risks may be encountered during renovation and demolition. Most common are asbestos, lead paint, and underground or aboveground storage tanks.

Excavation

The most common risk faced during excavation is underground storage tanks.

§14.04 Sources of Environmental Law

Originally, environmental problems were addressed by common law as disputes between private parties. One party would be held responsible to others for having breached a legal duty. The remedy afforded the injured party was usually money damages, and, in a few cases, injunctive relief. Traditionally, cases were based on nuisance, trespass, and negligence theories.[2] These theories, while still valid, are not used as often as they once were. Today, it is primarily through a statutory framework that environmental problems are addressed.

The passing of statutes in the environmental area was necessary because common law remedies were too narrow and courts were ill equipped to fashion remedies for communitywide harm. Statutory remedies are mostly prospective and address public rather than private harm. Typically, there is strict liability for violation of an environmental statute, regardless of intent or scienter. The rationale is that the substantial risk to public health created by a violation justifies this higher standard.

Environmental regulation occurs at every level of government—federal, state, and local. Where state and federal regulations apply, concurrent exercise of authority is allowed under the United States Constitution's Supremacy Clause, unless the federal government is deemed to have preempted the field. To determine whether a federal statute preempts a state statute, the following questions must be taken into account:

(1) Would it be a physical impossibility to comply with both? If so, federal law applies exclusively;

(2) Did Congress expressly or clearly intend to preempt a field of regulation? If so, federal law governs; and

(3) Does a congressional policy objective apply that has a regulatory scheme and requires a uniform national format? If so, a court may imply preemption.

---

[2] Boomer v Atlantic Cement Co, 26 NY2d 219, 257 NE2d 870, 309 NYS2d 312 (1970) (private nuisance suit against cement plant that released dirt and smoke into air and created ground vibrations); State v Monarch Chems, Inc, 90 AD2d 907, 456 NYS2d 867 (1982) (public nuisance suit against hazardous waste storage and ground water contamination).

In many instances, federal environmental laws govern in New York. Environmental quality statutes, such as the Clean Air Act, the Clean Water Act, and the Resource Conservation and Recovery Act (RCRA), preempt state environmental statutes and set out the terms under which the state can be authorized to administer federal programs. If the state does not take, or fails to qualify for, delegation, the United States Environmental Protection Agency (EPA) administers pollution controls directly. Programs that have been delegated to the state include RCRA,[3] the Clean Water Act,[4] and portions of the Clean Air Act.[5]

The federal Superfund and the Superfund Amendments and Reauthorization Act of 1986 are binding directly on the state and are not subject to delegation. Since there has not been an express preemption, however, there are parallel state laws on hazardous waste clean-up. Only if the state and federal laws are inconsistent is there a question of preemption.

Other federal laws apply directly in New York, including the asbestos enforcement program of the EPA. This program and others apply directly because the state of New York has declined to seek delegation.

§14.05 —Federal Legislation

The National Environmental Protection Act (NEPA) enacted in 1969 sets forth the commitment of the federal government to the environment. NEPA created the Council on Environmental Quality (CEQ), which was to advise the president on the state of the national environment annually. In addition, the CEQ was authorized to promulgate regulations for the implementation of the procedural requirements of the act.

Federal regulation of the environment is achieved primarily through the Clean Air Act, Clean Water Act, Superfund Laws, and asbestos regulation (discussed in §§14.28-14.31).

The Clean Air Act

The Clean Air Act[6] is a complex law, designed to provide significant federal control of the nation's air. The act may be enforced by state and federal environmental protection acts (EPAs). Further, the law gives a cause of action to private individuals to enforce its provisions. Sanctions for noncompliance include fines, criminal penalties, and injunctive relief.

---

[3] 42 USC §6926 *et seq.*

[4] 33 USC §1251 *et seq.*

[5] Clean Air Act, Prevention of Significant Deterioration, 40 CFR §52.21.

[6] 42 USC §§7401-7642. Comprehensive amendments to the Clean Air Act were made in 1990; *see* Pub L No 101-549, 104 Stat 2399 (1990).

The Clean Water Act

The Clean Water Act[7] relies on the issuance of permits for its effectiveness. Each person discharging pollution into a body of water must receive a permit to do so from the federal EPA or from a state with EPA permission to issue the same. A permit is required for any work that could release *toxic pollutants* into a body of water. The extent to which this act may govern construction projects has been increased by the broad definition accorded the term *toxic pollutant*. This term includes dredge spoil, solid waste, sewage, garbage, sludge, heat, wrecked or discarded equipment, rock, and sand.[8]

Dischargers using municipal treatment systems do not need to obtain permits. They must, however, meet certain pretreatment standards which, in many instances, require the dischargers to compile reports similar to those produced by permittees. The EPA also regulates the discharge of dredge-and-fill material and requires a permit for any construction work performed in navigable waters.

The Superfund Laws

In an effort to clean up toxic waste sites, the federal government enacted the Comprehensive Environmental Response, Compensation, and Liability Act (CERCLA). This act is commonly known as the Superfund Laws.

For many years, toxic waste was conveniently dumped in open pits or abandoned mines, or simply stockpiled. Since 1980, the EPA has been trying to see to it that these sites are cleaned up. The cost of removal, however, is staggering. The Superfund Laws permit the EPA to identify toxic waste sites and require their clean-up. The EPA may clean up a site itself and bill any of the parties named by the act as potentially responsible for the cost. Potentially responsible parties include: past and present owners; past and present operators; transporters of hazardous substances to the site; and generators of hazardous substances. The courts have interpreted CERCLA as providing for joint and several liability.

The liability imposed on property owners by the Superfund Laws poses a special problem for developers. In *New York v Shore Realty Corp*,[9] Shore Realty planned to build a condominium development on property that had been used as a toxic waste storage site. After purchasing the property, but prior to construction, Shore Realty was sued by the state of New York under state and federal Superfund Laws. The court held that both Shore Realty and its majority shareholder and officer were liable for the cost of clean-up. Faced with staggering clean-up costs, Shore Realty abandoned its construction plans and agreed to sell the property and give the sale proceeds to New York State as partial reimbursement to the state for the clean-up effort.

---

[7] 33 USC §1251 *et seq*. The Clean Water Act was formerly known as the Federal Water Pollution Control Act.

[8] 33 USC §1317(a). The list of toxic pollutants is defined in Table 1 of Committee of Public Works and Transportation of the House of Representatives Print Number 95-30, as amended by the Administrator of the EPA.

[9] 759 F2d 1032 (2d Cir 1985).

Developers are advised to investigate any property on which they intend to build *before* purchase. As *Shore Realty* makes clear, a landowner may be liable for the cost of toxic waste clean-up even though it may have had nothing to do with contaminating the site. Although the act was amended to include an exception to liability for innocent landowners, this exception is drawn very narrowly—the landowner must not have had *any* reason to know of the presence of the toxic waste and must have made a pre-purchase investigation of the site and its history.

§14.06 —State Legislation

New York extensively regulates the environment through several acts in the Environmental Conservation Law, including the State Environmental Quality Review Act,[10] the state Superfund Laws,[11] and state wetlands acts.[12] New York also has significant asbestos[13] and underground tank regulations.[14] Brief discussions of these laws are found in appropriate sections of this chapter.

§14.07 —Local Legislation

Although a substantial body of federal and state environmental law has developed, there is a growing volume of environmental law at the local level. Some relates to zoning, some to the exercise of specific police powers, such as the enactment of historical districts and landmark laws, and some to flood plain and wetlands restrictions.

All local governments within New York must comply with the State Environmental Quality Review Act. New York City has adopted a City Environmental Quality Act (CEQA) by Mayor's Executive Order No 91 of 1977. CEQA and the city's Uniform Land Use Review Procedures must be carefully examined if one is developing property within the city of New York. It is important that similar restrictions be examined at the outset for each locality.

§14.08 Managing Environmental Risks

Legislation, regulation, and case law place a heavy burden upon developers to preserve the environment and protect individuals from the adverse effects of hazardous substances. Each new project is affected in some way by these laws. Developers must identify each environmental risk associated with a proj-

---

[10] SEQRA; NY Envtl Conserv Law §§8-0101 to -0117 (McKinney 1984 & Supp 1992).

[11] NY Envtl Conserv Law, art 27, tit 13 (McKinney 1984 & Supp 1992).

[12] Tidal Wetlands Act, NY Envtl Conserv Law §25-0101 *et seq* (McKinney 1984 & Supp 1992); Freshwater Wetlands Act, NY Envtl Conserv Law §24-0101 *et seq* (McKinney 1984 & Supp 1992).

[13] NY Lab Law §30-900 *et seq* (McKinney 1988 & Supp 1992).

[14] NY Envtl Conserv Law §§17-0101 *et seq*, 40-0101 *et seq*, (McKinney 1984 & Supp 1992).

ect, thoroughly evaluate each, and, based on that evaluation, take steps necessary to allocate each to a particular party or to assume the risk itself.

As a rule, the owner or developer of a project—whether renovation, demolition, excavation, or new construction—should take responsibility for determining whether any hazardous substances are present on the project site. For example, if an owner is planning the construction of a new office building, a consultant might be retained to perform an environmental audit concerning the presence of underground storage tanks and hazardous substances in the soil or ground water. Similarly, if an owner is planning to renovate or demolish an existing structure, the owner should employ a knowledgeable consultant to determine whether hazardous chemicals, asbestos, or PCBs are present. When an owner takes the lead and thoroughly investigates and abates hazardous substances at the beginning of a project, and fully informs all concerned parties of these actions, the likelihood of a dispute relating to the presence of hazardous substances is greatly reduced.

The potential for problems on projects where the owner has not taken appropriate action during planning is considerably higher. Such projects can spell trouble for all parties involved—owners, contractors, and design professionals alike. For instance, if an owner and a contractor enter into a simple contract to demolish an old hotel and asbestos is encountered during demolition, work will be halted until the parties resolve the question of who will remove the asbestos and pay the cost thereof. Demolition work cannot resume until the asbestos remediation is complete and all regulations regarding asbestos removal have been complied with.

§14.09 Identifying Potential Risks

Identifying environmental risks on a potential project requires intricate knowledge of the site and applicable federal, state, and local statutes, regulations, and other rules that define the scope of potential liability. In each instance, the developer[15] must become familiar with these laws, regulations, and rules and determine the extent of its responsibility or potential exposure to liability.

In light of the potential liability created by environmental laws, developers, contractors, and architects/engineers are advised to compile a checklist of environmental concerns to address while initially planning a project. In all possible instances, an evaluation should be made *prior* to purchase, bidding, and contracting. Once the risks have been identified, the relative significance of each risk can be evaluated.

Assume that a developer intends to purchase a vacant city lot for the purpose of constructing a small commercial office building. The developer prepares a checklist of environmental concerns. See Appendix 14-1. Its decisions of

---

[15] *Developer* is used in this section to describe a person or firm intending to purchase and improve real property or that has already purchased property with the intention of improving it.

whether to purchase the lot and, if so, the cost and type of development best suited, will be informed, if based on the information obtained through the checklist.

Retaining an environmental engineer to perform a thorough preliminary site assessment—an *environmental assessment*—should be considered essential.[16] The engineer should know applicable laws and regulations and how and when environmental hazards are found and abated. Many environmental laws, such as the Superfund Laws, are essentially indifferent to the concept of fault. A current owner may be liable for cleaning up a site even though it had nothing to do with polluting it. Although those parties who owned the site at the time hazardous substances were deposited and those who actually polluted the site are primarily liable for clean-up costs, as a practical matter, they may be out of business or unable to contribute their fair share. In such cases, the current owner is responsible. Thus, the laws create an incentive, as well as a duty, for a developer to thoroughly investigate a site prior to purchase. In light of the staggering risk, it is probably unwise not to employ an experienced environmental engineer at an early stage.

Reconsider the list of inquiries that a developer might pursue prior to purchasing a vacant lot. (See Appendix 14-1.) A similar list should be compiled in connection with the demolition or renovation of an existing structure. The risk that the existing building may contain asbestos must be evaluated in much the same way as the possibility that a site for new construction may contain a hazardous substance. The evaluation process is intended to provide the developer with the necessary information to make a well-reasoned decision concerning each risk. Only after a risk is correctly evaluated may it be allocated or assumed effectively.

§14.10 Assigning and Assuming Risk

Once a developer has evaluated the environmental risks associated with a project, the next step is to determine what action should be taken with regard to each identified risk. In some instances, the developer may decide to allocate a certain risk to another party by contract. In others, the developer may decide to assume the risk itself.

A developer's initial retention of risk is probably the most sensible course for sites where environmental hazards have not yet been discovered. The developer, as the "moving force" behind the project (and, appropriately, the prime risk-taker), is in the best position to later allocate environmental risks if any are encountered.

---

[16] *See* 42 USC §9601(35)(B), which makes the CERCLA *diligent purchaser defense* available only to purchasers who made *appropriate inquiry* into the site's previous uses and ownership, including inspection. Further, at press time, two bills were pending before the New York legislature that would make seller disclosure of environmental contamination mandatory. *See* 1990 Assembly No 9676 (Attorney General's Bill) and 1989 Assembly No 1474-c (Governor's Bill).

By eliminating liability of the general contractor, subcontractor, or architect for the presence of yet-undiscovered asbestos or other hazardous substances, a developer enables those parties to estimate the value of their services accurately and, hopefully, from the developer's standpoint, at a lower price.

As a practical matter, general contractors, subcontractors, and architects usually are not equipped to abate hazardous substances. When unexpected environmental hazards are encountered, the most prudent course may be for the developer to seek a separate contractor who specializes in such removals. In theory, allocation of the risk to a highly specialized contractor results in more effective abatement at a reduced cost with diminution of the developer's liability.

For example, suppose that a developer, prior to contracting for demolition or renovation of an existing structure, hired an environmental engineer who discovered that the building's boiler pipes were insulated with an asbestos-containing material. Based on this information, the developer may decide to allocate the risk associated with the removal or stabilization of the asbestos to an asbestos abatement contractor, rather than to have its general contractor, who may be inexperienced in asbestos removal, attempt to handle the job.

The contract between the developer and the asbestos abatement contractor must clearly set forth the liability assumed by each party. It would be impractical for a developer who wishes to shift the risk associated with removing or stabilizing asbestos to enter into a contract under which the asbestos abatement contractor assumes no liability for the effectiveness of its services. If the contractor is willing to assume this risk, the contract must spell out the methods the contractor will employ and the expected results.

The contracts by which a developer allocates an environmental risk must be well tailored to the specific project. The risks are so substantial in many instances that a court may be unsympathetic to a developer's argument that boilerplate exculpatory language should shift the risk to the other party. When a developer allocates a risk under one contract, it should do so specifically, and should reflect that allocation in each of the remaining contracts for the project (architect/engineer, contractors, subcontractors, etc.).

§14.11 Owner-Contractor Agreement

Perhaps no contract should be more carefully drawn than the one between the owner and general contractor. Typical owner-contractor agreements contain broad clauses that appear to make the contractor wholly responsible for job completion, regardless of conditions encountered at the site. Broad language should be restricted and replaced with tailored language that addresses environmental concerns.

§14.12 —The Bid

When placing a bid on a site containing known hazardous waste or possessing another environmental problem, it is important that the bid documents be carefully dissected. Any attempt by an owner to step back from supporting the data it furnishes must be looked upon with suspicion. For example, contractors should be wary of bid documents that state that the information contained in the documents is not guaranteed. Specifications may state that the information given on the contract drawings is "from the best source available to the owner at the present time." This phrase may lead an unwary bidder to believe that there are no further sources available at the time. In fact, it may mean that the engineer or owner has not done thorough research. If this clause is combined with a site investigation clause, a contractor could be exposed to substantial liability for hazardous wastes found at the site. Similarly, it is essential that subsurface exploration be thorough and that the contractor attempt to avoid assuming subsurface risks.

Consider a project that requires subsurface exploration. The contractor should consider the effect on the project if some type of hazardous material is encountered. There are two traditional approaches:

(1) Include clauses that allow additional compensation for the handling of the waste; or

(2) Make sure that the contract documents specifically exclude excavation or removal of hazardous substances or toxic materials from the scope of the work to be performed. Even if compensation for the removal of hazardous materials is allowed, it may not be sufficient, as the contractor may not be equipped to handle a removal in terms of personnel, availability of support facilities, or know-how.

When placing a bid at a site where there is an environmental problem, a contractor should consider:

(1) The cost of disposal;

(2) That some contracts require the contractor to load hazardous substance after it has been properly packaged onto a transporter's vehicles for transportation to the disposal site, with all costs paid directly by the owner. Such an agreement may be satisfactory. Be wary, however, of agreeing to *transport* the waste as: (a) costs are significantly increased by the distance traveled; (b) it is necessary to know which disposal site will take the material and whether it will be available when needed; and, (c) when members of the public learn that hazardous waste will travel through their town, shipping may be affected—disruption, delay, and additional cost will result; take these factors into account in the contract and bid;

(3) The necessity and cost of hiring special consultants or contractors;

(4) The cost of required sampling;

(5) That expensive protective clothing must be utilized by workers;

(6) That local workers may be unwilling to work on a hazardous waste project, requiring the use of outside labor at additional cost;

(7) That employee health should be monitored on a hazardous waste job, making it difficult to shift labor back and forth among jobs;

(8) That insurance may be difficult or impossible to obtain;

(9) That sureties may refuse to issue bid, performance, and payment bonds;

(10) That loss of productivity may be caused by heavy protective clothing and other safety precautions;

(11) The termination for convenience clause should cover up-front costs;

(12) Clean-up activities are likely to result in cost-recovery legal actions; such issues as chain-of-custody of documents and samples, record keeping, and the authority to direct work activities should be addressed in the contract;

(13) The impact of incomplete field investigation data and the added burdens and liability that may result; and

(14) That due to the hazardous nature of the work, the parties should clearly allocate responsibility for site safety, materials and waste control at the site, and third-party liability, and the extent of the design professional's responsibility and liability for site activities.

It is also important that the contractor be aware of any land use impediments that have yet to be remedied by the developer, such as wetlands, air quality, or water quality restrictions. Failure of the developer to achieve regulatory sign-offs under such laws can delay substantially a project or keep it from being built in its bid form. The contractor should not bind itself to a price in the face of these potential delays; its bid should include a contingency to cover these risks.

§14.13 —The Contract

There are several typical clauses that appear in general contracts that, when read together, could be interpreted to require an unsuspecting contractor to abate an unknown hazardous substance. For example, assume that a general contractor agreed to renovate an entire structure under a contract containing the following clauses. After the start of construction it was determined that there was a considerable amount of asbestos in the building.

The site investigation clause read:

> The contractor represents that it has had an opportunity to examine and has examined carefully the plans and specifications and the contract and has acquainted itself with . . . all other conditions at the site of the project and its surroundings; and that it has made all investigations essential to a full understanding of the difficulties which may be encountered in the performance of the terms of this agreement. The contractor will, regardless of any such conditions relevant to the project, the site of the project, or its surroundings,

complete the project for the compensation stated herein and assume full and complete responsibility for completion of the project under any such conditions which may exist at the site of the project or its surroundings and all risks in connection therewith. In addition thereto, the contractor represents that it is qualified fully and able to complete the project in accordance with the terms of the contract and within the specified time.

The "all incidental and necessary work" clause read:

The construction documents are to be treated by contractor as "scope" documents which indicate the general scope of the project in terms of the architectural design concept, the overall dimensions, the type of structural, mechanical, electrical, utility, and other systems, and an outline of major architectural elements. As "scope" documents, the construction documents do not necessarily indicate or describe all items required for the full performance and proper completion of the work. This agreement is let with the understanding that contractor is to furnish for the contract sum all items required for proper completion of the work.

The compliance clause read:

The contractor shall comply with and give notices required by all federal, state, and local laws, ordinances, rules, regulations, and lawful orders of all public authorities having jurisdiction over the work.

Reading these clauses together, the owner might be able to successfully argue that the contractor is responsible for removing or stabilizing the asbestos-containing material.

If it were determined that the contractor is not responsible for the actual abatement work, it is likely that the entire job, or at least a portion of it, would be suspended until the asbestos is stabilized or removed. If the contract is not cost-reimbursable and includes a clause giving the owner the right to suspend the contractor's performance or a *no damage for delay* clause, the contractor could be required to expend unrecoverable substantial sums for remobilization and increased labor or materials prices.

A *changed conditions* or *equitable adjustment* clause may be sufficient to relieve the contractor of the responsibility for dealing with a hazardous substance or for absorbing resulting expenses. But as a general rule, the contractor may not rely on these provisions unless they specifically address environmental risks. An owner will argue that a changed condition clause applies only to traditional changed conditions, standard geotechnical problems, not hazardous wastes. On the other hand, a contractor will argue that an environmental risk is a changed condition. Such arguments can be avoided by specifying in the clause that it is or is not intended to include the discovery of hazardous materials.

A contractor who agrees to perform work outlined in an engineer's report should consider incorporating that report into its contract with the developer, thereby limiting the scope of its work and, presumably, its liability. In other words, if the engineer assumes responsibility for discovering asbestos in a building, the contractor should promise only to remove asbestos previously identified and should not guarantee the removal of all asbestos.

§14.14 —Clauses That Cause Trouble for Contractors

There are several clauses that seem innocent but, in an environmentally troubled project, can cause problems for contractors and subject them, unwillingly, to substantial risk. The most troublesome clauses are those concerning compliance with all laws and regulations, time extensions, delay damages, changed conditions, change orders, and site inspection.

Compliance with Laws and Regulations Clause

Contractors might wish to replace standard clauses that require them to comply with and give notices required by all federal, state, and local laws, ordinances, rules, regulations, and lawful orders of all public authorities having jurisdiction over the work, with a clause that limits a contractor's obligation to comply with laws and regulations to those that specifically address the scope, manner, or method of the contractor's work and that are in effect and actively enforced at the time the agreement is executed.

There are many laws and regulations that require an owner to notify a particular public agency of some environmental occurrence or require the owner to obtain a specialized permit. By employing the above-suggested limiting clause, a contractor will prevent the owner from claiming that it is the contractor's responsibility to make the required notification or obtain the specialized permit.

Many contracts require the contractor to obtain *all* permits. Such clauses might be tailored to relieve the contractor from responsibility for obtaining specialized permits more properly the responsibility of the owner.

In addition, laws and regulations that govern environmental hazards on construction sites are continually changing. If the contractor enters into an agreement containing the above limiting language and, after the start of construction, some new regulation governing the scope, manner, or method of the contractor's performance becomes effective, translating into additional costs to the contractor, the contractor could argue that the additional cost of compliance is an extra.

Time Extension Clauses

Many construction contracts set forth specific start and completion dates and contain language that permits a contractor to receive an extension of time under specified circumstances. A time extension clause can be modified to enable a contractor to obtain an extension of the completion time for delays resulting from environmental concerns outside its control, such as the discovery of hazardous substances or work stoppages ordered by environmental authorities.

Delay Damage Clauses

The right to merely suspend performance is not sufficient to protect the contractor against the added costs that may result from a work stoppage or the decreased productivity that may result from being required to perform work out of sequence. The contract might include a clause that requires the owner to compensate the contractor for all costs incurred due to the discovery and abatement of hazardous substances, including those incurred due to adverse impact on job progress. These costs should include demobilization and remobilization costs, lost productivity costs, and delay damages.

It should be noted that the addition of such a clause usually requires that other clauses be modified, including the following:

1. A clause that permits the owner to suspend the contractor's performance on the entire project or any portion thereof
2. A clause that permits the owner to alter the proposed sequencing of the work
3. A *no damage for delay* clause; and
4. A clause that permits the owner to employ independent contractors and requires the contractor to coordinate its work with the work of the independent contractors

Changed Conditions/Differing Site Conditions Clauses

The changed conditions or differing site conditions clause is most applicable to underground construction, although it can apply to conditions in existing buildings. Typically, an excavation contract indicates that if a previously undisclosed and uncontemplated subsurface condition is encountered during construction, the contractor will perform any necessary related work and receive additional compensation on a time and materials basis. If a contractor enters into a contract for excavation work ignorant of hazardous waste and later some is discovered, it may be obligated to perform remediation under a standard changed conditions clause. If the contractor is not adequately licensed or otherwise prepared to perform the work, this obligation can cause substantial expense and disruption to the contractor. A contractor is best advised to give itself the option to treat the contract as terminated upon its discovery of hazardous waste or to provide that the owner is directly responsible for abatement of the waste, including the cost.

The issue of whether an item of work qualifies as a changed condition may also be a problem. An owner may take the position that the contractor should have become aware of the condition through its pre-bid site inspection and should have included the condition in its lump sum bid.

Some lump sum contracts do not include provisions that allow a contractor to receive additional compensation when it discovers a changed condition. The rationale is that since everything was included in the lump sum price, the risk is on the contractor. It is imprudent for a contractor on a known or potentially hazardous site to enter into a contract without an appropriate changed conditions clause.

Change Order Clauses

In an environmentally troubled construction project, a contractor may be asked to perform an extra or change order it is not qualified to perform, perhaps due to a lack of experience handling hazardous materials or because it does not have a required license. In such cases, a contractor should be allowed to refuse the change order without sacrificing the rest of the job. The decision as to who should do abatement work should be the contractor's. If the contractor is experienced, willing, and able to perform the environmental remediation, it is probably in the best interests of both the contractor and the owner that it do so.

To protect both owners and contractors, a clear method for processing and pricing change orders must be included in the contract. The contract must include a clear definition of how change orders are to be calculated and a clear statement of what records are required to be kept so that later discrepancies and disputes may be avoided. Further, it should define under what circumstances a contractor may refuse an environmental remediation change order without jeopardizing its other performance under the contract.

Site Inspection Clauses

Typical site investigation clauses state that the contractor has visited the site and is familiar with it and the conditions under which the work is to be performed. These clauses attempt to place the burden of undiscovered or concealed conditions on the contractor. The contractor may choose to avoid wording that specifically requires it to inspect subsurface and concealed areas and, instead, to include language that specifically excludes any obligation to investigate, discover, or be responsible for hazardous materials. By doing this, it may be able to argue that it did not have the duty to perform such inspections and is not responsible for those subsurface and concealed conditions that are materially different from those one would reasonably expect to encounter.

§14.15 —Clauses That Are Helpful to Contractors

Just as there are clauses that do not favor contractors, so too are there clauses that do favor them and that should be considered for inclusion by contractors. Owners, for obvious reasons, may feel differently and avoid inclusion of these clauses.

Disclaimers for Hazardous Substances

A contractor entering into a contract for a site not known by it to have hazardous substances present might wish to include a clause that specifically states that the contractor takes no responsibility for toxic, hazardous, or other dangerous substances that may be found on the site. The clause might further state that any such substances are the responsibility of the owner.

Representations and Warranties

It is appropriate for an owner to expressly set forth what it knows about the site and that the contractor is entitled to rely on what the owner knows. It is unwise for a contractor to place a bid without receiving a statement from the owner of what it knows about the project site. Of course, it would be ideal if the owner would broadly warrant and represent that no hazardous substances are present on the site, but it is doubtful that any owner would or should agree to such a provision.

Indemnification

Owners do not like to indemnify contractors. A rational argument can be made, however, that an owner should not protest a clause requiring it to indemnify the contractor for all loss or expense incurred by the contractor relating to an environmental risk that was not caused by the contractor and that was not adequately disclosed in the construction documents.

§14.16 —Industry Standard Forms

The 1987 edition of the American Institute of Architects' (AIA) general conditions of the contract for construction (AIA Doc A201) includes a series of provisions that attempt to place responsibility for detecting and dealing with hazardous substances on owners. For instance, in clause 10.1.2, a contractor, upon encountering material it reasonably believes to be asbestos or PCBs that have not been rendered harmless, is to "immediately stop Work in the area affected and report the condition to the Owner and Architect in writing." Work in the area is not to be resumed until a written agreement is reached between the owner and contractor and the asbestos or PCBs have been removed or rendered harmless. Further, pursuant to clause 10.1.3, a contractor cannot be required to perform any work relating to asbestos or PCBs without its consent. Similar provisions appear in the AIA subcontract agreement (AIA Doc A401).

The following examples will serve to analyze the effectiveness of these clauses.

> Example 1: Contractor discovers material reasonably believed to contain asbestos or PCBs.

Clearly, the contractor has the right to stop work in the affected area and has no responsibility for removing or handling the material containing the asbestos or PCBs.

> Example 2: Contractor discovers material reasonably believed to be toxic and hazardous, such as lead, but which is not reasonably believed to be asbestos or PCBs.

Here, the responsibility of the contractor is not so clear. As a practical matter, the contractor will suspend performance in the affected area and contact the owner. But, the contractor's liability for removal or abatement of the nonclassified waste is not adequately covered by the agreement.

Example 3: Contractor removes asbestos-containing material in contravention of controlling regulations, but did not know or have reason to know that the material contained asbestos, and is faced with potential personal injury suits from workers and third parties.

Here, the contractor is likely to incur expense in defending suits and possibly paying any resulting judgments. In addition, the contractor may be fined by an appropriate regulatory agency. The AIA contracts permit the contractor to recover at least some of these costs from the owner under an indemnification clause, if the owner was partially or wholly responsible for the damages incurred.[17]

Example 4: Contractor innocently removes material that is toxic and hazardous but that is not asbestos or PCBs and is faced with potential suits from workers and third parties.

Here, the extent to which the contractor can recover its costs incurred is less clear. Under a strict reading of the clause, it probably would not be indemnified for any of its costs.

The Engineers Joint Contract Documents Committee (EJCDC) *Standard General Conditions of the Construction Contract* 1910-8 (1990 ed) goes further in extending protection to the contractor. The applicable provisions read as follows:

4.5 Asbestos, PCBs, Petroleum, Hazardous Waste or Radioactive Material:

4.5.1 OWNER shall be responsible for any Asbestos, PCBs, Petroleum, Hazardous Waste or Radioactive Material uncovered or revealed at the site which was not shown or indicated in the Drawings or Specifications or identified in the Contract Documents to be within the scope of the Work and which may present a substantial danger to persons or property exposed thereto . . . .

4.5.2 CONTRACTOR shall immediately: (i) stop all Work in connection with such hazardous condition and in any area affected thereby . . . . Contractor shall not be required to resume work in connection with such hazardous condition or in any such affected area until after OWNER has obtained any required

---

[17] AIA Doc A201, ¶10.1.4 (1987 ed). Reproduced by permission of The American Institute of Architects under license number 92095. Permission expires July 31, 1993. FURTHER REPRODUCTION IS PROHIBITED. Because AIA Documents are revised from time to time, users should ascertain from the AIA the current edition of this document. Copies of the current edition of this AIA document may be purchased from The American Institute of Architects or its local distributors. The text of this document is not "model language" and is not intended for use in other documents without permission of the AIA.

4.5.3   permits related thereto and delivered to CONTRACTOR special written notice: (i) specifying that such condition and any affected area has been rendered safe for the resumption of Work, or (ii) specifying any special conditions under which Work may resume safely. If the OWNER and CONTRACTOR cannot agree as to the entitlement to or the amount or extent of an adjustment, if any, in Contract Price or Contract Times as a result of such Work stoppage or such special conditions under which Work is agreed by CONTRACTOR to be resumed, either party may make a claim therefore as provided in Articles 11 and 12.

4.5.3   If after receipt of such special written notice CONTRACTOR does not agree to resume such Work based on a reasonable belief it is unsafe, or does not agree to resume such Work stoppage under such special conditions, then OWNER may order such portion of the Work that is in connection with such hazardous condition or in such affected area to be deleted from the Work....

4.5.4   To the fullest extent permitted by Laws and Regulations, OWNER shall indemnify and hold harmless CONTRACTOR ... against all claims, costs, losses and damages arising out of or resulting from such hazardous condition provided that: (i) any such claim, cost, loss or damage is attributable to bodily injury, sickness, disease or death, or to injury to or destruction of tangible property ... (the claimant's own negligence excludes indemnification). [Reprinted with permission.]

As with the AIA general conditions, the EJCDC provisions are designed to permit the contractor to stop work where hazardous materials have been discovered. The EJCDC provisions are broader than the AIA provisions in that the contractor is protected upon discovery of asbestos, PCBs, petroleum, hazardous waste, and radioactive materials. Additionally, the contractor may incorporate its own definition of hazardous waste into the agreement or utilize that which has been provided in various state and federal laws.

§14.17 Owner-Design Professional Agreement

Design professionals are not immune from liability for hazardous materials. Further, standard professional liability insurance does not cover hazardous materials. Under certain circumstances, design professionals may be responsible for removing and stabilizing hazardous materials. For example, suppose a designer agreed to prepare all plans and specifications for a renovation project for a stated sum. If standard contract language is used, an owner could make the argument that its designer is responsible for preparing the specifications for the abatement work.

A designer should not take comfort in the fact that it has a cost-plus fee contract. Although the designer could employ an independent environmental consultant to prepare and supervise the abatement work, the designer remains primarily responsible to the owner for the sufficiency of the specifications and any related supervisory efforts. The mark-up on the consultant's costs that the designer receives from the owner may not be sufficient to offset its increased exposure to liability.

Architects and engineers must carefully draft their contracts, paying strict attention to the scope of work and definition of their role. Generally, designers will wish to use standard form agreements prepared by the American Institute of Architects (AIA) as these agreements tend to favor designers and place responsibility for detecting and abating hazardous waste on owners.

§14.18 —Defining the Role

Whether an architect or an engineer is designing a new project or the renovation of an existing one, the contract should specifically spell out what its responsibilities and liabilities are with regard to hazardous substances. If the owner takes responsibility for knowledge of and dealing with hazardous wastes, the agreement should state this. Similarly, if the owner does not take responsibility and wishes its architect to detect and plan the abatement of any hazardous wastes, the agreement should state this, as well as the extent of the architect's liability for the abatement method and contractor chosen and their effectiveness.

When an engineer is hired specifically to address environmental issues, special attention must be given to the description of the scope of work to be performed. If the developer is knowledgeable in environmental hazards, it may need the engineer to conduct only an information study to determine which, if any, hazardous substances are present on the site. If, however, the developer has no experience concerning environmental hazards, it may require the engineer to suggest appropriate methods to dispose of or neutralize any hazardous substances found on the property. In either case, the developer and engineer must carefully draft a contract that delineates the potential liability and risk assumed by each party.

For example, suppose that a developer and an engineer enter into a contract by which the engineer agrees to conduct an informational study. The engineer should make sure that the agreement clearly sets forth the general types of hazardous substances it is being retained to investigate, the methods of investigation to be employed, and the anticipated reliability or accuracy of those methods.

If the engineer provides additional services to the owner, new questions of liability are raised. For example, if the engineer suggests a method to dispose of or neutralize a hazardous substance, what is the extent of the engineer's liability for the effectiveness of that method? Similarly, if the owner asks the engineer to recommend a hazardous waste contractor, to what extent is the engineer responsible for the contractor's performance? These questions must be addressed by clear and concise contract language.

§14.19 —Industry Standard Forms

The American Institute of Architects (AIA) standard form of agreement between owner and architect (AIA Doc B141) includes provisions that benefit the architect with respect to the presence of hazardous substances. For instance, an owner must furnish "the services of geotechnical engineers..." when requested by the architect, including evaluations of hazardous materials[18] and "air and water pollution tests, tests for hazardous materials, and other laboratory and environmental tests, inspections and reports required by law or the Contract Documents."[19] These services, information, surveys, and reports are furnished at the owner's expense. The architect is entitled to rely upon their accuracy and completeness.[20]

The contract also provides that the architect "shall have no responsibility for the discovery, presence, handling, removal, or disposal of or exposure of persons to hazardous materials in any form at the Project site, including... asbestos, PCBs or other toxic substances."[21]

In contrast to the AIA general contractor agreement, the architect's agreement makes it clear that the architect will not be responsible for the discovery or abatement of any hazardous substance. Further, the category of hazardous substances covered by the architect's agreement is much broader than the category of those substances covered by general conditions applicable to a contractor's work (AIA Doc A201). The architect's agreement concerns hazardous materials "including but not limited to" asbestos and PCBs, but the general conditions governing the contractor's work deal specifically with only asbestos and PCBs.

§14.20 Insurance

Another method for a developer, designer, or contractor to shift risk connected with subsequent discovery or handling of hazardous substances is through insurance. Practical considerations may counsel against this approach, however, as the premium may be too expensive, the coverage too limited, or the insurance simply unavailable.

Increased environmental regulation has led to a crisis in the insurance industry. Parties, faced with enormous environmental liability, have turned to their insurance companies to help relieve the financial burden. Insurance companies, however, have consistently resisted paying environmental claims, many of which are the result of actions taken years before claims were made. Today, the cost of environmental liability insurance, when available, has skyrocketed. For many businesses in the United States, insurance against environmental liability is unavailable. Construction companies must take measures to protect themselves as best they can. Various types of insurance provide different pro-

---

[18] AIA Doc B141, ¶4.6.
[19] *Id* ¶4.7.
[20] *Id* ¶4.9.
[21] *Id* ¶9.8.

tection and relief. A brief analysis of errors and omissions liability, comprehensive general liability, claims made and occurrence policies, and hazardous waste insurance follows in §§14.21-14.24.

§14.21 —Errors and Omissions Liability Insurance

Almost all errors and omissions policies contain an exclusion for claims arising out of a pollution incident,[22] except those due to a negligent professional act, an error, or an omission for described operations. This coverage is written on either a blanket/specified site or project-specific basis. A drawback of error and omissions liability insurance is that other forms of insurance must also be taken along with it. For example, when a consulting engineering firm hires a contractor and supervises asbestos abatement, the firm would be acting as general contractors for insurance purposes and would need general liability, contractor's pollution liability, or asbestos abatement liability policies for its protection in addition to errors and omissions.

There is asbestos consultant errors and omissions insurance that eliminates the pollution exclusion, thereby providing coverage for errors, acts, or omissions arising out of the *design* of asbestos abatement or hazardous waste projects. It has the potential to be redundant; consultants should check to see if this design work is covered in their engineer's pollution liability policy. Asbestos consultants errors and omissions policies tend to limit coverage to $1,000,000.

§14.22 —Comprehensive General Liability Insurance: Exclusions

Generally, contractor comprehensive general liability insurance is limited to $10,000,000 per occurrence. The problem is that typical contractor policies specifically exclude coverage for pollution incident claims at the job site relating to hazardous waste clean-up or asbestos removal. A standard "pollution exclusion" clause states:

> It is agreed that the insurance does not apply to bodily injury or property damage arising out of the discharge, dispersal, release or escape of smoke, vapors, soot, fumes, acids, alkalis, toxic chemicals, liquids or gases, waste materials or other irritants, contaminants or pollutants into or upon land, the atmosphere, or any watercourse or body of water; but this exclusion does not apply if such discharge, dispersal, release or escape is sudden and accidental.

Insurers and insureds debate the meaning and intent of this exclusion. The pollution exclusion clause purports to exclude all property damage or bodily

---

[22] Some policies delete the exclusion if the contract is for the design of drinking water systems or sewage treatment plants.

injury caused by the release or discharge of pollutants, except if the discharge is "sudden and accidental." This phrase is undefined and has caused much litigation. Insurers argue that the clause was intended to exclude all pollution damage with a narrow exception for pollution caused by releases or discharges that were both sudden in time and accidental, such as a tank rupture. Insureds argue that the phrase "sudden and accidental" is merely a reiteration of "unexpected and unintended" which appears in the definition of the policy term "occurrence" and, significantly, that the insurance industry originally advertised the exclusion as not reducing the scope of coverage.

The courts tend to focus on the nature of the discharge and not on the damage caused. "The relevant factor is not whether the policyholder anticipated or intended the resultant injury or damage, but whether the toxic material was discharged unexpectedly and unintentionally or knowingly and intentionally."[23] Thus, gradual pollution damage is excluded; the "sudden" requirement is unambiguous and includes a temporal element.[24] The minority view is that the exclusion is a clarification of the occurrence definition and that it is ambiguous and to be construed against the insurer, resulting in the exclusion barring coverage for only active polluters.[25]

Another exclusion often written into a comprehensive general liability policy is an "owned property" exclusion. Such a clause excludes coverage for property owned by, or under the care, custody, or control of, the insured. The applicability of this exclusion becomes an issue in environmental insurance coverage when contamination comes from the insured's facility. In construction, this exclusion may be relevant if remediation becomes necessary. It may be important for a contractor to know that remediation will not be funded by the owner's insurer if this exclusion applies.

Another exclusion contractors should be wary of—both in their own business insurance and in an owner's coverage—is called the "absolute" pollution exclusion for "property damage caused by seepage, pollution, or contamination of whatsoever nature or howsoever caused." This exclusion bars coverage for any and all pollution-related claims.

§14.23 —Claims Made v Occurrence Policies

Historically, most commercial general liability policies have been written on an *occurrence* basis. A claim is covered regardless of when filed so long as the occurrence took place during the policy period. As the courts began to interpret this policy language to cover situations that insurers never intended to be covered—such as asbestos-related personal and property damage claims—

---

[23] Technicon Elecs Corp v American Home Assurance Co, 141 AD2d 124, 533 NYS2d 91 (2d Dept 1988), *affd*, 74 NY2d 66, 542 NE2d 1048, 544 NYS2d 531 (1989).

[24] *Id*; EAD Metallurgical, Inc v Aetna Cas & Sur Co, 701 F Supp 399 (WDNY 1988), *affd*, 905 F2d 8 (2d Cir 1990) (discharges over seven-year period excluded).

[25] *See* Autotronics Sys v Aetna Life & Cas Co, 89 AD2d 401, 456 NYS2d 504 (3d Dept 1982); Niagara County v Utica Mut Ins Co, 80 AD2d 415, 439 NYS2d 538 (4th Dept), *appeal dismissed*, 54 NY2d 608, 443 NYS2d 1030 (1981).

underwriters reacted by offering certain coverage on a *claims made* basis (i.e., coverage is based on when the claim is made, rather than when the occurrence happened).

Claims made coverage causes a number of practical problems for parties involved in asbestos or other hazardous waste abatement. Since most of the health-related problems have a lag time of 10-to-40 years between the occurrence and the claim, an insured has little reason to believe that premiums paid today will offer any protection when a claim is likely to be made, many years in the future. Only if the policy is maintained through the years and the construction company and the insurance company are still viable will any protection be offered. Insureds are advised to keep copies of all old policies, as an insured seeking coverage many years after the policy period has passed must be able to identify who its insurer was for each potential period of injury or incident and discover the terms of its coverage during those periods. This process is made more difficult if the insured changed insurance carriers.

An insured must beware of what type of coverage it has. The fact that insurance is called *occurrence coverage* does not mean that it is any more helpful than claims made coverage. For example, insurers may offer occurrence coverage to asbestos abatement contractors, allowing them to issue certificates showing coverage. A review of a typical policy reveals an exclusion of coverage for "airborne mineral fibers" contained in the pollution liability exclusion. Asbestos is a mineral fiber and rarely causes problems until it is airborne. Further, some insurers include clauses in occurrence policies that provide that the policy reverts to claims made after several years.

§14.24 —Hazardous Waste Insurance Coverage

Due to general liability exclusions, a contractor who deals with hazardous wastes must procure a contractor's pollution liability policy that provides pollution liability coverage for bodily injury, property damage, clean-up, and defense costs for defined operations. However, a contractor's pollution liability policy rarely offers the protection an insured expects, especially if it is a *claims made* rather than an *occurrence* based policy.[26]

Since most environmental health hazards resulting from exposure do not manifest themselves for 10-to-40 years in the future, occurrence liability is the only true insurance available. True *occurrence* liability with no cut-off dates after five-or-more years (also called sunset clauses) covers health injuries discovered in the future, no matter how distant. In contrast, a *claims made* policy generally pays for claims submitted during the policy period or, if various extensions are available, for a very few years after the occurrence date.

Another drawback to many contractor's pollution liability policies is their monetary limits. Typical policies are limited in claims made form to $1,000,000 per occurrence and $5,000,000 in aggregate on a blanket basis covering all job sites or $5,000,000 per occurrence and in aggregate on a specific project

---

[26] *See* §14.23.

basis. These amounts easily can be inadequate in a large suit. Further, most insurers on group plan occurrence policies have set $1,000,000 limits to be shared among all plan participants. The danger to the insured is that a single large claim against any one participant could leave the others unprotected.

§14.25 Bonds

Environmental contractor performance bonds may be more difficult to obtain than insurance contracts due to two main concerns of sureties: (1) the experience level of the contractor, and (2) the potential for liability claims being made against the bond. The fields of asbestos abatement, hazardous waste removal, and other environmental clean-up are new and subject to rapid change in removal methods, effectiveness, and regulation. Further, clean-up, removal, and transport companies have been in business for a relatively short period of time. This combination of factors makes it difficult for surety bond underwriters to determine whether the abatement contractor is financially and technically capable of handling a particular job.

In addition, sureties are concerned that liability claims will be made against the bond. Assume that an abatement contractor fails to remove all asbestos from a building. Its performance bond surety may be viewed as a guarantor of the contractor's correct performance, not only its completion of the job. If so, the surety might be liable for property and personal injury damages in addition to completing the job that its principal failed to finish. Surety bonds are not and never were intended to be long-term insurance contracts. The liability of the surety should end when the project has been completed, all suppliers and subcontractors have been paid, and the bond limitation period has expired, typically two years after the job has been completed.

Given the concern of long-lasting liability upon performance bonds, sureties are reluctant to provide bonds to abatement contractors unless the contractors also maintain quality occurrence liability insurance.

§14.26 Superfund

The Superfund Laws[27] impose strict liability on those deemed *responsible;* a party's good intentions are irrelevant. To protect oneself, a landowner, an architect, an engineer, an operator, a contractor, a generator, or a transporter must inspect a site thoroughly. To gain knowledge about a prospective site, one might take the following steps:

1. Review official records and initiate formal and informal contacts with regulatory agencies at all government levels
2. Review past litigation and administrative proceedings related to the site
3. Review land ownership records; look for deed restrictions regarding land use, special use permits, variances, and other authorizations

---

[27] *See* §14.05.

4. Review corporate owner's reports which under federal and state securities laws must include a discussion of any contingent liabilities (which may include the costs of any required hazardous waste clean-up)
5. Review environmental reports and filings
6. Review the Environmental Protection Agency's (EPA) Hazardous Waste Site Lists

   —Is the site on the National Priority List? If so, the EPA has determined that a major response action is necessary.

   —Is the site carried on the Comprehensive Environmental Response Compensation and Liability Information System? The EPA maintains this list of more than 25,000 sites; inclusion is not proof that a site contains toxic waste, but is notice to a prospective buyer that further investigation should be undertaken.
7. Proximity to Nearby Sites—How close is the property to other industrial operations, including past operations? The potential for waste must be considered. Even though a property is not the source of waste, it may be required to be cleaned-up
8. Talk to adjacent landowners
9. Visit the site, walk over it or through it
10. Obtain a description of any and all waste produced on the site and how and where it is or was treated, managed, stored, and disposed of, including a description of facilities such as tanks, drainage systems, incinerators, etc
11. Obtain all regulatory information, such as permits, permit applications, notices to agencies, and monitoring reports concerning environmental matters
12. Obtain a history and explanation of all known spills, leaks, and disposal activities on the property
13. Obtain copies of all environmental risk assessments that have been performed on the property
14. Obtain copies of all insurance policies on the property

Businesspersons often attempt to balance environmental risk through a reduced purchase price. A court may consider a reduced purchase price for land containing hazardous waste as a buyer's acknowledgment that it was aware that the land contains such wastes.[28]

§14.27 —Reducing Superfund Risk

Architects, engineers, and contractors must take steps to ensure that they do not become, or appear to be, parties deemed responsible by the Superfund

---

[28] United States v Price, 523 F Supp 1055 (DNJ 1981), *affd,* 688 F2d 204 (3d Cir 1982).

516 ENVIRONMENTAL PROBLEMS

Laws.[29] The best ways to do this are: remain independent from responsible parties by not making operational decisions about the running of the site; have the contract explicitly state that the project is not a joint venture between the owner and contractor, architect, or engineer, and that the owner is responsible for keeping the plant in compliance with environmental regulations and has total control over the handling and disposal of hazardous substances; if the contractor, architect, or engineer must take responsibility for some waste control, it should maintain a veto over waste disposal practices; do not own or operate a dump site, transport waste to disposal sites, or arrange for disposal, treatment, or transportation of wastes; and, when doing on-site clean-up, have the owner make waste transportation and disposal arrangements.

Further, architects, engineers, and contractors should exercise great care to avoid releases of waste, including properly training their personnel and maintaining equipment. If a release occurs, it must be reported to the Environmental Protection Agency (EPA) within 180 days;[30] failure to do so may lead to penalties of up to $10,000 and a year in prison.

Another way to protect oneself is through an indemnification clause in the contract. An abatement architect's, engineer's, or contractor's exposure to liability arises, unless it is negligent, solely as a result of its agreement to deal with someone else's hazardous substance. Thus, it is reasonable that the contracting party agree to indemnify the architect, engineer, or contractor. An indemnification agreement has value only to the extent that the indemnitor can meet its obligations. Thus, besides being aware of the indemnitor's financial health, one might seek other protection, such as a surety bond or letter of credit.

Although it poses grave risks to architects, engineers, and contractors, Superfund offers an opportunity for lucrative work decontaminating hazardous waste sites. The architect, engineer, or contractor that examines the Comprehensive Environmental Response, Compensation, and Liability Act (CERCLA) carefully and takes positive steps to avert potential liabilities before they happen can greatly minimize its risks while enjoying the benefits that Superfund work offers.

§14.28 Asbestos Abatement

Airborne asbestos contamination in buildings is a significant environmental problem that has been linked to various diseases. The Environmental Protection Agency (EPA) estimates that asbestos-containing materials (ACMs) can be found in approximately 31,000 schools and 733,000 other public and commercial buildings in the United States.[31] Mere presence of asbestos in a building does not necessarily mean that a health hazard exists. As long as an ACM

---

[29] See §§14.05, 14.26.
[30] 40 CFR §112.
[31] United States EPA, Toxic Substances: Guidance for Controlling Asbestos Containing Materials in Buildings 5-1 (1985).

remains in good condition and is not disturbed, exposure is unlikely. Once an ACM is disturbed (often as a result of building maintenance, repair, renovation, or other activities), asbestos fibers are released, creating a potential hazard to building occupants. Soft or loosely bound fibers of ACMs that crack or crunch, releasing deadly asbestos into the air, are called *friable* asbestos. Friable ACM is the greatest health concern because it easily releases fibers. As the binders (such as plaster and cement) that hold asbestos fibers in place begin to deteriorate, the likelihood of fiber release increases. Examples of common friable ACMs are fireproofing on structural beams, sprayed-on asbestos ceiling insulation, and trowel-applied acoustical insulation.

Nonfriable, or *hard* asbestos, may also become a health hazard. Hard ACMs, in which asbestos fibers are firmly bound, such as vinyl floor tile, are generally difficult to expose. However, even nonfriable ACMs can release fibers and present a hazard if sanded, cut, ground, or otherwise disturbed. Thus, any material that contains asbestos has the potential to release fibers and become hazardous.

Federal, state, and local governments are faced with the problem of regulating asbestos. The following three sections contain a summary of federal, state, and local asbestos regulation. Each level of government has its own definition of what an asbestos project is; do not assume that what is or is not an asbestos project at the federal level will have the same status at the state or local level.[32]

§14.29 —Federal Law

At the federal level, asbestos is regulated primarily through the Environmental Protection Agency (EPA) and the Occupational Safety and Health Administration (OSHA) using the Clean Air Act, the National Emission Standards for Hazardous Air Pollutants (NESHAP), the Asbestos Hazard Emergency Response Act (AHERA),[33] and OSHA regulations.

The EPA has identified three classes of asbestos-containing materials (ACMs) based upon the location of the asbestos, the potential for damage to the material and release, and the mandatory reaction/response actions to control damaged material:

> *Surfacing ACM:* Sprayed-on or trowel-applied building interior surfaces and structures; these typically lack an outer layer or coat of protection. Includes sprayed-on structural steel fireproofing and acoustical ceiling plaster. Likely to release airborne particles when struck or damaged accidentally, or by construction, water leaks, deterioration, etc.
>
> *Thermal System Insulation:* Applied to boilers, breachings, tanks, pipes, ducts, etc., of heating, cooling, and plumbing systems, generally enclosed in a canvas or other physical cover. Likely to release airborne asbestos

---

[32] National Emission Standards for Hazardous Air Pollutants defines its coverage at 40 CFR pt 61; New York State, at NY Lab Law §901 (7); and the City of New York, at NYC Admin Code §C26-118.9 and in Dept of Envtl Protection Rules and Regulation §8100.

[33] 15 USC §2641 *et seq.*

when damaged or worked on to maintain or repair the system. They may be hazardous when the cover is struck, breached, or damaged, exposing friable ACM.

Miscellaneous ACM: All other asbestos-containing building materials, such as ceiling and floor tiles, wall plaster, or textured paints where the asbestos is contained in a cement or glue-like matrix. Likely to be released when the material is cut, sanded, drilled, or otherwise subdivided into small particles during construction or renovation work. Hazardous when physically disturbed, severely damaged, or badly deteriorated.

Currently, no law requires nonfriable asbestos to be removed from commercial buildings. There are laws that regulate when and how friable asbestos will be removed and that ban certain uses of asbestos. For instance, NESHAP regulations ban spray-applied, molded, and wet-applied asbestos-containing insulation, as well as fireproofing materials and decorative applications.[34] The EPA requires written notice for the renovation or demolition of any building that contains at least 160 square feet of asbestos-containing materials.[35]

AHERA requires the EPA to establish a comprehensive regulatory framework of inspection, management, planning, operation, and maintenance activities and appropriate abatement responses to control asbestos-containing materials in *schools*. Pursuant to AHERA, the EPA issued a set of guidelines which require all public and private elementary and secondary schools to inspect for friable and nonfriable materials containing more than one per cent asbestos and to take specified action if asbestos is found. No parallel rule applies to other public or commercial buildings.

OSHA regulations govern the handling and disposal of asbestos by private[36] and public[37] sector workers engaged in demolition of buildings, asbestos abatement, renovation projects, emergency clean-ups, and transportation and disposal of asbestos. These *construction standards* establish permissible exposure limits for workers, and standards for exposure monitoring, the removal and disposal of asbestos, communication of asbestos hazards to employees, medical surveillance requirements, and record keeping.

§14.30 —New York State Law

New York State's regulatory scheme centers on the requirement that all individuals who inspect, handle, or supervise the handling of asbestos be trained and certified. All contractors who remove or encapsulate asbestos must be

---

[34] *See* 44 Fed Reg 73127 (Dec 17, 1979) (codified in 40 CFR pt 763); 16 CFR ch II; Fed Reg 29461 (July 12, 1989).

[35] 40 CFR §61.145.

[36] OSHA tit 29 CFR pt 1926.58 (The Construction Standard).

[37] EPA tit 40 CFR pt 763 subpt G.

licensed to do so by the state[38] and must keep certain records for 30 years. The following is a *partial* list of the information that a contractor must record and maintain:

1. The name and address of the asbestos project supervisor
2. The location and description of the asbestos project
3. The amount of asbestos material that was removed, enclosed, encapsulated, or disturbed
4. The starting and completion date of the asbestos project
5. The name and address of the site on which the asbestos material was deposited
6. The name and address of the asbestos transporter; and
7. The name, address, and social security number of all persons who worked on the asbestos project[39]

Further, New York law requires contractors on an asbestos project to give prior written notice to the federal Environmental Protection Agency (EPA) as well as to the New York Department of Labor. The notice must contain, among other things:

1. The name, address, and asbestos-handling license number of the project contractor
2. The address and description of the building involved
3. The location of the asbestos material in the building; and
4. The procedures to be followed by the contractor[40]

As a general rule, the more asbestos involved in the project, the more stringent the regulations that govern its removal, encapsulation, and disposal. State law defines an *asbestos project* and provides narrow exclusions for owner-occupied single family dwellings and *in-plant operations.*[41]

A contractor found to be in violation of any provision of Article 30 §900 *et seq.* of the New York Labor Law may be liable for civil penalties of up to 25% of the contract price. A repeat offender may be liable for penalties of up to 50% of the monetary value of the contract. Each day a violation occurs may be considered a separate violation. The law does provide that consideration shall be given to the size of the contractor's business, its good faith, the gravity of the violation, and any prior violations.[42]

---

[38] NY Lab Law art 30 §900 (McKinney 1988 & Supp 1992).
[39] *Id* §904(1).
[40] *Id* §904(2).
[41] *Id* §901.
[42] *Id* §909(1).

§14.31 —Local Law

In addition to federal and state governments, local governments may regulate asbestos. For instance, in New York City, application of regulations concerning procedures to be followed on an asbestos project depend on the amount of asbestos involved. New York City Department of Environmental Protection regulations require contractors to determine whether a project is an asbestos project and, if it is, to classify it into one of three categories:

1. *Large Asbestos Project:* An asbestos project involving disturbance (e.g., removal, enclosure, or encapsulation) of 260 linear feet or more of friable asbestos-containing material or 160 square feet or more of friable asbestos-containing material

2. *Small Asbestos Project:* An asbestos project involving the disturbance of more than 25 but less than 260 linear feet or more than 10 but less than 160 square feet of friable asbestos-containing material

3. *Minor Asbestos Project:* An asbestos project involving the disturbance of more than three but less than 25 linear feet or more than three but less than 10 square feet of friable asbestos-containing material[43]

A contractor on a *small* or *large asbestos project* must submit an asbestos investigation report with its permit application.[44] This report must include a specific plan for handling the asbestos and a description of the work site, the scope of the work to be performed, and the name of the asbestos abatement contractor who will perform the work. As do state regulations, the city's regulations require that more stringent regulations be followed on projects involving more asbestos. Further, the New York City Department of Environmental Protection is in the process of promulgating more stringent regulations than either the federal or the state governments for the disclosure, certification, and handling of asbestos on demolition and renovation projects.[45]

§14.32 Other Indoor Pollution

Environmental scientists agree that there is roughly three times as much risk from breathing indoor air as there is from breathing outdoor air.[46] The materials within buildings that cause indoor pollution include: asbestos (used in sound and fire insulation), formaldehyde (used in office furniture and building materials), paint, wall, and ceiling materials, fiberglass, adhesives, and caulking. Natural sources of indoor pollution include radon and uranium. Indoor

---

[43] City of New York, Dept of Envtl Protection, Rules and Regulations of the New York City Asbestos Control Program §8100.

[44] NYC Admin Code §27-198.1.

[45] See proposed NYC Bill No 1164 (Introduction No 453 of 1990) and the mayor's version of the bill, Introduction No 471 of 1990.

[46] M. Diamond, *Liability in the Air: The Threat of Indoor Pollution*, ABAJ, Nov 1, 1987, at 78. (quoting Lance Wallace, an environmental scientist for the EPA).

pollution produces a wide range of health disorders from mere headaches, dizziness, and nausea to severe respiratory problems and cancer. These health problems are caused primarily by the known carcinogens: asbestos (discussed previously), radon, formaldehyde, and lead.

Radon

Radon is a radioactive gas that decays naturally. While decaying, radon atoms are transformed into other elements that usually are radioactive and subject to further decay. Radon and its progeny may pose severe health threats because they can continue to decay within the lungs after being inhaled. The Environmental Protection Agency (EPA) ranked radon emission as the greatest environmental cause of lung cancer, although more recent studies indicate that radon may not pose the threat originally believed and that tolerable levels should be modified upwards.[47]

Radon is found in most soils and creeps into homes from the ground. Radon may be present in concrete and brick made from affected rock and soil. Further, both water and natural gas used within homes and buildings may contain radon if they pass through underground areas that contain radon.

Formaldehyde

The main sources of formaldehyde in indoor air are urea formaldehyde insulation, particle board, and plywood. In addition, formaldehyde gas is released from combustion appliances, cigarettes, paper products, floor coverings, fabrics, and other consumer products.

At low levels of exposure, formaldehyde leads to rashes, irritation of the respiratory tract, nausea, headaches, dizziness, and lethargy. It also aggravates bronchial asthma. However, the biggest concern is that doctors suspect that formaldehyde causes cancer.

Lead

Lead contamination is a major indoor pollution concern. In the body it affects heme synthesis and kidney and central nervous system function. The primary concern with lead is when children inadvertently eat lead paint dust. Housing built before 1960 is likely to have lead-based paint on the walls, woodwork, and window frames.

Construction industry employees who work with paints, with solder, or in other occupations with suspected lead exposure should have regular health and safety training and, when removing lead paint, wear half-face respirators with dust filters and disposable coveralls at a minimum. Strict sampling and abatement regulations govern removal of lead paint from all housing controlled or financed by the department of Housing and Urban Development (HUD).

---

[47] Brody, *Some Scientists Say Concern over Radon is Overblown by EPA*, NY Times, Jan 8, 1991, §L (The Environment), at C4, col 1; Leary, *U.S. Study Finds a Reduced Cancer Danger from Radon in Homes*, NY Times, Feb 2, 1991, (National), at 10, col 1.

Grinding, sanding, cleaning, and other activities also release potentially hazardous chemicals into the air. Health hazards linked to chemical fumes range from simple headaches to nasal and respiratory cancer.

Parties Exposed to Liability

Five groups are potentially liable for indoor air pollution: (1) owner/sellers, (2) real estate agents, (3) engineers or land surveyors, (4) private house inspectors, and (5) construction contractors or builders. Although each of these groups may be appropriate defendants in indoor pollution cases, contractors seem to be the most likely defendants because they are most visible, although they are not necessarily in the best position to prevent high accumulations of radon, asbestos, formaldehyde, lead, and other pollutants in the buildings they build or renovate. Owners, architects, and engineers are better able to prevent these problems. The four common law theories typically involved in lawsuits against contractors for injuries resulting from indoor pollution are negligence, products liability,[48] ultrahazardous activity,[49] and implied warranty of habitability.[50]

§14.33 Underground Storage Tanks

Leaking underground storage tanks (USTs) and piping represent a serious and pervasive threat to ground water resources. Congress squarely addressed the environmental dangers associated with UST leaks with the Resource Conservation and Recovery Act (RCRA) Amendments of 1984.[51] These amendments set forth a comprehensive scheme to regulate USTs, including registration;[52] release detection, prevention, and correction;[53] and closure procedures.[54]

New York regulates the bulk storage of both petroleum[55] and hazardous substances.[56] New York's legislation is aimed at the prevention of leaks,[57] the regis-

---

[48] *See* Pearl v Allied Corp, 566 F Supp 400 (ED Pa 1984) (products liability claim based on continuous formaldehyde gas emission from foam insulation).

[49] A contractor may carry out an ultrahazardous activity by building on land with high levels of radon or uranium. *See* Rylands v Fletcher, IR 3 HL 330 (1868); Restatement (Second) of Torts §520 (1989).

[50] *See* Chandler v Madsen, 197 Mont 234, 642 P2d 1028 (1982) (contractor found liable under an implied warranty of habitability for undetected natural defects that caused high levels of indoor pollution in a home).

[51] 42 USC §§6991-6991(i).

[52] 1984 Amendments to RCRA §9002.

[53] 1984 Amendments to RCRA §9003.

[54] 1984 Amendments to RCRA §9003; 52 Fed Reg 48638 §281.33 (Dec 23, 1987).

[55] NY Envtl Conserv Law §17-1001 *et seq* (McKinney 1984 & Supp 1992).

[56] *Id* §40-0101 *et seq.*

[57] NY Comp Codes R & Regs tit 6, §613.3.

tration of facilities,[58] testing and monitoring,[59] proper tank closure,[60] and enforcement.[61]

Increased regulation of underground tanks has led to the repair and replacement of old tanks to meet tough standards of the Environmental Protection Agency (EPA). The building and installation of USTs is a lucrative field for contractors that know what they are doing. However, contractors that do not carefully limit their contractual liability can be held liable for damage to the environment, as well as to the tank, if their installation is faulty.

A contractor may become liable for a tank leak if its contract with the owner contains a broad indemnification clause. The challenge for an installation contractor is to satisfy legitimate requests for indemnification without subjecting itself to future liability for multimillion dollar corrective action projects or third-party tort judgments that may be based on leaks caused by things other than faulty installation. Such judgments may go beyond the cost of tank replacement and include damage caused to third parties and the cost of government-enforced corrective action. Contractors that design or install corrosion protection devices face an even greater risk of liability.

Another concern of excavation contractors is encountering hazardous materials in storage tanks. If the contract allows for termination upon the owner's convenience, such as when unforeseen hazardous wastes are found, the contractor could be out its up-front costs if not provided for in the contract. Excavation contractors would be wise to make sure that their contracts specifically exclude excavation or removal of hazardous wastes, no matter where found.

§14.34 Wetlands

Wetlands are the areas, either coastal or inland, between land and bodies of water. They include salt- and freshwater marshes, swamps, wet meadows, bogs, and flats. Government regulation of wetlands development was undertaken because of their environmental value and the fact that many wetlands are in desirable locations, making them attractive to developers. For instance, coastal wetlands attract water-dependent developments, like ports and industrial uses. Development of wetlands is accomplished through dredging and filling: wetland areas are dredged to provide water channels and the dredged material is used as a foundation for land development. Development of wetlands has become so prevalent that less than half of the country's original 215 million acres of wetlands remain. The EPA estimates that 300,000-to-450,000 acres of wetlands continue to be lost to development annually. In

---

[58] NY Envtl Conserv Law §40-0107 (McKinney 1984 & Supp 1992); NY Comp Codes R & Regs tit 6, §612.2.

[59] NY Envtl Conserv Law §40-0111 (McKinney 1984 & Supp 1992); NY Comp Codes R & Regs tit 6, §613.5.

[60] NY Envtl Conserv Law §17-1005 (McKinney 1984 & Supp 1992); NY Comp Codes R & Regs tit 6, §613.9.

[61] NY Envtl Conserv Law §§17-1941, 40-4303 and 4305 (McKinney 1984 & Supp 1992).

order to prevent the continued accelerated loss of wetlands, regulations at the federal, state, and local level have been enacted.

New York enacted a strict saltwater or Tidal Wetlands Act in 1973[62] and a parallel statute regulating freshwater wetlands in 1975.[63] These state laws precede federal statutes established in the 1977 Amendments to the Clean Water Act, which delegated the program to the states.[64] New York has not sought delegation, but has continued its own programs. Congress has encouraged state wetlands laws which are stricter than federal law, thus making it unlikely that preemption will be implied.[65]

While wetlands are often enticing areas to develop because of their relatively low purchase cost and easily converted topographies, they pose a great risk to the developer. A developer who builds upon a wetland without a required permit could be liable for restoring the area to its original condition, in addition to civil and criminal penalties for each day the wetland is violated. Thus, anyone considering development of wetland properties in New York must become familiar with the Freshwater Wetlands and Tidal Wetlands Acts, both of which use permit systems to regulate development. Many provisions of the two acts are parallel. One major difference is that the freshwater act is enforced by localities; the state steps in only if and when local authorities fail to enact an ordinance protecting their wetlands.[66] In contrast, the Tidal Wetlands Act is administered entirely by the State Department of Health.

Contractors, architects, and engineers must also be attuned to wetland regulation as they may be liable not only pursuant to statute or regulation, but also to a developer for professional malpractice or breach of contract if they design or construct without determining whether the property is a wetland.

Tidal Wetlands

Wetlands subject to regulation under the Tidal Wetlands Act are located in Nassau, Suffolk, Rockland, and Westchester counties and the five boroughs of New York City.[67] Tidal wetlands include not only marshes and salt meadows but also "those areas which border on or lie beneath tidal waters," including bogs, meadows, and "other lowlands subject to tidal action."[68] Artificially created tidal wetlands have been found not to be protected by this statute,[69]

---

[62] NY Envtl Conserv Law §25-0101 et seq (McKinney 1984 & Supp 1992).

[63] Id §24-0101 et seq.

[64] 33 USC §1344(g)(1).

[65] See New York Environmental Law Handbook 190 (N. Robinson ed 1988).

[66] See NY Envtl Conserv Law §24-0501 (McKinney 1984 & Supp 1992).

[67] NY Comp Codes R & Regs tit 6, §661.3.

[68] NY Envtl Conserv Law §25-0103(1) (McKinney 1984 & Supp 1992).

[69] State v Lang, 84 Misc 2d 106, 375 NYS2d 941 (Sup Ct 1975), affd, 52 AD2d 921, 383 NYS2d 400 (2d Dept 1976) (defendant's land was inundated at high tide due to a state-built drainage culvert).

although more recent cases allow their regulation.[70]

The New York Department of Environmental Conservation (DEC) was required to complete a tentative tidal wetlands map, hold public hearings on the tentative map, and issue a final tidal wetlands map for filing. These "final" wetlands inventory maps were adopted on September 14, 1977, and are available to the public at the DEC's regional offices.[71] Maps may be amended.[72]

The Tidal Wetlands Act regulates the following actions, whether directly or indirectly caused: draining, dredging, excavating, removal, dumping, filling, and depositing of any soil, stones, sand, gravel, mud, rubbish, or other aggregate; erection of structures or construction of facilities or roads, the driving of any pilings or placing of any other obstructions, whether or not changing the ebb and flow of the tide; any form of pollution; subdividing of land in any tidal wetland or adjacent area; and any other new activity within a tidal wetland or on an adjacent area which may "substantially alter or impair the natural condition or function of the tidal wetland."[73] Since basically all types of construction are covered by the Tidal Wetlands Act, a developer must know the locations of wetlands and applicable regulations and mappings of tidal wetlands at state, county, and local levels.

When considering development of a property, investigation is required to determine if the property is a tidal wetland or adjacent to one. If the property is designated as a wetland on the Tidal Inventory Map, the developer must either apply for a development permit or petition the DEC to remove the land from the wetland map. As DEC regulation of tidal wetlands does not preclude application of local statutes, local requirements must be adhered to as well.

A person wishing to undertake a regulated activity in a tidal wetlands area must obtain either a permit or a notification letter of approval from the DEC.[74] An activity that the DEC characterizes as *generally compatible* with the tidal wetland may require either a permit or a notification letter, depending upon the particular activity, while an activity designated as *incompatible* always requires

---

[70] Gazza v New York Dept of Envtl Conservation, 139 AD2d 647, 527 NYS2d 285 (2d Dept 1988); Jack Coletta, Inc v New York Dept of Envtl Conservation, 128 AD2d 755, 513 NYS2d 465 (2d Dept), *appeal denied* 70 NY2d 602, 512 NE2d 551, 518 NYS2d 1025 (1987).

[71] NY Envtl Conserv Law §25-0201 (McKinney 1984 & Supp 1992); NY Comp Codes R & Regs tit 6, §661.27(a).

[72] NY Envtl Conserv Law §25-0201(3)(5) (McKinney 1984 & Supp 1992); NY Comp Codes R & Regs tit 6, §661.27; *see* Merrick Jewish Centre, Inc v New York Dept of Envtl Conservation, 128 AD2d 877, 513 NYS2d 799 (2d Dept 1987) and Jack Coletta, Inc v New York Dept of Envtl Conservation, 128 AD2d 755, 513 NYS2d 465 (2d Dept), *appeal denied*, 70 NY2d 602, 512 NE2d 551, 518 NYS2d 1025 (1987) (DEC legally remapped a tidal wetlands map upon the discovery of tidal inundation and changes in vegetation); Thompson v New York Dept of Envtl Conservation, 130 Misc 2d 123, 495 NYS2d 107, *affd*, 132 AD2d 665, 518 NYS2d 36, *appeal denied* 71 NY2d 803, 522 NE2d 1067, 527 NYS2d 769 (1988) (DEC Commissioner possesses authority to alter a wetlands inventory map at any time; an applicant for a wetlands permit is subject to any duly revised boundaries).

[73] NY Comp Codes R & Regs tit 6, §661.4 (ee)(1) (1992).

[74] NY Envtl Conserv Law §25-0401(1) (McKinney 1984 & Supp 1992).

a permit.[75] Generally, every type of construction upon a tidal wetland requires a permit.

Freshwater Wetlands

The Freshwater Wetlands Act[76] calls for the balancing of critical environmental concerns for protecting freshwater wetlands with legitimate practical needs of economic, social, and agricultural development. Development is limited to *beneficial development,* i.e., it must benefit economic, social, or agricultural interests to offset environmental concerns.[77]

Freshwater wetlands include: marshes, swamps, sloughs, bogs, and flats[78] that are 12.4 acres or more or that have unusual local importance for one or more specific benefits.[79] Even if the property upon which development is planned is less than 12.4 acres—and, thus, may not be on state or local freshwater wetlands maps—it still may be regulated locally. The Freshwater Wetlands Act applies to artificially created and natural freshwater wetlands.[80]

Freshwater wetlands are subject to rigorous regulation, with certain uses permitted as of right and others allowed only by permit. Uses as of right include recreational or commercial fishing, aquaculture, hunting and trapping, grazing and watering livestock, harvesting natural products of the land, selective cutting of timber, and draining and other use of the land for growing agricultural products.[81] Activities upon wetlands not *expressly* allowed as of right may be conducted only by permit.[82]

The Freshwater Wetlands Act regulates the following actions, whether direct or indirect: draining, dredging, excavation, dumping, filling, erecting any structures, constructing roads, and driving pilings or placing any other obstructions, whether or not changing the ebb and flow of the water.[83]

There are final freshwater wetlands maps for all counties except the Adirondack Park, New York City, and Essex, Otsego, Suffolk, and Ulster counties.[84] Wetlands within the Adirondack Park are regulated separately.[85] In New York City, Staten Island is the only borough with a final freshwater wetlands map in place. The absence of a final map does not mean that the wetland is not subject to the act. Any landowner or contractor who is unaware of the status

---

[75] NY Comp Codes R & Regs tit 6, §661.5(a)(2), (3).

[76] NY Envtl Conserv Law §24-0101 *et seq* (McKinney 1984 & Supp 1992).

[77] *Id* §§24-0101, -0103; Spears v Berle, 48 NY2d 254, 397 NE2d 1304, 422 NYS2d 636 (1979).

[78] NY Envtl Conserv Law §24-0107 (McKinney 1984 & Supp 1992).

[79] *Id* §24-0301(1); Goldhirsh v Flacke, 114 AD2d 998, 495 NYS2d 436 (2d Dept 1985).

[80] *In re* Rappl & Hoening Co v New York Dept of Envtl Conservation, 61 AD2d 20, 401 NYS2d 346 (4th Dept 1978), *affd,* 47 NY2d 925, 393 NE2d 485, 419 NYS2d 490 (1979).

[81] NY Envtl Conserv Law §24-0701(3), (4) (McKinney 1984 & Supp 1992).

[82] *Id* §§24-0703(4), -0705(3).

[83] *Id* §24-0105; NY Comp Codes R & Regs tit 6, §663.2(Z).

[84] New York Environmental Handbook, *supra* note 65.

[85] *See* NY Envtl Conserv Law §24-0801 *et seq* (McKinney 1984 & Supp 1992).

of a particular parcel of land may make a written inquiry to the DEC, which, in turn, must respond, in writing, within 30 days.[86] Final maps are kept "in the office of the Clerk where each such wetland, or a portion thereof, is located."[87]

The Freshwater Wetlands Act requires that any person wishing to conduct a regulated activity in a freshwater wetland area obtain either a permit or a letter of permission.[88] Permits are required whether the wetland map is interim or final[89] or, indeed, whether or not there is a map. A locally declared freshwater wetlands area need not be designated on a map to be regulated locally.[90] Thus, before purchasing land or constructing upon suspected wetlands, it is wise to receive written approval from the local government.[91]

§14.35 Trial Preparation

Without thorough discovery and preparation, multiparty litigation, such as Superfund[92] and other environmental cases, easily flounders. Even when the federal government utilizes its substantial discovery and investigatory powers, the sheer number of parties and factual issues can gridlock case progress. Thus, it is important to carefully plan the prosecution and defense of such cases, closely monitor their progression, and avoid needless argument over barely relevant side issues that serve only to increase time and fees and fail to resolve the central issue of responsibility.

In order to avoid a case dragging on for years, the government or other major party should file a *case management order*. In the order, a party may seek bifurcation of liability and damages issues; a time limitation on discovery; a limit to the number of interrogatories each party may submit; a stay of discovery by third-party defendants against the government; and appointment of a committee of defendants to respond to generic issues. A comprehensive and ambitious case management order will include a complete pre-trial schedule setting out periods for discovery, requests for admissions, and filing of dispositive motions. In a complex case, a two-year pre-trial period is not unreasonable.

Generally, the government prefers an expeditious schedule, while defendants have little to gain by this approach; confusion and delay may be helpful to the defendants. Further, delay may provide a defendant with an opportunity to research the site more thoroughly. Typically, the government collects a formidable array of documentation before its complaint is filed. Conversely, many private parties are likely to know only their own small slice of site history.

---

[86] *Id* §24-0703(5).

[87] Id §24-0301(5).

[88] *Id* §24-0701(1).

[89] Wedinger v Goldberger, 71 NY2d 428, 522 NE2d 25, 527 NYS2d 180, *cert denied*, 488 US 850 (1988).

[90] Drexler v Town of New Castle, 62 NY2d 413, 465 NE2d 836, 477 NYS2d 116 (1984).

[91] NY Envtl Conserv Law §24-0501(4) (McKinney 1984 & Supp 1992); Drexler v Town of New Castle, 62 NY2d 413, 465 NE2d 836, 477 NYS2d 116 (1984).

[92] *See* §14.05.

Use of a special master is often wise, especially in a Superfund case, to avoid day-to-day dealings with the court. The government may oppose an appointment, often on grounds of cost. The expense of the special master is normally split between the parties.

The ability to limit issues is essential to the progress of the government's case; dispositive motions are often used in this regard. The three most commonly used motions are those to strike affirmative defenses, for summary judgment, and *in limine*.

§14.36 —Obtaining Documents

In addition to traditional discovery techniques available under the rules of civil procedure, records may be obtained from a government body or public authority through the use of the New York State Freedom of Information Law[93] and the Federal Freedom of Information[94] and Privacy Acts.[95] These acts are discussed more thoroughly in Chapter 16 on dispute resolution.

New York law provides that each agency shall make *all* records available for public inspection and copying, except those in specific categories.[96] Access to agency records is not affected by litigation between the government and the party requesting the records.[97] Federal laws also provide that all records shall be made available except those that have been exempted.[98]

§14.37 —Personal Liability for Environmental Risks

It has become clear that the Environmental Protection Agency (EPA) and other regulatory agencies have determined that enforcement efforts will be taken seriously only if officers and high-ranking employees of those regulated are held personally accountable. There are various ways personal civil and criminal liability may be found, including:

> 1. Under Federal Securities Laws: Liability derives from disclosure requirements regarding material legal proceedings and contingent liabilities in corporate annual financial statements. Failure of a corporation to disclose material environmental risks in its annual financial statements may lead to liability.[99]

---

[93] Article 6 of the NY Pub Off Law §84 *et seq.*

[94] 5 USC §552.

[95] *Id* §552a.

[96] The exceptions are listed in NY Pub Off Law §87(2).

[97] M. Farbman & Sons v New York City Health & Hosps, 62 NY2d 75, 464 NE2d 437, 476 NYS2d 69 (1984).

[98] The exemptions are listed at 5 USC §552(b).

[99] *See* Reg S-K, 17 CFR §229.

§14.37 PERSONAL LIABILITY   529

2. There are three other major ways an individual can become liable:[100]

a. Make a mistake: fail to do something required or do something that should not have been done:

(1) Innocently or intentionally ignore reporting requirements for discharges;

(2) Act as a facility operator when a spill was caused through direct action. Contractors and other construction parties may become individually liable as owners or operators if they are joint venturers in plants that discharge toxins[101] or developers of contaminated property.[102]

b. Be in charge: one in charge of a facility, regardless of knowledge, may be personally liable.[103]

c. Sign something:[104]

(1) Many businesses require environmental permits, most commonly for air or water discharges. The application for the permit and required related reports can give rise to personal liability if they contain false information or omit material information.[105]

(2) The courts have found a duty to inquire; personal liability

---

[100] Individuals may become liable without piercing the corporate veil under CERCLA, 42 USC §§9601(21), 9607(a), which provides for personal liability of those who participate in wrongful activity. *See also* United States v Northeastern Pharmaceutical & Chem Co, 810 F2d 726 (8th Cir 1986), *cert denied*, 484 US 848, 108 S Ct 146 (1987); New York v Shore Realty, 759 F2d 1032 (2d Cir 1985).

[101] Edward Hines Lumber Co v Vulcan Materials Co, 861 F2d 155 (7th Cir 1988).

[102] Tanglewood E Homeowners v Charles-Thomas, Inc, 849 F2d 1568 (5th Cir 1988).

[103] United States v Northeastern Pharmaceutical & Chem Co, 810 F2d 726 (8th Cir 1986), *cert denied*, 484 US 848, 108 S Ct 146 (1987) (corporate president and vice president, who were also major stockholders, found liable for arranging disposal and transportation of hazardous waste); United States v Pollution Abatement Servs, 763 F2d 133 (2d Cir) (officers found liable for clean-up of waste site when court found they had authority and responsibility to prevent and correct violations but failed to do so), *cert denied*, 474 US 1037, 106 S Ct 605 (1985); United States v Scardi, 20 Envt Rep Cas (BNA) 1753 (DNC 1984) (officer liable where he personally participated in hazardous waste disposal activities). In United States v Wade, 577 F Supp 1326 (ED Pa 1983), the court held that a corporate officer is personally liable if he or she participates in wrongful conduct. An employee need not have management responsibility to be criminally liable. *See* United States v Johnson & Towers, 741 F2d 662 (3d Cir 1984), *cert denied*, 469 US 1208, 105 S Ct 1171, 84 L Ed 321 (1985).

[104] 18 USC §1001 provides criminal sanctions for giving false information on items such as permit applications.

[105] Resource Conservation and Recovery Act §3008(d)(3), 42 USC §§6298(d)(3), 9603(d)(2).

may be found against a signatory for falsely certifying or failing to make proper inquiry.[106]

Criminal Liability

A corporate officer or other responsible person may be held criminally liable under the Clean Water Act for knowingly violating discharge requirements, knowingly making false statements or representations, and knowing endangerment (placing a person in imminent danger of serious bodily harm or death).[107] Similarly, under the Clean Air Act, an officer or other responsible person may be held criminally liable for knowing violation of emission limits and knowingly making false statements.[108] Criminal sanctions are also provided for in the Resource Conservation and Recovery Act,[109] Superfund,[110] and other federal and state laws.

In determining whether criminal liability should apply, prosecutors look at the company's past operations and the officer's involvement with the violation at issue,[111] although personal involvement is not required.[112]

§14.38 Superfund Litigation

Superfund[113] litigation typically is complex and involves multiple parties. Perhaps the most difficult and complex part of the Superfund action is locating potentially responsible parties. Often, a great deal of detective work is required before it can be determined who generated the waste and who transported it to the site. Incomplete records increase the difficulty of locating responsible parties, a difficulty often compounded if a site was abandoned years ago or a major party has dissolved or is bankrupt.

Once the government identifies and locates the parties, the Department of Justice will produce a complaint. A typical complaint will contain a cause of action for recovery of costs expended by the government in bringing the action

---

[106] 18 USC §1001 provides criminal sanctions for giving false information on items such as permit applications. *See also* United States v Park, 421 US 658, 95 S Ct 1903, 44 L Ed 2d 489 (1975); United States v Frezzo Bros, 602 F2d 1123 (3d Cir 1979), *cert denied*, 444 US 1074 (1980) (officers held vicariously liable under respondeat superior theory).

[107] Water Quality Act §312(c)(4) (1987); Clean Water Act §309.

[108] 42 USC §7413.

[109] *Id* §9603.

[110] *Id* §9612.

[111] In Illinois v O'Neil, 194 Ill App 3d 79, 550 NE2d 1090, *cert denied*, 553 NE2d 400 (1990), three corporate officials were convicted of manslaughter when the company failed to protect its workers from highly toxic fumes despite repeated warnings by regulatory officials.

[112] In United States v Park, 421 US 658, 95 S Ct 1903, 44 L Ed 2d 489 (1975), a corporate officer was criminally convicted even though he did not participate directly in the criminal acts. The Court established the following test for criminal liability of a corporate officer: the officer must be "responsible" for the action that constitutes the crime and must have had the ability to prevent the criminal action.

[113] *See* §§14.05, 14.26, and 14.27.

and for declaratory judgment; for costs it expects to expend in the future;[114] to obtain an order requiring that the defendants perform remedial action at the site;[115] and, possibly, for injunctive relief to abate any endangerment of the site.[116]

The government's case consists of background witnesses to explain the history of the site and the government's response to the problems at the site; fact witnesses to establish the linkage between the waste generator and the disposal at the site; and a summary expert witness to review the depositions, requests for admissions, and sampling data, and conclude that substances of the kind generated by the waste generator are found at the site. The government may also use specialty expert witnesses, such as hydrologists, soil scientists, and toxicologists, if it intends to prove public endangerment.[117] Further, if the government wishes to prove natural resource damage, it will use experts to prove the extent of the damage and the estimated cost of restoration.

§14.39 —Defenses

A limited number of defenses are available to potentially responsible parties in Superfund litigation.[118] These affirmative defenses include that the release or threatened release was caused by an act of God or war. Under such circumstances, neither the owners, operators, generators, nor transporters may be held liable. In addition, a "third party" defense is available, at least theoretically, to a party that can establish that it purchased property on which hazardous wastes were placed by others, that it did not add any further wastes, and that it used "due care."[119] Further, liability may be avoided if it can be established that the release was caused solely by "an act or omission of a third party other than an employee or agent of the defendant . . .," that the defendant "exercised due care with respect to the hazardous substance concerned . . .," and that the defendant "took precautions against foreseeable acts or omissions of any such third party and the consequences that could foreseeably result from such acts or omission."[120]

Another facet of the third party defense is the "good faith owner" defense. To determine whether an owner of land is a "good faith" owner under the statute, the courts have considered whether the present owner knew or had reason to know that the property held hazardous wastes. The courts' "had reason to know" language indicates a case-by-case consideration of what is required of the defendant, rather than a rigid rule which sets forth specific steps

---

[114] §107(a).

[115] §106(a).

[116] RCRA §7003.

[117] Id.

[118] See 42 USC §9607(b). See §§14.05, 14.26, 14.27, and 14.38.

[119] 42 USC §9607(b)(3); 15 Envtl L Rep (Envtl L Inst), at 20,994. This exception has been called the "innocent landowner" exception.

[120] 42 USC §9607(b)(3).

a party must take to avoid liability. First, the court looks to the circumstances of the case to determine what facts were known or reasonably should have been known by the defendant. Second, the court examines whether, in light of what a reasonably prudent defendant would know under the circumstances, the defendant in fact exercised the requisite due care.[121] The test is one of foreseeability.[122]

Other defenses include: that there is not a hazardous substance on the site;[123] that an action does not constitute a release or threatened release; that the site in question is not a facility; that the defendant is not a person whom the statute covers; and that the deposit was de minimis. None of these defenses has been particularly successful.[124]

In general, equitable factors are considered by the courts in the apportioning of liability between defendants, but not as a complete bar to a liability action.[125] Thus, while CERCLA does not *per se* prohibit the equitable defenses of waiver and laches, they are generally unavailable against the United States when the government is acting to enforce a public right.[126] Further, issues of innocence and clean hands are relevant only as to apportionment of costs and the amount of response costs that the government may recover, and will not bar a government claim, even where the government contributed to the waste.[127]

An indemnification clause will not affect the government's right to sue a liable party,[128] but may allow a party to recover from another party.[129] Thus, indemnification contracts may give a site buyer a cause of action against its seller for reimbursement of costs incurred due to the violation of an environmental statute.

Superfund Amendments and Reauthorization Act of 1986 §9619(a) does limit the liability of response action contractors to circumstances in which their "negligent, grossly negligent, or . . . intentional misconduct" causes the release of the hazardous substance. Nevertheless, contractors may be subject to strict

---

[121] Jersey City Redevelopment Auth v PPG Indus, 665 F Supp 1257 (DNJ 1987); *see* United States v Maryland Bank & Trust Co, 632 F Supp 573, 581 (D Md 1986); New York v Shore Realty Corp, 759 F2d 1033, 1049 (2d Cir 1985).

[122] *See* Gibney, *The Practical Significance of the Third Party Defense under CERCLA*, 16 BC Envtl Aff L Rev 383 (1988).

[123] 42 USC §§9601(14), 9607.

[124] *See* Gibney, *supra* note 122; *Superfund and SARA: Are There Any Defenses Left?*, 12 Harv Envtl L Rev 385 (1988).

[125] United States v Conservation Chem Co, 628 F Supp 391 (WD Mo 1985).

[126] United States v Dickerson, 640 F Supp 448 (D Md 1986); Mardan Corp v GGC Music, Ltd, 600 F Supp 1049 (D Ariz 1984), *aff'd*, 804 F2d 1454 (9th Cir 1986).

[127] United States v Conservation Chem Co, 628 F Supp 391 (WD Mo 1985); Chemical Waste Management, Inc v Armstrong World Indus, 669 F Supp 1285, 1292 (ED Pa 1987).

[128] 42 USC §9607(e)(1).

[129] Mardan Corp v GGC Music, Ltd, 600 F Supp 1049 (D Ariz 1984), *aff'd*, 804 F2d 1454 (9th Cir 1986).

liability under state law. State law liability may be mitigated, however, by indemnification from the federal government if the contractor is unable to obtain adequate liability insurance "at a fair and reasonable price."[130]

Bankruptcy generally does not insulate a party from Superfund liability. The United States Supreme Court held in *Ohio v Kovacs*[131] that *any* party in possession of property, including a bankruptcy trustee and receiver, has an affirmative obligation to comply with all laws respecting property that were designed to protect public health or safety. In *Midatlantic National Bank v New Jersey Department of Environmental Protection*,[132] the Court extended *Kovacs* by holding that a bankruptcy trustee cannot abandon a property that is in violation of laws designed to protect public health and safety. These two cases, in effect, require bankruptcy trustees to clean up hazardous waste situations created by a bankrupt.

§14.40 —Consent Decrees

The government may settle a Superfund[133] case through a consent decree. A consent decree is not an express confession of liability. There are two primary types of consent decrees: *cash outs* and *response action* agreements.[134]

In a *cash out* settlement, the defendant agrees to pay all or a portion of the cost of the response action that the government has determined is appropriate.

In a *response action* decree, the defendant agrees to partially or wholly clean up the site. These decrees are the most complex type of consent decree and require that certain related documents be drafted. These documents may include:

1. A "Work Plan" specifying the activities to be undertaken and a schedule of completion dates
2. A mechanism to pay abatement contractor(s)
3. A trust to oversee the work of the contractor(s)
4. A dispute resolution provision that provides a period in which the parties may resolve their dispute through negotiation; if a dispute is not resolved, then either party may petition the court for a hearing
5. A *force majeure clause* that narrowly defines those circumstances that will excuse performance; and
6. A covenant by the government not to sue a party[135]

---

[130] SARA §9619(a).
[131] 469 US 274, 105 S Ct 705, 83 L Ed 2d 649 (1985).
[132] 474 US 494, 106 S Ct 755, 88 L Ed 2d 859 (1986).
[133] See §§14.05, 14.26, 14.27, 14.38, and 14.39.
[134] *See* Jones, *Drafting CERCLA Consent Decrees*, 3 Nat Resources & Envt 31 (1988).
[135] SARA §9627(f).

§14.41 Alternative Dispute Resolution

With the passage of a massive volume of new environmental legislation and the development of common law doctrines that create new areas of environmental responsibility, federal and state courts might expect an onslaught of new and complex cases, many of which, in terms of the volume of documents, witnesses, and parties involved, resemble antitrust, construction contract, or other large and protracted commercial litigation.

There are problems and benefits associated with each form of dispute resolution, especially in the environmental area. At the outset, it is important to remember that if the parties do not select another method to resolve disputes, the disputes will be heard by a court. Almost any environmental matter is amenable to alternative dispute resolution, including: Superfund[136] and RCRA[137] clean-up determination of who is responsible and each party's clean-up liability; asbestos personal injury and property damage; land use planning issues, including whether a developer is allowed to build on a site and, if so, what the developer is allowed to build; government enforcement; and breach of contract claims concerning the obligations of parties who have contracted to abate a hazardous waste problem. The general pros and cons of various alternative dispute resolution techniques are discussed in Chapter 16.

§14.42 —The EPA

The Environmental Protection Agency (EPA) has recognized the value of alternative dispute resolution (ADR) and has taken steps to implement ADR procedures for handling agency cases. The following information was adapted from an article written by Terrell E. Hunt.[138]

The increasing number of cases on the EPA's enforcement and defensive litigation dockets, the long average life of a case, and the complexity of issues and interests being litigated suggest an urgent need for the EPA to find innovative ways to manage the case resolution process. Over the past 3 years, 95 per cent of all enforcement and defensive litigation cases have been resolved by negotiated settlement. Specific procedures have been adopted to foster settle-

---

[136] See §14.05.

[137] See §14.04.

[138] Mr. Hunt is a partner in the Houston, Texas office of Bracewell and Patterson. Before joining Bracewell and Patterson, Mr. Hunt worked for the EPA for 18 years where he served as Director of EPA's Office of Enforcement Policy, Associate Enforcement Counsel for Air Enforcement, Associate Enforcement Counsel for Criminal Enforcement, and in other capacities. A graduate of Brigham Young University and the Georgetown University Law Center, Mr. Hunt is an author and frequent lecturer on environmental compliance, criminal enforcement, and environmental risk management.

The article, Terrell E. Hunt, *Innovative Settlement Techniques: Use of Alternative Dispute Resolution Tools in Resolving Environmental Litigation*, was published in Envtl Mgmt Rev No 7 (1989), and is reprinted here with the permission of the author.

ment of cases before they are formally referred to the Department of Justice for filing.[139]

The EPA envisions using alternative dispute resolution in a broad range of litigation-related matters. Recent guidance instructed EPA regional officials to consider using neutral persons to resolve:

1. Defensive and enforcement litigation
2. Not yet filed and filed cases
3. Administrative and civil judicial cases
4. Technically complex and routine matters; and
5. Any case that appears to be at an impasse or is suffering from delay or inattention by the parties or court[140]

Cases That the EPA Deems Inappropriate for ADR

The government recognizes the important function of environmental litigation in clarifying legal requirements, prescribing what is and is not lawful conduct, and defining the rights and responsibilities of parties under the law.[141] Accordingly, the government will seek to obtain judicial rulings in a relatively select body of cases in which:

1. Precedential issues of regulatory policy, application of the law, or constitutionality are raised
2. Specific performance, injunctive, or other court-supervised relief is needed
3. Immediate action is required to prevent or abate conditions that may present an imminent hazard to health or the environment
4. Where ADR materially benefits one party by slowing the process because it is suggested at a time when it will cause a temporary hiatus in a case proceeding to resolution
5. Witness credibility is pivotal to understanding the facts of the case; or
6. The conduct of a party is so egregious as to warrant the imposition of harsh and visible sanctions[142]

---

[139] Memorandum, T.L. Adams, Jr., Process for Conducting Pre-referral Settlement Negotiations on Civil Judicial Enforcement Cases (Apr 13, 1988). Note that the EPA and DOJ are simultaneously considering the more aggressive use of a nonsettlement, "litigation track" for selected cases that raise policy or legal issues of first impression; whose facts are uniquely favorable to the government; or that reflect conduct that warrants harsh and uncompromising punishment.

[140] Memorandum, Thomas L. Adams, Jr., Follow-Up on ADR (Feb 12, 1988), at 2.

[141] See C. E. Dinkins, *Shall We Fight or Will We Finish: Environmental Dispute Resolution in a Litigious Society*, 14 Envtl L Rev 10398 (1984).

[142] Memorandum, T. Hunt, Proposed Elements of a Regional Pilot on Innovative Approaches to Dispute Resolution, (Mar 15, 1988), at 129; Mays, *Alternative Dispute Resolution and Environmental Enforcement*, 18 Envtl L Rev 10087 (1988).

The EPA's Program to Utilize ADR to Resolve Enforcement and Defensive Cases

The EPA issued final guidance encouraging agency enforcement staff to creatively consider the use of ADR in resolving enforcement actions.[143] This guidance provides criteria on the types of cases for which ADR may be appropriate, establishes internal procedures for the selection of ADR cases, sets detailed qualifications and ethical standards for the selection of neutrals, and provides for the payment of the EPA's share of the cost of ADR. It also includes, as appendices, detailed guidance on the use of each of the primary ADR techniques and provides model ADR agreements for each technique.

The guidance clearly points out that the EPA views ADR as a means of resolving enforcement disputes more efficiently. The EPA's willingness to consider ADR does *not* imply that it would settle a case using ADR on terms that are less favorable to the agency or less protective of the environment than it would accept if the case were resolved by the familiar approach of litigation and negotiation.

The following types of cases have been suggested for expedited handling.[144] None of these, or any other, types of cases have been designated by the EPA for presumptive ADR.

1. Small Superfund cost recovery cases. The 1986 Superfund amendments authorize the EPA to engage in arbitration to resolve cost recovery claims under $500,000.[145] This might best be used where the only issues are the amount and applicability of reimbursable costs and the allocation of such costs among a discrete group of parties.

2. "Routine" violations of National Pollutant Discharge Elimination System Permits discharge limits. Cases raising neither factual disputes nor issues of law or policy may not warrant the cost of protracted litigation.

3. Violations of preexisting settlement agreements by "nonmajor" municipalities.

4. Inactive or stalled cases in any substantive area.

5. Wetlands cases.

6. Instances of environmental noncompliance at federal facilities.

---

[143] Lee M. Thomas, *Final Guidance on the Use of Alternative Dispute Resolution in EPA Enforcement Cases*, Administrator, Aug 14, 1987.

[144] Mr. Hunt notes that of the case categories discussed, none has in fact been designated for presumptive handling through alternative means. At press time, the agency was in the process of identifying such categories and determining how a selected category might best be handled.

[145] 42 USC §9622(h)(2).

§14.43 —Using ADR in Environmental Litigation

Superfund and RCRA

In Superfund[146] and RCRA[147] multiple party clean-ups cases, alternative dispute resolution (ADR) is often appropriate as there are many parties involved who have not previously negotiated together, and there is typically a wide disparity of power and resources between the parties. It is anticipated that ADR will be utilized extensively in this field.

Asbestos Personal Injury Suits

The Asbestos Claims Facility has used ADR in a number of contexts, including helping to resolve disputes between producers and insurers. Plaintiffs submit their claims directly to the facility for possible settlement. Once a settlement offer is made, and rejected by the plaintiff, a variety of ADR procedures can be undertaken. A formal ADR procedure has been implemented for cases involving serious injury, total disability, and death. It should be kept in mind that punitive damages are excluded from this process. The Manville Personal Injury Settlement Trust provides for mediation and arbitration.

Asbestos Property Damage Suits

There is some doubt as to the effectiveness of ADR in property damage litigation. Asbestos property damage claims are relatively new and untried. Thus, many defendants are not inclined to settle these claims. Once more plaintiffs' verdicts are recovered for property damage, it is likely that ADR will be used more often. The chance for punitive damages may provide plaintiffs with an impetus to try these cases to conclusion.

Land Use Planning Disputes

ADR can be used to streamline the process by which developers and municipalities can determine whether a developer should be allowed to build at its chosen location and, if so, what it should be allowed to build. ADR can be used effectively to make decisions before a developer spends substantial sums on a project it may not be allowed to build.

§14.44 References

The volume of environmental material is immense. Some publications that are of use in construction-related environmental matters are listed here. This list is by no means exhaustive.

M. Glazerman, *Asbestos in Commercial Buildings: Obligations and Responsibilities of Landlords and Tenants*, 22 Real Prop, Prob, & Trade J 661 (1987)

---

[146] *See* §14.05.
[147] *See* §14.04.

Asbestos Monitor Newsletter

Boston College Environmental Affairs Law Review

F. Skillern, *Environmental Protection: The Legal Framework*, (McGraw-Hill, Inc 1981)

Harvard Environmental Law Review

T. Burke & L. Phillips, *Hazard Communication: An Interim Guide for the Construction Industry* (published by the American Subcontractors Association, Associated Builders and Contractors, & National Association of Home Builders, 1988)

Hazardous Waste Disposal and Underground Construction Law (R. Cushman & B. Ficken eds 1987)

L. Italiano, *Liability for Underground Storage Tanks* (1987) (PLI)

J. Machlin & T. Young, *Managing Environmental Risk Real Estate and Business Transactions* (1988)

New York State Environmental Law Handbook (N. Robinson ed 1988)

C. Schraff & R. Steinberg, *RCRA & Superfund: A Practice Guide with Forms* (1988)

Temple Environmental Law & Technology Journal

UCLA Journal of Environmental Law & Policy

Virginia Environmental Law Journal

Susan M. Cooke, *The Law of Hazardous Waste: Management, Cleanup, Liability and Litigation* (Matthew Bender 1991) (3 volumes)

Frank P. Grad, *Treatise on Environmental Law*, (Matthew Bender, 1991) (4 volumes)

Nicholas A. Robinson, *New York Environmental Law Handbook*, New York State Bar Assn (1988)

William A. Hancock, *Corporate Counsel's Guide to Environmental Law* (Business Laws, Inc 1990)

Robert F. Cushman & Bruce W. Ficken, *Hazardous Waste Disposal and Underground Construction Law* (John Wiley & Sons 1987)

Robert F. Cushman & John W. DiNicola, *Construction Renovation Formbook* (John Wiley & Sons 1991)

Nicholas A. Robinson, *Environmental Regulation of Real Property* (Law Journal Seminar Press 1990)

Marburg Associates & William P. Parkin, *Site Auditing: Environmental Assessment of Property* (STP Specialty Technical Publishers, Inc 1991)

Lawrence P. Postol, *Legal Guide to Handling Toxic Substances in The Workplace* (Business Laws, Inc 1990)

Berle, Kass & Case, *Environmental Law In New York Newsletter* (Matthew Bender 19__)

William A. Hancock, *Corporate Counsel's Guide: Environmental Law Newsletter* (Business Laws, Inc 19__)

Environmental Reporter: A Weekly Review of Pollution Control and Related Environmental Management Problems, (Bureau of National Affairs, Inc)

Toxic Law Reporter: A Weekly Review of Toxic Torts, Hazardous Waste and Insurance Litigation, (Bureau of National Affairs, Inc)

John E. Osborn & Paul R. Schreyer, *Dealing With Environmental Risks in Construction Contracts,* Construction Specifier 8 (July 1988)

John E. Osborn & Paul R. Schreyer, *Asbestos Abatement Contractor Agreements,* Natl Insulation & Abatement Contractors' Assn Outlook Mag, July 1989, at 29

John E. Osborn, *Voice: Developing A Standard Form of Asbestos Agreement,* Natl Insulation & Abatement Contractors' Assn Outlook Mag, Nov 1989, at 84

The ASIC Contract Reference Guide (2d ed 1986)

The NIAC Owner-Contractor Asbestos Agreement Guide (2d ed 1990)

John E. Osborn, *Alternative Dispute Resolution and Asbestos,* Natl Insulation & Abatement Contractors' Assn Outlook Mag, Apr 1990, at 48

Frank P. Grad, *Alternative Dispute Resolution in Environmental Law,* 14 Colum J Envtl L 157 (1989)

Gary F. Bennett, Frank S. Feates & Ira Wilder, *Hazardous Spills Handbook* (McGraw-Hill Book Company 1982)

The EPA maintains an extensive collection of EPA-authored publications that may be obtained from:

EPA Public Information Center
401 M Street, SW, (PM-211B)
Washington, DC 20460

Appendix 14-1

Developer's Environmental Risk Checklist

To evaluate the risk of the presence of hazardous substances on a vacant lot, a developer might do the following prior to purchasing the site:

1. Visit the site
2. Question prior owners concerning past uses of the property
3. Speak with adjacent landowners or occupants, local business owners, and others concerning past uses of the property
4. Determine whether the property is listed on any hazardous waste site register
5. Determine whether local regulations require underground tank registration, and if so, whether a tank has been registered in connection with the property
6. Engage an environmental engineering firm to investigate the site to determine whether any hazardous substance is present, and if so, to what degree

Remedies/Damages 15

§15.01 Article 78
§15.02 —Procedure
§15.03 —Article 78 in Construction Cases
§15.04 —Standard of Review
§15.05 Injunctions
§15.06 —Preliminary Injunctions
§15.07 —Permanent Injunctions
§15.08 Declaratory Judgment
§15.09 Accounting
§15.10 Breach of Contract v Quantum Meruit
§15.11 Fraud
§15.12 Punitive Damages
§15.13 —Public Contracts
§15.14 Attorneys' Fees
§15.15 Interest
§15.16 Noncontractual Limitations on Damages
§15.17 —Mitigation
§15.18 —Collateral Source Rule
§15.19 —Certainty
§15.20 —Economic Loss Rule
§15.21 UCC Damage and Remedy Provisions
§15.22 Contractual Limitations on Damages
§15.23 Contractual Provisions Regarding Remedies
§15.24 Specific Breaches by Contractor
§15.25 —Failure to Commence Performance
§15.26 —Partial Performance
§15.27 —Substantial Performance
§15.28 —Defective Performance

§15.29 —Cost of Completion v Diminution in Value
§15.30 Specific Breaches by Owner
§15.31 —Failure to Commence Project
§15.32 —Abandonment Following Start of Construction
§15.33 —Nonpayment
§15.34 Breach by Architect/Engineer
§15.35 Breach by Subcontractors
§15.36 Materialmen Remedies
§15.37 —Replevin
§15.38 —Account Stated
§15.39 Specific Performance
§15.40 Rescission and Restitution
§15.41 Reformation

§15.01 Article 78

Article 78 is a statutory means by which a party may seek relief that previously was obtained "by writs of certiorari to review, mandamus or prohibition...."[1] It is used to challenge actions by public entities, typically administrative bodies or personnel that have made determinations that adversely affect the petitioner. Article 78 replaces the old forms and provides one method by which aggrieved persons may challenge governmental decisions. While a petitioner no longer need worry whether it has couched its proceeding properly, its remedies are limited to what could have been accomplished under the old writs. Briefly,

> [c]ertiorari was designed to review judicial or quasi-judicial determinations of a body or officer made pursuant to statute. Mandamus, on the other hand, served two functions. It might be invoked to review administrative—as opposed to judicial—determinations, and it was also designed to compel action by a body or officer specifically enjoined by law. Prohibition was the writ employed to prevent bodies or officers which exercised judicial or quasi-judicial functions from acting without or in excess of their jurisdiction.[2]

The only questions that may be raised in an Article 78 proceeding are:

1. Whether the body or officer failed to perform a duty enjoined upon it by law
2. Whether the body or officer proceeded, is proceeding, or is about to proceed without or in excess of jurisdiction

---

[1] NY Civ Prac L & R 7801 (McKinney 1981 & Supp 1992).
[2] *Id* 7802, Practice Commentary C7802:1.

3. Whether a determination was made in violation of lawful procedure, was affected by an error of law, or was arbitrary and capricious or an abuse of discretion, including abuse of discretion as to the measure or mode of penalty or discipline imposed; or
4. Whether a determination made as a result of a hearing held, and at which evidence was taken, pursuant to direction by law is, on the entire record, supported by substantial evidence[3]

Article 78 may not be used to review an administrative agency's legislative actions, such as establishing standards or regulations or compiling and writing specifications;[4] a declaratory judgment action may be used to challenge legislative actions[5] or to declare a party in default under a contract.[6] Further, an Article 78 proceeding cannot be used to compel a public body to perform a contract; the proper remedy is a breach of contract action.[7]

Before resorting to an Article 78 proceeding, a party must exhaust its administrative remedies in most cases.[8] If, however, a determination is "patently erroneous as a matter of law," a party need not exhaust its administrative remedies.[9] Further, if the petitioner has sought relief in a civil action in which any Article 78 issue can be determined, it will not have a right to Article 78 relief.[10]

> **PRACTICE POINTER:**
>
> It is not advisable to rely upon the "patently erroneous as a matter of law" exception. If a court should decide that the determination was not patently erroneous as a matter of law, it will dismiss the Article 78 proceeding for failure to exhaust administrative remedies. The regulations governing the appropriate administrative remedy may contain time limitations, e.g., an administrative appeal must be taken within 30 days after the determination sought to be appealed was rendered. By the time the Article 78 proceeding is dismissed, these time limitations may have expired so that administrative relief is barred. Thus, the petitioner is left without a remedy. Therefore, it is better practice, even though one believes the "patently erroneous as a matter of law" exception to be applicable, both to pursue the administrative remedy

---

[3] *Id* 7803.

[4] Ludlow's Sand & Gravel Co v LaBella, 80 Misc 2d 997, 364 NYS2d 669 (Oneida 1974).

[5] Thompson Water Works Co v Diamond, 44 AD2d 487, 356 NYS2d 130 (4th Dept 1974).

[6] City of Rochester v Vanderlinde Elec Corp, 56 AD2d 185, 392 NYS2d 167 (4th Dept 1977).

[7] Lord Elec Co v Litke, 122 Misc 2d 112, 469 NYS2d 846 (NY 1983).

[8] Perosi Homes, Inc v Maniscalco, 15 AD2d 563, 223 NYS2d 173 (2d Dept 1961).

[9] Dobbs Ferry Hosp Assoc v Whalen, 62 AD2d 999, 403 NYS2d 304 (2d Dept 1978).

[10] Great Lakes Dredge & Dock Co v Wagner, 46 AD2d 721, 360 NYS2d 337 (4th Dept 1974).

> and to commence the Article 78 proceeding. That way, if the Article 78 proceeding is dismissed, the petitioner can commence a new Article 78 proceeding after the administrative remedies are exhausted.
>
> Particularly with local government bodies, it is sometimes very difficult to determine what administrative remedies are available, if any, and how one goes about pursuing an administrative remedy. In such circumstances, probably the best one can do is make a written demand on the government body for a copy of the applicable regulations. Such demands must be made promptly so that, if no administrative remedies are available, one still has time to commence the Article 78 proceeding. See §15.02 for a discussion of the short statute of limitation applicable to Article 78 proceedings. If the government body does not respond to the demand, commence the Article 78 proceeding timely and hope that the court will agree that the failure to exhaust administrative remedies was excused by the government body's inaction.

It is important that one understand the difference between issues that may be presented in a breach of contract action and in an Article 78 proceeding. The fact that a party may have a breach of contract claim does not mean that it has a right to Article 78 relief. Generally,

> violation by a governmental official or agency of a contractual obligation gives rise to a plenary action for violation of the contract, and not to an Article 78 proceeding seeking nullification of the governmental decision. . . . [A] claim that a public official or governmental unit has violated a contract will be adjudicated in accordance with traditional rules of contract law. . . . [A] claim for Article 78 relief necessarily rests upon the quite separate issue as to whether the challenged determination "was made in violation of lawful procedure, was affected by an error of law or was arbitrary and capricious or an abuse of discretion. . . ."[11]

§15.02 —Procedure

An Article 78 proceeding must be brought in the supreme court[12] and is initiated by the service of a notice of petition with a verified petition on the adverse party at least 20 days before the return date.[13] It is technically a special proceeding rather than an action. The notice of petition serves the dual function of both a summons and a notice of motion in a civil action and the petition is the equivalent of a complaint. If the proceeding is against a state body or offi-

---

[11] Goodstein Constr Corp v Gliedman, 117 AD2d 170, 502 NYS2d 136, 140 (1st Dept 1986), *affd mem*, 69 NY2d 930, 509 NE2d 350, 516 NYS2d 655 (1987) (quoting NY Civ Prac L & R 7803(3) (McKinney 1981)), *related breach of contract action*, Goodstein Constr Corp v City of NY, 111 AD2d 49, 489 NYS2d 175 (1st Dept 1985), *affd*, 67 NY2d 990, 494 NE2d 99, 502 NYS2d 994 (1986).

[12] NY Civ Prac L & R 7804(b) (McKinney 1981 & Supp 1992).

[13] *Id* 7804(c).

cer, the petition must be served on the state attorney general.[14] The statute of limitation for Article 78 proceedings depends upon the nature of the claim. Generally, they are governed by NY Civ Prac L&R 217, the four-month statute of limitation applicable to disputes with governmental entities.[15]

§15.03 —Article 78 in Construction Cases

In construction, Article 78 has many uses. It has successfully been used: to compel the state to pay a contractor money due on a terminated contract;[16] to annual a county's rejection of a bid;[17] to declare an award of contract illegal and void;[18] to review and overturn a decision of a superintendent of public works that the petitioner's materials did not conform to contract specifications;[19] to review and annul zoning and planning board decisions;[20] to compel issuance of a building permit and certificate of occupancy;[21] to review and overturn a health commissioner's decision to reject a hospital project;[22] to review a city council's issuance of change orders rather than letting work for public bid;[23] to compel certification that a proposed wage schedule complies with prevailing wage rates established pursuant to the Labor Law or to compel issuance of a wage schedule more reflective of the community;[24] and to challenge specifications that placed the burden of contract drawings' accuracy on contractors,[25] among numerous others. Article 78 is the only means by which a contractor can challenge a public officer's refusal to allow withdrawal of a bid.[26]

---

[14] *Id.*

[15] Mulvihill Elec Contracting Corp v Metropolitan Trans Auth, 167 AD2d 471, 562 NYS2d 144 (2d Dept 1990); McComb v Town of Greenville, 163 AD2d 369, 558 NYS2d 104 (2d Dept 1990).

[16] Fehlhaber Corp v O'Hara, 53 AD2d 746, 384 NYS2d 270 (3d Dept 1976).

[17] Angelo J. Martone & Son v County of Nassau, 42 Misc 2d 804, 249 NYS2d 353 (Nassau 1964).

[18] *In re* Gottfried Baking Co, 45 Misc 2d 708, 257 NYS2d 833 (Albany 1964).

[19] National Wire Prods Corp v McMorran, 23 AD2d 708, 257 NYS2d 71 (3d Dept 1965).

[20] Diocese of Rochester v Planning Bd, 1 NYS2d 508, 136 NE2d 827, 154 NYS2d 849 (1956).

[21] Davison v Flanagan, 273 AD 870, 76 NYS2d 849 (2d Dept 1948).

[22] Dobbs Ferry Hosp Assoc v Whalen, 62 AD2d 999, 403 NYS2d 304 (2d Dept 1978).

[23] Albert Elia Bldg Co v New York State Urban Dev Corp, 54 AD2d 337, 388 NYS2d 462 (4th Dept 1976).

[24] Gottlieb Contracting, Inc v Beame, 41 Misc 2d 1097, 247 NYS2d 237 (NY 1964).

[25] General Bldg Contractors, Inc v County of Oneida, 54 Misc 2d 260, 282 NYS2d 385 (Oneida 1967).

[26] TPK Constr Co v O'Shea, 69 AD2d 316, 419 NYS2d 279 (3d Dept 1979), *affd mem*, 50 NY2d 835, 407 NE2d 1331, 430 NYS2d 34 (1980).

§15.04 —Standard of Review

The standard of review in an Article 78 proceeding requires a two-step inquiry. If the act complained of required an exercise of discretion by the public officer, the standard of review is one of rationality, not equity. The issue is not whether the decision was wise, but whether there was *any* rational basis for the decision.[27] Only if an act or refusal to act is irrational, arbitrary, and capricious will it be overturned by the courts.[28] An arbitrary and capricious action is one taken without a sound basis in reason and with disregard for the facts.[29] Examples of discretionary acts include award of contracts,[30] allowing withdrawal of a bid, rejection of nonconforming bids,[31] determinations of responsibility,[32] a comptroller's power to approve a contract,[33] and a board's decision to reject all bids and readvertise.[34]

If the act or failure to act complained of is ministerial or determinative, the court will question whether the act was required and, if it was required, whether it was performed at all or properly; if not, the court will compel correct performance of the officer's statutory duty.[35] Examples of ministerial or determinative acts include whether the petitioner's materials conformed to contract specifications[36] and a contractor's right to payment where the parties had agreed on the amount due but the comptroller refused to pay it.[37]

---

[27] Zara Contracting Co v Cohen, 45 Misc 2d 497, 257 NYS2d 479 (Albany 1964), *affd*, 23 AD2d 718, 257 NYS2d 118 (3d Dept 1965) (*per curiam*).

[28] TPK Constr Co v O'Shea, 69 AD2d 316, 419 NYS2d 279 (3d Dept 1979), *affd mem*, 50 NY2d 835, 407 NE2d 1331, 430 NYS2d 34 (1980). The Third Department has criticized this limited review: "Apparently the Court of Appeals, by consigning these claims [bid mistakes] to Article 78 proceedings, in effect has predetermined that only outrageous inequitable results, i.e., those that are irrational, arbitrary and capricious, can be overturned by this court." 419 NYS2d at 281. *See also* Dierks Heating Co v Egan, 115 AD2d 836, 496 NYS2d 97 (3d Dept 1985), *appeal denied*, 67 NY2d 606, 501 NYS2d 1025 (1986).

[29] Pell v Board of Educ, 34 NY2d 222, 231, 313 NE2d 321, 325, 356 NYS2d 833, 839 (1974).

[30] *In re* Gottfried Banking Co, 45 Misc 2d 708, 257 NYS2d 833 (Albany 1964).

[31] *In re* K&M Turf Maintenance, 166 AD2d 445, 560 NYS2d 673 (2d Dept 1990).

[32] Callanan Indus v City of Schenectady, 116 AD2d 883, 498 NYS2d 490 (3d Dept 1986); Zara Contracting Co v Cohen, 45 Misc 2d 497, 257 NYS2d 479 (Albany 1964), *affd*, 23 AD2d 718, 257 NYS2d 118 (3d Dept 1965) (*per curiam*); Meyer v Board of Educ, 31 Misc 2d 407, 221 NYS2d 500 (Nassau 1961).

[33] Konski Engrs, PC v Levitt, 69 AD2d 940, 415 NYS2d 509 (3d Dept 1979), *affd mem*, 49 NY2d 850, 404 NE2d 1337, 427 NYS2d 796, *cert denied*, 449 US 840 (1980).

[34] Halpern v Hodgkiss, 89 NYS2d 451 (NY 1949).

[35] Fehlhaber Corp v O'Hara, 53 AD2d 746, 384 NYS2d 270 (3d Dept 1976); Angelo J. Martone & Son v County of Nassau, 42 Misc 2d 804, 249 NYS2d 353 (Nassau 1964).

[36] National Wire Prods Corp v McMorran, 23 AD2d 708, 257 NYS2d 71 (3d Dept 1965). (Here, the specifications required domestically manufactured or produced materials. Petitioner, a United States corporation, made steel mesh at its plant in the United States from foreign made steel. The court found the superintendent's decision that the materials did not conform to specifications to be unsupported by substantial evidence.)

[37] Fehlhaber Corp v O'Hara, 53 AD2d 746, 384 NYS2d 270 (3d Dept 1976).

§15.05 Injunctions

Injunctions are a means by which a party seeks to compel another party to take an action or to prevent it from taking another action. In construction, injunctions may be sought to prevent an owner from beginning construction, perhaps because a boundary is unclear or because the building will or does violate zoning ordinances.[38] Injunctions may also be sought to compel removal of structures.[39] Injunctions may be sought by any party aggrieved by another's actions where the danger is immediate and an adequate remedy at law does not exist. To obtain either a temporary restraining order (TRO) or a preliminary injunction, the plaintiff must show a likelihood of success on the merits.

There are frequently two, and often three, steps to obtaining a permanent injunction. First, the plaintiff might seek a TRO. Then, either after obtaining a TRO or as its first step, the plaintiff seeks a preliminary injunction. The final step is when the preliminary injunction is made permanent by the court or denied altogether.

§15.06 —Preliminary Injunctions

New York Civil Practice Law and Rules 6301 provides that a preliminary injunction may be obtained in two situations: (1) where it appears that the defendant threatens to do, is about to do, or is doing some act in violation of the plaintiff's rights respecting the subject of the action; or (2) in an action where the plaintiff has demanded and would be entitled to a permanent injunction restraining the defendant from causing some act to occur, which act would damage the plaintiff if committed during the pendency of the court action. The purpose of a preliminary injunction is to preserve the *status quo* until the main action can be resolved.

For instance, a party might seek a preliminary injunction if its neighbor threatens to build a house on what it believes to be its property, but which in fact belongs to the plaintiff. The plaintiff could seek a preliminary injunction to stop its neighbor from beginning construction until ownership of the land and proper location of the properties' boundaries can be determined by the court.

To obtain a preliminary injunction, a party must bring a motion, made on notice, which may be served at the time of the summons or at any time thereafter.[40] To apply for a preliminary injunction, an action must be pending. To be entitled to a preliminary injunction, a party must show at the hearing, by affidavit and other evidence, convincingly, that: (1) its claim falls within NY Civ Prac L&R §6301, i.e., it is either a cause of action concerning a specific,

---

[38] Little Joseph Realty, Inc v Town of Babylon, 41 NY2d 738, 363 NE2d 1163, 395 NYS2d 428 (1977); Malerba v Warren, 108 Misc 2d 785, 438 NYS2d 936 (Suffolk 1981), *affd as modified,* 96 AD2d 529, 464 NYS2d 835 (2d Dept 1983).

[39] Malerba v Warren, 108 Misc 2d 785, 438 NYS2d 936 (Suffolk 1981), *affd as modified,* 96 AD2d 529, 464 NYS2d 835 (2d Dept 1983).

[40] NY Civ Prac L & R 6311(1) (McKinney 1980 & Supp 1992).

identifiable subject, or a cause of action for a permanent injunction; (2) irreparable damage will occur if a preliminary injunction is not granted; (3) no adequate remedy at law exists (money damages are not sufficient); and (4) there is a high probability that the plaintiff will be successful in its main action.[41]

Prior to the injunction being implemented, the plaintiff must post a bond in an amount set by the court. The amount of the bond is supposed to be sufficient to compensate the defendant for any losses it might suffer if it is later determined that the plaintiff was not entitled to an injunction.[42]

Temporary Restraining Order

If a party believes that it will suffer "immediate and irreparable injury, loss or damages" unless the defendant is restrained before a hearing on a preliminary injunction can be held, it may seek a Temporary Restraining Order (TRO).[43] A TRO is granted without prior notice to the defendant. Further, it may be granted before an action has been commenced.

> **PRACTICE POINTER:**
>
> Although the request for a TRO is made without notice to the defendant, many courts have adopted the practice of not granting TROs against government bodies without their attorneys having the opportunity to argue against the TRO. It is therefore a wise practice to arrange for the government attorney to accompany you to court when presenting the TRO.

To obtain a TRO, a party must seek an order to show cause from the court. If the court grants the order, and hence the TRO, it must also set a hearing date for a preliminary injunction at the "earliest possible time." An executed order to show cause contains the same information as a notice of motion (the time and place of the preliminary injunction hearing); who must be served with the TRO; how the TRO must be served; and also the terms of the TRO. After it is executed by the court, the order to show cause, together with the papers on which it is based and the summons and complaint, is served on the defendant to prevent the defendant from action prior to the preliminary injunction hearing.

A bond is not mandatory for a TRO, although the court may require one, in its discretion.[44]

---

[41] *Id* 6312(a) (McKinney 1980).

[42] *Id* 6312(b).

[43] *Id* 6313(a) (McKinney 1980 & Supp 1992).

[44] *Id* 6313(c) (McKinney 1980).

PRACTICE POINTER:

In deciding whether to grant TROs or preliminary injunctions, courts often "balance the equities," i.e., weigh the prejudice to the plaintiff if the relief is not granted against the harm to the defendant if the relief is granted. Delay in applying for the relief may tip the balance in favor of the defendant. For instance, the failure to move to enjoin the award of a contract prior to award may lead the court to conclude that the defendant has adversely altered its position as a contract now exists and the defendant may have liability to the contractor. If construction has actually started, the harm to the defendant and to the contractor (which will probably seek to intervene in the action if not named as a party defendant) is even more apparent and may lead the court to deny the relief. If this happens, the whole action may be rendered moot as construction may be completed by the time the action is finally tried.

If the Court strikes the TRO from the order to show cause, ask that it set the preliminary injunction hearing for a date earlier than the normal return date required by the CPLR.

§15.07 —Permanent Injunctions

A temporary injunction may be made permanent following resolution of the action in which it was obtained. A permanent injunction is a court order that prohibits a party from doing an act in the future or compels a party to perform an act for or within a specified period of time.

§15.08 Declaratory Judgment

An action for a declaratory judgment asks the court to declare parties' rights and responsibilities in a particular matter. The only limitations on a declaratory judgment request are that a genuine, ripe controversy exists between the parties, that each has a stake in the outcome, and that a "justiciable controversy"[45] exists. It is not a means to obtain an advisory opinion. There is no laundry list of what matters may or may not be submitted for declaratory judgment. In the construction context, declaratory judgment is most often sought to determine parties' rights under a construction contract or an insurance policy. For instance, a party may bring an action asking the court to declare a contract void, a release binding,[46] that wage schedules issued by the Commissioner of Labor are null and void,[47] that award of a public contract was illegal,[48] or that

---

[45] NY Civ Prac L & R 3001 (McKinney 1991 & Supp 1992).

[46] See Central Hudson Gas & Elec Corp v Benjamin F. Shaw Co, 465 F Supp 331 (SDNY 1978).

[47] See Associated Gen Contractors of Am v Roberts, 122 AD2d 406, 505 NYS2d 220 (3d Dept 1986).

[48] See McComb v Town of Greenville, 163 AD2d 369, 558 NYS2d 104 (2d Dept 1990).

its insurer must defend it in a negligence action or provide coverage.[49]

A claim for declaratory judgment may be the only relief requested in the action or it may be coupled with a request for injunctive relief, damages, or any other relief to which a party believes itself entitled.[50] A declaratory judgment action may be brought despite the availability of other remedies,[51] including Article 78.[52]

A declaratory judgment action may be brought only in the supreme court.[53] It is not even appropriate in the court of claims.[54] The statute of limitation for a declaratory judgment action is determined by the substantive nature of the claim. Thus, if a party chooses to challenge a town's award of a contract through a declaratory judgment action, it must bring the action within four months, the limitations period applicable to an Article 78 proceeding to review or challenge government actions.[55]

> **PRACTICE POINTER:**
>
> If the petitioner/plaintiff brings the action in the wrong form, i.e., a declaratory judgment action when it properly should have been an Article 78 proceeding, or vice versa, the court has the power to "convert" it to the proper form if requested to do so and if there is no statute of limitation problem. But counsel should not count on a "conversion"; the proper form should be used in the first instance.

§15.09 Accounting

When discussing a claim for an accounting in construction cases, a distinction must be made between a common law accounting and an accounting under the Lien Law. They are distinct and separate remedies, each available only under certain circumstances.

---

[49] *See* Prince Carpentry, Inc v Cosmopolitan Mut Ins Co, 124 Misc 2d 919, 479 NYS2d 284 (NY 1984).

[50] NY Civ Prac L & R 3001, 3017(b) (McKinney 1991 & Supp 1992).

[51] Rockland Light & Power Co v City of NY, 289 NY 45, 43 NE2d 803 (1942); Davis Constr Corp v County of Suffolk, 112 Misc 2d 652, 447 NYS2d 355 (Suffolk 1982), *affd*, 95 AD2d 819, 464 NYS2d 519 (2d Dept 1983).

[52] *In re* Zuckerman v Board of Educ, 44 NY2d 336, 376 NE2d 1297, 405 NYS2d 652 (1978); Prince Carpentry, Inc v Cosmopolitan Mut Ins Co, 124 Misc 2d 919, 479 NYS2d 284 (NY 1984).

[53] NY Civ Prac L & R 3001 (McKinney 1991 & Supp 1992).

[54] Wikarski v State, 91 AD2d 1174, 459 NYS2d 143 (4th Dept 1983). The only exception to this rule is if a defendant in a pending court of claims action seeks a determination that its insurer must indemnify or defend the defendant. Court of Claims Act §9 (McKinney 1989 & Supp 1992).

[55] McComb v Town of Greenville, 163 AD2d 369, 558 NYS2d 104 (2d Dept 1990).

Common Law Accounting

A claim for an accounting seeks, through equity, a complete disclosure and explanation of what a defendant has done with money or property that the defendant controls or controlled. To be entitled to an equity accounting, a plaintiff must allege a fiduciary relationship between itself and the defendant[56] and a claim of wrongdoing by the defendant.[57] Further, the plaintiff must not have an adequate remedy at law.[58] The relationship must truly be fiduciary; a debtor-creditor relationship does not meet the test,[59] nor does an employee-employer relationship.[60] Rarely is a common law equity action for accounting used in construction in the absence of a joint venture or some other relationship akin to partnership.

Accounting under the Lien Law

The Lien Law provides that a contractor, a subcontractor, a materialman, or any other person with a claim to Lien Law trust funds may seek an accounting of the trust funds. To obtain an accounting under the Lien Law, the trust beneficiary need show only that it has not been paid moneys due.[61] Lien Law trust fund provisions and accounting are further discussed in Chapter 9.

§15.10 Breach of Contract v Quantum Meruit

If a contractor properly terminates a construction contract because of an owner's substantial material breach, such as failure to pay or interference with performance, it has the right of electing to sue on the contract or to rescind or abandon the contract and sue in quantum meruit.[62] The choice is the innocent party's; it cannot be forced to sue in contract.[63] If the contractor elects to sue on the contract, its measure of damages is the contract price less the payments made under the contract and less what it would have cost the contrac-

---

[56] Reichert v N. MacFarland Builders, Inc, 85 AD2d 767, 445 NYS2d 264 (3d Dept 1981).

[57] Brigham v McCabe, 27 AD2d 100, 276 NYS2d 328 (3d Dept 1966), affd, 20 NY2d 525, 232 NE2d 327, 285 NYS2d 294 (1967).

[58] Hermes v Compton, 260 AD 507, 23 NYS2d 126 (2d Dept), *modified on other grounds*, 260 AD 1027 (1940).

[59] Brigham v McCabe, 27 AD2d 100, 276 NYS2d 328 (3d Dept 1966), affd, 20 NY2d 525, 232 NE2d 327, 285 NYS2d 294 (1967).

[60] Reichert v N. MacFarland Builders, Inc, 85 AD2d 767, 445 NYS2d 264 (3d Dept 1981).

[61] Fentron Architectural Metals Corp v Solow, 48 AD2d 820, 370 NYS2d 58 (1st Dept 1975).

[62] New Era Homes Corp v Forster, 299 NY 303, 86 NE2d 757 (1949); Farrell Heating, Plumbing, Air Conditioning Contractors v Facilities Dev & Improvement Corp, 68 AD2d 958, 414 NYS2d 767 (3d Dept 1979); Paterno & Sons v Town of New Windsor, 43 AD2d 863, 351 NYS2d 445 (2d Dept 1974); Zadek v Olds, Wortman & King, 166 AD 60, 151 NYS 634 (1st Dept 1915).

[63] ST Grand, Inc v Cedar Bay Park Corp, 14 Misc 2d 428, 182 NYS2d 747 (NY 1958).

tor to complete the work.[64] In other words, the contractor is entitled to receive the contract value of the work completed plus the profit the contractor would have made on the uncompleted work. If the contractor elects to sue in quantum meruit, its damages are limited to the fair and reasonable value of work, labor, materials, and services furnished, including overhead and profit thereon; the contractor is not entitled to the profit it would have made on the work not performed, and the cost of completion is irrelevant.[65] A contractor would be wise to choose that measure of damages that provides it with the higher recovery. If the value of the uncompleted work were high, a contractor would want to seek recovery in quantum meruit.[66] Similarly, if the contractor had underbid the job, its quantum meruit recovery would probably exceed recovery based upon the contract price. Conversely, if the contractor had a large profit margin built into its contract and the cost of completion was not high, it probably would choose breach of contract.

If the breach occurs after contract performance is complete or if a contractor continues meaningful performance after an owner's breach, there can be no recovery in quantum meruit.[67] If a breach occurs during performance, the contractor may continue its performance under protest and recover breach of contract damages or may rescind, if warranted, and recover in quantum meruit.[68] It may not continue performance and recover in quantum meruit, although it may terminate the contract and choose between contract and quantum meruit.[69]

§15.11 Fraud

While the majority of claims between parties involved in a construction project are based in contract, fraud or misrepresentation claims are not uncommon. An attractive feature of a fraud claim is that it does not require privity. Often, negligent or intentional misrepresentation is claimed by a contractor that encounters unanticipated subsurface conditions. These claims are discussed in Chapter 5. As one court has aptly stated:

> The law recognizes two kinds of fraud—actual and constructive. In order to sustain an action for actual fraud the plaintiff must prove: (1) that the defendant made a representation, (2) as to a material fact, (3) which was false, (4) and known to be false by the defendant, (5) that the representation was made for the purpose of inducing the other party to rely upon it, (6) that the other party rightfully did so rely, (7) in igno-

---

[64] New Era Homes Corp v Forster, 299 NY 303, 86 NE2d 757 (1949).

[65] ST Grand, Inc v Cedar Bay Park Corp, 14 Misc 2d 428, 182 NYS2d 747 (NY 1958).

[66] *See* Farrell Heating, Plumbing, Air Conditioning Contractors v Facilities Dev & Improvement Corp, 68 AD2d 958, 414 NYS2d 767 (3d Dept 1979).

[67] Clark-Fitzpatrick, Inc v Long Island RR, 70 NY2d 382, 516 NE2d 190, 521 NYS2d 653 (1987).

[68] *Id.*

[69] Paterno & Sons v Town of Windsor, 43 AD2d 863, 351 NYS2d 445 (2d Dept 1974).

rance of its falsity (8) to his injury. Constructive fraud may be defined as a breach of a duty which, irrespective of moral guilt and intent, the law declares fraudulent because of its tendency to deceive, to violate a confidence or to injure public or private interests which the law deems worthy of special protection. The elements of a cause of action to recover for constructive fraud are the same as those to recover for actual fraud with the crucial exception that the element of *scienter* upon the part of the defendant, his knowledge of the falsity of his representation, is dropped and is replaced by a requirement that the plaintiff prove the existence of a fiduciary or confidential relationship warranting the trusting party to repose his confidence in the defendant and therefore to relax the care and vigilance he would ordinarily exercise in the circumstances.[70] (Citations omitted.)

Fraud may be in the inducement to contract or in the performance of the contract. For example, fraud in the inducement may occur if a party represents itself as an owner of the property to be improved and a contractor relies on that representation, when in fact it was a mere tenant without the right to improve the property. Fraud in performance was found and a contractor was held liable to individual cooperative apartment owners in fraud when it was discovered that the contractor had not connected kitchen and bathroom ventilation systems to any central exhaust duct or fan.[71] The contractor had installed dummy sheet metal ducts that led nowhere and simply ended in walls or ceilings.

§15.12 Punitive Damages

In New York, punitive damages are available in a limited number of instances, typically tort based. The wrong complained of must be "morally culpable" or "actuated by evil and reprehensible motives."[72] They are awarded to punish a defendant and to deter it and others from similar conduct.[73] They may only be awarded for

> [e]xceptional misconduct which transgresses mere negligence, as where the wrongdoer has acted "maliciously, wantonly, or with a recklessness that betokens an improper motive or vindictiveness" or has engaged in

---

[70] Brown v Lockwood, 76 AD2d 721, 432 NYS2d 186, 193-94 (2d Dept 1980).

[71] 17 E 80th Realty Corp v 68th Assocs, 173 AD2d 245, 569 NYS2d 647 (1st Dept 1991).

[72] Garrity v Lyle Stuart, Inc, 40 NY2d 354, 353 NE2d 793, 795, 386 NYS2d 831 (1976); (*quoting* Walker v Sheldon, 10 NY2d 401, 404, 179 NE2d 497, 498, 223 NYS2d 488, 490 (1961)).

[73] *Id.*

"outrageous or oppressive intentional misconduct" or with "reckless or wanton disregard of safety or rights."[74]

Punitive damages are not compensatory; they are a public, social remedy. Thus, they are not available for a simple breach of contract, as a breach of a contract is a private wrong between the parties to the contract and, generally, no public right is involved.[75] To recover punitive damages in a breach of contract action, it must be shown that the wrong was of a "continuous systematic nature" aimed at the public generally.[76]

Punitive damages have been awarded in construction cases where contractors have performed their contracts in a manner that totally ignored the owners' rights; the basis for the awards was not breach of contract but was intentional tort. In *Grau v Eljay Real Estate Corp*,[77] a home owner was unfortunate enough to have hired two contractors that exhibited outrageously unprofessional behavior. One contractor allowed its workmen to make personal use of the owner's apartment in ways wholly unrelated to the work; when the owner called the police, the workmen vandalized his apartment and threatened him with bodily harm. The owner's other contractor repeatedly allowed concrete to fall on his terrace and greenhouse. The court found these to be intentional torts of an extreme nature and allowed the owner's claim for punitive damages to withstand the contractors' motion to strike.

In other construction-related cases it has been held that an owner who diverted Lien Law trust funds may be liable for punitive damages if the beneficiary can prove that the owner flagrantly disregarded Lien Law trust fund provisions.[78] Punitive damages also may be appropriate in fraud and deceit actions, such as when one is fraudulently induced to enter into a contract.[79]

If an insured contractor, architect, owner, or other party can show that its insurer has engaged in a general pattern of unfair claim settlement practices, the insured may be able to recover punitive damages from its insurer.[80]

---

[74] Sharapata v Town of Islip, 56 NY2d 332, 437 NE2d 1104, 452 NYS2d 347 (1982) (quoting 9 Encyl NY, *Damages* §63 (1956 & Supp 1982) and Morris, *Punitive Damages in Personal Injury Cases*, 21 Ohio St LJ 216 (1961)).

[75] *Id*; Aetna Cas & Sur Co v City of NY, 160 AD2d 561, 554 NYS2d 210 (1st Dept 1990).

[76] Merrick v Four Star Stage Lighting, Inc, 60 AD2d 806, 400 NYS2d 543, 544 (1st Dept 1978).

[77] 162 AD2d 320, 556 NYS2d 898 (1st Dept 1990).

[78] Sabol & Rice, Inc v Poughkeepsie Galleria Co, 147 Misc 2d 641, 557 NYS2d 253 (Dutchess 1990), *affd*, 572 NYS2d 811 (3d Dept 1991). Lien Law trust fund provisions are found in Article 3-A of the Lien Law and are discussed in **ch 9**.

[79] Walker v Sheldon, 10 NY2d 401, 179 NE2d 497, 223 NYS2d 488 (1961).

[80] Belco Petroleum Corp v AIG Oil Rig Inc, 164 AD2d 583, 565 NYS2d 776 (1st Dept 1991).

Arbitration[81]

New York state courts will not uphold an arbitrator's award of punitive damages, regardless of the basis or merit of the award, and regardless of the parties' agreement to allow an arbitrator to award punitive damages.

> The power to punish has been a monopoly of the State, and not that of any private individual.... The law does not and should not permit private persons to submit themselves to punitive sanctions of the order reserved the State. The freedom of contract does not embrace the freedom to punish, even by contract.[82]

Recent New York cases hold to the rule that arbitrators may not award punitive damages.[83] Some jurisdictions allow arbitrators to award punitive damages, including California[84] and Texas.[85]

It is important to note that an arbitration award will not be considered punitive merely because the compensatory damages awarded are somewhat speculative. Arbitrators are not bound by the same evidentiary and proof of damage constraints that courts are and may make a compensatory damage award that would be too speculative for a court to make.[86]

§15.13 —Public Contracts

Punitive damages may not be awarded against the state of New York,[87] its political subdivisions, including some public benefit corporations,[88] or its cities[89] for the rather simple reason that punitive damages awarded against a pub-

---

[81] The power of arbitrators to award punitive damages is discussed in numerous articles, including Stewart, *Punitive Damages in Arbitration: Fish or Cut Bait*, NYLJ, Feb 21, 1991, at 5, col 1; Report on Punitive Damages in Commercial Arbitration, NY State Bar Assoc Rep (1989); Stipanowich, *Punitive Damages in Arbitration: Garrity v Lyle Stuart, Inc Reconsidered*, 66 Boston UL Rev 953 (1986); Note, *An Argument Against the Availability of Punitive Damages in Commercial Arbitration*, 62 St John's L Rev 270 (1988); Note, *Punitive Damages in Arbitration: The Search for a Workable Rule*, 63 Cornell L Rev 272 (1978).

[82] Garrity v Lyle Stuart, Inc, 40 NY2d 354, 353 NE2d 793, 797, 386 NYS2d 831 (1976).

[83] *E.g.*, Diker v Cathray Constr Corp, 158 AD2d 657, 552 NYS2d 37 (2d Dept 1990); Barbier v Shearson Lehman Hutton, Inc, 948 F2d 117 (2d Cir 1991).

[84] Baker v Sadick, 162 Cal App 3d 618, 208 Cal Rptr 676 (1984).

[85] Grisson v Greener & Sumner Constr, Inc, 676 SW2d 709 (Tex Ct App 1984).

[86] Board of Educ v Niagara-Wheatfield Teachers Assoc, 46 NY2d 553, 389 NE2d 104, 415 NYS2d 790 (1979).

[87] Sharapata v Town of Islip, 56 NY2d 332, 437 NE2d 1104, 452 NYS2d 347 (1982).

[88] Clark-Fitzpatrick, Inc v Long Island RR, 70 NY2d 382, 516 NE2d 190, 521 NYS2d 653 (1987).

[89] Berg-Bakis, Ltd v City of Yonkers, 90 AD2d 784, 455 NYS2d 645 (2d Dept 1982), *appeal dismissed*, 60 NY2d 664, 455 NE2d 658, 468 NYS2d 99 (1983).

lic entity would be paid, eventually, by innocent taxpayers, defeating the goals of punishment and deterrence.[90]

Not all public benefit corporations are to be treated like the state in all instances, and hence, not all are immune to punitive damages. One must inquire whether, for the specific purpose at issue, such special treatment is warranted. When considering punitive damages against a public benefit corporation, the main inquiries are whether it has an essential public function and the amount of its support from public funding.[91]

§15.14 Attorneys' Fees

Absent an agreement or statute allowing an award of attorneys' fees, they may not be awarded by a court[92] or in arbitration.[93] Indemnification agreements often provide that one party will indemnify another from "all losses" related to a contract. If the agreement does not expressly or impliedly include attorneys' fees, they may not be awarded to the party indemnified.[94] If, however, the agreement provides for indemnification of "all claims, damages, losses and expenses, including but not limited to attorneys' fees," the indemnified party is entitled to an award of its attorneys' fees incurred in defending against an indemnification claim, regardless of the success of that action.[95]

> **PRACTICE POINTER:**
>
> If the arbitration clause provides that the arbitration will be conducted in accordance with the rules of a particular organization and if those rules permit the arbitrators to award attorneys' fees, one seeking attorneys' fees can argue that the agreement for arbitration to be conducted in accordance with those rules constitutes the necessary agreement allowing an award of attorneys' fees.

§15.15 Interest

Interest is allowed on claims for money due under a contract as compensation for the debtor's delay in paying the money when due.[96] "Generally, where there is delay in the making of stipulated payments, the only recoverable damage accruing to the payee is interest at the legal or contractual rate for the time

---

[90] Clark-Fitzpatrick, Inc v Long Island RR, 70 NY2d 382, 516 NE2d 190, 521 NYS2d 653 (1987).

[91] *Id.*

[92] NY Civ Prac L & R 7513 (McKinney 1980 & Supp 1992); Fink v Friedman, 78 Misc 2d 429, 358 NYS2d 250 (Nassau 1974).

[93] Arthur Richards, Ltd v Brampton Textiles, Ltd, 59 AD2d 842, 399 NYS2d 111 (1st Dept 1977); Central School Dist No 1 v Double M Constr, 46 AD2d 800, 361 NYS2d 47 (2d Dept 1974); NY Civ Prac L & R 7513 (McKinney 1980 & Supp 1992).

[94] Golaszewski v Cadman Plaza N, Inc, 158 AD2d 670, 552 NYS2d 43 (2d Dept 1990).

[95] Estate of Nasser v Port Auth, 155 AD2d 250, 546 NYS2d 626 (1st Dept 1989).

[96] *In re* Burke, 191 NY 437, 84 NE 405 (1908).

of delay."[97] Indeed, "[c]ompensation to the plaintiff is incomplete, unless accompanied by interest. . . ."[98]

> While a failure by the [owner] to pay as agreed might have afforded plaintiff ground for rescinding the contract, he did not elect to do so. After having proceeded with the contract to completion, it would certainly be a novelty in the law if he could recover, beyond interest, damages for the city's failure to pay as and when agreed.[99]

Generally, on construction projects, interest should run from the date the moneys were due,[100] e.g., the date the project was substantially completed;[101] the owner delivered its final estimate of money due;[102] the owner accepted the project;[103] or the contract was breached.[104]

In most noncontractual matters, interest runs from the date of the award or, in case of a bifurcated trial, from the date of liability adjudication.[105]

Arbitrators may grant preaward interest if the agreement does not specifically exclude an award of interest.[106] If they do not grant preaward interest, interest runs from the date of the arbitration award, not the date the award is converted to a judgment in a court.[107] If the arbitrators do not grant preaward interest, the court, on a motion to confirm, cannot add it.

Some contracts provide that if a contractor refuses to accept an owner's tender of final payment (perhaps because the contract provides that the contractor's acceptance of final payment constitutes a release of all its claims against the owner and the contractor has some claims), the refusal is a waiver of interest on the final payment. Such clauses may be ineffective. It has been held that a contractor is entitled to interest on moneys owing it under the contract from

---

[97] O'Rourke Engg Constr Co v City of NY, 229 AD 261, 241 NYS 613, 619 (2d Dept 1930), (quoting Green Briar Drainage Dist v Clark, 292 F 828, 831 (7th Cir 1923)).

[98] General Supply & Constr Co v Goelet, 241 NY 28, 148 NE 778, 780 (1925).

[99] Ryan v City of NY, 159 AD 105, 111, 143 NYS 974, 980 (1st Dept 1913).

[100] NY Civ Prac L & R 5001(b) (McKinney 1992) provides that interest should run from the "earliest possible date the cause of action existed. . . ."

[101] Italian Economic Corp v Community Engrs, Inc, 135 Misc 2d 209, 514 NYS2d 630 (NY 1987).

[102] D'Angelo v State, 41 AD2d 77, 341 NYS2d 84 (3d Dept), *appeal dismissed*, 32 NY2d 896, 300 NE2d 155, 346 NYS2d 814 (1973), *order affd as modified*, 34 NY2d 641, 311 NE2d 509, 355 NYS2d 377 (1974).

[103] Rusciano & Son Corp v State, 201 Misc 690, 110 NYS2d 770 (Ct Cl), *affd per curiam*, 281 AD 733, 118 NYS2d 77 (3d Dept 1952).

[104] Hart v United Artists Corp, 252 AD 133, 298 NYS 1 (1st Dept 1937).

[105] Gunnarson v State, 70 NY2d 923, 519 NE2d 307, 524 NYS2d 396 (1987); Krause v City of NY, 152 AD2d 473, 544 NYS2d 126 (1st Dept 1989), *appeal denied*, 76 NY2d 714, 565 NE2d 1268, 564 NYS2d 717 (Bronx 1990).

[106] *In re* Burke, 191 NY 437, 84 NE 405 (1908).

[107] Board of Educ v Niagara-Wheatfield Teachers Assoc, 46 NY2d 553, 389 NE2d 104, 415 NYS2d 790 (1979); Yeroush Corp v Nhaissi, 164 AD2d 891, 559 NYS2d 569 (2d Dept 1990), *affd*, 78 NY2d 873, 573 NYS2d 65 (1991).

the date the moneys were due,[108] regardless of the good faith nature of the parties' dispute.

§15.16 Noncontractual Limitations on Damages

General common law rules regarding damages apply in construction cases as in any other case. These are common sense rules that serve to stop a party from taking advantage of the situation and recovering more damages than it suffered, is entitled to, or can prove. In addition to damage limitations due to a failure to mitigate, the collateral source rule, the doctrine of certainty, and the economic loss rule (all discussed in the following sections), damages are limited by the concept of foreseeability.

In the construction contract context, *foreseeability* means that the particular damages sought were "fairly within the contemplation of the parties to the contract at the time it was made"[109] and are the "direct, natural and immediate consequence of the breach."[110] To determine whether particular damages were foreseeable, courts will look to the parties' contract and its remedy provisions[111] as well as damages typically claimed and awarded in similar instances.

§15.17 —Mitigation

Once a party has been damaged by another's actions, it has a duty to use reasonable efforts to mitigate its damages.[112] A party does not have a right to leave a serious wound untreated and expect the responsible party to pay for complications that result because of the lack of treatment. In construction cases, reasonable steps in mitigation by an owner may include promptly engaging a completion contractor after terminating a nonperforming contractor or, on the part of a contractor, moving idle equipment and laborers to another job.[113] If a party does not mitigate its damages, its recovery is limited to what it would have been had there been mitigation.[114] The burden of proving a failure to mitigate is on the party that breached the contract.[115]

---

[108] Rusciano & Son Corp v State, 201 Misc 690, 110 NYS2d 770 (Ct Cl), *affd per curiam*, 281 AD 733, 118 NYS2d 77 (3d Dept 1952).

[109] Kenford Co v County of Erie, 67 NY2d 257, 261, 493 NE2d 234, 502 NYS2d 131, 132 (1986) (*per curiam*).

[110] American Standard, Inc v Schectman, 80 AD2d 318, 439 NYS2d 529 (4th Dept), *appeal denied*, 54 NY2d 604, 427 NE2d 512, 443 NYS2d 1027 (1981).

[111] Kenford Co v County of Erie, 67 NY2d 257, 493 NE2d 234, 502 NYS2d 131 (1986) (*per curiam*).

[112] Losei Realty Corp v City of NY, 254 NY 41, 171 NE 899 (1930).

[113] *See* McMaster v State, 108 NY 542, 15 NE 417, 423 (1888).

[114] *Id.*

[115] *Id.*

§15.18 —Collateral Source Rule

The collateral source rule provides that if an injured person receives funds from a source that is wholly independent from the tortfeasor, evidence to prove such source is admissible to reduce the injured person's damage recovery from the tortfeasor by the amount received or expected to be received from the collateral source, less premiums paid and to be paid by the injured person for the benefits.[116] The most typical types of collateral sources are health insurance, social security, workers' compensation, and employee benefit programs. Evidence of life insurance is not admissible.[117] In construction cases, the collateral source rule most often comes into play when persons are injured during construction or as a result of claimed defective design or construction.

§15.19 —Certainty

While in theory every wrong should have a remedy and every party that suffers monetary damage due to another's wrong should receive just compensation for its damages, in reality, damages, unless they can be proved with a reasonable degree of certainty, may not be awarded beyond a nominal amount. Damage awards

> may not be merely speculative, possible, or imaginary, but must be reasonably certain and directly traceable to the breach, not remote or the result of intervening causes. In addition, there must be a showing that the particular damages were fairly within the contemplation of the parties to the contract at the time it was made.[118]

Proof of damages need not be perfect, however. If it is certain that damages were caused by a breach of contract, damages should not be precluded only because their amount is somewhat uncertain. In such a case, the person seeking damages may offer proof of the consequences that flowed reasonably and naturally from the breach and leave it to the fact-finder to determine just compensation for the breach.[119] Unfortunately, there is no clear line between damages that are just certain enough to allow recovery and those that are just uncertain enough to prohibit recovery.

In construction cases, the degree of certainty required is no clearer than in any other area. There are some basic rules, however. For instance, a contractor's desired measure of delay damages was rejected as unrealistic when it claimed "that the correct measure of damages would be the difference between its estimated costs, based on established cost data, and the actual completion

---

[116] *See* NY Civ Prac L & R 4545 (McKinney 1992).

[117] *Id.*

[118] Kenford Co v County of Erie, 67 NY2d 257, 261, 493 NE2d 234, 502 NYS2d 131, 132 (1986) (*per curiam*).

[119] Najjar Indus v City of NY, 87 AD2d 329, 451 NYS2d 410 (1st Dept 1982), *affd*, 68 NY2d 943, 502 NE2d 997, 510 NYS2d 82 (1986).

costs."[120] The court rejected this proof of damages, commonly known as the *total cost method,* as improper and unrealistic because it failed to consider delay not caused by the owner and because the contractor's "estimated costs" were subprices used internally by the contractor to compute bid prices and included subjective computations by the contractor.[121] It is clear in New York that a contractor may not offer its bid estimate, without more, as proof of what a job should have cost and contrast it with what the job actually cost to prove delay damages.[122] This issue is further discussed in Chapter 7.

If the damages proof relies upon too many variables or assumptions, it will be too speculative and uncertain, no matter how reasonable the assumptions or variables are or how qualified the expert is who testifies in support of the statistical projections used to calculate the damages.[123] A party can present "massive quantities of expert proof"[124] and not meet the burden of proving its damages with certainty.

To prove damages, a contractor should, to the extent it can, show the actual number of hours expended by its laborers due to the breach, their wages on the dates in issue, the cost of materials by invoices or checks, and daily reports. Where it reasonably can be expected that such evidence will prove a contractor's damage with certainty, it must come forward with such evidence.[125]

An arbitrator's award is not bound by the same constraints of certainty that a court's is.[126]

Lost Profits

Lost profits on a project are discussed in Chapter 7. Loss of future profits is a different subject. To recover loss of future profits, the following three criteria must be met:

1. It must be demonstrated with some certainty that loss of future profits was caused by the breach
2. The loss must be provable with reasonable certainty; and

---

[120] Mount Vernon Contracting Corp v State, 56 AD2d 952, 392 NYS2d 726, 729 (3d Dept 1977).

[121] *Id; see also* Whitmyer Bros v State, 63 AD2d 103, 406 NYS2d 617 (3d Dept 1978), *affd mem,* 47 NY2d 960, 393 NE2d 1027, 419 NYS2d 954 (1979).

[122] Whitmyer Bros v State, 63 AD2d 103, 406 NYS2d 617 (3d Dept 1978), *affd mem,* 47 NY2d 960, 393 NE2d 1027, 419 NYS2d 954 (1979); Mount Vernon Contracting Corp v State, 56 AD2d 952, 392 NYS2d 726, 729 (3d Dept 1977).

[123] Kenford Co v County of Erie, 67 NY2d 257, 493 NE2d 234, 502 NYS2d 131 (1986) (*per curiam*).

[124] *Id* at 262, 493 NE2d at 236, 502 NYS2d at 133.

[125] Goldner v Doknovitch, 88 Misc 2d 88, 388 NYS2d 504 (App Term 1976).

[126] Board of Educ v Niagara-Wheatfield Teachers Assoc, 46 NY2d 553, 389 NE2d 104, 415 NYS2d 790 (1979).

3. The damages must have been within the contemplation of the parties at the time the agreement was made[127]

A claim of lost profits for a new business is subjected to an even higher level of certainty than other damages. A new business has no track record upon which to base projections of future profits. Further, comparisons to similar businesses are difficult because no two businesses are ever the same—different locations, personnel, reputations, etc.

Loss of Bondability

Often, when contractors are delayed on a job, they are unable to bid on other jobs because they cannot obtain bonds.[128] In New York, compensatory damages based on impaired bonding capacity and lost opportunity are not allowed as they are deemed to be too speculative and lacking in the necessary degree of certainty.[129]

> [T]he plaintiff's contention that the delay made it impossible for it to receive bonding to bid on a subsequent job, that if it had bid it would have been the low bidder and, furthermore, that it would have received the job and earned a profit of $800,000 are based on inferences piled upon inferences and, as a matter of law, are too speculative to give rise to the recovery of damages for lost profits.[130]

A party that has suffered loss of bondability due to a breach of contract may recover nominal damages.[131]

§15.20 —Economic Loss Rule

The economic loss doctrine or rule

> marks the fundamental distinction between the law of contracts, which is designed to enforce expectancy interests created through an agreement between private parties, and the law of tort, which seeks to protect citizens and their property by imposing a duty to use reasonable care to avoid

---

[127] Kenford Co v County of Erie, 67 NY2d 257, 493 NE2d 234, 502 NYS2d 131 (1986) (*per curiam*).

[128] See Gerald B. Kirksey & Ronald W. Routson, *Proving Damages: Loss of Profits Resulting from Loss of Bonding Capacity*, 1983-No 2 Construction L Adviser 1 (1983), for a discussion of proving loss of bondability.

[129] Hirsch Elec Co v Community Serv, Inc, 133 AD2d 140, 518 NYS2d 818 (2d Dept 1987), *affd as modified*, 145 AD2d 603, 536 NYS2d 141 (1988). *Contra* Tempo, Inc v Rapid Elec Sales & Serv, 132 Mich App 93, 347 NW2d 728 (1984); Laas v Montana State Highway Comm, 157 Mont 121, 483 P2d 699 (1971).

[130] Hirsch Elec Co v Community Serv, 145 AD2d 603, 536 NYS2d 141, 142 (2d Dept 1988).

[131] *Id* at 605, 536 NYS2d at 143.

physical harm to others. Simply stated, the doctrine holds that one may not recover "economic" losses under a theory of nonintentional torts.[132]

The economic loss rule generally provides "that if there is no contractual relationship and there is no personal injury or damage to property, one cannot recover financial losses."[133]

Economic losses are losses that are not due to physical harm to a person or tangible property. Economic loss in construction typically results because of such things as: delay; negligently performed testing that results in work being performed that is not necessary;[134] air conditioning systems failing to function as warranted;[135] roofs leaking without damage to any personal property;[136] or negligent misrepresentation by a design professional.[137] Generally, economic loss results because of delay or because the building or product is not of the quality expected or does not perform as expected. Elements of economic loss include diminution of value, repair or replacement costs, lost profits, lost overhead, business interruption, and loss of use damages.

It is important to remember that economic losses are recoverable in contract or if the relationship between the parties is so close as to be the "functional equivalent of contractual privity."[138] The economic loss rule bars recovery of damages that are solely economic absent privity or its "functional equivalent"; if the defendant's conduct caused physical harm to either a person or tangible property, other than the building or product itself, the damages are not considered to be solely economic and recovery may be had in tort. In other words, without an agreement to the contrary, economic loss can be recovered only in actions based in contract; economic loss cannot be recovered in negligence actions absent a contractual relationship.

The economic loss rule has been praised[139] and criticized.[140] Some commen-

---

[132] Barrett, *The Center Holds: The Continuing Role of the Economic Loss Rule in Construction Litigation*, 11 Construction 3 (1991).

[133] Tarullo, *The Good, The Bad, and Economic Loss Liability of a Design Professional*, 11 Construction L 10 (1991).

[134] Ossining Union Free School Dist v Anderson LaRocca Anderson, 73 NY2d 417, 539 NE2d 91, 541 NYS2d 335 (1989).

[135] Prudential-Bache Sec, Inc v Resnick Water St Dev Co, 161 AD2d 456, 555 NYS2d 367 (1st Dept 1990).

[136] Hudson City Bd of Educ v Sargent, Webster, Crenshaw, & Folley, 71 NY2d 21, 517 NE2d 1360, 523 NYS2d 475 (1987).

[137] Ossining Union Free School Dist v Anderson LaRocca Anderson, 73 NY2d 417, 539 NE2d 91, 541 NYS2d 335 (1989); Briar Contracting Corp v City of NY, 156 AD2d 628, 550 NYS2d 717 (2d Dept 1989).

[138] Ossining Union Free School Dist v Anderson LaRocca Anderson, 73 NY2d 417, 419, 539 NE2d 91, 541 NYS2d 335 (1989).

[139] House & Bell, *The Economic Loss Rule: A Fair Balancing of Interests*, 11 Construction L 1 (1991); Bertschy, *Negligent Performance of Service Contract and the Economic Loss Doctrine*, 17 J Marshall L Rev 249 (1984); *see also* Schiavone Constr Co v Elgood Mayo Corp, 81 AD2d 221, 227-34, 439 NYS2d 933, 937-41 (1st Dept 1981) (Silverman, J. dissenting), *revd in opinion adopting Silverman, J. dissent*, 56 NY2d 667, 436 NE2d 1322, 451 NYS2d 720 (1982).

tators see a national movement away from imposing the economic loss rule in construction cases towards allowing recovery of economic loss damages by third parties,[141] while others believe that the law has remained relatively constant since a brief series of inroads in the 1940s.[142] In reality, the country is fairly evenly split; some 23 jurisdictions have accepted the economic loss rule.[143]

"New York remains a jurisdiction in which courts have not extended tort liability to cover negligently caused economic loss unless the loss is coupled with physical injury or direct property damage."[144] There is one exception: if the injured party can show that its relationship with the defendant was the "functional equivalent" of privity of contract. In *Ossining Union Free School District v Anderson LaRocca Anderson*,[145] the Court of Appeals held that a school district, which contracted with an architect, could sue engineers hired by the architect for damages suffered as a result of the engineers' negligence and malpractice. The issue addressed by the court was whether, in a negligent misrepresentation case that produces only economic injury, privity of contract is required. The court held that what is required is not *actual* privity of contract but a relationship so close as to be the "functional equivalent of contractual privity."[146] This decision is discussed more completely in Chapters 8 and 11.

New York has only this one exception to the rule. It bars not only direct claims for economic loss but also statutory contribution[147] and common law indemnification claims[148] for economic loss due to breach of a construction contract. Of course, parties may provide in indemnification agreements that purely economic losses are recoverable.[149] Further, New York bars claims for economic loss due to breach of implied warranties unless the damaged party

---

[140] G.A. Smith, *The Continuing Decline of the "Economic Loss Rule" in Construction Litigation*, 10 Construction L 1 (1990).

[141] Forsten, *Delaware Joins in Rejecting the Economic Loss Rule in Construction Settings*, 11 Construction L 7 (1991); Smith, *supra* note 140.

[142] House & Bell, *supra* note 139; Barrett, *supra* note note 132; Barrett, *Recovery of Economic Loss in Tort for Construction Defects: A Critical Analysis*, 40 SC L Rev 892 (1989).

[143] House & Bell, *supra* note 139, at 29. Note 2 of the article lists those states and federal courts that have accepted the rule.

[144] Milliken & Co v Consolidated Edison Co, 119 AD2d 481, 501 NYS2d 23 (1st Dept 1986), *affd*, 69 NY2d 786, 787, 505 NE2d 624, 513 NYS2d 114 (1987).

[145] 73 NY2d 417, 539 NE2d 91, 541 NYS2d 335 (1989).

[146] *Id* at 419, 539 NE2d at 91, 541 NYS2d at 335.

[147] Hudson City Bd of Educ v Sargent, Webster, Crenshaw & Folley, 71 NY2d 21, 517 NE2d 1360, 523 NYS2d 475 (1987); Lawrence Dev Corp v Jobin Waterproofing, Inc, 167 AD2d 988, 562 NYS2d 902 (4th Dept 1990); Briar Contracting Corp v City of NY, 156 AD2d 628, 550 NYS2d 717 (2d Dept 1989); NY Civ Prac L & R 1401 (McKinney 1976 & Supp 1992).

[148] Prudential-Bache Sec, Inc v Resnick Water St Dev Co, 161 AD2d 456, 555 NYS2d 367 (1st Dept 1990); Briar Contracting Corp v City of NY, 156 AD2d 628, 550 NYS2d 717 (2d Dept 1989).

[149] Hudson City Bd of Educ v Sargent, Webster, Crenshaw & Folley, 71 NY2d 21, 517 NE2d 1360, 523 NYS2d 475 (1987).

is in privity of contract with the responsible party.[150] Thus, a building owner that suffers economic loss due to breach of an implied product warranty cannot recover from the manufacturer or the product's installer where the owner lacks privity of contract with both the manufacturer and the installer.[151] The owner's remedy is against its contractor, who would then seek recovery from the subcontractor. Similarly, a remote purchaser does not have a strict products liability claim against a manufacturer that made no representations to it and with whom it is not in privity of contract where its only damages are economic loss.[152]

§15.21 UCC Damage and Remedy Provisions

The Uniform Commercial Code (UCC) provides specific remedies and damages for contracts that primarily are for the sale of goods. These are discussed in Chapter 3.

§15.22 Contractual Limitations on Damages

It is not unusual for construction contracts to contain liquidated damages clauses under which an owner receives a per diem sum for every day the project is delayed beyond the completion date. Generally, if a contract contains a liquidated damages clause, an owner's remedy upon late completion is to recover the specified daily sum from the contractor; the owner may not also recover its actual damages as a result of the delayed completion.[153] This rule does not hold true if the contractor abandons the job. If the liquidated damages clause does not specify that it applies in the event of abandonment as well as delay, the owner may not recover liquidated damages, but is limited to its actual damages.[154] Further, if both parties are responsible for the delay, the general rule is that the liquidated damages clause is abrogated and the parties must resort to recovery of their actual damages.[155] Liquidated damages are discussed in depth in Chapter 7.

Another form of contractual damages limitation is an exculpatory clause, such as a *no damage for delay* clause, a site investigation clause, or a notice of

---

[150] Coffey v United States Gypsum Co, 149 AD2d 960, 540 NYS2d 92 (4th Dept), *appeal denied*, 74 NY2d 610, 545 NE2d 868, 546 NYS2d 554 (1989); Chenango Indus Agency v Lockwood Greene Engrs, Inc, 114 AD2d 728, 494 NYS2d 832 (3d Dept 1985), *appeal dismissed*, 67 NY2d 757, 490 NE2d 1233, 500 NYS2d 1027 (1986).

[151] Ralston Purina Co v Arthur G. McKee & Co, 158 AD2d 969, 551 NYS2d 720 (4th Dept 1990).

[152] Schiavone Constr Co v Elgood Mayo Corp, 81 AD2d 221, 227-34, 439 NYS2d 933, 937-41 (1st Dept 1981) (Silverman, J. dissenting), *revd in opinion adopting Silverman, J. dissent*, 56 NY2d 667, 436 NE2d 1322, 451 NYS2d 720 (1982).

[153] General Supply & Constr Co v Goelet, 241 NY 28, 148 NE 778 (1925).

[154] City of Elmira v Larry Walter, Inc, 76 NY2d 912, 564 NE2d 655, 563 NYS2d 45 (1990).

[155] Babylon Assocs v County of Suffolk, 101 AD2d 207, 475 NYS2d 869, 875 (2d Dept 1984).

claim requirement. These are discussed in various places throughout this book, including Chapters 5, 6, 7, and 12.

One limitation clause used by architects and engineers in an attempt to limit their liability provides:

> The client agrees to limit the consultant's liability to the client and to all contractors and subcontractors on the project, due to professional negligent acts, errors or omissions of the consultant to the sum of $50,000 or the consultant's fee, whichever is greater.[156]

Similar clauses attempt to limit an architect or engineer's potential liability to the amount the professional's insurance actually covers; such a clause was upheld as valid by the Southern District of the United States District Court of New York.[157] It is unclear whether New York state courts will allow or prohibit such clauses due to the effect of legislative prohibitions against liability exemptions and limitations in connection with construction.[158]

§15.23 Contractual Provisions Regarding Remedies

Generally, parties may limit or expand their available remedies under a contract as they choose. If the contract contains an exclusive remedies provision, the parties are limited to the remedies contained therein. For instance, in *Sevenson Environmental Services v New York State Thruway Authority*,[159] the contract required the contractor to use minority business enterprises in performance of the contract work and to use good faith efforts to attain the Minority/Women's Business Enterprise goals of the contract. The authority, during contract performance, determined that the contractor was not using good faith efforts to meet its affirmative action requirements and found it to be in breach of the contract. The contract provided that such a breach subjected the contractor to forfeiture of its deposit, possible termination, and possible disqualification from other authority work for up to three years. The authority did not seek any of these remedies against the contractor; instead, it deducted almost

---

[156] Ashcraft, *Limitation of Liability—The View after Markborough*, 11 Construction L 3 (Aug 1991), discussing the contract clause at issue in Markborough Cal, Inc v Superior Ct, 227 Cal App 3d 705, 277 Cal Rptr 919 (1991).

[157] *See* Long Island Lighting Co v IMO DeLaval, Inc, 668 F Supp 237 (SDNY 1987); Florida Power & Light Co v Mid-Valley, Inc, 763 F2d 1316 (11th Cir 1985).

[158] *See* NY Gen Oblig Law §5-323 (McKinney 1989 & Supp 1992). In St Vincent's Medical Center v Vincent E. Iorio, Inc, 78 Misc 2d 968, 358 NYS2d 993 (Richmond 1974), a trial court limited NY Gen Oblig Law §5-323 (McKinney 1989 & Supp 1992) to construction that is incidental to the installation or servicing of appliances and equipment. In Board of Educ v Delle Cese, 65 Misc 2d 473, 318 NYS2d 46 (Oneida 1971), a trial court found §5-323 to be much broader and applied it to a contract concerning new construction. *See also* Long Island Lighting Co v Imo Delaval, Inc, 668 F Supp 237 (SDNY 1987).

[159] 149 Misc 2d 268, 561 NYS2d 523 (Ct Cl 1990).

$90,000 from moneys due the contractor as the lost value of minority work on the project. The Court of Claims held the authority to be in breach of contract for this withholding, since the contract did not allow it to withhold money for the breach. Further, the authority did not prove that the parties contemplated at the time of contracting that a dollar amount would be paid for such a breach, nor could it show that it suffered any monetary damage. The court stated:

> The [Authority] having incorporated into the contract the remedies for relief in the event of breach of the contract by claimant as to M/WBE participation, and having failed to exercise these remedies, cannot now complain of denial of relief for alleged breach of said covenant when existing law prevents recovery under established principles of contract law.[160]

§15.24 Specific Breaches by Contractor

Breaches of construction contracts by contractors are discussed throughout this text in various chapters dealing with specific types of breach, such as delay or defects, or in chapters that deal with relationships, such as with sureties or subcontractors. Within those chapters and sections are discussions of remedies and damages available to owners, subcontractors, architects, and others when a contractor is in breach. The discussion in the following relevant sections is thus brief to avoid duplication of matters covered elsewhere.

§15.25 —Failure to Commence Performance

If a contractor fails to begin performance, the owner's measure of damages is the owner's actual cost to perform the contract work, including damages suffered because of the delay in the project, less the contract price (discussed in Chapter 7). If there is a performance bond, the owner may seek its damages and/or performance of the contract from the surety (discussed in Chapter 8). In addition, an owner may seek specific performance of the contract, discussed in **§15.39** and Chapter 7.

§15.26 —Partial Performance

Unless the contract provides otherwise, a party who has partly performed a contract and who has materially defaulted in completing it is not entitled to recover for his or her partial performance, unless he or she can establish a legal excuse for not completing the work.[161] The owner may recover the excess cost

---

[160] *Id* at 272-73, 561 NYS2d at 526.
[161] Waters v Glasheen, 103 AD2d 1043, 478 NYS2d 437 (4th Dept 1984) (citing Steel Storage & Elevator Constr Co v Stock, 225 NY 173, 121 NE 786 (1919)(; *see also* Triple M Roofing Corp v Greater Jericho Corp, 43 AD2d 594, 349 NYS2d 771 (2d Dept 1973) ("defendant is entitled to retain the benefits of plaintiff's partial performance without paying for it").

to complete the contractor's work and remedy any defects.[162]

It is normally held, however, that the defaulting contractor may be permitted to set off against the owner's damages the value of its part performance. The apparent conflict between (1) the doctrine of substantial performance and (2) the contractor's right to set off against the owner's damages any payments justly due for part performance is perhaps resolved by referring to the contract between the parties. Under the older cases, a contractor could have no recovery until substantial performance of the contract. In one case, the court observed:

> [w]e have the case of a contract for a lump sum, no part of which is to become due or payable until the completion of the contract, except that a percentage of the amount earned from time to time is to be advanced "in order to enable the contractor to prosecute the work advantageously." If nothing had been said about the advancements as work progressed, it would be quite clear that nothing would be due to the contractor until the completion of the contract.[163]

Modern contracts normally provide for periodic payments from the owner to the contractor to enable the contractor to maintain the progress of the construction.

In addition, American Institute of Architects (AIA) Document A201 provides that if the owner terminates the contract, and if the unpaid balance of the contract sum exceeds costs of finishing the work, then such excess shall be paid to the contractor.[164]

If the contractor's failure to perform is caused by the owner, the contractor may be permitted to recover payment for the partial performance and lost profits on the unperformed work.[165]

This issue is also discussed in Chapters 4 and 12.

§15.27 —Substantial Performance

If a contractor breaches after substantially performing its duties under the contract, it is entitled to be paid the contract price less payments made, less the cost of remedying any defects in its work or of achieving complete performance. The doctrine of substantial performance or completion is discussed in Chapter 12.

---

[162] Tri-Mar Contractors, Inc v Itco Drywall, Inc, 74 AD2d 601, 424 NYS2d 737 (2d Dept 1980); Condello v Stock, 285 AD 861, 136 NYS2d 507 (4th Dept 1955).

[163] Herman & Grace v City of NY, 130 AD 531, 114 NYS 1107 (1st Dept 1909).

[164] *General Conditions of the Contract for Construction*, AIA Doc A201, ¶14.2.4. (14th ed 1987); *See also* Al-Ev Constr Corp v Ahern Maintenance & Supply Corp, 141 AD2d 591, 529 NYS2d 354 (2d Dept 1988) (cost to complete was less than amount remaining in contract sum; owner entitled only to nominal damages for its counterclaim against defaulting contractor).

[165] *See* AIA Doc A201, ¶14.1.2; Langan Constr Corp v State, 110 Misc 177, 180 NYS 249 (Ct Cl 1920); Peru Assocs v State, 70 Misc 2d 775, 334 NYS2d 772 (Ct Cl 1971).

§15.28 —Defective Performance

An owner's remedies and damages for a contractor's defective performance are discussed throughout Chapter 12 on defects and failures, as are other parties' remedies and damages for a contractor's defective performance. Generally, an owner's measure of damages for defective performance is the reasonable cost to repair the defect or complete performance.[166] If the contract provides that the contractor shall fix the defect, it must do so and may be compelled to do so.[167]

§15.29 —Cost of Completion v Diminution in Value

Generally, the measure of damages for a contractor's breach is the cost to complete performance or of repair or replacement of the defect.[168] If, however, the contractor substantially performed the contract in good faith, but defects resulted, and the cost of completion, repair, or replacement is great and out of proportion to the benefit to be gained from correction, the measure of damages is the difference in value as constructed and the value if there had been proper performance. In other words, the measure of damages is the diminished value of the property due to the breach.[169]

This diminished value measurement is known as the *economic waste rule* and was first established in the landmark case of *Jacob & Youngs, Inc v Kent*,[170] also known as the "reading pipe case." As this rule benefits the wrongdoer somewhat, it is carefully applied. Not every claim of economic waste will result in a diminished value measure of damages. The defect must be irremediable or incapable of repair without substantial destruction of the property. The contractor's breach must not have been intentional and the contractor must show that its contract performance was in substantial good faith.[171] Further, the defect must not affect the structure's safety.[172] An example of a defect that would invoke the diminution in value rule (besides *Jacob & Youngs*) is a case where a contractor substituted floor materials. The substitution did not affect the building's safety and was not noticeable. The owner was awarded the difference in value of the materials used, not the replacement cost.[173]

---

[166] VanDeloo v Moreland, 84 AD2d 871, 444 NYS2d 744 (3d Dept 1981).

[167] A-1 Camp Chair Serv Co v William L. Crow Constr Co, 24 AD2d 623, 262 NYS2d 166 (2d Dept 1965).

[168] American Standard, Inc v Schectman, 80 AD2d 318, 439 NYS2d 529 (4th Dept), *appeal denied*, 54 NY2d 604, 427 NE2d 512, 443 NYS2d 1027 (1981).

[169] Jacob & Youngs, Inc v Kent, 230 NY 239, 129 NE 889 (1921); American Standard, Inc v Schectman, 80 AD2d 318, 439 NYS2d 529 (4th Dept), *appeal denied*, 54 NY2d 604, 427 NE2d 512, 443 NYS2d 1027 (1981).

[170] 230 NY 239, 129 NE 889 (1921).

[171] American Standard, Inc v Schectman, 80 AD2d 318, 439 NYS2d 529 (4th Dept), *appeal denied*, 54 NY2d 604, 427 NE2d 512, 443 NYS2d 1027 (1981).

[172] Ferrari v Barleo Homes, Inc, 112 AD2d 137, 490 NYS2d 827 (2d Dept 1985).

[173] *Id.*

In an unusual case, an owner was allowed to recover both the cost of repair and the diminished value of its building.[174] Structural and ventilation repairs were required for the building to comply with the New York City Building Code and for it to be used as intended. The necessary repairs would reduce the use of floor space and cover some windows, thus reducing the building's value. The court, upon awarding both measures of damage, acknowledged the lack of precedent for such an award but stated that "[i]f plaintiff is to be made whole, that is, to have what it contracted for or its equivalent, it is entitled to recover both the cost of repairing the building and the resultant diminution in its value subsequent to the repair."[175]

This issue is further discussed in Chapter 12.

§15.30 Specific Breaches by Owner

Breaches by owners are discussed throughout this book, primarily in Chapters 4 on default and termination, 7 on delays, and 9 on mechanics' liens.

§15.31 —Failure to Commence Project

If an owner fails to begin its project, its contractor is entitled to recover the profits it would have made had it performed the job.

§15.32 —Abandonment Following Start of Construction

If an owner prevents a contractor from performing its contract, the contractor may seek either a contract or a quantum meruit measure of damages. See discussion at §15.10.

Recovery of delay damages following abandonment is discussed in Chapter 7.

§15.33 —Nonpayment

Generally, an owner's failure to pay a contractor for work performed is a substantial breach of the contract that entitles the contractor to terminate the contract and seek breach of contract damages or quantum meruit recovery.[176] See §15.10. Nonpayment is discussed in Chapter 4.

---

[174] Italian Economic Corp v Community Engrs, Inc, 135 Misc 2d 209, 514 NYS2d 630 (NY 1987).

[175] *Id* at 216, 514 NYS2d at 630.

[176] New Era Homes Corp v Forster, 299 NY 303, 86 NE2d 757, 22 ALR2d 1338 (1949).

§15.34 Breach by Architect/Engineer

Generally, if an architect breaches its contract with an owner, the owner is entitled to recover the cost incurred as a result of the breach.[177] Breaches by architects and engineers are discussed in Chapter 11 on professional liability. Design defects are discussed in Chapter 12.

§15.35 Breach by Subcontractors

There is little that is unique about a subcontractor's breach of contract. Generally, subcontractors breach construction contracts in the same ways general contractors do—they fail to perform; their performance is defective; they are late or slow. The question that is somewhat unique to subcontractor breach is, who can recover from the breaching subcontractor? Obviously, the contractor that retained the subcontractor may sue it for breach of contract. The issue of concern for a subcontractor is whether the owner can recover directly from it.

A quick review of the issue may lead to the conclusion that, because a subcontractor generally cannot seek compensation directly from an owner, an owner should be barred from seeking damages from a subcontractor. Unfortunately for subcontractors, this is not always the case. If an owner can prove that it is a third-party beneficiary of the subcontract, it may be entitled to seek damage recovery from the subcontractor for breach of contract and breach of express warranty.[178]

This rule may seem simplistic, for what owner is not the intended beneficiary of the subcontractor's performance? Subcontractors do not perform work in a vacuum; their work is performed for a general contractor that is under contract to the owner. The courts, recognizing the reality of construction work, have invented a legal fiction that provides that, generally, a subcontractor's work is intended to benefit the contractor only, not the owner. In *Fourth Ocean Putnam Corp v Interstate Wrecking Co*,[179] the Court of Appeals adopted the test found in Restatement (Second) of Contracts, §302[2], which looks at circumstances surrounding the project, including contractual language, to determine whether the subcontractor intended to give the owner the benefit of its performance. An example of circumstances sufficient to make an owner an intended third-party beneficiary is found in *City of New York v Kalisch-Jarcho, Inc.*[180] In that case, the city decided to renovate an ice rink in Central Park. Long before the job was advertised, an ice rink manufacturer contacted city officials and invited them to inspect rinks it had built in Boston and provided preliminary budget and engineering information. The city's bid documents required that the gen-

---

[177] Schwartz v Kuhn, 71 Misc 149, 126 NYS 568 (App Term 1911).

[178] Ralston Purina Co v Arthur G. McKee & Co, 158 AD2d 969, 551 NYS2d 720 (4th Dept 1990); City of NY v Kalisch-Jarcho, Inc, 161 AD2d 252, 554 NYS2d 900 (1st Dept 1990).

[179] 66 NY2d 38, 485 NE2d 208, 495 NYS2d 1 (1985).

[180] 161 AD2d 252, 554 NYS2d 900 (1st Dept 1990).

eral contractor use the manufacturer's product. The subcontract between the general contractor and manufacturer incorporated the general contract and gave the city inspection and testing rights at the manufacturer's plant, provided warranties, and obligated the manufacturer to indemnify the general contractor and city against damages due to breach of warranty. Based on these facts, the appellate court found that the city had shown that it was an intended third-party beneficiary of the subcontract.[181]

To avoid inadvertently granting third-party beneficiary status to an owner, courts have suggested that subcontractors insist upon a subcontract clause that expressly negates any enforcement of the subcontract by a third party.[182] Of course, in the real world, a subcontractor that insists upon such a clause may find itself without work.

> **PRACTICE POINTER:**
>
> Under the appropriate circumstances, an owner may consider entering into a liquidating agreement with the general contractor as a means of reaching the subcontractors responsible for the damage. "Reverse liquidating agreements" have been upheld in New York and are governed by the same legal principles as are liquidating agreements between general contractors and subcontractors. Compliance with the strict requirements for a valid liquidating agreement are mandatory. These requirements are discussed in Chapter 3. If a lawsuit has been commenced at the time the liquidating agreement is executed by the owner and general contractor, the legal papers should be amended to conform to the provisions of the agreement. For guidance, see *Lambert Houses Redevelopment Company v. HRH Equity Corporation*, 117 A.D.2d 227, 502 N.Y.S.2d 433 (1st Dept. 1986).

Unless it is a third-party beneficiary of the subcontract, if an owner's losses due to subcontractor breach were economic only, i.e., it suffered no personal physical harm and none of its tangible property besides the subcontractor's work was damaged, it could not recover from the subcontractor without proving privity of contract.[183] The owner's remedy is to look to the general contractor, which, by most contracts, is wholly responsible for its subcontractor's performance.[184]

Damages and remedies due to a materialman's breach are discussed in Chapters 3 and 12.

---

[181] *Id.*

[182] *Id;* Edward B. Fitzpatrick Constr Corp v County of Suffolk, 138 AD2d 446, 525 NYS2d 863 (2d Dept 1988).

[183] Schiavone Constr Co v Elgood Mayo Corp, 81 AD2d 221, 227-34, 439 NYS2d 933, 937-41 (1st Dept 1981) (Silverman, J. dissenting), *revd in opinion adopting Silverman, J. dissent,* 56 NY2d 667, 436 NE2d 1322, 451 NYS2d 720 (1982). *But see* City of NY v Kalisch-Jarcho, Inc, 161 AD2d 252, 554 NYS2d 900 (1st Dept 1990).

[184] Babylon Assocs v County of Suffolk, 101 AD2d 207, 475 NYS2d 869 (2d Dept 1984).

§15.36 Materialmen Remedies

In addition to standard contract remedies, materialmen have two remedies that are somewhat unique to suppliers of goods: replevin and a suit on an account stated. These are discussed in the following two sections.

§15.37 —Replevin

A *replevin* is a means by which a materialman may physically recover possession of the goods delivered to another upon a promise to pay, but for which the materialman has not been paid.[185] Technically, replevin no longer exists in New York; the "new" term is an action for *seizure of a chattel*.[186] Regardless of its name, the action provides a supplier with a supposedly quick way to recover its property, without having to wait for a judgment following a full round of motions or a trial. In fact, due to procedural, notice, and bonding requirements and the idiosyncrasies, schedules, and fees of local sheriff departments, replevin is usually more work, time, and, hence, money than it is worth. Moreover, the person from whom the goods are replevined can rereplevin them from the materialman. Rarely do the authors advise replevin.

§15.38 —Account Stated

A suit on *account stated* is based on a creditor's invoices and statements relating to its transaction with the debtor.

> Generally, an account stated is defined as an agreement between the parties, who have had previous transactions of a monetary character that all the items of the account representing such transactions, and the balance struck, are correct, together with a promise, express or implied, for the payment of such balance.[187]

The elements of an account stated are:

1. Previous transactions between the parties that created the debt
2. An agreement as to amount due
3. Express or implied promise to pay; and

---

[185] NY Civ Prac L & R art 71, 7101-7112 (McKinney 1980 & Supp 1992) set forth, in detail, how physical possession of goods may be recovered.

[186] McLaughlin, *Practice Commentaries* to CPLR §7101, 7B McKinney's Consolidated Rules of NY 170 (McKinney 1980 & Supp 1992).

[187] 1A CJS 67 *Account Stated* §2(a) (1985); *see also* Corr v Hoffman, 256 NY 254, 176 NE 383 (1931).

4. The balance due[188]

Thus, an account stated claim may be proved by a showing that the defendant received and retained the plaintiff's bills and acknowledged them without objection.[189]

§15.39 Specific Performance

Despite many attorneys' and judges' beliefs, "there is no hard and fast rule against applying the remedy of specific performance to [construction] contracts, especially when the parties have by agreement provided for just that remedy."[190] While there is no rule that deprives equity of ordering specific performance of a building contract, a court does have the discretion either to refuse to award it or to award it and enforce such an award.[191] Further, a court will enforce an arbitration award of specific performance,[192] even if the court would not or could not have ordered specific performance.[193]

§15.40 Rescission and Restitution

Rescission is a drastic remedy that is properly granted only if: there is no adequate remedy at law;[194] the parties can be restored to the status quo;[195] and there was fraud in the inducement to contract, a mutual mistake of fact, a failure of consideration, an inability to perform the contract after it was made, or a substantial breach of the contract that defeated its purpose.[196] Generally, if a party has an adequate remedy at law, i.e., the recovery of money damages due to the breach, rescission will not be granted.[197]

---

[188] Franklin, Weinrib, Rudell & Vassallo, PC v Gruber, NYLJ, Jan 10, 1992, at p 21, col 2 (App Term 1st Dept 1992); Graham v Lansing Dev Corp, 56 Misc 2d 1064, 290 NYS2d 590 (Broome 1968).

[189] Franklin, Weinrib, Rudell & Vassallo, PC v Gruber, NYLJ, Jan 10, 1992, at p 21, col 2 (App Term 1st Dept 1992).

[190] Grayson-Robinson Stores, Inc v Iris Constr Corp, 8 NY2d 133, 136, 168 NE2d 377, 202 NYS2d 303 305 (1960).

[191] *Id.*

[192] *Id.*

[193] Staklinski v Pyramid Elec Co, 6 NY2d 159, 160 NE2d 78, 188 NYS2d 541 (1959) (employment contract).

[194] Tarleton Bldg Corp v Spider Staging Sales Co, 26 AD2d 809, 274 NYS2d 43 (1st Dept 1966).

[195] Rudman v Cowles Communications, Inc, 30 NY2d 1, 280 NE2d 867, 330 NYS2d 33 (1972); Fink v Friedman, 78 Misc 2d 429, 358 NYS2d 250 (Nassau 1974). This case provides a good summary of the law of rescission, 78 Misc 2d 429, 358 NYS2d at 258-59.

[196] Babylon Assocs v County of Suffolk, 101 AD2d 207, 475 NYS2d 869 (2d Dept 1984).

[197] *Id.*

574   REMEDIES/DAMAGES

Rescission is further discussed in Chapter 4. Rescission of bids is discussed in Chapter 2.

Restitution is another equitable remedy whereby a party can recover a thing of value it bestowed on another party. Neither party need have done anything wrong for restitution to be permitted. All that has to have occurred was that one person received something of value from another without paying for it, while the other gave something without receiving payment. If a court finds that unjust benefit and loss, respectively, will occur, it may order restitution. When the restitution is based upon a rescission, its goal is a return to the status quo for each party. The question in restitution is not what the cost of services or goods conferred was, but, rather, what value and actual benefit they are to the one who received the services or goods.[198] If it cannot be shown that the receiver benefited, there can be no restitution.[199]

§15.41   Reformation

The purpose of reformation is to change the contract judicially to reflect the parties' original intent. A court will not rewrite the agreement, but will correct any mistakes in its language that do not reflect the parties' true agreement. Consider, for instance, a subcontract to install doors in a hotel. The hotel has 100 rooms, but due to a typographical error, the contract specifies 1,000 doors. Reformation would correct the contract. In a somewhat unusual case, a lower New York court reformed a contract due to a substantial clerical bid error.[200] This case is unusual for two reasons: (1) the typical relief for a mistaken bid is withdrawal of the bid, not reformation of the contract, and (2) the public owner urged the court to reform rather than rescind the bid because, even with reformation, the bidder would be the lowest responsible bidder.

---

[198] Robbins v Frank Cooper Assocs, 19 AD2d 242, 241 NYS2d 259 (1st Dept 1963), *revd on other grounds*, 14 NY2d 913, 200 NE2d 860, 252 NYS2d 318 (1964).

[199] Naimoli v Massa, 81 Misc 2d 431, 366 NYS2d 573 (City Ct Geneva 1975).

[200] Iversen Constr Corp v Palmyra-Macedon Cent School Dist, 143 Misc 2d 36, 539 NYS2d 858 (Wayne 1989).

Dispute Resolution 16

§16.01 Introduction
§16.02 Notice of Claim Requirements
§16.03 Freedom of Information Laws
§16.04 Contract Scope of Work Disputes
§16.05 Informal Dispute Resolution
§16.06 —Dispute Review Boards
§16.07 —Mediation
§16.08 —Mediation and "Baseball Arbitration" in Construction Disputes
§16.09 —Minitrials
§16.10 Formal Dispute Resolution
§16.11 —Litigation
§16.12 —Arbitration
§16.13 —Federal Arbitration Act
§16.14 —Agreement to Arbitrate
§16.15 —Conditions Precedent to Arbitration
§16.16 —Arbitration: Is a Surety Bound?
Appendix 16-1 Selected References

§16.01 Introduction

There are many ways to resolve a dispute—from meeting face-to-face to work out an amicable solution to mediation to a full-blown jury trial with expert witnesses and scores of documents and exhibits. Obviously, the more simple the means chosen, the less costly it is to all parties in terms of time, effort, and, usually, money. The best way to resolve a dispute is to avoid getting into one in the first place. In a perfect world, owners, contractors, subcontractors, architects, and engineers carefully review all plans and specifications, discuss and clarify confusing items before bidding is had or work begins, confirm all orders in writing, maintain open and honest communications, bill and pay honestly and promptly, refuse to cut corners, and act fairly and reasonably, treating all parties with respect. While no job is perfect, the more steps the parties take to avoid disputes, the more successful the job will be from all parties' perspectives. If a dispute cannot be avoided or resolved amicably, consider all options for resolution and be thoroughly familiar with all options before embarking on a resolution course. Plan resolution carefully, avoiding unnecessary escalation of a dispute. Before claiming fraud, try sitting down with the other side and discussing the facts rationally; before filing suit, try mediation or a minitrial.

Ambrose Bierce once defined a lawsuit as "a machine which you go into as a pig and come out as a sausage."[1] This definition often holds true, whether a party wins or loses, especially in commercial cases. The expense, in time and money, of formal dispute resolution can be immense. Not only are there attorneys' fees, but also court and arbitration fees, discovery costs, expert witness fees, lost interest, loss of productive work time as litigants and their employees spend time reconstructing a past job rather than concentrating on present and future jobs, etc. For this reason, use of informal dispute resolution is urged. Parties should try all available means to informally resolve their disputes *before* resorting to third parties—i.e., the courts or arbitration—paying close attention, however, to contractual time limitations and applicable statutes of limitations.

Informal dispute resolution starts when the parties sit down together and discuss their differences without third parties. If no resolution is reached, it can progress to more structured methods, such as mediation, a minitrial, or using a dispute review board set up in the initial contract. Generally, the earlier and more simply parties can resolve their disagreements, the quicker and less expensive the resolution will be and the more likely it is that permanent damage will not be done to the parties' relationship.

> **PRACTICE POINTER:**
>
> Be wary when settling a dispute with a public entity—the settlement must be approved by someone with *actual* authority, such as a city comptroller. A party is presumed to know who has authority and who does not, since the extent of a public employee's authority is generally set forth in statutes and regulations.[2]

Formal dispute resolution means either litigation in court or private arbitration. Either means tends to be expensive and time consuming, although there are advantages and disadvantages to each.

Before the means of resolving a dispute can be addressed, one must consider three preliminary matters: notice of claim requirements, the Freedom of Infor-

---

[1] A. Bierce, The Devil's Dictionary 188 (1906).
[2] Walentas v New York City Dept of Ports, 167 AD2d 211, 561 NYS2d 718 (1st Dept 1990).

mation laws, and contract provisions for scope of work disputes. These are discussed in relevant sections following.

§16.02 Notice of Claim Requirements

Construction contracts often contain provisions that require written notice of any claim for extra work, changed condition, damage, delay, etc., within a specified period after the claim arises or accrues. The purported purpose of notice provisions is to provide an owner with an opportunity to investigate and determine the validity of the claim.[3] Typically, compliance with a notice provision is a condition precedent to a contractor's right to request an extension of time or adjustment of contract amount, to arbitration or litigation, and to recover damages.[4] These notice requirements should be complied with as closely as possible.

> **PRACTICE POINTER:**
>
> To help ensure notice requirement compliance, contractors might prepare a chart at the beginning of the project. The chart should list all notice requirements including the types of claims for which notice must be given, time periods, the content of the notice, to whom notice must be given, reply times, etc.

For public construction projects, notice requirements are often set forth in statutes in addition to the notice requirements found in the contract itself. For example, Education Law §§2562 and 3813 set forth requirements for the presentation of claims and bringing of suit against a school district.[5]

Education Law §3813 provides in part:

> 1. No action or special proceeding, for any cause whatever, except as hereinafter provided, relating to district property or property of schools . . . or claim against the district or any school, . . . shall be prosecuted or maintained against any school district, board of education, board of cooperative educational services, school . . . or any officer of a school district, . . . unless it shall appear by and as an allegation in the complaint

---

[3] Board of Educ v Wager Constr Corp, 37 NY2d 283, 333 NE2d 353, 372 NYS2d 45 (1975).

[4] Id; Vanderlinde Elec Corp v City of Rochester, 54 AD2d 155, 388 NYS2d 388 (1976).

[5] NY Educ Law §2562 (McKinney 1981) applies to boards of education of cities with populations of 400,000 or more. NY Educ Law §3813 (McKinney 1981 & Supplementary Pamphlet 1992) applies to all governing bodies of any school district and certain state-supported schools, including those school boards covered under NY Educ Law §2562 (McKinney 1981). A claim against a city of more than 400,000 must comply with both sections. See Crescent Elec Installation Corp v Board of Educ, 50 NY2d 780, 409 NE2d 917, 431 NYS2d 443, (1980).

Justice Shapiro analyzed the legislative history of NY Educ Law §§2562 and 3813 in H&J Floor Covering v Board of Educ, 66 AD2d 588, 413 NYS2d 414 (2d Dept 1979).

or necessary moving papers that a written verified claim upon which such action or special proceeding is founded was presented to the governing body of said district or school within three months after the accrual of such claim, and that the officer or body having the power to adjust or pay said claim has neglected or refused to make an adjustment or payment thereof for thirty days after such presentment.

2-a. Upon application, the court in its discretion, may extend the time to serve a notice of claim. The extension shall not exceed the time limited for the commencement of an action by the claimant against any district or any school. In determining whether to grant an extension, the court shall consider, in particular, whether the district or school or its attorney or its insurance carrier or other agent acquired actual knowledge of the essential facts constituting the claim within the time specified in subdivision one of this section or within a reasonable time thereafter. The court shall also consider all other relevant facts and circumstances, including:. . .; whether the claimant failed to serve a timely notice of claim by reason of his justifiable reliance upon settlement representations made by an authorized representative of the district or school or its insurance carrier; whether the claimant in serving a notice of claim made an excusable error concerning the identity of the district or school against whom the claim should be asserted; and whether the delay in serving the notice of claim substantially prejudiced the district or school in maintaining its defense on the merits.

An application for leave to serve a late notice shall not be denied on the ground that it was made after commencement of an action against the district or school.

2-b. Except as provided in subdivision two of this section, and notwithstanding any other provision of law providing a longer period of time in which to commence an action or special proceeding, no action or special proceeding shall be commenced against any entity specified in subdivision one of this section more than one year after the cause of action arose; provided, however, that nothing contained in this subdivision shall be deemed to modify of supersede any provision of law specifying a shorter period of time in which to commence an action or special proceeding against any such entity.

Similarly, State Finance Law §145 sets forth notice requirements for claims against the state. Statutory notice provisions are not consolidated in the statutes or indexes, but may be found in many different places. Local provisions may be even harder to find, thus deepening further the trap for the unwary. These statutes and their requirements are automatically part of every contract made by a school district or the state,[6] although they are rarely mentioned in the contract. Contractual terms specifying procedures for filing a claim do not replace statutory requirements as conditions precedent to maintenance of a

---

[6] Anderson Constr Co v Board of Educ, 229 NYS2d 337 (Suffolk 1962).

claim.[7] Compliance with statutory notice provisions is mandatory to maintain a claim[8] both in court and before arbitrators,[9] although a slight variation from statutory requirements will not always result in outright dismissal of a claim.[10]

> **PRACTICE POINTER:**
>
> Find out what statutory notice provisions are applicable early in a job. When certain that all notice provisions have been found, in both state and local legislation, ask the agency for its opinion of which statutory notice provisions apply. Do not rely on the agency opinion if it differs from what legal research has discovered. When in doubt, comply with every provision found that may apply.

The primary issues surrounding notice provisions are to whom the notice must be presented, when the notice must be presented, what the notice must contain, and how an owner waives a notice requirement. Notice requirements are also discussed in Chapters 5, 6, and 7.

Service of Notice

Relevant statutes and most contracts designate the person or entity upon whom service must be made. Such provisions must be complied with strictly; variance is rarely allowed. For instance, Education Law §3813 provides that notice must be served on the "governing body of said district or school." A contractor's claim was disallowed when it was served on the school board's architect rather than on the board, despite the fact that the contract specified that the architect was to receive first notification of contract disputes.[11] Similarly, a contractor's claim against the state Department of Transportation was denied because it served the Attorney General rather than the department as specified in the contract.[12] Perhaps the most shocking example of strict interpretation of the service requirement was when a contractor's claim was denied

---

[7] Public Improvements, Inc v Board of Educ, 81 AD2d 537, 438 NYS2d 305 (1981), affd, 56 NY2d 850, 438 NE2d 876, 453 NYS2d 170 (1982).

[8] Id.

[9] Board of Educ v Wager Constr Co, 37 NY2d 283, 333 NE2d 353, 372 NYS2d 45 (1975).

[10] See Nyack Bd of Educ v K. Capolino Design & Renovation, Ltd, 114 AD2d 849, 494 NYS2d 758 (1985), affd, 68 NY2d 647, 496 NE2d 233, 505 NYS2d 74, (1986) (late claim allowed); Almar Constr Corp v PM Hughes & Sons, 58 AD2d 615, 395 NYS2d 700 (1977) (requisition with copies of letters to board architect held to constitute notice of claim); McCullough v Board of Educ, 11 AD2d 740, 204 NYS2d 555 (1960) (later verification of claim allowed).

[11] Nyack Bd of Educ v K. Capolino Design & Renovation, Ltd, 114 AD2d 849, 494 NYS2d 758 (1985), affd, 68 NY2d 647, 496 NE2d 233, 505 NYS2d 74 (1986) (the contractor's claim was allowed under NY Educ L §3813(2-a), which provides for late claims in special circumstances).

[12] Fosco Fabricators, Inc v State, 94 AD2d 667, 462 NYS2d 662 (1983).

580 DISPUTE RESOLUTION

based on untimely notice when the contractor served the Board of Education's *admitted* business agent whose office was at the board's address, rather than addressing the notice to the Board itself.[13]

Compliance with a statutory notice requirement while ignoring contractual notice requirements would cause a problem. Comply with all notice provisions that may be applicable, no matter where found.

Time to Serve Notice

Typically, a notice of claim is due within a specified number of days after a claim arises. Contract notice provisions vary from as few as 5 days to as many as 90. Statutory notice provisions vary as well; contractors on state contracts have 40 days from the mailing of the final payment,[14] while contractors on school contracts have 3 months from the *accrual* of their claim.[15] It is important not to confuse the time when a claim accrues with the time when a cause of action arises or when arbitration may be demanded or litigation begun.[16] They are distinct and often separate events. To determine whether notice was timely given, it must be determined when the time frame for notice began to run. Sometimes this determination is simple, such as when the contract is one for state improvements. It is easy to count 40 days from the day the final payment was mailed.[17] More often, however, the time frame begins to run from the "accrual of the claim"[18] or the date the "claim arose."[19] A claim cannot accrue until damages are ascertainable.[20] Notice of a changed condition claim should be given immediately after the condition is discovered and before it is disturbed. Similarly, a claim for extra work accrues upon the completion of the extra work.[21] In a delay claim, the time of accrual is more difficult to ascertain. See Chapter 7 for a discussion of accrual of a delay claim.

School Contracts

Contractors on school contracts in cities with populations of more than 400,000 must comply with Education Law §2562 in addition to §3813.[22] Thus,

---

[13] Accen Constr Corp v Port Wash Union Free School Dist, 173 AD2d 753, 570 NYS2d 628, 68 Educ L Rep (West) 128 (2d Dept 1991).

[14] NY State Fin Law §145 (McKinney 1989 & Supp 1992).

[15] NY Educ Law §3813(1) (McKinney 1981 & Supplementary Pamphlet 1992).

[16] Board of Educ v Wager Constr Corp, 37 NY2d 283, 291, 333 NE2d 353, 372 NYS2d 45 (1975).

[17] NY State Fin Law §145.

[18] NY Educ Law §3813(1).

[19] Vanderlinde Elec Corp v City of Rochester, 54 AD2d 155, 388 NYS2d 388 (1976).

[20] Board of Educ v Wager Constr Corp, 37 NY2d 283, 333 NE2d 353, 372 NYS2d 45 (1975).

[21] Prote Contracting Co v Board of Educ, 135 AD2d 523, 521 NYS2d 752 (2d Dept 1987).

[22] Crescent Elec Installation Corp v Board of Educ, 50 NY2d 780, 409 NE2d 917, 431 NYS2d 443 (1980).

in addition to §3813's requirement that notice must be given within 3 months of accrual of the claim, Education Law §2562 requires that notice of the claim be given at least 30 days before any action may be commenced on the claim and that the school board must have refused or neglected to honor the claim within that 30-day period. Compliance with Education Law §§3813 and 2562, if applicable, must be affirmatively alleged in any complaint against a school board and proved at trial.

Late claims will not always be rejected, although their acceptance should not be expected. Pursuant to NY Educ Law §3813(2-a), the court may, in its discretion, extend the time to serve a notice of claim. The court is to consider whether the board had actual knowledge of the essential facts of the claim during the notice period and "all other relevant facts and circumstances," including the claimant's capacity, whether there was justifiable reliance on settlement representations made by an authorized representative of the board, and whether the delay in making the claim substantially prejudiced the board.[23] "[T]he absence of a reasonable excuse for the delay is not necessarily fatal to an application for leave to serve a late notice of claim."[24] Thus, a contractor's late notice was allowed when: the contractor was able to show that the board had actual knowledge of the essential facts of the claim; the parties, their attorneys, the contractor's surety, and project architects had corresponded and discussed the dispute in an attempt to resolve it and avoid termination of the contract and the discussions were held within the time frame; the contractor had sent an itemized bill to the board architect; and the board was unable to demonstrate prejudice.[25]

Too Early

Just as notice can be given too late, it can also be given too early on school contracts. Education Law §3813 provides that notice cannot be given until *after* the claim has accrued. Any formal claim made before it accrues is premature and may be denied.[26] No similar restriction is placed upon claims against the state; a notice of claim on a state contract may be made at any time, so long as it is no later than 40 days after mailing of final payment.[27]

Content

A notice of claim should contain all relevant information that the contractor has regarding its claim. State Finance Law §145 requires a "detailed and verified statement of claim" that should "specify the items upon which the claim

---

[23] NY Educ Law §3813(2-a) (McKinney Supplementary Pamphlet 1992).

[24] Quirk v Morrissey, 106 AD2d 498, 483 NYS2d 34, 36 (1984) (libel and slander action).

[25] Nyack Bd of Educ v K. Capolino Design & Renovation, Ltd, 114 AD2d 849, 494 NYS2d 758, *affd*, 68 NY2d 647, 496 NE2d 233, 505 NYS2d 74 (1986); *see also* Quirk v Morrissey, 106 AD2d 498, 483 NYS2d 34 (1984) (libel and slander action).

[26] Anderson Constr Co v Board of Educ, 229 NYS2d 337 (Suffolk 1962).

[27] NY State Fin Law §145; Pinto Equip Rental, Inc v State, 134 AD2d 905, 522 NYS2d 63 (1987).

will be based."[28] Education Law §3813 requires a "written verified claim." At a bare minimum, whether the claim is under a private or a public contract, it should:

1. Identify the contract
2. State original contract commencement and completion dates and actual dates
3. Identify the date, duration, and cause of damage
4. Identify all involved parties
5. Estimate or state the damage amount and how it was calculated
6. Request a specific amount of additional time, if appropriate; and
7. Be verified

> **PRACTICE POINTER:**
>
> When submitting a formal claim in compliance with contract requirements, consider including a narrative, similar to the example provided. The narrative not only clearly establishes your claim, but also may prove useful later when engaging in settlement negotiations or drafting trial memoranda.
>
> Sample claim narrative:
>
> The contract documents do not require new roofing on Building 133.
>
> Drawing A-8, rev. 1, the drawing in effect at the time of bidding, bears the notation at Building 133, "New Roofing See Alt. #5." There is no Alternate #5 in the bid documents. By contrast, other buildings bear only the notation "New Roofing" and refer to detail 4/A-8, which shows exactly how the new roofing is to be installed. Building 133, on the other hand, does not refer to that detail or to any other detail for roofing.
>
> In addition, the drawings for all other buildings where new roofing is required show restoration work on parapet walls. No such parapet work is shown for Building 133. In fact, no other contract work is shown on any plans for Building 133 except for mechanical work necessary for an adjacent building. In other words, *no* other restoration work is specified for Building 133. Site inspection would have revealed the deteriorated condition of the roof bulkheads, skylights, and parapet

---

[28] A claim that set out the following was held to be in compliance with NY State Fin Law §145: (1) a statement that the breach of contract was due to extraordinary delay caused by the misfeasance and malfeasance of the state; (2) a statement that the damages were increased costs of labor and materials; (3) the critical dates (the date the contract was signed, the date the contract work was supposed to have begun, the date it was actually done, the date the contract work was supposed to have been completed, and the date it actually was completed; and (4) a statement that the delays were due to the state's actions. *See* A&M Wallboard, Inc v Facilities Dev Corp, 97 Misc 2d 434, 411 NYS2d 492 (Albany 1978).

walls of Building 133. It would make no sense to put a new roof on the building without restoring those other elements of the roof as well.

Moreover, it was known that, after a prior bid letting for this project resulted in bids that exceeded the engineer's estimates, design changes were made to reduce costs. With this history, a bidder could reasonably have assumed that the designers had made an inadvertent error in failing to delete the notation "New Roofing See Alt. #5" on Building 133 plans when Alternate #5 itself was deleted. There was no detail to show what new roofing work was required and there was no other restoration work specified for this building. In particular, work on the bulkheads, skylights, and parapet walls would have been required along with new roofing, to make a watertight roof.

Based on the foregoing, it is reasonable for a contractor to have concluded that new roofing on Building 133 should not be included in its bid. Where work is shown on a plan but there is no specification as to how the work is to be performed, such work is not deemed to be a part of the contract. In this case, there is no detail or specification setting forth what the new roofing on Building 133 is to be. Therefore it is not required.[29]

It is best if the claim is set forth in a document or letter that clearly identifies it as a notice of claim. Verification is required in claims against a public entity,[30] although a court has the power to permit a claim to be amended by supplying verification that was omitted.[31] Notices containing less than what is recommended here have been accepted, however, as was done when notice was found in a contractor's submission to a board of copies of letters it originally sent to the board's architect along with requisitions incorporating those letters.[32]

Waiver of Notice

Generally, estoppel is not available against a public agency;[33] thus, a finding of waiver of notice provisions by a public entity is rare. This rule is best seen in *Public Improvements, Inc v Board of Education*,[34] where an electrical contractor's claim was barred for its failure to file its notice of claim within the three-month notice period required by statute. The electrical contractor argued that the board was estopped from asserting the notice provision because it had not enforced Education Law §3813 notice requirements in more than 40 years.

---

[29] Rubin, *Scope of Work Disputes*, in Construction Litigation 89, 109-11 (Practising Law Institute 1981) (reprinted with permission).

[30] *See* NY State Fin Law §145 (McKinney 1989 & Supp 1992) and NY Educ Law §3813 (McKinney 1981 & Supp 1992).

[31] McCullough v Board of Educ, 11 AD2d 740, 204 NYS2d 555 (1960); Boutelle v Central School Dist No 1, 2 AD2d 925, 156 NYS2d 358 (1956).

[32] Almar Constr Corp v PM Hughes & Sons, 58 AD2d 615, 395 NYS2d 700 (1977).

[33] Public Improvements, Inc v Board of Educ, 56 NY2d 850, 438 NE2d 876, 453 NYS2d 170 (1982), *affg* 81 AD2d 537, 438 NYS2d 305 (1981).

[34] *Id.*

The Court of Appeals rejected this argument and held that estoppel was not available against a public agency and that compliance with the statute was mandatory. Thus, waiver by a public entity cannot be presumed. A public entity waives notice provisions only if it "affirmatively agree[s] that the statutory notice clause is inapplicable"[35] or if the contract sets out detailed procedures that are "plainly inconsistent"[36] with statutory procedures.

Waiver of a statutory notice provision was found when a contractor presented its claim to the board of education, the board authorized payment and notified the contractor of its intent to pay (both events occurred within the notice period), and, later, after the notice period had expired, the board attempted to rescind its authorization because the claim was not verified. The court found that the board waived the lack of timely verification by its failure to return the unverified claim, its authorization of payment, and its notification to the contractor of the authorization.[37]

In a private contract, a notice requirement may be waived as may any other requirement. It may be waived orally or in writing.[38] Typically, waiver occurs in the course of performance, such as when an owner tells its contractor to perform extra work without worrying about the paper work, that it will be "worked out later." Chapter 6 discusses waiver more thoroughly.

§16.03 Freedom of Information Laws

Before beginning any sort of dispute resolution, it is helpful to know what one's strengths and weaknesses really are. For instance, when a contractor encounters unanticipated subsurface conditions that drastically affect its performance and costs, it wants to know whether the owner knew or should have known of the conditions. If the owner was innocently ignorant of the problem and the contractor had assumed the risk of unanticipated conditions, the contractor would stand to gain little, if anything, by pursuing formally its claims against the owner, and would lose the very dear cost of litigation or arbitration. On the other hand, if the owner failed to disclose all subsurface information that it possessed or misrepresented true conditions, the contractor would have a viable claim and a much improved bargaining position.

On a private job, a contractor has few means to discover what an owner knew without resorting to litigation and formal discovery. On a public project, however, a contractor, by using freedom of information laws, may discover substantial information about what the owner knew of the job and site, its plans, its concerns, and the problems encountered in planning the job. If the job was done by a public agency in New York, the contractor may use the New York

---

[35] Geneseo Cent School v Perfetto & Whalen Constr Corp, 53 NY2d 306, 311, 423 NE2d 1058, 441 NYS2d 229, 231 (1981) (construing AIA Standard Form Agreement Between Owner and Contractor).

[36] Id.

[37] Boutelle v Central School Dist No 1, 2 AD2d 925, 156 NYS2d 358 (1956).

[38] Corbin on Contracts §§722, 756 (1951 & Supp 1992).

Freedom of Information Law; if a federal project, the Freedom of Information Act.

State

Under the New York Freedom of Information Law (FOIL),[39] a contractor may obtain copies of any agency's records that are not exempt from disclosure. The contractor need not show that it needs the records, that its request is in good faith, or, indeed, that it has any legitimate purpose in requesting the records.[40] "Full disclosure by public agencies is, under FOIL, a public right and in the public interest, irrespective of the status or need of the person making the request."[41] It is immaterial that the person making the request is involved in or contemplating litigation against the agency.[42]

To obtain information, a requester must have "reasonably described"[43] the records it wishes in a written request to the agency. The description must be sufficient so the agency can locate and identify the documents sought. If a request is made for all records that relate to a job number and the agency maintains records by job name, the agency's search may lead to nothing. It is important to remember that, typically, the person who searches the agency records in response to a request was not involved in the project. The searcher, at a larger agency, may be a full-time records access officer, or, at a smaller agency, may be a file clerk or secretary. Thus, the more information the searcher is given, the more likely it is that the wanted information will be found. Agencies are required to maintain current subject matter lists that detail all records in their possession.[44] Review of this list can be helpful when compiling a request.

> **PRACTICE POINTER:**
>
> When making a FOIL request, a contractor might request the agency's subject matter list and copies of all records relating to a specific job number, job name, or job location. It is best to mention all possible ways the records may be classified.

When an agency receives a written request, it has 5 business days to make the record available, deny the request and state why, or acknowledge the request and state when it will be answered. In reality, the typical response time is much longer. Be patient and make constant but polite inquiry regarding your request. If denied access to a record, a requester may appeal the decision within 30 days to the agency head, chief executive, or governing body.[45] If the denial

---

[39] NY Pub Off Law §§84-90 (McKinney 1988 & Supp 1992).

[40] M. Farbman & Sons v New York City Health & Hosps Corp, 62 NY2d 75, 464 NE2d 437, 476 NYS2d 69 (1984).

[41] *Id* at 80, 464 NE2d at 439, 476 NYS2d at 71.

[42] *Id.*

[43] NY Pub Off Law §89(3) (McKinney 1988).

[44] *Id* §87(3)(c).

[45] *Id* §89(4)(a).

is upheld, the requester may bring an *Article 78* proceeding for court review of the agency determination.[46]

If an agency claims that the records are exempt from disclosure, it has the burden of proving the exemption.[47] Records are exempt if they are specifically exempt by virtue of a state or a federal statute;[48] if disclosure would invade personal privacy;[49] if disclosure would impair contract awards or negotiations;[50] if they are trade secrets or their disclosure would cause "substantial injury" to a business's competitive position;[51] if they are interagency or intraagency materials that are not data tabulations, staff instructions that affect the public, final agency policy or determinations, or external audits;[52] or if they are other types of records that do not concern construction projects.

Many state and local contracts are financed in part by federal funds. In such cases, federal files may contain valuable information regarding project feasibility, subsurface conditions, and so forth. If involved on such a project, make a request of the relevant federal agencies in addition to the state agencies.

> **PRACTICE POINTER:**
>
> When making a request, whether federal or state, ask for a list of those documents that are being withheld and for the basis for the withholding. This list is known as a *Vaughn* list.[53]

Federal

The Federal Freedom of Information Act (FOIA)[54] is very similar to New York's and can be the means to gain valuable information about an agency's knowledge of a job site, opinion of a design's feasibility, and evaluation of bids and choice of a contractor, and many other matters that can prove of use if a contractor is contemplating litigation. Relevant federal exemptions include classified documents, confidential business information, information exempt under other laws, and internal government communications.

FOIA provides that a request must "reasonably describe" the records sought. Each agency has issued its own FOIA regulations that describe its request process, including the form of the request, requirements, fees, and appeal processes. Agency FOIA regulations can be found in the Code of Federal Regulations.

FOIA provides that a request for records must be responded to within 10 business days after receipt. It provides for appeal of denials to the head of the

---

[46] *Id* §89(4)(b).
[47] Fink v Lefkowitz, 47 NY2d 567, 393 NE2d 463, 419 NYS2d 467 (1979).
[48] NY Pub Off Law §87(2)(a) (McKinney 1988).
[49] *Id* §§87(2)(b), 89(2).
[50] *Id* §87(2)(c).
[51] *Id* §87(2)(d) (McKinney 1988 & Supp 1992).
[52] *Id* §87(2)(g) (McKinney 1988).
[53] Vaughn v Rosen, 484 F2d 820 (DC Cir 1973), *cert denied*, 415 US 977 (1974).
[54] 5 USC §552.

agency; while FOIA does not prescribe an appeal time limit, an agency may. If an appeal is filed late, the matter is easily revived by submitting another request for the records; when that request is denied, an appeal may be made. If the administrative appeal is denied, a requester may appeal to the United States District Court in the district where the requester lives or where the documents are located, or in the District of Columbia.

> **PRACTICE POINTER:**
>
> If you are planning on making a FOIA request, consult *A Citizen's Guide on Using the Freedom of Information Act and the Privacy Act of 1974 to Request Government Records*, written by the House Committee on Government Operations, available from the Government Printing Office. The guide sets forth the laws in a simple manner and provides sample forms for requests and appeals.

§16.04 Contract Scope of Work Disputes

Most contracts provide an initial dispute resolution system by which the contractor presents its claim to the project architect, engineer, or other designated person who considers the claim and either decides that it is justified (and, thus, entitles the contractor to an adjustment of time or money) or decides that it is not justified and orders the contractor to proceed with its work. Under such clauses, if the contractor accepts the determination, the dispute is considered resolved. If the contractor does not, it must give notice of its disagreement and inform the owner and architect that it is continuing its work under protest. A failure to give notice that one is working under protest may bar a later attempt to pursue damages.

Such clauses make the architect or engineer an arbitrator for purposes of factual contract disputes.[55] Such clauses are valid and may make the decision of an architect/arbiter or engineer/arbiter conclusive and binding upon the parties and final as a matter of law, unless bad faith, fraud, or palpable mistake can be shown.[56] If the clause is very carefully drawn, it may vest final authority for all factual and *legal* determinations, including interpretation of the contract, with the architect or engineer. "The requirement of explicit and unequivocal agreement when there is to be mutually binding arbitration before a neutral arbitrator obviously takes on even greater significance when resolution of all disputes is to take place before the employee of one contracting party, and bind only the other."[57]

---

[55] *See* Dutchess Community College v Rand Constr Co, 57 AD2d 555, 393 NYS2d 77 (2d Dept 1977).

[56] Ardsley Constr Co v Port Auth, 54 NY2d 876, 429 NE2d 414, 444 NYS2d 907 (1981), *affg* 75 AD2d 760, 427 NYS2d 814 (1st Dept 1980).

[57] Thomas Crimmins Contracting Co v City of NY, 74 NY2d 166, 542 NE2d 1097, 544 NYS2d 580 (1989).

American Institute of Architects (AIA) forms have similar clauses that allow a contractor to appeal an architect/arbiter's decision to an independent arbitrator for a *de novo* review and decision.

Scope of work disputes is more fully discussed in Chapter 6.

§16.05 Informal Dispute Resolution

Informal dispute resolution takes many forms. The parties may do it themselves or rely on third parties to help. Typically, when faced with a dispute, most parties try to work it out themselves before involving third parties. When parties are unable to resolve their disputes, there are several structured yet informal means through which solutions may be offered and resolution reached; these are discussed in §§16.06-16.09. None of the informal dispute resolution procedures discussed here is binding on the parties or is final.

§16.06 —Dispute Review Boards

In a very large public or, more rarely, private construction project, a *contract review* or *dispute review board* may be established to review referred disputes and issue nonbinding recommendations. Typically, the board is established by the general contract and is comprised of one member selected by the owner, one selected by the contractor, and a third selected jointly by the other two members. The owner's member must be approved by the contractor, and vice versa.

The contractor and owner enter into a contract with the board members by which the members agree to consider impartially all disputes regarding the general contract work placed before them and to issue recommendations to resolve these disputes.[58] Board findings and recommendations may be either admissible or inadmissible as evidence in court or arbitration proceedings, depending upon the parties' agreement. Board members meet regularly to review the project status and potential problems. They visit the site regularly and, if possible, when specific problems arise.

Dispute review boards have the effect of encouraging cooperation and reasonableness by owners and contractors, even when no disputes are referred to the board. Perhaps the mere existence of a board provides the incentive needed to get the parties to resolve their disputes themselves. Further, when a dispute is resolved, parties tend to abide by it.

Dispute review boards have two great advantages to more formal methods of dispute resolution. First, they determine the facts contemporaneously with the problem and are able to see the problem firsthand and to discuss it with the parties while the facts are well known and several potential solutions may

---

[58] The American Society of Engineers, 345 East 47th Street, New York, NY 10014, has a form Disputes Review Board Three Party Agreement which is contained in Technical Committee on Contracting Practices, Underground Technology Research Council, *Avoiding and Resolving Disputes During Construction—Successful Practices and Guidelines* 52 (1991).

be available. Second, they tend to resolve disputes quickly, avoiding the intense adversarial relationship and exacerbations of other contract problems that can develop when a dispute is dragged out and allowed to interfere with the work.

Board members are paid for their time and expenses by the owner and the contractor. The cost of paying three well-qualified individuals to review disputes and keep abreast of a project's status tends to limit the use of such boards to major public works projects and very large private projects. In practice, however, the cost of boards on very large projects has been only $30,000 to $70,000, a range clearly affordable and practical for not-so-large projects.[59] The reluctance to take on the expense of a board may save pennies now but cost dollars later. If litigation can be avoided by using a dispute review board, its expense is minimal in the long run. Indeed, the effectiveness of dispute review boards cannot be questioned. Of 63 projects studied that had dispute review boards, *none* had disputes that ended up in court—an outstanding success rate.[60]

On smaller private jobs, owners and contractors may wish to investigate establishing a board where their designees volunteer, perhaps in exchange for the parties' promises to do the same for the designees, and only the third member must be paid. If all parties work in good faith and nominate members who will honestly and objectively perform their duties, a smaller job may have the benefits of a review board without its costs.

Recommendations of a review board are not final nor binding on the parties.

§16.07 —Mediation

A less costly approach to resolving a dispute is to resort to mediation, especially where there is a high level of distrust, the parties have reached an impasse, or the parties are hostile towards each other. Mediation is the attempt of one or more individuals to help parties reach a settlement of their dispute through direct negotiation. Typically, the mediator is an outside party with expertise in the industry. Its main function is to listen to each side's version of the dispute, review the documents, encourage and participate in negotiation, and, sometimes, recommend a settlement. A mediator guides the parties toward settlement of their differences; it does not dictate a resolution of them.

Mediation may be handled by the parties on their own or their attorneys may be involved. The process may be very simple with each party telling its version of the facts, or more complicated with attorneys and witnesses.

The American Arbitration Association (AAA) has promulgated Construction Industry Mediation Rules which the parties can choose to make applicable to their mediation. The AAA will administer a mediation at the parties' request and has trained mediators available. AAA fees depend on the amount of the claim and range from $150 to more than $850, plus mediator fees. If the parties do not wish to use the AAA's rules or the AAA, there are other private, for-

---

[59] *Id* 10.
[60] *Id* 16.

profit firms that provide mediation services; local yellow pages should list these firms. Parties may also develop their own process for mediation and find a mediator. Sources for mediators include professional societies, bar associations, and construction industry associations.

Generally, parties choose to make a mediation and its conclusions confidential and inadmissible as evidence, much like settlement discussions,[61] and to establish that all disclosures to the mediator are confidential and privileged. Of course, the conclusions are not final and are not binding on the parties.

§16.08 —Mediation and "Baseball Arbitration" in Construction Disputes

"Baseball arbitrations" between baseball players and team owners first came into vogue in the United States during the 1980s after free agency resulted in wide discrepancies between players' salary demands and the owners' willingness to pay. It is a form of "winner take all," with a twist. Each party puts its last best offer in writing. The arbitrator has limited authority: it must select one of the two offers. The arbitrator may not make a compromise award.

The effect is twofold. First, the parties have a strong incentive to make settlement offers and to settle the dispute among themselves prior to arbitration. Second, the time required to conduct the actual arbitration is significantly reduced. The sole issue to be resolved is which offer is more reasonable under the circumstances. A provision requiring payment of the winner's costs and reasonable attorneys' fees can create added incentive to settle.

The "baseball arbitration" concept is easily transferable to construction disputes. Coupled with mediation, resolution of a dispute can be expedited, resulting in significant savings in cost and time.

A "baseball arbitration" was recently completed involving a dispute between an owner and a contractor over a large contract that was terminated for the owner's convenience at an early stage in construction. The principal issue was the value of the contractor's efforts prior to the date of termination, much of which was in mobilization and preparatory work. Admittedly, very little physical work had been completed.

The contractor sought $2,500,000. The owner, however, believed that the contractor should receive $600,000. A single day's mediation brought the parties closer together, but not close enough to settle. The next step was "baseball arbitration." Each party put its last best offer in writing. The contractor reduced its demand to $1,455,000 and the owner increased its offer to $1,045,000. The gap had narrowed significantly. Then the parties agreed upon a single arbitrator, known to each of them and in whom each had great confidence. He was given position papers and copies of the relevant documents by the parties to study in advance.

The arbitration hearings were limited to two days. Fixed time periods were established for making presentations to the arbitrator and for the arbitrator

---

[61] White v Empire Mut Ins, 59 Misc 2d 527, 299 NYS2d 998 (Civ Ct 1969) (an Irving Younger decision).

and each side to ask questions. The arbitrator's award was rendered within a week.

Both parties "won." The difference between the contractor's demand and the owner's offer had been so reduced that neither party felt particularly "at risk" in allowing the arbitrator to make the final decision by choosing one or the other. The savings in time and expenses more than offset the potential loss or gain that could have been reasonably expected through conventional dispute resolution. Perhaps more importantly, the relationship between the parties was preserved because the acrimony normally engendered during a conventional arbitration or litigation procedure was minimized.

Perhaps the conventional forms of dispute resolution have gotten so out of hand that the time is ripe for alternatives. The 1980s may be characterized as the era of hardball litigation conducted by "pit bull" lawyers, encouraged by more than willing clients. It is hoped that this trend will be reversed in the 1990s through the use of innovative alternative dispute resolution techniques. Mediation coupled with "baseball arbitration" offers the potential of substantially reducing the time, cost, and acrimony of conventional dispute resolution procedures.

The results of "baseball arbitration" are final and binding on the parties.

§16.09 —Minitrials

A minitrial is similar to mediation but more structured. The parties, generally through their attorneys, present their views of the dispute to a third party who makes a written recommendation which the parties may use in reaching a settlement or may reject. The recommendation is confidential. The hearing is attended by principals of each party who have full settlement authority. It is best if the parties' representatives are not directly involved in the dispute.

The parties execute a minitrial agreement, which sets forth format, discovery limitations, participants, time periods and deadlines, relevant documents, length of presentations, etc. An agreement may also include sanctions if a party rejects a final settlement offer and later takes the matter to court or arbitration but does not improve its position by a specified amount, such as 10 per cent. Prior to the minitrial, the parties may conduct limited discovery and submit evidence to the neutral party as provided by the minitrial agreement. At the minitrial, each side makes a short and informal presentation of its case, including witnesses and the introduction of evidence. Generally, the right of cross-examination is limited to the neutral party.

Minitrials have been very successful, probably because the parties evince a genuine willingness to resolve their dispute informally by agreeing to participate. A construction contract may provide that a minitrial, or any other informal dispute resolution method, is a condition precedent to litigation or arbitration.

Results of minitrials are not binding on the parties nor final.

§16.10 Formal Dispute Resolution

Formal dispute resolution is justly dreaded by most contractors and owners. It is expensive and time consuming; worst of all, it is a great risk to allow an uncontrollable third party to make a final decision that will materially affect the parties involved. The thrill of "having one's day in court" can soon turn to despair when one considers the great expense of litigation and arbitration. A party can win and still be a loser when it considers how much time, money, and aggravation the process cost. What good does it do a contractor to spend $100,000 to recover $200,000 in court when the owner offered it $150,000 to settle two years earlier? When all else fails and the parties insist on resolving their disputes formally, they have two options: litigation through the court system or private arbitration; these are discussed in the relevant sections following. At that point, the choice is not always the parties'; if there is a binding agreement to arbitrate, they may not be able to choose to litigate.[62]

§16.11 —Litigation

A construction dispute is litigated in a trial court as is any other civil dispute. The same rules of discovery and evidence apply. In most cases, juries may be demanded as a matter of right.

There are advantages and disadvantages to litigation that are unique to construction law because of the often complex and technical issues involved. Typical judges and jurors have little or no experience in construction and can have trouble understanding who the various parties are—owners, engineers, contractors, subcontractors, etc.—and their relationship to each other, not to mention who is at fault, especially in a complex design failure case. They are unable to devote the time necessary to thoroughly understand the terminology used, much less the root of the problem. This ignorance generally works in favor of the contractor and against the owner or architect, especially if the jury perceives the contractor to be "the little guy." Similarly, if the case is one of compliance with contract notice requirements, including waiver, a jury may be more apt to side with the contractor and find waiver, while a judge may be more apt to strictly construe the contract and interpret the facts with a jaded view, more often finding in favor of the owner.

The formal discovery process afforded litigants is unmatched in most arbitration proceedings. In a concealed conditions case against a private owner, extensive pre-trial discovery may be necessary to prove that the owner knew of the condition but intentionally failed to reveal it. In litigation, the contractor may examine the owner's records and reports, question its employees, and request admissions from the owner to discover evidence sufficient to prove that the owner knew, or should have known, of the condition. In arbitration, however, in the absence of a clause allowing formal discovery, parties must subpoena records and witnesses to the hearing, conducting discovery as they make their cases.

---

[62] See discussion at **§16.14**.

Experts are essential in litigation of a construction case, no matter how simple the issue. Of course, a party can serve as its own expert and not only testify as to what happened but also give the party's opinion of why the problem developed, its consequences, and whether it could have been avoided. An expert is needed to establish whether the construction was or was not done with ordinary skill and workmanship or to local standards. In arbitration, experts are not necessarily needed as one or more of the arbitrators may know what community standards are and what ordinary skill and workmanship require. In fact, some arbitrators resent the use of experts, feeling it usurps one of their functions.

If a party requires special remedies, temporary or equitable, it may have to seek court relief. An arbitrator cannot issue a writ of attachment, enforce a mechanic's lien, or issue a restraining order. An arbitrator can order specific performance[63] or issue an injunction[64], which judgments the courts will enforce.

Litigation may be more advantageous to the party on the slow side of the case or who has the most money to spend, although litigation is not always more costly than arbitration. Litigation may also be preferred by a party if it believes that the case is appropriate for disposal by dismissal or summary judgment.

A distinct advantage to litigation is the ability to consolidate cases and join parties. These reliefs are not always available in arbitration. Assume that a contractor demands that the owner arbitrate an extra work claim. The owner, believing that the work was necessary due to an omission in the plans, might wish to join the architect or engineer that designed the plans. In litigation, joinder is generally a matter of right. In arbitration, it cannot be done as a matter of right (in fact, standard American Institute of Architects (AIA) forms—designed principally to protect the general interests of the architect—expressly forbid joinder of an architect in arbitration between an owner and contractor), leaving the potential for inconsistent results when the owner brings separate suit against the architect or engineer.[65]

Finally, a trial court's decision is always appealable while an arbitration panel's decision may only be set aside on very limited grounds.[66] "An arbitra-

---

[63] Grayson-Robinson Storage v Iris Constr Corp, 8 NY2d 133, 168 NE2d 377, 202 NYS2d 303 (1960).

[64] Park City Assocs v Total Energy Leasing Corp, 58 AD2d 786, 396 NYS2d 377 (1st Dept 1977); J. Brooks Secs, Inc v Vanderbilt Secs, Inc, 126 Misc 2d 875, 484 NYS2d 472 (NY 1985).

[65] *See* Mid-Atlantic Constr Corp v Guido, 30 AD2d 232, 291 NYS2d 501 (4th Dept 1968) (multiparty action in which owner, general contractor, and some subcontractors were held to their binding arbitration agreement, but other subcontractors were found not to have agreed to arbitration; court stayed the subcontractors' court action in hopes that resolution of the owner-general contractor dispute would lead to resolution of the subcontractors' disputes).

[66] NY Civ Prac L & R 7511 (McKinney 1980 & Supp 1992); 9 USC §10.

tion award is not subject to judicial review for merely erroneous findings of fact, unless the errors in question are completely irrational."[67]

New York Court of Claims

The New York Court of Claims has the sole jurisdiction to hear any claims against the state for breach of contract and torts of state officers or employees while acting in their official capacity.[68] Thus, controversies involving construction contracts with the state and some of its agencies[69] must be brought in the Court of Claims. Two of the agencies that must be sued in the Court of Claims are the New York State Thruway Authority[70] and the New York State Teachers' Retirement System.[71] The court has the power to consolidate related actions to which the state is not a party so there may be a complete determination of all claims and counterclaims.[72]

Federal Disputes

Before a federal contract dispute is ripe for litigation, the contractor must have complied with the Contract Disputes Act;[73] this act applies to every executive agency, independent establishment, military department, and wholly owned corporation of the United States government, and the Postal Service. If a contractor has a claim against the government, it must first submit its claim to the contracting officer for a decision. The officer's decision is final unless the contractor appeals to a Board of Contract Appeals within 90 days after its receipt or unless suit is brought in the United States Claims Court within 12 months after the officer's decision. A trial de novo is held in the claims court. The government must abide by the officer's decision; it may not appeal to a board or bring suit directly.

If the officer's decision is appealed to a Board of Contract Appeals, either the contractor or the government may appeal the board's decision within 120 days after its receipt. The board's decision is final on questions of fact, unless the decision is fraudulent, arbitrary, capricious, made in bad faith, or unsubstantiated. The board's decision is not final on issues of law.

---

[67] Lange v Sartorius, Inc, 160 AD2d 527, 554 NYS2d 179 (1st Dept 1990).

[68] Court of Claims Act §9(2) (McKinney 1989 & Supp 1992).

[69] Determining whether an agency is an arm of the state (and, thus, must be sued in the Court of Claims) is a question of law for the court. See Easley v New York State Thruway Auth, 1 NY2d 374, 135 NE2d 572, 153 NYS2d 28 (1956); Belscher v New York State Teachers' Retirements Sys, 45 AD2d 206, 357 NYS2d 241 (4th Dept 1974).

[70] Easley v New York State Thruway Auth, 1 NY2d 374, 135 NE2d 572, 153 NYS2d 28 (1956).

[71] East Hill, Inc v New York State Teachers' Retirements Sys, 80 AD2d 670, 436 NYS2d 392 (3d Dept), *appeal denied*, 53 NY2d 604, 422 NE2d 583, 439 NYS2d 1028 (1981).

[72] Court of Claims Act §9(6) & (7) (McKinney 1989 & Supp 1992).

[73] 41 USC §601 *et seq.*

§16.12 —Arbitration

Construction arbitration has some advantages over litigation. Perhaps the greatest advantage is that parties may select arbitrators who are experienced in the construction industry—architects, contractors, construction managers, engineers, and construction attorneys can make excellent arbitrators. They are familiar with most technical aspects of construction jobs, as well as with the true day-to-day operations on typical job sites as opposed to the ideal operations expressed in contracts. Skilled arbitrators can digest complex information and evidence more quickly and accurately than can an untrained judge or juror. On the other hand, arbitrators are not necessarily trained in the law and do not have to follow rules of law or evidence. Arbitrators tend to consider much irrelevant evidence, lengthening hearing time and considering evidence that would be inadmissible in court. Precise, complicated legal arguments and briefs may be meaningless to nonattorney arbitrators who may disregard them if they choose.

The American Arbitration Association (AAA) has formulated Construction Industry Arbitration Rules that parties may make applicable to their arbitration. The American Institute of Architects (AIA) General Conditions of the Contract for Construction call for administration of arbitration under AAA rules.[74] Under the AAA's unpublished guidelines, if the damage demand is for $200,000 or less, the AAA usually provides one arbitrator; if the demand is for more than $200,000, three arbitrators are provided. In the alternative, the contract may specify the number and qualifications of arbitrators.

It is a widely held belief that arbitration is less expensive than litigation. This is not always true. Attorneys' fees can be remarkably similar in litigation and arbitration. The time an attorney would have spent on discovery in litigation will be spent examining documents during the arbitration hearing. Often, more preparation time is needed for an arbitration hearing than for a trial because hearings are rarely held on consecutive days. Arbitrators are busy professionals who may be hard pressed to schedule 2 consecutive hearing days, let alone the 5 or 10 days needed for a somewhat complex matter and the upwards of 25 days for a truly complex matter. Attorneys thus must prepare and re-prepare numerous times over the several weeks, months, or years that it can take to schedule all needed hearing days, coordinating the calendars of three arbitrators, the parties, the parties' attorneys, and witnesses. Further, parties must pay the arbitrators' fees, the cost of a stenographer if one is used, the cost of a hearing room, and filing fees if the arbitration is done through the AAA. The AAA filing fee is dependent upon the amount of the claim and ranges from a minimum of $300 for a $10,000 claim to a maximum of $59,250 for a claim of $50,000,000 or more.[75] In addition, the AAA charges fees for postponements and for each hearing session after the first. In contrast, the court fee to initiate a case in the New York County Supreme Court is $245 and $50 for a jury demand, regardless of the amount of the claim.

---

[74] AIA Doc A201, ¶¶4.5, 13.1.1, 13.6.1 and 13.7.1 (1987 ed).

[75] *See* American Arbitration Association, Construction Industry Arbitration Rules, Administrative Fee Schedule (1991 ed).

596 DISPUTE RESOLUTION

The choice—if a party has one—between arbitration and litigation can only be made on a case-by-case basis. Generally, the larger the claim, the more economical litigation will be. Similarly, the more complex the matter, the more formal discovery will be helpful to one party and harmful to another. Both parties will benefit from an experienced and knowledgeable finder of fact. If a party seeks punitive damages, it must litigate its claim; an arbitrator cannot award punitive damages.[76] What do you do if you have a $30,000,000 case that involves sophisticated questions of design or construction failure and changed subsurface conditions? Settle the case; try mediation; have a minitrial; do *all* you can to avoid litigation or arbitration. If all else fails, evaluate each option carefully, discuss the case with colleagues, find out what their experiences have been with local arbitrators, consider whether the matter can be arbitrated without the AAA (and thus avoid their fees), all the while continuing settlement efforts.

Generally, an arbitration decision and award is final and conclusive. It is not subject to review for errors of law or fact[77] and cannot be set aside, unless there was a miscalculation of figures,[78] there was an abuse of discretion,[79] the arbitrator exceeded its powers,[80] the contractually specified method of selecting an arbitrator was not complied with,[81] an arbitrator appointed as a neutral was

---

[76] Garrity v Lyle Stuart, Inc, 40 NY2d 354, 353 NE2d 793, 386 NYS2d 831, 83 ALR3d 1024 (1976); Diker v Cathray Constr Corp, 158 AD2d 657, 552 NYS2d 37 (2d Dept 1990). *See also* Glower W. Jones, *Awarding Punitive Damages by Arbitration*, 7 Construction Law, Aug 1987, at 1. Other courts, however, have upheld the arbitrator's authority to award punitive damages. *See* Bonar v Dean Witter Reynolds, Inc, 835 F2d 1378 (11th Cir 1988) (Eleventh Circuit upheld a decision by the district court of Florida that a choice-of-law provision in a contract governed by the Arbitration Act does not prevent arbitrators from awarding punitive damages); Willoughby Roofing & Supply Co v Kajima Intl, Inc, 776 F2d 269 (11th Cir 1985) (United States Court of Appeals for the Eleventh Circuit held that the arbitrator has authority to award a particular remedy); Peabody v Rotan Mosle, Inc, A Subsidiary of Paine Weber, 677 F Supp 1135 (MD Fla 1987) (a district court in Florida found that the arbitration agreement included the power of the arbitrator to award punitive damages if the arbitrator believed such damages were appropriate.)

[77] SCM Corp v Fisher Park Lane Co, 40 NY2d 788, 358 NE2d 1024, 390 NYS2d 398 (1976), *limited on other grounds*, 428 NYS2d 906 (1980).

[78] Bay Ridge Medical Group v Health Ins Plan, 22 AD2d 807, 254 NYS2d 616 (2d Dept 1964).

[79] Omega Contracting, Inc v Maropakis Contracting, Inc, 160 AD2d 942, 554 NYS2d 664 (2d Dept 1990) (arbitrator refused to grant adjournment).

[80] Granite Worsted Mills v Aaronson Cowen, 25 NY2d 451, 255 NE2d 168, 306 NYS2d 934 (1969), *modified*, 26 NY2d 842, 309 NYS2d 589 (1970), *affd*, 473 NYS2d 779 (1984) (arbitrator ignored damage limitation clause in the contract without finding that clause was unconscionable); Arthur Richards, Ltd v Brampton Textiles, Ltd, 59 AD2d 842, 399 NYS2d 111 (1st Dept 1977); *see also* NY Civ Prac L & R §7511(c) (McKinney 1980) (arbitration award shall be modified by court if arbitrators awarded upon matter not submitted to them).

[81] Local 964, United Bhd of Carpenters & Joiners of Am v Shirl-Ann Constr Corp, 73 AD2d 968, 424 NYS2d 253 (2d Dept 1980).

§16.12 ARBITRATION   597

not really neutral,[82] an arbitrator failed to disclose its relationship with a party,[83] the award was based on the strength of the arbitrator's independent investigation,[84] or other factors existed that relate more to the arbitrator's conduct than to the validity of the decision reached. The discovery of new evidence is not grounds for vacatur of an arbitration award.[85] An arbitrator is not required to give a reason for its decision.[86]

In the absence of a clause that limits its powers, an arbitrator may decide the following issues in addition to factual issues and related issues of law:

1. Procedural issues, such as whether contractual time limitations have been complied with and whether the demand for arbitration was made properly[87]
2. The validity of releases that do not expressly cancel contractual arbitration provisions[88]
3. Whether the arbitration agreement was terminated by the parties[89]
4. Contract interpretation[90]
5. Whether a prior award was res judicata of the dispute under arbitration[91] or a prior decision collaterally estops a party[92]
6. The effect of a settlement agreement[93]
7. Venue;[94] and

---

[82] Koppel v Koppel, 52 AD2d 676, 382 NYS2d 143 (3d Dept 1976).

[83] JP Stevens & Co v Rytex Corp, 34 NY2d 123, 312 NE2d 466, 356 NYS2d 278 (1974); Colony Liquor Distribs v Local 669, Bhd of Teamsters, 34 AD2d 1060, 312 NYS2d 403 (3d Dept 1970), affd mem, 28 NY2d 596, 268 NE2d 645, 319 NYS2d 849 (1971).

[84] Goldfinger v Lisker, 68 NY2d 225, 500 NE2d 857, 508 NYS2d 159 (1986).

[85] Central Gen Hosp v Hanover Ins Co, 49 NY2d 950, 406 NE2d 739, 428 NYS2d 881 (1980).

[86] Bay Ridge Medical Group v Health Ins Plan, 22 AD2d 807, 254 NYS2d 616 (2d Dept 1964).

[87] County of Rockland v Primiano, 51 NY2d 1, 409 NE2d 951, 431 NYS2d 478 (1980). The court is to determine whether statutes of limitations have been complied with.

[88] In re Pile Found Co, 159 AD2d 352, 552 NYS2d 631 (1st Dept 1990).

[89] Ferran Concrete Co v Commerce Elec Inc, 118 AD2d 619, 499 NYS2d 769 (2d Dept 1986); Black & Pola v Manes Org, Inc, 72 AD2d 514, 421 NYS2d 6 (1979), affd mem, 50 NY2d 821, 407 NE2d 1345, 430 NYS2d 49 (1980).

[90] De Lillo Constr Co v Lizza & Sons, 7 NY2d 102, 164 NE2d 95, 195 NYS2d 825 (1959).

[91] Board of Educ v Patchogue-Medford Congress of Teachers, 48 NY2d 812, 399 NE2d 1143, 424 NYS2d 122 (1979).

[92] Citizens Day Care Center, Inc v Community & Social Agency Employees Union, 59 AD2d 845, 399 NYS2d 10 (1st Dept 1977).

[93] Opark Constr Corp v Eureka Constr, Inc, 42 NY2d 1031, 369 NE2d 9, 398 NYS2d 1009, (1977).

[94] DMC Constr Corp v Nash Steel Corp, 41 NY2d 855, 362 NE2d 260, 393 NYS2d 709 (1977).

598 DISPUTE RESOLUTION

8. Whether the contract has been abandoned[95]

Issues for the courts include:

1. Whether conditions precedent to arbitration have been met[96]
2. Whether a dispute is arbitrable under the agreement[97]
3. Fraud in the inducement of the agreement to arbitrate[98]
4. Compliance with statutes of limitations[99] and statutory notice of claims requirements[100]

If a party participates in arbitration despite the existence of one of these issues, it may be held to have waived its right to stay the arbitration and to have consented to submission of the issue to the arbitrators rather than the court.[101]

Arbitration of mechanic's lien claims is discussed in Chapter 9.

Public Contracts

Arbitration clauses are less often found in public works contracts. The reason for this difference is that public entities tend to believe that they will do better in court than in arbitration. Courts often give public entities a favored status, while arbitrators are much less likely to do so.

If a public works contract does contain an arbitration clause, its validity and meaning is interpreted by the courts in the same manner as is a private arbitration clause.[102] The courts' deference to arbitrated determinations applies equally to public and private arbitration clauses and decisions, so long as no issue of public policy is raised and is applicable.[103]

---

[95] RH Macy Co v National Sleep Prods, 39 NY2d 268, 347 NE2d 887, 383 NYS2d 562, (1976).

[96] Rosenbaum v American Sur Co, 11 NY2d 310, 183 NE2d 667, 229 NYS2d 375 (1962). Conditions precedent to arbitration are discussed in §16.15.

[97] AT&T Tech, Inc v Communication Workers of Am, 475 US 643, 106 S Ct 1415, 89 L Ed 2d 648 (1986).

[98] Prima Paint Corp v Flood Conklin Mfg Co, 388 US 395, 87 S Ct 1801, 18 L Ed 1270 (1967).

[99] County of Rockland v Primiano, 51 NY2d 1, 409 NE2d 951, 431 NYS2d 478 (1980); SCM Corp v Fisher Park Lane Co, 40 NY2d 788, 358 NE2d 1024, 390 NYS2d 398 (1976), *limited on other grounds,* 428 NYS2d 906 (1980).

[100] Board of Educ v Tracy Trombley Constr Co, 122 AD2d 421, 505 NYS2d 233 (1986).

[101] Milton L. Ehrlich, Inc v Swiss Constr Corp, 11 AD2d 644, 201 NYS2d 133 (1st Dept 1960); *see also* County of Rockland v Primiano, 51 NY2d 1, 431 NYS2d 478 409 NE2d 951, (1980) (dicta).

[102] Maross Constr, Inc v Central NY Regional Trans Auth, 66 NY2d 341, 488 NE2d 67, 497 NYS2d 321 (1985).

[103] *Id.*

§16.13 —Federal Arbitration Act

The Federal Arbitration Act[104] provides rules for arbitrations of disputes of actions that would have been tried in the United States District Courts or Claims Courts or that involve purely federal questions, regardless of where brought.[105] The federal act has the same standards as the New York act, but has different procedural rules. If faced with an arbitration subject to the federal act, it is essential that the parties' attorneys familiarize themselves with the federal rules.

Interstate Commerce

Section 2 of the Federal Arbitration Act states that a contractual arbitration agreement is subject to the Federal Arbitration Act if the contract "evidenc[es] a transaction involving" interstate or maritime commerce.[106] Excepted from the application of the statute, however, are employment contracts of seamen,[107] railroad workers,[108] postal workers,[109] or any other class of workers engaged in foreign or interstate commerce.[110]

In a case where a contract involved a multimillion dollar construction project to be built in New York by a Delaware corporation, involving engineers, contractors, and supplies from various states, the court held that the construction on the facility affected interstate commerce.[111]

In a case where the contractor's principal place of business was in California, various personnel of the contractor were intermittently sent from California to Indiana in connection with a university construction project, the contractor employed a Wisconsin firm as a subcontractor, the laboratory equipment provided by the contractor was manufactured outside of Indiana, and the architectural firm appointed to oversee the project had its principal office in Missouri, there was found to be sufficient evidence to demonstrate that the contract between the owner-university and lab equipment contractor involved interstate commerce.[112]

Under an agreement where the defendant sold a paint business, serving at least 175 wholesale clients in a number of states, and the plaintiff secured the defendant's assistance in arranging the transfer of manufacturing and selling

---

[104] 9 USC §1 et seq.

[105] A/S J. Ludwig Mowinckels Rederi v Dow Chem Co, 25 NY2d 576, 255 NE2d 774, 307 NYS2d 660 (case concerned interstate transaction and FAA), cert denied, 398 US 939 (1970).

[106] 9USC §2.

[107] Tenney Engg, Inc v United Elec Radio & Mach Workers of Am, Local 437, 207 F2d 450 (3d Cir 1953).

[108] Id.

[109] Bacashihua v United States Postal Serv, 859 F2d 402 (6th Cir 1988).

[110] Tenney Engg, Inc v United Elec Radio & Mach Workers of Am, Local 437, 207 F2d 450 (3d Cir 1953).

[111] Pennsylvania Engg Corp v Islip Resource Recovery Agency, 710 F Supp 456 (EDNY 1989).

[112] University Casework Sys v Bahre, 172 Ind App 624, 362 NE2d 155 (1977).

operations from New Jersey to Maryland, with the defendant to render consultation services, the court found that a transaction in interstate commerce had occurred.[113]

§16.14 —Agreement to Arbitrate

In the absence of an express, unequivocal agreement to arbitrate, no one can be forced to arbitrate a dispute.[114] The agreement to arbitrate need not be mutual; one party may reserve the right to arbitrate or litigate while the other has no choice.[115] An agreement to arbitrate must be written,[116] but need not be signed if the Uniform Commercial Code (UCC) applies[117] or the parties' conduct indicates an intent to be bound.[118] The typical agreement to arbitrate is made in the construction contract, long before a dispute has arisen. Agreement after the fact is rare; one party invariably believes that arbitration is not in its best interest. Parties should closely consider the advantages and disadvantages of arbitration *before* including an arbitration clause in their contracts. If the project could be a source of complex disputes involving large amounts of money and multiple parties, it might be best to include a clause requiring nonbinding mediation instead of an arbitration clause; this type of dispute may be best resolved through litigation if informal means fail.

Chapter 3 discusses the issue of whether a subcontract's incorporation by reference of a general contract that includes an arbitration clause binds the subcontractor to arbitration of its disputes with the general contractor. The general rule is that a subcontractor will not be required to arbitrate its claims unless the subcontract contains an arbitration clause or the incorporation by reference clause specifically mentions the arbitration clause.[119]

An agreement to arbitrate covers those matters that it claims to cover. If the clause limits arbitration to certain issues, a party cannot be compelled to arbitrate any issues but those specified.[120] If other issues exist, they may be volun-

---

[113] Prima Paint Corp v Flood & Conklin Mfg Co, 388 US 395, 87 S Ct 1801, L Ed 1270 (1967).

[114] Marlene Indus Corp v Carnac Textiles, Inc, 45 NY2d 327, 380 NE2d 239, 408 NYS2d 410 (1978).

[115] Sablosky v Edwards S. Gordon Co, 73 NY2d 133, 535 NE2d 643, 538 NYS2d 513 (1989), *overruling* Cored Panels, Inc v Meinhard Commercial Corp, 72 AD2d 544, 420 NYS2d 731 (2d Dept 1979); Hull Dye & Print Works, Inc v Riegel Textile Corp, 37 AD2d 946, 325 NYS2d 782 (1st Dept 1971).

[116] NY Civ Prac L & R 7501 (McKinney 1980 & Supp 1992).

[117] Trafalgar Square, Ltd v Reeves Bros, 35 AD2d 194, 315 NYS2d 239 (1st Dept 1970); UCC §2-201(2).

[118] Race Co v Oxford Hall Contracting Corp, 25 AD2d 665, 268 NYS2d 175 (2d Dept 1966).

[119] *See* ch 3.

[120] Walter A. Stanley & Son v Trustees of Hackley School, 42 NY2d 436, 366 NE2d 1339, 397 NYS2d 985 (1977).

tarily joined in the arbitration or brought separately in court. If the clause is broadly written, it may be interpreted to include resolution of unexpected claims, including, for example, one of damage to reputation.[121]

If a party asserts that there is not a binding agreement to arbitrate, it must avoid any participation in the arbitration, save giving the arbitrators and other party notice of a motion to stay arbitration. If a party is found to have participated in an arbitration, it may be held to have waived its right to contest the validity of the arbitration agreement.[122]

> **PRACTICE POINTER:**
>
> When faced with a situation where you cannot compel a party to arbitrate or participate in an arbitration with others, there is nothing to prevent you from "inviting" the reluctant party to participate voluntarily.
>
> For example, in an arbitration between a subcontractor and a general contractor over a contract balance due the subcontractor, the likelihood is that the subcontractor could not compel the general contractor's labor and material payment bond surety to arbitrate. However, the subcontractor could invite the surety to participate, setting the stage for a claim later that the surety is collaterally estopped from relitigating issues decided by the arbitration award. This can be effective in the situation where the general contractor fails to appear or defend itself at the arbitration. If the surety knew about the arbitration and had been invited by the subcontractor to participate, the surety will be hard pressed to argue later that it was prejudiced by its principal's default and/or failure to defend itself.

§16.15 —Conditions Precedent to Arbitration

Typically, arbitration may not be compelled unless the parties have complied with all conditions precedent required under the contract. For instance, American Institute of Architects (AIA) A201, General Conditions, states:

> A decision by the Architect [as to a contractor's claim] shall be required as a condition precedent to arbitration or litigation of a Claim between the Contractor and Owner as to all such matters arising prior to the date final payment is due, regardless of (1) whether such matters relate to execution and progress of the Work or (2) the extent to which the work has

---

[121] American Airlines v Licon Assocs, 56 AD2d 782, 392 NYS2d 457 (1st Dept 1977) (clause required arbitration of "all claims, disputes and other matters in questions arising under this contract or in breach thereof").

[122] National Cash Register Co v Wilson, 8 NY2d 377, 171 NE2d 302, 208 NYS2d 951 (1960) (participation in selection of arbitrators is sufficient participation to amount to waiver of issue of arbitrability); *see also* Mayfair Super Markets, Inc v Tantleff, 27 Misc 2d 599, 212 NYS2d 571 (NY) *aff'd*, 13 AD2d 488, 212 NYS2d 570 (1st Dept 1961).

been completed. The decision by the Architect in response to a Claim shall not be a condition precedent to arbitration or litigation in the event (1) the position of Architect is vacant, (2) the Architect has not received evidence or has failed to render a decision within agreed time limits, (3) the Architect has failed to take action required under Subparagraph 4.4.4 within 30 days after the Claim is made, (4) 45 days have passed after the Claim has been referred to the Architect or (5) the Claim relates to a mechanic's lien.[123]

Compliance with conditions precedent to arbitration is generally a question of law for the court to determine.[124] Only failure to comply with an *express* condition precedent will bar the right to compel arbitration.[125] Where a contract provision is not expressly made a condition precedent, the issues of whether a provision sets forth a condition precedent or a procedural requirement and of whether there has been compliance are for the arbitrator rather than the court, as the questions are really questions of contract construction or interpretation.[126]

Care must be taken not to confuse a condition precedent with a procedural hurdle, either of which may preclude a claim from arbitration. Typical procedural hurdles include time limitations[127] and requirements regarding manner of service and upon whom the demand for arbitration is to be made. Such matters are determined by the arbitrators. Conditions precedent are those requirements that are intended to be complied with before a party has a right to seek redress in arbitration; they are "prerequisites to entry into the arbitration process," not "procedural prescriptions for the management of that process."[128] Of course, the best source for determining whether a requirement is a condition precedent or a procedural requirement is the contract itself. If the contract says that the requirement is a condition precedent, it is, regardless of what general category or classification into which the required action is typically thought to fall.

In addition to contractual conditions precedent, there are statutory conditions precedent (as distinguished from statutory time limitations). For instance, compliance with applicable notice of claim laws on a public project is a condition precedent to arbitration or litigation and a question for the

---

[123] AIA Doc A201, ¶4.3.2 (1987 ed).

[124] County of Rockland v Primiano Constr Co, 51 NY2d 1, 409 NE2d 951, 431 NYS2d 478 (1980).

[125] Raisler Corp v New York City Auth Hous, 32 NY2d 274, 298 NE2d 91, 344 NYS2d 917 (1973).

[126] Pearl St Dev Corp v Conduit & Found Corp, 41 NY2d 167, 359 NE2d 693, 391 NYS2d 98 (1976).

[127] United Nations Dev Corp v Norkin Plumbing Co, 45 NY2d 358, 380 NE2d 253, 408 NYS2d 424 (1978).

[128] County of Rockland v Primiano Constr Co, 51 NY2d 1, 409 NE2d 951, 431 NYS2d 478 (1980).

court, not the arbitrators.[129]

§16.16 —Arbitration: Is a Surety Bound?

The law in New York used to be clear that a surety was not bound by an arbitration clause in the contract it assured unless it could be shown that the surety expressly agreed to participate in arbitration.[130] The Court of Appeals complicated the issue in the case of *Fidelity & Deposit Co v Parsons & Whittemore Contractors Corp*.[131] In *Fidelity*, the surety issued a performance bond assuring the performance of a subcontractor. The subcontract contained a broad arbitration clause that applied to disputes arising under the contract between the contractor and subcontractor. The performance bond incorporated the subcontract by reference, but did not contain an arbitration clause of its own. The Court of Appeals found that by incorporating the subcontract by reference,

> the surety company agreed that disputes arising under the subcontract between the general contractor and the subcontractor would be submitted to arbitration and *that it would be bound by the determinations made in such arbitration*. . . . It did not agree, however, that separate and distinct controversies, if any, which might arise under the terms of the performance bond between the general contractor as obligee thereunder and the surety company would be submitted to arbitration.[132]

The court's analysis of the issue of whether a surety is bound by its principal's agreement to arbitrate was based upon the "critical distinction" between disputes arising under the subcontract and those arising under the terms of the performance bond.[133] The court stated that an implicit corollary of the surety's acceptance of the subcontract was agreement by it that "for purposes of later determining its liability under its performance bond, it would accept and be bound by the resolution reached in the arbitration forum of any dispute between the general contractor and the subcontractor."[134] Thus, a surety is bound by an arbitration decision regarding disputes between the contractor and subcontractor, the surety's obligee and principal; such a decision will col-

---

[129] *See* Board of Educ v Wager Constr Corp, 37 NY2d 283, 333 NE2d 353, 372 NYS2d 45 (1975). §§**16.02** and **16.03** discuss statutory and contractual notice of claim requirements.

[130] *See* HH & FE Bean, Inc v Travelers Indem Co, 67 AD2d 1102, 415 NYS2d 144 (4th Dept 1979); Sherwood Village Coop, Inc v Had-Ten Estates Corp, 29 AD2d 771, 287 NYS2d 921 (2d Dept 1968); Transamerica Ins Co v Yonkers Contracting Co, 49 Misc 2d 512, 267 NYS2d 669 (NY 1966); Ledo Realty Corp v Continental Cas Co, 43 Misc 2d 380, 251 NYS2d 99 (Schenectady 1964).

[131] 48 NY2d 127, 397 NE2d 380, 421 NYS2d 869 (1979).

[132] *Id* at 129, 397 NE2d at 381, 421 NYS2d at 870.

[133] *Id* at 131, 397 NE2d at 382, 421 NYS2d at 871.

[134] *Id* at 131-32, 397 NE2d at 382, 421 NYS2d at 872.

laterally estop a surety.[135] Disputes regarding the performance bond are not subject to arbitration without express agreement. The court did not address whether a surety may be compelled to participate in arbitration between the contractor and subcontractor or whether it could demand the right to participate over the objection of one of the parties.[136]

---

[135] *See* Burdick Assocs Owners Corp v Indemnity Ins Co of N Am, 166 AD2d 402, 560 NYS2d 481 (2d Dept 1990).

[136] Chief Justice Cooke, in his dissent concurred with by Justice Gabrielli, stated that the majority's holding implies that the surety agreed to arbitrate contractual disputes, not just to be bound by arbitration decisions regarding contractual disputes. The dissent would have held that the incorporation of the subcontract and the language of the arbitration clause concerned require the surety to be a party to arbitration concerning the subcontractor's breach. 48 NY2d at 134, 397 NE2d at 384, 421 NYS2d at 873.

Appendix 16-1 Selected References

J. Acret, *Construction Arbitration Handbook* (Shepard's/McGraw-Hill 1985).

J. Acret, *Construction Litigation Handbook* (Shepard's/McGraw-Hill 1986).

K. Cushman, B. Ficken, & W. Sneed, *Construction Litigation* (1981).

Donovan Leisure Newton & Irvine, *ADR Practice Book* (J. Wilkinson, ed) (1990).

F. Sander & F. Snyder, *Alternative Methods of Dispute Settlement: A Selected Bibliography*, American Bar Association (1982).

M. & R. Schoenfield, *Legal Negotiations: Getting Maximum Results* (Shepard's/McGraw-Hill 1988).

T. Watts, *Arbitration, Mediation, and Other Forms of Alternate Dispute Resolution: A Selected Bibliography* (Vance Bibliographies 1987).

17

An Overview of the New York City Procurement Policy Board Rules*

§17.01 Negotiating the Maze
§17.02 PPB Rules Chapter Three: Methods of Source Selection
§17.03 PPB Rules Chapter Four: Contract Formation
§17.04 PPB Rules Chapter Five: Contract Award
§17.05 PPB Rules Chapter Six: Contract Administration
§17.06 PPB Rules Chapter Nine: Construction, Architecture, and Engineering Services
§17.07 PPB Rules Chapter Seven: Dispute Resolution
§17.08 —Bidding Disputes
§17.09 —Contract Disputes
§17.10 —Debarment and Suspension
§17.11 —Solicitation or Award of Contract in Violation of PPB Rules
§17.12 —Hearings on Borough President Complaints
§17.13 Questions and Suggestions for PPB Dispute Resolution
§17.14 —Delays
§17.15 —Finality of City Decisions
§17.16 —The Need for Fairness: Some Suggestions

§17.01 Negotiating the Maze

On September 1, 1990, New York City's first comprehensive set of rules governing the purchase of all goods, services, and construction by city agencies went into effect.[1] Modeled after the American Bar Association's Model Procurement Code for State and Local Governments, these rules will have a profound effect on the contractual relationships between the city and architects, engineers, construction managers, and contractors. The Procurement Policy Board (PPB) Rules are an improvement in that, finally, there are written stan-

---

[1] Procurement Policy Board Rules ch 1, §1-02(a).
* Reprinted with permission from *New York Construction News, Inc.*

dards against which to judge procurement decisions by city officials. However, the rules attempt to severely restrict a contractor's right to sue the city in court. In addition to establishing the standards under which the city will purchase construction and related services, the PPB Rules provide that the city will be the sole arbiter of most, if not all, disputes between the city and its contractors.

A thorough understanding of the PPB Rules is essential to obtain and successfully perform city contracts. When disputes arise, the contractor and its attorney must know what rules will apply to the substantive issues and what procedures will be followed to resolve the disputes.

The PPB Rules are divided into fifteen chapters, four of which are reserved for future use. Chapter One contains the general provisions on the purpose and the rules of construction, application, and definitions. Chapter Two sets forth the organization and authority of the Procurement Policy Board, as well as other officials, such as the mayor, agency heads, and specific agencies, with respect to the purchase of goods and services by the city.

Of particular significance to the construction industry are Chapter Three, "Methods of Source Selection," Chapter Four, "Contract Formation," Chapter Five, "Contract Award," Chapter Six, "Contract Administration," Chapter Nine, "Construction, Architecture, and Engineering Services," and, lastly, Chapter Seven, "Dispute Resolution." These are discussed in relevant chapters following.

§17.02   PPB Rules Chapter Three: Methods of Source Selection

For the most part, construction contracts will continue to be let to the lowest bidder after competitive sealed bidding. This method, mandated by state statute, is also the stated preference of the Procurement Policy Board (PPB) Rules.[2] Other methods included are competitive sealed bidding from prequalified vendors, competitive sealed proposals, negotiated acquisition, and sole source procurement. This list is not exclusive.[3] The use of a method other than competitive sealed bidding, except for small purchases, emergencies, and intergovernmental purchases, requires a "special case" determination, which must be based on 1 of 12 reasons set forth in the rules.[4]

Contractors will find that the rules on competitive sealed bidding do not significantly change current city practices. One change is found in §3-02(m), "Mistakes in Bid," subsection (3), "Confirmation of Bid."[5]

This section states that when the city official responsible for opening bids has reason to conclude that a mistake was made, the official should request the bidder to confirm the bid. An obvious error on the face of the bid or an unreasonably low bid are examples of situations when this could occur. If the

---

[2] PPB Rules ch 3, §3-01(b).

[3] *Id* ch 3, §3-01(a).

[4] *Id* ch 3, §3-01(e).

[5] *Id* ch 3, §3-02(m)(3).

bidder does not confirm the bid but alleges a mistake, the bid may be corrected or withdrawn upon conditions set forth in the PPB Rules. Generally, when a bid mistake is the result of an error in judgment, correction or withdrawal will not be allowed. If the mistake is nonjudgmental and clearly evident, or if the contractor can establish through clear and convincing evidence that a mistake was made, the bid may be corrected or withdrawn. In the past, it was usually incumbent on the bidder to raise the issue. Placing an affirmative duty on the city to review bids for potential mistakes is similar to the system used by the federal government.

Besides being low, a successful bid must also be responsive to the solicitation and the bidder must be responsible. The standards to determine whether a bid is responsive and the bidder responsible are set forth in Chapter Five, "Contract Award."[6] A bidder designated *nonresponsible* by the city, or whose bid is designated *nonresponsive*, may appeal under the procedure set forth in Chapter Seven, "Dispute Resolution."[7]

Section 3-11 of Chapter Three, entitled "Prequalification," describes when the city may limit bidders to a prequalified list, the procedure for a contractor to become prequalified, and the criteria for prequalification.[8] Because state statute limits those circumstances in which the city may prequalify bidders, this section will not have an immediate impact on the award of construction contracts. However, it is no secret that the city would prefer to be able to limit bidders to a prequalified list, a power currently enjoyed by the New York City School Construction Authority (SCA).[9] The statute that created the SCA allowed prequalification with the expectation that the SCA could limit bidders to the most qualified contractors without unduly limiting competition. If the SCA experience is successful, legislation will almost certainly be sought to expand the use of prequalification in public contracting.

A contractor's being prequalified by the city does not represent a determination of responsibility.[10] However, the criteria for each are not significantly different. A refusal to prequalify a contractor is appealable under the rules.[11] The criteria for determining responsibility is of more immediate concern to construction contractors and is discussed in §17.04 on PPB Rules Chapter Five.

§17.03 PPB Rules Chapter Four: Contract Formation

Chapter Four of the Procurement Policy Board (PPB) Rules explains how the city makes the initial decision and decides on the most appropriate method to contract out for goods or services. Once those decisions are made, the rules

---

[6] *Id* ch 5, §5-01 *et seq.*
[7] *Id* ch 7, §7-01 *et seq.*
[8] *Id* ch 3, §3-11.
[9] NY Pub Auth Law §1725 *et seq* (McKinney 1981 & Supp 1992).
[10] PPB Rules ch 3, §3-11(l).
[11] *Id* ch 3, §3-11(m); ch 7, §7-06.

§17.03 CONTRACT FORMATION 609

provide a procedure for selecting the type of contract, such as fixed price, fixed price-plus incentive, cost-plus incentive, or cost-plus a fixed fee.[12] The use of cost-plus contracts is strongly discouraged.[13] Chapter Four also defines the various types of contracts.[14]

Section 4-06 of Chapter Four, "Cost or Pricing Data and Analysis," directly impacts the way change orders are negotiated and paid.[15] Section 4-06 defines *price* analysis as "an evaluation of proposed prices without regard to the separate cost elements and proposed profit amount."[16] *Cost* analysis is defined as "a review and verification of cost data supporting each element of a proposed cost."[17] For smaller change orders, the contractor's proposal will be subjected to a price analysis. Cost analysis is recommended whenever possible and is required when change orders exceed $100,000,[18] except in limited circumstances. The rules also provide that contractors must certify, in writing, that the cost or pricing data submitted with change order proposals is accurate, complete, and current.[19]

The city is entitled to adjust the amount of a negotiated and agreed-upon change order to exclude any "significant sum" if it later determines that cost or pricing data were inaccurate or overstated.[20] This applies to unit price (for items for which the contract has no unit price), time and materials, and lump sum change orders.

Section 4-07 of Chapter Four sets forth the principles applied in any cost evaluation.[21] Section 4-07(h) lists certain allowable and unallowable costs.[22] For example, except where there is a contract clause removing the risk from the contractor for which a contingency factor is sought, providing for contingencies is not prohibited. Costs to compensate a contractor for the use of buildings, capital improvement, and equipment are allowable, while entertainment costs are not. Interest is generally not allowable. A loss incurred under one contract may not be charged to any other contract as a cost. Additional cost standards for time and material change orders and certain negotiated lump sum change orders are contained in Chapter Nine of the PPB Rules.[23]

When pricing change orders and preparing to negotiate with the city over the amount to be allowed, the contractor is well advised to be sure the proposal complies as closely as possible with the standards in Chapter Four and, where applicable, Chapter Nine of the PPB Rules.

---

[12] PPB Rules ch 4, §4-01 *et seq.*
[13] *Id* ch 4, §4-03(a).
[14] *Id* ch 4, §4-03(e)-(j).
[15] *Id* ch 4, §4-06(a).
[16] *Id* ch 4, §4-06(a)(1).
[17] *Id.*
[18] *Id* ch 4, §4-06(b).
[19] *Id* ch 4, §4-06(c).
[20] *Id* ch 4 §4-06(d).
[21] *Id* ch 4, §4-07.
[22] *Id* ch 4, §4-07(h).
[23] *Id* ch 9, §9-02(q).

§17.04 PPB Rules Chapter Five: Contract Award

Chapter Five of the Procurement Policy Board (PPB) Rules sets forth the standards by which bids are evaluated for responsiveness[24] and bidders evaluated for responsibility.[25] If a bid is designated *nonresponsive*, the decision is appealable, unless the determination is based on certain specific grounds set forth in the rules; in the latter case, the rejection of the bid is automatic with no right of appeal.[26] The notice sent to a bidder that its bid is nonresponsive will also let the bidder know whether the decision can be appealed.[27] A bidder whose bid is automatically rejected with no right of appeal is not expressly prohibited from suing in court. However, such actions are rarely practical, given that a court generally will not direct an award to a specific party, but rather will require a new round of bidding if there is a problem with the solicitation, the receipt of bids, or the selection process.

City officials have often complained that some of the problems they experience while building public facilities are due to the fact that the city cannot select contractors from those best qualified, as do private owners, and must generally award contracts to the lowest bidder. The PPB Rules attempt to address this problem by requiring contractors, and certain subcontractors, to "affirmatively demonstrate" their "responsibility."[28] Section 5-02 of Chapter Five sets forth the standards used to judge responsibility.[29] Some of the factors considered are financial resources, experience, organization and equipment, past performance, and compliance with minority business enterprises/women business enterprises regulations.

Information on contractor responsibility gathered by city agencies will be entered into a centralized database known as VENDEX.[30] In addition, prospective contractors will be required to complete and submit with their bids a questionnaire on background data on the companies and their principals, which will also be entered into the VENDEX database. The VENDEX will then be used by agencies during their investigation into a contractor's responsibility, which must be done before a contract is awarded.[31] If a bid is rejected on the basis that the bidder is not responsible, the bidder will be notified in writing and given an opportunity to appeal.[32]

Once a bid has been accepted, the agency must follow the procedures set forth in Chapter Five before actually awarding the contract.[33] There is also a

---

[24] PPB Rules ch 5, §5-01.
[25] *Id* ch 5, §5-02.
[26] *Id* ch 5, §5-01(c).
[27] *Id* ch 5, §5-01(f).
[28] *Id* ch 5, §5-02(a)(2).
[29] *Id* ch 5, §5-02(b)(1)-(2).
[30] *Id* ch 5, §5-02(e)(1).
[31] *Id* ch 5, §5-02(3).
[32] *Id* ch 5, §5-02(f)(2).
[33] *Id* ch 5, §5-03.

description of who can award contracts and the procedures they must follow.[34] Section 5-06 sets forth procedures to be followed where a public hearing is required before awarding certain types of contracts.[35]

Finally, §5-07 of Chapter Five sets forth the procedures for contract registration,[36] which is the process by which the comptroller of the city of New York approves the award of a contract and makes sure there is money available to pay the contractor.[37] The city cannot pay a contractor for its work until a contract and change orders are registered with the comptroller.[38]

§17.05 PPB Rules Chapter Six: Contract Administration

Chapter Six of the Procurement Policy Board (PPB) Rules covers the day-to-day administration of contracts, including the rules for change orders, extensions of time, stop work orders, terminations, and payment to contractors. In addition, this chapter sets forth the standards under which a contractor's performance will be evaluated.

To assist the city in weeding out what it considers to be nonresponsible contractors, Section 6-01 of Chapter Six sets forth a system under which a contractor's performance will be monitored, evaluated, and documented.[39] The data collected during this process will be entered into VENDEX, a centralized database.[40]

A contractor whose performance leads to an evaluation or report of unsatisfactory performance will get a copy of the evaluation and be given an opportunity to respond.[41] While the response will not necessarily change the evaluation, the response will be included in the contractor's file and, assumedly, VENDEX.

Section 6-02, "Contract Changes," deals with issuance and approval of change orders.[42] Pricing of change orders is dealt with in Chapter Four. In the past, the commissioner of the agency that let the contract had the authority to approve change orders for up to 10% of the contract price. Under the new rules, change orders that cumulatively exceed the greater of 10% *or* $50,000 must be approved, not only by the agency head, but also by the mayor's Office of Construction.[43] A contractor risks not being paid for change order work if

---

[34] *Id* ch 5, §5-04.
[35] *Id* ch 5, §5-06.
[36] *Id* ch 5, §5-07.
[37] *Id* ch 5, §5-07(a)(1).
[38] *Id* ch 5, §5-07(b).
[39] PPB Rules ch 6, §6-01(a).
[40] *See* §17.04.
[41] PPB Rules ch 6, §6-01(k).
[42] *Id* ch 6, §6-02.
[43] *Id* ch 6, §6-02(d)(2)(ii).

it does extra work without receiving all the requisite written approvals and confirmation that the change order has been *registered* with the comptroller.[44]

As in the past, change orders will be issued on the basis of an agreed fixed price, unit prices set forth in the contract, or on a time and material basis.[45] If a change order delays contract work, the contractor will be entitled to an adjustment of the contract time as well as price.[46]

Section 6-03 contains the rules by which a contractor may request an extension of time.[47] Most requests for extensions of time can be granted by each agency's chief contracting officer.[48] Extensions of time for substantial completion payments and final completion payments require the approval of a Board of Time Extension, comprised of the agency chief contracting officer, the corporation counsel, and the comptroller.[49]

Contractors should not anticipate time extension requests to be routinely granted unless they have complied with all the requirements set forth in the rules. A contractor should also expect the city to assess liquidated damages if the contractor does not finish on time and cannot justify an extension.[50] Finally, contractors' completing their contracts late can almost guarantee an unsatisfactory rating being placed into the VENDEX database.[51]

Section 6-05(b) and (c) contain rules for default terminations and terminations for the city's convenience.[52] Contractors will find that these rules are not significantly different from the termination clauses in standard city construction contracts.

What remains unclear is the extent to which city actions on extensions of time, liquidated damages, and default judgments are subject to the "Dispute Resolution" section of the PPB Rules. This is discussed in more detail in **§§17.14-17.15.**

Section 6-07, "Prompt Payment," states that "it is the policy of the City of New York to process contract payments efficiently and expeditiously, so as to assure payment in a timely manner...."[53] It remains to be seen whether there will be a radical departure from past practice with the city paying requisitions timely or interest to contractors on late payments. The rules require the city to pay interest if payments on "proper invoices" are not paid within 30 days, for regular progress payments, 60 days for change orders, and 120 days for

---

[44] *Id* ch 5, §5-07(d).
[45] *Id* ch 6, §6-02(e)(1)-(4).
[46] *Id* ch 6, §6-02(e).
[47] *Id* ch 6, §6-03.
[48] *Id* ch 6, §6-03(c).
[49] *Id* ch 6, §6-03(2)(iii).
[50] *Id* ch 6, §6-03(3).
[51] *See* **§17.04.**
[52] PPB Rules ch 6, §6-05(b)-(c).
[53] *Id* ch 6, §6-07(a).

substantial completion or final payments.[54] The clock begins to run when the city accepts the contractor's requisition and determines that it is "proper."[55] If there is a dispute over whether payment is due, the "interest clock" stops until the dispute is resolved.[56] In other words, if the city makes a conscious decision, valid or not, that it is not going to pay a requisition, no interest is due. Interest will be due only when the city intends to pay a requisition but, due to bureaucratic delays, does not.

The "prompt payment" section of the rules requires clauses in subcontracts obligating general contractors to pay each subcontractor not later than 7 days after the city pays the contractor. If a contractor is paid interest by the city, it must share that interest proportionately with each of its subcontractors.[57]

§17.06 PPB Rules Chapter Nine: Construction, Architecture, and Engineering Services

Chapter Nine of the Procurement Policy Board (PPB) Rules sets forth some rules peculiar to construction, architecture, and engineering. Some of these rules are a restatement of earlier rules with an emphasis on construction, such as the stated preference for procuring construction through competitive sealed bids and the use of lump sum or unit price as opposed to cost-plus contracts. The chapter also consists of definitions and sets forth requirements for preparing information for bidders, specifications, and contracts. The rules state a preference for construction projects to be fully designed before contracts for construction are awarded, which is referred to as "sequential construction."[58] An agency is permitted to use the "fast-track" method in limited circumstances and with prior approval of the mayor's Office of Construction.[59]

Of particular interest to contractors will be §§9-02(o), "Change Orders, General,"[60] 9-02(p), "Negotiated Change Orders,"[61] and 9-02(q), "Cost Standards for Time and Material Change Orders and Change Orders Negotiated Without Established Cost History."[62] In summary, these sections state that proposals for change orders should preferably be on a lump sum basis or on unit prices established by the contract. If the parties cannot agree on a lump sum, the change may be performed under a time and material basis if the city has staff on site to verify the contractor's work. The costs are subject to the cost

---

[54] Id ch 6, §6-07(c)(2).
[55] Id ch 6, §6-07(b)(ii).
[56] Id ch 6, §6-07(d)(2).
[57] Id ch 6, §6-07(e)(2).
[58] PPB Rules ch 9, §9-02(e)(1).
[59] Id ch 9, §9-02(e)(2).
[60] Id ch 9, §9-02(o).
[61] Id ch 9, §9-02(p).
[62] Id ch 9, §9-02(q).

principles in Chapter Four of the PPB Rules (§§4-06 & 4-07), and are subject to verification by post audit.[63]

Negotiated change orders must be supported by documented experience on similar work, documented unit price experience, or documented industry estimating publications supporting the reasonableness of the cost.[64] If there is no established "cost history," a negotiated change order must be supported by detailed information on labor rates and mark-up, crew sizes, compositions and production rates, equipment description and estimated usage, material volume, and cost.[65] All negotiated change orders having no cost history are subject to a post audit verification.[66] If the audit reveals that the contractor's costs were inaccurately stated, the agency is entitled to a reduction in the negotiated amount of the change order.[67] The phrase "inaccurately stated" is not defined and the circumstances under which the city would be entitled to reduce a negotiated lump sum change order are not clear. Section 4-06 of Chapter Four allows the city to adjust the price of change orders to exclude "significant sums" if an audit finds that the price was based on inaccurate cost data.[68] It would make sense to apply the same standard under §9-02(p)(2). Presumably, under such a standard, if the contractor based its lump sum change order on the work taking 2 men 10 days to complete and it actually takes 1 man 5 days, the city would be entitled to an adjustment. However, if the contractor claims an overhead rate that can be supported for the change order, the city should not be entitled to adjust a previously agreed-upon lump sum price by arguing that the overhead rate is more than it normally allows, which is 10 per cent of costs.

Time and material change orders and negotiated change orders without a cost history are subject to specific cost standards for equipment and labor rates. Allowances for material and insurance must be supported by business records.[69]

§17.07 PPB Rules Chapter Seven: Dispute Resolution

The "Executive Summary" to the Procurement Policy Board (PPB) Rules states that the rules place an emphasis on "treating contractors fairly by giving those who disagree with agency decisions a fair opportunity to be heard...."[70] A recent city notice sent to prospective bidders on city jobs told the bidders that there is now a place to go to resolve disputes "quickly and fairly."

---

[63] *Id* ch 9, §9-02(o)(3).

[64] *Id* ch 9, §9-02(p)(1).

[65] *Id* ch 9, §9-02(p)(1)(ii).

[66] *Id* ch 9, §9-02(p)(2).

[67] *Id.*

[68] *Id* ch 4, §4-06(d).

[69] *Id* ch 9, §9-02(q).

[70] "Executive Summary" to the PPB Rules, at 2.

Chapter Seven of the PPB Rules outlines the procedure by which the contractor will be "heard." Whether the rules will provide a fair opportunity to be heard remains to be seen. The fact is, the rules do not provide for procedural due process, that is, a hearing before an impartial tribunal with the opportunity to present evidence and confront adverse witnesses. Instead, they establish the city itself as judge, jury, and appellate court.

While these rules attempt to limit litigation between the city and contractors, it is anticipated that they will actually create litigation over the intent and effect of the rules.

§17.08 —Bidding Disputes

A contractor that disputes an appealable determination that its bid is nonresponsive may appeal to the agency head, whose decision is final. The contractor has no right to a hearing; in fact, it is within the sole discretion of the agency head whether the agency officials will meet with the bidder to discuss the merits of the appeal.[71] A determination of bidder nonresponsibility is also appealable to the agency head[72] and, subsequently, appealable to the mayor.[73] Again, there is no provision for procedural due process nor is there any procedure whereby the contractor can compel city officials to appear and give testimony explaining why the decision was made in the first instance. All documents generated during an appeal of nonresponsibility will end up in the VENDEX database.[74]

In both the case of an appeal of a determination of nonresponsiveness and the case of an appeal of a determination of nonresponsibility, the Procurement Policy Board (PPB) Rules provide that award of a contract is to be stayed pending a decision, unless there is a written determination that execution of the contract without delay is necessary to protect a substantial city interest.[75] Presumably, a contractor is not precluded from obtaining an order from a court staying award of the contract if the city does not stay the award. However, such orders are often difficult to obtain.

When the basis of a protest is other than a determination of nonresponsiveness or nonresponsibility, any actual or prospective bidder may lodge a protest about city procurement actions with the agency chief contracting officer.[76] There is no explicit provision for a taxpayer who is not a prospective bidder lodging a protest.

The protest must be submitted in writing within 10 days after publication of the notice of award and must state all the facts upon which the award is contested. Where the protest is made by a person who has not submitted a bid or proposal, the protest is limited to a challenge "of the notice procedures fol-

---

[71] Procurement Policy Board Rules ch 7, §7-02(c).
[72] Id ch 7, §7-03(c).
[73] Id ch 7, §7-03(e).
[74] See §17.04.
[75] PPB ch 7, §§7-02(c)(6), 7-03(d).
[76] Id ch 7, §7-07(a).

lowed by the contracting officer."[77] There is no definition or explanation as to exactly what "notice procedures" the rules are referring. Presumably, they are the procedures discussed in Chapter Fourteen of the Rules, entitled "Public Notice," which sets forth certain publication requirements for solicitations and awards of contracts.[78]

The agency chief contracting officer is required to make a "prompt written decision," but the rules set no time limit. The contracting officer may, but need not, "convene an informal conference" with the protester or other city agencies.[79] There are no provisions for a hearing where evidence is introduced or witnesses examined.

The protester must be notified of the decision in writing and the decision must state the reasons upon which it is based.[80]

The protester may appeal the decision to the agency head, provided it is done within five days of receipt of the decision. The agency head may also convene an informal conference,[81] but need not conduct any hearings.

The agency head's decision "shall be final."[82]

As with almost all other data and documents generated during the dispute process under the rules, copies of documents generated during a protest will be included in the VENDEX database.[83]

§17.09 —Contract Disputes

For nonconstruction-related contracts, the Procurement Policy Board (PPB) Rules make clear that the dispute resolution procedures in Chapter Seven apply to *all* disputes between the city and its contractors.[84] However, for "construction and construction-related" contracts, §7-05 limits the application of the dispute resolution procedure to disputes about the following:

1. The scope of work delineated by the contract
2. The interpretation of contract documents
3. The amount to be paid for extra work or disputed work
4. The conformity of the contractor's work to the contract, and
5. The acceptability and quality of the contractor's work.[85]

The procedure is a two-step process. After the agency's engineer renders a decision with which the contractor disagrees, the contractor must notify the

---

[77] *Id* ch 7, §7-07(a)(2).
[78] *Id* ch 14, §14-01.
[79] *Id* ch 7, §7-07(a)(3).
[80] *Id* ch 7, §7-07(a)(4).
[81] *Id* ch 7, §7-07(b)(3).
[82] *Id* ch 7, §7-07(b)(5).
[83] *Id* ch 7, §7-07(d). See §17.04.
[84] PPB Rules ch 7, §7-04(a).
[85] *Id* ch 7, §7-05(a).

§17.09 CONTRACT DISPUTES 617

agency head, in writing, of the dispute.[86] Within a specified amount of time, the contractor must submit a detailed, written statement setting forth all facts, evidence, documents, etc., upon which it will rely in support of its position. Thereafter, the city's engineer must submit to the agency head all materials that are deemed pertinent to the dispute. Though not expressly required, the implication is that the engineer must also provide the contractor with whatever it submits to the agency. Either party may then demand that the other produce documents not already produced that may be relevant. A "willful" failure by the contractor to produce any requested material will constitute a final waiver of its claim. There is no sanction for the agency's failure to produce relevant material.[87]

After all material has been produced, the agency head may, but is not obligated to, convene a conference with agency personnel and the contractor to resolve the dispute. The agency head may also seek such expertise as he or she deems appropriate, including the use of a "neutral mediator," which is not further defined. The rules do not address whether the agency head must disclose to the contractor its use of experts. The fact that the agency head may have participated in negotiations over the dispute does not affect its ability to act as the decider of the dispute.[88]

Either the agency or the contractor may compel the participation of any other contractor on the project in the dispute procedure, and any contractor brought into the proceedings will be bound by the decision rendered. This presumably includes architects, engineers, and construction managers under contract to the city.[89] Within a specified time after receipt of all materials, the agency head is required to render a decision in writing, which, unless appealed, is final and binding on the parties. A failure of the agency head to render a decision within the time allowed is deemed a rejection of the claim.[90]

If the contractor disagrees with the agency head's decision, it may appeal to the Contract Dispute Resolution Board (CDRB) established by the PPB Rules. The city may not appeal to the board, but if the contractor takes an appeal, the city may then appeal any portion of the decision with which it disagrees.[91] The board is composed of the city chief procurement officer or designee; the director or designee of the mayor's Office of Construction, and a neutral person with "appropriate experience."[92] The neutral person may not have a contract or dispute with the city or be regularly engaged in representing persons, companies, etc., having disputes with the city. The neutral person is to be paid on a per diem basis. The PPB Rules do not say how much the neutral person will be paid or who will pay him or her.[93]

---

[86] *Id* PPBR ch 7, §7-04(d)(1).
[87] *Id* ch 7, §7-05(d)(2).
[88] *Id* ch 7, §7-05(d)(3).
[89] *Id.*
[90] *Id* ch 7, §7-05(d)(4).
[91] *Id* ch 7, §7-05(d)(5).
[92] *Id* ch 7, §7-05(e).
[93] *Id* ch 7, §7-05(e)(3).

Prior to submitting its dispute to the CDRB, the contractor must submit its claim to the comptroller for review, investigation, and possible adjustment.[94] The PPB Rules set forth exactly what must be submitted to the comptroller, which may not include any evidence that was not presented to the agency head.[95] If the claim is not settled by the comptroller, the contractor may, by written petition, ask the CDRB to review the agency head's determination. The rules specify what must be contained in the petition, which includes all evidence submitted to the agency head. The petition must be served by the contractor on the agency head, the corporation counsel, and the comptroller. The agency must respond within 15 days and provide to the CDRB all evidence it submitted to the agency head.[96] There is no requirement that the agency response be served on the contractor, but basic fairness dictates that the agency do so. The contractor cannot submit any evidence to the CDRB not presented to the agency head or the comptroller. No similar prohibition is placed on the agency. The rules allow oral argument by the contractor to the CDRB as well as the submission of memoranda and briefs. However, there is no provision for a hearing where evidence is introduced and witnesses called. As allowed the agency head, the CDRB can seek technical or other expertise, but the rules do not address whether the use of such expertise must be disclosed to the parties.[97] Interestingly, the rules do not address the use of neutral mediators by the CDRB.

The CDRB has 45 days to render a decision and, in complex cases, may take up to 60 days. In reaching its decision, the CDRB is instructed not to rely on its past decisions.[98] The PPB Rules state that the CDRB's decision on a contractor's appeal is final and binding on the contractor and the city. The contractor is permitted to seek a review of the board's decision in court. However, the review by the court is limited to the question of whether the decision was obtained through or infected by fraud, bad faith, or palpable error. No evidence or information may be introduced or relied upon in court that was not presented to the CDRB during the dispute procedure. If a contractor seeks court review, the city may ask the court to reject any portion of the decision with which it disagrees.[99] It appears that the contractor has no right to demand a trial *de novo* on its claims.

§17.10 —Debarment and Suspension

Section 7-08 of the Procurement Policy Board (PPB) Rules outlines the grounds for debarment and suspension. The grounds for debarment include

---

[94] *Id* ch 7, §7-05(f).
[95] *Id* ch 7, §7-05(f)(1).
[96] *Id* ch 7, §7-05(g)(1).
[97] *Id* ch 7, §7-05(g)(2).
[98] *Id* ch 7, §7-05(g)(3).
[99] *Id* ch 7, §7-05(g)(5).

certain "acts or omissions on the part of the contractor or any of its officers, directors, partners, 5 per cent shareholders, principals or other persons substantially involved in its contracting activities."[100]

Examples of acts that are grounds for debarment include:

1. A criminal offense involving obtaining or attempting to obtain or performing a public or private contract
2. Fraud, embezzlement, theft, bribery, forgery, falsification or destruction of records, or receiving stolen property
3. A criminal violation of a state or federal antitrust statute
4. RICO violations involving submissions of bids or offenses indicating a lack of business integrity
5. Arrears on any debt or contract with the city
6. Violations of certain contract provisions[101]

This list is illustrative, but hardly exhaustive. The rules appear to allow the city to debar a contractor for any acts that reflect adversely on the integrity of the contractor or on the city for using a contractor with a less than sterling reputation.

Debarment proceedings are held before the Office of Administrative Trials and Hearings, which is an independent city agency established by the City Charter.[102] The fact that the city initiates a debarment proceeding will be included in the VENDEX database.[103]

An agency that has petitioned the Office of Administrative Trials and Hearings for debarment may suspend the contractor from consideration for award of contracts pending the debarment proceedings for a period not to exceed three months.[104] Since an agency may "in its exclusive discretion" suspend a contractor pending debarment, and any appeal of the suspension is to the agency head with no further right of appeal,[105] contractors should expect that suspensions will be automatic when debarment proceedings are commenced.

The rules call for the debarment process to be informal, yet consistent with principals of fundamental fairness and due process. The debarment can be for as long as a period of five years.[106]

The petition for debarment, as well as any documents relating to an agency-initiated suspension of a contractor, will be included in the VENDEX data-

---

[100] PPB Rules ch 7, §7-08(a).

[101] Id ch 7, §7-08(a)(i)(A)-(F).

[102] Id ch 7, §7-08(b)(1); New York City Charter & Code, ch 45, §1048 (New York Legal Publishing Corp 1990).

[103] Id. See §17.04.

[104] Id ch 7, §7-08(c).

[105] Id.

[106] Id ch 7, §7-08(d); (i)(4).

base.[107] Presumably, the existence of any past or pending debarment proceedings will factor into decisions on a contractor's "responsibility" and eligibility for other contracts. The PPB Rules also require the city to maintain and publish monthly in the City Record a list of suspended or debarred contractors, including a summary of each suspension or debarment.[108]

§17.11 —Solicitation or Award of Contract in Violation of PPB Rules

Section 7-09 of Chapter Seven of the Procurement Policy Board (PPB) Rules, entitled "Remedies," sets forth the procedure to be followed if a solicitation or an award is in violation of the PPB Rules. If at all possible, contracts awarded in violation will be canceled and solicitations will be revised. If a contract has been awarded and the contractor has not acted fraudulently or in bad faith, the contract may be ratified if it is in the best interests of the city to do so. Alternatively, the city may terminate the contract and compensate the contractor for the actual, direct out-of-pocket expenses incurred, not including overhead or profit.[109]

If the contractor awarded the contract has acted fraudulently or in bad faith, the contract may be declared null and void or, if it is in the city's best interests, the contract may be ratified, without prejudice to the city's right to collect damages.[110]

§17.12 —Hearings on Borough President Complaints

When New York City's Board of Estimate was declared unconstitutional,[111] in part because each borough president had one equal vote notwithstanding wide population disparities between the various boroughs, the borough presidents lost considerable power, including the power to award city contracts. That function will now be handled by administrators operating under the Procurement Policy Board (PPB) Rules. In order to make the adoption of the new city charter more palatable, the borough presidents were given an oversight function over city contracts which is codified in §7-10 of Chapter Seven of the PPB Rules.

Very simply, a borough president has the right to make certain recommendations concerning contracts being performed in his or her borough. These recommendations can range from modification of the contract to termination.[112]

---

[107] Id ch 7, §7-08(j). See **§17.04**.

[108] Id ch 7, §7-08(j)(2).

[109] PPB Rules ch 7, §7-09(b)(1)(ii).

[110] Id ch 7, §7-09(b)(2)(i)-(ii).

[111] Board of Estimates v Morris, 489 US 688, 109 S Ct 1433, 103 L Ed 2d 717 (1989).

[112] PPB Rules ch 7, §7-10(b).

Upon receipt of a recommendation from a borough president, the agency head is required to respond in writing setting forth what action, if any, the agency intends to take.[113] If the borough president is not satisfied with the agency's response, the borough president may demand a hearing on the subject before persons designated by the mayor.[114] The agency and the contractor "whose performance is being evaluated" have the right and, when requested, the duty to appear and give testimony.[115]

The hearings are to be expeditious and in no event to continue past 40 days after the borough president's demand.[116] At the conclusion of the hearings, the panel is to make a written recommendation. The rules do not state whether the panel's recommendation is binding on the agency head, the borough president, or the contractor, and the assumption must be that it is advisory only. Nor do the rules address whether evidence introduced in such a hearing is admissible in proceedings on disputes between the contractor and the agency.

There is no provision in the PPB Rules for compensating a contractor for costs incurred when a job is delayed by reason of a borough president's demand for hearing, nor do the PPB Rules state whether the contractor would be entitled to an extension of time.

§17.13 Questions and Suggestions for PPB Dispute Resolution

The Procurement Policy Board (PPB) dispute resolution rules themselves lead to questions about their scope—that is, what types of disputes will or will not be subject to the PPB dispute resolution procedures? Attempting to answer these questions leads to some suggestions regarding how the city might administer the rules so as to achieve their intended purpose—a fair resolution of disputes.

§17.14 —Delays

It is anticipated that the city will take the position that any claim by a contractor arising out of delays caused by the city may not be raised in the Procurement Policy Board (PPB) dispute process. Construction contracts will continue to contain a *no damage for delay* clause. The city apparently does not want to take the chance that a contractor will recover delay damages in the dispute resolution process, especially given its success in defeating delay claims in court. What is unclear is whether the denial of an extension of time requested by a contractor and an assessment against the contractor of liquidated damages are subject to the PPB dispute procedure.

---

[113] *Id* ch 7, §7-10(e).
[114] *Id* ch 7, §7-10(f)(1).
[115] *Id* ch 7, §7-10(f)(4).
[116] *Id* ch 7, §7-10(f)(6).

Granting extensions of time and assessment of liquidated damages are governed by Chapter Six of the PPB Rules. Section 6-03 provides that, in the first instance, decisions are made by the agency's chief contracting officer.[117] For long delays, as defined by the rules, and for extensions for substantial completion and final payment, the decisions on whether the delays are excusable must be approved by the Board of Time Extension.[118] What the rules do not make clear is whether a decision by this Board of Time Extension is appealable under §7-05 to the agency head and then to the Contract Dispute Resolution Board (CDRB). Further questions are raised by the language in §6-03(c)(3) that the failure to assess liquidated damages and the granting of an extension of time do not operate as a waiver of city claims against the contractor for actual or liquidated damage.[119]

Some questions are:

(1) Must the city assert these claims as part of the dispute resolution procedure?

(2) If a decision of the CDRB upholds a contractor's request for an extension of time, are the city's claims for liquidated or delay damages extinguished?

(3) If the city withholds payment to the contractor due to the assessment of liquidated damages, must this "dispute" be submitted to the agency head and appealed to the CDRB, or can the contractor sue in court?

(4) If the city wishes to recover liquidated damages that exceed any balance due on the contract, can it sue the contractor in court or must it first obtain a decision from the CDRB and then ask a court to confirm that decision and enter a judgment, much like an arbitration award?

(5) Conversely, if the agency head or the CDRB awards money to a contractor, must the contractor "confirm" that award in court before the city can be legally compelled to pay the contractor?

§17.15 —Finality of City Decisions

Certain langauge in the standard contract used by city agencies brings up the question of whether a decision by the Contract Dispute Resolution Board (CDRB) is, in fact, final and binding. The standard contract, which now makes reference to the Procurement Policy Board (PPB) Rules and incorporates wholesale some of the language in the rules, such as §7-05 on dispute resolution, continues to speak of the contractor being barred from "commencing an action for breach of contract" unless the contractor files a statement of claim within the time set forth in Article 44 of the standard contract. Article 53, entitled "Claims and Actions Thereon," speaks of an action against the city asserting claims for breach of contract, seeking compensation for extra work, to

---

[117] PPB Rules ch 6, §6-03(b)(1).

[118] *Id* ch 6, §6-03(c)(2)(ii).

[119] *Id* ch 6, §6-03(c)(3).

recover money deducted, retained, or withheld, or to challenge a declaration of default, and places time limits on when such actions must be commenced. These time limits do not appear to be consistent with the time limits established by the PPB dispute procedure.

At least some of these claims would appear to be subject to the "final and binding" dispute resolution procedure in the PPB Rules, such as claims for extra work and claims for money withheld due to an allegation of nonconformity of the work to the contract, or the acceptability and quality of the work.

Even a declaration of default would seem to be subject to the dispute resolution procedure. A declaration of default involves an interpretation of the contract documents—i.e., the contract documents impose certain obligations on the contractor, and, since the contractor has failed or refused without cause to fulfill these obligations, the contractor is in default.

§17.16 —The Need for Fairness: Some Suggestions

While the questions raised in this chapter about the Procurement Policy Board (PPB) dispute resolution procedure certainly should be examined and addressed, there is a much more significant issue. Will the PPB Rules lead to a fair and impartial hearing on disputes between the city and its contractors?

On their face, the PPB Rules create a kangaroo court where city officials will render decisions affecting contractors and then, when those decisions are questioned, decide whether the initial decisions are fair. If a contractor does not agree with the "second" decision, it can "appeal" to other city officials, whose responsibility it is to supervise, consult, and advise the official who made the initial decision. The system is fraught with conflicts of interest and conflicting loyalties. It is problematic to expect a city official to render impartial decisions on a dispute when it may not be in the city's, or that official's, best interests. For example, assume that a contractor's claim is valid in all respects. How does the agency head find for the contractor when to do so will not only create an unexpected burden on the agency's budget, but also suggests that some act or omission on the agency's part caused the problem in the first place. Or, consider the problems caused when the validity of the claim is questionable, but ruling against the contractor may affect its ability to complete the project or other work it is doing for the agency.

Precisely because of problems such as these, a judicial function is best given to someone with no stake in the outcome. Unfortunately, the reality is that New York City cannot afford an independent contract dispute agency staffed with individuals whose sole function is to act as impartial judges in disputes between the city and its contractors; thus, the system created by the PPB Rules. What, if anything, can be done to ensure that the PPB Rules do what they say is their intention—i.e., "treating contractors fairly and giving those who disagree with agency decisions a fair opportunity to be heard"?

The first thing is for the mayor's Office of Construction, the corporation counsel, and the comptroller to state unequivocally that they expect all decisions made under the PPB Rules to be based solely on their merits, and that city officials who make difficult or unpopular decisions will not suffer for them. City officials, or their subordinates, asked to sit as judges should not be concerned if, after considering all the evidence, they admit a mistake and rule against their agencies. Perhaps the City Council should consider protection similar to that afforded to "whistle blowers" for those asked to decide disputes under the PPB Rules. When an agency head or a member of the Contract Dispute Resolution Board (CDRB) feels that he or she is too close to the dispute to judge it fairly, he or she should be encouraged to recuse him- or herself.

The rules give great leeway to agency heads in determining exactly how they will gather the information necessary to reach a decision on a dispute. They should be encouraged to hold evidentiary hearings where witnesses testify and are cross-examined. Because of the powers given them by the rules, agency heads can impose limits on the presentation and the cross-examination so hearings do not drag on ad infinitum, which seems to be the case in some trials and arbitrations.

Since the rules do not require a hearing at all, no one should complain if the agency head elected to have one, perhaps, for example, limiting each witness to three hours of direct testimony, with no interruptions or objections allowed, and then allowing the other side one-and-one-half hours of cross-examination. These hour limits are arbitrary—it may be that the claimant's entire case should be limited to three hours, with the other side given an equal time for rebuttal. The point is that those with a dispute should be given an opportunity to be heard and, more important, to confront adverse witnesses.

The rules make no allowance for a contractor's reserving its right to present its claims until the end of the job. Rather, the rules seem to contemplate that each dispute will be processed as it occurs. The CDRB has the discretion to combine one or more disputes for a hearing, but has no obligation to do so. This may prove to be unduly burdensome to the contractor and the city as any contractor could have a number of disputes, each requiring a separate initial presentation and appeal. A fairer system would be to allow a contractor to elect to present all of its claims and disputes at the end of the job, provided that it has complied with the various notice provisions of the contract. If a particular dispute must be resolved during the job because of its impact on the work or financial impact on the contractor, the contractor could elect to have the dispute heard immediately. The city is protected since, in most instances, it can direct a contractor to proceed with disputed work under the terms of its contract.

The rule that directs the CDRB not to place any weight on past decisions should be scrapped. One of the most frequently heard complaints of contractors doing city work is that one of the few things one can depend on when dealing with the city is that decisions will be made arbitrarily. Being unable to predict, with any degree of certainty, how the city will act leads to large contingencies, or contractors simply avoiding certain agencies. One of the benefits of requiring the CDRB to establish precedents to follow is that it would allow the city to monitor the type of disputes that seem to recur frequently. Agencies can then attempt to prevent such disputes from occurring at all through better contract administration or a change in contract language.

§17.16 NEED FOR FAIRNESS: SUGGESTIONS

The concept of one party to a contract acting as the sole and final decider of disputes arising under the contract has come under attack in many cases. An appellate court in New Jersey has ruled that dispute resolution clauses, like that established by the PPB Rules, where one party to the contract acts as an arbitrator, are unenforceable and do not foreclose a contractor's right to sue in court.[120] In New York, the contractor may not fare as well.[121]

When the PPB Rules dispute resolution procedure is challenged, and it no doubt will be, the city will face an uphill battle due to the almost complete absence of any procedural due process safeguards in the PPB Rules. The city may be able to make up for this inherent defect by an enlightened administration of the PPB Rules and an overriding commitment to ensuring the absolute impartiality and integrity of the dispute resolution process. The city says it wants to treat contractors fairly. Whether it does so is up to the city.

---

[120] Gauntt Constr Co/Lott Elect Co v Delaware River & Bay Auth, 241 NJ Super 422, 575 A2d 70 (Burlington 1989), revd, 241 NJ Super 310, 575 A2d 13 (1990).

[121] Nab Constr Corp v Metropolitan Transp Auth, NYLJ, Feb 10, 1992, at 26, col 1 (AD 1st Dept).

Cases

A

A&E Plumbing, Inc v Biedoff, 66 AD2d 455, 413 NYS2d 776 (1979) §9.49

A&J Buyers, Inc v Johnson, Drake & Piper, Inc, 25 NY2d 265, 303 NYS2d 841 (1969) §9.08

A&M Wallboard, Inc v Facilities Dev Corp, 97 Misc 2d 434, 411 NYS2d 492 (Albany 1978) §§7.19, 16.02

A&R Constr Co v New York State Elec & Gas Corp, 23 AD2d 450, 261 NYS2d 482 (1965) §§5.12, 5.15, 5.18

Abele Tractor & Equip Co v Department of Pub Works, 74 AD2d 980, 426 NYS2d 186 (1980) §2.05

A. Burgart, Inc v Foster-Lipkins Corp, 63 Misc 2d 930, 313 NYS2d 831, *affd*, 38 AD2d 779, 328 NYS2d 856, *affd*, 30 NY2d 901, 287 NE2d 269, 335 NYS2d 562 (1970) §9.41

Accen Constr Corp v Port Wash Union Free School Dist, 173 AD2d 753, 570 NYS2d 628, 68 Educ L Rep (West) 128 (2d Dept 1991) §16.02

Ace Hardwood Flooring Co v Glazer, 74 AD2d 912, 426 NYS2d 69 (1980) §9.79

Aces Mechanical Corp v Cohen Bros Realty & Constr Corp, 136 AD2d 503, 523 NYS2d 824 (1st Dept 1988), *order modified as indicated*, 531 NYS2d 218 (1988) §2.31

Active Fire Sprinkler Corp v United States Postal Serv, 811 F2d 747 (2d Cir 1987) §8.43

Admiral Transit Mix Corp v Sagg-Bridgehampton Corp, 56 Misc 2d 47, 287 NYS2d 751 (Suffolk 1968) §9.26

Advanced Alarm Tech, Inc v Pavilion Assocs, 145 AD2d 582, 536 NYS2d 127 (1988) §§9.12, 9.26

AD Walker & Co v Shelter Programs Co, 84 AD2d 536, 443 NYS2d 96 (1981) §9.81

AE Ottaviano, Inc v State, 202 Misc 532, 110 NYS2d 99 (Ct Cl 1952) §7.64

Aetna Cas & Sur Co v BBB Constr Corp, 173 F2d 307 (2d Cir), *cert denied*, 337 US 917, 69 S Ct 1158, 93 L Ed 1726 (1949) §8.46

Aetna Cas & Sur Co v City of NY, 160 AD2d 561, 554 NYS2d 210 (1st Dept 1990) §§4.18, 15.12

Aetna Cas & Sur Co v Lumbermens Mut Cas Co, 136 AD2d 246, 527 NYS2d 143 (4th Dept 1988) §10.22

Aetna Ins Co v Hellmuth, Obata & Kassabaum, Inc, 392 F2d 472 (8th Cir 1968) §§8.50, 11.14

Affirmative Pipe Cleaning, Inc/Edenwald Contracting Co v City of NY, 159 AD2d 417, 553 NYS2d 324 (1st Dept 1990) §4.04

AG Concrete Breakers, Inc v State, 16 Misc 2d 511, 185 NYS2d 455 (Ct Cl), *affd*, 9 AD2d 995, 194 NYS2d 743 (3d Dept 1959) §§5.02, 5.12, 5.15, 5.18

AJ Beaudette Constr Co v City of Syracuse, 62 Misc 2d 564, 309 NYS2d 517 (Onondaga), *affd*, 313 NYS2d 356 (App Div 1970) §§2.05, 2.22

AJ Cianciulli, Inc v Town of Greenburgh, 12 Misc 2d 931, 172 NYS2d 233 (Westchester 1958) §6.07

Albany Builders Supply Co v Eastern Bridge & Structural Co, 235 NY 432, 139 NE 565 (1923) §9.30

Albany County Indus Dev Agency v Gastinger Ries Walker Architects, Inc, 144 AD2d 891, 534 NYS2d 823 (1988) §§9.05, 9.13

Albany Supply & Equip Co v City of Cohoes, 47 Misc 2d 312, 262 NYS2d 603 (Albany 1965), *affd*, 25 AD2d 700, 268 NYS2d 42, *affd*, 18 NY2d 968, 224 NE2d 716, 278 NYS2d 207 (1966) §2.11

ALB Contracting Co v York-Jersey Mortgage Co, 60 AD2d 989, 401 NYS2d 934 (1978) §9.71

Albert Elia Bldg Co v New York State Urban Dev Corp, 54 AD2d 337, 388 NYS2d 462 (4th Dept 1976) §§2.08, 6.04, 6.07, 15.03

Alco Standard Corp v Schmid Bros, 647 F Supp 4 (SDNY 1986) §4.04

Al-Ev Constr Corp v Ahern Maintenance & Supply Corp, 141 AD2d 591, 529 NYS2d 354 (2d Dept 1988) §15.26

Allen v Cloutier Constr Corp, 44 NY2d 290, 376 NE2d 1276, 405 NYS2d 630 (1978) §§13.03, 13.04, 13.06, 13.07, 13.13, 13.18

Allerton Constr Corp v Fairway Apts Corp, 26 AD2d 636, 272 NYS2d 867 (1966) §9.68

Allstate Ins Co v Kashkin, 130 AD2d 744, 516 NYS2d 43 (2d Dept 1987) §10.15

Almar Constr Corp v PM Hughes & Sons, 58 AD2d 615, 395 NYS2d 700 (1977) §16.02

Alside, Inc v Spancrete NE, Inc, 84 AD2d 616, 444 NYS2d 241 (3d Dept 1981) §11.22

Aluminum Fair, Inc v Abdella, 90 AD2d 603, 456 NYS2d 184 (3d Dept 1982) §9.49

Alvord & Swift v Stewart M. Muller Constr Co, 46 NY2d 276, 385 NE2d 1238, 413 NYS2d 309 (1978) §3.06

Amadeus, Inc v State, 55 Misc 2d 27, 284 NYS2d 620 (Ct Cl 1967), *affd as modified*, 36 AD2d 873, 320 NYS2d 677 (3d Dept), *appeal dismissed*, 29 NY2d 634, 324 NYS2d 458 (1971) §§6.01, 6.13, 6.24

Amedure v Standard Furniture Co, 125 AD2d 170, 512 NYS2d 912 (3d Dept 1987) §13.05

American Airlines v Licon Assocs, 56 AD2d 782, 392 NYS2d 457 (1st Dept 1977) §16.14

American Blower Corp v James Talcott, Inc, 18 Misc 2d 1031, 194 NYS2d 630 (NY 1959), *affd mem*, 11 AD2d 654, 203 NYS2d 1018 (1960), *affd*, 10 NY2d 282, 219 NYS2d 263 (1961) §§9.18, 9.76

American Bridge Co v State, 245 AD 535, 283 NYS 577 (3d Dept 1935) §§7.23, 7.38, 7.43

American Fidelity Fire Ins Co v Pavia-Byrne Engg Corp, 393 So 2d 830 (La Ct App 1981) §8.50

American Indus Contracting Co v Travelers Indem Co, 54 AD2d 679, 387 NYS2d 260 (1976), *affd*, 42 NY2d 1041, 369 NE2d 762, 399 NYS2d 206 (1977) §§8.33, 8.34, 8.37

American Motorists Ins Co v ER Squibb & Sons, 95 Misc 2d 222, 406 NYS2d 658 (NY 1978) §10.09

American Motorists Ins Co v Salvatore, 102 AD2d 342, 476 NYS2d 897 (1st Dept 1984) §10.15

American Sign Co v Rundback, 161 NYS 228 (1st Dept 1916) §6.22

American Standard, Inc v New York City Transit Auth, 133 AD2d 595, 519 NYS2d 701 (2d Dept 1987) §7.52

American Standard, Inc v Schectman, 80 AD2d 318, 439 NYS2d 529 (4th Dept), *appeal denied*, 54 NY2d 604, 427 NE2d 512, 443 NYS2d 1027 (1981) §§15.16, 15.29

American Tempering, Inc v Craft Architectural Metals Corp, 107 AD2d 565, 483 NYS2d 304 (1985) §3.29

Amerman v Lizza & Sons, 45 AD2d 996, 358 NYS2d 220 (2d Dept 1974) §§13.03, 13.04, 13.15

Anderman v 1395 E 52nd St Realty Corp, 60 Misc 2d 437, 303 NYS2d 474 (Sullivan 1969) §9.56

Anderson Constr Co v Board of Educ, 229 NYS2d 337 (Suffolk 1962) §§7.17, 7.18, 16.02

Anderson Constr Co v United States, 289 F2d 809 (Ct Cl 1961) §§6.01, 6.18, 6.29

Andrew Catapano Co v City of NY, 116 Misc 2d 163, 455 NYS2d 144 (NY 1980) §§2.36, 5.02, 5.03, 5.07, 5.08

Angelo J. Martone & Son v County of Nassau, 42 Misc 2d 804, 249 NYS2d 353 (Nassau 1964) §§15.03, 15.04

Antunes v 950 Park Ave Corp, 149 AD2d 332, 539 NYS2d 909 (1st Dept 1989) §13.05

A-1 Camp Chair Serv Co v William L. Crow Constr Co, 24 AD2d 623, 262 NYS2d 166 (2d Dept 1965) §§12.03, 15.28

Aquilino v United States, 10 NY2d 271, 219 NYS2d 254 (1961), *on remand from*, 363 US 509, 80 S Ct 1277, 4 L Ed 2d 1365 (1960) §9.68

Arc Elec Constr Co v George A. Fuller Co, 24 NY2d 99, 247 NE2d 111, 299 NYS2d 129 (1969) §12.03

Ardsley Constr Co v Port Auth, 54 NY2d 876, 429 NE2d 414, 444 NYS2d 907 (1981), *affg* 75 AD2d 760, 427 NYS2d 814 (1st Dept 1980) §§6.23, 16.04

Ardsley Constr Co v Port of NY Auth, 61 AD2d 953, 403 NYS2d 43 (1st Dept 1978) §3.23

Arrow Plumbing Co v Dare Constr Corp, 212 NYS2d 438 (Nassau 1961) §§6.08, 6.09

Arthur A. Johnson Corp v City of NY, 162 Misc 665, 295 NYS 547 (NY 1936), *affd*, 251 AD 811, 298 NYS 188 (1937) §§5.03, 5.08, 5.11

Arthur Richards, Ltd v Brampton Textiles, Ltd, 59 AD2d 842, 399 NYS2d 111 (1st Dept 1977) §§15.14, 16.12

A/S J. Ludwig Mowinckels Rederi v Dow Chem Co, 25 NY2d 576, 255 NE2d 774, 307 NYS2d 660, *cert denied*, 398 US 939 (1970) §16.13

AS Reynolds Elec Co v Board of Educ, 46 Misc 2d 140, 259 NYS2d 503 (Queens 1965) §2.09

Associated Builders & Contractors, Inc v City of Rochester, 67 NY2d 854, 492 NE2d 781, 501 NYS2d 653 (1986) §2.08

Associated Gen Contractors v Savin Bros, 45 AD2d 136, 139, 356 NYS2d 374 (3d Dept 1974), *affd*, 36 NY2d 957, 335 NE2d 859, 373 NYS2d 555 (1975) §7.72

Associated Gen Contractors of Am v Roberts, 122 AD2d 406, 505 NYS2d 220 (3d Dept 1986) §15.08

AS Wikstrom, Inc v State, 52 AD2d 658, 381 NYS2d 1010 (3d Dept 1976) §§5.10, 5.12

AT&T Tech, Inc v Communication Workers of Am, 475 US 643, 106 S Ct 1415, 89 L Ed 2d 648 (1986) §16.12

AT Morris & Co v Lumber Mut Cas Ins Co, 163 Misc 715, 298 NYS 227 (Queens 1937) §§10.09, 10.23

Ausable Chasm Co v Hotel Ausable Chasm & Country Club, 263 AD 486, 33 NYS2d 427 (1942) §9.01

Autotronics Sys v Aetna Life & Cas Co, 89 AD2d 401, 456 NYS2d 504 (3d Dept 1982) §14.22

Avon Elec Supplies, Inc v Goldsmith, 54 AD2d 552, 387 NYS2d 1 (1976) §9.26

B

Babylon Assocs v County of Suffolk, 101 AD2d 207, 475 NYS2d 869 (2d Dept 1984) §§15.22, 15.35, 15.40

Bacashihua v United States Postal Serv, 859 F2d 402 (6th Cir 1988) §16.13

Backstatter v Berry Hill Bldg Corp, 56 Misc 2d 351, 288 NYS2d 850 (Nassau 1968) §9.05

Bagwell Coatings, Inc v Middle S Energy, Inc, 797 F2d 1298 (5th Cir 1986) §11.19

Baker v Sadick, 162 Cal App 3d 618, 208 Cal Rptr 676 (1984) §15.12

Baker v State, 77 AD 528, 78 NYS 922 (3d Dept 1902) §§4.04, 4.21, 6.05

Balaban-Gordon Constr Co v Brighton Sewer Dist No 2, 41 AD2d 246, 342 NYS2d 435 (1973) §§2.19, 8.06, 8.07

Bank of NY, Albany v Hirschfeld, 59 AD2d 976, 399 NYS2d 329 (1977) §8.48

Banks v Demillo, 145 AD2d 903, 536 NYS2d 284 (4th Dept 1988) §12.08

Barbier v Shearson Lehman Hutton, Inc, 948 F2d 117 (2d Cir 1991) §15.12

Bargabos Constr Co v Realty Intl, Inc, 96 Misc 2d 1028, 410 NYS2d 263 (Onondaga 1978) §§9.36, 9.40

Barnes v MacBrown & Co, 264 Ind 227, 342 NE2d 619 (1976) §12.14

Barnes Constr Co, *In re* 131 Misc 2d 285, 499 NYS2d 867 (Cattaraugus 1986) §9.32

Barrett Paving Materials, Inc v United States Fidelity & Guar Co, 118 AD2d 1039, 500 NYS2d 413 (3d Dept 1986) §§3.31, 12.04, 12.07

Basic Adhesives, Inc v Robert Matzkin Co, 101 Misc 2d 283, 420 NYS2d 983 (Civ Ct NY 1979) §3.33

Bates & Rogers Constr Corp v Greeley & Hansen, 109 Ill 2d 225, 486 NE2d 902 (1985) §11.19

Bayridge Air Rights, Inc v Blitman Constr Corp, 160 AD2d 589, 554 NYS2d 528 (1st Dept 1990) §12.08

Bay Ridge Medical Group v Health Ins Plan, 22 AD2d 807, 254 NYS2d 616 (2d Dept 1964) §16.12

Beacon Constr Co v United States, 314 F2d 501 (Ct Cl 1963) §6.16

Beacon Plastic & Metal Prods, Inc v Corn Prods Co, 57 Misc 2d 634, 293 NYS2d 429 (App Term NY 1968) §3.31

Belco Petroleum Corp v AIG Oil Rig Inc, 164 AD2d 583, 565 NYS2d 776 (1st Dept 1991) §15.12

Bellevue S Assocs v HRH Constr Corp, 160 AD2d 189, 553 NYS2d 159 (1st Dept 1990) §12.04

Belscher v New York State Teachers' Retirements Sys, 45 AD2d 206, 357 NYS2d 241 (4th Dept 1974) §16.11

Ben Constr Co v Ventre, 23 AD2d 44, 257 NYS2d 988 (1965) §3.28

Benderson Dev Co v Schwab Bros Trucking, Inc, 64 AD2d 447, 409 NYS2d 890 (4th Dept 1978) §§2.48, 8.12

Bennett Bros v Bracewood Realty No 1, Inc, 31 Misc 2d 284, 220 NYS2d 38 (Queens 1961) §9.26

Berg-Bakis, Ltd v City of Yonkers, 90 AD2d 784, 455 NYS2d 645 (2d Dept 1982), *appeal dismissed*, 60 NY2d 664, 455 NE2d 658, 468 NYS2d 99 (1983) §15.13

Berger Mfg Co v City of NY, 206 NY 24, 99 NE 153 (1912) §§9.20, 9.33

Berkel & Co Contractors v Providence Hosp, 454 So 2d 496 (Ala 1984) §5.14

Berlanti, *In re*, 198 Misc 543, 103 NYS2d 418 (Westchester 1950) §9.03

Berley Indus v City of NY, 45 NY2d 683, 385 NE2d 281, 412 NYS2d 589, (1978) §7.60

Berndt v Aquavello, 139 AD2d 920, 527 NYS2d 910 (4th Dept 1988) §13.14

Bernmil Contracting Corp v City of NY, 80 AD2d 869, 437 NYS2d 17 (2d Dept 1981) §§7.05, 7.25, 7.66

Bero Constr Corp v State, 27 AD2d 974, 278 NYS2d 658 (4th Dept 1967) §7.05

Bethlehem Fabricators, Inc v Wills Taylor & Mafera, 248 AD 331, 289 NYS 96 (1936) §9.36

BG Equip Co v American Ins Co, 61 AD2d 247, 402 NYS2d 479, *affd*, 46 NY2d 802, 386 NE2d 833, 413 NYS2d 922 §§8.27, 8.39, 9.78

Biankanja v Irving, 49 Cal 2d 647, 320 P2d 16 (1958) §5.14

Biondo v City of NY, 18 AD2d 78, 238 NYS2d 7 (1963) §9.30

Birnant v Aetna Cas & Sur Co, 28 AD2d 978, 283 NYS2d 393 (1967) §8.12

Bistrian Gravel Corp v Wainscott NW Assocs, 116 AD2d 681, 497 NYS2d 748 (1986) §3.11

Black & Pola v Manes Org, Inc, 72 AD2d 514, 421 NYS2d 6 (1979), *affd mem*, 50 NY2d 821, 407 NE2d 1345, 430 NYS2d 49 (1980) §16.12

Blackman-Shapiro Co v Salzberg, 8 Misc 2d 972, 168 NYS2d 590 (Queens 1957) §9.26

Blair v Rosen-Michaels, Inc, 146 AD2d 863, 536 NYS2d 577 (3d Dept 1989) §§13.05, 13.14

Blakey v McMurray, 110 AD2d 998, 488 NYS2d 286 (3d Dept 1985) §2.25

Bland v Manocherian, 66 NY2d 452, 488 NE2d 810, 497 NYS2d 880 (1985) §13.05

Blandford Land Clearing Corp v Davidson, 62 AD2d 1007, 403 NYS2d 775 (1978) §2.08

Blatt Bowling & Billiard Corp v State, 14 AD2d 144, 217 NYS2d 766 (3d Dept 1961) §2.30

Blau Mech Corp v City of NY, 158 AD2d 373, 551 NYS2d 228 (1st Dept 1990) §§7.11, 7.37, 7.40

Blecick v School Dist No 18, 2 Ariz App 114, 406 P2d 746 (1965) §11.11

Board of Educ v Bernard Assocs No 3, 230 NYS2d 509 (Westchester 1962) §§6.06, 6.24

Board of Educ v Celotex Corp, 88 AD2d 713, 451 NYS2d 290 (3d Dept), *affd*, 58 NY2d 684, 444 NE2d 1006, 458 NYS2d 542 (1982) §§11.04, 11.23, 12.08

Board of Educ v Delle Cese, 65 Misc 2d 473, 318 NYS2d 46 (Oneida 1971) §15.22

Board of Educ v Matthew L. Carroll, Inc, 157 NYS2d 775 (Cattaraugus 1956) §§8.08, 8.18

Board of Educ v Niagara-Wheatfield Teachers Assoc, 46 NY2d 553, 389 NE2d 104, 415 NYS2d 790 (1979) §§15.12, 15.15, 15.19

Board of Educ v Patchogue-Medford Congress of Teachers, 48 NY2d 812, 399 NE2d 1143, 424 NYS2d 122 (1979) §16.12

Board of Educ v Sargent, Webster, Crenshaw & Folley, 71 NY2d 21, 517 NE2d 1360, 523 NYS2d 475 (1987) §§12.03, 12.10

Board of Educ v Thompson Constr Corp, 111 AD2d 497, 488 NYS2d 880 (3d Dept 1985) §§11.24, 12.08

Board of Educ v Tracy Trombley Constr Co, 122 AD2d 421, 505 NYS2d 233 (1986) §16.12

Board of Educ v Valden Assocs, 46 NY2d 653, 389 NE2d 798, 416 NYS2d 202 (1979) §3.13

Board of Educ v Wager Constr Corp, 37 NY2d 283, 291, 333 NE2d 353, 372 NYS2d 45 (1975) §16.02

Board of Educ v Wager Constr Corp, 37 NY2d 283, 333 NE2d 353, 372 NYS2d 45 (1975) §§7.17, 7.18, 16.02, 16.15

Board of Educ, *In re*, 226 NYS2d 300 (Westchester 1962) §6.32

Board of Estimates v Morris, 489 US 688, 109 S Ct 1433, 103 L Ed 2d 717 (1989) §17.12

Board of Managers v Vector Real Estate Corp, 172 AD2d 303, 568 NYS2d 391 (1st Dept), *appeal denied*, 78 NY2d 854, 578 NE2d 442, 573 NYS2d 644 (1991) §11.23

Bolander Co v United States, 186 Ct Cl 398 (1968) §5.02

Bonar v Dean Witter Reynolds, Inc, 835 F2d 1378 (11th Cir 1988) §16.12

Boomer v Atlantic Cement Co, 26 NY2d 219, 257 NE2d 870, 309 NYS2d 312 (1970) §14.04

Borgia v City of NY, 12 NY2d 151, 187 NE2d 777, 237 NYS2d 319 (1962) §11.24

Borough Constr Co v City of NY, 200 NY 149, 93 NE 480 (1910) §§5.16, 5.19, 6.04, 6.23, 6.34

Borysko, *In re*, 2 Misc 2d 621, 149 NYS2d 53 (Kings 1956) §9.35

Boutelle v Central School Dist No 1, 2 AD2d 925, 156 NYS2d 358 (1956) §16.02

Bradley v Kostanoski, 101 NYS2d 767 (Nassau 1950) §9.29

Bradley Envtl Constr v Village of Sylvan Beach, 98 AD2d 973, 470 NYS2d 214 (4th Dept 1983) §7.33

Bralus Corp, *In re*, 282 AD 959, 125 NYS2d 786 (1953), *affd*, 307 NY 626, 120 NE2d 829 (1954) §9.04

Brandt Corp v City of NY, 14 NY2d 217, 199 NE2d 493, 250 NYS2d 407 (1964) §6.33

Brauer v Central Trust Co, 77 AD2d 239, 433 NYS2d 304 (1980) §2.20

Braunstein v Jason Tarantella, Inc, 87 AD2d 203, 450 NYS2d 862 (2d Dept 1982) §2.28

Brecker v Mutual Life Ins Co, 120 AD2d 423, 501 NYS2d 879 (1st Dept 1986) §10.14

Brescia Constr Co v Walart Constr Co, 264 NY 260, 190 NE 484 (1934) §9.41

Bretzfelder v Froman, 76 Misc 2d 1063, 352 NYS2d 549 (Westchester 1973) §9.36

Brew v State Educ Dept, 73 AD2d 743, 423 NYS2d 271 (3d Dept 1979) §11.02

Brewster v Baltimore & Ohio RR, 167 AD2d 908, 562 NYS2d 277 (4th Dept 1990) §13.01

Briar Contracting Corp v City of NY, 156 AD2d 628, 550 NYS2d 717 (2d Dept 1989) §§11.14, 15.20

Brigham v McCabe, 27 AD2d 100, 276 NYS2d 328 (3d Dept 1966), *affd*, 20 NY2d 525, 232 NE2d 327, 285 NYS2d 294 (1967) §15.09

Bristol, Litynski, Wojcik, PC v Elliott, 107 Misc 2d 1005, 436 NYS2d 190 (Albany 1981) §§9.70, 9.71

Broadway Plus v Metro Transp Authority, 157 AD2d 453, 549 NYS2d 23 (1st Dept 1990) §2.16

Broderick v Cauldwell-Wingate Co, 301 NY 182, 93 NE2d 629 (1950) §13.04

Bronx Asphalt Corp v City of NY, 35 NYS2d 7 (App Term 1942) §6.33

Brook-Lea Country Club, Inc v Hanover Ins Co, 61 Misc 2d 896, 306 NYS2d 780 (Monroe 1969) §2.19

Brooklyn Ash Removal Co v O'Brien, 238 AD 647, 265 NYS 504 (1933) §2.08

Brooks v A. Gatty Serv Co, 127 AD2d 553, 511 NYS2d 642 (2d Dept 1987) §13.15

Brown v Lockwood, 76 AD2d 721, 432 NYS2d 186, (2d Dept 1980) §15.11

Brown v Two Exch Plaza Partners, 146 AD2d 129, 539 NYS2d 889

(1989), *affd*, 76 NY2d 172, 556 NE2d 430, 556 NYS2d 991 (1990) §3.13

Bruce Constr Corp v United States, 324 F2d 516 (Ct Cl 1963) §6.25

Bryant Equip Corp v A-1 Contracting Corp, 51 AD2d 792, 380 NYS2d 705 (1976) §9.36

Buckley & Co v City of NY, 121 AD2d 933, 505 NYS2d 140 (1st Dept 1986) §§5.17, 5.18, 5.20, 6.01, 6.09, 7.35, 7.37, 7.52

Buffalo Elec Co v State, 14 NY2d 453, 201 NE2d 869, 253 NYS2d 537 (1964) §6.33

Bujas v Katz, 133 AD2d 730, 520 NYS2d 18 (2d Dept 1987) §11.03

Bulova Watch Co v Celotex Corp, 46 NY2d 606, 389 NE2d 130, 415 NYS2d 817 (1979) §§12.04, 12.08, 12.09

Burdick Assocs Owners Corp v Indemnity Ins Co of N Am, 166 AD2d 402, 560 NYS2d 481 (2d Dept 1990) §16.16

Burke, *In re*, 191 NY 437, 84 NE 405 (1908) §15.15

Burmar Elec Corp v Starrett Bros, 60 AD2d 561, 400 NYS2d 346 (1977) §3.12

Bush Constr Co, ASBCA No 8573, 1963 BCA ¶3657 §6.01

BWA Corp v Alltrans Express USA, Inc, 112 AD2d 850, 493 NYS2d 1 (1st Dept 1985) §2.49

Byrne Constr Co v New York State Thruway Auth, 30 Misc 2d 980, 221 NYS2d 632 (Ct Cl 1961), *affd*, 19 AD2d 192, 241 NYS2d 58 (4th Dept 1963) §2.50

C

Cable Belt Conveyors, Inc v Alumina Partners, 717 F Supp 1021 (SDNY 1989) §3.23

Cabrini Medical Center v Desina, 64 NY2d 1059, 479 NE2d 217, 489 NYS2d 872 (1985) §12.08

Caceci v DiCanio Constr Corp, 132 AD2d 591, 517 NYS2d 753 (2d Dept 1987), *affd*, 72 NY2d 52, 526 NE2d 266, 530 NYS2d 771 (1988) §§12.02, 12.03, 12.14

Cadin Constr Corp v Adam Jay Assocs, 112 AD2d 395, 492 NYS2d 55 (1985) §9.75

Cadin Constr Corp v Adam Jay Assocs, 86 Misc 2d 407, 382 NYS2d 671 (Nassau 1976) §9.74

Caledonia Lumber & Coal Co v Chili Heights Apartments, 70 AD2d 766, 417 NYS2d 536 (1979) §§9.70, 9.71

Calla v Shulsky, 48 AD2d 60, 543 NYS2d 666 (1st Dept 1989) §13.01

Callanan Indus v City of Schenectady, 116 AD2d 883, 498 NYS2d 490 (3d Dept 1986) §15.04

Callanan Indus, *In re*, 88 Misc 2d 802, 389 NYS2d 80 (Albany 1975) §9.30

Callipari v 516 E 11th St Corp, 166 Misc 2d 79, 1 NYS2d 384 (NY 1937) §9.35

Camarco Contractors, Inc v State, 33 AD2d 717, 305 NYS2d 207 (3d Dept 1969), *affd as modified on other grounds*, 28 NY2d 948, 271 NE2d 917, 323 NYS2d 434 (1971) §§6.25, 6.27, 7.05, 7.08, 7.23

Cameron Equip Corp v People, 31 AD2d 299, 297 NYS2d 326 (1969), *affd mem*, 27 NY2d 634,

261 NE2d 668, 313 NYS2d 763 (1970) §§8.34, 9.03, 9.08
Camillo v Olympia & York Props Co, 136 Misc 2d 315, 518 NYS2d 702 (NY 1987) §13.05
Campagna Dev Corp v UCM Interior Designs, Inc, 75 Misc 2d 191, 347 NYS2d 253 (NY 1973) §9.04
Canton, Village of v Globe Indem Co, 201 AD 820, 195 NYS 445 (1922) §§8.15, 8.19, 8.26, 8.49
Capital Elec Co v United States, 729 F2d 743 (Fed Cir 1984) §7.60
Carboline Co v Gold, 94 AD2d 921, 463 NYS2d 341 (1983) §9.33
Caristo Constr Corp v Diners Fin Corp, 21 NY2d 507, 289 NYS2d 175 (1968) §§9.76, 9.79, 9.82
Carl A. Morse, Inc v Rentar Indus Dev Corp, 85 Misc 2d 304, 379 NYS2d 994 (Queens 1976), *affd*, 56 AD2d 30, 391 NYS2d 425 (1977), *affd*, 43 NY2d 952, 375 NE2d 409 (1978) §§9.03, 9.17
Carlo Bianchi & Co v State, 17 AD2d, 38, 230 NYS2d 471 (3d Dept 1962), *affd*, 28 NY2d 536, 268 NE2d 121, 319 NYS2d 439 (1971) §§7.05, 7.24, 7.42
Carmel Assocs v Turner Constr Co, 35 AD2d 157, 314 NYS2d 941 (1st Dept 1970) §1.25
Carollo v Tishman Constr & Research Co, 109 Misc 2d 506, 440 NYS2d 437 (NY 1981) §§13.12, 13.16
Carrols Equities Corp v Villnave, 57 AD2d 1044, 395 NYS2d 800 (1977) §§8.03, 8.08, 8.23, 8.26, 8.29, 8.48, 12.09, 12.12, 12.16
Carrols Equities Corp v Villnave, 76 Misc 2d 205, 350 NYS2d 90 (Onondaga 1973), *affd mem*, 49 AD2d 672, 373 NYS2d 1012 (4th Dept 1975) §§2.36, 4.10, 12.02, 12.03, 12.10
Carter v Blake, 63 AD2d 760, 404 NYS2d 728 (1978) §2.22
Casale v August Bohl Contracting Co, 26 AD2d 974, 275 NYS2d 140 (3d Dept 1966) §4.06
Castagne & Son v Board of Educ, 151 AD2d 392, 542 NYS2d 622 (1st Dept 1989) §§7.18, 7.40
Cauldwell-Wingate Co v State, 276 NY 365, 12 NE2d 443 (1938) §§5.03, 5.12, 5.13, 5.20, 7.37, 7.41
CD Perry & Sons v Sarkisian Bros, 53 AD2d 932, 385 NYS2d 191 (1976) §9.62
Celestine v City of NY, 86 AD2d 592, 446 NYS2d 131 (2d Dept 1982), *affd mem*, 59 NY2d 938, 453 NE2d 548, 466 NYS2d 319 (1983) §13.08
Central Gen Hosp v Hanover Ins Co, 49 NY2d 950, 406 NE2d 739, 428 NYS2d 881 (1980) §16.12
Central Hudson Gas & Elec Corp v Benjamin F. Shaw Co, 465 F Supp 331 (SDNY 1978) §15.08
Central School Dist No 1 v Double M Constr, 46 AD2d 800, 361 NYS2d 47 (2d Dept 1974) §15.14
Central School Dist No 1 v Double M Constr Corp, 41 AD2d 771, 341 NYS2d 905 (2d Dept 1973), *affd mem*, 34 NY2d 695, 312 NE2d 479, 356 NYS2d 296 (1974) §6.32
Central School Dist No 2 v Flintkote Co, 56 AD2d 642, 391 NYS2d 887 (2d Dept 1977) §11.08
Central Valley Concrete Corp v Montgomery Ward & Co, 34 AD2d 860, 310 NYS2d 925 (1970) §§9.05, 9.34, 9.50

Chandler v Madsen, 197 Mont 234, 642 P2d 1028 (1982) §14.32

Charlesbois v JM Weller Associates, 72 NY2d 587, 531 NE2d 1288, 535 NYS2d 356 (1988) §1.23

Charles E. Gates & Co v John F. Stevens Constr Co, 220 NY 38, 115 NE 22 (1917) §§9.18, 9.20

Charles S. Sells, Inc v New York State Thruway Auth, 27 AD2d 893, 278 NYS2d 162 (3d Dept 1967) §§7.22, 7.58

Charles S. Wood & Co v Alvord & Swift, 232 AD 603, 251 NYS 35 (1st Dept 1931), affd mem, 258 NY 611, 180 NE 354 (1932) §6.23

Chemical Bank v State, 64 AD2d 755, 406 NYS2d 633 (3d Dept 1978) §§5.04, 5.11

Chemical Waste Management, Inc v Armstrong World Indus, 669 F Supp 1285 (ED Pa 1987) §14.39

Chenango Indus Dev Agency v Lockwood Greene Engrs, Inc, 114 AD2d 728, 494 NYS2d 832 (3d Dept 1985), appeal dismissed, 67 NY2d 757, 490 NE2d 1233, 500 NYS2d 1027 (1986) §§12.04, 12.13, 12.15, 15.20

Chester, Town of v Republic Ins Co, 89 AD2d 959, 454 NYS2d 107 (1982) §§8.02, 8.08

Chittenden Lumber Co v Silberblatt & Lasker, Inc, 288 NY 396, 43 NE2d 459 (1942) §§8.32, 8.33

Christiana Point Dev, Inc v Galesi, 143 AD2d 717, 533 NYS2d 443 (2d Dept 1988) §2.47

CH Stuart, Inc, In re, 17 BR 400 (WDNY 1982) §9.70

Ciavarella v People, 36 Misc 2d 1083, 234 NYS2d 15 (Albany 1962) §9.74

Citizens Day Care Center, Inc v Community & Social Agency Employees Union, 59 AD2d 845, 399 NYS2d 10 (1st Dept 1977) §16.12

City & County Sav v Oakwood Holding Corp, 88 Misc 2d 198, 387 NYS2d 512 (Chemung 1976) §9.56

City School Dist v McLane Constr Co, 85 AD2d 749, 445 NYS2d 258 (3d Dept 1981) §§12.04, 12.07

CK Rehner, Inc, In re, 106 AD2d 268, 483 NYS2d 1 (1984) §2.15

Clark v Harris, 53 Misc 556, 103 NYS 785 (App Term 1907) §6.10

Clark Plastering Co v Seaboard Sur Co, 237 AD 274, 260 NYS 468 (1932) §§8.32, 8.40

Clark-Fitzpatrick, Inc v Long Island RR, 70 NY2d 382, 516 NE2d 190, 521 NYS2d 653 (1987) §§15.10, 15.13

Clemens v Benzinger, 211 AD 586, 207 NYS 539 (4th Dept 1925) §§12.05, 12.06

Clemente Contracting Co v State, 89 NYS2d 453 (Ct Cl 1944) §§6.15, 6.17

Clifford F. MacEvoy Co v United States ex rel Calvin Tomkins Co, 322 US 102, 64 S Ct 890, 88 L Ed 1163 (1944) §8.44

Clifton Steel Corp v General Elec Co, 80 AD2d 714, 437 NYS2d 734 (1981) §§2.28, 3.26, 9.24

Clyde-Savannah Cent School Dist v Naetzker, Thorsell & Dove, 73 AD2d 810, 424 NYS2d 67 (1979) §8.28

C. Norman Peterson Co v Container Corp of Am, 172 Cal App 3d 628, 218 Cal Rptr 592 (1985) §§6.04, 6.25

Cobleskill Sav & Loan Assn v Rickard, 15 AD2d 286, 223 NYS2d 246 (1962) §9.56

Coffey v United States Gypsum Co, 149 AD2d 960, 540 NYS2d 92 (4th Dept), *appeal denied,* 74 NY2d 610, 545 NE2d 868, 546 NYS2d 554 (1989) §§12.13, 12.15, 15.20

Coleman Capital Corp v Travelers Indem Co, 443 F2d 47 (2d Cir 1971) §§8.25, 8.47

Coley Props Corp, PSBCA 291, 75-2 BCA ¶11,514 (1975) §6.29

Collard v Incorporated Village of Flower Hills, 52 NY2d 594, 421 NE2d 818, 439 NYS2d 326 (1981) §§2.33, 2.47

Collins v State, 259 NY 200, 181 NE 357 (1932) §§5.04, 5.16, 6.04, 6.13

Colonial Roofing Corp v John Mee, Inc, 105 Misc 2d 140, 431 NYS2d 931 (Queens 1980) §3.18

Colony Liquor Distribs v Local 669, Bd of Teamsters, 34 AD2d 1060, 312 NYS2d 403 (3d Dept 1970), *affd mem,* 28 NY2d 596, 268 NE2d 645, 319 NYS2d 849 (1971) §16.12

Columbia Asphalt Corp v State, 70 AD2d 133, 420 NYS2d 36 (3d Dept 1979), *appeal denied,* 49 NY2d 702, 426 NYS2d 1027 (1980) §§7.23, 7.49, 7.50, 7.59

Comet Heating & Cooling Co v Modular Technics Corp, 57 AD2d 526, 393 NYS2d 573 (1st Dept 1977) §§3.12, 6.08

Commander Elec, Inc v Lerner, 54 AD2d 698, 387 NYS2d 294 (1976) §9.33

Commercial Mech Contractors, Inc, ASBCA 25695, 83-2 BCA ¶16768 §5.12

Commercial Union Ins Co v International Flavors & Fragrances, Inc, 822 F2d 267 (2d Cir 1987) §10.15

Commissioner of Welfare v Jones, 73 Misc 2d 1014, 343 NYS2d 661 (Queens 1973) §11.23

Community Science Tech Corp, ASBCA 20244, 77-1 BCA 12,352 (1977) §6.18

Concrete Constr Corp v Commercial Union Ins Co, 68 AD2d 866, 414 NYS2d 703 (1974) §8.37

Condello v Stock, 285 AD 861, 136 NYS2d 507 (4th Dept 1955) §15.26

Conduit & Found Corp v Metropolitan Transp Auth, 66 NY2d 144, 485 NE2d 1005, 495 NYS2d 340 (1985) §§2.15, 2.22

Conduit & Found Corp v State, 52 NY2d 1064, 420 NE2d 397, 438 NYS2d 516 (1981) §7.28

Conforti & Eisele, Inc v R. Salzstein & Co, 56 AD2d 292, 392 NYS2d 430 (1977) §9.74

Consolidated Sheet Metal Works, Inc v Board of Educ, 62 Misc 2d 445, 308 NYS2d 773 (Jefferson 1970) §2.05

Construction Management Corp v Brown & Root, Inc, 35 Misc 2d 223, 229 NYS2d 70 (NY 1962) §8.30

Contelmo's Sand & Gravel, Inc v J&J Milano, Inc, 96 AD2d 1090, 467 NYS2d 55 (1983) §§9.05, 9.26

Conti v Pettibone Cos, 111 Misc 2d 772, 445 NYS2d 943 (NY 1981), *affd mem,* 90 AD2d 708, 455 NYS2d 689 (1st Dept 1982) §§11.13, 13.11

Continental Cas Co v Chrysler Constr Co, 80 Misc 2d 552, 363 NYS2d 258 (Orange 1975) §8.48

Continental Ins Co v Colangione, 107 AD2d 978, 484 NYS2d 929, 930 (3d Dept 1985) §10.09

Contracting & Material Co v City of Chicago, 20 Ill App 3d 684, 314 NE2d 598 (1974), *revd,* 64 Ill 2d 21, 349 NE2d 389 (1976) **§7.47**

Conway v New York State Teachers' Retirement Sys, 141 AD2d 957, 530 NYS2d 300 (3d Dept 1988) **§§13.05, 13.14, 13.18**

Cooper v Emmanuele, 25 AD2d 809, 270 NYS2d 99 (1966) **§9.36**

Cooperstein v Patrician Estates, 117 AD2d 774, 499 NYS2d 423 (2d Dept 1986) **§§7.30, 7.69, 7.70, 7.73**

Coppola Bros Excavating Corp v Melnick & Co, 55 AD2d 522, 389 NYS2d 7 (1976), *affd as modified,* 56 AD2d 524, 391 NYS2d 121, *affd,* 43 NY2d 752, 372 NE2d 797, 401 NYS2d 1009 (1977) **§9.61**

Corinno Civetta Constr Corp v City of NY, 72 NY2d 737, 533 NE2d 258, 536 NYS2d 419 (1988) **§7.36**

Corinno Civetta Constr Corp v City of NY, 67 NY2d 297, 493 NE2d 905, 502 NYS2d 681 (1986) **§§7.33, 7.35, 7.36, 7.38, 7.39, 7.40, 7.41, 7.42**

Cornell v Barney, 94 NY 394 (1884) **§9.13**

Corr v Hoffman, 256 NY 254, 176 NE 383 (1931) **§15.38**

Cortland Asbestos Prods, Inc v J&K Plumbing & Heating Co, 33 AD2d 11, 304 NYS2d 694 (1969) **§§2.21, 3.02**

Costello v Geffen, 36 Misc 2d 895, 236 NYS2d 93 (Nassau 1962) **§§9.70, 9.81**

Country Excavation, Inc v State, 44 Misc 2d 1057, 255 NYS2d 708 (Ct Cl 1964) **§7.59**

Country Village Heights Condo v Mario Bonito, Inc, 79 Misc 2d 1088, 363 NYS2d 501 (Rockland 1975) **§§9.12, 9.36**

County Asphalt, Inc v State, 40 AD2d 26, 337 NYS2d 415 (3d Dept 1972) **§§5.03, 5.12, 5.13, 5.14, 5.16, 5.18, 5.19, 5.20**

County of Broome v Vincent J. Smith, Inc, 78 Misc 2d 889, 358 NYS2d 998 (Broome 1974) **§§11.24, 12.04**

County of Chenango v Lockwood Greene Engrs, Inc, 114 AD2d 728, 494 NYS2d 832 (1985) **§3.28**

County of Onondaga v Penetryn Sys, 84 AD2d 934, 446 NYS2d 693 (1981), *affd,* 56 NY2d 726, 436 NE2d 1340, 451 NYS2d 738 (1982) **§3.13**

County of Rockland v Aetna Cas & Sur Co, 129 AD2d 606, 514 NYS2d 102 (1987) **§8.17**

County of Rockland v Primiano Constr Co, 51 NY2d 1, 409 NE2d 951, 431 NYS2d 478 (1980) **§§11.11, 16.12, 16.15**

Cowen v Paddock, 137 NY 188, 33 NE 154 (1893) **§9.05**

Crawford v Leimzider, 100 AD2d 568, 473 NYS2d 498 (2d Dept 1984) **§13.05**

Credit Alliance Corp v Anderson & Co, 65 NY2d 536, 483 NE2d 110, 493 NYS2d 435 (1985) **§§5.14, 8.50, 11.14**

Crescent Elec Installation Corp v Board of Educ, 72 AD2d 760, 421 NYS2d 376 (2d Dept 1979), *affd,* 50 NY2d 780, 409 NE2d 917, 431 NYS2d 443 (1980) **§§7.18, 16.02**

Cromwell Towers Redev Co v City of Yonkers, 41 NY2d 1, 359 NE2d 333, 390 NYS2d 822 (1976) **§2.47**

Crown NW Equip, Inc v Donald M.
Drake Co, 49 Or App 679, 620
P2d 946 (1980) §2.20

Crown Plastering Corp v Elite
Assocs, 166 AD2d 495, 560
NYS2d 694 (2d Dept 1990) §3.18

Cubito v Kreisberg, 69 AD2d 738,
419 NYS2d 578 (2d Dept 1979),
affd mem, 51 NY2d 900, 415
NE2d 979, 434 NYS2d 991
(1980) §§11.13, 11.22, 11.23

Custer Builders, Inc v Quaker
Heritage, Inc, 41 AD2d 448, 344
NYS2d 606 (1973) §9.05

D

DaBolt v Bethlehem Steel Corp, 92
AD2d 70, 459 NYS2d 503 (4th
Dept), *appeal dismissed*, 60 NY2d
554, 467 NYS2d 1029 (1983)
§§13.03, 13.05

Dal Constr Corp v City of NY, 108
AD2d 892, 485 NYS2d 774 (2d
Dept 1985) §§7.33, 7.37

Dalrymple Gravel & Contracting
Co v State, 23 AD2d 418, 261
NYS2d 566 (3d Dept 1965), *affd
mem*, 19 NY2d 644, 225 NE2d
210, 278 NYS2d 616 (1967)
§6.33

D'Angelo v Cole, 67 NY2d 65, 490
NE2d 819, 499 NYS2d 900
(1986) §2.11

D'Angelo v State, 41 AD2d 77, 341
NYS2d 84 (3d Dept 1973), *appeal
dismissed*, 32 NY2d 896, 300 NE2d
155, 346 NYS2d 814 (1973), *order
affd as modified*, 34 NY2d 641, 311
NE2d 509, 355 NYS2d 377
(1974) §§7.49, 7.52, 7.60, 15.15

D'Angelo v State, 7 Misc 2d 783,
166 NYS2d 378 (Ct Cl 1957)
§§6.02, 6.24, 6.33

Danton Constr Corp v Bonner, 173
AD2d 759, 571 NYS2d 299 (2d
Dept 1991) §2.31

Dash Contracting Corp v Slater, 142
Misc 2d 512, 537 NYS2d 736
(NY 1989) §9.12

Daub v Board of Regents, 33 AD2d
964, 306 NYS2d 869 (3d Dept
1970) §11.02

Davidson & Jones, Inc v County of
New Hanover, 41 NC App 661,
255 SE2d 580, *cert denied*, 259
SE2d 911 (1979) §5.14

Davis v City of NY, 50 Misc 2d 275,
270 NYS2d 265 (NY 1966) §2.13

Davis v Lenox School, 151 AD2d
230, 541 NYS2d 814 (1st Dept
1989) §§13.11, 13.15

Davis Acoustical Corp v Hanover
Ins Co, 22 AD2d 843, 254
NYS2d 14 (1964) §8.21

Davis Co v Hoffman-LaRoche Chem
Works, 178 AD 855, 166 NYS
179 (1917) §3.31

Davis Constr Corp v County of
Suffolk, 149 AD2d 404, 539
NYS2d 757 (2d Dept 1989) §7.37

Davis Constr Corp v County of
Suffolk, 112 Misc 2d 652, 447
NYS2d 355 (Suffolk 1982), *affd*,
95 AD2d 819, 464 NYS2d 519
(2d Dept 1983) §15.08

Davis Lumber Co v Blanchard, 175
AD 256, 161 NYS 474 (1916)
§9.27

Davison v Flanagan, 273 AD 870,
76 NYS2d 849 (2d Dept 1948)
§15.03

Davis Wallbridge, Inc v Aetna Cas
& Sur Co, 103 AD2d 1010, 478
NYS2d 389 (1984) §§8.33, 8.40

Dawco Constr, Inc v United States,
18 Cl Ct 682 (1989), *modified on
other grounds*, 930 F2d 872 (Fed
Cir 1991) §§5.01, 5.03

640 CASES

Dawson Constr Co, GSBCA 3685, 72-2 BCA ¶9758 (1972) §6.18

DeBonis v Hudson Valley Community College, 55 AD2d 778, 389 NYS2d 647 (1976) §2.03

Debron Corp v National Homes Constr Corp, 493 F2d 352 (8th Cir 1974) §2.21

DeFoe Constr Corp v Beame, 75 Misc 2d 309, 347 NYS2d 626 (NY 1973) §6.27

De Foe Corp v City of NY, 95 AD2d 793, 463 NYS2d 508 (2d Dept 1983), *appeal dismissed*, 66 NY2d 759, 497 NYS2d 1028 (1985) §§6.04, 6.08

Degnon Contracting Co v City of NY, 235 NY 481, 139 NE 580 (1923), *affg in part & revg in part*, 202 AD 390, 196 NYS 63 (1st Dept 1922) §§3.23, 6.23

Del Balso Constr Corp v City of NY, 278 NY 154, 15 NE2d 559 (1938) §6.04

De Lillo Constr Co v Lizza & Sons, 7 NY2d 102, 164 NE2d 95, 195 NYS2d 825 (1959) §16.12

Della Corte v Incorporated Village of Williston Park, 60 AD2d 639, 400 NYS2d 357 (2d Dept 1977) §11.06

Delma Engg Corp v 6465 Realty Co, 39 AD2d 846, 332 NYS2d 841, *affd*, 31 NY2d 816, 291 NE2d 587, 339 NYS2d 464 (1972) §§5.03, 5.08, 5.13, 5.15

Delta Elec, Inc v Ingram & Greene, Inc, 123 AD2d 369, 506 NYS2d 594 (1986) §3.06

Dempsey v City Univ, 106 AD2d 486, 483 NYS2d 24 (2d Dept 1984) §2.30

DePalo v McNamara, 139 AD2d 646, 527 NYS2d 283 (1988) §9.35

Department of Health v East Minster Realty Corp, 53 Misc 2d 957, 280 NYS2d 63 (NY 1967) §9.37

Depot Constr Corp v State, 23 AD2d 707, 708, 257 NYS2d 230 (3d Dept 1965), *affd*, 19 NY2d 109, 224 NE2d 866, 278 NYS2d 363 (1967) §§2.36, 5.03, 5.07, 5.08, 5.10, 6.03, 6.27

Derion v Buffalo Crushed Stone, Inc, 135 AD2d 1105, 523 NYS2d 322 (4th Dept 1987) §13.03

DeRiso Bros v State, 161 Misc 934, 293 NYS 436 (Ct Cl 1937) §§7.23, 7.37, 7.38, 7.42

Dermott v Jones, 2 Wall (69 US) 1 (1864) §7.07

Derouin's Plumbing & Heating, Inc v City of Watertown, 71 AD2d 822, 419 NYS2d 390 (1979) §§2.19, 8.07

Desco Vitro Glaze, Inc v Mechanical Constr Corp, 159 AD2d 760, 552 NYS2d 185 (3d Dept 1990) §4.04

Deso v London & Lancashire Indem Co, 3 NY2d 127, 143 NE2d 889, 164 NYS2d 689 (1957) §10.15

Deverho Constr Co v State, 94 Misc 2d 1053, 407 NYS2d 399 (Ct Cl 1978) §§2.30, 2.47

DiCamillo v Navitsky, 90 Misc 2d 923, 396 NYS2d 585 (Putnam 1977) §9.36

Di-Com Corp v Active Fire Sprinkler Corp, 36 AD2d 20, 318 NYS2d 249 (1971) §§9.03, 9.36

Dierks Heating Co v Egan, 115 AD2d 836, 496 NYS2d 97 (3d Dept 1985), *appeal denied*, 67 NY2d 606, 501 NYS2d 1025 (1986) §§2.19, 8.07, 15.04

Diker v Cathray Constr Corp, 158 AD2d 657, 552 NYS2d 37 (2d Dept 1990) §§15.12, 16.12

DiNatale Management Co v Finney, 46 AD2d 827, 361 NYS2d 95 (1974) §2.05
Diocese of Rochester v Planning Bd, 1 NYS2d 508, 136 NE2d 827, 154 NYS2d 849 (1956) §15.03
Diocese of Rochester, NY v R-Monde Contractors, Inc, 148 Misc 2d 926, 562 NYS2d 593 (Monroe 1989) §§11.04, 11.08
DiPaolo v HBM Enters, 95 AD2d 794, 463 NYS2d 511 (1983) §9.26
DiPerna v Roman Catholic Diocese, 30 AD2d 249, 292 NYS2d 177 (3d Dept 1968) §§11.13, 12.02, 12.04, 12.05
Disalvatore v United States, 456 F Supp 1079 (ED Pa 1978) §13.16
DJL Gen Contractor, Inc v Harrison, NYLJ, Apr 9, 1991, at 29, col 6 (Nassau 1991) §11.03
DMC Constr Corp v A. Leo Nach Steel Corp, 50 AD2d 560, 375 NYS2d 18 (1975) §9.41
DMC Constr Corp v Nash Steel Corp, 41 NY2d 855, 362 NE2d 260, 393 NYS2d 709 (1977) §16.12
Dobbs Ferry Hosp Assoc v Whalen, 62 AD2d 999, 403 NYS2d 304 (2d Dept 1978) §§15.01, 15.03
Dolomite Prods Co v State, 258 AD 294, 17 NYS2d 48 (4th Dept 1939) §§5.14, 5.16
D'Onofrio Bros Constr Corp v Board of Educ, 72 AD2d 760, 421 NYS2d 377 (2d Dept 1979) §6.12
Dorn v Arthur A. Johnson Corp, 16 AD2d 1009, 229 NYS2d 266 (1962) §§1.14, 3.01, 9.03, 9.08
Dorrity v Rapp, 72 NY 307 (1878) §1.26
Doundoulakis v Town of Hempstead, 42 NY2d 440, 368 NE2d 24, 398 NYS2d 401 (1977) §§1.25, 12.02, 12.06
Drachman Structurals, Inc v Anthony Rivara Contracting Co, 78 Misc 2d 486, 356 NYS2d 974 (Nassau 1974) §9.60
Drake Constr Corp v Kenn Equip Co, 274 AD 809, 79 NYS2d 747 (1948) §9.37
Drennan v Star Paving Co, 51 Cal 2d 409, 333 P2d 757 (1958) §§2.21, 3.02
Drexler v Town of New Castle, 62 NY2d 413, 465 NE2d 836, 477 NYS2d 116 (1984) §14.34
Drzewinski v Atlantic Scaffolding & Ladder Co, 70 NY2d 774, 515 NE2d 902, 521 NYS2d 216 (1987) §11.22
Dube v Kaufman, 145 AD2d 595, 536 NYS2d 471 (2d Dept 1988) §13.03
Dunbar & Sullivan Dredging Co v State, 34 NYS2d 850 (Ct Cl 1942), *after remand from* 259 AD 440, 20 NYS2d 127 (4th Dept 1940), *revg* 34 NYS2d 848 (Ct Cl 1939) §§6.05, 6.25
Dunne v Robinson, 53 Misc 545, 103 NYS 878 (App Term 1907) §11.05
Dupack v Nationwide Leisure Corp, 73 AD2d 903, 424 NYS2d 436 (1980) §8.02
Durant v Grange Silo Co, 12 AD2d 694, 207 NYS2d 691 (3d Dept 1960) §12.08
Durham v Reidsville Engg Co, 255 NC 98, 120 SE2d 564 (1961) §§8.50, 11.14
Dutchess Community College v Rand Constr Co, 57 AD2d 555, 393 NYS2d 77 (2d Dept 1977) §16.04

E

E-J Elec Installation Co v Miller & Raved, Inc, 51 AD2d 264, 380 NYS2d 702 (1st Dept), *appeal dismissed*, 39 NY2d 898, 352 NE2d 584, 386 NYS2d 397 (1976) §9.49

EAD Metallurgical, Inc v Aetna Cas & Sur Co, 701 F Supp 399 (WDNY 1988), *affd*, 905 F2d 8 (2d Cir 1990) §14.22

Earthbank Co v City of NY, 145 Misc 2d 937, 549 NYS2d 314 (NY 1989) §§7.37, 7.41, 7.42

Easley v New York State Thruway Auth, 1 NY2d 374, 135 NE2d 572, 153 NYS2d 28 (1956) §16.11

East Coast Wholesalers, Inc v John J. Moran Co, 42 AD2d 605, 345 NYS2d 115 (1973) §9.74

Eastern Tunneling Corp v Southgate Sanitation Dist, 487 F Supp 109 (D Colo 1980) §§5.10, 5.14

East Hill, Inc v New York State Teachers' Retirements Sys, 80 AD2d 670, 436 NYS2d 392 (3d Dept), *appeal denied*, 53 NY2d 604, 422 NE2d 583, 439 NYS2d 1028 (1981) §16.11

EC Ernst, Inc v Manhattan Constr Co, 551 F2d 1026 (5th Cir 1977), *cert denied*, 434 US 1067 (1978) §11.11

Edenwald Contracting Co v City of New York, 86 Misc 2d 711, 384 NYS2d 338 (NY 1974), *affd*, 47 AD2d 610, 366 NYS2d 363 (1975) §2.08

Edgerton Estates, *In re* 78 Misc 2d 961, 359 NYS2d 88 (Onondaga 1974) §9.07

Edward B. Fitzpatrick Constr Corp v Country of Suffolk, 138 AD2d 446, 525 NYS2d 863 (2d Dept 1988) §15.35

Edward Hines Lumber Co v Vulcan Materials Co, 861 F2d 155 (7th Cir 1988) §14.37

Edward J. Dobson, Jr, Inc v Rutgers State Univ, 157 NJ Super 357, 384 A2d 1121 (1978), *affd*, 180 NJ Super 350, 434 A2d 1125 (1981), *affd*, 90 NJ 253, 447 A2d 906 (1982) §11.19

Edward Joy Co v Noise Control Prods, 111 Misc 2d 64, 443 NYS2d 361 (Onondaga 1981) §2.21

EG DeLia & Sons Constr Corp v State, 1 AD2d 732, 146 NYS2d 757 (3d Dept 1955) §6.27

EH Smith Contracting Co v City of NY, 240 NY 491, 148 NE 655 (1925) §§6.01, 6.23, 6.25, 6.27, 6.28

Eichleay Corp, ASBCA No 5183, 61-1 BCA ¶2894 (1960), *affg* ASBCA No 5183, 60-2 BCA ¶2688 (1960) §7.60

Eisenson Elec Serv Co v Wien, 30 Misc 2d 926, 219 NYS2d 736 (NY 1961) §9.05

Eisert v Ermco Erectors, Inc, 60 AD2d 903, 401 NYS2d 553 (1978) §§3.28, 3.32

EJ Dayton, Inc v Brock, 120 AD2d 560, 502 NYS2d 53 (1986) §9.51

EJ Eddy, Inc v Fidelity & Deposit Co, 265 NY 276, 192 NE 410 (1934) §8.10

Elden v Simmons, 631 P2d 739 (Okla 1981) §12.14

Electronic & Missile Facility, Inc, ASBCA 9031, 1964 BCA ¶4338 (1964) §7.46

Eli-Dorer Contracting Co v PT&L Constr Co, 85 AD2d 866, 446 NYS2d 457 (3d Dept 1981) §3.21

CASES 643

Eljam Mason Supply Co v Glazer, 74 AD2d 912, 426 NYS2d 69 (1980) §9.76

Eljam Mason Supply, Inc v IF Assocs Corp, 84 AD2d 720, 444 NYS2d 96 (1981) §9.69

Ell Dee Clothing Co v Marsh, 247 NY 392, 160 NE 651 (1928) §10.15

Elmira, City of v Larry Walter, Inc, 150 AD2d 129, 546 NYS2d 183 (3d Dept 1989), *affd*, 76 NY2d 912, 564 NE2d 655, 563 NYS2d 45 (1990) §§7.72, 15.22

Eminon Acoustical Contractor's Corp v Richkill Assocs, 89 Misc 2d 992, 392 NYS2d 1007 (Queens 1977) §9.72

Empire City Subway Co v Greater NY Mut Ins Co, 35 NY2d 8, 315 NE2d 755, 358 NYS2d 691 (1974) §10.15

Empire Pile Driving Co v Hylan Sanitary Serv, 32 AD2d 563, 300 NYS2d 434 (1969) §9.33

Employers-Commercial Union Ins Cos of Am v Buonomo, 41 AD2d 285, 342 NYS2d 447 (4th Dept 1973) §10.29

Empress Apts, Inc, *In re*, 26 Misc 2d 852, 203 NYS2d 972 (Kings 1960) §9.37

EM Substructures, Inc v City of NY, 73 AD2d 608, 422 NYS2d 444 (2d Dept 1979), *appeal dismissed*, 49 NY2d 878, 405 NE2d 233, 427 NYS2d 990 (1980) §6.32

Endicott, Village of v Parlor City Contracting Co, 51 AD2d 370, 381 NYS2d 548 (3d Dept 1976) §§12.02, 12.04, 12.07

Endres Plumbing Corp v State, 198 Misc 546, 95 NYS2d 574 (Ct Cl 1950), *affd mem*, 285 AD 1107, 139 NYS2d 319 (3d Dept 1955) §7.39

Engineering Corp v Scott-Paine, 29 Misc 2d 508, 217 NYS2d 919 (Columbia 1961) §9.03

Ennis v Hayes, 152 AD2d 914, 544 NYS2d 99 (4th Dept 1989) §13.09

Eno v Rapp, 169 Misc 473, 7 NYS2d 513 (NY 1938) §9.05

Entenman v Anderson, 106 AD 149, 94 NYS 45 (1905) §9.45

Erecto Corp v State, 29 AD2d 728, 286 NYS2d 562 (3d Dept 1968) §§7.05, 7.08, 7.30, 7.71

Esopus, Town of v Brinnier & Larios, PC, 135 AD2d 935, 522 NYS2d 337 (1987) §§8.27, 8.28

Ets-Hokin Corp v United States, 420 F2d 716 (Ct Cl 1970) §6.15

Euclid Concrete Corp, *In re*, 279 AD 594, 107 NYS2d 237 (1951) §9.37

Evans v Nab Constr Corp, 80 AD2d 841, 436 NYS2d 774 (2d Dept), *appeal dismissed*, 54 NY2d 605, 443 NYS2d 1027 (1981) §13.05

F

Faber v City of NY, 222 NY 255, 118 NE 609 (1918) §§5.03, 5.08, 5.10, 5.11

Fairbairn Lumber Corp v Telian, 92 AD2d 683, 460 NYS2d 194 (3d Dept 1983) §§3.11, 12.03

Farash Constr Corp v Standco Dev, Inc, 139 AD2d 899, 527 NYS2d 940 (4th Dept 1988), *appeal dismissed*, 73 NY2d 918, 539 NYS2d 301 (1989) §11.23

Farrell Heating, Plumbing & Air Conditioning Contractors v Facilities Dev & Improvement Corp, 68 AD2d 958, 414 NYS2d 767 (3d Dept 1979) §§4.14, 4.21, 7.05, 7.23, 7.52, 15.10

Farub Found Corp v City of NY, 138 Misc 636, 49 NYS2d 922 (NY 1944) §6.27

FD Rich Co v United States *ex rel* Indus Lumber Co, 417 US 116, 94 S Ct 2157, 40 L Ed 2d 703 (1974) §8.46

Federal Ins Co v Walker, 53 NY2d 24, 422 NE2d 548, 439 NYS2d 888 (1981) §§8.11, 8.24

Fehlhaber Corp v O'Hara, 53 AD2d 746, 384 NYS2d 270 (3d Dept 1976) §§15.03, 15.04

Fehlhaber Corp v State, 65 AD2d 119, 410 NYS2d 920 (3d Dept 1978) §§7.05, 7.24, 7.28, 7.52, 7.54, 7.55, 7.59, 7.64

Fehlhaber Corp v State, 69 AD2d 362, 419 NYS2d 773 (3d Dept 1979) §7.49

Fehlhaber Corp v Unicon Management Corp, 32 AD2d 367, 302 NYS2d 98 (1st Dept 1969), *affd*, 27 NY2d 828, 265 NE2d 257, 316 NYS2d 435 (1970) §3.06

Fehlhaber Pile Co v State, 265 AD 61, 37 NYS2d 928 (3d Dept 1942) §5.10

Feinberg v J. Bongiovi Contracting, Inc, 110 Misc 2d 379, 442 NYS2d 399 (Suffolk 1981) §§3.31, 3.35

Felix Contracting Corp v Oakridge Land & Prop Corp, 106 AD2d 488, 483 NYS2d 28 (2d Dept 1984), *appeal denied*, 66 NY2d 606, 519 NYS2d 1025 (1985) §4.14

Fentron Architectural Metals Corp v Solow, 101 Misc 2d 393, 420 NYS2d 950 (NY 1979) §§9.71, 9.78, 9.80

Fentron Architectural Metals Corp v Solow, 48 AD2d 820, 370 NYS2d 58 (1975) §§9.74, 9.82, 15.09

Ferguson Contracting Co v State, 202 AD2d 27, 195 NYS 901 (3d Dept 1922), *affd*, 237 NY 186, 142 NE 580 (1923) §6.13

Ferran Concrete Co v Commerce Elec Inc, 118 AD2d 619, 499 NYS2d 769 (2d Dept 1986) §16.12

Ferran Concrete Corp v Avon Elec Supplies Corp, 128 AD2d 527, 512 NYS2d 459 (1987) §9.30

Ferrante Equip Co v Charles Simkin & Sons, 30 AD2d 525, 290 NYS2d 246 (1968) §§8.25, 8.40

Ferrari v Barleo Homes, Inc, 112 AD2d 137, 490 NYS2d 827 (2d Dept 1985) §15.29

Fetterolf v S&L Constr Co, 175 AD 177, 161 NYS 549 (2d Dept 1916) §§6.01, 6.07, 6.08

Fett Roofing & Sheet Metal Co v Seaboard Sur Co, 294 F Supp 112 (ED Va 1968) §§8.50, 11.14

Fichtner v State Farm Fire & Cas Co, 148 Misc 2d 194, 560 NYS2d 94 (Cattaraugus 1990) §10.17

Fidelity & Deposit Co v Parsons & Whittemore Contractors Corps, 48 NY2d 127, 397 NE2d 380, 421 NYS2d 869 (1979) §16.16

Fifty States Management Corp v Niagara Permanent Sav & Loan Assn, 58 AD2d 177, 396 NYS2d 925 (4th Dept 1977) §7.02

Fink v Friedman, 78 Misc 2d 429, 358 NYS2d 250 (Nassau 1974) §§4.20, 15.14, 15.40

Fink v Lefkowitz, 47 NY2d 567, 393 NE2d 463, 419 NYS2d 467 (1979) §16.03

Firemen's Ins Co v State, 65 AD2d 241, 412 NYS2d 206 (1979) §8.14

First Bank, NA v Spaulding Bakeries, Inc, 117 Misc 2d 892,

459 NYS2d 696 (Broome 1983) §9.10
First Fed Sav & Loan Assoc v Burdett Ave Properties, Inc, 41 AD2d 356, 343 NYS2d 271 (1973) §9.36
First Natl Bank v Cann, 503 F Supp 419 (ND Ohio 1980), *affd*, 669 F2d 415 (6th Cir 1982) §11.16
Fischbach & Moore, Inc v New York City Transit Auth, 79 AD2d 14, 435 NYS2d 984 (1981) §§2.13, 2.33
530 E 89 Corp v Unger, 43 NY2d 776, 373 NE2d 276, 402 NYS2d 382 (1977), *affg* 54 AD2d 848, 388 NYS2d 284 (1st Dept 1976) §§11.04, 12.02
FJC Cavo Constr, Inc v Robinson, 81 AD2d 1005, 440 NYS2d 106 (1981) §9.35
Flans v Martini, 136 AD2d 498, 523 NYS2d 819 (1st Dept 1988) §10.29
Fleck v Perla, 40 AD2d 1069, 339 NYS2d 246 (1972) §9.79
Fleck v Putterman, 60 AD2d 904, 401 NYS2d 556 (1978) §9.82
Fleisher Engg & Constr Co v United States *ex rel* Hallenbeck, 311 US 15, 61 S Ct 81, 85 L Ed 12 (1940) §§8.25, 8.43, 8.45
Flemington Natl Bank & Trust Co v Domler Leasing Corp, 65 AD2d 29, 410 NYS2d 75 (1st Dept 1978), *affd*, 48 NY2d 678, 397 NE2d 393, 421 NYS2d 881 (1979) §2.49
Florida Power & Light Co v Mid-Valley, Inc, 763 F2d 1316 (11th Cir 1985) §15.22
FN Lewis Co v State, 132 Misc 688, 230 NYS 517 (Ct Cl 1928) §7.37
Fontaine Bleau Swimming Pool Corp v Aquarama Swimming Pool Corp, 27 Misc 2d 315, 210 NYS2d 634 (Nassau 1961) §9.74
Forest Elec Corp v Century Natl Bank & Trust Co, 70 Misc 2d 190, 333 NYS2d 644 (NY 1970) §9.81
Forest Elec Corp v State, 30 AD2d 905, 292 NYS2d 589 (3d Dept 1968) §§7.05, 7.09, 7.10, 7.22, 7.23
Forman v Pala Constr Co, 124 AD2d 453, 507 NYS2d 553 (1986) §§9.05, 9.26
Fosco Fabricators, Inc v State, 94 AD2d 667, 462 NYS2d 662 (1983) §16.02
Fosmire v National Sur Co, 229 NY 44, 127 NE 472 (1920) §8.10
Foulke v New York Consol RR, 228 NY 269, 127 NE 237 (1920) §7.39
Foundation Co v State, 233 NY 177, 135 NE 236 (1922) §§2.20, 5.08, 5.10, 5.11, 6.27
Fourth Ocean Putnam Corp v Interstate Wrecking Co, 66 NY2d 38, 485 NE2d 208, 495 NYS2d 1 (1985) §15.35
Fox v Jenny Engg Corp, 122 AD2d 532, 505 NYS2d 270 (4th Dept 1986), *affd mem*, 70 NY2d 761, 514 NE2d 1374, 520 NYS2d 750 (1987) §§13.08, 13.11, 13.15
Francavilla v Nagar Constr Co, 151 AD2d 282, 542 NYS2d 557 (1st Dept 1989) §13.18
Franchise Tax Bd v United States Postal Serv, 467 US 512, 104 S Ct 2549, 81 L Ed 2d 446 (1984) §8.43
Frank A. Scibetta Plumbing & Heating Corp v M&W Ltd Partnership, 90 AD2d 956, 456 NYS2d 544 (4th Dept 1982), *affd*, 58 NY2d 1092, 449 NE2d 742, 462 NYS2d 848 (1983) §6.21

Frank Buttermark Plumbing & Heating Corp v Sagarese, 119 AD2d 540, 500 NYS2d 551 (1986) §9.67

Franklin, Weinrib, Rudell & Vassallo, PC v Gruber, NYLJ Jan 10, 1992, at p 21, col 2 (App Term 1st Dept 1992) §15.38

Frank Nordone Contracting Co v City of NY, 269 AD 1035, 59 NYS2d 256 (1945), *affd*, 295 NY 985, 68 NE2d 61 (1946) §§5.03, 5.11

Frank Nowak Constr Co v County of Suffolk, 233 NYS2d 627 (Suffolk 1962) §§2.05, 8.05

Freedman v Chemical Constr Corp, 43 NY2d 260, 372 NE2d 12, 401 NYS2d 176 (1977) §2.27

Freeo v Victor A. Perosi, Inc, 54 AD2d 684, 387 NYS2d 268 (2d Dept 1976) §§3.10, 13.03, 13.04

Fremar Bldg Corp v Sand, 104 AD2d 1025, 480 NYS2d 945 (1984) §9.26

Frontier Excavating, Inc v Sovereign Constr Co, 30 AD2d 487, 294 NYS2d 994 (1968), *motion denied*, 24 NY2d 991, 250 NE2d 228, 302 NYS2d 820 (1969) §§9.72, 9.73, 9.74, 9.82

Frye v State, 192 Misc 260, 78 NYS2d 342 (Ct Cl 1948) §§2.46, 2.47, 2.48, 6.23

Fullilove v Klutznick, 448 US 448, 100 S Ct 2758, 65 L Ed 2d 902 (1980) §2.35

FW Carlin Constr Co v New York & Brooklyn Brewing Co, 149 AD 919, 134 NYS 493 (2d Dept 1912) §6.12

G

Gabriel v Attigliato, 60 Misc 2d 536, 303 NYS2d 399 (Rockland 1968) §10.15

Gallo v Supermarkets Gen Corp, 112 AD2d 345, 491 NYS2d 796 (2d Dept 1985) §13.03

Galuth Realty Corp v Greenfield, 103 AD2d 819, 478 NYS2d 51 (2d Dept 1984) §2.28

G&B Lab Installation, Inc v Beekman Downtown Hosp, 66 Misc 2d 441, 321 NYS2d 175 (NY 1971) §§9.70, 9.71, 9.74

G&R Elec Contractors, Inc v Egan, 85 AD2d 191, 448 NYS2d 850, *affd*, 57 NY2d 721, 440 NE2d 795, 454 NYS2d 710 (1982) §§2.12, 2.19, 8.06, 8.07

G&R Elec Contractors, Inc v State, 130 Misc 2d 661, 496 NYS2d 898, (Ct Cl 1985) §4.04

Gannon v New York Mut Underwriters, 78 AD2d 399, 435 NYS2d 163 (3d Dept), *affd mem*, 55 NY2d 641, 430 NE2d 1318, 446 NYS2d 265 (1981) §10.17

Garfinkel v Lehman Floor Covering Co, 60 Misc 2d 72, 302 NYS2d 167 (Nassau 1969) §3.31

Garrett v Holiday Inns, Inc, 58 NY2d 253, 447 NE2d 717, 460 NYS2d 774 (1983) §13.15

Garrity v Lyle Stuart, Inc, 40 NY2d 354, 353 NE2d 793, 386 NYS2d 831, 83 ALR3d 1024 (1976) §§15.12, 16.12

Gauntt Constr Co/Lott Elect Co v Delaware River & Bay Auth, 241 NJ Super 422, 575 A2d 70 (Burlington 1989), *revd*, 241 NJ Super 310, 575 A2d 13 (1990) §17.16

Gazza v New York Dept of Envtl Conservation, 139 AD2d 647,

527 NYS2d 285 (2d Dept 1988) §14.34

Gearty v Mayor of NY, 171 NY 61, 63 NE 804 (1902) §6.34

Geelan Mech Corp v Dember Constr Corp, 97 AD2d 810, 468 NYS2d 680 (1983) §3.28

Gem Drywall Corp v C. Scialdo & Sons, 42 AD2d 1045, 348 NYS2d 643 (4th Dept 1973), *affd mem*, 35 NY2d 781, 320 NE2d 867, 362 NYS2d 152 (1974) §§4.13, 12.03

Gem Jewelers, Inc v Dykman, 160 AD2d 1069, 553 NYS2d 890 (3d Dept 1990) §3.31

General Acc Ins Co of Am v Manchester, 116 AD2d 790, 497 NYS2d 180 (3d Dept 1986) §10.09

General Bldg Contractors, Inc v City of Syracuse, 40 AD2d 584, 334 NYS2d 730 (1972), *modified on other grounds*, 32 NY2d 780, 298 NE2d 122, 344 NYS2d 961 (1973) §§2.08, 2.09

General Bldg Contractors, Inc v County of Oneida, 54 Misc 2d 260, 282 NYS2d 385 (Oneida 1967) §15.03

General Crushed Stone Co v State, 23 AD2d 250, 260 NYS2d 32 (1965) §§9.78, 9.80

General Elec Co v New York State Dept of Labor, 936 F2d 1448 (2d Cir 1991) §2.35

General Motors Acceptance Corp v Kalkstein, 101 AD2d 102, 474 NYS2d 493 (1984) §8.30

General Supply & Constr Co v Goelet, 241 NY 28, 148 NE 778 (1925) §§4.16, 15.15, 15.22

Geneseo Cent School v Perfetto & Whalen Constr Corp, 53 NY2d 306, 423 NE2d 1058, 441 NYS2d 229 (1981) §16.02

George Hyman Constr Co v Precision Walls, Inc, 132 AD2d 523, 517 NYS2d 263 (2d Dept 1987) §§2.47, 3.06

Gernatt Asphalt Prod v Bensal Constr, Inc, 90 AD2d 993, 456 NYS2d 590 (1982), *affd as modified*, 60 NY2d 871, 458 NE2d 821, 470 NYS2d 362 (1983) §9.08

Gerosa Crane Serv v International Prods, 70 Misc 2d 176, 332 NYS2d 536 (Civ Ct NY 1972) §§8.37, 8.47

Gerosa Haulage & Warehouse Corp v Prospect Iron Works, Inc, 197 NYS2d 936 (Nassau 1959) §9.83

Gerrity Co v Bonacquisti Constr Corp, 136 AD2d 59, 525 NYS2d 926 (1988) §9.79

Gerzof v Sweeney, 22 NY2d 297, 239 NE2d 521, 292 NYS2d 640 (1968) §§2.07, 2.11

Gerzof v Sweeney, 16 NY2d 206, 211 NE2d 826, 264 NYS2d 376 (1965) §§2.07, 2.08, 2.11, 2.13, 2.15

Gifford Constr Co v Lever Management Corp, 78 AD2d 869, 432 NYS2d 897 (2d Dept 1980) §12.03

Gjertsen v Mawson & Mawson, Inc, 135 AD2d 779, 522 NYS2d 891 (1987) §§3.09, 3.10

Glantz Contracting Corp v 1955 Assocs, 20 AD2d 535, 245 NYS2d 129 (1963), *affd*, 14 NY2d 931, 200 NE2d 867, 252 NYS2d 328 (1964) §9.70

Glanzer v Shepard, 233 NY 236, 135 NE 275 (1922) §8.50

Glazer v Alison Homes Corp, 62 Misc 2d 1017, 309 NYS2d 381 (Kings 1970) §§9.70, 9.71, 9.81, 9.83

Glielmi v Toys "R" Us, Inc, 94 AD2d 663, 462 NYS2d 225 (1983), *affd*, 62 NY2d 664, 464 NE2d 981, 476 NYS2d 283 (1984) §3.13

Globe Indem Co v Southern Pac Co, 30 F2d 580 (2d Cir 1929) §8.26

Golaszewski v Cadman Plaza N, Inc, 158 AD2d 670, 552 NYS2d 43 (2d Dept 1990) §15.14

Goldfinger v Lisker, 68 NY2d 225, 500 NE2d 857, 508 NYS2d 159 (1986) §16.12

Goldhirsh v Flacke, 114 AD2d 998, 495 NYS2d 436 (2d Dept 1985) §14.34

Goldner v Doknovitch, 88 Misc 2d 88, 388 NYS2d 504 (App Term 1976) §15.19

Gomes v Ern-Roc Homes, Inc, 72 Misc 2d 410, 339 NYS2d 401 (Civ Ct Queens 1973) §12.15

Goodell v Harrington, 76 NY 547 (1879) §9.67

Goodman v Del-Sa-Co Foods, Inc, 15 NY2d 191, 257 NYS2d 142 (1965) §9.49

Goodstein Constr Corp v City of NY, 111 AD2d 49, 489 NYS2d 175 (1st Dept 1985), *affd*, 67 NY2d 990, 494 NE2d 99, 502 NYS2d 994 (1986) §§2.47, 15.01

Goodstein Constr Corp v Gliedman, 117 AD2d 170, 502 NYS2d 136 (1st Dept 1986), *affd mem*, 69 NY2d 930, 509 NE2d 350, 516 NYS2d 655 (1987) §15.01

Gordon v Adenbaum, 171 AD2d 841, 567 NYS2d 777 (2d Dept 1991) §11.03

Gordon v Holt, 65 AD2d 344, 412 NYS2d 534 (4th Dept), *appeal denied*, 47 NY2d 710, 419 NYS2d 1026 (1979) §§11.08, 11.14

Gottfried Banking Co, *In re*, 45 Misc 2d 708, 257 NYS2d 833 (Albany 1964) §§15.03, 15.04

Gottlieb Contracting, Inc v Beame, 41 Misc 2d 1097, 247 NYS2d 237 (NY 1964) §15.03

Gottlieb Contracting, Inc v City of NY, 86 AD2d 588, 446 NYS2d 311 (1st Dept 1982), *affd*, 58 NY2d 1051, 449 NE2d 422, 462 NYS2d 642 (1983) §§7.23, 7.38

Gould, Inc v Pension Benefits Guar Corp, 589 F Supp 164 (SDNY 1984) §8.42

Government Employees Ins Co v Elman, 40 AD2d 994, 338 NYS2d 666 (2d Dept 1972) §10.15

Graham v Lansing Dev Corp, 56 Misc 2d 1064, 290 NYS2d 590 (Broome 1968) §15.38

Granite Computer Leasing Corp v Travelers Indem Co, 702 F Supp 415 (SDNY 1988), *vacated on other grounds*, 894 F2d 547 (2d Cir 1990) §4.17

Granite Worsted Mills v Aaronson Cowen, 25 NY2d 451, 255 NE2d 168, 306 NYS2d 934 (1969), *modified*, 26 NY2d 842, 309 NYS2d 589 (1970), *affd*, 473 NYS2d 779 (1984) §16.12

Grau v Eljay Real Estate Corp, 162 AD2d 320, 556 NYS2d 898 (1st Dept 1990) §15.12

Grayson-Robinson Stores, Inc v Iris Constr Corp, 8 NY2d 133, 168 NE2d 377, 202 NYS2d 303 (1960) §§15.39, 16.11

Greater Johnstown City School Dist v Cataldo & Waters, Architects, 159 AD2d 784, 551 NYS2d 1003 (3d Dept 1990) §11.24

Great Lakes Dredge & Dock Co v Wagner, 46 AD2d 721, 360

NYS2d 337 (4th Dept 1974) §15.01

Green v City of NY, 283 AD 485, 128 NYS2d 715 (1st Dept 1954) §§2.08, 2.11, 2.50, 6.03, 6.18, 6.22

Greenberg v City of Yonkers, 45 AD2d 314, 358 NYS2d 453 (2d Dept 1974), *affd on opinion*, 37 NY2d 907, 340 NE2d 744, 378 NYS2d 382 (1975) §11.22

Green Briar Drainage Dist v Clark, 292 F 828 (7th Cir 1923) §15.15

Greene v Greene, 56 NY2d 86, 436 NE2d 496, 451 NYS2d 46 (1982) §11.24

Green Plumbing & Heating Co v Turner Constr Co, 500 F Supp 910 (ED Mich 1980), *affd*, 742 F2d 965 (6th Cir 1984) §11.19

Greenspan v Amsterdam, 145 AD2d 535, 536 NYS2d 90 (2d Dept 1988) §§4.12, 4.14

Gregory v General Elec Co, 131 AD2d 967, 516 NYS2d 549 (3d Dept 1987) §13.05

Griffin Bldg & Constr Corp v RHD Constr Corp, 133 Misc 2d 335, 507 NYS2d 116 (Albany 1986) §§9.26, 9.29

Grimpel v Hochman, 74 Misc 2d 39, 343 NYS2d 507 (Civ Ct NY 1972) §§3.11, 9.49, 12.03

Grisson v Greener & Sumner Constr, Inc, 676 SW2d 709 (Tex Ct App 1984) §15.12

Gross v Sweet, 49 NY2d 102, 400 NE2d 306, 424 NYS2d 365 (1979) §5.09

Grossman Steel & Aluminum Corp v Samson Window Corp, 78 AD2d 871, 433 NYS2d 31 (1980), *affd*, 54 NY2d 653, 426 NE2d 176, 442 NYS2d 769 (1981) §3.18

Grow Constr Co v State, 56 AD2d 95, 391 NYS2d 726 (3d Dept 1977) §§5.03, 5.13, 5.20, 7.02, 7.05, 7.10, 7.26, 7.27, 7.29, 7.50

Gruenberg v United States, 29 AD2d 527, 285 NYS2d 962 (1967) §9.75

Guaranty Trust Co v United States, 304 US 126 (1938) §11.23

Guidetti v Pratt Plumbing & Heating, Inc, 55 AD2d 720, 389 NYS2d 170 (3d Dept 1976) §§3.11, 12.05

Gunnarson v State, 70 NY2d 923, 519 NE2d 307, 524 NYS2d 396 (1987) §15.15

H

Hadley v Baxendale, 156 Eng Rep 145, 9 Ex 341 (Ex 1854) §11.23

Haimes v New York Tel Co, 46 NY2d 132, 385 NE2d 601, 412 NYS2d 863 (1978) §§13.03, 13.04, 13.05, 13.08

Hall v Blumberg, 26 AD2d 64, 270 NYS2d 539 (1966) §§9.70, 9.83

Hall v Thomas, 111 NYS 979 (NY 1908) §9.26

Hall v Union Indem Co, 61 F2d 85 (8th Cir), *cert denied*, 287 US 663, 53 S Ct 222, 77 L Ed 572 (1932) §8.50

Hall & Co v Continental Cas Co, 34 AD2d 1028, 310 NYS2d 950 (1970), *affd*, 30 NY2d 517, 280 NE2d 890, 330 NYS2d 64 (1972) §§8.02, 8.07, 8.47

Halpern v Hodgkiss, 89 NYS2d 451 (NY 1949) §15.04

Hamill v Foster-Lipkins Corp, 41 AD2d 361, 342 NYS2d 539 (3d Dept 1973) §§11.13, 13.15

Hammond v Bechtel, Inc, 606 P2d 1269 (Alaska 1980) §13.16

H&J Floor Covering v Board of Educ, 66 AD2d 588, 413 NYS2d 414 (2d Dept 1979) §16.02

Hansen Excavating Co v Benjamin, 36 Misc 2d 686, 233 NYS2d 589 (Nassau 1962) §§3.07, 9.49

Hansen Excavating Co v Comet Constr Corp, 14 AD2d 911, 222 NYS2d 233 (1961) §9.74

Harlem Plumbing Supply Co v Handelsman, 40 AD2d 768, 337 NYS2d 329 (1972) §9.36

Harman v Fairview Assocs, 25 NY2d 101, 302 NYS2d 791 (1969) §§9.71, 9.81

Harper, Inc v City of Newburgh, 159 AD 695, 145 NYS 59 (1913) §2.19

Harry J. Kangieser, Inc v Palm Beach Realty Co, 223 NYS2d 38 (Suffolk 1961) §9.74

Hart v United Artists Corp, 252 AD 133, 298 NYS 1 (1st Dept 1937) §15.15

Hartford Fire Ins Co v Masternak, 55 AD2d 472, 390 NYS2d 949 (4th Dept 1977) §10.27

Haseley Trucking Co v Great Lakes Pipe Co, 101 AD2d 1019, 476 NYS2d 702 (4th Dept 1984) §11.05

Hawkins v Mapes-Reeve Constr Co, 178 NY 236, 70 NE 783 (1904) §9.44

Headen v Progressive Painting Corp, 160 AD2d 319, 553 NYS2d 401 (1st Dept 1990) §13.13

Heath v Soloff Constr, Inc, 107 AD2d 507, 487 NYS2d 617 (4th Dept 1985) §13.05

Heating Maintenance Corp v State, 206 Misc 605, 134 NYS2d 71 (Ct Cl 1954) §2.50

Hedden Constr Co v Rossiter Realty Co, 136 AD 601, 121 NYS 64 (1st Dept 1910), *affd mem*, 202 NY 522, 95 NE 1130 (1911) §§6.01, 6.08

Hempstead Resources Recovery Corp v Peter Scalamandre & Sons, 104 Misc 2d 278, 428 NYS2d 146 (Nassau 1980) §§9.07, 9.15

Henningsen v United States Fidelity & Guar, 208 US 404, 28 S Ct 389, 52 L Ed 547 (1908) §8.51

Henry & John Assoc v Demile Constr Corp, 137 Misc 2d 354, 520 NYS2d 341 (Queens 1987) §9.17

Herbert G. Martin, Inc v City of Yonkers, 54 AD2d 971, 388 NYS2d 673 (2d Dept 1976), *appeal dismissed*, 43 NY2d 946, 374 NE2d 1246, 403 NYS2d 895 (1978) §§7.05, 7.30

Herman v Lancaster Homes, Inc, 145 AD2d 926, 536 NYS2d 298 (4th Dept 1988) §§13.03, 13.04, 13.19

Herman & Grace v City of NY, 130 AD 531, 114 NYS 1107 (1st Dept 1909) §15.26

Hermes v Compton, 260 AD 507, 23 NYS2d 126 (2d Dept), *modified on other grounds*, 260 AD 1027 (1940) §15.09

Hertz Commercial Leasing Corp v Transportation Credit Clearing House, 59 Misc 2d 226, 298 NYS2d 392 (Civ Ct NY 1969), *revd on other grounds*, 64 Misc 2d 910, 316 NYS2d 585 (1970) §3.28

Herzog v Williams, 139 Misc 2d 18, 526 NYS2d 329 (Ossining Justice Ct 1988) §6.03

HH & FE Bean, Inc v Travelers Indem Co, 67 AD2d 1102, 415 NYS2d 144 (4th Dept 1979) §16.16

Hirsch Elec Co v Community Serv, Inc, 133 AD2d 140, 518 NYS2d 818 (2d Dept 1987), *affd as modified*, 145 AD2d 603, 536 NYS2d 141 (1988) §§7.49, 7.62, 15.19

HNC Realty Co v Bay View Towers Apts, Inc, 64 AD2d 417, 409 NYS2d 774 (1978) §8.32

Hodge & Hammond, Inc v Burns, 23 Misc 2d 318, 202 NYS2d 133 (Nassau 1960) §2.08

Hollerbach v United States, 233 US 165, 34 S Ct 553, 58 L Ed 898 (1915) §§5.09, 5.11, 5.14

Home Indem Co v Wachter, 115 AD2d 590, 496 NYS2d 252 (1985) §8.48

Home Owners Loan Corp v Vangerow, 277 AD 774, 96 NYS2d 861 (1950) §9.67

Honeywell, Inc v Trico Sheet Metal, Inc, 60 Misc 2d 1049, 304 NYS2d 330 (Albany 1969) §8.33

Horgan & Slattery v City of NY, 114 AD 555, 100 NYS 68 (1st Dept 1906) §§11.04, 11.07

Horn Waterproofing Corp v Bushwick Iron & Steel Co, 66 NY2d 321, 488 NE2d 56, 497 NYS2d 310 (1985) §6.33

Horn Waterproofing Corp v Horn Constr Co, 104 AD2d 851, 480 NYS2d 367 (1984) §3.33

Hotel Utica, Inc v Armstrong, 62 AD2d 1147, 404 NYS2d 455 (4th Dept 1978) §§11.04, 12.02

Houseknecht v Reeve, 108 NYS2d 917 (Oneida 1951) §§9.26, 9.33

Houston Fire & Cas Ins Co v EE Cloer Gen Contractor, Inc, 217 F2d 906 (5th Cir 1954) §8.43

Howdy Jones Constr Co v Parklaw Realty, Inc, 76 AD2d 1018, 429 NYS2d 768 (3d Dept 1980), *affd mem*, 53 NY2d 718, 421 NE2d 846, 439 NYS2d 354 (1981) §§6.10, 6.12

Huber Lathing Corp v Aetna Cas & Sur Co, 132 AD2d 597, 517 NYS2d 758 (1987) §8.33

Hubert v Aitken, 2 NYS 711 (CP 1888), *affd on reargument*, 5 NYS 839 (CP 1889), *affd mem*, 123 NY 655 (1890) §11.08

Hub Oil Co v Jodomar, Inc, 176 Misc 320, 27 NYS2d 370 (Monroe 1941) §§8.33, 8.37

Hudson City Bd of Educ v Sargent, Webster, Crenshaw & Folley, 71 NY2d 21, 517 NE2d 1360, 523 NYS2d 475 (1987) §§11.22, 15.20

Hudson Demolition Co v Ismor Realty Corp, 62 AD2d 980, 403 NYS2d 327 (1978) §9.26

Hull Dye & Print Works, Inc v Riegel Textile Corp, 37 AD2d 946, 325 NYS2d 782 (1st Dept 1971) §16.14

Hunt v Bankers & Shippers Ins Co, 73 AD2d 797, 423 NYS2d 718 (1979), *affd*, 50 NY2d 938, 409 NE2d 928, 431 NYS2d 454 (1980) §§8.15, 8.20, 8.23, 8.29

Hunt v Bankers & Shippers Ins Co, 60 AD2d 781, 400 NYS2d 645 (1977) §§8.11, 8.26

Hunt v Ellisor & Tanner, Inc, 739 SW2d 933 (Tex Ct App 1987) §11.04

Hurley v Tucker, 128 AD 580, 112 NYS 980 (1908), *affd*, 198 NY 534 (1910) §9.29

Hurley Sand & Gravel Co v Italian-American Civil Rights League, 76 Misc 2d 305, 350 NYS2d 837 (Ulster 1973) §9.44

I

I. Burack, Inc v Simpson Factors Corp, 21 AD2d 481, 250 NYS2d 989 (1964), *affd*, 16 NY2d 604, 261 NYS2d 58 (1965) §9.01

Iervolino v Best Built Homes Holding Corp, 56 Misc 2d 343, 288 NYS2d 724 (Kings 1968) §4.14

Illinois v O'Neil, 194 Ill App 3d 79, 550 NE2d 1090, *cert denied*, 553 NE2d 400 (1990) §14.37

Illinois Sur Co v John David Co, 244 US 376, 37 S Ct 614, 61 L Ed 1206 (1917) §8.46

Industrial Automated & Scientific Equip Corp v RME Enters, 58 AD2d 482, 396 NYS2d 427 (1977) §3.28

Industrial Temperature Sys v Tishman Interiors, NYLJ, Nov 8, 1991, at 22, col 2 (Sup Ct 1991) §11.14

Ingalls Iron Works Co v Fehlhaber Corp, 29 AD2d 29, 285 NYS2d 369 (1967), *affd mem*, 24 NY2d 862, 301 NYS2d 95 (1969) §9.30

Ingalls Iron Works Co v Golden, 32 Misc 2d 426, 224 NYS2d 158 (NY 1961) §8.33

Ingram & Greene, Inc v Wynne, 47 Misc 2d 200, 262 NYS2d 663 (Queens 1965) §9.13

Inman v Binghamton Hous Auth, 3 NY2d 137, 143 NE2d 895, 164 NYS2d 699 (1957) §§11.13, 12.02, 12.03, 12.11

Interboro Mut Indem Ins Co v Karpowic, 116 Misc 2d 947, 456 NYS2d 967 (Kings 1982) §10.30

International Paper Co v Continental Cas Co, 35 NY2d 322, 320 NE2d 619, 361 NYS2d 873 (1974) §10.18

International Paper Co v Rockefeller, 161 AD 180, 146 NYS 371 (1914) §3.31

Ippolito-Lutz, Inc v Cohoes Hous Auth, 22 AD2d 990, 234 NYS2d 783 (3d Dept 1964) §§3.22, 7.33, 7.35

Isadore Rosen & Sons v Conforti & Eisele, Inc, 40 AD2d 794, 338 NYS2d 39 (1972) §9.74

Italian Economic Corp v Community Engrs, Inc, 135 Misc 2d 209, 514 NYS2d 630 (NY 1987) §§11.05, 15.15, 15.29

Iversen Constr Corp v Palmyra-Macedon Cent School Dist, 143 Misc 2d 36, 539 NYS2d 858 (Wayne 1989) §15.41

J

Jack Coletta, Inc v New York Dept of Envtl Conservation, 128 AD2d 755, 513 NYS2d 465 (2d Dept), *appeal denied*, 70 NY2d 602, 512 NE2d 551, 518 NYS2d 1025 (1987) §14.34

Jackson v State, 210 AD 115, 205 NYS 658 (4th Dept 1924), *affd mem*, 241 NY 563, 150 NE 556 (1925) §§5.03, 5.08, 5.10, 5.12, 5.16, 5.19

Jacob & Youngs, Inc v Kent, 230 NY 239, 129 NE 889 (1921) §§12.04, 15.29

Jaffie Contracting Co v Board of Educ, 90 AD2d 163, 456 NYS2d 375 (1st Dept 1982) §§7.02, 7.21, 7.25

JA Jones Constr Co v United States, 390 F2d 886 (Ct Cl 1968) §§5.05, 5.12

James H. Merritt Plumbing, Inc v City of NY, 55 AD2d 552, 390 NYS2d 65 (1976) §§2.13, 2.20

James King & Sons v DeSantis
 Constr No 2 Corp, 97 Misc 2d
 1063, 413 NYS2d 78 (NY 1977)
 §2.21
Jandous Elec Equip Co v State, 158
 Misc 238, 285 NYS 385 (Ct Cl
 1936) §6.21
J&J Tile Co v Feinstein, 43 AD2d
 529, 348 NYS2d 783 (1973)
 §8.10
Janice v State, 201 Misc 915, 107
 NYS2d 674 (Ct Cl 1951) §13.03
Jannotta v Noslac Realty Corp, 231
 AD 864, 246 NYS 510 (1930)
 §9.26
Janowitz Bros Venture v 25-30
 120th St Queens Corp, 75 AD2d
 203, 429 NYS2d 215 (2d Dept
 1980) §7.02
Jarcho Bros, Inc v State, 179 Misc
 795, 39 NYS2d 867 (Ct Cl 1943)
 §§5.04, 5.12, 5.16
Jaroszewicz v Facilities Dev Corp,
 115 AD2d 159, 495 NYS2d 498
 (3d Dept 1985) §§13.11, 13.15
Jarvis & Spitz, Inc v Federation, 14
 AD2d 833, 220 NYS2d 680
 (1961), *appeal dismissed*, 11 NY2d
 765, 227 NYS2d 15 (1962) §3.10
JA Valenti Elec Co v Board of Educ,
 56 AD2d 884, 392 NYS2d 482
 (1977) §2.09
J. Brooks Secs, Inc v Vanderbilt
 Secs, Inc, 126 Misc 2d 875, 484
 NYS2d 472 (NY 1985) §16.11
JC Whritenour Co v Colonial
 Homes Co, 209 AD 676, 205
 NYS 299 (1924) §9.01
JD Hedin Constr Co v United
 States, 347 F2d 235 (Ct Cl 1965)
 §§7.20, 7.28, 7.60
Jered Contracting Corp v New York
 City Transit Auth, 22 NY2d 187,
 239 NE2d 197, 292 NYS2d 98
 (1968) §§2.03, 2.11

Jericho Jewish Center, *In re*, 28 Misc
 2d 458, 210 NYS2d 77 (1960)
 §9.36
Jersey City Redevelopment Auth v
 PPG Indus, 665 F Supp 1257
 (DNJ 1987) §14.39
Jewish Bd of Guardians v Grumman
 Allied Indus, 96 AD2d 465, 464
 NYS2d 778 (1983), *affd*, 62 NY2d
 684, 465 NE2d 42, 476 NYS2d
 535 (1984) §3.34
JGA Constr Corp v Charter Oak
 Fire Ins Co, 66 AD2d 315, 414
 NYS2d 385 (4th Dept 1979)
 §§10.19, 10.27
JI Hass Co v Frank A. Kristal
 Assocs, 127 AD2d 541, 512
 NYS2d 104 (1st Dept), *appeal
 denied*, 69 NY2d 611, 517 NYS2d
 1025 (1987) §12.08
JL Young Engg Co v United States,
 98 Ct Cl 310 (1943) §§7.53, 7.55
J. McKinney & Son v Lake Placid
 1980 Olympic Games, Inc, 92
 AD2d 991, 461 NYS2d 483 (3d
 Dept 1983), *affd as modified*, 61
 NY2d 836, 462 NE2d 137, 473
 NYS2d 960 (1984) §§11.14,
 11.21
JN Futia v Schenectady Mun House
 Auth, 33 AD2d 591, 304 NYS2d
 358 (1969) §3.07
JN Futia v State Office of Gen
 Servs, 39 AD2d 136, 332 NYS2d
 261 (1972) §2.04
Jobco, Inc v County of Nassau, 129
 AD2d 614, 514 NYS2d 108
 (1987) §§2.19, 8.06, 8.07
John Arborio, Inc v State, 41 Misc
 2d 145, 245 NYS2d 274 (Ct Cl
 1963) §§5.01, 5.02, 5.03, 5.04,
 5.05, 5.09, 5.11, 5.12, 5.13, 5.14
John Grace & Co v State Univ
 Constr Fund, 99 AD2d 860, 472
 NYS2d 757 (3d Dept 1984)
 §§11.04, 11.05

John T. Brady & Co v Board of Educ, 222 AD 504, 226 NYS 707 (1st Dept 1928) §§7.24, 7.34, 7.35, 7.39

John Johnston Concrete Gutter Co v Amercian Empire Ins Co, 81 AD2d 1004, 440 NYS2d 107 (1981) §§8.10, 8.25, 8.47

John Kennedy & Co v New York World's Fair 1939, Inc, 260 AD 386, 22 NYS2d 901 (1940), *affd*, 288 NY 494, 41 NE2d 789 (1942) §§9.07, 9.10, 9.15

Johnson v City of NY, 191 AD 205, 181 NYS 137, *affd*, 231 NY 564, 132 NE 890 (1920) §§7.37, 7.42

Johnson v State, 5 AD2d 919, 172 NYS2d 41 (3d Dept 1958) §§7.05, 7.23, 7.38

Johnson, Drake & Piper, Inc v State, 31 AD2d 980, 297 NYS2d 754 (3d Dept 1969) §§7.23, 7.28, 7.58

Johnson Serv Co v EH Monin, Inc, 253 NY 417, 171 NE 692, *remanded for remittitur*, 254 NY 551, 173 NE 862 (1930) §8.10

John W. Cowper Co v Buffalo Hotel Dev Venture, 115 AD2d 346, 496 NYS2d 127 (4th Dept 1985), *affd*, 72 NY2d 890, 528 NE2d 1214, 532 NYS2d 742 (1988) §§11.08, 12.16

John W. Cowper Co v Buffalo Hotel Dev Venture, 99 AD2d 19, 471 NYS2d 913 (1984) §9.51

John W. Cowper Co v CDC-Troy, Inc, 50 AD2d 1076, 376 NYS2d 754 (4th Dept 1975) §2.33

John West & Sons v West Street Improvement Co, 149 AD 504, 134 NYS 39 (1912) §2.20

John W. Johnson, Inc v Basic Constr Co, 292 F Supp 300 (DDC 1968), *affd*, 429 F2d 764 (DC Cir 1970) §6.14

Joseph Davis, Inc v Merritt-Chapman & Scott Corp, 27 AD2d 114, 276 NYS2d 479 (4th Dept 1967) §§6.03, 6.21, 6.23

Joseph F. Egan, Inc v City of NY, 17 NY2d 90, 215 NE2d 490, 268 NYS2d 301 (1966) §6.09

Joyce v Rumsey Realty Corp, 17 NY2d 118, 216 NE2d 317, 269 NYS2d 105 (1966) §13.06

JP Stevens & Co, v Rytex Corp, 34 NY2d 123, 312 NE2d 466, 356 NYS2d 278 (1974) §16.12

JR Stevenson Corp v County of Westchester, 113 AD2d 918, 493 NYS2d 819 (2d Dept 1985) §§7.33, 7.41

JV Vrooman Sons Co v Pierce, 179 AD 436, 165 NYS 929 (1917) §9.60

JW Bateson Co v United States *ex rel* Bd of Trustees, 434 US 586, 98 S Ct 873, 55 L Ed 2d 50 (1978) §8.44

K

Kaiser Indus Corp v United States, 340 F2d 322 (Ct Cl 1965) §§5.02, 5.04, 5.19

Kalisch-Jarcho, Inc v City of NY, 135 AD2d 262, 525 NYS2d 190 (1st Dept), *revd*, 72 NY2d 727, 533 NE2d 258, 536 NYS2d 419 (1988) §§6.04, 6.13

Kalisch-Jarcho, Inc v City of NY, 58 NY2d 377, 448 NE2d 413, 461 NYS2d 746 (1983) §§2.35, 5.09, 7.33, 7.35, 7.36, 7.39, 7.40

Kalwall Corp v K. Capolino Design & Renovation, 54 AD2d 941, 388 NYS2d 346 (1976) §3.18

K&M Turf Maintenance, *In re*, 166 AD2d 445, 560 NYS2d 673 (2d Dept 1990) §15.04

Kapilow Constr Corp v Prince, 52 AD2d 620, 382 NYS2d 349 (2d Dept 1976) §2.30

Kelly v Diesel Constr Div of Carl Morse, Inc, 35 NY2d 1, 315 NE2d 751, 358 NYS2d 685 (1974) §13.18

Kelly v St Michael's Roman Catholic Church, 148 AD 767, 133 NYS 328 (2d Dept 1912) §6.07

Kemp v Lakelands Precast, Inc, 55 NY2d 1032, 434 NE2d 1077, 449 NYS2d 710 (1982) §3.13

Kenford Co v County of Erie, 67 NY2d 257, 493 NE2d 234, 502 NYS2d 131, (1986) §§15.16, 15.19

Kennedy v McKay, 86 AD2d 597, 446 NYS2d 124 (2d Dept 1982) §§13.03, 13.05

Kennedy Elec Co v United States Postal Serv, 508 F2d 954 (10th Cir 1974) §8.43

Kenneth Reed Constr Corp v United States, 475 F2d 583 (Ct Cl 1973) §6.20

Kenny v George A. Fuller Co, 87 AD2d 183, 450 NYS2d 551 (2d Dept 1982) §§13.12, 13.16, 13.18

Kerr v Rochester Gas & Elec Corp, 113 AD2d 412, 496 NYS2d 880 (4th Dept 1985) §§13.08, 13.11

Ketcham v Newman, 141 NY 206 (1894) §1.26

Keyway Contractors, Inc v Leek Corp, 189 Ga App 467, 376 SE2d 212, *cert denied*, 189 Ga App 912 (1988) §4.17

Kick v Regan, 110 AD2d 934, 487 NYS2d 403 (3d Dept 1985) §2.33

Kim Kevin Corp v A&A Gibel Co, 20 AD2d 807, 248 NYS2d 741 (1964) §9.37

Kings Bay Buses, Inc v Aiello, 100 Misc 2d 1, 418 NYS2d 284 (Kings 1979) §2.22

Kingsley v City of Brooklyn, 78 NY 200 (1879) §§6.05, 6.27

Kingston Trust Co v Catskill Land Corp, 43 AD2d 995, 352 NYS2d 514 (1974) §9.70

Kingston Trust Co v State, 57 Misc 2d 55, 291 NYS2d 208 (Ulster 1968) §9.17

Kinney v GW Lisker Co, 76 NY2d 215, 556 NE2d 1090, 557 NYS2d 283 (1990) §3.13

Kinser Constr Co v State, 204 NY 381, 97 NE 871 (1912) §§6.02, 6.04, 6.05

Klein v Young, 168 NYS 526 (1st Dept 1918) §§7.05, 7.10

Kleinhans v State, 17 AD2d 905, 233 NYS2d 134 (4th Dept 1962) §7.09

Klien v General Foods Corp, 148 AD2d 968, 539 NYS2d 604 (4th Dept 1989) §13.05

Knapp v Cirillo, 133 NYS2d 356 (Westchester 1954) §1.26

Koch, *In re*, 98 NYS2d 109 (Erie 1950) §9.26

Kojic v City of NY, 76 AD2d 828, 428 NYS2d 305 (2d Dept 1980) §§13.03, 13.05

Kole v Brown, 13 AD2d 920, 215 NYS2d 876 (1st Dept 1961) §§6.25, 6.34

Konski Engrs, PC v Levitt, 69 AD2d 940, 415 NYS2d 509 (3d Dept 1979), *affd mem*, 49 NY2d 850, 404 NE2d 1337, 427 NYS2d 796, *cert denied*, 449 US 840 (1980) §15.04

Kooleraire Serv & Installation Corp v Board of Educ, 28 NY2d 101, 268 NE2d 782, 320 NYS2d 46 (1971) §§2.13, 2.32

Koppel v Koppel, 52 AD2d 676, 382 NYS2d 143 (3d Dept 1976) §16.12

Koumianos v State, 141 AD2d 189, 534 NYS2d 512 (3d Dept 1988) §§13.05, 13.14

Krause v City of NY, 152 AD2d 473, 544 NYS2d 126 (1st Dept 1989), *appeal denied*, 76 NY2d 714, 565 NE2d 1268, 564 NYS2d 717 (Bronx 1990) §15.15

L

Laas v Montana State Highway Comm, 157 Mont 121, 483 P2d 699 (1971) §15.19

LaBarge Bros Co v Town of Cicero, 104 Misc 2d 764, 429 NYS2d 140 (Onondaga 1979) §§2.05, 8.05

La Casse v Blaustein, 93 Misc 2d 572, 403 NYS2d 440 (Civ Ct NY 1978) §3.34

Lacille v Feldman, 44 Misc 2d 370, 253 NYS2d 937 (NY 1964) §9.12

LaCroix v J. Migliore Constr Co, 142 AD2d 980, 530 NYS2d 401 (4th Dept 1988) §§13.04, 13.18

Lagzdins v United Welfare Fund-Sec, Div Marriott Corp, 77 AD2d 585, 430 NYS2d 351 (2d Dept 1980) §§13.04, 13.05, 13.17

Lake v McElfatrick, 139 NY 349, 34 NE 922 (1893) §12.03

Lake Steel Erection, Inc v Egan, 61 AD2d 1125, 403 NYS2d 387 (4th Dept), *appeal dismissed*, 44 NY2d 848, 378 NE2d 124, 406 NYS2d 761 (1978) §§4.08, 7.02, 7.05, 7.30, 7.69

La May & Poudrier, Inc v Smith, 3 Misc 2d 843, 150 NYS2d 71 (Suffolk 1956) §9.43

Lambert Hous Redev Co v HRH Equity Corp, 117 AD2d 227, 502 NYS2d 433 (1986) §3.23

Lamparter Acoustical Prods v Maryland Cas Co, 64 AD2d 693, 407 NYS2d 579 (1978) §§8.12, 8.17, 8.19

Langan Constr Corp v State, 110 Misc 177, 180 NYS 249 (Ct Cl 1920) §§4.03, 6.04, 6.05, 6.14, 15.26

Lange v Blake, 58 AD2d 1034, 397 NYS2d 290 (4th Dept 1977) §12.13

Lange v Sartorius, Inc, 160 AD2d 527, 554 NYS2d 179 (1st Dept 1990) §16.11

Langley v Rouss, 185 NY 201, 77 NE 1168 (1906) §§6.07, 6.08, 6.09

LA Rose v Backer, 11 AD2d 314, 203 NYS2d 740 (3d Dept), *judgment amount modified*, 11 AD2d 969, 207 NYS2d 258 (3d Dept 1960), *aff'd*, 11 NY2d 760, 226 NYS2d 695 (1962) §§6.02, 6.34

Lasa Corp, *In re*, 27 Misc 2d 495, 203 NYS2d 731 (Queens 1960) §9.37

LA Storch & Co v Marginal Realty Corp, 109 Misc 669, 180 NYS 661 (NY 1919) §9.26

LA Swyer Co v John W. Cowper Co, 55 AD2d 774, 389 NYS2d 197 (3d Dept 1976) §3.06

Laura Roofing & Renovating Co v Board of Educ, 57 AD2d 586, 393 NYS2d 593 (2d Dept 1977) §§5.04, 5.09, 5.11

Lawrence Dev Corp v Jobin Waterproofing, Inc, 167 AD2d 988, 562 NYS2d 902 (4th Dept 1990) §15.20

LB Foster Co v Terry Contracting, 34 AD2d 638, 310 NYS2d 76 (1970) §9.23

Leary v City of NY, 222 NY 337, 118 NE 849 (1918) (actual) §6.27

Leary v City of Watervliet, 222 NY 337, 118 NE 849 (1918) §§5.08, 5.09, 5.19

LeCesse Bros Contracting v Egan, 89 AD2d 640, 453 NYS2d 82 (1982) §§2.05, 2.15

LeCesse Bros Contracting v Town Bd, 62 AD2d 28, 403 NYS2d 950 (1978), *affd*, 46 NY2d 960, 388 NE2d 737, 415 NYS2d 413 (1979) §§2.05, 2.13

Ledo Realty Corp v Continental Cas Co, 43 Misc 2d 380, 251 NYS2d 99 (Schenectady 1964) §16.16

Lee Turzillo Contracting Co v State, 24 AD2d 548, 261 NYS2d 387 (4th Dept 1965) §7.27

Leghorn v Ross, 53 AD2d 560, 384 NYS2d 830 (1976), *affd*, 42 NY2d 1043, 369 NE2d 763, 399 NYS2d 206 (1977) §8.48

Lehigh Portland Cement Co v City of NY, 179 AD 368, 166 NYS 454 (1917) §9.30

Lehmann v Kingston Plaza, Inc, 44 Misc 2d 63, 252 NYS2d 964 (Albany 1964) §9.45

Leonard v Brooklyn, 71 NY 498 (1877) §9.07

Lewis v Axinn, 100 AD2d 617, 473 NYS2d 575 (2d Dept 1984) §§11.23, 12.08

Lewis v Barsuk, 55 AD2d 817, 389 NYS2d 952 (4th Dept 1976) §12.03

LG Defelice & Son v Globe Indem Co, 189 F Supp 455 (SDNY 1960) §8.18

LG DeFelice & Son v State, 63 Misc 2d 257, 313 NYS2d 21 (Ct Cl 1970) §§6.25, 6.27, 7.07, 7.09, 7.22, 7.26, 7.28, 7.58, 7.60

Lichtenstein v Grossman Constr Corp, 221 AD 527, 225 NYS 118, *modified on other grounds*, 248 NY 390, 162 NE 292 (1928) §9.26

Liles Constr Co v United States, 455 F2d 527 (Ct Cl 1972) §6.17

Lincoln First Bank, NA v Spaulding Bakeries, Inc, 117 Misc 2d 892, 459 NYS2d 696 (Broome 1983) §9.07

Lindeberg v Hodgens, 89 Misc 454, 152 NYS 229 (App Term 1st Dept 1915) §§11.04, 11.08

Litchfield Constr Co v City of NY, 244 NY 251, 155 NE 116 (1926) §§6.04, 7.26, 7.53, 7.55, 7.64

Little Joseph Realty, Inc v Town of Babylon, 41 NY2d 738, 363 NE2d 1163, 395 NYS2d 428 (1977) §15.05

LI Waldman & Co v State, 41 NYS2d 704 (Ct Cl 1943) §§5.03, 5.08, 5.14, 5.19, 5.20

Local 964, United Bd of Carpenters & Joiners of Am v Shirl-Ann Constr Corp, 73 AD2d 968, 424 NYS2d 253 (2d Dept 1980) §16.12

Locke v Goode, 10 Misc 2d 65, 174 NYS2d 435 (1957) §9.29

Lockwood v National Valve Mfg Co, 143 AD2d 509, 533 NYS2d 44 (4th Dept 1988) §13.05

LoForte v Omel, 50 Misc 2d 178, 269 NYS2d 924 (Erie 1966) §9.26

Long v Forest-Fehlhaber, 55 NY2d 154, 433 NE2d 115, 448 NYS2d 132 (1982) §§13.06, 13.14

Long Island Lighting Co v IMO DeLaval, Inc, 668 F Supp 237 (SDNY 1987) §15.22

Long Island Signal Corp v County of Nassau, 51 Misc 2d 320, 273 NYS2d 188 (Nassau 1966) §2.04

Lord Elec Co v Litke, 122 Misc 2d 112, 469 NYS2d 846 (NY 1983) §§2.04, 15.01

658 CASES

Lori-Kay, Inc v Lassner, 61 NY2d 722, 460 NE2d 1097, 472 NYS2d 612 (1984) §8.48

Losei Realty Corp v City of NY, 254 NY 41, 171 NE 899 (1930) §15.17

L. Rosenman Corp v State, 32 AD2d 603, 299 NYS2d 652 (3d Dept 1969) §6.33

Louis N. Picciano & Son v Olympic Constr Co, 112 AD2d 604, 492 NYS2d 476 (3d Dept), *appeal dismissed*, 66 NY2d 854, 489 NE2d 253, 498 NYS2d 366 (1985) §§4.17, 6.10

Luboil Heat & Power Corp v Pleydell, 178 Misc 562, 34 NYS2d 587 (NY 1942) §2.15

Ludlow's Sand & Gravel Co v LaBella, 80 Misc 2d 997, 364 NYS2d 669 (Oneida 1974) §15.01

Luria Bros & Co v United States, 369 F2d 701 (Ct Cl 1966) §§6.04, 6.21, 6.29, 7.60

Lutes v Briggs, 64 NY 404 (1876) §6.07

Lutzken v City of Rochester, 7 AD2d 498, 184 NYS2d 483 (4th Dept 1959) §6.07

Lycee Francais de NY, *In re*, 26 Misc 2d 374, 204 NYS2d 490 (NY 1960) §9.32

M

Mack v Altmans Stage Lighting Co, 98 AD2d 468, 470 NYS2d 664 (2d Dept 1984) §§13.03, 13.05, 13.14

Mack v State, 122 Misc 86, 202 NYS 344 (Ct Cl), *affd without opinion*, 211 AD 825, 206 NYS 931 (1923) §7.39

MacKnight Flintic Stone Co v Mayor of NY, 160 NY 72, 54 NE 661 (1899) §§2.36, 4.10, 6.18, 6.22, 12.02, 12.03, 12.06, 12.15

Macro M. Frisone, Inc v Paul Borg Constr Co, 40 AD2d 589, 334 NYS2d 590 (1972) §9.62

Magowan, *In re*, 203 NYS2d 35 (Suffolk 1960) §9.04

Magrath v L. Migliore Constr Co, 139 AD2d 893, 527 NYS2d 892 (4th Dept 1988) §§13.04, 13.13

Major v Leary, 241 AD 606, 268 NYS 413 (2d Dept 1934) §§11.05, 12.01

Malerba v Warren, 108 Misc 2d 785, 438 NYS2d 936 (Suffolk 1981), *affd as modified*, 96 AD2d 529, 464 NYS2d 835 (2d Dept 1983) §15.05

Maltin v Maryland Cas Co, 24 AD2d 419, 260 NYS2d 194 (1965) §§8.15, 8.19

Mann v Helmsley-Spear, Inc, 177 AD2d 147, 581 NYS2d 16 (1st Dept 1992) §2.27

Manniello v Dea, 92 AD2d 426, 461 NYS2d 582 (3d Dept 1983) §12.02

Manshul Constr v Board of Educ, 551 NYS2d 497 (App Div 1st Dept 1990) §6.07

Manshul Constr Corp v Dormitory Auth, 79 AD2d 383, 436 NYS2d 724 (1st Dept 1981) §§7.49, 7.50, 7.53, 7.55, 7.58, 7.60

Manton v Brooklyn & Flatbush Realty Co, 217 NY 284, 111 NE 819 (1916) §9.29

Maple Farms, Inc v City School Dist, 76 Misc 2d 1080, 352 NYS2d 784 (Chemung 1974) §3.31

Marchionne v New York State Dept of Transp, 88 AD2d 655, 450

NYS2d 529 (1982) §§2.08, 2.13, 2.15, 8.05

Mardan Corp v GGC Music, Ltd, 600 F Supp 1049 (D Ariz 1984), *affd*, 804 F2d 1454 (9th Cir 1986) §14.39

Marine Midland Servs Corp v Samuel Kosoff & Sons, 60 AD2d 767, 400 NYS2d 959 (4th Dept 1977) §§10.19, 10.27

Mario Bonito, Inc v Country Village Heights Condo, 79 Misc 2d 1094, 363 NYS2d 508 (Rockland 1975) §9.70

Markborough Cal, Inc v Superior Ct, 227 Cal App 3d 705, 277 Cal Rptr 919 (1991) §15.22

Marlene Indus Corp v Carnac Textiles, Inc, 45 NY2d 327, 380 NE2d 239, 408 NYS2d 410 (1978) §16.14

Mar-Mes Constr Co v Gitlow, 24 AD2d 481, 260 NYS2d 703 (2d Dept 1965) §2.22

Maross Constr, Inc v Central NY Regional Transp Auth, 66 NY2d 341, 488 NE2d 67, 497 NYS2d 321 (1985) §§6.23, 16.12

Mars Assocs v City of NY, 70 AD2d 839, 418 NYS2d 27 (1st Dept 1979), *affd*, 53 NY2d 627, 420 NE2d 971, 438 NYS2d 779 (1981) §§7.21, 7.51

Mars Assocs v New York City Educ Constr Fund, 126 AD2d 178, 513 NYS2d 125 (1st Dept 1987) §3.23

Marshall Constr Co v Brookdale Hosp Center, 68 Misc 2d 20, 324 NYS2d 806 (Kings 1971) §9.26

Martin Mech Corp v Mars Assocs, 158 AD2d 280, 550 NYS2d 681 (1st Dept 1990) §§3.23, 7.32, 7.33, 7.36

Martin Mech Corp v PJ Carlin Constr Co, 132 AD2d 688, 518 NYS2d 166 (2d Dept 1987) §§7.08, 7.38, 7.40

Martirano Constr Corp v Briar Contracting Corp, 104 AD2d 1028, 481 NYS2d 105 (1984) §9.36

Marvec-All State, Inc v Purcell, 110 Misc 2d 67, 441 NYS2d 618 (Nassau 1981), *affd*, 87 AD2d 593, 450 NYS2d 411 (1982) §2.07

Maryland Cas Co v Straubinger, 19 AD2d 26, 240 NYS2d 228 (1963) §8.48

Matco Prods v Boston Old Colony Ins Co, 104 AD2d 793, 480 NYS2d 134 (1984) §10.15

Mathies Wheel & Pump Co, v Plainview Jewish Center, 42 Misc 2d 569, 248 NYS2d 441 (Nassau 1964) §9.05

Matnel Constr Corp v Robert Homes, Inc, 221 NYS2d 889 (Nassau 1961) §§9.70, 9.73

Mayfair Kitchen Center, Inc v Nigro, 139 AD2d 885, 527 NYS2d 613 (3d Dept 1988) §§12.03, 12.04

Mayfair Super Markets, Inc v Tantleff, 27 Misc 2d 599, 212 NYS2d 571 (NY) *affd*, 13 AD2d 488, 212 NYS2d 570 (1st Dept 1961) §16.14

Mazzola v County of Suffolk, 143 AD2d 734, 533 NYS2d 297 (2d Dept 1988) §2.47

McArdle v Board of Estimate, 74 Misc 2d 1014, 347 NYS2d 349 (Westchester 1973), *affd*, 357 NYS2d 1009 (App Div 1974) §2.07

McCaffrey v Strainer, 81 AD2d 977, 439 NYS2d 773 (3d Dept), *appeal dismissed*, 55 NY2d 700, 431 NE2d 308, 446 NYS2d 947 (1981) §2.27

McComb v Town of Greenville, 163 AD2d 369, 558 NYS2d 104 (2d Dept 1990) §§15.02, 15.08

McCoy v Bailey, 24 Misc 2d 875, 209 NYS2d 550 (Nassau 1960) §9.67

McCullough v Board of Educ, 11 AD2d 740, 204 NYS2d 555 (1960) §16.02

McEligot v State, 246 AD 121, 284 NYS 646 (3d Dept 1936) §6.18

McGroarty v Great Am Ins Co, 36 NY2d 358, 329 NE2d 172, 368 NYS2d 485 (1975) §§10.07, 10.09, 10.27, 10.31

McGurk v Turner Constr Co, 127 AD2d 526, 512 NYS2d 71 (1st Dept 1987) §§3.13, 13.18

McKay Constr Co v City of Oneida Hous Auth, 70 AD2d 993, 417 NYS2d 808 (3d Dept 1979) §§7.02, 7.25

McMaster v State, 108 NY 542, 15 NE 417 (1888) §§6.04, 6.05, 6.25

M. Crist, Inc v State Office of Gen Servs, 42 AD2d 481, 349 NYS2d 191 (1973) §2.04

Meaott Constr Corp v Ross, 76 AD2d 137, 431 NYS2d 207 (3d Dept 1980) §2.35

Mechanic's Bank v City of NY, 164 AD 128, 149 NYS 784 (2d Dept 1914) §7.37

Melniker v Grae, 82 AD2d 798, 439 NYS2d 409 (1981) §9.36

Melwood Constr Corp v State, 126 Misc 2d 156, 481 NYS2d 289 (Ct Cl 1984), affd, 119 AD2d 734, 501 NYS2d 604 (1986) §§7.30, 7.67, 7.72

Mendel-Mesick-Cohen-Architects v Peerless Ins Co, 74 AD2d 712, 426 NYS2d 124 (1980) §8.02

Menorah Nursing Home, Inc v Zukov, 153 AD2d 13, 548 NYS2d 702 (2d Dept 1989) §8.52

Meo v Skellyway Constr Co, 30 AD2d 606, 290 NYS2d 516 (1968) §9.26

Merchants Mut Cas Co v United States Fidelity & Guar Co, 253 AD 151, 2 NYS2d 370 (4th Dept 1938) §8.10

Mercury Paint Corp v Seaboard Painting Corp, 112 Misc 2d 529, 447 NYS2d 191 (NY 1981) §§9.44, 9.56

Merit Plumbing & Heating v Eastern Natl Bank, 221 NYS2d 143 (Suffolk 1961) §9.78

Merrick v Four Star Stage Lighting, Inc, 60 AD2d 806, 400 NYS2d 543 (1st Dept 1978) §15.12

Merrick Jewish Centre, Inc v New York Dept of Envtl Conservation, 128 AD2d 877, 513 NYS2d 799 (2d Dept 1987) §14.34

Merritt-Chapman & Scott Corp v State, 54 AD2d 37, 386 NYS2d 894 (3d Dept 1976), affd, 43 NY 690, 371 NE2d 790, 401 NYS2d 28 (1977) §7.44

Merritt-Chapman & Scott Corp v United States, 458 F2d 42 (Ct Cl 1972) §6.16

Merv Blank, Inc v Dwyer, 50 AD2d 563, 374 NYS2d 676 (1975) §9.74

Messersmith v Amercian Fidelity Co, 232 NY 161, 133 NE 432 (1921) §10.09

Met Painting Co v Dana, 90 Misc 2d 289, 394 NYS2d 392 (Civ Ct NY 1977) §9.05

Metropolitan Paving Co v United States, 163 Ct Cl 420 (1963) §7.26

Metropolitan Sewage Comm v RW Constr, Inc, 72 Wis 2d 365, 241 NW2d 371 (1976) §5.01

Meyer v Board of Educ, 31 Misc 2d 407, 221 NYS2d 500 (Nassau 1961) §§2.04, 2.15, 15.04

M. Farbman & Sons v New York City Health & Hosps, 62 NY2d 75, 464 NE2d 437, 476 NYS2d 69 (1984) §§14.36, 16.03

Michael J. Torpey, Inc v Consolidated Edison Co, 99 AD2d 484, 470 NYS2d 426 (1984), *appeal dismissed*, 66 NY2d 915, 489 NE2d 773, 498 NYS2d 1027 (1985) §§5.09, 5.11

Michael Mazzeo Elec Corp v Murphy, 137 Misc 2d 853, 522 NYS2d 798 (NY 1987) §2.03

Mid-Atlantic Constr Corp v Guido, 30 AD2d 232, 291 NYS2d 501 (4th Dept 1968) §16.11

Midatlantic Natl Bank v New Jersey Dept of Envtl Protection, 474 US 494, 106 S Ct 755, 88 L Ed 2d 859 (1986) §14.39

Midtown Contracting Co v Goldsticker, 165 AD 264, 150 NYS 809 (1st Dept 1914) §§4.06, 4.07, 4.08

Milau Assocs v North Ave Dev Corp, 42 NY2d 482, 368 NE2d 1247, 398 NYS2d 882 (1977) §§3.11, 3.28, 11.04, 11.05

Milbank-Frawley Hous Dev Fund Co v Marshall Constr Co, 71 Misc 2d 42, 335 NYS2d 598 (NY 1972) §§9.07, 9.36

Miliken Bros v City of NY, 201 NY 65, 94 NE 196 (1911) §§9.30, 9.36

Miller v McMahon, 135 AD2d 1030, 523 NYS2d 185 (3d Dept 1987) §6.11

Miller v TA & JM Gen Contractors, Inc, 124 Misc 2d 273, 476 NYS2d 449 (Kings 1984) §§9.37, 9.45

Miller v Town & Country, Inc, 74 Misc 2d 1038, 346 NYS2d 555 (Suffolk 1973) §2.36

Milliken & Co v Consolidated Edison Co, 119 AD2d 481, 501 NYS2d 23 (1st Dept 1986), *affd*, 69 NY2d 786, 505 NE2d 624, 513 NYS2d 114 (1987) §15.20

Millington v Rapoport, 98 AD2d 765, 469 NYS2d 787 (1983) §9.03

Milton L. Ehrlich, Inc v Swiss Constr Corp, 11 AD2d 644, 201 NYS2d 133 (1st Dept 1960) §16.12

Mineola Rd Oil Corp v Walsh, 137 NYS2d 342 (Suffolk 1954) §§9.01, 9.32

MJ Posner Constr Co v Valley View Dev Corp, 118 AD2d 1001, 499 NYS2d 997 (3d Dept 1986) §4.20

M. Leiken & Sons, *In re*, 39 Misc 2d 156, 240 NYS2d 73 (Queens 1963) §9.74

Mobil Chem Co v Blount Bros Corp, 809 F2d 1175 (5th Cir 1987) §7.44

Modern Scaffold Co v Karell Realty Corp, 28 AD2d 581, 279 NYS2d 436 (3d Dept 1967) §10.05

Mojave Enters v United States, 3 Cl Ct 353 (1983) §§5.02, 5.10, 5.12, 5.13

Monroe Sav Bank v Stark-Center Corp, 79 Misc 2d 952, 361 NYS2d 839 (Seneca 1974) §9.53

Moore Golf, Inc v Lakeover Golf & Country Club, Inc, 49 AD2d 583, 370 NYS2d 156 (1975) §9.66

Morsillo, *In re*, 17 AD2d 894, 233 NYS2d 689 (1962) §9.56

Mortise v 55 Liberty Owners Corp, 102 AD2d 719, 477 NYS2d 2, *affd*, 63 NY2d 743, 469 NE2d 529, 480 NYS2d 208 (1984) §9.03

Morton v Tucker, 145 NY 244, 40 NE 3 (1895) §§9.36, 9.44

Moshiko, Inc v Seiger & Smith, Inc, 137 AD2d 170, 529 NYS2d 284 (1st Dept), *affd mem*, 72 NY2d 945, 529 NE2d 420, 533 NYS2d 52 (1988) §10.15

Mosler Safe Co v Maiden Lane Safe Deposit Co, 199 NY 479, 93 NE 81 (1910) §7.72

Mount Vernon Contracting Corp v State, 56 AD2d 952, 392 NYS2d 726 (3d Dept 1977) §§7.05, 7.10, 7.11, 15.19

Moxley v Laramie Builders, Inc, 600 P2d 733 (Wyo 1979) §12.14

Moyer v City of Little Falls, 134 Misc 2d 299, 510 NYS2d 813 (Herkimer 1986) §3.31

Muhlstock & Co v Amercian Home Assurance Co, 117 AD2d 117, 502 NYS2d 174 (1st Dept 1986) §10.27

Mulvihill Elec Contracting Corp v Metropolitan Trans Auth, 167 AD2d 471, 562 NYS2d 144 (2d Dept 1990) §15.02

Municipal Consultants & Publishers, Inc v Town of Ramapo, 47 NY2d 144, 390 NE2d 1143, 417 NYS2d 218 (1979) §§2.24, 2.25

N

Nab Constr Corp v Metropolitan Transp Auth, 579 NYS2d 375 (1st Dept) §17.16

Naclerio Contracting Co v EPA, 86 AD2d 793, 447 NYS2d 4 (1st Dept 1982) §§7.21, 7.51

Nadal Baxendale, Inc v Iannace, 12 AD2d 785, 209 NYS2d 615 (2d Dept 1961) §2.31

Naetzker v Brocton Cent School Dist, 50 AD2d 142, 376 NYS2d 300 (4th Dept 1975), *revd on other grounds*, 41 NY2d 929, 363 NE2d 351, 394 NYS2d 627 (1977) §§11.04, 11.24

Nager Elec Co v State Otfice of Gen Servs, 56 Misc 2d 975, 290 NYS2d 943 (Albany 1967), *affd*, 30 AD2d 626, 290 NYS2d 947, *appeal denied*, 22 NY2d 645, 295 NYS2d 1026 (1968) §2.09

Naimoli v Massa, 81 Misc 2d 431, 366 NYS2d 573 (City Ct Geneva 1975) §15.40

Najjar Indus v City of NY, 87 AD2d 329, 451 NYS2d 410 (1st Dept 1982), *affd*, 68 NY2d 943, 502 NE2d 997, 510 NYS2d 82 (1986) §15.19

Najjar Indus v City of NY, 86 AD2d 573, 446 NYS2d 302 (1st Dept), *affd*, 57 NY2d 647, 439 NE2d 874, 454 NYS2d 65 (1982) §6.32

Nassau Suffolk White Trucks, Inc v Twin County Transit Mix Corp, 62 AD2d 982, 403 NYS2d 322 (1978) §§3.31, 3.33

Nasser, Estate of v Port Auth, 155 AD2d 250, 546 NYS2d 626 (1st Dept 1989) §15.14

National Bank of Commerce v City of Watervliet, 97 Misc 121, 160 NYS 1072 (Albany 1916), *affd mem*, 178 AD 944, 164 NYS 1103 (3d Dept 1917) §§6.09, 6.11

National Cash Register Co v Wilson, 8 NY2d 377, 171 NE2d 302, 208 NYS2d 951 (1960) §16.14

National Plumbing Supply Co v Castellano, 118 Misc 2d 150, 460 NYS2d 248 (Westchester 1983) §3.34

National Shawmut Bank v New Amsterdam Cas Co, 411 F2d 843 (1st Cir 1969) §8.51

National Wire Prods Corp v McMorran, 23 AD2d 708, 257 NYS2d 71 (3d Dept 1965) §§15.03, 15.04

Navajo Circle, Inc v Development Concepts, 373 So 2d 689 (Fla Dist Ct App 1979) §§8.50, 11.14

Neil Plumbing & Heating Constr Co v Providence Wash Ins Co, 125 AD2d 295, 508 NYS2d 580 (2d Dept 1986) §10.03

Nelson v Schrank, 273 AD 72, 75 NYS2d 761 (1947) §9.29

New Again Constr Co v City of NY, 76 Misc 2d 943, 351 NYS2d 895 (Kings 1974) §§7.20, 7.21, 7.25, 7.51

Newark, Village of v James F. Leary Constr Co, 118 Misc 622, 194 NYS 212 (Wayne 1922) §8.26

New Era Homes Corp v Forster, 299 NY 303, 86 NE2d 757, 22 ALR2d 1338 (1949) §§4.21, 15.10, 15.33

New York v Shore Realty Corp, 759 F2d 1033 (2d Cir 1985) §§14.05, 14.37, 14.39

New York Artcrafts, Inc v Marvin, 29 Misc 2d 774, 215 NYS2d 788 (Nassau 1961) §9.04

New York City Charter, Inc v Fabber, 73 Misc 2d 859, 343 NYS2d 33 (NY), *affd*, 41 AD2d 821, 343 NYS2d 558 (1973) §2.03

New York Plumbers Specialties Co v Columbia Cas Co, 13 AD2d 449, 211 NYS2d 824 (1961) §§8.10, 8.33

New York Tel Co v Jamestown Tel Corp, 282 NY 365, 26 NE2d 295 (1940) §4.04

New York Tel Co v Schumacher & Forelle, Inc, 60 AD2d 151, 400 NYS2d 332 (1977) §3.06

Niagara County v Utica Mut Ins Co, 80 AD2d 415, 439 NYS2d 538 (4th Dept), *appeal dismissed*, 54 NY2d 608, 443 NYS2d 1030 (1981) §14.22

Niagara Mohawk Power v Graver Tank & Manu Co, 470 F Supp 1308 (NDNY 1979) §4.04

Niagra Venture v Sicoli & Massaro, Inc, 77 NY2d 175, 565 NYS2d 449 (1990) §§9.05, 9.26

Niaztat Iron Works, Inc v Tri-Neck Constr Corp, 62 Misc 2d 228, 308 NYS2d 427 (Kings 1970) §§9.68, 9.71, 9.75

Nieman-Irving & Co v Lazenby, 263 NY 91, 188 NE 265 (1933) §11.08

Niewenhous Co v State, 248 AD 658, 288 NYS 22 (3d Dept), *affd*, 272 NY 484, 3 NE2d 880 (1936) §§5.08, 5.13

Nimke v Inta-State, Inc, 34 AD2d 675, 310 NYS2d 462 (1970) §9.26

Noel J. Brunell & Son v Town of Champlain, 95 Misc 2d 320, 407 NYS2d 376 (Clinton 1977), *affd*, 64 AD2d 757, 407 NYS2d 447, *revd*, 47 NY2d 745, 390 NE2d 1178, 417 NYS2d 254 (1979) §2.35

Norcross v Wills, 198 NY 336, 91 NE 803 (1910) §7.12

Norelli & Oliver Constr Co v State, 30 AD2d 992, 294 NYS2d 35 (3d Dept 1968), *affd*, 32 NY2d 809, 298 NE2d 691, 345 NYS2d 556 (1973) §§7.08, 7.23, 7.24

Norman Co v County of Nassau, 27 AD2d 936, 278 NYS2d 719 (2d Dept 1967), *on remand*, 63 Misc 2d 965, 314 NYS2d 44 (Nassau 1970) §§7.23, 7.26

Norris v Depew Paving Co, 14 AD2d 117, 217 NYS2d 203

(1961), *affd*, 11 NY2d 812, 182 NE2d 109, 227 NYS2d 436 (1962) §§8.15, 8.29, 8.35, 8.37, 8.38

North Am Iron & Steel Co v Isaacson Steel Erectors, Inc, 36 AD2d 770, 321 NYS2d 254 (2d Dept 1971), *affd mem*, 30 NY2d 640, 331 NYS2d 667 (1972) §10.23

Northern Structures, Inc v Union Bank, 57 AD2d 360, 394 NYS2d 964, *amended as to judgment amount*, 396 NYS2d 1021 (1977) §§9.75, 9.78, 9.81

Northern Tree Serv v Donovan Tree Serv, 36 AD2d 22, 318 NYS2d 638 (3d Dept 1971) §9.49

Northrup Contracting, Inc v Village of Bergen, 139 Misc 2d 435, 527 NYS2d 670 (Monroe 1986), *affd mem as modified on other grounds*, 129 AD2d 1002, 514 NYS2d 306 (4th Dept 1987) §§11.05, 11.14

Novak & Co v Facilities Dev Corp, 116 AD2d 891, 498 NYS2d 492 (3d Dept 1986) §§6.30, 7.49, 7.53, 7.63

Novak & Co v New York City Hous Auth, 108 AD2d 612, 485 NYS2d 68 (1st Dept 1985), *appeal dismissed*, 67 NY2d 1027, 494 NE2d 457, 503 NYS2d 326 (1986), *second appeal dismissed*, 72 NY2d 1002, 531 NE2d 297, 534 NYS2d 665 (1988) §7.40

Novak & Co v Travelers Indem Co, 56 AD2d 418, 392 NYS2d 901 (1977) §§8.03, 8.19, 8.31

Nowak v Smith & Mahoney, PC, 110 AD2d 288, 494 NYS2d 449 (3d Dept 1985) §§13.04, 13.07

NW Developers, Inc v Jeremiah Burns, Inc, 55 AD2d 580, 389 NYS2d 865 (1976) §9.30

NY, City of v Kalisch-Jarcho, Inc, 161 AD2d 252, 554 NYS2d 900 (1st Dept 1990) §§12.03, 15.35

NY, City of v Local 333, Marine Div, Intl Longshoremen's Assn, 79 AD2d 410, 437 NYS2d 98 (1st Dept 1981), *affd*, 55 NY2d 898, 433 NE2d 1277, 449 NYS2d 29 (1982) §§7.05, 7.09

NY, City of v United States Fidelity & Guar Co, 119 Misc 2d 725, 464 NYS2d 659 (NY 1983) §§2.13, 8.06

NY, City of v Unsafe Bldg & Structure No 97, Columbia Heights, 113 Misc 2d 246, 448 NYS2d 938 (NY 1982) §2.14

Nyack Bd of Educ v K. Capolino Design & Renovation, Ltd, 114 AD2d 849, 494 NYS2d 758 (2d Dept 1985), *affd*, 68 NY2d 647, 496 NE2d 233, 505 NYS2d 74 (1986) §§7.18, 16.02

O

Oakhill Contracting Co v City of NY, 262 AD 530, 30 NYS2d 567 (1st Dept 1941) §6.33

O'Brien v Fago, 54 Misc 2d 203, 282 NYS2d 295 (Erie 1967) §8.14

Ogdensburg Urban Renewal Agency v Moroney, 42 AD2d 639, 345 NYS2d 169 (3d Dept 1973) §4.15

Ohio v Kovacs 469 US 274, 105 S Ct 705, 83 L Ed 2d 649 (1985) §14.39

O'Leary v Raymond LeChase, Inc, 125 AD2d 991, 510 NYS2d 389 (4th Dept 1986) §13.06

Olsen v Chase Manhattan Bank, 10 AD2d 539, 205 NYS2d 60 (2d Dept 1960), *affd mem*, 9 NY2d

829, 175 NE2d 350, 215 NYS2d 773 (1961) §§13.03, 13.11

O'Mara Org, Inc v Plehn, 579 NYS2d 48 (1st Dept 1992) §11.15

Omega Contracting, Inc v Maropakis Contracting, Inc, 160 AD2d 942, 554 NYS2d 664 (2d Dept 1990) §16.12

101 Park Ave Assoc v Trane Co, 99 AD2d 428, 470 NYS2d 392, *affd mem*, 62 NY2d 734, 465 NE2d 359, 476 NYS2d 820 (1984) §9.36

O'Neill, *In re*, 182 Misc 828, 45 NYS2d 564 (Wayne 1943) §§9.26, 9.33

Onondaga Commercial Dry Wall Corp v Clinton St, Inc, 25 NY2d 106, 250 NE2d 211, 302 NYS2d 795 (1969) §§9.70, 9.71, 9.83

Onondaga Commercial Dry Wall Corp v Sylvan Glen Co, 26 AD2d 130, 271 NYS2d 523 (1966), *affd*, 21 NY2d 739, 234 NE2d 840, 287 NYS2d 886 (1968) §9.71

Opark Constr Corp v Eureka Constr, Inc, 42 NY2d 1031, 369 NE2d 9, 398 NYS2d 1009, (1977) §16.12

Orange Front Paint Supply, Inc v Scaramuccia, 59 AD2d 894, 399 NYS2d 52 (1977) §2.06

O'Rourke Engg Constr Co v City of NY, 229 AD 261, 241 NYS 613 (2d Dept 1930) §15.15

Ortiz v Uhl, 39 AD2d 143, 332 NYS2d 583 (4th Dept 1972), *affd mem*, 33 NY2d 989, 309 NE2d 425, 353 NYS2d 962 (1974) §§13.03, 13.06

Osborne v McGowan, 1 AD2d 924, 149 NYS2d 781 (1956) §9.05

Oscar Daniels Co v City of NY, 196 AD 856, 188 NYS 716 (1st Dept 1921) §§6.23, 6.33

Ossining Union Free School Dist v Anderson LaRocca Anderson, 73 NY2d 417, 539 NE2d 91, 541 NYS2d 335 (1989) §§5.14, 8.50, 11.06, 11.14, 15.20

Oster, *In re*, 31 Misc 2d 253, 219 NYS2d 988 (Oneida 1961) §9.36

Otis v Dodd, 90 NY 336 (1882) §9.05

Outdoor Scenes, Inc v Anthony Grace & Sons, 111 Misc 2d 36, 443 NYS2d 583 (Queens 1981) §§3.11, 3.28

Owens v Patent Scaffolding Co, 50 AD2d 866, 376 NYS2d 948 (1975), *revg* 77 Misc 2d 992, 354 NYS2d 778 (Kings 1974) §3.28

P

Paccione v Board of Educ, 20 Misc 2d 896, 195 NYS2d 593 (NY 1959) §2.04

Paedergat Boat & Racquet Club, Inc v Zarrelli, 83 AD2d 444, 445 NYS2d 162 (1981), *revd*, 57 NY2d 966, 443 NE2d 477, 457 NYS2d 229 (1982) §§9.05, 9.13, 9.15

Page v Krekey, 137 NY 307, 33 NE 311 (1893) §8.26

Pallette v State, 266 AD 490, 43 NYS2d 553 (3d Dept 1943), *affd*, 292 NY 657, 55 NE2d 518 (1944) §2.50

Palm Beach Realty Co v Harry J. Kangieser, Inc, 36 Misc 2d 1058, 233 NYS2d 641 (NY 1962), *affd*, 19 AD2d 862, 243 NYS2d 413 (1963) §9.82

Palsgraf v Long Island RR, 248 NY 339, 162 NE 99 (1928) §11.23

Park City Assocs v Total Energy Leasing Corp, 58 AD2d 786, 396 NYS2d 377 (1st Dept 1977) §16.11

Pashen Contractors, Inc v John J.
Colnan Co, 13 Ill App 3d 485,
300 NE2d 795 (1973) §11.11

Paterno & Sons v Town of New
Windsor, 43 AD2d 863, 351
NYS2d 445 (2d Dept 1974)
§§4.17, 4.21, 15.10

Pathman Constr Co, ASBCA 14285,
71-1 BCA ¶8905 (1971) §7.46

Pavarini Constr Co v Liberty Mut
Ins Co, NYLJ, Dec 21, 1990, at
23, col 4 §10.27

Paver & Wildfoerster v Catholic
High School Assoc, 38 NY2d
669, 345 NE2d 565, 382 NYS2d
22 (1976) §§11.04, 11.23

PC Chipouras & Assocs v 212
Realty Corp, 156 AD2d 549, 549
NYS2d 55 (2d Dept 1989)
§§11.02, 11.03

P. Delay & Co v Duvoli, 278 NY
328, 16 NE2d 354 (1938) §9.05

Peabody v Rotan Mosle, Inc, A
Subsidiary of Paine Weber, 677 F
Supp 1135 (MD Fla 1987) §16.12

Pearl v Allied Corp, 566 F Supp
400 (ED Pa 1984) §14.32

Pearl St Dev Corp v Conduit &
Found Corp, 41 NY2d 167, 359
NE2d 693, 391 NYS2d 98 (1976)
§§3.06, 16.15

Pecker Iron Works, Inc v Sturdy
Concrete Co, 96 Misc 2d 998,
410 NYS2d 251 (Queens 1978)
§3.28

Peckham Rd Co v State, 32 AD2d
139, 300 NYS2d 174 (3d Dept
1969), affd, 28 NY2d 734, 269
NE2d 826, 321 NYS2d 117
(1971) §§7.24, 7.37

Pell v Board of Educ, 34 NY2d 222,
313 NE2d 321, 356 NYS2d 833,
(1974) §15.04

Pennsylvania Engg Corp v Islip
Resource Recovery Agency, 710
F Supp 456 (EDNY 1989) §16.13

People v John W. Rouse Constr Co,
26 AD2d 405, 274 NYS2d 981
(1966) §§2.12, 8.07

People v Massachusetts Bonding &
Ins Co, 182 AD 122, 169 NYS
693 (1918) §§8.08, 8.27

People v Rallo, 46 AD2d 518, 363
NYS2d 851 (1975), affd, 39 NY2d
217, 347 NE2d 633, 383 NYS2d
271 (1976) §§9.70, 9.78

People v Rosano, 50 NY2d 1013,
409 NE2d 1357, 431 NYS2d 683
(1980) §9.73

People v Rosano, 69 AD2d 643, 419
NYS2d 543 (1979) §9.79

Perosi Homes, Inc v Maniscalco, 15
AD2d 563, 223 NYS2d 173 (2d
Dept 1961) §15.01

Perrin v Stempinski Realty Corp, 15
AD2d 48, 222 NYS2d 148 (1961)
§9.26

Perry v Levenson, 82 AD 94, 81
NYS 586 (1st Dept 1903), affd,
178 NY 559, 70 NE 1104 (1904)
§6.11

Persichilli v Triborough Bridge &
Tunnel Auth, 16 NY2d 136, 209
NE2d 802, 262 NYS2d 476
(1965) §13.03

Peru Assocs v State, 70 Misc 2d
775, 334 NYS2d 772 (Ct Cl
1971), affd mem, 335 NYS2d 373
(3d Dept 1972) §§4.21, 15.26

Peter A. Camilli & Sons v State, 41
Misc 2d 218, 245 NYS2d 521 (Ct
Cl 1963) §§6.12, 7.24, 7.43

Peter K. Freuh, Inc v Kass, 120
Misc 2d 330, 465 NYS2d 841
(Albany 1983) §9.56

Petersen v Rawson, 34 NY 370
(1866) §§11.08, 12.03

Petluck v McGolrick Realty Co, 240
AD 61, 268 NYS 782 (1st Dept
1934) §§13.03, 13.04

Pettinelli Elec Co v Board of Educ,
56 AD2d 520, 391 NYS2d 118

(1st Dept), *affd mem*, 43 NY2d 760, 372 NE2d 799, 401 NYS2d 1011 (1977) §4.03

Philan Dept of Borden Co v Foster-Lipkins Corp, 39 AD2d 633, 331 NYS2d 138 (1972) §9.50

Phillips Constr Co v City of NY, 61 NY2d 949, 463 NE2d 585, 475 NYS2d 244, *reargument denied*, 62 NY2d 646, 464 NE2d 990, 476 NYS2d 1028 (1984) §§8.28, 12.08

Phoenix Contracting Corp v New York City Health & Hosp Corp, 118 AD2d 477, 499 NYS2d 953 (1st Dept), *appeal denied*, 68 NY2d 606, 498 NE2d 151, 506 NYS2d 1031 (1986) §7.37

Picone v City of NY, 176 Misc 967, 29 NYS2d 539 (NY 1941) §2.04

Piland Corp v REA Constr Co, 672 F Supp 244 (ED Va 1987) §2.21

Pile Found Co, *In re*, 159 AD2d 352, 552 NYS2d 631 (1st Dept 1990) §16.12

Pilgrim Homes & Garages, Inc v Fiore, 75 AD2d 846, 427 NYS2d 851 (2d Dept), *appeal dismissed*, 51 NY2d 702, 431 NYS2d 1030 (1980) §§4.13, 12.03

Pinckney, *In re*, 13 AD2d 806, 216 NYS2d 19 (1961) §§9.23, 9.35

Pinto Equip Rental, Inc v State, 134 AD2d 905, 522 NYS2d 63 (1987) §16.02

Pipe Welding Supply Co v Haskell, Conner & Frost, 61 NY2d 884, 462 NE2d 1190, 474 NYS2d 472 (1984) §11.07

Piston v Lincoln Supply Co, 37 Misc 2d 1003, 239 NYS2d 20 (Onondaga 1963) §9.36

PJ Carlin Constr Co v A to Z Equip Corp, 31 AD2d 546, 295 NYS2d 239 (1968) §9.04

PJ Carlin Constr Co v Whiffen Elec Co, 66 AD2d 684, 411 NYS2d 27 (1st Dept 1978) §§2.25, 2.27

PJ Panzeca, Inc, *In re*, 56 Misc 2d 460, 288 NYS2d 813 (Nassau), *affd*, 30 AD2d 640, 292 NYS2d 1007 (1968) §8.07

PJ Panzeca, Inc v Alizio, 52 AD2d 919, 383 NYS2d 396 (2d Dept 1976) §9.49

Plumbing Contractors Assoc v City of Buffalo, 70 Misc 2d 412, 334 NYS2d 9 (Erie 1972) §2.09

Poirier & McLane Corp v State, 13 Misc 2d 858, 178 NYS2d 925 (Ct Cl 1958) §6.33

Poly Constr Corp v Oxford Hall Co, 44 Misc 2d 82, 252 NYS2d 971 (Kings 1964) §9.74

Pomperaug Realty Corp v Schulte Real Estate Co, 182 Misc 1080, 50 NYS2d 238 (NY 1944) §9.66

Poughkeepsie Iron & Metal Co v Ermco Erectors, Inc, 79 Misc 2d 142, 359 NYS2d 634 (Duchess 1974) §9.82

Power Auth v Westinghouse Elec Corp, 117 AD2d 336, 502 NYS2d 420 (1st Dept 1986) §10.15

Prairie State Bank v United States, 164 US 227, 17 S Ct 142, 41 L Ed 412 (1896) §§8.49, 8.51

Premier Elec Constr Corp v Security Natl Bank, 39 AD2d 967, 334 NYS2d 199 (1972) §9.81

Premier Elec Installation Co v Board of Educ, 20 Misc 2d 286, 191 NYS2d 187 (Suffolk 1959) §2.18

Price v Lawrence-Van Voast, Inc, 58 AD2d 727, 396 NYS2d 296 (3d Dept 1977) §10.15

Prima Paint Corp v Flood & Conklin Mfg Co, 388 US 395, 87 S Ct 1801, 18 L Ed 1270 (1967) §§16.12, 16.13

Primiano Constr Co, *In re*, 117 Misc 2d 523, 458 NYS2d 147 (Nassau 1982) §9.68

Prince Carpentry, Inc v Cosmopolitan Mut Ins Co, 124 Misc 2d 919, 479 NYS2d 284 (NY 1984) §15.08

Progressive Dietary Consultants, Inc v Wyoming County, 90 AD2d 214, 457 NYS2d 159 (1982) §2.08

Prosper Contracting Co v Board of Educ, 73 Misc 2d 280, 341 NYS2d 196 (App Term 1973), *affd*, 43 AD2d 823, 351 NYS2d 402 (1974) §§2.07, 2.11

Prote Contracting Co v Board of Educ, 135 AD2d 523, 521 NYS2d 752 (2d Dept 1987) §16.02

Prudential-Bache Sec, Inc v Resnick Water St Dev Co, 161 AD2d 456, 555 NYS2d 367 (1st Dept 1990) §15.20

PS Griswold Co v Cortland Glass Co, 138 AD2d 869, 525 NYS2d 973 (3d Dept 1988) §3.21

PT&L Constr Co v Winnick, 59 AD2d 368, 399 NYS2d 712 (1977) §9.01

Public Constructors, Inc v State, 55 AD2d 368, 390 NYS2d 481 (3d Dept 1977) §§5.08, 5.12, 5.13

Public Improvements, Inc v Board of Educ, 81 AD2d 537, 438 NYS2d 305 (1st Dept 1981), *affd*, 56 NY2d 850, 438 NE2d 876, 453 NYS2d 170 (1982) §§7.17, 16.02

Putnins Contracting Corp v Winston Woods, Inc, 72 Misc 2d 987, 340 NYS2d 317 (Nassau), *affd*, 43 AD2d 667, 349 NYS2d 652 (1973), *affd*, 36 NY2d 679, 365 NYS2d 853 (1975) §9.81

Q

Quain v Buzzetta Constr Corp, 69 NY2d 376, 507 NE2d 294, 514 NYS2d 701 (1987) §3.13

Quaker-Empire Constr Co v DA Collins Constr Co, 88 AD2d 1043, 452 NYS2d 692 (3d Dept 1982) §§3.09, 7.05, 7.27, 7.37, 7.43

Queensbury Union Free School Dist v Jim Walter Corp, 101 AD2d 992, 477 NYS2d 475 (3d Dept 1984), *affd mem*, 64 NY2d 964, 477 NE2d 1106, 488 NYS2d 652 (1985) §§12.09, 12.16

Queensbury Union Free School Dist v Jim Walter Corp, 82 AD2d 204, 442 NYS2d 650 (3d Dept), *appeal dismissed*, 55 NY2d 745, 431 NE2d 642, 447 NYS2d 157 (1981) §§12.04, 12.08

Queensbury Union Free School Dist v Jim Walter Corp, 91 Misc 2d 804, 398 NYS2d 832 (Warren 1977) §11.04

Quirk v Morrissey, 106 AD2d 498, 483 NYS2d 34 (1984) §16.02

R

Race Co v Oxford Hall Contracting Corp, 25 AD2d 665, 268 NYS2d 175 (2d Dept 1966) §16.14

Radory Constr Corp v Arronbee Constr Corp, 24 AD2d 573, 262 NYS2d 389 (1965) §9.74

Rainbow Elec Co v Bloom, 132 AD2d 539, 517 NYS2d 273 (2d Dept 1987) §6.09

Raisler Corp v New York City Auth Hous, 32 NY2d 274, 298 NE2d 91, 344 NYS2d 917 (1973) §16.15

Raisler Corp v Uris 55 Water St Co, 91 Misc 2d 217, 397 NYS2d 668

(NY 1977) §§9.68, 9.69, 9.73, 9.76, 9.80
Ralston Purina Co v Arthur G. McKee & Co, 158 AD2d 969, 551 NYS2d 720 (4th Dept 1990) §§12.03, 12.04, 12.13, 15.20, 15.35
Ramos v Shumavon, 21 AD2d 4, 247 NYS2d 699 (1st Dept), *affd mem*, 15 NY2d 610, 203 NE2d 912, 255 NYS2d 658 (1964) §§11.13, 13.15
Ramos v Wheel Sports Center, 96 Misc 2d 646, 409 NYS2d 505 (Civ Ct NY 1978) §3.34
Randy Knitwear, Inc v Amercian Cyanamid Co, 11 NY2d 5, 181 NE2d 399, 226 NYS2d 363 (1962) §12.15
Rao Elec Equip Co v State, 36 AD2d 1019, 321 NYS2d 670 (4th Dept 1971) §§7.05, 7.10, 7.28, 7.43
Rappl & Hoening Co v New York Dept of Envtl Conservation, *In re*, 61 AD2d 20, 401 NYS2d 346 (4th Dept 1978), *affd*, 47 NY2d 925, 393 NE2d 485, 419 NYS2d 490 (1979) §14.34
Rarick v Samal Constr Co, 137 Misc 2d 953, 522 NYS2d 829 (Albany 1987) §13.02
Raymond Intl, Inc, ASBCA 13121, 70-1 BCA ¶8341 (1970) §7.46
Reading, City of v Rae, 106 F2d 458 (3d Cir), *cert denied*, 308 US 607, 60 S Ct 145, 84 L Ed 508 (1939) §§5.14, 5.16
Realty Adv & Supply Co v Hickson, 184 AD 168, 171 NYS 455 (1st Dept 1918) §4.16
RE Crist, Inc v Lasker-Goldman Corp, 27 Misc 2d 552, 203 NYS2d 493 (NY 1960) §9.44
Redarowicz v Ohlendorf, 92 Ill 2d 171, 441 NE2d 324 (1982) §12.14
Reeve Serv Corp v Raab, 64 AD2d 826, 407 NYS2d 315 (1978) §9.41
Refrod Realty Corp, *In re*, 216 NYS2d 564 (Kings 1961) §9.26
Reichert v N. MacFarland Builders, Inc, 85 AD2d 767, 445 NYS2d 264 (3d Dept 1981) §15.09
Reiss v Pacific Steel Pool Corp, 73 Misc 2d 78, 341 NYS2d 364 (Albany 1973) §3.35
Reister v Town of Fleming, 32 AD2d 733, 302 NYS2d 176 (4th Dept 1969) §2.22
Reliable Constr Corp v Relide Realty Corp, 6 Misc 2d 857, 162 NYS2d 550 (NY 1957) §9.39
Reliance Ins Co v Garsart Bldg Corp, 131 AD2d 828, 517 NYS2d 189 (2d Dept 1987) §2.08
Resco Equip & Supply Corp v City Council, 34 AD2d 1088, 313 NYS2d 74 (1970) §§2.08, 2.11
Reynolds Metals Co v People, 41 Misc 2d 694, 245 NYS2d 890 (NY 1963), *affd mem*, 259 NYS2d 1006 (1965) §9.30
RG Equip Corp v Gursha, 60 Misc 2d 240, 303 NYS2d 275 (Montgomery 1969) §9.26
RH Baker Co v State, 267 AD 712, 48 NYS2d 272 (3d Dept 1944), *affd*, 294 NY 698, 60 NE2d 847 (1945) §§7.23, 7.38
RH Bowman Assocs v Danskin, 74 Misc 2d 244, 338 NYS2d 224 (Schenectady 1972), *affd mem*, 43 AD2d 621, 349 NYS2d 655 (3d Dept 1973) §11.06
RH Cunningham & Sons Co v State, 52 NYS2d 65 (Ct Cl 1944), *affd*, 270 AD 864, 60 NYS2d 206 (3d Dept 1946) §6.07

RH Macy Co v National Sleep
Prods, 39 NY2d 268, 347 NE2d
887, 383 NYS2d 562 (1976)
§16.12

Rhodes-Haverty, Etc v Robert & Co,
163 Ga App 88, 293 SE2d 876
(1982), *affd*, 250 Ga 680, 300
SE2d 503 (1983) §5.14

Richmond, City of v JA Croson Co,
488 US 469, 109 S Ct 706, 102 L
Ed 2d 854 (1989) §2.35

Ring 57 Corp v Litt, 28 AD2d 548,
280 NYS2d 330 (2d Dept 1967)
§7.02

Riva Ridge Apts v Robert G. Fisher
Co, 745 P2d 1034 (Colo Ct App
1987) §11.17

Robbins v Frank Cooper Assocs, 19
AD2d 242, 241 NYS2d 259 (1st
Dept 1963), *revd on other grounds*,
14 NY2d 913, 200 NE2d 860,
252 NYS2d 318 (1964) §15.40

Robbins v Melbrook Realty Co, 28
Misc 2d 1076, 213 NYS2d 403
(Queens 1961) §8.21

Robert Mfg Co v South Bay Corp,
82 Misc 2d 250, 368 NYS2d 413
(Nassau 1975) §3.31

Robert M. Padden Constr, Inc v
Reitkopf, 146 Misc 2d 272, 550
NYS2d 523 (Suffolk 1989)
§§11.02, 11.03

Rochester, City of v Holmsten Ice
Rinks, Inc, 155 AD2d 939, 548
NYS2d 959 (4th Dept 1989)
§12.10

Rochester, City of v Vanderlinde
Elec Corp, 56 AD2d 185, 392
NYS2d 167 (4th Dept 1977)
§§6.04, 15.01

Rochester Plumbing & Supply Co v
Burgart, Inc, 49 AD2d 78, 370
NYS2d 716 (1975) §2.21

Rockefeller Center, *In re*, 238 AD
736, 265 NYS 546 (1933) §9.36

Rockland Light & Power Co v City
of NY, 289 NY 45, 43 NE2d 803
(1942) §15.08

Rocovich v Consolidated Edison Co,
78 NY2d 509, 577 NYS2d 219
(1991) §13.05

Rodin v Director of Purchasing, 38
Misc 2d 362, 238 NYS2d 2
(Nassau 1963) §2.14

Rosen, *In re*, 172 Misc 134, 13
NYS2d 1019 (Queens 1939)
§9.37

Rosenbaum v Amercian Sur Co, 11
NY2d 310, 183 NE2d 667, 229
NYS2d 375 (1962) §16.12

Rottcamp v Young, 21 AD2d 373,
249 NYS2d 330 (2d Dept 1964),
affd, 15 NY2d 831, 205 NE2d
866, 257 NYS2d 944 (1965)
§12.03

Roy v Poquette, 147 Vt 332, 515
A2d 1072 (1986) §13.15

RS Noonan, Inc v Morrison-
Knudsen Co, 522 F Supp 1182
(ED La 1981) §11.19

Rubin v Coles, 142 Misc 139, 253
NYS 808 (City Ct Kings 1931)
§§12.02, 12.03, 12.06

Rudman v Cowles Communications,
Inc, 30 NY2d 1, 280 NE2d 867,
330 NYS2d 33 (1972) §15.40

Rusciano & Son Corp v State, 201
Misc 690, 110 NYS2d 770 (Ct
Cl), *affd per curiam*, 281 AD 733,
118 NYS2d 77 (3d Dept 1952)
§15.15

Rusciano Constr Corp v State, 37
AD2d 745, 323 NYS2d 21 (3d
Dept 1971) §§5.03, 5.09, 5.10,
5.12, 7.05, 7.24, 7.27, 7.29, 7.49,
7.50

Russin v Louis N. Picciano & Son, 54 NY2d 311, 429 NE2d 805, 445 NYS2d 127 (1981) §§13.07, 13.10

Ryan v City of NY, 159 AD 105, 143 NYS 974 (1st Dept 1913) §§7.37, 15.15

Rye, City of v Public Serv Mut Ins Co, 34 NY2d 470, 315 NE2d 458, 358 NYS2d 391 (1974) §7.72

Rylands v Fletcher, IR 3 HL 330 (1868) §14.32

S

Sablosky v Edwards S. Gordon Co, 73 NY2d 133, 535 NE2d 643, 538 NYS2d 513 (1989), *overruling* Cored Panels, Inc v Meinhard Commercial Corp, 72 AD2d 544, 420 NYS2d 731 (2d Dept 1979) §16.14

Sabol & Rice, Inc v Poughkeepsie Galleria Co, 147 Misc 2d 641, 557 NYS2d 253 (Dutchess 1990), *affd*, 572 NYS2d 811 (3d Dept 1991) §§9.79, 15.12

Samson Elec Co v Buffalo Elec Co, 234 AD 521, 256 NYS 219 (1932) §§8.10, 8.33

S&M Traylor Bros, *In re*, ENG BCA Nos 3878, 3943, 32-1 BCA ¶15,484 §5.02

San Marco Constr Corp v Gillert, 15 Misc 2d 208, 178 NYS2d 137 (Westchester 1958) §§9.26, 9.33

Savin Bros v State, 62 AD2d 511, 405 NYS2d 516 (4th Dept 1978), *affd mem*, 47 NY2d 934, 393 NE2d 1041, 419 NYS2d 969 (1979) §§2.36, 5.03, 5.09, 6.01, 6.02, 6.03, 6.23, 6.34

Savino v Merchants Mut Ins Co, 44 NY2d 625, 378 NE2d 1038, 407 NYS2d 468 (1978) §10.17

Sawyer v Camp Dudley, 102 AD2d 914, 477 NYS2d 498 (1984) §3.28

Sbarro Holding Corp v Lamparter Acoustical Prods, 87 Misc 2d 556, 386 NYS2d 920 (Nassau 1976) §9.33

Scales-Douwes Corp v Paulaura Realty Corp, 24 NY2d 724, 249 NE2d 760, 301 NYS2d 980 (1969) §8.10

Schaff v William C. Maunz Co, 144 AD2d 109, 534 NYS2d 447 (3d Dept 1988) §13.02

Scheck v Francis, 26 NY2d 466, 260 NE2d 493, 311 NYS2d 841 (1970) §2.25

Schenectady Homes Corp v Greenside Painting Corp, 37 NYS2d 53 (Schenectady 1942) §9.22

Schenectady Steel Co v Bruno Trimpoli Gen Constr Co, 43 AD2d 234, 350 NYS2d 920 (3d Dept 1974), *affd mem*, 34 NY2d 939, 316 NE2d 875, 359 NYS2d 560 (1974) §§3.28, 4.08, 4.16

Schiavone Constr Co v County of Nassau, 717 F2d 747 (2d Cir 1983) §2.36

Schiavone Constr Co v Elgood Mayo Corp, 81 AD2d 221, 439 NYS2d 933 (1st Dept 1981), *revd in opinion adopting Silverman, J. dissent*, 56 NY2d 667, 436 NE2d 1322, 451 NYS2d 720 (1982) §§12.03, 12.04, 15.20, 15.35

Schneider v Rola Constr Co, 16 Misc 2d 556, 183 NYS2d 955 (Suffolk 1959) §4.16

Schooley Enters v Paso Contracting Corp, 33 AD2d 981, 307 NYS2d 388 (1970) §§8.26, 8.47

Schreiber Hauling Co v Schwab Bros Trucking, 54 Misc 2d 395, 283 NYS2d 69 (Erie 1967) §9.76

Schroeder v City & County Sav Bank, 293 NY 370, 57 NE2d 57 (1944) §13.17

Schubtex, Inc v Allen Snyder, Inc. 49 NY2d 1, 399 NE2d 1154, 424 NYS2d 133 (1970) §2.50

Schuler-Haas Elec Co v Aetna Casualty & Sur Co, 474 US 494, 106 S Ct 755, 88 L Ed 2d 859 (1986) §3.18

Schuster v City of NY, 5 NY2d 75, 154 NE2d 534, 180 NYS2d 265 (1958) §12.14

Schwadron v Freund, 69 Misc 2d 342, 329 NYS2d 945 (Rockland 1972) §§9.71, 9.73, 9.80

Schwartz v Kuhn, 71 Misc 149, 126 NYS 568 (App Term 1911) §§11.08, 15.34

Schwartz & Co v Aimwell Co, 204 AD 769, 198 NYS 838, *affd*, 236 NY 672, 142 NE 330 (1923) §9.13

SCM Corp v Fisher Park Lane Co, 40 NY2d 788, 358 NE2d 1024, 390 NYS2d 398 (1976), *limited on other grounds*, 428 NYS2d 906 (1980) §16.12

SCM Corp v Hudson Overlook Co, 58 AD2d 578, 395 NYS2d 663 (1977) §9.39

Scribner v Cottone, 284 AD 1007, 135 NYS2d 280 (3d Dept 1954) §6.09

Scriven v Maple Knoll Apts, Inc, 46 AD2d 210, 361 NYS2d 730 (1974) §§9.26, 9.82

Seaboard Pools, Inc v Freeman, 46 Misc 2d 508, 259 NYS2d 999 (Nassau 1965) §9.05

Seaboard Sur Co v Massachusetts Bonding & Ins Co, 17 AD2d 795, 232 NYS2d 809 (1962) §§9.69, 9.70

Seacoast Constr Corp v Lockport Urban Renewal Agency, 72 Misc 2d 372, 339 NYS2d 188 (Erie 1972) §§2.04, 2.15

Sears, Roebuck & Co v Enco Assocs, 83 Misc 2d 552, 370 NYS2d 338 (Westchester 1975), *affd*, 54 AD2d 13, 385 NYS2d 613 (2d Dept 1976), *affd as modified as to unrelated issue*, 43 NY2d 389, 372 NE2d 555, 401 NYS2d 767 (1977) §§2.47, 11.04, 11.23, 12.02, 12.08, 12.12

Security Ins Co v United States, 428 F2d 838 (Ct Cl 1970) §8.49

Security Mut Ins Co v Acker-Fitzsimons Corp, 31 NY2d 436, 293 NE2d 76, 340 NYS2d 902 (1972) §§10.03, 10.15

Seebold v Halmar Constr Corp, 146 AD2d 886, 536 NYS2d 871 (3d Dept 1989) §§6.01, 6.27

Seglin-Harrison Constr Co v State, 267 AD 488, 46 NYS2d 602 (3d Dept), *affd*, 293 NY 782, 58 NE2d 521 (1944) §§6.18, 6.21, 6.23, 6.25, 12.02

Seglin-Harrison Constr Co v State, 30 NYS2d 673 (Ct Cl 1941), *affd as modified on other grounds*, 264 AD 466, 35 NYS2d 940 (1942) §§7.05, 7.23, 7.37, 7.38

Seid, *In re*, 31 Misc 2d 316, 219 NYS2d 962 (Onondaga 1961) §9.35

Selwyn Realty Corp, *In re*, 184 AD 355, 170 NYS 491 (1st Dept), *affd*, 224 NY 559, 120 NE 876 (1918) §§9.37, 9.39

Serena Constr Corp v Valley Drywall Serv, 45 AD2d 896, 357 NYS2d 214 (3d Dept 1974) §4.17

Servidone Constr Corp v Security Ins Co, 64 NY2d 419, 477 NE2d

441, 488 NYS2d 139 (1985) §10.27
Sevenson Envtl Serv v New York State Thruway Auth, 149 AD 504, 134 NYS 39 (1912) §15.23
17 E 80th Realty Corp v 68th Assocs, 173 AD2d 245, 569 NYS2d 647 (1st Dept 1991) §15.11
Seville Iron Works, Inc v Devine Constr Co, 32 Misc 2d 797, 224 NYS2d 321 (Queens 1962) §9.68
Shaheen v IBM Corp, 157 AD2d 429, 557 NYS2d 972 (3d Dept 1990) §§13.03, 13.05
Shalman v Board of Educ, 31 AD2d 338, 297 NYS2d 1000 (3d Dept 1969) §§7.18, 7.23, 7.38, 7.43, 7.52
Shames v Abel, 141 AD2d 531, 529 NYS2d 344 (2d Dept 1988) §2.47
Shank-Artukovich v United States, 13 Cl Ct 346 (1987), affd, 848 F2d 1245 (Fed Cir 1988) §§5.02, 5.14
Shapiro v Board of Regents, 29 AD2d 801, 286 NYS2d 1001 (3d Dept 1968) §11.02
Sharapata v Town of Islip, 56 NY2d 332, 437 NE2d 1104, 452 NYS2d 347 (1982) §§15.12, 15.13
Shawangunk, Town of v Goldwill Properties, Inc, 61 AD2d 693, 403 NYS2d 784 (1978) §§8.02, 8.08
Sherman v Freuhaff, 177 Misc 2d 727, 32 NYS2d 945 (Queens 1941) §9.45
Sherwood Village Coop, Inc v Had-Ten Estates Corp, 29 AD2d 771, 287 NYS2d 921 (2d Dept 1968) §16.16
Shields v City of NY, 84 AD 502, 82 NYS 1020 (1st Dept 1903) §6.01
Shilowitz v Wadler, 237 AD 330, 261 NYS 351 (1932) §§9.52, 9.54

Shore Bridge Corp v State, 186 Misc 1005, 61 NYS2d 32 (Ct Cl), affd, 271 AD 811, 66 NYS2d 921 (1946) §§7.02, 7.59
Sica & Sons v Ciccolo, 39 Misc 2d 698, 241 NYS2d 923 (Westchester 1963) §9.04
Sieburg v Paddell, 134 NYS 403 (NY 1912) §9.36
Silverstein, In re, 30 Misc 2d 510, 219 NYS2d 389 (Queens 1961) §9.74
Simon v Schenectady N Congregation of Jehovah's Witnesses, 132 AD2d 313, 522 NYS2d 343 (3d Dept 1987) §13.06
Sinclairs Deli, Inc v Associated Mut Ins Co, 163 AD2d 296, 559 NYS2d 15 (2d Dept 1990) §10.17
Sinram-Marnis Oil Co v City of NY, 139 AD2d 360, 532 NYS2d 94 (1st Dept 1988), affd, 74 NY2d 13, 542 NE2d 337, 544 NYS2d 119 (1989) §§2.12, 2.33
Siragusa v State, 117 AD2d 986, 499 NYS2d 533 (4th Dept 1986) §§13.03, 13.14
SJ Groves & Sons v LM Pike & Son, 41 AD2d 584, 340 NYS2d 230 (4th Dept 1973) §§2.24, 2.25
Sklar Door Corp v Locoteta Homes, Inc, 33 Misc 2d 299, 224 NYS2d 294 (Nassau 1961) §3.16
Slattery Assocs v City of NY, 98 AD2d 686, 469 NYS2d 758 (1st Dept 1983) §§7.05, 7.11, 7.40
Slattery Contracting Co v State, 56 Misc 2d 111, 288 NYS2d 126 (Ct Cl 1968) §7.28
S. Leo Harmonay, Inc v Binks Mfg Co, 597 F Supp 1014 (SDNY 1984), affd, 762 F2d 990 (2d Cir 1985) §§3.06, 3.09, 7.64
Smathers' Will, In re, 249 AD 523, 293 NYS 314 (2d Dept 1937),

limited on other grounds, 262 NYS2d 352 §11.23

Smith v Fleischman, 23 AD 355, 48 NYS 234 (1897) §9.38

Smith v Jesus People, 113 AD2d 980, 493 NYS2d 658 (3d Dept 1988) §13.05

Smith v Vail, 53 AD 628, 65 NYS 834 (1st Dept 1900), *affd*, 166 NY 611, 59 NE 1125 (1901) §§7.10, 7.12, 7.20

Solow v Bethlehem Steel Corp, 60 AD2d 826, 401 NYS2d 227 (1978) §9.35

Sosnow v Paul, 43 AD2d 978, 352 NYS2d 502 (2d Dept 1974), *affd mem*, 36 NY2d 780, 330 NE2d 643, 369 NYS2d 693 (1975) §11.23

Soundwall Constr Corp v Moncarol Constr Corp, 290 NYS2d 363 (1968) §9.49

Sousie v Williams, 97 Misc 2d 532, 411 NYS2d 861 (Rensselaer 1979) §9.71

Spancrete NE, Inc v Travelers Indem Co, 112 AD2d 571, 491 NYS2d 848, *appeal dismissed*, 66 NY2d 909, 489 NE2d 762, 498 NYS2d 793 (1985) §§8.14, 8.22, 8.29, 8.30

Spano v Perini Corp, 25 NY2d 11, 250 NE2d 31, 302 NYS2d 527 (1969) §§1.25, 12.06

Spears v Berle, 48 NY2d 254, 397 NE2d 1304, 422 NYS2d 636 (1979) §14.34

Spence v Ham, 163 NY 220, 57 NE 412 (1900) §12.03

Sperber v Penn Cent Corp, 150 AD2d 356, 540 NYS2d 877 (2d Dept 1989) §13.08

Sperry v Millar, 23 AD2d 418, 261 NYS2d 566 (3d Dept 1965), *affd mem*, 19 NY2d 644, 225 NE2d 210, 278 NYS2d 616 (1967) §9.35

Spitz v M. Brooks & Sons, 210 AD 438, 206 NYS 313 (1924) §9.44

Sprickerhoff v Gordon, 120 AD 748, 105 NYS 586 (1907), *affd*, 194 NY 77, 88 NE 1132 (1909) §9.26

SSDW Co v Feldman-Mistopoulos Assocs, 151 AD2d 293, 542 NYS2d 565 (1989) §8.52

SSI Investors, Ltd v Korea Tungsten Mining Co, 80 AD2d 155, 438 NYS2d 96 (1981), *affd*, 55 NY2d 934, 434 NE2d 242, 449 NYS2d 173 (1982) §§2.02, 2.22

Stage v Whitehouse, 43 Misc 2d 703, 252 NYS2d 142 (Broome 1964) §2.05

St John's College, Fordham v Aetna Indem Co, 201 NY 335, 94 NE 994 (1911) §8.26

St Paul Fire & Marine Ins Co v State, 99 Misc 2d 140, 415 NYS2d 949 (Ct Cl 1979) §9.71

St Vincent's Medical Center v Vincent E. Iorio, Inc, 78 Misc 2d 968, 358 NYS2d 993 (Richmond 1974) §15.22

Staklinski v Pyramid Elec Co, 6 NY2d 159, 160 NE2d 78, 188 NYS2d 541 (1959) §15.39

Stanley R. Benjamin, Inc v Fidelity & Cas Co, 72 Misc 2d 742, 340 NYS2d 578 (Nassau 1972) §8.28

Staples v Town of Amherst, 146 AD2d 292, 540 NYS2d 926 (4th Dept 1989) §13.05

State v Lang, 84 Misc 2d 106, 375 NYS2d 941 (Sup Ct 1975), *affd*, 52 AD2d 921, 383 NYS2d 400 (2d Dept 1976) §14.34

State v Lundin, 91 AD2d 343, 459 NYS2d 904 (3d Dept), *affd*, 60 NY2d 987, 459 NE2d 486, 471

NYS2d 261 (1983) §§11.23, 11.24, 12.08

State v Malvaney, 221 Miss 190, 72 So 2d 424 (1954) §11.10

State v Monarch Chems, Inc, 90 AD2d 907, 456 NYS2d 867 (1982) §14.04

State v Peerless Ins Co, 108 AD2d 385, 489 NYS2d 213 (1985), *affd,* 67 NY2d 845, 492 NE2d 779, 501 NYS2d 651 (1986) §§8.02, 8.11

State *ex rel* Natl Sur Corp v Malvaney, 221 Miss 190, 72 So 2d 424 (1954) §§8.49, 8.50

Staten Island Supply Co v Beverly-Glenwood Richmond Corp, 96 AD2d 553, 465 NYS2d 232 (2d Dept 1983) §7.02

State Farm Mut Auto Ins Co v Romero, 109 AD2d 786, 486 NYS2d 297 (2d Dept 1985) §10.15

State Univ Constr Fund v United Tech Corp, 78 AD2d 748, 432 NYS2d 653 (3d Dept 1980) §11.22

Steiner v Wenning, 43 NY2d 831, 373 NE2d 366, 402 NYS2d 567 (1977) §§11.04, 11.09

Stewart M. Muller Constr Co v Alvord & Swift, 50 AD2d 572, 375 NYS2d 27 (1975) §9.74

ST Grand, Inc v Cedar Bay Park Corp, 14 Misc 2d 428, 182 NYS2d 747 (NY 1958) §15.10

ST Grand, Inc v City of NY, 32 NY2d 300, 298 NE2d 105, 344 NYS2d 938 (1973) §§2.07, 2.11

Stisling Elec, Inc v Albany Co, 97 AD2d 631, 469 NYS2d 154 (1983) §2.22

Strand Bldg Corp v Russell & Saxe, Inc, 36 Misc 2d 339, 232 NYS2d 384 (Kings 1962), *affd mem,* 240 NYS2d 948 (2d Dept 1963) §4.20

Straus v Buchman, 96 AD 270, 89 NYS 226 (1st Dept 1904), *affd mem,* 184 NY 545, 76 NE 1109 (1906) §11.08

Sturdy Concrete Corp v Nab Constr Corp, 65 AD2d 262, 411 NYS2d 637 (2d Dept 1978), *appeal dismissed,* 46 NY2d 938, 388 NE2d 349, 415 NYS2d 212 (1979), *appeal after remand,* 89 AD2d 588, 452 NYS2d 252 (1982) §§3.12, 3.20, 6.34

Stuyvesant Dredging Co v United States, 11 Cl Ct 853, *affd,* 834 F2d 1576 (Fed Cir 1987) §§5.07, 5.13, 5.16

Suffolk County Water Auth v JD Posillico, Inc, 145 AD2d 623, 536 NYS2d 149 (2d Dept 1988) §12.08

Sullivan Highway Prods Corp v Edward L. Nezelek, Inc, 52 AD2d 986, 383 NYS2d 463 (1976) §§8.32, 8.40

Sun Ins Co v Diversified Engrs, Inc, 240 F Supp 606 (D Mont 1965) §8.43

Superior Hydraulics, Inc v Town Bd, 88 AD2d 404, 453 NYS2d 711 (1982) §8.05

Susskind v 1136 Tenants Corp, 43 Misc 2d 588, 251 NYS2d 321 (Civ Ct NY 1964) §9.12

Sutton v East River Sav Bank, 55 NY2d 550, 435 NE2d 1075, 450 NYS2d 460, (1982) §2.47

Syracuse, City of v Sarkisian Bros, 87 AD2d 984, 451 NYS2d 945, *affd,* 57 NY2d 618, 439 NE2d 880, 454 NYS2d 71 (1982) §8.07

T

Tager v Healy Ave Realty Corp, 14 AD2d 584, 218 NYS2d 679 (1961) §9.66

Tanglewood E Homeowners v Charles-Thomas, Inc, 849 F2d 1568 (5th Cir 1988) §14.37

Tarelton Bldg Corp v Spider Staging Sales Co, 26 AD2d 809, 274 NYS2d 43 (1st Dept 1966) §§4.20, 15.40

Taylor & Jennings, Inc v Bellino Bros Constr Co, 106 AD2d 779, 483 NYS2d 813 (1984) §8.27

Taylor & Jennings, Inc v Bellino Bros Constr Co, 57 AD2d 42, 393 NYS2d 203 (1977) §8.30

Taylor-Fichter Steel Constr Co v Niagara Frontier Bridge Commn, 261 AD 288, 25 NYS2d 437 (1st Dept), *affd*, 287 NY 669, 39 NE2d 290 (1941) §7.38

Taylor-Warner Corp v Minskoff, 167 AD2d 382, 561 NYS2d 797 (2d Dept 1990) §4.04

Teal v Place, 85 AD2d 788, 445 NYS2d 309 (3d Dept 1981) §§2.48, 2.49

Tebbutt v Niagara Mohawk Power Corp, 124 AD2d 266, 508 NYS2d 69 (3d Dept 1986) §§2.25, 2.33

Tech Heating & Mechanical, Inc v First Downstream Serv Corp, 126 Misc 2d 85, 481 NYS2d 201 (NY 1984) §9.05

Technicon Elecs Corp v Amercian Home Assurance Co, 141 AD2d 124, 533 NYS2d 91 (2d Dept 1988), *affd*, 74 NY2d 66, 542 NE2d 1048, 544 NYS2d 531 (1989) §14.22

Tedesco v Niagara Power Corp, 142 AD2d 932, 530 NYS2d 357 (1988) §3.13

Teman Bros v New York Plumbers' Specialties Co, 109 Misc 2d 197, 444 NYS2d 337 (NY 1981) §§9.68, 9.72, 9.83

Tempo, Inc v Rapid Elec Sales & Serv, 132 Mich App 93, 347 NW2d 728 (1984) §15.19

Tenney Engg, Inc v United Elec Radio & Mach Workers of Am, Local 437, 207 F2d 450 (3d Cir 1953) §16.13

Tenney Engg, Inc, ASBCA 7352, 1962 BCA ¶6189 §6.16

Terlinde v Neely, 275 SC 395, 271 SE2d 768 (1980) §12.14

Terry Contracting, Inc v State, 42 AD2d 619, 344 NYS2d 583 (3d Dept 1973) §7.09

TGI E Coast Constr Corp v Fireman's Fund Ins Co, 534 F Supp 780 (SDNY 1982) §3.23

Thomas Crimmins Contracting Co v City of NY, 74 NY2d 166, 542 NE2d 1097, 544 NYS2d 580 (1989) §§6.23, 16.04

Thomason & Perry, Inc v State, 38 AD2d 609, 326 NYS2d 246 (3d Dept 1971), *affd*, 30 NY2d 836, 286 NE2d 465, 335 NYS2d 81 (1972) §§7.34, 7.35

Thomassen v J&K Diner, Inc, 152 AD2d 421, 549 NYS2d 416 (2d Dept 1989), *appeal dismissed*, 76 NY2d 771, 559 NE2d 673, 559 NYS2d 979 (1990) §§12.02, 12.03, 12.11

Thompson v New York Dept of Envtl Conservation, 130 Misc 2d 123, 495 NYS2d 107, *affd*, 132 AD2d 665, 518 NYS2d 36, *appeal denied*, 71 NY2d 803, 522 NE2d 1067, 527 NYS2d 769 (1988) §14.34

Thompson v Taylor, 72 NY 32 (1878) §8.48

Thompson Water Works Co v Diamond, 44 AD2d 487, 356 NYS2d 130 (4th Dept 1974) §15.01

Thrasher v United States Liab Ins Co, 19 NY2d 159, 225 NE2d 503, 278 NYS2d 793 (1967) §10.29

Tibbetts Contracting Corp v O&E Contracting Co, 15 NY2d 324, 206 NE2d 340, 258 NYS2d 400 (1965) §§7.05, 7.08, 9.05

Timberline Elec Supply Corp v Insurance Co of N Am, 72 AD2d 905, 421 NYS2d 987 (1979), *affd,* 52 NY2d 793, 417 NE2d 1248, 436 NYS2d 707 (1980) §§8.10, 8.28

Ting-Wan Liang v Malawista, 70 AD2d 415, 421 NYS2d 594 (2d Dept 1979) §§12.07, 12.12

Tisdale Lumber Co v Read Realty Co, 154 AD 270, 138 NYS 829 (1912) §9.03

TJ Picozzi Constr Co v Exchange Mut Ins Co, 138 AD2d 907, 526 NYS2d 652 (3d Dept 1988) §§10.09, 10.27

TJW Corp v Board of High Educ, 251 AD 405, 296 NYS 693 (1st Dept 1937), *affd,* 276 NY 644, 12 NE2d 800 (1938) §5.08

TNT Coatings, Inc v Nassau, 114 AD2d 1027, 495 NYS2d 466 (1985) §9.05

Tombigbee Constructors v United States, 420 F2d 1037 (Ct Cl 1970) §6.22

Toop v Smith, 181 NY 283, 73 NE 1113 (1905) §9.26

Topping v Swords, 1 ED Smith 609 (CP 1852) §§2.17, 2.22

Torncello v United States, 681 F2d 756 (Ct Cl 1982) §4.04

Tougher Heating & Plumbing Co v State, 73 AD2d 732, 423 NYS2d 289 (3d Dept 1979) §§1.22, 2.47

TPK Constr Co v O'Shea, 69 AD2d 316, 419 NYS2d 279 (3d Dept 1979), *affd mem,* 50 NY2d 835, 407 NE2d 1331, 430 NYS2d 34 (1980) §§15.03, 15.04

Trafalgar Square, Ltd v Reeves Bros, 35 AD2d 194, 315 NYS2d 239 (1970) §§3.29, 3.35, 16.14

Transamerica Ins Co v Yonkers Contracting Co, 49 Misc 2d 512, 267 NYS2d 669 (NY 1966) §§3.06, 16.16

Travelers Indem Co v Buffalo Motor & Generator Co, 58 AD2d 978, 397 NYS2d 257 (1977) §8.06

Travelers Indem Co v Central Trust Co, 47 Misc 2d 849, 263 NYS2d 261 (Monroe 1965), *affd,* 27 AD2d 803 (4th Dept 1967) §9.80

Travers v Kronenberg's, Inc, 32 Misc 2d 141, 230 NYS2d 768 (Erie 1961) §9.74

Travis v Nansen, 176 Misc 44, 26 NYS2d 590 (Broome 1941) §9.56

Trentacosti v Materesa, 67 AD2d 1025, 413 NYS2d 236 (3d Dept 1979) §12.03

Triangle Erectors, Inc v James King & Son, 41 Misc 2d 12, 244 NYS2d 433 (Suffolk 1963) §8.40

Triangle Sheet Metal Works, Inc v James H. Merritt & Co, 79 NY2d 801, 588 NE2d 69, 580 NYS2d 171 (1991) §§3.22, 3.23

Triangle Steel, Inc v Sarkisian Bros, 70 AD2d 698, 416 NYS2d 391, *appeal denied,* 47 NY2d 710, 393 NE2d 1050, 419 NYS2d 1027 (1979) §§5.05, 5.07

Triangle Underwriters, Inc v Honeywell, Inc, 604 F2d 737 (2d Cir 1979) §3.28

Tri-City Elec Co v People, 96 AD2d 146, 468 NYS2d 283 (1983) §9.70

Tri-Mar Contractors, Inc v Itco Drywall, Inc, 74 AD2d 601, 424 NYS2d 737 (2d Dept 1980) §§4.17, 4.21, 15.26

Trimpoli v State, 20 AD2d 933, 249 NYS2d 154 (3d Dept 1964) §§6.01, 6.02, 6.04

Trinity Universal Ins Co v United States, 382 F2d 317 (5th Cir 1967), *cert denied*, 390 US 906 (1968) §8.49

Triple M Roofing Corp v Greater Jericho Corp, 43 AD2d 594, 349 NYS2d 771 (2d Dept 1973) §§4.07, 4.08, 4.13, 15.26

Tri-Quality Mechanical Corp v Chappastream Corp, 138 AD2d 610, 526 NYS2d 194 (1988) §9.33

Troy Pub Works v City of Yonkers, 207 NY 81, 100 NE 700 (1912) §9.19

Truax & Hovey, Ltd v Aetna Cas & Sur Co, 122 AD2d 563, 504 NYS2d 934 (4th Dept 1986) §10.18

Trustees of Columbia Univ v Mitchell/Giurgola Assocs, 109 AD2d 449, 492 NYS2d 371 (1st Dept 1985) §12.10

Trustees of Hanover Square Realty Investors v Weintraub, 52 AD2d 600, 382 NYS2d 110 (1976) §§9.34, 9.36, 9.50

Tufano Contracting Co v State, 25 AD2d 329, 269 NYS2d 564 (3d Dept 1966), *affd*, 26 NY2d 823, 257 NE2d 901, 309 NYS2d 355 (1970) §6.27

Tufano Contracting Corp v Port of NY Auth, 18 AD2d 1001, 238 NYS2d 607 (2d Dept), *affd mem*, 13 NY2d 848, 192 NE2d 270, 242 NYS2d 489 (1963) §§6.23, 6.25

Tufano Contracting Corp v Port of NY Auth, 33 Misc 2d 1028, 227 NYS2d 707 (Queens 1962), *affd*, 18 AD2d 832, 237 NYS2d 562 (2d Dept 1963) §6.33

Tufaro Transit Co v Board of Educ, 79 AD2d 376, 436 NYS2d 886 (1981) §§2.13, 2.22

Tully & DiNapoli, Inc v State, 34 AD2d 439, 311 NYS2d 941 (3d Dept 1970) §7.50

Tumac Realty Corp, *In re*, 203 Misc 649, 123 NYS2d 642 (Kings 1952) §9.36

Tupper v Wade Lupe Constr Co, 39 Misc 2d 1053, 242 NYS2d 546 (Schenectady 1963) §§4.08, 7.02, 7.30, 7.73

Turk v Look, 53 AD2d 709, 383 NYS2d 937 (3d Dept 1976) §§4.13, 4.17, 6.34, 12.03

Twin County Transit Mix, Inc v Ingula Builders Corp, 27 AD2d 939, 278 NYS2d 990 (1967) §9.26

Twin Village Constr Corp v State, 53 NY2d 724, 421 NE2d 827, 439 NYS2d 335 (1981) §§5.08, 5.14

Tynan Incinerator Co v International Fidelity Ins Co, 117 AD2d 796, 499 NYS2d 118 (1986) §§8.13, 8.18, 8.21, 8.23, 8.29

U

Ulster Elec Supply Co v Maryland Cas Co, 35 AD2d 309, 316 NYS2d 159 (1970), *affd*, 30 NY2d 712, 283 NE2d 622, 332 NYS2d 648 (1972) §§8.25, 8.40

Umbaugh Builders, Inc v Parr Co, 86 Misc 2d 1036, 385 NYS2d 698 (Suffolk 1976) §§9.01, 9.05

Union Free School Dist No 1 v Gumbs, 20 Misc 2d 315, 191 NYS2d 183 (Suffolk 1958) §2.19

United Nations Dev Corp v Norkin Plumbing Co, 45 NY2d 358, 380 NE2d 253, 408 NYS2d 424 (1978) §16.15

United States v Conservation Chem Co, 628 F Supp 391 (WD Mo 1985) §14.39

United States v Dickerson, 640 F Supp 448 (D Md 1986) §14.39

United States v Fidelity & Deposit, 690 F Supp 905 (D Haw 1988) §8.46

United States v Frezzo Bros, 602 F2d 1123 (3d Cir 1979), *cert denied*, 444 US 1074 (1980) §14.37

United States v Glens Falls Ins Co, 534 F Supp 109 (NDNY 1981) §8.15

United States v Johnson & Towers, 741 F2d 662 (3d Cir 1984), *cert denied*, 469 US 1208, 105 S Ct 1171, 84 L Ed 321 (1985) §14.37

United States v Maryland Bank & Trust Co, 632 F Supp 573 (D Md §14.39

United States v Munsey Trust Co, 332 US 234, 67 S Ct 1599, 91 L Ed 2022 (1947) §§3.21, 8.49

United States v Northeastern Pharmaceutical & Chem Co, 810 F2d 726 (8th Cir 1986), *cert denied*, 484 US 848, 108 S Ct 146 (1987) §14.37

United States v Park, 421 US 658 95 S Ct 1903, 44 L Ed 2d 489 (1975) §14.37

United States v Pollution Abatement Servs, 763 F2d 133 (2d Cir), *cert denied*, 474 US 1037, 106 S Ct 605 (1985) §14.37

United States v Price, 523 F Supp 1055 (DNJ 1981), *affd*, 688 F2d 204 (3d Cir 1982) §14.26

United States v Rice, 317 US 61, 63 S Ct 120, 87 L Ed 53 (1942) §§6.01, 6.29, 8.46

United States v Scardi, 20 Envt Rep Cas (BNA) 1753 (DNC 1984) §14.37

United States v Seaboard Sur Co, 817 F2d 956 (2d Cir), *cert denied*, 484 US 855, 108 S Ct 161 (1987) §§1.16, 8.03

United States v Spearin, 248 US 132 (1918) §2.36

United States v Wade, 577 F Supp 1326 (ED Pa 1983) §14.37

United States *ex rel* Consol Pipe & Supply Co v Morrison-Knudsen Co, 687 F2d 129 (6th Cir 1982) §8.44

United States *ex rel* Edwards v Thompson Constr Corp, 273 F2d 873 (2d Cir 1959), *cert denied*, 362 US 951, 80 S Ct 864, 4 L Ed 2d 869 (1960) §8.45

United States *ex rel* Harris Paint Co v Seaboard Sur Co, 437 F2d 37 (5th Cir 1971) §8.45

United States *ex rel* Hasco Elec Corp v Reliance Ins Co, 390 F Supp 158 (EDNY 1975) §8.44

United States *ex rel* I. Burack, Inc v Sovereign Constr Co, 338 F Supp 657 (SDNY 1972) §§8.45, 8.46

United States *ex rel* JA Edward & Co v Peter Reiss Constr Co, 273 F2d 880 (2d Cir 1959), *cert denied*, 362 US 951, 80 S Ct 864, 4 L Ed 2d 869 (1960) §§8.40, 8.45

United States *ex rel* JP Byrne & Co v Fire Assoc, 260 F2d 541 (2d Cir 1958) §8.46

United States *ex rel* Magna Masonry, Inc v RT Woodfield, Inc, 709 F2d 249 (4th Cir 1983) §§8.40, 8.45

United States *ex rel* Mariana v Piracci Constr Co, 405 F Supp 904 (DDC 1975) §8.46

United States *ex rel* Otis Elevator Co v Piracci Constr Co, 405 F Supp 908 (DDC 1975) §8.46

United States *ex rel* Powers Regulator Co v Hartford Accident & Indem Co, 376 F2d 811 (1st Cir 1967) §8.44

United States *ex rel* Sherman v Carter, 353 US 210, 77 S Ct 793, 1 L Ed 2d 776 (1957) §8.46

United States *ex rel* Wellman Engg Co v MSI Corp, 350 F2d 285 (2d Cir 1965) §8.44

United States Fidelity & Guar Co v A&A Mach Shop, Inc, 330 F Supp 1403 (SD Tex 1971) §8.43

United States Fidelity & Guar Co v Amercian State Bank, 372 F2d 449 (10th Cir 1967) §8.43

United States Steel Corp v Missouri Pac RR, 668 F2d 435 (8th Cir 1982) §§7.23, 7.38, 7.43

United States Steel Corp v Turner Constr Co, 560 F Supp 871 (SDNY 1983) §3.06

Unity Sheet Metal Works, Inc v Farrell Lines, Inc, 101 NYS2d 1000 (NY 1950), *revd*, 108 NYS2d 919 (1st Dept 1951), *affd*, 304 NY 639, 107 NE2d 164 (1952) §11.10

University Casework Sys v Bahre, 172 Ind App 624, 362 NE2d 155 (1977) §16.13

Upstate Builders Supply Corp, *In re*, 63 Misc 2d 35, 310 NYS2d 862 (Onondaga 1970) §§9.26, 9.33

US Indus, Inc v Blake Constr Co, 671 F2d 539 (DC Cir 1982) §7.43

Utica Plumbing Supply Co v Home Owner's Loan Corp, 267 AD 779, 45 NYS2d 452 (1943) §9.05

V

Valente v Two Guys from Harrison, NY, Inc, 35 AD2d 862, 315 NYS2d 220 (3d Dept 1970) §§6.03, 6.08

Van Amerogen v Donnini, 78 NY2d 880, 573 NYS2d 443 (1991) §13.09

Van Clif v Van Vechten, 130 NY 571, 29 NE 1017 (1892) §§9.34, 9.50

VanDeloo v Moreland, 84 AD2d 871, 444 NYS2d 744 (3d Dept 1981) §§12.03, 12.07, 15.28

Vanderlinde Elec Corp v City of Rochester, 54 AD2d 155, 388 NYS2d 388 (1976) §§7.17, 7.18, 7.33, 16.02

Vanoni v New York State Gas & Elec Corp, 141 Misc 2d 680, 533 NYS2d 846 (Niagara 1988) §13.05

Van Opdorp v Merchants Mut Ins Co, 55 AD2d 810, 390 NYS2d 279 (4th Dept 1976) §10.29

Vaughn v Rosen, 484 F2d 820 (DC Cir 1973), *cert denied*, 415 US 977 (1974) §16.03

VC Vitanza Sons v Murray, 90 Misc 2d 873, 396 NYS2d 305 (Albany 1977) §2.09

Vereinigte Osterreichische Eisen & Stahlwerke, AG v Modular Bldg & Dev Corp, 64 Misc 2d 1050, 316 NYS2d 812 (NY 1970), *affd as modified*, 37 AD2d 525, 322

NYS2d 976 (1st Dept 1971) §11.02

Victor v Turner, 113 AD2d 490, 496 NYS2d 761 (2d Dept 1985) §10.17

Video Corp of Am v Frederick Flatto Assocs, 58 NY2d 1026, 448 NE2d 1350, 462 NYS2d 439 (1983) §12.08

Vigliarolo Bros v Lanza Contracting Corp, 127 Misc 2d 965, 487 NYS2d 979 (Civ Ct NY 1985) §§8.39, 8.40

Vincenty v Davis, 43 AD2d 534, 349 NYS2d 376 (1st Dept 1973) §13.05

V. Zappala & Co v Pyramid Co, 81 AD2d 983, 439 NYS2d 765 (1981) §3.31

W

Walcutt v Clevite Corp, 13 NY2d 48, 191 NE2d 894, 241 NYS2d 834, *remittur amended*, 13 NY2d 903, 193 NE2d 511, 242, NYS2d 903 (1963) §8.30

Waldman v New Phone Dimensions, Inc, 109 AD2d 702, 487 NYS2d 29 (1st Dept 1985) §2.47

Walentas v New York City Dept of Ports, 167 AD2d 211, 561 NYS2d 718 (1st Dept 1990) §16.01

Walker v Sheldon, 10 NY2d 401, 179 NE2d 497, 223 NYS2d 488 (1961) §15.12

Walsh v Morse Diesel, Inc, 143 AD2d 653, 533 NYS2d 80 (2d Dept 1988) §§3.13, 13.18

Walter v Horowitz, 60 NYS2d 327 (Westchester), *affd*, 271 AD 802, 65 NYS2d 672 (2d Dept 1946) §6.07

Walter A. Stanley & Son v Trustees of Hackley School, 42 NY2d 436, 366 NE2d 1339, 397 NYS2d 985 (1977) §16.14

Walter E. Heller & Co v American Flyers Airline Corp, 459 F2d 896 (2d Cir 1972) §7.72

Walter Sign Corp v State, 31 AD2d 729, 297 NYS2d 45 (4th Dept 1968) §§7.05, 7.10, 7.26

Wappinger, Town of v Republic Ins Co, 89 AD2d 621, 452 NYS2d 674 (1982) §8.48

Warebak Realty Corp v Enros Constr Co, 39 Misc 2d 298, 240 NYS2d 193 (1963) §9.74

Waring v Burke Steel Co, 69 NYS2d 399 (Monroe 1947) §9.04

Warren Bros Co v Craner, 30 AD2d 437, 293 NYS2d 763 (1968) §§2.08, 2.15

Warren Bros Co v New York State Thruway Auth, 34 AD2d 97, 309 NYS2d 450 (3d Dept 1970), *affd*, 34 NY2d 770, 314 NE2d 878, 358 NYS2d 139 (1974) §§2.36, 5.03, 5.08, 5.10, 5.13

Warwick, Village of v Republic Ins Co, 104 Misc 2d 514, 428 NYS2d 589 (Orange 1980) §§8.14, 8.25

Waters v Glasheen, 103 AD2d 1043, 478 NYS2d 437 (4th Dept 1984) §§4.17, 15.26

Wayne County Vinegar & Cider Corp v Schorr's Famous Pickled Prods, 118 Misc 2d 52, 460 NYS2d 209 (Kings 1983) §7.60

Wear v Koehler, 168 AD 115, 153 NYS 773 (1st Dept 1915) §1.26

Websco Constr Corp v State, 57 Misc 2d 9, 292 NYS2d 315 (Ct Cl 1966) §7.23

Webster v Culver Roadways, Inc, 79 Misc 2d 256, 359 NYS2d 863 (Monroe 1974) §7.70

Wedinger v Goldberger, 71 NY2d 428, 522 NE2d 25, 527 NYS2d

180, *cert denied*, 488 US 850 (1988) §14.34

Weeks Dredging & Contracting, Inc v United States, 13 Cl Ct 193 (1987), *affd mem*, 861 F2d 728 (Fed Cir 1988) §§5.13, 5.14

Welch v Grant Dev Co, 120 Misc 2d 493, 466 NYS2d 112 (Bronx 1983) §§11.08, 13.11, 13.15

Wells & Newton Co v Craig, 232 NY 125, 133 NE 419 (1921) §7.39

Welsch v Gindell & Johnson, 50 AD2d 971, 376 NYS2d 661 (3d Dept 1975) §6.32

Westcott v State, 264 AD 463, 36 NYS2d 23 (3d Dept 1942) §§6.04, 6.29, 7.49

Westerhold v Carroll, 199 F Supp 951 (D Minn 1961) §8.50

Westmount Intl Hotels, Inc v Sear-Brown Assocs, 65 NY2d 618, 480 NE2d 739, 491 NYS2d 150 (1985) §11.04

Weston v State, 262 NY 46, 186 NE 197, 88 ALR 1219 (1933) §§5.01, 5.03, 5.09, 5.11, 5.16

Westpac Banking Corp v Deschamps, 66 NY2d 16, 484 NE2d 1351, 494 NYS2d 848 (1985) §8.50

West, Weir & Bartel, Inc v Mary Carter Paint Co, 25 NY2d 535, 255 NE2d 709, 307 NYS2d 449 (1969), *remittitur amended*, 26 NY2d 969, 259 NE2d 483, 311 NYS2d 13 (1970) §2.48

Whitacre Constr Specialties, Inc v Aetna Cas & Sur Co, 86 AD2d 972, 448 NYS2d 287 (1982), *affd*, 57 NY2d 1018, 443 NE2d 953, 457 NYS2d 479 (1984) §8.28

White v Empire Mut Ins, 59 Misc 2d 527, 299 NYS2d 998 (Civ Ct 1969) §16.07

Whitmore v Fago, NYS2d 672 (Steuben 1949) §1.26

Whitmyer Bros v State, 63 AD2d 103, 406 NYS2d 617 (3d Dept 1978), *affd mem*, 47 NY2d 960, 393 NE2d 1027, 419 NYS2d 954 (1979) §§3.23, 6.02, 6.25, 7.49, 7.52, 15.19

Whitney Bros Plumbing & Heating, Inc, ASBCA 16876, 72-1 BCA 9448 (1972) §6.18

Wikarski v State, 91 AD2d 1174, 459 NYS2d 143 (4th Dept 1983) §15.08

Wilder v Crook, 250 Ala 424, 34 So 2d 832 (1938) §11.11

Willets Point Contracting Corp v Hartford Ins Group, 75 AD2d 254, 429 NYS2d 230 (2d Dept 1980), *affd mem*, 53 NY2d 881, 423 NE2d 42, 440 NYS2d 619 (1981) §§10.27, 10.31

Willets Point Contracting Corp v Town Bd, 141 AD2d 735, 529 NYS2d 592, *appeal denied*, 72 NY2d 810, 534 NYS2d 938 (1988) §2.05

William Iselin & Co v Landau, 71 NY2d 420, 522 NE2d 21, 527 NYS2d 176 (1988) §8.50

William J. Morris, Inc v Lanzilotta & Teramo Constr Corp, 63 AD2d 969, 405 NYS2d 508 (1978), *affd*, 47 NY2d 901, 393 NE2d 488, 419 NYS2d 494 (1979) §8.07

Williamson & Adams, Inc v McMahon-McEntegart, Inc, 256 AD 313, 10 NYS2d 37 (1939) §9.60

Williams Press, Inc v State, 45 AD2d 397, 357 NYS2d 920 (3d Dept 1974) §3.21

William S. Van Clief & Sons v City of NY, 141 Misc 216, 252 NYS 402 (NY 1931) §8.10

Willoughby Roofing & Supply Co v Kajima Intl, Inc, 776 F2d 269 (11th Cir 1985) §16.12

Wilson & English Constr Co v New York Cent RR Co, 240 AD 479, 269 NYS 874 (2d Dept 1934) §§7.35, 7.37

Wilton Coach Co v Central High School Dist No 3, 36 Misc 2d 637, 232 NYS2d 876 (Nassau 1962) §2.10

Wineman v Blueprint 100, Inc, 75 Misc 2d 665, 348 NYS2d 721 (Civ Ct NY 1973) §§11.02, 11.03

WL Waples Co v State, 178 AD 357, 164 NYS 797 (3d Dept 1917) §7.38

Wolf v Amercian Tract Socy, 164 NY 30, 58 NE 31 (1900) §13.17

Wolf v New York State Elec & Gas Corp, 142 Misc 2d 774, 538 NYS2d 188 (Niagara 1989) §13.03

Wolff & Munier, Inc v Whiting-Turner Contracting Co, 946 F2d 1003 (2d Cir 1991) §7.44

Wormuth v Lower Eastside Action Project, Inc, 71 Misc 2d 314, 335 NYS2d 896 (App Term 1st Dept 1972) §§11.02, 11.03

WPC Enter v United States 323 F2d 894 (Ct Cl 1963) §6.16

Wrecking Corp of Am v Memorial Hosp for Cancer & Allied Diseases, 63 AD2d 615, 405 NYS2d 83 (1st Dept), *appeal dismissed*, 45 NY2d 774, 380 NE2d 335, 408 NYS2d 509 (1978) §§5.07, 5.08, 5.13

Wright v Belt Assocs, Inc, 14 NY2d 129, 198 NE2d 590, 249 NYS2d 416 (1964) §13.04

Wright & Kremers, Inc v State, 263 NY 615, 189 NE 724 (1934) §7.37

Wynkoop v Mintz, 17 Misc 2d 1093, 192 NYS2d 428 (Kings 1958) §9.81

X

XLO Concrete Corp v John T. Brady & Co, 104 AD2d 181, 482 NYS2d 476 (1st Dept 1984), *affd mem*, 66 NY2d 970, 489 NE2d 768, 498 NYS2d 799 (1985) §§2.47, 7.72

Y

Yaeger v New York Tel Co, 148 AD2d 308, 538 NYS2d 526 (1st Dept 1989) §§13.03, 13.05, 13.06

Yager v Rubymar Corp, 34 Misc 2d 704, 216 NYS2d 577 (Kings 1961) §2.47

Yeroush Corp v Nhaissi, 164 AD2d 891, 559 NYS2d 569 (2d Dept 1990), *affd*, 78 NY2d 873, 573 NYS2d 65 (1991) §15.15

Yeshiva Univ v Fidelity & Deposit Co, 116 AD2d 49, 500 NYS2d 241 (1986) §8.28

Yonkers Contracting Co v New York State Thruway Auth, 25 AD2d 811, 270 NYS2d 16 (4th Dept 1966), *affd*, 23 NY2d 856, 245 NE2d 800, 298 NYS2d 67 (1969) §§6.03, 6.27

York Concrete Corp v Northwood Projects, Inc, 57 AD2d 950, 395 NYS2d 98 (1977) §8.28

York Corp v 1955 Assocs, 20 AD2d 538, 245 NYS2d 131 (1963) §9.70

Young v Casabonne Bros, 145 AD2d 244, 538 NYS2d 348 (3d Dept 1989) §13.05

Young v Whitney, 111 AD2d 1013, 490 NYS2d 330 (3d Dept 1985) §§4.08, 7.02

Young Fehlhaber Pile Co v State, 265 AD 61, 37 NYS2d 928 (3d Dept 1942) §§2.50, 5.03, 5.08, 5.09, 5.12, 5.13, 5.14

Z

Zadek v Olds, Wortman & King, 166 AD 60, 151 NYS 634 (1st Dept 1915) §§4.02, 4.12, 4.14, 15.10

Zahn v Pauker, 107 AD2d 118, 486 NYS2d 422 (3d Dept 1985) §13.09

Zandri Constr Co v Firemen's Ins Co, 81 AD2d 106, 440 NYS2d 353 (3d Dept), *affd mem*, 54 NY2d 999, 430 NE2d 922, 446 NYS2d 45 (1981) §§10.18, 10.19

Zara Contracting Co v Cohen, 45 Misc 2d 497, 257 NYS2d 479 (Albany 1964), *affd*, 23 AD2d 718, 257 NYS2d 118 (3d Dept 1965) §§2.04, 15.04

Zimmer v Chemung County Performing Arts, Inc, 65 NY2d 513, 482 NE2d 898, 493 NYS2d 102 (1985) §§13.05, 13.14

Zipp v Fidelity & Deposit Co, 73 AD 20, 76 NYS 386 (1902) §8.35

Zuckerman v Board of Educ, In re 44 NY2d 336, 376 NE2d 1297, 405 NYS2d 652 (1978) §15.08

Zulferino v State Farm Auto Ins Co, 123 AD2d 432, 506 NYS2d 736 (2d Dept 1986) §10.17

Philip Zweig & Sons v Tuscarora Constr Co, 50 AD2d 1069, NYS2d 761 (4th Dept 1975) §7.07

Statutes

United States Code

5 USC §522a §14.36
5 USC §552 §§14.36, 16.03
5 USC §552(b) §14.36
9 USC §1 et seq §16.13
9 USC §2 §16.13
9 USC §10 §16.11
11 USC §365 §4.11
15 USC §2641 et seq §14.29
18 USC §1001 §14.37
26 USC §6323 §9.56
28 USC §1295 et seq §7.60
29 USC §651 et seq §13.19
29 USC §653(b)(4) §13.19
30 USC §401(1) §9.01
33 USC §1251 et seq §§14.04, 14.05
33 USC §1317(a) §14.05
33 USC §1344(g)(1) §14.34
39 USC §401 et seq §8.43
40 USC §270(b) §8.43
40 USC §§270a-270f §§8.40, 8.43
40 USC §§270a §9.01
40 USC §270a(a)(1) §8.43
40 USC §270a(a)(2) §8.43
40 USC §270a(b) §8.43
40 USC §270a(c) §8.43
40 USC §270a(d) §8.46
40 USC §270b(a) §8.45
40 USC §270b(b) §8.45
40 USC §270e §8.43
40 USC §270f §8.43
41 USC §601 et seq §16.11
42 USC §6298(d)(3) §14.37
42 USC §6926 et seq §14.04
42 USC §§6991-6991(i) §14.33
42 USC §§7401-7642 §14.05
42 USC §7413 §14.37
42 USC §9601(14) §14.39
42 USC §9601(21) §14.37
42 USC §9601(35)(B) §14.09
42 USC §9603 §14.37
42 USC §9607 §14.39
42 USC §9607(a) §14.37
42 USC §9607(b) §14.39
42 USC §9607(b)(3) §14.39
42 USC §9607(e)(1) §14.39
42 USC §9612 §14.37
42 USC §9622(h)(2) §14.42
45 USC §51 et seq §13.02
46 USC §1101 et seq §8.43
49 USC §§1671-1684 §1.27
50 USC app §1735 et seq §8.43

State Statutes

NY Canal Law §30(6) (McKinney 1939 & Supp 1992) §8.32
NY Canal Law §32 §4.04

NY City Admin Code §20-387 (1991) §§1.24, 2.28
NY City Admin Code §26-142 (1986) §1.24
NY City Admin Code §26-154 (1986) §1.24
NY City Admin Code §26-166 (1986) §1.24
NY City Admin Code §27-132(a) (1991) §1.28
NY City Admin Codes §27-198.1 §14.31
NY City Admin Code §27-586, Tables 10-1, 10-2 §1.28
NY City Admin Code §27-721 §1.28
NY City Admin Code §27-724 §1.28
NY City Admin Code §27-730 (1986) §12.02
NY City Admin Code §27-3017 (1986) §1.24
NY City Admin Code §§C26-71.0(b), §1.26
NY City Admin Code §C26-118.9 §14.28
NY City Admin code §C26-1903.1(b)(1) §1.26
NY City Admin Code §C26-1903.1(b)(2) §1.26
NY City Charter §643 (1990) §1.28
NY Civ Prac L & R 201 (McKinney 1990 & Supp 1992) §11.23
NY Civ Prac L & R 213 (McKinney 1990 & Supp 1992) §§10.28, 12.12
NY Civ Prac L & R 213(2) (McKinney 1990 & Supp 1992) §8.28
NY Civ Prac L & R 214 (McKinney 1990 & Supp 1992) §11.23
NY Civ Prac L & R 214(4) (McKinney 1990) §11.23
NY Civ Prac L & R 214(6) (McKinney 1990 & Supp 1992) §11.23
NY Civ Prac L & R 304 §9.39

NY Civ Prac L & R 1401 (McKinney 1976 & Supp 1992) §§12.10, 15.20
NY Civ Prac L & R 1402 (McKinney 1976 & Supp 1992) §12.10
NY Civ Prac L & R 3001 (McKinney 1991 & Supp 1992) §15.08
NY Civ Prac L & R 3017(b) (McKinney 1991 & Supp 1992) §15.08
NY Civ Prac L & R 4545 (McKinney 1992) §15.18
NY Civ Prac L & R 5001(b) §15.15
NY Civ Prac L & R 6301 §15.06
NY Civ Prac L & R 6311(1) (McKinney 1980 & Supp 1992) §15.06
NY Civ Prac L & R 6312(a) (McKinney 1980) §15.06
NY Civ Prac L & R 6312(b) (McKinney 1980) §15.06
NY Civ Prac L & R 6313(a) (McKinney 1980 & Supp 1992) §15.06
NY Civ Prac L & R 6313(c) (McKinney 1980) §15.06
NY Civ Prac L & R art 71, §§7101-7112 (McKinney 1980 & Supp 1992) §15.37
NY Civ Prac L & R 7501 (McKinney 1980 & Supp 1992) §16.14
NY Civ Prac L & R 7511 (McKinney 1980 & Supp 1992) §16.11
NY Civ Prac L & R 7511(c) (McKinney 1980) §16.12
NY Civ Prac L & R 7513 (McKinney 1980 & Supp 1992) §15.14
NY Civ Prac L & R 7801 (McKinney 1981 & Supp 1992) §15.01
NY Civ Prac L & R 7802 (McKinney 1981), Practice Commentary C7802:1 §15.01
NY Civ Prac L & R 7803 (McKinney 1981) §15.01
NY Civ Prac L & R 7803(3) (McKinney 1981) §15.01

NY Civ Prac L & R 7804(b)
(McKinney 1981 & Supp 1992)
§15.02
NY Civ Prac L & R 7804(c)
(McKinney 1981 & Supp 1992)
§15.02
NY Comp Codes R & Regs tit 12,
§82.3 §1.24
NY Comp Codes R & Regs tit 6,
§612.2 §14.33
NY Comp Codes R & Regs tit 6,
§613.3 §14.33
NY Comp Codes R & Regs tit 6,
§613.5 §14.33
NY Comp Codes R & Regs tit 6,
§613.9 §14.33
NY Comp Codes R & Regs tit 6,
§661.27 §14.34
NY Comp Codes R & Regs tit 6,
§661.27(a) §14.34
NY Comp Codes R & Regs tit 6,
§661.3 §14.34
NY Comp Codes R & Regs tit 6,
§661.4 (ee)(1) §14.34
NY Comp Codes R & Regs tit 6,
§661.5(a)(2) §14.34
NY Comp Codes R & Regs tit 6,
§661.6(a)(3) §14.34
NY Comp Codes R & Regs tit 6,
§663.2(Z) §14.34
NY Coop Corp Law §14(o)
(McKinney 1951 & Supp 1992)
§9.12
NY Coop Corp Law §14(q)
(McKinney 1951 & Supp 1992)
§9.12
NY Coop Corp Law §14(r)
(McKinney 1951 & Supp 1992)
§9.12
NY County Law §625 (McKinney
1991) §2.03
NY Educ Law §458 (McKinney
1988) §2.09
NY Educ Law §2562 (McKinney
1981) §16.02

NY Educ Law §3813 (McKinney
1981 & Supplementary Pamphlet
1992) §§7.19, 16.02
NY Educ Law §3813(1) (McKinney
1981 & Supplementary Pamphlet
1992) §§7.18, 16.02
NY Educ Law §3813(2)(a)
(McKinney Supplementary
Pamphlet 1992) §7.18
NY Educ Law §3813(2-a)
(McKinney Supplementary
Pamphlet 1992) §16.02
NY Educ Law §6218 (McKinney
1988) §2.03
NY Educ Law §7201 *et seq*
(McKinney 1985) §1.24
NY Educ Law §7201 (McKinney
1985 & Supp 1992) §§1.05, 11.02
NY Educ Law §7202 (McKinney
1985) §1.23
NY Educ Law §7203 (McKinney
1985) §1.23
NY Educ Law §7204 (McKinney
1985) §1.24
NY Educ Law §7206 (McKinney
1985 & Supp 1992) §1.05
NY Educ Law §7207 (McKinney
1985 & Supp 1992) §11.02
NY Educ Law §7208(p) (McKinney
1985) §11.02
NY Educ Law §7209(4) (McKinney
1985) §1.23
NY Educ Law §7301 *et seq*
(McKinney 1985) §1.24
NY Educ Law §7301 (McKinney
1985 & Supp 1992) §§1.04, 11.02
NY Educ Law §7304 (McKinney
1985 & Supp 1992) §1.04
NY Educ Law §7305 (McKinney
1985 & Supp 1992) §11.02
NY Educ Law §7306(1)(g)
(McKinney 1985) §11.02
NY Envtl Conserv Law §§8-0101 to
-0117 (McKinney 1984 & Supp
1992) §14.06

NY Envtl Conserv Law §§17-0101 et seq (McKinney 1984 & Supp 1992) §14.06
NY Envtl Conserv Law §17-1001 et seq §14.33
NY Envtl Conserv Law §17-1005 (McKinney 1984 & Supp 1992) §14.33
NY Envtl Conserv Law §17-1941 (McKinney 1984 & Supp 1992) §14.33
NY Envtl Conserv Law §24-0101 et seq (McKinney 1984 & Supp 1992) §§14.06, 14.34
NY Envtl Conserv Law §24-0103 (McKinney 1984 & Supp 1992) §14.34
NY Envtl Conserv Law §24-0105 (McKinney 1984 & Supp 1992) §14.34
NY Envtl Conserv Law §24-0107 §14.34
NY Envtl Conserv Law §24-0301(1) (McKinney 1984 & Supp 1992) §14.34
NY Envtl Conserv Law §24-0301(5) (McKinney 1984 & Supp 1992) §14.34
NY Envtl Conserv Law §24-0501 (McKinney 1984 & Supp 1992) §14.34
NY Envtl Conserv Law §24-0501(4) (McKinney 1984 & Supp 1992) §14.34
NY Envtl Conserv Law §24-0701(1) (McKinney 1984 & Supp 1992) §14.34
NY Envtl Conserv Law §24-0701(3) (McKinney 1984 & Supp 1992) §14.34
NY Envtl Conserv Law §24-0701(4) (McKinney 1984 & Supp 1992) §14.34
NY Envtl Conserv Law §24-0703(4) (McKinney 1984 & Supp 1992) §14.34
NY Envtl Conserv Law §24-0703(5) (McKinney 1984 & Supp 1992) §14.34
NY Envtl Conserv Law §24-0705(3) (McKinney 1984 & Supp 1992) §14.34
NY Envtl Conserv Law §24-0801 et seq (McKinney 1984 & Supp 1992) §14.34
NY Envtl Conserv Law §25-0101 et seq (McKinney 1984 & Supp 1992) §§14.06, 14.34
NY Envtl Conserv Law §25-0103(1) (McKinney 1984 & Supp 1992) §14.34
NY Envtl Conserv Law §25-0201 (McKinney 1984 & Supp 1992) §14.34
NY Envtl Conserv Law §25-0201(3) (McKinney 1984 & Supp 1992) §14.34
NY Envtl Conserv Law §25-0201(5) (McKinney 1984 & Supp 1992) §14.34
NY Envtl Conserv Law §25-0401(1) (McKinney 1984 & Supp 1992) §14.34
NY Envtl Conserv Law §40-0101 et seq (McKinney 1984 & Supp 1992) §14.06, §14.33
NY Envtl Conserv Law §40-0107 (McKinney 1984 & Supp 1992) §14.33
NY Envtl Conserv Law §40-0111 (McKinney 1984 & Supp 1992) §14.33
NY Envtl Conserv Law §40-4303 (McKinney 1984 & Supp 1992) §14.23
NY Envtl Conserv Law §40-4305 (McKinney 1984 & Supp 1992) §14.33
NY Envtl Conserv Law, art 27, tit 13 (McKinney 1984 & Supp 1992) §14.06

NY Gen Bus Law §482 (McKinney 1984) §1.24
NY Gen Bus Law §§770-776 (McKinney Supp 1992) §1.10
NY Gen Bus Law §777 *et seq* (McKinney 1984 & Supp 1992) §12.14
NY Gen Bus Law §777(3) (McKinney 1984 & Supp 1992) §12.14
NY Gen Bus Law §777(6) §12.14
NY Gen Bus Law §777-a(1) (McKinney 1984 & Supp 1992) §12.14
NY Gen Bus Law §777-a(1)(a) §12.14
NY Gen Bus Law §777-a(1)(b) §12.14
NY Gen Bus Law §777-a(1)(c) §12.14
NY Gen Bus Law §777-a(2)(a) (McKinney 1984 & Supp 1992) §12.14
NY Gen Bus Law §777-a(2)(b) (McKinney 1984 & Supp 1992) §12.14
NY Gen Bus Law §777-a(4)(a) (McKinney 1984 & Supp 1992) §12.14
NY Gen Bus Law §777-a(4)(b) (McKinney 1984 & Supp 1992) §12.14
NY Gen Bus Law §777-b(3) §12.14
NY Gen Mun Law §101 (McKinney 1986) §2.09
NY Gen Mun Law §103 (McKinney 1986 & Supp 1992) §§2.07, 2.08, 2.22
NY Gen Mun Law §103 n 131-137, 146 (McKinney 1986 & Supp 1992) §2.16
NY Gen Mun Law §103(4) (McKinney 1986 & Supp 1992) §2.14
NY Gen Mun Law §103(5) (McKinney 1986 & Supp 1992) §2.08
NY Gen Mun Law §105 (McKinney 1986 & Supp 1992) §§2.12, 8.07
NY Gen Mun Law §106-b (McKinney 1986) §1.08
NY Gen Mun Law §120-w (McKinney 1986) §2.09
NY Gen Oblig Law §5-322.1 (McKinney 1989) §§3.13, 11.22
NY Gen Oblig Law §5-322.2 §3.05
NY Gen Oblig Law §5-322.2(1)(a) (McKinney 1989) §3.05
NY Gen Oblig Law §5-322.2(1)(b) (McKinney 1989) §3.06
NY Gen Oblig Law §5-322.2(1)(c) §3.05
NY Gen Oblig Law §5-322.2(2) (McKinney 1989) §3.06
NY Gen Oblig Law §5-322.2(4) §3.05
NY Gen Oblig Law §5-322.3 (McKinney 1989 & Supp 1992) §8.32
NY Gen Oblig Law §5-323 (McKinney 1989 & Supp 1992) §15.22
NY Gen Oblig Law §5-324 §§2.36, 11.22
NY Gen Oblig Law §5-701 §2.27
NY Gen Oblig Law §5-703 §2.27
NY Gen Oblig Law §7-301 (McKinney 1989 & Supp 1992) §§8.06, 8.14, 8.15, 8.23, 8.29, 8.42
NY Gen Oblig Law §15-301 §2.27
NY Gen Oblig Law §17-103(1) (McKinney 1989 & Supp 1992) §12.08
NY Gen Oblig Law §17-103(2) §12.08
NY High Law §193 (McKinney 1979 & Supp 1992) §8.32
NY Ins Law §2502 (McKinney 1982) §10.31

NY Ins Law §2502(c) (McKinney 1982) §10.10
NY Ins Law §2504 (McKinney 1982) §§10.10, 10.31
NY Ins Law §2505(a) (McKinney 1982) §10.10
NY Ins Law §2505(b) (McKinney 1982) §10.10
NY Ins Law §3425 (McKinney 1985 & Supp 1992) §10.17
NY Ins Law §3426 (McKinney 1985 & Supp 1992) §§10.14, 10.17
NY Ins Law §3426(b) (McKinney 1985 & Supp 1992) §10.17
NY Ins Law §3427 (McKinney 1985 & Supp 1992) §10.17
NY Ins Law §3429 (McKinney 1985 & Supp 1992) §10.17
NY Ins Law §3431 (McKinney 1985 & Supp 1992) §10.17
NY Lab Law §200 §§13.03, 13.14
NY Lab Law §220 (McKinney 1986 & Supp 1992) §2.35
NY Lab Law §240 §§13.02, 13.03, 13.04, 13.05, 13.07, 13.08, 13.09, 13.10, 13.11, 13.12, 13.13, 13.18
NY Lab Law §240(1) (McKinney 1986 & Supp 1992) §§13.09, 13.11, 13.14
NY Lab Law §240(2) (McKinney 1986 & Supp 1992) §13.05
NY Lab Law §240(3) (McKinney 1986 & Supp 1992) §13.05
NY Lab Law §241 §§13.02, 13.03, 13.04, 13.06, 13.07, 13.08, 13.09, 13.10, 13.11, 13.12, 13.13, 13.18
NY Lab Law §241(1) §13.14
NY Lab Law §241(2) §13.14
NY Lab Law §241(3) §13.14
NY Lab Law §241(4) §13.14
NY Lab Law §241(5) §13.14
NY Lab Law §241(6) (McKinney 1986 & Supp 1992) §§3.09, 3.10, 13.03, 13.06, 13.09, 13.14
NY Lab Law §241(7) (McKinney 1986 & Supp 1992) §13.06
NY Lab Law §241(8) (McKinney 1986 & Supp 1992) §13.11
NY Lab Law §902 (McKinney 1988 & Supp 1992) §1.24
NY Lab Law art 30 §900 et seq (McKinney 1988 & Supp 1992) §14.06
NY Lab Law art 30 §900 (McKinney 1988 & Supp 1992) §14.30
NY Lab Law art 30 §901 (McKinney 1988 & Supp 1992) §14.30
NY Lab Law art 30 §904(1) (McKinney 1988 & Supp 1992) §14.30
NY Lab Law art 30 §904(2) (McKinney 1988 & Supp 1992) §14.30
NY Lab Law art 30 §909(1) (McKinney 1988 & Supp 1992) §14.30
NY Lien Law §§1 through 79-a §9.01
NY Lien Law §2(2) (McKinney 1966 & Supp 1992) §9.14
NY Lien Law §2(3) (McKinney 1966 & Supp 1992) §§9.04, 9.11, 9.13
NY Lien Law §2(4) (McKinney 1966 & Supp 1992) §§9.03, 9.04, 9.09, 9.22
NY Lien Law §2(5) (McKinney 1966) §§9.21, 9.22, 9.62, 9.75
NY Lien Law §2(5-a) (McKinney 1966) §9.21, 9.22
NY Lien Law §2(6) §9.07
NY Lien Law §2(7) (McKinney 1966) §§1.08, 9.07
NY Lien Law §2(8) (McKinney 1966) §§1.09, 9.02
NY Lien Law §2(9) (McKinney 1966) §§1.10, 9.03, 9.08
NY Lien Law §2(10) (McKinney 1966) §§1.14, 9.03, 9.08
NY Lien Law §2(11) (McKinney 1966) §§9.03, 9.08, 9.31

NY Lien Law §2(12) (McKinney 1966) §§1.15, 8.38, 9.03, 9.08, 9.19
NY Lien Law §2(13) §9.53
NY Lien Law §2(14) §9.53
NY Lien Law §3 (McKinney 1966 & Supp 1992) §§9.02, 9.03, 9.04, 9.05, 9.06, 9.18, 9.21, 9.22, 9.62
NY Lien Law §4 §§9.34, 9.44, 9.50
NY Lien Law §4(2) §9.14
NY Lien Law §4(4) §9.14
NY Lien Law §5 (McKinney 1966 & Supp 1992) §§9.07, 9.08, 9.10, 9.25, 9.62
NY Lien Law §7 §9.54
NY Lien Law §8 (McKinney 1966 & Supp 1992) §9.27
NY Lien Law §9 §§9.22, 9.26, 9.36
NY Lien Law §9(2) §9.26
NY Lien Law §9(4) §9.26
NY Lien Law §9(6) (McKinney 1966 & Supp 1992) §9.26
NY Lien Law §9(7) (McKinney 1966 & Supp 1992) §9.26
NY Lien Law §10 (McKinney 1966 & Supp 1992) §§9.29, 9.52
NY Lien Law §10(2) (McKinney 1966 & Supp 1992) §9.26
NY Lien Law §11 (McKinney 1966 & Supp 1992) §§9.25, 9.31, 9.36
NY Lien Law §11-a §9.30
NY Lien Law §11-a(4) (McKinney 1966 & Supp 1992) §9.30
NY Lien Law §11-b (McKinney 1966 & Supp 1992) §9.31
NY Lien Law §11-c (McKinney 1966 & Supp 1992) §9.31
NY Lien Law §12 (McKinney 1966 & Supp 1992) §§9.22, 9.27, 9.30, 9.36
NY Lien Law §12-a(1) §9.33
NY Lien Law §12-a(2) §9.33
NY Lien Law §13(1) §§9.52, 9.54, 9.56
NY Lien Law §13(1-a) §§9.52, 9.55
NY Lien Law §13(2) §§9.52, 9.54, 9.57
NY Lien Law §13(3) §§9.52, 9.53, 9.54
NY Lien Law §13(4) §9.52
NY Lien Law §13(6) §§9.52, 9.55
NY Lien Law §15 §§9.55, 9.77
NY Lien Law §15(2) §9.55
NY Lien Law §17 (McKinney 1966 & Supp 1992) §§9.32, 9.40
NY Lien Law §18 §§9.32, 9.40
NY Lien Law §19 §9.36
NY Lien Law §19(1) §9.36
NY Lien Law §19(2) §9.36
NY Lien Law §19(4) §9.36
NY Lien Law §19(5) §9.36
NY Lien Law §19(6) §9.36
NY Lien Law §20 §9.36
NY Lien Law §20(2) §9.36
NY Lien Law §21 §9.36
NY Lien Law §21(1) §9.36
NY Lien Law §21(3) 9.36
NY Lien Law §21(4) §9.36
NY Lien Law §21(5) §9.36
NY Lien Law §21(7) §9.36
NY Lien Law §21-a §9.37
NY Lien Law §22 §9.53
NY Lien Law §23 (McKinney 1966 & Supp 1992) §§9.01, 9.26
NY Lien Law §25 §9.59
NY Lien Law §25(1) §9.59
NY Lien Law §25(2) §9.59
NY Lien Law §25(3) §9.52
NY Lien Law §25(4) §§9.52, 9.56
NY Lien Law §25(5) §9.59
NY Lien Law §26 §§9.55, 9.58
NY Lien Law §29 §9.58
NY Lien Law §31 §9.58
NY Lien Law §33 §9.58
NY Lien Law §34 (McKinney 1966 & Supp 1992) §§2.28, 3.26, 9.24
NY Lien Law §35 §9.41
NY Lien Law §37 §9.36
NY Lien Law §37(1) §9.36
NY Lien Law §38 §9.35

NY Lien Law §39 (McKinney 1966 & Supp 1992) **§9.26, 9.49**
NY Lien Law §39-a (McKinney 1966 & Supp 1992) **§9.26, 9.49**
NY Lien Law §41 **§§9.38, 9.42**
NY Lien Law §42 (McKinney 1966 & Supp 1992) **§§9.38, 9.43, 9.44**
NY Lien Law §43 **§§9.43, 9.61**
NY Lien Law §44(1) **§9.44**
NY Lien Law §44(2) **§§9.44, 9.51**
NY Lien Law §44(3) **§9.44**
NY Lien Law §44(4) **§§9.44, 9.51**
NY Lien Law §44(5) **§§9.46, 9.51**
NY Lien Law §44(6) **§9.44**
NY Lien Law §45 **§9.51**
NY Lien Law §§46-53 **§9.43**
NY Lien Law §46 **§9.43**
NY Lien Law §53 **§9.62**
NY Lien Law §54 **§9.51**
NY Lien Law §55 **§9.36**
NY Lien Law §56 **§§9.52, 9.60**
NY Lien Law §57 **§9.61**
NY Lien Law §58 **§9.66**
NY Lien Law §59 **§§9.36, 9.37**
NY Lien Law §60 **§9.61**
NY Lien Law §62 **§9.44**
NY Lien Law §63 **§9.46**
NY Lien Law §70(1) **§9.70**
NY Lien Law §70(2) **§9.71**
NY Lien Law §70(3) **§9.69**
NY Lien Law §70(4) **§9.68**
NY Lien Law §70(5) **§9.70**
NY Lien Law §70(6) **§9.70**
NY Lien Law §70(7) **§9.70**
NY Lien Law §71 **§9.76**
NY Lien Law §71(1) **§9.75**
NY Lien Law §71(2) **§§9.71, 9.75**
NY Lien Law §71(3) **§9.71**
NY Lien Law §71(3)(a) **§9.75**
NY Lien Law §71(3)(b) **§9.75**
NY Lien Law §71(4) **§9.71, 9.75**
NY Lien Law §71-a **§9.75**
NY Lien Law §72(1) (McKinney 1966 & Supp 1992) **§9.78**
NY Lien Law §72(2) **§9.71**
NY Lien Law §72(3)(a) **§9.72**
NY Lien Law §73(1) (McKinney 1966 & Supp 1992) **§9.76**
NY Lien Law §73(2) (McKinney 1966 & Supp 1992) **§9.76**
NY Lien Law §73(3)(a) (McKinney 1966 & Supp 1992) **§9.76**
NY Lien Law §73(3)(b) (McKinney 1966 & Supp 1992) **§9.76**
NY Lien Law §73(3)(c) (McKinney 1966 & Supp 1992) **§9.76**
NY Lien Law §73(3)(d) (McKinney 1966 & Supp 1992) **§9.77**
NY Lien Law §73(4) (McKinney 1966 & Supp 1992) **§9.76**
NY Lien Law §74(1) (McKinney 1966 & Supp 1992) **§§9.72, 9.83**
NY Lien Law §75 **§9.74**
NY Lien Law §75(1) **§9.73**
NY Lien Law §75(3)(A) **§9.73**
NY Lien Law §75(3)(B) **§9.73**
NY Lien Law §75(3)(C) **§9.73**
NY Lien Law §75(3)(D) **§9.73**
NY Lien Law §75(3)(E) **§9.73**
NY Lien Law §75(4) **§9.73**
NY Lien Law §76(1) **§9.74**
NY Lien Law §76(2) **§9.74**
NY Lien Law §76(5) **§9.74**
NY Lien Law §76(6) **§9.74**
NY Lien Law §77 **§9.74**
NY Lien Law §77(1) (McKinney 1966 & Supp 1992) **§9.81**
NY Lien Law §77(3)(ii) **§9.82**
NY Lien Law §77(3)(iii) (McKinney 1966 & Supp 1992) **§9.82**
NY Lien Law §77(3)(iv) **§9.82**
NY Lien Law §77(3)(a)(i) (McKinney 1966 & Supp 1992) **§§9.79, 9.82**
NY Lien Law §77(3)(a)(v) (McKinney 1966 & Supp 1992) **§9.82**
NY Lien Law §77(3)(a)(vi) (McKinney 1966 & Supp 1992) **§9.82**

STATUTES 693

NY Lien Law §77(3)(a)(viii)
(McKinney 1966 & Supp 1992)
§9.82
NY Lien Law §77(3)(a)(ix) **§9.82**
NY Lien Law §77(3)(b) (McKinney
1966 & Supp 1992) **§9.81**
NY Lien Law §77(7) **§9.81**
NY Lien Law §77(8) (McKinney
1966 & Supp 1992) **§9.83**
NY Lien Law §77(8)(a) (McKinney
1966 & Supp 1992) **§9.83**
NY Lien Law §77(8)(b) (McKinney
1966 & Supp 1992) **§9.83**
NY Lien Law §77(8)(c) (McKinney
1966 & Supp 1992) **§9.83**
NY Lien Law §77(8)(d) (McKinney
1966 & Supp 1992) **§9.83**
NY Lien Law §78 (McKinney 1966)
§9.84
NY Lien Law §79 (McKinney 1966
& Supp 1992) **§9.84**
NY Lien Law §79-a (McKinney 1966
& Supp 1992) **§9.79**
NY Lien Law §79-a(2) (McKinney
1966 & Supp 1992) **§9.80**
NY Lien Law §79-a(3) **§9.73**
NY Priv Hous Fin Law §650
(McKinney's 1991) **§9.07**
NY Pub Auth Law §1045-i
(McKinney Supplementary
Pamphlet 1992) **§2.09**
NY Pub Auth Law §1048-i
(McKinney Supplementary
Pamphlet 1992) **§2.09**
NY Pub Auth Law §1209 (McKinney
1982 & Supp 1992) **§2.16**
NY Pub Auth Law §1209(5)(a)
§2.16
NY Pub Auth Law §1725 *et seq*
(McKinney 1981 & Supp 1992)
§§2.09, 17.02
NY Pub Auth Law §1779 (McKinney
1981) **§2.03**
NY Pub Auth Law §1974(4)
(McKinney 1981) **§2.03**

NY Pub Auth Law §2312 (McKinney
1981) **§2.03**
NY Pub Auth Law §2466(6)(a)
(McKinney 1981) **§2.03**
NY Pub Auth Law §2466(6)(b)
(McKinney 1981) **§2.03**
NY Pub Auth Law §2620(1)
(McKinney 1981 & Supp 1991)
§2.03
NY Pub Auth Law §2620(2)
(McKinney 1981 & Supp 1991)
§2.03
NY Pub Auth Law §2722 (McKinney
Supplementary Pamphlet 1992)
§2.09
NY Pub Auth Law §2768 (McKinney
Supplementary Pamphlet 1992)
§2.09
NY Pub Hous Law §151-a
(McKinney 1989) **§2.09**
NY Pub Off Law §§84-90
(McKinney 1988 & Supp 1992)
§16.03
NY Pub Off Law §84 art 6 *et seq*
§14.36
NY Pub Off Law §87(2) **§14.36**
NY Pub Off Law §87(2)(a)
(McKinney 1988) **§16.03**
NY Pub Off Law §87(2)(b)
(McKinney 1988) **§16.03**
NY Pub Off Law §87(2)(c)
(McKinney 1988) **§16.03**
NY Pub Off Law §87(2)(d)
(McKinney 1988 & Supp 1992)
§16.03
NY Pub Off Law §87(2)(g)
(McKinney 1988) **§16.03**
NY Pub Off Law §87(3)(c)
(McKinney 1988) **§16.03**
NY Pub Off Law §89(2) **§16.03**
NY Pub Off Law §89(3) (McKinney
1988) **§16.03**
NY Pub Off Law §89(4)(a)
(McKinney 1988) **§16.03**
NY Pub Off Law §89(4)(b)
(McKinney 1988) **§16.03**

NY Real Prop Law §294 (McKinney 1989 & Supp 1991) §9.57
NY Real Prop Law, art 9-B, §§339-d through 339-ii §9.12
NY Real Prop Act Law §231 §§9.63, 9.64, 9.67
NY Real Prop Act Law §1351 (McKinney 1979 & Supp 1992) §9.61
NY Real Prop Act Law §1353 §9.64
NY Real Prop Acts Law §1354 §§9.62, 9.65
NY Real Prop Act Law §1361 §9.65
NY Real Prop Act Law §1371 §9.66
NY Real Prop Act Law §1371(3) §9.66
NY State Fin Law §112 (McKinney 1989 & Supp 1992) §2.32
NY State Fin Law §112(2) (McKinney 1989) §2.30
NY State Fin Law §135 (McKinney 1989 & Supp 1992) §§2.03, 2.09
NY State Fin Law §136-a (McKinney 1989 & Supp 1992) §2.14
NY State Fin Law §136-a(2) §2.14
NY State Fin Law §137 (McKinney 1989 & Supp 1992) §§1.08, 8.25, 8.28, 8.32, 8.34, 8.37, 8.40, 8.41, 8.44, 8.46
NY State Fin Law §137(3) (McKinney 1989 & Supp 1992) §8.40
NY State Fin Law §137(4)(c) (McKinney 1989 & Supp 1992 §8.41
NY State Fin Law §140 (McKinney 1989 & Supp 1992) §§2.12, 8.07
NY State Fin Law §145 (McKinney 1989 & Supp 1992) §§6.33, 7.18, 7.19, 16.02
NY Town Law §122 (McKinney 1987) §§2.03, 2.07
NY Unconsol Law §6261 (McKinney 1979) §2.09
NY Unconsol Law §9606 (McKinney 1974) §2.03
NY Village Law §17-1718(5) (McKinney 1973 & Supp 1992) §8.32
NY Work Comp Law §1 *et seq* (McKinney 1965 & Supp 1992) §13.02

Uniform Commercial Code

UCC §1-203 (McKinney 1964) §3.28
UCC §1-204(2) (McKinney 1964 & Supp 1992) §3.30
UCC §1-207 §6.33
UCC §2-201 (McKinney 1964 & Supp 1992) §3.29
UCC §2-201(1) (McKinney 1964) §2.27
UCC §2-201(2) §§2.27, 16.14
UCC §2-201(3)(a) §2.27
UCC §2-201(3)(b) §2.27
UCC §2-201(3)(c) §2.27
UCC §2-207 (McKinney 1964 & Supp 1992) §3.29
UCC §2-305 (McKinney 1964 & Supp 1992) §§3.32, 3.28
UCC §2-307 (McKinney 1964 & Supp 1992) §3.32
UCC §2-308 (McKinney 1964 & Supp 1992) §§3.28, 3.30, 3.34
UCC §2-309 (McKinney 1964 & Supp 1992) §3.30
UCC §2-309(1) (McKinney 1964 & Supp 1992) §3.28
UCC §2-310 (McKinney 1964 & Supp 1992) §3.32
UCC §2-313 §3.33, §12.13
UCC §2-314 §12.13
UCC §2-314(3) §§3.33, 12.13
UCC §2-315 §§3.33, 12.13
UCC §2-316(2) §3.33
UCC §2-316(3)(a) (McKinney 1964 & Supp 1992) §3.33
UCC §2-503 (McKinney 1964 & Supp 1992) §3.30

UCC §2-509 (McKinney 1964 & Supp 1992) §3.34
UCC §2-615 (McKinney 1964 & Supp 1992) §3.28
UCC §2-615(a) (McKinney 1964 & Supp 1992) §3.31
UCC §2-708 (McKinney 1964 & Supp 1992) §3.35
UCC §2-712 (McKinney 1964 & Supp 1992) §3.35
UCC §2-713 (McKinney 1964 & Supp 1992) §3.35
UCC §2-714(2) (McKinney 1964 & Supp 1992) §3.31
UCC §718(2) (McKinney 1964 & Supp 1992) §3.35
UCC §2-719 (McKinney 1964 & Supp 1992) §3.35
UCC §2-725 §12.12
UCC §2-725(1) §3.35
UCC §2-725(2) (McKinney 1964 & Supp 1992) §3.35

Regulations

Code of Federal Regulations

16 CFR ch II §14.29
17 CFR pt 229 §14.37
29 CFR §1926.58 §14.29
40 CFR §52.21 §14.04
40 CFR 112 §14.27
40 CFR pt 61 §14.28

40 CFR §61.145 §14.29
40 CFR pt 763 subpt G §14.29
48 CFR ch 1 §4.04
48 CFR §28.203 §8.43
48 CFR §52.212-6 §7.14
48 CFR §52.243.5 §§5.01, 5.02, 5.18
48 CFR §52.249-14 §7.14

Procurement Policy Board Rules

ch 1, §1-02(a) §17.01
ch 3, §3-01(a) §17.02
ch 3, §3-01(b) §17.02
ch 3, §3-01(e) §17.02
ch 3, §3-02(m)(3) §17.02
ch 3, §3-11 §17.02
ch 3, §3-11(m) §17.02
ch 4, §4-01 *et seq* §17.03
ch 4, §4-03(a) §17.03
ch 4, §4-03(e)-(j) §17.03
ch 4, §4-06(a) §17.03
ch 4, §4-06(a)(1) §17.03
ch 4, §4-06(b) §17.03
ch 4, §4-06(c) §17.03
ch 4, §4-06(d) §§17.03, 17.06
ch 4, §4-07 §17.03
ch 4, §4-07(h) §17.03
ch 5, §5-01 *et seq* §17.02
ch 5, §5-01 §17.04
ch 5, §5-01(c) §17.04
ch 5, §5-01(f) §17.04
ch 5, §5-02 §17.04
ch 5, §5-02(a)(2) §17.04
ch 5, §5-02(b)(1)-(2) §17.04
ch 5, §5-02(e)(1) §17.04
ch 5, §5-02(f)(2) §17.04
ch 5, §5-02(3) §17.04
ch 5, §5-03 §17.04
ch 5, §5-04 §17.04
ch 5, §5-06 §17.04

ch 5, §5-06(f) §17.04
ch 5, §5-07 §17.04
ch 5, §5-07(a)(1) §17.04
ch 5, §5-07(b) §17.04
ch 5, §5-07(d) §17.05
ch 6, §6-01(a) §17.05
ch 6, §6-01(k) §17.05
ch 6, §6-02 §17.05
ch 6, §6-02(d)(2)(ii) §17.05
ch 6, §6-02(e) §17.05
ch 6, §6-02(e)(1)-(4) §17.05
ch 6, §6-03 §17.05
ch 6, §6-03(2)(iii) §17.05
ch 6, §6-03(b)(1) §17.14
ch 6, §6-03(c) §17.05
ch 6, §6-03(c)(2)(ii) §17.14
ch 6, §6-03(c)(3) §17.14
ch 6, §6-03(3) §17.05
ch 6, §6-05(b)-(c) §17.05
ch 6, §6-07(a) §17.05
ch 6, §6-07(b)(ii) §17.05
ch 6, §6-07(c)(2) §17.05
ch 6, §6-07(d)(2) §17.05
ch 6, §6-07(e)(2) §17.05
ch 7, §7-01 *et seq* §17.02
ch 7, §7-02(c) §17.08
ch 7, §7-02(c)(6) §17.08
ch 7, §7-03(c) §17.08
ch 7, §7-03(d) §17.08
ch 7, §7-03(e) §17.08

ch 7, §7-04(a) §17.09
ch 7, §7-04(d)(1) §17.09
ch 7, §7-05(a) §17.09
ch 7, §7-05(d)(2) §17.09
ch 7, §7-05(d)(3) §17.09
ch 7, §7-05(d)(4) §17.09
ch 7, §7-05(d)(5) §17.09
ch 7, §7-05(e) §17.09
ch 7, §7-05(e)(3) §17.09
ch 7, §7-05(f) §17.09
ch 7, §7-05(f)(1) §17.09
ch 7, §7-05(g)(1) §17.09
ch 7, §7-05(g)(2) §17.09
ch 7, §7-05(g)(3) §17.09
ch 7, §7-05(g)(5) §17.09
ch 7, §7-06 §17.02
ch 7, §7-07(a) §17.08
ch 7, §7-07(a)(2) §17.08
ch 7, §7-07(a)(3) §17.08
ch 7, §7-07(a)(4) §17.08
ch 7, §7-07(b)(3) §17.08
ch 7, §7-07(b)(5) §17.08
ch 7, §7-07(d) §17.08
ch 7, §7-08(a) §17.10
ch 7, §7-08(a)(i)(A)-(F) §17.10
ch 7, §7-08(b)(1) §17.10
ch 7, §7-08(c) §17.10
ch 7, §7-08(d) §17.10
ch 7, §7-08(i)(4) §17.10
ch 7, §7-08(j) §17.10
ch 7, §7-08(j)(2) §17.10
ch 7, §7-09(b)(1)(ii) §17.11
ch 7, §7-09(b)(2)(i)-(ii) §17.11
ch 7, §7-10(b) §17.12
ch 7, §7-10(e) §17.12
ch 7, §7-10(f)(1) §17.12
ch 7, §7-10(f)(4) §17.12
ch 7, §7-10(f)(6) §17.12
ch 9, §9-02(e)(1) §17.06
ch 9, §9-02(e)(2) §17.06
ch 9, §9-02(o) §17.06
ch 9, §9-02(o)(3) §17.06
ch 9, §9-02(p) §17.06
ch 9, §9-02(p)(1) §17.06
ch 9, §9-02(p)(1)(ii) §17.06
ch 9, §9-02(p)(2) §17.06
ch 9, §9-02(q) §§17.03, 17.06
ch 14, §14-01 §17.08

Authorities

A

J. Acret, *Architects and Engineers* (Shepard's/McGraw-Hill 2d ed 1984) §§8.50, 11.01

13 Am Jur 2d *Building & Constr Contracts* §52 (1964) §7.32

17 Am Jur 2d *Contractor's Bonds* §31 (1990) §8.26

II Am Socy of Civil Engineers, Construction Risks and Liability Sharing 2 (1980) §2.40

Annotation, 62 ALR3d 288 (1975) §9.05

Ashcraft, *Limitation of Liability—The View after Markborough*, 11 Constr L 3 (Aug 1991) §15.22

Avoiding Liability in Architecture, Design and Construction (R. Cushman ed 1983) §11.01

B

Barrett, *The Center Holds: The Continuing Role of the Economic Loss Rule in Construction Litigation*, 11 Constr 3 (1991) §15.20

Barrett, *Recovery of Economic Loss in Tort for Construction Defects: A Critical Analysis*, 40 SC L Rev 892 (1989) §15.20

Bertschy, *Negligent Performance of Service Contract and the Economic Loss Doctrine*, 17 J Marshall L Rev 249 (1984) §15.20

A. Bierce, The Devil's Dictionary (1906) §16.01

P. Blawie, *Legal Liability of Building Officials for Structural Failures*, 57 Conn BJ 211 (1983) §12.03

Brody, *Some Scientists Say Concern over Radon is Overblown by EPA*, NY Times, Jan 8, 1991, §L (The Environment), at C4, col 1 §14.32

Maurice Brunner, Annotation, "*Validity and Construction of "No Damage" Clause With Respect to Delay in Building or Construction Contract,*" 74 ALR3d 187 (1976) §7.33

C

L. Cantor, *The Application of Statutory Limitation Periods on Latent Construction Defects*, 18 NY St BA

Real Prop L Sec Newsl 13 (July 1990) §12.08

Richard H. Clough, *Construction Contracting* 205 (4th ed 1981) §10.31

Michael Chapman, *The Liab of Design Professionals to the Surety*, 20 Forum 591 (1984-85) §8.50

1A CJS 67 *Account Stated* §2(a) (1985) §15.38

72 CJS *Principal & Surety* §257 (1987) §8.48

Construction Litigation: Representing the Owner 278, §126 (Practising Law Institute R. Cushman & K. Cushman eds 1984) §5.06

1 Corbin, Contracts §§95-100 (1952) §2.24

Cushman & Carpenter, Proving and Pricing Construction Claims 136 (1990) §7.49

R. Cushman & T. Bottum, Architect and Engineer Liability: Claims Against Design Professionals §11.6 (1987) §8.50

R. Cushman & C. Meeker, Constr Defaults: Rights, Duties, and Liabilities §§1.11, 6.8 (1984) §8.49

D

Dealing with Damages 388 (Itzkoff ed 1983) §7.49

Department of Gen Services, City of New York, Permit Construction Handbook 11 (1985) §1.28

M. Diamond, *Liability in the Air: The Threat of Indoor Pollution*, ABAJ, Nov, 1987, at 78 §14.32

C.E. Dinkins, *Shall We Fight or Will We Finish: Environmental Dispute Resolution in a Litigious Society*, 14 Envtl L Rev 10398 (1984) §14.42

C.T. Drechsler, Annotation, *Scope and Effect of Clause in Liability Policy Excluding from Coverage Liability Assumed Under Contract Not Defined in Policy, Such as One of Indemnity*, 63 ALR2d 1122 (1959) §10.22

E

9 Encyl NY, *Damages* §63 §15.12

C.A. Erikson & M.J. O'Connor, Construction Contract Risk Assignment, Technical Rep P-101, Construction Engineering Research Laboratory, Rep No CERL-TR-P-101, at 9 (1979) §2.39

J. Ernstrom & K. Essler, *Beyond the Eichleay Formula: Resurrecting Home Office Overhead Claims*, 3 Constr Law 1 (1982) §7.60

F

Lloyd E. Ferguson, *Gupta v Ritter Homes, Inc: Extending the Implied Warranty of Habitability to Subsequent Purchasers—An Honorable Result Based on Unsound Theory*, 35 Baylor L Rev 670 (1983) §12.14

C. Ferguson, *Lender's Liability for Construction Defects*, 11 Real Est LJ 310 (1983) §12.03

Forsten, *Delaware Joins in Rejecting the Economic Loss Rule in Construction Settings*, 11 Constr L 7 (1991) §15.20

J. Forster, *Sign the Contract; Then Provide the Service*, Consulting Engineer, 1983, at 106-08 §2.30

C.A. Foster, *Construction Management and Design-Build/Fast Track Construction*, 46 Law & Contemp Probs 95 (1983) §11.15

G

Gibney, *The Practical Significance of the Third Party Defense under CERCLA*, 16 BC Envtl Aff L Rev 383 (1988) §14.39

M. Greenberg, *Problems Relating to Changes and Changed Conditions on Public Contracts*, 3 Pub Cont LJ 135 (1970) §5.01

J. Grubin, *No-Damage-For-Delay Clauses: Fair or Foul—The Owner's Perspective*, 78 Mun Engineer's J issue 2, at 1 (1990) §7.32

H

Hart, *The Ripple Effect: Proving Contractor's Losses*, 3 Litig 12 (1976) §6.29

House & Bell, *The Economic Loss Rule: A Fair Balancing of Interests*, 11 Constr L 1 (1991) §15.20

Terrell E. Hunt, *Innovative Settlement Techniques: Use of Alternative Dispute Resolution Tools in Resolving Environmental Litigation*, Envtl Mgmt Rev No 7 (1989) §14.42

I

Impact of Various Construction Types and Clauses on Project Performance, Constr Industry Inst Rep 10 (1986) §§2.40, 2.43

J

Bruce M. Jervis & Paul Levin, Construction Law Principles and Practice 25 (McGraw-Hill, Inc Book Co 1988) §2.08

J.M.H., Annotation, *Right to Mechanics' lien against fee for work or material furnished under contract with, or consent of, life tenant*, 97 ALR 870 (1935) §9.05

Jones, *Drafting CERCLA Consent Decrees*, 3 Nat Resources & Envt 31 (1988) §14.40

Glower W. Jones, *Awarding Punitive Damages by Arbitration*, 7 Constr Law (Aug 1987) §16.12

K

Gerald B. Kirksey & Ronald W. Routson, *Proving Damages: Loss of Profits Resulting from Loss of Bonding Capacity*, 1983-No 2 Constr L Adviser 1 (1983) §15.19

L

Latent Defects in Home Construction: The Illinois Supreme Court Redefines Legal Options for the Subsequent Purchaser, 59 Chi-Kent L Rev 1099 (1983) §12.14

Leary, *U.S. Study Finds a Reduced Cancer Danger from Radon in Homes*, NY Times, Feb 2, 1991, (National), at 10, col 1 §14.32

M

Donald S. Malecki & Jack P. Gibson, The Additional Insured Book 1 (1991) §10.31

E. Marks, Jensen on the Mechanics' Lien Law (4th ed 1963, Supp 1983) §9.11

G.E. Mason, A Quantitative Risk Management Approach to the Selection of Construction Contract Provisions, Technical Rep No 173, The Constr Institute, Dept of Civil

Engineering, Stanford Univ at 26-61 (April 1973) §2.39

Mays, *Alternative Dispute Resolution and Envtl Enforcement*, 18 Envtl L Rev 10087 (1988) §14.42

M. McElroy, Construction Litigation §11.0.2[2][a][ii] (S. Stein ed 1987) §7.60

McLaughlin, *Practice Commentaries* to CPLR §7101, 7B McKinney's Consol Rules of NY 170 §15.37

Memorandum, T. Hunt, Proposed Elements of a Regional Pilot on Innovative Approaches to Dispute Resolution (Mar 15, 1988) at 129 §14.42

Memorandum, T.L. Adams, Jr., Process for Conducting Pre-referral Settlement Negotiations on Civil Judicial Enforcement Cases (Apr 13, 1988) §14.42

Memorandum, Thomas L. Adams, Jr., Follow-Up on ADR (Feb 12, 1988), at 2 §14.42

Morris, *Punitive Damages in Personal Injury Cases*, 21 Ohio St LJ 216 (1961) §15.12

N

Ralph C. Nash, Jr, Govt Contract Changes 233 (1981) §6.16

New York Envtl Law Handbook 190 (N. Robinson ed 1988) §14.34

10 NY Jur §284 (1960) §6.27

Note, *An Argument Against the Availability of Punitive Damages in Commercial Arbitration*, 62 St John's L Rev 270 (1988) §15.12

Note, *Construction Manager's Liability for Job-Site Safety*, 8 U Bridgeport L Rev 105 (1987) §11.15

Note, *Professional Construction Management: Developments in Legal Liability*, 32 Loy L Rev 447 (1986) §§11.15, 11.19

Note, *Punitive Damages in Arbitration: The Search for a Workable Rule*, 63 Cornell L Rev 272 (1978) §15.12

O

Ostrower, *The Absolutely Worst Contract I Ever Saw*, Consulting Engr 24 (July 1985) §13.15

P

Partridge & Noletto, *Construction Management: Evolving Roles and Exposure of Construction Managers and Architects/Engineers*, 12 Am J Trial Advoc 55 (1988) §11.15

William J. Postner, Robert A. Rubin & Lisa A. Banick, *Fixing the Failure and Settling the Dispute*, in Constr Failures 313 (Cushman, Richter, & Rivelis eds 1989) §12.10

R

Report on Punitive Damages in Commercial Arbitration, NY State Bar Assoc Rep (1989) §15.12

Restatement (Second) of Agency §7 (1958 & 1984) §2.30

Restatement (Second) of Contracts §90 (1982) §2.21

H. Reynolds, *Is Eichleay the Answer? An In-Depth Look at Home Office Overhead Claims*, 7 Constr Law 1 (1987) §7.60

Rubin, *Scope of Work Disputes*, in Constr Litigation 89-114 (Practising Law Institute K. Cushman ed 1981) §§3.07, 6.22, 16.02

Robert A. Rubin & Lisa A. Banick
The Hyatt Regency Decision—One View, 6 Constr Law 1 (Aug 1986) §12.01

Robert A. Rubin, Sammie D. Guy, Alfred C. Maevis & Virginia Fairweather, Construction Claims: Analysis, Presentation, Defense (Van Nostrand Reinhold 2d ed 1992) §§6.15, 6.19, 6.22, 7.72, 7.59

S

School Subs Decry "Abuse", Engg News Record, Mar 11, 1991, at 11 §2.09

Schreyer, *Construction Managers' Liab for Job-Site Safety*, 8 U Bridgeport L Rev 105, 116-19 (1987) §§13.16, 11.15

T. Shea, *Proving Productivity Losses in Govt Contracts*, 18 Pub Cont LJ 414 (Mar 1989) §7.55

W.E. Shipley, Annotation, *Liability of Architect or Engineer for Improper Issuance of Certificate*, 43 ALR2d 1227 §11.10

M. Simon, Construction Contracts and Claims (McGraw-Hill Book Co 1979) §§5.01, 7.49

G.A. Smith, *The Continuing Decline of the "Economic Loss Rule" in Construction Litigation*, 10 Constr L 1 (1990) §15.20

J. Smyth, *Behavioral Differing Site Conditions Claims*, 11 Constr Litig Rep 158 (1990) §5.02

Sneed, *What Is My Liability as Construction Manager?*, in Avoiding Liab in Architecture, Design and Constr 111 (R. Cushman ed 1983) §§11.15, 11.16, 11.20

Stein, *Construction Law* 11, ¶11.02 [6][c] (1991) §7.70

Stewart, *Punitive Damages in Arbitration: Fish or Cut Bait*, NYLJ, Feb 21, 1991, at 5, col 1 §15.12

Stipanowich, *Punitive Damages in Arbitration: Garrity v Lyle Stuart, Inc Reconsidered*, 66 Boston UL Rev 953 (1986) §15.12

H. Streeter, Professional Liab of Architects and Engineers (1988) §11.01

Superfund and SARA: Are There Any Defenses Left?, 12 Harv Envtl L Rev 385 (1988) §14.39

J. Sweet, Legal Aspects of Architecture, Engineering and the Construction Process (1985) §11.01

T

Tarullo, *The Good, The Bad, and Economic Loss Liability of a Design Professional*, 11 Constr L 10 (1991) §15.20

Technical Comm on Contracting Practices, Underground Technology Research Council, Avoiding and Resolving Disputes During Construction—Successful Practices and Guidelines 52 (1991) §16.06

Lee M. Thomas, Administrator, Final Guidance on the Use of Alternative Dispute Resolution in EPA Enforcement Cases (Aug 14, 1987) §14.42

Richard Gary Thomas & Fred D. Wilshusen, *How to Beat a 'No Damage For Delay' Clause*, 9 Constr Law (1989) §7.36

U

United States EPA, Toxic Substances: Guidance for

Controlling Asbestos Containing Materials in Buildings 5-1 (1985) §14.28

V

Matthew A. Victor, *The Hyatt Collapse—A Post Mortem*, 10 Constr Law 7 (1990) §12.01

W

Wickwire & Smith, *The Use of Critical Path Method Techniques in Contract Claims*, 7 Pub Cont LJ 1 (1974) §§6.29, 7.04

Wickwire, Hurlbut, & Lerman, *Use of Critical Path Method Techniques in Contract Claims: Issues and Developments, 1974 to 1988*, 18 Pub Cont LJ 338 (1989) §§6.29, 7.04

1 Williston, Contracts §§38-48 (3d ed 1964) §2.24

Index

A

ABANDONMENT OF CONTRACT
  Bonds §8.19
  Changes/extra work §§6.04, 6.05
  Delays §7.39
  Specific breaches by owner, remedies/damages §5.32
ABNORMALLY DANGEROUS ACTIVITIES
  Introductory material §1.25
ABOVE-GROUND CONDITIONS
  Changed conditions §5.04
ABSOLUTE POLLUTION EXCLUSION
  Environmental problems §4.22
ACCELERATION
  See DELAYS
ACCEPTANCE
  Bidding and contract formation §2.24
  Mechanics' liens §9.30
ACCEPTANCE OF SUPPLY CONTRACT TERMS
  Subcontracts §3.31
ACCEPTED STANDARDS OF ARCHITECTURAL AND ENGINEERING PRACTICE
  Professional's role and liability §11.04
ACCEPTING A CARDINAL CHANGE
  Changes/extra work §6.04
ACCEPTING BIDS
  Public contracts, bidding and contract formation §2.10
ACCESS TO JOB SITE
  Subcontracts §3.22
ACCIDENTAL RESULTS FROM INTENTIONAL CAUSES
  Insurance §10.09
ACCIDENTS
  Coverage, insurance §10.06
  Definition, insurance §10.09
ACCORD
  Claims preservation and defense, changes/extra work §6.33
ACCOUNTING
  Remedies/damages §5.09
  Trust funds, mechanics' liens §9.75
ACCRUAL OF CLAIM
  Dispute resolution §6.02
ACCURACY OF DATA
  Contract clauses, changed conditions §5.09
ACM
  See ASBESTOS-CONTAINING MATERIALS

ACQUIESCENCE
  Waiver of writing requirement, changes/extra work §6.11
ACTION TO COMPEL PAYMENT
  Bonds §8.45
ACTIVE INTERFERENCE
  Delays §7.23
  Exceptions to enforcement of no damages for delay clauses §§7.38, 7.42
ACTS OF GOD
  Excusable delay §7.08
  Superfund litigation, environmental problems §4.39
ACTS OF WAS
  Superfund litigation, environmental problems §4.39
ACTUAL ACCELERATION
  Delays §7.45
ACTUAL AND APPARENT AUTHORITY
  Bidding and contract formation §2.30
ACTUAL CONSENT
  Mechanics' liens §9.05
ACTUAL DAMAGES
  Delays §7.68
ACTUAL DELAY DAMAGES
  Bonds §8.19
ACTUAL FRAUD
  Remedies/damages §5.11
"ACTUATED BY EVIL AND REPREHENSIBLE MOTIVES"
  Punitive damages, remedies/damages §5.12
ADA
  Environmental problems §§4.41-14.43
ADDITIONAL COMPENSATION
  Delays §7.22
  Subcontracts §3.08
ADDITIONAL WORK VS EXTRA WORK
  Changes/extra work §6.01

"ADDITIONS-DEDUCTIONS-DEVIATIONS" CLAUSE
  Changes/extra work §6.02
ADJUSTMENTS TO CHANGE ORDERS
  Procurement Policy Board (PPB) Rules §7.03
ADMINISTERING CONTRACTS
  Procurement Policy Board (PPB) Rules §7.05
ADMINISTRATIVE REMEDIES
  Remedies/damages §5.01
ADMINISTRATIVE RULES
  Construction safety §3.06
ADMISSION OF LIABILITY
  Bonds §8.48
ADVANCE PAYMENT
  Bonds §8.26
ADVANCES
  Mechanics' liens §9.59
ADVERTISING
  Defects and failures §2.15
ADVERTISING BIDS
  Public contracts, bidding and contract formation §2.07
ADVOCATE VS COUNSELOR
  Risk allocation, bidding and contract formation §2.44
AFFIRMATIVE DEFENSES
  Statutory liability, construction safety §3.14
AGENCY
  Bidding and contract formation §2.30
  Changes/extra work §§6.07, 6.09
  Insurance §10.15
  Mechanics' liens §9.05
AGENTS
  Liability
  —construction safety §3.10
  —constructions safety. See CONSTRUCTION SAFETY
  Policy requirements, insurance §10.15

INDEX

AGREEMENTS TO SUBORDINATE
  Mechanics' liens §9.58
AGREEMENT TO ARBITRATE
  Dispute resolution §6.14
AGREEMENT TO WAIVE, EXTEND, OR POSTPONE STATUTES OF LIMITATIONS
  Defects and failures §2.08
AHERA
  See ASBESTOS HAZARD EMERGENCY RESPONSE ACT
ALL INCIDENTAL AND NECESSARY WORK CLAUSE
  Environmental problems §4.13
ALLOCATION OF RISK
  Bidding and contract formation §2.36
  Environmental problems §4.10
  Risk allocation. See BIDDING AND CONTRACT FORMATION
ALLOWABLE COSTS
  Procurement Policy Board (PPB) Rules §7.03
ALTERATION OF OBLIGATIONS
  Bonds §8.07
ALTERNATIVE DISPUTE RESOLUTION (ADA)
  See ADA
AMBIGUITY
  Bidding and contract formation §§2.26, 2.47, 2.48
  Bonds §8.02
  Constructive changes, changes/extra work §6.16
AMENDMENTS
  Mechanics' liens §9.33
  Payment requests, subcontracts §3.16
AMERICAN ARBITRATION ASSOCIATION (AAA)
  Dispute resolution §§6.07, 16.12
AMERICAN INSTITUTE OF ARCHITECTS (AIA) CONTRACT
  Default/termination §4.03

AMERICAN INSTITUTE OF ARCHITECTS (AIA) CONTRACT, *continued*
  Environmental problems §§4.16, 14.19
  Standard contract forms, bidding and contract formation §2.46
AMERICAN SOCIETY OF FOUNDATION ENGINEERS (ASFE)
  Bidding and contract formation §2.46
AMERICAN SUBCONTRACTORS ASSOCIATION (ASA)
  Bidding and contract formation §2.46
AMOUNT DUE OR TO BECOME DUE
  Mechanics' liens §9.27
AMOUNT OF JUDGMENT
  Mechanics' liens §9.62
AMOUNT OWED
  Mechanics' liens §9.26
ANALYSIS OF BOILERPLATE
  Bidding and contract formation §2.34
ANSWERS TO DEPENDENT LIENORS
  Enforcement, mechanics' liens §9.46
APPEAL
  Dispute resolution §6.11
  Procurement Policy Board (PPB) Rules §§7.04, 17.08
APPLICABLE LAW
  UCC, subcontracts §3.28
APPORTIONMENT OF LIABILITY
  Defects and failures §2.10
  Superfund litigation, environmental problems §4.39
APPORTIONMENT OF RESPONSIBILITY
  Delays §7.50

APPROPRIATE EXPERIENCE
  Procurement Policy Board (PPB)
    Rules §7.09
APPROPRIATION AMOUNT
  Bidding and contract formation
    §2.13
ARBITRARY ACTS
  Article 78, remedies/damages
    §5.04
ARBITRATION
  Attorneys' fees, remedies/
    damages §5.14
  Certainty, remedies/damages
    §5.19
  Dispute resolution §§6.11-16.14,
    16.16
  Enforcement, mechanics' liens
    §9.41
  Interest, remedies/damages §5.15
  Procurement Policy Board (PPB)
    Rules §7.01
  Professional's role and liability
    §11.11
  Punitive damages, remedies/
    damages §5.12
  Specific performance,
    remedies/damages §5.39
  Subcontracts §§3.06, 3.35
ARBITRATION VS LITIGATION
  Dispute resolution §6.12
ARCHITECT BIAS
  Bidding and contract formation
    §2.46
ARCHITECT/ENGINEER
  Acts and omissions, professional's
    role and liability §11.11
  Agents' liability, construction
    safety §3.11
  Approval, default/termination
    §4.05
  Breach, remedies/damages §5.34
  Claims by surety against, bonds
    §8.50
  Default, default/termination §4.19
  Defects and failures §§2.08, 12.11

ARCHITECT/ENGINEER, *continued*
  Environmental problems §§4.02,
    14.17-14.19
  Liability. See PROFESSIONAL'S
    ROLE AND LIABILITY
  Liability limitation, remedies/
    damages §5.22
  Negligence, liability in §3.15
  Protected persons, bonds §8.36
ARCHITECT INTERFERENCE
  Contractor defenses, default/
    termination §4.14
ARCHITECTS
  Mechanics' liens §9.03
ARCHITECTURAL SERVICES
  Bidding and contract formation
    §2.14
  Procurement Policy Board (PPB)
    Rules §7.06
ARTICLE 78
  See REMEDIES/DAMAGES
ASBESTOS
  Abatement. See
    ENVIRONMENTAL PROBLEMS
  Assigning and assuming risk,
    environmental problems §4.10
  Claims made coverage,
    environmental problems §4.23
  Owner-contractor agreements,
    environmental problems §4.13
  Personal injury suits,
    environmental problems §4.43
  Property damage suits,
    environmental problems §4.43
ASBESTOS CONSULTANT ERRORS
  AND OMISSIONS INSURANCE
  Environmental problems §4.21
ASBESTOS-CONTAINING MATERIALS
  (ACMS)
  Environmental problems §4.29
ASBESTOS HAZARD EMERGENCY
  RESPONSE ACT
  Environmental problems §4.29
ASBESTOS INVESTIGATION REPORT
  Environmental problems §4.31

INDEX

ASBESTOS PROJECTS
  Environmental problems §§4.30, 14.31
ASCERTAINABLE DAMAGES
  Delays §7.18
ASSETS
  Trust funds, mechanics' liens §9.70
ASSIGNEES
  Trust funds, mechanics' liens §9.75
ASSIGNING RISK
  Environmental problems §4.10
ASSIGNMENT
  Liens, mechanics' liens §9.03
  Moneys due, mechanics' liens §9.55
ASSOCIATED GENERAL CONTRACTORS OF AMERICA, INC (AGC)
  Bidding and contract formation §2.46
ASSUMING RISK
  Environmental problems §4.10
ATTACHMENT
  Funds, mechanics' liens §9.07
  No funds available, mechanics' liens §9.50
  Obtaining judgments, mechanics' liens §9.61
  Real property, mechanics' liens §9.06
ATTORNEYS' FEES
  Bonds §§8.41, 8.48
  Claims by obligee, bonds §8.21
  Dispute resolution §§6.08, 16.12
  Liens, mechanics' liens §9.79
  Miller Act bonds, bonds §8.46
  Professional's role and liability §11.22
  Remedies/damages §5.14
  Subcontracts §3.25
  Trust funds, mechanics' liens §9.79

AUTHORITY
  Architect or engineer, dispute resolution §6.04
  Bidding and contract formation §2.30
  Changes/extra work §6.07
  Contracting (capacity), bidding and contract formation §2.29
  Dispute resolution §6.01
  Enforcing safety standards, construction safety §3.08
  Stopping work, construction safety §3.15
  Supervision and control, construction safety §§3.10, 13.11, 13.15
AVAILABILITY OF RECORDS TO CLAIMANTS
  Trust funds, mechanics' liens §9.74
AVAILABLE DEFENSES
  Surety's defenses, bonds §8.47
AWARDING BIDS
  Public contracts, bidding and contract formation §2.13
AWARDING CONTRACTS
  Procurement Policy Board (PPB) Rules §§7.04, 17.11

B

BACK CHARGES
  Subcontracts §3.20
BAD FAITH
  Bonds §8.22
  Procurement Policy Board (PPB) Rules §7.11
  Professional's role and liability §11.21
BALANCING OF EQUITIES
  Injunctions, remedies/damages §5.06

BANKRUPTCY
Contractor default, default/termination §4.11
Superfund litigation, environmental problems §4.39

BAR CHART
Delays §7.04
Swimming pool construction, fig. 7-2

BARGAINING POWER
Subcontracts §3.08

"BASEBALL" ARBITRATION
Dispute resolution §6.08

BASIC CLAUSE COVERAGE
See CHANGES/EXTRA WORK

BEATING A NO DAMAGES FOR DELAY CLAUSE
Delays §7.36

BEHAVIORAL CHANGED CONDITIONS
Changed conditions §5.02

BENEFICIAL DEVELOPMENT
Wetlands, environmental problems §4.34

BENEFICIARIES
Trust funds, mechanics' liens §9.71

BETTER RISK ALLOCATION
Bidding and contract formation §2.43

BID BONDS
See BONDS

BIDDERS LISTS
Bidding and contract formation §2.06

BIDDING AND CONTRACT FORMATION
Generally §2.01
Analysis of boilerplate §2.34
Bidding §2.02
Contract formation
–generally §2.23
–actual and apparent authority §2.30

BIDDING AND CONTRACT FORMATION, *continued*
–authority to contract (capacity) §2.29
–certainty of terms §2.26
–illegal contracts §2.28
–mutual assent/intent to be bound §2.25
–offer and acceptance §2.24
–statute of frauds §2.27
Delays §3.35
Disputes, Procurement Policy Board (PPB) Rules §7.08
Evaluating risks and responsibilities
–generally §2.36
–pricing risks §2.37
Evaluating special terms §2.35
Execution of contract §2.32
Incorporation by reference §2.51
Interpreting contracts
–generally §2.47
–contracts vs other documents §2.49
–extrinsic evidence/parol evidence rule §2.48
–plans vs specifications §2.50
Letter of intent §2.31
Mistakes
–generally §2.18
–mutual mistakes §2.20
–unilateral mistakes §2.19
Negotiating terms and conditions §2.33
Private contracts §2.17
Public contracts
–generally §2.03
–accepting bids §2.10
–advertising bids §2.07
–awarding bid §2.13
–challenging award or rejection of bid §2.15
–compliance with bid documents, responsiveness §2.05
–exceptions to bidding rules §2.14

BIDDING AND CONTRACT FORMATION, *continued*
  –illegal bids and contracts §2.11
  –lowest responsible bidder §2.04
  –prequalification of bidders §2.06
  –public agencies exempt from competitive bidding requirements §2.16
  –specifications §2.08
  Wicks Law, separate specifications §2.09
  –withdrawal of bid §2.12
  Rejection of bids §2.22
  Risk allocation
  –generally §2.38
  –better risk allocation and total project cost reductions §2.43
  –options for allocating risks §2.41
  –philosophies for dealing with risks §2.40
  –risk allocation language in contract §2.42
  –role of counsel §2.44
  –types of risk §2.39
  Standard contract forms §2.46
  Subcontractor bids §2.21
  Subcontract terms and conditions §2.45
BIDS
  Changes/extra work §6.04
  Contract clauses, changed conditions §5.08
  Disputes, Procurement Policy Board (PPB) Rules §7.08
  Documents, bidding and contract formation §2.08
  Instructions, bidding and contract formation §2.05
  Mistakes, Procurement Policy Board (PPB) Rules §7.02
  Owner-contractor agreement, environmental problems §4.12
  Subcontracts §3.02
BIERCE, AMBROSE
  Dispute resolution §6.01

BINDING SURETY TO ARBITRATION CLAUSE
  Dispute resolution §6.16
BLANKET LIENS
  Mechanics' liens §9.12
  Waivers
  –mechanics' liens §9.24
  –subcontracts §3.26
BLASTING
  Introductory material §1.25
BOARD OF CONTRACT APPEALS
  Contract disputes §6.11
BOARD OF ESTIMATE
  Procurement Policy Board (PPB) Rules §7.12
BODILY INJURY
  Insurance, environmental problems §4.24
BOILERPLATE
  Analysis, bidding and contract formation §2.34
  Subcontracts §3.05
BONDS
  Attorneys' fees §8.41
  Bid bonds
  –generally §8.05
  –releasing sureties §8.07
  –surety's liability §8.06
  Bonds vs insurance §8.01
  Claims against, defects and failures §2.09
  Claims by obligee
  –generally §8.17
  –attorneys' fees §8.21
  –cost of completion §8.18
  –incidental and consequential damages §8.20
  –interest §8.23
  –liquidated and delay damages §8.19
  –punitive damages §8.22
  Claims by surety
  –generally §8.48
  –against architect/engineer §8.50
  –against lending institutions §8.51

BONDS, *continued*
  –against obligee §8.49
  –against subcontractors, their sureties, and their insurers §8.52
  Construing bonds §8.02
  Defenses. See SURETY'S DEFENSES, this heading
  Environmental problems §4.25
  Guaranty and completion bonds §8.09
  Interest §§8.23, 8.42
  Items covered
  –generally §8.37
  –materials §8.38
  –rental equipment §8.39
  Miller Act bonds
  –generally §8.43
  –claimable items §8.46
  –notice of claim and limitation of action §8.45
  –persons protected §8.44
  Notice of claim §8.40
  Parties to surety relationships §8.03
  Payment bond notice provisions app 8-1
  Payment bonds §8.32
  Performance bonds §8.08
  Preliminary injunctions §5.06
  Surety's defenses
  –generally §8.24
  –available defenses §8.47
  –discharge by fraud §8.27
  –discharge by modification or breach of contract §8.26
  –lack of or untimely notice §8.25
  –liability in excess of penal sum §8.29
  –party not protected by bond §8.31
  –principal's defenses and claims §8.30
  –untimely claim §8.28
  Surety's obligations and options
  –generally §8.12

BONDS, *continued*
  –penal sum paid to obligee §8.16
  –work completion by obligee §8.15
  –work completion by surety or with substitute contractor §8.14
  –work completion with original contractor §8.13
  Third-party beneficiaries and combination bonds §8.10
  Types and terms §8.04
  Who is protected
  –generally §8.33
  –architects/engineers §8.36
  Miller Act bonds §8.44
  –subcontractors §8.34
  –suppliers and materialmen §8.35
  –third-party beneficiaries and combination bonds §8.10
BONDS VS INSURANCE
  Bonds §8.01
BOROUGH PRESIDENT COMPLAINTS
  Procurement Policy Board (PPB) Rules §7.12
BREACH
  Architect/engineer, remedies/damages §5.34
  Specific breaches by owner. See REMEDIES/DAMAGES
  Subcontractors, remedies/damages §5.35
BREACH OF CONTRACT
  Changed conditions §5.16
  Changes/extra work §§6.04, 6.35
  Constructive changes. See CHANGES/EXTRA WORK
  Delays §7.01
  Discharge, bonds §8.26
  Distinguished from Article 79, remedies/damages §5.01
  Exceptions to enforcement of no damages for delay clauses §7.42

BREACH OF CONTRACT, *continued*
  Professional's role and liability §11.23
  Subcontracts §§3.25, 3.35

BREACH OF CONTRACT VS QUANTUM MERUIT
  Remedies/damages §5.10

BREACH OF EXPRESS WARRANTY
  Professional's role and liability §11.04

BREACH OF IMPLIED WARRANTY
  Changed conditions §5.16

BREACH OF TRUST
  Trust funds, mechanics' liens §9.79

BREACH OF WARRANTY VS BREACH OF CONTRACT
  Defects and failures §2.16

BROKERS
  Insurance §10.15

BUILDING LOAN CONTRACTS AND MORTGAGES
  Mechanics' liens §9.53

BURDEN OF PROOF
  Bidding and contract formation §2.15
  Construction safety §3.17
  Defects and failures §§2.03, 12.08
  Delays §7.49

C

CALCULATION OF DAMAGES
  Changed conditions §5.19

CALL BEFORE YOU DIG
  Introductory material §1.27

CANCELLATION OF CONTRACTS
  Procurement Policy Board (PPB) Rules §7.11

CANCELLATION OF DELIVERY
  Supply contract, subcontracts §3.31

CAPRICIOUS ACTS
  Article 78, remedies/damages §5.04

CARDINAL CHANGE
  Changes/extra work §§6.04, 6.13, 6.35

CARE, CUSTODY, OR CONTROL EXCLUSION
  Insurance §10.23

CARRYOVER OF PAYMENTS
  Subcontracts §3.16

CASE MANAGEMENT ORDER
  Trial preparation, environmental problems §4.35

CASH-OUT
  Superfund litigation, environmental problems §4.40

CATASTROPHE INSURANCE
  Wrap-up insurance §10.11

CAUSE
  Contractual right of termination, default/termination §§4.03, 4.05

CAUSE OF ACTION FOR RECOVERY OF COSTS
  Superfund litigation, environmental problems §4.38

CAUSES OF DELAY
  Delays §7.05

CAVEAT EMPTOR RULE
  Defects and failures §2.14

CDRB
  See CONTRACT DISPUTE RESOLUTION BOARD

CEASING WORK
  Bonds 8.26

CERCLA
  Environmental protection §4.05

CERTAINTY
  Remedies/damages §5.19

CERTAINTY OF TERMS
  Bidding and contract formation §2.26

CERTIFICATE OF INSURANCE, NECESSITY
  Insurance §10.31
CERTIFICATES OF INTEREST
  Professional's role and liability §11.08
CERTIFICATION
  Contracts, bidding and contract formation §2.32
  Progress reports, professional's role and liability §§11.10, 11.20
  Work done, subcontracts §3.16
CERTIORARI
  Remedies/damages §5.01
CHALLENGING AWARDS
  Public contracts, bidding and contract formations §2.15
CHANGED CIRCUMSTANCES
  Default/termination §4.04
CHANGED CONDITIONS
  Generally §5.01
  Claims
  –generally §5.17
  –notice and documentation §5.18
  Clauses, environmental problems §4.14
  Compensable delay §7.29
  Contract clauses
  –generally §5.06
  –changed condition clauses §5.07
  –disclaimer clauses §5.08
  –exculpatory clauses §5.09
  Contractor's duty to perform §5.15
  Damages
  –generally §5.19
  –impact costs §5.20
  Definition
  –generally §5.02
  –latent above-ground conditions §5.04
  –miscellaneous causes §5.05
  –subsurface conditions §5.03
  Delays §7.37

CHANGED CONDITIONS, *continued*
  Dispute resolution §6.02
  Owner-contractor clause, environmental problems §4.13
  Owner's misrepresentation
  –generally §5.10
  –fraud, concealment, and reckless representation §5.12
  –innocent misrepresentation §5.11
  Reliance on owner's data §5.14
  Remedies §5.16
  Site investigation §5.13
CHANGE ORDERS
  Adjustments, Procurement Policy Board (PPB) Rules §7.03
  Bidding and contract formation §2.43
  Changes/extra work §§6.05, 6.06, 6.29
  Clauses, environmental problems §4.14
  Delays §7.37
  Procurement Policy Board (PPB) Rules §§7.03, 17.05, 17.06
  Subcontracts §3.12
CHANGE-RELATED COSTS
  Pricing, changes/extra work §6.26
CHANGES/EXTRA WORK
  Authority to make changes §6.07
  Basic clause coverage
  –generally §6.02
  –cardinal change doctrine §6.04
  –contract scope of work §6.03
  –deductive changes vs convenience terminations §6.05
  Claims preservation and defense
  –generally §6.32
  –accord and satisfaction §6.33
  Constructive changes
  –generally §6.15
  –defective specifications §6.18
  –dictating performance methods §6.21
  –duty to seek clarification §6.16
  –overmeticulous inspection §6.20

CHANGES/EXTRA WORK, *continued*
–owner interference with work §6.17
–owner nondisclosure of information §6.19
Duty to proceed with disputed work
–generally §6.13
–failure to proceed with disputed work §6.14
Exculpatory clauses §6.31
Issuing change orders §6.06
Notice, protest, and record keeping requirements §6.24
Origin of changes §6.01
Performance specifications vs detailed specifications §6.22
Price adjustments for changed work
–generally §6.25
cost reimbursement contracts §6.28
–impact costs §6.29
–pricing change-related costs §6.26
–proving costs §6.30
–unit price §6.27
Remedies §6.34
Scope of work disputes §6.23
Waiver of writing requirement
–generally 6.09
–acquiescence §6.11
–conduct §6.12
–oral order §6.10
Writing requirement §6.08

CHECKLIST, DEVELOPER'S
Payment bond notice provisions app 8-1

CHECKLIST OF ENVIRONMENTAL CONCERNS
Environmental problems §4.09

CHECKS CASHED UNDER PROTEST
Changes/extra work §6.34

CITY ENVIRONMENTAL QUALITY ACT (CEQA)
Environmental problems §4.07

CIVIL LIABILITY
Trial preparation, environmental problems §4.37

CIVIL PENALTIES
Asbestos abatement, environmental problems §4.30

CLAIMABLE ITEMS
Miller Act bonds, bonds §8.46

CLAIMS
Against bond, defects and failures §2.09
Changed conditions. See CHANGED CONDITIONS
Changes/extra work §§6.29, 6.32-6.34
Disruption/interference vs delay §7.43
Narrative, dispute resolution §6.02
New York court of claims, dispute resolution §6.11
By obligee. See BONDS
Principals defenses and claims, bonds §8.30
Relief, mechanics' liens §9.82
By surety. See BONDS
Unexpected, dispute resolution §6.14

CLAIMS MADE VS OCCURRENCE POLICIES
Environmental problems §§4.23, 14.24
Insurance §10.04

CLARIFICATION, DUTY TO SEEK
Changes/extra work §6.16

CLEAN AIR ACT
Environmental problems §4.05

CLEAN HANDS
Superfund litigation, environmental problems §4.39

CLEAN WATER ACT
Environmental problems §5.05

716 INDEX

CLOSE-TO-PRIVITY RELATIONSHIP
  Bonds §8.50
CODES
  Introductory material §1.24
  Subcontracts §3.11
COLLAPSE
  Insurance §10.21
COLLATERAL SOURCE RULE
  Remedies/damages §5.18
COMBINATION BONDS
  Third-party beneficiaries, bonds §8.10
COMMENCING ACTION ON FORECLOSURES
  Mechanics' liens §9.39
COMMENCING PROJECTS
  Failure, remedies/damages §§5.25, 15.31
COMMERCIAL PRACTICE
  Relevant contract clauses, delays §7.16
COMMON ELEMENTS CHARGES
  Trust funds, mechanics' liens §9.70
COMMON LAW ACCOUNTING
  Remedies/damages §5.09
COMMON LAW INDEMNITY OR CONTRIBUTION
  Insurance §10.22
  Subcontracts §3.13
COMMON LAW OBLIGATIONS
  Contractor's obligations §3.04
  Owner's obligations §3.03
COMMUNITY STANDARDS
  Defects and failures §2.03
COMPARATIVE NEGLIGENCE
  Construction safety §3.14
COMPENSABLE DELAY
  Delays. See DELAYS
  Excusable delay §7.07
COMPENSATED SURETIES
  Bonds §8.03

COMPENSATION
  Procurement Policy Board (PPB) Rules §§7.11, 17.12
COMPETITIVE BIDDING STATUTES
  Changes/extra work §6.04
COMPETITIVE SEALED BIDDING FROM PREQUALIFIED VENDORS
  Procurement Policy Board (PPB) Rules §7.02
COMPETITIVE SEALED PROPOSALS
  Procurement Policy Board (PPB) Rules §7.02
COMPLAINTS
  Borough presidents, Procurement Policy Board (PPB) Rules §7.12
  Form, mechanics' liens §9.45
  Superfund litigation, environmental problems §4.38
COMPLEMENTARY SPECIFICATIONS
  Changes/extra work §6.22
COMPLETE FORFEITURE
  Bidding and contract formation §2.11
COMPLETION
  Bonds §8.09
  Delays §7.02
  Mechanics' liens §§9.29, 9.30
  Professional's role and liability §11.08
  Tasks, subcontracts §3.16
COMPLIANCE
  Bid documents, bidding and contract formation §2.05
  Laws and regulations clause, environmental problems §4.14
  Owner-contractor agreement, environmental problems §4.13
  Specifications, bidding and contract formation §2.08
COMPREHENSIVE ENVIRONMENTAL RESPONSE, COMPENSATION, AND LIABILITY ACT (CERCLA)
  See CERCLA

INDEX

COMPREHENSIVE GENERAL LIABILITY INSURANCE: EXCLUSIONS
Environmental problems §4.22

COMPTROLLER
Bidding and contract formation §2.30

CONCEALED CONDITIONS
Changed conditions. See CHANGED CONDITIONS
Dispute resolution §6.11

CONCEALMENT
Owner's misrepresentation, changed conditions §5.12

CONCRETE
Defects and failures §2.07

CONCURRENT DELAY
Delays §7.31
Delays, figs. 7-3, 7-4, 7-5

CONCURRENT EXERCISE OF AUTHORITY
Environmental problems §4.04

CONDITIONS PRECEDENT
Bidding and contract formation §§2.13, 2.32
Bonds §8.06
Dispute resolution §§6.02, 16.15
Distinguished from procedural hurdles, dispute resolution §6.15
Subcontracts §3.18

CONDOMINIUMS
Lienable property, mechanics' liens §9.12
Trust funds, mechanics' liens §9.70

CONDUCT
Waiver of writing requirement, changes/extra work §6.12

CONFIRMATION OF BID
Procurement Policy Board (PPB) Rules §7.02

CONFLICT OF INTEREST
Procurement Policy Board (PPB) Rules §7.16
Professional's role and liability §11.11

CONSENT DECREES
Superfund litigation, environmental problems §4.40

CONSEQUENTIAL DAMAGES
Claims by obligee, bonds §§8.15, 8.20

CONSIDERATION
Bidding and contract formation §2.21

CONSOLIDATION OF CASES
Dispute resolution §6.11

CONSPICUOUS WRITING
Supply contract, subcontracts §3.33

CONSTRUCT CONCEPTS
New designs, insurance §10.33

CONSTRUCTION CASES
Article 78, remedies/damages §5.03

CONSTRUCTION CHANGE DIRECTIVE
Changes/extra work §6.02

CONSTRUCTION DEFECTS
Defects and failures §2.03

CONSTRUCTION INDUSTRY ARBITRATION RULES
Dispute resolution §6.12

CONSTRUCTION INDUSTRY MEDIATION RULES
Dispute resolution §6.07

CONSTRUCTION INSURANCE
Insurance §10.01

CONSTRUCTION MANAGEMENT ASSOCIATION OF AMERICA (CMAA)
Bidding and contract formation §2.46

CONSTRUCTION MANAGEMENT SERVICES EXCLUSION
Insurance §10.07
CONSTRUCTION MANAGERS
Agents' liability, construction safety §3.12
Continuous treatment doctrine, professional's role and liability §11.24
Environmental problems §4.02
Insurance §§10.07, 10.35
Introductory material §1.13
Licensing, professional's role and liability §11.02
Mechanics' liens §9.03
Negligence, liability in §3.16
Professional's role and liability. See PROFESSIONAL'S ROLE AND LIABILITY
CONSTRUCTION MEANS OR METHODS
Professional's role and liability §11.04
CONSTRUCTION PROJECTS OUTSIDE THE STATE
Construction safety §3.01
CONSTRUCTION RISK
Bidding and contract formation §2.39
CONSTRUCTION SAFETY
Generally §3.01
Affirmative defenses to statutory liability §3.14
Agents' liability
–generally §3.10
–architect/engineer §3.11
–construction manager §3.12
–subcontractors §3.13
Architect/engineer liability in negligence §3.15
Construction manager liability in negligence §3.16
Contractor's obligations §3.04
Contribution/indemnification §3.18

CONSTRUCTION SAFETY, *continued*
General contractor's liability §3.07
Labor law §240 13.05, 241 13.06
Negligence
–architect/engineer liability §3.15
–construction manager liability §3.16
OSHA §3.19
Owner's liability
–generally §3.08
–residential dwelling exception §3.09
Owner's obligations §3.03
Res ipsa loquitur §3.17
Statutory liability, affirmative defenses to §3.14
Workers' compensation laws §3.02
CONSTRUCTION SERVICES
Procurement Policy Board (PPB) Rules §7.06
CONSTRUCTIVE ACCELERATION
Delays §7.46
CONSTRUCTIVE CHANGES
See CHANGES/EXTRA WORK
CONSTRUCTIVE FRAUD
Remedies/ damages §5.11
CONSTRUING BONDS
Bonds §8.02
CONTEMPLATION
Delays §7.37
CONTENT
Notice of claim, bonds §8.40
Notice requirements
–delays §7.19
–dispute resolution §6.02
CONTINGENCIES
Bidding and contract formation §2.35
CONTINGENCY FAILURE
Supply contract, subcontracts §3.31

CONTINGENT PAYMENT CLAUSES
Subcontracts §3.18
CONTINUOUS TREATMENT
DOCTRINE
Defects and failures §2.08
Professional's role and liability
§11.24
CONTRACT-BASED CLAIMS
Professional's role and liability
§11.04
CONTRACT DISPUTE
Procurement Policy Board (PPB)
Rules §7.09
CONTRACT DISPUTE RESOLUTION
BOARD (CDRB)
Procurement Policy Board (PPB)
Rules §7.09
CONTRACT DISPUTES ACT
Dispute resolution §6.11
CONTRACTOR DAMAGE RECOVERY
Delays §7.65
CONTRACTORS
Acts or omissions, professional's
role and liability §11.04
Contractor's damages for delay.
See DELAYS
Default/termination. See
DEFAULT/TERMINATION
Defenses. See
DEFAULT/TERMINATION
Delays caused by §7.05
Duties, subcontracts §3.09
Duty to perform, changed
conditions §5.15
Environmental problems §4.02
Introductory material. See
INTRODUCTORY MATERIAL
Mechanics' liens §§9.03, 9.05
Nonexcusable delay §7.30
Obligations, construction safety
§3.04
Responsibilities, defects and
failures §2.03
Types of delay caused by §7.05

CONTRACTOR'S OTHER REMEDIES
Delays §7.66
CONTRACTOR'S OWN WORK
Insurance §10.19
CONTRACTORS' POLLUTION
LIABILITY POLICY
Insurance, environmental
problems §§420-424
CONTRACTOR'S TRUST
Mechanics' liens §9.70
CONTRACT/OTHER DOCUMENTS
CONFLICT
Bidding and contract formation
§2.49
CONTRACT REVIEW BOARD
See DISPUTE REVIEW BOARD
CONTRACTS
Changes
–compensable delay §7.28
Procurement Policy Board (PPB)
Rules §7.05
Clauses
–changed conditions. See
CHANGED CONDITIONS
–relevant contract clauses. See
DELAYS
Damages, mechanics' liens §9.22
Description, mechanics' liens
§9.27
Disputes, Procurement Policy
Board (PPB) Rules §7.09
Formation
–bidding and contract formation.
See BIDDING AND CONTRACT
FORMATION
Procurement Policy Board (PPB)
Rules §7.03
Interpretations, changes/extra
work §6.23
Liability, professional's
role and liability
§§11.04, 11.14
Owner-contractor agreement,
environmental problems §4.13

CONTRACTS, *continued*
  Procurement Policy Board (PPB) Rules. See PROCUREMENT POLICY BOARD (PPB) RULES
  Registration, Procurement Policy Board (PPB) Rules §7.04
  Third parties, professional's role and liability §11.14
CONTRACT SCOPE OF WORK
  Changes/extra work §6.03
  Dispute resolution §6.04
CONTRACTUAL INDEMNIFICATION/ CONTRIBUTION
  Defects and failures §2.11
  Insurance §10.22
CONTRACTUAL LIABILITY
  Insurance §10.22
CONTRACTUAL LIMITATIONS ON DAMAGES
  Remedies/damages §5.22
CONTRACTUAL PROVISIONS REGARDING REMEDIES
  Remedies/damages §5.23
CONTRACTUAL RIGHT OF TERMINATION
  See DEFAULT/TERMINATION
CONTRACTUAL RISK
  Bidding and contract formation §2.39
CONTRACTUAL TERMINATION PROCEDURES
  Notice requirements, default/termination §4.06
  Owner's failure to follow, default/termination §4.18
CONTRACTUAL WARRANTY OF GUARANTEE PERIOD
  Defects and failures §2.12
CONTRIBUTION/INDEMNIFICATION
  Construction safety §§3.08, 13.10, 13.12, 13.18
  Defects and failures §§2.10, 12.11

CONTRIBUTION/INDEMNIFICATION, *continued*
  Professional's role and liability §11.22
CONTROL
  Insurance §10.23
CONTROLLED INSPECTIONS
  Introductory material §1.24
CONTROLLING CLAUSES
  Subcontracts §3.06
CONVENIENCE TERMINATIONS
  Contractual right of termination, default/termination §4.04
  Distinguished from deductive changes, changes/extra work §6.05
CONVERSION
  Remedies/damages §5.08
COOPERATION WITH INSURANCE COMPANY
  Insurance §§10.16, 10.29
COOPERATIVES
  Lienable property, mechanics' liens §9.12
COORDINATION
  Delays §7.23
  Professional's role and liability §§11.09, 11.18
CORRECTING DEFECTIVE WORK
  Default/termination §4.10
CORRECTION OF BIDS
  Procurement Policy Board (PPB) Rules §7.02
COST ANALYSIS
  Procurement Policy Board (PPB) Rules §7.03
COST DETERMINATION
  Introductory material §1.03
COST EFFECTIVE RISK ALLOCATION LANGUAGE
  Integration into contract, bidding and contract formations §2.42

COST ESTIMATES
  Professional's role and liability §§11.07, 11.17
COST EVALUATION
  Procurement Policy Board (PPB) Rules §7.03
COST HISTORY
  Procurement Policy Board (PPB) Rules §7.06
COST OF COMPLETION
  Claims by obligee, bonds §8.18
  Distinguished from diminuation in value, remedies/damages §5.29
COST OR PRICING DATA AND ANALYSIS
  Procurement Policy Board (PPB) Rules §7.03
COST-PLUS
  Contracts
  –changes/extra work §6.28
  –owner-design professional agreement, environmental problems §4.17
  –procurement Policy Board (PPB) Rules §7.03
  –supply contract, subcontracts §3.32
  Fixed fee, introductory material §1.21
  Incentive fee, introductory material §1.21
  Percentage of cost contract, introductory material §1.21
  Reimbursable contracts, introductory material §1.21
COST REDUCTION
  Risk allocation, bidding and contract formation §2.43
COST REIMBURSEMENT
  Contracts, changes/extra work §6.28
  Method, introductory material §1.03
COSTS
  Introductory material §1.21

COSTS OF IMPROVEMENT
  Trust funds, mechanics' liens §9.75
COUNCIL ON ENVIRONMENTAL QUALITY (CEQ)
  Environmental problems §4.05
COUNSEL, ROLE OF
  Risk allocation, bidding and contract formation §2.44
COURSE OF DEALING
  Supply contract, subcontracts §3.33
COURTS OF RECORD AND NOT OF RECORD
  Enforcement, mechanics' liens §9.43
COVERAGE
  See INSURANCE
COVERED ITEMS
  Bonds §§8.37-8.39
CREDIT
  Changes/extra work §6.01
CREDIT VS RISK
  Bonds §8.01
CRIMINAL LARCENY
  Trust funds, mechanics' liens §§9.79, 9.80
CRIMINAL LIABILITY
  Trial preparation, criminal liability §4.37
CRITERIA FOR ABNORMALLY DANGEROUS MATERIAL
  Introductory material §1.25
CRITICAL PATH
  Delays §§7.07, 7.08, 7.46
CRITICAL PATH METHOD (CPM)
  Delays §7.04
  Schedule, fig. 7-1
CUSTODY
  Insurance §10.23
CUSTOM AND USAGE
  Bidding and contract formation §2.48

CUT-OFF DATES
  Insurance, environmental problems §4.24

D

DAILY SUM OF LIQUIDATED DAMAGES
  Subcontracts §3.22
DAMAGES
  Additional work, changed conditions §5.16
  Bonds §8.17
  Changed conditions §§5.09, 5.19, 5.20
  Changes/extra work §6.04
  Contractor recovery, delays §7.65
  Contractor's damages for delay. See DELAYS
  Delay damages. See DELAY DAMAGES
  Insurance §10.19
  Mechanics' liens §9.49
  Mistakes, bidding and contract formation §2.19
  Offsets, subcontracts §3.21
  Remedies/damages. See REMEDIES/DAMAGES
  Subcontracts §3.35
  Supply contracts, subcontracts §3.31
DAMAGE TO REPUTATION
  Dispute resolution §6.14
DATES OF PERFORMANCE
  Mechanics' liens §9.26
45-DAY PERIOD
  Bidding and contract formation §2.12
DEADLINE TO COMMENCE ACTION
  Enforcement, mechanics' liens §9.39
DEBARMENT
  Procurement Policy Board (PPB) Rules §7.10

DECEPTION
  Contract clauses, changed conditions §5.08
DECLARATORY JUDGMENT
  Insurance §10.27
  Remedies/damages §5.08
DECONTAMINATION OF WASTE SITES
  Environmental problems §4.27
DEDUCTIBLES
  Insurance §10.10
DEDUCTIONS
  Supply contract, subcontracts §3.32
DEDUCTIVE CHANGES
  Cardinal change, changes/extra work §6.04
  Distinguished from convenience terminations, changes/extra work §6.05
DEFAULT/TERMINATION
  Generally §4.01
  Architect/engineer default §4.19
  Changes/extra work §6.14
  Contractor default
  –generally §4.07
  –failure to correct defective work §4.10
  –failure to pay subcontractors and suppliers §4.09
  –failure to prosecute work §4.08
  –insolvency or bankruptcy §4.11
  Contractor defenses
  –generally §4.12
  –impossibility §4.15
  –non-payment §4.17
  –owner failure to follow procedure §4.18
  –owner or architect interference §4.14
  –substantial performance §4.13
  –waiver and estoppel §4.16
  Contractual right of termination
  –generally §4.02

DEFAULT/TERMINATION, *continued*
–architect/engineer approval §4.05
–for cause §4.03
–for convenience §4.04
Notice requirements §4.06
Procurement Policy Board (PPB) Rules §§7.05, 7.15
Remedies/damages §5.26
Rescission §4.20
Subcontracts §3.24
Wrongful termination §4.21

DEFECTIVE DESIGN
Collateral source rule, remedies/damages §5.18
Compensable delay §7.27

DEFECTIVE LIENS
Enforcement, mechanics' liens §9.48

DEFECTIVE PERFORMANCE
Remedies/damages §5.28

DEFECTIVE SPECIFICATIONS
Changes/extra work §6.18

DEFECTIVE WORK
Failure to correct, default/termination §4.10
Insurance §10.19

DEFECTS AND FAILURES
Generally §2.01
Claims against bond §2.09
Construction defects §2.03
Design defects §2.02
Divided responsibility §2.06
Faulty materials §2.04
Improper installation §2.05
Indemnification and contribution
–generally §2.10
–contractual indemnification and contribution §2.11
Mechanics' liens §9.36
Professional's role and liability §§11.08, 11.14
Statute of limitations §2.08
Waiver of defects §2.07
Warranty (guarantee) clauses

DEFECTS AND FAILURES, *continued*
–generally §2.12
–exclusive remedy §2.16
–express warranties §2.15
–implied warranties §2.13
–implied warranties in new home sales §2.14

DEFECTS ON THE FACE
Mechanics' liens §9.36

DEFENSE AND COUNTERCLAIM
Mechanics' liens §9.49

DEFENSE COSTS
Insurance §10.12

DEFENSES
Claims preservation and defense. See CHANGES/EXTRA WORK
Contractor defenses. See DEFAULT/TERMINATION
Diversion, mechanics' liens §9.76
Foreclosure actions, mechanics' liens §9.47
Insurance §10.07
Principals, bonds §8.30
Superfund litigation, environmental law §4.38
Surety's defenses. See BONDS

DEFENSIVE CASES
Alternative dispute resolution, environmental cases §4.42

DEFICIENCY JUDGMENTS
Sale upon execution, mechanics' liens §9.66

DEFINITION
See CHANGED CONDITIONS

DELAY AND DISRUPTION CLAUSES
Delays §7.05

DELAY DAMAGES
Changed conditions §5.20
Claims by obligee, bonds §8.19
Clauses, environmental problems §4.14
Default/termination §4.16
Miller Act bonds, bonds §8.46
Remedies/damages §5.15
Subcontracts §§3.22, 3.25, 3.35

DELAYED NOTICE TO PROCEED
  Compensable delay §7.25
DELAY OR CANCELLATION OF DELIVERY
  Supply contract, subcontracts §3.31
DELAYS
  Generally §7.01
  Acceleration
  –generally §7.44
  –actual acceleration §7.45
  –constructive acceleration §7.46
  –right to relief §7.47
  Apportionment of responsibility §7.50
  Burden of proof
  –generally §7.49
  –jury-verdict method §7.49
  –total cost method §7.49
  Causes §§7.05, 7.06
  Change orders, Procurement Policy Board (PPB) Rules §7.05
  Claim, dispute resolution §6.02
  Compensable delay
  –generally §7.22
  –changed conditions §7.29
  –contract changes and extras §7.28
  –defective design §7.27
  –delayed notice to proceed §7.25
  –denial of access §7.24
  –inspection/approval delays §7.26
  –owner interference §7.23
  Concurrent delay §7.31
  Contractor damage recovery §7.65
  Contractor's damages for delay
  –generally §7.52
  –field overhead §7.58
  –financing costs §7.61
  –home office overhead §7.60
  –idle equipment §7.59
  –impact costs §7.57
  –inability to take on other work §7.62
  –interest §7.64

DELAYS, *continued*
  –labor escalation §7.53
  –loss of productivity §7.55
  –material escalation §7.54
  –procurement costs §7.56
  –profit §7.63
  Contractor's other remedies §7.66
  Delay and disruption clauses §7.05
  Determination §7.02
  Disruption/interference §7.43
  Effect of excuse §7.20
  Enforceability of no damage for delay clauses §7.33
  Exceptions to enforcement of no damages for delay clauses
  –generally §7.36
  –active interference §7.38
  –breach of contract §7.42
  –fraud or bad faith §7.41
  –uncontemplated delay §7.37
  –unreasonable delay and abandonment §7.39
  Excusable delay
  –generally §7.07
  –acts of God/force majeure §7.08
  –owner-caused delay §7.10
  –sovereign and other interfering acts §7.11
  –strikes and labor disputes §7.09
  –subcontractor and supplier delays §7.12
  General vs specific no damage for delay clauses §7.34
  Liquidated damages §7.72
  No damages for delay provisions §7.32
  Noncompensable delay §7.21
  Nonexcusable delay §7.30
  Notice requirements
  –generally §7.17
  –content §7.19
  –time of notice §7.18
  Owner's damages for delay
  –generally §7.67
  –actual damages §7.68

DELAYS, *continued*
  –interest §7.70
  –loss of use §7.69
  –professional fees §7.71
  Owner's other remedies §7.73
  Procurement Policy Board (PPB) Rules §7.14
  Relevant contract clauses
  –generally §7.13
  –commercial practice §7.16
  –federal contracts §7.14
  –state and local contracts §7.15
  Remedies §7.48
  Risk, bidding and contract formation §3.35
  Scheduling procedures/progress schedules §7.04
  Time-money relationship §7.03
  Types of delay §7.06
  Typical no damages for delay clauses
  Waiver §7.51
DELIVERY OF GOODS
  Mechanics' liens §9.18
  Supply contract, subcontracts §3.34
DEMANDS
  Foreclosure, mechanics' liens §9.37
  Statement, mechanics' liens §9.35
DEMOBILIZATION, DELAY, AND REMOBILIZATION COSTS
  Delays §7.59
  Subcontracts §3.25
DEMOLITION
  Environmental problems §4.03
DENIAL OF ACCESS
  Compensable damages §7.24
DEPARTMENT OF BUILDINGS
  Introductory material §1.28
DESCRIPTIONS
  Contract, mechanics' liens §9.27
  Public property, mechanics' liens §9.27

DESIGN
  Professional's role and liability §§11.05, 11.16
DESIGN-BUILD
  Introductory material §1.21
DESIGN DEFECTS
  Defects and failures §2.02
  Professional's role and liability §11.13
DESIGNER FEES
  Introductory material §1.03
DESIGN PROFESSIONALS
  Defects and failures §2.02
  Insurance §10.11
  Introductory material. See INTRODUCTORY MATERIAL
DETAILED SPECIFICATIONS
  Distinguished from performance specifications §6.22
DETAIL OF THE WORK
  Construction safety §3.03
DETERMINATIVE ACTS
  Article 78, remedies/damages §5.04
DETERMINING DELAY
  Delays §7.02
DETERMINING EMPLOYEE STATUS
  Construction safety §3.02
DEVELOPERS
  Environmental checklist app 14-1
  Environmental problems §4.02
DEVIATIONS BY CONTRACTORS OR MATERIALMEN
  Professional's role and liability §11.05
DICTATING PERFORMANCE METHODS
  Changes/extra work §6.21
DIFFERING SITE CONDITIONS
  Changed conditions. See CHANGED CONDITIONS
  Clauses, environmental problems §4.14

DIMINUATION IN VALUE
  Distinguished from cost of completion, remedies/damages §5.29

DIRECT DISBURSEMENT
  Subcontracts §3.16

DIRECTORS
  Environmental problems §4.04
  Insurance §10.25

DISCHARGE
  Enforcing trust funds, mechanics' liens §9.81
  Fraud, bonds §8.27
  Mechanics' liens §9.36
  Modification or breach of contract, bonds §8.26

DISCHARGE OF POLLUTANTS, NATURE OF
  Environmental problems §4.22

DISCLAIMERS
  Contract clauses, changed conditions §§5.07, 5.08
  Hazardous substances, environmental problems §4.15
  Insurance §§10.29, 10.30
  Owner's data, changed conditions §5.14

DISCOVERABLE PATENT DEFECTS
  Defects and failures §2.14

DISCOVERY
  Dispute resolution §6.11

DISCRETION BY PUBLIC OFFICERS
  Article 78, remedies/damages §5.04

DISMISSAL
  Dispute resolution §6.11

DISPOSITIVE MOTIONS
  Trial preparation, environmental problems §4.35

DISPUTED CONTRACTS
  Procurement Policy Board (PPB) §7.09

DISPUTED WORK
  Duty to proceed, changes/extra work §§6.13, 6.14

DISPUTE RESOLUTION
  Generally §6.01
  Contract scope of work disputes §6.04
  Formal dispute resolution
  –generally §6.10
  –agreement to arbitrate §6.14
  –arbitration §6.12
  –conditions precedent §6.15
  Federal Arbitration Act §6.13
  –litigation §6.11
  –surety and arbitration clause §6.16
  Freedom of information laws §6.03
  Informal dispute resolution
  –generally §6.05
  –mediation §6.07
  –mediation and "baseball" arbitration §6.08
  –mini-trials §6.09
  –review boards §6.06
  Notice requirements §6.02
  Procedure, Procurement Policy Board (PPB) Rules §§7.09, 7.15
  Procurement Policy Board (PPB) Rules. See PROCUREMENT POLICY BOARD (PPB) RULES
  Professional's role and liability §11.11
  Questions and suggestions for PPB dispute resolution. See PROCUREMENT POLICY BOARD (PPB) RULES
  Selected references §6.17

DISRUPTION CLAUSES
  Delays §7.05

DISRUPTION/INTERFERENCE
  Delays §7.43

DISTRIBUTION OF PROCEEDS
Sale upon execution, mechanics' liens §9.65
DIVERSION
Trust funds, mechanics' liens §§9.68, 9.73, 9.76-9.80
DIVIDED RESPONSIBILITY
Defects and failures §2.06
DOCUMENTATION
Claims, changed conditions §5.18
DOMINANT PURPOSE RULE
Bonds §8.10
DOUBLE RECOVERY
Insurance §10.05
DUE CARE
Professional's role and liability §11.13
Superfund litigation, environmental problems §4.39
DUE PROCESS
Procedural due process. See PROCEDURAL DUE PROCESS
Procurement Policy Board (PPB) Rules §7.10
DUPLICATIVE COVERAGE
Insurance §§10.05, 10.10
DURATION
Mechanics' liens §9.32
Trust funds, mechanics' liens §9.69
DUTY OF COOPERATION
Insurance §§10.16, 10.29
DUTY OF DEFENSE
Insurance §§10.07, 10.18, 10.27
DUTY TO PERFORM
Contractors, changed conditions §5.15
DUTY TO PROCEED WITH DISPUTED WORK
Changes/extras work §§6.13, 6.14
DUTY TO SEEK CLARIFICATION
Changes/extra work §6.16

E

EARLY NOTICE
Dispute resolution §6.02
ECONOMIC LOSS
Damages, defects and failures §2.13
Rule, remedies/damages §5.20
ECONOMIC WASTE RULE
Remedies/damages §5.29
ECONOMY CHANGES
Default/termination §4.04
EDUCATION LAW
Dispute resolution §6.02
EDUCATION LAW §3813
Dispute resolution §16.02
EFFECT OF EXCUSE
Delays §7.20
EICHLEAY FORMULA
Delays §7.60
ELEMENTS OF PROPER LIEN NOTICE
Mechanics' liens §§9.26, 9.27
ELEVATED HEIGHTS
Construction safety §3.05
EMBEZZLEMENT
Insurance §10.24
EMERGENCIES
Bidding and contract formation §2.14
EMPLOYEE BENEFITS
Collateral source rule, remedies/damages §5.18
Lienable items, mechanics' liens §9.21
EMPLOYEE STATUS, DETERMINATION OF
Construction safety §3.02
EMPLOYMENT TAXES
Mechanics' liens §9.71
ENFORCEABILITY
No damage for delay clauses §7.33

ENFORCEMENT
    Alternative dispute resolution, environmental problems §4.42
    Enforcing trust funds. See MECHANICS' LIENS
    Exceptions to no damages for delay clauses. See DELAYS
    Mechanics' liens. See MECHANICS' LIENS
    No damages for delay clauses §§7.32, 7.33

ENGINEERING SERVICES
    Bidding and contract formation §2.15
    Procurement Policy Board (PPB) Rules §7.06

ENGINEERS
    Final decision on factual issues, changes/extra work §§6.23, 6.25
    Introductory material §1.05
    Mechanics' liens §9.03

ENGINEERS JOINT CONTRACT DOCUMENTS COMMITTEE (EJCDC)
    Bidding and contract formation §2.46

ENGINEER'S POLLUTION LIABILITY POLICY
    Environmental problems §4.21

ENGINEER'S REPORT
    Owner-contractor agreement, environmental problems §4.13
    Standard general conditions of the construction contract, environmental problems §4.16

ENVIRONMENTAL AUDIT
    Environmental problems §4.09

ENVIRONMENTAL ENGINEERS
    Environmental problems §4.09

ENVIRONMENTAL LITIGATION
    Alternative dispute resolution, environmental problems §4.43

ENVIRONMENTAL PROBLEMS
    Generally §4.01

ENVIRONMENTAL PROBLEMS, *continued*
    Alternative dispute resolution (ADR)
    –generally §4.41
    EPA §4.42
    –using ADR in environmental litigation §4.43
    Asbestos abatement
    –generally §4.28
    –federal law §4.29
    –local law §4.31
    New York state law §4.30
    Assigning and assuming risk §4.10
    Bonds §4.25
    Developer's environmental checklist app 14-1
    Identifying potential risks §4.09
    Insurance
    –generally §4.20
    –claims made vs occurrence policies §4.23
    –comprehensive general liability insurance: exclusions §4.22
    –errors and omissions liability insurance §4.21
    –hazardous waste insurance coverage §4.24
    Managing environmental risks §4.08
    Other indoor pollution §4.32
    Owner-contractor agreement
    –generally §4.11
    –bids §4.12
    –contracts §4.13
    –helpful clauses for contractors §4.15
    –industry standard forms §4.16
    –troublesome clauses for contractors §4.14
    Owner-design professional agreement
    –generally §4.17
    –industry standard forms §4.19
    –role definition §4.18

ENVIRONMENTAL PROBLEMS, *continued*
   References §4.44
   Sources of environmental law
     –generally §4.04
     –federal legislation §4.05
     –local legislation §4.07
     –state legislation §4.06
   Superfund
     –generally §4.26
     –reducing risk §4.27
   Superfund litigation
     –generally §4.38
     –consent decrees §4.40
     –defenses §4.39
   Trial preparation
     –generally §4.35
     –obtaining documents §4.36
     –personal liability for environmental risks §4.37
   Types of projects affected §4.03
   Underground storage tanks §4.33
   Wetlands §4.34
   Who should be concerned §4.02
ENVIRONMENTAL PROBLEMS
   Default/terminations §4.02
ENVIRONMENTAL PROTECTION AGENCY
   See EPA
ENVIRONMENTAL QUALITY STATUTES
   Environmental problems §4.04
EPA
   Alternative dispute resolution, environmental problems §4.42
   Environmental problems §4.05
EQUIPMENT
   Idle equipment, delays §7.59
   Insurance §10.10, 10.26
   Specifications, bidding and contract formation §2.08
EQUITABLE ADJUSTMENT
   Changes/extra work §§6.25, 6.29
   Owner-contractor agreement, environmental problems §4.13

EQUITABLE APPORTIONMENT OF INCREASED COSTS
   Owner's misrepresentation, changed conditions §5.11
EQUITABLE DECISIONS
   Article 78, remedies/ damages §5.04
EQUITABLE DEFENSES
   Superfund litigation, environmental problems §4.39
EQUITY ACCOUNTING
   Remedies/damages §5.09
ERRORS AND OMISSIONS LIABILITY INSURANCE
   Environmental problems §4.21
ESCALATION CLAUSES
   Supply contract, subcontracts §3.32
ESTIMATES VS BIDS RECEIVED
   Professional's role and liability §11.07
ESTOPPEL
   Contractor defenses, default/termination §4.16
EVALUATING PERFORMANCE
   Procurement Policy Board (PPB) Rules §7.05
EVALUATING RISKS AND RESPONSIBILITIES
   See BIDDING AND CONTRACT FORMATION
EVALUATING SPECIAL TERMS
   Bidding and contract formation §2.35
EXAMINATION OF BOOKS
   Trust funds, mechanics' liens §9.74
EXCAVATION
   Environmental problems §4.03
EXCEPTIONS
   Bidding rules, bidding and contract formation §2.14
   General obligation rule, construction safety §3.03

EXCEPTIONS, *continued*
　Liability for innocent landowners, environmental problems §4.05
　No damages for delay clauses. See DELAY
EXCESS EXCAVATION
　Changes/extra work §6.03
EXCLUSIONS
　See INSURANCE
EXCLUSIVE REMEDY
　Defects and failures §12.16
　Remedies/damages §5.23
EXCULPATORY CLAUSES
　Changes/extra work §§6.04, 6.31
　Contract clauses, changed conditions §5.09
　Delays §7.07
　No damages for delay clauses. See NO DAMAGES FOR DELAY CLAUSES
　Owner's data, changed conditions §5.14
　Professional's role and liability §11.04
　Remedies/damages §5.22
EXCUSABLE BIDDING ERROR
　Bonds §8.07
EXCUSABLE DELAY
　Commercial practice, delays §7.16
　Delays. See DELAYS
　Effect, delays §7.20
　Federal contracts, delays §7.14
　State and local contracts, delays §7.15
EXCUSABLE UNILATERAL MISTAKES
　Bidding and contract formation §2.19
EXCUSE, EFFECT OF
　Delays §7.20
EXECUTION
　Contracts, bidding and contract formation §2.32
　Mechanics' liens §9.07, 9.63
　Sale upon execution. See MECHANICS' LIENS

EXECUTORY CONTRACT VENDEES
　Trust funds, mechanics' liens §9.71
EXEMPTION FROM COMPETITIVE BIDDING REQUIREMENTS
　Public agencies, bidding and contract formation §2.16
EXEMPTION FROM DISCLOSURE
　Freedom of information laws, dispute resolution §6.03
EXPEDITED HANDLING
　Alternative dispute resolution, environmental problems §4.42
EXPERTS
　Defects and failures §2.03
　Dispute resolution §6.11
　Superfund litigation, environmental problems §4.38
EXPIRED LIENS
　Enforcement, mechanics' liens §9.48
EXPLOSION
　Insurance §10.21
EXPRESS CONDITIONS PRECEDENT
　Dispute resolution §6.15
EXPRESS WARRANTIES
　Defects and failures §§2.12, 12.15
　Subcontracts §3.11
　Supply contract, subcontracts §3.33
EXTENDED OVERHEAD
　Delays §7.60
EXTENDED REPORTING PERIOD
　Insurance §10.04
EXTENSION OF LIEN
　Mechanics' liens §9.32
EXTENSION OF STATUTE OF LIMITATIONS
　Defects and failures §2.08
EXTENSION OF TIME
　See TIME EXTENSION
EXTRAORDINARY BAD FAITH
　Bonds §§8.22, 8.29

EXTRAS
Bidding and contract formation §2.08
Changed conditions §5.15
Changes/extra work. See CHANGES/EXTRA WORK
Compensable delay §7.28
Definition §6.01
Dispute resolution §6.02
Lienable items, mechanics' liens §9.23
Mechanics' liens §9.35
Subcontracts §3.12

EXTRINSIC EVIDENCE
Bidding and contract formation §2.48

F

FAILURES
Awarding contracts, bonds §8.07
Commencing project, remedies/damages §§5.25, 15.31
Correcting defective work, default/termination §4.10
Defects and failures. See DEFECTS AND FAILURES
Following contractual termination procedure, default/termination §4.18
Joining necessary parties, mechanics' liens §9.44
Licensing, professional's role and liability §11.03
Paying subcontractors and suppliers, termination/default §4.09
Proceeding with disputed work, changes/extra work §6.14
Prosecuting work, default/termination §4.08

FAIRNESS
Procurement Policy Board (PPB) Rules §§7.16, 17.10

FAST-TRACK METHOD
Procurement Policy Board (PPB) Rules §7.06

FAULT
Environmental problems §4.09

FAULTY MATERIALS
Defects and failures §2.04

FAULTY PLANS AND SPECIFICATIONS
Bidding and contract formation §2.36

FAULTY REPORTS
Professional's role and liability §11.06

FEDERAL ACQUISITION REGULATION (FAR)
Delays §7.14

FEDERAL ARBITRATION ACT
Dispute resolution §6.13

FEDERAL CONTRACTS
Default/termination §4.04
Relevant contract clauses, delays §7.14

FEDERAL DISPUTES
Formal dispute resolution, dispute resolution §6.11

FEDERAL ENVIRONMENTAL LAWS
Environmental problems §4.04

FEDERAL FREEDOM OF INFORMATION LAWS
Dispute resolution §6.03

FEDERAL HOUSING ADMINISTRATION (FHA) INSPECTION AND EXAMINATION FEES
Trust funds, mechanics' liens §9.75

FEDERAL LAW
Asbestos abatement, environmental problems §4.29

FEDERAL LEGISLATION
Source of environmental law, environmental problems §4.05

FEES
Dispute resolution §§6.07, 16.12
FIDELITY INSURANCE
Insurance §10.24
FIDUCIARY RELATIONSHIP
Trust funds, mechanics' liens §9.72
FIELD OVERHEAD
Delays §7.58
FILING LOCATIONS
Mechanics' liens §9.30
FILING NOTICE OF PENDENCY
Enforcement, mechanics' liens §9.40
FILING OF BOND OR DEPOSIT
Bonds §8.32
Mechanics' liens §9.36
FILING OF LIEN NOTICE
Mechanics' liens. See MECHANICS' LIENS
FINALITY OF CITY DECISIONS
Procurement Policy Board (PPB) Rules §7.15
FINAL PAYMENT
Changes/extra work §6.34
Procurement Policy Board (PPB) Rules §7.05
Subcontracts §3.19
FINAL PERFORMANCE
Mechanics' liens §9.29
FINAL SETTLEMENT
Enforcing trust funds, mechanics' liens §9.82
FINANCING
Costs, delays §7.61
Failure, default/termination §4.04
FIRST PERSON COVERAGE
See PROPERTY COVERAGE
FITNESS FOR PARTICULAR PURPOSE
Supply contract, subcontracts §3.33
FIXED/LUMP SUM PRICE
Procurement Policy Board (PPB) Rules §7.05

FIXED PRICE CONTRACTS
Mechanics' liens §9.35
Supply contract, subcontracts §3.32
FLOW CHARTS
Delays §7.04
FLOW DOWN CLAUSES
See INCORPORATION BY REFERENCE
FORCE MAJEURE
Excusable delay §7.08
FORECLOSURES
Defenses to action, mechanics' liens §9.47
Demand, mechanics' liens §9.37
Enforcement, mechanics' liens §9.41
Obtaining executions and judgments, mechanics' liens §§9.61-9.63
Sale upon execution, mechanics' liens §§9.64-9.67
Trial, mechanics' liens §9.51
FORESEEABILITY
Noncontractual limitations on damages, remedies/damages §5.16
Superfund litigation, environmental problems §4.39
FORMALDEHYDE
Indoor pollution, environmental problems §4.32
FORMAL DISCOVERY
Dispute resolution §6.11
FORMAL DISPUTE RESOLUTION
See DISPUTE RESOLUTION
FORMATION
Subcontracts §3.02
FORM OF COMPLAINT
Enforcement, mechanics' liens §9.45
FORMS, STANDARD
Bidding and contract formation §2.46

FORMS, STANDARD, *continued*
  Subcontracts §3.03
FORUM SELECTION CLAUSES
  Subcontracts §3.06
FRAUD
  Default/termination §4.20
  Defects and failures §2.08
  Discharge, bonds §8.27
  Owner's misrepresentation, changed conditions §§5.12, 5.16
  Procurement Policy Board (PPB) Rules §7.11
  Professional's role and liability §11.11
  Remedies/damages §5.11
FREAK ACCIDENTS
  Construction safety §§13.03, 13.04
FREEDOM OF INFORMATION ACT (FOIA)
  Dispute resolution §6.03
  Trial preparation, environmental problems §4.36
FREEDOM OF INFORMATION LAW, NEW YORK LAW
  Trial preparation, environmental problems §4.36
FREEDOM TO CONTRACT
  Introductory material §1.08
FRESHWATER WETLANDS
  Environmental problems §4.34
FUNCTIONAL EQUIVALENT OF CONTRACTUAL PRIVITY
  Professional's role and liability §11.14
  Remedies/damages §5.20
FUTURE HEALTH PROBLEMS
  Insurance, environmental problems §4.24

G

GAPS IN COVERAGE
  Insurance §10.04
GARNISHMENT
  Mechanics' liens §9.61
GAS
  Lienable property, mechanics' liens §9.14
GENERAL CONTRACTORS
  Introductory material §1.11
  Liability, construction safety §3.07
GENERAL LIABILITY INSURANCE: EXCLUSIONS
  Environmental problems §4.22
GENERALLY COMPATIBLE ACTIVITIES
  Wetlands, environmental problems §4.34
GENERAL VS SPECIFIC NO DAMAGES FOR DELAY CLAUSES
  Delays §7.34
GLOSSARY OF COMMON CONSTRUCTION INSURANCE TERMS
  Mechanics liens app 10-2
GOOD FAITH AND FAIR DEALING
  Bidding and contract formation §2.31
  Default/termination §4.04
  Subcontracts §3.23
GOOD FAITH OWNER DEFENSE
  Superfund litigation, environmental litigation §4.39
GOVERNMENT ACTS
  Delays §7.11
GUARANTEED MAXIMUM PRICE CONTRACTS
  Introductory material §1.22
  Professional's role and liability §11.17

GUARANTEES
Warranty clauses. See DEFECTS AND FAILURES
GUARANTY BONDS
Bonds §8.09
Defects and failures §2.09

H

HAD REASON TO KNOW LANGUAGE
Superfund litigation, environmental problems §4.39
HARD MONEY CONTRACT
See FIXED PRICE CONTRACT
HAZARDOUS SUBSTANCES
Chapter 14, generally §4.18
Disclaimers, environmental problems §4.15
HAZARDOUS WASTE INSURANCE COVERAGE
Claims made coverage, environmental problems §4.43
Insurance, environmental problems §4.24
HEALTH INSURANCE
Collateral source rule, remedies/damages §5.18
HEARINGS
Bidding and contract formation §2.15
Borough president complaints, Procurement Policy Board(PPB) Rules §7.12
Procurement Policy Board (PPB) Rules §7.08
HELPFUL CLAUSES FOR CONTRACTORS
Owner-contractor agreement, environmental problems §4.15
HIGHER STANDARDS OF CARE
Defects and failures §2.02
"HIS SUBCONTRACTOR"
Mechanic's liens §9.08
HOLD HARMLESS CLAUSE
Subcontracts §3.13
HOME OFFICE OVERHEAD
Delays §7.60
HONEST ERRORS
Bidding and contract formation §2.19
HOUSING AND URBAN DEVELOPMENT (HUD) PROJECTS
Introductory material §1.23
HOUSING MERCHANT WARRANTY
Defects and failures §2.14
HYBRID CONTRACTS
Supply contracts, subcontracts §3.28

I

IDENTIFICATION
Owner, mechanics' liens §9.26
Party for whom work performed, mechanics' liens §9.26
Potential risks, environmental problems §4.09
Property improved, mechanics' liens §9.26
IDENTIFYING POTENTIAL RISKS
Environmental problems §4.09
IDENTITY OF INTEREST
Insurance §10.05
IDLE EQUIPMENT
Delays §7.59
ILLEGAL BIDS
Public contracts, bidding and contract formation §2.11
ILLEGAL CONTRACTS
Bidding and contract formation §§2.11, 2.28
IMPACT COSTS
Changes/extra work §6.26, §6.29
Damages, changed conditions §5.20
Delays §7.57

IMPARTIALITY
  Trust funds, mechanics' liens §9.72
IMPLIED CONSENT
  Mechanics' liens §9.05
IMPLIED WARRANTIES
  Changed conditions §5.16
  Defects and failures §2.13
  New home sales, defects and failures §2.14
  Subcontracts §3.11
  Supply contract, subcontracts §3.33
IMPOSSIBILITY
  Contractor defenses, default/termination §4.15
IMPROPER INSTALLATION
  Defects and failures §2.05
IMPROVEMENT AS A REQUIREMENT
  Public sector, mechanics' liens §§9.04, 9.09
IMPROVEMENT OF REAL PROPERTY
  Mechanic's liens §9.02
INABILITY TO TAKE ON OTHER WORK
  Delays §7.62
INADEQUACY OF SALE
  Mechanics' liens §9.67
INADEQUATE SAFETY DEVICES
  Construction safety §3.05
INADVERTENT CONSTRUCTIVE ACCELERATION
  Delays §7.46
INAPPROPRIATE CASES FOR ALTERNATIVE DISPUTE RESOLUTION
  Environmental problems §4.42
INCOMPATIBLE ACTIVITIES
  Wetlands, environmental problems §4.34
INCORPORATION BY REFERENCE
  Bidding and contract formation §2.51
  Dispute resolution §§6.14, 16.16

INCORPORATION BY REFERENCE, *continued*
  Subcontracts §§3.06, 3.11
INCREASED COSTS
  Bonds §8.46
INDEFINITE SPECIFICATIONS
  Bidding and contract formation §2.08
INDEMNIFICATION
  Attorneys' fees, remedies/damages §5.14
  Bidding and contract formation §2.36
  Bonds §8.48
  Construction safety §§3.03, 13.08, 13.10, 13.12, 13.18
  Defects and failures §§2.10, 12.11
  Environmental problems §§4.02, 14.15, 14.27
  Limitations, subcontracts §3.13
  Professional's role and liability §11.22
  Remedies/damages §5.20
  Subcontracts §§3.13, 3.23
  Superfund litigation, environmental problems §4.39
  Underground storage tanks, environmental problems §4.33
INDEMNITORS
  Bonds §§8.03, 8.48
INDEPENDENT PRIME CONTRACTORS
  Introductory material §1.12
INDOOR POLLUTION
  Asbestos abatement. See ENVIRONMENTAL PROBLEMS
  Other indoor pollution, environmental problems §4.32
INDUCEMENT TO CONTRACT
  Fraud, remedies/damages §5.11
INDUSTRY STANDARD FORMS
  Owner-contractor agreement, environmental problems §4.16

INDUSTRY STANDARD FORMS, *continued*
   Owner-design professional agreement, environmental problems §4.19

INEXPERIENCED OWNERS
   Introductory material §1.09

INFORMAL DISPUTE RESOLUTION
   See DISPUTE RESOLUTION

INJUNCTIONS
   Dispute resolution §6.11
   Remedies/damages. See REMEDIES/DAMAGES

INJURED WORKERS
   Professional's role and liability §11.13

INJURIES
   Subcontracts §3.13

IN LIMINE
   Trial preparation, environmental problems §4.35

INNOCENCE
   Superfund litigation, environmental problems §4.39

INNOCENT MISREPRESENTATION
   Changed conditions §5.11

IN-PLANT OPERATIONS
   Asbestos abatement, environmental problems §4.30

INQUIRY
   Safety devices, construction safety §3.05

INSOLVENCY
   Contractor default, default/termination §4.11

INSPECTION
   Professional's role and liability §§11.06, 11.08, 11.18

INSPECTION, OVERMETICULOUS
   Changes/extra work §6.20

INSPECTION/APPROVAL DELAYS
   Delays §7.26

INSURANCE
   Bodily injury, environmental problems §4.24
   Certificate of insurance, necessity §10.31
   Construction insurance §10.01
   Coverage
   –generally §10.06
   –accident defined §10.09
   –liability coverage §10.07
   –occurrence defined §10.09
   –property coverage §10.08
   Disclaimers §10.30
   Distinguished from bonds, bonds §8.01
   Duty of cooperation §10.29
   Duty of defense §10.27
   Environmental problems. See ENVIRONMENTAL PROBLEMS
   Exclusions
   –generally §10.18
   –care, custody, or control §10.23
   –contractor's own work §10.19
   –contractual liability §10.22
   –explosion, collapse, and underground damage §10.21
   –pollution §10.20
   Fidelity insurance §10.24
   Limitation of actions §10.28
   Motor vehicles and equipment §10.26
   Obtaining needed insurance
   –generally §10.03
   –claims made vs occurrence policies §10.04
   –duplicative coverage §10.05
   Officer's and director's insurance §10.25
   Policies app 10-1
   Policy limits §10.12
   Policy requirements
   –generally §10.13
   –notice to insurers §10.15
   –premiums §10.14
   Procedure on occurrence §10.16

INSURANCE, *continued*
Professional liability insurance §10.11
Professional's role and liability §11.25
Special insurance problems
–generally §10.32
–construction managers §10.35
–design build contracts §10.33
–joint ventures §10.34
Supply contract terms, subcontracts §3.34
Termination §10.17
Understanding insurance policies §10.02
What to do on occurrence §10.16
Wrap-up insurance §10.10

INSURANCE SERVICES ORGANIZATION (ISO)
Insurance §10.02

INSURERS
Claims by surety against, bonds §8.52
Environmental problems §4.02
Introductory material §1.17
Punitive damages, remedies/damages §5.12

INSURE VS INDEMNIFY
Subcontracts §3.13

INTENTIONAL SUBMISSION OF LOW BIDS
Changes/extra work §6.16

INTENTIONAL TORT
Construction safety §3.02

INTENTIONAL WRONGDOING
Delays §7.36

INTENT TO BE BOUND
Bidding and contract formation §2.25

INTEREST
Bonds §8.42
Claims by obligee, bonds §8.23
Delays §7.64
Miller Act bonds, bonds §8.46

INTEREST, *continued*
Overdue bills, mechanics' liens §9.75
Owner's damages for delay §7.70
Procurement Policy Board (PPB) Rules §7.05
Remedies damages §5.15
Subcontracts §3.25

INTERFERENCE
Owners, changes/extra work §6.17
Owners or architects, default/termination §14.14
Professional's role and liability §11.04

INTERPLEADING OF PENAL SUM
Bonds §8.42

INTERPRETATION OF PLANS AND SPECIFICATIONS
Defects and failures §2.03

INTERPRETING CONTRACTS
See BIDDING AND CONTRACT FORMATION

INTERSTATE COMMERCE
Dispute resolution §6.13

INTRODUCTORY MATERIAL
Abnormally dangerous activities §11.25
Call before you dig §1.27
Contractors
–generally §1.10
–construction managers §1.13
–general contractors §1.11
–independent prime or trade contractors §1.12
–subcontractors §1.14
Design professionals
–generally §1.02
–architects §1.04
–designer fees §1.03
–engineers §1.05
–subconsultants §1.06
Insurers §1.17
Licenses and codes §1.24
Owners

INTRODUCTORY MATERIAL, *continued*
   –generally §1.07
   –private owners §1.09
   –public owners §1.08
   Parties §1.01
   Special problems in New York City §1.28
   Suppliers and materialmen §1.15
   Sureties §1.16
   10-foot rule, lateral support §1.26
   Turnkey/design-build §1.23
   Types of contracts
   –generally §1.18
   –cost-plus reimbursable contracts §1.21
   –fixed price contracts §1.19
   –guaranteed maximum price contracts §1.22
   –unit price contracts §1.20

INVESTIGATIONS
   Bidding and contract formation §2.15

INVITEES
   Construction safety §3.04

IRRATIONAL ACTS
   Article 78, remedies/damages §5.04

ISSUES DECIDED BY ARBITRATORS
   Dispute resolution §6.12

ITEMIZATION
   Mechanics' liens §9.35

ITEMS COVERED
   See BONDS

J

JOB SITE
   Subcontracts §3.10

JOINDER
   Dispute resolution §6.11

JOINING NECESSARY PARTIES
   Mechanics' liens §9.44

JOINT AND SEVERAL LIABILITY
   Environmental problems §4.05

JOINT VENTURES
   Accounting, remedies/damages §5.09
   Environmental problems §4.27
   Insurance §10.34

JUDGMENTS
   Enforcing trust funds, mechanics' liens §9.84
   Obtaining judgments. See MECHANICS' LIENS
   Priority, mechanics' liens §9.56

JURISDICTION
   Enforcement, mechanics' liens §9.42

JURY QUESTION
   Delays §7.07

JURY-VERDICT METHOD
   Delays §7.49

JUSTIFIABLE CONTROVERSY
   Remedies/damages §5.08

K

KNOWLEDGE
   Trust funds, mechanics' liens §9.79

KNOWN PERSON TEST
   Professional's role and liability §11.14

KNOWN UNSAFE CONDITIONS
   Construction safety §3.04

L

LABOR
   Bonds §8.37
   Lienable items, mechanics' liens §9.17
   Miller Act bonds, bonds §8.46

LABOR DISPUTES
   Excusable delay §7.09

LABORERS
Mechanics' liens §§9.03, 9.17
LABOR ESCALATION
Delays §7.53
LABOR LAW §240
Construction safety §3.05
General contractor liability, construction safety §3.07
Owner liability, construction safety §§3.08, 13.09
LABOR LAW §241
Construction safety §3.06
General contractor liability, construction safety §3.07
Owner liability, construction safety §§3.08, 13.09
LACHES
Superfund litigation, environmental problems §4.39
LACK OF COORDINATION
Delays §7.23
LACK OF NOTICE
Surety's defenses, bonds §8.25
LANDSCAPE GARDENERS
Mechanics' liens §9.03
LAND USE IMPEDIMENTS
Environmental problems §4.11
LAND USE PLANNING DISPUTES
Alternative dispute resolution §4.43
LANGUAGE CONTROLLING OR SPECIFIC DOCUMENT
Bidding and contract formation §2.49
LARCENY
Trust funds, mechanics' liens §§9.79, 9.80
LARGE ASBESTOS PROJECTS
Environmental problems §4.31
LATE CLAIMS
Delays §7.18
Dispute resolution §6.02

LATE COMPLETION
Procurement Policy Board (PPB) Rules §7.05
LATENT ABOVE-GROUND CONDITIONS
Changed conditions §§5.02, 5.04
LATENT DEFECTS
Defects and failures §§2.01-12.03, 12.05, 12.08
Insurance §10.04
Professional's role and liability §11.13
LATERAL SUPPORT
10-foot rule, introductory material §1.26
LAW OF CONTRACTS VS LAW OF TORTS
Remedies/damages §5.20
LAWS AND REGULATIONS CLAUSE
Compliance, environmental problems §4.14
LEAD
Indoor pollution, environmental problems §4.32
LEASED EQUIPMENT
Bonds §8.39
Supply contracts, subcontracts §3.28
LEASEHOLD INTERESTS
Lienable property, mechanics' liens §9.13
LEGAL FEES
Trust funds, mechanics' liens §9.75
LEGALITY OF SPECIFICATIONS
Bidding and contract formation §2.08
LEGAL OBLIGATION
Changes/extra work §6.07
LENDERS
Trust funds, mechanics' liens §§9.75, 9.76

LENDING INSTITUTIONS
  Claims by surety against, bonds §8.51
LESSEES
  Mechanics' liens §9.05
LETTER OF INTENT
  Bidding and contract formation §2.31
LIABILITY
  Insurance §§10.06, 10.07. See ENVIRONMENTAL PROBLEMS
  Professional's role and liability. See PROFESSIONAL'S ROLE AND COVERAGE
LIABILITY FOR DIVERSION
  Trust funds, mechanics' liens §9.79
LIABILITY IN EXCESS OF PENAL SUM
  Surety's defenses, bonds §8.29
LIABILITY IN NEGLIGENCE
  Architect/engineer, construction safety §3.15
  Construction manager, construction safety §3.16
  Professional's role and liability §§11.04, 11.13
LIABILITY INSURANCE, PROFESSIONAL
  Insurance §§10.10-10.12, 10.35
LIABILITY OF SURETY
  Bid bonds, bonds §§8.06, 8.48
LIABILITY VS NEGLIGENCE
  Subcontracts §3.13
LICENSES AND CODES
  Introductory material §1.24
  Professional's role and liability §§11.02, 11.03
LIENABLE ITEMS
  See MECHANICS' LIENS
LIENABLE PROPERTY
  See MECHANICS' LIENS
LIEN FUND
  Mechanics' liens §§9.50, 9.60

LIEN LAW
  Accounting, remedies/damages §5.09
  Bonds §§8.33, 8.35, 8.37
LIEN NOTICE
  Filing lien notice. See MECHANICS' LIENS
LIEN WAIVERS
  Subcontracts §3.26
LIFE INSURANCE
  Collateral source rule, remedies/damages §5.18
LIMITATION OF ACTIONS
  Insurance §10.28
  Miller Act bonds, bonds §8.45
LIMITATION PERIODS
  Bonds §§8.10, 8.24
LINKING TO RELIANT PERSON
  Professional's role and liability §11.14
LIQUIDATED DAMAGES
  Delays §7.72
  Procurement Policy Board (PPB) Rules §§7.05, 17.14
  Remedies/damages §5.22
  Subcontracts §§3.22, 3.35
LIQUIDATING AGREEMENTS
  Delays §7.52
  Subcontracts §3.23
LITIGATION
  Dispute resolution §6.11
  Environmental problems §4.43
  Procurement Policy Board (PPB) Rules §7.07
  Professional's role and liability §11.11
  Superfund. See ENVIRONMENTAL PROBLEMS
LOCAL CONTRACTS
  Relevant contract clauses, delays §7.15
LOCAL LAW
  Asbestos abatement, environmental problems §4.31

INDEX

LOCAL LEGISLATION
Sources of environmental law, environmental problems §4.07

LOSS OF BONDABILITY
Certainty, remedies/damages §5.19
Delays §7.62

LOSS OF FUTURE PROFITS
Certainty, remedies/damages §5.19

LOSS OF LICENSE
Professional's role and liability §11.02

LOSS OF PRODUCTIVITY
Delays §7.55

LOSS OF USE
Owner's damages for delay §7.69

LOST PROFITS
Bonds §8.15
Certainty, remedies/damages §5.19
Changes/extra work §§6.04, 6.05, 6.14
Default/termination §4.21
Delays §§7.63, 7.69
Lienable items, mechanics' liens §9.22
Miller Act bonds, bonds §8.46
Subcontracts §§3.24, 3.25

LOST USE OF PREMISES
Bonds §8.15

LOW BID REDUCTION
Bidding and contract formation §2.13

LOWEST RESPONSIBLE BIDDER
Introductory material §1.08
Public contracts, bidding and contract formation §2.04

LUMP SUM METHOD
Changes/extra work §6.28
Fixed price contract. See FIXED PRICE CONTRACT
Mechanics' liens §9.35

LUMP SUM METHOD, *continued*
Procurement Policy Board (PPB) Rules §7.06

M

MALFEASANCE
Professional's role and liability §11.13

MALPRACTICE
Professional's role and liability §§11.04, 11.23

MANAGING RISK
Bidding and contract formation §§2.38-2.44
Environmental problems §4.08

MANDAMUS
Remedies/damages §5.01

MANUSCRIPT POLICIES
Insurance §§10.32, 10.33

MATERIAL ESCALATION
Delays §7.54

MATERIALITY
Changed conditions §5.02

MATERIALMEN
Contractors and subcontractors, subcontracts §3.10
Demands, excusable delay §7.12
Environmental problems §4.02
Failure to pay, default/termination §4.09
Introductory material §1.15
Mechanics' liens §9.03
Remedies/damages §§5.36-15.38
Subcontracts §3.14

MATERIAL NONCOMPLIANCE
Waiver, bidding and contract formation §2.05

MATERIALS
Bonds §8.37
Items covered, bonds §8.38
Lienable items, mechanics' liens §9.18
Miller Act bonds, bonds §8.46

MEASURE OF DAMAGES
  Bonds §8.50
  Defects and failures §2.04
MECHANICS' LIENS
  Generally §9.01
  Amendment of lien §9.33
  Bonds §§8.37, 8.38
  Duration and extension of lien §9.32
  Elements of proper lien notice
  –private improvements §9.26
  –public improvements §9.27
  Enforcement
  –generally §9.38
  –answers to defendant lienors §9.46
  –courts of record and courts not of record §9.43
  –deadline to commence action §9.39
  –defective and expired liens §9.48
  –defendant lienors' answers §9.46
  –defenses to foreclosure action §9.47
  –filing notice of pendency §9.40
  –form of complaint §9.45
  –lien foreclosure and arbitration §9.41
  –necessary parties §9.44
  –no fund to which lien can attach §9.50
  –venue and jurisdiction of action §9.42
  –willful exaggeration §9.49
  Enforcing trust funds
  –generally §9.81
  –claims for relief §9.82
  –judgment §9.84
  –priority and preference §9.83
  Filing of lien notice
  –private improvement liens §9.29
  –public improvement liens §9.30
  –time and place §9.28
  Foreclosure trial §9.51
  Lienable items
  –generally §9.16

MECHANICS' LIENS, *continued*
  –appendix 9-2
  –extras §9.23
  –labor §9.17
  –lost profits and contract damages §9.22
  –materials §9.18
  –overhead and employee benefits §9.21
  –rental equipment §9.19
  –temporary works §9.20
  Lienable property
  –generally §9.11
  –condominiums and cooperatives §9.12
  –leasehold interests §9.13
  –oil and gas §9.14
  Obtaining executions §9.63
  Obtaining judgments
  –generally §9.61
  –amount of judgment §9.62
  Owner's response to notice of lien
  –generally §9.34
  –demand for statement §9.35
  –demand to foreclose §9.37
  –discharge of lien §9.36
  Parity and preference among mechanic's lienors §9.60
  Priority of private improvement liens
  –generally §9.52
  –agreements to subordinate §9.58
  –assignment of moneys due §9.55
  –building loan contracts and mortgages §9.53
  –miscellaneous liens §9.56
  –mortgages §9.54
  –subsequent purchasers §9.57
  Priority of public improvement liens §9.59
  Private improvements, proper lien notice for §9.27
  Private sector §9.02
  Private vs public works liens app 9-1

MECHANICS' LIENS, *continued*
Public property §9.15
Public sector
–generally §9.07
–improvement as a requirement §9.09
–securing interest in funds §9.10
–who may file §9.08
Sale upon execution
–generally §9.64
–deficiency judgments §9.66
–distribution of proceeds §9.65
–setting aside sales §9.67
Service of lien notice §9.31
Should you file a lien §9.25
Trust funds
–generally §9.68
–assets §9.70
–availability of records to claimants §9.74
–diversion §9.78
–duration §9.69
–enforcement, See ENFORCING TRUST FUNDS, this heading
–fiduciary relationship §9.72
–liability for diversion §9.79
–notice of assignment §9.77
–notice of lending §9.76
–parties involved §9.71
–proper application §9.75
–record keeping requirements §9.73
–restoration after diversion §9.80
Waivers §9.24
Who may file
–generally §9.03
–improvement as a requirement §§9.04, 9.09
–lien attachment to real property §9.06
–owner's consent §9.05

MEDIATION
Dispute resolution §§6.07, 16.08

MERCHANTABILITY
Supply contract, subcontracts §3.33

METHOD OF WORK PERFORMED
Construction safety §3.04

METHODS OF SOURCE SELECTION
Procurement Policy Board (PPB) Rules §7.02

MILLER ACT BONDS
See BONDS

MINISTERIAL ACTS
Article 78, remedies/damages §5.04

MINI-TRIALS
Dispute resolution §6.09

MINOR ASBESTOS PROJECTS
Environmental problems §4.31

MINORITY BUSINESS ENTERPRISES (MBES)
Bidding and contract formation §2.35

MISCELLANEOUS ACM
Environmental problems §4.29

MISCELLANEOUS CONDITIONS
Changed conditions §5.05

MISCELLANEOUS LIENS
Mechanics' liens §9.56

MISLEADING BID DOCUMENTS
Professional's role and liability §11.14

MISREPRESENTATION
Defects and failures §2.07
Delays §§7.41, 7.42
Owners, changed conditions §§5.10-5.12

MISTAKES
See BIDDING AND CONTRACT FORMATION

MISTAKES IN BID
Procurement Policy Board (PPB) Rules §7.02

MISUNDERSTANDING
Contract clauses, changed conditions §5.08

MITIGATION
Remedies/damages §5.17

MIX AND MATCH CONTRACTS
Introductory material §1.18
MODIFICATIONS OF CONTRACT
Changed conditions §5.18
Discharge, bonds §8.26
MONETARY LIMITS
Insurance, environmental problems §4.24
MONEYS DUE
Assignment, mechanics' liens §9.55
MORAL CULPABILITY
Punitive damages, remedies/damages §5.12
"MORALLY CULPABLE AND ACTUATED BY EVIL AND REPREHENSIBLE MOTIVES"
Bonds §§8.22, 8.29
MORTGAGES
Mechanics' liens §§9.53, 9.54
MOTION TO STAY ARBITRATION
Dispute resolution §6.14
MOTOR VEHICLES
Insurance §10.26
MULTIPARTY LITIGATION
Trial preparation, environmental problems §§4.35, 14.38
MULTI-PRIME CONSTRUCTION PROJECT
Bonds §8.19
MUNICIPALITY
Bidding and contract formations §2.03
MUNICIPAL TREATMENT SYSTEMS
Environmental problems §4.05
MUTUAL ASSENT
Bidding and contract formation §2.25
MUTUAL CONSENT CLAUSE
Changes/extra work §6.02
MUTUAL MISTAKES
Bidding and contract formation §2.20
Changed conditions §5.16

N

NARRATIVE
Dispute resolution §6.02
NATIONAL ENVIRONMENTAL PROTECTION ACT (NEPA)
Environmental problems §4.05
NECESSARY PARTIES
Enforcement, mechanics' liens §9.44
NECESSITY
Changes/extra work §6.02
Notice, bonds §8.40
NECESSITY OF NOTICE
Bonds §8.40
NEGLIGENCE
Architect/engineer liability, construction safety §3.15
Bonds §§8.07, 8.48, 8.50
Construction manager liability, construction safety §3.16
Defects and failures §2.08
Environmental problems §4.04
Presumption, construction safety §3.17
Professional's role and liability §§11.04, 11.13, 11.24
Subcontracts §3.13
Third-parties, professional's role and liability §11.13
NEGLIGENT INTERPRETATION
Professional's role and liability §11.14
NEGLIGENT MISREPRESENTATION
Professional's role and liability §11.14
NEGLIGENT PERFORMANCE OF CONTRACT
Professionals' role and liability §11.23
NEGLIGENT SUPERVISION AND INSPECTION
Professional's role and liability §11.14

INDEX

NEGOTIATED ACQUISITION
Procurement Policy Board (PPB) Rules §7.02

NEGOTIATED CHANGE ORDERS
Procurement Policy Board (PPB) Rules §7.06

NEGOTIATING MAZE
Procurement Policy Board (PPB) Rules §7.01

NEMO POTEST ESSE SIMUL ACTOR ET JUDEX
Professional's role and liability §11.11

NEUTRAL MEDIATOR
Procurement Policy Board (PPB) Rules §7.09

NEUTRAL PERSONS
Alternative dispute resolution, environmental problems §4.42
Procurement Policy Board (PPB) Rules §7.09

NEW AGREEMENTS
Changes/extra work §6.04

NEW CONSTRUCTION
Environmental problems §4.03

NEW DESIGN, CONSTRUCT CONCEPTS
Insurance §10.33

NEW YORK CITY SCHOOL CONSTRUCTION AUTHORITY (SCA)
Procurement Policy Board (PPB) Rules §7.02

NEW YORK COURT OF CLAIMS
Formal dispute resolution, dispute resolution §6.11

NEW YORK FREEDOM OF INFORMATION LAW (FOIL)
Dispute resolution §6.03

NEW YORK RULE
Owner's misrepresentation, changed conditions §5.11

NEW YORK STATE LAW
Asbestos abatement, environmental problems §4.30

NO DAMAGES FOR DELAY CLAUSES
Changed conditions §5.20
Changes/extra work §6.04
Enforceability, delays §7.33
General vs specific, delays §7.34
Introductory material §1.12
Noncompensable delay, delays §7.21
Procurement Policy Board (PPB) Rules §7.12
Professional's role and liability §11.19
Provisions, delays §7.32
Subcontracts §§3.06, 3.08, 3.22
Typical clauses, delays §7.35

NO FUND FOR ATTACHMENT
Enforcement, mechanics' liens §9.50

NO LIEN CONTRACT CLAUSES
Mechanics' liens §9.24
Subcontracts §3.26

NON-BINDING RECOMMENDATIONS
Dispute resolution §6.06

NONCOMPENSABLE DELAY
Delays §7.21

NONCOMPLEMENTARY SPECIFICATIONS
Changes/extra work §6.22

NONCOMPLIANCE
Bidding and contract formation §§2.05, 2.07

NONCONSTRUCTION-RELATED CONTRACTS
Procurement Policy Board (PPB) Rules §7.09

NONCONTRACTUAL LIMITATIONS ON DAMAGES
See REMEDIES/DAMAGES

NONCOOPERATION
  Insurance §10.29
NONDELEGABLE DUTIES
  Construction safety §§3.03, 13.04, 13.06, 13.08, 13.18
NONDISCLOSURE OF TECHNICAL INFORMATION
  Constructive changes, changes/extra work §6.19
NONEXCUSABLE DELAY
  Delays §7.30
NONEXCUSABLE UNILATERAL MISTAKES
  Bidding and contract formation §2.19
NONFEASANCE
  Professional's role and liability §11.13
NONLIABILITY
  Insurance §10.15
NONMATERIAL ERRORS
  Bonds §8.05
NONPAYMENT
  Contractor defenses, default/termination §4.17
  Remedies, subcontracts §3.25
  Specific breaches by owner, remedies/damages §5.33
NONRESPONSIBILITY
  Bidders, Procurement Policy Board (PPB) Rules §7.02
  Contractors, Procurement Policy Board (PPB) Rules §§7.05, 17.08
NONRESPONSIVE BIDDERS
  Procurement Policy Board (PPB) Rules §§7.02, 17.04, 17.08
NOTICE, LACK OF OR UNTIMELY
  Surety's defenses, bonds §8.25
NOTICE OF ASSIGNMENT
  Trust funds, mechanics' liens §§9.75, 9.77
NOTICE OF CANCELLATION
  Insurance §10.14

NOTICE OF CLAIM
  See NOTICE REQUIREMENTS
NOTICE OF LENDING
  Trust funds, mechanics' liens §§9.75-9.77
NOTICE OF LIEN
  Mechanics' lien §§9.29, 9.30
  Owner's response to. See MECHANICS' LIEN
NOTICE OF PENDENCY
  Filing, mechanics' liens §9.40
NOTICE OF PETITION
  Article 78, remedies/damages §5.02
NOTICE OF SALE
  Mechanics' liens §9.63
NOTICE REQUIREMENTS
  Appendix 8-1
  Asbestos abatement, environmental problems §4.30
  Bidding and contract formation §2.21
  Bonds §§8.10, 8.11, 8.25, 8.40
  Changes/extra work §§6.13, 6.24, 6.32
  Claims, changed conditions §5.18
  Default/termination §§4.04, 4.06
  Defects and failures §2.14
  Delays. See DELAYS
  Dispute resolution §6.02
  Elements of proper lien notice, mechanics' liens §§9.26, 9.27
  Insurance §§10.14, 10.15
  Miller Act bonds, bonds §8.45
  Procurement Policy Board (PPB) Rules §7.08
  Statutory notice requirements. See STATUTORY NOTICE REQUIREMENTS
  Subcontracts §3.20
  Time of the essence, delays §7.02
  Working under protest, dispute resolution §6.04
NOTICE TO INSURERS
  Insurance §10.15

INDEX

NOTICE TO PROCEED
Compensable damages §7.25
Delays §7.25
NUISANCE
Environmental problems §4.04
NURSERYMEN
Mechanics' liens §9.03

O

OBJECTIVE MANIFESTATIONS OF INTENT
Bidding and contract formation §2.25
OBLIGATIONS
Alteration, bonds §8.07
Common law obligations. See COMMON LAW OBLIGATIONS
Construction safety §§3.03, 13.04
Contractor's obligations. See CONTRACTOR'S OBLIGATIONS
Obligees, bonds §8.11
Owner's obligations. See OWNER'S OBLIGATIONS
Statutory obligations. See STATUTORY OBLIGATIONS
Surety's obligations and options. See BONDS
OBLIGEES
Bonds §§8.03, 8.10, 8.11
Claims by surety against, bonds §8.49
Penal sum payment, bonds §8.16
Priority, bonds §8.33
Work completion, bonds §8.15
OBSERVATION CLAUSES
Professional's role and liability §11.08
OBTAINING DOCUMENTS
Trial preparation, environmental problems §4.36
OBTAINING EXECUTIONS
Mechanics' liens §9.63

OBTAINING NEEDED INSURANCE
See INSURANCE
OCCUPATIONAL SAFETY AND HEALTH ACT
See OSHA
OCCURRENCE DEFINED
Coverage, insurance §10.09
Insurance §10.02
OCCURRENCE POLICIES
Distinguished from claims made §§10.04, 14.23
OFFER AND ACCEPTANCE
Bidding and contract formation §2.24
OFFICE OVERHEAD RATES
Bidding and contract formation §2.43
OFFICERS
Environmental problems §4.02
Insurance §10.25
OFFSETS
Insurance §10.12
Subcontracts §3.21
OIL
Lienable property, mechanics' liens §9.14
OMISSIONS
Errors and omissions liability insurance, environmental problems §4.21
ONE CALL PROGRAMS
Introductory material §1.27
ONE-YEAR RULE
Bidding and contract formation §2.27
ON TIME COMPLETION OF PROJECTS
Delays §7.02
OPPORTUNITY TO BE HEARD
Procurement Policy Board (PPB) Rules §7.07
OPPORTUNITY TO CURE
Defects and failures §2.14
Subcontractors §3.20

OPTIONS FOR ALLOCATING RISKS
Bidding and contract formation §2.41
ORAL CONTRACT
Bidding and contract formation §2.25
ORAL ORDER
Waiver of writing requirement, changes/extra work §6.18
ORDINARY AND REASONABLE SKILL TEST
Professional's role and liability §§11.04, 11.05
ORIGINAL CONTRACTOR
Work completion, bonds §8.13
ORIGIN OF CHANGES
Changes/extra work §6.01
OSHA
Asbestos abatement, environmental problems §4.29
Construction safety §3.19
OTHER INDOOR POLLUTION
Environmental problems §4.32
OTHER SUBCONTRACTORS
Subcontracts §3.15
OUT OF SEQUENCE WORK
Changes/extra work §6.29
OVERHEAD
Bidding and contract formation §2.43
Expense books, mechanics' liens §9.73
Field overhead, delays §7.58
Home office overhead, delays §7.60
Lienable items, mechanics' liens §9.21
Subcontracts §3.24
OVERLOOKING CONTRACT TERMS
Bidding and contract formation §2.19
OVERMETICULOUS INSPECTION
Changes/extra work §6.20

OVERVIEW
See INTRODUCTORY MATERIAL
OWNED PROPERTY EXCLUSION
Environmental problems §4.22
OWNER CAUSED DELAY
Delays §§7.05, 7.10
OWNER-CONTRACTOR AGREEMENT
See ENVIRONMENTAL PROBLEMS
OWNER-DESIGN PROFESSIONAL AGREEMENT
See ENVIRONMENTAL PROBLEMS
OWNER-OCCUPIED SINGLE FAMILY DWELLINGS
Asbestos abatement, environmental problems §4.30
OWNERS
Consent, mechanics' liens §§9.05, 9.12
Damages for delay. See DELAYS
Environmental problems §4.02
Identification, mechanics' liens §9.26
Interference
–changes/extra work §6.17
–compensable delays §7.23
–default/termination §4.14
–types of delays caused by §7.05
Introductory material. See INTRODUCTORY MATERIAL
Liability, construction safety §§3.08, 13.09
Misrepresentation, changed conditions §§5.10-5.12
Nondisclosure of technical information, changes/extra work §6.19
Obligations, construction safety §3.03
Other remedies, delays §7.73
Protection, construction safety §3.08
Specific breaches. See REMEDIES/DAMAGES

OWNER'S RESPONSE TO NOTICE
   OF LIEN
   See MECHANICS' LIENS
OWNER'S TRUST
   Mechanics' liens §9.70

P

PARITY
   Mechanics' liens §9.60
PAROL EVIDENCE RULE
   Bidding and contract formation
      §2.48
PARTIAL PERFORMANCE
   Specific breaches by contractor,
      remedies/damages §5.26
PARTICULAR PERSON TEST
   Professional's role and liability
      §11.14
PARTIES
   Introductory material §1.01
   Liability exposure, environmental
      problems §4.32
   Not protected by bond, bonds
      §8.31
   Surety relationships, bonds §8.03
   Trust funds, mechanics' liens
      §9.71
PARTNERSHIPS
   Accounting, remedies/damages
      §5.09
PASS THROUGH CLAUSES
   See INCORPORATION BY
      REFERENCE
PATENT DEFECTS
   Defects and failures §2.01
   Professional's role and liability
      §11.13
"PATENTLY ERRONEOUS AS A
   MATTER OF LAW" EXCEPTION
   Remedies/damages §5.01
PAYING SUBCONTRACTORS AND
   SUPPLIERS, FAILURE
   Default/termination §4.09

PAYMENT
   Delay, remedies/damages §5.15
   Mechanics' liens §9.36
   Procurement Policy Board (PPB)
      Rules §7.05
PAYMENT BONDS
   Bonds §§8.04, 8.32
   Introductory material §1.08
   Notice provisions, bonds app 8-1
PAYMENT FOR WORK DONE
   Bonds §8.26
PAYMENT REQUISITIONS
   Subcontracts §3.16
PAYMENT SCHEDULES
   Bonds §8.26
PAYMENT TERMS
   Subcontracts §3.06
PENAL SUM
   Bonds §§8.06, 8.08, 8.13, 8.18,
      8.42
   Liability in excess of, bonds §8.29
   Obligee payments, bonds §8.16
PENDENCY
   Filing notice, mechanics' liens
      §9.40
PERCENTAGE OF CONSTRUCTION
   COST METHOD
   Introductory material §1.03
PERCENTAGE OF WORK DONE
   Subcontracts §3.16
PER DIEM VALUE FOR EXTENDED
   PROJECT TIME
   Bidding and contract formation
      §2.43
PERFORMANCE BONDS
   Bonds §§8.04, 8.08
   Dispute resolution §6.16
   Environmental problems §4.25
PERFORMANCE EVALUATION
   Procurement Policy Board (PPB)
      Rules §7.05
PERFORMANCE SPECIFICATIONS
   Changes/extra work §6.22

PERFORMING WORK UNDER PROTEST
Changes/extra work §§6.02, 6.04, 6.13, 6.24, 6.31
Dispute resolution §6.04

PERMANENT CHANGE OF PROPERTY
Mechanics' liens §§9.04, 9.05

PERMANENT INJUNCTIONS
Remedies/damages §5.07

PERMITS
Environmental problems §§4.14, 14.34
Introductory material §1.24

PERSONAL INJURY
Alternative dispute resolution, environmental problems §4.43
Third parties, defects and failures §2.02

PERSONAL LIABILITY FOR ENVIRONMENTAL RISKS
Trial preparation, environmental problems §4.37

PERSONS PROTECTED
Miller Act bonds, bonds §8.44

PHILOSOPHIES FOR DEALING WITH RISKS
Bidding and contract formation §2.40

PHYSICAL INJURY
Professional's role and liability §11.13
Remedies/damages §5.20

PLACE FOR FILING LIEN NOTICE
Mechanics' liens §9.28

PLANS/SPECIFICATIONS CONFLICT
Bidding and contract formation §2.50

PLANTS AND EQUIPMENT
Insurance §10.10

POLICY LIMITS
Insurance §10.12

POLICY REQUIREMENTS
See INSURANCE

POLLUTION
Exclusions, environmental problems §§4.02, 14.22
Insurance §10.20

POSTBID NEGOTIATIONS
Bidding and contract formation §2.13

POSTCONSTRUCTION ACTIVITIES
Professional's role and liability §11.24

POSTPONING STATUTE OF LIMITATIONS
Defects and failures §2.08

POTENTIALLY RESPONSIBLE PARTIES
Environmental problems §§4.05, 14.38

POTENTIAL RISKS
Identification, environmental problems §4.09

PPB
See PROCUREMENT POLICY BOARD (PPB) RULES

PREAWARD INTEREST
Remedies/ damages §5.15

PRECAUTIONS
Introductory material §1.23

PRECLUSION OF EQUIVALENT EQUIPMENT OR MATERIALS
Bidding and contract formation §2.08

PRECLUSION OF RECOVERY FOR SERVICES
Professional's role and liability §11.03

PRECONDITIONS TO CONTRACT AWARD
Bidding and contract formation §2.08

PREDEFINED ADJUSTMENT EQUATIONS AND PROCEDURES
Bidding and contract formation §2.43

INDEX

PREEMPTION
  Environmental problems §4.04
PREFERENCE
  Enforcing trust funds, mechanics' liens §9.83
  Mechanics' liens §9.60
  Procurement Policy Board (PPB) Rules §7.06
PREJUDICING RIGHTS OF INSURANCE COMPANY
  Insurance §10.16
PRELIMINARY INJUNCTIONS
  Remedies/damages §5.06
PREMATURE CLAIMS
  Delays §7.18
PREMIUMS
  Bonds §8.01
  Insurance §10.14
PREPARATION WORK
  Subcontracts §3.09
PREQUALIFICATION OF BIDDERS
  Procurement Policy Board (PPB) Rules §7.02
  Public contracts, bidding and contract formation §2.06
PRESERVATION OF CLAIMS
  Changes/extra work §§6.33, 6.34
PRESERVATION OF RIGHT TO SUE
  Insurance §10.16
PRESUMPTIVE ADR
  Environmental problems §4.42
PREVAILING RATE OF WAGE
  Bidding and contract formation §2.35
PRICE
  Supply contract, subcontracts §3.32
  Work performed, mechanics' liens §9.26
PRICE ADJUSTMENTS FOR CHANGED WORK
  See CHANGES/EXTRA WORK

PRICE ANALYSIS
  Procurement Policy Board (PPB) Rules §7.03
PRICING CHANGE-RELATED COSTS
  Changes/extra work §6.26
PRICING RISKS
  Bidding and contract formation §2.37
PRINCIPALS
  Bonds §§8.03, 8.10
  Defenses and claims, bonds §8.30
PRIORITY
  Enforcing trust funds, mechanics' liens §9.83
  Public improvement liens, mechanics' liens §9.59
PRIORITY OF PRIVATE IMPROVEMENT LIENS
  See MECHANICS' LIENS
PRIVACY ACT
  Trial preparation, environmental problems §4.36
PRIVATE CONTRACTS
  Bidding and contract formation §2.17
PRIVATE IMPROVEMENTS
  Attachment, mechanics' liens §9.06
  Elements of proper lien notice, mechanics' liens §§9.26, 9.27
  Filing of lien notice, mechanics' liens §9.29
  Priority, mechanics' liens §§9.52-9.58
PRIVATE OWNERS
  Introductory material §1.09
PRIVATE PAYMENT BONDS
  Bonds §8.40
PRIVATE PROPERTY
  Mechanics' liens §§9.11-9.14
PRIVATE REJECTION OF BID
  Bidding and contract formation §2.22

PRIVATE SECTOR
Mechanics' liens §9.02
PRIVATE VS PUBLIC WORKS LIENS
Mechanics' liens, app 9-1
PRIVITY OF CONTRACT
Bonds §8.50
Defects and failures §§2.13, 12.16
Mechanics' liens §9.08
Professional's role and liability §§11.05, 11.13, 11.14
Remedies/damages §§5.11, 15.20, 15.35
Subcontracts §3.06
PROCEDURAL DEFECTS
Mechanics' liens §9.36
PROCEDURAL DUE PROCESS
Procurement Policy Board (PPB) Rules §§7.07, 17.08
PROCEDURE
Article 78, remedies/damages §5.02
PROCEDURE ON OCCURRENCE
Insurance §10.16
PROCUREMENT COSTS
Delays §7.56
PROCUREMENT POLICY BOARD (PPB) RULES
Construction, architecture, and engineering services §7.06
Contract
–administration §7.05
–award §7.04
–disputes §7.09
–formation §7.03
Delays §7.14
Dispute resolution
–generally §7.07
–bidding disputes §7.08
–contract disputes §7.09
–debarment and suspension §7.10
–hearings on borough president complaints §7.12
–solicitation or award of contract in violation of PPB rules §7.11
Methods of source selection §7.02

PROCUREMENT POLICY BOARD (PPB) RULES, *continued*
Negotiating maze §7.01
Questions and suggestions for PPB dispute resolution
–generally §7.13
–delays §7.14
–fairness §7.16
–finality of city decisions §7.15
PRODUCTS LIABILITY
Defects and failures §2.04
Professional's role and liability §11.04
PROFESSIONAL FEES
Owner's damages for delay §7.71
PROFESSIONAL LIABILITY INSURANCE
Insurance §§10.10-10.12, 10.35
PROFESSIONAL'S ROLE AND LIABILITY
Generally §11.01
Architect/engineer liability
–generally §11.04
–certification of progress payments §11.10
–cost estimates §11.07
–design §11.05
–dispute resolution §11.11
–scheduling and coordination §11.09
–supervision and inspection §11.08
–testing §11.06
–third parties. See THIRD PARTIES
Construction managers
–generally §11.15
–certification of progress payments §11.20
–cost estimates §11.17
–design §11.16
–scheduling and coordination §11.19
–supervision and inspection §11.18
–third parties §11.20

PROFESSIONAL'S ROLE AND
LIABILITY, *continued*
  General principles
    –continuous treatment doctrine
      §11.24
    –indemnification and contribution
      §11.22
    –statutes of limitations §11.23
  Insurance §11.25
  Licensing and qualifying to do
    business
    –generally §11.02
    –failure to license §11.02

PROFIT
  Delays §7.63

PROGRAM EVALUATION AND
REVIEW TECHNIQUE (PERT)
CHARTS
  Delays §7.04

PROGRESS PAYMENTS
  Improper certification, bonds
    §8.50
  Introductory material §1.03
  Subcontracts §§3.16, 3.17

PROGRESS REPORTS
  Certification, professional's role
    and liability §§11.10, 11.20

PROGRESS SCHEDULES
  Delays §7.04

PROHIBITION
  Remedies/damages §5.01

PROJECTS OUTSIDE OF STATE
  Construction safety §3.01

PROMISSORY ESTOPPEL
  Bidding and contract formation
    §2.21

PROMPT PAYMENT
  Procurement Policy Board (PPB)
    Rules §7.05

PROOF OF JUDGMENT
  Bonds §8.48

PROOF OF SERVICE
  Mechanics' liens §9.31

PROPER APPLICATION
  Trust funds, mechanics' liens
    §9.75

PROPERTY COVERAGE
  Insurance §§10.06, 10.08

PROPERTY DAMAGE
  Professional's role and liability
    §11.13

PROPERTY DAMAGE SUITS
  Alternative dispute resolution,
    environmental problems §4.43

PROS AND CONS OF NO
DAMAGES FOR DELAY
CLAUSES
  Delays §7.32

PROSECUTION OF WORK
  Default/termination §4.08

PRO TANTO RELEASE
  Bonds §8.26

PROTECTED PERSONS
  Bonds §§8.10, 8.33-8.36
  Miller Act bonds, bonds §8.44

PROTEST REQUIREMENTS
  Changes/extra work §§6.02, 6.03,
    6.13, 6.24, 6.31
  Dispute resolution §6.04
  Procurement Policy Board (PPB)
    Rules §7.08

PROVING COSTS
  Changes/extra work §6.30

PROVISIONS
  See SUBCONTRACTS

PROXIMATE CAUSE
  Construction safety §§3.06, 13.14

PUBLIC AGENCIES
  Exemption from competitive
    bidding requirements, bidding
    and contract formation §2.16

PUBLICATION REQUIREMENTS
  Procurement Policy Board (PPB)
    Rules §§7.08, 7.10

PUBLIC CONTRACTS
    Bidding and contract formation. See BIDDING AND CONTRACT FORMATION
    Formal dispute resolution, dispute resolution §6.12
    Punitive damages, remedies/damages §5.13
    Standard contract forms, bidding and contract formation §2.46

PUBLIC CORPORATION
    Introductory material §1.08
    Mechanics' liens §9.07

PUBLIC HARM
    Environmental problems §4.04

PUBLIC HEARINGS
    Procurement Policy Board (PPB) Rules §7.04

PUBLIC IMPROVEMENTS
    Description, mechanics' liens §9.27
    Elements of proper lien notice, mechanics' liens §9.27
    Filing of lien notice, mechanics' liens §9.30
    Introductory material §1.08
    Mechanics' liens §9.07
    Priority, mechanics' liens §9.59

PUBLIC INTEREST
    Bidding and contract formation §2.03

PUBLIC OWNERS
    Introductory material §1.08

PUBLIC PROPERTY
    Mechanics' liens §9.15

PUBLIC REJECTION OF BID
    Bidding and contract formation §2.22

PUBLIC SECTOR
    See MECHANICS' LIENS

PUBLIC WORKS CONTRACTS
    Statutes of limitations, professional's role and liability §11.23

PUNITIVE DAMAGES
    Bonds §8.29
    Claims by obligee, bonds §8.22
    Remedies/damages §§5.12, 15.13
    Trust funds, mechanics' liens §9.79

PURCHASE MONEY MORTGAGE
    Priority, mechanics' liens §9.54

PURCHASE ORDERS
    Supply contracts, subcontracts §3.27

"PURPOSE OF THE CONTRACT" BASIS
    Default/termination §4.03

Q

QUALIFYING TO DO BUSINESS
    Professional's role and liability §§11.02, 11.03

QUALITY OCCURRENCE LIABILITY INSURANCE
    Bonds, environmental problems §4.25

QUANTITATIVE VS QUALITATIVE CHANGE
    Changes/extra work §6.27

QUANTUM MERUIT
    Changes/extra work §§6.04, 6.27, 6.35
    Default/termination §§4.17, 4.21
    Delays §7.52
    Distinguished from breach of contract, remedies/damages §5.10
    Nonpayment, remedies/damages §5.33

QUESTIONS AND SUGGESTION
    See PROCUREMENT POLICY BOARD (PPB) RULES

R

RADON
Indoor pollution, environmental problems §4.32

RATIONALITY OF DECISIONS
Article 78, remedies/damages §5.04

RCRA
Alternative dispute resolution, environmental problems §4.43

READVERTISING
Bidding and contract formation §§2.08, 2.13, 2.15

REAL PROPERTY ACTIONS AND PROCEEDINGS LAW
Mechanics' liens §§9.61, 9.63

REASONABLE COST
Price adjustments, changes/extra work §6.25

REASONABLE TIME OF COMPLETIONS
Delays §7.02

REASONABLE UNDER ALL CIRCUMSTANCES
Policy requirements, insurance §10.15

REASONABLY PRUDENT CONTRACTOR STANDARD
Owner's misrepresentation, changed conditions §5.10

REBATES
Supply contract, subcontracts §3.32

RECEIVERS
Mechanics' liens §9.05

RECKLESS REPRESENTATION
Owner's misrepresentation, changed conditions §5.12

RECORD KEEPING REQUIREMENTS
Changes/extra work §§6.24, 6.30, 6.31
Trust funds, mechanics' liens §9.73

RECOVERY IN CONTRACT
Default/termination §§4.17, 4.21
Owner's misrepresentation, changed conditions §5.11
Remedies/damages §5.20

RECOVERY OF LOSSES
Bonds §§8.48, 8.49

REDUCING SUPERFUND RISK
Environmental problems §4.27

REDUCTION OF RETAINAGE
Subcontracts §3.17

REFERENCES
Bidding and contract formation §2.04
Environmental problems §4.44

REFORMATION
Remedies/damages §5.41

REFUSAL TO USE SAFETY EQUIPMENT
Construction safety §§3.05, 13.14

REGISTRATION OF CONTRACT
Bidding and contract formation §2.32
Procurement Policy Board (PPB) Rules §7.04

REGULATORY PROVISIONS
Construction safety §3.06

REIMBURSEMENT
Bonds §8.48
Subcontracts §3.23

REJECTION OF BIDS
Bidding and contract formations §§2.15, 2.22

REJECTION OF SUPPLY CONTRACT TERMS
Subcontracts §3.31

RELATIONS WITH OTHER SUBCONTRACTORS
Subcontracts §3.15

RELEASES OF WASTE
Environmental problems §4.27

RELEASING SURETIES
Bid bonds, bonds §8.07

RELIANCE ON OWNER'S DATA
  Changed conditions §5.14
RELIEF
  Enforcing trust funds, mechanics' liens §9.81
  Right to, delays §7.47
REMEDIAL WORK
  Changes/extra work §6.03
  Defects and failures §2.07
REMEDIES
  Changed conditions §5.16
  Changes/extra work §6.34
  Delays §§7.48, 7.73
  Nonpayment, subcontracts §3.25
  Procurement Policy Board (PPB) Rules §7.11
REMEDIES/DAMAGES
  Accounting §5.09
  Article 78
  –generally §5.01
  –construction cases §5.03
  –procedure §5.02
  –standard of review §5.04
  Attorneys' fees §5.14
  Breach by architect/engineer §5.34
  Breach by subcontractors §5.35
  Breach of contract vs quantum meruit §5.10
  Contractual limitations on damages §5.22
  Contractual provisions regarding remedies §5.23
  Declaratory judgment §5.08
  Fraud §5.11
  Injunctions
  –generally §5.05
  –permanent injunctions §5.07
  –preliminary injunctions §5.06
  Interest §5.15
  Materialmen remedies
  –generally §5.36
  –account stated §5.38
  –replevin §5.37

REMEDIES/DAMAGES, *continued*
  Noncontractual limitations on damages
  –generally §5.16
  –certainty §5.19
  –collateral source rule §5.18
  –economic loss rule §5.20
  –mitigation §5.17
  Punitive damages
  –generally §5.12
  –public contracts §5.13
  Reformation §5.41
  Rescission and restitution §5.40
  Specific breaches by contractor
  –generally §5.24
  –cost of completion vs diminution in value §5.29
  –defective performance §5.28
  –failure to commence performance §5.25
  –partial performance §5.26
  –substantial performance §5.27
  Specific breaches by owner
  –generally §5.30
  –abandonment following start of construction §5.32
  –failure to commence project §5.31
  –nonpayment §5.33
  Specific performance §5.39
  UCC damage and remedy provisions §5.21
REMOBILIZATION
  Delays §7.59
  Subcontracts §3.23
REMOTE PURCHASERS
  Defects and failures §2.04
REMOTE USER'S INJURIES
  Professional's role and liability §11.13
RENOVATION
  Environmental problems §4.03
RENTAL EQUIPMENT
  Delays §7.59
  Items covered, bonds §8.39

RENTAL EQUIPMENT, *continued*
  Lienable items, mechanics' liens §9.19
REPAIR AND MAINTENANCE BONDS
  See GUARANTY BONDS
REPAIR BONDS
  Defects and failures §2.16
REPLACEMENT CONTRACTORS
  Subcontracts §3.24
REPRESENTATION OF FACT
  Owner's misrepresentation, changed conditions §§5.11, 5.12
REPRESENTATIONS
  Environmental problems §4.15
REPRESENTATIVE ACTIONS
  Enforcement of trust funds, mechanics' liens §9.81
REPUDIATION
  Changed conditions §5.15
  Supply contract, subcontracts §3.31
REQUESTING INFORMATION
  Subcontracts §§3.16, 3.17
REQUIRED EQUIPMENT
  Bidding and contract formation §2.08
REQUIREMENTS
  Construction safety §3.06
  Mistakes, bidding and contract formation §2.19
  Notice, protest, and record keeping, changes/extra work §6.24
  Writing, changes/extra work §6.08
RESCISSION
  Changed conditions §5.16
  Default/termination §4.20
  Remedies/damages §5.40
RESERVING RIGHT TO MAKE CLAIM
  Changes/extra work §§6.13, 6.34

RESIDENTIAL DWELLING EXCEPTION
  Owner liability, construction safety §3.09
RES IPSA LOQUITUR
  Construction safety §3.17
RESOLVING FACTUAL DISPUTES
  Changes/extra work §6.23
RESOURCE CONSERVATION AND RECOVERY ACT
  See RCRA
RESPONSE ACTION DECREE
  Superfund litigation, environmental problems §4.40
RESPONSIBILITIES
  Evaluating risks and responsibilities. See BIDDING AND CONTRACT FORMATION
RESPONSIBILITY
  Apportionment, delays §7.50
  Bidding and contract formation §§2.05, 2.13, 2.15
  Defects and failures §§2.01, 12.03, 12.06
  Procurement Policy Board (PPB) Rules §§7.02, 17.04, 17.10
RESPONSIBILITY FOR GOODS
  Supply contract, subcontracts §3.34
RESPONSIVENESS
  Procurement Policy Board (PPB) Rules §§7.02, 17.04
  Public projects, bidding and contract formation §2.05
RESTITUTION
  Remedies/damages §5.40
RESTORATION AFTER DIVERSION
  Trust funds, mechanics' liens §9.80
RESTRAINING ORDERS
  Delays §7.11
RESULTS
  Insurance §10.09

758 INDEX

RETAINAGE
  Bonds §§8.26, 8.48
  Interest, delays §7.64
  Premature release
  –bonds §8.50
  –professional's role and liability §11.10
  Subcontracts §3.17
RETAINERS
  Introductory material §1.03
REVERSE LIQUIDATING AGREEMENTS
  Remedies/damages §5.35
REVIEW BOARDS
  Dispute resolution §6.06
REVISION OF CONTRACTS
  Procurement Policy Board (PPB) Rules §7.11
RIGHTS AND RESPONSIBILITIES
  Remedies/damages §5.08
RIGHT TO RELIEF
  Acceleration, delays §7.47
RIPENESS OF CLAIM
  Changes/extra work §6.35
RISK
  Allocation. See BIDDING AND CONTRACT FORMATION
  Categories §2.42
  Delays §3.35
  Distinguished from credit, bonds §8.01
  Evaluating risks and responsibilities. See BIDDING AND CONTRACT FORMATION
  Management consultants, insurance §10.03
  Risk allocation. See BIDDING AND CONTRACT FORMATION
  Superfund, environmental problems §4.27
RISK/INJURY
  Insurance §10.02

ROLE DEFINITION
  Owner-design professional agreement, environmental problems §4.18
ROLE OF COUNSEL
  Risk allocation, bidding and contract formation §2.44
ROOTS OF DEFECTS AND FAILURES
  Defects and failures §2.01
RULES
  See PROCUREMENT POLICY BOARD (PPB) RULES
RULES OF CONTRACT INTERPRETATION
  Scope of work disputes, changes/extra work §6.23

S

SAFE ACCESS
  Construction safety §3.04
SAFE PLACE TO WORK DOCTRINE
  Construction safety §3.03
SAFETY
  Construction safety. See CONSTRUCTION SAFETY
  Devices, construction safety §§3.04, 13.05
  Subcontracts §3.10
SALE OF GOODS
  Subcontracts §§3.11, 3.28
SALES LITERATURE
  Defects and failures §2.15
SALE UPON EXECUTION
  See MECHANICS' LIENS
SARA
  Superfund litigation, environmental problems §4.39
SATISFACTION
  Claims preservation and defense, changes/extra work §6.33
  Judgments, mechanics' liens §9.36

SCAFFOLDING
Construction safety §3.05
SCHEDULING
Professional's role and liability §§11.09, 11.19
SCHEDULING PROCEDURES
Delays §3.35
SCHOOL CONTRACTS
Dispute resolution §6.02
SCOPE DOCUMENTS
Environmental problems §4.13
SCOPE OF WORK
Changes/extra work §§6.03, 6.23
Dispute resolution §6.04
Subcontracts §3.07
Terms, subcontracts §3.07
SECOND NOTICE OF LENDING
Trust funds, mechanics' liens §9.76
SECOND TIER SUBCONTRACTORS
See SUB-SUBCONTRACTORS
SEIZURE
Mechanics' liens §9.07
SEIZURE OF CHATTEL
Remedies/damages §5.37
SELECTED REFERENCES
Dispute resolution §6.17
SEPARATE BOOKS
Trust funds, mechanics' liens §9.73
SEPARATE SPECIFICATION FOR CERTAIN TYPES OF WORK
Public contracts, bidding and contract formation §2.09
SEQUENCING OF CONSTRUCTION
Subcontracts §§3.08, 3.09
SEQUENTIAL CONSTRUCTION
Procurement Policy Board (PPB) Rules §7.06
SERVICE CONTRACTS
Supply contracts, subcontracts §3.28

SERVICE OF NOTICE
Dispute resolution §6.02
Mechanics' liens §9.31
SERVICES VS SALES OF GOODS
Subcontracts §3.11
SET OFF
Specific breaches by contractor, remedies/damages §5.26
SETTING ASIDE SALES
Sale upon execution, mechanics' liens §9.67
SHARED RISKS
Bidding and contract formation §2.36
SHAREHOLDERS
Environmental problems §4.02
SHIFTING LIABILITY
Environmental problems §4.01
SHIPPING
Supply contract terms, subcontracts §3.34
SHOULD YOU FILE A LIEN
Mechanics' liens §9.25
SHOWING CAUSE
Injunctions, remedies/damages §5.06
SIGNIFICANT DELAY
Supply contract, subcontracts §3.32
SISTERSHIP CLAUSE
Insurance §10.18
SITE INSPECTION CLAUSES
Environmental problems §4.14
SITE INVESTIGATION
Changed conditions §5.13
Contract clauses, changed conditions §5.08
Owner-contractor agreement, environmental problems §4.13
Superfund, environmental problems §4.26
SMALL ASBESTOS PROJECTS
Environmental problems §4.31

SOCIAL SECURITY DEDUCTIONS
Trust funds, mechanics' liens §9.71

SOCIAL SECURITY PAYMENTS
Collateral source rule, remedies/damages §5.18

SOLE CONTROL
Construction safety §3.17

SOLE SOURCE PROCUREMENT
Procurement Policy Board (PPB) Rules §7.02

SOLE SOURCE SUBCONTRACTORS
Subcontracts §3.08

SOLICITATION OF CONTRACTS
Violation of PPC rules, Procurement Policy Board (PPB) Rules §7.11

SOURCE SELECTION
Methods, Procurement Policy Board (PPB) Rules §7.02

SOURCES OF ENVIRONMENTAL LAW
See ENVIRONMENTAL PROBLEMS

SOVEREIGN AND OTHER INTERFERING ACTS
Excusable delay §7.11

SPECIAL CASE DETERMINATION
Procurement Policy Board (PPB) Rules §7.02

SPECIAL CONCERNS
See INTRODUCTORY MATERIAL

SPECIAL INSURANCE PROBLEMS
See INSURANCE

SPECIALLY RESERVED CLAIMS
Changes/extra work §6.29

SPECIAL MASTERS
Trial preparation, environmental problems §4.35

SPECIAL ORDERS
Subcontracts §3.35

SPECIAL PROBLEMS IN NEW YORK CITY
Introductory material §1.28

SPECIAL REMEDIES
Dispute resolution §6.11

SPECIAL TERMS
Evaluation, bidding and contract formation §2.35

SPECIALTY SUBCONTRACTORS
Subcontracts §§3.08, 3.11

SPECIFICALLY MANUFACTURED MATERIALS
Mechanics' liens §§9.04, 9.09

SPECIFICATIONS
Bidding and contract formation §§2.08, 2.50
Changed conditions §5.02
Changes/extra work §§6.18, 6.21, 6.22
Conflict with plans, bidding and contract formation §2.50
Supply contract, subcontracts §3.33

SPECIFIC BREACHES BY CONTRACTOR
See REMEDIES/DAMAGES

SPECIFIC BREACHES BY OWNER
See REMEDIES/DAMAGES

SPECIFIC CONDITIONS CONTROLLING
Bidding and contract formation §2.47

SPECIFIC DOCUMENT OR LANGUAGE CONTROLLING
Bidding and contract formation §2.49

SPECIFIC PERFORMANCE
Delays §7.73
Dispute resolution §6.11
Remedies/damages §5.39

SPECIFIC RISK INSURANCE
Insurance §10.05

SPECIFIED MATERIALS
Bidding and contract formation §2.08

SPECULATIVE PROFITS
Delays §7.69

STANDARD FORMS
  Bidding and contract formation §2.46
  Subcontracts §3.03
STANDARD OF PROFESSIONAL CARE
  Defects and failures §2.02
  Professional's role and liability §§11.04, 11.15
STANDARD OF REVIEW
  Article 78, remedies/damages §5.04
STANDARD POLICIES
  Insurance §10.02
STANDARDS OF COMMUNITY
  Defects and failures §3.03
START-UP EXPENSES
  Default/termination §4.21
STATE
  Mechanics' liens §9.07
STATE CONTRACTS
  Relevant contract clauses §7.15
STATE ENVIRONMENTAL QUALITY REVIEW ACT
  Environmental problems §4.07
STATE FREEDOM ON INFORMATION LAW
  Dispute resolution §6.03
STATE LAW
  Asbestos abatement, environmental problems §4.30
STATE LEGISLATION
  Source of legislation, environmental problems §4.06
STATING WORK PERFORMED AND PRICE
  Mechanics' liens §9.26
STATUTE OF FRAUDS
  Bidding and contract formation §2.27
STATUTES OF LIMITATIONS
  Article 78, remedies/damages §5.02

STATUTES OF LIMITATIONS, *continued*
  Declaratory judgments, remedies/damages §5.08
  Defects and failures §§2.08, 12.12
  Professional's role and liability §11.23
  Supply contracts, subcontracts §§3.28, 3.29
STATUTES OF REPOSE
  Defects and failures §2.08
STATUTORY AGENT
  Construction safety §§3.10, 13.13
STATUTORY CONDITIONS PRECEDENT
  Dispute resolution §6.15
STATUTORY LIABILITY
  Affirmative defenses, construction safety §3.14
STATUTORY NOTICE PROVISIONS
  Claim preservation, changes/extra work §6.32
  Dispute resolution §6.02
  Waiver, dispute resolution §6.02
STATUTORY OBLIGATIONS
  Contractor's obligations §3.04
  Owner's obligations §3.03
STAYING CONTRACTS
  Procurement Policy Board (PPB) Rules §7.08
STOPPING WORK
  Environmental problems §4.16
  Subcontracts §3.25
STRICTISSIMI JURIS
  Bonds §8.02
STRICT PRODUCTS LIABILITY CLAIM
  Professional's role and liability §14.04
STRIKES
  Excusable delay §7.09
STRIKING AFFIRMATIVE DEFENSE
  Trial preparation, environmental problems §4.35

STRUCTURAL DAMAGE TO
    NEIGHBORING PROPERTIES
  Introductory material §1.26
SUBCONSULTANTS
  Introductory material §1.06
SUBCONTRACTORS
  Agents' liability §3.13
  Bids, bidding and contract
    formation §2.21
  Bonds §§8.10, 8.33, 8.44
  Certification of work,
    professional's role and liability
    §11.10
  Claims by surety against, bonds
    §8.52
  Defects and failures §2.07
  Demands, excusable delay §7.12
  Environmental problems §4.02
  Failure to pay,
    default/termination §4.09
  Introductory material §1.14
  Mechanics' liens §§9.03, 9.05
  Protected persons, bonds §8.34
SUBCONTRACTOR'S TRUST
  Mechanics' liens §9.70
SUBCONTRACTS
  Generally §3.01
  Actions for breach and damages
    §3.35
  Applicable law - UCC §3.28
  Breach, remedies/damages §5.35
  Formation §3.02
  Provisions
  –back charges §3.20
  –boilerplate §3.05
  –change orders and extras §3.12
  –contingent payment clauses
    §3.18
  –contractor's duties §3.09
  –default/termination §3.24
  –delay damages §3.22
  –final payment §3.19
  –hold harmless and
    indemnification clauses §3.13
  –incorporation by reference §3.06

SUBCONTRACTS, *continued*
  –job site §3.10
  –lien waivers §3.26
  –liquidating agreements §3.23
  –offsets §3.21
  –other subcontractors §3.15
  –progress payments §3.16
  –remedies for non-payment §3.25
  –retainage §3.17
  –scope of work §3.07
  –sub-subcontractors and
    materialmen §3.14
  –time of performance §3.08
  –warranties §3.11
  Purchase orders and supply
    contracts §3.27
  Standard forms §3.03
  Supply contract terms
  –generally §3.29
  –acceptance and rejection §3.31
  –insurance and shipping §3.34
  –price and terms of payment
    §3.32
  –time of performance §3.30
  –warranties §3.33
  Terms and conditions, bidding
    and contract formation §2.45
SUBMISSION OF CLAIMS
  Procurement Policy Board (PPB)
    Rules §7.09
SUBORDINATION
  Mechanics' liens §9.58
SUBPOENAS
  Dispute resolution §6.11
SUBSEQUENT PURCHASERS
  Mechanics' liens §9.57
  Warranty clauses, defects and
    failures §2.14
SUBSTANTIAL COMPLETION
  Delays §§7.02, 7.18
  Payments, Procurement Policy
    Board (PPB) Rules §7.05
SUBSTANTIAL COMPLIANCE
  Notice requirements, delays §7.17

SUBSTANTIAL PERFORMANCE
   Contractor defenses §4.13
   Defects and failures §§2.03, 12.08
   Specific breaches by contractor, remedies/damages §5.27

SUBSTITUTE CONTRACTOR
   Work completion, bonds §8.14

SUB-SUBCONTRACTORS
   Bonds §8.34
   Introductory material §1.14
   Subcontracts §3.14

SUB-SUB-SUBCONTRACTORS
   Mechanics' liens §9.09

SUBSURFACE CONDITIONS
   Changed conditions §§5.02, 5.03
   Dispute resolution §6.03
   Environmental problems §4.03

SUCCESSORS IN INTEREST
   Mechanics' liens §9.03

SUDDEN AND ACCIDENTAL DISCHARGE
   Environmental problems §4.22

SUMMARY JUDGMENT
   Dispute resolution §6.11
   Trial preparation, environmental problems §4.35

SUNSET CLAUSE
   Insurance §10.04

SUPERFUND
   Environmental problems. See ENVIRONMENTAL PROBLEMS
   RCRA, environmental problems §4.43
   Sources of environmental law, environmental problems §4.05

SUPERVISION AND COORDINATION
   Mechanics' liens §9.17
   Separate prime contracts, bidding and contract formation §2.09

SUPERVISION AND INSPECTION
   Professional's role and liability §§11.08, 11.18

SUPPLEMENTAL AGREEMENTS
   Changed conditions §5.18

SUPPLEMENTAL PERFORMANCE
   Defects and failures §2.12

SUPPLIERS
   See MATERIALMEN

SUPPLY CONTRACT
   Formation, subcontracts §3.02
   Purchase orders, subcontracts §3.27
   Subcontracts. See SUBCONTRACTS

SURETIES
   Bid bonds, bonds §8.07
   Binding to arbitration clause, dispute resolution §6.16
   Bonds §8.03
   Claims by surety against, bonds §8.52
   Environmental problems §4.02
   Expenses. See BONDS
   Introductory material §1.16
   Liability, bonds §8.06
   Obligations and options, bonds §§8.12-8.16
   Work completion, bonds §8.14

SURETY'S EXPENSES
   See BONDS

SURFACING ACM
   Environmental problems §4.29

SURPLUSAGE
   Mechanics' liens §9.26

SURPRISE
   Changed conditions §5.02

SURVEYING SERVICES
   Bidding and contract formation §2.14
   Professional's role and liability §11.06

SURVEYORS
   Mechanics' liens §9.03

SUSPENSION
   Clauses, default/termination §4.04

SUSPENSION, *continued*
   Procurement Policy Board (PPB)
      Rules §7.10

T

TAXES
   Miller Act bonds, bonds §8.46
TAX LIENS
   Mechanics' liens §9.56
TECHNICAL INFORMATION
   Changes/extra work §6.19
TECHNICAL NONCOMPLIANCE
   Waiver, bidding and contract
      formation §2.05
**TEMPORARY RESTRAINING ORDER
   (TRO)**
   Injunctions, remedies/damages
      §§5.05, 15.06
TEMPORARY WORKS
   Lienable items, mechanics' liens
      §9.20
10-FOOT RULE
   Lateral support, introductory
      material §1.26
TERMINATION
   Damages, changes/extra work
      §§6.05, 6.14
   Deductive changes vs convenience
      terminations, changes/extra
      work §6.05
   Default/termination. See
      DEFAULT/TERMINATION
   Delays §§7.18, 7.66, 7.73
   Insurance §10.17
   Procurement Policy Board (PPB)
      Rules §§7.05, 17.10
   Professional relationship,
      professional's role and liability
      §11.23
   Remedies/damages §5.10
   Subcontracts §§3.24, 3.25
TERMS
   Bonds §8.04

TERMS AND CONDITIONS
   Subcontracts, bidding and
      contract formation §2.45
TERMS OF PAYMENT
   Supply contract, subcontracts
      §3.32
TESTING
   Professional's role and liability
      §11.06
   Work, subcontracts §3.17
THERMAL SYSTEM INSULATION
   Environmental problems §4.29
THIRD PARTIES
   Architect/engineer liability
      –generally §11.12
      –contracts §11.14
      –negligence §11.13
   Bonds §§8.03, 8.19, 8.31, 8.33,
      8.48
   Completion bonds, bonds §8.10
   Construction manager liability
      §11.21
   Construction safety §§3.10, 13.16
   Owners as third-party
      beneficiaries, remedies/
      damages §5.35
   Personal injury, defects and
      failures §2.02
   Protected persons, bonds §8.10
THIRD-PARTY COVERAGE
   See LIABILITY COVERAGE
THIRD PARTY DEFENSE
   Superfund litigation,
      environmental problems §4.39
**THIRD PERSON'S REASONABLE
   PERCEPTION**
   Bidding and contract formation
      §2.30
THREE-PARTY CONTRACTS
   Bonds §8.01
TIDAL WETLANDS
   Environmental problems §4.34
TIME AND EXPENSES
   Introductory material §1.03

INDEX

TIME AND MATERIALS
  Change orders, Procurement Policy Board (PPB) Rules §7.06
  Contracts
    –introductory material 1.21
    –procurement Policy Board (PPB) Rules §7.05

TIME EXTENSIONS
  Clauses, environmental problems §4.14
  Delays §§7.08, 7.10, 7.13, 7.14, 7.21, 7.22, 7.28
  Procurement Policy Board (PPB) Rules §§7.05, 17.12, 17.14

TIME LIMITATION
  Enforcement of trust funds, mechanics' liens §8.81
  Insurance §10.28
  Procurement Policy Board (PPB) Rules §7.15

TIMELY NOTICE
  Insurance §10.16

TIME/MONEY RELATIONSHIP
  Delays §7.03

TIME OF NOTICE
  Delays §7.18
  Mechanics' liens §9.28
  Notice of claim, bonds §8.40

TIME OF PAYMENT
  Subcontracts §3.24

TIME OF PERFORMANCE
  Subcontracts §3.08
  Supply contract terms, subcontracts §3.30

TIME OF THE ESSENCE
  Delays §7.02

TIME TO SERVE NOTICE
  Dispute resolution §6.02

TOOLS AND EQUIPMENT
  Construction safety §3.03

TORT-BASED CLAIMS
  Professional's role and liability §11.04

TOTAL COST METHOD
  Delays §7.49
  Remedies/damages §5.19

TOTAL PROJECT COST REDUCTION
  Risk allocation, bidding and contract formation §2.42

TOXIC POLLUTANTS
  Environmental problems §4.05

TRADE CONTRACTORS
  Introductory material §1.12

TRADE CUSTOM AND USAGE
  Contract clauses, changed conditions §5.09

TRANSACTION AS A WHOLE TEST
  Insurance §10.09

TRANSFER OF RISKS
  Bidding and contract formation §2.41

TRESPASSERS
  Construction safety §3.04
  Environmental problems §4.04

TRIALS
  Foreclosures, mechanics' liens §9.51
  Trial preparation. See ENVIRONMENTAL PROBLEMS

TROUBLESOME CLAUSES
  Owner-contractor agreement, environmental problems §4.14

TRUST BOOK ENTRIES
  Mechanics' liens §9.73

TRUST COVENANT CLAUSE
  Priority, mechanics' liens §§9.57, 9.59
  Trust funds, mechanics' liens §9.76

TRUSTEES
  Mechanics' liens §§9.71, 9.72

TRUST FUNDS
  Beneficiaries, mechanics' liens §9.71
  Enforcement, mechanics' liens §§9.81-9.84

766 INDEX

TRUST FUNDS, *continued*
  Lien law accounting, remedies/damages §5.09
  Mechanics' liens. See MECHANICS' LIENS

TURNKEY/DESIGN-BUILD
  Introductory material §1.23

TWO-PARTY CONTRACTS
  Bonds §8.01

TYPE I AND TYPE II CHANGED CONDITIONS
  Changed conditions §§5.02, 5.07

TYPES OF BONDS
  Bonds §8.04

TYPES OF CONTRACTS
  Introductory material. See INTRODUCTORY MATERIAL
  Price adjustments, changes/extra work §6.25
  Procurement Policy Board (PPB) Rules §7.03

TYPES OF DELAY
  Delays §§7.05, 7.06

TYPES OF PROJECTS AFFECTED
  Environmental problems §4.03

TYPES OF RISK
  Bidding and contract formation §2.39

TYPICAL NO DAMAGES FOR DELAY CLAUSES
  Delays §7.35

U

UCC
  See UNIFORM COMMERCIAL CODE

UNABSORBED OVERHEAD
  Delays §7.60

UNALLOWABLE COSTS
  Procurement Policy Board (PPB) Rules §7.03

UNAMBIGUOUS CONTRACTS
  Bidding and contract formation §2.47

UNANTICIPATED CONDITIONS
  See CHANGED CONDITIONS

UNCOMPENSATED SURETIES
  Bonds §8.03

UNCONTEMPLATED CAUSE
  Delays §7.42

UNCONTEMPLATED DELAY
  Exceptions to enforcement of no damages for delay clauses §7.37

UNDERCERTIFICATION OF PAYMENTS DUE
  Bonds §8.50

UNDERGROUND DAMAGE
  Insurance §10.21

UNDERGROUND STORAGE TANKS (USTS)
  Environmental problems §§4.03, 14.33

UNDERGROUND UTILITIES
  Introductory material §1.27

UNDERSTANDING INSURANCE POLICIES
  Insurance §10.02

UNEMPLOYMENT INSURANCE
  Mechanics' liens §9.71

UNEXCUSABLE ERRORS
  Bonds §8.06

UNEXPECTED CLAIMS
  Dispute resolution §6.14

UNFORESEEN CONDITIONS
  Bidding and contract formation §2.36
  Changed conditions. See CHANGED CONDITIONS

UNFORESEEN DIFFICULTIES
  Delays §7.07
  Weather, delays §§7.08, 7.09

UNFORESEEN OCCURRENCES
  Bidding and contract formation §2.14

UNIFORM COMMERCIAL CODE (UCC)
Bidding and contract formation §2.27
Defects and failures §2.13
Remedies/damages §5.21
Subcontracts §§3.11, 3.28

UNILATERAL MISTAKES
Bidding and contract formation §2.19

UNIQUE PROJECTS AND SOLUTIONS
Special insurance problems §§10.32-10.35

UNIT PRICE
Changes/extra work §§6.26-6.28
Contracts, introductory material §1.20
Price adjustments for changed work, changes/extra work §6.27
Procurement Policy Board (PPB) Rules §§7.05, 17.06

UNKNOWN CONDITIONS
See CHANGED CONDITIONS

UNREASONABLE DELAY AND ABANDONMENT
Exceptions to enforcement of no damages for delay clauses §7.39

UNSATISFACTORY PERFORMANCE
Procurement Policy Board (PPB) Rules §7.05

UNTIMELY CLAIM
Surety's defenses, bonds §8.28

UNTIMELY NOTICE
Surety's defenses, bonds §8.25

UNUSUAL WEATHER
Delays §7.08

USAGE OF TRADE
Supply contract, subcontracts §3.33

USERS OF BUILDINGS
Professional's role and liability §11.04

USING ADR IN ENVIRONMENTAL LITIGATION
Environmental problems §4.43

USUAL DANGERS OF CONSTRUCTION
Construction safety §3.06

V

VAUGHN LIST
Dispute resolution §6.13

VENDEE IN POSSESSION
Mechanics' liens §9.05

VENDEES
Priority, mechanics' liens §9.57

VENDEX
Procurement Policy Board (PPB) Rules §§7.04, 15.08, 17.05, 17.10

VENUE
Enforcement, mechanics' liens §9.42
Enforcing trust funds, mechanics' liens §9.81

VERIFICATION
Dispute resolution §6.02
Post audits, Procurement Policy Board (PPB) Rules §7.06

VERIFIED TRUSTEE STATEMENTS
Mechanics' liens §9.74

VICARIOUS LIABILITY
Subcontracts §3.13

VIOLATION, STATUTORY
Construction safety §3.14

VIOLATION OF PPB RULES
Procurement Policy Board (PPB) Rules §7.11

VISITORS
Construction safety §3.03

VISITORS, *continued*
   Professional's role and liability §11.04

VOLUNTEERS
   Bonds §8.24

W

WAIVERS
   Arbitration, dispute resolution §6.14
   Bonds §8.05
   Claims preservation and defense, changes/extra work §6.34
   Contractor defenses, default/termination §4.16
   Damages
   –changes/extra work §6.32
   –subcontracts §3.06
   Defects and failures §2.07
   Delays §§7.02, 7.21, 7.51
   Interest, remedies/damages §5.15
   Liens, subcontracts §3.26
   Material noncompliance, bidding and contract formation §2.05
   Mechanics' liens §9.24
   Notice requirements, dispute resolution §6.02
   Owner's misrepresentation, changed conditions §5.12
   Procurement Policy Board (PPB) Rules §§7.09, 17.14
   Right to claim, changed conditions §5.18
   Statute of limitations, defects and failures §2.08
   Superfund litigation, environmental problems §4.39
   Technical noncompliance, bidding and contract formation §2.05
   Writing requirement, changes/extra work §§6.08-6.12

WARRANTIES
   Bidding and contract formation §2.36
   Defects and failures §§2.12-12.16
   Environmental problems §4.15
   Express warranties. See EXPRESS WARRANTIES
   Implied warranties. See IMPLIED WARRANTIES
   Subcontracts §3.11
   Supply contract terms, subcontracts §3.33

WARRANTY BASED CLAIMS
   Professional's role and liability §11.04

WEATHER CAUSED DELAY
   Delays §7.08

WETLANDS
   Environmental problems §4.34

WHAT TO DO ON OCCURRENCE
   Insurance §10.16

WHISTLEBLOWERS
   Procurement Policy Board (PPB) Rules §7.16

WHO CAN BIND WHOM
   Bidding and contract formation §2.30

WHO IS PROTECTED
   See BONDS

WHO MAY FILE
   Mechanics' liens. See MECHANICS' LIENS
   Public sector, mechanics' liens §9.09

WHO SHOULD BE CONCERNED
   Environmental problems §4.02

WICKS LAW
   Bidding and contract formation §2.09
   Introductory material §1.12

WILLFUL EXAGGERATION
   Enforcement, mechanics' liens §9.49

WILLFUL FAILURE TO PRODUCE REQUESTED MATERIAL
Procurement Policy Board (PPB) Rules §7.09

WINNER'S COSTS
Dispute resolution §6.08

WITHDRAWAL OF BIDS
Bidding and contract formation §2.12
Procurement Policy Board (PPB) Rules §7.02

WITHHOLDING TAXES
Mechanics' liens §9.71

WORK
Bonds §8.26

WORK COMPLETION
Obligees, bonds §8.15
Original contractor, bonds §8.13
Surety or substitute contractor, bonds §8.14

WORK DISPUTES
See DISPUTE RESOLUTION

WORKER NEGLIGENCE
Construction safety §3.06

WORKERS' COMPENSATION
Collateral source rule, remedies/damages §5.18
Laws, construction safety §3.02
Premium refunds, insurance §10.10

WORKERS INJURED ON JOB SITE
Professional's role and liability §11.04

WORKING UNDER PROTEST
Changes/extra work §§6.02, 6.04, 6.13, 6.24, 6.31
Dispute resolution §6.04

WORK PERFORMED AND PRICE
Mechanics' liens §9.26

WORK STOPPAGE
Default/termination §4.03

WRAP-UP INSURANCE
Insurance §10.10

WRITING REQUIREMENT
Bidding and contract requirements §2.27
Changes/extra work §§6.02, 6.08, 6.24, 6.31
Waiver, changes/extra work §§6.06-6.12

WRITTEN AGREEMENTS
Bidding and contract formation §§2.25, 2.27

WRONGFUL TERMINATION
Default/termination §4.21

X

"X, C, U" EXCLUSION
Insurance, app 10-2

Z

ZEALOUS ADVOCACY
Bidding and contract formation §2.44